THE OFFICIAL
AUTOGRAPH
COLLECTOR
PRICE GUIDE

Third Edition

by Kevin Martin

"Trusted by Collectors and Dealers"

ODYSSEY PUBLICATIONS

A Collectors Universe Company

NASDAQ: CLCT

www.AutographCollector.com

The official autograph
collector price guide

Publisher: Odyssey Publications
Publisher: A Collectors Universe Company
Publisher: NASDAQ: CLCT

Cover Design: Jackie Floyd, Type "F"
Author: Kevin Martin
Sports Author: Joe Orlando, *Sports Market Report* Magazine
Book Author: Tim Miller
Edited By: Ev Phillips

Printed in the United States of America
First Edition, First Printing
10 9 8 7 6 5 4 3 2 1

ISBN# 0-9669710-5-1

Library of Congress Catalog Card Number: 2001094910

Odyssey Publications
A Collectors Universe Company
510-A So. Corona Mall
Corona, CA 92879-1420

1-800-996-3977 or (909)734-9636

www.AutographCollector.com

Printed in the United States

FOREWARD

Since our last price guide, we have seen a continued interest in the hobby of autograph collecting. No dramatic downturns in spite of what some see as a weakening economy and, based on what we see, solid growth in sales and increasing values of good material are likely to continue.

The Internet continues to play a role in our hobby, although many are reporting that the competition between traditional autograph sales and online sales has cooled off somewhat, in favor of the traditional dealer. Online sales through the large Internet auction sales continue to be strong, but largely for lower priced autographs. This could be due to the fact that many buyers are simply not comfortable with making significant purchases with the relative anonymity the online auctions afford. In short, there is a larger potential for things to go wrong. After all, in the days before the Internet, you could always pick up a phone or even visit a dealer if there was a problem with a particular purchase.

Direct sales of autographs through print publications and printed catalogs still account for the vast majority of the many millions of dollars in sales in our hobby. Serious collectors still like to peruse catalogs and ads; they like to be able to speak with a real live person and have their questions answered in seconds, not hours or days as can happen when buying online. We predict that these traditional sales vehicles will continue to grow, and dealers who offer good quality material will continue to prosper.

Overall, values in the (non-sports) autograph market have increased steadily over the past few years, with no across the board downturns. Autographs have either kept their value or increased in value. Dealers haven't been forced to slash prices on good material, and, in fact, based on demand have steadily increased prices on the vast majority of pieces in their inventories.

This, of course, bodes well for dealer and collector alike. If you're a dealer, you're enjoying the fruits of your labor and the constant hunt for unearthing good material. If you're a collector, you may be able to sell many of your autographs at a profit over what you originally paid. While we don't advocate buying collectibles as an investment vehicle, the record shows that collectors of autographs have done pretty well from that standpoint.

What we do recommend is to buy and collect those autographs from personalities who have truly touched your world or influenced history in a way that you admire. Are you a big fan of Abraham Lincoln, or Marilyn Monroe or Albert Einstein? If you are, it is possible for you to possess your very own letter, photo or document actually touched and signed by these historical greats!

So, as we often advocate, keep collecting for your own personal satisfaction and enjoyment. Buy only what you like and buy from reputable dealers who not only will help you build your collection, but also educate and accompany you on this wonderful journey.

Bill Miller
Darrell Talbert
Odyssey Publications

TABLE OF CONTENTS

PRICING
(OR ... "ONCE MORE WITH FEELING!")

It is so frustrating to hear people quote incorrectly from this guide because they forgot the information in this introductory chapter (or never read it in the first place) on HOW we determined the prices contained herein.

I have had COUNTLESS dealers and collectors call me during the year to say something like, "I think the price for a signed photo of Elizabeth Montgomery is too low." I invariably end up saying something like, "Is the photo in question a shot of her from *Bewitched?*" They almost always say yes, and I have to remind them that the prices shown in the signed photo section of this guide are for commonly encountered PORTRAITS of the person – no special meaning, long inscriptions, special scene, larger size, not signed by the photographer, etc. In other words, they are for basic, NO CONTENT photos.

Likewise, the TLS and ALS sections are for NON-content letters like "Thanks for the dinner invitation, but I just can't find the time – Sincerely, Albert Einstein" as opposed to "I really don't care what you think about $E=mc^2$ ... I happen to think it works!"

So why isn't the $E=mc^2$ letter priced in this guide? Because one-of-a-kind content items will always sell for whatever the market, auction crowd, etc. decides they are worth at any given time – and that variation can be as wide as the Mississippi. It is impossible to quantify in a guide. However, letters like "Thanks, but I can't make it" come up often enough that we can, with a high degree of accuracy, give you average prices for them. And that's what we have done in this guide.

So remember, even if you have a Bert Lahr signed photo as the Cowardly Lion from *The Wizard of Oz* – the last one at auction brought nearly $10,000 – your portrait is still worth only $400 like the guide says. (Sorry about that.)

So, to wrap it up, this guide is just that – a guide. It starts off by giving you what an average, no-content, run-of-the-mill SP, DS, TLS, etc. is worth today. If it has something special to recommend it, then I suggest you decide on your own if the extra price the dealer has added to it warrants the extra kick. But if you are building a set of signatures of the Declaration Signers, cast members of a TV show or Supreme Court justices, then don't pay more than the prices in this guide, because that's what they've been selling for – all year long.

Happy Collecting!

– Kevin Martin

WHO DO YOU TRUST?

by Kevin Martin

In any field where authenticity is important, there is always the inevitable clashing of educated opinions, the jealousy of one "expert" aimed at another with the poor collector caught in the middle, and the unscrupulous dealer who will kill one dealer's sale to make his own. Ugly? Sure, but as long as flawed human beings are involved, these things will occur.

So what can you do? Where do you go? You go where the autographs are – dealers, of course!

But understand this one fact: All dealers are not alike, just as not all doctors are alike. Ask yourself this question: If you had to be treated for a disease or undergo an important operation, which doctor would you choose and why?

Hopefully you would pick one with experience dealing with your particular situation, one that had seen your problem before (hopefully many times). And you may even pay a bit more for his or her experience.

Can they still make a mistake? Of course they can. But you are paying them for their knowledge and experience in the belief that MOST of the time they are correct.

If you have a heart problem, you don't ask your barber what he thinks of it, right? (Nod your head.) But unfortunately, that is sometimes what happens in our hobby. A well-meaning (perhaps) historical dealer tells someone their Marilyn Monroe looks bad to them (and maybe it does ... to them). Should that shake your trust in the original purchase? No, but why ask them in the first place? If you feel unsure of your dealer, the bottom line is you shouldn't be dealing with them. In reality, you are wasting your time and theirs. No one wins. TRUST ME on this. As a dealer myself, I know I only want to deal with happy customers. And while it is my responsibility to educate my client to whatever extent I can, it should not be my job to constantly hold their hand after the sale. A case in point was a client who just bought a video of the collected films of Audrey Hepburn, and the fascimile signature on the box didn't match the one I sold him. (True story.) By the way, the box art featured a secretarial signature because it was more legible. But then again, I don't put together video retrospectives. (They did a great job ... I saw it.) But I do authenticate entertainment autographs.

So pick someone you trust and have a good rapport with, hopefully someone who has been around a while in this business. In other words, look for all the things you'd look for in a good doctor. Then go ahead with confidence and enjoy the wonderful hobby of autograph collecting!

A MILLION MILES AND THIRTY YEARS AGO

AUTOGRAPHS FROM SPACE
by Kim Poor

Imagine that your ultimate autograph wish list was not restricted by funds, availability, or time. Who would you collect? Moses? Jesus? Alexander the Great? Caesar? Da Vinci? Joan of Arc? Mozart? Shakespeare? Columbus?

There are a few people walking the Earth today whose accomplishments are as legendary as any of those that changed the course of civilization – the early astronauts.

It's been 30 years since the moon landings ... time enough to look back at what superhuman feats we accomplished in only a few short years. Sure, space flight still takes place. It's risky, and the program is always pushing ahead. But in the 1960s it was new, more dangerous, and the exclusive realm of a handful of rugged pioneers in the Mercury, Gemini and Apollo programs. The goal was to put the first man on an alien world.

Postal Cover flown to the surface of the moon on Apollo 15

The Space Race

The social, political and economic climate of that tiny slice of human history was so unique that it will be written about for centuries. Only 12 years spanned the launch of the first Soviet satellite (Sputnik) and the first U.S. moon landing.

The world's two great superpowers, with fiercely competing ideologies, pushed their resources to the limit in a do-or-die race to the moon to show the rest of the world whose system was best. As an adjunct, technology, communications, (and weaponry) took a huge leap forward. Mankind also gained the confidence that anything was possible given enough money and national will. "If we can put a man on the moon" is still a common preface to many sentences. Although history tends to repeat itself, that magic mixture of political and technological goals probably will never happen again.

Signed Buzz Aldrin footprint photo

Can we do it again? No. We lack the hardware, personnel, money and commitment. We'd have to start over. The space shuttle might be modified to fly to the moon, but it couldn't land. At least we know that it could be done, many years ago. That makes it very special.

The Apollo moon landings mark a significant passage of human evolution. Surely the future includes man's spread into space. Our fragile Earth is the "cradle of mankind ... but one cannot stay in the cradle forever" (Tsiolkovsky). We will have to colonize new worlds to survive and flourish. We'll use up the Earth if we don't. In this context, our first steps on another world have paramount significance. Ships, cities, planets and even stars will be named after the pioneer astronauts.

Collecting Space Autographs

Most autograph buffs collect the celebrities of the day; sports figures, music and movie stars. They are accessible, inexpensive, and they need fans to perpetuate and fuel their success. Historical figures, on the other hand, have a different agenda, personal goals, duty or political. They do not require – and sometimes eschew – fame. Getting their autographs is a privilege, not a right.

Although some astronauts like Neil Armstrong have stopped signing altogether and make few appearances, others keep an unbelievably hectic schedule of public events despite their advanced ages. Apollo astronauts are deluged with speaking invitations and autograph requests from all over the world. Most still sign, though only a few do so for free.

Print signed by the Mercury Seven Astronauts

Relatively few have passed on, moonwalkers Jim Irwin, Alan Shepard and Pete Conrad among them. Many astronauts express a desire to slow down, but haven't. Realistically, though, within a few years, their public appearances should slack off, and more will leave Earth permanently. We must savor their remaining time here. One aging Gemini and Apollo veteran told us during a recent visit, "I feel fine, but like many of the other guys, I'm getting my estate in order."

Extremely gratifying to astronauts and eyewitness baby-boomers alike, is the enthusiastic response of the younger generation. Although they missed the firsthand excitement of the experience, their enthusiasm for the early space program belies their age. Many can quote chapter and verse facts and figures like a baseball buff. These young people are voracious autograph collectors and some are actually acknowledged experts, advising and authenticating autographs for much older collectors who may just be starting.

Signed & inscribed beta cloth patch flown to the moon on Apollo 8

The space autograph demand is worldwide, though only two countries took part in the moon race. Europeans, Japanese and Australians are especially enthusiastic – much more so than Americans, who may not realize it is the space program and not our superpower status or our wealth that are the source of international admiration and awe for our country.

There are three main reasons for collecting autographs: fandom, historical and financial. Astronaut autographs satisfy all aspects. For space buffs who collect astronaut autographs and artifacts, they help preserve and perpetuate the significance of an era that took humanity a "giant leap" forward. Financially, astronaut autographs are the closest to a "sure thing" you may ever find. Valuations and prices have skyrocketed in recent years and command some of the highest prices of living persons, with only brief dips occurring during hiccups in the economy, but there are still bargains to be found.

Where?

As with other autographs, the sources are similar: mail-in directly, auctions and dealers.

Most astronauts still sign their books for free, and you can sometimes catch one at a public appearance. A few still sign for free through the mail. Others charge

Apollo 11 signed crew photo

fees. Mailing to NASA will usually get you an autopen, but occasionally the real thing comes from current astronauts.

Astronaut autographs are a staple of online auction sites, but these sites are an easy refuge for forgers and scoundrels. With entertainment, sports and astronaut autographs, the lure of easy cash and the relative anonymity of sellers make it a dangerous place for the inexperienced to buy. That being said, there are some incredible bargains to be found, and good, honest sellers. We personally feel that a good seller should have other business avenues, such as a store, catalog or Web site that makes them legitimate and locatable should there be a problem. Traditional auction houses also have space memorabilia events, though only once or twice a year.

Dealers are a reliable, safer source of material, although only a few dealers specialize in astronaut autographs. With the widespread use of autopens (every astronaut is issued one) and forgeries – especially Neil Armstrong and rare signatures – it pays to go through a knowledgeable dealer with a space specialty. As with any business, look for a long track record and good word-of-mouth reputation.

Various dealers have various specialties. Some provide unsigned NASA photographs for collectors, some may specialize in Mercury, Gemini or Apollo; some deal exclusively with certain astronauts; some like inscribed photos, others do not. Most of the dozen-odd astronaut autograph dealers' specialties overlap, but all have something unique to offer.

Novaspace Galleries started as an art gallery 23 years ago to showcase the astronomical art of owner

Signed Neil Armstrong photo

Kim Poor. Gradually colleagues were added to the mix, including Alan Bean, who coincidentally was the fourth of the 12 Apollo moonwalkers. Bean had quit NASA in 1981 to try his hand as a professional artist, painting his own brand of space art. Novaspace quickly became his largest gallery. Alan began having his astronaut buddies co-sign his art prints, and introducing Kim to this exclusive club of lunar explorers.

Today, Novaspace Galleries is by far the largest source for pioneer astronaut autographs and space art, not only handling autographed NASA photos, but also autographed space art prints and posters. Novaspace is trusted by these astronauts so completely that, with little more than a handshake, they consign their precious artifacts that were flown to the moon, a million miles and 30 years ago! If you've ever seen an Apollo spacecraft, you'll appreciate how little room for souvenirs existed and how a mission patch, miniature flag, or dollar bill taken along to the moon becomes the ultimate collectible. Certificates of Authenticity are signed by the astronauts themselves for flown items.

Novaspace represents some astronauts exclusively, and even though located in a small city, organizes book and memorabilia signings with moonwalkers and famous astronauts that draw customers from all over the globe for the rare chance to meet a space hero close-up. These Bacchanalian galas have become legendary among space collectors. The astronauts sign, speak, pose for photos with guests and hobnob for a weekend with those fortunate enough to be invited.

As a gallery, one of the unique services Novaspace can provide is custom archival framing. The staff of master framers can flatter as well as preserve autographed treasures.

Novaspace also has one of the largest and oldest retail Web sites on the Internet, which is maintained by Kim himself, with secure online ordering. The Web site began in 1995, before there were any Web site designers, as one of the first Web sites to appear. The site has grown to more than 1,450 pages at www.novaspace.com.

The spacious gallery is open to the public Monday through Saturday, and several different catalogs are published and sent to the customer list each year. However, the Novaspace e-mail list is used to announce astronaut events, special promotions and new and rare items.

Alan Bean- "Right Stuff Field Geologists"

COLLECTING CASTS

by Kevin Martin

For those of us who can't afford all the U.S. presidents, Signers of the Constitution or Declaration of Independence, how about collecting your favorite movie or TV cast members?

Who among us doesn't have a favorite movie or TV series? As a child I absolutely loved *The Wild, Wild West* starring Ross Martin and Robert Conrad. Easy cast to collect you say? Well, they are fairly available, but I'm still looking for Michael Dunn, who played a recurring villain in the series. However, I do have Victor Buono, who played another villain.

Like many people, a friend of mine collects people associated with the *Batman* TV series, which goes far beyond the regular cast into villains and special guest appearances.

On the big screen, the two most collected films are undoubtedly *Gone with the Wind* and *The Wizard of Oz*. However, I have seen nearly every film collected ... so collect what you like!

It seems to be true that any decent-sized TV or movie cast has that one star who either hated to sign or perhaps died before signing very much. (How rude!)

The good news is that once these "keys" are filled, your collection will come together much more easily. But remember, much of the joy is in looking for the keys in the first place.

Here are a few of the key people in TV and movie casts and some tips on what to expect when collecting them. Maybe you've been looking for one of these slippery fellows, and now you'll understand you're not alone in your pursuit!

I apologize if space doesn't permit me to mention your favorite show or movie, but here are a few that collectors have been in hot pursuit of lately, along with some of the main obstacles you'll encounter in collecting each.

Let's start with TV first ...

M*A*S*H – One of the longest running and most watched TV shows in history. Overall it's a large, but fairly easy cast to collect except for three people. The first is McLean Stevenson, who played Lt. Col. Henry Blake. Stevenson died in 1996 and signed only sporadically, but his signature can be found. The second is Larry Linville (Maj. Frank Burns), who died in 2000 and is uncommon. However, the third and most difficult to obtain is very much alive and still active in films. He's David

Ogden Stiers, who played Maj. Winchester. Stiers hates to sign, and usually is missing (or forged) in a cast situation, so beware!

The Munsters – The spooky family from 1313 Mockingbird Lane is easy to collect, with all of but one of the cast members still alive and willing. The star of the show, Fred Gwynne, who played Herman Munster, died in 1993. Gwynne hated to sign *Munsters* material, so beware of secretarials and forgeries like the F. Gwynne signatures that have popped up recently. When Gwynne did sign, he always signed in FULL.

The Beverly Hillbillies – Those crazy Hillbillies are fun to collect. Max Baer (Jethro) is very much alive and a bit uncommon, but still available. The tough one in the main cast is character actress Irene Ryan (Granny), who died in 1973. However, she was a good signer, so her autograph is available.

The rarest cast members here are Raymond Bailey (bank president Milburn Drysdale) and Harriett MacGibbon, who played his wife Margaret. My advice is to buy these two whenever you have a chance.

Gilligan's Island – Another fun cast to collect – and easy, too – with the exception of The Skipper, Alan Hale Jr., who died in 1990. He signed a lot of pieces at a seafood restaurant he owned near the end of his life and often wrote "Skipper" after his name. But watch for Hale forgeries on cast photos, as the rest are fairly easy to obtain.

Bewitched – A lot of toughies here. Elizabeth Montgomery is the easiest, even though she's been gone since 1995. However, getting her and the main cast members in character is tougher.

Dick Sargent and Dick York are easier to find in signatures, letters or documents than on photos from the series.

Agnes Moorehead (d. 1974) is rare in character as Samantha's mother Endora, and is easier on album pages or in letters. David White as Larry Tate is uncommon, as are Irene Vernon and Kasey Rogers, who played Larry's wife Louise. A lot of people collect the more famous recurring witch and warlock roles such as Dr. Bombay, played by Bernard Fox, who still signs at celebrity shows. Others like the first Gladys Kravitz – played by Alice Pearce, who died in 1966 – and her replacement Sandra Gould are quite rare. George Tobias as Abner Kravitz also is rare, but easier in signatures alone. Marion Lorne as Aunt Clara and Reta Shaw as head of the witches' council are rare. Paul Lynde (d. 1982) as Samantha's Uncle Arthur is uncommon, while Alice Ghostly is easy to obtain.

Bonanza – This is a fun and relatively easy to collect cast consisting of four main signatures and sometimes five. Pernell Roberts is scarce, with Michael Landon

(d. 1991) and Lorne Greene (d. 1987) available but getting more uncommon. The key here is Dan Blocker (d. 1972), who played Hoss on the show. Victor Sen Yung also is fun to go after as the cook Hop Sing, but is mainly available in signatures only.

The Andy Griffith Show – The main cast is fairly easy here, although Aunt Bea played by Frances Bavier (d. 1989) is tough but obtainable. Andy Griffith hates to sign autographs, but his personal checks and other items are available. Don Knotts, Ron Howard, George Lindsey and Jim Nabors are all easy to find and inexpensive. The rarest cast member is Howard McNear, who played Floyd the barber. He hardly ever shows up at events, so jump on him whenever you get a chance.

And finally ... Hugh Beaumont is nearly impossible for you *Leave it to Beaver* fans, George Reeves on a Superman photo will set you back $2,500, but Batman Adam West has practically made a living out of signing ($20 a pop). And Bruce Lee as Cato from *The Green Hornet?* Forget about it!

Movies

The Wizard of Oz – There is much to collect here. The list includes directors Victor Fleming (RARE), Mervyn LeRoy and King Vidor, art director Sir Cedric Gibbons (Scarce), Composers like E.Y. Harburg and Harold Arlen and, of course, those great cast members.

Frank Morgan or Bert Lahr in character as well as Billie Burke are very rare. But fortunately for us fans the Wicked Witch (Margaret Hamilton), the Tin Man (Jack Haley), the Scarecrow (Ray Bolger) and a host of Munchkins are all available.

Ironically, the rarest of all *in character* is Judy Garland herself!

Casablanca – A fantastic film full of great actors and actresses like Humphrey Bogart and Ingrid Bergman, the rarest here are character actors Conrad Veidt and Sydney Greenstreet.

Gone with the Wind - Clark Gable and Vivien Leigh are available as Rhett and Scarlett, but not for the faint of pocketbook! Once again there are a host of character actors who are rare and only available in signature or letter form. They include Alicia Rhett, Oscar Polk, Lillian Kemble-Cooper, Harry Davenport and literally dozens of others who make collecting this cast a lifelong affair!

A rare name need not be expensive, as there are hundreds to choose from. The signatures of these people may set you back only a few dollars, but may take years to find!

The search is where your fun begins.

Happy Collecting!

PROFESSIONAL

AUTOGRAPH

ORGANIZATIONS

IACC/IADA

Established in 1997, the International Autograph Collectors Club (IACC) and Dealers Alliance (IADA) is the first autograph organization of its kind. The IACC/DA is a nonprofit organization whose primary purpose is to accurately educate the autograph community around the world and, above all, to assure collectors that IADA members stand out above the rest in terms of credentials and adherence to the hobby's strictest code of ethics.

The club is unique, as its sole focus is on the field of autograph collecting.

Educational courses are given during our regional shows held around the United States. Notables in our field such as Bill Butts, Gil Griggs, Christopher Jaeckel, Steve Koschal, Ken Laurence, Kevin Martin, Bill Miller, Kenneth Rendell, John Reznikoff and Daniel Weinberg have taught these complimentary courses. Each person taking a course receives a certificate of completion signed by the club president and instructor.

To join, collectors need only to fill out a simple application. Our membership dues are the lowest in the hobby.

Not every person who sells autographs can become an IADA member. An existing member must sponsor potential dealer members. They must also have at least two references, which are thoroughly checked. In some cases their material is examined before the membership committee votes on their application.

Most importantly, the IACC/DA assures each member that should an ethics complaint arise against any member, that complain will be acknowledged and acted upon by our ethics board.

Every IADA member must offer their customers a Lifetime Guarantee with every item sold and a receipt at the time of purchase.

The club is the only one in existence today with a physical headquarters where all members are welcome to visit.

Each club member receives:

a) A membership card

b) A copy of our Code of Ethics

c) The Annual IADA Dealers Directory, called by many "The Who's Who In Professional Autograph Dealers."

d) A major signature study. The 1998 study was on Gerald R. Ford, praised by the former president himself. The 1999 study was on Robert F. Kennedy, praised by the John F. Kennedy Library, *Autograph Collector* magazine and hundreds of collectors. The 2000 study was on Neil Armstrong.

Our club publishes six magazines a year called *The Eyes, Ears And Voice Of The Hobby,* which is sent free to our members. It contains up to date information on autographs, timely articles, signature studies and educational information. Each member can place a free 35-word ad in the Bulletin Board section. An unofficial poll ranked our magazine "The BEST educational and informative club magazine in the hobby."

Special private signings are held from time to time, and members can purchase these autographs at below market prices.

All members have access to a large autograph reference library used by scholars, librarians, collectors and dealers from around the world.

The IACC/DA is the only organization that offers a club authentication service. Items are examined by a minimum of three experts and a certificate is issued.

You will not simply be joining an autograph club; you will be enjoying an entire autograph experience! To become part of the IACC or IADA family, write for an application to:

IACC/DA
P.O. Box 848486
Hollywood, Florida 33084
USA
or visit our Web site at: www.iacc-da.org

THE MANUSCRIPT SOCIETY

THE MANUSCRIPT SOCIETY was founded in 1948 as the *National Society of Autograph Collectors*, and has grown to an international membership of more than 1,800 including dealers, private collectors, scholars, authors, and caretakers of public collections such as librarians, archivists, and curators. There are also many historical societies, museums, special libraries and academic libraries that are institutional members.

The Society publishes two quarterly publications, *MANUSCRIPTS* and *THE MANUSCRIPT SOCIETY NEWS*, which are sent to each member without charge. *MANUSCRIPTS* is a journal with an established reputation for excellent scholarly and collector articles reflecting the diverse interests in the field of autographs and manuscripts. Issues offer views on the principal areas of historical and literary collecting, present auction results, list new members and publicize sources of autographs through dealer and auctioneer advertisements. The *NEWS* features information on the whole contemporary world of autographs, including important discoveries, acquisitions, trends, disasters, preservation, upcoming sales, legal questions, thefts, forgeries, replevin actions and exhibits, as well as news about the Society and its members. Collectors and scholars seeking or offering manuscript material are permitted to place their notices in a special section.

The Society's chief activity is a five-day annual meeting, held in a community offering good manuscript resources for viewing. The programs feature exhibitions, panel discussions, speakers of note, tours and social occasions for fellowship and interchange of ideas. Major cities have alternated with smaller communities as the locales for these meetings so as to provide a varied view of the manuscript resources available. Five annual meetings have been held abroad: London in 1970 and 1986, Ottawa in 1978, Dublin in 1991 and Edinburgh in 1996.

Local chapters in the Twin Cities, Washington and Southern California offer members a chance to meet with others in their area. All members in good standing may belong to a chapter.

A comprehensive monograph titled *AUTOGRAPHS AND MANUSCRIPTS: A COLLECTOR'S MANUAL*, was published under the auspices of The Manuscript Society by Charles Scribner's Sons in 1978. Its long definitive articles on many aspects of collecting, arranging and preserving manuscript material – all of them written by experts in their fields – have caused the book to be hailed as a classic treatment of the subject. In 1984 Greenwood Press published *MANUSCRIPTS: THE FIRST TWENTY YEARS*, an anthology of 50 memorable articles from the Society's journal. THE *AUTOGRAPH COLLECTOR'S CHECKLIST* was published by the Society in 1990, providing lists to aid collectors in a number of popular collecting fields. HISTORY IN YOUR HANDS, a 50-year history of the Society and autograph collecting in general, was published in 1997.

To celebrate the bicentennial of the United States, in 1975 and 1976 a traveling exhibit was sponsored by the Society in cooperation with the Smithsonian Institution. It consisted of documents written during the early months of the Revolution, which were loaned to the exhibit by members of the Society from their own collections. The Society also has aided members involved in litigation over contested ownership of manuscript material where the rights of individuals to own historic documents have been questioned.

The Manuscript Society welcomes new members. The annual individual or institutional membership fee is $45. Contributing memberships at $100, sustaining memberships at $250, benefactor memberships at $500, and life memberships at $2,000 help to further Society interests. Memberships are on a calendar year basis; new members joining after July 1 may pay half the annual rate. All monies go to support the publication program, to aid in the defense of individuals against government agencies in replevin suits, and to maintain the expenses of managing Society affairs.

The Manuscript Society
Edward C. Oetting
Executive Director
1960 E. Fairmont Drive
Tempe, AZ 85282-2844
Visit our Web site at: http://www.manuscript.org

PADA

The Professional Autograph Dealers Association, Inc. (PADA) is an organization of knowledgeable, experienced, and ethical dealers in historic autograph material. Established in 1995 by many of the nation's leading dealers, PADA is dedicated to maintaining the highest standards of business ethics, professionalism and service in the autograph industry. Its members seek to establish a marketplace for autographs, in which collectors can buy and sell with confidence and receive informed, accurate advice.

PADA has a stringent code of ethics to which its members must adhere. PADA dealers are required to provide a money-back guarantee of authenticity on all the autographs they sell. In addition, they must conscientiously authenticate and accurately describe all autographs; they must conduct their businesses honestly, fairly, and with integrity; and they must make every effort to promote customer satisfaction.

Membership in PADA is limited to dealers who abide by its code of ethics and who have demonstrated expertise and integrity in buying and selling autographs. All applicants for membership are carefully screened. Applicants must have been in the autograph business for at least three years; most PADA members have far more experience than this.

PADA also seeks to encourage interest in, and appreciation of, autographs. It maintains an informational Web site (www.padaweb.org) where its complete code of ethics can be found. The site also presents the Monthly Catalog, a new list every month of autographs offered by PADA members. The Monthly Catalog provides an excellent sampling of the fine and varied autograph material handled by PADA dealers. The Web site also lists all PADA members, along with their areas of special expertise, and contains links to their individual e-mail addresses and Web sites. Further expansion of PADA's Web site is planned, including the addition of a library of information that will be helpful to autograph collectors.

Every April PADA holds an autograph show in New York City that is considered by many the nation's premier autograph show. The organization is planning other shows across the country, and details about all PADA shows can be found on its Web site. PADA also plans to issue publications on autographs that will be useful to collectors.

PADA dealers are an unrivaled source for autographs. Collectively, they offer a large and diverse assortment of material in all price ranges. Among the specialties of PADA members are U.S. history, including presidents and military leaders; world history; music; literature; the fine and performing arts; science and medicine; exploration; aviation; business and finance; and vintage theater and entertainment.

PADA members can provide collectors with other valuable services. With their many years of experience, they can answer questions about autograph collecting and offer advice on all aspects of the field. They can discuss proper methods for storing and displaying autographs and can help locate an expert conservator, when one is needed. Individual members of PADA offer authentication services and appraisals of autographs. They can act as agents for collectors and libraries at auctions.

PADA dealers also represent a significant market for purchasing autographs, whether single items or entire collections. They buy autographs outright, offering a fair price and immediate payment. PADA dealers also take autographs on consignment, acting as agents for their sale. PADA's code of ethics requires members to adhere to the highest professional standards when they are buying autographs, assuring the seller of courteous and honest treatment.

Whether you are buying or selling autographs, if you do business with a PADA member, you can be sure that you are dealing with a reliable individual who has a commitment to quality, service and integrity. PADA dealers look forward to sharing with you the excitement and rewards of autograph collecting and helping you find the autographs that you will treasure for years to come.

For a free brochure and membership directory, write to:
The Professional Autograph Dealers Association, Inc.
P.O. Box 1729, Murray Hill Station
New York, NY 10156
Visit our Web site at: www.padaweb.org

UACC

The Universal Autograph Collectors Club, Inc. (UACC) is the world's largest organization for autograph collectors with over 2,000 members in more than 27 countries. Founded in 1965, the UACC is a federally approved nonprofit organization whose purpose is to educate members and the public about all aspects of autograph collecting through its publications, shows, conventions and seminars. Unlike other organizations, the UACC Executive Board is not made up of dealers but, rather, of collectors. They are elected by the membership.

By joining the UACC, you will receive our renowned 64-page bimonthly journal, *The Pen and Quill,* which features articles and news on autographs in all areas. These include our famous signature studies (articles on authentic, secretarial, autopen, rubber-stamped, facsimile and forged signatures), as well as interesting historical footnotes using collectors' documents and stories of in-person encounters with the celebrities of the time. This information gives the collector better information in order to make decisions in purchasing good quality material.

To this end, the UACC also boasts the largest Autograph Dealer's registry, known as UACC Registered Dealers. These 150+ individuals or companies have provided information regarding their business for publication, including how long they have been involved in the field and if they have any ethics violations. This information is posted on the UACC Web site at www.uacc.org along with other important information you should know about each dealer. These dealers are the leaders in the field of autographs and, as such, they fully support the UACC and its goals. Each year we give a Distinguished Dealer Award to one of our dealers that excels in service to the industry.

Speaking of the Internet, the UACC was the first organization to establish a fully interactive Web site, which includes autograph news, membership information, Registered Dealer information, the Hall of Shame, Constitution and Code of Ethics, show schedules and more.

The UACC was also the first organization to institute a Code of Ethics by which each member agrees to abide as a condition of membership. Our code is the toughest in the industry and has resolved over 95% of the complaints filed by the membership. Our extensive ethics files have been used and applauded by numerous law enforcement agencies. Our active Ethics Board works for the protection of the membership.

Each year the UACC presents a number of awards to individuals that have given of themselves each year for the betterment of the hobby. These include literary awards, collector of the year awards, the president's quality award and the coveted UACC Distinguished Service Award.

Our members are also given FREE classified ads in our journal as well as opportunities to purchase uncommon autographic material and reference works at affordable prices. There is also our annual auction that benefits the membership.

We sponsor shows around the United States and in England, as well as a yearly convention, and are the only organization that accepts Visa and Mastercard for membership or anything else for that matter.

Our best resource is our membership. When shared, the combined knowledge and experience of our members makes the UACC the best organization for the informed collector.

To learn more about the UACC, write for a brochure and membership information to:
UACC
P.O. Box 6181
Washington, DC 20044-6181
or visit our Web site at: www.uacc.org
We hope you will join our universe of fellow collectors soon.

UNIVERSAL AUTOGRAPH COLLECTORS CLUB

HOW TO USE THIS GUIDE

Please read and understand the next couple of pages so you get the most out of using this guide.

CONTENT is the single most important factor after condition to determining value of an item autographed and CONTENT applies to photographs, letters, documents and even in some rare cases, signatures.

Content varies from item to item so it would be inaccurate to try and quantify it in a price guide so we have not tried!

Instead, in each of our fields we have given you the ACTUAL accurate CURRENT recorded average price that the signed piece goes for with NO regard to content.

What exactly does this mean?

Let's say for example you are looking to buy a George Reeves signed photograph and you look in a dealers catalog and see a lovely 8x10 signed photograph in character as Superman, one of his most famous roles, offered for $2,500.

You then pull out our trusty guide only to find the George Reeves listing for a signed photograph is $1,500 ... Which is more accurate? The dealer or us?

The answer is BOTH of us are dead on accurate. How?

Our guide lists average, routinely encountered NON CONTENT items in the marketplace. In the case of signed photographs our prices represent an 8x10 black and white signed PORTRAIT like was commonly signed for fans BUT if the star wrote something extraordinary or the image was 11x14 not 8x10 or the image was of their "signature role" that would constitute CONTENT and be worth more.

Content pieces are the best buy if you can afford them and should be bought when encountered because they won't last long in the hot market of today!

The same would be true in our document section with a signed typed letter or document concerning a routine invitation, thank you note, tax document, etc., being the items we have averaged and placed in our guide under that heading. But, if the document using the above example, were Reeves original contract to play Superman you would throw the guide out the window and hope and pray you can obtain the piece before anyone else calls the dealer! A one of a kind item by definition, may never come you way again ... and on such items using a price guide of the past averages would be pointless.

In our remarks column we have listed career highlights and other comments that will help you determine what may constitute content in that person's life. Under Einstein we list that he was known obviously for his physics theories for one example and note signed $E=MC2$ would be worth more than a full letter declining a dinner invitation.

When in doubt, just buy what you like ... that way even if it does not appreciate in value it will still always be appreciated – by you!

- Kevin Martin

KEY TO ABBREVIATIONS

SIG

A single signature in ink (pencil is worth approximately 25% less). Uninscribed on a piece of paper or cut from a document or letter. Capable of being properly matted and not irregular, smeared or in any other way unattractive.

DS

A document signed. Checks that have been found in small quantities fall into this category.

TLS

A typed letter signed by the person. Prices run parallel with DS in this guide.

FDC

A First Day Cover ... a special postal envelope honoring various events.

SP

A signed photograph. For our purposes, an uninscribed 8x10 portrait signed in ink with good contrast between the signature and surface of the photograph.

MQS

A musical quote signed. Often done by composers as a souvenir for fans. Consists of a few words and/or bars of music from one of their works.

Inscribed

Means that the item has been personalized, i.e. "To John," etc.

LS

A letter signed by the person in question, but written by someone else such as a secretary. For LS values use the DS column.

ALS

A handwritten letter signed and written entirely in the hand of the celebrity in question.

Name	Field	SIG	DS	ALS	SP	Remarks
Aadland, Beverly	Ent	10	25		25	
Aaker, Lee	Ent	10	15		25	
Aames, Willie	Ent	15	25		25	Eight is Enough
Abba	Music	60	150		125	Signed by all Four
Abbado, Claudia	Music	20			50	Opera
Abbey, Edwin Austin	Art	20		50		
Abbott and Costello	Ent	450	800		1,300	Signed by both.
Abbott, Bessie	Music	25			50	Opera
Abbott, Bud 1895-1974	Ent	250	400	450	450	Abbott and Costello
Abbott, George	Ent	50		100	100	Director/Producer
Abbott, Henry L.	Civil War	100				Union General/1842-1864
Abbott, John	Ent	15			30	
Abdul, Paula	Music	20	75	75	50	
Abel, Walter 1898-1987	Ent	20	45	50	50	
Abercrombie, John J.	Civil War	50	75	150		Union General/1798-1877
Aberdeen, Fourth Earl	Political	50		100		British Prime Minister
Abernathy, Ralph D.	Political	35		100	75	Civil Rights Leader
Abraham, F. Murray	Ent	20	45	50	40	Amadeus/AA Winner
Abruzzo, Ben A.	Aviation	35			100	
Abt, Franz	Music	100		200		Composer
Abzug, Bella	Political	10		25	20	Congresswoman
AC/DC	Music	50	100		100	Signed by Entire Group
Acheson, Dean	Military	35			100	
Acosta, Bert	Aviation	50		125	100	
Acuff, Roy	Music	20	45		40	Country
Adair, John	Political	50		100		KY Governor
Adam 12	Ent	25			45	Signed by both
Adam, Adolphe-Charles	Music	50		150	100	Opera/Composer
Adams, Abigail	First Lady	750	2,500	5,000		
Adams, Andrew	RevWar	150		300		Continental Congress
Adams, Ansel 1902-84	Art	100	200	300	200	Photographer
Adams, Brooke	Ent	5		20	15	
Adams, Bryan	Music	20			50	
Adams, Clara	Aviation	65		150	125	1st woman on Zeppelin
Adams, Daniel	Civil War	200		600		CSA General/1821-1872
Adams, Don	Ent	10	25	25	25	Get Smart
Adams, Edie	Ent	5	15	20	15	
Adams, Joey	Ent	5	15		15	
Adams, John	Civil War	250				CSA General/1825-1864
Adams, John	President	1,500	3,000	4,500		
Adams, John C.	Science	50		100		Discovered Neptune
Adams, John Quincy	President	450	850	1,600		

Name	Field	SIG	DS	ALS	SP	Remarks
Adams, Julie	Ent	10	20		20	Creature/Black Lagoon
Adams, Louisa Catherine	First Lady	250	500	750		1775-1852
Adams, Maud	Ent	15			30	James Bond's Octopussy
Adams, Maude	Ent	50			100	1872-1953
Adams, Nick	Ent	150	300	350	350	TV's "Rebel"/Died Young
Adams, Samuel	RevWar	750	2,000	3,500		Signer/1722-1803
Adams, Stanley	Music	15	25		25	Composer
Adams, William Wirt	Civil War	300	500			CSA General/1819-1888
Addams, Charles	Cartoonist	75		250	250	Addam's Family
Addams, Jane	Political	75			200	Nobel Peace/Social Ref.
Adelaide, HRH (Queen)	Royalty	50		100		Queen of William IV
Adenhauer, Konrad	Political	50		150	150	Ist Chan. Fed Rep/Ger.
Ader, Rose	Music	35			75	Opera
Adjani, Isabelle	Music	35			75	Opera
Adler, Alfred 1870-1937	Science	100	400	600	200	Psychiatrist
Adler, Buddy	Ent	25			50	Producer
Adler, Luther	Ent	15	25	30	30	1903 - 1984
Adler, Richard	Music	20			35	
Adoree, Renee	Ent	35			75	
Adrian, Edgar Lord	Science	35			75	Nobel/Physiology
Adrian, Iris	Ent	10	20		20	
Aerosmith	Music	100	250		200	Signed by All Five
Affleck, Ben	Ent	25			50	
Aga Khan III	Royalty	125				
Aga Khan IV	Royalty	15		45	35	
Agar, John	Ent	5	15	15	15	
Agassi, Andre	Sports	25			60	Tennis
Agassiz, Jean Louis	Science	100		250	600	Zoologist
Agnew, Spiro	Vice Pres	25	100		75	
Aguilera, Christina	Music	25			50	
Aguinaldo, Emilio	Political	100			150	Phillipine Leader
Agutter, Jenny	Ent	5			15	
Aherne, Brian	Ent	15		45	45	1902 - 1986
Aiello, Danny	Ent	20	30		40	
Aiken, Conrad	Author	30			50	(Am) Pulitzer Winner
Airy, George	Science	50		150		British Astronomer
Aitken, Robert Ingersoll	Art	35		100		Sculptor (Am)
Akers, Elizabeth	Author	5		15	15	
Akihito	Royalty	400		600		
Akin, Warren 1811-1877	Civil War	50		100		Confederate Congressman
Akins, Claude	Ent	10	25		35	
Alabama	Music	35	75		75	Signed by All Four
Alba, Jessica	Ent	25			50	TV's Dark Angel
Albanese, Licia	Music	35			75	Opera
Albee, Edward	Author	30			75	Pulitzer Winner
Alberghetti, Anna	Ent	35			75	Scarce
Albert I (Belgium)	Royalty	25		100	50	

Name	Field	SIG	DS	ALS	SP	Remarks
Albert III (Monaco)	Royalty	100		200	150	
Albert Victor, Duke	Royalty	200			500	Oldest Son of Edward VII
Albert, Don	Music	25			50	Bandleader
Albert, Eddie	Ent	10	25	30	30	Green Acres
Albert, Herb	Music	10	20		25	Trumpet
Albert, Prince (Monaco)	Royalty	25			50	
Albert, Prince (Victoria)	Royalty	150		450		
Albertson, Jack	Ent	30	40		55	Chico & the Man
Albertson, Joseph	Business	10			20	Grocer
Albright, Lola	Ent	10	20		20	
Albright, Madeleine	Political	15			30	Sect State
Albury, Charles	Aviation	25		50	50	
Alcock, John William	Aviation	300	500		600	Pioneer Aviator/1892-1919
Alcorn, James Lusk	Civil War	75		200		CSA General/1816-94
Alcott, Louisa May	Author	275		500		Little Women/1832-88
Alda, Alan	Ent	25	50		55	MASH/Hawkeye Pierce
Alda, Frances	Music	30			75	Opera
Alda, Robert	Ent	10		25	25	1914-1986
Aldred, Joel	Aviation	25			50	Canadian WWII Ace
Aldrich, Thomas Bailey	Author	50		200	150	1836 - 1907
Aldrin, Edwin "Buzz"	Space	50	200	250	150	Second Moonwalker
Alexander I (Russian)	Royalty	300	750	900		1777 - 1825
Alexander II (Russian)	Royalty	350	750	900		Assasinated
Alexander III (Russian)	Royalty			500		
Alexander, Barton S.	Civil War	50		100		Union General/1819-78
Alexander, Ben	Ent	50			125	Dragnet
Alexander, Edward P.	Civil War	300	600	900		CSA General/1835-1910
Alexander, George	Ent	5		15	15	
Alexander, Harold	Military	75		150		Alexander of Tunis (WWII)
Alexander, Jane	Ent	10	20	20	25	
Alexander, Jason	Ent	25	50	50	50	Seinfeld/George
Alexander, John	Ent	20			40	
Alexander, William	RevWar	300	600	1,200		Gen. in Continental Army
Alexandra (Edward VII)	Royalty	150			500	Queen of Edward VII
Alexandra (Nich II)	Royalty	100			200	Russian
Alexis, Kim	Ent	15	30	35	30	Model/Actress
Alfieri, Carlo	Music	15			30	Opera
Alfonso, Kristian	Ent	5			15	
Alfonso, XIII	Royalty	200		550	500	
Alfred, Prince	Royalty	30		75		Son of Queen Victoria
Alfven, Hannes	Science	20		50	35	Nobel/Physics
Alger, Horatio	Author	125		250	250	1832-1899/Rags to Riches
Alger, Russell Alexander	Civil War	50		100	100	Union General/1836-1907
Ali Khan, Prince	Royalty	25		75		
Ali Khan, Princess	Royalty	20		50		
Alice in Chains	Music	50			100	Signed by Entire Group
Alice, Princess	Royalty	15		45	25	

Name	Field	SIG	DS	ALS	SP	Remarks
All in the Family	Ent	60			125	Signed by All Four
Allen, Barbara Jo	Ent	50	100		85	Disney Voice
Allen, Bob	Ent	25	50		60	Western Star
Allen, Debbie	Ent	10	20		20	Fame star
Allen, Elizabeth	Ent	10			20	
Allen, Ethan 1738-89	RevWar	750	1,500	2,500		Col. Green Mtn Boys
Allen, Fred	Ent	50		100	100	Radio Star
Allen, Ginger Lynn	Ent	10			30	
Allen, Gracie	Ent	100	200		200	Of Burns and Allen
Allen, Henry T.	Military	25		75	50	General WWI
Allen, Henry Watkins	Civil War	300		600		CSA General/1820-1866
Allen, Irwin	Ent	25	60		50	Producer/Director
Allen, Karen	Ent	10	25	25	30	Indiana Jones star
Allen, Marty	Ent	5			10	Comedian
Allen, Nancy	Ent	20			50	
Allen, Peter	Music	40			75	Composer
Allen, Rex	Ent	15	35	40	35	Cowboy Star
Allen, Robert	Civil War	50		100		Union General/1811-86
Allen, Steve	Ent	20	40	50	50	
Allen, Tim	Ent	25	50		50	Home Improvement
Allen, William Wirt	Civil War	175		450		CSA General/1835-1894
Allen, Woody	Ent	20	50		50	Director/Actor
Allenby, Edmund	Military	50		150		Br. Field Marshal/1861-36
Allende Gossens, Sal	Political	40		150	75	President of Chile
Alley, Kirstie	Ent	25	50		50	Cheers/Veronica's Closet
Allgood, Sara	Ent	20		50	50	
Allingham, Margery	Author	50		150		Mystery Author
Allison, Bobby	SPorts	10			25	Auto Racing
Allison, Davey	Sports	50			150	Auto Racer/Killed in crash
Allison, May	Ent	20		45	50	
Allizard, Adolphe	Music	20			50	Opera
Allman Brothers	Music	50	100		100	Signed by Both
Allman, Greg	Music	25	50		50	
Allred, Gloria	Ent	10			25	
Allston, Washington	Art	300		700		Landscape Artist/1799-43
Allyson, June	Ent	15	20	25	20	
Alma-Tadema, Lawrence	Art	25		75		Br. Painter
Almonte, Juan N.	Military	100		250		Mexican General/1804-69
Alonso, Maria Conchita	Ent	15	30		30	
Alt, Carol	Ent	10		25	25	
Altman, Robert	Ent	15		30	30	
Alvarez, Luis W.	Science	15		50	30	Nobel Physics
Alvary, Lorenzo	Ent	10		25	25	
Alvord, Benjamin	Civil War	30		75		Union General/1813-1884
Alyn, Kirk	Ent	20	45		45	First Movie Superman
Amara, Lucine	Music	20			45	Opera
Amato, Pasquale	Music	50			125	Opera

Name	Field	SIG	DS	ALS	SP	Remarks
Ambler, Eric	Author	50		150		Br. Novelist
Ambrose, Bert	Music	15			45	Bandleader/1896-1971
Ameche, Don 1908-93	Ent	25	50	65	55	
Ames, Adelbert	Civil War	100		200		Union General/1835-1933
Ames, Ed	Ent	10	25		25	
Ames, Fisher 1758-1808	Political	150		450		Federalist party
Ames, Leon	Ent	15			35	
Ames, Oakes	Business	150	450	1,500		Fndr Union Pacific RR
Ames, Oliver	Business	175	750	2,000		Union Pacific RailRoad
Amherst, Jeffrey	RevWar	400	600	900		1717-97
Amin Dada, Idi	Political	50			100	Uganda
Amis, Kingsley	Author	25		75	50	Watership Down
Amis, Suzy	Ent	25			50	Titanic
Ammen, Daniel	Civil War	35	75	100		Union General
Ammen, Jacob	Civil War	25	50	75		Union General/1806-1894
Amos and Andy	Ent	150	250		300	Signed by Corell/Gosden
Amos, John	Ent	15	35		35	Good Times
Amos, Tori	Music	25		50	50	
Amos, Wally	Business	5		15	15	Famous Amos Cookies
Ampere, Andre Marie	Science	300		1,000		
Amsden, Ben	Aviation	15		30	30	
Amsterdam, Morey	Ent	25	40	45	50	Dick Van Dyke Show
Amundsen, Roald	Explorer	150		300	400	
Anders, Luana	Ent	15			25	
Anderson, Bill	Music	5			15	Country
Anderson, Brad	Cartoonist	15			25	Marmaduke
Anderson, Bronco Billy	Ent	150		400	450	
Anderson, C.E. Bud	Aviation	15		45	35	Ace
Anderson, Carl	Cartoonist	25	75	75		Henry
Anderson, Carl David	Science	35			75	Nobel in Physics/1936
Anderson, Clifford	Civil War	50	100			CSA Congress
Anderson, Eddie	Ent	75		200	200	Rochester"/1905-77
Anderson, George B.	Civil War	200	450			CSA General/1831-1862
Anderson, George T.	Civil War	125		300	250	CSA General/1824-1901
Anderson, Gillian	Ent	25			50	X-Files
Anderson, Hans Christian	Author	500		1,250	1,500	Fairy Tales
Anderson, Harry	Ent	20	40		45	Night Court
Anderson, James P.	Civil War	400		2,500		CSA General/1822-1872
Anderson, Joseph	RevWar	75	225	300		1757 - 1837
Anderson, Joseph R.	Civil War	200	450	600		CSA General/1813-92
Anderson, Judith Dame	Ent	25			50	1898 - 1992
Anderson, Loni	Ent	5	15	20	15	WKRP in Cincinatti
Anderson, Louie	Ent	10	20		20	Comedian
Anderson, Lynn	Music	10			20	Country and Western
Anderson, Pamela	Ent	25			50	Baywatch
Anderson, Poul	Author	15	35		45	Sci-Fi Author
Anderson, Richard Dean	Ent	25			50	MacGuyver/Stargate

Name	Field	SIG	DS	ALS	SP	Remarks
Anderson, Richard Heron	Civil War	75	150	250		CSA General/1821-1879
Anderson, Robert	Civil War	150	300	500	1,500	Cmdr Ft. Sumter/1805-71
Anderson, Samuel R.	Civil War	125	250	350		CSA General/1804-1883
Anderson, Willie	Aviation	10			30	WWII ACE
Andre, John	RevWar	1,200	3,000	7,000		Br.Officer/Hung as a Spy
Andress, Ursula	Ent	25			55	James Bond Girl
Andretti, Mario	Sports	15			45	Auto Racing
Andrew Sisters	Music	75			150	Signed by all Three
Andrews, Chris	Civil War	35	75	200		Union General/1829-1922
Andrews, George L.	Civil War	35	75	100		Union General/1828-99
Andrews, Julie	Ent	20	45	50	50	Sound of Music/Mary Popp
Andrews, Tige	Ent	15			30	
Andrews, V.C.	Author	10			20	Horror
Angel, Heather	Ent	15			35	
Angeli, Pier	Ent	50		150	100	
Angelou, Maya	Author	25		50	50	Poet
Animals, The	Music	100	200		200	Signed by entire group
Aniston, Jennifer	Ent	25			50	FRIENDS
Anka, Paul	Music	10		20	20	
Ankers, Evelyn	Ent	50	125		150	Horror star
Anna Ivanovna	Royalty	350	900	1,500		Empress of Russia
Annabella	Ent	20	30		45	
Annaloro, Antonio	Music	15		35	40	Opera
Anne, Princess	Royalty	100	200		150	Elizabeth II Daughter
Anne, Queen (Eng)	Royalty	500	1,500	2,000		1665 - 1714
Annseau, Fernand	Music	25			75	Opera
Anouilh, Jean	Author	30	75	100	50	
Ansara, Michael	Ent	10	25	25	25	
Anselmi, Giuseppe	Music	50			125	Opera
Ant, Adam	Music	25			50	
Anthony, HRH	Royalty	50	100			King of Saxony
Anthony, Lysette	Ent	20			45	
Anthony, Ray	Music	5		20	15	Big Band Leader
Anthony, Susan B.	Political	200		600	1,200	Women's Rights/1820 - 06
Antokolski, Mark M.	Art	50	75	150		Russ. Sculp. 1843-1902
Anton, Susan	Ent	10	20	20	20	
Antonelli, Laura	Ent	25		50	50	
Antonioni, Michelangelo	Ent	50			150	Director
Anwar, Gabrielle	Ent	25			50	
Apollo 10	Space				400	Signed by entire crew
Apollo 11	Space				1,500	Signed by all three
Apollo 12	Space				275	Signed by entire crew
Apollo 13	Space				1,400	Signed by all three
Apollo 15	Space				500	Signed by entire crew
Apollo 16	Space				300	Signed by entire crew
Apollo 17	Space				300	Signed by entire crew
Apollo 8	Space	250			500	Signed by entire crew

Name	Field	SIG	DS	ALS	SP	Remarks
Apollo 9	Space				300	Signed by all three
Apollonia	Ent	25			50	Singer/Actress w/Prince
Apollo-Soyuz	Space	200			400	Signed by entire crews
Applegate, Christina	Ent	25	50		50	Married with Children
Appleton, Edward, Sir	Science	25		50	50	Nobel Physics
Aquino, Corazon	Political	25			50	Pres. Philippines
Arafat, Yassir	Political	100			200	PLO Leader
Araisa, Francisco	Music	15			35	Opera
Arbuckle, Roscoe 'Fatty'	Ent	450	600	800	900	
Arcaro, Eddie	Sports	20			45	Jockey
Archer, Anne	Ent	15			30	
Archer, James J.	Civil War	200	350	600		CSA General/1817-64
Archer, Jeffrey	Author	5	15		15	
Arden, Elizabeth	Business	30	75	150	50	Founder/Eliz. Arden Co.
Arden, Eve	Ent	20	25	40	40	1912 - 1990
Argyll, 9th Duke	Political	30	50	75		Gov Gen. Canada
Arkin, Adam	Ent	10	15	20	20	
Arkin, Alan	Ent	10	25		25	
Arledge, John	Ent	40			65	
Arlen, Harold	Music	200	300		400	Wizard of Oz
Arlen, Richard	Ent	25			65	1899 - 1976
Arletty	Ent	25			75	
Arliss, George 1868-46	Ent	50	60	75	100	AA Winner
Armani, Giorgio	Business	15			35	Fashion Designer
Armendariz, Pedro	Ent	35	50		75	
Armetta, Henry	Ent	25		50	50	1888 - 1945
Armistead, Lewis A.	Civil War	550				CSA General/1817-63
Armour, Philip D.	Business	250	1,000	1,500	450	Meat Packing. Armour & Co.
Armstead, Henry Hugh	Art	15		35		Br. Sculptor
Armstrong, Louis	Ent	175	400	600	400	Satchmo" 1900 - 1971
Armstrong, Bess	Ent	15			30	
Armstrong, Edw. R.	Science	50		150		Inventor Seadrome
Armstrong, Edwin H.	Science	75	200			Invented FM Broadcasting
Armstrong, Frank C.	Civil War	300				CSA General/1835-1909
Armstrong, Harry	Music	100		200		Composer
Armstrong, John	Political	75	200	400		Sect. of War/1758-1843
Armstrong, Neil A.	Space	200	600	600	400	First Moonwalker
Armstrong, Robert	Ent	75			200	
Armstrong, Samuel C.	Civil War	75	150	250		Cmdr Black Regiments
Arnaz, Desi 1917-86	Ent	65	150	200	200	Lucy and Desi
Arnaz, Lucie	Ent	5			20	Lucy's Daughter
Arness, James	Ent	25	100		60	Gunsmoke
Arnett, Peter	Ent	5			10	CNN News
Arnheim, Gus	Music	15			45	Bandleader
Arno, Peter	Cartoonist	15		50	25	The New Yorker
Arno, Sig	Ent	10			25	
Arnold, Archibald	Military	20	50	75		

Name	Field	SIG	DS	ALS	SP	Remarks
Arnold, Benedict 1741-01	RevWar	1,500		4,000		Am. Army Officer. Traitor
Arnold, Eddy	Music	10			30	
Arnold, Edward	Ent	30			60	
Arnold, Edwin, Sir	Author	50	100	150	100	Br. Poet/Journalist
Arnold, Fred	Aviation	20	35		50	WWII ACE
Arnold, Henry 'Hap'	Military	75	150	250	175	Air Force Gen. WWII
Arnold, Leslie P.	Aviation	15			30	'24 Round the World Flight
Arnold, Lewis Golding	Civil War	50	100	200		Union General/1817-1871
Arnold, Matthew	Author	50	75	100		British Poet
Arnold, Tom	Ent	20	40		40	
Arquette, Cliff	Ent	20			40	
Arquette, David	Ent	25			50	
Arquette, Patricia	Ent	25			50	
Arquette, Roseanna	Ent	25	45		50	
Arrhenuis, Svante A.	Science	150	300	450		Nobel Chemistry 1903
Arthur, Beatrice	Ent	10	25	25	25	Maude/Golden Girls
Arthur, Chester A.	President	275	850	750	600	1830-1886
Arthur, Duke/Connought	Political	10		25		Prime Minister
Arthur, Ellen Lewis	First Lady	600		1,200		
Arthur, George K.	Ent	5			10	
Arthur, Jean	Ent	100	150	200	200	1905 - 1991
Arthur, Julia	Ent	15			25	
Artot, Desiree	Music	35			75	Opera
Asboth, Alexander S.	Civil War	75		150		Union General/1811-68
Ash, Roy L.	Business	10	25		35	
Ashby, Hal	Ent	10			20	
Ashby, Turner 1828-62	Civil War	350		900		CSA General
Ashcroft, Dame Peggy	Ent	25			60	
Ashe, Arthur	Sports	50			100	Deceased Tennis star
Ashe, John	RevWar	100	200	300		General
Ashford and Simpson	Music	20			45	Singing Duo
Ashley, Alfred 1835-1913	Author	25			50	British Poet Laureatte
Ashley, Elizabeth	Ent	10	20		25	
Asimov, Isaac 1920-92	Author	35	75	150	75	Sci-Fi Author
Asner, Ed	Ent	10	20	25	25	Mary Tyler Moore
Asquith, Herbert H.	Political	35	75		125	Prime Minister
Assante, Armand	Ent	20			45	
Astaire and Rogers	Ent	175			350	Signed by Both
Astaire, Adele	Ent	45			100	Fred's Dancing Sister
Astaire, Fred 1899-1987	Ent	75	200	200	200	
Asther, Nils	Ent	35	75	75	100	
Astin, John	Ent	10	25	25	25	Addam's Family TV/Gomez
Astin, Sean	Ent	20			35	
Astley, Rick	Music	15			35	
Aston, Francis W.	Science	50		150		Nobel Chemistry 1922
Astor, John Jacob	Business	500	2,000	3,500		Fur Trader/1763-1848
Astor, John Jacob Jr.	Business	200	500	750		Union General/1822-90

Name	Field	SIG	DS	ALS	SP	Remarks
Astor, John Jacob Mrs.	Business	35		75		
Astor, Mary	Ent	45			125	AA Winner
Astor, John Jacob III	Business	200	500	700		Grandson of Founder
Astor, John Jacob IV	Business	400	900	1,500		Died on the Titanic
Astor, Waldorf 1879-1952	Political	15		50	45	British M.P.
Astor, William						
Backhouse 1792-1875	Business	250	800	1,200		Son of John Jacob
Astor, William Waldorf	Business	100		300		Financier
Asturias, Miquel Angel	Author	75		200		Nobel Literature
Atchison, David Rice	President	400	750	900		President for One Day
Ates, Roscoe	Ent	40			75	
Atherton, Gertrude	Author	35		125	75	Am. Novelist
Atkins, Chet	Music	10			20	Country
Atkins, Christopher	Ent	10	25	25	25	Blue Lagoon
Atlas, Charles	Business	20		50	45	Mail Order Muscles
Atlee, Clement 1883-1967	Political	75	150			Br. Prime Minister
Attenborough, Richard	Ent	25	45		50	AA Winner
Atterbury, William W.	Military	25		50		General WWI/1866-35
Attlee, Clement	Political	35	100		75	Prime Minister
Atwill, Lionel	Ent	100	250		225	1885 - 1946
Auber, Daniel Francois	Music	100		150		Father of Fr. Opera
Auberjonois, Rene	Ent	10	25		20	Star Trek/Benson
Aubry, Cecile	Ent	15			25	French actress
Auchincloss, Louis	Author	15	35	50	30	American novelist
Auchinleck, Claude J.E.	Military	50			100	Br Fld Mar. WWII
Auckland, Baron	Political	50		100		Gov-Gen India
Auden, Wystan Hugh	Author	200		500	550	Pulitzer
Audran, Edmond	Music	50		150		Fr. Operettas
Audran, Marius	Music	35		75		Opera
Audubon, John J.	Science	750		2,500		Ornithologist/1785-1851
Auel, Jean M.	Author	10		30	30	Clan of the Cave Bear
Auer, Leopold	Music	25			45	Violinist
Auer, Mischa	Ent	20			50	1905 - 1967
Auger, Christopher C.	Civil War	50		150		Union General/1821-98
Auger, Claudine	Ent	20			50	James Bond babe
Augereau, P.F.C. de	Military	150	300	450		Marshal of Napoleon
Augusta, Queen/Prussia	Royalty	100	150			Empress of Germany
Augustus I, Duke of Sax	Royalty	2,000				1526-1586
Augustus III	Royalty	150		300		King Poland
Aumont, Jean Pierre	Ent	20	25	25	75	
Aust, Abner	Aviation	10			20	Am. ACE
Austen, Jane	Author	600	1,500			Pride & Prejudice
Austin, Bobby	Music	10			20	
Austin, Moses 1761-1821	Business	500	1,500	2,000		Texas Founder
Austin, Stephen F.	Western	750	2,000	4,000		1793 - 1836/Texas
Autry, Gene 1907 - 1998	Ent	30	100	125	75	Singing Cowboy
Avalon, Frankie	Ent	15	35		35	

Name	Field	SIG	DS	ALS	SP	Remarks
Avebury, John Lubbock	Science	25		100		Paleontologist
Avedon, Richard	Art	50		125	100	Photographer
Average White Band	Ent	25			50	Entire Group
Averell, William W.	Civil War	75	150	200		Union General/1832-1900
Avery, John, Jr.	RevWar	35	75			
Avery, Tex	Cartoonist	75	150	150	150	Warner Brothers
Avery, William W.	Civil War	75	150			CSA Congress
Axelrod, Julius	Science	35		75	50	Nobel Medicine
Axtell, George	Aviation	15			35	Marine ACE
Axton, Hoyt	Music	10	20		20	Country
Aykroyd, Dan	Ent	25			50	Sat Nite Live alumni
Ayres, Agnes	Ent	75		150	125	Silent Film Star
Ayres, Lew	Ent	10	20	30	25	Dr. Kildare
Ayres, Romeyn Beck	Civil War	50	75	125		Union General/1825-88
Ayub Khan, General	Political	35		75	100	Afghan Prince

B

Name	Field	SIG	DS	ALS	SP	Remarks
B 52's	Music	35			75	Entire Group
Babbage, Charles	Science	200		500		Computer Pioneer
Babcock, Orville E.	Civil War	35	75	150		Union General/1845-84
Baby Peggy	Ent	10			25	
Bacall, Lauren	Ent	10	35		35	Mrs. Humphrey Bogart
Baccaloni, Salvatore	Music	20			50	Opera
Bach, Barbara	Ent	20	45	45	50	James Bond Girl
Bach, Catherine	Ent	20	40	45	45	Dukes of Hazzard
Bach, Johann Sebastian	Music	7,500	25,000	35,000		RARE
Bach, Richard	Author	35	75	125		Jonathan Livingston Seagull
Bacharach, Burt	Music	15	25	30	25	Composer
Back, George, Sir	Explorer	25	75	125		Arctic Navigator
Backhaus, Wilhelm	Music	50			100	Ger. Concert Pianist
Backstreet Boys	Music	75			150	Signed by entire group
Backus, Jim	Ent	35	55	75	75	Gilligans Island/Mr.Magoo
Bacon, Francis, Sir	Author	6,000	12,000	15,000		Br. Statesman
Bacon, Kevin	Ent	25	60		50	Footloose
Bacon, Lloyd	Ent	15			25	Film Director
Bacon, Peggy	Art	35	75	125		
Bad Co.	Music	50			100	Signed by Entire Band
Baddeley, Hermione	Ent	15			30	
Badeau, Adam	Civil War	35	75	150		Union General/1831-95
Baden-Powell, Robert	Military	125	250	300	450	Br Founder of Boy Scouts
Bader, Douglas, Sir	Aviation	50	125		100	British ACE
Badger, Charles J.	Military	20	40		35	US Navy Admiral
Badger, Oscar C.	Miltary	25			50	Adm. US Navy WWII
Badham, John	Ent	25			50	Director
Badler, Jane	Ent	10		25	25	
Badoglio, Pietro	Political	35			75	Suceeded Mussolini
Badu, Erykah	Music	25			50	
Baekeland, L. H. Dr.	Science	50		125		Inventor Bakelite
Baer, Arthur "Bugs"	Cartoonist	10			30	Columnist/Cartoonist
Baer, George F.	Business	10	25		30	Pres. Reading Railroad
Baer, Max, Jr.	Ent	35	75		60	Beverly Hillbillies/Jethro
Baez, Joan	Music	10	25		30	
Bahlou, Charles	Military	35	75			WWI General
Bailey, Buster	Music	35			75	Jazz
Bailey, F. Lee	Business	15	25		25	Famous Attorney (OJ)
Bailey, James Anthony	Ent	500	900	RARE	RARE	Barnum & Bailey Circus
Bailey, Joseph 1825-67	Civil War	100	200			
Bailey, Mildred C.	Military	25			75	Brig General
Bailey, Pearl	Music	25	50	75	60	1918 - 1990

Name	Field	SIG	DS	ALS	SP	Remarks
Bailey, Raymond	Ent	100			200	Beverly Hillbillies
Bailey, Theodorus	Civil War	35	75	150		Union Naval Officer
Baillie, Joanna 1762-51	Author	25	50	100		Scottish Poet
Bain, Barbara	Ent	25	50	50	50	Mission Impossible
Bain, Conrad	Ent	10	25		20	Mork and Mindy
Bainbridge, William	Military	150	300	500		Officer War 1812/1774-33
Bainter, Fay	Ent	55	100	100	100	1892 - 1968
Baio, Scott	Ent	10	25		25	Happy Days/ChaChi
Baird, Absalom	Civil War	35		75		Union General/1824-1905
Baker, Alpheus	Civil War	150	300	450		CSA General/1828-1891
Baker, Anita	Music	20			45	
Baker, Art	Ent	10			20	
Baker, Benny 1907-94	Ent	10			25	
Baker, Blanche	Ent	10			20	
Baker, Bob	Ent	50	100		100	Singing Cowboy 1930's
Baker, Bonnie Wee	Music	5			15	Big Band Vocalist
Baker, Carroll	Ent	25		50	60	
Baker, Chauncey	Military	10			15	General WW I
Baker, Diane	Ent	10			20	
Baker, Edward D.	Civil War	150	450	600		Union General/1811-61
Baker, George 1915-75	Cartoonist	50		100	150	
Baker, Janet, Dame	Music	15	25		35	Opera
Baker, Josephine	Ent	150	350	350	400	1906 - 1975
Baker, Kathy	Ent	15			30	
Baker, Kenny	Ent	15			35	R2-D2 in Star Wars
Baker, LaFayette Curry	Civil War	100	150	200		Union General/1826-68
Baker, Laurence S.	Civil War	100	150	250		CSA General/1830-97
Baker, LaVerne	Music	30			60	Jazz Vocalist
Baker, Mark	Music	15			25	Opera
Baker, Newton D.	Political	20		60	50	Wilson Sect. of War
Baker, Royal N.	Aviation	25		75	50	Air Ace Korea, WW II
Baker, Samuel, Sir	Explorer	40	90	150		Found Source of Nile River
Bakewell, William	Ent	25		60	55	GWTW
Bakst, Leon 1868-1924	Art	150		500		Russian Painter
Bakula, Scott	Ent	25	60		50	Quantum Leap
Balanchine, George	Ent	125		250	250	Ballet/1904-83
Balbo, Italo	Aviation	125		200	200	It Air Marshall
Balck, Hermann	Military	25			75	Ger. Panzer General
Baldwin, Abraham	Political	RARE	RARE	RARE	RARE	Signer Constitution
Baldwin, Alec	Ent	25	60		50	
Baldwin, Faith	Author	35		60	60	Novelist
Baldwin, Henry	SuprCt	25	50	100		
Baldwin, James	Author	100		250	200	
Baldwin, Roger Sherman	Political	35		75		
Baldwin, Stanley	Political	50	100	125	125	British P.M./1867-57
Baldwin, Stephen	Ent	20	50		50	
Baldwin, William	Ent	20	50		50	

Name	Field	SIG	DS	ALS	SP	Remarks
Baldwin, William E.	Civil War	350	600	1,000		CSA General/1827-64
Balfour, Arthur J.	Political	50	100	125	100	Br. P.M./1848-30
Balin, Ina	Ent	25			50	Black Orchid/Actress
Balk, Fairuza	Ent	25			50	
Ball, Albert	Aviation	125	200	250	250	Brit. RAF ACE WW I
Ball, Lucille	Ent	200	400	500	450	Full Signature/1910-1989
Ball, Lucille (Lucy)	Ent	80		225	175	Signed "Love, Lucy"
Ballantine, Carl	Ent	15	45		40	McHales Navy/Magician
Ballard, Kaye	Ent	15	25	25	25	
Ballard, Robert, Dr.	Science	20		50	50	Found Titanic
Balsam, Martin	Ent	20	50		50	
Balzac, Honore de	Author	600		1,500		Fr. Novelist/1799-50
Bampton, Rose	Music	20	35	50	50	Opera
Bananarama	Music	40	75		75	Signed by All Four
Bancroft, Anne	Ent	15			35	
Bancroft, George	Political	50	100	150		Polk Sect of Navy
Bancroft, George	Ent	25	40	50	75	1882-1956
Band,The	Music	60	150		125	Signed by entire group
Bandaranike, S.W.R.D	Political	15	25	50	30	Prime Minister Sri Lanka
Banderas, Antonio	Ent	25			50	
Bangles, The	Music	50			100	Signed by All Four
Bankhead, Tallulah	Ent	75	125	200	175	1903 - 1968
Banks, Billy	Ent	100			250	Jazz
Banks, Joseph, Sir	Explorer	50	100			Sailed w/Capt. Cook
Banks, Leslie	Ent	20			40	
Banks, Nathaniel P.	Civil War	75	150	250		Union General/1816-94
Banks, Tyra	Ent	25			50	Supermodel
Banky, Vilma	Ent	50	100		150	
Banner, John 1910-73	Ent	100	200		200	Hogans Heroes/Sgt.Shultz
Banning, Henry B.	Civil War	25	75			Union General
Banting, Frederick G.	Science	600	1,000	1,250	1,000	Discoverd Insulin with Best
Bara, Theda	Ent	125		200	250	
Baranski, Christine	Ent	25	50		50	Cybil
Barbarin, Paul	Music	25		50		Bandleader/Drummer
Barbeau, Adrienne	Ent	10	20		25	Maude
Barbe-Marbois, Francois de	Political	35	75	150		Louisiana Purchase
Barber, Rex T.	Aviation	20	35	50	35	Am. ACE
Barber, Samuel 1910-81	Music	40		150	75	Opera
Barber, William	Military	35			75	
Barbera, Joe	Cartoonist	40	125		100	Hanna and Barbera
Barbier, George	Ent	15			35	
Barbieri, Fedora	Music	25			75	Opera
Barbour, Dave	Music	20			40	Jazz Guitar
Barbour, Philip	SuprCt	RARE	RARE	RARE	RARE	
Bardeen, John	Science	25	50	100	35	Nobel
Bardot, Brigitte	Ent	25	60	75	60	
Bardshar, F.A.	Aviation	10	30		35	Navy Ace WWII

Name	Field	SIG	DS	ALS	SP	Remarks
Bari, Lynn	Ent	10			20	
Baring, Alexander	Business	200		500		1774-1848
Baring, Francis, Sir	Business	25		75		Dir East India Co.
Baring-Gould, Sabine	Author	35		150	75	Onward Christian Soldiers
Barishnikov, Mikhail	Ent	50	100		100	
Barker, Bob	Ent	5	15		15	The Price is Right
Barker, Clive	Author	15	30		35	Br. Horror Novelist
Barker, Lex 1919-1973	Ent	100	150	200	200	Tarzan
Barker, William George	Aviation	150	225	350	300	Canadian ACE, WW I
Barkhorn, Gerhard	Aviation	75			125	Ger. ACE, #2 Worldwide
Barkin, Ellen	Ent	20			50	
Barkley, Alban W.	Vice Pres	30	75	150	75	Truman VP/1877-56
Barkley, Charles	Sports	20			40	Basketball
Barks, Carl	Cartoonist	50			100	Disney Duck Artist
Barksdale, William	Civil War	500		1,500		CSA General. KIA1821-63
Barlow, Francis C.	Civil War	75	225	235		Union General/1834-96
Barlow, Howard	Music	25			45	
Barnabee, Henry Clay	Ent	5	15	25	15	Operatic Comedian
Barnaby, Ralph S.	Aviation	25			45	
Barnard, Christian, Dr.	Science	25		75	50	Heart Specialist
Barnard, Frederick A.P.	Political	75	150	250		Educator
Barnard, John Gross	Civil War	35	75			Union General/1815-82
Barnes, Binnie	Ent	10			25	
Barnes, James	Civil War	50	100	150		Union General/1801-69
Barnes, Joanna	Ent	10			20	
Barnes, Joseph K.	Civil War	150	400	500		Union Surg. Gen./1817-83
Barnes, Priscilla	Ent	10	20		25	
Barnet, Charlie	Music	15			30	Big Band Leader
Barnette, Vince	Ent	15	30		45	
Barney, Natalie 1876-72	Author	150	300	400		Am. Poet
Barnum, Henry A.	Civil War	50	100	150		Union General/1833-92
Barnum, Phineas T.	Business	200	600	500	900	1810-1891
Baronova, Irina	Ent	35		125	100	Rus.-Br. Ballerina
Barr, Candy	Ent	10		30	30	Famous Stripper
Barr, Doug	Ent	5			15	
Barr, Roseanne	Ent	25	75	125	50	Roseanne
Barrett, John	Military	25		50		WWI Victoria Cross
Barrett, Lawrence	Civil War	25			50	Union Officer/1838-91
Barrett, Majel	Ent	10	30	30	25	Star Trek/Roddenberry's Wife
Barrett, Rona	Ent	5			15	Gossip
Barrett, Wilson 1846-1904	Ent	25		75	60	Br Playwright
Barrie, Barbara	Ent	5	20		15	
Barrie, James M, Sir	Author	100	250	250	400	Peter Pan/1860-1937
Barrie, Wendy	Ent	15	25	30	45	1912 - 1978
Barringer, Rufus	Civil War	150	300	400		CSA General/1821-95
Barron, Clarence	Business	25			50	Editor/Publisher Barron's
Barrow, John, Sir	Political	75	200	300		Explorer/Author/1764-1848

Name	Field	SIG	DS	ALS	SP	Remarks
Barrow, Clyde 1909-34	Criminal	2,500	7,500	10,000	RARE	ALS often signed w/pen names
Barry, Charles, Sir	Science	25	50	100		1795-1860
Barry, Dan	Cartoonist	15			35	Flash Gordon
Barry, Dave	Author	10			20	Creator Dave's World
Barry, Don 'Red'	Ent	25			60	
Barry, Gene	Ent	10			25	TV's Bat Masterson
Barry, John	RevWar	1,000	2,000			Ir. Born US Naval Officer
Barry, John Decatur	Civil War	150		450		CSA General/1839-67
Barry, Thomas	Military	50		150		General WW I
Barry, Jack	Ent	10			20	
Barry, Wm. Farquhar	Civil War	75	150	200		Union General/1818-79
Barrymore, Diana	Ent	30		75	75	1921 - 1960
Barrymore, Drew	Ent	25	75		50	
Barrymore, Ethel	Ent	100	150		200	1898 - 1959
Barrymore, John	Ent	150	250	300	450	1882-1942
Barrymore, Lionel	Ent	75	150		150	1978-1954
Bartel, Jean	Ent	5			15	Miss America/1943
Barth, John	Author	30	50	75	50	Am. Novelist
Barthelmess, Richard	Ent	25	50	75	75	
Bartholdi, Fred, Auguste	Art	350	750	500	800	Statue of Liberty/1834-04
Bartholomew, Freddie	Ent	25	50	60	75	Child Star/1924 - 1992
Bartlett, Joseph Jackson	Civil War	50	100			Union General/1834-93
Bartlett, Josiah 1729-95	RevWar	250	500	750		
Bartlett, Paul Wayland	Art	15		35		Sculptor
Bartlett, Robert Abram	Explorer	50	150	125		
Bartlett, William F.	Civil War	50	100	150		Union General/1840-76
Bartok, Bela 1881-1945	Music	300	500			Pianist/Composer
Bartok, Eva	Ent	5			15	Actress
Barton, Clara 1821-1912	Political	175	450	550	800	Founder Am. Red Cross
Barton, Derek H.R, Sir	Science	20	30	40	40	Nobel Chemistry
Barton, Seth Maxwell	Civil War	100		300		CSA General
Bartow, Francis Stebbins 1816-61	Civil War	100		250		CSA Congress/1816-61
Barty, Billy	Ent	25	50		50	Midget Actor
Baruch, Bernard M.	Business	100	300	400	250	Financier/1870-1965
Baryshnikov, Mikail	Ent	75		150	200	Ballet
Basehart, Richard	Ent	25	50		50	Voyage to Btm of the Sea
Basie, Wm, 'Count'	Music	100	200		200	Big Band Leader
Basil, Toni	Music	15			25	Mickey
Basinger, Kim	Ent	25	60		50	
Baskett, James	Ent	250			600	Song of the South
Basov, Nickolay	Science	20	45		40	Rus. Nobel Physicist
Bassett, Angela	Ent	25	50		50	
Bassett, Charles A.	Space	40			75	Astronaut
Bassett, Leslie	Music	20	40	50		Pulitzer
Bassett, Richard	RevWar	350	700			SignerConstitution
Bassi, Amedeo	Music	50			125	Tenor

Name	Field	SIG	DS	ALS	SP	Remarks
Bate, William Brimage	Civil War	75	125	175		CSA General/1826-05
Bateman, Jason	Ent	15	30		30	
Bateman, Justine	Ent	20	30		40	Family Ties
Bates, Alan	Ent	10			20	British Actor
Bates, Edward	Political	50	150	225	350	Lincoln Att'y Gen.
Bates, John C.	Civil War	35		100		Union General
Bates, Katharine Lee	Author	100		300		
Bates, Kathy	Ent	25	50		50	AA Winner
Bathori, Jane 1876-1970	Music	75			125	Opera
Batista, Fulgencio	Political	125	275	350	175	Cuban Dictator-Pre Castro
Batiuk, Tom	Cartoonist	5			20	Funky Winkerbean
Battaglia, Franco	Music	25			50	Opera
Battaille, Charles 1822-72	Music	25		50		Opera
Batten, Hugh	Aviation	10	25		30	Navy Ace WWII
Batten, Jean	Aviation	50	75			Pioneer Aviatrix
Battle, Cullen Andrews	Civil War	200	400			CSA General/1829-1905
Battu, Marie 1838-88	Music	25		75		Opera
Batz, Willhelm	Aviation	35			100	Ger. ACE, #7 Worldwide
Baudelaire, Charles-P.	Author	300	900	1,500		Poet/1821-67
Baudouin, King	Royalty	50	100	200	125	King of Belgium
Bauduc, Ray	Music	10			25	Big Band
Bauer, Harold	Music	50	100			Pianist
Bauer, Steven	Ent	10			20	
Baum, L. Frank	Author	1,750	3,000	5,000	RARE	The Wizard of Oz books
Baum, Maud	Author	200	450	750		Wife of Frank L. Baum (Oz)
Baumer, Steven	Ent	10			25	
Baur, Hans	Aviation	25	75	100	100	Hitler's Pilot
Baur, Harry	Ent	50			150	
Bavier, Frances	Ent	100	200		200	Aunt Bee/Andy Griffith
Baxter, Anne	Ent	20		50	50	AA Winner
Baxter, Henry	Civil War	50	100	150		Union General/1821-1873
Baxter, Les	Music	25			50	Composer
Baxter, Warner	Ent	75	125		175	1889 - 1951
Baxter-Birney, Meredith	Ent	10			20	
Bayard, George Dashiell	Civil War	150		450		Union General
Bayard, John	RevWar	75		200		Continental Congress
Bayard, William	RevWar	100	200	400		
Bayne, Beverly	Ent	10			20	
Beach Boys	Music	200	400		400	Orig five members
Beach, Amy M.	Music	100		300	250	Composer
Beach, Rex	Author	25	50	75	75	Am. Novelist
Beacham, Stephanie	Ent	5			10	
Beadle, George Wells	Science	20	30	50	40	Nobel Medicine
Beal, George Lafayette	Civil War	50	100		250	Union General/1825-96
Beal, John	Ent	15		25	25	
Beale, Richard Lee	Civil War	75	100	200		1819-93. CSA General
Beall, William N.	Civil War	175	300	600		CSA General/1825-83

Name	Field	SIG	DS	ALS	SP	Remarks
Beals, Jennifer	Ent	25			50	Flashdance
Bean, Alan L.	Space	50	150		100	Moonwalker
Bean, L.L. 1872-1967	Business	200	300			Scarce
Bean, Roy, Judge	Western	2,000	5,000	7,500		Western Law
Beard, "Stymie"	Ent	125	200		250	Our Gang
Beard, Charles A.	Author	15	30	50		Am. Historian/1874-1948
Beard, Daniel C. 1850-41	Author	125	300	200	200	Fndr Boy Scouts/America
Beardslee, Lester A.	Military	35		100		Adm. Span -Am War
Beardsley, Aubrey	Art	175	350	450		Br Illustrator
Bearse, Amanda	Ent	15			35	
Beastie Boys	Music	35			75	Signed by entire band
Beatles, The	Music	1,800	7,500		3,500	Four on one piece
Beaton, Cecil 1904-80	Art	100	200	200	350	
Beatrice, Princess	Royalty	30	125	100	100	Daughter Q. Victoria
Beatrix, Queen	Royalty	150		450		Netherlands
Beatty, Clyde 1903-1965	Business	50	100	150	150	
Beatty, David, Adm.	Military	35	75	100	100	
Beatty, Ned	Ent	10			20	
Beatty, Samuel	Civil War	25	50	75		Union General/1820-85
Beatty, John	Civil War	25	50			Union General/1828-1914
Beatty, Warren	Ent	25	75		50	
Beauharnais, Eugene de	Royalty	100	350	450		Son of Josephine, Adopted
Beauharnais, Hortense	Royalty	75				Wife of Louis Bonaparte
Beaumont, Hugh	Ent	400	600		600	Leave it to Beaver/Dad
Beauregard, P.G.T.	Civil War	350	750	900	1,000	CSA General/1818-93
Beauvoir, Simone de	Author	25	50	100		Fr. Novelist. Existentialist
Beaux, Cecilia 1855-1942	Art	75				Am. Portrait Painter
Beaver, James A.	Civil War	35	75	100		Union General/1837-1914
Beavers, Louise	Ent	100			250	
Bechet, Sidney 1897-59	Music	125	275		175	Jazz
Bechi, Gino	Music	25			60	Opera
Beck, Dave 1894-1993	Political	25	50	50	50	
Beck, John	Ent	5			10	
Beck, C.C	Cartoonist	20			50	Capt. Marvel
Beck, Jeff	Music	25			50	Guitarist
Beckett, Samuel 1906-89	Author	150		350		Nobel
Beckett, Scotty	Ent	30			75	
Beckwith, Edward G.	Civil War	50				Union General/1818-81
Beckwith, Geo. Sir	RevWar	200	400			RevWar Br Gen/1753-23
Beckwith, J. Carroll	Art	50	75	125		
Becquerel, Edmond	Science	RARE	RARE	RARE	RARE	Fr. Physicist/1820-91
Becquerel, Henri	Science	175	400	500		Nobel Curies' Radioactivity
Bedelia, Bonnie	Ent	10			20	
Bedford, Brian	Ent	15			35	Disney Voice/Actor
Bedford, Gunning, Jr.	RevWar	350	700			Signer of Constitution
Bedford, Gunning, Sr.	RevWar	175	350			Cousin of Above
Bee Gees	Music	100	200		200	Signed by Three

Name	Field	SIG	DS	ALS	SP	Remarks
Bee, Barnard E.	Civil War	300	700	1,500		CSA General/1824-61
Bee, Hamilton P.	Civil War	100		300		CSA General/1822-97
Beebe, Charles William	Explorer	25	75	100	75	1877-1962
Beebe, Marshall	Aviation	25		50	50	WWII ACE
Beech, Olive Ann	Aviation	25			50	Beechcraft Airplane Mfg.
Beecher, Henry Ward	Clergy	100		200		
Beems, Patricia	Ent	5			10	
Beene, Geoffrey	Business	20		30	40	Fashion Designer
Beerbohm, Max	Author	40		125	75	Humorist, Caricaturist
Beery, Noah 1884-1946	Ent	75			175	Scarce
Beery, Noah Jr.	Ent	20	30	45	40	
Beery, Wallace	Ent	100	150	200	200	AA Winner/1885-1949
Beeson, Jack	Music	15	35	50	30	Composer
Beethoven, Ludwig van	Music	RARE	27,500	50,000	RARE	Composer
Begin, Menachem	Political	75		200	150	Prime Minister Israel
Begley, Ed, Jr.	Ent	5			15	
Begley, Ed, Sr.	Ent	25	50		75	
Behan, Brendan F.	Author	150	400	550		Playwright/Author
Behrman, S. N.	Author	15	25	50	25	Am. Playwright
Beichel, Rudolph	Science	25			50	Rocket Pioneer/von Braun
Beiderbecke, Bix	Music	RARE	RARE	RARE	RARE	Jazz Musician
Beinhorn, Elly	Aviation	15		45	40	Ger. Aviation Pioneer
Beith, Ian Hay	Author	10	30	30	20	Br. Novelist/Playwright
Beke, Charles Tilstone	Explorer	25	50	100		Nile Geographer
Bekins, Milo	Business	35		100	75	Bekins Van & Storage Co.
Bel Geddes, Barbara	Ent	20			35	
Bel Geddes, Norman	Art	20		75	35	Scenic Designer Theater
Belafonte, Harry	Music	20	45		40	
Belafonte, Shari	Music	10		25	20	
Belasco, David	Ent	35	50	60	75	Theatrical Producer
Belcher, Edward, Sir	Military	15	35	45		
Belcher, Jonathan	Political	225	325	550		Colonial Gov. MA, NH, NJ
Belimer, Hans 1902-75	Art	75	150			Ger. Surrealist
Belknap, George	Civil War	25		50		Union Naval Officer
Belknap, William W.	Civil War	75		150		Union General, Sec'y War
Bell, Alexander Graham	Science	500	1,200	2,000	2,500	Telephone/1847-1922
Bell, Charles H.	Civil War	50	100	150		Union Naval Captain
Bell, Eric Temple	Author	30			50	
Bell, Henry H. 1808-1868	Civil War	75	150			Rear Adm under Farragut
Bell, Herbert A.	Business	15	25	75	50	
Bell, John	Political	100	150			Harrison/Tyler Sect. War
Bell, Lauralee	Ent	5			15	
Bell, Rex	Ent	50			100	
Bell, Tyree Harris	Civil War	75	125	200		CSA General/1815-1902
Bellamy, Edward	Author	25	75	150		Novelist
Bellamy, Madge	Ent	15	25	35	35	
Bellamy, Ralph 1904-91	Ent	20	30	45	40	

Name	Field	SIG	DS	ALS	SP	Remarks
Bellanca, Giuseppe M.	Aviation	50	75	150	125	Bellanca Aircraft
Bellaver, Henry	Ent	10			20	
Belleri, Marguerite	Music	10		30	25	Opera
Belliard, A.D. (Count)	Military	25	50	150		Fr. Gen under Napoleon
Bellincioni, Gemma	Ent	35		125	100	It. Soprano
Belloc, Hilaire 1870-1953	Author	25	50	150	50	Versatile Novelist, Poet
Belloc-Lowndes, Marie	Author	15	45	100	30	Br.Author/Historical Works
Bellon, Leoncadia	Music	15			45	Opera
Bellonte, Maurice	Aviation	100	150	225	300	
Bellow, Saul	Author	20	75	75	50	Nobel/Novelist
Bellows, George	Art	100	200	300		
Bellson, Louis	Music	25		50	75	Jazz Drummer
Belmondo, Jean Paul	Ent	25			50	
Belmont, August	Business	200	750	900	400	Banker/Belmont Park
Belmont, August, Jr.	Business	50	125			
Belushi, James	Ent	10	30		35	
Belushi, John	Ent	200	500		450	Sat Nite Live/Blues Bros.
Belzer, Richard	Ent	15			35	
Bemelmans, Ludwig	Author	50	100		100	
Benacerraf, Barui	Science	30	50		50	Nobel Medicine-Physiology
Benatar, Pat	Music	20	50		50	
Benben, Brian	Ent	15			30	
Benchley, Peter	Author	20	45	50	50	Jaws
Benchley, Robert	Author	25	75	125	75	
Bendix, William 1906-64	Ent	60	125		175	
Benederet, Bea	Ent	90	200		200	Petticoat Junction
Benedict XV Pope	Clergy	175		350	450	
Benedict, Dirk	Ent	10	30		30	Battlestar Gallactica
Benedict, Julius, Sir	Music	15			25	Br. Pianist
Benedict, William	Ent	25			60	
Beneke, Tex	Music	30			50	Big Band/Sax for Miller
Benes, Eduard	Political	75	100	150	200	PM. & President Czech.
Benet, Stephen Vincent	Author	100	150	175	150	Pulitzer
Ben-Gurion, David	Political	300	900	900	600	1st Prime Minister of Israel
Benham, Henry W.	Civil War	50	125	150		Union General
Bening, Annette	Ent	25	75		50	
Benjamin, Judah P.	Civil War	300	800	900		CSA General/1811-84
Benjamin, William, Jr.	SuprCt	40			60	
Bennett, Arnold	Author	50	150			Br. Novelist
Bennett, Bruce	Ent	15	30		30	Tarzan
Bennett, Constance	Ent	30	60	100	65	
Bennett, Floyd	Aviation	300	350	750	500	Byrd/North Pole
Bennett, James Gordon	Business	50	150			Financed Stanley-Livingstone
Bennett, Joan 1910-90	Ent	20	40	50	50	Dark Shadows
Bennett, Richard	Ent	15			35	Stage & Silent Films
Bennett, Robert Russell	Music	50			100	Great Broadway Composer
Bennett, Samuel F.	Music	50	100	150		In the Sweet Bye & Bye

Name	Field	SIG	DS	ALS	SP	Remarks
Bennett, Tony	Ent	10			25	
Benning, Henry Lewis	Civil War	150	250	300		CSA General/1814-75
Benny, Jack 1894-1974	Ent	80	175		200	
Benois, Alexander	Art	50	150			Costume & Set Designer
Benson, Edward F.	Author	15	35	60		
Benson, Egbert	RevWar	35	75	125		Continental Congress
Benson, Frank Robert	Ent	15	20	30	20	British Actor
Benson, George	Music	15			25	
Benson, Jodi	Ent	15			35	Disney Voice/Ariel
Benson, Robby	Ent	15			35	Actor/Disney Voice
Benson, William S.	Military	10	20	30	25	Adm. USN WW I
Benteen, Frederick W.	Civil War		3,500		2,500	Scarce
Benton, Barbi	Ent	5		20	15	
Benton, Robert	Ent	10			20	AA Winning Director
Benton, Samuel	Civil War	300	500			CSA General/1820-64
Benton, Thomas H.	Art	100	250	450		
Benton, Thomas H.	Political	100		200		Senator
Benton, William P.	Civil War	75	125			Union General/1828-67
Benzell, Mimi	Music	15			35	Opera
Ben-Zvi, Itzhak 1884-1963	Political	75	200	250	150	2nd President Israel
Berenger, Tom	Ent	20			45	
Berenson, Marisa	Ent	10			25	
Berenstain, Stan	Cartoonist	20			50	Bearenstein Bears
Beresford, Charles,						
Lord 1846-1919	Military	25	35	100	75	British Admiral
Berg, Alban	Music	150	300			Composer
Berg, Gertrude	Ent	15			35	
Berg, Paul	Science	25		75	50	Nobel Chemistry
Berganza, Teresa	Music	15			35	Opera
Bergen, Candace	Ent	20	50		50	Murphy Brown
Bergen, Edgar 1903-78	Ent	50	100		150	Ventriloquist
Bergen, Frances	Ent	5			15	
Bergen, Polly	Ent	10			20	
Berger, Erna	Music	10			30	Opera
Berger, Gottlob	Military	50	100	200	75	
Berger, Senta	Ent	10		35	30	
Bergere, Lee	Ent	10			20	
Bergman, Ingmar	Ent	50	100		150	
Bergman, Ingrid 1915-82	Ent	125	200	250	300	AA Winner/Casablanca
Bergner, Elizabeth	Ent	15	35	50	35	1898-1968
Bergonzi, Carlo	Music	35			65	Opera
Bergson, Henri 1859-1941	Author	50	125			Nobel/Literature
Berio, Luciano	Music	25	45	75		Composer
Berjerac, Jacques	Ent	20		60	40	French Actor
Berkeley, Busby 1895-76	Ent	100	200	250	300	Choreagrapher/Director
Berkley, Elizabeth	Ent	20			50	Showgirls
Berkowitz, David	Criminal	75		200		Son of Sam - Killer

Name	Field	SIG	DS	ALS	SP	Remarks
Berle, Milton	Ent	15	30	35	35	Mr. Television
Berlier, Jean Baptiste	Science	15	30	45		French Engineer
Berlier, Theophile	Military	50	150	200		
Berlik, Jan	Music	25			50	Opera Tenor
Berlin, Irving 1888-1990	Music	150	550		800	Composer
Berlinger, Warren	Ent	10			20	
Berlioz, Hector 1803-69	Music	250	750	1,000		Composer
Berlitz, Charles	Business	15			35	
Berman, Eugene	Art	50	100	200		
Berman, Pandro S.	Ent	50			100	Producer
Berman, Shelley	Ent	10			20	
Bernadotte, Jean-Baptiste	Royalty	150	450	550		Marshal of Napolean
Bernard, Claude 1813-78	Science	150		600		
Bernard, Crystal	Ent	20			45	Wings
Bernard, Francis,1712-79	Political	175	400	650		Gov of Mass Bay Colony
Bernard, Simon	Civil War	50	100			Engineer
Bernardi, Herschel	Ent	25			50	
Berndt, Walter	Cartoonist	15			35	Smitty
Bernhard, Sandra	Ent	5			15	Comedian
Bernhardt, Sarah d.1923	Ent	150	300	400	600	Early Stage star
Bernie, Ben	Music	20		35	50	Big Band Leader
Bernsen, Corbin	Ent	15			45	
Bernstein, Elmer	Music	25			50	Composer
Bernstein, Leonard	Music	150	450	600	250	Composer
Berosini, Josephine	Ent	10			30	
Berringer, Tom	Ent	20			50	
Berry, Chuck	Music	35			75	
Berry, Halle	Ent	25	50		50	
Berry, Hiram G. 1824-63	Civil War	400	600			Union General/KIA
Berry, Ken	Ent	5	20	20	20	Mama's Family
Berry, Lucien	Military	20	50			General WW I
Berryman, Clifford	Art	50	75	100		Created the "Teddy" bear
Bertelson, Richard L.	Aviation	15		35	30	WWII Navy ACE
Berthier, L. Alexandre	Military	100	200	300		Marshal of Napoleon
Berthold, Rudolf	Aviation	200	350	500	450	WWI Ace
Berthollet, Claude-Louis	Science	75	150	200		French Chemist
Bertinelli, Valerie	Ent	5	30		25	
Bertolucci, Bernardo	Ent	15			35	Director
Berwick, Duke	Military	150	350			Gen. of Louis XIV
Berzelius, Jons Jacob	Science	100	200	400		Chemist
Besant, Walter 1836-1901	Author	50	125	175		
Beser, Jacob	Aviation	50	100		100	Enola Gay member
Bess, Gordon	Cartoonist	10			20	Redeye
Bessemer, Henry	Science	35	75	150	100	Invented Blast Furnace
Besser, Joe	Ent	50	100		100	Three Stooges
Bessieres, Jean-Baptiste	Military	175	350			Marshal of Napoleon
Best, Charles H.	Science	50	150	200	125	Co-"Discoverer of Insulin

Name	Field	SIG	DS	ALS	SP	Remarks
Best, Edna	Ent	15		30	45	
Best, James	Ent	5			15	
Best, Pete	Music	25			60	Pre-Ringo Beatle's Drummer
Best, Willie	Ent	50			150	
Bestor, Don	Music	20				Jack Benny Bandleader
Bethe, Hans, Dr.	Science	35	50		75	Nobel Physics
Bethune, Mary McLeod	Political	125	250	400	200	Black Teacher, Activist.
Bettelheim, Bruno	Science	35	75		150	Psychiatrist
Bettger, Lyle	Ent	10			20	
Betz, Carl	Ent	50			75	
Beugnot, J.C., Count	Military	100	150			
Beverage, John	Civil War	45	100			Union General
Bevin, Ernest	Political	25	50	100	50	(Br.) Union Leader
Bewick, Thomas	Art	100	250	500		Illustrator/Wood Engraver
Bey, Turhan	Ent	20			40	
Bhutto, Zullikar Ali	Political	25			75	Pakistan President
Biasini, Piero	Music	15			35	Opera
Bickel, Theodore	Ent	15			35	
Bickford, Charles	Ent	35	50	75	100	
Biddle, Clement	RevWar	275	550	750		Rev Officer/Businessman
Biddle, Clement Carroll	Military	25	50	75		Col. of lst Inf. PA.
Biddle, George	Art	35	75	150		
Biddle, Nicholas	Business	150	450	600		Financier
Bidwell, Daniel D.	Civil War	250		600		Union General/1819-64
Bidwell, John	Western	25	100			California Pioneer
Biehn, Michael	Ent	15			40	
Bierce, Ambrose	Author	275	450	500		Short Stories
Bierstadt, Albert	Art	125	225	400		
Bigard, Barney	Music	75			150	Jazz Clarinet, Ten. Sax
Bigelow, Erastus B.	Business	100	200	450		Power Looms for Weaving
Bigelow, John 1817-1911	Business	5		30	15	Editor NY Evening Post
Bigelow, Poultney	Author	10		20		Journalist
Biggers, Earl Derr	Author	150		300	350	Am.Mystery Writer
Biggs, Asa	Civil War	25	75			CSA Judge
Bikel, Theodore	Ent	5			15	Actor/Singer
Bill, Tony	Ent	10			20	
Billings, Josh 1818-85	Author	25	75	150	50	American Humorist.
Billingsley, Barbara	Ent	5	20		20	Leave it to Beaver/Mom
Billo, James D.	Aviation	15		35	30	Navy ACE, WWII
Billroth, Theodor 1829-94	Science	75	200	250		Surgeon/Use of Antisepsis
Binci, Mario	Music	15			45	Opera
Bing, Herman	Ent	30			60	Disney Voice
Bing, Rudolph	Music	15	25	35	35	Metropolitan Opera Leader
Bingham, Henry	Civil War	100		150		Union General
Bingham, John A.	Political	25	45	100		Lincoln Judge Adv.
Bingham, Judson David	Civil War	50	150	200		Union General/1831-1909
Bingham, William	RevWar	125	250	300		Continental Congress

Name	Field	SIG	DS	ALS	SP	Remarks
Binnig, Gerd, Dr.	Science	25	75		50	Nobel Physics
Binoche, Juliette	Ent	25			50	
Birch, Thora	Ent	25			50	
Birds, The	Music	150	250		300	Signed by Entire Group
Birdseye, Clarence	Business	250	400	500	350	Birdseye Frozen Foods
Birdwood, William, Sir	Military	50	150			Br. Fid. Marshal, WW I
Birendra, Bir B.	Political	10			20	Prime Minister Nepal
Birney, David	Ent	10			20	
Birney, David Bell	Civil War	200	300	600		Union General/1825-64
Birney, William	Civil War	50	100	100		Union General
Bisbee, Horatio, Jr.	Civil War	25	50	100		Union Officer
Bishop, Elizabeth 1911-79	Author	45	125			Am. Poet/Pulitzer Prize '55
Bishop, J. Michael. Dr.	Science	25	50		50	Nobel Medicine
Bishop, Joey	Ent	10	20	20	20	Rat Pack member
Bishop, Julie	Ent	5			15	
Bishop, Stephen	Music	15			35	
Bishop, Wm. 'Billy'	Aviation	150	250	300	250	ACE, WWI w/72 Kills
Bismark, Prince Otto von	Royalty	250	600	700	800	The Iron Chancellor
Bispham, David	Music	50	100	100	100	Opera
Bissell, Clayton L.	Aviation	25	50	100		
Bissell, Whit	Ent	10			20	
Bisset, Jacqueline	Ent	10			20	The Deep...
Bissett, Josie	Ent	15			45	Melrose Place
Bissit, J.E.	Military	10		25	15	Comdr. HMS Queen Eliz.
Bitter, Karl Theodore	Art	35	75	125	100	Am. Sculptor
Bittrich, Wilhelm	Military	30	75	125	75	
Bixby, Bill	Ent	40	75		75	Incredible Hulk...
Bizet, Georges 1838-75	Music	350		900		Composer
Bjoerling, Jussi 1911-69	Ent	500	650	900	900	
Bjork	Music	25			50	
Bjornson, Bjornstjerne	Author	50	75	150		Nobel/Literature
Bjornstad, Alfred	Military	15	25	35		General WWI
Black Crowes	Music	75			125	Signed by Entire Group
Black Sabbath	Music	50			100	Signed by Entire Group
Black, Clint	Music	25	50		50	
Black, Hugo 1886-1966	SuprCt	50	125	200	100	
Black, Jeremiah	Political	25	50	100		Att'y General (Buchanan)
Black, John Charles	Civil War	50	125	150		Union General/18399-1915
Black, Karen	Ent	5			15	TV's Room 222
Black, Richard B.	Military	10	25	40		
Black, William	Military	25			50	General WWI
Blackburn, John T.	Aviation	15		45	30	WWII ACE
Blackett, Patrick M.	Science	20	45	50	40	Nobel Physics
Blackman, Honor	Ent	10	25		25	James Bond Girl
Blackmer, Sidney	Ent	25	50	50	50	1895 - 1973
Blackmore, Richard D.	Author	25	50	100		Br. Novelist. Lorna Doone
Blackmun, Harry A.	SuprCt	50	150	200	100	

Name	Field	SIG	DS	ALS	SP	Remarks
Blackstone, Harry	Ent	150		450	350	Magician
Blackstone, Harry, Jr.	Ent	45			100	Magician
Blackwell, Mr.	Business	5			15	Fashion Critic
Blackwell, Otis	Music	35	75	125		Composer
Blaine, James G. 1830-93	Political	35	75	100	60	Sen.&Garfield's Sec'y St.
Blaine, Vivian	Ent	10		25	25	
Blair, Charles	Aviation	45			75	
Blair, Francis P. Jr.	Civil War	50	100	150		Union General/1825-1875
Blair, Janet	Ent	15			30	
Blair, John	SuprCt	250	600	900		Signer of Constitution
Blair, Linda	Ent	10	25	25	25	The Excorsist
Blair, Montgomery	Political	100	200	400		Counsel to Dred Scott
Blair, Selma	Ent	25			50	
Blake, Amanda	Ent	50	75	125	100	Gunsmoke's Miss Kitty
Blake, Bud	Cartoonist	5			20	Tiger
Blake, Eubie 1883-1983	Music	50		125	100	Composer
Blake, Madge	Ent	200	RARE	RARE	450	TV Batman's Aunt Harriet
Blake, Robert	Ent	15	30		30	Baretta
Blake, Whitney	Ent	15			35	
Blakely, Susan	Ent	10			20	
Blakeslee, Don	Aviation	10	25	35	30	WWII ACE
Blanc, Mel 1908-89	Ent	75	175	200	250	Man of 1,000 Voices
Blanchard, Albert G.	Civil War	100	250			CSA General/1810-91
Blanchard, Nina	Ent	5			15	
Blandick, Clara	Ent	750	1,500	RARE	1,800	Autnie Em/Oz
Blane, Ralph	Music	10			30	Composer
Blane, Sally	Ent	5			15	
Blasco-Ibanez, Vicente	Author	150			450	Sp. Novelist. Self Exiled
Blasiev, Lisabeth	Music	10			25	Opera
Blass, Bill	Business	10			25	Fashion Designer
Blatchford, Samuel	SuprCt	50	125	150		1820 - 1893
Blatty, William Peter	Author	20	50		50	The Exorcist
Bledsoe, Tempest	Ent	15			45	The Cosby Show
Bleeth, Yasmine	Ent	15			45	Baywatch
Blenker, Louis	Civil War	100	200			Union General/1812-63
Blennerhassett, Harman	RevWar	125	250	450		Burr Conspiracy
Bleriot, Louis 1872-1936	Aviation	300	500	600	600	Ist To Fly English Channel
Bless, Frederick	Aviation	15		35	35	Korean ACE
Bligh, William, Capt.	Military	1,500	3,500	7,500		Br. Adm/Capt. HMS Bounty
Bliss, Arthur, Sir	Music	45		150		Br. Opera
Bliss, George Jr.	Civil War	10		25		
Bliss, Tasker H.	Military	15	25	45	25	US Gen.Cmdr. War College
Bliss, William Wallace S.	Military	150	300	450		Pvt. Sec'y Zachary Taylor
Bliss, Zenas R.	Civil War	35	100	150		Union Officer
Blitzstein, Marc	Music	75	150	225		Opera/Composer
Blixen, Karen (Isak Dinesen)	Author	100		200	200	Out of Africa
Bloch, Ernest 1880-1959	Music	100		300	250	Composer, Teacher

Name	Field	SIG	DS	ALS	SP	Remarks
Bloch, Felix	Science	25	50	100	50	Nobel Physics
Bloch, Konrad, Dr.	Science	20	30	45	30	Nobel Medicine
Bloch, Raymond	Music	10	20	35	20	Composer
Bloch, Robert	Author	25	50	75	50	
Block, Henry W.	Business	20	45		35	H & R Block
Block, Richard	Business	20	35	75	35	H & R Block
Blocker, Dan	Ent	200	300		400	Bonanza's "Hoss"
Blodget, Samuel Jr.	RevWar	350	750	1,200		Inventor/Judge
Bloembergen, Nicolaas	Science	20	35	40	35	Nobel Physics
Blomberg, Werner Von	Military	45	75	150	125	Ger. Fld. Marshal WWII
Blondell, Gloria	Ent	10			25	
Blondell, Joan	Ent	35	50	75	50	
Blood, Sweat and Tears	Music	50	100		100	Signed by Entire Band
Bloom, Claire	Ent	10			25	
Bloomer, Amelia	Political	250	350			Social Reformer
Bloomfield, Joseph	RevWar	45	100	150		
Bloomfield-Zeisler, F.	Music	25			75	Concert Pianist
Blossom Rock	Ent	100	150		200	Addam's Family Grandma
Blount, James H.	Civil War	25	50			CSA Officer
Blount, William	Political	300	650			Continental Congress
Blucher, Gebhard L. von	Military	200	450	Scarce		Pruss/Fld.Marshal vs Napoleon
Blue, Ben 1901-75	Ent	25	40	75	50	
Blue, Monte 1880-1963	Ent	25		50	75	Silent Star
Blues Traveller	Music	50			100	Signed by Entire Group
Blum, Leon	Political	25	45	100	45	Pres. France during WWII
Blum, Norbert	Political	5			10	Ger. Minister/Statesman
Blumberg, Baruch S.	Science	20	35	50	25	Nobel Medicine
Blumenfeld, Felix	Music		150		300	Russ. Conductor
Blumenthal, Jacques	Music	50		150		Composer/Pianist
Blunt, Asa P.	Military	25		200		General
Blunt, James G. Dr.	Civil War	50	75			Union General/1826-81
Blyden, Larry	Ent	15			35	Whats My Line?
Blyth, Ann	Ent	10			20	
Blythe, Betty	Ent	45		75	150	Silent Star
Blyton, Enid	Author	200		500		
Boardman, Eleanor	Ent	10		25	25	
Boardman, Russell	Aviation	25	50	100	100	
Bob & Ray	Ent	25			50	Comedy Team
Bochco, Steven	Ent	15			35	TV Producer
Bock, Feodor von	Military	100	250		200	Ger.Gen. WWII
Bock, Jerry	Music	30		50	75	
Bodenschatz, Karl	Aviation	45	75	125	100	
Bogart, Humphrey	Ent	800	1,400	2,200	2,500	1899 - 1957
Bogdonavich, Peter	Ent	15	35		35	Director
Boggs, Charles	Civil War	50	100	100		Union Admiral
Boggs, William R.	Civil War	100	200	300		CSA General/1829-1911
Bohm, Karl	Music	35		75	100	Conductor

Name	Field	SIG	DS	ALS	SP	Remarks
Bohr, Aage Niels 1922-	Science	25			50	Nobel Physics 1975
Bohr, Niels H.D. 1885-62	Science	250	500			Danish Physicist/Nobel '22
Boito, Arrigo	Music	50	100	225		Composer
Bok, Edward W.	Author	30	75	125	50	Pulitzer
Bokor, Margit	Music	15			30	Hungarian Soprano
Boland, Mary	Ent	30	75		75	1880 - 1965
Bolcom, William	Music	15	25	45		Composer/Pulitzer
Boles, John	Ent	30	45	45	50	1895 - 1969
Bolet, Jorge	Music	35			125	Pianist
Bolger, Ray 1904-87	Ent	65	200	275	225	Scarecrow in Wiz of Oz
Bolingbroke, Henry	Author	50	150	200		1st Viscount
Bolivar, Simon	Political	900	2,500	4,000		Statesman/RevWar Leader
Boll, Heinrich	Author	35		100	50	Nobel Lit./Novelist/ Poet
Bologna, Joseph	Ent	15			30	
Bolt, John	Aviation	15	30	50	50	ACE, WWII & Korea
Bolton, Guy	Author	25	75			Playwright
Bolton, James	Science	25	75		50	Sewing Machine
Bolton, Michael	Music	25			50	
Bolton-Jones, Hugh	Art	15	45	45		Am. Landscape Painter
Bombeck, Erma	Author	25		50	50	Humorist
Bomford, George	Military	100	200			Howitzer Gun
Bon Jovi, Jon	Music	25	100		50	
Bonaduce, Danny	Ent	10			25	Partridge Family
Bonaparte, Elise	Royalty	250		500		Oldest Sister of Napoeon
Bonaparte, Eugene Nap.	Royalty	100	200	300		Adopted by Napoleon
Bonaparte, Jerome	Royalty	75	150	225		Brother of Napoleon
Bonaparte, Joseph	Royalty	150	250	350		Elder Brother of Napoleon
Bonaparte, Letizia	Royalty		1,500	2,500		Mother of Napoleon
Bonaparte, Lucien	Royalty	50	100	150		Brother
Bonaparte, Marie Louise	Royalty	200	550			Wife of Napoleon
Bonaparte, Napoleon	Royalty					See Napolean
Bonci, Alessandro	Music	45			125	Opera
Bond, Carrie Jacobs	Music	35	100	150	75	Composer
Bond, Charles	Aviation	15		45	35	ACE - WWII/Flying Tigers
Bond, Johnny	Music	10			25	
Bond, Tommy "Butch"	Ent	10			25	Our Gang child star
Bond, Ward 1903-60	Ent	100	150	200	200	Western star & GWTW
Bond, William C.	Science	50	150	250		Am. Astronomer..
Bondi, Beulah	Ent	50	100		100	1904 - 1987
Bonerz, Peter	Ent	5			15	Bob Newhart Show
Bonesteel, Charles H.	Military	25	45	50		
Bonet, Lisa	Ent	10			25	
Bong, Richard	Aviation	500	1,200	2,000	1,800	ACE - WWII/Top U.S. Ace
Bonham, Milledge L.	Civil War	100	200			CSA General/1813-90
Bonheur, Rosa 1822-1899	Art	100	200	300		
Bonnard, Pierre	Art	125	250	450		Fr. Post-impressionist
Bonneville, Benj. L. E. de	Western	250	500	750		Pioneer of the NW Territory

Name	Field	SIG	DS	ALS	SP	Remarks
Bonney, Barbara	Music	15			30	Opera
Bono,Sonny	Ent	50	75		100	Sonny and Cher
Bonstelle, Jessie	Ent	25		45		Actress/Producer
Bontemps, Arna	Author	45	100			(Am.) Novels/Poetry
Book, Sorrell	Ent	5			15	
Booker T and the MG's	Music	50			125	Signed by Entire Group
Boone, Daniel 1734-1820	Western	4,500	9,000	RARE	RARE	American Pioneer
Boone, Debbie	Music	5			20	
Boone, Pat	Music	5			10	
Boone, Richard	Ent	75	150		150	Palladin
Boone, Squire	RevWar	Scarce	Scarce	Scarce	Scarce	Father of Daniel
Boosler, Elayne	Ent	10			20	Stand Up Comedy
Booth, Adrian	Ent	10			20	
Booth, Edwin 1833-93	Ent	125		300	250	
Booth, Evangeline	Political	35	100		75	Salvation Army
Booth, John Wilkes	Criminal	7,500	12,500	25,000	RARE	Assassin of Lincoln
Booth, Junius Brutus, Jr. 1821-83	Ent	35	75			Actor Brother of JW Booth
Booth, Maude 1865-1948	Political	50	100	200		
Booth, Shirley	Ent	35		100	75	TV's Hazel
Booth, William 1829-1912	Political	125	150	250	175	Founder of Salvation Army
Booth, William Bramwell	Political	35	75	100	75	Eldest Son & Organizer
Boothe, Powers	Ent	10	20		20	
Bor, Tadeusz	Military	25	45	75		
Bordaberry, Juan M.	Political	10	20	25	20	Uraguay
Bordelon, Guy	Aviation	15		35	25	ACE, Korea
Borden, Lizzy	Criminal	1,800	RARE	RARE	RARE	Alleged Ax Murderess
Borden, Olive	Ent	45	75	75	150	
Bordoni, Irene	Ent	20		50	50	1895 - 1953
Borge, Victor	Music	20			40	Pianist/Comedian
Borges, Jorge Luis	Author	125	350			
Borglum, Gutzon	Art	225	375	550	800	Creator Mt. Rushmore
Borglum, Lincoln	Art	25	50	75		Son of Gutzon. Sculptor
Borgnine, Ernest	Ent	10	25	25	25	AA Winner/McHales Navy
Bori, Lucrezia 1887-1960	Music	35	100		100	Opera
Boring, Wayne	Cartoonist	30			50	Superman
Boris III	Royalty	100			200	King & Dictator Bulgaria
Borkh, Inge	Music	10			25	Opera
Borlaug, Norman, Dr.	Science	20	35	75	35	Nobel Peace Prize
Borman, Frank	Space	40			125	Astronaut
Bormann, Martin 1900-45	Military	350	750	1,000	750	Nazi Private Sec'y to Hitler
Born, Max 1882-70	Science	175	350	450		Nobel/Physicist
Borne, Hermann von	Military	25	50	75		
Borno, Louis	Political	25	75			Pres. Haiti
Borodin, Alexander	Music	250	450	750		Russian Composer
Borowski, Felix	Music	20	45	100	50	Composer
Borso, Umberto	Music	15			45	It. Tenor

Name	Field	SIG	DS	ALS	SP	Remarks
Borzage, Frank	Ent	75	150		150	Director-Producer
Bose, Jagadis, Sir	Science	30	45	150		Indian Physicist
Bosley, Tom	Ent	10	25		25	Happy Days
Bostwick, Barry	Ent	25	50		50	Rocky Horror Pix Show
Bostwick, George	Aviation	15	25	45	30	WWII ACE
Boswell, Connie	Ent	5		20	10	
Bosworth, Hobart	Ent	25	45	45	75	
Botha, Louis	Political	50	100	100		So.African Soldier
Bottoms, Joseph	Ent	5			15	
Bottoms, Timothy	Ent	10			20	
Boudin, Eugene-Louis	Art	100	200	400		Fr. Sea & Beach Scenes
Boudinot, Elias 1740-1821	RevWar	250		550		Washington's Att'y Gen.
Boudinot, Elias C.	Civil War	150	250	Scarce	Scarce	Cherokee Leader/1835-90
Boulanger, Nadia	Music	125			300	Composer
Boulard, Georges	Aviation	15		45	35	
Boulle, Pierre	Author	35	75	100		
Boult, Adrian, Sir	Music	35	45	100	75	Conductor (Br)
Bourbon-Parma, Zita	Royalty	Scarce	Scarce	Scarce	Scarce	Last Austrian Empress
Bourguiba, Habib	Political	15	45	75	25	Pres. Tunisia
Bourke-White, Margaret	Art	75	75	150		1904-1971
Bourmont, Louis A.V.	Military		75	150		General under Napoleon
Bourrienne, L.A.F. de	Military	50	75	125		Pvt. Sec'y to Napoleon
Bouton, Chas, Marie	Art	100	150	300		
Boutwell, George S.	Political	15	45	150	45	Grant Sec'y Treasury
Bow, Clara 1905-1965	Ent	225	400	500	600	It Girl
Bowditch, Nathaniel	Science	150	300	450		Astronomer/Mathematician
Bowen, Elizabeth	Author	25	75	125	50	
Bowen, John S.	Civil War	125	200	400		CSA General
Bowen, Thomas Meed	Civil War	50				Union General/1835-1906
Bowie, David	Music	30			60	
Bowie, James (Jim)	Military	RARE	15,000	RARE	RARE	Alamo Hero
Bowler, Metcalf	Political	50	125	250		Opposed Stamp Act
Bowman, Lee	Ent	10	20	25	25	
Boxcar Willie	Music	10	25		25	
Boxleitner, Bruce	Ent	10			35	
Boy George	Music	25	75		55	
Boyd, Belle	Civil War	3,000	10,000	RARE	10,000	Confederate Spy
Boyd, Jimmy	Ent	20			45	
Boyd, William	Ent	200	350		400	Hopalong Cassidy
Boyer, Charles	Ent	45	75		100	1897 - 1978
Boyer, Jean-Pierre	Political	45	125			President of Haiti
Boyington, "Pappy"	Aviation	75	150	200	175	WWII Marine ACE/Gregory
Boyle, Lara Flynn	Ent	25			50	
Boyle, Peter	Ent	20	40		40	Young Frankenstein
Boynton, Henry Van Ness	Civil War	45	75	150		Union Officer
Boys II Men	Music	60			125	Signed by all
Brabazon-Moore, John T.	Aviation	25	50	75	50	lst Licensed. WW I Pilot

Name	Field	SIG	DS	ALS	SP	Remarks
Bracco, Lorraine	Ent	25			45	
Bracken, Eddie	Ent	5			10	
Brackett, Charles	Ent	25			60	Producer/AA Screenwriter
Bradbury, Ray	Author	25	125	150	50	Am. Sci-Fi Writer
Bradford, Gamaliel	Author	10	25	35		Am. Biographer
Bradford, William	Political	125	250	400		G. Washington Att'y Gen'l
Bradlee, Ben	Author	15			35	Editor/Washington Post
Bradley, Ed	Ent	5			10	TV News
Bradley, James	Military	20	35	45		
Bradley, John H.	Military	35	75		75	Iwo Jima Flag Raiser
Bradley, Joseph P.	SuprCt	50	100	150		
Bradley, Kathleen	Ent	5			10	Price is Right Model
Bradley, Omar N. 1893-81	Military	100	225	300	200	5 Star General WWII
Bradley, Tom	Political	5	15	30	15	Mayor Los Angeles
Bradstreet, John	Military	150	350	400		British Major General
Brady, Alice	Ent	75		125	150	1892 - 1939
Brady, James B.	Business	600	1,200	1,500	900	Diamond Jim
Brady, Mathew S.	Art	350	750	2,000		Photographer
Brady, Pat	Ent	100			250	1914 - 1972
Brady, Scott	Ent	15		25	35	
Brady, William A.	Ent	25			50	
Braga, Sonia	Ent	10		30	30	
Bragg, Braxton	Civil War	365	600	900	900	CSA General
Bragg, Edward S.	Civil War	50	75	125		Union General
Bragg, Thomas	Civil War	125	225			CSA Att'y General/1810-72
Bragg, Wm. Henry, Sir	Science	50	100			Nobel Physics w/son Wm. L.
Bragg, Wm. Lawrence	Science	50	100			Nobel Physics w/Father Wm
Braham, John (Abraham) 1774-1856	Music	35		100		Opera
Brahms, Johannes	Music	1,000	2,000	3,500	4,500	Composer
Brailowsky, Alexander	Music	50			100	Concert Pianist
Braithwaite, Wm. Stanley	Author	35	100	200	75	
Branagh, Kenneth	Ent	25	50		50	
Branch, John 1782-1863	Political	25	75	125		Sec'y Navy
Branch, Lawrence O.	Civil War	200	400			CSA General/KIA/1820-62
Brand, Christopher Q.	Aviation	75	150	300	200	ACE WWI/Only night Ace
Brand, Harry	Ent	10			20	Producer
Brand, Max 1892-1944	Author	50			150	Dr. Kildare
Brand, Neville	Ent	75			150	
Brand, Vance D.	Space	25	50		150	Apollo Soyuz
Brandauer, Klaus Maria	Ent	20	75	75	50	James Bond Villain
Brandegee, Augustus	Civil War	15	45	125		
Brandeis, Louis D.	SuprCt	200	400	650	1,000	Ist Jewish Supr. Ct. Judge
Brando, Marlon	Ent	200	550		600	AA Winner
Brandt, Marianne	Music	25		75	75	Opera
Brandt, Willy 1913-92	Political	35	150	200	75	Ger.Chancellor
Brandy	Music	25			50	

Name	Field	SIG	DS	ALS	SP	Remarks
Branigan, Laura	Music	15			35	
Branly, Edouard 1844-40	Science			550	475	Fr. Physicist/Inventor
Brant, Joseph 1742-1807	Western	RARE	RARE	5,000	RARE	Mohawk Indian Chief
Branzell, Karin	Music	50			150	Opera
Braque, Georges	Art	400	600	1,000		Developed Cubism w/ Picasso
Bratt, Benjamin	Ent	25			50	Law and Order
Brattain, Walter	Science	25	50	100	50	Nobel Physics.
Bratton, John, Dr.	Civil War	100	225	300		CSA General/1831-98
Brauchitsch, Walter von	Military	75	150	200	125	Hitler Fld.Marshall
Braun, Eva	Military	1,000		2,500	RARE	Hitler's Mistress-Wife
Braun, Wernher von	Science					see Von Braun
Brautigan, Richard	Author	50	150			Beat author
Braxton, Carter 1736-97	RevWar	275	550	1,200		Signer/Decl of Independence
Braxton, Toni	Music	25			50	
Brayman, Mason	Civil War	35	75			Union General/1813-95
Brayton, Charles Ray	Civil War	50	75	100		Union General/1840-1910
Brazzi, Rossano 1916-95	Ent	15			35	
Bread	Music	50			100	Signed by Entire Band
Brearley, David	RevWar	400	800			Continental Congress
Breathed, Berke	Cartoonist	35		75	75	Bloom County/Outland
Brecht, Bertolt	Author	400	1,200	2,000		Playwright, Poet
Breckinridge, John C.	Civil War	200	400	750		CSA General/1821-75
Breckinridge, Joseph C.	Military	25	50			
Breckinridge, Wm. C.	Civil War	100	250	275		CSA Officer
Breen, Bobby	Ent	10		35	25	Child Star
Breese, Lou	Music	5			15	Big Band Leader
Breese, Vance	Aviation	30	100		50	Aviator & Aircraft Designer
Brendel, El 1890-1964	Ent	15	35		50	
Breneman, Tom	Ent	15		30	25	
Brennan, Eileen	Ent	10			35	
Brennan, Walter 1894-74	Ent	100	150	250	175	AA Winner
Brennan, William J. Jr.	SuprCt	50	100	150	100	
Brenner, David	Ent	15			25	Comedian
Brenner, Victor D.	Art	250		550		Design Lincoln Penny/VDB
Brent, Evelyn	Ent	15		25	35	
Brent, George	Ent	25		35	50	
Brent, George Wm.	Civil War	100	200	300		
Brent, Joseph Lancaster	Civil War	100	150	250		CSA Colonel
Brent, Robert	Military	35	100	150		
Brereton, Lewis Hyde	Aviation	50	150		75	Cmdr.1st Allied Airborne
Breslau, Sophie	Music	45			100	Opera
Bresser-Gianoli, Clotilde	Music	25			50	Opera
Breton, Andre	Author	75	175	275		Poet/Essayist/Critic
Brett, George H.	Military	50	125			Air Corps General WWII
Brett, Jeremy 1935-95	Ent	35			100	Played Sherlock Holmes
Brewer, David J.	SuprCt	75	100	150		
Brewer, Teresa	Music	5			15	Big Band Singer

Name	Field	SIG	DS	ALS	SP	Remarks
Brewster, David, Sir	Science	30	50	125		Invented Kaleidoscope
Breyer, Stephen	SuprCt	25			45	
Brezhnev, Leonid	Political	275	600		400	Soviet Comm. Party Leader
Brian, Mary	Ent	10			25	
Brice, Benjamin W.	Civil War	15	45			Union Paymaster General
Brice, Fanny 1891-1951	Ent	100	200	300	300	
Brickell, Edie	Ent	10			30	
Brico, Antonia, Dr.	Music	25			60	Female Conductor
Bridges, Beau	Ent	15	30		35	
Bridges, Harry	Political	75	125		150	Pres. Longshoreman Union
Bridges, Jeff	Ent	15	30		35	
Bridges, Lloyd	Ent	30	50		50	SeaHunt TV star
Bridges, Todd	Ent	15			35	Different Strokes
Briggs, Austin	Cartoonist	25			75	Flash Gordon
Briggs, Charles F.	Author	15	45	125		Editor NY Times
Briggs, Claire	Cartoonist	20			50	Mr. & Mrs.
Briggs, Roxanne Dawson	Ent	15			40	Star Trek Voyager
Bright, John	Political	35	50	125		
Brightman, Sarah	Music	25			50	Phantom of the Opera
Brimley, Wilford	Ent	10			30	
Brinegar, Paul	Ent	10		20	25	
Brinkley, Christie	Ent	15	45		45	Super Model
Brinkley, David	Ent	5			15	News Anchor
Brisbane, Arthur	Author	15	35	75	35	Influential Editorial Writer
Brisson, Carl	Ent	15		25	25	Danish Actor
Bristol, Henry Platt	Business	250	500	600		Founder of Bristol-Myers
Bristol, Mark	Military	20		35		Admiral WWI
Bristow, Benjamin Helm	Civil War	20	75	100		Civil War Comdr of 25th KY
Britt, Maurice L.	Military	20	45			WWII Hero & Football Star
Britt, May	Ent	15			30	
Brittany, Morgan	Ent	10		25	30	
Britten, Benjamin	Music	100	300	400	200	Br. Conductor
Britton, Barbara	Ent	10			25	
Brix, Herman	Ent					SEE Bruce Bennett
Broadhead, James O.	Political	25		75		Att'y Friend of Lincoln
Broccoli, Cubby	Ent	50	100	125	100	Producer/007 films
Brochier, Jan	Music	15			35	Opera
Brockett, Don	Ent	15			25	
Broderick, Helen	Ent	25			75	
Broderick, Matthew	Ent	20	50		50	
Brodie, Benjamin C.	Science		50	100		Br. Orthopedic Surgeon
Broglie, Duke	Political	125	250	450		French Politician
Broglie, Louis Victor de	Science	35	75	125	250	Nobel Physics
Brokow, Tom	Ent	5			15	TV News Anchor
Brolin, James	Ent	20			40	JAG
Bromberg, J. Edward	Ent	35			75	
Bromfield, John	Ent	10			25	

Name	Field	SIG	DS	ALS	SP	Remarks
Bromfield, Louis	Author	35	75	150	75	Am. Novelist. Pulitzer
Bronson, Betty	Ent	35			75	
Bronson, Charles	Ent	15	45	60	45	Death Wish movies
Bronte, Charlotte	Author	RARE	RARE	RARE	RARE	Br. Novelist. Jane Eyre
Brook, Alexander	Art	25	50	75		
Brook, Clive 1887-1974	Ent	50		75	100	
Brooke, Alan, Fld Mar	Military	50	100	200	75	Cmdr. Br.Corps WWII,Dunkirk
Brooke, John Rutter	Civil War	50	75	175		Union General/1838-1926
Brooke, Rupert	Author	450	550	750		Br. Poet
Brooke-Popham, Robert	Military	30	75	100	50	Br, Air Chief Marshal WWII
Brooks and Dunn	Music	25			50	Country Duo
Brooks, A. Raymond	Aviation	35	50	100	75	Bi-Plane ACE, WWI
Brooks, Albert	Ent	10			20	
Brooks, Avery	Ent	25	50		50	Star Trek Deep Space Nine
Brooks, Foster	Ent	10			25	
Brooks, Garth	Music	25	100		50	
Brooks, Geraldine	Ent	20			45	Actress
Brooks, Gwendolyn	Author	20	45		40	Poet
Brooks, James L.	Ent	15			30	
Brooks, John	Military	75	125	250		Am. Revolution General
Brooks, Leslie	Ent	10			25	
Brooks, Louise 1906-1985	Ent	150	400	450	550	
Brooks, Mel	Ent	15	40	50	35	Actor/Director AA Winner
Brooks, Phillips 1835-93	Author	50	125	125	75	0 Little Town of Bethlehem
Brooks, Rand	Ent	15	35		30	GWTW
Brooks, Randi	Ent	5			15	
Brooks, Richard	Ent	20	30		50	AA Film Director
Brooks, Wm. Thos. H.	Civil War	50	75	100		Union General/1821-70
Broom, Jacob	RevWar	350	750	1,500		Continental Congress
Brophy, Ed	Ent	25			45	
Brosnan, Pierce	Ent	25			50	James Bond
Brothers, Joyce	Science	5			15	Early TV Psychiatrist
Brougham, Henry, Lord	Political	100		250		
Brougham, John	Ent	15			30	Actor/Playwright
Broun, Heywood 1888-39	Author	15	35	60	35	
Browder, Earl	Political	15	30	50	30	US Comm. Party Leader
Brown, A. Roy	Aviation	250	Scarce	Scarce	Scarce	Can ACE/Downed RedBaron
Brown, Aaron V. 1795-59	Political	50	125			
Brown, Albert Gallatin	Political	50	75	100		CSA Senator
Brown, Alice	Author	15	35			Novelist/Poet
Brown, Arthur Whitten	Aviation	300	400	575	575	Alcock & Brown
Brown, Blair	Ent	5			15	
Brown, Bothwell	Ent	10		25	25	
Brown, Charles B.	Author	1,000	RARE	RARE	RARE	Father of American Novel
Brown, Clarence	Ent	10			25	
Brown, David	Ent	10			20	Producer/AA Winner
Brown, Harry Joe	Ent	25	50	75		Producer/Director

Name	Field	SIG	DS	ALS	SP	Remarks
Brown, Helen Gurley	Author	5		20	15	Editor/Publisher
Brown, Henry B.	SuprCt	75	150	200		
Brown, Henry W.	Aviation	15	45	45	30	ACE, WWII
Brown, Herbert C., Dr.	Science	25		45	40	Nobel Chemistry
Brown, Jacob	Military	50	100			General/ War 1812
Brown, James	Ent	5			15	Actor
Brown, James	Music	25	75		50	
Brown, Joe E. 1892-1973	Ent	35	50	60	75	
Brown, John 1800-1859	Political	800	1,500	2,500	2,500	Abolitionist
Brown, John Calvin	Civil War	125	150	300		CSA General/1827-89
Brown, Johnny Mack	Ent	50	100		150	Cowboy Actor
Brown, Joseph Emerson	Civil War	50	75	100		Civil War Governor of GA.
Brown, Julie	Ent	5			10	
Brown, Les	Music	15			35	Big Band Leader
Brown, Lt. John	RevWar	100	175	350		
Brown, Moses	RevWar	75		200		Naval Commander
Brown, Nicholas 1729-91	RevWar	35	50	150		
Brown, Peter	Ent	10			25	
Brown, Phyllis George	Ent	5			15	
Brown, Preston	Military	20	45		45	General VWWI/Chief of Staff
Brown, Robert	Military	25		75	125	General WWI
Brown, Robert	Science	150		500		Botanist
Brown, Ruth	Music	20			50	
Brown, Sam J.	Aviation	20	50	50	45	WWII ACE
Brown, Tom	Ent	10		25	25	
Browne, Chris	Cartoonist	20			35	Hagar
Browne, Dik	Cartoonist	25			75	Hagar
Browne, Hablot Knight	Art	25	75	150		Illustrator Dickens
Browne, Jackson	Music	20			50	
Browne, Leslie	Ent	5			10	
Brownell, Herbert Jr.	Political	15		40		Att'y Gen., Eisenhower
Browning, Eliz. Barrett	Author	750		2,500	2,500	
Browning, George	Business	200	500			Browning Arms Mfg.
Browning, John B.	Business	50	125		75	Pres. Browning Arms Co.
Browning, John Moses	Science	200		450		Inventor, Designer of Fire Arms
Browning, Ricou	Ent	15		40	35	Creature of Black Lagoon
Browning, Robert 1812-89	Author	250	450	900	1,200	Br. Poet
Browning, Tod	Ent	150			350	
Brownlee, John	Music	15		45	30	Opera/Baritone
Brownsville Station	Music	25			50	Signed by Entire Band
Brubeck, Dave	Music	10		25	25	Jazz
Bruce, Andrew D.	Military	50	150			Gen. 77th Infantry Div
Bruce, Blanche K.	Political	250	400			1st Afr-Am.Full Term Sen.
Bruce, Carol	Music	10			30	
Bruce, David	Ent	15			25	
Bruce, Lenny 1925-66	Ent	250	500	1,200	900	Stand-Up Comedian
Bruce, Nigel 1895-1953	Ent	150		300	350	Dr. Watson in films

Name	Field	SIG	DS	ALS	SP	Remarks
Bruce, Thos, (7th Earl)	Political	50	150	250		
Bruce, Virginia	Ent	15			25	
Bruce, Wallace	Author	35		125		
Bruch, Max 1838-1920	Music	75	200	350	125	Opera
Bruckner, Josef Anton	Music	1,200	2,500	3,500	2,500	Composer
Brummel, Geo. B. 'Beau'	Business	100	250	500		Br. Man of Fashion
Bruna Rasa, Lina	Music	75			250	Opera
Brune, G.M.A. 1763-1815	Military	100	250	350		Marshal of Nap. Assassinated
Brunel, Marc Isambard	Science	75	150	250		French engineer
Brunet, Isambard Kingdom	Science	50	150	250		Eng. of Broad Gauge RR
Bruning, Heinrich 1885-71	Political	100			350	Ger. Chancellor. Fled to U.S.
Bruscantini, Sesto	Music	10			25	Opera
Bruson, Renato	Music	10			30	Opera
Bryan, George	RevWar	125	350	550		Jurist.Proposed Abolition 1777
Bryan, Goode	Civil War	150		450		CSA General/1812-85
Bryan, William E.	Aviation	15		45	35	ACE, WWII
Bryan, William						
Jennings 1860-1925	Political	125		350	400	3x Pres. Nominee
Bryant, Alys McKay	Aviation	50	75	150	75	Canadian 1st Woman Flier
Bryant, Anita	Music	5			15	
Bryant, William Cullen	Author	100	250	350	750	Poet/1794-78
Brynner, Yul 1915-85	Ent	50	75	100	150	AA Winner
Buchan, John, Lord	Author	50	150			
Buchanan, Edgar	Ent	75	100		100	Petticoat Junction
Buchanan, Franklin	Civil War	150		350		CSA Admiral/1800-74
Buchanan, James	President	350	750	900	750	1791 - 1868
Buchanan, James M.	Science	30	50	75	50	Nobel Economics
Buchanan, Patrick	Political	10			30	Political Commentator
Bucher, Lloyd M.	Military	35	75	150	100	Captured Capt.USS Pueblo
Buchwald, Art	Author	5	20	25	25	Syndicated Humor.Column
Buck, Frank 1888-1950	Explorer	50	75	125	100	Bring'Em Back Alive
Buck, Pearl S. 1892-1973	Author	50	150	150	100	Am,Novelist/Pulitzer/Nobel
Buck, Peter	Ent	15			35	
Buckingham, Catharinus						
P. 1808-88	Civil War	35		100		Union General/1808-88
Buckingham, William A.	Civil War	40	75	150		Civil War Gov. CT.
Buckland, Ralph P.	Civil War	125		250		Union General/1812-92
Buckley, Betty	Ent	20			45	Eight is Enough
Buckley, William F. Jr.	Author	10		35	20	
Buckner, Simon B.	Civil War	200		375		CSA General/1823-1914
Buell, Don Carlos	Civil War	75	150	250	150	Union General/1818-98
Buffett, Jimmy	Music	25			50	
Buffington, Thomas M.	Western	350	550			Chief of Cherokee Nations
Buford, Abraham	Civil War	175		550		CSA General/1820-84
Buford, John	Civil War	300				Union General/1826-63
Buford, Napoleon B.	Civil War	75	150	300		Union General/1807-83
Buick, David D.	Business	200	600	550	350	Buick Motor Co.

Name	Field	SIG	DS	ALS	SP	Remarks
Bujold, Genevieve	Ent	10			25	
Bulfinch, Charles	Science	125	300			
Bulfinch, Thomas	Author	20	50	100		Bulfinch's Mythology
Bulkley, John D.	Military	20	75		45	Adm. USN WWII
Bull, John S.	Space	15			25	Astronaut
Bull, Ole B.	Music	45		125	125	Violin Virtuoso
Bull, William	Political	75		150		Governor SC 1760
Bullard, Robert Lee	Military	25	75	125	100	General WW I
Bullard, William	Military	15	35			Admiral WW I
Buller, Redvers, Sir	Military	40	125	200	75	Cmdr-in-Chief South Africa
Bulloch, Terrence	Aviation	20			45	Br. Aviator WWII
Bullock, Jim J.	Ent	15			35	Too Close for Comfort
Bullock, Sandra	Ent	25	75		50	
Bulow, Bernhard H.M.K.	Political	15	35	75	45	Prussian Imperial Chancellor
Bulwer-Lytton, Edward	Author	75	200	400		
Bumbry, Grace	Music	25			65	Opera
Bunce, Francis M.	Military	25	50	125	75	Admiral Span-Am War
Bunche, Ralph J. 1904-71	Political	50	125	225	125	Nobel Peace Prize
Bundy, McGeorge	Political	20	35	45	30	Director FBI
Bundy, Omar	Military	35	75		50	General WW I
Bunner, Henry C. 1855-96	Author	50	75	125		Editor Puck Magazine
Bunny, John	Ent	100	150	150	200	Comedian
Bunsen, Robert W.	Science	175	400	900	1,250	Ger. Chemist/Bunsen Burn
Buntline, Ned 1823-86	Author	150		250	550	
Buono, Victor	Ent	75	100		125	Character Actor
Burbank, Luther 1849-26	Science	125	250	300	175	Experimental Botanist
Burdette, Robert J.	Author	20	50	125	50	
Burger, Warren E.	SuprCt	50	150	200	75	Chief Justice
Burgess, Anthony	Author	50	75		150	Clockwork Orange
Burgess, Bobby	Ent	10			25	Mouseketeer
Burgess, Thornton W.	Author	50	150	200		Peter Rabbit
Burghoff, Gary	Ent	15			35	Radar on MASH
Burgoyne, John 1722-92	RevWar	850	1,500	2,500		Br. Gen. vs Am. Colonies
Burke, Billie 1885-1970	Ent	200	300	400	200	Glenda in Wizard of Oz
Burke, Delta	Ent	15	25		40	Designing Woman
Burke, Selma	Art	10	20	45	25	
Burke, Arleigh 1901-1996	Military	35	75	100	100	Adm. USN WWII
Burleigh, Harry Thacker	Music	35		150		
Burmester, Willy	Music	100		225		German Violinist
Burne - Jones, Edward	Art	125	200	350		Pre-Raphaelite Painter
Burnet, David G. 1788-70	Political	275	550	900		Ist Pres. Republic TX
Burnet, William 1688-28	Political	150	450			
Burnett, Carol	Ent	10	30	35	35	
Burnett, Frances H.	Author	50	150	250		Little Lord Fauntleroy
Burnett, Peter H,	Western	200		500		California Pioneer/Ist Gov.
Burnette, Johnny	Music	50				
Burnette, Smiley	Ent	60	125		100	

Name	Field	SIG	DS	ALS	SP	Remarks
Burney, Cecil, Sir	Military	15	35			Br. Adm. WW I
Burnham, Hiram	Civil War	75	200			Union General
Burns & Allen	Ent	200	450		400	Both Signed
Burns, Bob	Ent	25	25	45	45	Bazooka
Burns, Edmund	Ent	35			75	Silent Screen Star
Burns, Edward	Ent	25			50	
Burns, George 1896-1996	Ent	25	75		50	
Burns, James MacGregor	Author	20		45		Educator, Political Science
Burns, John 1791-1872	Civil War	350			1,250	Vet. War 1812. Vol. Gettysburg
Burns, Ken	Ent	10	25		20	Documentary Film Maker
Burns, Robert 1759-96	Author	500	1,500	2,500		Scottish Poet
Burns, William J.	Business	35		150		Chief FBI 1921-24, Det. Agency
Burns, William Wallace	Civil War	35	75	100	150	Union General/1825-92
Burnside, Ambrose E.	Civil War	125	275	350	650	Union General/1824-81
Burpee, David	Business	25	35	75	45	Burpee Seed Co.
Burpee, Jonathan	Business	10	25	50	25	Burpee Seed Co.
Burr, Aaron 1756-1836	Vice Pres	400	650	750		
Burr, Raymond 1917-93	Ent	45	75	100	75	Ironsides/Perry Mason
Burritt, Elihu 1810-79	Political	25		100		
Burroughs, Edgar Rice	Author	250	400	675	600	Tarzan/1875-1950
Burroughs, John 1837-21	Author	100		200	450	Am. Naturalist
Burrows, Abe	Author	10		25	20	Playwright, Pulitzer
Burstyn, Ellen	Ent	15			35	
Burton, Harold H.	SuprCt	50	150	100	100	
Burton, Isabel, Lady	Author	25	75	150		
Burton, LeVar	Ent	25	75		50	Star Trek/Roots
Burton, Richard F.	Explorer	125	225			1821-1890
Burton, Richard Sir	Ent	100	200		200	1925 - 1984
Burton, Tim	Ent	25	50		50	Director
Buscalia, Leo	Author	10	25	35	20	Educator, Author, Lecturer
Busch, Adolphus	Business	450	2,500	3,500		Anheuser-Busch
Busch, August A.	Business	25	100	150	50	Anheuser-Busch Brewery
Busch, Fritz	Music	75		125	250	Ger. Conductor
Busch, Niven	Author	15		30		Dramatist, Screenwriter
Busch, Wilhelm 1832-08	Art	Scarce	Scarce	Scarce	Scarce	Painter & Poet.
Busell, Darcey	Music	15			45	Ballet
Busey, Gary	Ent	15	45		35	
Bush, Barbara	First Lady	50	150		100	
Bush, George H. 1924-	President	100	300	450	200	
Bush, George W.	President	85	325	350	300	
Bush, Owen	Ent	5			15	
Bush, Vannevar	Science	50	150	200	125	Pioneer Analog Computer
Bushman, Francis X.	Ent	45		125	100	Silent Star of Ben Hur
Bushmiller, Ernie	Cartoonist	20			50	Nancy
Bushnell, David	Science	250	750	1,250		Invented 1st Submarine
Busoni, Ferruccio	Music	125		275	375	Pianist/1899-1924
Busse, Henry	Music	20			50	Big Band Leader

Name	Field	SIG	DS	ALS	SP	Remarks
Bute, John Stuart	Royalty	100	125			Earl of Bute
Butenandt, Adolf F.J.	Science	20		45	25	Nobel Chemistry
Butheiezi, Gatsha M.	Political	20			45	Chief of Zulu Nation
Butler, Benjamin F.	Civil War	150	250	250	500	Union General/1818-93
Butler, Brett	Ent	15			35	Grace Under Fire
Butler, Daws	Ent	50	75	100	75	Man of many Voices
Butler, Ellis Parker	Author	25	50	75	50	1869-1937
Butler, John	RevWar	75	150	300		Am. Loyalist.Butler's Rangers
Butler, Matthew C.	Civil War	100	200	300		CSA General/1836-1909
Butler, Pierce	SuprCt	35	100	175	50	
Butler, Pierce 1744-1822	RevWar	75	150	300		Signer of Constitution
Butler, Samuel 1835-1902	Author	35	75	125		
Butler, Smedley D.	Military	15	35	75	35	
Butler, Walter 1752-81	RevWar		500	675		
Butler, William Orlando	Military	50	200			Hero Battle of New Orleans
Butler, Yancy	Ent	25			45	
Butler, Zebulon	Military	100	200			Col. Revolutionary War
Butt Rumford, Clara	Music	50			150	Opera
Butterfield, Billy	Music	25			50	Jazz Trumpet, Bandleader
Butterfield, Daniel	Civil War	75		225		Union Gen/ Composed Taps
Buttons, Red	Ent	10			25	
Buttram, Pat	Ent	45	75		75	Green Acres
Butts, Alfred M.	Science	50				Inventor of Scrabble game
Buzzi, Ruth	Ent	5	20	20	15	Laugh In
Byers, Samuel Hawkins	Author	25	50	75		Union Soldier-Author
Byington, Spring	Ent	20			50	
Byner, John	Ent	5			15	Comedian
Byng, Geo. Viscount	Military	25	75			Br. Adm.Destroyed Sp.Fleet 1719
Byrd, Charlie	Music	15			25	Jazz Guitar
Byrd, Ralph	Ent	100	150		300	
Byrd, Richard E. 1888-57	Aviation	75	275	450	325	Adm. USN, Polar Expl.
Byrds, The	Music	100	250		200	Entire Group Signed
Byrne, Gabriel	Ent	25			50	
Byrnes, James F.	SuprCt	35	125	200	75	
Byron, Arthur	Ent	15			35	
Byron, Geo, G. Lord	Author	1,500		2,750		Scarce

Name	Field	SIG	DS	ALS	SP	Remarks
Caan, James	Ent	10	30		30	
Cabal, Bob	Ent	10			25	
Cabell, Earle	Political	15		35		Dallas Mayor/JFK Assas.
Cabell, James B.	Author	35	125	150		
Cabell, William L.	Civil War	175	350			CSA General/1827-1911
Cable, Geo.Washington	Author	35	50	75	75	CSA Soldier/Writer
Cabot, Bruce 1904-72	Ent	75		100	150	King Kong
Cabot, George 1751-1823	Political	25	50	100		
Cabot, Sebastian	Ent	50	75		100	Disney Voice/Family Affair
Caceres, Andreas A.	Political	10	25	45	25	Peru
Cadbury, George	Business	35		150	50	Cadbury Chocolate Mfg.
Cadbury, Richard	Business	30	75	150	50	Cadbury Chocolate Mfg.
Cade, Robert, Dr.	Business	15			25	Inventor of Gatorade
Cadman, Chas. W.	Music	50	200	300	100	Composer
Cadmus, Paul	Art	35	75	125		
Cadwalader, George	Civil War	50	100	150		Union General/1830-79
Cadwalader, Lambert	RevWar	50	150	250		Continental Congress
Cady, Frank	Ent	45	75		75	Green Acres
Caesar, Irving	Music	25	50	125	50	Lyricist (Tea for Two)
Caesar, Sid	Ent	10	25		25	Your Show of Shows
Cage, John M. 1912-92	Music	50	100	200		Composer
Cage, Nicholas	Ent	25	75		50	AA Winner
Cagney and Lacy	Ent	25			50	Signed by both stars
Cagney, James 1899-86	Ent	100	200	250	250	AA Winner
Cahier, Madame Charles	Music	25			75	Opera
Cahn, Sammy 1913-93	Music	20	75	125	50	Composer
Cain, Dean	Ent	25			45	TV's Superman
Cain, James	Author	40	75	100		
Caine, Michael	Ent	25	50		50	
Caine, Thos. Hall	Author	15	45	50	25	Br. Novelist
Calamity Jane	Western	RARE	20,000	35,000	RARE	
Calder, Alexander	Art	125	225		200	Sculptor/1898-1976
Caldwell, Erskine	Author	35	125	175	75	Tobacco Road
Caldwell, John Curtis	Civil War	35	75		100	Union General
Caldwell, Sarah	Music	15			20	1st Woman Conductor NY Met.
Caldwell, Taylor	Author	35	150	200	75	
Caldwell, Zoe	Ent	10	25	25	25	
Calhern, Louis	Ent	25		50	50	1895 - 1956
Calhoun, John C.	Vice Pres	150	300	450	400	Andrew Jackson VP
Calhoun, Rory	Ent	10	45		25	
Callaghan, James	Political	40	75	150	50	Br. Prime Minister
Callahan, Laurence K.	Aviation	10	20	45	30	

Name	Field	SIG	DS	ALS	SP	Remarks
Callas, Charlie	Ent	10			20	
Callas, Maria 1923-77	Music	300	750	750	1,000	Opera
Calleia, Frank	Ent	25		50	45	
Calleia, Joseph	Ent	25			50	
Calley, William	Military	25	45	45	50	My Lai, Viet Nam
Calloway, Cab 1907-95	Music	35	75	100	100	Big Band Leader
Calve, Emma	Music	50	100	150	250	Opera
Calvert, Louis	Ent	5		20	15	
Calvert, Phyllis	Ent	5			15	
Calvet, Corinne	Ent	10			20	
Calvin, John	Clergy	7,500	15,000	30,000		RARE
Calvin, Melvin, Dr.	Science	25	50	50	45	Nobel Chemistry
Camacho, Manuel Avila	Political	25		60	35	Pres. Mexico
Camargo, Alberto	Political	10		30	20	Columbia
Cambern, Donn	Ent	10			20	
Cambon, Jules	Political	20	25	35		Fr. Ambassador to US
Cambridge, Godfrey	Ent	35			75	
Cameron, George	Military	25		45		General WWI
Cameron, James	Political	30		50		Senator PA. Sec'y War
Cameron, Kirk	Ent	15	30		35	Growing Pains
Cameron, Robert	Civil War	35	75			Union General/1828-94
Cameron, Rod	Ent	10			25	
Cameron, Simon 1800-89	Civil War	75	125	175	300	Lincoln Sec'y War
Cammaerts, Emile	Author	10		30	25	Poet/Writer
Camp, Colleen	Ent	10			25	
Campanini, Italo	Ent	50	75	175		
Campbell, Archibald	RevWar	100	250			Br. General.
Campbell, Archie	Music	10			25	
Campbell, Beatrice	Ent	20	35	45	45	1865-1940
Campbell, Bruce	Ent	25			45	
Campbell, Chas Thomas	Civil War	35	75	100		Union General/1823-95
Campbell, Colin	Military	15	45	75		Br. Gen during War of 1812
Campbell, Douglas	Aviation	45	75	100	100	WWI Bi-Plane ACE
Campbell, Glen	Music	10			30	
Campbell, John	RevWar	75	150	250		Br. General
Campbell, John A.	SuprCt	100	150	200		1811 - 18889
Campbell, Mary	Ent	25		75		Miss America 1922-23
Campbell, Naomi	Ent	20			50	SuperModel
Campbell, Neve	Ent	25			50	
Campbell, Patrick, Mrs.	Ent	35	75		75	
Campbell, William (Bill)	Ent	25			50	Rocketeer
Campbell, William B.	Civil War	50	75	100		Union General/1807-67
Campbell-Bannerman, H.	Political	20	50	100		Prime Minister
Campora, Giuseppe	Music	15			40	Tenor - Opera
Camus, Albert 1913-1960	Author	75	200	400		Nobel
Canary, David	Ent	10			20	
Canby, Edward R.	Civil War	75	200	325		Union General/1817-73

Name	Field	SIG	DS	ALS	SP	Remarks
Cander, John	Music	50				Composer
Candler, Asa Griggs	Business	750	2,000	2,500		Founder of Coca Cola
Candy, John	Ent	50	100		100	Died Young
Canetti, Elia	Author	75	200	300		
Canfield, Dorothy (Fisher)	Author	50	100	200		1879 - 1958
Canham, Erwin	Author	10	20			Christian Science Monitor
Caniff, Milton 1907-88	Cartoonist	35	100	100	125	Terry & Steve Canyon
Caniglia, Maria	Music	25			75	Opera
Canned Heat	Music	45			75	Signed by Entire Band
Cannell, Stephen J.	Ent	5			10	TV Producer
Canning, Charles John	Political	15		75	45	lst Viceroy of India
Canning, Effie	Author	100		300		
Canning, George	Political	50	100	150		Prime Minister
Cannon, Dyan	Ent	10	25	25	30	
Cannon, George Q.	Political	50	150	200		Utah's lst Congressman
Cannon, Jos. G.	Political	20	45	100	45	Speaker of the House
Cannon, Martha H., Dr.	Science	25	30	50	40	
Canova, Antonio 1757-22	Art	100	250	450		Italian Sculptor
Canova, Diana	Ent	10			20	
Canova, Judy	Ent	10	15	20	25	
Cantinflas	Ent	35			100	
Cantor, Eddie 1892-1964	Ent	75	150		150	
Canutt, Yakima	Ent	25		75	75	AA Winner
Capers, Ellison	Civil War	75				CSA General
Caperton, William	Military	25			50	WWI Admiral
Capone, Al	Criminal	3,500	8,000	RARE	RARE	Gangster
Capote, Truman 1924-84	Author	125	250		250	In Cold Blood"
Capp, Al	Cartoonist	50			125	Lil Abner
Capra, Frank 1897-1991	Ent	35	150		125	AA Winning Director
Capshaw, Kate	Ent	20			45	
Captain & Tennile	Music	25	50		50	Signed by Both
Capucine	Ent	25	50	50	50	
Cara, Irene	Music	20	45		40	
Caraway, Hattie 1878-50	Political	25	50	45	45	1st Woman US Senator
Cardigan, 7th Earl	Military	75	175	250	150	Br.Gen. Charge of Lt Brigade
Cardinale, Claudia	Ent	15			45	James Bond Girl
Cardozo, Benjamin N.	SuprCt	200	350	550	650	
Carere, Christine	Ent	10			20	
Carerre, Tia	Ent	20			50	
Carey, Drew	Ent	25			50	Drew Carey Show
Carey, Harry Jr.	Ent	10	30		20	
Carey, Harry Sr.	Ent	100		175	250	
Carey, Macdonald	Ent	15			30	
Carey, Mariah	Music	25			50	
Carey, Michele	Ent	10			25	
Carey, Ron	Ent	10			20	Barney Miller TV series
Carias, Andino, Tiburcio	Political	40	125		75	Pres. Honduras

Name	Field	SIG	DS	ALS	SP	Remarks
Carl XIV Johan 1763-1844	Royalty	200	450			King Sweden
Carl XV 1826-72	Royalty	150	400			King of Sweden & Nor. from 1859
Carl XVI Gustaf	Royalty	50	150			King Sweden
Carl, Marion	Aviation	15		50	45	WWI 1st Marine ACE
Carle, Frankie	Music	15			35	Big Band Leader
Carleton, Guy 1724-1808	Military	250	500	700		Br. Commander-in-Chief
Carleton, James H.	Civil War	35		100		Union General/1814-73
Carleton, Will 1845-1912	Author	15	50	100	25	Ir. Novelist
Carlin, George	Ent	10	25		25	
Carlisle, 7th Earl	Author	20	50	100		Poet/Orator
Carlisle, Belinda	Music	25	50		50	Go-Go's Lead Singer
Carlisle, Kitty	Music	10			30	
Carlisle, Mary	Ent	10		25	20	
Carlo Alberto 1798-1849	Royalty	75	150	275		King of Sardinia
Carlotta (Marie-Charlotte-Amalie)	Royalty	375	700	1,500		Empress of Mex. Became Insane
Carlson, Richard	Ent	20			45	
Carlton, Guy 1724-1808	RevWar	Scarce	Scarce	Scarce	Scarce	British General
Carlyle, Russ	Music	5			15	Bandleader
Carlyle, Thomas	Author	75	225	450	125	Br. Philosopher, Social Critic
Carmen, Jean	Ent	5			10	
Carmer, Carl	Author	20	50	125		
Carmichael, Hoagy	Music	75	200		200	Composer/1899-1991
Carnarvon, Henry IV Earl	Political	25	50	75		Created Fed. Dom/Canada
Carne, Judy	Ent	10			20	Laugh In
Carnegie, Andrew	Business	350	1,250	1,250	1,250	Carnegie Steel
Carnegie, Dale 1888-1955	Author	50			100	How to Win Friends and...
Carnes, Kim	Music	15			35	
Carney, Art	Ent	10	30	35	25	Honeymooners
Carney, Robert B.	Military	10	20	25		
Carnot, Lazare N.M.	Military	75	200	300		Min. of War. Exiled
Carnot, Marie Francois S	Political	75		150		Pres. France/Assasinated
Carnovsky, Morris	Ent	15		45	45	
Caroline (Geo. IV-Eng)	Royalty	100	150	200		Estranged Queen
Caroline (Monaco)	Royalty	25			75	Princess/Graces Daughter
Caroline 1768-1821	Royalty			450		Estranged Queen George IV
Caroline 1776-1841	Royalty		100	150		2nd Queen of Maximilian I
Caroline of Anspach	Royalty	300	450	900		Queen of George II (Eng)
Caron, George R.	Aviation	35		100	100	Enola Gay Tail gunner
Caron, Leslie	Ent	25	50		50	
Carpenter, Charisma	Ent	25			50	
Carpenter, John	Ent	10			25	Director/Writer
Carpenter, Karen	Music	150	250		300	
Carpenter, Mary-Chapin	Music	20			45	
Carpenter, Richard	Music	15	45		45	
Carpenter, Scott	Space	25	75	125	100	Mercury 7 Astronaut
Carpenter, William B.	Explorer	15	30	50		Br. Physiologist

Name	Field	SIG	DS	ALS	SP	Remarks
Carpenter, William S.	Military	10		45	30	
Carpenters, The	Music	250	400		400	Signed by Both
Carr, Eugene Asa	Civil War	35	75		175	Union General/1820-1910
Carr, Gerald P.	Space	5			15	Astronaut
Carr, Jane	Ent	5			15	
Carr, Tommy	Ent	15			35	
Carr, Vicki	Music	5			15	
Carradine, David	Ent	25	50		50	Kung Fu
Carradine, John	Ent	100	100	150	200	Dracula
Carradine, Keith	Ent	10			25	
Carradine, Robert	Ent	10			25	
Carranza, Venustiano	Political	75	150	300		Murdered Mexican Pres.
Carrel, Dr. Alexis	Science	75	200	300	125	Nobel Medicine
Carreno, Terresa	Music	25		125	100	Pianist
Carrera, Barbara	Ent	15			40	James Bond Girl
Carrere, Christine	Ent	5			15	French Actress
Carrey, Jim	Ent	30	100		65	
Carrillo, Leo 1880-1961	Ent	60	100		125	
Carroll, Charles 1737-32	RevWar	275	550	750		Signer
Carroll, Daniel	RevWar	200	475	700		Continental Congress
Carroll, Diahann	Ent	10			300	
Carroll, John	Ent	10		25	35	
Carroll, Leo G. 1892 - 72	Ent	75			150	Man from UNCLE
Carroll, Lewis	Author					See C.L. Dodgson
Carroll, Madeleine	Ent	25			50	1906 - 1987
Carroll, Mickey	Ent	10	30		30	Wizard of Oz Munchkin
Carroll, Nancy	Ent	10		20	35	
Carroll, William	Military	25		75		Gen. TN Militia
Carroll, William H.	Civil War	75	150			CSA General/1810-68
Cars, The	Music	50			100	Signed by entire group
Carson, Christopher "Kit"	Western	6,000	RARE	40,000	15,000	Scout/Indian Trader/Fur
Carson, Jack	Ent	20			50	
Carson, John	Military	10			35	General WW I
Carson, Johnny	Ent	20	50		50	Tonight Show Host
Carson, Leonard Kit	Aviation	15		45	35	WWII ACE
Carson, Rachel 1907-1964	Science	75	150	225	250	
Carson, Sunset	Ent	30		75	60	Western Star
Carter, Ann S.	Aviation	25	45		45	1st Woman Helicopter Pilot
Carter, Ben	Ent	100			250	
Carter, Benny	Music	50	100	100	100	Jazz
Carter, Betty	Music	15			35	Lionel Hampton Vocalist
Carter, Carlene	Ent	10			25	
Carter, Dixie	Ent	15			35	Designing Women
Carter, Elliot	Music	25		100		Pulitzer/Composer
Carter, Helen	Music	10			20	
Carter, Helena Bonham	Ent	25			50	
Carter, Howard	Science	1,500	RARE	2,500	RARE	Found King Tut's Tomb

Name	Field	SIG	DS	ALS	SP	Remarks
Carter, Jack	Ent	10			20	
Carter, Jimmy	President	45	200	400	125	
Carter, Leslie, Mrs.	Ent	25	75	100	75	
Carter, Lynda	Ent	10		25	25	Wonder Woman
Carter, Mother Maybelle	Music	45			100	Country
Carter, Nell	Ent	10	25		25	Gimme a Break
Carter, Rosalynn	First Lady	25	75	100	50	
Carter, Terry	Ent	10			20	
Carteret, George 1610-80	Military	Scarce	Scarce	Scarce	Scarce	Br. Naval Off/Fndr NJ
Cartland, Barbara	Author	20	45	75	75	Romance Novelist
Cartwright, Angela	Ent	10			30	Lost in Space TV series
Cartwright, Nancy	Ent	15			35	Voice of Bart Simpson
Carty, John J.	Science	75	150	250	150	Telephone Pioneer. AT&T
Caruso, Anthony	Ent	25			50	
Caruso, David	Ent	25			50	NYPD Blues
Caruso, Enrico 1873-1921	Music	250	500	700	750	
Carver, Geo.						
Washington 1864-1943	Science	300		700	1,500	Botanist/1864-43
Carvey, Dana	Ent	25			50	Sat Nite Live alumni
Casadesus, Robert, Dr.	Music	50		100	100	Pianist/Composer
Casals, Pablo 1876-1973	Music	100	150	300	350	Spanish Cellist
Casanovo, Giacomo	Author	150	450	750		
Case, Allen	Ent	10			20	
Case, Jerome	Business	35	75	150		Case Tractors & Farm Implements
Caselia, Alfredo	Music	35	125	200		Composer/Pianist
Casellato, Renzo	Music	10			20	Opera
Caselotti, Adriana	Ent	25	75	75	60	Voice of Snow White
Casement, Jack	Civil War	50	150			Union General
Casey, Silas 1807-82	Civil War	50	100	150		Union General/1807-82
Cash, Johnny	Music	25	150		75	
Cash, June Carter	Music	10			25	
Cash, Rosanne	Ent	10			25	
Casimir-Perier, Jean P.	Political	50		150		Pres. France 1894-95
Cass, Lewis 1782-1866	Political	50	100	150		Jackson Sec'y War
Cass, Peggy	Ent	10			20	
Cassatt, Mary	Art	225	450	750		
Cassavetes, John	Ent	20		35	45	Actor/Director
Cassidy, David	Ent	20	50		45	Partridge Family
Cassidy, Jack	Ent	30			65	
Cassidy, Joanna	Ent	10			25	
Cassidy, Shaun	Ent	15			35	Hardy Boys/Singer
Cassidy, Ted	Ent	150	300		450	Addams Family/Lurch
Cassin, Jimmy	Music	10	30			Composer
Cassin, Rene	Political	35	75	150	75	Founder UNESCO/Nobel
Cassini, Oleg	Business	20			45	Fashion Designer
Casson, Mel	Cartoonist	10			20	Redeye
Castagna, Bruna	Music	25			75	Opera

Name	Field	SIG	DS	ALS	SP	Remarks
Castanzo, Jack	Music	10			30	Jazz
Castelnuovo-Tedesco, M.	Music	75		250	125	Composer
Castle, Irene	Ent	50		75	75	
Castle, Peggy	Ent	10			25	
Castle, Vernon	Ent	50			150	
Castle, William	Ent	75			150	Director
Castro, Fidel	Political	600	750		900	Cuban Premier
Cates, Clifton B.	Military	10	25	40	25	
Cates, Phoebe	Ent	20			50	
Cather, Willa 1873-1947	Author	200	400	550		
Catherine I (Rus)	Royalty	900	2,000	4,500		
Catherine II (The Great)	Royalty	600	1,200	2,200		Empress of Russia
Catlett, Walter	Ent	45			100	
Catlin, George 1796-1872	Art	100	250			Indian Scenes
Catlin, Isaac	Civil War	50	100	250		Union General
Catt, Carrie Chapman	Political	75	125	250		Suffragette Leader
Catton, Bruce	Author	50	150	150	100	Historian/Pulitzer
Caulfieid, Joan	Ent	20			40	1922 - 1991
Caulfield, Maxwell	Ent	15			30	
Cavalieri Muratore, Lina	Music	100			200	Opera
Cavallaro, Carmen	Music	15			35	Big Band Leader
Cavanagh, Paul	Ent	10			25	
Cavell, Edith 1865-1915	Science	225	375	575		
Cavett, Dick	Ent	10			25	
Cavour, Camillo, Count	Political	175	400			Architect of It. Unification
Cayce, Edgar	Author	100	225			Psychic?
Ceausecu, Nicolae	Political	50	250		125	Romanian Pres/Assas.
Cech, Thomas R., Dr.	Science	20	45		45	Nobel Chemistry
Celi, Adolfo	Ent	35			75	Largo" in James Bond film
Cellini, Benvenuto	Art	1,000	4,000	RARE	RARE	Goldsmith and Sculptor
Cello, Aldo	Business	5			15	
Cerf, Bennett	Author	15		30	25	Random House Editor
Cermak, Anton J.	Political	35	50	75	100	Assas. Mayor of Chicago
Cernan, Eugene A.	Space	35			100	Moonwalker Astronaut
Cervantes, Miguel de	Author	7,500	10,000	RARE	RARE	Don Quioxte
Cesky, Charles J.	Aviation	15		35	30	WWII ACE
Cezanne, Paul	Art	1,000	2,300	RARE	RARE	Fr Impressionist
Chabas, Paul Emile	Art	35	75	125		
Chabert, Lacey	Ent	25			50	Child Actress
Chabot, Phillipe de Brion	Military	Scarce	Scarce	Scarce	Scarce	Fr.Cmdr.In Chief
Chabrier, Alexis E.	Music	100	250	400		Opera/Composer
Chadwick, James, Sir	Science	100	200	400		Discovered Neutron/Nobel
Chaffee, Adna R.	Civil War	45	75	125		
Chaffee, Roger	Space	200			400	Died in Apollo Fire (1-27-67)
Chagall, Marc 1887-1985	Art	200	350	Scarce	350	
Chaka Kahn	Music	20			45	
Chakiris, George	Ent	10		25	25	

Name	Field	SIG	DS	ALS	SP	Remarks
Chaliapin, Feodor	Music	200	250	500	550	Opera
Chalker, Jack	Author	15		45	30	
Chalmers, James R.	Civil War	150	350			CSA General/1831-98
Chamberlain, Austen	Political	35	100	100	100	Nobel Peace Prize
Chamberlain, Joseph A.	Political	50	100	100	100	Statesman/Nobel
Chamberlain, Joshua L.	Civil War	700	1,250	1,800		Union General/1828-1914
Chamberlain, Neville	Political	75	300	400	150	Prime Minister
Chamberlain, Owen, Dr	Science	25	45	75	45	Nobel Physics
Chamberlain, Richard	Ent	20		30	45	
Chamberlaine, William	Military	10		35	25	General WW I
Chamberlin, Clarence	Aviation	100	250		250	Record Non-Stop Flight NY-Ger.
Chambers, Marilyn	Ent	15			35	Porn Star
Chambers, Robert Wm.	Author	10		25		Life Mag Illustrator
Chambers, Whittaker	Author	15	50	100	25	Journalist
Chaminade, Cecile	Music	100	200	300	225	Composer/1857-1944
Champion, Gower	Ent	25	45	50	60	Dancer
Champion, Marge	Ent	15	45		45	Dancer
Chan, Jackie	Ent	25			50	Martial Arts Film Star
Chancellor, John	Ent	15			30	News Anchor
Chandler, Jeff	Ent	75	150	150	150	1918 - 1961
Chandler, Lane	Ent	20			40	
Chandler, Norman	Business	15	35	75	30	L.A. Times
Chandler, Otis	Business	20	45	100	45	Founder L.A. Times
Chandler, Raymond	Author	500	1,200	RARE	RARE	Detective Novelist
Chandler, William E.	Political	25	45	75		Sect. Navy
Chandler, Zachariah	Political	25	50	50		Sec'y Int./Att'y Gen'l
Chanel, Coco	Business	50	100	200	100	Fashion Designer
Chaney, Lon, Jr. 1906-73	Ent	350	650	Scarce	600	Wolfman ...
Chaney, Lon, Sr.	Ent	1,000	2,500	Scarce	1,750	Man of a 1000 Faces
Chang	Ent	25			75	Chinese Giant
Channing, Carol	Ent	5			10	Hello Dolly/Broadway
Channing, Stockard	Ent	5			15	
Channing, William Ellery	Author	50	75	125		Clergy
Chapin, Harry	Music	100			250	Scarce
Chapin, Lawrence	Ent	15			35	
Chaplin, Charles	Ent	300	600	Scarce	700	1889 - 1977
Chaplin, Geraldine	Ent	10		30	30	
Chaplin, Lita Grey	Ent	20	25	45	25	
Chaplin, Sydney	Ent	15		35	30	
Chapman, Graham	Ent	15	20	25	30	
Chapman, Leonard, Jr.	Military	15	30		50	USMC General, WWII
Chapman, Marguerite	Ent	10			20	
Chapman, Mark David	Criminal	75		200		Murdered John Lennon
Chapman, Oscar L.	Political	15		30	35	Sec'y Interior 1849
Chappell, William	Business	20	50	100	50	Music Publisher
Chaptal, Jean Antoine	Political	125	200			Min Agriculture/Interior
Charcot, Jean Martin	Science	100	225	450		Fr. Neurologist

Name	Field	SIG	DS	ALS	SP	Remarks
Charisse, Cyd	Ent	10			35	
Charlemagne	Royalty	75,000	RARE	RARE	RARE	Institutionalized
Charles & Diana	Royalty				3,500	Prince and Princess
Charles Albert (Sardinia)	Royalty			250		Count of Savoy
Charles Edw, Stuart	Royalty	150	350	600		Bonnie Prince Charlie
Charles Emmanuel I	Royalty	500	900			1562-1630
Charles Emmanuel I	Royalty		400			King of Sardinia
Charles I (Eng) 1600-49	Royalty	750	1,750	4,000		
Charles II (Eng) 1630-85	Royalty	1,000	2,000	2,500		
Charles II (SP)	Royalty	275	450			
Charles IV (Eng)	Royalty	350	900			
Charles IV (Sp)	Royalty	200		600		
Charles IX (Fr) 1560-74	Royalty	350	1,000	1,500		
Charles V (Charles II)	Royalty	750	1,800	3,500		
Charles VI (Charles III)	Royalty	400	1,200			
Charles X (Fr)	Royalty	150	450	600		
Charles XIV John (Swe)	Royalty	250	475	750		
Charles XV (Swe-Nor)	Royalty	50	150	300		
Charles, Prince of Wales 1948-	Royalty	400		1,500	600	Philip Arthur George
Charles, Ray	Music	200	250		Scarce	Blind
Charles, Suzette	Ent	10			20	Miss American 1984
Charlie's Angels	Ent	50			100	Signed by all three orig. stars
Charlotte, Grand Duchess	Royalty	25	75	150	50	Luxembourg
Charlotte, Sophia	Royalty	150	275	450		Queen of George III (Eng)
Charo	Music	5			10	
Charpentier, Gustave	Music	100	250	300	300	1880-1956
Charteris, Leslie	Author	40	75	125	125	The Saint
Chartoff, Melanie	Ent	10			25	
Charvet, David	Ent	25			45	Baywatch
Chase, Charley	Ent	35			100	
Chase, Chevy	Ent	10			35	Sat Nite Live
Chase, Ilka	Ent	15			25	Author
Chase, Mary	Author	45	100	150		Harvey" and others...
Chase, Salmon P.	SuprCt	100	150	300	300	Chief Justice
Chase, Samuel	RevWar	275	550	1,200		Signer
Chase, William C.	Military	10		35		
Chase, William Merritt	Art	100				US Painter/Western Scenes
Chateaubriand, Francois	Author	125	250	450		Fr. Novelist
Chatterton, Ruth	Ent	25			50	
Chauncey, Isaac	Military	35	100	100		Am. Naval - War 1812
Chausson, Ernest	Music	50	150	300		Opera
Chauvel, Henry, Sir	Military	25	75			Aussie General WW I
Chavez, Carlos	Music	15	35	75	50	Conductor/Composer
Chavez, Cesar E. 1927-93	Political	50			100	Migrant Labor Organizer
Chavez, George A.	Aviation	50		150	100	
Chayefsky, Paddy	Author	75	150	250	125	

Name	Field	SIG	DS	ALS	SP	Remarks
Cheap Trick	Music	50			100	Signed by Entire Band
Cheatham, Benj. F.	Civil War	225	400			CSA General/1820-86
Checker, Chubby	Music	20	50		45	The Twist
Cheech n' Chong	Ent	25			60	Signed by both
Cheers	Ent				350	Signed Cast/All Six
Cheever, Charles A, Dr.	Science	35	100		75	
Cheever, John	Author	50	125	250	100	Novelist/Pulitzer
Chekhov, Anton 1860-04	Author	Scarce	2,000	4,500	7,500	Russian Novelist
Chen, Joan	Ent	15			45	
Cheney, Sherwood	Military	10		25		General WW I
Chennault, Claire L.	Aviation	400		750	550	Flying Tigers. USAAF Gen.
Cher	Music	25	75		50	Sonny and Cher
Cherkassky, Shura	Music	25			60	Opera
Chernov, Vladimir	Music	15			30	Opera
Cherubini, Luigi	Music	175	250	500		Opera Composer
Chesebrough, Robert	Business	15		50		Vaseline Products
Cheshire, Leonard	Military	15	50	75	45	Br. RAF
Chester, Bob	Music	20			45	Big Band Leader
Chester, Colby M.	Business	15			45	CEO General Foods
Chester, John	RevWar	35	75			Continental Army. Judge
Chesterton, Gilbert Keith	Author	75	300	300	150	Father Brown, Detective
Chestnut, James	Civil War	250				CSA General/1815-85
Chestnutt, Mark	Music	15			30	
Chevalier, Albert	Music	10	25	45	25	Composer
Chevalier, Maurice	Ent	35		150	125	
Chevrolet, Louis 1879-41	Business	800	3,500	RARE	RARE	Chevrolet Auto Mfg
Chicago	Music	50			100	Signed by Entire Band
Chichester, Francis, Sir	Aviation	35	100	150	75	Aviator, Sailed Gypsy Moth IV
Chickering, Thos.E.	Civil War	75	125	175		Union General/1824-71
Chiklis, Michael	Ent	10			25	
Child, Julia	Author	5			15	TV Chef. Cookbook Author
Child, Lydia Maria	Author	35	75	150		Abolitionist/Reformer
Childress, Alvin	Ent	50			125	
Childs, George Wm.	Author	10		25		Publisher
Chiles, Lois	Ent	10			25	James Bond Girl
Chilton, Robert H.	Civil War	200				CSA General/1816-79
Chirac, Jacques	Political	25	75	150	50	French Prime Minister
Chirico, Giorgio de	Art			600		Major Italian Surrealist
Cho, Margaret	Ent	10			25	Comedian
Choate, Joseph H.	Political	15	45	75	25	Prosecuted Tweed Ring
Chong, Rae Dawn	Ent	15			35	
Chopin, Frederic	Music	1,500	3,500	8,000		Composer
Chou En-Lai	Political	1,250	RARE	RARE	2,500	Chinese Premier
Chouteau, Auguste	RevWar	300	600	900		Am. Fur Trader/Pioneer
Christian IX (Den)	Royalty	100	250			1818-1906
Christian VII 1749-1808	Royalty	125	275	550		King of Denmark
Christian, Claudia	Ent	10			25	

Name	Field	SIG	DS	ALS	SP	Remarks
Christianson, Helena	Ent	15			30	
Christie, Agatha	Author	150	400	Scarce	Scarce	1891 - 1976
Christie, Julie	Ent	10	15	30	55	
Christina, Queen (Swe)	Royalty	450	1,500	2,250		
Christo	Art	25			75	
Christophe, Henry	Political	1,200				Haitian Revolution/1767-20
Christopher, William	Ent	5	25		20	MASH
Christy, Eileen	Ent	10			25	Vintage Actress
Christy, Howard Chandler	Art	100	200	250	400	Book Illustrator/1873-52
Christy, June	Music	10			20	Stan Kenton Vocalist
Chrysler, Walter P.	Business	400	1,000	1,500	900	Chrysler Motors/1879-40
Chung, Connie	Ent	5			15	TV News Anchor
Church, Benjamin	RevWar	200	500	900		Am. Physician & Spy
Church, Frederick E.	Art	150	375	750		Am. Landscapes/1826-00
Church, Frederick S.	Art	40	75	125		
Church, Thomas Hayden	Ent	20			45	Wings
Churchill, Clementine	First Lady	75	150	200	150	Wife of Winston
Churchill, John 1650-1722	Military	1,100				Ist Duke of Marlborough
Churchill, Randolph	Political	50	100	250		Father of Winston S.
Churchill, Sarah	Ent	30	65		60	Daughter of Winston S.
Churchill, Thomas J.	Civil War	75	100	200		CSA General/1824-1905
Churchill, Winston	Author	15	35	50	35	
Churchill, Winston S.	Political	800	1,600	3,000	2,750	PM During WWII/1874-65
Ciano, Galeazzo, Conte	Royalty	100	300			Son-in-Law of Mussolini
Cigna, Gina	Music	50	75			Opera
Cimaro, Pietro	Music	10	25	50		It. Conductor
Cimino, Michael	Ent	10		20	20	Director
Citroen, Andre 1878-1935	Business	100	350		700	Citroen Auto Mfg.
Clair, Rene 1898-1981	Ent	100		300		Fr. Filmaker
Clairborne, Liz	Business	10			20	Clothing Designer
Claire, Ina	Ent	15		35	25	
Claire, Marion	Music	10			25	Am. Soprano
Clampett, Bob	Cartoonist	100	200		300	Beany & Cecil/Warner Bros
Clancy, Tom	Author	15		50	35	Am. Novelist
Clanton, Jimmy	Music	20			45	Rock
Clapton, Eric	Music	30	125	200	60	
Clark, Abraham 1726-94	RevWar	350	750			Signer Decl. of Indepen.
Clark, Bruce C.	Military	5		25	15	
Clark, Buddy	Music	10			25	40's Singer
Clark, Candy	Ent	5			15	American Grafitti
Clark, Carol Higgins	Author	10		35	25	Mystery Novelist
Clark, Charles	Civil War	125	275	350		CSA General/1811-77
Clark, Cottonseed	Music	15			30	
Clark, Dick	Ent	10	25	30	25	
Clark, Edward	Civil War	75	200			CSA General/1815-80
Clark, Fred	Ent	25			50	
Clark, George Rogers	RevWar	750	2,250	3,500		General, Frontier Leader

Name	Field	SIG	DS	ALS	SP	Remarks
Clark, James B. Champ	Political	50		150	100	Speaker of the House
Clark, James, Sir	Science	25		75		Dr. to King and Queen
Clark, John Bullock,Sr.	Civil War	100	200			CSA General/1831-1903
Clark, L. Gaylord	Author	20	35	75		Editor Knickerbocker Mag
Clark, Marcia	Celebrity	15			35	OJ Simpson Trial
Clark, Marguerite	Ent	20			50	Stage
Clark, Mark W. 1896-1984	Military	35		200	100	Gen. WWII 5th Army.
Clark, Mary	Military	5		15	15	
Clark, Mary Higgins	Author	15	25		25	Suspense Novels
Clark, Petula	Music	10			25	
Clark, Roy	Music	5			15	
Clark, Susan	Ent	5			15	
Clark, Tom C.	SuprCt	50	100	125	125	
Clark, Walter J.	Aviation	10		35	30	WWII ACE
Clark, William 1770-1838	Western	400	1,500	2,000		Lewis & Clark Expedition
Clark, William A.	Business	45	125	200		Railroad & Mining Magnate
Clarke, Arthur C.	Author	15	35	75	45	Sci-Fi Author
Clarke, Charles M.	Science	25	50	125		Br. Obstetrician
Clarke, Henri J.G. Duc	Military	75	250	350		Marshal of Napoleon
Clarke, Ken	Ent	10			25	
Clarke, Mae	Ent	35		75	75	Frankenstein
Clarke, Thomas	RevWar	150	450			
Clarkson, Mathew	RevWar	50	100	175		
Clary, Robert	Ent	10	25	35	25	Hogans Heroes
Clavell, James	Author	10	25	50	25	
Clay, Andrew Dice	Ent	15			35	
Clay, Cassius Marcellus	Civil War	100	200	450		Union General/1810-1903
Clay, Henry 1777-1852	Political	125	300	750		Sec'y State
Clay, Lucius D. 1897-1978	Military	35	125	145	100	Gen.WWII
Clayburgh, Jill	Ent	5			20	
Clayton, Jan	Ent	5			15	
Clayton, John M.	Political	35	75	150		Taylor Sec'y State
Clayton, Joshua	RevWar	225	425			First DE Governor
Clear Sky, Chief	Western	25			50	Iroquois Chief
Cleaveland, Moses	RevWar	200				Cleveland, Ohio Namesake
Cleburne, Patrick R.	Civil War	1,000	1,750			CSA General/1828-64
Cleese, John	Ent	20	45	50	45	Monty Python member
Clem, John L.	Civil War	150	250	350	RARE	Union Drummer
Clemenceau, Georges	Political	100	150	175		Prime Minister France
Clemens & Twain	Author	1,200			RARE	Dual Signed
Clemens, Orion	Western	125		200		Sect of Nevada Territory
Clemens, Samuel L.	Author	750	1,500	2,000		Mark Twain/1835-1910
Clement VI II, Pope	Political	550	1,200			
Clements, John	Ent	25			45	Br. Director/Actor
Cleveland, Frances F.	First Lady	50	75	150	200	1864-1957
Cleveland, Grover	President	200	375	600	500	1837-1905
Clewes, Henry	Business	25	45			Banker

Name	Field	SIG	DS	ALS	SP	Remarks
Cliburn, Van	Music	25		50	75	Pianist
Clifford, Nathan 1803-81	SuprCt	75	175	200	150	Att'y Gen., Ambassador
Clift, Montgomery	Ent	225	350	600	750	1920 - 1966
Clifton, Joseph C.	Aviation	15	35	60	40	
Cline, Patsy	Music	450	1,750	2,000	1,500	Scarce in All Forms
Clingman, Thomas Lanier	Civil War	100	250	350		CSA General/1812-97
Clinton, De Witt 1769-28	Political	100	300	500		Mayor NYC
Clinton, George1739-1812	Vice Pres	150		300		
Clinton, Henry, Sir	RevWar	400	800	1,750		Br. Soldier
Clinton, Hillary Rodham	First Lady	200	450	Scarce	450	
Clinton, James	RevWar	200	450			General Revolutionary War
Clinton, William J. "Bill"	President	350	750	900	450	42nd U.S. President
Clive, Colin	Ent	225			400	
Clive, E.E.	Ent	20			50	
Clive, Robert	Military	250	600	900		Baron Clive of Plassey
Cloggers, Stoney Mtn.	Music	35			75	
Clokey, Art	Cartoonist	25			50	Gumby
Clooney, George	Ent	25			50	ER/Batman
Clooney, Rosemary	Ent	25			50	
Close, Glenn	Ent	25			50	
Clostermann, Pierre	Military	50	100	125	75	
Clover, Richardson	Military	35	125			USN Admiral
Clovio, Giorgio Guilio	Art	650	1,250	1,750		It. Miniaturist/1498-1578
Clyde, Andy	Ent	75			150	
Clymer, George 1739-13	RevWar	125	450	750		Signer Decl. of Indepen.
Coates, Eric	Music	25	50	75	125	Composer
Coates, Phyllis	Ent	15			25	
Coats, Bob	Aviation	10	20	35	30	WWII ACE
Cobain, Kurt	Music	125			250	Nirvana/Suicide
Cobb, Calvin H.	Military	15	45	75		
Cobb, Howell	Civil War	100	200	400		CSA General/1815-68
Cobb, Irvin S. 1876-1944	Author	25	50	150	100	
Cobb, Jerrie	Aviation	10		25		
Cobb, Lee J.	Ent	50	50	75	100	1911 - 1976
Cobb, Sylvanus 1823-87	Author	15		40		
Cobb, Thos. Reade R.	Civil War	500	1,500	2,000		CSA General/KIA/1823-62
Cobb, Ty	Sports	500	1,000	1,500	1,500	1936 HOF Baseball
Cobham, Alan J., Sir	Aviation	25	50	75	50	Br. Aviation Pioneer
Coburn, Charles 1877-61	Ent	50	100	150	125	AA
Coburn, James	Ent	10		25	25	
Coca, Imogene	Ent	15			25	
Cochran, Eddie 1938-60	Music	300	600		575	Dead at age 22
Cochran, Jacqueline	Aviation	50	150		150	Record Speed Holder
Cochran, Johnnie	Celebrity	15	45		35	OJ Simpson Trial
Cochran, Steve	Ent	15		30	30	
Cochrane, Basil, Sir	Military	15	25	30		
Cochrane, John	Civil War	30	50	100		Union General/1813-98

Name	Field	SIG	DS	ALS	SP	Remarks
Cockburn, George, Sir	Military	50	100	150		Br. Admiral War 1812
Cockcroft, John Douglas	Science	50	100	225	75	Nobel Physics
Cocke, Philip St. George	Civil War	Scarce	Scarce	Scarce	Scarce	CSA General/1809-61
Cocker, Joe	Music	25	50		50	
Cockrell, Francis Marion	Civil War	75	125	200		CSA General/1834-1915
Coco, James	Ent	15		25	35	
Cocteau, Jean	Author	125		600	600	
Coda, Eraldo	Music	10			25	Opera
Cody, Iron Eyes	Ent	25	50		50	Cherokee Indian Actor
Cody, Lew	Ent	15		25	35	
Cody, William F.	Western	750	1,500	2,000	4,500	Buffallo Bill
Coffin, Charles C.	Civil War	100				
Coffin, Isaac, Sir 1759-39	Military	25		75		Boston Born Br. Naval Officer
Coffin, John 1756-1838	RevWar	175	450			Loyalist General
Coffin, Tris	Ent	20			35	
Coffyn, Frank	Aviation	40	75		100	
Coghlan, Frank, Jr.	Ent	10	25		25	GWTW
Coghlan, Joseph B.	Military	25			50	Adm USN-Spanish American War
Cogswell, William	Civil War	15	35	75		
Cohan, George M.	Music	100	175	200	200	Composer/1878-1942
Cohen, Octavus Roy	Author	15	30	45	25	Novels and Screenplays
Cohen, Stanley, Dr.	Science	20	35		25	Nobel Medicine
Cohn, Harry	Business	35	75	150	75	Co-Founder Columbia Pix
Cohn, Jack	Business	25	75	150	50	Co-Founder Columbia Pix
Coit, James Brolles	Civil War	25		125		Union General
Coke, Edward, Sir	Political		2,000	3,500		Jurist/Lord Chief Justice
Colbert, Claudette	Ent	50	125		100	1905 - 1997
Colby, Leonard	Military	50	100			General. Indian Fighter
Colden, Cadwallader	RevWar	100	225			Am. Colonialist
Cole, Nat King 1919-65	Music	175	300		350	
Cole, Natalie	Music	15	45		45	
Cole, Tommy	Ent	25			45	
Coleman, Dabney	Ent	10			25	Nine to Five
Coleman, Gary	Ent	10	25		35	
Coleman, George	Music	20			45	Jazz Sax
Coleridge, Samuel T.	Author	325	575	1,250		Br. Poet and Critic
Coleridge-Taylor, S.	Music	25	75	150	50	Composer/1875-1912
Colette, Sidonie-Gabrielle	Author	100	250	350	600	French Novelist
Colfax, Schuyler	Vice Pres	75	125		250	Grants VP
Colgate, James C.	Business	25	25	50	50	Colgate University. Donor
Colgrass, Michael	Music	20	35	75		Composer/Pulitzer
Collective Soul	Music	25			45	Signed by all
Collier, Constance	Ent	25			75	British Actress
Collier, Peter F.	Business	15	35	75		
Collins, J. Lawton	Military	15	50	75	35	General WWII
Collins, Jackie	Author	10		20	15	
Collins, Joan	Ent	10	25	35	25	

Name	Field	SIG	DS	ALS	SP	Remarks
Collins, Judy	Music	10			25	
Collins, Michael	Space	100	150	250	150	Astronaut
Collins, Phil	Music	30	75		50	Genesis
Collins, Ray	Ent	50	75	150	175	
Collins, Wilkie	Author	100	300	450	1,250	Br. Novelist
Collis, Charles	Civil War	25		75		Union General
Collishaw, Raymond	Aviation	100	175	375	225	Brit. ACE, WW I
Collyer, June	Ent	15			35	
Colman, Ronald	Ent	75	125		175	AA Winner/1891-1958
Colman, Samuel	Art	25		100		
Colombo, Scipio	Music	10			30	Opera
Colonna, Jerry 1903 - 86	Ent	20			35	Comedian/Disney Voice
Color Me Badd	Music	35			65	Entire Group
Colquitt, Alfred H.	Civil War	100	150	275	250	CSA General/1824-94
Colston, Raleigh E.	Civil War	100	350			CSA General/1825-96
Colt, Samuel 1814-1862	Business	750	2,000	2,750		Founder Colt Firearms
Coltrane, John	Music	RARE	RARE	RARE	RARE	Jazz
Colum, Padraic	Author	30	150		75	Irish Poet & Playwright
Columbo, Russ	Ent	75	150	200	200	
Combs, Holly Marie	Ent	25			50	
Combs, Sean "Puffy"	Music	20			50	
Comden, Betty & Green, A.	Music	10	45		35	Broadway Composers
Commager, Henry S.	Civil War	25	60	100		Union General/1825-67
Commodores	Music	35	100		75	Entire Group
Como, Perry	Music	15			40	
Compson, Betty	Ent	15	30	50	75	
Compton, Arthur H.	Science	100	200	275	150	Nobel Physics. Atom Bomb
Compton, Fay	Ent	5			15	
Compton, Joyce	Ent	10			20	
Compton, Karl T.	Science	100	200		150	Physicist, Pres. M.I.T.
Conant, A. Roger	Aviation	10		35	30	ACE/WWII/Marine Ace
Conati, Lorenzo	Music	25			65	Opera
Conaway, Jeff	Ent	15			35	Taxi/Grease
Conchita, Maria	Ent	5			10	
Conde', Louis II 1621-86	Military		750			French General
Condon, Eddie	Music	40			75	Composer
Condon, Richard	Author	5		35	10	
Cone, Fairfax M.	Business	10	35	45	25	Foote,Cone & Belding, Adv.
Cone, Hutchinson	Military	25	35			Admiral WW I
Congreve, William	Author	200	450	750		1670-1729
Coningham, Sir Arthur	Aviation	35	75			Cmdr. RAF lst Tactical
Conklin, Chester	Ent	100	150	225		
Conklin, Hal	Ent	10			25	
Conlee, John	Ent	5			10	
Conley, Eugene	Music	20	30		50	Opera
Conley, Joe	Ent	5			10	
Connally, John B.	Political	25	50	100	50	Gov. TX, Sec'y Treasury

Name	Field	SIG	DS	ALS	SP	Remarks
Connelly, Christopher	Ent	10			25	
Connelly, Jennifer	Ent	20			50	
Connelly, Marc 1890-1980	Author	20	75	75	35	Am. Dramatist. Pulitzer
Connelly, Matthew J.	Political	10	25	35	25	Pres. Truman Aide
Conner, James	Civil War	100	200	250		CSA General. lst Bull Run
Conner, Nadine	Music	10			35	Opera/Radio
Connery, Sean	Ent	50	125		125	James Bond
Connick, Harry, Jr.	Music	25			45	
Conniff, Ray	Ent	25	35	75	50	
Connolly, Walter	Ent	50		100	75	
Connor, Harry P.	Aviation	15	30		50	
Connor, James	Civil War	100	200	250		CSA General/18829-83
Connor, Patrick Edward	Civil War	35	75			Union General/1820-91
Connors, Chuck	Ent	35	75	100	75	The Rifleman
Connors, Mike	Ent	10	25		25	Mannix
Conquest, Ida	Ent	15		25	30	
Conrad, Charles Jr.	Space	40	100		100	3rd Moonwalker.
Conrad, Charles Magill	Political	50		175		Sec'y War/1804-1878
Conrad, Joseph 1857-24	Author	350	900	1,400	1,250	Br. Novelist. Lord Jim etc.
Conrad, Michael	Ent	15		45	35	
Conrad, Robert	Ent	20	50		50	Wild,Wild,West
Conrad, William	Ent	35	50		65	Cannon
Conried, Hans	Ent	25	50		50	Disney Voice/Actor
Conroy, Kevin	Ent	10			20	Voice of Animated Batman
Conroy, Pat	Author	25			50	Great Santini,Prince of Tides
Constable, John 1776-37	Art	300	550	1,500		Br. Landscapes, Rural Life
Constantine I, 1868-1923	Royalty	100				King of Greece. Resigned
Constantino, Florencio	Music	100			300	Opera
Conte, John	Ent	5			15	
Conte, Richard	Ent	15			25	1911 - 1975
Conti, Bill	Music	25	75	100	50	Composer
Convy, Bert	Ent	20			25	
Conway, Henry Seymour	Military	25	75	125		Br. Fld. Marshal. /1721-95
Conway, Pat	Ent	10			25	
Conway, Shirl	Ent	10			25	
Conway, Thomas	RevWar	50	100	225		Maj. Gen. Rev, War
Conway, Tim	Ent	5		15	20	Carol Burnett Show
Conway, Tom	Ent	50			100	The Saint
Coogan, Jackie 1914-84	Ent	35	75		75	Fester/Addams Family
Coogan, Richard	Ent	5			20	
Cook, Ann T.	Ent	10			25	Model For Gerber Baby Products
Cook, Elisha Jr. 1902-95	Ent	75	100		100	Character Actor
Cook, Eliza	Author	25		75		Poet
Cook, Everett R.	Aviation	10		50	50	ACE WW I
Cook, Francis Augustus	Military	35		50	75	Spanish American War
Cook, Frederick Albert	Explorer	75	150	175	150	Claimed lst at North Pole
Cook, James, Capt.	Military	4,000	9,000	RARE	RARE	Captain Cook

Name	Field	SIG	DS	ALS	SP	Remarks
Cook, Philip	Civil War	150	300	400		CSA General/1817-94
Cook, Robin	Author	10			25	Coma,Sphinx...
Cook, Thomas	Business	35	100			Fndr Br Tourist Comm.
Cook, Tommy	Ent	20			45	Child Actor
Cook, Walter V.	Aviation	15		45	30	ACE/WWII
Cooke, Alistair, Sir	Ent	25	100	150	75	TV Host. Masterpiece Theatre
Cooke, Jack Kent	Business	10			15	
Cooke, Jay 1821-1905	Business	300	1,200	2,000		Banker, Financier
Cooke, Nicholas	RevWar	Scarce	700	1,000	Scarce	Rev-War Gov. RI
Cooke, Sam	Music	250	750		500	Died Young
Cooley, Denton A., Dr.	Science	15		60	50	Heart Transplant Surgeon
Cooley, Lyman E.	Science	10		35		Civil Engineer
Cooley, Spade	Music	15			35	King of Western Swing
Coolidge, Calvin	President	150	400	900	450	
Coolidge, Grace	First Lady	90	250	175	175	
Coolidge, Rita	Music	10			25	
Coolidge, William David	Science	50	100	150	125	GE Researcher/Inventor
Coolio	Music	20			50	
Coombs, Patricia	Art	10	20	35	15	
Cooper, Alice	Music	20			55	
Cooper, Emil	Music	35	150	100	75	Russian Composer
Cooper, Gary 1901-61	Ent	125	300	450	400	
Cooper, Gladys, Dame	Ent	35		75	50	1888 - 1971
Cooper, Gordon	Space	35	75		75	Mercury 7 Astronaut
Cooper, Jackie	Ent	25	25	35	60	Child Actor
Cooper, James Fenn	Author	100	200			Am. Novelist/1789-1851
Cooper, Leon N., Dr.	Science	20	35	75	45	Nobel Physics
Cooper, Leroy, Jr.	Space	50				Apollo VII (Early Sig.)
Cooper, Merian C.	Ent	150	300		250	King Kong
Cooper, Miriam	Ent	35			75	
Cooper, Peter 1791-1883	Business	150	500	750		Am. Inventor, Philanthropist
Cooper, Samuel	Civil War	125	250	450		CSA General/1798-1876
Cooper, Thos. Sidney	Art	10	20	35		
Coors, W. K.	Business	20	75	100	50	Coors Brewery
Coots, J. Fred	Music	35	45	100	40	Composer
Copage, Marc	Ent	10			25	
Copas, Cowboy	Music	100			225	
Copeland, L. du Pont	Business	25		50		
Copland, Aaron 1900-90	Music	75	150	300	150	Composer
Copley, John Singleton	Art	350	700	RARE		1738-1815
Copley, Teri	Ent	5			15	
Coppens, Willy (Baron)	Aviation	20	45	125	50	
Copperfield, David	Ent	20	50		50	Magician
Coppola, Francis Ford	Ent	35	75	100	75	AA Film Director
Coquelin, Benoit-Const	Ent	25	50	75		
Corbett, Boston	Assasin	1,000	RARE	2,000	RARE	Shot John Wilkes Booth
Corbin, Bary	Ent	10			25	

Name	Field	SIG	DS	ALS	SP	Remarks
Corbin, Henry Clarke	Civil War	50		100		Union General
Corbusier, Le 1887-1965	Science	200	450		575	Jeanneret, Charles Edouard
Corby, Ellen	Ent	25	45		50	The Waltons
Corcoran, Michael	Civil War			1,500		Union General/1827-63
Corcoran, William W.	Business	150	600	1,200		Banker, Philanthropist
Cord, Alex	Ent	10			15	
Corden, Henry	Ent	15			35	2nd Voice/Fred Flintstone
Corea, Chick	Ent	15			35	
Corelli, Franco	Music	25		100	100	Opera
Corelli, Marie 1855-1924	Author	35	75	75	75	English Novelist
Corena, Fernando	Music	20			50	Opera
Corey, Elias	Science	20	35		30	Nobel Chemistry
Corey, Jeff	Ent	5			15	
Corey, Wendell	Ent	35	75	75	75	
Cori, Carl F.	Science	15	25	45	30	Nobel Medicine
Corio, Ann	Ent	15		20	30	
Corlett, Irene	Ent	5			10	
Cormack, Allan M.	Science	20	35	50	25	Nobel Medicine
Corman, Roger	Ent	10			30	
Cornbury, Edward Hyde	Political	200	450			Ist Colonial Gov. NJ
Cornelius, Don	Ent	10			20	
Cornelius, Peter	Music	100		250		Opera
Cornell, Ezekiel	Military	75	200			Brig. Gen. American Rev.
Cornell, Ezra	Business	35	75	150	75	Western Union Financier
Cornell, Joseph 1903-72	Art	250	750	600		Am. Surrealist Sculptor
Cornell, Katharine	Ent	20		75	75	1898-1974
Cornell, Lydia	Ent	5			15	
Corner, George W.	Science	75	150		100	
Cornfeld, Bernard	Business	10		50	45	
Cornforth, John W., Sir	Science	15	35	45	30	Nobel Laureate/Chemistry
Corning, Erastus 1794-72	Business	75	175	250		Pres. NY Central RR
Cornwallis, Charles E.	RevWar	175	500	1,200		Br. General RevWar
Corot, J.B. Camille	Art	250	500	900	2,000	Impressionist
Corrigan, Douglas	Aviation	50	75	200	100	Wrong Way
Corrigan, Mairead	Political	35	50	100	50	Nobel Peace Prize 1976
Corrigan, Ray Crash	Ent	50			150	
Corsaut, Aneta	Ent	50	100	100	100	Andy Griffith Show
Corse, John Murray	Civil War	50	100	100		Union General/1835-93
Corse, Montgomery D.	Civil War	125		275		CSA General/1816-95
Cortez, Hernando	Explorer	6,000	20,000	RARE	RARE	Sp. Conqueror of Mex.
Cortez, Ricardo	Ent	25			45	
Cortina, Juan	Military	Scarce	Scarce	Scarce	Scarce	Mexican General
Corwin, Thomas	Political	35	75	100		Fillmore Sec'y Treasury
Cosby, Bill	Ent	10	30	40	30	
Cosby, George B.	Civil War	75	125	200		CSA General/1831-1909
Cosell, Howard	Ent	25	50	75	50	Radio-TV Sports News
Cosgrave, William T.	Political	75	150	275		Sinn Fe'in Easter Uprising.

Name	Field	SIG	DS	ALS	SP	Remarks
Coslow, Sam	Music	75	200	300	350	AA Winning Composer
Cossotto, Fioranza	Music	10			30	Opera
Cossutta, Carlos	Music	10			25	Opera
Costa Lo Giudice, Silvio	Music	50			100	Opera
Costa, Michael, Sir	Music	15	45	75	25	Br. Conductor.Opera
Costas, Bob	Ent	5			10	TV Host & Sports Commentator
Coste, Dieudonne	Aviation	125	200	350	275	
Costello, Delores	Ent	30	50	75	75	
Costello, Elvis	Music	15			45	
Costello, Lou 1906-59	Ent	200	250	400	400	Abbott and Costello
Costner, Kevin	Ent	25	75		50	AA Winner
Coswell, Henry T.	Aviation	50	100	150		Ist Balloon ascent 1844
Cotten, Joseph 1905-94	Ent	25	45		45	
Cotton, Carolina	Music	15			30	
Coty, Frangois	Business	100	300	450		Coty Perfume & Cosmetics
Couch, Darius Nash	Civil War	50	75	150		Union General/1822-97
Coulouris, George	Ent	10			25	Character Actor
Coulter, Jessie	Music	10			25	
Coulter, Richard	Civil War	50	75	100		Union Bvt. General
Couples, Fred	Sports	15			30	Golfer
Courbet, Jean D. Gustave	Art	225	500	900		Leader of Realist School
Couric, Katie	Ent	5			15	TV Host of Today Show
Court, Hazel	Ent	10			35	
Courtney, Inez	Ent	15			35	
Cousins, Norman	Author	10		45	25	Saturday Review Editor
Cousteau, Jacques	Science	100	175	175	150	Underwater Explorer, Films
Cousteau, Jim (Son)	Science	25			75	Underwater Explorer
Couter, John B.	Military	15	45			
Coward, Noel, Sir	Author	100	200	300	275	1899-1973
Cowl, Jane	Ent	20		35	45	
Cowles, Gardner	Business	10		25	15	Publisher
Cox, George H.	Author	5		30		Br. Historical Writer
Cox, Jacob D.	Civil War	25		75		Union General/1828-1900
Cox, Samuel S. 1824-89	Political	35		125		Civil War Repr. OH
Cox, Wally	Ent	30	50		60	
Cox, William R.	Civil War	50	75	100		CSA General/1832-1919
Cox, Archibald	Political	15		50	25	Att'y Gen/Watergate
Cox, Courtney	Ent	25	50		50	Friends
Cox, Nikki	Ent	25			50	
Cox, Palmer	Cartoonist	100		300	250	Brownies
Coxe, Tenche	RevWar	50	100	150		Continental Congress
Coyote, Peter	Ent	15			35	
Crabbe, Buster 1909-83	Ent	35	75		75	Flash Gordon/Tarzan
Crabbe, Cullen	Ent	15			35	
Crabtree, Lotta	Ent	25	75	100	100	
Craddock, "Crash" Billy	Music	10			25	
Craig, Edward Gordon	Ent	15	45	150	200	

Name	Field	SIG	DS	ALS	SP	Remarks
Craig, James	Civil War	50	75	100		Union General/1820-88
Craig, Jenny	Business	5			10	Diet Guru
Craig, Yvonne	Ent	10	20		20	TV's Batgirl
Crain, Jeanne	Ent	15		45	45	
Cram, Donald J., Dr.	Science	20	35		30	Nobel Chemistry
Cramer, Floyd	Music	5			15	
Crampton, Barbara	Ent	15			25	
Cranch, Christopher P.	Art	5		25	35	1813-1892
Crane, Bob	Ent	150	250	Scarce	300	Hogan of Hogans Heroes
Crane, Charles Henry	Civil War	35	175	200		Union General.Surgeon
Crane, Fred	Ent	35		75	75	GWTW
Crane, Hart	Author	150	450	Scarce	350	Am. Poet, The Bridge
Crane, John	Military	100	250			RevWar General
Crane, Richard	Ent	20			45	
Crane, Roy	Cartoonist	30			75	Wash Tubbs, B. Sawyer
Crane, Stephen	Author	1,500	RARE	4,500	RARE	Red Badge of Courage
Crane, Walter 1845-1915	Art	75	150	250		Br. Painter-Illustrator.
Crane, William H	Ent	30	45	75	50	1845-1928
Crass, Franz	Music	10			25	Opera
Craven, Frank	Ent	20			50	
Craven, John	Ent	10			25	
Craven, Wes	Ent	10			25	Director
Cravens, Jordan E.	Civil War	25		75		CSA Officer
Crawford, Broderick	Ent	35	75		100	
Crawford, Christina	Ent	5		30	15	Daughter of Joan Crawford
Crawford, Cindy	Ent	25			50	Model
Crawford, Francis M.	Author	15		25		Am. Novelist/1854-1909
Crawford, J. W. Capt.	Military	75		250		Indian Wars Scout
Crawford, Joan 1904-77	Ent	75	175	250	225	
Crawford, Johnny	Ent	10			25	The Rifleman
Crawford, Michael	Ent	25			50	Phantom of the Opera
Crawford, Samuel W.	Civil War	50	75	200		Union General/1829-92
Crawford, William H.	Political	50	150	150		Madison Sect of War
Crawford-Frost, Wm. A.	Business	15	25	50	30	
Cream	Music	75			150	Signed by All Three
Credence Clearwater	Music	50	150		100	Signed by All
Credence Clearwater	Music	125	300		250	Signed by entire band
Creeley, Robert	Author	5			10	
Cregar, Laird 1916-44	Ent	100		200	300	Character Actor/Dead at 28
Creighton, Johnston	Civil War	100	350			Union Admiral
Cremer, Peter Erich	Military	75		125		
Crenna, Richard	Ent	10	25		35	Rambo
Cresap, Mark	Business	5			10	
Creston, Paul	Music	35			125	Composer
Crews, Laura Hope	Ent	200	300		350	Aunt Pittypat-GWTW
Crichton, Michael	Author	25	100		75	Jurassic Park. etc.
Crick, Francis, Dr.	Science	50	75			Nobel in Medicine, DNA

Name	Field	SIG	DS	ALS	SP	Remarks
Crier, Katherine	Ent	5			10	TV Commentary
Crippen, Robert L.	Space	15			50	Shuttle Orbiter 102 Crew
Cripps, Richard Stafford	Political	35	100	200		Br.Economist
Crisp, Donald	Ent	50	75	100	150	
Cristal, Linda	Ent	10		30	20	
Crittenden, John J.	Political	25	50	125		Attorney General/Senator
Crittenden, Thomas L.	Civil War	50	125	250	250	Union General/1819-93
Croce, Benedetto	Author	35	75	75		
Croce, Jim	Music	150	300		450	Died Young
Crocker, Charles	Business	500	2,000	3,000		Am. Financier/RARE
Crockett, David 1786-36	Military	6,000	9,000	20,000		Died at Alamo
Crockett, Samuel R.	Author	10		35		
Croft, Dwayne	Music	10			25	Opera
Croghan, George	Business	200	400	800		Indian Treaty Maker/Trader
Croker, Richard Boss	Political	25	50	75		Tammany Hall Leader
Crompton, Richmal	Author	15	45	75	45	
Cromwell, James	Ent	15			45	
Cromwell, Oliver 1599-58	Political	1,200	RARE	RARE		Named Lord Protector Eng.
Cromwell, Richard	Ent	5			15	
Cronenberg, David	Ent	10			25	Film Director
Cronin, A. J.	Author	25	75	150	45	Br. Physician-Novelist.
Cronin, Hume	Ent	15		30	35	1911 - 1997
Cronin, James W.	Science	15	25	35	20	Nobel Physics
Cronkite, Walter	Ent	10	25	50	25	TV News Anchor
Crook and Chase	Ent	15			25	Lorianne & Charlie
Crook, George	Civil War	150	400	400	400	Union General/1818-90
Crookes, William, Sir	Science	125		200		Nobel Chemistry/1832-19
Crooks, Richard	Music	20		50	50	Opera
Crosby, Bing 1901-77	Ent	75	200	300	200	
Crosby, Bob	Music	15			25	Big Band Leader
Crosby, Cathy Lee	Ent	10			25	
Crosby, Denise	Ent	15			40	Star Trek Next Generation
Crosby, Gary	Ent	5			10	
Crosby, J.T.	Aviation	10		45	30	ACE/WWII/Navy Ace
Crosby, Kathryn	Ent	10		25	25	
Crosby, Mary	Ent	5		10	15	
Crosby, Norm	Ent	5		15	10	
Crosby, Percy	Cartoonist	40			75	Skippy
Crosby, Stills & Nash	Music	75	125		125	
Crosley, Powel Jr.	Business	20	75	100	45	Crosley Radio Corp.
Crosman, George H.	Civil War	25		75	50	Union General/1798-1882
Crosman, Henrietta	Ent	10			25	
Cross, Christopher	Music	15			30	
Cross, Marcia	Ent	25			50	Melrose Place
Crosse, Andrew 1784-55	Science			165		Br. Electrical Pioneer
Crossfield, A. Scott	Aviation	15	30	45	50	Ist U.S. Test Pilot of X-15
Crothers, Rachel	Author	5	30	40	20	Am. Playwright.

Name	Field	SIG	DS	ALS	SP	Remarks
Crothers, Scatman	Ent	35	45		75	Disney Voice/Actor
Crouse, Russell	Author	10		45	60	Playwright. Life With Father
Croves, H. (B.Traven)	Author	250	600			Ger. Novelist
Crow, Sheryl	Music	25			50	
Crowe, Russell	Ent	25			50	Gladiator
Crowe, William	Military	15	45		25	Admiral U.S. Navy
Crowell, Rodney	Ent	15			30	
Crowley, Pat	Ent	5			15	
Crowninshield, Benj. W.	Political	30	75	150		Sec'y Navy 1814
Crozier, William	Military	35			75	General WWI, Inventor
Cruger, Henry	Business	250	Scarce	Scarce		1739-1827 Amer. Merchant
Cruikshank, George	Art	150	150	350	400	Illustrator,Caricaturist
Cruise, Tom	Ent	35	200	Scarce	75	
Crumb, George	Music	25			45	Composer/Pulitzer
Crumb, Robert	Cartoonist	25			75	Underground Comic Books
Cruz, Brandon	Ent	15			35	Courtship of Eddie's Father
Cruzen, Richard H.	Explorer	20		50	75	Adm. Arctic-Antarctic/Byrd
Cruz-Romo, Gilda	Music	15			30	Opera
Cryer, Jon	Ent	25	50		50	Breakfast Club
Crystal, Billy	Ent	20	50		45	
Cudahy, Michael F.	Business	25	75	125	50	Meat Packer. Refrigeration
Cugat, Xavier	Music	20		35	100	Big Band Rhumba King
Cui, Cesar 1835-1918	Music	100	200	450		Composer
Cukor, George	Ent	45	100		100	Stage and Screen Director
Culbertson, Ely 1891-55	Author	25	75		150	Bridge Championship
Culkin, Macaulay	Ent	25	50		50	Home Alone
Cullen, Bill	Ent	10			30	Game Show Host
Cullen, Countee 103-46	Author	200	400	400		Am. Black Poet
Cullum, George W.	Civil War	25		75		Union General/1809-92
Culp, Julia	Music	35			150	Opera
Culp, Robert	Ent	10	30		25	I Spy
Cumming, Alfred	Civil War	100	250	300		CSA General/1829-1910
Cummings, E.E.	Author	200	350	500	750	Am. Poet, Painter
Cummings, Homer	Political	25	50	75	125	FDR Att'y Gen./1870-56
Cummings, Robert	Ent	15			35	1908 - 1990
Cunard, Samuel, Sir	Business	100	125	200		Br. Shipowner.Cunard Line
Cunningham, Andrew B. 1883-1963	Military	50	100	200		Br. Adm. S. Afr, & WW I
Cunningham, E.V.	Author	20			45	Howard Fast
Cunningham, Merce	Ent	50		150	75	Dancer/Choreographer
Cunningham, R. Walter	Space	10	20	30	25	Astronaut
Cunningham, Randy D	Aviation	15	25	45	35	ACE, Nam, Only Navy Ace
Cuomo, Mario	Political	15	35		50	Governor NY
Curbs, Samuel Ryan	Civil War	50		150		Union General/1817-66
Curie, Marie 1867-1934	Science	1,000	1,500	2,250	Scarce	
Curie, Pierre 1859-1906	Science	400	800	RARE	RARE	
Currie, Donald, Sir	Business	10	25	45		Scot. Shipowner

Name	Field	SIG	DS	ALS	SP	Remarks
Currier, Nathaniel	Art	250	600	600		Currier & Ives, Lithographers
Curry, B.	Civil War	30	75			CSA Officer
Curry, George	Military	30	75			Ist Territorial Gov. NM
Curry, Jabez L.M.	Civil War	15		40		CSA Congress/1825-1903
Curry, John Stewart	Art	75		300		
Curry, Tim	Ent	25			50	Rocky Horror Show
Curtin, Jane	Ent	20	45	45	45	Sat Nite Live
Curtis, Alan	Ent	10		35	25	
Curtis, Benjamin R.	SuprCt	35	150	200		Resigned in Protest
Curtis, Charles	Vice Pres	50	125	175	100	
Curtis, Cyrus H. K.	Business	35	75	150	100	Curtis Publishing Co.
Curtis, Edward Sheriff	Art	Scarce	500	RARE	1,300	Photographer/1868-52
Curtis, George Wm.	Author	50	125	75		Editor Harper's Weekly
Curtis, Jamie Lee	Ent	25	100		50	
Curtis, Ken 1916-91	Ent	35	100	100	75	Festus on Gunsmoke
Curtis, Newton M.	Civil War	30	75			Union General/1835-1910
Curtis, Robin	Ent	10		25	30	Star Trek movie
Curtis, Tony	Ent	10	30	30	30	
Curtis, Verna Maria	Music	10			30	Am. Soprano
Curtis, Wilfred A.	Aviation	10	25		25	
Curtiss, Glenn	Aviation	300	500	600	750	Pioneer Aircraft
Curtiz, Michael	Ent	35	75		100	Director
Cusack, Joan	Ent	20			45	
Cusack, John	Ent	25			50	
Cushing, Caleb 1800-79	Political	25	50	100		Pierce Att'y Gen., Diplomat
Cushing, Harvey, Dr.	Science	175	350	550		Specialist in Neurosurgery
Cushing, Peter	Ent	50	100	125	100	Horror star
Cushing, Thomas	Military	450	900			Patriot/1725-88
Cushman, Charlotte S.	Ent	25		45	45	
Custer, Elizabeth	Author	100	200	Scarce	375	Wife of George A. Custer
Custer, George A.	Civil War	3,500	7,500	10,000	15,000	Union General/1839-76
Custine, Adam Philippe	RevWar	100	350			Fr.Gen.in RevWar
Cutler, Lysander	Civil War	100	200	250		Union General/1806-66
Cutler, Manasseh 1742-23	RevWar	425	550			Am.Clergyman
Cuvier, Georges, Baron	Science	100	250	350		Fr. Comparative Anatomy
Cuyler, Theodore L.	Author	10		35		
Cyrus, Billy Ray	Music	20			40	
Czerny, Carl	Music	100	200	400		Composer
Czerny, Vincenz	Science	125				Pioneer/Abdominal Surgery

Name	Field	SIG	DS	ALS	SP	Remarks
D'Abo, Maryan	Ent	25			45	
D'Abo, Olivia	Ent	25			45	
Dache, Lilly	Business	50	75	125	150	Coutourier.Specialty-Hats
Dafoe, Allan Roy, Dr.	Science	75	100	125	225	Delivered Dionne Quintuplets
Dafoe, Willem	Ent	15	50		45	
Dagmar	Ent	20			35	
Dagover, Lil	Ent	100			200	
Daguerre, Louis	Science	250	450	1,250		Fr. Inventor Daguerreotype
Dahl, Arlene	Ent	10			20	
Dahl, Perry	Aviation	10		35	35	ACE/WWII
Dahl, Roald	Author	50	150		100	Childrens Books
Dahlberg, Edward	Author	15	25	35	20	Am. Writer & Critic
Dahlberg, Ken	Aviation	15	30	50	40	WWII ACE
Dahlgren, John A.	Civil War	100	300	400		Adm. Union Navy/1809-70
Dahlgren, Ulric	Civil War	350		1,200		Planned Jeff Davis Capture
Dailey, Dan	Ent	15	25	45	45	1914 - 1978
Dailey, Janet	Author	5		25	15	
Daily, Bill	Ent	10			20	
Dal Monte, Toti	Music	35			100	Opera
Daladier, Edouard	Political	30	75	150	50	
Dalai Lama XIV	Political	75	150	200	100	Tibetan Religious Leader
D'Albert, Eugene	Music	100	200		200	Opera
Daley, Cass	Ent	5		25	15	
Daley, Richard J.	Political	20	50	75	50	Mayor Chicago
Daley, Richard M.	Political	5			10	Mayor Chicago
Dali, Salvador 1904-89	Art	200	450	600	750	Sp. Surrealist Painter
Dallapozza, Adolf	Music	10			25	Vienna Operettas
Dallas, Alexander J.	Political	45	150	175		Madison Sec'y Treasury
Dallas, George M.	Vice Pres	75	200	300		Dallas Named for Him
Dalmores, Charles	Music	25			85	Opera
Dalton, Dorothy	Ent	20		65	60	
Dalton, Lacy J.	Music	5			15	
Dalton, Emmett 1871-37	Western	800	1,600	3,500	Scarce	Western Train Robber
Dalton, Frank	Western	850	2,500			U.S.Marshal-Old West
Dalton, John	Science	150	450	750		Br. Chemist & Philosopner
Dalton, Tristan	Military	600		2,000		Am. Patriot/1738-1817
Dalton,Timothy	Ent	25			50	James Bond
Daltry, Roger	Music	35	75		65	Lead singer of the Who
Daly, James	Ent	5			15	
Daly, John Charles	Ent	5			10	Broadcaster
Daly, Timothy	Ent	20			45	Wings
Daly, Tyne	Ent	10	25		25	Cagney and Lacey

Name	Field	SIG	DS	ALS	SP	Remarks
Damita, Lili	Ent	30	75	100	100	
Damon, Cathryn	Ent	10			20	
Damon, Les	Ent	15			45	The Thin Man
Damon, Matt	Ent	25			50	
Damone, Vic	Music	5			10	Singer
Damrosch, Walter	Music	50	150	125	200	Composer/1862-1950
Dana, Charles A. 1819-97	Business	20	35	75	45	Owner & Editor NY Sun
Dana, James D.	Science	15		45		
Dana, James Jackson	Civil War	50	150			Union General
Dana, Napoleon J.T.	Civil War	30	75			Union General/1822-05
Dana, Richard Henry, Jr.	Author	50	200	200		1815-1882
Dandridge, Dorothy	Ent	100	200		300	1923-1965
Dandridge, Ruby	Ent	35			75	
Dandy, George B.	Civil War	50	100			Union General/1830-1911
Dane, Karl	Ent	10			15	
Dane, Nathan	RevWar	25	75	125		Continental Congress
Dane, Taylor	Music	20			45	
Danes, Claire	Ent	25			50	
Danforth, Thomas	Political	300	500			Deputy Governor MA
D'Angelo, Beverly	Ent	15			30	
Dangerfield, Rodney	Ent	10		25	25	
Danges, Henry 1870-1948	Music	35				Opera
Daniel, Peter Vivian	SuprCt	50	125	200		
Daniell, Henry	Ent	50			150	Character Actor
Daniels, Babe	Ent	20		50	75	
Daniels, Billy	Music	10			20	
Daniels, Charlie	Music	10			20	
Daniels, Jeff	Ent	15			45	
Daniels, Josephus	Political	25		150	125	Sec'y Navy WWI
Daniels, William	Ent	10			25	
Danilova, Alexandra	Music	20	45	50	75	Rus-Am Ballerina, Teacher
Dannay, Frederick	Author	75	200	300 Scarce		Ellery Queen
Dannay, Frederick	Author	75	150	300		ELLERY QUEEN
Dannenberg, Konrad	Science	20			50	Rocket Pioneer/von Braun
Danner, Blythe	Ent	10			25	
Danning, Sybil	Ent	10			25	
D'Annunzio, Gabriele	Author	75	175	150	350	It Writer/1863-1938
Dano, Royal	Ent	30		75	60	Hawaii 5-0
Danson, Ted	Ent	25	50		50	Cheers
Dantine, Helmut	Ent	15			45	
Danton, Georges-Jacques	Military	1,000	2,500			Guillotined Leader of Rev.
Danton, Ray	Ent	10			15	
Danza, Tony	Ent	10		30	30	Taxi and Who's the Boss
Darby, Kim	Ent	15			35	
Darcel, Denise	Ent	25			50	Actress
Darcy, Emery	Music	15			45	Met Tenor
Darin, Bobby	Music	150		300	400	1936 - 1973

Name	Field	SIG	DS	ALS	SP	Remarks
Darion, Joe	Music	10			30	Composer
Darlan, Francois 1881-42	Military			450		Fr. Adm. Vichy. Assassinated
Darling, J.N. "Ding"	Cartoonist	25			75	Political Cartoonist
Darlington, William	Science	35		125		Naturalist/1782-1863
Darnell, Linda 1923-65	Ent	75	150		200	Died Tragically in Fire
Darrah, Thomas	Military	25	50			General WW I
Darrall, Chester B.	Civil War	15	45	50		Union Surgeon CW
Darrell, Johnny	Music	10			20	
Darren, James	Ent	10			20	
Darro, Frankie	Ent	75	125		150	Disney Voice/Child actor
Darrow, Charles B.	Business	400	RARE	1,000	RARE	Inventor of Monopoly
Darrow, Clarence	Political	450	1,500	2,000	1,250	Scopes Trial Lawyer
Dart, Justin	Business	50	100	200	100	
D'Artagnan, Comte de	Military	RARE	RARE	6,500	RARE	Capt.Louis XIV Musketeers
Darwell, Jane 1880-1967	Ent	100	200	250	200	GWTW
Darwin, Charles 1809-92	Science	750	1,500	1,750	RARE	Theory of Evolution
Dassin, Jules	Ent	20			45	Director
Daubigny, Charles F.	Art	100	300	400		Fr. Landscape Painter
Daudet, Alphonse	Author	35	75	175		
Daugherty, Harry M.	Political	25	50	125	50	Attorney General
Daumier, Honore	Art	250	500	1,000		Fr. Caricaturist
Dauphin, Claude	Ent	35			75	
Dausset, Jean, Prof.	Science	20	45		30	Nobel Medicine
Dave Clarke Five	Music	100	150		200	Signed by Entire Band
Davenport, Addington	RevWar	150	250	500		Am. Colonial Jurist1670-36
Davenport, Fanny	Ent	25			50	
Davenport, Harry	Ent	150			275	1866 - 1949
Davenport, Homer C.	Cartoonist	30	75	125		Uncle Sam cartoonist
David, Felicien-Cesar	Music	100	300			Composer/1810-76
David, Ferdinand	Music	50		175		Ger. Violinist
David, Hal	Music	20		65	35	Composer
David, Jacques Louis	Art	175	350	500		Fr. Classical Painter
David, Mack	Music	20			40	Lyricist
Davidson, Allen Turner	Civil War	25	75	125		CSA Congress
Davidson, Arthur d.1950	Business	Scarce	2,000	Scarce	Scarce	RARE/Harley Davidson
Davidson, Gordon	Business	Scarce	2,750	Scarce	Scarce	One of Harley-Davidson Founders
Davidson, Jo	Art	35	75	125		Am. Sculptor
Davidson, John	Ent	5			10	
Davidson, William H.	Business	Scarce	3,000	4,000		Harley-Davidson Pres./Scarce
Davies, Gail	Music	5			10	
Davies, Marion	Ent	30	50	150	125	
Davies, Peter Maxwell	Music	30			100	Opera
Davies, Rhys John	Ent	15		50	45	
Davies, William	RevWar	35		150		VA Sec'y War
Davis, Ann B.	Ent	10			25	Brady Bunch
Davis, Benjamin O. Jr	Aviation	20	35	75	50	WWII ACE

Name	Field	SIG	DS	ALS	SP	Remarks
Davis, Bette 1908-89	Ent	100	200	350	200	
Davis, Brad	Ent	30			45	
Davis, Charles Henry	Civil War	30	75	100		Union Admiral/1807-77
Davis, Clifton	Ent	5			15	
Davis, David/1815-1886	SuprCt	75	200	225		Sen. IL. Pres Pro Tem
Davis, Dwight F.	Political	25	75	150	75	Sec'y War
Davis, Fay	Ent	5			10	
Davis, Gail	Ent	15	20	25	35	
Davis, Geena	Ent	20	50		50	AA Winner
Davis, Henry Greene	Civil War	50	125			Union General
Davis, James J.	Political	20	50	100	75	Sec'y Labor
Davis, Jefferson 1808-89	Civil War	550	1,500	1,750	2,500	President of the CSA
Davis, Jefferson C.	Civil War	50	100	100		Union General/1828-79
Davis, Jim	Cartoonist	35	75	225	175	Garfield
Davis, Jim	Ent	45	50	75	100	
Davis, Jimmie	Political	30	45		75	Gov. LA
Davis, Joan	Ent	25			50	
Davis, John 1761-1847	Author	45	175	250		US Treasury Comptroller
Davis, John 1787-1854	Political	25	50	75		Gov. MA
Davis, John William	Political	20	35	75	50	Dem. Presidential Candidate
Davis, Mack	Music	10			20	
Davis, Meyer	Music	15			35	
Davis, Miles	Music	125	250		300	Jazz Trumpet
Davis, Nancy (Reagan)	First Lady	100			225	Scarce as Davis
Davis, Nelson H.	Civil War	25	50	75		Union General/1821-90
Davis, Ossie	Ent	10			25	
Davis, Patti (Reagan)	Ent	10			25	
Davis, Phil	Cartoonist	30			75	Mandrake the Magician
Davis, Phyllis	Ent	10		20	25	
Davis, Reuben	Civil War	75		200		CSA General/1813-90
Davis, Rich'd Harding	Author	10	25	40	25	
Davis, Robert	Military	10		25		General WW I
Davis, Rufe	Ent	25			50	
Davis, Sammy, Jr.	Ent	50	75	150	150	
Davis, Varina	First lady	150	250	500	750	Mrs. Jefferson Davis
Davison, Bruce	Ent	10			20	
Davison, Wild Bill	Music	30			75	Jazz Cornet-Bandleader
Davisson, Clinton Joseph	Science	25	75			Nobel Physics
Davout, Louis Nicolas	Military	75	150	200		Marshal of Napoleon
Davy, Humphry Sir	Science	125	250	500		
Dawber, Pam	Ent	10	25		30	Mork and Mindy
Dawes, Charles G.	Vice Pres	50	150	300	275	Nobel Peace Prize
Dawes, William 1745-99	RevWar	Scarce	20,000	3,000	RARE	Rode w/ Revere
Dawson-Briggs, Roxanne	Ent	15			35	Star Trek Voyager
Day, Chon	Cartoonist	10	30		50	Brother Sebastian
Day, Dennis	Music	10		25	30	
Day, Doris	Ent	10	45		35	

Name	Field	SIG	DS	ALS	SP	Remarks
Day, Linda (George)	Ent	5		20	15	
Day, William R. d.1923	SuprCt	50	100	125	75	Sec'y State
Day, Loraine	Ent	10			45	
Dayan, Moshe 1915-1981	Military	125	225	275	250	Israeli Soldier, Politician
Dayan, Yael	Author	10			25	
Day-Lewis, Daniel	Ent	30			60	AA Winner
Daymond, Gus	Aviation	15		50	45	ACE/WWII Eagle Squadron
Dayne, Taylor	Music	15			45	
Dayton, Elias	RevWar	100	200	350		Gen. Continental Congress
Dayton, Jonathan	RevWar	175	450	600		Continental Congress
Dayton, William L.1807-67	Political	25	50	125		
De Luca, Giuseppe	Music	25	50	100	175	Opera
De Palma, Brian	Ent	15			45	Film Director
De Quincey, Thomas	Author	150	300			
De Reszke, Edouard	Music	75			150	Opera/1853-1917
De Reszke, Jean 1850-25	Music	100	150		300	Opera
De Rita, Joe Curly	Ent	35	75		75	Three Stooges
De Almeida, Antonio	Music	10			45	
De Beauvoir, Simone	Author	35	100	200		
De Bono, Emilio	Military	75	225		375	
De Bray, Xavier B.	Civil War	125				CSA General/1818-95
De Corsia, Ted	Ent	20			40	
De Duve, Christian R.	Science	10			40	Nobel
De Falla, Manuel 1876-46	Music	425	900			Composer
De Forest, Lee, Dr.	Science	350	900	1,200	1,500	1873-1961
De Gaulle, Charles	Political	375	1,000	1,500	2,500	1890-1969
De Havilland, Geoffrey	Aviation	75	150	200	125	De Havilland Aircraft Co.
De Kooning, Elaine	Art	75			250	
De Kooning, Willem	Art	100	250	450	150	
De La Cierva, Juan	Aviation	100		250	350	Inventor Autogyro
De La Mare, Walter	Author	20	50	75	45	
De La Renta, Oscar	Business	10		35	20	Fashion Designer
De Lancey, Stephen	RevWar	75	150	225		
De Leo, Sarafina	Music	15			40	Opera
De Mornay, Rebecca	Ent	10	25		35	
De Peyster, John W. Jr.	Civil War	10	25	45		Aide to Gen.Kearny
De Ridder, Anton	Music	10		45	35	Opera
De Russy, Gustavus	Civil War	75	200	250		Union General/1818-91
De Seversky, Alex.	Aviation	100	200	200	225	1894-1973
De Toth, Andre'	Ent	10			20	Film Director
De Trobriand, P. R.	Civil War	100	275	325		Union General/1816-97
De Valera, Eamon	Political	50	125	200	100	Pres.PM/1882-1975
De Vere, Aubrey T.	Author	25	50	125		
De Wilde, Brandon	Ent	100	200		250	Child Actor
De Windt, Harry 1856-33	Explorer	30		75	50	Br. Explorer
Deacon, Richard	Ent	45	100		100	Dick van Dyke Show
Dean, Billy	Music	10			20	

Name	Field	SIG	DS	ALS	SP	Remarks
Dean, Donald J.	Military	15	45			WW I Victoria Cross
Dean, Eddie	Music	10		20	25	
Dean, James 1931-55	Ent	1,800	6,000	RARE	6,000	
Dean, Jimmy	Music	5			20	
Dean, John W.	Political	10		25	75	Legal Counsel to Nixon
Dean, William F.	Military	15	35	45	35	Gen.WWII
Deane, Silas	RevWar	225	550	800		
Dearborn, Henry	Political	100	400	550		RevWar/Jeffersons Sect
Dearborn, Henry A.S.	Political	75	175	250		1783-1851
Debakey, Michael, Dr.	Science	20			35	Ist Coronary Artery Bypass Op.
Debeck, Billy	Cartoonist	35			75	Barney Google & Snuffy Smith
DeBlanc, Jeff	Aviation	15		45	45	WWII ACE
DeBray, Xavier B.	Civil War	100		200		CSA General/1818-95
Debs, Eugene	Political	75	225	250	150	U.S. Socialist Leader.
Debussy, Claude 1862-18	Music	400		1,200		
DeButts, John D.	Business	10		45	25	
Debye, Peter J.W.	Science	50	100	175		Nobel/Discovered Rayon
Decamp, Rosemary	Ent	10			40	Am.Radio & Film Star
DeCarlo, Yvonne	Ent	10	30		30	Munsters/Lily
Decatur, Stephen	Military	1,000	2,000	4,500		American Naval Hero, War 1812
DeCisneros, Eleanora	Music	50			175	Opera
DeCordova, Fred	Ent	5			15	
Dee, Francis	Ent	5			25	
Dee, Ruby	Ent	5			20	
Dee, Sandra	Ent	10			35	
Deems, 'Cousin'	Music	5			15	
Deep Purple	Music	75			125	Signed by Entire Group
Deere, Allan Christopher	Aviation	15	45	50		Nazi Ace WWII, 22 Kills
Deere, John 1804-86	Business	500	1,500	1,500		
Deering, James	Business	10	25	45	25	
Deering, Olive	Ent	15			35	
Dees, Rick	Music	5		20	15	
Defoe, Daniel 1660-1731	Author	1,500	Scarce	Scarce	Scarce	
DeFore, Don	Ent	10			15	
DeFranco, Buddy	Music	15			25	Bandleader
Degas, Edgar 1831 - 17	Art	750		2,000		Fr.Impressionist
DeGeneres, Ellen	Ent	25	45		45	
DeHart, John	RevWar	35	75	150		
DeHaven, Gloria	Ent	10			25	
DeHaven, Robert	Aviation	10		40	30	WWII ACE
DeHavilland, Olivia	Ent	30	75	75	55	GWTW
Dehmelt, Hans G., Dr.	Science	20	35		30	Nobel Physics
Deisenhofer, Johann	Science	25			35	Nobel
Dekker, Albert	Ent	20			45	
DeKlerk, F.W.	Political	75	150		150	Nobel Peace/Pr.Minister
DeKoven, Reginald	Music	25	50	150	100	Composer/1859-1920
Del Monaco, Mario	Music	50	75	125	175	Opera

Name	Field	SIG	DS	ALS	SP	Remarks
Del Rio, Delores	Ent	30		50	75	
Del Tredici, David	Music	15	45	75		Composer/Pulitzer
Delacroix, F.V. Eugene	Art	200	375	550		Murals/1798-1886
Delafield, Richard	Civil War	50	75	100		Union General. Engineer
DeLagnel, Juius A.	Civil War	100		200		CSA General/1827-1912
DeLancie, John	Ent	15			45	Star Trek's "Q"
DeLand, Margaret	Author	15		75	25	Am. Novelist
Delaney, Dana	Ent	10			35	China Beach
Delaney, Kim	Ent	10			25	
Deledda, Grazia	Author	75	100	250		Nobel Literature 1926
Delibes, Leo	Music	100	200	300		Opera
Delius, Frederick 1862-34	Music	300	450	650		Composer
Dell, Gabriel	Ent	15		25	35	
Dell, Myrna	Ent	5			10	
Della Casa, Lisa	Music	10			25	Opera
Della Chiesa, Vivian	Music	5			15	Soprano
Della Joio, Norman	Music	35	125	200	75	Pulitzer/Composer
Delna, Marie	Music	35			100	Opera
DeLong, Phillip C.	Aviation	10	25	40	30	WWII ACE
Deluise, Dom	Ent	10	20		20	
DeMarco, Antonio	Ent	10	25			Producer
DeMarco, Tony	Ent	10	25			Dancer
Demarest, William	Ent	30		60	65	My Three Sons/1881-59
DeMille, Agnes	Ent	75	150		150	Dancer/Choreographer
DeMille, Cecil B. 1881-59	Ent	100	250	450	300	Director/Producer
DeMille, Katherine	Ent	10			25	
DeMille, William C.	Ent	25	50		50	Director/Producer
Demme, Jonathan	Ent	20			40	
DeMornay, Rebecca	Ent	20			45	
Dempsey, Patrick	Ent	10			25	
Dench, Dame Judi	Ent	15			35	James Bond's "M"
Deneuve, Catherine	Ent	10		25	35	
Denfeld, Louis E.	Military	10	25	45	25	Adm.Chief Naval Operations WWII
DeNiro, Robert	Ent	30	100		60	
Denman, G. Tony	Aviation	10		35	25	ACE, WWII, Navy Ace
Denman, Thomas, 3rd Baron	Political	10		35		Gov. General Australia
Dennehy, Brian	Ent	15	35		25	
Denning, Richard	Ent	5			15	
Dennis, Sandy	Ent	35	45		75	
Dennison, Anthony	Ent	10			25	
Dennison, Jo Carroll	Ent	5			10	
Dennison, William	Political	150		450		Lincoln P.M.
Denny, Reginald	Ent	35		100	75	Mary Poppins
Denslow, W.W.	Cartoonist	75			175	Illustrator Of Wizard Of Oz
Dent, Elliott	Aviation	10		35	30	WWII ACE
Dent, Frederick T.	Civil War	35	100	175		Union General/1821-92
Denton, Jeremiah A., Jr.	Military	10		30	20	WWII Admiral

Name	Field	SIG	DS	ALS	SP	Remarks
Denver, Bob	Ent	10	30	45	30	Gilligans Island
Denver, James W.	Civil War	100	200	400		Union General/1817-92
Denver, John	Music	35	75		75	Died in Plane Crash
Depardieu, Gerard	Ent	20			50	
Depeche Mode	Music	50			100	Signed by Entire Band
Depew, Chauncey M.	Business	150	450	750	500	NY Central Railroad
Depp, Johnny	Ent	25			50	
Derain, Andre'	Art	125	200	400		
Derby,14th Earl	Political	50	50	100		Br. Prime Minister
Derek & the Dominoes	Music	50			150	Signed by Entire Group
Derek, Bo	Ent	25			50	
Derek, John	Ent	25	50		50	
Deringer, Henry 1786-68	Business	2,000	RARE	6,500	RARE	Invented Derringer Pistol
Derleth, August	Author	25	75			
Dern, Bruce	Ent	15			35	
Dern, Laura	Ent	15			35	Jurassic Park...
Dershowitz, Alan M.	Political	15			30	Trial Attorney
Desai, M.R.	Political	5		25		Prime Minister India
Descartes, Rene	Science	RARE	17,500	20,000	RARE	Mathematician
Deschanel, Paul Eugene	Political	30		100		President France
Descher, Sandy	Ent	15			35	Child Actress
DeSilva, Howard	Ent	10		20	25	
Desmond, Johnny	Music	5			10	
Desmond, Shaw 1877-60	Author	25	75			Irish Playwright
Desmond, William	Ent	40			75	
Despretz, Cesar	Science	10		30		Inventor Electric Arc Furnace
D'Estaing,V. Gistard	Political	20	45	100	75	Pres. France
Destinn, Emmy 1878-1930	Music	100		225	200	Czech Soprano
Detaille, Edwouard	Art	125		325		Fr. Military & Portr. Painter
DeTreville, Yvonne	Music	35			75	Opera
Deutekom, Cristina	Music	15			35	Soprano
Deutsch, Patti	Ent	10			20	
DeVane, William	Ent	10		20		
Devens, Charles, Jr.	Military	30	50	150	150	Union Gen.-Att'y Gen.
Devereux, James P.S.	Military	35	75	100	150	WWII General
Devers, Jacob L.	Military	10	25		35	WWII General
Devine, Andy 1905-77	Ent	75	150		150	Roy Rogers Sidekick
DeVito, Danny	Ent	25	50		50	Taxi...
Devo	Music	35	100		75	Signed by all five
DeVos, Rich	Business	15			25	Founder Amway
DeVries, William, Dr.	Science	15	25	35	25	
Dewey, George	Military	100	150	200	300	Span-Am Admiral
Dewey, John	Author	50	125	250	75	Philosopher
Dewey, Thomas E.	Political	40	75	150	100	Presidential Candidate
Dewhurst, Colleen	Ent	25		75	60	1926 - 1991
DeWitt, Joyce	Ent	15	30		35	Three's Company
DeWolf, H.G.	Military	10	25		20	Canadian Adm. WWII

Name	Field	SIG	DS	ALS	SP	Remarks
DeWolfe, Billy 1907-74	Ent	25	50	50	50	
Dey, Susan	Ent	10	20	35	25	Partridge Family
Di Stefano, Giuseppe	Music	25		75	75	It. Opera
Diaghilev, Sergei 1872-29	Music	600		1,800		Ballet Impresario
Diamond Rio	Music	15			45	
Diamond, Bobby	Ent	15			30	
Diamond, David	Music	25		45		Composer
Diamond, Neil	Music	25	75		50	
Diamond, Selma	Ent	30		50	75	
Diana, Princess (Eng)	Royalty	975	RARE	4,000	3,000	Princess Di
Diaz, Armando Vittorio	Military	35	100	175	125	It. General WWI
Diaz, Cameron	Ent	25			50	
Diaz, Porfirio	Political	100	200	250	225	Dictatorial Pres. of Mexico
Dibrell, George Gibbs	Civil War	150	300	300		CSA General/1822-88
Dicaprio, Leonardo	Ent	30			65	Titanic
Dick, Douglas	Ent	10			25	
Dick, Fred	Aviation	15		40	30	ACE, WWII
Dick, Samuel	RevWar	50	150	225		Continental Congress NJ
Dickens, Charles 1812-70	Author	550	1,200	1,500	Scarce	Christmas Carol ...
Dickens, Jimmy	Music	5	20		15	
Dickenson, Don M.	Political	15		45	20	P.M. General 1888
Dickerson, Mahlon	Political	25	75	150		Jackson Sec'y Navy
Dickey, James	Author	15	35	50	50	Am.Poet
Dickinson, Angie	Ent	5	20		20	Police Woman
Dickinson, Anna Eliz.	Author	25	75	150		Abolitionist-Lecturer
Dickinson, Emily	Author	850	2,500	RARE	RARE	
Dickinson, Jacob M.	Political	25	50	125		Taft Sec'y of War
Dickinson, James S.	Civil War	25	50	75		CSA Congressman
Dickinson, John P.	RevWar	200	575			Continental Congress
Dickison, J. J.	Civil War	75	150	200		CSA Cav'ry Off.
Diddley, Bo	Music	25	50		50	
Diefenbaker, John	Political	15	35		20	Prime Minister Canada
Diem, Ngo Dinh	Political	50				Pres. So. Viet Nam
Diemer, Walter E.	Business	35		75	100	Inventor Dubble Bubble Gum
Diesel, Rudolf	Science	900		2,500		Ger. Mech. Engineer
Diesenhofer, Johann, Dr.	Science	20	25		50	Nobel Chemistry
Dieterle, William	Ent	30			75	Director
Dietl, Eduard	Military	75			150	German Military
Dietrich, Marlene 1901-92	Ent	75	150	300	175	
Dilke, Charles W.	Author	15	25	45		Br. Travel Books, Politician
Diller, Phyllis	Ent	5			15	
Dillinger, John	Criminal	5,000		15,000		1902-1934
Dillman, Bradford	Ent	5		20	15	
Dillon, Kevin	Ent	15			30	
Dillon, Matt	Ent	10	25		35	
Dimitrova, Ghana	Music	15			35	Opera
D'Indy, Vincent 1851-1931	Music	45	125			Composer

Name	Field	SIG	DS	ALS	SP	Remarks
Dinesen, Isak	Author	150	500		500	Out of Africa/1885-1962
Dion	Music	15			25	
Dion, Celine	Music	25			50	
Dior, Christian	Business	125	350		225	Fashion Designer
Dippel, Andreas	Music	35			125	Opera
Dire Straits	Music	35	100		75	Entire Band
Dirks, Rudolph 1877-1968	Cartoonist	75		175	150	Katzenjammer Kids
Disney, Roy E.	Business	25	75		50	Brother of Walt
Disney, Walter E.	Cartoonist	1,200	2,500	RARE	3,750	Mickey Mouse/1901-66
Disraeli, Benjamin	Political	175	350	900		Prime Minister
Disraeli, Isaac	Author	25	75	150		
Divine	Ent	50	100		100	Drag Queen
Divine, M.J. 'Father'	Clergy	125	350	500	200	Fndr. Communal Society
Dix, Dorothy	Author	15	30	45	25	Am. Journalist
Dix, Dorothea L. 1802-87	Civil War	100	200	350		
Dix, John Adams	Civil War	75	200	150	450	Union General/1798-1879
Dix, Richard	Ent	20	40	75	65	1894 - 1949
Dix, Robert	Ent	10			25	
Dixey, Henry E. 1859-43	Ent	10		30	25	Ist Success as Adonis
Dixon, Donna	Ent	10	20		25	
Dixon, Jeane	Ent	10			15	Syndicated Columnist
Dixon, Thomas	Author	150		450		Birth of a Nation
Dixon, Willie	Music	50			100	Blues
Dmytryk, Edward	Ent	20			40	Film Director
Dobbin, James C.1814-57	Political	30	75	150		Pierce Sec'y Navy
Dobbin, John F.	Aviation	25	50	75	50	ACE, WWII, Marine Ace
Dobehoff, F.L.	Aviation	25			75	
Dobie, J. Frank	Author	25	50	125	75	Western Author
Dobrinyin, Anatole	Political	35	125	275	75	U.S.S.R. Political Power
Dobson, Kevin	Ent	5			15	
Dockery, Thomas P.	Civil War	100		300		CSA General/1833-98
Doctorow, E. L.	Author	15	35	75	30	Am. Novelist. Ragtime
Dodd, Jimmie	Ent	30	75		75	Mouseketeer
Dodd, William E.	Political	15	50	75	25	Ambassador to Nazi Germany
Dodge, Charles C.	Civil War	40				Union General/1841-1910
Dodge, Grenville M.	Civil War	200	500	750	375	Union General/1831-1916
Dodge, Grenville M.	Civil War	300	900	1,200		Union General/War Dated
Dodge, Joseph M.	Business	10	25	50		Banker, Built Jap. Economy
Dodge, Mary Abigail	Author	10	20			
Dodge, Mary Mapes	Author	15	45	75	30	Children's Books.
Dodge, William Earl	Business	150	450	800		
Dodge, William G.	Civil War	25	50	75		
Dodgson, Charles L.	Author	400	900	1,500		Alice in Wonderland
Dodson, Jack	Ent	25	50		60	Andy Grifith Show
Doefflinger, Joseph	Aviation	15		50	45	
Doenitz, Karl 1891-1980	Military	75	200	250	175	Ger. Adm/WWII
Doering, Arnold	Aviation	10		35	25	

Name	Field	SIG	DS	ALS	SP	Remarks
Doherty, Shannen	Ent	25			50	Beverly Hills 90210
Dohnanyi, Erno von	Music	50	125	225		Composer/Conductor
Doisy, Edward A.	Science	20	50	150	45	Nobel Medicine. Vitamin K
Dolby, Ray	Science	20	35		50	Inventor Dolby Sound
Dolby, Thomas	Music	20			40	
Dole, Elizabeth	Political	10			25	
Dole, James D.	Business	50	150	225	75	Fdr.Hawaiian Pineapple Industry
Dole, Robert "Bob"	Political	30			50	
Dole, Sanford B. 1844-26	Business	50	200	300	100	Pres. Repub. HI.
Dolenz, Mickey	Music	10		25	35	Monkees
Dolin, Anton	Music	25	50	100	75	Ballet
Dollar, Robert	Business	25	50	100	50	Dollar Steamship Line.
Domingo, Placido	Music	20		50	50	Opera
Domino, Fats	Music	10	50		25	
Donahue, Al	Music	15			45	Big Band Leader
Donahue, Archie	Aviation	15		50	35	WWII ACE in one Day
Donahue, Elinor	Ent	5			15	
Donahue, Phil	Ent	15			30	TV Talk Show Host
Donahue, Troy	Ent	5	20		25	
Donaldson, Jesse M.	Political	10		35	15	Ist Postman Becomes P.M. Gen.
Donaldson, Sam	Ent	5			15	TV News Anchor
Donat, Robert 1905-1958	Ent	75	150	150	200	Academy Award Winner
Doniphan, Alexander W.	Military	125	250	400		
Donizetti, Gaetano	Music	500	800	1,500		Composer/1797-1848
Donlevy, Brian	Ent	25			55	1899 - 1972
Donnell, Jeff	Ent	5			10	
Donnelly, Ruth	Ent	10		25	25	
Donner, Clive	Ent	10			25	Film Director
Donner, Richard	Ent	10			20	
Donohue, Amanda	Ent	10			25	
Donovan, King	Ent	15			35	
Donovan, Tate	Ent	10			25	Voice of Disney's Hercules
Donovan, Wm. J.	Military	50	200	300	100	Fighting 69th,OSS-CIA
Doobie Brothers	Music	50	100		100	Signed by entire band
Doohan, James	Ent	15		45	45	Star Trek
Dooley, Paul	Ent	5			15	
Dooley, Thomas A., Dr.	Science	125	200	300	125	1927-1961
Doolittle, Hilda	Author	75	200	400		1886-1961
Doolittle, James H.	Aviation	50	150	200	75	Gen. WWII/Bombed Tokyo
Doors & Jim Morrison	Music	1,500	2,500		2,500	
Doors, The w/o Morrison	Music	75	150		100	
Dor, Karin	Ent	25			60	James Bond Girl
Doraine, Lucy	Ent	20			45	Actress
Doran, Ann	Ent	15		25	20	
Dorati, Antal	Music	25			75	Conductor
Dore, Paul Gustave	Art	75	150	450		
Dorff, Stephen	Ent	20			45	

Name	Field	SIG	DS	ALS	SP	Remarks
Dornberger, Walter R.	Military	40	100	125	75	Rocket Engineer
Dors, Diana	Ent	35			125	
D'Orsay, Alfred, Count	Political	25	75	175		Fr. Artist
D'Orsay, Fifi	Ent	15		25	35	
Dorsey, Jimmie	Music	50	150		250	Big Band/1904 - 1957
Dorsey, Tommy 1905-56	Music	75	150		200	Big Band
Dortch, William T.	Civil War	25	50	75		CSA Senator NC
Dostoevsky, Fyodor	Author	1,500	5,000	RARE	RARE	Crime & Punishment
Doubleday, Abner	Civil War	500	2,000	1,500		Union General/1819-93
Doubleday, Frank N.	Business	75	150	350		Book Publisher
Douglas, Beverly B.	Civil War	30		75		CSA Officer
Douglas, Chas. W.H.	Military	25	75	200		Br. Gen./1850-1914
Douglas, Donald W. Jr.	Business	25	75		50	Douglas Aircraft
Douglas, Donald W. Sr.	Aviation	150	300	450	350	Pioneer Aircraft Mfg.
Douglas, Donna	Ent	5		20	20	Beverly Hillbillies
Douglas, Eric	Ent	10			20	Son of Kirk Douglas
Douglas, Kirk	Ent	25	75	75	50	
Douglas, Lloyd C.	Author	25	50	75	50	
Douglas, Melvyn	Ent	30			75	1901 - 1981
Douglas, Michael	Ent	25	50		50	Son of Kirk
Douglas, Mike	Ent	5			15	Singer. Early TV Host
Douglas, Paul	Ent	15			35	
Douglas, Paul P.	Aviation	10		45	35	WWII ACE
Douglas, Robert	Ent	10			25	
Douglas, Stephen A.	Political	100	225	450	225	Pres. Candidate/1813-61
Douglas, William O.	SuprCt	75	175	150	200	1898 - 1980
Douglass, Frederick	Political	250	450	RARE	RARE	Author/Educator/1817-95
Doulton, Henry, Sir	Business	20	45	75		Royal Doulton China
Doumer, Paul 1857-1932	Political	50		100		Pres. France 1931-32. Assassinated
Doumergue, Gaston	Political	75		200		Pres. France. P.M. France
Dove, Billie	Ent	15		45	60	
Dow, Neal	Civil War	50		300		Union General/1804-97
Dow, Tony	Ent	15	45		40	Leave it to Beaver
Dowden, Edward	Author	10		25		Ir. Critic, Editor, Professor
Dowling, Eddie	Ent	20		50	50	1895-1975
Down, Lesley-Anne	Ent	10			30	
Downey, Morton	Ent	10		20	25	
Downey, Robert, Jr.	Ent	25			50	Actor
Downey, Roma	Ent	25			50	Touched by an Angel
Downing, Big Al	Ent	5			15	
Downing, George, Sir	Political	Scarce	Scarce	Scarce	Scarce	1623-84
Downs, Hugh	Ent	10		25	25	TV Co-Host 20/20
Downs, Johnny	Ent	50			100	Our Gang
Doyle, Arthur Conan, Sir	Author	400	750	1,250	1,750	Sherlock Holmes/1859-30
Doyle, David	Ent	15			45	Charlie's Angels
Dr. Seuss	Cartoonist	75	250	400	250	Cat in the Hat etc...

Name	Field	SIG	DS	ALS	SP	Remarks
Dragonette, Jessica	Music	20			45	Soprano
Dragoni, Maria	Music	10			30	Opera
Drake, Alfred	Music	15			30	
Drake, Frances	Ent	10			25	
Drake, Michele	Ent	5			15	
Drake, Samuel Adams	Civil War	50		75		Union General
Drake, Stan	Cartoonist	20			45	Blondie
Draper, Polly	Ent	10			25	
Draper, Ruth	Ent	25	50	75	50	Am. Monologuist
Draper, William F.	Civil War	25	75			Union General/1842-1910
Drayton, Gracie	Cartoonist	25			75	Campbell Soup Kids
Drayton, Thomas F.	Civil War			200		CSA General/1808-91
Drees, Willem	Political	25	50	100		Survivor Buchenwald
Dreiser, Theodore	Author	75	200	300	300	1871-1945
Drescher, Fran	Ent	20			50	The Nanny
Dresser, Louise	Ent	30			60	
Dressler, Marie	Ent	125			250	AA Winner/1869 - 1934
Drew, Ellen	Ent	5			10	
Drew, John 1853-1927	Ent	50	75	200	100	
Drexel, Anthony	Business	45	75	150		Philanthropist
Drexel, J. A.	Aviation	43	50	100	75	
Dreyfus, Alfred 1859-1935	Military	150	250	750		
Dreyfus, Julia Louis	Ent	25			50	Seinfeld
Dreyfuss, Henry	Business	10		25		
Dreyfuss, Richard	Ent	25			50	AA Winner
Dribrell, George G.	Civil War	100	250	300		
Drinkwater, John	Author	20	50	125	45	Poet/1882-1937
Driscoll, Bobby	Ent	150			450	Child star/Disney Voice
Driver, Minnie	Ent	25			50	Good Will Hunting
Dru, Joanne	Ent	10			25	
Druckman, Jacob	Music	25	50	100		Pulitzer/Composer
Drum, Hugh A. Lt.Gen	Military	25	50	100	50	General WW 1, WW II
Drum, Richard C.	Civil War	30	50	80		
Drury, Allen	Author	10	30	75	45	
Drury, Frank	Aviation	10	25	45	45	ACE, WWII Marine Ace
Drury, James	Ent	15			35	The Virginian
Dryer, Fred	Ent	10			25	Hunter
Du Barry, Jeanne, C.	Political	300	900	1,200		Arrested/Guillotined
Du Chaillu, Paul B.	Explorer	35	75	75	75	1831-1903
Du Maurier, Daphne	Author	50	150	150	50	Rebecca
Du Maurier, George	Author	25	45	125		And Illustrator of Punch
Du Pont, Henry A.	Business	150	450	750		1838-1926
Du Pont, Lammot	Business	25			50	CEO Du Pont Chemical
Du Pont, Pierre S.	Business	400	1,250	2,000		Du Pont Chemical
Du Pont, Pierre-Samuel	Business	50	100	225		Progenitor of Du Pont's
Du Pont, R.	Aviation	50	100			Am Aviation Exec
Du Pont, Samuel F.	Civil War	150	200	450		Union Admiral

Name	Field	SIG	DS	ALS	SP	Remarks
Du Vigneaud, Vincent	Science	25	50	150	50	Nobel/Synthz.Penicillin
Duane, James 1733-1797	RevWar	125	325	750		1st Continental Congress
Dubcek, Alexander	Political	75	150			Czech. Reformer
DuBois, W. E. B.	Author	300	750		425	Black Rights
Dubose, Dudley	Civil War	100	275			CSA General/1834-83
DuBridge, Lee, Dr	Science	30	100	150	50	Pres. Cal-Tech
Dubuffet, Jean 1931-85	Art	150	400	950		Swiss proponent of raw art
Duchamp, Marcel 1887-68	Art	125	350	575		Fr. Avante Garde Artist
Duchin, Eddie	Music	25	45		125	Big Band Leader, Pianist
Duchin, Peter	Music	5		20	15	Pianist, Band Leader
Duchovny, David	Ent	30			60	X-Files
Duckworth, John T.Sir	Military	50	150			Br. Admiral
Ducos, Jean Francois	Military	35	100	175	75	Pres.Chechen Republic
Dudley, Joseph 1647-1720	Political	400	800	1,000		Col,Gov.MA
Duesenberg, Frederick	Business	500	1,250			
Duff, Arthur, Sir	Military	15	45	75		Br. Admiral
Duff, Howard	Ent	15		25	35	
Duffer, Candy	Music	20			45	
Duffie, Alfred Napoleon	Civil War	35	75	100		Union Calv. Gen./1835-80
Duffy, Julia	Ent	10			25	Newhart
Duffy, Patrick	Ent	15			30	Step by Step/Dallas
Dufy, Raoul 1877-1953	Art	300	450	750	500	Fr. Impressionist, Fauvism
Duggan, Andrew	Ent	15			25	
Dukakis, Olympia	Ent	15	25	35	30	
Dukas, Paul 1865-1935	Music	50	150	275		Composer
Duke, Basil Wilson	Civil War	100	200	500		CSA General/1838-1916
Duke, Charles M., Jr.	Space	35	150		75	Moonwalker
Duke, Patty	Ent	20		35	45	
Duke, Vernon 1903-69	Music	25	50	150		Composer
Dulbecco, Renato	Science	25	50	75		Nobel Physiology-Medicine
Dulles, Allen W.	Political	30	150	200	75	Stae Department
Dulles, John Foster	Political	35	125	150	75	Sec'y State, Diplomat, UN
Dumas, Alexandre (Pere)	Author	100	225	450	750	Fr.Novelist/3 Musketeers
Duna, Steffi	Ent	10			25	
Dunagin, Ralph	Cartoonist	5			20	The Middletons
Dunaway, Faye	Ent	15	30		30	
Dunbar, Bonnie J.	Space	5			15	Astronaut
Dunbar, Dixie	Ent	5		15	15	
Dunbar, Paul Lawrence	Author	750	Scarce	Scarce	Scarce	Afro-Am. Poet, Novelist etc.
Duncan, James 1811-49	Military	75				Mexican War Hero
Duncan, Johnny	Music	10			20	
Duncan, Isadora 1878-27	Ent	400		1,000	1,000	Am. Interpretive Dancer
Duncan, Sandy	Ent	10	20		20	
Duncan, Thomas	Civil War	25	50	75		Union General
Duncan, Todd	Music	35			100	First Porgy
Dunlap, John	Business	150	450			1st to Print Decl of Indep.
Dunn, Artie	Music	15			45	The Three Sons
Dunn, Emma	Ent	20			35	

Name	Field	SIG	DS	ALS	SP	Remarks
Dunn, Holly	Music	10			25	
Dunn, James	Ent	45			125	1905 - 1967
Dunn, William McKee	Civil War	25	50	75		Union General
Dunne, Dominick	Author		30		35	
Dunne, Griffin	Ent	15			30	
Dunne, Irene	Ent	15	25	35	50	1901 - 1990
Dunne, Phillip	Author	5	20	35	20	
Dunnock, Mildred	Ent	15			25	1904 - 1991
Dunsany, Edw.J.Plunkett	Author	50		225	125	
Dunst, Kirsten	Ent	25			50	
DuPonceau, Pierre	Military	25	50	125		
Dupre, Marel	Music	45			125	Organist
Duran Duran	Music	50			100	Entire Band Signed
Durand, Asher Brown	Art	100	175	200		Hudson River School
Durant, Don	Ent	10			25	
Durant, William C.	Business	250	750	900		Durant Motor Car. GM, Chevrolet
Durante, Jimmy 1893-80	Ent	35	100		100	
Durbin, Deanna	Ent	25	50		50	
Durer, Albrecht	Art	3,000	RARE	RARE	RARE	Foremost Ger.Renaissance Artist
Durham, Bobby	Music	10			20	
Durning, Charles	Ent	10			25	
Duroc, Geraud C.M.	Military	25	75	150		Napol. Grand Marshal
Durrell, Lawrence	Author	25	75	150	50	Br-ir Poet,Playwright,Travel
Duryea, Charles E.	Science	150	450	Scarce	RARE	Built lst Am.Gas Motor Car
Duryea, Dan	Ent	15		30	35	
Duryea, Hiram	Civil War	Scarce	Scarce	Scarce	Scarce	Union General
Duse, Eleanore 1859-1924	Ent	200	400	750	575	
Dussault, Nancy	Ent	5			10	
Dussek, Jan L 1760-1812	Music	35	100	150		
Dustinn, Emmy	Music	35			125	Opera
Dutra, Enrico Gaspar	Political	10		50	35	Pres. Brazil
Dutton, Charles	Ent	15			30	
Duv, Christian de, Dr.	Science	20	35		30	Nobel Medicine
Duval, Gabriel	SuprCt	50	100	200		
Duvalier, Francois	Political	75			150	Papa Doc. Haitian President
Duvall, Robert	Ent	25	50		550	
Duvall, Shelley	Ent	10			25	
Dvorak, Antonin	Music	475	900	1,500		Composer
Dwight, Theodore	Author	35	50	150		1764 - 1846
Dwight, Timothy 1752-17	Author	20	50			Yale President
Dyer, Edward 1543-1607	Author	Scarce	Scarce	Scarce	Scarce	Br Poet
Dyer, George C.	Military	15	45	75		Admiral USN
Dyer, Nehemiah 1839-10	Military	25				Admiral
Dyke, Leroy Van	Music	5			15	
Dylan, Bob	Music	175	350	600	450	
Dylan, Jakob	Music	20			45	

E

Name	Field	SIG	DS	ALS	SP	Remarks
Eads, James Buchanan	Civil War	100	300	450		Shipbuilder for the Union
Eagles	Music	100			250	All signed
Eagleston, Glenn	Aviation	25	50	75	50	WWII ACE
Eaker, Ira	Aviation	35	75	100	150	WW II Air Force Cmdr
Earhart, Amelia	Aviation	400	1,750	RARE	1,500	1897 - 1937 ?
Early, Jubal A.	Civil War	500	800	1,000		CSA General/1816-94
Earp, Virgil	Western	2,000	4,500	7,500		US Marshal
Earp, Wyatt	Western	5,000	15,000	30,000		Gunfighter/All pieces Rare
East, James	Western	250	750			Cowboy
Eastlake, Charles L., Sir	Art	75	150	350		Pres. of Royal Academy
Eastman, George	Business	350	1,200	3,000	1,500	Fndr Eastman Kodak.
Eastman, John	Art	50		150		American Artist
Eastman, Max	Author	35	75	100		Editor-Fdr. The Masses
Easton, Florence	Music	50			150	Opera
Easton, Sheena	Music	25			50	
Eastwood, Clint	Ent	35	150	150	65	AA Winner
Eaton, Amos Beebe	Civil War	25	50	100		Union General/1806-77
Eaton, Dorman 1823-99	Political	10	25	50		Nat'l Civil Service Act
Eaton, John Henry	Political	25	50	100		Sect War
Eaton, Shirley	Ent	10			25	Golden girl in "Goldfinger"
Eaton, William 1764-1811	Military	35		75		
Eban, Abba	Political	25	75	75	65	
Ebb, Fred	Music	10		35	25	Composer/"NY,NY"
Ebbets, Charles H.	Business	150			250	Brooklyn Dodgers Field
Eberhart, Richard	Author	10	20	45	45	Poet/Pulitzer
Eberly, Bob	Music	20			40	
Eberly, Ray	Music	20			45	
Ebert, Roger	Ent	10			35	Movie critic
Ebsen, Buddy	Ent	10	30		35	Beverly Hillbillies
Eccles, John C.	Science	20	30	40	30	Nobel Medicine
Echols, John	Civil War	100	200	300		CSA General
Eckener, Hugo von	Aviation	200	400	550	550	Built Graf Zeppelin
Eckert, Thomas T.	Civil War	475				Union Gen.Telegraph Giant
Eckstine, Billy	Music	25			50	Bandleader
Eddington, Arthur	Science	25	125	150		Mathemetician
Eddy, Duane	Music	35			75	
Eddy, Mary Baker	Clergy	1,250	2,500	Scarce	Scarce	
Eddy, Nelson	Ent	50	75		100	1901 - 1967
Edelman, Herb	Ent	10			20	
Eden, Anthony, Sir	Political	50	150	200	100	Prime Minister
Eden, Barbara	Ent	10	40		35	I Dream of Jeannie
Ederle, Gertrude Trudy	Ent	25			50	

Name	Field	SIG	DS	ALS	SP	Remarks
Edeson, Robert	Ent	20			45	Silent Star
Edison, Thomas Alva	Science	475	800	1,500	2,000	Am. Inventor/1847-31
Edmonds, Walter D.	Author	10	25	45	25	
Edmundson, Henry A.	Civil War	50	75	75		CSA Officer
Edward III (Reign of ...)	Royalty	RARE	RARE	RARE	RARE	
Edward IV (England)	Royalty	25,000	RARE	RARE	RARE	1442-83
Edward VI (Reign of ...)	Royalty	RARE	RARE	RARE	RARE	
Edward VII (Eng) (As King)	Royalty	75	200			King From 1901-10
Edward VIII 1894-1972	Royalty	300	750	650	750	
Edward VIII, as Prince	Royalty	150	475	550	675	
Edward VII (England)	Royalty	150	275	300	600	Queen Victoria's Eldest Son
Edward, Duke of Kent	Royalty	50	125	250		Father of Queen Victoria
Edward, Duke Windsor	Royalty	200	600		600	1894-1972
Edwards, Anthony	Ent	25			50	ER
Edwards, Blake	Ent	25	45		45	Producer/Director
Edwards, Clarence	Military	35				General WW I
Edwards, Cliff	Ent	75			125	Voice of Jimminy Cricket
Edwards, Douglas	Ent	5			15	Radio-TV News
Edwards, Joan	Ent	5			10	
Edwards, Oliver	Civil War	25	50	100		Union General/1835-1904
Edwards, Ralph	Ent	5	25		15	This Is Your Life
Edwards, Tommy	Music	25	75			
Edwards, Vince	Ent	10			25	Dr. Ben Casey
Egan, Richard	Ent	5			15	
Eggar, Samantha	Ent	10			20	
Eggert, Nicole	Ent	25			50	Baywatch
Eggerth, Marta	Music	15			45	Opera
Eggleston, Edward	Author	10		30		Am Novelist/1837-02
Eggleston, Geo. C.	Author	15	25			1839-1911
Eglevsky, Andre	Music	35	50	100	75	Ballett Teacher
Ehrlich, Paul, Dr.	Science		1,250	1,850	1,250	Nobel. Diphtheria, Syphillis
Eichelberger, Robert L.	Military	25	50	75	50	WWII General
Eichelbrenner, E. A.	Science	50	100	200		
Eichmann, Adolf	Military	275	500	1,250	750	
Eiffel, Gustave 1832-23	Science	300	600	900	1,250	Architect/Eiffel Tower
Eigar, Edward, Sir	Music	150	350	675	525	Composer/1867-1934
Eigen, Manfred	Science	20	35	75	45	Nobel Chemistry
Eilers, Sally	Ent	15		30	45	
Einstein, Albert 1879-55	Science	900	1,800	3,500	2,750	
Eisele, Donn F.	Space	50			100	Astronaut
Eisenberg, Maurice	Music	10			20	Cellist
Eisenhower, Arthur B.	Business	5			10	Brother to Ike. Banker
Eisenhower, Barbara	Political	5			10	Daughter-in Law to Ike
Eisenhower, Dwight D.	President	200	550	Scarce	450	1890-1969
Eisenhower, Edgar N.	Political	5			15	Brother & Lawyer to Ike
Eisenhower, John S. D.	Military	10	20	35	20	General & Only Son of Ike
Eisenhower, Julie Nixon	Political	5		25	25	Daughter & Inlaw To Ike

Name	Field	SIG	DS	ALS	SP	Remarks
Eisenhower, Mamie	First Lady	50	125	150	50	
Eisenhower, Milton	Political	10	30		30	Brother. Pres. Penn. State U.
Eisenstaedt, Alfred	Art	15	45		125	
Eisley, Anthony	Ent	10			15	
Eisner, Michael O.	Business	25	75		50	CEO Walt Disney Co.
Eizey, Arnold	Civil War	350		1,400		CSA General
Ekberg, Anita	Ent	10			20	
Ekland, Britt	Ent	10		25	30	
El Fadil, Siddig	Ent	20			50	Star Trek Deep Space Nine
Elam, Jack	Ent	5			15	
Elbert, Samuel 1743-1788	RevWar		100	150		
Elder, Ruth	Aviation	100	200	300	350	Pioneer Aviatrix
Elder, Will	Cartoonist	30			75	Lil Annie Fanny
Eldridge, Florence	Ent	10			35	
Eldridge, Roy	Music	30			75	Jazz Trumpet
Electra, Carmen	Ent	25			50	
Electric Light Orchestra	Music	50			100	Signed by entire band
Eleniak, Erika	Ent	25			50	Baywatch
Elfman, Jenna	Ent	25			50	Dharma and Greg
Elg, Taina	Ent	10			30	Ballet-Actress/Gene Kelly
Elgart, Les	Music	35			75	Bandleader
Elijah, Muhammad	Political	175	275		425	Religious Activist
Elion, Gertrude, Dr.	Science	20	75		45	Nobel Medicine
Eliot, George (Pseud.)	Author	150	450	1,200		British Novelist
Eliot, T(homas) S.	Author	175	400	Scarce	750	British Poet/1888-1965
Elizabeth 1 1533-1603	Royalty	5,500	12,000	30,000	RARE	
Elizabeth II & Philip	Royalty		750		900	
Elizabeth, II	Royalty	350	775	800	775	
Elizabeth, Queen Mother	Royalty	100	350	450	500	Queen of George VI
Elizondo, Hector	Ent	15			30	
Ellerbee, Linda	Ent	10	25		15	TV News, Commentator
Ellery, William 1727-1820	RevWar	175	350	650		Signer Decl. of Indepen.
Ellicott, Andrew	RevWar	75	200	300		Surveyor, Mathematician
Ellington, Duke 1899-74	Music	200	500		450	Composer
Elliott, Bill	Sports	10			25	Auto Racing
Elliott, Bob	Ent	5			10	
Elliott, Carter	Music	50	125	250		Composer
Elliott, Cass (Mama)	Music	200	400		450	Mamas and Papas
Elliott, Denholm	Ent	35			75	Indiana Jones
Elliott, Maxine	Ent	35	50	75	75	
Elliott, Sam	Ent	20			50	
Elliott, Washington L.	Civil War	35				Union General/1825-88
Elliott, Wild Bill	Ent	75			150	
Ellis, F. H.	Aviation	15	35		30	
Ellis, Havelock 1859-1939	Science	35		150	275	Br. Pioneer in Sex Ed.
Ellis, Robert H.	Military	10	25	45		
Ellison, James	Ent	10			30	

Name	Field	SIG	DS	ALS	SP	Remarks
Ellison, Ralph W. 1914-94	Author	50	150			Invisible Man
Ellsberg, Daniel	Political	25	35	50	45	Leaked Pentagon Papers
Ellsworth, Ephriam E.	Civil War	500	1,250	2,500		Union Zouave Col./1837-61
Ellsworth, Oliver 1745-07	SuprCt	100	275	575		Chief Justice
Elman, Mischa 1891-1967	Music	35	175		75	Russian/American Violinist
Elman, Ziggy	Music	25			75	Trumpet
Elmore, E.C.	Civil War	50	100			CSA Treasurer
Eluard, Paul	Author	100	225	350		Fr Poet
Elvira	Ent	15			45	
Elwes, Cary	Ent	15			35	
Ely, Paul, General	Military	75		150	100	Fr. Cmdr. Indochina
Ely, Ron	Ent	25	45		45	Tv's Tarzan
Emberg, Kelly	Ent	10			25	Model
Embry, Joan	Ent	5			20	Zoologist
Emerson, Faye	Ent	5			30	
Emerson, George	Ent	10			30	
Emerson, Lake & Palmer	Music	35	125		100	Signed by All Three
Emerson, Ralph Waldo	Author	200	300	450 Scarce		1803-1882
Emery, Ralph	Ent	5			10	TV Host
Emma, Queen	Royalty	100				Wife of King Kamehameha IV
Emmett, Daniel D.	Music	300	425	600		Ist Minstral Show. Dixie
Emmons, Ebenezer	Science	25	50	75		Natural History Proff.
Emory, William H.	Civil War	75	150	300		Union General/1811-87
Empey, James W.	Aviation	15	25			WWII ACE
Enders, John Franklin	Science	25	75	100	50	Nobel Medicine.
Endicott, William C.	Political	25		50	50	Sec'y War/1826-1900
Enesco, Georges	Music	125	275	450	550	Composer
Engel, Georgia	Ent	10			20	Mary Tyler Moore Show
Engel, Samuel G.	Ent	10			15	Producer
Engle, Frederick	Civil War	45				Union Commodore
Engle, Joe Henry	Space	15			45	Astronaut
Engler, Irvin	Author	10	25	30		Poet
English, Thos. Dunn	Author	25	30	45		Poet/Lawyer/1819-1902
Englund, Robert	Ent	10			30	Freddy
Ennis, Skinnay	Music	25			65	Bandleader
Enos, Roger 1729-1808	Military	75	175	275		General
Enriquez, Rene	Ent	15			35	
Ensor, James Sydney	Art	50	150	300		Belgian Painter
Ephron, Nora	Author	15			35	
Ephron, Phoebe	Author	15			25	Playwright Mother of Nora
Epp, Franz Xaver von	Military	15	50		75	WWI General
Epstein, Brian	Music	350	600	750		Beatles Manager
Epstein, Jacob, Sir	Art	150	250	375		Br/Am Sculptor
ER (Cast)	Ent	100			200	All Six Signed
Erdrich, Louise	Author	5			10	Novelist. The Bingo Palace
Erhard, Ludwig	Political	20	75	150	50	Chancellor W. Germany
Erickson, Leif 1911-86	Ent	20			50	

Name	Field	SIG	DS	ALS	SP	Remarks
Ericsdotter, Siw	Music	25			60	Opera
Ericson, B.A.	Aviation	10	25			Piloted XC-99
Ericsson, John 1803-89	Civil War	100	200	400		Designed & Built Monitor
Ernest Augustus	Royalty	100		300		Ist Hanover King
Erni, Hans	Art	75		225		
Ernouf, Manuel L.J	Military	35	75	150		
Ernst, Max 1891-1976	Art	200	300	575		Surrealist-Dada Movement
Errol, Leon	Ent	35			75	
Erskine, Graves B.	Military	15	35	50	45	Led Marines at Iwo Jima
Erskine, John 1879-1951	Author	35	125	175		Novelist
Erte	Art	125	275	450		
Erwin, James	Military	45				General WW I
Erwin, Sam J.	Political	25	75			Watergate Investigation
Erwin, Stuart	Ent	20			45	1903 - 1967
Esaki, Leo	Science	20		50	45	Nobel Physics
Escobedo, Mariano	Military	75	200			Captured Maximillian
Eshkol, Levi 1895-1969	Political	200	250	450		PM of Israel
Esnault-Pelterie, Robert	Aviation	100	250			Pioneer Aviator
Esperian, Kalen	Music	10			30	Opera
Estaing, Charles Hector	RevWar	175	450	750		Fr.Gen-Adm. Pro American Hero
Este, Isabella	Royalty	RARE	4,000	RARE	RARE	Art Patron
Estefan, Gloria	Music	25			50	
Esterhasy, Gunt A.	Political	25	75			Austria
Esterhazy, Prince Pal A.	Political	25		75		Austro-Hung. Diplomat
Estevez, Emilio	Ent	15	35		45	
Estrada, Erik	Ent	10	25	30	25	CHIPS
Etheridge, Melissa	Music	20			45	
Etter, Philippe	Political	15	50			Switzerland
Etting, Ruth	Ent	25			55	
Eubanks, Bob	Ent	5			15	Game Show Host
Eubanks, Kevin	Music	15			30	Jay Leno's Tonight Show
Eugenie, Empress	Royalty	200	300	375		
Eurythmics	Music	45			75	Signed by both
Eustis, Abraham	Military	75		300		War 1812. Br. Gen.
Eustis, William 1753-1825	Political	35	125	175		Sect War
Evangelista, Linda	Ent	10			25	
Evans, Clement A.	Civil War	100		300		CSA General/1833-1911
Evans, Dale	Ent	30		75	60	
Evans, De Lacy	Military	150	200			Br. Col./Burned White House
Evans, Edith, Dame	Ent	15	30		35	1888-1976
Evans, Edw. R.G.	Explorer	35			75	Admiral, Arctic Explorer
Evans, Gene	Ent	5		15	30	
Evans, Geraint, Sir	Music	10			35	Opera
Evans, Joan	Ent	5		15	10	
Evans, Linda	Ent	5			25	Big Valley
Evans, Lt. Col. D. M	Civil War	15	25	45		
Evans, Madge	Ent	15		35	30	1909 - 1981

Name	Field	SIG	DS	ALS	SP	Remarks
Evans, Maurice	Ent	60	100		100	Bewitched
Evans, Nathan G.	Civil War	175		475		CSA General/1824-68
Evans, Ray	Music	15	35	45	45	Composer
Evans, Robley D.	Civil War	30	75	100	150	Capt. USN, Fight'n Bob
Evans, Ronald E.	Space	50			100	Astronaut
Evans, William M.	Political	30	100	150	50	Attorney General/1818-01
Everest, F.K. 'Pete'	Aviation	15		45	35	
Everett, Chad	Ent	5			20	
Everett, Edward 1794-65	Political	75	150	175	100	Fillmore Sec'y State
Everett, Rupert	Ent	25	50		50	My Best Friends Wedding
Everhart, Angie	Ent	15			35	
Everly Brothers	Music	35			75	
Evers, Medgar 1925-63	Political	RARE	RARE	RARE	RARE	Civil Rights
Evigan, Greg	Ent	10			25	My Two Dads/TekWar
Ewell, I.R.L.	Civil War	200	400			
Ewell, Rich'd Stoddert	Civil War	375	550	900		CSA General/1817-72
Ewell, Tom	Ent	10			25	
Ewing, James	Military	50	125			Officer Am. Revolution
Ewing, Thomas 1789-71	Political	50	100	225		
Exelmans, Rene' J.	Military	35	75	125		Marshal of France
Exile	Music	25			50	All Four Signed
Extreme	Music	40			75	Signed by Entire Band
Eyre, Edward John	Explorer	50		150		Gov. Australia. Eyre Rock
Eytinge, Rose 1838-1911	Ent	25		50	50	

Name	Field	SIG	DS	ALS	SP	Remarks
Fabares, Shelley	Ent	5	20		20	Coach
Faber, John Eberhard	Business	150	500	700		Eberhard Faber Pencil Co.
Fabian	Music	10			20	
Fabio	Ent	15			35	Male Model
Fabray, Nanette	Ent	5			25	
Factor, Max	Business	25	125	175	75	Cosmetic Mfg.
Factor, Max Jr.	Business	10	30	45	45	Cosmetic Mfg.
Fagan, James F.	Civil War	Scarce	Scarce	Scarce	Scarce	CSA Gen.& U.S.Marshal
Fagerbakke, Bill	Ent	15			35	Coach
Fagoaga, Isidodo	Music	15			50	Opera
Fahey, Jeff	Ent	10			25	The Marshal
Faick, Wolfgang	Aviation	20	45	50	45	
Fair, James G.	Political	30	125	100		Mining/CA Developer
Fairbank, Calvin	Political	50	75	150		Freed Fugitive Slaves
Fairbanks, Charles W.	Vice Pres	50	100	275	150	T. Roosevelt VP
Fairbanks, Douglas, Jr.	Ent	20	50		50	
Fairbanks, Douglas, Sr.	Ent	150			300	Silent Film Swashbuckler
Fairchild, David G.	Science	5		20	10	Am Botanist
Fairchild, Lucius	Civil War	20	45	75		Union General/1831-96
Fairchild, Morgan	Ent	10		25	25	
Fairchild, Sherman	Business	25	50	100	50	Fairchild Camera & Equipment Co
Fairfax, George Wm.	Political	75	200	300		
Fairless, Benjamin F.	Business	35	100	200	75	CEO US Steel
Faisal, King	Royalty	25	50	100	125	King Saudi Arabia
Faith, Percy	Music	35			150	Conductor-Arranger
Faithfull, Emily	Business	25	50	50		Br Painter
Falana, Lola	Ent	10			25	
Falconer, William	Author	50	200			Br Poet/1732-69
Falk, Peter	Ent	10	25		30	Columbo
Falkenburg, Jinx	Ent	5			25	
Fall, Albert B.	Political	50	75	150	75	Sec'y Interior.Teapot Dome
Fall, Leo 1873-1925	Music	35			100	Composer
Falla, Manuel de 1876-46	Music	175	450		900	Composer
Falstaff, John, Sir	Military	RARE	RARE	RARE	RARE	
Faneuil, Peter	RevWar	125	225	450		Faneuil Hall, Boston
Fantin-Latour, Henri	Art	35	100	175		Fr. Illustrator, Lithographer
Faraday, Michael 1791-67	Science	175		450	650	Br Chemist
Farentino, James	Ent	15			30	
Fargo, Donna	Music	10			20	
Fargo, James C.	Business	450	1,200			Founder Wells Fargp
Fargo, William G. 1818-81	Business	450	900			Wells-Fargo, Am. Expr
Farina, Dennis	Ent	15	35		35	

Name	Field	SIG	DS	ALS	SP	Remarks
Farley, Chris	Ent	50			90	Died Young/Sat Nite Live
Farley, James A.	Political	15	45	75	35	FDR P.M. General
Farman, Henri	Aviation	75	125	175	175	Pioneer Aviator/Manftg
Farman, Maurice	Aviation	75		150		Pioneer Aviator
Farmer, Art	Music	10			25	Jazz Fluegelhorn-Trumpet
Farmer, Fannie Merritt	Author	150			250	
Farmer, Frances	Ent	150	200	300	500	1914 - 1970
Farnsworth, Charles	Military	25			75	General WW I
Farnsworth, John F.	Civil War	50	100			Union General
Farnsworth, Philo T.	Science	RARE	RARE	RARE	RARE	Invented first TV camera
Farnsworth, Richard	Ent	10			20	
Farnum, Dustin	Ent	50		100	125	The Virginian
Farnum, William	Ent	50			175	
Farr, Jamie	Ent	5	20		20	MASH/Klinger
Farragut, David G.	Civil War	175	450	750		Union Admiral/1801-70
Farrakhan, Louis	Political	75			150	Leads Nation of Islam
Farrar, Geraldine 1882-67	Music	75		125	125	Opera, Concert
Farrell, Charles	Ent	15		30	45	
Farrell, Eileen	Music	25			100	Opera
Farrell, Glenda	Ent	25	35		75	1904 - 1971
Farrell, Mike	Ent	5	20		20	MASH
Farrentino, Deborah	Ent	10			25	
Farrow, Mia	Ent	20			50	
Fassbaender, Brigitte	Music	10			25	Ger. Mezzo Soprano,Opera
Fast, Howard	Author	15			35	
Faulkner, William	Author	350	1,500	2,500	Scarce	Nobel Lit/Pulitzer Fiction
Fauquier, Francis	Political	200	450			Colonial Administrator
Faure, Felix 1841-99	Political	35		125		Pres. France 1895-99
Faure, Gabriel 1845-1924	Music	100	200	200	550	Composer. French
Fausto, Cleva	Music	30			75	Opera
Faversham, William	Ent	25			45	1868-1940
Fawcett, Edgar	Author	50	100	225		
Fawcett, Farrah	Ent	20	50		45	Sig in full/Charlies Angels
Fawcett, Millicent, Dame	Political	35		100		Womens Suffrage
Fay, Frank	Ent	15		45	45	
Faye, Alice	Ent	20			45	1912 - 1998
Faye, Julia	Ent	5			15	
Faylon, Frank	Ent	45			75	
Fazenda, Louise	Ent	25			75	
Featherston, Winfield S.	Civil War	75	225	225		CSA General/1819-91
Fegelein, Hermann Otto	Military	500				Ger. SS Gen. WWII
Feinhals, Fritz	Music	30			50	Ger. Baritone, Opera
Feld, Fritz	Ent	10			20	
Feldany, Eric	Ent	5			10	
Feldman, Charles K.	Business	10	20	40	20	Fndr. Famous Artists Corp.
Feldman, Marty	Ent	50	100		100	
Feldon, Barbara	Ent	5	20		20	Get Smart

Name	Field	SIG	DS	ALS	SP	Remarks
Feliciano, Jose	Music	10			20	Guitar-Vocalist
Felix, Maria	Ent	10			30	
Fellini, Frederico 1920-93	Ent	50	150		100	AA Film Director-Producer
Fellows, Edith	Ent	10			20	
Fels, Joseph	Business	100	200	400		Fels Naptha Soap
Felt, Harry, Adm.	Military	10	30	50	25	
Fenn, Sherilyn	Ent	15			40	
Fenneman, George	Ent	15			45	Announcer/You Bet Your Life
Fenton, Ruben E.	Civil War	30	50	75		Civil War Gov. NY
Feoktistov, Konstantin	Space	25			75	Pioneer Russian Cosmonaut
Ferber, Edna 1887-1968	Author	150	350	450		Novelist/Pulitzer
Ferdinand I 1503-1564	Royalty	400	1,200			Holy Roman Emperor
Ferdinand I 1793-1875	Royalty	100	200			Emperor of Austria
Ferdinand I 1865-1927	Royalty				450	King of Roumania
Ferdinand I, III, IV	Royalty	RARE	3,500	RARE	RARE	King of Naples
Ferdinand II 1578-1637	Royalty	150	450			Holy Roman Emperor
Ferdinand II, The Catholic	Royalty	450	1,700	3,500		Spain
Ferdinand V 1452-1516	Royalty		2,750			King of Spain
Ferdinand VII (Sp)	Royalty	125	450			
Ferebee, Thomas	Aviation	50	125	250	100	Bombadier of Enola Gay
Ferenczi, Sandor	Science	75	150	350		
Ferguson, Maynard	Music	10			30	Trumpet Player
Ferguson, Miriam A. 'Ma'	Political	75	150			Governor TX
Ferguson, Samuel W.	Civil War	200	350	550		CSA General/1834-1917
Ferguson, William J.	Ent	175	225	425		
Ferlinghetti, Lawrence	Author	20	75	100	25	Poet/Beat Movement
Fermi, Enrico 1901-1954	Science	500	1,500	2,000		
Ferrar, Geraldine	Music	35			125	Opera
Ferrara, Franco	Music	50			250	Conductor
Ferrare, Cristina	Ent	5			15	Model
Ferrari, Enzo 1898-1988	Business	300	550		550	Auto Mfg. Race Car Driver
Ferrer, Jose	Ent	20	25	50	50	AA Actor
Ferrer, Miguel	Ent	5			15	
Ferrero, Edward	Civil War	75	150	225		Union General
Ferrigno, Lou	Ent	10	25		25	Incredible Hulk
Ferry, Orris S.	Civil War	50	75	150	300	Union General/1823-75
Fesch, Cardinal	Political		225	450		Married Napoleon & Josephine
Fessenden, Francis	Civil War	50	100	200		Union General/1839-1906
Fessenden, James	Civil War	25	50	70		Union General/1833-82
Fessenden, William P.	Political	50	75	175		Lincoln Sec'y Treasury
Fetchit, Stepin	Ent	50			150	
Few, William	RevWar	200	450	750		Continental Congress
Feynman, Richard P.	Science	25	50	75	45	Nobel Physics
Fidler, Jimmy	Ent	5			15	Gossip Columnist
Fiedler, Arthur	Music	30			50	Conductor Boston Pops
Fiedler, John	Ent	5			20	Voice of Disney's Piglet
Field, Cyrus W. 1819-92	Business	150	450	900		Atlantic Cable, Financier

Name	Field	SIG	DS	ALS	SP	Remarks
Field, Eugene 1850-95	Author	100	200	400	200	Children's Poet, Journalist
Field, Marshall, III	Business	100	150	350		Communications Empire
Field, Marshall, Jr.	Business	35	100	150	75	1916-1965
Field, Marshall, Sr.	Business	400	1,000	1,500	650	Marshall Field & Co.
Field, Rachel	Author	20	100			Am Novelist
Field, Sally	Ent	10	25		30	AA Winner
Field, Stephen J.	SuprCt	75	150	250	225	
Field, Virginia	Ent	5			15	
Fields, Debbi	Ent	5			10	
Fields, Gracie	Music	20	35	50	75	1898 - 1979
Fields, James T. 1817-81	Author	10	20	35		Publisher
Fields, Shep	Music	15			40	Big Band Leader
Fields, Stanley	Ent	15		35	40	
Fields, W. C. 1879-1946	Ent	275	550	775	1,500	
Fiennes, Ralph	Ent	25			50	
Fieseler, Gerhard	Aviation	25	50	75	75	
Figueres, Jose	Political	15	45	100	35	
Filacuridi, Nicola	Music	15			45	Opera
Filippeschi, Mario	Music	25			75	Opera
Fillmore, Caroline	First Lady	600	900	900		
Fillmore, Millard 1800-74	President	250	900	1,200	RARE	
Finch, Peter	Ent	75		150	150	AA Winner
Findlay, William 1768-46	Political	50		100		Gov PA
Fine, Larry	Ent	100	250		350	Three Stooges
Finegan, Bill (William J.)	Music	20			40	Big Band Leader
Finkel, Fyvush	Ent	10			20	Picket Fences
Finlay, Frank	Ent	5			15	
Finley, Jesse J.	Civil War	75	125	200		CSA General/1812-1904
Finney, Albert	Ent	9		20	25	
Finnie, Linda	Music	10			30	Opera
Finston, Nat W.	Music	10			20	Conductor-Violinist
Fiorentino, Linda	Ent	25			50	
Fio-Rito, Ted	Music	15			35	Big Band Leader
Firestone, Harvey S.	Business	450	1,200	1,500	750	Founder Firestone Tire
Firestone, Jr., Harvey S.	Business	25	50	75	35	Pres. CEO Firestone Tire....
Firestone, Leonard K.	Business	15	45	75	25	
Fischer, Edmond H., Dr.	Science	20	45		30	Nobel Medicine
Fischer, Harold E.	Aviation	10	25	45	35	ACE, Korea, Double Ace
Fischer, Siegfried	Aviation	10		25	15	
Fish, Hamilton 1808-1893	Political	25		100		Gov/Senator
Fish, Nicholas	RevWar	50	125	250		Aide-de-Camp Gen. Scott
Fishburne, Lawrence	Ent	20			50	
Fishel, Danielle	Ent	25			50	Boy Meets World
Fisher, Bud (Harry C.)	Cartoonist	75	125		150	Mutt & Jeff
Fisher, Carrie	Ent	20	50		50	Star Wars
Fisher, Eddie	Ent	5		20	25	
Fisher, Frances	Ent	25			50	Titanic

Name	Field	SIG	DS	ALS	SP	Remarks
Fisher, Fred J.	Business	100				Mfg, Auto Body. Gen'l Motors
Fisher, Gail	Ent	10			25	
Fisher, Ham	Cartoonist	100		225	150	Joe Palooka
Fisher, Harrison	Art	40				
Fisher, Joely	Ent	20			40	
Fisher, John, Lord	Military	15	25			Brit, Adm. of the Fleet 1905
Fisher, Lawrence P.	Business	100	150	350		Co-Founder Fisher Body
Fisk, Clinton B.	Civil War	50	75	100		Union General/1828-90
Fisk, James 1834-1872	Business	1,000	RARE	RARE	2,500	Robber Baron/RARE
Fiske, Bradley	Military	15		35		Admiral WW I
Fitch, Val L., Dr.	Science	20	35		30	Nobel Physics
Fitz, Reginald H. 1843-13	Science	100		300		Physician
FitzGerald, Edward	Author	90	250	600		Poet/Translator
Fitzgerald, Barry	Ent	125	150	200	250	
Fitzgerald, Ella	Music	30	50	75	75	
Fitzgerald, F. Scott	Author	450	1,500	Scarce	Scarce	1896-1940
Fitzgerald, Geraldine	Ent	15	35		50	1912 - 1992
Fitzgerald, John	RevWar	35	100	200		
Fitzsimmons, Thomas	RevWar	200	300	400		Continental Congress
Five Presidents	President	1,500			4,500	5 Presidents on One Piece
Fix, Paul	Ent	25			75	
Fixx, Jim	Author	15	35			
Flack, Roberta	Music	20			45	
Flagg, Fannie	Ent	5		20	15	Author/Actress
Flagg, James Montgomery	Art	75	175	250	250	
Flagler, D. W.	Military	15		25	20	
Flagler, Henry M.	Business	Scarce	2,500	6,500	3,000	Standard Oil Pioneer
Flagstad, Kirsten	Music	100			200	Nor. Soprano/1895-62
Flammarion, Nicolas-C..	Science	50	75	150		Fr. Astronomer
Flamsteed, John 1646-19	Science	800	975			Br. Ist Astronomer Royal
Flanagan, Edward, Fr.	Political	50	125		250	Boy's Town Founder
Flannery, Sean Patrick	Ent	20			50	Young Indiana Jones
Flatt and Scruggs	Music	50			125	Earl and Lester
Flaubert, Gustave	Author	175	550	1,250		Fr. Novelist. Realist School
Fleetwood Mac	Music	125	250		275	Signed by All 6
Fleetwood, Mick	Music	30			50	Fleetwood Mac
Fleischer, Charles	Ent	10			25	Voice of Roger Rabbitt
Fleischer, Leonora	Author	15			30	Shadowlands
Fleischer, Max 1883-1972	Cartoonist	250			450	Created Betty Boop
Fleischer, Richard	Ent	10			20	Film Director
Fleischmann, Charles L.	Business	100	300			Fleischmann's Yeast
Fleming, Alexander, Sir	Science	225	600	750	900	Nobel for Penicillin
Fleming, Art	Ent	10			25	
Fleming, Eric	Ent	150	250		300	Original Rawhide
Fleming, Francis	Aviation	10		40	30	ACE/WWII
Fleming, Ian	Author	575	1,500	Scarce	1,800	Creator of James Bond
Fleming, John Ambrose	Science	25	75	150		Br. Electrical Engineer

Name	Field	SIG	DS	ALS	SP	Remarks
Fleming, Rhonda	Ent	10		25	45	
Fleming, Victor	Ent	450	900		900	Director GWTW and OZ
Fleming-Sandes, Alfred	Military	15	50			WW I Victoria Cross
Fleta, Miguel	Music	75			250	Opera
Fletcher, Bramwell	Ent	45			100	1904 - 1988
Fletcher, Frank Jack	Military	25		100	75	
Fletcher, Harvey 1884-81	Science	225				Stereo Sound 1934
Fletcher, John Gould	Author	15		100		Pulitzer Poet
Fletcher, Louise	Ent	10			25	AA Winner
Flint, Austin 1812-86	Science	75	225	400		Eminent Physician-Teacher
Flint, Lawrence	Aviation	10		35	25	
Flippen, Jay C.	Ent	25			50	
Flockhart, Calista	Ent	25			50	Ally McBeal
Floege, Ernest	Military	25	45		75	
Floren, Myron	Music	5			10	Lawrence Welk
Florence, William J.	Ent	15	25	45	75	Actor/Playwright
Florey, Howard Walter	Science	25	45	75	45	Nobel Medicine, Penicillin
Florey, Robert	Ent	15			35	
Flory, Paul J., Dr.	Science	20	35	75	45	Nobel Chemistry
Flotow, Frederich von	Music	75	150	450		Composer
Flower, Wm.Henry, Sir	Science	10	25	50		Br.Zoologist
Flowers, Bess	Ent	5			15	
Flowers, Wayland	Ent	25			50	Marionette Artist/Madame
Floyd, John Buchanan	Civil War	175	300	400		CSA General/1806-63
Floyd, William 1734-21	RevWar	450	1,250	1,500		Signer Decl. of Indepen.
Fluckey, Gene	Military	45		100	100	Top US Submarine Cmdr.
Flynn, Errol 1909-59	Ent	250	500	750	550	
Flynn, Joe	Ent	50	75	100	125	
Flynt, Larry	Business	5			15	Hustler Magazine
Foch, Ferdinand	Military	50	125	250	200	Fr. General WWI, Marshal
Foch, Nina	Ent	10			20	
Fogelberg, Dan	Music	15			35	
Fogerty, John	Music	25			50	CCR
Fokker, Anthony	Aviation	200	300	450	500	Am Aircraft Designer
Foley, Red	Music	30			75	
Follett, Ken	Author	5			15	Br. Mystery Novelist
Folsom, Nathaniel	RevWar	125		450		Am General
Foltz, Frederick	Military	25			100	General WW I
Fonck, Paul-Rene'	Aviation	1,000	2,000			WWI Top Allied ACE/Fr
Fonda, Bridget	Ent	25			50	
Fonda, Henry 1905-1982	Ent	75	150		175	AA Winner
Fonda, Jane	Ent	15	45		50	
Fonda, Jelles	RevWar	50	150	225		RevWar Officer
Fonda, Peter	Ent	15			45	Easy Rider
Fonda, Ten Eyck H.	Civil War	50		100		Military Telegrapher Hero
Fong, Benson	Ent	25			50	
Fontaine, Frank	Ent	10			20	

Name	Field	SIG	DS	ALS	SP	Remarks
Fontaine, Joan	Ent	15			45	
Fontanne, Lynn	Ent	15			45	
Fonteyn, Margot 1919-91	Music	50		125	200	Premier Ballerina
Foo Fighters	Music				75	Signed by Entire Group
Foote, Andrew Hull	Civil War	50	100	300		Union Admiral/1806-63
Foote, Arthur	Music	35	75	150		Composer
Foote, Henry S.	Civil War	25	50	75		Senator
Foote, Horton	Author	5			15	Playwright, Scriptwriter
Foote, Shelby	Author	15	35			
Foran, Dick	Ent	15		35	45	
Foray, June	Ent	5			20	Voice of Rocky & Bullwinkle
Forbes, Bertie Chas.	Business	35	150		75	Founder Forbes Magazine
Forbes, M. Steve	Business	5			15	Presidential Candidate
Forbes, Malcolm S.	Business	35	75	150	75	Publisher
Forbes, Ralph	Ent	15		30	25	
Forbes, Scott	Ent	10			25	
Forbes-Robertson, John	Ent	25		125	50	1853-1957
Force, Manning F.	Civil War	25		100		Union General/1824-99
Ford, Benson	Business	5		25	15	Ford Motor Car
Ford, Betty	First Lady	35	100		75	
Ford, Edsel 1893-1943	Business	250	500		500	Ford Motor Co.
Ford, Edsel II	Business	5		20	15	Ford Motor Co.
Ford, Eileen	Business	5			15	Ford Modelling Agency
Ford, Elaine	Business	20			40	
Ford, Gerald R.	President	50	200	400	75	
Ford, Glenn	Ent	35			75	
Ford, Harrison	Ent	50	100		100	Indiana Jones/Star Wars
Ford, Henry 1863-1947	Business	900	2,500	3,750	2,500	Pioneer Auto Mfg.Important
Ford, Henry II	Business	15		30	45	Ford Motor Co.
Ford, John	Ent	150	250	400	300	Western Film Director
Ford, John Thompson	Ent	450	600	750		Ford's Theater, Wash. D.C.
Ford, Lita	Music	15			45	Singer
Ford, Paul	Ent	15			35	
Ford, Ross	Ent	10			20	
Ford, Sewell 1868-1946	Author	10		35		Short Story Writer
Ford, Tennessee Ernie	Music	15			45	
Ford, Wallace	Ent	25			50	
Foreignor	Music	50	150		100	Signed by Entire Band
Forepaugh, Adam	Business	75				Early Circus Owner
Forester, C[ecil] S[cott]	Author	75		100	100	Novelist
Forman, Milos	Ent	25			75	AA Winning Director
Forman, Thomas M.	RevWar	50	100			
Formica, Fern	Ent	15	25		45	Munchkin, Wizard of Oz
Forney, John H.	Civil War	Scarce	Scarce	Scarce	Scarce	CSA General/1829-1902
Forney, William H.	100	90	150	300		CSA General/1823-94
Forrest, Edwin 1806-1972	Ent	45	75	125	150	Early Great Am. Actor
Forrest, Frederick	Ent	5			15	Actor

Name	Field	SIG	DS	ALS	SP	Remarks
Forrest, French 1796-66	Civil War	100	150	175		CSA Naval Commander
Forrest, Hal	Cartoonist	25			75	Tailspin Tommy/Tarzan
Forrest, Nathan B.	Civil War	575	Scarce	Scarce	RARE	CSA General/1821-1877
Forrest, Sally	Ent	5			15	
Forrest, Steve	Ent	5			15	
Forrestal, James 1892-49	Political	50	100		45	Sec'y Navy/Sec'y Defense/Suicide
Forster, Edw. Morgan	Author	75	200	300		Br. Novelist. Howard's End
Forster, John 1812-76	Author	20		50		Br. Historian, Biographer
Forster, Robert	Ent	5			15	
Forsyth, Frederick	Author	20		75	35	Spy Novelist.
Forsyth, James William	Civil War	35	100	175		Union General/1835-1906
Forsyth, John 1780-1841	Political	25	50	150		Sec'y of State (Jackson)
Forsythe, John	Ent	15			40	Dallas
Fort, Luigi	Music	20			45	Opera
Fortas, Abe	SuprCt	25	150	200		Resigned from Court
Forte, Fabian (Fabian)	Ent	5		25	20	
Forti, Carmen Fiorella	Music	25			60	Opera
Forward, Walter 1786-52	Political	20	50	75		Sec'y Treasury 1841
Foss, Joe	Aviation	30	75	75	50	WWII ACE
Foss, Sam Walter	Author	5		20	15	
Fosse, Bob 1927-1987	Ent	35	125	100	75	AA Winning Choreagrapher
Foster, Abiel 1735-1806	Political	125	275			Cont. Congress
Foster, Charles 1828-04	Political	35	75	100		Gov Ohio
Foster, Dianne	Ent	10			20	
Foster, Jodie	Ent	35	75		75	AA Winner
Foster, John Gray	Civil War	35	40	65		Union General/1823-74
Foster, John W. 1836-17	Political	25		50	125	Sect State/1892
Foster, Lafayette S.	Political	25	50	100		Civil War Senator CT
Foster, Myles B.	Art	20	50	75		
Foster, Norman	Ent	15		35	45	Directer
Foster, Preston	Ent	25	75		75	1901 - 1970
Foster, Stephen	Music	1,000	3,500	RARE	RARE	Composer/Scarce
Foster, Susanna	Ent	15			35	
Fountain, Pete	Music	5		20	25	Jazz-Dixieland Clarinetist
Four Non Blondes	Music	35			75	Signed by Entire Band
Four Presidents	President	1,000			2,500	Four Signed on One Piece
Four Seasons, The	Music	75	150		125	Signed by all four
Four Tops	Music	50			100	Signed by entire group
Fournier, G.	Military	50	100			
Fowler, Gene	Author	25	75		45	
Fowler, William, Dr.	Science	20		45	45	Nobel Physics
Fowles, John	Author	30	75	100	35	Br Novelist
Fowley, Douglas	Ent	10			30	
Fox, Charles 1749-1806	Political	30	75	150		Br Reformer
Fox, Edward	Ent	5			15	
Fox, Fontaine T.	Cartoonist	35			150	Toonerville Trolley
Fox, Fred S.	Ent	15		45		

Name	Field	SIG	DS	ALS	SP	Remarks
Fox, Michael J.	Ent	25	50		50	Spin City/Family Ties
Fox, Samantha	Music	15			45	
Fox, Vivica	Ent	20			50	
Fox, William	Business	200	400		400	Founder Fox Film Corp.
Foxworth, Robert	Ent	5			10	
Foxworthy, Jeff	Ent	15			35	Comedian
Foxx, Redd	Ent	25	50		50	Sanford and Son
Foy, Eddie, Jr.	Ent	20	45	45	45	
Foy, Eddie, Sr.	Ent	25			50	
Foy, Maximilian S.	Military	15	45	75		General at Waterloo
Fradona, Ramone	Cartoonist	15			50	Brenda Starr
Frakes, Jonathan	Ent	15			45	Star Trek Next Generation
Frampton, George	Art	15		35		Br Sculptor/1860-28
Frampton, Peter	Music	25			50	
France, Anatole	Author	75	125	200	250	Novelist
Franchetti, Alberto	Music	35		125	100	Wrote 9 Operas
Franchi, Sergio	Ent	15			45	
Franciosa, Anthony	Ent	5			15	
Francis I 1494-1547	Royalty	500	750			France
Francis I 1777-1830	Royalty		200			King Two Sicilies
Francis II 1768-1835	Royalty	100	300	425		Last Hooly Roman Emperor
Francis V 1819-75	Royalty	50	100			Duke of Modena
Francis, Anne	Ent	5			20	
Francis, Arlene	Ent	5		15	10	
Francis, Connie	Music	5			15	
Francis, Dick	Author	25		75	45	Mystery Writer
Francis, Genie	Ent	5			15	General Hospital
Francis, Kay	Ent	30		75	100	
Franciscus, James	Ent	10			20	
Franck, Cesar 1822-1920	Music	350	750	700		Composer
Franco, Francisco	Political	175	750	900	275	Sp. Soldier & Dictator
Frank, August	Military	10	30	45		
Frank, Hans	Military	275	500			Nazi Lawyer
Frank, Otto	Military	300	550			Ann Franks father
Franken, Rose	Author	10	25	45		Playwright
Frankenheimer, John	Ent	10		30	25	Film Director
Frankfurter, Felix	SuprCt	250	900	900	750	Founder Am. Civil Liberties Un,
Franklin, Aretha	Music	20			45	
Franklin, Benjamin 1706 - 1790	RevWar	9,000	16,000	RARE		
Franklin, Bonnie	Ent	5			20	One Day at a Time
Franklin, Herbert H, 1867-1956	Business	35	125			Pioneer Auto Manufacturer
Franklin, Jane 1792-1875	Author	100		395		
Franklin, John, Sir	Political	125	250	450		Proved NW Passage
Franklin, William	Political	150	450	750		Brit. Gov. NJ, Son of Benj.
Franklin, Wm. Buell	Civil War	75	150	175	200	Union General
Frann, Mary	Ent	15			45	Newhart
Frantz, Charton C.	Business	10	35	45	25	

Name	Field	SIG	DS	ALS	SP	Remarks
Franz Josef II	Royalty	40	75	150	75	Liechtenstein
Franz Joseph I 1830-16	Royalty	175	450	750		Emperor of Austria
Franz, Arthur	Ent	10			20	
Franz, Dennis	Ent	15			45	NYPD Blue
Fraser, Brendan	Ent	25			50	
Fraser, Elizabeth	Ent	10			30	
Fraser, James Earle	Art	450	650			Sculptor/Buffalo Nickel
Fraser, Malcolm	Political	10			30	Prime Minister/Australia
Fraser, Peter	Political	10	25		20	Prime Minister/New Zealand
Frasier	Ent	100			200	Signed by All Five
Frawley, William	Ent	250	400	550	450	I Love Lucy
Frazer, John Wesley	Civil War	150	250			
Frazer, Joseph W.	Business	275	550			Kaiser-Frazer Auto Mfg.
Frazetta, Frank	Cartoonist	50			100	Johnny Comet
Freddy & The Dreamers	Music	100	150			Signed by Entire Group
Frederic, Harold	Author	10	35	75		Novelist
Frederic, Prince	Royalty	10	25			The Just Saxony
Frederick Augustus I	Royalty		275			1750-1827
Frederick Augustus II	Royalty		175			King Saxony/1797-1854
Frederick I	Royalty	25	75			Wurtemburg
Frederick II, The Great	Royalty	400	1,200	2,000		1712-86
Frederick III 1831-1888	Royalty	150	275	400	500	Prussia
Frederick IV 1671-1730	Royalty		350	750		Denmark
Frederick IX 1899-1972	Royalty	50	175	300		Denmark
Frederick V 1723-66	Royalty	100	250	500		Denmark
Frederick VI 1768-1839	Royalty	100	225			Denmark
Frederick VII 1808-63	Royalty	50	150			Denmark
Frederick Wm. I 1688-40	Royalty	150	450			Prussia
Frederick Wm. II	Royalty	100	300	450		Prussia/1770 - 1840
Frederick Wm. IV	Royalty	100	375	750		Prussia. Insane/1795 - 61
Frederick, Pauline	Ent	15	30		75	Silent Cinema Star
Fredericks, Fred	Cartoonist	20		75	50	Mandrake The Magician
Frederique	Ent	20			40	
Freeland, Paul van	Political	10			20	Prime Minister
Freeman, Kathleen	Ent	5			15	
Freeman, Mona	Ent	5			15	
Freeman, Morgan	Ent	20	50		50	
Freeman, Samuel	RevWar	15	50	100		Rev. War Patriot
Freleng, Friz 1906 - 95	Cartoonist	40			75	Looney Tunes/Pink Panther
Fremont, Jessie Benton	Author	35	75	200		Wife of John C.
Fremont, John C.	Civil War	200	600	750		Union General/1813-80
Fremstad, Olive	Music	125			275	Opera
French, Daniel Chester	Art	75	175	225	125	Sculptor, Lincoln Memorial
French, Samuel Gibbs	Civil War	150	300	300		CSA General/1818-1910
French, Victor	Ent	15			45	
French, William H.	Civil War	45	125	250		
Freni, Mirelia	Music	10			40	Opera

Name	Field	SIG	DS	ALS	SP	Remarks
Freron, Louis M.S.	RevWar	20	50	100		
Fresnay, Pierre	Ent	15			45	Fr. Actor/Director
Freud, Anna 1895-1982	Science		450	450		Daughterof Sigmund Freud
Freud, Sigmund 1856-39	Science	1,750	3,500	4,500	6,000	
Frey, Richard	Aviation	25	50	100	75	
Friant, Louis, Count	RevWar	35	75	150		
Frick, Henry Clay	Business	200		900		Carnegie Steel
Fricke, Janie	Music	5			10	
Fricker, Brenda	Ent	20			45	
Friedman, Jerome I.	Science	20			45	Nobel Physics
Friends (Cast)	Ent	100			200	Cast of 6
Friml, Rudolf 1879-1972	Music	100	200	300	250	Composer
Frisch, Karl von	Science	15		45	25	Nobel Medicine
Fritchle, Barbara	Civil War	RARE	RARE	RARE	RARE	PatrioticHeroine
Frith, William P.1819-09	Art	25	50	100		
Fritsch, Werner von	Military	50	150	200	175	
Frizzell, Lefty	Music	25			75	
Frobe, Gert	Ent	75			150	Goldfinger
Frohman, Daniel	Ent	15	45		50	Dean/Am Theatre Producers
Froman, Jane 1907-80	Music	15		20	45	
Fromm, Erich	Science	50	150		75	Psychoanylyst/Philosopher
Fromme, Lynette	Political	50		150		Charles Manson Follower
Frondizi, Arturo	Political	15	35	75	50	PresidentArgentina
Frontiersmen, The	Music	25			50	
Frost, A.B.	Cartoonist	50			125	Illustrator
Frost, Daniel Marsh	Civil War	175	275	450		CSA General/1823-1900
Frost, David	Ent	5			15	
Frost, Edwin B.	Science	10		45		Am. Astronomer
Frost, Lindsay	Ent	15			25	
Frost, Robert 1874-1963	Author	150	600	1,000	750	Pulitzer in Poetry 4x
Fry, Christopher	Author	35	100	150		
Fry, James Barnet	Civil War	30		100		Union General/1827-94
Frye, Dwight	Ent	1,200		1,800	2,000	Character Actor/RARE
Fuchida, Mitsuo	Aviation	300		500		Led Attack on Pearl Harbor
Fuchs, Rutger	Military	50	125	200	100	
Fuchs, Vivian E. Sir	Explorer	25	75	150		Br. Antarctic Expl.
Fuentes, Daisey	Ent	25			50	
Fukuda, Takeo	Political	15		50	30	Prime Minister Japan
Fukui, Kenichi	Science	20		45	35	Nobel Chemistry
Fulbright, James W.	Political	20		100	50	AR Senator
Fulgham, Robert	Author	5			15	
Fuller, Alfred C.	Business	125			150	Founder Fuller Brush Co.
Fuller, Buckminster R.	Science	30	75	150	175	Architectural Engineer
Fuller, Delores	Ent	20			50	
Fuller, Margaret 1810-50	Political	150	250	450		Feminist
Fuller, Melville W.	SuprCt	50	150	275	175	1839 - 1910
Fuller, Robert	Ent	5			10	

Name	Field	SIG	DS	ALS	SP	Remarks
Fuller, Sam	Ent	35			75	Film Director
Fulton, Robert 1765-1815	Science	325	1,250	2,500	RARE	Submarine, Steamboat
Funicello, Annette	Ent	50	100		100	Full Signature/Less if not
Funk, Isaac K.	Author	25	75	125		Funk & Wagnalls Dictionary
Funk, Larry	Music	15			30	Bandleader
Funston, Frederick	Military	75	150	300		Span Am War
Funt, Alan	Ent	15	50		45	Candid Camera
Furlong, Edward	Ent	25			50	T2
Furness, Betty	Ent	15			25	1916 - 1994
Furrer, Reinhard	Space	25			75	German Astronaut
Furstenberg, Betsy von	Business	5			10	Fashion Designer
Furtwangler, Wilhelm	Music	400		800	775	German Conductor
Fuseli, Henry 1741-1825	Art	200	450			Br/Swiss Painter

G

Name	Field	SIG	DS	ALS	SP	Remarks
Gable, Clark 1901-60	Ent	350	450	Scarce	900	
Gable, Kay	Ent	10			25	Wife of Clark
Gabor, Eva	Ent	35	75		75	Green Acres
Gabor, Zsa Zsa	Ent	5			15	
Gabreski, Frances	Aviation	35	100	125	100	ACE, WW 11, #3 US
Gabriel, Peter	Music	25			50	
Gabrielle, Monique	Ent	20			45	
Gabrilowitsch, Ossip	Music	75	125	200	125	Pianist, Conductor
Gacy, John Wayne	Criminal	75	125	150	175	Serial Killer
Gadsden, James	Political	175	350	550		Gadsden Purchase
Gadski-Tauscher, Johan	Music	50		75	100	
Gagarin, Yuri 1934-68	Space	400			1,500	First Man in Space
Gage, Thomas	RevWar	225	450	750		British General
Gagnon, Ren, A.	Military	25			50	Iwo Jima Flag Raising
Gail, Max	Ent	10			20	Barney Miller
Gailand, Adolf	Aviation	50	75	150	125	German WWII ACE
Gainsborough, Thomas	Art	275	550	1,200		Br, Portraitist. Landscapes
Gajdusek, D. Carleton	Science	20			30	Nobel Medicine
Galbraith, John Ken	Author	15	35		35	Author Books Economics
Gale, Zona 1874-1938	Author	10	45	75	25	Am. Novelist
Galer, Robert E., Jr.	Aviation	15			50	WWII General
Galileo 1564-1642	Science	RARE	25,000	50,000	RARE	It. Astronomer
Gallagher, Megan	Ent	15			45	
Gallagher, Peter	Ent	15			45	
Gallatin, Albert 1761- 49	Political	75	275	375		
Galle, Emile 1846-1904	Art	100	325	600		Fr. Artist in Glass
Gallico, Paul W.	Author	25	100		45	Am.Novelist
Galli-Curci, Amelita	Music	75	150	250	200	Opera/1889-1963
Gallo, Ernest & Julio	Business	40			75	Gallo Winery, Sonoma, CA
Gallo, Gustavo	Music	25			50	Opera
Gallo, Robert, Dr.	Science	20	50		50	Co-Discoverer HIV Virus
Galloway, Don	Ent	10			25	
Galloway, Joseph	RevWar	Scarce	3,500	Scarce	Scarce	Continental Congr.& Army
Gallup, Benadam	Military	25	75	100		French and Indian War
Gallup, George, Jr.	Business	10			25	Gallup Poll
Galsworthy, John	Author	35	75	175	225	Br. Novelist, Playwright
Gamble, Hamilton R.	Civil War	25		100		Civil War Governor
Gance, Abel 1889-1981	Ent		200	500		Director. Fr.
Gandhi, Indira 1917-84	Political	150	350	350	Scarce	Assassinated P.M. India.
Gandhi, Mohandas K.	Political	550	1,200	1,500	Scarce	Spiritual Leader India
Gandhi, Rajiv	Political	35		75	150	P.M. of India, Assasinated
Gann, Ernest K.	Author	10		35		

Name	Field	SIG	DS	ALS	SP	Remarks
Gannett, Frank E.	Business	20	45		45	Newspapers
Ganz, Rudolph	Music	15			45	Conductor
Garafalo, Janeane	Ent	25			50	
Garat, Pierre (Pere)	Music	125		300		French Tenor
Garber, Jan	Music	15			35	Big Band Leader
Garbo, Greta 1905-91	Ent	1,200	2,200	3,000	12,000	RARE in Authentic SP
Garcia, Andy	Ent	25			50	
Garcia, Jerry	Music	150	300		300	Grateful Dead
Garcia-Robles, Alfonso	Political	35		125	75	Nobel Peace Prize
Gardanne, Gaspard A.	Military	50	125	250		
Garden, Mary 1874-1967	Music	25		75	125	Opera
Gardiner, Reginald	Ent	20			45	1903 - 1980
Gardner, Ava 1922-90	Ent	50	75		125	
Gardner, Erle Stanley	Author	75	200	300	200	1889-1970
Gardner, Franklin	Civil War	225	200	750		CSA General/1823-73
Gardner, John L.	Civil War	35		125		Union General/1813-69
Garfield, James A.	President	250	600	1,200	2,000	Union General/1831-81
Garfield, James R.	Political	20	35	75	35	Sec'y Interior 1907
Garfield, John 1913-1952	Ent	75			275	
Garfield, Lucretia R.	First Lady	100	200	150		1832-1918
Garfunkel, Art	Music	20			45	Simon and Garfunkel
Gargan, William	Ent	15		35	45	1905 - 1979
Garibaldi, Giuseppe	Political	150	300		550	1807-1882
Garland, Augustus H.	Political	75	150	200		Att'y Gen. & CSA Congress
Garland, Beverly	Ent	10			20	
Garland, Hamlin	Author	25		50	75	Pulitzer. Novelist, Essayist
Garland, Judy 1922-69	Ent	325	750	Scarce	700	
Garner, Erroll	Music	75			150	Jazz Pianist
Garner, James	Ent	5	20		20	Rockford Files/Maverick
Garner, John Nance	Vice Pres	50	150	225	175	FDR VP
Garner, Peggy Ann	Ent	35			75	
Garnett, Francis H.	Author	25	50	125		
Garnett, Richard Brooke	Civil War	650	450	550		1817-1863
Garnett, Tay	Ent	10	25		30	Director-Producer
Garr, Teri	Ent	10			30	
Garrard, Kenner	Civil War	50	75	150		Union General/1828-79
Garrett, Patrick R. (Pat)	Western	Scarce	2,500	3,000		Killed Billy the Kid
Garrett, Thomas	Political	100	250	350		Chief Engineer Underground RR
Garrison, Lindley M.	Political	25	75	150	50	Sec'y War 1913
Garrison, Vermont	Aviation	15	25	45	35	ACE, WWII & Korea
Garrison, Wm. Lloyd	Political	100	125	250	200	1805-1879
Garros, Roland	Aviation	125			425	French ACE
Garroway, Dave	Ent	10			25	
Garson, Greer 1908 - 96	Ent	35	75	100	75	AAWinner
Garth, Jennie	Ent	25			50	
Gartrell, Lucius J.	Civil War	100	250	300		CSA General/1821-91
Gary, Elbert Henry	Business	125	450	650	250	U.S.Steel, Gary, Ind.

Name	Field	SIG	DS	ALS	SP	Remarks
Gasser, Heber S.	Science	20	35		50	Nobel Medicine
Gassman, Vittorio	Ent	25			75	
Gately, George	Cartoonist	10			20	Heathcliff
Gates, Bill	Business	25			50	Microsoft
Gates, Daryl	Political	15			30	Chief Police of L.A.
Gates, Horatio 1727 - 06	RevWar	275	550	1,200		General, Continental Army
Gates, John W.	Business	500	1,000			Bet a Million Gates
Gates, Larry	Ent	10			20	
Gates, Seth 1800-77	Political	25		75		Anti-Slavery Repr. from NY
Gatlin, Larry & Brothers	Music	10			20	
Gatlin, Richard C.	Civil War	100	225			CSA General/1809-96
Gatling, Richard J.	Science	400	1,200	2,500		Inventor of Gatling Gun
Gatti-Casazza, Giulio	Music	75	150	250		Opera
Gatty, Harold	Aviation	75	275	450	175	Australian, Wiley Post Navigator
Gaugin, Paul	Art	600	1,200	2,500		Fr. Post-impressionist
Gautier, Dick	Ent	5			15	Get Smart
Gavarni, Paul	Art	100		300		
Gavaudan, Pierre	Music			135		Opera. Tenor/1772-1840
Gavin, James M. 1907-93	Military	50	100	250	125	WWII General
Gavin, John	Ent	25			55	Actor
Gaxton, William	Ent	10		25	25	
Gay, George A.	Civil War	15		45		
Gaye, Marvin	Music	150	200		200	Killed by His Father
Gayle, Crystal	Music	5			15	
Gaynor, Janet	Ent	25		50	75	1906 - 1984
Gaynor, Mitzi	Ent	20			45	
Gazzara, Ben	Ent	5			15	
Geary, Anthony	Ent	5			15	General Hospital
Geary, Cynthia	Ent	15			35	
Geary, John W.	Civil War	75	125	250	250	Union General/1819-73
Gedda, Nicolai	Music	15			35	Opera
Geer, Will	Ent	30			75	Waltons
Geffrard, Nicholas Fabre	Political	45	125			Pres. Haiti
Gehlen, Reinhard	Military	15	45	45		
Gehrig, Lou	Sports	800			3,500	1939 Baseball HOF
Geiger, Johannes H.	Science	125	350	750		Geiger Counter
Geisel, Theodore	Cartoonist					SEE Dr. Seuss
Gell, William, Dr.	Science	25	45			Br. Archaeologist
Geller, Sarah Michelle	Ent	20			50	
Gelston, David	RevWar	75	150			
Genesis	Music	75			100	Entire Band
Genet, Edmond Citizen	Military	75	150			Ist Fr. Minister to U.S.
Gentilini, Amerigo	Music	15			45	Opera
Gentry, Bobbie	Music	5			15	
George (Pr. Denmark)	Royalty	100	275			Consort of Queen Anne
George I (Eng) 1660-1727	Royalty	225	1,000	2,500		
George I (Gr) 1845-1913	Royalty	50	100	125		

Name	Field	SIG	DS	ALS	SP	Remarks
George II (Eng) 1683-60	Royalty	400	550	1,200		
George II (Greece)	Royalty	50	100	200	400	
George III (Eng) 1738-20	Royalty	200	400	Scarce		
George IV (Eng) 1762-30	Royalty	125	275	450		
George V (Eng) 1865-36	Royalty	125	350	700	600	
George V And Queen	Royalty	250			750	Queen Mary of Tack
George VI (Eng) 1895-52	Royalty	200	400	300	450	
George VI and Queen E.	Royalty	275	550		1,200	Queen Elizabeth
George, Alexander	Ent	10			20	
George, Boy	Music	25			50	Culture Club
George, Christopher	Ent	20		75	75	
George, Gladys	Ent	50	100		100	1900 - 1954
George, Grace	Ent	25			50	
George, Harold L.	Military	35	75	150	75	
George, Henry	Author	30		200	75	Author, Reformer, Editor
George, Phyllis	Ent	5			10	Miss America
George, Susan	Ent	5			15	
Gerard, Francis R.	Aviation	10		35	35	Ace/WWII
Gerard, Gil	Ent	15			30	Buck Rogers in 25th Century
Gerard, Richard	Music	50	100	150		Composer
Gerardo	Ent	15			35	
Gerardy, Jean	Music	125			200	Belg. Violin-Cellist
Gere, Richard	Ent	35	125		75	
Gerlache de Gomery, A.	Explorer	75	150	300		Belg. Naval Offr., Antarctic
Gerland, Alfred	Aviation	15	35	50	45	
German, Edward, Sir	Music	35	100	175	75	Operettas/1862-36
Gernreich, Rudi	Business	10		40	25	Fashion Designer
Geronimo	Western	5,500	RARE	RARE	RARE	1829 - 1909
Gerry, Elbridge 1744-14	RevWar	300	600	Scarce		Signer Decl. of Indep.
Gersel Cemal	Political	25	50	150	45	Turkey
Gershon, Gina	Ent	25			50	Showgirls
Gershwin, George	Music	675	1,200	RARE	2,750	Composer/1898 - 1937
Gershwin, Ira 1896-1983	Music	75	150	250	200	Composer
Gerson, Betty Lou	Ent	25			55	Voice of Cruella DeVil
Gertz, Jamie	Ent	15			35	
Gervais, John L. 1753-98	RevWar	25		100		Continental Congress
Gerville-Reache, Jeanne	Music	100			250	Opera
Gessendorf, Mechthild	Music	10			25	Opera
Get Smart	Ent	25			50	Signed by Feldon and Adams
Getty, Estelle	Ent	10			25	Golden Girls
Getty, George W.	Civil War	30	50			Union General/1819-1901
Getty, J. Paul 1892-1976	Business	150	575	900	375	Billionaire Oil Mogul.
Getz, Stan	Music	100			225	Am. Jazz Saxophonist
Ghali, Boutros Boutros	Political	10			30	Pres. U.N.
Gholson, Samuel J.	Civil War	150	350	450		CSA General/1808-83
Ghostley, Alice	Ent	5			20	Bewitched
Giannini, A. P.	Business	150	300	500		Bank of America Founder

Name	Field	SIG	DS	ALS	SP	Remarks
Gibb, Andy	Music	75	200		150	Overdosed young
Gibb, Cynthia	Ent	10			35	
Gibbon, Edward	Author	300	750	1,500		Decline/Fall Roman Empire
Gibbon, John	Civil War	150		750		Union General/1827-96
Gibbons, Barry	Business	5			20	Founder Burger King
Gibbons, Cedric	Ent	100	225	450		AA Winning Director
Gibbons, Floyd 1887-39	Aviation	75	175	300	150	Pioneer Aviator
Gibbons, Leeza	Ent	5			15	
Gibbs, Alfred	Civil War	30	75	100		Union General/1823-68
Gibbs, Georgia	Music	15			35	Big Band Vocalist
Gibbs, Marla	Ent	10	20		25	Jeffersons/227
Gibran, Kahlil	Author	125	300	750	200	Syrian Poet
Gibson, Charles Dana	Art	100	200	200	300	Illustrator-Gibson Girl
Gibson, Debbie	Music	25			50	
Gibson, Hoot 1892 - 62	Ent	125	200		250	Film Cowboy
Gibson, Horatio G.	Civil War	50				Union General/1828-1924
Gibson, James	Military	75	200	375		Officer War 1812. Wounded, Died
Gibson, Mel	Ent	35			75	
Gibson, Randall Lee	Civil War	100	300	600		CSA General/1832-1892
Gide, Andre	Author	175	350	600		Nobel/Literature
Gielgud, John, Sir	Ent	25	50		50	
Gieseking, Walter	Music	35			125	Concert Pianist
Gifford, Francis	Ent	5			10	
Gifford, Kathie Lee	Ent	5			20	
Gifford, Walter S.	Business	5		25	15	Pres. AT&T 1925-48
Gigli, Beniamino 1890-57	Music	100	200	300	300	Opera
Gilbert, A. C.	Business	75	125	175		Inventor Erector Set.
Gilbert, Billy	Ent	25	45	45	55	Disney Voice
Gilbert, Cass	Science	20	60		35	Architect
Gilbert, John	Ent	125		250	250	
Gilbert, L. Woolfe	Music	15	45	75	45	Composer
Gilbert, Melissa	Ent	15	45		45	
Gilbert, Sara	Ent	15			45	Roseanne
Gilbert, William S.	Music	175	350	700	700	Gilbert & Sullivan
Gill, Eric	Art	35	75	150		Br. Sculptor
Gill, Vince	Music	35			50	
Gillespie, Darlene	Ent	15			35	Mouseketeer
Gillespie, Dizzy 1917-93	Music	50	100		100	Jazz. Trumpet
Gillette, Anita	Ent	5			15	
Gillette, King Camp	Business	250	750	RARE	500	Gillette Co. (Safety Razor)
Gillette, William 1855-37	Ent	75	175	200	150	Portrayed Sherlock Holmes Originally
Gilley, Mickey	Music	5			20	Country
Gillmore, Quincy A.	Civil War	35	75	150		Union General/1825-88
Gilman, John T. 1753-28	RevWar	50	100	150		Cont. Congr.Gov. NH
Gilman, Nicholas	RevWar	100	300	500		Continental Congress
Gilmer, Jeremy F.	Civil War	150		400		CSA General/1818-83

Name	Field	SIG	DS	ALS	SP	Remarks
Gilmer, John H.	Civil War	35		75		CSA Congress from NC
Gilmer, Thomas W.	Political		100	150		Tyler Sec'y Navy
Gilmore, James R.	Author	25	50	150		Merchant/1822-1903
Gilmore, Joseph A.	Civil War	35	125			Gov. NH
Gilmore, P.S.	Music	35	75	150		Composer
Gilmore, Virginia	Ent	10		30	30	
Gilpin, Peri	Ent	25			50	Frasier
Gimbel, Bernard F.	Business	50	175	275	100	Gimbel Bros, Dept. Stores
Giminez, Eduardo	Music	10			30	Opera
Gingold, Hermione	Ent	10			25	1897-1987
Gingrich, Newt	Political	10	45		40	Congressman
Ginsberg, Allen	Author	35	200	200	75	Beat Poet
Ginsberg, Ruth Bader	SuprCt	30	45		40	
Giordano, Umberto	Music	250	400	475	700	Opera Composer
Girard, Stephen 1750-31	RevWar	125	350	325		Merchant
Gish, Annabeth	Ent	20			40	
Gish, Dorothy 1898 - 1968	Ent	55			125	Lillians acting sister
Gish, Lillian 1896-1993	Ent	30	75	75	75	Silent Star
Gissing, George Robert	Author	50	175	345		Br.Novelist./1857-03
Gist, States Rights	Civil War	450	900	1,200		CSA General/1831-64
Given, Robin	Ent	15			35	Head of the Class
Givenchy, Hubert de	Business	35	75	100		Fashion Designer
Gladden, Adley H.	Civil War	450	900			CSA General/1810-62
Gladstone, William E.	Political	75	100		100	Prime Minister/1809-98
Glaser, Donald A.	Science	20		75	45	Nobel Physics
Glaser, Paul Michael	Ent	15			45	Miami Vice
Glasgow, Ellen	Author	50	150			Novelist. Pulitzer. VA Life
Glashow, Sheldon Lee	Science	15			30	Nobel Physics
Glaspell, Susan	Author	25	75	100		Am. Playwright. Pulitzer
Glass, Philip	Music	50			150	Opera
Glass, Ron	Ent	10			25	Barney Miller
Glassman, Alan	Music	10			25	Opera
Glazer, Tom Paul	Music	15			30	
Glazunov, Alexander	Music	200	350	550	350	Russian Composer
Gleason, Jackie 1916-87	Ent	75	175	225	175	The Honeymooners
Glenn, John	Space	40	150	Scarce	100	1st To Orbit Earth
Glenn, Scott	Ent	10			30	
Gless, Sharon	Ent	10	25		25	Cagney and Lacey
Glossop, Peter	Music	10			30	Opera
Gloucester, Henry Wm.	Royalty	10	20	50	30	
Glover, Danny	Ent	15	45		45	Lethal Weapon films
Glover, John	RevWar	300	600	1,200		Gen. Continental Army
Glubb, John, Sir Pasha	Military	20	45	55	35	Br. General
Gluck, Alma	Music	20	35	45	100	Opera
Glyn, Elinor	Author	20	75	150	50	Br. Novelist, Film Scenarios
Gnys, Wladek	Aviation	50			150	Shot Dwn 1st Plane/WWII
Gobbi, Tito	Music	25			75	Opera

Name	Field	SIG	DS	ALS	SP	Remarks
Gobel, George 1918-91	Ent	10			25	
Godard, Benjamin	Music	75	125	225	150	Opera
Godard, Louis	Aviation	200	475			
Goddard, Paulette	Ent	35			100	1911 - 1990
Goddard, Robert H.	Science	550	1,250	1,500	Scarce	Am. Rocket Pioneer
Goderich, Fred. John R.	Political	15	45	100		Br PM
Godey, Louis A. 1804-78	Author	50	100	150		Godey's Ladies Book
Godfrey, A. Earl	Aviation	30		100	75	
Godfrey, Arthur	Ent	15	50	55	35	
Godfrey, Capt. Johnny	Aviation	50			150	Ace/29 Victories
Godolphin, Sidney	Political	75	200			PM. Eng.Queen Anne
Godoy, Manuel de	Political	300				Prime Minister
Godt, Eberhard	Military	25		75		
Godunov, Alexander	Music	45			75	Ballet/Defected
Goebbels, Joseph	Military	350	750	900	1,250	Nazi Minister of Propaganda
Goebel, Arthur	Aviation	50			100	Pioneer Aviator
Goering, Hermann W.	Military	550	1,750	2,400	1,500	Marshal of the Reich
Goethals, George W.	Military	175	450			Panama Canal
Goethe, Johann W. von	Author	1,200	2,500	Scarce		German Novelist/Poet
Gogh, Vincent van	Art	4,000	RARE	RARE	RARE	
Gogol, Nicholai	Author	750	2,500	5,500		Father of Rus. Realistic Lit.
Go-Go's	Music	35			75	Signed by all four
Going, Joanna	Ent	20			45	
Golan, Menahem	Ent	5			15	Film Producer
Gold, Missy	Ent	10			35	Benson
Gold, Tracy	Ent	10			35	Growing Pains
Goldberg, Arthur J.	SuprCt	50	150		125	Resigned
Goldberg, Reiner	Music	15			30	Opera
Goldberg, Rube 1883-70	Cartoonist	50	100		150	Ike & Mike, Boob McNutt
Goldberg, Stan	Cartoonist	10			30	Archie
Goldberg, Whoopi	Ent	25			50	
Goldblum, Jeff	Ent	25	50		50	
Golden Girls, The	Ent	50			100	Signed by All Four
Goldenson, Leonard H.	Business	10		30	25	TV Broadcasting Exec.
Golding, Louis	Author	50	75	125	75	Novels
Golding, William 1911-94	Author	50	200	450	100	Nobel Lit.,Lord of the Flies
Goldman, Edwin Franco	Music	25	50	75		Bandmaster
Goldman, Emma	Author	50	225	450	75	Deported. Author-Editor
Goldman, William	Author	50		125		Princess Bride etc..
Goldmark, Peter C.	Science	25		50		Invented LP Records
Goldowsky, Boris	Music	15			35	Opera Coach
Goldsboro, Bobby	Music	5			15	Singer
Goldsborough, Louis M.	Civil War	75	125	200		Rear Admiral USN
Goldschmidt, Berthold	Music	75			175	His work Banned by Nazis
Goldschmidt, Richard	Science	20		45		World Famous Geneticist
Goldsmith, Jerry	Ent	5			10	
Goldwater, Barry	Political	10			30	Presidential Candidate

Name	Field	SIG	DS	ALS	SP	Remarks
Goldwyn, Sam	Ent	100	150	250	200	Goldwyn Studios
Goldwyn, Sam, Jr.	Ent	5			15	Producer
Goldwyn, Tony	Ent	10			25	
Golino, Valerie	Ent	15			45	
Gollob, Gordon	Aviation	75	150		200	WWII German ACE
Gombell, Minna	Ent	25		50	50	
Gomes, Carlos 1836-96	Music	35		150		Opera
Gomes, Francisco	Political	15	50	125	30	
Gomez, Aurea	Music	10			20	Opera/Soprano
Gomez, Thomas	Ent	30			50	1905 - 1971
Gompers, Samuel	Political	150	225	450		Fndr Pres AFL-CIO
Goodacre, Jill	Ent	25			45	Victoria's Secret model
Gooding, Cuba Jr.	Ent	25			50	Jerry McGuire
Goodman, Al	Music	15			45	Bandleader
Goodman, Benny 1909-86	Music	50	150		150	Big Band Leader-Clarinetist
Goodman, Dody	Ent	5			10	
Goodman, John	Ent	20	45		45	Roseanne
Goodpaster, Andrew	Military	15	35	50	25	Gen.WWII
Goodson, Mark	Ent	10			30	Producer TV
Goodwin, Hugh H.	Military	25	75	125	50	
Goodwin, Nat C.	Ent	20			30	
Goodyear, Charles	Science	400	2,000	RARE	RARE	Rubber Vulcanization
Goodyear, Charles Jr.	Business	25	50	150	45	Goodyear Tire & Rubber
Goosens, Eugene, Sir	Music	15	45	75	75	Conductor/Composer
Gorbachev, Mikhail	Political	300		900	575	Russian President
Gorcey, Leo	Ent	125			175	1915 - 1969
Gordon, Alex., 4th Duke	RevWar	20		35		
Gordon, Anita	Ent	10			25	
Gordon, Bruce	Ent	10			20	
Gordon, Charles G.	Military	150	350	750	600	
Gordon, Gale	Ent	25	75		75	Lucy Show
Gordon, Gavin 1901-83	Ent	50				
Gordon, George H.	Civil War	35	75	100		Union General/1823-86
Gordon, George W.	Civil War	225	350	475		CSA General/1836-11
Gordon, Huntley 1897-56	Ent	15	30		45	
Gordon, John Brown	Civil War	150	200	400		CSA General/1832-1904
Gordon, Mack	Music	30	75	125	45	Lyricist
Gordon, Ruth 1896 - 85	Ent	20		45	45	AA Winner
Gore, Albert A., Jr.	Vice Pres	25			75	Vice President
Gorgas, Josiah	Civil War	200	400			CSA General/1813-83
Gorgas, William C., Dr.	Science	125	225	325		Eradicated Yellow Fever
Gorham, Nathaniel	RevWar	375	425	900		Pres. Continental Congress
Goritz, Otto 1873-1929	Music	35			75	Operatic Baritone
Gorky, Maxim 1868-1936	Author	400	900	1,200	1,200	Russian/Novelist
Gorman, Margaret	Ent	40			75	Ist Miss America 1921
Gorshin, Frank	Ent	10			35	
Gosfield, Maurice	Ent	15			30	

Name	Field	SIG	DS	ALS	SP	Remarks
Gosse, Edmund, Sir	Author	20		50	45	Br. Poet, Man of Letters
Gossett, Louis, Jr.	Ent	20			50	
Gottfrederson, Floyd	Cartoonist	100	200		200	Mickey Mouse Strip Art
Gotti, John	Criminal	150			350	Mafia Boss
Gottschalk, Louis M.	Music	500	1,200	1,600	Scarce	Composer
Goudal, Jetta	Ent	15		30	40	
Goudsmit, Samuel A.	Science	15	25	45	20	Atomic Physicist
Gould, Chester	Cartoonist	50			150	Dick Tracy
Gould, Elliott	Ent	10			20	
Gould, George	Business	100	150	250	175	Son of Jay Gould
Gould, Gordon	Science	15	45			Commercial Laser Inventor
Gould, Harold	Ent	5		15	15	
Gould, Jay 1836-92	Business	250	550	1,500	1,200	Financier, Pres. Erie RR
Gould, John 1804-81	Science	150		450		Br. Ornithologist
Gould, Morton	Music	20	50	75	45	Composer
Gould, Robert Simonton	Civil War	25	75	100		CSA Commander
Goulet, Robert	Music	10			30	
Gounod, Charles 1818-93	Music	150	350	500	550	Composer
Gouraud, Henri-Joseph	Military	50	150		75	Fr. Gen. WW I
Govan, Daniel C.	Civil War	100		400		CSA General/1829-1911
Goya, Francisco	Art	2,500	RARE	RARE	RARE	Painter
Grabe, Ronald J.	Space	5			20	Astronaut
Grable, Betty 1916-73	Ent	100	150	200	200	WWII Pin Up Girl
Grace de Monaco	Royalty	150	300	450	300	Signed as Princess
Grace, Eugene G.	Business	25	50	125	50	
Grace, William R.	Business	15	30	45	45	Mayor NYC
Grace/Prince Rainier	Royalty	175	300		350	
Gracen, Elizabeth Ward	Ent	5			10	Miss America '82
Grady, Don	Ent	5			25	
Graf, Herman	Aviation	35			75	Ger. ACE. #9 Worldwide
Graham, Billy	Clergy	35	100		100	Evangelist
Graham, Donald	Business	10	25	45	25	
Graham, George 1772-30	Military	20	50	75		Monroe Sec. War
Graham, Heather	Ent	20			50	Lost in Space movie
Graham, John 1774-1820	Political	75	200	400		Jefferson/Madison
Graham, Katherine	Author	15		50	30	Chm. CEO Washington Post
Graham, M. Gordon	Aviaton	25			50	WWII ACE
Graham, Martha 1895-86	Music	100	300	400	300	Dancer/Teacher
Graham, Sheila	Author	25		40	35	Journalist, Gossip Columnist
Graham, Virgnia	Ent	5			10	TV Host
Graham, William A.	Political	25	45	75		Fillmore Sec. Navy 1850
Grahame, Gloria	Ent	50	100		150	AA Winner
Grahame, Kenneth	Author	75	125	200		Wind in the Willows
Grahame-White, Claude	Aviation	75	100	250	125	Ist Br. School of Aviation
Grainger, Percy	Music	50	100	200	125	Composer
Gramegna, Anna	Music	45			100	Opera
Grammer, Kelsey	Ent	25			50	Cheers/Frasier

Name	Field	SIG	DS	ALS	SP	Remarks
Grandi, Dino, Count	Political	50	45	90	40	Mussolini Cabinet
Grandval, Marie F.C.	Music	20		75		Fr. Woman Composer
Grandy, Fred	Ent	15	40		40	Love Boat
Grange, E. R.	Aviation	10		45	35	
Granger, Farley	Ent	15			35	
Granger, Gideon	Political	75	100	250		P.M. General 1801
Granger, Gordon	Civil War	50	100	150		Union General/1822-76
Granger, Robert S.	Civil War	35		75		Union General/Captured
Granger, Stewart	Ent	25			50	
Granit, Ragnar	Science	20	45	80	35	Nobel Medicine
Granlund, Nils T.	Ent	20			40	Producer
Grant, Amy	Music	10			30	
Grant, Cary 1904-86	Ent	200	450		400	AA Winner
Grant, Duncan 1885-1978	Art	100		300		Impressionist
Grant, Frederick Dent	Military	20		50		Son Of U.S. Grant
Grant, Hugh	Ent	25	50		50	
Grant, Julia Dent 1826-02	First Lady	150	300	600		
Grant, Kirby	Ent	15			35	Western star
Grant, Lee	Ent	10			30	
Grant, U.S. III	Military	10		50		
Grant, Ulysses S. 1822-85	President	500	1,000	1,500	2,500	
Grant, William T.1876-72	Business	50	125	350	275	WT Grant Dept Stores
Granville, Bonita	Ent	15		20	35	1923 - 1988
Grapewin, Charles	Ent	350	700		600	Uncle in "Wizard of Oz"
Grass Roots, The	Music	125	200		200	All Five Signed
Grass, Gunter	Author	50	125	200	125	German Novelist
Grasser, Hartmann	Aviation	15		50	35	
Grassi, Rinaldo	Music	35		100		Opera
Grateful Dead	Music	200	450		450	Entire Band signed
Gratiot, Charles	Military	125	250			War 1812/General
Gratz, Barnard	RevWar	75	200	400		
Graue, Dave	Cartoonist	25			60	Alley Oop
Grauman, Sid	Ent	35	75	100	75	Owner of Opulent Theaters
Graveline, Duane E.M.D.	Space	5			20	Astronaut
Graves, Peter	Ent	15	35		35	Mission Impossible
Graves, Robert	Author	50	175	250	100	Br. Poet/Novelist
Graves, Teresa	Ent	10			20	
Graves, William	Military	50				General WW I
Gray, Asa 1810-88	Science	35	75	175		Am Botanist
Gray, Billy	Ent	10			20	
Gray, Charles	Ent	35			75	Blofeld/James Bond film
Gray, Colin	Aviation	35		75		Top New Zealand ACE
Gray, Colleen	Ent	15		45	30	
Gray, Delores	Music	40			75	Am. Singer, Dancer
Gray, Elisha 1835-1901	Science	250	900	Scarce	Scarce	Telephone Pioneer
Gray, Erin	Ent	10	25		25	Buck Rogers/25th Century
Gray, Gilda 1901-59	Ent	50			100	Popularized the Shimmy

Name	Field	SIG	DS	ALS	SP	Remarks
Gray, Glen	Music	15			35	Big Band Leader
Gray, Harold	Cartoonist	100			200	Little Orphan Annie
Gray, Horace	SuprCt	50	150	250	100	1828 - 19022
Gray, Jack Stearns	Aviation	150				
Gray, Linda	Ent	10			20	Dallas
Gray, Thomas 1716-71	Author	1,000	2,000	Scarce		Br. Poet
Grayco, Helen	Music	5			15	Vocalist & Wife Spike Jones
Grayson, Kathryn	Ent	15			30	
Greco, Jose	Ent	10			40	Dance
Greeley, Horace 1811-72	Western	125	275	300	550	Go West, Young Man...
Greely, Adolphus W.	Explorer	100	200	200	150	Union General/Explorer
Green, Adolph	Music	10			20	Collaborated/Betty Comden
Green, Al	Music	10			20	
Green, Anna Katherine	Author	50	75			1846-1935
Green, Charles 1785-1870	Aviation	50	100	250		Br. Balloonist
Green, Dorothy	Ent	5			15	
Green, Herschel	Aviation	15	30	50	35	ACE/WWII/Triple Ace
Green, John(ny)	Music	25	75	150	75	Composer
Green, Mitzi 1920-69	Ent	20	45		40	
Green, Richard	Ent	30			75	
Green, Thomas 1814-64	Civil War	100	200			CSA General/KIA
Green, William F.	Political	50	100	200	125	Pres AFL/Labor Leader
Greenaway, Kate	Art	1,000	1,500			1846 - 1901
Greene, George S.	Civil War	35	75			Union General/1801-99
Greene, Graham 1904-91	Author	150	350	600	600	Br Novelist
Greene, Lorne 1915-87	Ent	50	100		100	Bonanza
Greene, Michele	Ent	5		25	20	
Greene, Nathaniel	RevWar	900	1,800	2,500		Am RevWar/1742-86
Greene, Richard	Ent	20			45	1914 - 1985
Greene, Sarah Pratt	Author	20				
Greene, Shecky	Ent	5			15	
Greenspan, Alan	Business	15	30		35	Chairman Fed. Reserve Bd.
Greenstreet, Sidney	Ent	225	400		475	Casablanca/1879-1954
Greenwood, Charlotte	Ent	20			40	1893-1978
Greenwood, Edward D.	Science	10		35		
Greenwood, Lee	Music	5			10	
Greer, Jane	Ent	5			15	
Gregg, David M.	Civil War	45	75	150	125	Union General/1933-1916
Gregg, John 1828-64	Civil War	RARE	RARE	RARE	RARE	CSA General/KIA
Gregg, John R.	Business	75	125	150	100	Inventor Gregg Shorthand
Gregg, Maxcy 1814-62	Civil War	400	600			CSA General/KIA
Gregg, Virginia	Ent	10		25	25	
Gregor XVI, Pope	Clergy		1,200			Catholic Pope 1831-46
Gregory, Dick	Ent	20			40	
Gregory, F.H.	Civil War	25		75		Union General
Gregory, James	Ent	5			15	
Gregory, Thomas W.	Political	20			45	Attorney General/Wilson

Name	Field	SIG	DS	ALS	SP	Remarks
Greico, Richard	Ent	20			45	
Grenfell, Wilfred T.	Author	35	75	75	125	Medical Missionary
Grenville, George	Political	200	550			Br PM/Stamp Act
Grenville, Wm. W.	Political	125	250	500		Roman Catholic
Gresham, Walter Q.	Civil War	45	75	100		Union General/1832-95
Gretchaninoff, Alex	Music	75	150	300		Composer
Grevy, Jules 1807-91	Political	40				Pres. France 1879-87
Grew, Joseph C.	Political	10	25		35	Ambassador Japan 1931-41
Grey, Chas. 2nd Earl of	Political	50	75	150		Prime Minister
Grey, George Sir 1799-82	Political	15	25	50		Br. Statesman
Grey, Jennifer	Ent	25	50		50	Dirty Dancing
Grey, Joel	Ent	15			30	Cabaret
Grey, Virginia	Ent	10		20	20	
Grey, Zane 1875-1939	Author	100	200	400	400	
Gridley, Chas. V.	Military	250	400	750		Cmdr. of Adm. Dewey Flagship
Gridley, Richard 1711-96	RevWar	225	450	600		Gen.Continental Army, Artillery
Grieco, Richard	Ent	20			45	
Grieg, Edvard 1843-1907	Music	350	600	900	900	Composer
Grier, Pam	Ent	10			25	
Grier, Robert C. 1794-70	SuprCt	75	175	250		
Grierson, Benjamin H.	Civil War	75		225		Union General/1825-1911
Griesbach, Franz	Military	25			50	Ger. Infantry General
Griffes, Charles T.	Music	175	350			Composer
Griffin, Charles 1826-67	Civil War	50	125			Union General
Griffin, Chris	Music	10			25	Jazz Trumpet
Griffin, Cyrus	RevWar	350	750			Continental Congress
Griffin, Merv	Ent	5			15	
Griffin, W.E.B.	Author	5			10	Fiction
Griffith, Andy	Ent	30	75	75	60	Andy Griffith Show
Griffith, Corinne	Ent	35	50	100	100	
Griffith, D.W 1874-1948	Ent	350	550	Scarce	1,100	Producer/Director
Griffith, Hugh 1912-80	Ent	200	300		450	Scarce
Griffith, Melanie	Ent	25	50		50	
Griggs, John W.	Political	15	45	100		Politician-Jurist, Gov. NJ
Griggs, S. David	Space	75	150		150	Astronaut
Grimes, Tammy	Ent	5			15	
Grimm, Jacob	Author	750	1,750	3,000		Grimm's Fairy Tales
Grimm, Wilhelm	Author	750	1,500	2,750		Grimm's Fairy Tales
Grinnell, Henry 1799-74	Business	50	150			Financed Arctic Expeditions
Grinnell, Moses H.	Business	25	75	125		Merchant
Gris, Juan 1887-1927	Art	200				Cubist Painter
Grisham, John	Author	50	150		75	The Firm/Pelican Brief...
Grisi, Giulia	Ent	125		300	200	It. Ballerina
Grissom, Virgil I.'Gus'	Space	350	700		1,200	Astronaut/1922-67
Griswald, O.W.	Military	15	35			
Griswold, Putnam	Music	25			50	Opera
Grizzard, George	Ent	5			15	

Name	Field	SIG	DS	ALS	SP	Remarks
Grizzard, Lewis	Author	25			50	Southern humorist
Grodin, Charles	Ent	5		20	15	
Groener, Harry	Ent	10			30	
Groening, Matt	Cartoonist	50			125	Simpsons
Grofe, Ferde	Music	100	200	250	125	Composer
Gromyko, Andrei A.	Political	125	150	250	150	Russian Ambassador to U.S.
Gronau, Wolfgang von	Aviation	75	125	225	200	
Groom, Victor	Aviation	25	50	75	50	
Groom, Winston	Author	35	125		75	Forrest Gump
Gropius, Walter 1883-69	Science	125	150	450	400	
Gropper, William	Art	50	100	200		Am. Social Protest Artist
Gross, Arye	Ent	25			50	Ellen
Gross, Chaim	Art	50	75	150		
Gross, Clayton K.	Aviation	10		30	25	WWII ACE
Gross, Courtlandt	Business	5		15	15	
Gross, Milt	Cartoonist	20			50	Nize Baby
Grosser, Heinz	Science	15			45	Rocket Pioneer/von Braun
Grossinger, Jennie	Business	25	75	125	50	Grossinger's Hotel,Catskill Mts
Grossmith, George	Ent	10			25	1874-1935
Grosvenor, Charles H.	Civil War	25	50	50		Union General/1833-1917
Grosvenor, Gilbert H.	Business	75	100	200	100	Pres.National Geographic
Grosz, George 1893-1959	Art	75	250	250		
Grouchy, Marquis E. de	Military	100	250			Marshal of Napoleon, Exiled
Grover, Cuvier	Civil War	35	75	75		Union General/1828-85
Groves, Leslie R.	Military	50	150	200	100	General WWII
Grow, Galusha A.	Political	15	125	150	35	Speaker of the House
Gruberova, Edita	Music	15			45	Opera
Gruelle, Johnny	Cartoonist	35			100	Raggedy Ann & Andy
Gruen, George John	Business	30	75	150	50	Chm. Gruen Watch Co
Gruenther, Alfred M.	Military	15		30	25	WWII General
Grumman, Leroy R.	Business	50	150		75	Grumman Aircraft
Guden,Hilde	Music	25		75	50	Opera
Guderian, Heinz	Military	50	175	250	450	WWII German Panzer
Gudunov, Alexander	Ent	15		40	35	Rus. Ballet
Guelfi, Piero	Music	10			25	Opera
Guerin, Jules	Art	10		35		Muralist
Guest, Edgar A.	Author	25	75	150	50	Am Journalist
Guest, Winston Mrs.	Business	5			10	
Guevaro, Ernesto Che	Military	300	600			Aide to Castro in Cuba
Gueymard-Lautiers, P.	Music	35		125		Opera
Guggenheim, Daniel	Business	25	100	75	45	Guggenheim Foundation
Guggenheim, Harry F.	Aviation	30	75			
Guggenheim, Peggy	Business	15	25	50	35	Patron of Arts/Collector
Guggenheim, William	Business	50	125		75	Industrialist/Philanthropist
Guilbert, Yvette	Ent	50	100	125	150	
Guillaume, Robert	Ent	10		20	25	Benson/Disney Voice
Guillemin, Roger C.L.	Science	20	50	100	45	Nobel Medicine

Name	Field	SIG	DS	ALS	SP	Remarks
Guillotin, Joseph-Ignace	Science	275	Scarce	Scarce	Scarce	Fr Dr./Supported Guillotine
Guiney, Louise Imogene	Author	100		300		Poet
Guingand, Francis	Military	15	35	50		Fr. General
Guinness, Alec, Sir	Ent	25	75		60	AA Winner/Star Wars
Guinness, Benjamin L.	Business	35	75	100		Guinness Brewing Co.
Guinness, Edward C.	Business	15		45	35	Guinness Brewing Co.
Guisewite, Cathy	Cartoonist	25			45	Cathy
Guiteau, Charles 1842-82	Criminal	400	900	1,800	Scarce	Shot Pres. Garfield
Gumbel, Bryant	Ent	5			10	
Guns 'N Roses	Music	65			125	Signed by entire Band
Gunsche, Otto	Military	50		75	50	
Gur, Mordechai	Military	25	75			Israeli General
Gurie, Sigrid	Ent	20		50	50	
Gusmeroli, Giovanni	Music	5			15	Opera
Gustavus III (Swe)	Royalty	150	450	750		
Gustavus IV Adolphus	Royalty	150				
Gustavus V (Swe)	Royalty	100			300	
Gustavus, Adolphus	Military	450	1,500	2,250		Saved Protestantism/Ger.
Guston, Philip 1913-80	Art	75		175		Canadian-born Am. Painter
Guthrie, Arlo	Music	5			15	
Guthrie, James 1792-69	Political	25	50	75		Pierce Sec'y Treas.
Guthrie, Woody	Ent	300	Scarce	Scarce	Scarce	Folksinger/Songwriter
Guttenberg, Steve	Ent	10			35	
Guy, Buddy	Ent	25			50	
Guy, Jasmine	Ent	20			45	Different World
Guynemer, Georges	Aviation	225	400	650	500	WWI ACE
Guyot, Arnold 1807-1884	Science	25	50	150		Geographer, Mapmaker
Guyot, Pierre	Military	25	50	125		French Revolution
Guyton-Morveau, L.B.	Science	20	50	100		Fr. Chemist
Gwenn, Edmund 1875-59	Ent	75	125		175	Miracle 34th Street
Gwinnett, Button	RevWar	85,000	150,000	RARE	RARE	Signer/RARE
Gwynne, Anne	Ent	10			25	
Gwynne, Fred	Ent	75	150		200	Munsters/Herman

Name	Field	SIG	DS	ALS	SP	Remarks
Haab, Robert	Political	25	75			Switzerland
Haag, Carl 1820-1915	Art		35	75		Ger.-Born Br. Court Painter to Victoria
Haakon VII (Nor)	Royalty	125	200			1st Indep King of Sweden
Haakon VII and Maud	Royalty	200			450	King & Queen of Norway
Habberton, John	Author	10		25		
Habersham, Joseph	RevWar	100	250	500		Continental Congress
Hack, Shelley	Ent	5			15	
Hackett, Bobby	Music	20			45	
Hackett, Buddy	Ent	5			20	
Hackett, Joan	Ent	10		25	25	
Hackman, Gene	Ent	25	50		50	
Hadley, Jerry	Music	15			35	Opera
Hadley, Reed	Ent	15			30	
Haenschen, Gus	Music	15		25	30	Big Band
Hagar, Sammy	Music	25			50	
Hagegard, Hakan	Music	15			30	Opera
Hagen, Jean	Ent	10			25	
Hagen, Johannes 1847-30	Science	15	45	100		
Hagen, Uta	Ent	10			20	
Haggard, Henry Rider	Author	100	125	275	275	King Solomon's Mines
Haggard, Merle	Music	10			35	Country
Haggerty, Dan	Ent	5		20	15	
Hagman, Larry	Ent	15	30	45	30	I Dream of Jeannie/Dallas
Hagood, Johnson	Civil War	100	200	300		CSA General/1829-98
Hahn, Jessica	Ent	10			25	Playboy
Hahn, Otto 1879-1968	Science	150	300	Scarce	350	German Nobel Chemistry
Hahn, Reynaldo	Music	75	150			Opera/Composer
Haider, Michael	Business	15			45	Pres. Standard Oil NJ
Haig, Alexander M.	Military	20	45	50	45	Gen. WWII/Sec'y State
Haig, Douglas. Ist Earl	Military	25	75	125	75	Br General
Haim, Corey	Ent	10	30		30	
Haines, Connie	Music	20			50	Big Band Vocalist
Haines, Daniel 1801-1877	Political	30	45	75		
Haines, William 1900-73	Ent	15		35	45	
Hairston, Jester	Ent	15			30	
Haise, Fred W. Jr.	Space	15			75	Astronaut
Halban, H.H., Dr.	Science	30	65			Fr. Pioneer Of Uranium Fission
Haldane, John B.S.	Science		125	200		Br. Geneticist & Author
Haldeman, George W.	Aviation	30	50	100	75	
Haldeman, H. R	Political	10		45	25	Nixon-Watergate
Halder, Franz	Military	50	100	150	125	
Hale, Alan Jr.	Ent	85	125		125	Gilligans Island

Name	Field	SIG	DS	ALS	SP	Remarks
Hale, Alan Sr.	Ent	50	75	100	100	
Hale, Barbara	Ent	10		25	35	Perry Mason
Hale, Edward Everett	Author	75	150	200	200	Author Man Without a Country
Hale, George E.	Science	25	100			Invented Spectroheliograph
Hale, John Parker	Political	15	45	100		Abolitionist/1806-73
Hale, Monte	Ent	10	25	25	25	Big Time Cowboy Star
Hale, Nathan	Political	15,000	RARE	RARE	RARE	
Hale, Richard	Ent	5			15	
Hale, Robert	Music	15			30	Opera
Hale, Sarah J. B.	Author		150	225		Mary Had a Little Lamb
Halevy, Jacques 1799-62	Music	45	75	125		Opera
Halevy, Ludovic	Author	25	75	125		Novels, Libretti For Operas
Haley, Alex 1922-92	Author	50	125	150	150	Am Novelist/Roots, Hotel...
Haley, Bill	Music	275	550		450	Rock Around the Clock
Haley, Jack 1899-1979	Ent	125	200		250	Wiz of Oz/Tin Man
Hall and Oates	Music	25			50	Signed by Both
Hall, Arsenio	Ent	15			30	TV Talk Show Host
Hall, Deidre	Ent	10			30	
Hall, Fawn	Ent	10			25	
Hall, Gus	Political	30	50	100	50	US Communist Party Leader
Hall, Harry	Ent	5			10	
Hall, Huntz	Ent	15		25	45	
Hall, Jerry	Ent	10			30	
Hall, Jon	Ent	30	45	75	50	1913 - 1979
Hall, Josephine	Ent	5			15	
Hall, Joyce C.	Business	100	400	400	250	Hallmark Greeting Cards
Hall, Juanita	Ent	75			125	1901 - 1968
Hall, Lyman 1724-90	RevWar	2,000	2,500	3,500		Signer Decl. of Indepen.
Hall, Monty	Ent	10	20		20	Let's Make a Deal
Hall, Nathan	Political	20	35	75		Fillmore P.M. General
Hall, Pauline	Ent	10			30	Vintage Actress
Hall, Radclyffe	Author		50	125		Well of Loneliness
Hall, Thurston	Ent	10			25	
Hall, Tom T.	Music	5			15	
Hall, William	Civil War	50		100		Union General
Hallam, Henry 1777-1859	Author	35	125	175		Br. Historian
Halleck, Fitz-Greene	Author	25	75			Poet/1790-1867
Halleck, Henry Wager	Civil War	125	250	550		Union General/1815-1872
Hallett, Mal	Music	20			35	Big Band Leader
Halliburton, Richard	Author	30			50	World Traveller, Lecturer
Halop, Billy	Ent	75		125	150	Dead End Kids
Halop, Florence	Ent	15			25	
Halpin, Luke	Ent	15			35	
Halpine, Charles G.	Author	20	35	75		
Halsey, Wm. F. 'Bull'	Military	75	175	225	200	WWII Admiral/1882-1959
Halstead, Murat	Author	10		35		Journalist
Halston	Business	15		40	30	Designer

Name	Field	SIG	DS	ALS	SP	Remarks
Halstrom, Holly	Ent	5			10	Price is Right Model
Hamblen, Stewart	Music	15			30	
Hamel, Veronica	Ent	5		20	20	
Hamer, Frank	Military	100				
Hamer, Rusty	Ent	35		50	75	
Hamil, Veronica	Ent	15			35	
Hamill, Mark	Ent	20	50		50	Star Wars
Hamilton, Alex. Jr.	Military	25		100		Officer War 1812
Hamilton, Alexander	Political	800	2,500	2,750		Washington Sect Treasury
Hamilton, Andrew J.	Civil War	Scarce	Scarce	Scarce	Scarce	Union General/1815-75
Hamilton, Charles Smith	Civil War	30	75	100		Union General/1822-91
Hamilton, Donald	Author	10			20	
Hamilton, Gail	Author					See Dodge, Mary A.
Hamilton, George	Ent	10	25		30	
Hamilton, Ian, Sir	Military	50				Br. General VWW I
Hamilton, James	Political	75	150			Colonial Gov. PA
Hamilton, John	Ent	250	400		450	Superman
Hamilton, Linda	Ent	25			50	Terminator
Hamilton, Margaret	Ent	100	250	350	225	Wiz of Oz/Wicked Witch
Hamilton, Neil	Ent	50	100	125	100	Batmans Comm Gordon
Hamlin, Hannibal	Vice Pres	100	250	300		Lincoln VP
Hamlin, Harry	Ent	10			30	
Hamlin, V.T.	Cartoonist	50			125	Alley Oop
Hamlisch, Marvin	Music	10		45	35	Composer
Hammarskjold, Dag	Political	175	350	475		Sec'y Gen. United Nations
Hammer, Armand	Business	50		275	150	Occidental Petroleum
Hammer, MC	Music	25			50	
Hammerstein, Oscar II	Music	125	250		250	Composer/1895 - 1960
Hammett, Dashiell	Author	550	1,500	RARE	Scarce	Hardboiled Mystery Genre
Hammond, James B.	Science	25	100			Typewriter
Hammond, James H.	Political		50	100		US Senator/1807-1867
Hammond, William A.	Civil War	50	125	250		Union General/1828-1900
Hampden, Walter	Ent	20		45	45	
Hampson, Thomas	Music	15			40	Opera
Hampton, Hope	Ent	40			75	
Hampton, Lionel	Music	40			75	Big Band Leader-Vibes
Hampton, Wade	Civil War	300	550	900		CSA General/1818-02
Hamsun, Knut	Author	50	75	125	75	Nobel/Literature
Hanami, Kohei	Military	100	250			
Hancock, Herbie	Music	20			45	
Hancock, John 1737-93	RevWar	2,200	4,500	6,000		First Signer
Hancock, Winfield Scott	Civil War	125	200	300	700	Union General
Hand, Edward	RevWar	200	475	900		
Handel, George F.	Music	1,500	5,500	RARE	RARE	Composer
Handelman, Stanley M.	Ent	5			10	
Handler, Ruth	Business	35		75	75	Creator/Barbie
Handy, W. C. 1873-1958	Music	250	475	Scarce	450	Composer

Name	Field	SIG	DS	ALS	SP	Remarks
Hanks, Tom	Ent	35			65	AA Winner
Hanna & Barbera	Cartoonist	75	200		150	Jetsons,Flinstones etc..
Hanna, Bill	Cartoonist	35	150		75	Jetsons, Flinstones etc..
Hanna, Marcus A.	Business	25			45	1837 - 1904
Hannah, Daryl	Ent	20	50		50	
Hansen, William	Ent	5			15	
Hanson	Music	65			100	Signed by All Three
Hanson, Howard	Music	15		75		Pulitzer. Dir.Eastman Sch.
Hanson, John	RevWar	2,250	Scarce	Scarce	Scarce	Pres. Continental Congress
Harbach, Otto 1873-1963	Music	125			175	Playwright
Harbison, John	Music	25		75		Pulitzer/Composer
Harbord, James G.	Military	75	150	200	125	WWI Chief of Staff
Harburg, E. Y. 'Yip'	Music	200	400			Composer/Over the Rainbow
Hardee, William J.	Civil War	300	650	900	900	CSA General/1815-73
Hardenberg, K.A. von	Political	20	50	125		Prussian Politician
Hardie, James Allen	Civil War	75	200	250		Union General/1823-1876
Hardie, James Allen	Civil War	50	150			Union General
Hardie, Russell	Ent	10		25	25	
Hardin, Gus	Music	5			10	
Hardin, John Wesley	Western	1,800	3,600	9,000	RARE	Gunslinger/1853 - 1895
Hardin, Ty	Ent	10			20	
Harding, Ann	Ent	15		35	30	
Harding, Florence Kling	First Lady	75	175		125	
Harding, Warren G.	President	125	250	750	450	1865-1923
Hardinge, Chas., Ist Bar	Political	10		35	25	Br.Viceroy India
Hardinge, Henry, Sir	Military			500		Br. Field Marshal/1785-56
Hardwicke, Cedric, Sir	Ent	75	150		150	1893 - 1964
Hardy, Oliver 1892-1957	Ent	250	300	500	550	
Hardy, Thomas 1840-28	Author	275		1,250	1,400	Br. Novelist/Poet
Hardy, Thomas M.	Military	75	250			1769-1839 Br. Adm./Nelson
Hare, John, Sir	Ent	20			50	
Haring, Keith	Art	25	40	100	200	Pop Artist
Harkins, Paul	Military	15	30	50	30	
Harlan, John Marshall	SuprCt	50	100	175		1833-1911
Harland, Marion	Author	10		20		
Harley, William S.	Business	1,000	3,500	RARE	RARE	Co-Fndr, Harley-Davidson
Harlin, Renny	Ent	20			45	Director
Harlow, Jean	Ent	1,250	2,500	3,000	3,500	1911 - 1937
Harman, Fred	Cartoonist	45			125	Red Ryder
Harmon, Angie	Ent	25			50	
Harmon, Mark	Ent	15			30	
Harmonica Rascals	Music	10			25	
Harned, Virginia	Ent	15			35	
Harney, William	Civil War	75		250		Union General
Harper, Robert G.	RevWar	75		150		General RevWar
Harper, Tess	Ent	10		20	25	
Harper, Valerie	Ent	10			25	Rhoda, MTM Show

Name	Field	SIG	DS	ALS	SP	Remarks
Harrel, Scotty	Music	5			15	
Harrelson, Woody	Ent	25			50	Cheers
Harridge, Will 1883-1971	Business		125			Pres./American League
Harries, George	Military	20	45	75		General WW I
Harriman, Edw. Henry	Business	200	750			US RR Magnate
Harriman, Edward R.	Business	20	50	125	50	CEO Union Pacific RR
Harriman, W. Averell	Political	25	75	100	50	1891-1986
Harrington, Pat	Ent	5			15	One Day at a Time
Harris, Arthur T, Sir	Military	30	75	100	150	Cmdr.-in-Chief RAF WWII
Harris, Barbara	Ent	5			15	
Harris, Cecil	Aviation	15	25	50	45	WWII ACE
Harris, Ed	Ent	15	45		35	
Harris, EmmyLou	Music	10			35	Country
Harris, Isham 1818-97	Civil War	50	75			Governor Tennessee
Harris, Jean	Criminal	50	75			Killed/Dr. Herman Tarnower
Harris, Joel Chandler	Author	250	450	750		Uncle Remus
Harris, John 1726-91	Western	125	250	550		Founder Harrisburg, PA
Harris, Jonathan	Ent	10	25		20	Lost in Space/Doctor
Harris, Julie	Ent	20			35	
Harris, Mel	Ent	10			40	
Harris, Neil Patrick	Ent	20			45	Doogie Howser
Harris, Paul Percy	Business	20	45		25	Fndr. & Pres. Emeritus Rotary
Harris, Phil	Ent	40	65		75	Disney Voice/BandLeader
Harris, Richard	Ent	25			50	
Harris, Robert	Author	20	50			
Harris, Thomas	Author	30	50	125		Silence of the Lambs
Harris, Thomas S.	Aviation	15	45			WWII ACE & Test Pilot
Harrison, Anna Symmes	First Lady	675	975	2,500		
Harrison, Benjamin	President	200	300	700		1833-1901
Harrison, Benjamin	RevWar	450	675	1,800		Signer Decl. of Indepen.
Harrison, Caroline Scott	First Lady	150	250	750	750	1832-1892
Harrison, Carter H.	Political	15		45		Mayor Chicago 1897
Harrison, George	Music	200	450	575	400	Beatle
Harrison, George	Civil War	100		275		CSA General/1841-1922
Harrison, Gregory	Ent	5			15	
Harrison, Helen	Aviation	50	125			Am Aviatrix
Harrison, Jenilee	Ent	10	30		35	Three's Company
Harrison, Linda	Ent	15			25	Planet of the Apes
Harrison, Mary Lord	First Lady	75	125	175	125	1858-1948
Harrison, Noel	Ent	5			15	
Harrison, Rex 1908-90	Ent	35	75		75	Br. My Fair Lady
Harrison, Richard B.	Ent	25	75		150	1865-1935
Harrison, Robert Hanson	RevWar	200	400	750		Sec'y to G. Washington
Harrison, William Henry	President	550	950	1,500		President Only 1 Month
Harrold, Kathryn	Ent	15			30	
Harry, Debbie	Music	25			50	Blondie
Harry, Jackee	Ent	15			30	

Name	Field	SIG	DS	ALS	SP	Remarks
Harryhausen, Ray	Ent	15			35	Film Director
Harshaw, Margaret	Music	25		50	75	Opera
Hart, Corey	Music	15			35	
Hart, Dolores	Ent	10			25	
Hart, Dorothy	Ent	15		25	35	
Hart, John	Ent	10			25	Lone Ranger
Hart, John 1711-1879	RevWar	350	600	1,200		Signer Decl. of Indepen.
Hart, Johnny	Cartoonist	35			75	B.C. & Wizard Of Id
Hart, Lorenz	Music	500	RARE	RARE	RARE	Composer w/Rogers
Hart, Mary	Ent	5			15	Entertainment Tonite host
Hart, Melissa Joan	Ent	25			50	TV's Sabrina
Hart, Moss	Author	35	50	100	75	1904 - 1961
Hart, Paul	Ent	5			15	
Hart, Thomas C.	Military	35			75	WWII Admiral
Hart, Veronica	Ent	10		35	35	
Hart, William S.	Ent	150	200	250	400	1870 - 1946
Harte, Francis Brett	Author	75	150	150		Frontier Life/1836-1902
Hartford, George L.	Business	75	200	250		Great Atlantic & Pacific Tea Co
Hartford, Huntington	Business	15	30	45	30	Patron of the Arts
Hartford, John	Music	15	45	75		Composer
Hartley, Mariette	Ent	5			20	
Hartley, Nina	Ent	20			45	
Hartline, Haldan K.	Science	25	75	125	45	Nobel Medicine
Hartman, David	Ent	5			10	Good Morning America host
Hartman, Don	Ent	10			35	Producer
Hartman, Lisa (Black)	Ent	5	20		20	
Hartman, Paul	Ent	10			20	
Hartman, Phil	Ent	40			75	Sat Nitle Live alumni/Murdered
Hartmann, Erich	Aviation	125			300	WWII German ACE
Hartranft, John F.	Civil War	75	125	150		Union General/1830-89
Harts, William	Military	15		35		General WWI
Hartsuff, George L.	Civil War	50	75	100		Union General/1830-74
Hartwell, Alfred S.	Civil War	25	75	100		Union General
Harvey, George B. M.	Author	25	75		100	Fostered W. Wilson Nomination
Harvey, Lawrence	Ent	100			150	
Harvey, Lilian	Ent	10			25	
Harvey, Paul	Author	10	25	35	25	
Harvey, Steve	Ent	15			30	
Harvey, William 1578-57	Science	750	2,500	Scarce	Scarce	Ist Theory Blood Circulation
Hasbrouck, Robert W.	Military	50	150		75	Am. Gen. WWII
Hasen, Irwin	Cartoonist	10			20	Dondi
Haskell, James K.	Ent	10		30	25	
Haskell, Peter	Ent	5			10	Actor
Haskin, Joseph Abel	Civil War	50				Union General/1817-74
Hassam, Childe 1859-35	Art	150	350	500		Foremost in Am. Impressionism
Hassam, Crown Prince	Royalty	15	35	75	50	Morocco
Hasselhoff, David	Ent	25			50	Baywatch

Name	Field	SIG	DS	ALS	SP	Remarks
Hasso, Signe	Ent	10			25	
Hastings, Bob	Ent	10			25	
Hastings, Warren 1732-18	Political	75	150	225		Gov Gen India
Haswell, Charles H.	Civil War	25		50		Union Naval Architect
Hatch, John Porter	Civil War	30	50	75	75	Union General/1822-1901
Hatcher, Teri	Ent	25			50	Lois & Clark/James Bond
Hatfield, Hurd	Ent	15		30	35	
Hatfield, Lansing	Music	25			75	Opera
Hathaway, Henry	Ent	45			100	
Hatlo, Jimmy 1898-1963	Cartoonist	25	50		75	Little Iodine
Hatton, Raymond	Ent	50			125	
Hatton, Robert	Civil War	125	250	350		RARE
Hauer, Rutger	Ent	20	50		50	LadyHawke
Haught, Helmut	Aviation	10			20	
Haupt, Herman 1817- 05	Civil War	35				Union General
Hauptman, Herbert A.	Science	20	35		30	Nobel Chemistry
Hauptmann, Bruno R.	Criminal	450	Scarce	Scarce	Scarce	Lindbergh Baby Kidnapper
Hauptmann, Gerhart	Author	100	300	450	375	Nobel Prize Literature 1912
Havel, Vaclav	Political	20			45	Czech.
Haven, Annette	Ent	10			25	
Havens, Beckwith	Aviation	20		50	50	
Havoc, June	Ent	5			15	
Hawes, Elizabeth	Art	10		35		
Hawke, Ethan	Ent	25	50		50	
Hawke, Robert	Political	15		75	25	Prime Minister Australia
Hawkins, Anthony Hope	Author	30		100		Prisoner of Zenda...
Hawkins, Coleman	Music	125			250	Jazz Tenor Sax
Hawkins, Jack	Ent	50			100	
Hawkins, John	Civil War	35		125		Union General/1830-1914
Hawkins, William	Political	35	75			Governor NC. War 1812
Hawks, Frank Monroe	Aviation	75	125	225	250	Pioneer Aviator/1897-38
Hawks, Howard	Ent	100	200		250	Director
Hawley, Joseph R.	Civil War	45	75	125		Union General/1826-1905
Hawn, Goldie	Ent	20	50		50	Laugh In
Haworth, Jill	Ent	5			10	
Hawthorn, Alex. Travis	Civil War	175	300	400		CSA General/1835-99
Hawthorne, Julian	Author	50		150		Son of Nathaniel Hawthorne
Hawthorne, Nathaniel	Author	400	900	1,500		Novelist/1804-65
Hay, John H.	Military	5		15		
Hay, John Milton	Political	50	150	225	150	1838-1905
Hay, William Henry	Military	5		30		
Hayakawa, Sessue	Ent	125			250	
Hayden, Charles 1870-37	Business	25	50			
Hayden, Russell	Ent	25			75	
Hayden, Sterling	Ent	25			50	1916 - 1986
Haydn, Joseph Franz	Music	3,500	RARE	RARE	RARE	Composer
Haydon, Benj. R. 1786-46	Art	75		200		Br Painter

Name	Field	SIG	DS	ALS	SP	Remarks
Hayek, Salma	Ent	25	50		50	
Hayes, George 'Gabby'	Ent	125	250		450	1885 - 1969
Hayes, Helen 1900-94	Ent	25		50	75	
Hayes, Ira H., Corporal	Military	400	Scarce	Scarce	Scarce	Iwo Jima Flag Raising
Hayes, Isaac Israel	Civil War	100	200	275		
Hayes, Joseph	Civil War	50	100	150	150	
Hayes, Lucy Webb	First Lady	250		400	700	
Hayes, Margaret	Ent	10			15	
Hayes, Roland	Music	100			250	Am Tenor
Hayes, Rutherford B.	President	200	500	600	1,200	Union General/1822-93
Haynes, Linda	Ent	5			10	
Hays, Frank A.	Aviation	35	50	100	75	German SS ACE
Hays, Harry Thompson	Civil War	200	450			CSA General/1820-76
Hays, Robert	Ent	5			15	
Hays, Will H. 1879-1859	Ent	30	45		50	
Hays, William	Civil War	35	75	150		Union General/1819-75
Hayward, George	Science	10		35	15	
Hayward, Louis	Ent	10		25	50	
Hayward, Susan 1918-75	Ent	125	200	450	375	
Haywood, Thomas	Military	5		15	10	
Hayworth, Rita 1918-87	Ent	150	250	Scarce	475	
Hazelwood, John	RevWar	75	200	325		1726 - 1800
Hazen, Wm. Babcock	Civil War	25	50	100		Union General/1830-87
Head, Edith	Ent	35			125	Costumer/AA Winner 8x
Headle, Marshall	Aviation	25	75		75	Lockheed Chief Test Pilot
Healey, George	Art	125	250	450		19th Century Portrait Artist
Healey, Robert C.	Author	10		25		
Healy, Ted	Ent	75			150	
Hearst, George 1820-91	Business	300		950		Newspaper Dynasty
Hearst, Patricia	Political	250		400		
Hearst, Phoebe A.	Business	20	50	75		
Hearst, Wm. Randolph	Business	150	550	900	750	Publisher/1863-1951
Hearst, Wm. Randolph Jr	Business	10		45	20	
Heart	Music	40			75	Signed by both
Heath, Edward	Political	40		100	50	Br.Prime Minister
Heath, William 1737-1814	RevWar	150	450	900		General Continental Army
Heatherton, Joey	Ent	10		20	25	
Hebert, Louis	Civil War	100	250			CSA General
Hebert, Paul O.	Civil War	100	175	250		CSA General/1818-80
Hecht, Ben 1894-1964	Author	15	45		45	AA.Playwright, Novelist, Newsman
Heckart, Eileen	Ent	15			15	
Heckerling, Amy	Ent	5			15	
Heckman, Charles A.	Civil War	30	75			Union General/1826-96
Hedi, Walter	Music	15	45	75		Composer
Hedin, Sven	Explorer	75		150	125	Swe. Asian Explorer
Hedison, David	Ent	5			15	Voyage to the Btm of Sea
Hedman, Robert Duke	Aviation	20	45	75	45	WWII ACE Flying Tigers

Name	Field	SIG	DS	ALS	SP	Remarks
Hedren, Tippi	Ent	10	25		25	The Birds
Hedrick, Roger	Aviation	15	25	40	35	WWII ACE
Heflin, Van 1910-71	Ent	30	75	75	75	
Hefner, Christie	Business	10		30	20	Publisher/Playboy
Hefner, Hugh	Business	20			45	Founder Playboy
Heft, Bob	Art	20			45	Designed US 50 Star Flag
Hefti, Neal	Music	20	35	50	40	Composer
Hegel, Geo. Wilhelm F.	Political	850	1,500	2,000		Ger. Idealist Philosopher
Heggie, O.P.	Ent	400	750		750	Character Actor
Heidt, Horace	Music	20			40	Big Band Leader
Heifetz, Jascha 1901-87	Music	150			450	Violin Virtuoso
Heimlich, Henry Jay, Dr.	Science	20		45	45	Created Heimlich Maneuver
Heine, Heinrich 1797-56	Author	Scarce	Scarce	6,500	Scarce	German Poet/Critic
Heinlein, Robert A.	Author	50	175	350		Sci-Fi Fiction
Heinrich, Albert H.	Aviation	35		125		
Heintzelman, Samuel P.	Civil War	50	125	200		Union General/1805-80
Heinz, Henry John	Business	150		550	350	A Founder H.J. Heinz Co.
Heinz, Henry John II	Business	35			50	Food Manufacturer
Heisenberg, Werner, Dr.	Science	75	225	500		Nobel Physics
Helbig, Joachim	Aviation	10		35	25	
Held, Anna	Ent	45	75	125	100	Mrs. Florenz Ziegfield
Held, John, Jr. 1889-1958	Cartoonist	150			250	Created the Flapper
Heldy, Fanny	Music	50			125	Opera
Helena, Princess	Royalty	10		50	30	Third Daughter Queen Victoria
Helgenberger, Marg	Ent	15			35	
Heller, John R., Dr.	Science	10			20	
Heller, Joseph	Author	20		45	45	Catch 22
Helletsgruber, Luise	Music	25			75	Opera
Hellinger, Mark	Author	35	100	200	75	Columnist, Playwright
Hellman, Lillian 1905-84	Author	50	150		100	Am Dramatisit
Helm, Benj. Hardin	Civil War	200	250			CSA General/1830-63
Helm, Fay	Ent	25			50	Actress
Helmond, Katherine	Ent	10			35	Soap
Helmsley, Leona	Business	10			35	Hotel Magnate
Helnwein, Gottfried	Art	20			50	
Heloise	Author	5			10	Columnist.
Helps, Arthur, Sir	Author	10		40		1817 - 1875
Helton, Percy	Ent	20			50	
Hemingway, Ernest	Author	1,000	2,000	3,000	2,500	Nobel Literature/1899-61
Hemingway, Margaux	Ent	40			75	Daughter E. Hemingway
Hemingway, Mariel	Ent	10			50	Daughter E. Hemingway
Hempel, Frieda	Music	25			75	German Soprano/Opera
Hemsley, Sherman	Ent	10	25		30	Jeffersons
Hench, Philip S.	Science	20	50	75	25	Nobel Medicine
Henderson, Archibald	Military	75	200			Marine General War 1812
Henderson, Fletcher	Music	15			35	Bandleader
Henderson, Florence	Ent	5	20		20	Brady Bunch

Name	Field	SIG	DS	ALS	SP	Remarks
Henderson, J. Pinckney	Political	300	500			Gen. TX Army, Gov. Texas
Henderson, Marcia	Ent	10			20	
Henderson, Skitch	Music	15			35	Composer
Hendricks, Barbara	Music	10			30	Opera
Hendricks, Thos. A.	Vice Pres	50	200	200	75	Cleveland VP/1819-95
Hendrix, Jimi 1942-1970	Music	775	1,750	Scarce	2,250	
Hendrix, Wanda	Ent	10			35	
Hendry, Gloria	Ent	15			35	Bond girl
Heney, Hugh	Western	325	750			Scout for Lewis & Clark
Henie, Sonja 1910 - 1969	Ent	75	100		175	Olympic Gold Medal
Henley, Don	Music	25			50	The Eagles
Henner, Marilu	Ent	10	25		25	Taxi
Henning, Paul	Ent	20			45	TV Producer
Henreid, Paul	Ent	75	125		100	Casablanca
Henri, Robert	Art	75	175	200		Portrait Painter
Henrikson, Lance	Ent	15			30	
Henry II	Royalty	400	900	2,000		France
Henry III	Royalty	250	550	1,200		France
Henry IV (Fr) 1553-1610	Royalty	250	700	Scarce		And Navarre. Assassinated
Henry IV (Sp)	Royalty		1,750			King of CastileThe Impotent
Henry V (Fr)	Royalty	50	75	150		Pretender to Throne
Henry VI	Royalty	200	450	900		England
Henry VII (Eng)	Royalty	1,200	RARE	RARE		
Henry VIII 1491-1547	Royalty	3,500	15,000	RARE	RARE	
Henry, Bill	Aviation	10	25	40	30	WWII ACE
Henry, Bill	Ent	15		35	30	
Henry, Buck	Ent	10			20	
Henry, Gloria	Ent	5			15	
Henry, John 1750-1798	RevWar	35	125	225		Continental Congress.
Henry, Joseph 1797-1878	Science	75	200	250		First Electric Motor
Henry, O.	Author					SEE W.S. Porter
Henry, Patrick 1736-99	RevWar	1,000	1,500	1,800		
Henschel, George, Sir	Music	75			150	Composer/Conductor
Henshaw, David	Political	20	75	100		Tyler Sec'y Navy
Henson, Jim 1936-90	Ent	75	150		225	Created the Muppets
Henson, Matthew A.	Explorer	125	275			Afro-Am. Arctic Explorer
Henstridge, Natasha	Ent	25			50	
Henze, Hans Werner	Music	50			150	German Opera Star
Henze, Karl	Aviation	15	45	75	45	
Hepburn, Audrey 1929-93	Ent	125	400	500	275	AA Winner/My Fair Lady
Hepburn, Katharine	Ent	125	250	450	600	AA Winner
Hepworth, Barbara	Art	75	150		125	Br Sculpture
Herbeck, Ray	Music	5			15	Big Band
Herbert, Don	Ent	10			25	
Herbert, F. Hugh	Author	10		30	20	Am. Playwright, Producer
Herbert, Frank	Author	15	20	35	20	Am. Sci-Fi. Dune Trilogy
Herbert, Geo.E.	Science	25	50	100		With Carter, King Tut Tomb

Name	Field	SIG	DS	ALS	SP	Remarks
Herbert, Hugh	Ent	30		75	75	
Herbert, P.O.	Civil War	100		375		
Herbert, Sidney	Ent	15	25	30	25	
Herbert, Victor 1859-1924	Music	100	200	375	350	Composer
Herdman, George	Cartoonist	100			250	Krazy Kat
Hergesheimer, Joseph	Author	25	75	125	75	Am. Psychological Novels
Herget, Wilhelm	Aviation	20		50		
Hering, Constantine	Science	15	25	50		lst Homeopathic School
Herkimer, Nicholas	RevWar	RARE	3,500	RARE	RARE	General of Militia.
Herkomer, Hubert von	Art	30	75	125		Br. Portrait Painter
Herman, Jerry	Music	25	75	75	50	Composer/Hello Dolly
Herman, Pee Wee	Ent	25		50		
Herman, Woody	Music	25	75		75	Big Band
Hermann, Bernard	Music	Scarce	550	Scarce	Scarce	Composer/1911-1975
Hermann, Hajo	Aviation	25	50		50	
Herndon, William	Political	200	450	900		Lincolns Law Partner
Herring, John F. 1795-65	Art	75		275		Br.Race Horses
Herriot, Edouard 1872-57	Political	35	75	175		Premier of Fr., Nazi Prisoner
Herriot, James (Wight)	Author	15	50	75	25	
Herrmann, Adelaide	Ent	50			150	Magicians/and Al
Herrmann, Bernard	Music	Scarce	875	Scarce	Scarce	Film Composer
Herron, Francis J.	Civil War	45	75	125		Union General/1837-1902
Herschbach, Dudley, Dr.	Science	25	45		45	Nobel Chemistry
Herschel, John Fred. Wm.	Science	150	250	275	Scarce	Br Astronomer
Herschel, William, Sir	Science	150	450	600		Discovered Uranus
Hersey, John 1914-93	Author	20	75	100	45	Bell for Adano Pulitzer
Hershey, Alfred D., Dr.	Science	20	30	45	30	Nobel Medicine
Hershey, Barbara	Ent	20			45	
Hershey, Lewis B.	Military	15			25	General
Hersholt, Jean 1886-1956	Ent	25		75	75	
Hertz, Alfred	Music	45			125	Conductor
Hervey, Irene	Ent	15			35	
Herzberg, Gerhard, Dr.	Science	25	50		35	Nobel Chemistry
Herzner, Hans-Albrecht	Military	700	Scarce	Scarce	Scarce	1st Ger engaged in WWII
Herzog, Chaim	Political	30	75	175	75	Pres. Israel
Hess, Myra, Dame	Music	20		75	45	Br. Pianist
Hess, Rudolf	Military	175	450	750	750	Nazi WWII 2nd to Hitler
Hess, Victor F.	Science	20		50	35	Nobel Physics
Hess, Walter R.	Science	20		50	25	Nobel Medicine
Hesse, Hermann 1877-62	Author	100	500	550	400	German Artist/Author
Hesseman, Howard	Ent	5		20	15	WKRP in Cincinatti
Heston, Charlton	Ent	10			35	
Heth, Henry	Civil War	300	450	600		CSA General
Hewes, Joseph 1730-80	RevWar	2,500	6,000	8,500		Signer Decl. of Indepen.
Hewish, Anthony	Science	20		75	45	Nobel Physics. Pulsars
Hewitt, Abram S.	Business	35	50	75		Iron Manafacturing
Hewitt, H.K.	Military	20	50	75		

Name	Field	SIG	DS	ALS	SP	Remarks
Hewitt, Jennifer Love	Ent	20			50	
Hewlett, William R.	Business	25	75	150	45	Hewlett-Packard
Hexum, Jon-Erik	Ent	100	200		200	
Heydrich, Reinhard	Military	200		1,200	600	Specialist in Nazi Terror
Heydt, Louis Jean	Ent	100	200		200	GWTW Star
Heyerdahl, Thor	Explorer	30	50	75	50	
Heyse, Paul	Author	45	125	250		German Novelist/Nobel
Heyward, Dorothy	Author	75	200			Co-writer of Porgy & Bess
Heyward, DuBose	Author	150	300	450		Co-Writer of Porgy & Bess
Heyward, Thomas Jr.	RevWar	600	1,200	1,500		Signer Decl. of Indepen.
Heywood, Anne	Ent	10			20	
Heywood, Eddie	Music	35			100	Big Band Leader-Piano
Hichens, Robert S.	Author	15	45			Br. Novelist.Garden of Allah
Hickenlooper, Andrew	Civil War	30	50	75		Union General/1837-1900
Hickman, Dwayne	Ent	5			15	
Hickman, Ron	Science	20	50			Black and Decker
Hicks, Catherine	Ent	10		25	25	
Hidalgo, Miguel C.	Military	1,500	Scarce	Scarce	Scarce	Mex Revolutionary
Higgins, Andrew Jackson	Business	25		50		
Higgins, Charles	Science	15	35			
Higginson, Henry L,	Business	10		35		
Higginson, Thos. W.	Civil War	100		200		Antislavery Writer
Hildebrand, Samuel	Civil War	Scarce	1,750	Scarce	Scarce	Quantrill Raider-Murderer
Hildegarde	Ent	5			10	
Hill, Ambrose Powell	Civil War	2,000	3,000	Scarce	Scarce	CSA General KIA/1825-65
Hill, Archibald V.	Science	25	45		35	Nobel Medicine 1922
Hill, Arthur	Ent	5			15	
Hill, Benjamin H. 1823-82	Civil War	75	150	225		Signed CSA Constitution
Hill, Benjamin J. 1825-80	Civil War	100	200	300		CSA General
Hill, Benny	Ent	30	75		60	
Hill, Dana	Ent	5			15	
Hill, Daniel Harvey	Civil War	320	500	600		CSA General/1821-89
Hill, David Lee Tex	Aviation	15	30	45	35	WWII Flying Tigers ACE
Hill, Faith	Music	15			45	
Hill, George Roy	Ent	10			25	AA
Hill, George Washington	Business	75	200			American Tobacco Co.,Pres.
Hill, Grace Livingston	Author	25	45	75		Am. Novelist
Hill, James J.	Business	400	1,500	2,000	950	RR Executive/Financier
Hill, Napoleon	Author	75	300			Think & Grow Rich
Hill, Rowland, Sir	Science	150	300	450		Originator of Penny Postage
Hill, Teresa	Ent	15			45	
Hill, Tiny	Ent	5			15	
Hill, Walter	Ent	10			25	Director
Hill, William	Ent	5			10	
Hillary, Edmund, Sir	Explorer	75	150	275	125	Ist To Climb Mt.Everest
Hillegas, Michael	RevWar	225	500			U.S. Treasurer 1777
Hillegess, C.K. Cliff	Author	15			30	Cliff's Notes

Name	Field	SIG	DS	ALS	SP	Remarks
Hiller, Arthur	Ent	5			25	Film Director
Hiller, Ferdinand	Music	40	75	125		Conductor, Pianist
Hiller, Frank, Jr,	Aviation	75	150	250	150	
Hiller, Wendy	Ent	20		35	40	AA
Hillerman, John	Ent	15	25		40	Magnum PI
Hilliard, Harriet	Ent	20			35	Harriet Nelson/Maiden Name
Hilliard, Henry W.	Civil War	35	75	100		
Hilliard, Robert	Ent	20			40	
Hillig, Otto	Aviation	40	75	150	125	
Hillis, Marjorie	Author	5	20			
Hilton, Barron	Business	10		25	25	
Hilton, Conrad	Business	75	100	200	125	Fndr. Hilton Hotel Dynasty
Hilton, James, Sir	Author	35	125	200	75	Lost Horizon
Himmler, Heinrich	Military	250	750	1,500	750	Nazi Head of the Gestapo
Hinckley, John, Jr.	Criminal	35	150	200		Attempt on Pres. Reagan
Hindemith, Paul	Music	100	250	400		German Teacher/Theorist
Hindenburg, Paul von	Political	150	300	400	575	1847-1934
Hindman, Thomas C.	Civil War	300				CSA General/1818-68
Hines, Duncan	Business	75	200		150	Duncan Hines
Hines, Earl K. Fatha	Music	125			250	Pianist/Composer
Hines, Gregory	Ent	15			35	
Hines, Herm	Music	10			25	Jazz Sax
Hines, Jerome	Music	20			45	Opera
Hingle, Pat	Ent	5			15	
Hinks, Edward W.	Civil War	50	150			Union General/1830-94
Hinshelwood, Cyril N.	Science	20	45		35	Nobel Chemistry
Hinton, Walter	Aviation	40	75	125	100	NC-4 Pilot
Hippel, Hans Joachim	Aviation	10			35	WWI and II Fighter Pilot
Hirohito	Political	2,000	RARE	RARE	12,000	RARE
Hirsch, Judd	Ent	15			35	Taxi
Hirschfeld, Al	Art	45			125	
Hirshfield, Harry	Cartoonist	25			75	Able The Agent
Hirt, Al	Music	10			25	Trumpet
Hiss, Alger	Political	50	75	200		Spy
Hitchcock, Alfred	Ent	200	400	575	700	1899-1980
Hitchcock, Ethan Allen	Civil War	50	150	200		Union General/1798-1870
Hitchcock, Raymond	Ent	20			35	
Hitchings, George, Dr.	Science	20		75	35	Nobel Medicine
Hite, Les	Music	100			275	Saxophone
Hitler, Adolf 1889-1945	Political	1,500	2,000	RARE	2,500	
Hittorff, Jacques 1792-67	Science	10	20	30		Fr. Architect
Hitzfeld, Otto Maximilian	Military	20			50	Ger, Infantry General
Hix, John	Author	20	50			Strange as it Seems
Ho Chi Minh	Political	600	1,200	2,000	2,400	Vietnam
Ho, Don	Music	5			15	
Hoagland, Everett	Ent	20			50	Bandleader
Hoban, James	RevWar	250	500			Architect White House

Name	Field	SIG	DS	ALS	SP	Remarks
Hobart, Garret A.	Vice Pres	75	200	300	200	
Hobart, Rose	Ent	10			25	
Hobbes, Halliwell	Ent	25			45	
Hobson, Richard P.	Military	100	250			Span Am War/1870-37
Hobson, Richmond P.	Military	75	200	300	150	Admiral/Blew up Merrimac
Hobson, Valerie	Ent	25			50	
Hoche, Lazare	Military	200	450			General French Republic
Hockney, David	Art	50		75		
Hodes, Art	Music	10			25	Pianist-Bandleader
Hodge, Al	Ent	25			100	
Hodges, Courtney	Military	15	100		25	WWII General
Hodgkin, Dorothy C.	Science	25		45		Nobel Chemistry
Hodiak, John	Ent	20		45	45	
Hoe, Richard M.	Business	100	300	500		Invented Rotary Press
Hoest, Bill	Cartoonist	10		35	40	The Lockhorns
Hoey, Dennis	Ent	75			200	1893 - 1960
Hofer, Andreas	Military	Scarce	3,000	Scarce	Scarce	Patriot/Executed
Hoffa, James R.	Political	275	450		400	Teamsters Union (disappeared)
Hoffman, Dustin	Ent	25			50	AA Winner
Hoffman, Gaby	Ent	15			30	Blossom
Hoffman, Kurt-Caesar	Military	25			50	
Hoffman, Paul G.	Business	10		35	20	Auto Mfg.-Studebaker Cars
Hoffmann, Peter	Music	25			50	Opera
Hoffmann, Roald, Dr.	Science	20		45	25	Nobel Chemistry
Hofmann, Josef 1876-57	Music	40	100	125	150	Composer/Pianist
Hofstadter, Robert	Science	20		45	25	Nobel Physics
Hogan, Ben	Sports	125	250	300	250	1974 Golf HOF
Hogan, Paul	Ent	10		20	25	Dundee
Hogarth, Burne	Cartoonist	25			75	Tarzan-2nd Artist
Hogarth, Wm. 1697-1764	Art	500	1,500	2,500		Br. Painter-Engraver.
Hogeback, Hermann	Aviation	15			40	Ger. Bomber Pilot.
Hoimquest, Donald L.	Space	10			20	Astronaut
Hoiris, Holger	Aviation	40	75	150	100	
Hoistrom, E.W. 'Brick'	Military	15	35	75	25	
Hoke, Robert Frederick	Civil War	100		300		CSA General/1837-1912
Hokinson, Helen	Cartoonist	25			75	Magazine Cartoonist
Holbrook, Hal	Ent	10			25	Barney Miller
Holden, Fay	Ent	20			50	
Holden, William 1918-81	Ent	100	200		200	
Holder, Geoffrey	Ent	20			50	James Bond villain
Holiday, Billie 1915-59	Music	450	800	Scarce	1,500	Jazz Singer
Holladay, Ben	Business	125	250	450		Indian Trade
Holland, Edmund M.	Ent	15			45	
Holland, John Philip	Science	75	150	250		Internal Combustion Engine
Holland, Josiah Gilbert	Author	25	75	100		Co-Founder Scribners
Hollen, Andrea Lee	Military	10		35	25	
Holley, Marietta 1836-26	Author	10		35		Am. Humorist

Name	Field	SIG	DS	ALS	SP	Remarks
Holley, Robert, Dr.	Science	15		35	20	Nobel Chemistry
Holliday, Judy	Music	100	200		250	
Holliday, Polly	Ent	10			20	Alice/Flo
Holliman, Earl	Ent	5			15	
Holliman, John	Ent	5			15	TV News Commentator
Hollins, Geo. Nichols	Civil War	275	450			Commodore CSA Navy
Holloway, Stanley	Ent	35			75	
Holloway, Sterling	Ent	75			150	Voice of Winnie the Pooh
Hollowell, George	Aviation	10	25	35	30	ACE/WWII/Marine Ace
Holly, Buddy 1936-1959	Music	750	900	5,000	2,000	
Holly, Lauren	Ent	20			45	
Holm, Celeste	Ent	5			25	
Holm, Eleanor	Ent	10			30	
Holman, Libby	Music	10	35		75	Singer
Holmes, Augusta 1847-03	Music	25		75		Composer
Holmes, Burton 1870- 58	Author	15		45	25	
Holmes, Christopher	Space	15	25		25	Astronaut
Holmes, Oliver W., Jr.	SuprCt	250	300	550	600	1841 - 1935
Holmes, Oliver W., Sr.	Author	75	200	300		1809 - 94
Holmes, Theophilus H.	Civil War	200	250			CSA General/1804-1880
Holst, Gustav	Music	50	100	300		Composer
Holt, Jack	Ent	45	75		100	
Holt, Jennifer	Ent	5			10	
Holt, Joseph 1807-94	Civil War	75		250		Union General
Holt, Tim	Ent	75			150	
Holt, Victoria	Author	5			15	
Holten, Samuel 1738-16	RevWar	100	200			Patriot/Statesman
Holyoake, Keith, Sir	Political	50	100	125	50	NZ Prime Minister
Holzer, Helmut	Science	20			50	Rocket Pioneer/von Braun
Home, A. Douglas	Political	45	75	150	150	Br. Prime Minister
Homer, Louise	Music	35			75	Opera. Am Mezzo
Homer, Winslow 1836-10	Art	350	500	750		Seascapes/Landscapes
Homesteaders, The	Music	25			50	
Homma, Masaharu	Military	75	200	300	200	Jap.Gen,Invasion of Philippines
Honda, Soichiro 1904-94	Business	Scarce	Scarce	Scarce	Scarce	Founder Honda Motor
Honeymooners, The	Ent	200			400	Signed by all four
Honnegger, Arthur	Music	45	125	200	100	Composer
Hood, Alexander Sir	Military	75	150	250		Accompanied Capt. Cook
Hood, Arthur Wm.	Military	25				Admiral, Ist Baron
Hood, Darla	Ent	150		200	350	Our Gang member
Hood, John Bell	Civil War	800	1,500	1,600	1,000	CSA General/1831-79
Hood, Samuel, Sir	Military	35	75	125		Br. Adm. with Lord Nelson
Hood, Sir Arthur W.	Military	25				Ist Baron, Admiral
Hood, Thomas	Author	50	150	275		Br. Humorist, Poet
Hook, James Clarke	Art	25		75		Brit. Royal Academy
Hooker, John Lee	Music	50	100		100	Jazz
Hooker, Joseph M.	Civil War	200	450	600		Union General/1814-79

Name	Field	SIG	DS	ALS	SP	Remarks
Hooks, Jan	Ent	10			25	Sat Nite Live alumni
Hooks, Kevin	Ent	10			20	
Hooper, William 1742-90	RevWar	Scarce		3,000	Scarce Scarce	Signer Decl of Indep
Hooten, Ernest A.	Science	25	75	150		Anthropologist
Hootie and the BlowFish	Music	65			100	Signed by Entire Group
Hoover, Herbert 1874-64	President	125	175	450	325	
Hoover, J. Edgar 1895-72	Political	75	150	225	150	FBI Director for 48 Years
Hoover, Lou Henry	First Lady	50	100	200		
Hope, Bob	Ent	35	100		75	
Hopf, Hans	Music	25			65	Opera
Hopkins, Anthony	Ent	25			50	AA Winner
Hopkins, Bo	Ent	10			20	
Hopkins, Claude	Music	30			60	Composer
Hopkins, Esek 1718-1802	Military	200				Cont Navy
Hopkins, Frederick G.	Science	50	125	200		Nobel Medicine 1929
Hopkins, Johns 1795-73	Business	175	500			Financier, Phiianthropist
Hopkins, Miriam	Ent	35	50		75	1902 - 1972
Hopkins, Samuel 1721-03	RevWar	100	200	350		Cont Army Officer
Hopkins, Stephen	RevWar	250	600	900		Signer/1707-85
Hopkinson, Francis	RevWar	250	450	900		Signer, Author, Composer
Hopkinson, Joseph	Author	100	200			1770-1842
Hopper, Bill	Ent	10			20	
Hopper, Dennis	Ent	15			45	
Hopper, DeWolfe	Ent	25		50	75	1858 - 1935
Hopper, Hedda	Ent	20			30	1890 - 1966
Hordern, Michael, Sir	Ent	10			35	
Horenstein, Jascha	Music	75				Conductor
Horina, Louise	Music	15			45	Opera
Hormel, Jay C.	Business	50	100	150	100	
Hornberger, H. Richard	Author	20		30	45	
Horne, L. Donald	Business	5			10	CEO Mennen Co.
Horne, Lena	Ent	15	25		35	Singer/Actress
Horne, Marilyn	Music	15			35	Opera
Horner, H. Mansfield	Business	5			10	Aircraft Exec.
Hornsby, Bruce	Music	20			40	and the Range
Horowitz, Vladimir	Music	100			175	Piano Virtuoso/1903-89
Horrocks, Gen. Sir Brian	Military	15	25	45	25	Cmdr. XIII Corps WWII
Horsford, Eben N. 1818-74	Science	25	50	75		Am. Analytical Chemist
Horsley, John Calcott	Art	45				Brit. Royal Academy
Horsley, Lee	Ent	10			25	Matt Houston
Horthy, Miklos, Adm.	Political	75	200	400	150	Hungarian Admiral
Horton, Edw. Everett	Ent	30	45		45	1886-1970
Horton, Peter	Ent	20			40	
Horton, Robert	Ent	5			15	
Horwich, Frances	Ent	10			25	
Hoskins, Bob	Ent	15			35	Roger Rabbit
Hosmer, Titus 1736-80	RevWar	35	100	200		Continental Congress

Name	Field	SIG	DS	ALS	SP	Remarks
Hotchkiss, Benjamin J.	Civil War			900		Union Arms Supplier
Hotchkiss, Charles T.	Civil War	50		100		
Houdini, Harry	Ent	1,000	2,250	4,500	3,000	Magician / 1874 - 1926
Houghton, Katharine	Ent	45			100	
Hounsfield, Godfrey	Science	20	30	40	25	Nobel Medicine
House, Edw. M.'Colonel'	Political	35	100		75	Confidant of Pres.Wilson
Houseman, John	Ent	25			60	Actor/Director
Housman, Alfred Edward	Author	75	225	450		Br. Poet, Scholar
Houssay, Bernando A.	Science	50	125	175	100	Nobel in Medicine/1947
Houston, David	Music	5			10	Country
Houston, Sam 1793-1863	Military	600	1,500	2,000		Pres. Repub. Texas
Houston, Temple	Western	375	Scarce	Scarce	750	Son of Sam Houston
Houston, Whitney	Music	25			50	
Houston, William C.	RevWar	35		125		Continental Congress, etc.
Hovey, Alvin	Civil War	25	50	75		Union General/1821-91
Hovis, Larry	Ent	25	50		50	Hogans Heroes
Howard, James H.	Aviation	15	30	45	45	WWII Flying Tigers ACE
Howard, John	Ent	15	25		45	
Howard, Ken	Ent	5			15	
Howard, Clint	Ent	10			25	
Howard, Curly	Ent	450	900	Scarce	900	Three Stooges
Howard, Leslie	Ent	250	275	Scarce	400	GWTW/1890-1943
Howard, Moe 1895-1975	Ent	200	275	600	450	Three Stooges
Howard, Oliver Otis	Civil War	100	200	250		Union General/1830-1909
Howard, Robert, Sir	Author	100	300			1626-1698
Howard, Ron	Ent	25	50		50	Actor/Director
Howard, Shemp 1891-55	Ent	450	600	Scarce	575	Three Stooges
Howard, Sidney	Author	150	250	350	250	Am. Playwright. Pulitzer
Howard, Trevor	Ent	10			35	
Howard, Willie	Ent	10			20	
Howe, Albion P.	Civil War	35	100			Union General/1818-97
Howe, Elias 1819-67	Science	400	Scarce	Scarce	Scarce	Invented Sewing Machine
Howe, James Wong	Ent	40			75	Director
Howe, Julia Ward	Author	100	150	300		Battle Hymn of Republic
Howe, Richard	RevWar	150	450	600		Br. Adm.Rev. War.
Howe, William, Sir	RevWar	250	850			Cmdr-in-Chief Br. Forces in Am.
Howell, C.Thomas	Ent	10	30		25	
Howells, William Dean	Author	75	200			Novelist, Critic, Editor
Howes, Barbara	Author	5			10	
Howland, Beth	Ent	10			20	Alice/Vera
Howlin, Olin	Ent	125			250	GWTW star
Hoyle, Edmond 1671-69	Author	175	550	750		Established Card Rules
Hoyt, John W.	Political	50	75			Governor Wy Territory
Hubbard, Elbert	Author	50	150	275	150	
Hubbard, L. Ron 1911-86	Author	250	750	Scarce	Scarce	Religious Activist
Hubbard, Thomas H.	Civil War	15	35			Union General/1838-1915
Hubble, Edwin P.	Science	20	50			Am. Astronomer.

Name	Field	SIG	DS	ALS	SP	Remarks
Hubel, David H., Dr.	Science	20		45	25	Nobel Medicine
Hubley, Adam	RevWar	75	200			Officer Cont. Army
Hudson, George	Business	10		35		Controlled 1,000 Miles Railrd
Hudson, Kate	Ent	25			50	Goldie Hawns Daughter
Hudson, Rochelle	Ent	35		45	45	1914 - 1972
Hudson, Rock 1925-85	Ent	60	100		125	
Hudson, W.H.	Author		125	300		Green Mansions
Huemer, Dick	Cartoonist	15			45	Disney Artist
Huerta, Victoriano	RevWar	75	250	500	125	Mex. General/Exiled
Huger, Benjamin 1805-77	Civil War	100	250	300		CSA General
Huger, Isaac 1742-97	RevWar	100	200	450		General Continental Army
Huggins, Charles, Dr.	Science	25			35	Nobel Medicine
Huggins, Roy	Ent	15			25	TV Producer
Huggins, William, Sir	Science	35	100	200	45	Br.Astron, Stellar Spectroscope
Hughes, Barnard	Ent	15			30	
Hughes, Charles E.	SuprCt	50	150		250	Cheif Justice
Hughes, Howard	Business	1,250	2,000	3,500	2,750	1905 - 1976
Hughes, Langston	Author	200	350	750	550	Afro-Am.Poet/1902-67
Hughes, Mary Beth	Ent	10			20	
Hughes, Richard	RevWar	25	50			Br. Adm. during Rev. War
Hughes, Rupert	Author	15	50	75		Poet, Author, Historian
Hughes, Sarah T.	Political	45	100			Judge/Swore In L.BJ in '63
Hughes, Thomas	Author	40		125		Tom Brown's School Days
Hughs, Finola	Ent	15			35	
Hugo, Victor 1802-85	Author	200	375	650	975	Novelist-Politician-Poet
Hulce,Tom	Ent	20			40	Disney Voice
Hull, Cordell 1871-1955	Political	50	125		125	Nobel, Father Fed.Income Tax
Hull, Henry	Ent	60	100		125	1890 - 1977
Hull, Isaac 1773-1843	Military	200	400	550		Cmdr. War of 1812
Hull, Josphine 1884-1957	Ent	150		300	300	
Hull, Warren	Ent	30			50	1903 - 1974
Hull, William	Military	150	350	700		Revolutionary War Gen.
Humble Pie	Music	75			150	Signed by all
Humboldt, Alexander	Science	75	125	300		German Naturalist
Hume, Joseph 1777-1855	Political	15	45	75		Br.Physician
Humes, William Y.	Civil War	150	225	400		CSA General
Hummel, Johann N.	Music	150	200	400		Piano Virtuoso
Humperdinck, Engelbert	Music	100	225	375	250	Composer
Humphrey, Hubert H.	Vice Pres	50	150		65	1911-1978
Humphreys, Andrew A.	Civil War	75	150	250		Union General/1810-1883
Humphreys, David	RevWar	50	150	200		
Hunt, Bonnie	Ent	15			30	
Hunt, E. Howard	Political	15	25	75	35	CIA/Watergate
Hunt, H. L.	Business	100	350	450	175	Texas Oil King
Hunt, Helen	Ent	25			50	AA Winner/Mad About You
Hunt, Henry J. 1819-89	Civil War	50	75	125		Union General
Hunt, James Bunker	Business	10		35	25	

Name	Field	SIG	DS	ALS	SP	Remarks
Hunt, Leigh 1784-1859	Author	30				Br. Poet
Hunt, Linda	Ent	25			75	AA Winner
Hunt, Marsha	Ent	10			30	
Hunt, Nelson Bunker	Business	10		45	25	
Hunt, Pee Wee	Music	15			45	Trombone-Vocalist
Hunt, Ward	SuprCt	75	125	175		
Hunt, William Holman	Art	75	150	250		Br. Pre-Raphaelite Painter
Hunt, William Morris	Art	100	200	400		American Portraitist
Hunter, David 1802-86	Civil War	75	150	175	250	Union General
Hunter, Holly	Ent	25			50	AA Winner
Hunter, Ian	Music	15			30	
Hunter, Jeffrey	Ent	100	150		100	Brief Star Trek Captain
Hunter, Jim	Sports	10			25	Catfish"/Baseball
Hunter, Kim	Ent	5		25	20	AA Winner/Planet of Apes
Hunter, R. M. T. 1809-87	Civil War	100	200	200		CSA Sec'y State, US Sen.
Hunter, Rachel	Ent	10			25	Model
Hunter, Robert	RevWar	250	500	750		Br. Gen. Colonial Gov.
Hunter, Tab	Ent	25	50		50	
Hunter, William 1774-49	Political	50	75	125		Statesman, Senator RI
Huntington, Agnes	Music	45			125	Opera
Huntington, Benjamin	RevWar	75	175	275		Continental Congress
Huntington, Collis P.	Business	125	450	Scarce	750	Pioneer Am. Railroad Builder
Huntington, Daniel	Art	75	150	250		PortraitPainter
Huntington, Ebenezer	RevWar	125	250	300		Statesman, Army General
Huntington, Henry E.	Business	75	125	200		Railroad Magnate
Huntington, Jabez W.	Political	25	30	45		Senator CT 1840
Huntington, Jedediah	Military	75	125	225		Gen. Revolutionary War
Huntington, Samuel	RevWar	250	750	1,000		Signer Decl. of Indepen.
Hunton, Eppa	Civil War	125	250			CSA General/1823-1908
Huppert, Isabelle	Ent	15			35	
Hurd, Peter	Art	100	200	300		
Hurlbut, Stephen A.	Civil War	75	125	300		Union General/1815-82
Hurley, Elizabeth	Ent	25			50	
Hurst, Fannie 1889-1968	Author	25	50	150	75	Novelist
Hurt, John	Ent	10			30	
Hurt, Mary Beth	Ent	5			15	
Hurt, William	Ent	20		50	50	
Husa, Karel	Music	15	30	50		Composer/Pulitzer
Hussein, King	Royalty	75	125	250	100	King of Jordan
Hussey, Olivia	Ent	10			20	
Hussey, Ruth	Ent	15			25	
Huston, Anjelica	Ent	10			30	AA Winner
Huston, John 1906-87	Ent	30		50	75	AA Film Director-Actor
Huston, Walter 1884-1950	Ent	75		150	175	AA Winner
Hutchence, Michael	Ent	20			50	
Hutchins, Will	Ent	10			15	
Hutchinson, Frederick S.	Civil War	45		125		Union Officer

Name	Field	SIG	DS	ALS	SP	Remarks
Hutchinson, John W.	Music	15		50		Composer
Hutchinson, Josephine	Ent	10		25	25	
Hutchinson, Thomas	Political	200	400			Royal Gov. MA. Exiled
Hutton, Betty	Ent	10			25	
Hutton, Gunilla	Music	5			10	
Hutton, Jim	Ent	40		100	100	
Hutton, Lauren	Ent	10		25	25	Model/Actress
Hutton, Robert	Ent	25		100	100	
Hutton, Timothy	Ent	25			45	AA Winner
Huxley, Aldous 1894-63	Author	100	300	350	350	Br. Novelist.
Huxley, Julian Sorell	Science	50	150	175		Br Biologist/1887-1975
Huxley, Thomas Henry	Science	75	150	225		Br. Biologist/1825-1895
Hyams, Leila	Ent	25		50	45	
Hyde-White, Wilfrid	Ent	15		35	35	
Hyer, Martha	Ent	5			25	
Hylton, Jack 1892-1965	Music	25			75	Br. Bandleader
Hynde, Chrissie	Music	25			50	The Pretenders
Hyndman, Henry M.	Political	75				Br. Marxist-Socialist

Name	Field	SIG	DS	ALS	SP	Remarks
Iacocca, Lee A.	Business	15	50		35	CEO Chrysler Motors
Ian, Janis	Music	10	40		30	
Ibert, Jacques-Francois	Music	75		226		Composer
Ibsen, Henrik 1828-1906	Author	200	600	900	1,200	
Icart, Louis 1888-1950	Artist	250		750		FR. Art Deco
Ice Cube	Music	20			45	
Ice T	Music	20			50	
Ickes, Harold L.	Political	20		50	35	Roosevelt Sec'y Interior
Idol, Billy	Music	25			45	
Iglesias, Julio	Music	25			50	
Ikeda, Hayato	Political	20		50		Japan
Iman	Ent	25			50	Super Model
Imboden, John Dan'l	Civil War	165	400			CSA General/1823-1895
Imbruglia, Natalie	Music	25			50	
Immelmann, Max	Aviation	200	425	700	500	1st German ACE in WWII
Ince, Thomas H.	Ent	50			125	Film Dir. Civil War Epics
Indiana, Robert	Art	45	100	150	125	
Indigo Girls	Music	30			75	Signed by all
Ingalls, Laura	Aviation	100	250			1st Non-Stop Trans. Flight
Ingalls, Rufus 1818-93	Civil War	35	75	125		Union General
Inge, William	Author	50	125	175		Am. Playwright. Pulitzer
Ingels, Marty	Ent	10			15	Comedian
Ingersoll, Jared 1749-22	RevWar	100	250	400		Signer Constitution
Ingersoll, Robert Green	Civil War	30	75	75	50	
Ingersoll, Robert H.	Business	100	175	300	225	Ingersoll Watch Co.
Ingham, Samuel D.	Political	50	125	150	100	Sec'y Treasury 1829
Ingle, Red	Business	10			20	Ingles Grocery Chain
Ingle, Robert P	Business	5		25		
Ingraham, Duncan N.	Civil War	150				Capt.CSA Navy
Ingram, Rex	Ent	125			300	1895 - 1969
Ingres, Jean-Auguste-D.	Art	250		900		
Ingrid, Victoria (Fred. IX)	Royalty	15	45			
Ink Spots, The	Music	150			250	Signed by Four Originals
Inman, Henry	Art	125	250	450		American Portraitist
Inman, Jerry	Music	10			20	
Inness, George 1824-94	Art	75	225	400		Amercian Painter
Inskeep, Jonathan	RevWar	75	175			Pvt. Sec'y Edison.
Insull, Samuel 1859-1938	Business	150	750	1,200		Financier
INXS	Music	35			75	Signed by all
Ionesco, Eugene	Author	50	125	200		
Ireland, Jill	Ent	25	50		75	
Ireland, Kathy	Ent	15			45	Super Model

Name	Field	SIG	DS	ALS	SP	Remarks
Irish, James M.	Military	10		50		
Irons, Jeremy	Ent	25			50	
Irvin, James B. "Jim"	Space	50	150	250	125	Moonwalker/1930-1991
Irvine, James 1735-1819	Military	50	125	250		Gen. Militia. Cmdr. Fort Pitt
Irvine, William 1741-1804	RevWar	150	500	600		Gen./Continental Congress
Irving, Amy	Ent	10			25	
Irving, Clifford	Author	15	50	100	25	
Irving, Henry, Sir	Ent	30	50	75	75	1838 - 1905
Irving, John	Author	25			75	World According to Garp
Irving, Margaret	Ent	10			20	
Irving, Washington	Author	150	350	450		Rip Van Winkle
Irwin, May	Ent	25			45	First Film Kiss
Irwin, Will 1873-1948	Author	20		40		War Correspondent
Isabella I, Of Castile	Royalty	850	2,500	5,000		Sp Queen/Columbus
Isabella II 1830-1904	Royalty	175	400	600		Spain.Abdicated
Isabey, Jean-Baptiste	Art		150	350		Court Painter to Napoleon
Ish Kabibble	Music	15			25	Kay Kyser Novelty Singer
Isherwood, Christopher	Author	50	150	225	300	Br. Novelist, Playwright
Ishiguro, Kazuo	Author	25			50	Remains of the Day
Ismay, Hastings Lionel	Military	20	35	75		Churchill Chief-of-Staff WWII
Israels, Jozef	Art	75	150	300		
Ito, Hirobumi (Prince)	Political	75	125			Japan/Prime Minister 1886
Ito, Lance	Political	50			75	O.J. Trial Judge
Ito, Robert	Ent	10			25	Quincy
Iturbi, Jose	Music	20			50	Classical Pianist
Iturbide, Augustin de	Political		875			Emperor of Mexico
Ivan IV, The Terrible	Royalty	35,000	75,000	RARE	RARE	
Iverson, Alfred, Jr.	Civil War	150	300	500		CSA General/1829-1911
Ives, Burl 1909 - 1997	Ent	25	45		45	AA Winner
Ives, Charles E. 1874-54	Music	250	750	1,500	500	Tonal Experimentation
Ivey, Judith	Ent	15			35	
Ivogun, Maria	Music	50			175	Opera
Izak, Edouard	Military	25	45			

Name	Field	SIG	DS	ALS	SP	Remarks
Jabotinsky, Vladimir	Political	45	125	250	75	Zionist Leader WW I
Jack, Thomas M. 1831-80	Civil War	45				CSA Colonel
Jackson, Alan	Music	25	50		50	Country
Jackson, Alfred Eugene	Civil War	Scarce	Scarce	950	Scarce	CSA General
Jackson, Andrew	President	550	1,200	2,500		1767-1845
Jackson, Anne	Ent	5			15	
Jackson, Charles T.	Science	200				Co-Discoverer of Ether
Jackson, Clairborne F.	Civil War		150	200		CSA General
Jackson, Eugene P.	Ent	10			20	Our Gang
Jackson, Glenda	Ent	15			35	AA Winner
Jackson, Gordon	Ent	15		50	50	Upstairs, Downstairs
Jackson, Helen Hunt	Author	15	35	50	25	Am.Novelist, Poet. Ramona
Jackson, Henry R.	Civil War	100	200	300		CSA General/1820-98
Jackson, Howell E.	SuprCt	50			100	
Jackson, James S.	Civil War	200	Scarce	Scarce	Scarce	Union General/KIA
Jackson, James, Dr.	Science	10			25	Ist Am. to Perform Vaccinations
Jackson, Janet	Music	35			75	
Jackson, Jesse	Political	15		45	35	
Jackson, Joe	Music	20			45	
Jackson, Kate	Ent	20	45		45	Charlie's Angels
Jackson, LaToya	Ent	20		45	45	
Jackson, Mahalia	Music	75			150	Gospel Singer
Jackson, Maynard	Music	5		20	15	Trumpet
Jackson, Michael	Music	125	300	Scarce	250	
Jackson, Rachel	First Lady	575	Scarce	Scarce	Scarce	
Jackson, Robert H.	SuprCt	75	200		125	Chief Prosec/Nuremberg
Jackson, Samuel L.	Ent	25			50	
Jackson, Samuel M.	Civil War	Scarce	Scarce	600	Scarce	Union General
Jackson, Sherry	Ent	10			20	
Jackson, Stonewall	Civil War	4,000	10,000	20,000	RARE	CSA General/1824-1863
Jackson, Stonewall	Civil War	5,500	12,000	24,000	RARE	CSA General/War Dated
Jackson, Victoria	Ent	10			25	Sat Night Live
Jackson, Wanda	Music	10			25	
Jackson, William 1759-28	RevWar	125	350	750		Gen. Washington Aide
Jackson, William Henry	Art	50	100			Photographer/1843-1944
Jackson, Wm. Hicks	Civil War	100	200	250		CSA General/1835-1903
Jacob, Francois	Science	20		50	40	Nobel Medicine 1965
Jacob, Irene	Ent	15			25	
Jacobi, Derek	Ent	5			15	
Jacobs, Josef	Aviation	30		75	50	
Jacobs, Lou	Ent	50	100		100	Clown
Jacobs, William W.	Author	10		50		Br. Monkey's Paw

Name	Field	SIG	DS	ALS	SP	Remarks
Jacobsen, Fritz	Aviation	10		35	40	Ace WW I
Jacquet, Illinois Jean	Music	35			75	Jazz Sax, Bandleader
Jadlowker, Hermann	Music	100			250	Opera
Jaeckel, Richard	Ent	10			20	
Jaeger, James A.	Aviation	10		30		
Jaehnert, Erhard	Aviation	5		20	15	
Jaffe, Sam 1893-1984	Ent	25			45	Gunga Din
Jagger, Bianca	Music	10			25	
Jagger, Dean	Ent	15	25		35	1903 - 1991/AA Winner
Jagger, Mick	Music	60	200	Scarce	125	Rolling Stones
Jakes, John	Author	20	50	75	50	Holiday for Havoc
James I & VI (Eng)	Royalty	800	1,200	RARE	RARE	
James II (Eng) 1633-1701	Royalty	550	1,200	1,500		
James, Daniel, Jr.	Military	20	35	75	45	1st Black 4 Star General.
James, Etta	Music	20			40	
James, Frank 1844-1915	Western	1,000	1,500	2,500		
James, Harry	Music	20		50	50	Big Band
James, Henry 1811-82	Author	75		200		
James, Henry 1843-1916	Author	150	300	550		
James, Manley	Military	10		45		WW I Victoria Cross
James, P.D.	Author	20	65			Br. Mystery Author
James, Rick	Music	20			45	
James, Sheila	Ent	10			20	
James, Sonny	Music	15			30	
James, Will	Author	75	250	400	600	Illustrated Western Novels
James, William 1842-10	Science	100	350	450	175	Psychologist
Jameson, House	Ent	10			20	
Jan & Dean	Music	20			45	
Janes Addiction	Music	25			50	Signed by Entire Band
Janis, Conrad	Ent	10			35	Mork and Mindy
Janis, Elsie	Ent	25	50		50	
Janney, Leon	Ent	35			75	Our Gang
Janowitz, Gundula	Music	25			50	Opera
Jansen, Marie	Music	15			40	Opera
Janssen, David	Ent	75	100		150	TV's "The Fugitive
Janssen, Famke	Ent	20			45	James Bond Girl
January, Lois	Ent	5			15	
Jardine, William	Political	10	25	45	20	Sec'y Agriculture 1925
Jarman, Claude, Jr.	Ent	20	60		50	
Jarman, Maxie	Business	15			45	Jarman Shoes
Jaroff, Serge	Ent	15			35	Jaroff Ballet
Jarreau, Al	Music	20			40	
Jarrett, Art	Music	15			30	Bandleader
Jarriel, Tom	Ent	5			10	TV News
Jarvik, Robert, Dr.	Science	15	35	50	35	Inventor Artificial Heart
Jarvis, Anna M.	Political	75	175			Mothers Day Sponsor
Jarvis, Gregory B.	Space	100			275	Astronaut

Name	Field	SIG	DS	ALS	SP	Remarks
Jarvis, Howard	Political	5		30	15	Sponsor Proposition 13
Jason, Rick	Ent	5			15	
Jason, Sybil	Ent	10		25	25	Child Star
Jawlensky, Aleksey von	Art	Scarce	Scarce	600	Scarce	Russian Painter
Jaworski, Leon	Political	10		45	15	Dir.Watergate Prosecution Force
Jay, James, Sir 1732-15	Science	100	275	400		Phys. to G. Washington
Jay, John 1745-1829	SuprCt	550	1,750	2,250		
Jay, John (Grandson)	Political	15	25	40		Opposed Slavery
Jean, Gloria	Ent	10		20		
Jean, Norma	Music	10			20	
Jeans, James, Sir	Science	10	30	50	25	Br. Physicist
Jedlichka, Ernest	Music	75			200	Rus-Pol Pianist
Jeffers, Robinson 1887-62	Author	75	350	450	150	Prize Winning Poet
Jeffers, William M.	Business	25	75	125	50	Union Pacific RR
Jefferson Airplane	Ent	125	300		250	Signed by Entire Band
Jefferson, Joe 1829-1905	Ent	30	75	125	75	
Jefferson, Martha W.	First Lady	RARE	RARE	RARE	RARE	
Jefferson, Thomas	Ent	50			125	Silent Film Star
Jefferson, Thomas	President	2,500	3,500	7,500		1743-1826
Jeffreys, Anne	Ent	15			30	
Jellicoe, John R.	Military	20	75	125	50	WWI Br Admiral
Jenckes,Joseph	Political	100	250			Colonial Governor RI
Jeni, Richard	Ent	10			25	Comedian
Jenkins, Allen	Ent	25			45	
Jenkins, Butch	Ent	10			25	
Jenkins, Thornton Alex.	Military	10	25	35		Chief-of Staff Farragut Squad.
Jenner, Bruce	Sports	10			25	Olympic Star
Jenner, Edward, Dr.	Science	450	850	Scarce	Scarce	Smallpox Vaccination
Jenner, William, Sir	Science	35	100	250		Phys. to Queen Victoria
Jennings, Emil	Ent	200			350	Ist Academy Award Winner
Jennings, Peter	Ent	5		25	15	TV News Anchorman
Jennings, Waylon	Music	10			20	
Jennison, Ralph D.	Business	10	35	45	20	
Jensen, Karen	Ent	5			10	
Jensen, Maren	Ent	10			25	
Jepson, Helen	Music	15			40	Opera
Jeritza, Maria 1887-1984	Music	35			90	Opera
Jernstedt, Ken	Aviation	10		40	30	WWII Flying Tigers ACE
Jerome, Jerome K.	Author	35	75	100		Humorist, Playwright
Jerusalem, Siegfried	Music	15			45	Opera
Jessel, George	Ent	30	75		100	1898 - 1981
Jesup, Thomas S.	Military	50	125	200		General/1788-1860
Jesup, William H.	Military	5		25		
Jeter, Michael	Ent	10			25	Evening Shade
Jethro Tull	Music	45			75	By Entire Band
Jett, Joan	Music	20			45	and the Blackhearts
Jewel	Music	25			50	

Name	Field	SIG	DS	ALS	SP	Remarks
Jewell, Marshall	Political	50	75	200		Governor/Cabinet Member
Jewett, Sarah Orne	Author	75	200	300		1849-1909
Jewison, Norman	Ent	10			20	Director
Jillian, Ann	Ent	10			25	
Jimenez, Enrique A.	Political	10		25	20	Panama
Jimenez, Marcos P.	Political	10	25	50	20	Venezuela
Joachim, Joseph 1831-07	Music	100	150	275	225	Violinist/Composer
Jodl, Alfred	Military	150	500	550	250	Chief-of-Staff To Keitel
Joel, Billy	Music	25			50	
Joffre, Joseph Jacques C.	Military	75	150	250	225	Marshal of France WW I
Johann, Zita	Ent	35			75	The Mummy
John II (King Castile)	Royalty	RARE	RARE	RARE	RARE	Patron of Literature &Arts
John of Austria	Royalty	150				1629-1679
John XXIII, Pope	Clergy	500			650	Angelo Giuseppe Roncalli
John, Augustus	Art	50	125	250		Welch. Portraits, Landscapes
John, Elton	Music	30	100		75	
Johns, Glynis	Ent	15			30	
Johns, Jasper	Art	20	50		30	Am. Pop Artist
Johnson, Amy (Mollison)	Aviation	75	100	125	200	Aviation Pioneer
Johnson, Andrew	President	400	1,200	Scarce	2,500	1808-1875
Johnson, Art	Aviation	10		40	30	USAF WWII ACE
Johnson, Arte	Ent	5			15	Laugh In
Johnson, Ben	Ent	35	75		75	Western star
Johnson, Ben 1572-1637	Author	450	1,500			Br. Playwright and Poet
Johnson, Betty	Ent	5			10	
Johnson, Brad	Ent	10			20	
Johnson, Bradley T.	Civil War	100	250	300		CSA General/1829-1903
Johnson, Bunk	Music	200			550	Jazz Trumpet
Johnson, Bushrod Rust	Civil War	150	300			CSA General/1817-1880
Johnson, Cave 1793-1866	Political	50	100	200		PM General
Johnson, Chic	Ent	45			75	(Olsen & Johnson)
Johnson, Crockett	Cartoonist	50			150	Barnaby
Johnson, Don	Ent	25			50	Miami Vice
Johnson, Eastman	Art	75		150	300	Am. Portrait & Genre Artist
Johnson, Edward	Music	25			75	Canadian Tenor
Johnson, Eliza M.	First Lady	750	1,500			
Johnson, Fred	Cartoonist	15			35	Moon Mullins
Johnson, Gerald	Aviation	15	30	50	40	WWII ACE
Johnson, Gorgean	Ent	10			20	
Johnson, H. Hank	Business	5			15	Pres. Spiegel
Johnson, Harold K.	Military	15	35	50	30	WWII Four Star General
Johnson, Henry A.	Business	5			15	CEO Spiegel Inc.
Johnson, Herschel	Civil War	40	100			GA Governor
Johnson, Hiram W.	Political	25	50			Senator CA/1866-1945
Johnson, Howard S.	Business	15	30		35	
Johnson, Hugh S.	Political	15	75	125	25	
Johnson, James Johnnie	Aviation	30	75	125	100	WWII Br RAF Top ACE

Name	Field	SIG	DS	ALS	SP	Remarks
Johnson, James K.	Aviation	10	25	45	35	ACE, Korea, Double Ace
Johnson, James Weldon	Author	30	100	225		
Johnson, Jesse G.	Military	35	75	150		WWII Admiral
Johnson, John H.	Business		50		65	Ebony/Jet...
Johnson, Jonathan E.	Art	25	150			Am. Portrait Painter
Johnson, June	Ent	10			25	
Johnson, Lady Bird	First Lady	40	100		100	
Johnson, Leon W.	Military	10		35		
Johnson, Lyndon B.	President	200	450	RARE	500	1908-1973
Johnson, Lynn	Cartoonist	10			25	For Better Or Worse
Johnson, Lynn-Holly	Ent	10			25	
Johnson, Martin 1884-37	Art	15	40			Wildlife Photographer
Johnson, Nunnally	Author	20	50		50	Am Playwright
Johnson, Osa	Explorer	15		35	30	Wild Animal Films
Johnson, Philip	Science	25			125	Early Skyscrapers
Johnson, Reverdy	Political	25	100	100		Attorney General
Johnson, Richard L.	Aviation	15		30	20	
Johnson, Richard M.	Vice Pres	100	200	350	400	Van Buren Vice Pres.
Johnson, Robert S.	Aviation	25		50	75	ACE, WWII #5 US
Johnson, Russ	Ent	5			10	
Johnson, Samuel C.	Business	5			10	Pres. Johnson's Wax
Johnson, Samuel, Dr.	Author	1,750	Scarce	Scarce	Scarce	Lexicographer, Critic
Johnson, Van	Ent	15	35		35	
Johnson, William B.	Business	5			10	CEO Railway Express
Johnson, William Cost	Political	10	20	35		MOC MD 1833
Johnson, William Sam'l	RevWar	150	375	675		Continental Congress
Johnston, Albert Sidney	Civil War	300	1,200	1,500		CSA General/1803-1862
Johnston, Frances	Art	10	25			Photographer/1864-1952
Johnston, George D.	Civil War	100	250	300		CSA General/1832-1910
Johnston, Harriet Lane	First Lady	200		600		Buchanan's Niece
Johnston, J. Lawson	Business	15	35	75		
Johnston, Johnny	Aviation	20	50		50	
Johnston, Joseph E.	Civil War	300	600	750	1,500	CSA General/1807-91
Johnston, Richard M.	Author	5		20		
Jolie, Angelina	Ent	20			50	
Joliot-Curie, Frederic	Science			500		Fr. Chem.Nobel '35.
Joliot-Curie, Irene	Science	75		200		1897-1956
Jolson, Al 1886-1950	Ent	150	250		275	Star of 1st Talkie Film
Jones, Allan 1908 - 1992	Music	15		35	30	Film & Concert Singer
Jones, Anne	Music	10			20	
Jones, Annisa	Ent	200	300		350	Buffy on "Family Affair"
Jones, Anson	Political	350		1,200		President of Texas Republic
Jones, Anthony A.	Music	10			20	
Jones, Barry	Ent	20			40	Br. Actor
Jones, Buck 1889-1942	Ent	175	250	Scarce	350	Vintage Film Cowboy
Jones, Carolyn	Ent	100	200		300	TV Addams Family/Morticia
Jones, Casey	Aviation	50	100	175	150	

Name	Field	SIG	DS	ALS	SP	Remarks
Jones, Catherine-Zeta	Ent	25			50	
Jones, Chuck	Cartoonist	35	125		100	Warner Bros. Animator
Jones, Claude A.	Military	40	75			
Jones, David (Davy)	Music	25			45	The Monkees
Jones, David R. 1825-63	Civil War	300	800	RARE	RARE	CSA General
Jones, Dean	Ent	10		20	20	
Jones, Dick	Ent	10			35	
Jones, Edward F.	Civil War	50	100	150	150	Union Officer
Jones, George	Music	10			25	
Jones, Gordon	Ent	10			20	
Jones, Grace	Ent	20			40	
Jones, Grandpa	Music	25			45	Country
Jones, Gwyneth	Music	15			40	Opera
Jones, Henry	Ent	5			15	
Jones, Howard	Ent	10			20	
Jones, Isham	Music	15			40	Vintage Big Band
Jones, J. Carey	Military	20	45			Admiral WWII
Jones, Jack	Ent	10			25	
Jones, James	Author	50	150			From Here to Eternity
Jones, James Earl	ENt	10			30	Voice of Darth Vader/CNN
Jones, Janet	Ent	10		30	30	
Jones, Jeffrey	Ent	20			40	
Jones, Jennifer	Ent	125	175		250	AA Winner
Jones, Jenny	Ent	10			20	Talk Show Host
Jones, Jim	Clergy	250	375	650	850	
Jones, John Marshall	Civil War	225	650			CSA General/1821-64
Jones, John Paul	RevWar	8,000	25,000	65,000	RARE	Naval Hero
Jones, Louis R.	Military	10	30			
Jones, Mary H. 'Mother'	Political	75	150	300		Labor Organizer
Jones, Quincy	Music	15		35	30	Composer
Jones, Rickie Lee	Music	20			45	
Jones, Samuel 1819-87	Civil War	100	300			CSA General
Jones, Shirley	Ent	10	25		25	Partridge Family
Jones, Spike 1911 - 1965	Music	30			75	Big Band Leader
Jones, Thomas V.	Business	15	30		25	
Jones, Tom	Music	10			20	
Jones, Tommy Lee	Ent	25	75		50	
Jones, William E.1824-64	Civil War	150	250	600		CSA General/KIA
Jong, Erica	Author	10		20	20	Fear of Flying Novel
Jongkind, Johan	Art	200	450	750		1819-1891
Jope, Bernhard	Aviation	15	25	45	35	
Joplin, Janis 1943-70	Music	750	1,500	3,500	1,750	
Joplin, Scott	Music	750	1,200	2,000		Rag Time Composer
Jordan, Dorothy	Ent	15		35	30	
Jordan, Hamilton	Political	5		20	15	Chief of Staff Carter Admin.
Jordan, Jim (Fibber)	Ent	15	20	35	25	
Jordan, Louis	Music	25			75	Big Band Leader

Name	Field	SIG	DS	ALS	SP	Remarks
Jordan, Thomas 1819-95	Civil War	100	250	350		CSA General
Jordanaires, The	Music	35			75	All Four
Jordon, Richard	Ent	15		25	30	
Jorn, Carl	Music	30			75	Opera
Jory, Victor 1902-82	Ent	50	75		100	
Jose, Richard J.	Music	10			25	
Joseffy, Raphael	Music	25			125	Pianist, Pupil of Llszt
Joseph II 1741-1790	Royalty	125	350	750		German King
Josephine, Empress	Royalty	750	1,500	2,500		Fr. Wife of Napoleon
Joslyn, Allyn	Ent	25			50	
Joswig, Wilhelm	Aviation	10			30	
Jouett, James	Civil War	25	50	125		Union Naval Officer
Jouhaux, Benjamin	Political	25	75	150	50	Nobel Peace Prize 1951
Jourdan, Jean B., Count	Military	100	250	300		Marshal of Napoleon
Jourdan, Louis	Ent	15			25	1919 - 1993
Journey	Music	50			100	Signed by Entire Band
Jovavich, Milla	Ent	25			50	Fifth Element
Joy, Leatrice	Ent	15			30	
Joyce, Alice 1890-1955	Ent	15	25		45	Silent Star
Joyce, Elaine	Ent	5			15	
Joyce, James 1882-1941	Author	450	600	Scarce	RARE	Ir. Novelist/Poet/Playwright
Joyce, Richard	Military	50	100	175		
Juan Carlos, King	Royalty	50	125	250	150	Spain
Juarez, Benito 1806-1872	Political	425	1,200	1,500	1,500	Pres. Mexico
Judas Preist	Music	35			75	Signed by entire Group
Judd, Ashley	Ent	25			50	
Judd, Naomi & Wynona	Music	35			75	
Judd, Wynonna	Music	25			50	
Judge, Arline	Ent	15		35	30	
Julia, Raul	Ent	35	75		75	Addams Family Gomez
Julian, George W.	Political	15		75		Co-Founder Free Soil
PartyJuliana, Queen	Royalty	100	250	450	150	Netherlands
Jump, Gordon	Ent	10			25	WKRP in Cincinatti
Jung, Carl Gustav	Science	750	1,500	2,500		Swiss Psychiatrist
Junkers, Hugo	Science	100		300		Ger. Airplane Designer
Junot, Andache, Duc A.	Military	75	225			Fr. Gen., Sec'y to Napoleon
Junot, Jean Androche	Military	50	100	200		French Revolution
Jurgens, Curt	Ent	30			75	
Jurgens, Dick	Music	20			45	Big Band Leader
Jusserand, Jean Jules	Author	20		45		Pulitzer Prize/1855-32
Justice, Bill	Cartoonist	35			75	The Chipmunks

Name	Field	SIG	DS	ALS	SP	Remarks
Kabaiwanska, Raina	Music	15			35	Opera
Kabalevsky, Dmitri	Music	75	300	250		Composer
Kabasta, Oswald	Music	125				Conductor/Suicide
Kadar, Janos	Political	50	125			
Kaelin, Kato	Ent	25		75	45	Houseguest 0 J. Simpson
Kafka, Franz	Author	1,250	RARE	RARE	RARE	German Novelist
Kahn, Madeline	Ent	25	50		50	
Kahn, Otto H. 1867-1934	Business	30		100	75	Banker, Patron of the Arts
Kahn, Yahya	Political	30			50	Pakistan
Kahoutek, Lubos	Science	5		30	15	Am. Astronomer
Kaiser, Henry J.	Business	200	900		375	
Kai-Shek, Chiang	Political	100	200	450	700	Republic of China
Kai-Shek, Mayling S.	Author	50	125		100	Madame Chiang
Kalakaua, David 1836-91	Royalty	150	425	750	1,500	King Hawaii
Kallen, Kitty	Music	10			25	Big Band Vocalist
Kaltenborn, H. V.	Ent	5	15	30	15	Radio Commentator
Kaltenbrunner, Ernst	Military	100	450		175	Guilty of Nazi Atrocities
Kamburg, Arthur, Dr.	Science	10	20			Nobel
Kamehameha IV 1824-63	Royalty		2,500			King of Hawaii
Kamehameha, Liholiho	Royalty	1,000	RARE	RARE	RARE	King Hawaii/1797-1824
Kamehamehal, K.	Royalty	750	1,500			King Hawaii
Kamen, Milt	Ent	15			35	
Kaminsky, Max	Music	10			30	Dixieland Jazz Bandleader
Kamio, Mitsuomi	Military	100		200		
Kammhuber, Josef	Aviation	20		65	35	Ger. Air Defense Gen. WWII
Kanaly, Steve	Ent	10			20	
Kander, John	Music	5	20	25	10	Composer
Kandinski, Vasili 1866-44	Art	200	500			Russian Painter
Kane, Bob	Cartoonist	75			150	Batman Creator
Kane, Carol	Ent	10			25	Taxi
Kane, Elisha Kent	Explorer	100	200	450		Grinnell Arctic Expedition
Kane, Helen 1904-1966	Ent	35			75	Boop Boop a Doop Girl
Kane, Richard	Military	25			75	
Kane, Thomas L.	Civil War	50	100			Union General/1822-83
Kanin, Garson	Author	25			50	
Kansas	Music	35			75	Signed by Entire Group
Kant, Immanuel 1724-04	Author	1,000				German Philosopher
Kantor, MacKinlay	Author	15			25	Pulitzer
Kaper, Bronislaw	Music	10			15	Composer
Kaplan, Gabe	Ent	20	45		50	Welcome Back Kotter
Kaplan, Gilbert	Music	5			15	Conductor
Kaplioani 1834-1899	Royalty	Scarce	Scarce	Scarce	1,200	Queen of Hawaii

Name	Field	SIG	DS	ALS	SP	Remarks
Karas, Alex	Ent	5			15	
Karas, Anton	Music	25			100	Composer
Karloff, Boris 1887-1969	Ent	275	450	750	550	Frankenstein
Karman, Theodore von	Business	25			50	Designed Karman Ghia
Karns, Roscoe	Ent	35			75	
Karpis, Alvin	Criminal	75			100	Public Enemy Number One
Karsavina, Tamara	Ent	100			300	Russian Dancer
Karsh, Yousuf	Art	35			75	Photographer
Kasavubu, Joseph	Political	20			50	Rep of Congo
Kaschmann, Guiseppe	Music	75			300	Baritone
Kasem, Casey	Ent	15			25	Radio/Voice of Shaggy
Kasem, Jean	Ent	10			25	
Kasha, Al	Music	15			45	Composer
Kashfi, Anna	Ent	10			35	
Kassell, Art	Music	20			50	Bandleader
Kastler, Alfred	Science	15			45	Nobel
Kasznar, Kurt	Ent	25			50	Land of the Giants
Katchinsky, Victorin	Aviation	20			45	
Katt, William	Ent	10			25	
Katz, Bernard	Science	15			35	Nobel/Medicine
Katzenberg, Jeffrey	Business	15	45		35	Dreamworks Executive
Katzir, Ephraim	Political	10			45	Pres of Israel
Kaufman, Andy	Ent	100	200		200	Taxi/Died young
Kaufman, George S.	Author	35			75	1889 - 1961
Kaunda, Kenneth	Political	40			70	First Pres. of Zambia
Kavner, Julie	Ent	20			45	Voice of Marge Simpson
Kawato, Masajiro	Aviation	50			150	WWII Ace/Shot Boyington
Kay, Beatrice	Ent	10			25	
Kay, Diane	Ent	5			15	
Kay, Herbie	Music	10			30	Bandleader
Kay, Mary	Business	5			15	Cosmetics Empire
Kaye, Danny	Ent	65	100		100	1913 - 1987
Kaye, Sammy	Music	15			45	Big Band Leader
Kaye, Stubby	Ent	10			25	
Kazan, Elia	Ent	15	45		35	Director/Producer
Keach, Stacey	Ent	10			20	
Keane, Bill	Cartoonist	10			25	The Family Circus
Keane, Edward	Ent	10			25	
Keane, Jane	Ent	5			15	
Kearny, Philip	Civil War	350	650	850		Union General/KIA
Kearny, Stephen	Military	100	225	350		War of 1812/First Gov. CA.
Keaton, Buster	Ent	250	400	Scarce	675	1895 - 1966
Keaton, Diane	Ent	20	50		50	
Keaton, Michael	Ent	20			50	Batman in Movies
Kedrova, Lila	Ent	15			40	
Keel, Howard	Ent	5			15	
Keeler, Ruby	Ent	35			55	

Name	Field	SIG	DS	ALS	SP	Remarks
Keene, Carolyn	Author	50		150	150	Nancy Drew Mysteries
Keene, Charles	Ent	10			25	
Keene, Tom	Ent	25			50	
Keeshan, Bob	Ent	10			25	Capt. Kangaroo
Keitel, Harvey	Ent	25			50	
Keitel, Wilhelm (d.1946)	Military	350	575		650	WWII Ger. Field Marshal
Keith, Brian	Ent	25	45		55	Family Affair
Keith, David	Ent	15			30	
Keith, George Keith	Military	45	125	150		British Admiral 1746-1823
Keith, Ian	Ent	15			35	
Keith, William	RevWar	150		550		Colonial Lt. Gov of PA/DE
Kelland, Clarence B.	Author	20			30	Am. Novelist
Kellar, Harry	Ent	250	Scarce	750	900	Magician
Kellard, Ralph	Ent	10			25	
Kellaway, Cecil	Ent	25			75	
Keller, Helen 1880-1968	Author	200	400	Scarce	800	Blind, Deaf, Mute
Kellerman, Annette	Ent	45				Dancer and Swimming Star
Kellerman, Sally	Ent	10			25	
Kelley, Deforest	Ent	35	75	100	75	Star Trek
Kelley, Kitty	Author	10			20	Celebrity Biographer
Kellogg, Frank 1856-1937	Political	35			35	Nobel Peace Prize
Kellogg, John Harvey	Business	50	150			Cereal/Health Reformer
Kellogg, Ray	Ent	5			15	
Kellogg, W.K.	Business	125	250	400	250	Founder WK Kellogg Co.
Kelly, Brian	Ent	10			25	
Kelly, Emmett Sr.	Ent	75	150	150	200	Famous Clown
Kelly, Gene	Ent	30	125	150	75	AA Winner/1912-1996
Kelly, Grace 1928-1982	Ent	250	550	750	500	Signed "Grace Kelly"
Kelly, Jack	Ent	15			45	
Kelly, John 1840-64	Civil War	475	Scarce	Scarce	Scarce	CSA Gen./Youngest Killed
Kelly, Moira	Ent	20			50	
Kelly, Nancy	Ent	10			25	
Kelly, Patsy	Ent	30			75	
Kelly, Paul	Ent	25			50	
Kelly, Paula	Ent	5			15	
Kelly, Sheila	Ent	10			25	
Kelly, Thomas	Military	10			15	General/Deseet Storm
Kelly, Walt	Cartoonist	75	175			Pogo
Kelsey, Linda	Ent	5			15	
Kelton, Pert	Ent	15			45	
Kelvin, William T.	Science	100			175	Kelvin Scale
Kemble, Edward W.	Art	50			175	Am. Illustrator (1861-1933)
Kemmer, Ed	Ent	10			20	
Kemp, Hal	Music	15			45	Big Band Leader
Kemper, James L.	Civil War	200				CSA General/1823-95
Kendall, Cy	Ent	25			50	
Kendall, Edward	Science	30			45	Nobel Medicine 1950

Name	Field	SIG	DS	ALS	SP	Remarks
Kendall, Henry	Science	20			30	Nobel Physics 1990
Kendren, John	Science	15			20	
Keneally, Thomas	Author	10			20	Schindlers List
Kennedy, Adam	Ent	10			20	
Kennedy, Anthony	SuprCt	30			50	
Kennedy, Arthur	Ent	35			75	1914 - 1990
Kennedy, Caroline	Political	25		75		JFK's Daughter
Kennedy, Douglas	Music	5			15	AKA Keith Douglas
Kennedy, Edgar	ENt	125			250	
Kennedy, Edward (Ted)	Political	15	25		25	
Kennedy, Ethel	Political	15	45		35	Mrs. Robert Kennedy
Kennedy, George	Ent	15			45	AA Winner
Kennedy, George C.	Aviation	50			200	
Kennedy, Jacqueline	First Lady	400	1,200	1,500	900	Value Higher if As 1st Lady
Kennedy, Jayne	Ent	5			15	
Kennedy, John F.	President	1,150	1,700	4,500	2,500	1917-1963
Kennedy, John F. Jr.	Political	50			100	Publisher of "George"
Kennedy, Joseph P.	Political	75			150	Kennedy Family Father
Kennedy, Madge	Ent	15			30	
Kennedy, Robert F.	Political	200	675		675	
Kennedy, Rose F.	Political	100	150		100	Kennedy Family Mother
Kennedy, Tom	Ent	50			100	
Kenney, George	Military	25			50	WWII General USAF
Kenny G.	Music	20			45	
Kenny, Bill	Music	25			50	Ink Spots Lead Singer
Kenny, Elizabeth	Science	175			275	Polio Treatments
Kenny, Nick	Music	20			40	Ink Spots Singer
Kensit, Patsy	Ent	20			50	
Kent, Atwater	Business	50	175	Scarce	Scarce	Radio Manafacturer
Kent, Edward Augustus	Royalty	50				Son of George III
Kent, Ford J.	Military	100				Gen. Took San Juan Hill
Kent, Jack	Cartoonist	10			30	King Aroo
Kent, James	RevWar	100		250		
Kent, Rockwell	Art	50			100	1882-1971
Kent, Walter	Music	40			65	Composer
Kenton, Simon	Western	400				Spy/General/Trapper
Kenton, Stan	Music	35			100	Big Band Leader
Kenyatta, Jomo	Political	125			150	PM of Kenya
Kenyon, Doris	Ent	15			45	
Kepford, Ira	Aviation	15			45	WWII Ace
Kepner, William	Military	15			25	
Kerbs, Edwin	Science	20			40	Nobel Medicine
Kercheval, Ken	Ent	10			20	
Kerensky, Alexander	Political	200			450	Russ.Politican
Kern, Jerome	Music	250	650	Scarce	2,000	Composer. (1885-1945)
Kerns, Joanna	Ent	10			30	Growing Pains
Keroauc, Jack	Author	400	1,500	RARE	RARE	Beat Generation Poet

Name	Field	SIG	DS	ALS	SP	Remarks
Kerr, Deborah	Ent	10			30	
Kerr, Ruth	Business	25			75	Kerr Glass Co.
Kerrigan, Warren	Ent	25			60	
Kershaw, Joseph B.	Civil War	200		900		CSA General/1822-94
Kesey, Ken	Author	20	50		50	One Flew Over the Cukoo's Nest
Kesselring, Albrecht	Military	100			175	WWII Ger Field Marshal
Kestnbaum, Meyer	Business	20	30		25	
Ketcham, Hank	Cartoonist	25	75		75	Dennis the Menace
Ketcham, John H.	Civil War	65				Union General/1832-1906
Ketelby, Albert W.	Music	25		75		Composer
Kettering, Charles F.	Science	100	150	325	150	
Kevorkian, Jack, Dr.	Science	25			75	Dr. assists in suicides
Key, David M. 1824-1900	Civil War	30	50	100		P.M. General. CSA Officer
Key, Francis Scott	Author	450	750	950		1779-1843
Key, Ted	Cartoonist	20		50	50	Hazel
Keyes, Erasmus D.	Civil War	50	125	300		Union General/1810-95
Keyes, Evelyn	Ent	15		45	35	GWTW star
Keyes, Roger J.B.	Military	15	30	55	25	Boxer Rebellion
Keynes, John Maynard	Science	75		400	225	Br. Economist
Keys, Ancel	Science	5		25	15	
Khachaturian, Aram	Music	200		675	650	Composer
Khalid, King	Royalty	20	75	125	50	Saudi Arabia
Khambatta, Persis	Ent	35			75	Star Trek:Motion Picture
Khan, Chaka	Music	25			50	
Khan, Mohammad Ayub	Political	30	75			
Khanh, Nguyen, Gen.	Political	20	50	175	45	
Khomeini, Ruhollah	Political	500	RARE	RARE	RARE	Iranian Moslem Leader
Khorana, Har G., Dr.	Science	15	25	45	35	Nobel Medicine 1968
Khruschchev, Nikita	Political	300	400	550	1,200	Premier Soviet Union
Kiam, Victor	Business	10		25	25	Remington Razor Co.
Kibbee, Guy	Ent	25			50	
Kidder, Margot	Ent	25			50	Movie "Lois Lane"
Kidman, Nicole	Ent	35	75		75	
Kiel, Richard	Ent	10	25		30	Jaws" in Bond films
Kielmansegg, Graf J.A.	Military	15			35	Gen. German Army
Kienzl, Wilhelm 1857-41	Music	15		50		Composer
Kiepura, Jan	Music	45			125	Opera
Kilban, B.	Cartoonist	10	25		100	New Yorker Cartoonist
Kilbride, Percy 1888 - 64	Ent	175			350	Ma and Pa Kettle films
Kilby, J. S. Jack	Science	15	35	50	30	Inventor of Micro Chip
Kiley, Richard	Ent	10			25	
Kilgallen, Dorothy	Ent	15			25	
Kilgore, Merle	Music	10			20	
Kilian, Victor	Ent	10		20	25	
Kilmer, Joanne Whalley	Ent	20			40	
Kilmer, Joyce	Author	200	450			Poet
Kilmer, Val	Ent	25	75		50	Batman

Name	Field	SIG	DS	ALS	SP	Remarks
Kilpatrick, Hugh J.	Civil War	150	225	400	400	Union General/1836-1881
Kimball, J. Golden	Political	25	150			Pioneer Mormon Leader
Kimball, John W.	Civil War	45		200		Union Officer
Kimball, Spencer W.	Political	25		35	30	Morman Leader
Kimball, Ward	Cartoonist	35	75		75	Disney Cartoonist
Kimberly, John W.	Political	20	45	100		
Kimberly, R. Lewis	Civil War	25	40	50		Union General
Kimbrough, Charles	Ent	20			45	Murphy Brown
Kimbrough, Emily	Author	10		45	15	
Kimmel, Husband E.	Military	400	RARE	RARE	650	US Cmdr at Pearl Harbour
Kindelberger, James H.	Business	45			75	
Kindermann, K. B.	Aviation	5			10	
Kindler, Hans	Music	15			45	Conductor
King, Alan	Ent	5			15	
King, Andrea	Ent	10			20	
King, B.B.	Music	25	50		50	
King, Ben E.	Music	20		75	50	Stand by Me
King, Cammie	Ent	10			30	GWTW Star
King, Carole	Music	15			25	
King, Charles	Author	50		150		During Civil War
King, Coretta Scott	Political	25	75	125	45	Mrs. Martin Luther King, Jr.
King, Ernest J. 1878-1956	Military	35	100		125	Adm Comdr US Fleet
King, Frank	Cartoonist	35			75	Gasoline Alley
King, Henry	Ent	30			75	Director
King, Horatio 1811-1897	Political	50	150			P.M. General 1861
King, John 'Dusty'	Ent	25	35	45	50	
King, Larry	Ent	10	20	35	25	Talk Show Host
King, MacKenzie	Political	50	50	100	75	Prime Minister Canada
King, Martin Luther, Jr.	Clergy	1,500	2,750	3,500	3,000	Assasinated
King, Martin Luther, Sr.	Clergy	35	75	75	75	
King, Pee Wee	Music	5			15	Bandleader/Composer
King, Perry	Ent	10			20	
King, Rufus 1755-1827	RevWar	250	400	450		Continental Congress
King, Rufus 1814-76	Civil War	35	100			Union General
King, Stephen	Author	60	200	400	125	Horror Author
King, Walter Woolf	Music	20			50	Broadway Star
King, Wayne	Music	15			20	Big Band Leader
King, William R.	Vice-Pres	200	300			Pierces VP
King, Wm. L. Mackenzie 1874-1950	Political		50	250		Prime Minster/Canada
Kingman, Dong	Art	25	50	100		
Kingsford-Smith, Charles	Aviation	75	250		200	
Kingsley, Ben	Ent	10		20	35	AA Winner
Kingsley, Charles 1819-75	Author	50	100	150		British Novelist
Kingston, William H.	Author	25		100		
Kinks	Music	40			100	Five current Lineup
Kinnear, Greg	Ent	25	50		50	As Good as it Gets
Kinsey, Alfred, Dr.	Science	150	225	350	250	1894-1956

Name	Field	SIG	DS	ALS	SP	Remarks
Kinskey, Leonid	Ent	10			25	
Kinski, Klaus	Ent	20		35	45	
Kinski, Natassia	Ent	15	45		45	
Kipling, Rudyard 1865-36	Author	200	550	700	900	Nobel Prize in Literature
Kiplinger, Austin	Business	10		45	25	
Kipnis, Alexander	Music	35	75		75	Opera
Kirby, Durwood	Ent	10			20	
Kirby, George	Ent	5			15	
Kirby, Jack	Cartoonist	25			50	Comic Book Artist/Creator
Kirby, Rollin	Cartoonist	25			50	
Kirby-Smith, Edmund	Military	75	150	250		CSA General
Kirk, Florence	Music	10			30	Opera
Kirk, George	Aviation	10		35	30	WWII ACE
Kirk, Norman T.	Military	40				U.S. Gen. WWII
Kirk, Phyllis	Ent	20			45	
Kirk, Tommy	Ent	15	35		25	Child Star
Kirkby-Lunn, Louise	Music	30			100	Opera
Kirkconnell, Clare	Ent	5			10	
Kirkham, Ralph W.	Civil War	30	50	75		Union General/1821-93
Kirkland, Sally	Ent	10			20	
Kirkwood, Joe, Jr.	Ent	45	75	150	100	
Kirsten, Dorothy	Music	20			50	Soprano/Opera
Kiss	Music	75			125	Signed by All Four
Kissinger, Henry A.	Political	35	125		75	Sec'y State
Kistiakowsky, G.B., Dr.	Science	50	125			Nobel Chemistry
Kitchener, Horatio H.	Military	75	200	300	200	Ir.-born Br. Field Marshal
Kitt, Eartha	Ent	10	30	35	35	TV's Catwoman
Kittinger, Joe	Aviation	25	45			
Kittredge, Walter	Music	30				Composer
Kleber, Jean-Baptiste	Military	150	400	750		French General
Klee, Paul	Art	200	600	1,500		Swiss Surrealist Painter
Klein, Calvin	Business	10		35	25	Fashion Designer
Klein, Robert	Ent	5			15	
Klemperer, Otto	Music	50			150	German Conductor
Klemperer, Werner	Ent	10	25		25	Col. Klink/Hogan's Heroes
Klimt, Gustav 1862-1918	Art	150	450	800		Murals
Kline, Kevin	Ent	25	50		50	AA Winner
Klose, Margarete	Music	25			75	Opera/1902 - 1968
Kluge, Hans Gunther von	Military	75		250		Ger.Gen.WWII (Suicide)
Klugman, Jack	Ent	10	25		25	Odd Couple
Knern, H.H.	Cartoonist	35			75	Katzenjammer Kids
Knievel, Evel	Ent	10	25	40	45	Daredevil Motorcycle Rider
Knight, Fuzzy	Ent	50			150	
Knight, Gladys	Music	15	45	60	45	
Knight, Jordan	Ent	15			45	
Knight, June	Ent	10		20	25	
Knight, Laura, Dame	Art	75	100	175		British/1877-1970

Name	Field	SIG	DS	ALS	SP	Remarks
Knight, Phil	Business	20	35	45	25	Nike Athletic Shoes Etc.
Knight, Shirley	Ent	10		20	25	
Knight, Ted	Ent	35	50		75	Mary Tyler Moore Show
Knight, Wayne	Ent	25			50	Seinfeld/Third Rock...
Knopf, Alfred A.	Business	10		35		Knopf Publishing
Knopfler, Mark	Music	25			50	Dire Straits
Knote, Heinrich	Music	25			50	Opera
Knott, Walter	Business	150			400	Founder Knott's Berry Farm
Knotts, Don	Ent	10	25	30	25	Barney Fife
Knowles, James S.	Author	15	25	45		
Knowles, Patrick	Ent	10			25	
Knox, Alexander	Ent	20		30	35	
Knox, Elyse	Ent	10		35	25	
Knox, Frank 1874-1944	Political	50	100	100	100	Sec'y Navy
Knox, Henry 1750-1806	RevWar	150	300	550		
Knudsen, William S.	Business	20	35	75	50	Pres. GM During WWII
Koch, Edward	Political	10		35	15	Mayor NYC
Koch, Heinrich H. Robert	Science		1,200	2,200	1,500	Nobel Medicine/1905
Koch, Howard W.	Ent	10			25	
Koch, Robert, Dr. 1843-10	Science			1,200	2,250	Fndr. Modern Bacteriology
Kodaly, Zoltan	Music	125	250	450	450	Composer/1882 - 1967
Koehl, Herman	Aviation	75			250	
Koehler, Armin	Aviation	10		35	25	
Koening, Walter	Ent	15	40	45	35	Star Trek
Kohl, Helmut	Political	15		50	25	Chancellor Germany
Kohler, Walter J.	Business	10	30			Founder Kohler Corp.
Kohner, Susan	Ent	10			20	
Kokoschka, Oskar	Art	100		350	275	1886-1980
Kolff, Willem J., Dr.	Science	15	50		50	Created Artificial Kidney
Kolker, Henry	Ent	10			20	
Kolleck, Teddy	Political	15	25		35	Mayor of Jerusalem
Kollo, Rene	Music	10		35	25	Opera
Kollwitz, Kathe	Art	75		300		Ger. Sculptor/1867 - 1945
Komarov, Vladimir	Space	125			200	Cosmonaut
Konetzni, Anny	Music	35			75	Opera
Konya, Sandor	Music	15			45	Opera/Tenor
Koontz, Dean	Author	25	75		75	Horror
Koop, C. Everett, Dr.	Military	10		50	30	Adm/US Surgeon General
Kopell, Bernie	Ent	10	20		20	Love Boat Doctor
Koppel, Ted	Ent	10		30	20	TV News
Korda, Alexander	Ent	50		100	75	1893 - 1956
Koren, Edward	Cartoonist	25			50	New Yorker Cartoonist
Korman, Harvey	Ent	10	20	20	25	Carol Burnett Show
Kornberg, Arthur	Science	20	30	45	25	Nobel Medicine
Kornby, Arthur	Science	15		20		
Korngold, Erich W.	Music	75	200	350	100	Opera/Composer
Korolyov, Sergei	Science		1,500	2,000		1906 - 1966

Name	Field	SIG	DS	ALS	SP	Remarks
Korvin, Charles	Ent	5			10	
Kosciusko, Thaddeus	RevWar	350	750	2,000		Patriot
Kosleck, Martin	Ent	15			35	
Kossa, Frank R.	Military	10			10	
Kossuth, Lajos 1802-94	Political	100	600	450	150	Hungarian Patriot
Kostal, Irwin	Music	5		20	10	Composer
Kostelanetz, Andre	Music	15	25	45	25	Conductor/1901-1980
Koster, Henry	Ent	15	35		40	Director
Kosygin, Aleksei	Political	275		550	500	Premier of Soviet Union
Kotto, Yaphet	Ent	35	75		75	James Bond Villain
Kovack, Nancy (Mehta)	Ent	5			10	
Kovacs, Ernie	Ent	200	400		400	Scarce
Kovansky, Anatol	Art	15		40	25	
Kove, Martin	Ent	5			15	
Kowarski, L.	Science	10	25	50		
Kozky, Alex	Cartoonist	10			20	
Kozlovsky, Ivan	Music	RARE	RARE	RARE	1,500	Tenor
Kraft, James L.	Business	30	100	175	50	Founder Kraft Foods Co.
Kramer, Stanley	Ent	15	45		45	Director/Producer
Kramer, Stephanie	Ent	10			30	
Krantz, Judith	Author	25		45	35	Novelist
Krasner, Milton	Ent	20			45	AA Winning Director
Kraus, Alfredo	Music	15			35	Opera
Kraus, Clemens	Music	75			200	Austrian Conductor
Kraus, Robert	Art	10	25	50	25	
Kravitz, Lenny	Music	25			50	
Krebs, Hans Adolf, Sir	Science	15		45	20	Nobel Medicine
Kreisler, Fritz 1875-1962	Music	100	150	300	225	Violinist
Kremer, Andrea	Ent	5			15	ESPN News
Krenek, Ernst	Music	15	35	75	50	Composer
Krenn, Fritz	Music	15			35	Opera
Kresge, S. S.	Business	150	250	300	200	Kresge Stores
Kretschmer, Otto	Military	50	150		200	U-Boat Commander
Kreutzer, Conradin	Music	125	300	550		Ger. Composer/Conductor
Krige, Alice	Ent	15			35	
Kristel, Sylvia	Ent	20			45	
Kristofferson, Kris	Ent	10		35	30	Actor/Singer
Kroc, Ray A.	Business	75		200	175	McDonalds
Krock, Arthur	Author	10		40	15	Columnist NY Times
Kroesen, Fred J.	Military	5		20	10	
Kroft, Steve	Ent	5			15	60 Minutes
Kroll, Gustov	Science	10			30	Rocket Pioneer/von Braun
Kropotkin, PeterA.	Political	30	75			Russian Prince
Kruger, Kurt	Ent	10			35	
Kruger, Otto 1885-1974	Ent	30			75	
Kruger, Paul	Political	75	250		175	
Kruger, Stephanus J.P.	Political	125	450		650	Krugerrand Named For Him

Name	Field	SIG	DS	ALS	SP	Remarks
Krupa, Gene 1909-73	Music	40	150		100	Big Band Leader-Drums
Krupinski, Walter	Aviation	20	45	50	75	WWII German ACE
Krupp, Alfred	Business	150	450	500		Founder Krupp Works
Krupp, Friedrich Alfred	Business	125	350			Arms Manufacturer
Krylov, Ivan A.	Author	15	45	50	30	Russian Fables
Kschessinska, Matilda	Music	150		400		Prima Ballerina
Kubelik, Jan	Music	50	125	225	225	Violinist
Kubelik, Rafael	Music	25	50		50	Conductor
Kubitschek, Juscelino	Political	10	35	75	25	Brazilian Head of State
Kubrick, Stanley	Ent	75	150		150	Director
Kuchta, Gladys	Music	10			30	Opera
Kudrow, Lisa	Ent	25			50	FRIENDS
Kulp, Nancy	Ent	45	100		100	Miss Jane/Beverly Hillbillies
Kuncewiczowa, Maria	Author	150		300		Escaped Nazi German
Kunstler, William	Political	20	35	75	25	
Kupka, Frantisek 1871-57	Art	100	225	350		Czech Abstract Artist
Kuralt, Charles	Ent	10	20	30	20	TV News Commentator
Kurtz, Swoosie	Ent	15			40	
Kusch, Polykarp, Dr.	Science	20	50		25	Nobel Physics
Kwan, Nancy	Ent	20			45	
Ky, Nguyen Cao	Political	30	100		75	
Kyne, Peter B.	Author	5	15	30	10	
Kyser, Kay	Music	15			30	Big Band Leader
L A Law	Ent	100			200	Cast signed by Ten

Name	Field	SIG	DS	ALS	SP	Remarks
La Belle, Patti	Music	15			35	
La Cava, Gregory	Ent	20			45	Director
La Forge, Frank	Music	15			45	
La Revelliere-Lepaux,L.	Political	25	75	150		French Revolution
La Rocque, Rod	Ent	20		50	50	
La Rue, Jack	Ent	20			40	Western Star
La Verne, Lucille	Ent	75			150	Disney Voice
LaBeauf, Sabrina	Ent	15			25	Cosby Show
Labouisse, Eve Curie	Science	15	45	75	35	
Lacepede, Bernhard de	Science	35	75	150		Fr. Naturalist
Lachaise, Gaston	Art	75	125	250		Sculptor/1882 - 1935
Laciura, Anthony	Music	10			25	Opera
Ladd, Alan 1913-64	Ent	50	100		175	
Ladd, Cheryl	Ent	10	20		25	Charlie's Angels
Ladd, David	Ent	10			25	Producer
Ladd, Diane	Ent	5			15	
Ladd, Sue Carol	Ent	5			15	
Laemmle, Carl	Business	100	250	500	700	Founder Universal Studios
Laennec, Rene T.H.	Science	3,500	3,500	6,500		Invented Stethoscope
LaFarge, John 1835-1910	Art	50	100	175		Am Landscape Painter
Lafayette, Marquis de	RevWar	400	800	1,500		
Lagerkvist, P.	Author	30	75	175	100	Nobel Literature 1951
Lagerlof, Selma 1858-40	Author	100	250		150	Nobel Literature 1909
LaGuardia, Fiorello	Political	35	100	125	150	Reform Mayor NYC
Lahm, Frank	Aviation	35	75	150	100	
Lahr, Bert 1895-1967	Ent	275	450		550	Wiz of Oz/Cowardly Lion
Lahti, Christine	Ent	5			20	
Laine, Frankie	Ent	5	20		15	
Laine, J.L.J.Viscount	Military	30	75	175		French Revolution
Lake, Arthur	Ent	50			75	Dagwood (Blondie)
Lake, Ricki	Ent	20			40	TV Talk Show Hostess
Lake, Simon 1866-1945	Science	75	150	450		Submarine
Lake, Veronica 1919-73	Ent	150	250	300	400	Scarce
Lakes, Gary	Music	15			30	Opera
LaLanne, Jack	Ent	10		30	25	TV Body Builder
Lalique, Rene 1860-1929	Art	250		750		Glass Artist
Lamar, Joseph R.	SuprCt	50	100	200		
Lamar, Lucius Q.C.	SuprCt	75		200		CSA Officer/1825-1893
Lamar, Mirabeau B.	Political	100	300			1789-1859
LaMarck, Jean Baptiste	Science	400	900	1,000		Forerunner of Darwin
LaMarr, Hedy	Ent	45	100		90	
LaMartine, Alphonse de	Author	100	200	225		Fr Poet/Statesman

Name	Field	SIG	DS	ALS	SP	Remarks
Lamas, Fernando	Ent	35		75	75	
Lamas, Lorenzo	Ent	10		20	25	
Lamb, Charles	Author	125	250	450		Br. Essayist, Critic
Lamb, Gil	Ent	10			20	Dancer/Comic
Lambert, Christopher	Ent	25			50	Highlander
Lambert, William C.	Aviation	75	125	175	150	WWI ACE
Lammers, Hans	Military	150	450			Hitlers Legal Advisor
Lamond, Frederic	Music	25		75	100	Pianist/Composer
Lamont, Forrest	Music	25			75	Opera
Lamont, Thomas	Political	15		50		Lincoln Pvt. Sec'y
LaMotta, Vikki	Ent	5		20	10	
Lamour, Dorothy	Ent	25	50		50	
L'Amour, Louis 1908-88	Author	100	200	RARE	200	Old West Novelist
Lancaster, Burt	Ent	50	150		90	1913 - 1996
Lanchester, Elsa 1902-86	Ent	75	125		150	Bride of Frankenstein
Land, E. S.	Military	25	50		35	WWII Admiral
Land, Edwin H.1909-92	Science	100	225		175	Polaroid Camera Inventor
Landau, Martin	Ent	25	50		50	AA Winner
Lander, Frederick West	Civil War	150	225	375		Union General/1821-62
Landers, Ann	Author	10		30	20	Advice Columnist
Landers, Audrey	Ent	5	20	20	15	
Landers, Harry	Ent	10			20	
Landers, Judy	Ent	5		20	15	
Landesberg, Steve	Ent	15			25	Barney Miller
Landi, Bruno	Music	25			50	Opera
Landi, Elissa	Ent	45	30		75	
Landis, Carole 1919-48	Ent	75			175	Suicide at 29
Landis, Jessie Royce	Ent	30			75	1904 - 1972
Landis, John	Ent	15			25	Director
Lando, Joe	Ent	15			35	Dr. Quinn
Landon, Alfred M.	Political	25	75	100	50	1887-1987
Landon, Michael	Ent	100	125		200	
Landseer, Charles	Art	30		75		Keeper of Royal Academy
Landseer, Edwin H., Sir	Art	35	75	200		Landscape Painter
Landseer, John	Art	25		125		Father of Edwin H.
Landseer, Thomas	Art	25	50	75		Brother of E. H.
Landsteiner, Karl, Dr.	Science	50	100	175		Nobel Medicine
Lane, Abbe	Music	15			20	Vocalist
Lane, Allan Rocky	Ent	100			250	Voice of Mr. Ed
Lane, Christy	Music	5			15	Gospel Singer
Lane, Diane	Ent	10	20		25	
Lane, Evelyn	Ent	10			25	Brit. Actress. Vintage
Lane, Harriet	First Lady	100	250	375		Actg. lst Lady, Buchanan
Lane, James H. 1814-66	Civil War	100	150	300		Union General/Suicide
Lane, James Henry	Civil War	100	200	300	950	CSA General/1833-1907
Lane, Joseph	Political	50	75	125		First US Senator
Lane, Nathan	Ent	25	50		50	Actor/Disney Voice

Name	Field	SIG	DS	ALS	SP	Remarks
Lane, Priscilla	Ent	10	20	25	25	
Lane, Rosemary	Ent	15	25	35	35	
Lang, Anton	Ent	25	25	45	45	
Lang, Fritz	Ent	100	300		175	Director/Metroplis...
Lang, K. D.	Music	25	45		50	
Lang, Rosa	Ent	5			10	
Lang, Sebastian	Ent	20	25	45	45	
Lang, Walter	Ent	35	45		75	Director
Langan, Glenn	Ent	10		35	25	
Langdon, Harry	Ent	100			225	
Langdon, John	RevWar	200	400	1,200		Signer Constitution
Langdon, Sue Anne	Ent	10			20	
Lange, David	Political	5		30	15	New Zealand
Lange, Hope	Ent	10			30	
Lange, Jessica	Ent	15			45	AA Winner
Lange, Ted	Ent	10			30	Love Boat Bartender
Langella, Frank	Ent	25	50		50	Dracula
Langford, Frances	Music	10			20	Big Band
Langley, Samuel P.	Aviation	250		600		Aeronautical Pioneer
Langmuir, Irving	Science	35	75	125		Nobel Chemistry 1932
Langtry, Lillie 1852-1929	Ent	350		550		Actress/Mistress/Edw VII
Lanier, Sidney	Author	300	500	900		Poet
Lanphier, Thomas G., Jr.	Aviation	40	75	125	100	WWII ACE
Lansbury, Angela	Ent	10		30	25	Murder She Wrote
Lansing, Robert	Political	50	125			Sec'y State
Lansky, Meyer 1902-83	Criminal	300	1,000			Mafia Boss
Lantieri, Rita	Music	10			20	Opera
Lantz, Walter 1900-94	Cartoonist	50	100	100	100	Woody Woodpecker
Lanza, Mario 1921-1959	Music	150			550	Tenor/Died Young
LaPaglia, Anthony	Ent	15			30	
LaPlace, P.M.,Marquis	Science	500				Fr. Astronomer
Lapoype, J.F.C., Baron	Military	25		125		French Revolution
Lara, Joe	Ent	25			45	Tarzan
Lardner, Dionysius	Author	50	175			
Lardner, James L.	Civil War	35	75	125		Union Naval Commodore
Lardner, Ring 1885-1933	Author	75	200	300	75	Am Humorist
Lardner, Ring Jr.	Author	10		35	15	
Laredo, Ruth	Ent	15		30	35	
LaRocca, D.J. Nick	Music	75			200	Composer
Larrey, Dominick Baron	Military	75	150	250		French Revolution
Larroquette, John	Ent	15	25		35	Night Court
Larsen-Todsen, Nanny	Music	25			50	Opera
Larson, Gary	Cartoonist	20			45	Far Side
Larson, Leonard, Dr	Science	5		25	15	
LaRue, Lash	Ent	30		75	60	
Lasker, Mary	Business	5			10	
Lasky, Jesse L.	Ent	50	100	150	85	Pioneer Film Producer

Name	Field	SIG	DS	ALS	SP	Remarks
Lasser, Louise	Ent	10			25	
Laswell, Fred	Cartoonist	25			50	B.Google & Snuffy Smith
Latham, Hubert	Aviation	25		75	75	
Latham, Louise	Ent	10			20	
Lathrop, George P.	Author	25	50	150		Am. Journalist, Writer
Latifah, Queen	Music	20			45	
Latour-Maubourg, M.	Military	25		75		Cavalry Gen.
Latrobe, Benjamin H.	Art	RARE	500	RARE	RARE	Architect of White House
Lattimore, Richard	Author	10		25	15	
Lauck, Chet	Ent	25	75			Radio. Lum & Abner
Lauder, Estee	Business	10			30	Cosmetics
Lauder, Harry, Sir	Ent	50	100	150	75	
Lauer, Matt	Ent	15			25	
Laughton, Charles	Ent	75	125		275	AA Winner/1899-1962
Lauper, Cyndi	Music	25	35	75	50	
Laurants, Arthur	Author	5			20	Playwright
Laurel, Stan 1890-1965	Ent	200	400	550	400	
Laurel,Stan/Hardy,Oliver	Ent	600	1,000		1,200	Signed by Both
Lauren, Ralph	Business	10	20	40	25	Fashion Designer.
Laurencin, Marie	Art	125		450		Fr. Painter & Printmaker
Laurens, Henry 1724-92	RevWar	800	1,200	1,600		Pres. Continental Congress
Laurie, Piper	Ent	5		15	20	
Lauter, Harry	Ent	5			15	
Lauterbach, Johann C.	Music	35	100	200		Ger. Violinist
Lavin, Linda	Ent	20	45		45	Alice
Lavoisier, Antoine L. de	Science	750	RARE	RARE	RARE	Fr. Fndr Modern Chemistry
Law, Andrew Bonar	Political	35	75	125		Br. Prime Minister
Law, Evander McIvor	Civil War	100	250	500		CSA General/1836-1920
Law, John 1671-1729	Political	150				Economist
Law, John Phillip	Ent	10			25	Barbarella
Law, Ruth	Aviation	35			100	
Lawford, Peter 1923 - 84	Ent	55	125		150	Rat Pack member
Lawler, Michael K.	Civil War	35	100			Union General/1814-1882
Lawless, Lucy	Ent	25			50	Xena, Warrior Princess
Lawrence, Barbara	Ent	10			20	
Lawrence, Carol	Ent	5		20	15	
Lawrence, D. H.	Author	300	600	2,000		Lady Chatterly's Lover
Lawrence, Elliot	Music	20			40	Big Band Leader
Lawrence, Ernest	Science	100	275	400	200	Nobel Physics
Lawrence, Gertrude	Ent	20	50		45	1902-1952
Lawrence, Herbert A.	Military	10		50	25	
Lawrence, Ist Baron	Political	10		75		India
Lawrence, Jacob	Art	15	25			
Lawrence, Joey	Ent	20	45		45	Brotherly Love
Lawrence, John	RevWar	35	100	175		Ct Statesman
Lawrence, Marc	Ent	10		25	25	
Lawrence, Marjorie	Music	25			90	Opera

Name	Field	SIG	DS	ALS	SP	Remarks
Lawrence, Sharon	Ent	25			50	NYPD Blue
Lawrence, Steve	Ent	5			15	
Lawrence, Thomas	Art	150	225	200		Br. Portrait Painter
Lawrence, Thos-E.	Author	650	1,250	RARE	RARE	Lawrence of Arabia
Lawrence, Tracy	Music	15			30	
Lawrence, Vicki	Ent	10		20	25	Carol Burnett Show
Lawson, Ted	Aviation	15	30		40	
Lawton, Alexander R.	Civil War	125	300	350		CSA General/1818-96
Lay, Herman W.	Business	10	25	50	35	Lay's Potato Chips
Lazarev, Alexander	Music	25			75	Conductor
Lazarus, Emma 1849-87	Author	RARE	2,000	RARE	RARE	Poem on Statue of Liberty
Lazarus, Mel	Cartoonist	5			20	Miss Peach/Momma
Lazarus, S. Ralph	Business	5			5	Pres.Benrus Watch
Lazenby, George	Ent	25	75		55	James Bond
Lazzari, Virgillo	Ent	15			45	
Lea, Homer	Military	50	150			
Leachman, Cloris	Ent	15	30	35	35	AA Winner
Leadbetter, Danville	Civil War	150	450			CSA General/1811-66
Leahy, William Daniel	Military	35		100	175	
Leake, J. B.	Civil War	25	50	75		
Leakey, Louis B.	Science	50	125	225	75	Anthropologist, Archaeologist
Leakey, Mary D.	Science	15	25	50	30	Anthropologist, Archaeologist
Leakey, Meave, Dr.	Science	20	50			
Leakey, Richard, Dr.	Science	125				Br. Anthropologist
Lean, David, Sir	Ent	50			75	Director
Lear, Edward	Art	150		450		Br. Painter/Poet
Lear, Norman	Ent	10		45	30	TV Producer
Lear, Tobias	RevWar	75	250	325		Pvt Sect to Washington
Lear, William P. Sr.	Business	30	100	150	100	Lear Jet Aircraft
Learned, Michael	Ent	10		20	25	
Leary, Timothy, Dr.	Political	35	75		75	
Leavenworth, Henry	Military	250		750		Frontier Soldier, General
LeBlanc, Matt	Ent	25	75		50	Friends
LeBrock, Kelly	Ent	10	25		35	
Lebrun, Albert 1871-1950	Political	30	50	125	45	
Lebrun, Chas. F. Duc de	Military	50	100	150		3rd Consul/Bonaparte
LeCarre, John	Author	25	75	100	75	Br. Realistic Spy Novels
Lecuona, Ernesto	Music	150			300	Composer
Led Zeppelin	Music	200	400		450	Signed by Entire Band
Ledbetter, Huddie	Music	RARE	RARE	4,000	RARE	RARE/"Leadbelly"/Jazz
Lederer, Francis	Ent	10			25	
Lederman, Leon M., Dr.	Science	15	25	50		Nobel in Physics
Ledger, Heath	Ent	25			50	
Ledoux, Harold	Cartoonist	10			25	Judge Parker
Ledyard, John 1751-89	Explorer		475			Accompanied Capt.Cook
Lee, Anna	Ent	5			15	
Lee, Bernard	Ent	75	150		125	Bond films as M

Name	Field	SIG	DS	ALS	SP	Remarks
Lee, Brandon 1964-93	Ent	200	450	RARE	400	Bruce Lee's Son
Lee, Brenda	Music	5			15	
Lee, Bruce	Ent	600	900	1,500	1,250	Photo/Letters are Scarce
Lee, Canada	Ent	55			125	
Lee, Charles (1731-82)	Military	RARE	RARE	2,000	RARE	Turncoat Gen. Rev. War
Lee, Charles (1758-1815)	Political	125	250	500		Washington's Att'y Gen.
Lee, Christopher	Ent	30	75	75	60	Dracula
Lee, Dr.Tsung-Dao	Science	20		45	25	Nobel Physics
Lee, E. Hamilton	Aviation	15	25	50	35	
Lee, Edwin G.	Civil War	125	250	400		CSA General/1835-70
Lee, Fitzhugh 1835-1905	Civil War	150	200	300	500	CSA General
Lee, Francis Lightfoot	RevWar	600	1,200	2,400		Signer Decl. of Indepen.
Lee, Geo. Wash. Custis	Civil War	150		400		CSA General/1832-1913
Lee, Gypsy Rose 1913-70	Ent	100	200		300	Burlesque Queen
Lee, Harper	Author	75	200		200	To Kill a Mocking Bird
Lee, Henry 1756-1818	RevWar	200	500	500		Light-Horse Harry
Lee, Jason Scott	Ent	15			35	The Bruce Lee Story
Lee, Manfred	Author	125	300	450	RARE	Ellery Queen
Lee, Mary Custis	Civil War	150		500	450	Mrs. Robert E. Lee
Lee, Michelle	Ent	5		15	15	
Lee, Peggy	Music	15	35		45	
Lee, Pinkie	Ent	15			35	
Lee, Richard Henry	RevWar	500	1,600	2,250		Signer Decl. of Indepen.
Lee, Robert E.	Civil War	2,000	3,500		6,500	CSA General/1807-1870
Lee, Robert E.	Military	3,000	7,500	12,500	7,500	CSA General/War Dated
Lee, Ruta	Ent	5			10	
Lee, Samuel P.	Civil War	75	200	275		Union Admiral
Lee, Sheryl	Ent	10			25	
Lee, Spike	Ent	10	25		25	Director
Lee, Stephen Dill	Civil War	125	325	400		CSA General/1833 - 1908
Lee, Tommy	Music	25			50	
Lee, William H. 1837-91	Civil War	200		550		CSA General
Lee, William Raymond	Civil War	15	45	75		Union General/1804-91
Lee, Yuan T., Dr.	Science	20	35	45	30	Nobel Chemistry
Leech, Richard	Music	15			35	Opera
Leeds, Andrea	Ent	10			25	
Leese, Oliver, Sir	Military	20	50		35	WWII Br. General
Leeves, Jane	Ent	25			50	Frasier
Lefebvre, F.J., Duke	Military	150	300			Marshal of Napoleon
LeGallienne, Eva	Ent	10	25	50	35	
LeGallienne, Richard	Author	25	50	75		Brit. Man of Letters
Leger, Fernand	Art	100	250	500		Fr. Abstract Painter
Leggett, Mortimer D.	Civil War	20		75		Union General/1821-96
Legrand, Michel	Music	10	50		25	Composer
Leguizamo, John	Ent	20			45	
LeHand, M. A. (Missy)	Political	20	75	125	45	FDR's Personal Sect.
Lehar, Franz 1870-1948	Music	100	200	550	350	Composer/Merry Widow

Name	Field	SIG	DS	ALS	SP	Remarks
Lehmann, Ernst August	Aviation	100		300		Ger. Aeronautical Engineer
Lehmann, Lilli 1848-1929	Music	150				German Soprano
Lehmann, Lotte	Music	50	75	150	125	Opera
Lehmann, Marie	Music	50			175	
Lehr, Lew	Ent	15		35	30	
Leibman, Ron	Ent	10		20	20	
Leider, Frida	Music	50			150	Opera
Leiferkus, Sergei	Music	10			25	Opera
Leigh, Janet	Ent	5		20	20	Psycho Star
Leigh, Jennifer Jason	Ent	25			50	
Leigh, Vivien 1913-67	Ent	350	450	650	750	Gone with the Wind
Leighton, Frederic	Art	50		150		Pres. Br.Royal Academy
Leighton, Laura	Ent	25			50	Melrose Place
Leinsdorf, Erich	Music	25			75	Austro-Amer Conductor
Leisure, David	Ent	10		35	30	Empty Nest
Lejeune, John Archer	Military	35	75	150	75	Us Marine Corps Cmndr
Leland, Henry M. 1843-32	Business	900	2,500	RARE	RARE	Lincoln Motor Co.
Leland, W. C.	Business	20	50	150	50	
Leloir, Luis Frederico	Science	20	40	50	25	Nobel Chemistry
LeMaire, Charles	Ent	15			25	Director
Lemass, Sean	Political	10	25	50	30	Prime Minister Ireland
LeMay, Curtis S.	Military	30	75		75	AF Gen./WWII/SAC
Lemeshev, Sergei	Music	Scarce	Scarce	Scarce	500	Opera/Russian Tenor
Lemmon, Jack	Ent	25	50	60	50	AA Winner
Lemnitz, Tiana	Music	50			125	Opera
Lemnitzer, Lyman L.	Military	30	50	75	45	WWII Supreme Allied Cmdr
Lemon, Mark 1809-70	Author	15		35		Br Playwright
Lemonheads	Music	25			50	Signed by all
L'Enfant, Pierre Charles	Aviation	400	750	900		
Lenin, Vladimir Ilyich	Political	RARE	RARE	RARE	RARE	
Lennon Sisters, The	Music	20			45	
Lennon, Janet	Ent	15			30	
Lennon, John 1940-1980	Music	475	2,000	1,750	900	Assasinated Beatle
Lennon, Julian	Music	20			45	Johns singing son
Lennon, Kathleen	Ent	10			25	
Lennon, Peggy	Ent	10			25	
Lennox, Annie	Music	25			50	Eurythmics
Lennox, Vera	Ent	10			20	
Leno, Jay	Ent	10			35	Tonite Show Host
Lenoir, William B.	Space	10			20	Astronaut
Lenormand, Rene	Music	50			150	Composer
Lenox, Lucie	Ent	15			40	
Lenske, Rule	Ent	5			15	
Lenya, Lotte	Ent	100	200		200	James Bond Villainess
Leonard, Elmore	Author	15			25	Get Shorty,...
Leonard, Gloria	Ent	5			15	
Leonard, Sheldon	Ent	5			15	

Name	Field	SIG	DS	ALS	SP	Remarks
Leoncavallo, Ruggiero	Music	175	500	500	675	Composer
Leone, Sergio	Ent	100	200	RARE	400	Director of Westerns
Leoni, Tia	Ent	25			50	
Leonov, Aleksei	Space	125	175		275	Cosmonaut/1st Space Walk
Leontif, Wassily, Dr.	Science	20	45		40	Nobel Economics
Leontovich, Eugenie	Ent	15		30	45	
Leopardi, Giacomo	Author	100	300	450		
Leopold I	Royalty	105	475			Belgium
Leopold I	Royalty	100	375	625		Hungary
Leopold II	Royalty	100	300	500		Belgium
Lermontov, Mikhail	Author	750	RARE	RARE	RARE	Novelist/Poet-Killed in Duel
Lerner, Alan Jay 1918-96	Music	50	100		125	Composer
Lerner, Max	Author	10	30	50	25	
LeRoy, Hal	Ent	10			25	Director
LeRoy, Mervyn	Ent	35	50		75	Director
Leslie, Frank 1821-80	Business	100				Fndr Illustrated Newspaper
Leslie, Frank, Mrs.	Business	20		75	75	Leslie's Magazine
Leslie, Joan	Ent	10		20	20	
Leslie, Thomas J.	Civil War	10		35		Union General
Lesseps, Ferdinand, de	Political	150	225	400	450	Engineer/Suez Canal
Lester, Buddy	Ent	5			15	
Lester, Jerry	Ent	15			25	
Lester, Tom	Ent	15	30		30	Green Acres
Lesters, The	Music	10			25	
Leszczynski, Stanislaus	Royalty	575				Stanislaw I, King of Poland
Letcher, John 1813-84	Civil War	100	200	200		CW Gov. VA
Leto, Jared	Ent	25			50	
Letterman, David	Ent	25	50		50	Late Nite Show Host
Letterman, Jonathan	Civil War	100	175			Medical Services
Leutze, Emanuel	Art	75		200		Washington Crossing DE
Levant, Oscar	Ent	20			45	
Levenson, Sam	Ent	10	25		15	Radio, TV Comic
Leventhrope, Collett	Civil War	100	175			CSA General/1815-89
Lever, Lord	Business	35	100	175	75	Br. Soap/Lever Brothers
Levi-Montalcini, Rita, Dr.	Science	20	75			Nobel Medicine
Levin, Ira	Author	25	35		30	Rosemary's Baby
Levine, David	Cartoonist	15			45	Caricaturist
Levine, Irving R.	Ent	5			10	TV News Commentator
Levine, James	Music	15		35	25	Conductor
Levinson, Barry	Ent	10	20		20	
Levy, David H.	Science	15			20	Discovered Meteor Crater
Lewes, Lauren	Ent	10	20	25	20	Love Boat
Lewinsky, Monica	Celebrity	35			75	Mistress Clinton
Lewis, Al	Ent	10	20		20	GrandPa Munster
Lewis, C(live) S(taples)	Author	300	600	1,250		Lion, Witch, Wardrobe ...
Lewis, Cathy	Ent	10			25	
Lewis, Daniel Day	Ent	25			50	

Name	Field	SIG	DS	ALS	SP	Remarks
Lewis, David 'Duffy'	Aviation	15		50	40	
Lewis, Emmanuele	Ent	10	25		25	Webster
Lewis, Francis	RevWar	450	1,250	2,500		Signer Decl. of Indepen.
Lewis, Geoffrey	Ent	5			10	
Lewis, George	Ent	10			20	
Lewis, Huey	Music	25			50	And the News
Lewis, J. C.	Music	10			25	Blues Drummer
Lewis, James	Ent	15		30	25	
Lewis, Jerry	Ent	15	25		30	
Lewis, Jerry Lee	Music	30	100	RARE	65	
Lewis, Joe E.	Ent	20	30	45	40	
Lewis, John	Political	5	15			Civil Rights Leader
Lewis, John L. 1880-1969	Political	50	75	150	100	AFL-CIO Labor Leader
Lewis, Juliette	Ent	25			50	
Lewis, Meriwether	Explorer	RARE	6,000	11,500	RARE	Lewis & Clark Expedition
Lewis, Morgan	RevWar	50	75	100		
Lewis, Ramsey	Music	25			50	Pianist-Composer
Lewis, Richard	Ent	10			20	
Lewis, Shari	Ent	20	40		45	Puppet/Vetriloquist
Lewis, Sinclair 1885-1951	Author	100	300	450	300	First Nobel for Literature
Lewis, Ted	Ent	20	25		75	
Lewis, William Arthur	Science	20	25		25	Nobel Economics
Lewis, William H.	Aviation	10	20	40	30	WWII ACE
Lewishon, Ludwig	Author	20		25		German Author
Lewisohn, Adolph	Business	20	50	75	25	Mining
Lewitt, Sal	Art	25			50	
Ley, Bob	Ent	5			10	ESPN News
Ley, Willy	Science	25	75	150	45	Rocker Expert
Li, Jet	Ent	25			50	
Libby, Willard F.	Science	20	35	50	35	Nobel Chemistry
Liberace	Ent	75	150		150	
Liberace, George	Ent	15	35		35	Liberaces Brother
Lichtenstein, Roy	Art	30	75	150	75	
Liddy, G. Gordon	Political	10	20	45	30	Watergate/Convicted
Lie, Jonas	Author	15	45	75		
Lie, Trygve 1896-1968	Political	50	150	250	175	1st Sect Gen/UN
Lieber, Fritz	Ent	45			100	
Liebermann, Max	Art	125		250		Ger. Impressionist/1847-35
Liebig, Justus von	Science	200				German Chemist
Lieck, Hudson	Ent	25			50	Xena
Liggett, Hunter	Military	15		75	45	Gen. WW I
Liggett, Louis Kroh	Business	100	200	350		Liggett's Drug Store Chain
Light, Judith	Ent	15	20	25	30	
Lightner, Winnie	Ent	20	25	45	45	
Ligi, Josella	Music	10			25	Opera
Liles, Brooks	Aviation	10	20	35	25	USAF WWII ACE
Lilienthal, David E.	Business	15	30		20	

Name	Field	SIG	DS	ALS	SP	Remarks
Lilienthal, Otto 1848-96	Science	RARE	RARE	2,500	RARE	Aeronautical Engineer
Liliuokalani, Lydia K.	Royalty	150	400	750	475	Queen Hawaii
Lillie, Beatrice 1894-1989	Ent	20		60	35	
Lillie, Gordon W.	Western	275	550	750	500	Buffalo Bill's Partner
Limbaugh, Rush	Ent	20			50	Radio/TV Commentator
Lin, Y. S. Maya	Art	25	75			Designed Viet Nam Wall
Lincke, Paul	Music	75	200	325		Composer
Lincoln, Abraham	President	3,000	5,000	9,500	RARE	1809-1865
Lincoln, Benjamin	Military	100	175	500		RevWar General
Lincoln, Benjamin	Political	50	150			Father of Gen. Lincoln
Lincoln, Elmo	Ent	500	RARE	RARE	1,500	First to Play Tarzan
Lincoln, Evelyn	Political	15	25	45	35	JFK Presidential Sec'y
Lincoln, Joseph	Author	15	20	30		
Lincoln, Levi	Political	35	75	125		Memb. Continental Congr
Lincoln, Mary Todd	First Lady	350	900	1,500	RARE	
Lincoln, Robert Todd	Political	100	200	300		Capt. CW.
Lincoln, Rufus	RevWar	RARE	1,650	RARE	RARE	
Lind, Jenny	Ent	100	300	300	750	Opera/1820-87
Lindberg, Charles W.	Military	25	50		50	Iwo Jima Flag Raiser
Lindbergh, Anne Morrow	Author	15	45	75	45	Am. Writer-Poet.
Lindbergh, Charles A.	Aviation	575	1,250	2,400	2,500	1902-1974
Linden, Hal	Ent	10	20		20	Barney Miller
Lindfors, Viveca	Ent	15			45	
Lindholm, Bent	Music	10			25	Opera
Lindley, Audra	Ent	20			40	Three's Company
Lindsay, E. Lin	Aviation	10	20	35	30	ACE, WWII USAAF Ace
Lindsay, Howard	Ent	10		25	25	Theatrical Producer
Lindsay, John	Political	5			10	Mayor NYC
Lindsay, Margaret	Ent	15	25	45	50	
Lindsay, Vachel	Author	50	150	350	150	Poet/Artist
Lindsey, George	Ent	10	20		25	Andy Griffith Show
Lindstrom, Pia	Ent	5			15	TV News
Linkletter, Art	Ent	10	25		15	Radio-TV MC,
Linnaeus, Carolus von	Science	900	RARE	RARE	RARE	Botanist
Linn-Baker, Mark	Ent	15	35		35	Perfect Strangers
Linville, Larry	Ent	30	50		50	MASH
Liotta, Ray	Ent	25			50	
Lipchitz, Jacques	Art	125	200	225		Cubist Sculptor
Lipfert, Helmut	Aviation	35			75	German ACE
Lipkovska, Lydia	Music	100			300	Rus. Soprano
Lipman, Clara	Ent	10			20	Stage Actress
Lipmann, Fritz A.	Science	25	45	75	40	Nobel Medicine 1953
Lippman, Walter	Author	25	75		30	Journalist, Editor, Pulitzer
Lipscomb, William N.	Science	20	35		30	Nobel Chemistry
Lipsner, B.B.	Aviation	30	75		100	Pioneer Air Mail Pilot
Lipton, Peggy	Ent	15	45		45	Mod Squad
Lipton, Thomas, Sir	Business	125	550	900	400	Br. Tea Merchant

Name	Field	SIG	DS	ALS	SP	Remarks
List, Emanuel	Ent	35			75	
Lister, Joseph, Lord	Science	225	400	600		1827-1912
Liston, Robert 1794-1847	Science	15	30	50		Skilled Scottish Surgeon
Liszt, Franz 1811-86	Music	450	650	950	1,600	Composer
Litchfield, Grace D.	Author	10		25		1849-1944
Litel, John 1892-1964	Ent	15		35	35	
Lithgow, John	Ent	25	50		50	Third Rock from the Sun
Little Richard	Music	35	125		75	Penniman
Little River Band	Music	35	100		75	Signed by Entire Band
Little, Cleavon	Ent	45			100	Blazing Saddles
Little, Little Jack	Music	15			35	Big Band Leader
Little, Rich	Ent	5			10	
Littlejohn, Dewitt C.	Civil War	40	75	125		Union Officer/1818-1892
Litvinov, Maksim M.	Political	50		100	75	Soviet Foreign Minister
Liu, Lucy	Ent	25			50	
Livermore, Mary A.	Political	50	75	125		Womans Suffrage
Liverpool, 2nd Earl	Political	100	150	200		
Livingston, Alan	Music	15	50			Composer
Livingston, Edward	Political	30	75	150		Sec'y of State 1831
Livingston, Henry B.	SuprCt	100	300	600		1757 - 1823
Livingston, Jay	Music	15	50	75	50	Composer
Livingston, Margaret	Ent	10			25	
Livingston, Mary	Ent	15	25	45	40	
Livingston, Philip	RevWar	300	900	1,200		Signer Decl. of Indepen.
Livingston, Robert	Ent	35			75	
Livingston, Robert	RevWar	175	350	400		1742-94
Livingston, Robert R.	RevWar	200	400	900		Continental Congress
Livingston, Stanley	Ent	15			35	
Livingston, William	RevWar	300	900	1,500		Continental Congress
Livingstone, David	Explorer	400	800	1,500		1813-187
LL Cool J	Music	25			50	
Llewelyn, Desmond	Ent	25			60	Q" in James Bond films
Lloyd, Christopher	Ent	20	50		50	Taxi
Lloyd, Emily	Ent	15			40	
Lloyd, Frank	Ent	35	75			AA Winning Director
Lloyd, Harold 1894-1971	Ent	200	275		400	
Lloyd, Jake	Ent	25			55	Star Wars/Anakin
Lloyd-George, David	Political	100	250	400	250	Br. Prime Minister, lst Earl
Lo Giudici, Franco	Music	50			150	Opera
Loan, Nguyen Ngoc	Military	150			375	Gen. Viet Nam
Locane, Amy	Ent	25			50	Melrose Place
Locke, John 1632-1704	Author	700	1,750	RARE	RARE	
Locke, Sandra	Ent	10		20	30	
Locke, William John	Author	20	35	75	35	Br. Novelist
Lockhart, Gene	Ent	20			50	
Lockhart, June	Ent	10	25		35	Lost in Space/Lassie
Lockheed, Alan	Aviation	75	150	250	150	Aviator/Plane Designer

Name	Field	SIG	DS	ALS	SP	Remarks
Locklear, Heather	Ent	10	20	25	35	
Lockwood, Belva A.	Political	225	325	700		
Lockwood, Gary	Ent	10			25	
Lockwood, Margaret	Ent	15		45	55	1916-1990
Lodge, Henry Cabot	Political	45	150	200	100	
Lodge, Henry Cabot, Jr.	Political	25	50	75	45	Ambassador UN, Diplomat
Lodge, Oliver J., Sir	Science	75	125	225	250	Br. Physicist, Spiritualist
Loeb, William	Business	15	30	50	35	
Loesser, Frank	Music	125				Broadway Composer
Loew, Marcus	Business	30		75	50	
Loewe, Frederick	Music	35	75	150	50	Composer/1901-1988
Loewy, Raymond	Business	35	100	150	75	Designer
Lofting, Hugh 1886-1947	Author	100				
Logan, Benjamin 1752-02	Military	350	560	675		Pioneer Hero
Logan, Ella	Ent	5		20	15	
Logan, John A. 1826-86	Civil War	100	200	250		Union General
Logan, Josh(ua) 1908-88	Ent	30	50		50	Producer/Director
Logan, Olive	Author	25	35			
Logan, Thomas M.	Civil War	100	225	400		CSA General/1840-1919
Loggia, Robert	Ent	5	20		20	
Loggins and Messina	Music	25	50		50	
Loggins, Kenny	Music	20			45	
Lolobrigida, Gina	Ent	10			35	
Lom, Herbert	Ent	25			45	
Lomax, Lunsford Lindsey	Civil War	100	250	350		CSA General/1835-1913
Lombard, Carole	Ent	275	750	RARE	750	1908 - 1942
Lombardi, Vince	Sports	200	300		450	1971 HOF/Coach
Lombardo, Guy 1902-77	Music	25	75	125	100	Big Band Leader
London, George	Music	35			75	Opera
London, Jack 1876-1916	Author	400	750	RARE	RARE	Novelist (Am)
London, Julie	Ent	5			15	
London, Tom	Ent	50			100	
Long, Armistead L.	Civil War	75	100	350		CSA General/1825-91
Long, Huey P.	Political	75	175			Sen/Gov LA
Long, Johnny	Music	25			50	Big Band. Violinist
Long, Lotus	Ent	10			30	
Long, Pierse 1739-89	RevWar	30	75	150		Continental Congress
Long, Richard	Ent	25			75	
Long, Shelley	Ent	20	45		50	Cheers
Longacre, James B.	Political	150		400		Chief Engr. of US Mint
Longfellow, Henry W.	Author	175		600	950	Poet/1807-1882
Longstreet, James	Civil War	400	900	1,200	900	CSA General/1821-1904
Loo, Richard	Ent	25			50	
Loomis, Gustavus	Civil War	35	75	100		Union General/1789-1872
Loos, Anita	Author	15	35	75	35	Am Novelist
Loos, Walter	Aviation	10		35	25	
Loper, Don	Business	5	15	25	10	Fashion Designer

Name	Field	SIG	DS	ALS	SP	Remarks
Lopez, Jennifer	Ent	25			50	Selena
Lopez, Vincent	Music	20			50	Big Band Leader
Loraine, Robert	Aviation	20		50		
Lorca, Frederico Garcia	Author	400	1,200	RARE	RARE	Poet
Lord, Jack	Ent	35	75		75	Hawaii 5-0
Lord, Marjorie	Ent	10			25	Danny Thomas Show
Lord, Walter	Author	5			10	
Lords, Traci	Ent	15	40	40	40	
Loren, Sophia	Ent	10	30		30	
Lorengar, Pilar	Music	20			40	Opera
Lorillard, Peter	Business	125	250	450		Tobacco Industry
Loring, Gloria	Ent	5	15		15	
Loring, Wm. Wing	Civil War	125	250	300	425	CSA General/1818-86
Lorne, Marion	Ent	100	150		200	Bewitched's Aunt Clara
Lorre, Peter	Ent	150	250		300	1904 - 1964
Losey, Joseph	Ent	15			45	Director
Lott, Felicity	Music	15			35	Opera
Loubet, Emile Frangois	Political	25		125		Pres. France 1899-1906
Loughlin, Lori	Ent	20			45	
Louis Philippe (Fr)	Royalty	75	200	350		Citizen King Duc D'Orleans
Louis XII (Fr)	Royalty	800	1,500	RARE		King of France
Louis XIII (Fr)	Royalty	500	900	RARE		King of France
Louis XIV (Fr)	Royalty	450	1,000	RARE		The Sun King
Louis XV	Royalty	750	900	RARE		King of France
Louis XVI	Royalty	375	600			King of France. Guillotined
Louis XVIII (Fr) 1755-1824	Royalty	200	400	1,250		Louis Stanislas Xavier
Louise Caroline Alberta	Royalty	25		75	175	4th Daugfhter of Queen
Louise, Anita	Ent	25			45	1915 - 1970
Louise, Tina	Ent	10			30	Gilligans Island/Ginger
Louise, Victor	Royalty	35		100	150	Princess Royal
Love, Bessie	Ent	25	50		60	
Love, Courtney	Music	25			50	Hole
Love, Montagu	Ent	20			50	
Love, Mother	Ent	5			15	
Lovecraft, H. P.	Author	500	RARE	1,250	RARE	Horror Writer
Lovejoy, Frank	Ent	25			50	
Loveless, Patty	Music	15			45	
Lovell, Bernard Dr.	Science	15		40	20	
Lovell, James	RevWar	75	200	450		Continental Congress
Lovell, James A. Jr.	Space	45	125		125	
Lovell, Mansfield 1822-84	Civil War	100	250	300		CSA General
Loverboy	Music	25			50	
Lovett, Lyle	Music	25			50	
Low, David, Sir	Cartoonist	25	50	100	150	
Low, Nicholas	RevWar	100	250	450		Backed Revolution
Low, Seth 1819-1916	Political	15		45		Mayor NYC
Lowe, Ed	Science	20			45	Kitty Litter Inventor

Name	Field	SIG	DS	ALS	SP	Remarks
Lowe, Edmund	Ent	45		75	75	1890 - 1971
Lowe, Hudson, Sir	Military	200		500		Last custodian of Napoleon
Lowe, Rob	Ent	20			45	
Lowe, Thaddeus S.	Civil War	200	325	500		Aeronaut/Ballonist
Lowell, Amy	Author	45	125	250		Poet/Critic
Lowell, Carey	Ent	10	20		25	James Bond Girl/Law & Order
Lowell, James Russell	Author	75	150	225	350	Poet
Lowell, John H.	Aviation	15	25	40	35	WWII ACE
Lowell, Percival	Science	20	45	75		Am. Astronomer, Author
Lowell, Robert	Author	50	150			Pulitzer Poetry
Lowery, Robert	Ent	75	150		125	Serial Batman
Loy, Myrna 1905-93	Ent	25	50	50	60	
Lubbock, Francis R.	Civil War	150	185	295	350	CSA Governor TX
Lubin, Arthur	Ent	25			75	Director
Lubin, Germaine	Music	100			275	Opera
Lubitsch, Ernst	Ent	65			125	Director
Lubke, Heinrich	Political	10		25		Pres. Ger. Fed. Repub.
Lucas, George	Ent	35	150		75	Director/Star Wars...
Lucca, Pauline	Music	30	75	100		Opera
Lucci, Susan	Ent	5		20	20	Soap Star
Luce, Clare Boothe	Author	30	100	150	45	Ambassador, Playwright
Luce, Henry R.	Business	40	100		50	Time, Life, Fortune, Sports
Luce, Stephen Bleecker	Military	10	35	75	30	
Luckinbill, Laurence	Ent	20			50	Star Trek Movies
Luckner, Felix, von	Military	75	200	200	100	The Sea Devil WWII
Luckner, Nicholas	Military	225	550			
Ludden, Allen	Ent	10			25	
Ludde-Neurath, Walter	Military	15			45	Aide-de-camp to Donitz
Ludendorff, Erich von	Military	100	225	350	275	WWI German General
Ludin, Hanns	Military	130	350			WWII Germ Storm Trooper
Ludlington, Marshall	Civil War	75	125	200		Union Officer
Ludlum, Robert	Author	15		45	30	Super Spy novels
Ludwig I 1786-1868	Royalty	100	300	450		King of Bavaria
Ludwig II	Royalty	100	250	400		King of Bavaria
Ludwig, Emil	Author	50	125	200		
Lufbery, Raoul	Aviation	125	350	550	400	WWI ACE
Luft, Lorna	Ent	10			20	Judy Garlands Daughter
Lugosi, Bela 1882-1956	Ent	350	1,750	RARE	1,200	SP as Dracula - 2500
Lukas, Foss	Music	25			75	Composer
Lukas, Paul	Ent	50			100	AA Winner/1887-1971
Luke, Frank	Aviation	150	400	600	500	WWI ACE
Luke, Keye	Ent	25	50		50	Charlie Chan films/Kung Fu
Luks, George Benjamin	Art	20	50	200		1867-1933
Lum & Abner	Ent	40	100		75	Both
Lumet, Sidney	Ent	30	50		75	TV Director
Lumiere, Louis 162-1954	Science	175		500	375	Cinematographe Projector
Lumley, Joanna	Ent	5	20		15	

Name	Field	SIG	DS	ALS	SP	Remarks
Luna, Barbara	Ent	10	25	25	25	
Lunceford, Jimmie	Music	50			125	Big Band Leader
Lund, John	Ent	5	15		15	
Lunden, Joan	Ent	10			20	TV Host
Lundgren, Dolph	Ent	20			40	
Lundigan, William	Ent	15			30	
Lunney, G.	Space	5			15	Astronaut
Lunt, Alfred & Fontaine	Ent	45			100	
Lupino, Ida	Ent	25	75	75	75	1914 - 1995
Lupino, Stanley 1893-42	Ent	15			35	
Lupton, John	Ent	10			20	
Lupus, Peter	Ent	10			25	TV's Mission Impossible
Luria, Salvador F.	Science	20	35	50	45	Nobel Medicine
Lurie, Bob	Business	10		45	25	
Luse, Harley	Music	10			20	
Luther, Hans	Political	40	50	75		Chancellor Ger., Ambass
Luther, Martin	Clergy	15,000	40,000	55,000	RARE	
Lutzow, Gunther	Aviation	175		445	450	
Lvov, Alexis	Music	75		200		Russian Composer
Lyautey, Louis	Military	15	50	75	35	Marshal of France
Lyell, Charles, Sir	Science	100		350		Br Fndr Modern Geology
Lyman, Abe	Music	15			45	Big Band Leader
Lynch, David	Ent	25			50	TV Director
Lynch, John R.	Political		250			
Lynch, Kelly	Ent	20			50	
Lynch, Thomas Jr.	RevWar	20,000	35,000	RARE	RARE	Signer
Lynde, Paul	Ent	35	50		75	Bewitched's Uncle Arthur
Lynen, Feodor	Science	20	40		35	Nobel Medicine
Lynley, Carol	Ent	20		45	45	
Lynn, Diana 1926-1971	Ent	45			75	Bedtime for Bonzo
Lynn, Jeffrey	Ent	10			25	
Lynn, Loretta	Music	5	25		20	Country
Lynn, Vera Dame	Music	25			75	Br. WW II Singing Star
Lyon, Ben	Ent	15			35	
Lyon, Nathaniel 1818-61	Civil War	350	RARE	RARE	RARE	Union General. KIA
Lyon, Sue	Ent	10			25	
Lyons, Lord Admiral	Military	25		125		
Lyons, Richard B.P.	Royalty	25		100		1st Earl
Lytell, Bert	Ent	30	50	100	75	
Lytton, E. George B.	Author	50	100	200		

Name	Field	SIG	DS	ALS	SP	Remarks
Ma, Yo Yo	Music	30			60	Cellist
Mabley, Jackie Moms	Ent	75			200	
MacArthur, Arthur	Military	50	100	125	75	Span - Am War General
MacArthur, Charles	Author	15	30		25	Playwright
MacArthur, Douglas	Military	225	600	750	500	Five Star General/WWII
MacArthur, James	Ent	15			35	
MacArthur, Jean	Military	15		25	20	Mrs. Douglas MacArthur
MaCartney, George	Political	10	35	75		
MaCaulay, (Emilie) Rose	Author	10	20	35		Br. Novelist and Critic
MaCaulay, Thos. B. Lord	Author	50	75	100		Historian/Poet
Macbeth, Florence	Music	20			50	Am. Soprano
Macchio, Ralph	Ent	25	50		50	Karate Kid
MacDonald, Charles H.	Aviation	15		50	45	WWII ACE
MacDonald, J. Farrell	Ent	25			50	
MacDonald, J. Ramsey	Political	45	125	175	250	British Prime Minister
MacDonald, Jacques E.J.	Military	75	100	250		Marshal of Napoleon
MacDonald, Jeanette	Ent	75	175	275	175	
MacDonald, John A.	Political	35	75			Ist Prime Minister/Canada
MacDonald, Ross	Author	50	150	250		Mystery Writer
MacDonogh, P. M. W.	Military	10		25		
MacDonough, Thomas	Military	100	300	600		
MacDowell, Andie	Ent	20	45		45	
MacDowell, Edward	Music	150	300	600	400	Composer
MacDowell, Melbourne	Ent	15			40	
MacFadden, Bernarr	Business	15	45	75	35	Publisher
MacGraw, Ali	Ent	15	30		25	
Machado, Anesia P.	Aviation	35	50	75	75	
Machiavelli, Niccolo	Author	500	1,250	RARE	RARE	1469-1527
Mack, Helen	Ent	10			30	
Mack, Marion	Ent	10		45	35	
Mack, Ted	Ent	10			25	Amateur Hour
Mackaill, Dorothy	Ent	20	35	75	75	
MacKall, William W.	Civil War	125	250			CSA General/1816-91
Mackay, John William	Business	50	100	200		Founder Postal Telegraph
MacKaye, Percy 1875-56	Author	40	100	150		Am. Poet
Mackensen, August von	Military	20		50	75	WWI Ger Field Marshal
Mackenzie, Morell, Sir	Science	75	175	350		
Mackie, Bob	Business	5		25	15	Fashion Designer
MacLachlan, Kyle	Ent	10			30	
MacLaine, Shirley	Ent	15		35	50	
MacLane, Barton	Ent	50			125	Maltese Falcon...
MacLaren, Donald M.	Military	25	50	100	75	

Name	Field	SIG	DS	ALS	SP	Remarks
MacLeish, Archibald	Author	30	100	125	50	Am Poet
MacLeod, Gavin	Ent	5		20	20	Love Boat Captain
MacInnes, Helen	Author	10		20		Novelist
MacMahon, Aline	Ent	25			75	
MacMahon, Marie E.P.	Political	35	100	200		Fr.Soldier, Marshal
MacMillan, Donald B.	Explorer	50	75	150		Am. w/Peary /North Pole
MacMillan, Harold	Political	25	75	150	50	British Prime Minister
MacMurray, Fred	Ent	25	75		50	1907 - 1991
MacNee, Patrick	Ent	20	40	50	40	The Avengers
MacNelly, Jeff	Cartoonist	25			50	Shoe
MacPherson, Elle	Ent	25			45	Super Model
MacRae, Gordon	Ent	20			35	1921 - 1986
MacRae, Meredith	Ent	5			15	
MacRae, Sheila	Ent	5			15	
MacReady, George	Ent	20			40	
MacReady, William C.	Ent	15			45	
MacVeagh, Franklin	Political	10	25	50	25	Sec'y Treasury
MacVeagh, Wayne	Political	50		100		Attorney General
Macy, Bill	Ent	5	20		15	Maude
Macy, William	Ent	25			50	
Madden, Charles Edw.	Military	35	100	200	100	British Admiral
Madeira, Jean	Music	15			40	Am. Contralto
Madigan, Amy	Ent	15			40	
Madison, Dolley Payne	First Lady	RARE	RARE	12,000	RARE	1768-1849
Madison, Guy	Ent	15			35	
Madison, James	President	550	1,000	3,000	2,500	1751-1836
Madonna	Music	150	600	900	250	
Madriguera, Enric	Music	15			30	Big Band Leader
Madsen, Chris	Western	RARE	RARE	RARE	RARE	Outlaw & Indian Fighter
Madsen, Michael	Ent	15			30	
Madsen, Virginia	Ent	10			25	
Maeterlinck, Maurice	Author	35	100	200	425	Nobel in Literature
Magnani, Anna	Ent	275			450	1908 - 1973
Magrath, Andrew G.	Civil War	35	75	75		CSA Governor of SC
Magritte, Renb 1898-1967	Art	200	350	900		Surrealist Painter
Magruder, John B.	Civil War	275	525	475		CSA General/1807-71
Magsaysay, Ramon	Political	25	50	150	45	Pres. Philippines
Maguire, Toby	Ent	25			50	
Maguire, W.A Cpt.	Military	25	50	75	50	
Mahan, Alfred Thayer	Military	50	75	100		US Naval Officer
Maharis, George	Ent	10		25	20	
Mahen, Robert A.	Business	15	30	70	40	
Mahendra Bir Bikram	Royalty	35	50	125	50	King, Leader Nepal
Mahler, Alma	Author	35		125		
Mahler, Gustav 1860-1911	Music	550	1,200	3,500	RARE	Austrian Composer
Mahone, William	Civil War	125	250	350		CSA General/1826-95
Mahoney, Jock	Ent	25	50	50	50	

Name	Field	SIG	DS	ALS	SP	Remarks
Mahoney, John	Ent	20			45	Frasier
Mahurin, Walker M.	Aviation	20	35	50	40	WWII ACE
Maiakovski, Vladimir V.	Author	300	600	RARE	RARE	
Mailer, Norman	Author	35	125	175	75	
Maillol, Aristide	Art	200	400	800		Fr Sculptor
Main, Marjorie	Ent	100	250		250	
Maintenon, Francoise	Royalty			900		2nd Wife Louis XIV
Maison, Nicholas J.	Military	45	150	175		General under Napoleon
Maison, Rene	Music	35			65	Opera
Maitland, Lester J.	Aviation	20		40		
Major, John	Political	10			30	Br. Prime Minister
Majors, Lee	Ent	10	25		30	Six Million Dollar Man
Makarios III, Mikhail	Political	50	75	150	75	Cyprus
Makarova, Natalia	Music	10			15	Ballet
Malamud, Bernard	Author	25	50	100	30	Am. Novelist, Pulitzer
Malcolm X 1925 - 1965	Political	1,250	4,000	14,000	RARE	Playboy Interview - 3000
Malden, Karl	Ent	10	25		25	
Malenkov, Georgi M.	Political	175	350		250	Union Sov. Russia
Malet, C. Francois de	Military	125	250			Gen/Court martial/Shot
Malher, J.P.F.	Military	25	75			French Revolution
Malis, David	Music	10			25	Opera
Malko, Nicolai	Music	75			225	Russian Conductor
Malkovich, John	Ent	25	50		50	
Mallarme, Stephane	Author	150				French Poet
Malle, Louis	Ent	30			75	Director
Mallory, Charles M.	Aviation	10	25	35	30	WWII ACE
Mallory, Stephen R.	Civil War	125	225	240		CSA Sec'y of Navy.
Malmesbury, Ist Earl	Political	15		45		
Malone, Dorothy	Ent	35	50		75	
Malten, Therese	Music	35			125	Opera
Malthus, Thomas Robert	Author	300	900			Educator, Author
Mamas and the Papas	Music	350	750		775	Signed by all four members
Mamet, David	Ent	10			25	DIrector
Mamoulian, Rouben	Ent	35			125	Director
Mana-Zucca	Music	35			100	Composer/Singer
Manchester, Melissa	Music	20			40	
Manchester, William	Author	5		20	15	
Mancini, Henry	Music	30	75		75	Composer/Conductor
Mandel, Howie	Ent	10			20	
Mandela, Nelson	Political	200	RARE	RARE	375	
Manderson, Charles	Civil War	70	100	150		Union General/1837-1911
Mandrell, Barbara	Music	10			25	Country
Mandylor, Costas	Ent	20			40	
Manet, Edouard 1832-83	Art	RARE	2,000	RARE	RARE	Impressionist School Fndr
Maney, George E.	Civil War	150				CSA General/1826-1901
Manfrini, Luigi	Music	45			125	Opera
Mangano, Silvana	Ent	25	35	50	50	

Name	Field	SIG	DS	ALS	SP	Remarks
Mangione, Chuck	Music	5	20		20	Trumpet
Manhattan Transfer	Music	35			75	Signed by Entire Band
Manheim, Camryn	Ent	25			50	
Manigault, Arthur M.	Civil War	125	250			CSA General/1824-86
Manilow, Barry	Music	25	50		50	
Mankiewicz, Joseph L.	Ent	20		50	50	AA Winning Director
Mankiller, Wilma	Author	5			20	
Manley, N. W.	Political	10		25	25	Prime Minister Jamaica
Mann, Delbert	Ent	20			45	Director
Mann, Hank	Ent	100				Keystone Kop
Mann, Heinrich	Author	35	125	200		German Novelist
Mann, Horace 1796-1859	Political	35	125	250		Education Reformer
Mann, Iria	Ent	10			20	
Mann, Manfred	Music	100			175	Signed by entire group
Mann, Orrin L.	Civil War	20	45	50		Union Officer
Mann, Thomas	Aviation	15	25	50	50	WWII Double ACE
Mann, Thomas 1875-1955	Author	200	450	900	1,100	Novelist/Nobel
Manne, Shelly	Music	15			45	Drummer
Mannerheim,C. Gustave	Political		300	750	775	Pres. Finland
Mannering, Mary	Ent	15			25	
Manners, David	Ent	45	75		75	
Manning, Irene	Ent	5			10	
Manning, Stephen H.	Civil War	30	50	100		Union Officer
Manoff, Dinah	Ent	10	30		30	Empty Nest
Manone, Wingy	Music	20			50	Jazz Trumpet
Mansfield, Joseph K.F.	Civil War	150	300	400		Union General/1803-62
Mansfield, Jayne	Ent	175	350		400	1933 - 1967
Mansfield, Joseph K.	Civil War	275	RARE	RARE	RARE	Union Gen.KIA 1862
Mansfield, Richard	Ent	50		150		
Manship, Paul Howard	Art	75	275	450		Am Sculptor
Manson, Charles	Criminal	75	250	350	200	Murderer, Cult Figure
Manson, Marilyn	Music	40			80	Signed by Entire Group
Manson, Marilyn	Music	25			50	
Manstein, Erich von	Military	25	75	100	75	Planned Assault vs France WWII
Mantegna, Joe	Ent	15			35	
Mantell, Gideon A .	Science	10	25	40		Paleontologist
Mantelli, Eugenia	Music	25			65	Opera
Manteuffel, Edwin F.	Military	150	300	400		WWII Pruss Field Marshal
Manteuffel, Hasso von	Military	50	150	200	100	Ger. Tank Commander
Mantle, Mickey	Sports	75			150	Baseball/1974 HOF
Mantovani	Music	10			20	Conductor-Arranger
Manuel, Lisa	Business	100	300			Fur Trader
Mao, Tse Tung	Political	3,000	RARE	RARE	RARE	Chinese Communist Leader
Maples, Marla	Ent	10			25	
Mapleson, James H.	Music	75				Opera
Marat, Jean-Paul	Military	RARE	RARE	4,500	RARE	
Marbot, J.B.A.M.	Military	25	75	125		Napoleonic General

Name	Field	SIG	DS	ALS	SP	Remarks
Marceau, Marcel	Ent	25	75		95	Mime
Marceau, Sophie	Ent	30			60	James Bond Girl
March, Fredric 1897-1975	Ent	35	75	100	100	AA Winner
Marchesi, Mathilde	Music	50		160	175	Ger. Mezzo-Sopr. Teacher
Marciano, Rocky	Sports	250			600	Boxer
Marconi, Guglielmo	Science	300	750	1,250	750	Inventor/Nobel 1874-1937
Marcos, Ferdinand E.	Political	50	125		125	Pres. Philippines
Marcos, Imelda	Political	15	35		25	Phillipines
Marcus, Rudolph A.	Science	20	35		30	Nobel Chemistry
Marcus, Stanley	Business	25	75	150	50	Merchant. Nieman-Marcus
Marcy, Randolph B.	Civil War	60		150		Union General/1812-87
Marcy, William L.	Political	50	150	225		Sec'y War, State
Maren, Jerry	Ent	15	45		35	Oz Munchkin
Marescot, Armand S.	Military	50		150		French Revolution
Maressyev, Alexei	Aviation	125				Russian ACE
Maret, Hugues B.	Military	75	150	300		Napoleans Advisor
Maret, Hugues B.	Military	100	200			PM/Napolean Advisor
Margie	Cartoonist	25			75	Little Lulu
Margret, Ann	Ent	15			35	
Marguerite De Valois	Royalty		1,750			Queen of France
Maria (Castile)	Royalty		2,500			Queen of Alfonso V
Maria Theresa 1717-80	Royalty	200	600	900		
Mariborough,John C.	Military	220	700			British General
Marie Amelie	Royalty	175	250	500		Queen of Louis Phillippe I
Marie Antoinette (Fr)	Royalty	1,200	4,850	RARE	RARE	Queen of Louis XVI France
Marie of Modena	Royalty	350	550			Queen of James II
Marie of Naples	Royalty	20		75		Queen of King Louis-Phillipe I
Marie of Romania	Royalty	75	125	250	100	
Marin, John	Art	100	225	450		Am. Watercolorist
Marinaro, Ed	Ent	5			15	
Marion, Francis 1732-95	RevWar	4,000	7,500	12,500	RARE	The Swamp Fox
Mariscal, Don Ignacio	Political	20	35	50		VP/Mexico
Markey, Enid 1890 - 1981	Ent	150	Scarce	Scarce	Scarce	First Jane/Tarzan
Markham, Edwin	Author	35	125	140	75	The Man With The Hoe
Markham, William	Political	150	400			Colonial Gov. PA
Markova, Alicia	Music	20			50	Ballet
Markowitz, Harry M., Dr.	Science	20	35	45		Nobel Economics
Marks, Johnny	Music	35	75	125	50	Composer
Marks, William, Jr.	Political	35	150			PA Senator
Marley, Bob	Music	600	RARE	RARE	RARE	Rock HOF
Marlin, Mahlon F.	Business	50	125	200		Pres/Marlin Firearms
Marlow, Lucy	Ent	5			15	
Marlowe, Hugh	Ent	25			50	
Marlowe, Julia	Ent	25	35	75	75	
Marmaduke, John	Civil War			2,400		CSA General
Marmont, A.F.L.V. Duke	Military	50	100			Marshal of France
Marquand, John P.	Author	40	125	150	50	Am. Novelist. Pulitzer

Name	Field	SIG	DS	ALS	SP	Remarks
Marques, Antonio	Music	35			75	Opera
Marquez, Gabriel	Author	100			200	Nobel Prize Winner
Marriott, J.	Business	20	35	75	45	Marriott Hotel Chain
Marryat, Frederick	Military	35	100	200		Br. Naval Cmmdr. Novelist
Marsala, Joe	Music	30			75	Composer
Marsalis, Branford	Music	10			25	Conductor
Marsalis, Wynton	Music	15			30	Trumpet
Marsh, Jean	Ent	10			20	
Marsh, Joan	Ent	15		40	35	
Marsh, Mae	Ent	30	50	75	50	
Marsh, Marion	Ent	15			40	
Marsh, Ngaio, Dame	Author	20		50	40	
Marshall, Catherine	Author	75	100	150	125	
Marshall, E. G.	Ent	10			25	
Marshall, George C.	Military	200	300	500	400	WWII Chief of Staff
Marshall, George E.	Ent	35			75	Director
Marshall, Herbert	Ent	35	75		75	1890 - 1966
Marshall, Humphrey	Civil War	200	300			CSA General/1812-72
Marshall, John	SuprCt	750	1,250	2,500		Chief Justice
Marshall, John, Sir	Political	10		35	20	Prime Minister/New Zealand
Marshall, Margaret	Music	10			25	Opera
Marshall, Penny	Ent	20	50		50	Actress/Director
Marshall, Peter	Ent	20			40	Hollywood Squares
Marshall, Thomas R.	Vice Pres	75	175	400	175	Wilson VP
Marshall, Thurgood	SuprCt	100	200		175	Ist Afro-Am. Justice
Marshall, William	Civil War	25	50	75		Union General/1825-96
Marshall, William	Ent	15			25	Director
Marston, Gilman 1811-90	Civil War	30	75			Union General
Marterie, Ralph	Music	10			20	Big Band Leader
Martin & Lewis	Ent	150	450		250	Both Signed
Martin, Andrea	Ent	10			20	
Martin, Chris Pin	Ent	50		100		
Martin, Dean 1917-95	Ent	35	75		100	
Martin, Dean Vincent	Ent	5			15	
Martin, Dewey	Ent	10			25	
Martin, Dick	Ent	10			25	Laugh In
Martin, Frank 1890-1974	Music	20			75	Swiss Composer
Martin, Freddie	Music	35			75	Big Band Leader-Pianist
Martin, George	Music	25			75	Beatle's Producer
Martin, Glenn L.	Aviation	75	150	250	250	Aeronautical Pioneer
Martin, James Green	Civil War	100	225			CSA General/1819-78
Martin, Kellie	Ent	10			25	
Martin, Luther	RevWar	100	175	300		Continental Congress
Martin, Mary 1913-1990	Ent	35	50		60	Peter Pan on Broadway
Martin, Pamela Sue	Ent	15	30		25	Nancy Drew
Martin, Ricardo	Music	15			45	Opera
Martin, Ricky	Music	25			50	

Name	Field	SIG	DS	ALS	SP	Remarks
Martin, Ross	Ent	50	75		100	Wild,Wild West
Martin, Steve	Ent	15	45		45	
Martin, Struther	Ent	35			80	
Martin, Theodore, Sir	Author	5		25	10	
Martin, Tony	Ent	10			25	
Martin, William T.	Civil War	100	250	400		CSA General/1823-1910
Martinelli, Giovanni	Music	30	50		75	Opera/Tenor
Martini, Nino	Music	15			45	Opera/Tenor
Martini, Steve	Author	5			10	
Martino, Al	Ent	5			10	
Martino, Donald	Music	20	35	75		Pulitzer
Marton, Eva	Music	20			50	Opera
Marvin, Lee	Ent	100	150		200	
Marx Brothers	Ent	1,250	1,450		2,500	Four Brothers
Marx Brothers	Ent	900	1,250		2,000	Chico,Groucho,Harpo (3)
Marx, Chico	Ent	125	200	350	400	
Marx, Groucho	Ent	200	400		400	1890 - 1977/Full Signature
Marx, Harpo	Ent	400	550		750	Scarcest Brother
Marx, Karl 1818-83	Author	750	1,500	RARE	RARE	Ger. Political Philosopher
Marx, Richard	Music	20			50	
Marx, Zeppo 1901-79	Ent	75	125		125	Fifth Marx Brother
Mary (of Teck) 1867-1953	Royalty	125	200	200	300	Queen of George V (Eng.)
Mary Adalaide	Royalty	25	75	150		Duchess of Teck
Mary I 1516-58	Royalty	1,000	3,000	RARE		
Mary II (Eng)	Royalty	400	1,200	RARE	RARE	
Masaryk, Jan	Political	75	150	275	450	Pres. Czechoslovakia
Masaryk, Thomas G.	Political	100	250	500	600	Czech First President
Mascagni, Pietro 1863-45	Music	165	375	500	600	Composer
Mascherini, Enzo	Music	20			50	Opera
Masefield, John 1878-67	Author	35	75	200	75	Br. Poet Laureate
MASH (Cast)	Ent	150			500	Eight Main Characters
Maskelyne, Nevil	Science	100	250	400		Br. Astronomer
Mason, George	RevWar	RARE	4,500	RARE	RARE	
Mason, Jackie	Ent	10	20		20	
Mason, James	Ent	40	75	75	90	1909 - 1984
Mason, James M.	Civil War	50	100	150		CSA Diplomat
Mason, LeRoy	Ent	50			150	
Mason, Marsha	Ent	10			25	
Massena, Andre Duke	Military	100	300	400		Napolean General
Massenet, Jules 1842-12	Music	75	150	250	275	Composer
Massey, Daniel	Ent	10			20	
Massey, Gerald 1828-1907	Author	25	75	100		Poet
Massey, Illona	Ent	20		30	40	1912 - 1974
Massey, Louise & Curt	Music	25			45	Country Western
Massey, Raymond	Ent	30			60	1896 - 1983
Massie, Paul	Ent	5			10	
Massine, Leonide	Music	35			75	Dancer/Choreagrapher

Name	Field	SIG	DS	ALS	SP	Remarks
Masson, Andre	Art	40	50	75		
Masters and Johnson	Science	35	100		75	Sex Researchers
Masters, Edgar Lee	Author	50	150	250	75	Poet/1869-1950
Masters, Frankie	Music	10			25	Big Band Leader
Masterson, Mary Stuart	Ent	25			50	
Masterson, Wm. "Bat"	Western	5,000	RARE	RARE	RARE	Sheriff/Gambler
Mastroantonio, Mary E.	Ent	15	25		45	
Mastroianni, Marcello	Ent	20			45	
Mata Hari (M.G. Zelle)	Military	450	900	RARE	RARE	WWI/Spy/Executed
Mather, Cotton	RevWar	900	1,750	2,500		Author
Mathers, Jerry 'Beaver'	Ent	20	45		45	Leave it to Beaver/Beaver
Matheson, Tim	Ent	15			35	
Mathews, George	RevWar	100	175			General/1739-1812
Mathews, Larry	Ent	10			20	
Mathewson, Christy	Sports	1,200			3,500	1936 Baseball HOF
Mathis, Johnny	Music	15	35		30	
Mathis, Samantha	Ent	30			75	
Matisse, Henri 1869-1954	Art	550	750	1,200	RARE	Dr Painter and Sculptor
Matlack, Timothy	RevWar	100	250	400		Continental Congress
Matlin, Marlee	Ent	20		50	50	AA Winner
Matoni, Walter	Aviation	10			35	WWII German ACE
Matsushita, Konosuke	Business	25	75	150	40	Japanese Electronic Giant
Mattea, Kathy	Music	5		50	15	Country
Mattern, Jimmie	Aviation	15		50	35	
Matthau, Walter	Ent	25	60	75	55	AA Winner
Matthews, DeLane	Ent	10			30	Dave's World
Matthews, Jessie	Ent	15			30	
Matthews, Stanley	SuprCt	50	150	275		
Mattingly, Thos. Ken	Space	35			100	Astronaut
Mattson, Conrad	Aviation	10		30	25	WWII ACE
Mature, Victor	Ent	20			40	
Matzky, Gerhard	Military	20	60			WWII Nazi General
Maugham, W. Somerset	Author	100	250	350	400	Br. Novelist and Playwright
Mauldin, Bill	Cartoonist	25			50	Willie & Joe
Maupassant, Guy de	Author	275	700	900		French Short Story Writer
Maura, Antonio	Political	100	175			
Mauro, Ermanno	Music	15			40	Opera
Maurois, Andre	Author	35	75	125		Fr. Biographer, Novelist
Maury, Dabney H.	Civil War	100		350		CSA General/1822-1900
Maury, Matthew F.	Civil War	200		600	1,250	CSA Naval Cmdr/1806-73
Mawson, Douglas, Sir	Explorer	75	150	300		Australian Polar Explorer
Max, Peter	Art	150	350			Am. Contemporary Art.
Maxey, Samuel Bell	Civil War	125	225	250		CSA General/1825-95
Maxey, Virginia	Ent	5			10	
Maxim, Hiram Percy	Science	50	250			Inventor Maxim Gun Silencer
Maxim, Hiram Stevens	Science	100	200	375	300	Inventor Maxim Machine Gun
Maxim, Hudson 1853-27	Science	75	150	175	175	Inventor Smokeless Powder

Name	Field	SIG	DS	ALS	SP	Remarks
Maximilian II	Royalty	150	400	750		Holy Roman Emperor
Maximilian, Ferdinand	Royalty	350	675	1,250		Emperor Mexico
Maxon, R.	Cartoonist	25			50	Tarzan
Maxwell, Lois	Ent	10			45	Moneypenny in James Bond
Maxwell, Marilyn	Ent	10			35	1921 - 1972
Maxwell, Robert	Aviation	10	25	30	25	WWII ACE
Maxwell, Robert	Business	50			125	Publisher/Died Mysteriously
May, Edna	Ent	20		30	30	
May, Marty	Ent	10			20	
Mayall, John	Ent	10			30	
Mayer, Louis B.	Ent	75	150	275	225	MGM Film Studio
Mayer, Maria, Dr.	Science	30	75		50	Nobel Physics
Maynard, Ken 1895-1973	Ent	100		150	175	Cowboy Star
Maynor, Dorothy	Ent				275	
Mayo, 6th Earl	Political	10		30		
Mayo, Charles H., Dr.	Science	150	300	350	475	Co-Founder Mayo Clinic
Mayo, Charles W., Dr.	Science	75	150	225	350	Surgeon Mayo Clinic
Mayo, Henry Thomas	Military	15	50	75	40	
Mayo, Virginia	Ent	10			25	
Mayo, William J., Dr.	Science	100	300	350	475	Co-Founder Mayo Foundation
Mayron, Melanie	Ent	15			40	
Maytag, Frederick L.	Business	100	275	750	200	Maytag Appliances
Mazurski, Paul	Ent	20	50		50	Director
Mazzini, Joseph	RevWar	50	150	400		Italian Patriot
Mazzoleni, Ester	Music	75			200	Opera
McAdam, John	Science	RARE	850	RARE	RARE	
McAdoo, William G.	Political	25	75	150	50	Wilson Sec'y Treasury
McAllister, Lon	Ent	15			30	
McArdle, Andrea	Ent	5		15	15	
McArthur, John 1826-06	Civil War	40				Union General
McAuliffe, Anthony A.	Military	85	175	175	350	WWII General
McAuliffe, Christa	Space	450	1,000	1,250	800	Died in Challenger Disaster
McAvoy, May	Ent	10			25	
McBain, Diane	Ent	5		15	10	
McBain, Ed	Author	15	30	50	30	
McBride, Martina	Ent	15			45	Country
McCaffrey, Anne	Author	5			20	
McCain, John N.	Military	15	35			WWII Admiral
McCalla, Irish	Ent	10		25	25	Sheena of the Jungle
McCallister, Lon	Ent	10			30	
McCallum, David	Ent	15	45	50	40	Man from UNCLE
McCambridge, Mercedes	Ent	50			100	Voice in Excorcist
McCampbell, David S.	Aviation	15	25	45	75	WWII Top Navy ACE
McCann, Chuck	Business	5		30	10	
McCarey, Leo	Ent	35			65	Director/Producer
McCarthy, Andrew	Ent	25			40	
McCarthy, Jenny	Ent	25			50	

Name	Field	SIG	DS	ALS	SP	Remarks
McCarthy, Joe 1908-1957	Political	35	150		100	Senator WI. McCarthyism
McCarthy, Kevin	Ent	10			30	
McCarthy, Mary	Author	50	100		50	Novelist
McCarthy, Michael W.	Business	5			10	
McCartney, Paul	Music	150	400	RARE	300	Beatle
McCauley, Rose, Dame	Author	25			45	
McCay, Peggy	Ent	15			35	
McCay, Winsor	Cartoonist	50			250	Little Nemo
McClanahan, Rue	Ent	10			35	Golden Girls
McClellan, George B.	Civil War	200	250	500		Union General/1826-85
McClernand, John A.	Civil War	50	100	175		Union General/1812-1900
McClintock, Francis Leopold	Explorer		50	100	200	Br. Adm., Arctic Navigator
McClintock, John	Space	5	15		20	Astronaut
McClinton, Delbert	Music	10			25	
McCloskey, Lee	Ent	5	15		15	
McClure, Doug	Ent	10			30	
McClurg, Alexander C.	Civil War	50	75			Union Officer/1832-1901
McColpin, Carroll W.	Military	25	50	75	50	WWII ACE
McComb, Wm. 1828-18	Civil War	100	225	350		CSA General
McConaughey, Matthew	Ent	20			50	
McConnell, Joseph, Jr.	Aviation	75	150	175	150	Top Korean ACE
McCoo, Marilyn	Music	5		15	15	Fifth Dimension
McCook, Alex. M. D.	Civil War	35	75	125		Union General/1831-1903
McCook, Anson	Civil War	30	50			Union Officer/1835-1917
McCord, Kent	Ent	10			25	Adam 12
McCormack, John	Music	50	150	300	125	Tenor
McCormack, John W.	Political	10		75		Speaker of the House
McCormack, Patty	Ent	5		20	15	
McCormic, Mary	Music	20			45	Opera
McCormick, Anne O'Hare	Author	30	45	100	50	lst Pulitzer Woman Journalist
McCormick, Cyrus H.	Science	350	850	2,000		Invented the Reaper
McCormick, Myron	Ent	20	25	45	40	1907 - 1962
McCormick, Nettie F.	Business	25		75		Mrs. Cyrus McCormick
McCormick, Robert R.	Business	35	150	200	75	Editor Chicago Tribune
McCown, John P.	Civil War	250	750	RARE	RARE	CSA General/War Date
McCown, John Porter	Civil War	100	300			CSA General/1815-79
McCoy, Charles B.	Business	25		75	45	Pres. DuPont Co.
McCoy, Clyde	Ent	5	20		15	
McCoy, Tim	Ent	75	150		150	1891-1978
McCoy, Wilson	Cartoonist	15			50	Phantom
McCrea, Joel	Ent	15			45	
McCreary, Richard L.	Military	30	75		50	WWII British General
McCudden, James T.B.	Aviation	125	225	350	300	WWI ACE
McCullers, Carson	Author	50	150	350	75	Am. Novelist/1917-67
McCulloch, Ben 1811-62	Civil War	150	450	550		CSA General
McCulloch, Henry E.	Civil War	150	350			CSA General
McCulloch, Hugh 1808-95	Political	50	150	150		

Name	Field	SIG	DS	ALS	SP	Remarks
McCullough, Colleen	Author	35	100	200	75	Novelist/The Thorn Birds
McCullough, John	Ent	10			35	1832-1885
McCullough, Julie	Ent	10			25	Growning Pains/Playboy
McCutcheon, John T.	Cartoonist	10			30	Pulitzer Political Cartoonist
McDaniel, Hattie	Ent	600	1,250	RARE	1,500	AA Winner/GWTW
McDermott, Dylan	Ent	15			35	
McDevitt, Ruth	Ent	10			20	
McDivitt, James A.	Space	30			35	Astronaut
McDonald, John D.	Author	150	600	Scarce	Scarce	Travis McGee novels
McDonald, M. Nick	Political	15	45		25	Captured LHarvey Oswald
McDonald, Marie	Ent	45	75	100	100	1923-1965
McDonald, Richard J.	Business	75	250		250	McDonalds
McDonald, Skeets	Music	10			20	
McDonnell, James S.	Business	20	50	100	45	Fndr. McDonnell Aircraft
McDonnell, Mary	Ent	20			50	
McDougall, Alexander	RevWar	100	200	400		Gen Continental Army
McDougall, Clinton	Civil War	35	75			Union General
McDowell, Andre	Ent	10			30	
McDowell, Irvin 1818-85	Civil War	75		250		Union General
McDowell, Malcolm	Ent	20			50	
McDowell, Roddy	Ent	30	50		60	Planet of the Apes
McEntire, Reba	Music	25		60	50	
McFadden, Gates	Ent	15			40	Star Trek:Next Generation
McFarland, Spanky	Ent	40	100		75	Little Rascals/Our Gang
McGarru, William D.	Aviation	15		45	40	WWII Flying Tigers ACE
McGavin, Darren	Ent	25			50	The Night Stalker
McGee,Don	Aviation	25				WWII ACE
McGillis, Kelly	Ent	15			45	Top Gun
McGinley, Phyllis	Author	10		45	20	Poet/Pulitzer Prize Winner
McGoohan, Patrick	Ent	20			45	TV's The Prisoner
McGovern, Elizabeth	Ent	10			20	
McGovern, George	Political	10			25	
McGovern, John	Author	25				
McGregor, Ewan	Ent	30			60	Star Wars
McGuire, Barry	Music	10			25	New Christy Minstrels
McGuire, Dorothy	Ent	15			30	
McGuire, Phyllis	Music	5			10	McGuire Sisters
McGuire, Thomas B.	Aviation	150	300	650	450	WWII/ACE #2 in US
McGwire, Mark	Sports	100			250	Baseball
McHenry, James	Military	200	275	RARE		Signer Constitution
McHugh, Frank	Ent	20	25	65	60	
McHugh, Jimmy	Music	25	75			Composer
McIntire, John	Ent	20			50	
McIntosh, Lachlan	RevWar	550	750	1,250		Killed Button Gwinett/Duel
McKay, Gardner	Ent	5		15	20	
McKean, Thomas	RevWar	250	475	750		Signer/1734-1817
McKeever, Chauncey	Civil War	50		175		

Name	Field	SIG	DS	ALS	SP	Remarks
McKellan, Ian	Ent	15			30	
McKenna, Joseph	SuprCt	35	50	75	50	Att'y General
McKenna, Siobhan	Ent	15			35	
McKenzie, Fay	Ent	5			15	
McKeon, Nancy	Ent	10			30	Facts of Life
McKeon, Phillip	ENt	15			35	Alice
McKern, Leo	Ent	15			40	
McKinley, Ida S.	First Lady	400	600	900	550	
McKinley, Ray	Music	25			75	Bandleader
McKinley, William	President	250	375	750	900	Assassinated by Anarchist
McKinly, John	RevWar	75	175			First Gov. DE
McKone, John R,	Military	10		40	30	
McKuen, Rod	Author	20	25	35	50	Poet
McLaglin, Andrew V.	Ent	10		25		
McLaglin, Victor	Ent	125			275	AA Winner/1886-1959
McLain, Raymond S.	Military	30			45	WWII General
McLane, Louis	Business	45	150			Pres. Wells Fargo & Co.
McLane, Louis 1786-1857	Political	15	45	50		Jackson Sec'y Treasury
McLane, Robert	Political	35	75	125		US Minister to Japan
McLaughlin, E.A.	Business	10	35		25	
McLaughlin, Kyle	Ent	25			75	
McLaws, Lafayette	Civil War	175	300	400		CSA General/1821-97
McLean, Don	Music	20			45	American Pie
McLean, John 1785-1861	SuprCt	100	200	300		
McLean, Nathaniel C.	Civil War	50	75	125		Union General/1815-1905
McLeod, Archibald N.	Business	RARE	2,500	RARE	RARE	Hudson's Bay Co.
McLeod, Catherine	Ent	5			15	
McMahon, Ed	Ent	10			25	The Tonight Show
McMahon, Horace	Ent	20			50	
McManus, George	Cartoonist	50			125	Bringing Up Father
McMichael, Morton	Author	50	100			1st Ed. Sat Eve Post
McMillan, Edwin M.	Science	20		50	30	Nobel Chemistry 1952
McMillan, James W.	Civil War	40				Union General/1825-1903
McMillan, Terry	Ent	10			25	
McMullen, Clements	Military	50	175			WWII General
McNair, Howard	Ent	500	RARE	RARE	RARE	Andy Griffith Show
McNair, Leslie J.	Military	45	100	150	100	WWI General
McNair, Ronald E.	Space	100			275	Died in Challenger Crash
McNally, Stephen	Ent	10			20	
McNamara, Robert S.	Political	15	45		30	
McNamara, William	Ent	10		25	25	
McNarney, Joseph T.	Military	20	50			WWII General
McNaughton, Kenneth	Military	5			10	
McNeill, Don	Ent	10			20	
McNichol, Kristy	Ent	20	45		45	Family/Empty Nest
McPartland, Jimmy	Music	30	50		75	Jazz Trumpet
McPhatter, Clyde	Music	400		800		Scarce

Name	Field	SIG	DS	ALS	SP	Remarks
McPhearson, Elle	Ent	15			45	
McPherson, Aimee S.	Clergy	100	300	400	350	
McPherson, James B.	Civil War	125	225	300		Union General/1828-64
McQuade, James	Civil War	25	75	175		Union General/1829-85
McQueen, Butterfly	Ent	55	85	100	75	GWTW "Prissy"/1911-97
McQueen, Steve 1930-80	Ent	200	325	400	325	
McRaney, Gerald	Ent	15			45	Major Dad
McReynolds, James C.	SuprCt	30	125	150	100	Wilson Att'y Gen.
McShane, Ian	Ent	10		20	25	
McShann, Jay	Music	50			125	Jazz Pianist
McVey, Patrick	Ent	10			20	
McWethy, John	Ent	5			20	ABC News
McWhorter, Hamilton	Aviation	15	25	45	35	WWII ACE
McWilliams, Caroline	Ent	5			10	
Mead, Margaret 1901-78	Science	75	125	175	225	
Meade, George G.	Civil War	300	400		450	Union General/1815-72
Meade, George G.	Civil War	650	900	RARE	RARE	Union GeneralWar Dated
Meadows, Audrey	Ent	25	50		65	HoneyMooners
Meadows, Jayne	Ent	10	25	30	25	
Meagher, Thomas F.	Civil War	75	175	250		Union General/1823-67
Meaney, Colm	Ent	15			35	Star Trek : Next Generation
Meany, George	Political	15	30		75	Pres. AFL-CIO
Meara, Anne	Ent	5			15	
Meat Loaf	Music	20			45	
Medawar, Peter B., Sir	Science	20		60	25	Nobel Medicine 1960
Medici, Cosimo I. de	Royalty	375	900			Duke of Florence
Medici, Fernando de	Royalty	450	1,250	RARE		Great Duke
Medicis, Catherine de	Royalty	300	800	RARE		Queen of Henry II of France
Medicis, Francesco de	Royalty	100	200	500		
Medicis, Marie de	Royalty	350	950	RARE		Queen of Henry IV (Fr)
Medill, Joseph	Author	125		250		A founder Repub. Party
Medina, Patricia	Ent	5			15	
Medley, Bill	Music	10			20	
Meeker, Ralph	Ent	25			40	
Meese, Edwin III	Political	10		35	25	Att'y General
Mehta, Zubin	Music	20			50	Conductor
Meier, Waltraud	Music	15			35	Opera
Meighan, Tom	Ent	35			75	
Meigs, Montgomery C.	Civil War	50	120	150	200	Union General/1816-92
Meigs, Return J., Jr.	Military	100	200	325		Monroe P.M. General
Meinl, Tanaka	Music	35			75	Opera
Meir, Golda 1898-1979	Political	125	250	450	300	
Melba, Nellie 1859-1931	Music	75	125	250	450	Opera/Soprano
Melbourne, Wm. Lamb	Political	50	75	150		
Melchior, Lauritz	Music	35	75		150	Opera/Tenor
Melis, Carmen	Music	35			75	Opera
Mellencamp, John C.	Music	25			50	

Name	Field	SIG	DS	ALS	SP	Remarks
Mellnik, Steve	Military	10		35		
Mellon, Andrew 1855-37	Business	250	750	1,200	400	
Melton, James	Music	25			50	Opera Tenor
Melvill, Thomas	RevWar	100	250	450		Memb. Boston Tea Party
Melville, George W.	Military	50	100	150		Union Admiral
Melville, Herman	Author	750	2,000	RARE	RARE	Moby Dick/1819-91
Melville, Sam	Ent	10			25	
Memminger, Christopher	Civil War	150	450	550		CSA Sec'y of Treasury
Mencken, Henry L.	Author	100	225	350	450	1880-1956
Mendel, Gregor Johann	Science	400	850	2,000		
Mendeleyev, Dmitry	Science	RARE	RARE	1,650	RARE	
Mendelssohn-Bartholdy	Music	600		3,000	RARE	Composer
Mendes, Abraham C.	Author	15	35	100		Fr. Poet
Mengelberg, Willem	Music	75			200	Dutch Conductor
Menjou, Adolphe	Ent	20	25		75	1890-1963
Menkes, Sara	Music	25			50	Opera
Mennin, Peter	Music	20		50		Composer
Menninger, Karl	Science	30		75	75	Menninger Clinic
Menninger, Roy	Science	10	25	50	30	
Menninger, William C.	Science	15		75	35	Psychiatrist
Menocal, Mario G.	Political	25			40	Pres. Cuba 1913-21
Menon, V. Krisna	Political	20		25		Ambassador Gr. Britain
Menotti, Gian Carlo	Music	150	250	450	350	Composer
Menuhin, Yehudi	Music	40	75		125	Concert Violinist
Menzies, Robert, Sir	Political	15	50	75	30	Australian Prime Minister
Mercadante, Saverio	Music	150		450		Composer
Mercer, Frances	Ent	5			15	
Mercer, Hugh W.	Civil War	100	175			CSA General/1808-77
Mercer, John Francis	Military	75		125		Aide-de-Camp Gen Lee
Mercer, Johnny	Music	50			125	
Mercer, Marian	Ent	10			35	
Merchant, Natalie	Music	20			45	
Mercouri, Melina	Ent	25		45	75	
Mercury, Freddie	Music	150	350		300	Lead singer of Queen
Meredith, Burgess	Ent	25	50	60	50	Batman/Penguin 1908-98
Meredith, Samuel	Political	100	200	300		RevWar General
Meredith, Solomon	Civil War	150		450		Union General/1810-75
Merivale, Philip	Ent	10		25	25	
Meriwether, Lee	Ent	5		20	20	Catwoman/Barnaby Jones
Merkel, Una	Ent	15			35	1903-1986
Merli, Francesco	Music	25			75	Opera/Tenor
Merli, Gino J.	Military	10	25			WWII
Merlin de Douai, P.A.	Military	50		150		French Revolution
Merlin, Jan	Ent	10			20	
Merman, Ethel	Ent	25	50		50	1909-1984
Merrick, David	Ent	50			100	Theatrical Producer/Scarce
Merrick, Samuel V.	Business	50	175			Financier

Name	Field	SIG	DS	ALS	SP	Remarks
Merrill, Dina	Ent	5	20	20	15	
Merrill, Frank D.	Military	225		325		General WWII/1903-55
Merrill, Gary 1914-90	Ent	15		45	35	
Merrill, Henry T.	Aviation	30	45	100	100	
Merrill, Lewis	Civil War	75	175			Union Officer/1834-96
Merrill, Richard Dick	Aviation	35	50	100	75	
Merrill, Robert	Music	30			50	
Merrill, Stuart	Author	30		125		American Poet
Merriman, Nan	Music				75	Opera
Merritt, Chris	Music	10			30	Opera
Merritt, Wesley 1834-10	Civil War	100	300	200		Union General
Merton, Thomas	Author	375	900			Priest/Poet
Mesmer, F. Anton, Dr.	Science	125	250	450		1734-1815
Messerschmitt, Wilhelm	Aviation	125	275		450	Ger. Aircraft Designer-Mfg.
Messiaen, Olivier	Music	75	200			Composer
Messick, Dale	Cartoonist	15			45	Brenda Starr
Messick, Don	Ent	30			60	Many Cartoon Voices
Messing, Debra	Ent	20			45	Will and Grace
Messmer, Otto	Cartoonist	75			200	Felix The Cat
Mesta, Perie	Business	25		75	45	Washington Hostess
Metallica	Music	50			100	Signed by Entire Band
Metcalf, Laurie	Ent	25			50	Roseanne
Metcalf, Victor H.	Political	20		100		Sect Navy
Metchnikoff, Elie	Science	50	100		150	Nobel Physiology 1908
Metternich, Prince	Political	75	250	400		
Meusel, Lucille	Music	10			25	Soprano
Mewman, Larry	Aviation	25			75	
Meyer, E. C.	Military	10		30	20	
Meyerbeer, Giacomo	Music	175	250	400	300	German Composer
Miaskovsky, Nikolai	Music	125				
Michael, George	Music	30			60	Wham/Later Solo Artist
Michaels, Barbara	Author	5	20		25	
Michaels, Bret	Music	10	20	50	45	
Michaels, Marilyn	Ent	5		25	20	
Michelangelo	Art	RARE	RARE	RARE	RARE	
Michele, Denise	Ent	5			10	
Michelet, Jules	Author	50		75		1798-1874
Michelson, Albert A.	Science	125		450		Nobel Physics 1907
Michener, James A.	Author	50	250	300	125	Am. Novelist. Pulitzer
Middleton, Arthur	RevWar	5,000	12,000	25,000	RARE	Signer Decl. of Indepen.
Middleton, Charles	Ent	150	RARE	RARE	300	Ming the Merciless
Middleton, Henry	RevWar	RARE	4,500	RARE	RARE	President of Congress
Middleton, Robert	Ent	50			150	
Middleton, Velma	Music	30			75	Jazz Vocalist
Midler, Bette	Ent	25		75	50	
Mielziner, Jo	Ent	15			35	Director
Mifflin, Thomas	RevWar	150	450	600		General/1744-1800

Name	Field	SIG	DS	ALS	SP	Remarks
Mifune, Toshiro	Ent	15	25		40	
Migenes, Julia	Music	15			35	Opera
Mihalovivi, Marcel	Music	30			150	
Miklas, Wilhelm 1872-56	Political	35				Pres. Austria
Milano, Alyssa	Ent	20	50		50	Who's the Boss
Milanov, Zinka	Music	35			125	Metropolitan Opera
Milch, Erhard	Aviation	100	250	400	175	
Miles, Josephine	Author	10		25	10	
Miles, Nelson A. 1839-25	Civil War	125	250	350		Union General
Miles, Sarah	Ent	10		25	25	
Miles, Sylvia	Ent	10		35	35	
Miles, Vera	Ent	20	50		50	
Milestone, Lewis	Ent	45			75	Director
Milhaud, Darius 1892-74	Music	150	250	300	450	Composer
Mill, James	Author	75	250	450		Scot.Philosopher,Historian
Mill, John Stuart	Author	150	400	850		Economist
Millais, John Everett, Sir	Art	50	75	250		Pre-RaphaelitePainter
Milland, Ray	Ent	30	50		75	1905-1986
Millay,Edna St. Vincent	Author	150	300	800	1,200	American Poet/1892-1950
Miller, Alice Duer	Author	15	25	45		Novelist
Miller, Ann	Ent	10			30	
Miller, Arthur	Author	50	100	200	100	Pulitzer/Am. Playwright
Miller, Caroline	Author	10			30	Pulitzer
Miller, Charles Henry	Art	25			100	Landscape Painter
Miller, Denny	Ent	10			25	Tarzan
Miller, Eddie	Music	20			45	Big Band Tenor
Miller, Frederick C.	Business	15		50	25	Miller Beer
Miller, Glenn 1904-44	Music	200	400	600	450	Big Band Tenor
Miller, Henry	Ent	35		75	70	
Miller, Henry V. 1891-80	Author	75	150	350	150	Tropic of Cancer
Miller, Jason	Ent	10			25	
Miller, Joaquin	Author	50		125		American Poet
Miller, John	Civil War	35	50	75		Union General/1831-86
Miller, Ken	Ent	10			20	Child Actor
Miller, Marilyn	Ent	75			200	Ziegfield Dancing Star
Miller, Marvin	Ent	10			25	
Miller, Mitch	Music	5			15	Conductor, Arranger
Miller, Patsy Ruth	Ent	25	35	50	45	
Miller, Penelope Ann	Ent	20			50	
Miller, Roger	Music	35			50	
Miller, Samuel F.	SuprCt	100	200	250		1816-1890
Miller, Stanley	Science	15	35	75	30	
Miller, Stephen	Civil War	100	200	300		Union General/1816-81
Millerande, Alexandre	Political	40		75	75	Pres of France 1920-24
Milles, Carl	Art	30	50	100		Sculptor
Millet, Jean Frangois	Art	200	450	RARE	RARE	Fr Classical/Religious
Millikan, Robert A., Dr.	Science	100	200	400	200	Nobel Physics

Name	Field	SIG	DS	ALS	SP	Remarks
Millinder, Lucky	Music	50			125	Bandleader
Millo, Aprile	Music	15			35	Opera
Mills Brothers	Music	100			200	Signed by All Four
Mills, Darius Ogden	Business	250	750	2,000		Merchant,Banker, Philan.
Mills, Donna	Ent	10			30	Producer
Mills, Earle W.	Military	10			30	
Mills, Hayley	Ent	15			35	The Parent Trap
Mills, John, Sir	Ent	20			35	
Mills, Juliette	Ent	10			20	
Mills, Roger Q.	Civil War	25	35	50		CSA Colonel
Milne, A. A. 1882-1956	Author	225	450	750	550	Winnie the Pooh Creator
Milner, Martin	Ent	5			20	Adam 12
Milnes, Sherrill	Music	10			25	Opera
Milosz, Czeslaw, Dr.	Author	45	100		50	Nobel Literature
Milroy, Robert H. 1816-90	Civil War	25	75			Union General
Milsap, Ronnie	Music	5			15	
Milstein, Nathan	Music	35			75	Rus. Violinist
Miltonberger, Butler	Military	35	75			
Mimieux, Yvette	Ent	5			20	
Mincus, Leon	Music	100			375	Composer
Mindil, George W.	Civil War	50		200		Union Officer
Minelli, Liza	Ent	15	50		30	
Mineo, Sal 1939-76	Ent	200	250		300	Murdered at 37
Mingus, Charlie	Music	RARE	RARE	RARE	RARE	Jazz Musician
Minh, Duong Van Gen.	Military	15		75	40	
Minh, Ho Chi	Political	500	1,500	RARE	1,500	Pres. & Fndr N. Vietnam
Minich, Peter	Music	10			20	Opera
Minnelli, Vincente	Ent	30	75		75	AA Film Director
Minter, Mary Miles	Ent	100	150	175	200	1902-1984
Minton, Sherman	SuprCt	50	150	250	100	
Minton, Yvonne	Music	10			25	Opera
Minvielle, Gabriel	Military	850	RARE	RARE	RARE	French Revolution
Miollis, S.A.F.	Military	100	200			French Revolution
Mirabeau, Gabriel H.R	Military	100	275	475		Diplomat/Statesman
Miramon, Miguel (Mex)	Military	25	75	150		Cmdr. Army vs Juarez.
Miranda, Carmen	Ent	100	200		350	1913-1955
Miranda, Isa	Ent	35			75	
Miro, Juan 1893-1983	Art	200	575	700	300	
Mister Mister	Music	25			50	
Mistral, Frederic	Author	30	75		50	Nobel Literature 1904
Mistral, Gabriela	Author	20	35		25	Nobel Literature in 1943
Mitchel, Ormsby M.	Science	125		475		Union General
Mitchell, Billy (William)	Aviation	200	900	975	1,200	WWI General
Mitchell, Cameron	Ent	15			40	
Mitchell, Don	Ent	10			20	
Mitchell, Edgar D.	Space	30		150	100	Moonwalker. Apollo 14
Mitchell, Grant	Ent	35			75	

Name	Field	SIG	DS	ALS	SP	Remarks
Mitchell, John Grant	Civil War	30	50	125		Union General/1838-94
Mitchell, John N. 1913-88	Political	75			275	Attorney General
Mitchell, John W.	Aviation	15		40	35	WWII ACE
Mitchell, Joni	Music	10			25	
Mitchell, Maggi 1832-18	Ent	25			50	
Mitchell, Margaret	Author	750	1,750	3,000	RARE	Pulitzer/1900-1949
Mitchell, Maria	Science	75	175	275		Astronomer
Mitchell, Ormsby M.	Civil War	RARE	RARE	1,000	RARE	Union General
Mitchell, Silas Weir	Science	35	75			Civil War Surgeon
Mitchell, Stephen Mix	RevWar	75	200			
Mitchell, Thomas	Ent	200	350		500	GWTW/Scarce
Mitchum, Robert	Ent	20	45		50	
Mitford, Jessica	Author	20			20	
Mitropoulous, Dimitri	Music	35	50		135	Greek Conductor
Mitscher, Marc A.	Military	375			550	WWII Admiral/RARE
Mitterand, Francois	Political	15		45	25	Pres. France
Mittford, Mary Russell	Author	15		40		Poet
Mix, Tom 1880-1940	Ent	150			400	
Mobley, Mary Ann	Ent	5			15	
Modesti, Giuseppe	Music	15			35	Opera
Modigliani, Amedeo	Art	275	700	1,400		
Modine, Matthew	Ent	10			35	
Moessbauer, Rudolf, Dr.	Science	25			50	Nobel
Moffett, W.A., Adm.	Military	15			50	
Moffo, Anna	Music	15			35	Opera
Mohler, A. L.	Business	10		40	25	
Mohnke, Wilhelm	Military	50			150	German General SS
Moholy-Nagy, Laszlo	Art	100	200			Painter/Photographer
Mohr, Gerald	Ent	35			75	
Mojica, Jose	Music	75			225	Opera
Molders, Werner	Aviation	175	275	400	325	WWII ACE
Molinari, Al	Ent	15			35	Happy Days
Molitor, Gabriel J.J.	Military	75	175	250		Napolean Gen/Fr Marshal
Moll, Kurt	Music	15			35	Opera
Moll, Richard	Ent	10			25	Night Court
Mollet, Guy	Political	25		75		Socialist Premier France
Molnar, Ferenc 1878-52	Author	75	150	275		Playwright,Novelist
Moltke, H. Johann L.	Military	15		50	30	Nephew Helmuth
Moltke, Helmuth von	Military	100		400	300	Prussian Field Marshal
Momaday, N. Scott	Author	10			15	
Momo, Giuseppe	Music	15			35	Opera
Monaghan, Tom	Business	10		35	20	Domino's Pizza
Moncada, Rivera y	Military	RARE	4,500	RARE	RARE	
Moncey, Bon-Adrien J.	Military	50	125	150		Marshal of France
Monck, George 1608-70	Military	100				
Mondale, Walter	Vice Pres	25			45	
Mondrian, Piet	Art	225	675	1,400		Dutch.Traditional-Cubism

Name	Field	SIG	DS	ALS	SP	Remarks
Monet, Claude 1840-1926	Art	450	1,200	1,500	RARE	Fr. Impressionist
Monk, Thelonious	Music	50			150	Jazz Musician
Monkees	Music	75			150	Signed by all four
Monroe, Bill	Music	50		150		Father of Blue Grass Music
Monroe, Elizabeth	First Lady	RARE	RARE	RARE	RARE	
Monroe, James	President	450	900	2,000		1758-1831
Monroe, Marilyn	Ent	4,000	10,000	15,000	RARE	Signed Norma Jean
Monroe, Marilyn 1926-62	Ent	1,800	3,500	9,000	7,000	
Monroe, Vaughn	Ent	15	25		30	
Montagu, Edwin Samuel	Political	15	50	75	35	Br. Statesman
Montagu, John	Political	75	200	400		Earl of Sandwich
Montalban, Ricardo	Ent	10		25	25	Fantasy Island
Montalivet, J.P.B. Count	Military	35	100	200		
Montana, Ashley	Ent	15			35	
Montana, Bob	Cartoonist	50			125	Archie
Montana, Bull	Ent	25			50	
Montana, Patsy	Music	15			35	
Montand, Yves	Ent	10			35	
Montcalm, Louis J.	Military	750	1,500	2,500		Marquis
Montefiore, Moses, Sir	Political	50		175		
Montenegro, Conchita	Ent	10			20	
Montessori, Maria	Science	300		900		Ist Italian Woman Doctor
Monteux, Pierre	Music	25	50		45	Conductor
Monteverde, Alfred de	Aviation	25	50		50	
Monteverde, George de	Aviation	25	50	75	50	
Montez, Lola	Explorer	200		500		
Montez, Maria	Ent	50			100	1920-1951
Montgolfier, Jacques-E.	Aviation	RARE	RARE	1,800	RARE	1st Hot Air Balloonist
Montgolfier, Joseph	Aviation	RARE	RARE	RARE	RARE	
Montgomery, Bernard L.	Military	75	225		350	Br. WWII General
Montgomery, Douglass	Ent	10			25	
Montgomery, Elizabeth	Ent	60	75		100	Bewitched/Samantha
Montgomery, George	Ent	10			25	
Montgomery, John M.	Ent	15			25	
Montgomery, Melba	Music	10			25	
Montgomery, Ray	Ent	10			25	
Montgomery, Robert	Ent	20		50	45	1904-1981
Monti, Carlotta	Ent	15			40	W.C. Fields Mistress
Monti, Nicola	Music	35			75	Opera
Montoya, Carlos	Music	10			25	Classical Guitarist
Moody Blues	Music	125			200	Signed by All Five
Moody, Dwight L.	Clergy	50	100	200	125	Evangelist
Moody, William H.	SuprCt	50	125	175	100	
Moody, William V.	Author	35	75	125		Poet. Playwright
Moog, Bob	Science	50		100	75	Inventor. Synthesizer
Moon, Keith	Music	175	250	RARE	350	Deceased Who member
Mooney, Art	Music	10			20	Big Band Leader

Name	Field	SIG	DS	ALS	SP	Remarks
Moore, Alfred	SuprCt	3,000	RARE	RARE	RARE	
Moore, Alvy	Ent	10			20	Green Acres
Moore, Andrew B.	Civil War	50	100			CSA Governor/1806-73
Moore, Clayton	Ent	20	75	60	50	The Lone Ranger
Moore, Clement C.	Author	200	500	RARE	RARE	'Twas the Night Before ....
Moore, Colleen 1900-88	Ent	10	25		35	Silent Screen Major Star
Moore, Constance	Ent	10			20	
Moore, Demi	Ent	35	150		75	
Moore, Dick	Ent	10			15	
Moore, Dudley	Ent	25			50	Arthur, 10
Moore, Foster	Cartoonist	20			50	Napoleon
Moore, Francis D., Dr.	Science	10		45	25	
Moore, Gary	Ent	10			25	
Moore, George	Author	50		125		Irish Novelist
Moore, Grace 1901-47	Music	75	100		150	Opera/Deceased
Moore, Henry	Art	50	200	450	100	Br. Sculptor. The Thinker
Moore, Jeremy, Sir	Military	5			15	General
Moore, Joanna	Ent	10			25	
Moore, John Bassett	Political	75		200		International Lawyer
Moore, John, Sir 1761-09	Military	75		300		
Moore, Julianne	Ent	15			30	
Moore, Marianne C,	Author	75	150		75	Am. Poet. Pulitzer
Moore, Mary Tyler	Ent	10			35	
Moore, Mary Tyler Show	Ent				250	Six Main Characters
Moore, Ray	Cartoonist	25			50	Phantom
Moore, Roger	Ent	25			500	James Bond
Moore, Roy D.	Business	10			20	
Moore, Samuel P.	Civil War	450	600	800		Surgeon General CSA
Moore, Sara Jane	Criminal	30	75	200		Attempted Ford Assasinat
Moore, Sydenham	Civil War	35		100		CSA Officer
Moore, Terry	Ent	15			45	
Moore, Thomas	Civil War		400			CSA Gov. of LA/1803-76
Moore, Thomas 1779-52	Author	50	100	475		Irish Poet
Moore, Victor	Ent	25			50	
Moore, William	Political	100	200			
Moorehead, Agnes	Ent	50	75	75	100	Endora on Bewitched
Moorer, Thomas	Military	75	150		100	Admiral
Moores, Dick	Cartoonist	10			30	Gasoline Alley
Morales, Ramon V.	Political	15	30			Ecuador
Moran, Erin	Ent	20	75		50	Happy Days
Moran, Lois	Ent	5			15	
Moran, Thomas	Art	100	225	350		American Western
Moranis, Rick	Ent	10			30	
Moranville, H. Blake	Aviation	10		40	30	WWII Naval ACE
More, Thomas, Sir	Author	25,000	RARE	RARE	RARE	
Moreau, Jean-Victor	Military	100		300		Fr. General/Napoleon
Morehead, James B.	Aviation	10		35	25	USAF WWII ACE

Name	Field	SIG	DS	ALS	SP	Remarks
Moreland, Mantan	Ent	100	125		200	
Morell, George W.	Civil War	35		100		Union General/1815-89
Moreno, Anthony	Ent	5			10	
Moreno, Bertha	Music	35			100	Opera
Moreno, Buddy	Music	15			45	Bandleader
Moreno, Rita	Ent	10		25	20	
Morgan, Charles L.	Author	25	50	75		British Novelist
Morgan, Dennis	Ent	10			15	
Morgan, Edward J.	Ent	10			25	
Morgan, Edwin Denison	Civil War	50	75	100		Union General/1811-83
Morgan, Frank 1890-1949	Ent	375	575	RARE	600	Wizard of OZ
Morgan, George	RevWar	125	425	675		Indian Agent
Morgan, George W.	Civil War	RARE	RARE	RARE	RARE	Union General/1820-93
Morgan, Harry	Ent	10	25	30	25	MASH/Dragnet
Morgan, Helen 1900-1941	Ent	50	175		200	
Morgan, Henry	Ent	10			20	
Morgan, Jane	Ent	10			20	
Morgan, Jaye P.	Music	5			15	
Morgan, John Hunt	Civil War	800	1,200	1,750		CSA General/1825-64
Morgan, John P. II	Business	275				Financier, Banker
Morgan, John Pierpont	Business	300	900	2,500	1,200	Banker,Financier/1837-13
Morgan, John Tyler	Civil War	125	200	350		CSA General/1824-1907
Morgan, Lorrie	Ent	10			25	
Morgan, Michele	Ent	10			25	
Morgan, Ralph	Ent	35			75	1882-1956
Morgan, Russ	Music	25			65	Big Band
Morgan, Sydney, Lady	Author	15		45		The Wild Irish Girl
Morgan, Thomas H.	Science	100	200	375	150	Nobel Medicine 1933
Morgan, Thos. Jeff.	Civil War	75	100	125		Union General/1839-1902
Morgan, Wm. H.	Civil War	25	50	75		Union Officer
Morganna	Ent	5		20	15	The Kissing Bandit
Morgenthau, Henry Jr.	Political	35	75	150	75	FDR Sec'y Treasury
Moriarty, Cathy	Ent	25			50	
Moriarty, Michael	Ent	25			50	Law and Order
Morini, Erica	Music	20			50	Austrian-born Violinist
Morisette, Alanis	Music	25			50	
Morison, Patricia	Ent	15		30	25	
Morita, Pat	Ent	15	35		35	Karate Kid
Mork and Mindy	Ent	25			50	Signed by Dawber/Williams
Morley, Christopher	Author	50	100	150		Am. Writer, Editor
Morley, Robert 1908-92	Ent	25	50		75	Noted Br. Actor
Morrill, Justin Smith	Political	50	75	100		1810-98
Morris, Anita	Ent	10			20	
Morris, Charles	Military	20	50			Commodore USN
Morris, Chester	Ent	25	45		75	1901-1970
Morris, Felix J.	Ent	15			45	
Morris, Garrett	Ent	15			35	Sat Nit Live alumni

Name	Field	SIG	DS	ALS	SP	Remarks
Morris, Gouverneur	RevWar	200	450	550		Continental Congress
Morris, Greg	Ent	25			50	Mission Impossible
Morris, Howard	Ent	10			25	Andy Griffith Show
Morris, James	Music	10			25	Opera
Morris, Lewis 1726-98	RevWar	675	975	1,500		Signer Decl. of Indepen.
Morris, Lewis, Sir	Author	5		20		
Morris, Robert 1734-1806	RevWar	325	750	750		Signer
Morris, Thomas A.	Civil War	RARE	RARE	3,500	RARE	Union General/1811-1904
Morris, Wayne	Ent	25			50	
Morris, William 1834-96	Art	125	275	550		British Poet
Morris, William Walton	Civil War	25	50	75		Union General/1801-65
Morrison, Herb	Aviation	50	75	150	100	Reporter/Hindenburg Crash
Morrison, Jim 1943-71	Music	750	1,500	7,500	1,750	Lead Singer/The Doors
Morrison, Toni	Author	35		75	45	Nobel/Literature
Morrison, Van	Music	25	50		45	
Morrison, William Ralls	Civil War	25		75		Union Officer
Morrow, Dwight W.	Political	10	35			Ambassador to Mexico
Morrow, Jeff	Ent	5			15	
Morrow, Pat	Ent	10			20	
Morrow, Rob	Ent	15			45	
Morrow, Vic 1932-82	Ent	100	150		200	Died Filming Movie
Morse, Barry	Ent	10			20	
Morse, Carleton E.	Author	20	25		30	Radio Writer/Producer
Morse, Jedediah	Science		75	125		Father Modern Geography
Morse, Samuel F. B.	Science	550		1,250	RARE	Telegraph/1791-1872
Mortier, Edouard A.C.J.	Military	35	100	200		French Revolution
Morton, J. Sterling	Political	25	50	125	75	Father Arbor Day
Morton, John 1724-77	RevWar	500	1,200	1,400		Signer Decl. of Indepen.
Morton, Levi 1824-1920	Vice Pres	75		200	250	
Morton, Wm. Thos.	Science	200	450	750		1st to use Ether
Mosby, John S.	Civil War	450	900	2,000	2,750	Mosbys Rangers/1833-16
Moscona, Nicola	Music	30			45	Opera
Mosconi, Willie	Sports	30			75	Billiard Legend/Deceased
Moseley, George Van H.	Military	25	100			MacArthur's Chief of Staff
Moser, Edda	Music	10			25	Opera
Moses, Anna Mary R.	Art	175	500	700	600	Grandma Moses
Moses, Robert 1888-1981	Political	15	35	75		Dominated NY Politics
Mosley, Jack	Cartoonist	25			75	Smilin' Jack
Mosley, Oswald, Sir	Political	25	75		150	
Moss, Kate	Ent	20			50	Super-Model
Mossadegh, Muhammad	Political	45	75	150		Iranian Premier
Mossbauer, Rudolf L.	Science	25	50	75	45	Nobel Physics
Mossman, Doug	Ent	10			20	
Mostel, Zero 1915-77	Ent	50	100		100	Stage, Film Comedy Star
Moszkowski, Moritz	Music	50		150		Ger. Pianist
Motherwell, Robert	Art	75	225	300		Am. Abstract Expressionist
Motley Crue	Music	45			100	Signed by Entire Group

Name	Field	SIG	DS	ALS	SP	Remarks
Motley, John Lothrop	Author	25	50	125		Historian
Mott, Charles S.	Business	25				Pioneer Auto. Exec.
Mott, Frank L.	Author	10		35	25	Pulitzer
Mott, Gershom 1822-84	Civil War	25		50		Union General
Mott, John R.	Clergy	30		75	100	Nobel Peace Prize
Mott, Lucretia	Political	75	150	375	250	Reformer, Abolitionist
Mott, Neville F. Dr.	Science	20		50	25	Nobel Physics
Moulton, Louise C.	Author	25	75	125		1835-1908
Moulton, William	RevWar	25	125			
Moultrie, William 1730-05	RevWar	150	300			Revolutionary War Gen.
Mountbatten, Louis, Lord	Military	100	175	250	200	Admiral of Fleet/1900-79
Mountevens, Baron	Military	25	75		225	Br. WW I Naval Hero
Moutrie, Alexander	RevWar	35		200		
Mowbray, Alan	Ent	45			75	
Mowbray, H. Siddons	Art	25		75		Muralist
Mower, Joseph A.	Civil War	35	100	125		Union General
Moyers, Bill	Author	5		25	15	TV Host
Mozart, Wolfgang A.	Music	RARE	RARE	75,000	RARE	Composer
Mubarak, M. Hosni	Political	50	100	225	100	President Egypt
Mucha, Alphonse	Art	150	RARE	400	RARE	Czech Painter & Illustrator
Muck, Karl, Dr.	Music	20			50	Conductor
Mudd, Roger	Ent	5		30	20	Radio-TV News
Muhammed, Elijah	Political	100	250			
Muhlenberg, John Peter	RevWar	150	250	RARE	RARE	General Continental Army
Muir, Jean	Ent	10			20	
Muir, John 1838-1914	Science	600	1,450	200		Naturalist
Muldaur, Diana	Ent	20			45	
Muldoon, Robert	Political	10		30	20	Prime Minister New Zealand
Mulgrew, Kate	Ent	20			45	Star Trek : Voyager
Mulhare, Edward	Ent	20			45	Ghost and Mrs. Muir
Mulheen, R.J.	Business	5			10	CEO Boston & Maine RR
Mull, Martin	Ent	10	25		30	Roseanne
Muller, Herman J.	Science	20		75	25	Nobel Medicine 1946
Muller, Hermann	Political	50		200		1876-1931
Mulligan, Gerry	Music	10			25	
Mulligan, James A.	Civil War	225				Union Col. KIA Irish Brig
Mulligan, Richard	Ent	10			30	Empty Nest/Soap
Mulliken, Robert S., Dr.	Science	30		75	50	Nobel Chemistry
Mullowney, Deborah	Ent	5			15	
Mulrooney, Dermot	Ent	20			40	
Mumy, Bill	Ent	10			25	Lost in Space
Munch, Charles	Music	10			35	Ger. Conductor
Munch, Edvard 1863-44	Art	75	250			Nor.Painter-Printmaker
Mundelein, George Wm.	Clergy	50	100	200	100	Cardinal
Munford, Thomas T.	Civil War	125		225		CSA General/1831-1918
Muni, Paul 1895-1967	Ent	100		125	175	AA Winner
Munro, Caroline	Ent	10			30	Bond Girl

Name	Field	SIG	DS	ALS	SP	Remarks
Munro, Peter Jay	Political	30	75	150		Nephew of John Jay.
Munsel, Patrice	Ent	20			50	
Munson, Ona	Ent	125		250	200	GWTW/1906-1955
Munster, Earl of	Military	10		40		
Munteanu, Petre	Music	50	100	150		Opera
Muntz, Earl 'Madman'	Business	10		25	20	Pioneer TV Advertiser
Murat, Joachim 1767-15	Military	150	500	500		Napolean Marshall
Murchison, Clint	Business	10		25	20	TX Oil Entrepreneur
Murchison, Clint, Jr.	Business	5		20	15	
Murdoch, Rupert	Business	15			45	
Murphy Brown	Ent				200	Seven Main Characters
Murphy, Audie 1924-71	Military	125	175	300	350	
Murphy, Ben	Ent	5			15	
Murphy, Eddie	Ent	25			50	
Murphy, Frank 1890-1949	SuprCt	75	200	250	150	
Murphy, George L.	Ent	15			25	1902-1992
Murphy, John Cullen	Cartoonist	20			35	Prince Valiant
Murphy, Turk	Music	20			50	Composer/BandLeader
Murphy, William P., Dr.	Science	30	75	125	50	Nobel Medicine 1934
Murray, Anne	Music	10			30	
Murray, Arthur	Business	10			25	Ballroom Dance Studios
Murray, Bill	Ent	25			50	Sat Night Live
Murray, Bob	Aviation	15			30	WWII ACE
Murray, Don	Ent	5			20	
Murray, Eli	Civil War	30				Union General/1844-96
Murray, Jan	Ent	5			10	
Murray, Joseph E., Dr.	Science	20			25	Nobel Medicine
Murray, Ken	Ent	15			30	1903-1988
Murray, Mae	Ent	30		75	75	
Murray, Philip	Political	25	50	75	50	
Murray, Stuart S.	Military	25	75		45	
Murray, William Vans	RevWar	25	50	100		Diplomat
Murrow, Edward R.	Ent	45			100	News Anchor
Murrow, Edward R.	Author	125	300		250	You Can Hear(See) It Now
Mussolini, Benito 1883-45	Political	300	450	RARE	1,200	Fascist Italian Dictator
Myers, Mike	Ent	25			50	Austin Powers
Myers, Russell	Cartoonist	10		25	35	Broom Hilda
Myerson, Bess	Ent	10		30	25	Miss America

Name	Field	SIG	DS	ALS	SP	Remarks
Nabokov, Vladimir	Author	325			900	Novelist
Nabors, Jim	Ent	10		25	20	Gomer Pyle
Nache, Maria Luise	Music	20			45	Opera
Nadar (F. Tournachon)	Art	100	175	300		Caricaturist
Nader, George	Ent	15		45	45	
Nadir Shah, Mohammed	Royalty	75				King Afghanistan. Assass.
Nafta, Giulio	Science	25	35	75		Nobel Chemistry 1963
Nagaoka, Guishi	Military	RARE	RARE	RARE	RARE	Father/Japanese Aviation
Nagel, Anne 1912-66	Ent	25			50	
Nagel, Conrad	Ent	20	25	45	65	1897 - 1970/AA Winner
Naglee, Henry M.	Civil War	30	65			Union General/1815-1886
Nagy, Imre	Political	50	150			Hungarian Prem./Executed
Naish, J. Carrol	Ent	50			100	
Najimy, Kathy	Ent	25			50	Veronica's Closet
Nakasone, Y.	Political	25	35	75	35	Japan
Naldi, Nita	Ent	40			75	1899 - 1961
Nansen, Fridtjof 1861-30	Explorer	175	475	375	450	Zoologist
Napavilova, Zofie	Music	25			75	Opera
Napier, Alan	Ent	45	75	150	75	Alfred on TV's Batman
Napier, Chas, James, Sir	Military	15		75		Br. Gen. vs U.S. War 1812
Napier, Robert C.	Military	45	35	125		Field Marshal/1810-90
Napier, Sir Wm. F.P.	Military	20	50	75		British General
Napoleon I	Royalty	700	2,000	RARE	RARE	
Napoleon II	Royalty	300	700	2,000		
Napoleon III, Emperor of	Royalty	150	400	500		Nephew of Napolean
Napoleon, Eugene L.	Military				575	
Narz, Jack	Ent	10			20	
Nash, Clarence	Ent	125			175	Voice of Donald Duck
Nash, Graham	Music	15			45	
Nash, Johnny	Music	25			50	
Nash, Ogden	Author	50		100	75	Poet
Nash, Walter	Political	15		45	25	P.M. New Zealand
Nasir-edun Shah Qajar	Royalty	750		3,500		King (Shah) Persia
Nasmyth, James 1808-90	Science	100				Steam Hammer
Nasser, Garnet Abdel	Political	75	400	350	275	President Egypt
Nast, Thomas 1840-1902	Cartoonist	125	350	300	RARE	Political Cartoonist.
Nathan, George Jean	Author	10		35	15	Drama Critic
Nathans, Daniel, Dr.	Science	25	35	45	35	Nobel Medicine
Nation, Carry 1846-1911	Clergy	75	150	200	RARE	Temperance Agitator
Natividad, Kitten	Ent	10			25	Model
Natwick, Mildred	Ent	25	35		45	1908 - 1998
Navon, Yitzhak	Political	20			50	Israel

Name	Field	SIG	DS	ALS	SP	Remarks
Nazimova, Alla	Ent	75			100	1879 - 1945
Neagle, Anna, Dame	Ent	10	25		30	1904-1986
Neal, Bob	Aviation	15	35	45	40	WWII ACE/Flying Tigers
Neal, Patricia	Ent	5	20	25	20	AA Winner
Neal, Sam	Ent	20			45	Jurassic Park
Neal, Tom	Ent	10			20	
Neale, Bob	Aviation	25			75	WWII Flying Tiger
Nebel, Rudolf	Science	50	100			
Neblett, Carol	Music	15			35	Opera
Necker, Jacques	Military	125	350			Fr. Financier & Statesman
Needham, Hal	Ent	10			20	Director
Neel, Louis Eugene F.	Science	20		45	25	Nobel Physics
Neeson, Liam	Ent	25			60	Darkman/Star Wars
Negley, James S.	Civil War	40	75	100		Union General/1826-1901
Negri, Joe	Ent	10			20	
Negri, Pola	Ent	35	75		125	
Nehru, B.K.	Political	10			20	Ambassador
Nehru, Jawaharlal	Political	125	350	600	400	Assasinated PM/1889-64
Neidlinger, Gustav	Music	15			40	Opera
Neil, Vince	Music	20			50	
Neill, James	Ent	15			35	
Neill, Noel	Ent	10			20	TV's first Lois Lane
Neiman, LeRoy	Art	40	150	150	75	Sports Artwork
Nelligan, Kate	Ent	10		25	20	
Nelson, Barry	Ent	15			35	
Nelson, Craig T.	Ent	15			45	Coach
Nelson, David	Ent	15			45	Ozzie & Harriett
Nelson, Ed	Ent	10			25	
Nelson, Gene 1920-96	Ent	20			50	
Nelson, Harriet Hilliard	Music	25			50	Singer/TV star
Nelson, Horatio 1758-05	Military	800	1,600	3,000		Br. Admiral
Nelson, John	Political	20		100		Tyler Att'y General
Nelson, Lori	Ent	5			15	
Nelson, Ozzie	Ent	35			75	Ozzie and Harriet Fame
Nelson, Ozzie & Harriet	Ent	100	200			Signed by Both
Nelson, Rick	Music	100	300	RARE	275	
Nelson, Samuel	SuprCt	50	150	200		1792 - 1873
Nelson, Thomas Jr.	RevWar	550		2,500		Signer
Nelson, Willie	Music	15			45	Country
Nemerov, Howard	Author	10			25	3rd Poet Laureate US
Nemeth, Maria	Music	25			50	Opera
Nero, Peter	Music	5			15	Jazz Pianist
Nesbit, Wilbur	Author	10		30		
Nesbitt, Cathleen	Ent	15			30	
Nesmith, Michael	Music	25			50	The Monkees
Ness, Eliot	Political	375	800	RARE	RARE	
Nethersole, Olga	Ent	15			45	

Name	Field	SIG	DS	ALS	SP	Remarks
Nettleton, Lois	Ent	5			15	
Neubert, Frank	Aviation	25	75			
Neurath, Constantin von	Political	50	75	150	100	
Nevelson, Louise	Art	50		150	100	Am Sculptor/Large Pieces
Neville, Aaron	Music	10			25	
Neville, Henry	Music	10			25	
Nevin, Ethelbert	Music	75	150	300	100	Composer
New Kids on the Block	Music	50			150	Signed by All in the Group
Newcomb, Simon	Science	75	200	300		Am. Astronomer
Newell, David	Ent	10			20	
Newhart, Bob	Ent	5		25	20	Newhart
Newhouse, Samuel	Business	15		45	25	Newspaper-Radio-TV
Newley, Anthony	Music	5			15	
Newman, Barry	Ent	5			10	
Newman, Paul	Ent	100	200	RARE	250	
Newman, Randy	Music	10	25		25	
Newmar, Julie	Ent	10	25	35	25	Catwoman on TV's Batman
Newsom, Tommy	Music	10			20	Bandleader/Tonite Show
Newton - John, Olivia	Ent	25	50		50	Singer-Actress
Newton, Huey P.	Political	100			350	Afro-Am. Activist
Newton, Isaac, Sir	Science	4,000	12,000	25,000	RARE	
Newton, John 1823-95	Civil War	75		300		Union General
Newton, Juice	Music	10			35	
Newton, Robert	Ent	50	75	100	75	
Newton, Thandie	Ent	25			50	Mission Impossible II
Newton, Wayne	Ent	10			35	
Ney, Michael	Military	125	250	500		Marshal of France
Ney, Richard	Ent	15			35	
Ngo, Dinn Diem	Political	100				South Vietnamese Pres.
Niarchos, Stavro	Business	50	125	150	75	
Nicholas I 1796-1855	Royalty		1,200			Czar of Russia
Nicholas II 1868-1918	Royalty		2,500	RARE		Last Czar of Russia
Nicholas, Denise	Ent	5			15	
Nicholas, Prince & King	Royalty	25	50	150		Greece
Nicholls, Francis R. T.	Civil War	75	125	175		CSA General/1834-1912
Nichols, Barbara	Ent	35			75	
Nichols, Ebenezer B.	Business	50	150			Early TX Banker
Nichols, Mike	Ent	35			100	Film Director
Nichols, Nichelle	Ent	15			35	Star Trek
Nichols, Red	Music	35			75	Jazz Instrumentalist
Nichols, Ruth Roland	Aviation	125	250		250	
Nichols, William A.	Civil War	25	75			Union Officer/1818-69
Nicholson, Jack	Ent	25	100	RARE	50	Joker in Batman Movie
Nicholson, John 1783-46	Military	30		175		Commodore U.S. Navy
Nicholson, Meredith	Author	20	50	125	50	
Nickerson, Franklin S.	Civil War	25	50	75		Union General
Nicks, Stevie	Music	25		100	50	Fleetwood Mac

Name	Field	SIG	DS	ALS	SP	Remarks
Nicol, Alex	Ent	10			25	
Nicolai, Elena	Music	30			75	Opera
Nicolay, John G.	Civil War	50	150	250		Lincoln Personal Sec'y.
Nicollet, Joseph N.	Explorer	100	225	300		
Nielsen, Alice 1876-1943	Music	50			150	Opera
Nielsen, Asta	Music	20			50	Opera
Nielsen, Brigitte	Ent	10			25	
Nielsen, Carl	Music	200	450	750		Danish Composer
Nielsen, Gertrude	Ent	10			25	
Nielson, Leslie	Ent	10	25		20	
Niemack, Horst	Military	20			50	Ger. General Major
Niesen, Gertrude	Music	10			15	
Nietzsche, Friedrich	Author	475	775	RARE	RARE	German Poet
Nigh, William	Ent	15			30	
Nightingale, Florence	Science	450	750	750		1820-1910
Nijinsky, Vaslav 1890-50	Music	500		RARE	RARE	Ballet
Nikisch, Artur	Music	35		85		Hungarian Conductor
Nikolayev, Andryan G.	Space	150			200	Russian Cosmonaut
Niles, Wendell	Ent	10			20	
Nillson, Christine	Music	50		175		Opera
Nilssen, Anna Q.	Ent	15			45	
Nilsson, Birgit	Music	15			35	Opera
Nilsson, Harry	Music	50	100		100	
Nimersheim, Jack	Author	5		20	20	Campbell Award nominee
Nimitz, Chester W.	Military	125	300	350	400	1885-1966
Nimoy, Leonard	Ent	35	75		75	Spock on Star Trek
Nin, Anais	Author	50	125	200	100	
Nirenberg, Marshall W.	Science	15		45	35	Nobel Medicine 1968
Nirvana	Music	175	400		350	Signed by All Three
Nissen, Greta	Ent	10			25	
Nitty Gritty Dirt Band	Music	35			65	Signed by all
Niven, David 1909-83	Ent	40		125	75	AA Winner
Nixon, John 1733-1808	RevWar	125	275			
Nixon, Marni	Ent	10			30	
Nixon, Patricia 1912-92	First Lady	45	75	250	175	
Nixon, Richard M.	President	200	600	RARE	300	1913-1994
No Doubt	Music	50			100	Signed by Entire Group
Nobel, Alfred	Science	250	400		450	
Nobile, Umberto 1885-78	Aviation	75	200	300	175	
Noble, Chelsea	Ent	15			45	
Noble, James	Ent	5			15	
Noble, John W. 1831-12	Civil War	35	50	125	100	Union General
Noel-Baker, Philip	Political	30		100	25	Nobel Peace Prize
Noguchi, Isamu	Art	25		75		Am. Sculptor
Noir, Haing S.	Ent	50	75		100	Murdered AA winner
Nolan, Kathleen	Ent	5			15	
Nolan, Lloyd 1902-85	Ent	25	50		50	

Name	Field	SIG	DS	ALS	SP	Remarks
Nolin, Gene Lee	Ent	25			50	Baywatch
Nolte, Nick	Ent	20			50	
Nono, Luigi 1924-90	Music	100			175	Composer/Opera
Noonan, Fred J. 1893-37	Aviation	RARE	RARE	RARE	RARE	
Noone, Peter	Music	25			50	Lead/Hermans Hermits
Noor, Queen	Political	25		100	75	Queen of Hussein (Jordan)
Nordau, Simon Max	Science	50	100		75	1849-1923
Nordenskjoid, Nils Adolf	Explorer	200			350	
Nordenskjoid, Nils Otto	Explorer	200			300	Led Antarctic Expedition
Nordhoff, Charles	Author	25		50		Mutiny on Bounty w/
Nordhoff, Heinz, Dr.	Business	25			50	Auto Mfg.-VW
Nordica, Lillian 1859-14	Music	75			250	Am. Soprano
Noriega, Manuel A.	Political	75	100		100	
Norman, Jessye	Music	30			45	Opera
Normand, Mabel	Ent	150			400	Scarce
Norris, Chuck	Ent	15	40		40	Walker, Texas Ranger
Norris, Frank 1870-1902	Author	125	275	450		War Correspondent
Norris, Kathleen	Author	20		50	25	Prolific Am. Novelist
Norstad, Lauris	Military	20			45	Gen.WWII
North, Frederick, Lord	Political	150	300	500		1732-1792
North, Jay	Ent	10			25	Denace the Menace
North, John Ringling	Business	50	100		100	Ringling Brothers Circus
North, Oliver L.	Military	35	100	175	75	Marine Colonel
North, Sheree	Ent	5			15	
North, William 1755-1836	Military	75	150	400		Gen. Cont. Army
Northbrook, Lord	Political	15		50		
Northrop, John H.	Science	50	150		100	Nobel Chemistry 1946
Northrop, John K.	Business	50	125	250	100	Founder Northrop Aircraft
Northumberland, 2nd Dk	RevWar	50	150	225		
Norton, Edward	Ent	25			50	
Norton, Oliver P.	Civil War	20		45		Civil War Governor
Norton-Taylor, Judy	Ent	10			20	
Norville, Deborah	Ent	5			15	TV News Anchor
Norvo, Red	Music	15			45	Bandleader
Norworth, Jack	Music	125		250		Take Me Out to BallGame
Nourse, Joseph	Military	500	900	RARE		1754-1841
Novak, Kim	Ent	25	50		75	
Novak, Vitezslav	Music	50			150	Czech. Composer
Novarro, Ramon	Ent	50	100		100	Mexican Actor/1899-1968
Novatna, Jarmila	Music	15			35	Czech. Soprano
Novello, Ivor	Music	25		75	75	Composer
Nowak, Max	Science	15			45	Rocket Pioneer/von Braun
Noyce, Phillip	Ent	10			20	Director
Noyes, Alfred	Author	15		45	35	British Poet
Nucci, Danny	Ent	25			50	Titanic
Nugent, Elliott	Ent	5			15	
Nugent, Ted	Music	25		50	50	

Name	Field	SIG	DS	ALS	SP	Remarks
Nungesser, Charles	Aviation	125	225	300	300	
Nureyev, Rudolf 1938-93	Music	75	125	200	150	Dancer/Choreagrapher
Nurmella, Kari	Music	15			30	Opera
Nuyen, France	Ent	10			255	
Nye, Bill (Edgar Wilson)	Author	25		75		Humorist
Nye, James W.	Political	75	125	175		
Nyerere, Julius	Political	10		50	30	Tanzania

O

Name	Field	SIG	DS	ALS	SP	Remarks
Oak Ridge Boys, The	Music	25			45	
Oakes, Randi	Ent	5			15	
Oakie, Jack	Ent	25	75		50	
Oakley, Annie 1860-1926	Western	2,500	6,000	9,000	7,500	Am. Markswoman
Oakley, Violet	Art	35	75			
Oates, Joyce Carol	Author	20		50	30	American Novelist
Oates, Warren	Ent	25			50	
Ober, W.O. 'Willy'	Aviation	25		50		
Oberhardt, William	Art	35	75	125		
Oberon, Merle	Ent	50			75	1911 - 1979
Oberth, Hermann, Dr.	Science	75	200		250	Early Rocket Pioneer
Oboler, Arch	Ent	10		35	25	Writer-Producer
Obratszova, Elena	Music	15			45	Opera
O'Brien, Conan	Ent	10			25	Late Night TV Host
O'Brien, Cubby	Ent	5			20	Mickey Mouse Club
O'Brien, Edmond	Ent	20			50	AA
O'Brien, George	Ent	20			45	
O'Brien, Hugh	Ent	25	50		50	TV Wyatt Earp
O'Brien, James	Business	5			15	
O'Brien, Lawrence F.	Political	10			20	JFK Adviser-Strategist.P.M.
O'Brien, Margaret	Ent	15			35	
O'Brien, Pat	Ent	45	100		100	
O'Brien, Virginia	Ent	5			15	
Ocasek, Ric	Music	25			50	The Cars
O'Casey, Sean l880-1964	Author	100	275	400	300	Irish Playwright
Ochoa, Severo, Dr.	Science	20		75	30	Nobel Physiology
Ochs, Adolph S. 1858-35	Business	150				Founder NY Times
O'Connell, Arthur	Ent	35			75	
O'Connell, Charles	Business	10		30	200	
O'Connell, Daniel	Political	75	250			Irish Nationalist Leader
O'Connell, Helen	Ent	15			25	
O'Connell, Jerry	Ent	25			50	
O'Conner, Flannery	Author	300	750			Am Author/Died Young
O'Connor, Carroll	Ent	10	25		25	All in the Family
O'Connor, Donald	Ent	10			30	Singing in the Rain
O'Connor, Glynnis	Ent	5			15	
O'Connor, Rene	Ent	25			60	Xena : Warrior Princess
O'Connor, Sandra Day	SuprCt	25	125	200	50	
O'Connor, Una	Ent	40			75	
O'Connor,Thos. P.	Author	50	100			Irish Journalist
Odd Couple (Movie)	Ent	25			75	Sgnd by Mathau/Lemmon
Odd Couple (TV)	Ent	25			50	Sgnd by Klugman/Randall
Odell, George C.D.	Author	5		30		Educator, Theatre Arts
Odets, Clifford	Author	50	100	175	150	Playwright.Golden Boy, etc.

Name	Field	SIG	DS	ALS	SP	Remarks
O'Donald, Emmett	Aviation	15		50	35	
O'Donnell, Chris	Ent	25			50	'Robin' in Batman
O'Donnell, Rosie	Ent	25	50		50	
O'Driscoll, Martha	Ent	5			10	
Oersted, Hans Christian	Science	2,500	RARE	RARE	RARE	Electromagnatism
Oesau, Walter'Gulle'	Aviation	150		400	275	
Offenbach, Jacques	Music	150	250	450	275	1819-1880
Offenhauser, Fred	Science	125	300			Automobile/Racing Engine
O'Flaherty, Liam	Author	100	275			Ir. Novelist
O'Flynn, Damien	Ent	10			20	
Ogden, Aaron	RevWar	50	100	225		Rev War Soldier
Ogden, Francis B.1783-57	Military	15	45	75		Steam Engine Pioneer
Ogden, Thomas L.	Political	20		45		
Oglesby, Richard J.	Civil War	50		100	150	Union General/1824-99
O'Grady, Gail	Ent	10			25	NYPD Blue
O'Hara, Geoffrey	Music	20	45		25	Composer
O'Hara, John	Author	150	450	600		Am. Novelist, Short Stories
O'Hara, Mary (Alsop)	Author	20	50	75		Novelist/My Friend Flicka
O'Hara, Maureen	Ent	15			20	
O'Higgins, Harvey	Author	10		50	25	Novelist
Ohms, Elizabeth	Music	50			150	Opera
O'Keefe, Dennis	Ent	5			20	
O'Keefe, Georgia	Art	350		750		Scarce
O'Keeffe, Adrian	Business	5			10	CEO First National Stores
Oland, Warner 1880-1938	Ent	150	200		250	Charlie Chan
O'Laughlin, Gerald S.	Ent	10			20	
Olcott, Chauncey	Music	50	100	150	100	My Wild Irish rose...
Oldenburg, Claes Thure	Art	15		75	35	Sculptor
Older, Charles H.	Aviation	15		45	35	WWII ACE/Flying Tigers
Older, Charles S.	Civil War	25		50		
Oldman, Gary	Ent	25			50	Dracula
Olds, Ransom E. 1864-50	Business	350	1,200			Oldsmobile Motors
Olds, Robin	Aviation	15		45	35	WWII ACE/Korea/Vietnam
Olin, Ken	Ent	5			10	
Olin, Lena	Ent	20			50	
Oliphant, Laurence	Author	10		50		Br Writer/Cape Town
Oliphant, Pat	Cartoonist	10			25	Political Cartoonist
Olitzka, Rosa	Music	50			125	Pol./Ger. Mezzo
Oliver, Andrew	RevWar	75	150	225		Am, Colonial Politician
Oliver, Edna May	Ent	50			125	
Oliver, Henry W., Jr.	Business	50	75			Iron & Steel Tycoon
Oliver, Jane	Ent	5			15	
Oliver, Paul A.	Civil War	25	50	75		Union Off/Inv. of Dynamite
Oliver, Sy	Music	35			75	Trumpet/Composer
Olivero, Magda	Music	25			50	Opera
Olivier, Laurence, Sir	Ent	75	125		175	1907-1969
Olmos, Edward James	Ent	10			25	
Olmstead, Frederick L.	Science	100	175	300		Landscape architect
Olsen & Johnson	Ent	35			75	Hellzapoppin

Name	Field	SIG	DS	ALS	SP	Remarks
Olsen, Merlin	Ent	10			25	
Olsen, Ole	Ent	25			50	
Olson, Nancy	Ent	5			15	
O'Malley, J. Pat	Ent	25			50	
Onassis, Aristotle	Business	175	300		225	Shipping Magnate
Onassis, Jacq. Kennedy	Political	375	750	1,500	900	
O'Neal, Ralph A.	Military	25		75	75	
O'Neal, Ryan	Ent	10			35	
O'Neal, Tatum	Ent	15	35		45	AA Winner
O'Neil, Barbara	Ent	150	RARE	RARE	350	GWTW star/1908-1980
O'Neill, Charles	Military	10		45		Adm. USN
O'Neill, Eugene 1888-53	Author	200	350		RARE	Playwright/Nobel/Pulitzer
O'Neill, Henry 1891-1964	Ent	20			50	
O'Neill, James	Ent	20		45	45	
O'Neill, Jennifer	Ent	5			15	
O'Neill, Peggy	Ent	5			15	
O'Neill, Thomas 'Tip'	Political	15	30		45	Speaker of the House. MA
Ono,Yoko	Music	45		75	75	
Ontkean, Michael	Ent	5			15	
Opatoshu, David	Ent	15			25	
Opp, Julie	Music	10			25	Opera
Oppenheimer, Rob't, Dr.	Science	450	RARE	RARE	RARE	Dir. Manhatten Project
Opper, Frederick Burr	Cartoonist	25		75	125	Happy Hooligan
Orbach, Jerry	Ent	10	25		30	Law and Order
Orbison, Roy	Music	125	200		250	
Orczy, Emmuska	Author	35		100	125	Br. Novelist
Ord, E.O.C. 1818-83	Civil War	100	150	400		Union Gen-Indian Fighter
Orff, Carl 1895-1982	Music	45			150	Ger. Carmina Burana
Orgonotzova, Ludmilia	Music	10			25	Opera
Orita, Zenji	Military	50	150		100	
Orlando, Vittorio E.	Political	75	125	250		It Prime Minister
Ormandy, Eugene	Music	25		100	75	Hungarian Conductor
Ormond, Julia	Ent	25			50	
Orpen, William, Sir	Art	50	175		350	
Orr, William T.	Ent	25	50			Film Director-Producer
Ory, Edward Kid	Music	100			200	Bandleader
Osborn, Joan	Music	15			45	
Osborn, Super Dave	Ent	10			20	
Osborne, Baby Marie	Ent	10			20	
Osborne, John 1929-94	Author	10		45	20	Br. Playwright, Screenwriter
Osborne, Ozzy	Music	20			45	
Oscar I, Joseph-Francois	Royalty	100	200	400		King Sweden & Norway
Oscar II	Royalty	35	75	150		King Sweden & Norway
Osgood, Charles	Ent	5			15	TV News, Host
Osgood, Samuel	RevWar	125	300	500		
O'Shea, Michael	Ent	10			25	
Oslin, K.T.	Music	5			20	
Osmena, Sergio	Political	75	150			Pres. Philippines 1944-46
Osmond Brothers	Music	50	100		75	Signed by all Five

Name	Field	SIG	DS	ALS	SP	Remarks
Osmond, Donny	Music	15	40		35	
Osmond, Ken	Ent	10			20	
Osmond, Marie	Music	10		25	25	
Osten, Hans Georg von	Aviation	30			75	German WWI ACE
Ostenso, Martha	Author	25		70		Novelist/Poet
Oster, William, Dr.	Science	350	500	1,500		Medical Historian
Osterhaus, Peter J.	Civil War	35	75	100		Union General/1823-1917
Osterkamp, Theo	Aviation	35		125	75	
Osterman, Kathryn	Ent	20			50	
O'Sullivan, Gilbert	Music	25	75			
O'Sullivan, Maureen	Ent	20			45	Tarzan's Jane
Osvoth, Julia	Music	25			45	Opera
Oswald, Lee Harvey	Criminal	RARE	7,500	12,000	RARE	Murdered John F. Kennedy
Oswald, Mark	Music	10			25	Opera
Otis, Elita Proctor	Ent	10	25		25	
Otis, Elwell S.	Civil War	25	50	75		Union General/1838-1909
Otis, James 1725-83	RevWar	250	475	650		
Otis, Johnny	Ent	25			45	Director/Producer
O'Toole, Annette	Ent	10			30	
O'Toole, Peter	Ent	25			50	Lawrence of Arabia
Otto I (Othon I) 1815-67	Royalty	100	300	250		Greece
Otto I (The Great)	Royalty	2,000	RARE	RARE	RARE	King of Germany
Oudinot, Charles N. Duc	Military	75	150			Marshal of Napoleon
Ouida (Louise dela Ram)	Author	25	75	100		Br Novelist
Ould, Robert 1820-82	Civil War	75	125			CSA Colonel
Ouspenskaya, Maria	Ent	225	400	RARE	400	1876 - 1949
Outcault, Richard	Cartoonist	125			275	Yellow Kid, Buster Brown
Outlaw, Edward C.	Aviation	15		45	35	WWII ACE in One Day
Overall, Park	Ent	10			20	Empty Nest
Overman, Lynn	Ent	15			45	Character Actor
Overmyer, Robert	Space	25			50	2nd Space Shuttle Flight
Ovington, Earle	Aviation	50			200	Pilot 1st Air Mail Plane
Owen, Joshua T.	Civil War	75		225		Union General/War Dated
Owen, Joshua T. 1821-87	Civil War	35	125			Union General
Owen, Reginald	Ent	35			75	
Owen, Robert 1771-1858	Political			250		Br. Utopian Socialist
Owen, Robert Dale	Political	25		125		1801-1877
Owen, Ruth Bryan	Political	25			50	
Owens, Buck	Aviation	15			30	Marine WWII ACE
Owens, Buck	Music	5			15	
Owens, Tex	Music	10			20	
Oxenberg, Catherine	Ent	25			40	
Oz, Frank	Ent	25			45	Voice of Miss Piggy/Yoda
Ozbourne, Ozzy	Music	25			50	

P

Name	Field	SIG	DS	ALS	SP	Remarks
Paar, Jack	Ent	25			50	
Pabst, Fred	Business	150	450		400	Pabst Brewing Co.
Paca, William 1740-99	RevWar	750	1,500	2,500		Signer
Pacetti, Iva	Music	25			75	Opera
Pache, Jean Nicholas	Military	25		150		French Revolution
Pacino, Al	Ent	25	100		50	Godfather
Pack, Denis, Sir	Military	25	75	125		
Packard, David	Business	20		50	50	Co-Fndr Hewlett-Packard
Packard, James Ward	Business	RARE	RARE	5,000	RARE	Fndr. Packard Automobile
Packard, Kelly	Ent	15			30	
Packard, Vance	Author	10		40	20	Am. Nonfiction Writer
Packwood, Bob	Political	10			35	Senator OR
Paderewski, Ignace J.	Music	175		550	450	Composer
Paduca, Duke of	Music	20			40	
Paer, Ferdinando	Music	50	100	200		Composer
Pafti, Amalia	Ent	50		125	150	Opera
Paganini, Nicolo	Music	450	RARE	RARE	RARE	1782-1840
Page, Anita	Ent	10			15	
Page, Bettie	Ent	25			75	Model
Page, Geraldine	Ent	30			75	AA Winner/1924-1987
Page, Lawanda	Ent	10			25	Sanford and Son
Page, Patti	Ent	5			15	
Page, Richard Lucian	Civil War	100	175	450		
Page, Thomas Nelson	Author	15		45		Novelist
Page, William 1811-85	Art	150		350		Am. Portrait Painter
Paget, Debra	Ent	25			50	
Pagliughi, Lina	Music	50			125	Opera
Pahlavi, Mohammed R.	Political	125	200	300	300	Shah of Iran/1919-80
Paige, Janis	Ent	10			15	
Paige, Mabel	Ent	10			25	Vintage Radio
Paine, John Knowles	Music	15		50		Composer
Paine, Robert Treat	RevWar	250	450	900		Signer/1731-1814
Paine, Thomas	RevWar	3,500	RARE	RARE	RARE	Am. Philosopher-Author
Pakula, Alan J.	Ent	5			15	Director
Pal, George	Ent	75			125	
Palacio, Ernesto	Music	15			30	Opera
Palade, George E., Dr.	Science	20			25	Nobel Medicine 1974
Palance, Jack	Ent	35	75		75	AA Winner/Scarce
Palet, Jose	Music	75			175	Opera
Paley, William S.	Business	15	35	75	35	Founded CBS in 1928
Palfrey, F.W.	Civil War	25		75		Union General/1834-1906
Pallette, Eugene	Ent	50			75	

Name	Field	SIG	DS	ALS	SP	Remarks
Palma, Tomas Estrada	Political	20		45		1st President Cuba
Palmenteri, Chaz	Ent	20			50	
Palmer, Gregg	Ent	15			35	
Palmer, Innis N. 1824-00	Civil War	45				Union General
Palmer, Jimmy	Music	15			40	Bandleader
Palmer, John McCauley	Civil War	75	125	175		Union General/1817-1900
Palmer, Lilli	Ent	15			65	1911 - 1986
Palmer, Potter	Business	225	750	1,250	450	Palmer House Hotel
Palmer, Robert	Music	25			50	
Palmerston, Henry J.T.	Political	50		150		Prime Minister Eng.
Paltrow, Gwyneth	Ent	25			50	
Pan, Hermes	Music	35	75		75	Choreographer
Panerai, Rolando	Music	10			25	Opera
Pangborn, Clyde	Aviation	75	150		250	Aviation Pioneer
Pangborn, Franklin	Ent	35			75	Comedic Character Actor
Pankhurst, Christabel	Political	25	75	150		
Pankhurst, E. Sylvia	Political	75	150	250		1882-1960
Pankhurst, Emmeline	Political	50	125	200		
Pantoliano, Joe	Ent	10			20	
Papen, Franz von	Military	50	150	200	150	Hitlers Vice-Chancellor
Papp, Joseph	Ent	30			50	Theatre Producer
Paquin, Anna	Ent	35			75	AA Winning child actress
Paris, Joel B., III	Aviation	15			35	WWII ACE
Park, Ray	Ent	20			50	Star Wars/Darth Maul
Parke, John Grubb	Civil War	50	150	150		Union General/1827-1900
Parker, Charlie 1920-55	Music	400	800	RARE	RARE	Alto Sax Jazz Musician
Parker, David	Military	15		50		
Parker, Dorothy	Author	30		75	50	Poet/1893-1967
Parker, Edward P.	Business	75	150			Parker Bros. Pen Co.
Parker, Eleanor	Ent	5			15	
Parker, Ely Samuel	Civil War	300				Union General/Seneca Chf.
Parker, Fess	Ent	10	35	35	25	Davy Crockett
Parker, Frank	Music	15			35	Jack Benny's Ist Vocalist
Parker, Gilbert 1861-1921	Author	15		45		
Parker, Graham	Ent	20			35	
Parker, Isaac 1768-1830	Political	25		100		
Parker, Isaac C. 1838-96	Western	500	1,500			The Hanging Judge
Parker, Jameson	Ent	10			25	
Parker, Jean	Ent	15			30	
Parker, Joel 1816-1888	Civil War	15		45		Civil War Gov. NJ
Parker, John	Civil War		750			Captured by Commanches
Parker, Mary Louise	Ent	20			45	
Parker, Roy, Jr.	Music	5			15	
Parker, Sarah Jessica	Ent	20			45	
Parker, Suzy	Ent	5			15	
Parker, Thomas	RevWar	50	100	150		Continental Army General
Parker, Tom, Colonel	Ent	25	50		50	Elvis' Manager

Name	Field	SIG	DS	ALS	SP	Remarks
Parker, Trey	Cartoonist	20			50	Co-Creator of South Park
Parker, Willard	Ent	10			25	
Parkins, Barbara	Ent	10			20	
Parkinson, Dian	Ent	5			15	Price is Right Model
Parkman, Francis	Author	25	75	150		Historian. The Oregon Trail
Parks, Bert	Ent	10			30	
Parks, Gordon	Author	20	50		50	Photographer
Parks, Larry	Ent	30			50	1914-1975
Parks, Rosa L.	Political	40			100	Civil Rights, Bus Boycott
Parks, Trina	Ent	25			50	James Bond Girl
Parr, Ralph	Aviation	15		45	30	Korean Double ACE
Parrish, Anne 1888-1957	Author	15	30			Novelist
Parrish, Helen	Ent	10			20	
Parrish, Julie	Ent	5			10	
Parrish, Maxfield 1870-66	Art	175	500	750		Checks - 250
Parry, Charles Hubert H.	Music	15		50		Historian
Parseval, August von	Aviation	100				Ger. Aeronautical Engineer
Parsons, Albert Ross	Music	5			10	
Parsons, Estelle	Ent	10			20	
Parsons, Louella	Ent	20		75	50	1893 - 1972
Parsons, Mosby M.	Civil War	200				CSA General/1819-65
Parsons, Samuel H.	RevWar		300	450		Continental General
Parton, Dolly	Music	15			45	Country
Parton, Stella	Music	5			10	
Partridge, Bernard, Sir	Art	25		45		Brit. Punch Cartoonist
Partridge, Wm. Ordway	Art	10			30	Am. Sculptor
Parvis, Taurino	Music	40			100	Opera
Pasero, Tancredi	Music	35			75	Opera
Paskalis, Kostas	Music	15			45	Opera
Pasternak, Boris 1890-60	Author	350	750	1,500		Dr. Zhivago
Pasternak, Joe	Ent	35	75	100	75	Director
Pasteur, Louis 1822-1895	Science	500	900	1,750	RARE	Pasteurization, Vaccines
Pastor, Tony	Music	10			35	Big Bandleader
Pastorelli, Robert	Ent	15			35	Murphy Brown
Patch, Alexander M.	Military	75	150	300	200	Am. General WWII
Pate, Michael	Ent	5			15	
Paterson, John	RevWar	75	200	300		1744 - 1808
Paterson, William	SuprCt	RARE	RARE	RARE	RARE	
Patinkin, Mandy	Ent	20			40	
Paton, Alan	Author	50	100	200		South African Author
Patric, Jason	Ent	15			35	
Patrick, Butch	Ent	5		25	20	Eddie Munster
Patrick, Dennis	Ent	5			10	
Patrick, Gail	Ent	10			15	
Patrick, Marsena R.	Civil War	35	50	75		Union General/1811-88
Patten, Gilbert	Author	35	75	150	50	
Patten, Luana	Ent	35			75	

Name	Field	SIG	DS	ALS	SP	Remarks
Patterson, Daniel Tod	Military	50	150	200		
Patterson, Robert	Civil War	25	50	75		Union General/1792-1881
Patti, Adelina (Niccolini)	Music	150	200	350	375	Opera
Patton, George S. III	Military	10		35	20	Son of WWII General
Patton, George S. Jr.	Military	1,000	2,000	3,500	5,000	1885-1945/General
Paul I & Frederica	Royalty	150			250	King & Queen of Greece
Paul I, Pavel Petrovich	Royalty	225	450	1,200		Emperor of Russia
Paul II, Pope	Clergy		400			
Paul III, Pope	Clergy		1,200			
Paul VI, Pope	Clergy	300	475	900	600	Giovanni Battista Montini
Paul VI, Pope 1897-1978	Clergy		500		900	
Paul, Adrian	Ent	25			50	TV's Highlander
Paul, Alexandra	Ent	20			45	Baywatch
Paul, Les	Music	25	35		45	
Paul, Wolfgang	Science	10			30	Nobel Physics 1989
Paulding, Hiram	Civil War	25	50	75		Commanded Navy Yard NY
Paulding, James Kirke	Author	35	75	150		Van Buren Sec'y Navy
Pauley, Jane	Ent	5			15	
Paulham, Louis	Aviation	35	75	125	75	
Pauling, Linus 1901-94	Science	75	250	400	125	Nobel in Chemistry
Paulsen, Valademar	Science	50	125			
Paulson, Pat	Ent	15			35	
Paulton, Harry	Ent	5			10	
Paulucci, Jeno F.	Business	15		35	30	
Pauly, Rose	Music	25			50	Opera
Pavarotti, Luciano	Music	35		100	75	Opera
Pavie, Auguste-Jean-Ma	Political	50	125	200		French Explorer
Pavlov, Ivan 1849-1936	Science	RARE	RARE	3,500	RARE	Rus. Physiologist
Pavlova, Anna 1882-1931	Music	350		450	550	Russian Ballerina
Pawnee Bill (Lillie,G.A.)	Western					See Lillie, Gordon A.
Paxinou, Katina	Ent	150		300	250	
Paxton, Bill	Ent	25			45	
Paxton, Elisha F.	Civil War	750	RARE	RARE	RARE	CSA General/1828-63
Paycheck, Johnny	Music	10			25	Country
Payer, Julius von	Explorer	100	200		275	North Polar Expedition
Payne, Eugene B.	Civil War	25	50	75		Union Officer
Payne, Freda	Music	10			20	
Payne, Henry C.	Political	15		35		P.M. General 1902
Payne, John 1912-89	Ent	20		50	60	
Payne, John Howard	Music	100	250	400		
Payne, William H.	Civil War	100	200	300		CSA General/1830-1904
Pays, Amanda	Ent	15			45	
Peabody, Charles, Dr.	Science	10		25		
Peabody, Eddie	Ent	15		35	30	
Peabody, George	Business	50	150	400		Merchant/1795-1869
Peabody, George F.	Business	50	100	300		Merchant/1852-1938
Peale, Chas. Wilson	Art	250	450	750		Portrait Painter

Name	Field	SIG	DS	ALS	SP	Remarks
Peale, Norman Vincent	Author	20	50	100	50	Clergy
Peale, Rembrandt	Art	250	475	1,200		Am. Portrait Artist
Peale, Titian 1799-1885	Art		225	750		
Pearce, Alice	Ent	100	150		250	Bewitched
Pearce, Richard	Ent	10			20	Director
Pearl Jam	Music	75			150	Signed by Entire Group
Pearl, Minnie	Music	25			45	Country
Pearson, Lester B.	Political	25	75	150	50	Nobel Peace Prize
Peary, Harold	Ent	20			45	
Peary, Robert E. 1856-20	Explorer	150		450	600	Adm. Arctic Explorer
Peck, Gregory	Ent	25	75		60	AA Winner
Peck, Robert Newton	Author	10		25		Am. Novelist
Peckham, Rufus W.	SuprCt	75	125	250	125	1838 - 1909
Peckinpah, Sam	Ent	100	200		200	Director
Peddie, G.	Military	15		45		Gen.WWII
Pederson, Monte	Music	15			30	Opera
Pederzini, Gianna	Music	25			75	Opera
Pedro II	Royalty	100	200	300		Emperor Brazil
Peel, Robert, Sir	Political	50	100	150		Prime Minister/1788-1850
Peeples, Nia	Ent	15			25	
Peerce, Jan 1904-84	Music	30			75	Opera
Pegler, Westbrook	Author	15		35	30	Journalist
Pegram, John 1832-65	Civil War	600	800	900		CSA General
Pei, I.M.	Science	35	75	150		Architect
Peirce, Benjamin	Science	20		60		Astronomer/1809-1880
Pelham, Henry	Political	50	150	250		Prime Minister/1696-1754
Pelham-Holies,Thomas	Political	50	100	175		Prime Minister
Pellegrini, Margaret	Ent	15			35	Munchkin, Wizard of Oz
Pelletier, St. Marie E.	Clergy			2,500		Saint Canonized 1940
Pelouze, Louis H.	Civil War	75	175	200		Union General/1831-78
Pemberton, John C.	Civil War	150	350	400	500	CSA General/1814-81
Pemsel, Max	Military	20			45	Nazi General
Pena, Elizabeth	Ent	10			20	
Pender, William Dorsey	Civil War	400				CSA General/1834-63
Penderecki, Krzysztof	Music	25		75		Opera
Pendergast, Thomas J.	Political	20	50	75	45	
Pendleton, Alex	Civil War	200	400	475		CSA Star Officer
Pendleton, Edmund	RevWar	350	600	900		Continental Congress
Pendleton, George Hunt	Political	25		75		Presidential Candidate
Pendleton, Karen	Ent	10			25	
Pendleton, Nat	Ent	30			50	
Pendleton, William N.	Civil War	300		500	900	CSA General/1809-83
Penn & Teller	Ent	20			45	Magicians/Signed by Both
Penn, Arthur	Ent	10			20	
Penn, John 1741-88	RevWar	750	1,500	RARE	RARE	Signer
Penn, Sean	Ent	20			50	
Penn, William 1644-1718	Political	1,500	3,500	7,500	RARE	Founder PA

Name	Field	SIG	DS	ALS	SP	Remarks
Pennell, Joseph	Art	50	150	250		Am. Artist/Printmaker
Penner, Joe	Ent	20			45	Comedian
Penney, J. C. 1875-1971	Business	100	300	400	300	Founder of J.C. Penney
Pennington, Ann	Ent	25		50	75	Ziegfield Star
Penny, Joe	Ent	10			25	Jake and the Fat Man
Pennypacker, Galusha	Civil War	75	150	225		Union General/1844-1916
Penske, Thomas H.	Business	10			20	
Penzias, Arno, Dr.	Science	15		50	25	Nobel Physics
Peppard, George	Ent	30	50		75	A-Team/1929 - 1994
Pepper, Art	Music	30			75	Bandleader
Pepper, Claude 1900-89	Political	15	20		20	
Pepperell, William, Sir	Military	125	250	400		American General
Pepys, Samuel	Author	550				Br. Sec'y of the Navy
Pequet, Henri	Aviation	15		35		
Perceval, Spencer	Political	125	250			Br. P.M. Assasinated
Percival, John	Military	50	100	150		Am. Navy 1812
Percy, Walker	Author	75		200		Am. Novelist
Perelman, S.J.	Author	50		150		Humorist
Peres, Shimon	Political	25	100		75	Israeli Statesman
Perez, Mariano	Political	15			20	President Colombia
Perez, Rosie	Ent	20	50		50	
Perez, Vincent	Ent	25			50	The Crow II
Perier, Jean	Music	25			75	French Baritone
Perignon, D.C. Marquis	Military	75	200	375		Marshal of Napoleon
Perkins, Anthony	Ent	75	100		100	Psycho/1932-1992
Perkins, Carl	Music	25	50	150	50	Blue Suede Shoes...
Perkins, Elizabeth	Ent	10			25	
Perkins, Frances	Political	25	75		75	
Perkins, Millie	Ent	10			30	
Perkins, Osgood	Ent	35			75	
Perlman, Itzhak	Music	20		60	45	Am. Violinist
Perlman, Rhea	Ent	15			40	Cheers
Perlman, Ron	Ent	20			45	Beauty and the Beast
Peron, Eva (Evita)	Political	400		600		Argentina
Peron, Juan & Eva	Political	600	800			
Peron, Juan Domingo	Political	125	300	500	600	President Argentina
Perot, H. Ross	Business	30			100	Presidential Candidate
Perrault, Charles	Author	RARE	RARE	RARE	RARE	Fr Poet/1628-1703
Perrin, Jean 1870-1942	Science	75				Nobel Prize '26 Physics.
Perrine, Valerie	Ent	10	30		25	
Perris, Adriana	Music	10			30	Opera
Perry, Alexander J.	Civil War	25				Union Officer/1829-1913
Perry, Lucas	Ent	20			45	
Perry, Matthew	Ent	25			50	Friends
Perry, Matthew C.	Military	450	775	1,400		Opened Japan/Trade
Perry, Nora	Author	5		20		Novelist
Perry, Oliver H.	Military	675		950		

Name	Field	SIG	DS	ALS	SP	Remarks
Perry, Ralph Barton	Author	10		35		Philosopher, Pulitzer Prize
Pershing, John J. 1860-48	Military	100		300	400	Comm-in-Chief AEF WWI
Persichetti, Vincent	Music	10		45	25	Composer
Pertile, Aureliano	Music	45			125	Opera
Perulli, Franco	Music	20			50	Opera
Perutz, Max	Science	20			30	Nobel Chemistry 1962
Pesci, Joe	Ent	20			50	AA Winner
Petain, Henri-Phillippe	Political	35	75		50	Hero WWI/Treason WWII
Peter & Gordon	Music	75			125	Signed by Both
Peter I	Royalty	100	225	400		King of Serbs, Croats
Peter I, The Great	Royalty	RARE	5,500	7,500	RARE	Czar of Russia
Peter, Paul & Mary	Music	20	45		35	Signed by All Three
Peters, Bernadette	Ent	5	20		20	
Peters, Brock	Ent	5			15	
Peters, Jean	Ent	50			75	
Peters, Mike	Cartoonist	10			25	Mother Grimm
Peters, Richard Jr.	RevWar	50	100	150		Soldier
Peters, Roberta	Music	10			25	Opera
Peters, Susan	Ent	75			100	
Petersen, Paul	Ent	5			15	
Peterson, Chesley	Aviation	15		45	40	WWII ACE
Peterson, Oscar	Music	25			45	Jazz Pianist
Peterson, Paul	Ent	10			20	
Peterson, Roger Tory	Author	20	35		25	
Petiet, Claude	Military	125	225			French Revolution
Petion, Alexandre	Political	275	400			Haitian General, President
Petrella, Clara	Music	20			50	Opera
Petrie, Wm. Matthew F.	Science	100	200			Egyptologist
Petrillo, James C.	Political	25	50			Czar of Musician's Union
Petroff, Paul	Music	30			75	Am. Ballet Dancer-Teacher
Petrova, Olga	Ent	35			75	Silent Films
Pettigrew, James	Civil War	375	RARE	RARE	RARE	CSA General/War Dated
Pettigrew, James J.	Civil War	150	500			CSA General/1828-63
Pettit, Charles	RevWar	75	150	300		Continental Congress
Pettus, Edmund W.	Civil War	75	150	300		CSA General/1821-1907
Petty, Lori	Ent	20			40	
Petty, Tom	Music	25			50	
Peugeot, Eugene	Business	75	125	250		Fndr. Peugeot Automobile
Pfeiffer, Michelle	Ent	35	100		75	
Pflug, Jo Ann	Ent	5			15	
Phelps, John Smith	Civil War	25		100		Union General/1814-86
Phelps, John Wolcott	Civil War	50	125	200		Raised Ist Negro Troops
Phelps, Noah 1740-1809	Military	50	150			Soldier, Patriot, Spy
Philbin, Mary	Ent	25			50	
Philbin, Regis	Ent	5			10	TV Host
Philip (Duke Edinburgh)	Royalty	125	200	300	350	Prince Consort ElizabethII
Philip II (Sp)	Royalty	250				

Name	Field	SIG	DS	ALS	SP	Remarks
Philip III (Sp) Philip II	Royalty	250	750			
Philip IV (Sp),III (Port)	Royalty	250	450	900		
Philip V (Sp)	Royalty	150	350			Founder Bourbon Dynasty
Philippe II	Royalty		500			Regent of Fr. for Louis XV
Philippi, Alfred	Military	15				German Gen WWII
Phillip, Jack W.	Military	25	75			Captain USN
Phillips, Chynna	Music	25			50	Wilson Phillips
Phillips, John	Music	15			35	Mamas and Papas
Phillips, Julianne	Ent	25			45	
Phillips, Lee	Ent	10			25	
Phillips, Lou Diamond	Ent	15			45	
Phillips, Mackenzie	Ent	10			35	One Day at a Time
Phillips, Michelle	Music	10			35	
Phillips, Phil	Music	15			35	
Phillips, Wendell	Political	35	50	100	50	Abolitionist/1811-84
Phillips, William	RevWar	200	500	700		Br. Major General
Phillpotts, Eden	Author	15		45		Br Novelist
Phipps, Spencer	Political	200	800	1,000		Br. Colonial Gov. MA
Phoenix, Joaquin	Ent	20			50	Rivers Younger Brother
Phoenix, River	Ent	175	450		300	Died Young
Piaf, Edith	Ent	150	300		250	
Piaget, Jean 1896-1980	Science		400			Swiss Psychologist
Piatigorsky, Gregor	Music	125	200	300	300	Rus./Am. Cellist
Piazza, Marguerite	Music	10			30	American Soprano
Picard, Emile	Science	75	200	400		Fr. Mathematician
Picasso, Pablo 1881-1973	Art	750	1,500		1,500	
Picasso, Paloma	Art	25			50	Daughter of Pablo/Designer
Piccaluga, Nino	Music	35			75	Opera
Piccard, Auguste	Science	35	100	150	100	Physicist. Bathyscaphe
Piccard, Jacques	Science	15		50	25	
Piccard, Jean-Felix	Science	75	150		125	Chemist, Aeronautical Eng.
Piccaver, Alfred	Music	75			200	Opera
Piccolomini, Marietta	Music	100	250		275	It. Soprano
Pichegru, Charles	Military	35	100	150		Fr Gen/Killed in Prison
Pick, Lewis A.	Military	35	100		50	Gen.WWII
Pickens, Francis W.	Civil War	35	75	150		CSA Gov SC/1805-69
Pickens, Jane	Ent	25			50	
Pickens, Slim	Ent	100			200	Scarce
Pickens, T. Boone	Business	25	50		50	
Pickering, John 1737-05	Political	175	250			
Pickering, Thomas	Political	10			20	Ambassador to Russia
Pickering, Timothy	Political	250	750	1,500		1745-1829
Pickering, William, Dr.	Science	15	35	50	25	Astronomer
Pickett, Cindy	Ent	5			10	
Pickett, George Edward	Civil War	600	1,200	2,000		CSA General/1825-75
Pickford, Jack	Ent	50			150	
Pickford, Mary 1893-1979	Ent	50		200	150	Co-Fndr United Artists

Name	Field	SIG	DS	ALS	SP	Remarks
Picon, Molly 1898-1992	Ent	15			45	Yiddish Stage & Film Star
Pidgeon, Walter	Ent	25	75		75	1897-1984
Pied Pipers, The	Music	20			50	Big Band Singing Group
Pierce, Benjamin	RevWar	75	125	200		Gov. NH
Pierce, Benjamin 1809-80	Science	35		75		Am. Math.& Astronomy
Pierce, David Hyde	Ent	20			45	Frasier/Niles Crane
Pierce, Franklin 1804-69	President	400	700	950		
Pierce, James	Ent	45	125		100	Early Tarzan
Pierce, Jan	Music	20			50	Opera
Pierce, Jane M.	First Lady	200	500	900		
Pierce, N. B.	Civil War	35	75	100		
Pierce, Web	Music	5			10	
Pierne, H.C. Gabriel	Music	15		100	200	Conductor
Pierrepont, Edwards	Political	15	45	75		Att'y General 1875
Pierson, Roland	Aviation	10		35	30	
Pigni, Renzo	Music	15			35	Opera
Pike, Albert 1809-91	Civil War	100	175	250		CSA General/1809-91
Pike, Christopher	Author	5			10	Novelist
Pike, James A.	Clergy	75	150	275	125	Bishop
Pike, Zebulon 1751-1834	RevWar	40	75	125		Officer Revolutionary Army
Pike, Zebulon M.1779-13	Military	225	600	900		Discovered Pike's Peak
Pilatre De Rozier, Jean	Aviation	125		500		Pioneer Balloonist
Pillow, Gideon J.	Civil War	100		350		CSA General/1806-78
Pillow, Gideon J.	Civil War	150	400	500		CSA General/War Dated
Pillsbury, George A.	Business Scarce		1,250	2,000		Founder of Flour Co.
Pillsbury, John S.	Business	100	400			Pillsbury Flour
Pilsudski, Joseph K.	Military	125	300	450	275	
Pinay, Antoine (Fr)	Political	15		50		France
Pinchback, Pinckney	Political	125	350	450		
Pinchot, Bronson	Ent	20	45		45	Perfect Strangers
Pinchot, Gifford	Political	35	75	125		Governor PA, Forester
Pinckney, Charles	RevWar	450		1,200		Continental Congress
Pinckney, Charles C.	RevWar	175		500		Diplomat/XYZ Affair
Pinckney, Thomas	RevWar	200	450			Continental Army
Pincus, Harry	Art	15		50		
Pine, Phillip	Ent	5			15	
Pinero, Arthur Wing, Sir	Author	15	35		45	British Actor
Ping, Deng Xiao	Political	200	RARE	RARE	RARE	China
Pingel, Rolf	Aviation	10			25	
Pink Floyd	Music	75	250		150	Signed by Five
Pinkerton, Allan 1819-84	Business	300	750	1,200	RARE	Pinkerton Detective Agency
Pinkerton, Robert A.	Business	35	100	200	75	CEO Pinkerton's Inc.
Pinkerton, William A.	Civil War	100	200			US Secret Service
Pinkett, Jada	Ent	20			40	
Pinkney, William	Political	100		200		Attorney General
Pinochet, Augusto	Political	25	100	200	50	Chilean Mil. Leader
Pinza, Ezio	Music	50			125	Opera/1893 - 1957

Name	Field	SIG	DS	ALS	SP	Remarks
Pioneers, Sons of the	Music	150			300	Five Signatures
Piper, William Thomas.	Aviation	175	350			Founder Piper Aircraft Corp.
Pirandello, Luigi 1867-36	Author	75	175	300	375	Nobel/Literature
Pirchoff, Nelly	Music	10			30	Opera
Piscopo, Joe	Ent	10			35	Sat Nite Live
Pissarro, Camile 1830-03	Art	250		1,200		Fr. Impressionist
Piston, Walter	Music	75	200	400	100	Pulitzer/Music
Pitney, Gene	Ent	10			25	
Pitney, Mahlon	SuprCt	20	50	125	45	
Pitt William (Elder)	Political	150	300			The Great Commoner
Pitt, Brad	Ent	25	75		50	
Pitt, Ingrid	Ent	10	25		30	Hammer Horror Star
Pitt, John, Sir 1756-1835	Military	45		100		
Pitts, Zazu	Ent	35			75	1890 - 1963
Pius IX, G.M. Mastori	Clergy	175	250	400		G. M. Mastori
Pius IX, Pope	Clergy	50	150	250		
Pius VII, Pope	Clergy		1,500			
Pius X, Pope 1835-1914	Clergy		700		RARE	Giuseppe MelchiorreSarto
Pius XI, Pope	Clergy	450	950	RARE		A.D. Achille Ratti
Pius XII, Pope	Clergy		1,500			Eugenio Pacelli
Plainsmen, The	Music	25			50	Signed by Entire Group
Planck, Max 1858-1947	Science	200	400	750	RARE	Nobel Physics 1918
Plancon, Pol	Music	150			400	Opera
Plant & Page	Music	75			125	Both Signed/Led Zeppelin
Plant, Robert	Music	30			60	
Plato, Dana	Ent	25			45	Different Strokes
Platt, Ed	Ent	75			150	Chief/Get Smart
Platters, The	Music	125	250		250	Signed by all Five
Playfair, Lyon, lst Baron	Science	10		40		Modern Sanitation
Pleasanton, Alfred	Civil War	35		100		Union General/1824-97
Pleasence, Donald	Ent	45	100		100	
Pleshette, Suzanne	Ent	15			35	Bob Newhart Show
Plimpton, George	Author	10	25		20	
Plimpton, Martha	Ent	20			40	
Plishka, Paul	Music	10			25	Opera
Plitsetskaya, Maya	Music	15			40	Ballet
Plowright, Joan	Ent	10	25		25	
Plummer, Amanda	Ent	15			35	
Plummer, Christopher	Ent	10			25	
Poe, Edgar Allan	Author	RARE	15,000	RARE	RARE	1809-1849
Pogany, Willy	Art	75	150			Muralist/Illustrator
Poggi, Gianni	Music	10			25	Opera
Poindexter, John	Military	50			150	US Adm. Iran-Contra
Poinsett, Joel R.	Political	75	250	250		1779-1851
Pointer Sisters	Music	35	75		75	Signed by All Three
Poitier, Sidney	Ent	25	50		60	AA Winner
Polando, John	Aviation	30			75	

Name	Field	SIG	DS	ALS	SP	Remarks
Polanski, Roman	Ent	30			75	Director
Polaski, Deborah	Music	10			25	Opera
Police, The	Music	75			125	Signed by entire group
Polk, James K.	President	350	1,500	3,000		1795-1849
Polk, Leonidas	Civil War	500	650	RARE	RARE	CSA General/War Dated
Polk, Leonidas 1806-64	Civil War	300				CSA General KIA
Polk, Sarah Childress	First Lady	400	600	900	1,200	
Poll, Afro	Music	15			45	Opera
Pollack, Sidney	Ent	10			25	AA Director-Actor
Pollard, Snub	Ent	75			200	Keystone Cop
Pollen, Tracy	Ent	10			35	
Pollock, Channing	Author	30	50		50	Am. Playwright
Pollock, Kevin	Ent	15			35	
Pompadour, Mme	Royalty	150	400	900		Louis VI Mistress
Pompidou, Georges	Political	10	25		20	Premier, President France
Ponce, Poncie	Ent	10			20	
Ponchielli, Amilcare	Music	250				Opera/Ballets
Pond, Julian	Science	100		300		
Poniatowski, Jozef A.	Military	500	RARE	RARE	RARE	Napolean Marshal
Pons, Juan	Music	10			25	Opera
Pons, Lily	Music	50			125	Soprano
Ponselle, Carmela	Music	25				Opera
Ponselle, Rosa	Music	25		75		Opera
Ponti, Carlo	Ent	15			30	It. Film Producer
Ponty, Jean-Luc	Ent	5			15	
Pool, Tilaman E.	Aviation	10			30	WWII Navy ACE
Poor, Enoch	RevWar	175	550	875		General. Patriot, Hero
Pope Pius X	Clergy	500			1,500	Giuseppe Melchiorre Sarto
Pope, A.J.	Aviation	20	35			American WWII ACE
Pope, Alexander	Author	600	RARE	RARE	RARE	Br. Poet
Pope, Alexander	Art	150	300	600		
Pope, John	Civil War		450	RARE	RARE	Union General/War Dated
Pope, John 1822-92	Civil War	80	125	300	450	Union General
Popham, William	RevWar	175		350		1752-1847
Popovich, Pavel	Space	50			175	Rus. Cosmonaut
Popp, Lucia	Music	20			50	Opera
Porizkova, Paulina	Ent	25			50	Model/Actress
Porsche, Ferdinand, Dr.	Business	225	450		550	Designer VW & Porsche
Portal, Charles	Aviation	25		75	50	
Porter, Cole 1891-1964	Music	225	450		650	Composer
Porter, David 1780-1843	Military	50	125	250		Am. Naval Officer
Porter, David Dixon	Civil War	150		450		Union Admiral/1813-91
Porter, Don	Ent	5			15	
Porter, Fitz-John	Civil War	50	100	400	RARE	Union General/1822-1901
Porter, Gene Stratton	Author	50	150	250	100	Am. Novelist
Porter, George, Sir	Science	15		75	35	Nobel Chemistry 1967
Porter, Horace 1837-1921	Civil War	50	175	300		Union General

Name	Field	SIG	DS	ALS	SP	Remarks
Porter, James M.	Political	25	75	125		Sec'y War 1843
Porter, Jane 1776-1850	Author	100		300		Br. Novelist
Porter, Katherine Anne	Author	75	125	300	150	Pulitzer/Amercian Author
Porter, Peter 1773-1844	Political	75	150	175		Sec'y War J.Q.Adams
Porter, William Sidney	Author	350	750	1,500		
Portes-Gil, Emilio	Political	40		75		President Mexico
Portland, 3rd Duke	Political	50	200			Prime Minister
Portman, Eric	Ent	35			75	
Portman, Natalie	Ent	25			50	The Professional
Portsmouth, Duchess	Royalty	75	200	450		Louise-Renee' Keroualle
Posey, Parker	Ent	20			50	
Poshetko, Joseph	Aviation	10		25	30	WWII Flying Tiger Ace
Possart, Ernst	Music	20			50	Classical Musician
Post, Augustus	Aviation	25	45		50	Pioneer Aviator, Balloonist
Post, Emily 1873-1960	Author	65		125		US Ettiquette
Post, Marjorie M.	Business	15		50	25	Postum Cereal
Post, Markie	Ent	15	30		35	Night Court
Post, Wiley 1900-35	Aviation	350		650	750	I st Solo Around the World
Poston, Tom	Ent	10			30	Newhart
Potter, Beatrix	Author	250		750		Childrens Author
Potter, Cora	Ent	10		30	25	
Potts, Annie	Ent	10	25		30	Designing Women
Poulenc, Francis-Jean	Music	125	275	450		
Poulter, Thomas C.	Explorer	20	40			2nd Arctic Expedition
Pound, Ezra 1885-1972	Author	250	675	900		Poet
Poundstone, Paula	Ent	5			15	Standup Comedienne
Povey, Len	Aviation	10			20	
Povich, Maury	Ent	10			20	TV Host
Powderly, Terence V.	Political	30	75		50	Am. Labor Leader
Powell, Adam Clayton	Political	30		50	35	
Powell, Colin L.	Military	35	100		100	Chmn. Joint Chiefs of Staff
Powell, Dick	Ent	35	50	75	65	1904-1963
Powell, Eleanor	Ent	20	35		60	Film Dancer/1910-1982
Powell, Jane	Ent	10			25	
Powell, Lewis F. Jr.	SuprCt	30	100			
Powell, Maud	Music	30			90	Violinist
Powell, Max	Music	10			20	
Powell, Robert	Ent	5			10	
Powell, Ross E.	Military	10		30		
Powell, Talmage	Author	10		40	20	Am. Novelist Mysteries
Powell, William	Ent	40			90	
Power, Tyrone	Ent	75	100		200	1913 - 1958
Powers, Francis Gary	Aviation	50			100	U2 Pilot/Shot Down/USSR
Powers, Hiram	Art	50	150	250	150	19th Cent. Major Sculptor
Powers, Preston	Art	25	75	150		
Powers, Stephanie	Ent	15			35	Hart to Hart
Pownall, Thomas	Political	250	600	900		Colonial Gov. MA

Name	Field	SIG	DS	ALS	SP	Remarks
Powter, Susan	Author	5			10	Excercise and Diet
Powys, Llewelyn	Author	30	65	90	45	Novelist
Powys, Theodore F.	Author	100		300		Br. Allegorical Novels
Poynter, Edward John	Art	25		75		Pres. Royal Academy
Pozzo de Borgo, Chas.	Political	50		200		Opponent of Napoleon
Prado, Perez	Music	25			75	Bandleader
Pratt, Francis & Whitney	Science		450			Pratt & Whitney Engine
Preble, George H.	Civil War	25	50	75		
Preddy, George E.	Aviation	15		45	30	
Preger, Kurt	Music	10			20	Opera
Preminger, Otto 1906-86	Ent	40	75		75	Director
Prentice, John	Cartoonist	15			40	Rip Kirby
Prentiss, Paula	Ent	10			20	
Prescott, Oliver	RevWar	75	175	400		Shays Rebellion
Prescott, Wm. Hickling	Author	30	75			
Presley, Elvis 1935-77	Music	575	1,400	RARE	900	
Presley, Priscilla	Ent	10		30	25	
Preston, Kelly	Ent	25			50	
Preston, Robert	Ent	40			90	1918 - 1987
Preston, William	Civil War	150	600			CSA General/War Dated
Preston, William 1816-87	Civil War	100	400			CSA General
Preston, William Ballard	Civil War	25	50	100		CSA Governor
Pretenders	Music	35			75	Signed by Entire Group
Pretty Things, The	Music	45			75	Signed by Entire Group
Preuss, Georg	Military	20		50		
Previn, Andre	Music	20		75	75	Conductor
Previn, Dorey	Music	5			10	Composer
Prevost, Eugene-Marcel	Author	10	25	45		Fr. Moralist, Feminist Fiction
Prey, Hermann	Music	10			30	Opera
Price, Leontyne	Music	25		50	75	Opera
Price, Margaret	Music	15			45	Opera
Price, Ray	Music	5			15	Country
Price, Sterling	Civil War	350		RARE	RARE	CSA General/War Dated
Price, Sterling 1809-67	Civil War	200	350			CSA General
Price, Vincent 1911-93	ENt	50	100	150	100	
Pride, Charley	Music	5			15	
Prien, Guenther	Military	300			750	
Priest, Pat	Ent	10			25	Munsters
Priest, Royce W.	Aviation	10		35	30	USAF WWII ACE
Priestley, J. B. 1894-1984	Author	50	75	175	125	Playwright, Novelist
Priestley, William O. Sir	Science	50	100	200		Obstetric Physician
Priestly, Jason	Ent	25	50		50	
Priestly, Joseph	Science	350	900	1,400		Br. Chemist
Prieur-Duvernois, Claude	Military	35	125			Fr. Revolutionary
Prigogine, Ilya	Science	20		45	25	Nobel Chemistry 1977
Prima, Louis	Ent	35			75	BandLeader/Disney Voice
Primrose, William	Music	75			225	Violinist

Name	Field	SIG	DS	ALS	SP	Remarks
Prince	Music	75	200		200	Scarce
Prince, Harold 'Hal'	Ent	15			30	
Prince, Henry	Civil War	35	75	75		
Principal, Victoria	Ent	15			35	
Pringle, Aileen	Ent	15		35	30	
Prinz, Rosemary	Ent	5			10	
Prinze, Freddie	Ent	75	100		150	Suicide Young
Pritchard, John, Sir	Music	15			45	Opera
Procol Harum	Music	35			75	Signed by Entire Group
Proctor, Edna Dean	Author	35		75		Am. Poet
Proctor, Redfield	Political	10		50	30	1831-1908
Proctor, Richard Anthony	Science	10		35		Br. Astonomer
Profumo, John	Political	50			100	
Profumo, Valerie	Ent	10	25		25	British film star
Prokofieff, Serge	Music	400	750	1,200	950	1891-1953
Prosky, Robert	Ent	5			15	
Protti, Aldo	Music	10			20	Opera
Prouse, Juliet	Ent	10			40	
Proust, Marcel 1871-1922	Author	500	875	1,600	RARE	
Provost, Jon	Ent	10	25		25	Timmy in "Lassie"
Prowse, Dave	Ent	15	45		30	Darth Vader in Star Wars
Prowse, Juliet	Ent	10			20	
Pryce, Jonathan	Ent	25			50	
Pryor, Richard	Ent	30	60		75	Scarce
Pryor, Roger	Ent	15			45	
Pryor, Roger A. 1828-19	Civil War	100	250	300		CSA General
Pucci, Emilio	Business	10		40	25	It. Fashion Designer
Puccini, Giacomo	Music	500	750	1,250	950	Composer
Puck, Wolfgang	Business	5			15	Owner of Spago
Puente, Tito	Music	15			45	Bandleader
Pulitzer, Joseph 1847-11	Business	125	350	500		Pulitzer Pr. Editor
Pulitzer, Joseph, Jr.	Business	15			20	Editor-Publisher
Pulitzer, Ralph 1879-1939	Business	75		250		Journalist/Publisher
Pulitzer, Roxanne	Ent	5			20	
Pullman, Bill	Ent	20			45	
Pullman, George M.	Business	225	450	500		Pullman RR Cars
Puma, Salvatore	Music	10			20	Opera
Pupin, Michael, Dr.	Science	100	300	300	225	Physicist-Inventor-Author
Purcell, Edward M., Dr.	Science	20	30	45	25	Nobel Physics 1952
Purcell, Lee	Ent	5			10	
Purcell, Sarah	Ent	5		20	10	
Purdy, James	Author	20	50			
Purl, Linda	Ent	10			20	
Purvis, Melvin	Western	25	100	150	100	
Purvis, Robert	Political	25	50	75		Underground Railroad
Pushkin, Alexander	Author	825	2,400	RARE	RARE	Russ. Poet/Author
Pusser, Buford	Political	125	250			Tennessee Sheriff/Slain

Name	Field	SIG	DS	ALS	SP	Remarks
Putnam, George Palmer	Business	15		75	35	Book Publisher, Author
Putnam, Israel 1718-90	RevWar	200		750		Dont Fire Until You See....
Putnam, Rufus	RevWar	175	400	650		General. Ohio Pioneer
Puzo, Mario	Author	35	75		75	Novelist/Godfather
Py, Gilbert	Music	10			25	Opera
Pyle, Denver	Ent	10			20	
Pyle, Ernie	Author	200	300	450	350	WWII Correspondent
Pyle, Howard 1853 - 1911	Art	175	300		600	Am.Art Nouveau Illustrator
Pynchon, John 1621-1703	Military	RARE	RARE	3,750	RARE	Stateman/Soldier

Name	Field	SIG	DS	ALS	SP	Remarks
Qaddafi, Muammar	Political	100		500	200	Libyan-Arab Republic
Quackenbush, Stephen	Civil War	50		175		Union Admiral
Quaid, Dennis	Ent	20			50	
Quaid, Randy	Ent	25			50	
Quale, Anthony	Ent	20			45	
Quang, Thich Tri	Political	35		125		
Quantrill, Wm. C.	Military	1,000		3,500		CSA Army Guerilla Leader
Quarles, William A.	Civil War	75	225			CSA General
Quarry, Robert	Ent	10			25	
Quasimodo, Salvatore	Author	25		50	35	Nobel Literature 1959
Quayle, Dan	Vice Pres	25			45	
Quayle, Marilyn	Political	25			50	
Queen	Music	200	400		450	Signed by Entire Group
Quesada, E,R, 'Pete'	Military	15			25	
Quesada, Elwood R.	Aviation	15	30	45	30	
Questel, Mae	Ent	75	150			Voice Betty Boop/Olive Oyl
Quincy, Josiah	Political	125		200		1772 - 1864
Quine, Richard	Ent	10			20	Actor/Director
Quinn, Anthony	Ent	15			45	AA Winner
Quinn, Martha	Music	5			10	MTV V-Jay
Quinn, Aida	Ent	15			25	
Quintard, Charles Todd	Civil War	75	100	150		
Quirk, Michael J.	Aviation	15		45	30	WWII ACE
Quiros, Jean B.	Political	45	75			
Quisling, Vidkun	Military	125	200	350	450	
Quitman, John A.	Military	25				General/1799-1858

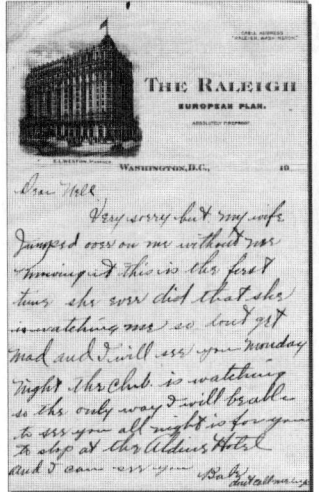

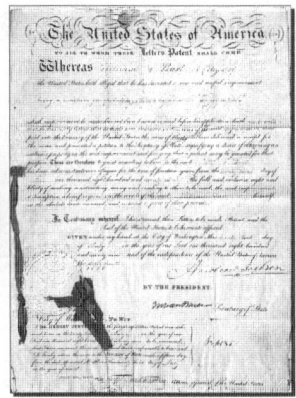
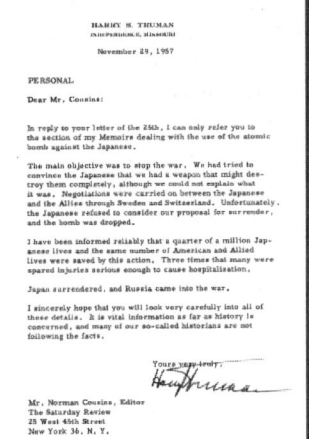

R

Name	Field	SIG	DS	ALS	SP	Remarks
Raab, Julius	Political	5			15	Chancellor Austria
Raabe, Meinhardt	Ent	15			35	Munchkin in Wiz of Oz
Rabaud, Henri	Music	50			150	Composer/1873 - 1949
Rabi, Isador	Science	25		75	50	Nobel Physics 1944
Rabin, Yitzhak	Political	150	250	350	450	PM Israel/Assasinated
Raboy, Mac	Cartoonist	20			45	Flash Gordon
Rachmaninoff, Sergei	Music	225	600	775	475	Composer/1873-1943
Racine, Jean 1639-99	Author	4,500	RARE	RARE	RARE	
Rackham, Arthur	Art	100	200	400		Illustrator Children's Books
Radford, William	Military	125		350		Naval Officer/1808-1890
Radhakrishnan, Sarvepa	Political	45	150	300	75	Pres. India
Radner, Gilda	Ent	75	150		150	Sat Nite Live
Rae, Cassidy	Ent	10			30	
Rae, Charlotte	Ent	10			30	
Raeder, Erich	Military	75	175	400	125	German Naval Commdr
Raff, Joseph Joachim	Music	45		150		Composer
Rafferty, Frances	Ent	5			10	
Raffin, Deborah	Ent	5			15	
Rafko, Kaye Lani	Ent	10			15	Miss America 1988
Raft, George	Ent	50	100	125	125	1895 - 1980
Ragsland, Rags	Ent	45			75	
Rahman, Abdul	Political	10			25	Ambassador
Raimondi, Ruggero	Music	25			50	Opera
Rainer, Luise	Ent	15		40	45	
Raines, Ella	Ent	10			20	
Rainey, Ford	Ent	5			10	
Rainger, Ralph	Music	20			40	Composer
Rainier, Prince	Royalty	75		200	125	Monaco
Rain-in-the-Face	Western	13,000	RARE	RARE	RARE	Indian Chief
Rains, Claude	Ent	125	250		275	1889 - 1967
Rainwater, Leo James	Science	20		45	30	Nobel Physics 1975
Rainwater, Marvin	Music	15			30	
Raisa, Rosa 1893-1963	Music	30			75	Opera
Raisch, Bill	Ent	10			20	
Raitt, Bonnie	Music	15			45	
Raitt, John	Ent	5			15	
Rall, Guenther	Military	45	75	125	100	WWII German ACE
Ralston, Esther	Ent	10	25	35	30	
Ralston, Vera H.	Ent	10			25	
Ralston, William	Business	50	100	150		Founder Bank of California
Rama VI	Royalty	150				King Siam (Thailand)
Rambeau, Marjorie	Ent	25			45	

Name	Field	SIG	DS	ALS	SP	Remarks
Rambo, Dirk	Ent	20			40	
Ramey, Samuel	Music	15			35	Opera
Ramirez, Carlos	Music	10			25	Baritone
Ramos, Mel	Art	20			40	
Rampling, Charlotte	Ent	10			20	
Ramsay, William, Sir	Science	150	300	450		Nobel Chemistry 1904
Ramseur, Stephen	Civil War	RARE	RARE	RARE	RARE	CSA General
Ramsey, Norman F., Dr.	Science	10			20	Nobel Physics 1989
Rand, Ayn 1905-82	Author	400	2,000		1,250	Atlas Shrugged...
Rand, Sally	Ent	25			75	
Randall, James R.	Music	75				Composer
Randall, Tony	Ent	10		25	20	Odd Couple
Randolph, Beverly	Revwar	100	250			Virginia Governor
Randolph, Boots	Music	5			15	
Randolph, Charles D.	Western	100	200	300		
Randolph, Edmund J.	RevWar	200	450	550		Secretary of State
Randolph, George W.	Civil War	250	400	550		CSA General/1818-67
Randolph, John	RevWar	100	225	375		Senator VA
Randolph, Joyce	Ent	10	25	30	20	Honeymooners
Randolph, Lillian	Ent	100			250	
Randolph, Peyton	RevWar	400				1st Pres Cont Congress
Randolph, Thos. Mann	Political	75	225			
Rank, J. Arthur, Ist Baron	Business	25		75	50	Br. Film Magnate
Rank, Otto	Science	200		400		Austrian Psychoanalyst
Rankin, Jeannette	Political	100	200			1880-1973
Rankin, Nell	Music	15			25	Am. Contralto
Rankin, Robert J.	Aviation	15		40	35	WWII ACE in one day
Ransom, John Crowe	Author	45	100	200		Am Poet
Ransom, Matt W.	Civil War	100	275			CSA General/1826-1904
Ransom, Robert, Jr.	Civil War	250				CSA General/1828-92
Rapaport, Lester	Art	10		30	15	
Rapee, Erno	Music	15			45	
Raphael	Art	3,500	9,000	RARE	RARE	
Raphael, Sally Jessy	Ent	5			20	TV Talk Show Hostess
Rapper, Irving	Ent	15			35	40's Film Director
Rappold, Marie	Music	35			75	Opera
Rashad, Phylicia	Ent	15			35	Cosby Show
Raskob, John J.	Business	10			15	CEO General Motors
Rasmussen, Knud J.V.	Explorer	150		300	250	Danish Arctic Explorer
Rasputin, Gregori E.	Clergy	2,000	4,500	6,000		Rus. Mystic. Assassinated
Rathbone, Basil	Ent	200	450	450	500	Sherlock Holmes/1872-16
Ratoff, Gregory	Ent	20			50	Film Director
Ratzenberger, John	Ent	15			35	Cheers
Raum, Green B.	Civil War	30	75			Union General/1829-1909
Ravel, Maurice	Music	450			1,500	Composer/1875-1937
Rawdon, Francis I732-97	RevWar	150		450		Br. Gen'l Rev. War.
Rawdon-Hastings, F.	RevWar	25		100		Br. Off'r. Bunker Hill

Name	Field	SIG	DS	ALS	SP	Remarks
Rawlings, Marjorie K.	Author	50		150		Am. Pulitzer. The Yearling
Rawlins, John A.	Civil War	75	150	225		Union General/1831-69
Rawlinson, Herbert	Ent	15			50	1886-1953
Rawls, Lou	Music	15	45		35	
Rawson, Edward	Political	125	250	450		1615-93
Ray, Aldo	Ent	5			15	
Ray, James Earl	Criminal	75		200		Shot Martin Luther King, Jr.
Ray, Johnny	Ent	15			40	
Ray, Leah	Ent	10			15	
Ray, Man (Rudnitsky)	Art	250	450			Painter/Photographer
Raye, Collin	Music	10			25	
Raye, Martha	Ent	20			45	
Raymond, Alex	Cartoonist	50			100	Flash Gordon/Rip Kirby...
Raymond, Gene	Ent	10			25	
Raymond, Henry J.	Business	50		150		Fndr./New York Times
Raymond, Jim	Cartoonist	15			35	Blondie
Raymond, Paula	Ent	5			15	
Razaf, Andy	Music	50		175		Lyricist Ain't Misbehavin'
Rea, Steven	Ent	20			45	
Read, Albert Cushing	Aviation	50		150	125	
Read, George 1733-98	RevWar	350	450	1,250		Signer Decl. of Indepen.
Read, T. Buchanan	Art	20		45		
Reade, Charles	Author	50	75	125		Br. Novelist, Dramatist
Reagan, John H.	Civil War	150	450	600		CSA Postmaster General
Reagan, Maureen	Political	5			15	Daughter of President
Reagan, Nancy	First Lady	35		100	75	
Reagan, Ron, Jr.	Ent	10			30	Dancer
Reagan, Ronald 1911-	President	200	450	850	300	
Real, Pierre F., Count	Military	20		50		French Revolution
Reale, Antenore	Music	25			50	Opera
Ream, Vinnie	Art	200		400		Am. Sculptor/Scarce
Reason, Rex	Ent	10			20	
Reasoner, Harry	Ent	15			40	60 Minutes
Rector, Henry M.	Civil War	200	450			CSA Governor
Red Hot Chili Peppers	Music	35			75	Signed by all four
Reddy, Helen	Music	10		25	25	
Redenbacker, Orville	Business	10		30	30	Popcorn King/1907-95
Redford, Robert	Ent	45	150		100	The Sting/Butch Cassidy
Redgrave, Lynn	Ent	10			25	
Redgrave, Michael, Sir	Ent	20			40	
Redgrave, Vanessa	Ent	20			45	
Redman, Don	Music	20			45	Jazz Musician
Redmond, John E.	Political	5		30	15	
Redon, Odilon	Art	75		275		Lithographer & Engraver
Redout, Pierre Joseph	Art	250	600	900		Fr. Painter/Lithographer
Reed, Alan	Ent	60	100		150	Orig.Voice/Fred Flinstone
Reed, Carol, Sir 1906-76	Ent	50			150	Br. Director

Name	Field	SIG	DS	ALS	SP	Remarks
Reed, Donna 1921-86	Ent	100	125		175	Its a Wonderful Life
Reed, Jerry	Music	5	20		15	Singer/Actor
Reed, John	Author	200			300	Radical Am.Journalist
Reed, Joseph 1741-85	RevWar	75	200	350		
Reed, Lou	Music	20			50	
Reed, Oliver	Ent	15			30	
Reed, Phillip	Ent	15	25		30	
Reed, Rex	ENt	5			15	
Reed, Robert	Ent	50	75		100	Brady Bunch/Dad
Reed, Roland	Ent	15			35	
Reed, Shanna	Ent	15			25	
Reed, Stanley 1884-1980	SuprCt	50	75	150		
Reed, Thomas Brackett	Political	15		45		Speaker of the House
Reed, Walter	Ent	10			25	
Reed, Walter 1851-1902	Science	400	750	RARE	675	Yellow Fever
Rees, Roger	Ent	10			20	
Rees, Thomas	Business	10		45	25	
Reese, Della	Ent	15			40	Touched by an Angel
Reeve, Christopher	Ent	75	150		150	Superman/Paralyzed
Reeves, George	Ent	850	1,500	RARE	1,500	50's Superman TV Star
Reeves, Keanu	Ent	25	50		50	Speed
Reeves, Martha	Music	5			20	Composer
Reeves, Ronna	Music	5			10	
Reeves, Steve	Ent	15			35	
Reeves-Smith, Olive	Ent	5			15	
Regan, Donald	Political	10			30	Sec'y Treasury
Regan, Phil	Ent	15	45		25	
Reger, Max	Music	75	200	450		German Composer
Reginald, Lionel	Ent	10			20	
Regnaud de Saint-Jean	Military	30		75		French Revolution
Rehan, Ada	Ent	20			40	
Rehm, Dan	Aviation	15		45	30	WWII ACE
Rehnquist, William H.	SuprCt	50	150	175	100	Chief Justice
Reich, Wilhelm	Science	125	300	450		Austr. Psychoanalyst
Reichers, Lou	Aviation	35		75	75	
Reid, Tara	Ent	25			50	
Reid, Tim	Ent	5			15	
Reid, Wallace	Ent	200			550	
Reid, Whitelaw	Author	30	75		50	
Reik, Theodor 1888-1969	Science	100	250	450		Austrian Psychoanalyst
Reilly, Charles Nelson	Ent	5			10	
Reinburg, J. Hunter	Aviation	15		50	40	WWII Marine ACE
Reinecke, Karl	Music	75	150	225	250	
Reiner, Carl	Ent	10		30	25	
Reiner, Fritz	Music	75	150		200	Hungarian Conductor
Reiner, Rob	Ent	10			25	Director
Reinert, Ernst Wilhelm	Aviation	25			50	German ACE

Name	Field	SIG	DS	ALS	SP	Remarks
Reinhardt, Max 1873-43	Ent	100	175	400	275	Austrian Director
Reinhold, Judge	Ent	15			30	
Reinking, Ann	Ent	5		20	15	
Reisch, Walter	Ent	10			20	Director
Reiser, Paul	Ent	25			50	Mad About You
Reiserer, Russell	Aviation	15		45		WWII ACE
Reitsch, Hanna	Aviation	75	150	250	150	Flew lst Practical H'Copter.
Reitz, Francis W.	Political	50	125			South Africa
Remarque, Erich Maria	Author	40	125	250	75	All Quiet on Western Front
Rembrandt van Rijn	Art	3,000				Dutch Painter-Etcher
Remer, Otto	Military	25			65	WWII SS General
Remick, Lee	Ent	30			75	1935 - 1991
Remington, Eliphalet Jr.	Business	250	450			Remington Guns Co.
Remington, Frederic	Art	600	1,200		1,750	Sculptor/Writer/1861-1909
Remington, Samuel	Business	Scarce	1,250			Fndr Remington Gun CO.
Renaldo, Duncan	Ent	45		100	125	Cisco Kid/1904-1980
Renaud, Maurice	Music	50			175	Opera
Renaud, Paul	Political	50			100	Premier France
Renault, Louis	Political	35	75	125		Nobel Peace Prize 1907
Renner, Karl, Dr.	Political	25	50	100	50	
Rennie, John 1761-1821	Science			600		Eng. Built Waterloo Bridge
Rennie,Michael	Ent	100			200	1909 - 1971
Reno, Jean	Ent	20			40	
Reno, Marcus A.	Military	1,000	2,750			Battle of Little Big Horn
Renoir, Jean	Ent	125	275			French Filmaker
Renoir, Pierre-Auguste	Art	300	700	1,500	RARE	
Renquist, William	SuprCt	75			150	Chief Justice
Renwick, Edward S.	Science	25		75		Father Modern Poultry Ind.
REO Speedwagon	Music	35			75	Signed by Entire Group
Resnick, Mike	Author	10		30	20	
Resnick, Regina	Music	25			75	Opera
Resnik, Judith	Space	100	250		200	Astronaut
Respighi, Oftorino	Music	100	200	450		Italian Opera
Reston, John 'Scotty'	Author	10		35	15	Journalist
Rethberg, Elisabeth	Music	45			125	Opera
Rethy, Ester	Music	10		35	30	Opera
Rettig, Tommy	Ent	10			25	Lassie
Reuther, Walter P.	Political	25		75	35	
Revelle, Hamilton	Ent	5			10	
Revels, Hiram Rhoades	Political	500				lst Black U.S. Senator
Revere, Anne	Ent	25			75	AA Winner/1903 - 1990
Revere, Paul 1735-1818	RevWar	2,500	5,500	9,000	RARE	
Rey, Alvino	Music	10			25	Big Band Leader
Reybold, E.	Military	15	35	45		Gen. WWII Engineer Corps
Reymann, Hellmuth	Aviation	30		75		
Reynolds, A.W.	Civil War	75	150	175		CSA General/1817-76
Reynolds, Albert	Political	15			25	P.M. Ireland

Name	Field	SIG	DS	ALS	SP	Remarks
Reynolds, Burt	Ent	10			20	Smokey and the Bandit
Reynolds, Craig	Ent	10			25	
Reynolds, Daniel H.	Civil War	100		350		CSA General/1832-1902
Reynolds, Debbie	Ent	10		25	20	
Reynolds, Donn	Music	10			20	
Reynolds, Gene	Ent	5			15	
Reynolds, John Fulton	Civil War	350	RARE	RARE	RARE	Union General/KIA
Reynolds, Joseph Jones	Civil War	45	125	175		Union General/1822-99
Reynolds, Joshua, Sir	Art	200	300	550		Br Portrait
Reynolds, Marjorie	Ent	30	75		75	GWTW
Reynolds, R.J.	Business	250	600			Founder Tobacco Empire
Reynolds, Richard S.	Business	50	125	225	75	Reynolds Aluminum Co.
Reynolds, William	Ent	5			15	
Rhames, Ving	Ent	25			50	
Rhee, Syngman 1875-65	Political	175			250	Ist Pres. So. Korea
Rheims, Bettina	Art	35			100	
Rhett, Alicia	Ent	200	RARE	RARE	RARE	RARE GWTW Star
Rhett, Robert Barnwell	Civil War	150	300	450		CSA General/1800-76
Rhodes, Billie	Ent	15			35	
Rhodes, Cecil John	Political	125	250	400	600	1853-1902
Rhys-Davies, John	Ent	25			75	Indiana Jones Films
Ribbentrop, Joachim von	Military	200	450	550	325	Hitlers Foreign Affairs Adv.
Ribbentrop, Rudolf von	Military	75		150		
Ricci, Christina	Ent	20	50		50	Addams Family movies...
Ricciarelli, Katia	Music	10			25	Opera
Rice, Alice C.	Author	75		225		
Rice, Anne	Author	25			45	Novelist
Rice, Dan	Business	75	100	300		Circus Clown & Owner
Rice, Donna	Ent	15			30	
Rice, Elmer 1882-1967	Author	100	250		150	Pulitzer Prize. Playwright
Rice, Grantland	Author	25			75	Sportswriter
Rice, Tim	Music	10		75	30	Composer/Disney
Rich, Buddy 1917-87	Music	35			125	Big Bandleader-Drummer
Rich, Irene	Ent	5			15	
Richards, Ann	Political	10			20	Governor TX
Richards, Cliff	Music	15			40	
Richards, Denise	Ent	20			45	
Richards, Dickinson W.	Science	25	35	50	35	Nobel Medicine 1956
Richards, Jeff	Ent	10			20	Child Star
Richards, Keith	Music	50	175		100	Rolling Stones Guitarist
Richards, Michael	Ent	25	50		50	Kramer on "Seinfeld"
Richardson, Dorothy	Author	50	125	250		
Richardson, Elliot	Political	10		35	20	Attorney General
Richardson, Ian	Ent	5			15	
Richardson, John, Sir	Science	20		125		Surgeon
Richardson, Michael	Ent	25			50	Sieinfeld/Kramer
Richardson, Miranda	Ent	25			50	Br. Actress

Name	Field	SIG	DS	ALS	SP	Remarks
Richardson, Natasha	Ent	20			50	
Richardson, Patricia	Ent	25			50	Home Improvement
Richardson, Ralph, Sir	Ent	20		50	45	
Richardson, Robert V.	Civil War	450	750			CSA General
Richardson, Tony	Ent	15			25	Director
Richardson, William A.	Political	25	45	75		Sec'y Treas.1873
Richelieu, Armand E. du	Political	100	225	300		Prime Minister France
Richelieu, Armand-Jean	Political	300	750	1,500		
Richey, Helen	Aviation	25	50		50	
Richie, Lionel	Music	20	75		50	Composer-Singer-Arranger
Richman, Harry	Aviation	15			35	
Richter, Burton, Dr.	Science	20		50	35	Nobel Physics 1976
Richter, Charles, Dr.	Science	25			75	Devised Richter Scale
Richter, Hans	Music	150		450		German Conductor
Richthofen, Manfred von	Aviation	2,000	RARE	RARE	6,500	WWI ACE/Red Baron
Rickenbacker, Edw V.	Aviation	100	200	450	275	WWI ACE
Rickles, Don	Ent	5	20		15	
Rickover, Hyman G.	Military	100	200	350	250	Father of Atomic Sub
Riddle, George	Music	10			20	
Ride, Sally K.	Space	15	45		35	Ist US Woman in Space
Ridgway, Matthew B.	Military	75	200	175	125	Supreme Allied Cmdr. WWII
Riefenstahl, Leni	Art	30		75	75	Hitler's Photographer
Rieger, Vince	Aviation	10		35	30	WWII Navy ACE
Riegger, Wallingford	Music	20		100	35	Composer
Rigal, Delia	Music	15			45	Opera
Rigg, Diana	Ent	20	45		45	Avengers TV Series
Riggs, Clinton E.	Science	20			40	Created Yield Sign
Riggs, Tommy	Ent	5			15	
Righteous Brothers	Music	45			100	Signed by Both
Riis, Jacob A. 1849-1914	Author	20		75		Journalist
Riley, James Whitcomb	Author	100		450	225	Poet/1849-1916
Riley, Jeannie C.	Music	5			15	Harper Valley PTA
Riley, Larry	Ent	5			10	
Rilke, Rainer Maria	Author	150	300			German Poet
Rimes, Lee Ann	Music	25			50	
Rimsky-Korsakov, N.	Music	750	1,500	2,500	1,500	Russian Composer
Rinehart, Mary Roberts	Author	25		75	75	Mystery Writer
Ringling, Albert C.	Business	150	400			Ringling Bros/Barnum...
Ringling, Chas. 1863-26	Business	125	300			Ringling Bros/Barnum..
Ringling, Henry	Business	125	350			Ringling Bros/Barnum...
Ringling, John 1866-1936	Business	125	600			Ringling Bros/Barnum...
Ringling, Otto 1858-1911	Business	250	550			Ringling Bros/Barnum ...
Ringo, John	Western	2,000	RARE	RARE	RARE	Cowboy Gunslinger
Ringwald, Molly	Ent	20			50	
Ripley, Eleazar W.	Military	75		225		General War 1812
Ripley, George	Political	150	325	575		
Ripley, James Wolfe	Civil War	75	150	200		Union General/1794-1870

Name	Field	SIG	DS	ALS	SP	Remarks
Ripley, Robert 1893-1949	Cartoonist	100		225	250	Believe It Or Not
Ripley, Roswell 1823-87	Civil War	175		400		CSA General
Ritchard, Cyril 1896-1977	Ent	20			50	Br. Dancer & Comedian
Ritchie, Adele	Ent	15		50	40	
Ritchie, Neil, Sir	Military	15		50	30	General
Ritchie, Steve	Aviation	15		45	40	
Ritt, Martin	Ent	35			75	Director
Rittenhouse, David	Science	750	1,250	RARE	RARE	Am Astronomer
Ritter, John	Ent	15			35	Three Company
Ritter, Tex	Music	75			225	1907 - 1974
Ritter, Thelma	Ent	50			150	
Ritterscheim, Karl	Music	10			30	Opera
Ritz Brothers, The	Music	75			150	Jimmy, Al, Harry
Ritz, Jimmy	Music	15			40	
Rivera, Diego	Art	300	550	750	1,200	Political-Social Muralist
Rivera, Geraido	Ent	15			30	TV Host
Rivers, Joan	Ent	5			15	
Rivers, Larry	Art	45	75	150		Pop Art Movement
Rivington, James 1724-02	RevWar	100	200			Journalist-Publisher-Spy
Roach, Hal, Jr.	Ent	5			15	
Roach, Hal, Sr.1892-1992	Ent	100	300		175	AA Film Pioneer. Our Gang
Roarke, Hayden	Ent	60	100		75	Dr. Bellows/Jeannie
Robards, Jason	Ent	15			30	AA Winner
Robbins, Frederick C.	Science	20		45	25	Nobel Medicine 1954
Robbins, Gale	Ent	15		35	30	
Robbins, Harold	Author	20	75		35	The Carpetbaggers
Robbins, Jay T.	Aviation	15		40	35	WWII ACE
Robbins, Jerome	Music	40	75		75	Ballet Dancer
Robbins, Marty	Music	25			50	Country
Robbins, Reg. L.	Aviation	25			50	Pioneer Aviator
Robbins, Tim	Ent	25			50	
Roberti, Margherita	Music	15			30	Am. Soprano
Roberts, Cokie	Ent	5			15	TV-Radio Journalist
Roberts, David	Art	50	100	175		Scottish Painter
Roberts, Doris	Ent	5			15	
Roberts, Eric	Ent	10			25	
Roberts, Frederick S.	Military	50			100	Field Marshal
Roberts, Jack	Music	10			20	
Roberts, Jonathan	Political	75		250		1771-1854
Roberts, Julia	Ent	35	150		75	
Roberts, Kenneth	Author	75	150	200		Am. Historical Novels
Roberts, Lee S.	Music	35	75	Scarce	Scarce	Composer
Roberts, Oral	Clergy	20		50	35	Am. Evangelist
Roberts, Owen J.	SuprCt	50	150	200	100	
Roberts, Pernell	Ent	75	100		150	Bonanza
Roberts, Ray	Ent	10			20	
Roberts, Tanya	Ent	15	25		25	Charlie Angels

Name	Field	SIG	DS	ALS	SP	Remarks
Roberts, Tony	Ent	5			15	
Roberts, William P.	Civil War	125				Youngest in CSA/1841-10
Roberts, Xavier	Business	15		35	25	
Robertson, Beverly H.	Civil War	75	150			CSA General/1826-1910
Robertson, Cliff	Ent	20			40	AA Winner
Robertson, Dale	Ent	15			35	
Robertson, James	RevWar			900		Br Gen in RevWar
Robertson, Morgan	Author	25		75		Sea Stories
Robertson, Pat, Rev.	Clergy	15		45	30	
Robeson, George M.	Political	25	50	75		Sec'y Navy 1869
Robeson, Paul 1898-1976	Ent	125	200	250	500	Singer/Actor
Robespierre, Maximilien	Military	1,250	2,500	RARE	RARE	French Revolution
Robin, Mado	Music	50			175	Opera
Robinson, Bill Bojangles	Ent	100	250	450	400	Dancer in Films
Robinson, Dwight P.	Business	5		20	15	
Robinson, Edward	Science		200	400		Archaeologist
Robinson, Edward G.	Ent	75	125		200	1893-1973
Robinson, Holly	Ent	10			20	
Robinson, John 1761-28	RevWar	75	150	275		Soldier/Merchant
Robinson, John C.	Civil War	75	150	200		Union General/1817-97
Robinson, Smokey	Music	25	50		45	of the Miracles
Robson, Flora, Dame	Ent	30			75	1902 - 1984
Robson, May	Ent	40			75	1858 - 1942
Robson, Stuart	Ent	20			45	
Rocco, Alex	Ent	10			20	
Rochambeau, Count de	RevWar	300		750		Fr. Gen. in Am. Revolution
Roche, James M.	Business	10		30	20	Pres. Ford Motor Co.
Rochefort, Henri	Author	20		50		Fr. Journalist
Rochford, Leonard	Aviation	20	40			WWI Br. ACE
Rock, Blossom	Ent	150	200	RARE	300	Addams Family
Rockefeller, Abby A.	Business	15	30	45	25	
Rockefeller, David	Business	15	35	45	25	Banker
Rockefeller, Happy	Business	5		20	10	Wife of Nelson Rockefeller
Rockefeller, John D.	Business	500	1,500	2,250	1,500	Standard Oil. Philantropist
Rockefeller, John D., Jr.	Business	35	125	175	75	Rockefeller Ctr
Rockefeller, Laurance	Business	5		25	10	Philanthropist
Rockefeller, Nelson A.	Vice Pres	30	75		45	Governor NY
Rockwell, George L.	Political	50	100	200	100	Am. Nazi Party
Rockwell, Norman	Art	150	250	475	400	Am. Illustrator-Artist
Rockwell, Robert	Ent	10	25		25	
Roddenberry, Gene	Ent	100	175	RARE	200	Creator of Star Trek
Roddey, Philip D.	Civil War	100	300	400		CSA General/1826-97
Roden, George	Civil War	30	45	75		
Rodenburg, Carl	Military	15			40	Ger General
Roderick, Milton David	Business	5			10	CEO U.S. Steel
Rodes, Robert E.	Civil War	1,000	RARE	RARE	RARE	CSA General
Rodes, Robert Emmett	Civil War	400		950		CSA General/Scarce

Name	Field	SIG	DS	ALS	SP	Remarks
Rodgers & Hammerstein	Music	500				Signed together
Rodgers and Hart	Music	650	1,250			Signed by Both
Rodgers, Geo. W.	Military	50	100	200		Naval Officer War of 1812
Rodgers, John	Aviation	65	125	225	135	
Rodgers, John 1771-1838	Military	100	300	200		
Rodgers, John 1812-82	Civil War	125	300	450		
Rodgers, Richard 1902-79	Music	75	250		225	Composer/Pulitzer
Rodin, Auguste	Art	250	450	475	RARE	1840 - 1917
Rodney, Caesar 1728-84	RevWar	500	900	2,000		Signer Decl. of Indepen.
Rodriguez, Chi Chi	Sports	10			25	1992 Golf HOF
Rodzinski, Artur	Music	35	75		75	Polish Conductor
Roe, Edward Payson	Author	15	25	35		Novelist
Roe, Tommy	Music	25	45		45	
Roebling, John A.	Science	75	175	275		Designer/Brooklyn Bridge
Roebling, Washington A.	Science	100	225	400		Builder of Brooklyn Bridge
Roebuck, Alva Curtis	Business		1,500		375	Co-Fndr. Sears & Roebuck
Roederer, Pierre C.	Military	25	50	75		French Revolution
Roell, Werner	Aviation	10			20	
Roentgen, Wilhelm	Science	650	1,300	2,400		Ist Nobel in Physics
Roethke, Theodore	Author	35	125	275	40	Am. Poet. Pulitzer
Rogatchewsky, Joseph	Music	25			75	
Rogers, Bernard W.	Military	10	25		40	
Rogers, Buddy	Ent	10		30	30	
Rogers, Fred	Ent	5			15	Mr. Rogers
Rogers, Ginger 1911-95	Ent	50	150		150	AA Winner
Rogers, Jean	Ent	25			50	
Rogers, Jimmy	Music	75			150	
Rogers, John	Military	150	350	350		
Rogers, Joseph W.	Aviation	15		45	35	
Rogers, Kenny	Music	20	45		45	
Rogers, Mimi	Ent	20			40	
Rogers, Randolph	Art	20		35		Sculptor/1825-1892
Rogers, Robert	RevWar	400	900	RARE	RARE	Frontier Soldier
Rogers, Roy	Ent	50	200		100	
Rogers, Samuel	Author	15	30			Br. Poet
Rogers, Wayne	Ent	10	25		25	MASH
Rogers, Will 1879-1935	Ent	250			700	
Rogers, William F.	Civil War	15	25	35		Union Officer
Roget, Peter M., Dr.	Author	30	75	125		Rogets Thesaurus
Rohmer, Eric	Ent	50	175			Fr. Director
Rohmer, Sax (A.S.Ward)	Author	75	225	250	100	Fu Manchu
Roland de La Platiere	Military	30	75	150		Fr. Statesman/Suicide
Roland, Gilbert 1909-94	Ent	20			45	
Roland, Ruth	Ent	25	35		45	
Roldan, Salv. C.	Political	10		35	20	Columbia
Rolland, Romain	Author	30	75	100	45	Nobel/Literature in 1915
Rolle, Esther	Ent	10	25		20	Good Times

Name	Field	SIG	DS	ALS	SP	Remarks
Rolling Stones	Music	275			600	Signed by all Five
Rollins, Sonny	Music	30			50	Jazz Tenor Sax
Rolls, Charles S.	Business	300		600		Roll-Royce Motors
Roman, Ruth	Ent	10			25	
Romanoff, Michael	Business	30	65	125	55	Romanoffs Restaurant
Romanov, Stephanie	Ent	15			40	
Rombauer, Irma S.	Author	5		30	10	The Joy of Cooking
Romberg, Sigmund	Music	75	200	300	225	Composer/1887-1951
Rome, Harold	Music	15	50	75	30	Composer
Romero, Cesar 1907- 93	Ent	35			65	TV's Batman/Joker
Romjin, Rebecca	Ent	20			40	
Rommel, Erwin 1891- 44	Military	750	1,150	RARE	1,500	Ger. Field Marshal WWII
Romney, George 1734-02	Art	150	375	450		
Romney, George W.	Business	15	30	50	25	Pres. American Motors.
Romulo, Carlos P.	Political	25		75	50	
Ronne, Finn	Explorer	20		70		Proved Antarctic/Continent
Ronstadt, Linda	Music	20			45	
Rooney, Mickey	Ent	10	30	35	25	
Roosa, Stuart R.	Space	15			30	Astronaut
Roosevelt, Alice	Political	40				Presidents Daughter
Roosevelt, Edith Kermit	First Lady	75	200	250	350	1861-1948
Roosevelt, Eleanor	First Lady	75	200	400	250	1884-1962
Roosevelt, Franklin D.	President	300	900	1,400	900	1882-1945
Roosevelt, Franklin Jr.	Political	10			20	
Roosevelt, James	Political	10	25	45	15	
Roosevelt, John A.	Political	20	35			FDR's Son
Roosevelt, Nicholas J.	RevWar	25		125		Inventor
Roosevelt, Sarah D.	Political	40	100	75	50	FDR's Mother
Roosevelt, Theodore	President	250	600	1,200	1,200	1858-1919
Roosevelt, Theodore, Jr.	Military	20	50	75	40	Gov Puerto Rico
Root, Elihu 1845-1937	Political	75			150	Secretary of War
Root, George F.	Music	50	125	150		Composer
Root, Jesse	RevWar	25		100		Continental Congress
Rops, Felicien 1833-98	Art	75	150	350		
Rorem, Ned	Music	25		100		Composer/Pulitzer
Rosas, Juan M.	Political	15	25	40		Argentina
Rose Marie	Ent	10	20		20	Dick VanDyke Show
Rose, Axl	Music	25			50	Guns and Roses
Rose, Billy	Ent	25		75	50	Producer
Rose, David	Music	10		35	20	Composer
Rose, Fred	Music	30			60	
Rosebery, Archibald P.	Political	35	75	125		Prime Minister
Rosecrans, William S.	Civil War	75	175	250		Union General/1819-98
Rosenberg, Alfred	Military	175	350		450	Nazi Head of Foreign Policy
Rosendahl, Charles E.	Aviation	75	160	200	200	
Rosenquist, James	Art	25	50	100		Am Pop Art
Rosenthal, Joe	Art	75	200	250	250	

Name	Field	SIG	DS	ALS	SP	Remarks
Rosenthal, Laurence	Music	5		20	10	Composer
Rosenwald, Julius	Business	400	1,200			1862-1932
Ross, David 1755-1800	RevWar			400		Cont'l Army & Congress
Ross, Diana	Music	25	75		60	of the Supremes
Ross, Edmund G.	Political	35	100			KS Sen/Impeachment Trial
Ross, George 1730-79	RevWar	250	450	950		Signer Decl. of Independ.
Ross, Joe E.	Ent	100			250	
Ross, John	Western	350	600	1,000		Chief Cherokee Nation
Ross, John, Sir 1777-1856	Explorer	65	150	250		Arctic Expeditions
Ross, Katharine	Ent	20			40	
Ross, Lawrence Sullivan	Civil War	175	550			CSA General/Texas Gov.
Ross, Marion	Ent	15	25	25	25	Happy Days / Mom
Ross, Nellie Tayloe	Political	35	75	125		1st US Woman Governor
Ross, Ronald 1857-1932	Science	75	125	250		
Rosselini, Isabella	Ent	20			45	
Rosser, Thomas L.	Civil War	125	250	350	350	CSA General/1836-1910
Rossetti, Christina	Author	50	125	245		Br Poet. Sister of Dante
Rossetti, Dante Gabriel	Art	150	225	550		Br. Poet & Painter
Rossetti, Wm. M, 1829-19	Author	75		350		Pre-Raphaelite Art Critic
Rossi, Dick	Aviation	10		45	30	WWII Flying Tigers ACE
Rossini, Gioacchino	Music	RARE	1,000	1,750	RARE	Composer
Rossmann, Edmund	Aviation	20			50	Ger. Ace WWII
Rostand, Edmond	Author	75	200	400	775	Fr. Playwright. Cyrano de....
Rostropovich, Mstislav	Music	25	75	100	75	Cello Virtuoso, Conductor
Roth, David Lee	Music	25	75		50	Formerly w/ Van Halen
Roth, Lillian 1910-1980	Music	40		75	75	
Roth, Philip	Author	15	35	45	25	Portnoys Complaint
Roth, Tim	Ent	20			45	
Rothafell, S. L. 'Roxy'	Business	15	25		45	Theatre Owner
Rothenstein, William	Art	25	50	75		WWI and II Artist
Rothschild, Alix de	Business	100	200	375		Banker
Rothschild, Amschel M.	Business	RARE	1,000	RARE	RARE	1733-1855
Rothschild, Guy de	Business	25		75	75	
Rothschild, Jakob	Business	200	600			1792 - 1868
Rothschild, Leopold	Business	35		125		Grandson of Nathan Mayer
Rothschild, Lionel N.	Business	25	75	125	45	Son of Nathan Mayer
Rothschild, Mayer A.	Business	150	350	550		Fndr House of Rothschild
Rothschild, Nathan	Business	50	150			Eldest son of Lionel
Rothschild, Nathan M.	Business	275	850			Founder London Bank
Rouault, Georges	Art	200	475	750	900	Landscapes,Clowns.
Rouget de Lisle, Claude	Military	125	275	775		Composed La Marseillaise
Roundtree, Richard	Music	10			25	Opera
Rourke, Mickey	Ent	20			50	
Rous, F. Peyton, Dr.	Science	20		45	30	Nobel Medicine 1966
Rousseau, Jean-Jacques	Author	300		RARE	RARE	Fr. Philosopher
Rousseau, Lovell H.	Civil War	50	75			Union General/1818-69
Rousseau, Theodore	Art	75	175	475		Fr. Leader of Barbizon

Name	Field	SIG	DS	ALS	SP	Remarks
Roux, Pierre Paul Emile	Science	20			40	French Bacteriologist
Rovero, Ornella	Music	20			45	Opera
Rowan, Andrew S.	Military	35	75	150	75	
Rowan, Dan	Ent	25	50	50	40	Laugh In
Rowan, John 1773-1853	Political	100	250			
Rowan, Stephen C.	Civil War	35		150		Union Naval Commodore
Rowe, Misty	Ent	10			20	
Rowland, David	Political	50	150			
Rowland, Gena	Ent	10			25	
Rowlandson, Thomas	Art	250	500	800		Br. Caricaturist, Illustrator
Rowling, William E.	Political	10	15		20	New Zealand
Roxas, Manuel	Political	35		100	75	Ist Pres. Philippines
Roxette	Music	25			50	Signed by leads
Royce, F. Henry, Sir	Business	600		1,200		Founder Rolls-Royce, Ltd.
Roze, Marie	Music	50			145	Opera
Rubattel, Rudolph	Political	30	50			Switzerland
Rubens, Alma 1899-1931	Ent	50	75	150	150	Actress
Rubens, Peter Paul	Art	2,000	RARE	RARE	RARE	Flem.Baroque Landscapes
Rubik, Erno	Science	35	75	75	50	Rubik's Cube/Hungarian
Rubinoff, David	Music	20			40	Rubinoff & His Violin
Rubinstein, Anton	Music	75	200	300	400	Composer/1829-1894
Rubinstein, Artur 1887-83	Music	50	125	250	175	Pianist
Rubinstein, Helena	Business	75	150	225	350	Cosmetics
Rubinstein, Ida	Ent	150			500	Russian Ballerina
Rubio, P. Ortiz	Political	40				Pres. Mex. 1930-32
Ruby, Harry	Music	30		125	50	Composer
Ruby, Jack 1911-67	Criminal	200	400	RARE	RARE	Killed Lee Harvey Oswald
Rucker, Daniel H.	Civil War	25	65	75	100	Union Col/Brvt. General
Rudel, Hans-Ulrich	Aviation	150	300	RARE	350	German ACE
Rudner, Rita	Ent	5			15	Stand-Up Comedian
Rudolf I (Hapsburg)	Royalty			750		(Aus)
Rudorffer, Erich	Aviation	40			75	German ACE (#7)
Ruehl, Mercedes	Ent	25			50	AA Winner
Ruff, Charles F.	Civil War	25	50	60		Union General/1817-85
Ruffo, Titta 1887-1953	Music	100	RARE	RARE	400	Italian Baritone
Ruge, Friedrich	Military	75			175	German Vice Admiral
Ruger, Thomas H.	Civil War	30		75		Union General/1833-1907
Ruggles, Charles	Ent	35			70	
Ruggles, Daniel	Civil War	150	600	950		CSA General/War Dated
Ruggles, Daniel 1810-97	Civil War	100	300	600		CSA General
Ruggles, Wesley	Ent	20			45	Director
Rulter, John	SuprCt	RARE	RARE	RARE	RARE	
Rumpler, Edward	Aviation	25		75	50	
Rumsfeld, Donald	Political	10		45	20	Sec'y Defense
Rundstedt, Karl R. Gerd	Military	200		350	275	Ger Field Marshal
Runyon, Damon 1884-46	Author	125	275	350	225	Sports Writer
Rush	Music	75			125	Signed by Entire Group

Name	Field	SIG	DS	ALS	SP	Remarks
Rush, Barbara	Ent	5			15	
Rush, Benjamin	RevWar	750		2,250		Signer Decl. of Indepen
Rush, Isadore	Ent	10			30	
Rush, Richard 1780-1859	Political	75	150	275		Attorney General
Rusk, Dean	Political	25			50	Sec'y State
Rusk, Jeremiah M.	Civil War	25	50	100		Union General/1830-93
Rusk, Thos. Jefferson	Military	350		700		TX Provisional Governor
Ruskin, John 1819-1900	Art	75	125	275		British Painter
Rusling, James F.	Civil War	15	30	40		Union Officer
Russell, Bertrand	Author	85	275	450	250	Math/Nobel/1872-1970
Russell, Bruce	Cartoonist	25			50	Political Cartoonist
Russell, Charles M.	Art	250	750	1,500		Western Artist
Russell, George W.	Author	35	100		75	
Russell, Harold	Ent	10		30	25	Military Hero/AA
Russell, Jane	Ent	15	40		35	The Outlaw
Russell, John	Ent	20			45	
Russell, John, Lord	Political	35	75	125		Br. Prime Minister, 1864-65
Russell, Johnny	Music	5			15	
Russell, Jonathan	Political	400	750			1771-1832
Russell, Keri	Ent	25			50	TV's "Felicity"
Russell, Kurt	Ent	25			50	Tombstone
Russell, Lillian 1861-1922	Music	100	150	275	400	Operetta Star
Russell, Mark	Ent	5			10	
Russell, Nipsey	Ent	10			20	
Russell, Rosalind	Ent	35	45		80	MAME/1908-1976
Russell, Theresa	Ent	10	15	30	25	
Russo, Rene	Ent	20			45	
Rust, Albert 1818-70	Civil War	75	150			CSA General
Rustin, Bayard	Political	15	35		25	
Rutan, Dick	Aviation	15			30	
Rutgers, Henry	RevWar	100	250	325		1745 - 1830
Rutherford, Ann	Ent	10	20	25	20	
Rutherford, Ernest	Science	150	350	RARE	225	Physicist/Nobel
Rutherford, Kelly	Ent	15			30	
Rutherford, Margaret	Ent	75		150	175	Dame
Rutledge, Edward	RevWar	200	500	750		Signer
Rutledge, John	SuprCt	200	600	1,200		Continental Congress
Rutledge, Wiley B.	SuprCt	30	100	250	50	
Ruttan, Susan	Ent	5			15	
Ryan, Irene	Ent	100	150		200	Granny/Bev Hillbillies
Ryan, Jeri	Ent	20			40	Star Trek : Voyager
Ryan, Meg	Ent	30			60	Scarce Signer
Ryan, Peggy	Ent	10	15	35	30	
Ryan, Robert	Ent	15	30		50	
Ryan, Sheila	Ent	5	15		15	
Ryan, T. Claude	Aviation	100			225	Ryan Aircraft Mfg
Rydell, Bobby	Music	15			30	

Name	Field	SIG	DS	ALS	SP	Remarks
Ryder, Albert P. 1847-17	Art	100	250	450		Am. Landscapes
Ryder, Winona	Ent	35			55	
Ryle, Martin, Sir	Science	30	100	150	45	Nobel Physics 1974

S

Name	Field	SIG	DS	ALS	SP	Remarks
Saarinen, G. Eliel	Science	20	75	100	40	Am. Architect
Sabatier, Paul	Science	75		150		Fr. Chem. Nobel 1912
Sabatini, Rafael	Author	25	50	75		
Sabato, Antonio Jr.	Ent	15			30	
Sabin, Albert Bruce, Dr.	Science	35		150	150	Polio Vaccine
Sabin, Florence R.,Dr.	Science	25		125		1871-1953
Sabine, Edward, Sir	Military	50		175		Br. General/1788-1833
Sablon, Jean	Music	20	25	40	45	French Singer
Sabu 1924-63	Ent	50			150	Child Star
Sacco, Nicola	Criminal	RARE	RARE	3,700	RARE	With Vanzetti
Sacher-Masoch, Leopold	Author	150	275	400		
Sacks, Oliver, Dr.	Science	15			30	Awakenings"/ Neurologist
Sadat, Anwar 1918-81	Political	100		300	500	Assassinated Pres/ Egypt
Sade	Music	25			45	
Sade, Marquis de	Author	250	750	1,500		
Safer, Morley	Ent	5	20	25	15	60 Minutes
Sagan, Carl, Dr.	Science	15	30	45	30	Am. Astronomer/Pulitzer
Sage, Russell 1816-1906	Business	200	750	1,500		Financier/Jay Gould
Sagendorf, Bud 1915-94	Cartoonist	35			75	Popeye (After Segar)
Sager, Carole Bayer	Music	10	25		25	
Saget, Bob	Ent	10	20		20	Full House
Sahl, Mort	Ent	5			15	Political Humorist
Said, Nuri	Political	5		35	10	Pr. Minister Iraq
Saint Hilaire, L.V, Jos.	Military	30	75	155		French Revolution
Saint James, Susan	Ent	15			35	
Saint Laurent, Yves	Business	25	35	50	45	Fashion Designer
Saint, Eva Marie	Ent	15	25		30	AA Winner
Saint-Cyr, Gouvion	Military	50	150	175		Fr. Minister of War
Saint-Exupery, Antoine	Aviation	50	125	175	125	Fr. Aviator and Author
Saint-Gaudens, Augustus	Art	200		900	1,200	Monuments...
Saint-Just, Louis	Military	375	750			French Revolution
Saint-Saens, Camille	Music	150	300	400	400	Opera/1835-1921
Saito, Makoto, Baron	Political	100	200	300		Prime Minister Japan
Sakai, Saburo	Aviation	50			100	3rd Highest Japanese Ace
Sakharov, Andrei	Science	300		RARE		Nobel Physics
Salalm, Abdus	Science	20	30	45	25	Nobel Physics 1979
Salan, Raoul	Military	20	50	75	50	
Sale, Chic 1885-1937	Ent	25	35		75	Comedian-Actor
Sales, Soupy	Ent	5		20	15	
Saleza, Albert	Music	15			45	Opera
Salinger, J[erome] D.	Author	RARE	3,000	4,500	RARE	Catcher in the Rye
Salinger, Pierre	Political	20		45	45	Press Sec'y Pres. JFK

Name	Field	SIG	DS	ALS	SP	Remarks
Salisbury, 3rd Marquis	Political	40		75		Prime Minister
Salisbury, Frank	Art	25	75	100		Br. Portrait Painter
Salk, Jonas, Dr. 1914-93	Science	50	150	250	200	Polio Vaccine
Salling, John	Civil War	15		50		
Salt, Titus, Sir 1803-76	Business	10	25	40		Pioneer Wool Industry
Salten, Felix 1870-1946	Author	75	100	200		Bambi
Sam the Sham	Music	25	50		50	and the Pharoahs
Samaroff-Stokowski	Music	25			75	Pianist/Teacher
Sambora, Richie	Music	20			40	
Samms, Emma	Ent	15	25	30	30	
Samples, Candy	Ent	25			55	
Samples, Junior	Ent	10			20	
Sampson, Will	Ent	75		150	200	Scarce/Cukoos Nest...
Sampson, William T.	Military	30	75	125	75	Adm. Sp.- Am. War
Samuelson, Paul A., Dr.	Science	25	40		35	Nobel Economics
San Giacomo, Laura	Ent	20	40		45	Just Shoot Me
San Juan, Olga	Ent	5			10	
San Martin, Jose de	Political	500	750	RARE	RARE	Soldier Hero of Argentina
Sand, George 1804-76	Author	100	200	400		
Sandburg, Carl	Author	100	225	300	400	1878 - 1967
Sanders, Deion	Sports	10			35	Football
Sanders, George	Ent	75			150	AA Winner
Sanders, Harland	Business	50		150	125	KFC Colonel Sanders
Sanders, Horace T.	Civil War	20		50		Union Officer
Sanderson, Julia	Ent	15			35	Radio
Sandoz, Marie	Author	25	50	100	50	
Sands, Julia	Ent	10			25	
Sands, Tommy	Ent	10			15	
Sandwich, 4thEarl	Political	125	300	400		
Sanford, Edw. Terry	SuprCt	75	150			
Sanford, Isabel	Ent	10			20	Weezy on the "Jeffersons"
Sanger, Frederick	Science	20	35	50	35	Nobel Chemistry 1958
Sanger, Margaret	Political	50	200	250	100	Birth Control Advocate
Sangster, Margaret E.	Author	30	75	125		Journalist, Poet, Editor
Santa Anna, Antonio L.	Political	400	1,100	1,400	675	Pres of Mexico
Santa Cruz, Andres	Political	100	225			Pres. Bolivia/Exiled
Santa Rosa, Annibale S.	Military	25		125		
Santana, Carlos	Music	20			50	
Santayana, George	Author	75	175	275		Poet, Philosopher, Critic
Santley, Charles, Sir	Music	50			150	Baritone
Santos-Dumont, A.	Aviation	300		600	750	Brazil/Pioneer Aeronaut
Santunione, Orianna	Music	10			20	Opera
Saperstein, Abe	Business	RARE	RARE	RARE	175	Coach/Harlem Globetrotters
Sara, Mia	Ent	20			50	
Sarandon, Susan	Ent	25	50		50	
Sarasate, Pablo de	Music	100		250		Violin Virtuoso
Sardi, Vincent	Business	5		20	10	Fndr. Sardi's Restaurant

Name	Field	SIG	DS	ALS	SP	Remarks
Sardou, Victorien	Author	25	45	100	125	Playwright/1831-1908
Sarett, Lew	Author	75	100			
Sarfatti, Margherita	Author	10	30	50		
Sarg, Tony 1882-1942	Art	25			75	
Sargent, Dick	Ent	35	50		65	Darren/Bewitched
Sargent, John G.	Political	15	30	50	25	Att'y General 1925
Sargent, John Singer	Art	100	250	350		1856-1925/Am. Portraitist
Sargent, Kenny	Music	20			45	Big Band Singer
Sargent,Winthrop	RevWar	30	100	240		1st Gov Miss.Territory
Sarnoff, David 1891-1971	Business	75	400	750	150	Broadcasting Pioneer
Sarocco, Suzanne	Music	10			25	Opera
Saroyan, William	Author	50	150	200	100	Pulitzer
Sartain, John 1808-97	Art	25		100		
Sartre, Jean-Paul	Author	100	300	400		1905 - 1980
Sassoon, Beverly	Ent	5			15	
Sassoon, Siegfried	Author	75	150	300		Br. Poet.Anti-War Verse
Sassoon, Vidal	Business	15	20	25	25	Hair Design & Products
Satie, Erik	Music	300	700	1,250		
Sato, Eisaku	Political	20	50	100	35	Premier Japan
Sauckel, Fritz	Military	75	200			Nazi War Criminal. Hanged
Sauer, Emil	Ent	15	25	60	30	
Sauguet, Henri	Music	75		250		Opera/Ballet
Saumarez, James, Sir	Military	100	250	450		Br. Adm./Battle of the Nile
Saunders, Alvin	Political	15	35	50		
Saunders, Hugh W.	Aviation	5		20	15	
Saunders, Lori	Ent	5			15	
Savage, Fred	Ent	20			45	Wonder Years/Working
Saval, Dany	Ent	10		25	20	French Actress
Savalas, Telly	Ent	25	45		45	Kojak
Savannah	Ent	75			150	Deceased porn star
Savitch, Jessica	Author	75			150	TV News
Savitt, Jan	Music	15			45	Bandleader
Savoia, Attilio	Art	15	35	50		
Sawyer, Diane	Ent	10	20		25	TV Broadcast Journalist
Sawyer, Joe	Ent	75			200	
Sax, Adolphe	Science	75	150	300		Inventor of the Saxophone
Saxbe, William B.	Political	5		20	15	Att'y General 1974
Saxe, John G.	Author	10	30	45	30	
Saxon, John	Ent	5			15	
Saxon, Rufus, Jr.	Civil War	25	45	65		
Sayao, Bidu	Music	25			75	Opera Soprano
Sayers, Dorothy 1893-57	Author	200	350	475		Br. Mystery Novelist
Scacchi, Greta	Ent	15			40	
Scacchi, Greta	Ent	15			30	
Scaggs, Boz	Music	15			35	
Scagliarini, Eleanora	Music	15			40	Opera
Scales, Alfred M.	Civil War	175		350		CSA General/1827-92

Name	Field	SIG	DS	ALS	SP	Remarks
Scalia, Antonin	SuprCt	30	75		55	
Scalia, Jack	Ent	10			25	
Scammell, Alexander	RevWar	350		1,200		1746-81
Scancarelli, Jim	Cartoonist	10			30	Gasoline Alley
Scarlatti, Alessandro	Music	RARE	RARE	20,000	RARE	Opera/1660-1725
Schacht, Hjalmar	Military	75	150	300		Nazi Minister WWII
Schaeffer, Rebecca	Ent	75			150	Murdered by fan
Schafer, Natalie	Ent	35			60	Mrs Howell/Gilligans Island
Schaffner, Franklin J.	Ent	30			75	
Schaffner, Hans	Political	10			20	Pres. Austria
Schally, Andrew V., Dr.	Science	20	30	45	30	Nobel Medicine 1977
Schanberg, Sydney, H.	Author	10	30	50	15	
Scharwenka, Franz X.	Music	25		75	150	Pianist
Schary, Dore 1905 - 1980	Ent	15		25	35	Producer, Director, Writer
Schawlow, Arthur L., Dr.	Science	20	30	35	35	Nobel Physics 1981
Scheer, Reinhard	Military	20	45	100	45	Ger. Admiral/1863-1928
Scheff, Fritzi 1882-1954	Ent	20		30	25	Silent Films
Scheider, Roy	Ent	25	50		50	Jaws/SeaQuest DSV
Schell, Maria	Ent	5		20	15	
Schell, Maximillian	Ent	10		35	30	AA Winner
Schenck, Robert C.	Civil War	35	45	75		Union General/1809-90
Schick, Bela, Dr.	Science	50	100	200	75	Schick Test for TB
Schiffer, Claudia	Ent	25			50	SuperModel
Schifrin, Lalo	Music	10		25	25	Composer
Schildkraut, Joseph	Ent	75	150		150	1895 - 1964
Schiller, Hans von	Aviation	20		45		
Schilling, David	Aviation	20		50	45	WWII ACE
Schipa, Tito	Music	45			125	Opera
Schirra, Walter M.	Space	25	75	150	75	Mercury 7 Astronaut
Schlafly, Phyllis	Political	10		35	25	Activist, Feminist
Schlesinger, Arthur Jr.	Author	10	30	50	20	
Schlesinger, John	Ent	20			50	Director
Schley, Winfield Scott	Military	100	200	300	350	Arctic rescue of Greely
Schliemann, Heinrich	Science	250		RARE	RARE	Archaeology
Schmalz, Wilhelm	Military	15	40	50	30	
Schmidt, Helmut	Political	15	25	40	20	
Schmidt, Joseph	Music	150			400	Opera Singer/RARE
Schmidt, Maarten, Dr.	Science	10	25	30	20	
Schmidtmer, Christiane	Ent	5			15	German Actress
Schmitt, Harrison H.	Space	25	125		75	Apollo 17 Moonwalker
Schmitt-Walter, Karl	Music	10			35	Opera
Schnabel, Artur	Music	50	125	200		Austrian Pianist
Schnaut, Gabriella	Music	10			25	Opera
Schneider, John	Ent	15			35	Dukes of Hazzard
Schneider, Romy	Ent	75			125	
Schoenberg, Arnold	Music	300			600	Composer/1874-1951
Schoene, Heinrich	Military	125	250		200	Ger. Gen. Storm Trooper

Name	Field	SIG	DS	ALS	SP	Remarks
Schoenebeck, Karl	Aviation	30	75		75	
Schoenert, Rudolf	Aviation	10	25	40	25	
Schoepfel, Gerhard	Aviation	5		25	15	
Schofield, John M.	Civil War	50	75	150		Union General/1831-1906
Schopenhauer, Arthur	Author	1,500	RARE	RARE	RARE	Ger. Philosopher
Schorner, Ferdinand	Military	50		125		
Schrader, Paul	Ent	10			20	Director
Schramm, Margit	Music	5			15	Opera
Schreiber, Avery	Ent	5			15	Comedian
Schrieffer, John R.	Science	10		35	15	Nobel Physics 1972
Schriver, Edmund	Civil War	50	100	125		Union General/1812-99
Schroder, Ricky	Ent	20			45	Child Star/Silver Spoon
Schroeder-Feinen, U.	Music	10			30	Opera
Schroer, Werner	Aviation	30			65	WWII German ACE
Schubert, Franz	Music	2,500	5,000	RARE	RARE	Composer
Schuk, Walter	Aviation	25	50		75	German ACE
Schulberg, Budd	Author	5	35		15	Novelist
Schulz, Charles	Cartoonist	100	225	RARE	250	PEANUTS
Schulze, William	Science	15			45	Rocket Pioneer/von Braun
Schuman, William	Music	20	35	50	50	Composer
Schumann, Clara	Music	75	150	300	650	Pianist/Composer
Schumann, Elizabeth	Music	40			125	Opera
Schumann, Robert	Music	1,000	RARE	RARE	RARE	Composer/1810-56
Schumann-Heink, E.	Music	50			150	Opera
Schurz, Carl 1829-1906	Civil War	45	100	150		Union General
Schuschnigg, Kurt von	Political	50	75	150	75	
Schuyler, Philip J.	RevWar	200	450	750		Soldier, Statesman
Schwab, Charles M.	Business	125	350	750	250	Pres Carnegie/US Steel
Schwab, Frank X.	Political	5	20			Mayor Buffalo, NY
Schwantner, Joseph	Music	15		50	40	Pulitzer
Schwartz, Melvin, Dr.	Science	25			30	Nobel Physics 1988
Schwarzenegger, Arnold	Ent	40	200		75	
Schwarzkopf, Elizabeth	Music	20			50	Opera
Schwarzkopf, Norman	Military	35		125	75	Gen. Desert Storm
Schweickart, Russell L.	Space	10			25	
Schweitzer, Albert, Dr.	Science	150		550	750	Nobel/1875-1965
Schwimmer, David	Ent	25			50	Friends
Schwinger, Julian, Dr.	Science	15	30	45	25	Nobel Physics 1965
Sciorra, Annabella	Ent	15			30	
Sciorra, Annabelle	Ent	10			30	
Scobee, Dick	Space	50			175	Challenger Victim
Scofield, Paul	Ent	20	40		35	AA Winner
Scoggins, Tracy	Ent	10		25	20	
Scolari, Peter	Ent	10			20	Newhart
Scopes, John T. 1900-70	Political	300		RARE	1,500	Defendant In Monkey Trial
Scorpions, The	Music	25			50	Signed by all
Scorsese, Martin	Ent	25			50	Director

Name	Field	SIG	DS	ALS	SP	Remarks
Scorupco, Izabella	Ent	20			45	
Scott, Campbell	Ent	15			30	
Scott, Charles	RevWar	100	200	300		General/Indian Fighter
Scott, Charles Wm. A.	Aviation	25	50	75	50	Br. Won Harmon Trophy
Scott, David R.	Space	50			200	Moonwalker
Scott, Eric	Ent	5			10	
Scott, Fred	Ent	25	50	75	50	Western Star
Scott, George C.	Ent	25	50		50	AA Winner
Scott, Gordon	Ent	15			30	Tarzan actor
Scott, Gustavus	RevWar	35	75			Lawyer, Patriot (MD)
Scott, Hazel	Ent	35			125	
Scott, Jerry	Cartoonist	10			30	Nancy
Scott, John Morin	RevWar	35	75	150		General and Patriot
Scott, Lizabeth	Ent	10			20	
Scott, Martha	Ent	10			20	
Scott, Randolph	Ent	50	100		100	1898-1987
Scott, Raymond	Music	25	50	75	50	Composer/Big Bandleader
Scott, Robert Falcon	Explorer	100	250	500	200	Br. Arctic Expeditions
Scott, Robert Kingston	Civil War	50				Union General/1826-1900
Scott, Robert L., Jr.	Aviation	15		45	35	WWII Flying Tiger ACE
Scott, Walter, Sir 1771-32	Author	150	500	900		Poet/Novelist
Scott, Willard	Ent	5			10	
Scott, Winfield 1786-1866	Civil War	125	300	550	450	Union General
Scott, Zachary	Ent	25			50	
Scotto, Renata	Music	25			50	Opera
Scowcroft, Brent	Military	10			20	
Scriabin, Alexander	Music	1,000	3,500	RARE	RARE	Composer/1872-1915
Scribe, Eugene 1791-61	Author	20		60		
Scribner, Charles	Business	200	900			Fndr Publishing Co.
Scripps, William E.	Aviation	15	50		40	
Scuderi, Sara	Music	35			75	Opera
Scullin, James H.	Political	45				P.M. Australia
Scully, Thomas	Art	200	375	550		
Seaborg, Glenn	Science	40	75	150	75	Nobel Chemistry 1951
Seaforth, Susan	Ent	10			20	
Seagal, Steven	Ent	25			50	Action/Martial Arts Star
Seal	Music	25			50	
Seals, Dan	Music	5			15	
Sears, Richard Warren	Business	RARE	RARE	6,000	RARE	Founder of Sears/Roebuck
Seaton, George	Ent	35			75	Director
Seaver, Tom	Sports	15			35	1992 Baseball HOF
Seawell, Molly Elliot	Author	5		30	10	
Sebastini, H.F.B.	Military	75		150		Gen Under Napolean
Seberg, Jean	Ent	75			150	Suicide
Sechelles, Marie - Jean	Military			900		Att'y to Louis XVI
Sedaka, Neil	Music	10			20	
Seddon, James A.	Civil War	250	500	RARE	RARE	CSA Sect of War//1815-80

Name	Field	SIG	DS	ALS	SP	Remarks
Seddon, Margaret R.	Space	10			20	
Sedgewick, John	Civil War	125	350			Union General (Uncle John)
Sedgwick, Catherine M.	Author	10		45		Am. Novelist
Sedgwick, John 1813-64	Civil War	250	750			Union General/KIA
Sedgwick, Kyra	Ent	20			50	
See, Elliot M. Jr.	Space	175			250	Astronaut
Seeburg, Justus Percival	Business	50	125	200		
Seeger, Pete	Music	20	50	75	40	
Seeley, Jeannie	Music	10			20	
Segal, Erich	Author	20				Love Story
Segal, George	Ent	10			35	Just Shoot Me
Seger, Bob	Music	30			60	and Silver Bullit Band
Seger, Elzie C.	Cartoonist	125			275	Popeye
Segovia, Andres	Music	100		300	150	Classical Guitar Virtuoso
Segre, Emilio, Dr.	Science	20	35	50	30	Nobel Physics 1959
Segura, Wiltz	Aviation	15	25	40	30	USAF WWII ACE
Segurola, Andres de	Music	50			150	
Seidel, Toscha	Music	25			75	Russian/American Violinist
Seidelman, Susan	Ent	5			10	Director
Seignolle, Claude	Author	100	175	200		
Seinfeld	Ent	150			300	Signed by Four
Seinfeld, Jerry	Ent	25			55	Scarce Signer
Seipel, Ignas Dr.	Political	15	30	60	40	
Selassie, Haile 1891-1975	Political	200	300	550	750	Emperor of Ethiopia
Selena	Music	200			400	Murdered pop star
Selfridge, Thos.	Civil War	40	75	125		Union Naval Commander
Sellecca, Connie	Ent	10	20		30	
Selleck, Tom	Ent	25			50	Magnum PI
Sellers, David Foote	Military	20	50	75	50	
Sellers, Peter 1925-80	Ent	100	150	250	175	Pink Panther Movies
Sellers, Winfield S.	Military	15		75	45	
Selman, John	Western	1,200	2,500			
Selznick, David O.	Ent	125	350		275	Film Producer (GWTW)
Selznick, Irene	Ent	10			20	Film Executive
Sembrich, Marcella	Music	100		200	200	Opera
Semenov, Nikolai	Science	35	100		75	Rus.Chem/Physicist/Nobel
Semmelwels, Ignaz	Science	500	900	RARE	RARE	Obstetrician/Antisepsis
Semmes, Paul J. 1815-63	Civil War	700	900	900		CSA General
Semmes, Raphael	Civil War	300	750	1,400	1,500	CSA Admiral/1809-77
Sen Young, Victor	Ent	75			200	Hop Sing on "Bonanza"
Senechal, Michel	Music	10			25	Opera
Senn, Nicholas	Civil War	35		125		Union Surgeon
Sennett, Mack 1880-1960	Ent	300	550		750	
Sergievsky, Boris	Aviation	75			150	
Serkin, Rudolf	Music	50		150	125	Piano
Serling, Rod	Ent	125	200		450	Outer Limits/Night Gallery
Serurier, Jean M.P.	Military	50	125	200		Marshal of Napoleon

Name	Field	SIG	DS	ALS	SP	Remarks
Service, Robert VV.	Author	75		200	400	Canadian Poet
Sessions, Roger	Music	15		90		Composer/Pulitzer
Seton, Ernest Thompson	Author	50	100	175	100	Co-Fndr Boy Scouts
Seuss, Dr.	Author	75			250	Theodore Gieisel
Severance, Joan	Ent	10			25	
Severeid, Eric	Ent	10			25	
Severeid, Susanne	Ent	5			15	
Severinson, Doc	Music	10			20	Tonite Show
Sevier, John 1745-1815	RevWar	600		750		
Sewall, David	RevWar	25	50	100		
Sewall, Samuel 1652-30	Political	350		950		Salem Witchcraft Trials
Sewall, Samuel 1757-14	Political	25		50		
Seward, Frederick Wm.	Political	25	50	75		Ass't Sec'y State
Seward, William H.	Political	75	125	150		1801-72
Sewell, William J.	Civil War	50	100	125		Union General/1835-1901
Sexton, Walton R.	Military	10		45	30	Adm. US Navy. WWII
Seymour, Jane	Ent	15			40	Dr. Quinn
Seymour, Stephanie	Ent	20			45	Super-Model
Seymour, Truman	Civil War	75	100	200		Union General/1824-91
Shackelford, Ted	Ent	5			15	
Shackleton, Ernest H.	Explorer	200		400	450	Br Antarctic Explorer
Shaffer, Paul	Music	5			15	David Letterman Show
Shaffer, Peter L.	Author	10	20		15	
Shafter, William R.	Civil War	15	40	75		Union General/1835-1906
Shafter, William R.	Civil War	35	75	125	150	Union General/War Dated
Shaftesbury, A.A.C.	Political	25	75	150		
Shah, Zahir	Royalty	50				King Afghanistan
Shahn, Ben	Art	50	125	200	150	Am.Painter-Graphic Artist
Shalamar	Music	20	50		50	
Shaler, Alexander	Civil War	35	50	100		Union General
Shalikashvilli, John	Military	10	25		20	Chm. Joint Chiefs of Staff
Shamir, Yitzhak	Political	25			75	Prime Minister Israel
Shamroy, Leon	Ent	25				Director
Shandling, Gary	Ent	25	50		50	Larry Sanders Show
Shannon, Del	Music	35	60		75	
Shannon, Wilson	Political	25		100		
Shapiro, Karl	Author	10		50	20	
Shapiro, Robert	Political	15			35	OJ Simpson Attorney
Shapley, Alan	Military	15	35	50		
Shapley, Harlow	Science	50	150	150		Astronomer
Sharan, Shri C.	Political	25			75	Pres. India
Sharett, Moshe (Shertok)	Political	50		200		Israeli Prime Minister
Sharif, Omar	Ent	25	25		75	
Sharkey, Ray	Ent	10			30	
Sharnova, Sonia	Music	10			25	Am. Contralto
Sharon, Ariel	Military	20	50	75	50	Israeli General
Sharon, William	Business	50	100	200		Banker and Financier

Name	Field	SIG	DS	ALS	SP	Remarks
Sharp, U. S. Grant	Military	10	25	35	15	
Sharp, William	Art	15	45	90		
Sharpe, George H.	Civil War	20	45			Union General/1828-1900
Sharpe, William, Dr.	Science	15	30		25	Nobel Enconomics 1990
Shatner, William	Ent	30	75		65	Star Trek's Captain Kirk
Shaud, Grant	Ent	20			45	Murphy Brown
Shaunessy, Charles	Ent	5		25	20	
Shaw, Anna Howard	Political	35	75	150		1847-1919
Shaw, Artie	Music	25			75	Big Band Leader
Shaw, Bernard	Ent	10			25	TV Broadcast Journalist
Shaw, George Bernard	Author	400	650	800	1,500	Ir. Playwright/Nobel
Shaw, Irwin	Author	25	50		45	Am. Novelist
Shaw, Lemuel	RevWar	15		75		
Shaw, Leslie M. 1848-32	Political	30		50		Sec'y Treasury 1902
Shaw, Robert	Ent	60			150	Jaws/The Sting
Shaw, Robert	Ent	65			125	Jaws/James Bond/...
Shaw, T.E.	Author	150			500	Real Life Lawrence of Arabia
Shawn, Dick	Ent	50			100	
Shawn, Ted	Ent	50			100	Am. Dancer-Choreographer
Shay, John	Ent	5			10	
Shayne, Robert	Ent	10			30	
Shazar, Zalman	Political	25			60	Israel
Shea, John	Ent	10			25	
Shear, Rhonda	Ent	5			10	Up All Night host
Shearer, Moira	Ent	25	50		75	Ballet
Shearer, Norma 1902-83	Ent	100	200		275	AA Winner
Shearing, George	Music	20			45	Jazz Pianist
Sheedy, Ally	Ent	10			25	
Sheehan, John	Ent	10			25	
Sheen, Charlie	Ent	10	25		25	
Sheen, Martin	Ent	15	30		30	AA Winner
Sheffer, Chris	Ent	10			15	
Sheffield, Johnny	Ent	10			20	Boy/Bomba
Shelby, Isaac 1750-1826	RevWar	300	350	500		
Shelby, Joseph 0.	Civil War	300		1,200	2,000	CSA General/1830-97
Sheldon, Gene	Ent	10			20	
Sheldon, Sidney	Author	5		25	15	Am. Novelist
Shelley, Mary W.	Author	900		1,750		Frankenstein
Shelley, Percy Bysshe	Author	1,200		2,000		
Shelton, Deborah	Ent	10			20	Miss USA
Shepard, Alan B.	Space	50	150		125	Moonwalker
Shepherd, Cybill	Ent	20	50		50	Cybil/Moonlighting
Sheridan, Ann	Ent	35			75	
Sheridan, Nicollette	Ent	20			45	SuperModel
Sheridan, Philip H.	Civil War	200	600	600	1,750	Union General/1831-88
Sheridan, Philip H.	Civil War	300	1,200	RARE	2,400	Union General/War Dated
Sheridan, Richard B.	Author	75	125	250		Ir. Dramatist

Name	Field	SIG	DS	ALS	SP	Remarks
Sherman, Allan	Ent	10			20	
Sherman, Forrest P.	Military	20	50	75	50	WWII Adm.
Sherman, Frederick C.	Military	20	45		35	
Sherman, George	Ent	10			25	
Sherman, James S.	Vice Pres	75	175	275	200	
Sherman, John 1823-00	Political	100	450	750	200	Sherman Anti-Trust Act
Sherman, Roger 1721-93	RevWar	200	600	900		
Sherman, Thomas West	Civil War	30	50	75		Union General/1813-79
Sherman, William T.	Civil War	400	550	750	1,250	Union General/1820-91
Sherriff, Robert C.	Author	45		125	80	Playwright/Novelist
Sherwood, Bobby	Ent	5			15	
Sherwood, Madeleine	Ent	10			20	
Sherwood, Percy	Music	25			60	German Composer
Sherwood, Robert E.	Author	30	75	125	50	Plays/Speeches FDR
Shields, Brooke	Ent	20	50		50	Suddenly Susan
Shields, James	Civil War	50	75	125		Union General/1806-79
Shillaber, Benjamin P.	Author	25	50	100		Humorist-Editor/1814-90
Shimmerman, Armin	Ent	15	25		25	Star Trek DS9/Quark
Shippen, Edward	RevWar	50		150		Chief Justice PA.
Shiras, George, Jr.	SuprCt	100	250	350		
Shire, Talia	Ent	15			35	
Shirer, William L.	Author	15	35		20	
Shirley, Anne	Ent	15		35	30	
Shirley, William 1693-71	Political	350	1,000	1,200		Colonial Gov. MA
Shockley, William, Dr.	Science	45	100	150	100	Nobel Physics 1956
Shoma, William	Aviation	15	35	50	45	WWII ACE
Shoop, Pamela Susan	Ent	5	20		15	
Shor, Bernard Toots	Business	20	45	50	35	
Shore, Dinah	Ent	25		100	50	Singer-Actress-TV Host
Shore, Pauly	Ent	15			25	
Short, Bobby	Music	10			20	
Short, Martin	Ent	20	45		50	Sat Nite Live
Shostakovich, Dmitri	Music	300	575	850	RARE	Composer
Shoumatoff, Elizabeth	Art	25	50	75		
Shoup, David M.	Military	15	35	60	35	
Shoup, Francis, A.	Civil War	100		300		CSA General/1834-96
Show, Grant	Ent	10			20	
Shrimpton, Jean	Ent	5	20		10	
Shriner, Herb	Ent	5			15	
Shriver, Edmund	Civil War	20	40			
Shriver, Maria	Ent	5			15	Broadcast Journalist
Shriver, Sargent	Political	10		25	20	Created Job Corps
Shroyer, Sonny	Ent	5			10	
Shrum, Cal	Ent	5			25	Cowboy Actor
Shubert, John	Ent	5			15	
Shubert, Lee 1873-1953	Ent	25	60	75	40	Theatrical Mgr.-Producer
Shue, Andrew	Ent	15			35	

Name	Field	SIG	DS	ALS	SP	Remarks
Shue, Elizabeth	Ent	25			50	AA Winner
Shugart, Alan	Science	10	20		20	Computer Disk Drive
Shulman, Max	Author	10			20	Creator Dobie Gillis
Shultz, George P.	Political	10	25	50	30	Sec'y State 1982
Shuman, Eleanor J.	Celebrity	75				Titanic Survivor
Shuster, W, Morgan	Business	10		35	15	
Sibelius, Jan 1865-1957	Music	400	750	1,250	1,000	Composer
Sibley, Henry H.	Civil War	150	300	450		Union General/1811-1891
Sickles, Daniel E.	Civil War	75	125	150	175	Union General/1825-1914
Siddons, F. Scott, Mrs.	Ent	25			50	
Siddons, Sarah Kemble	Ent	200		600		
Sidmouth, Viscount	Political	35		100		Prime Minister
Sidney, George	Ent	25			50	Director
Sidney, Sylvia	Ent	10	25		25	
Siegbahn, Kai Manne	Science	30	50	100	100	Nobel Physics 1981
Siegbahn, Karl Manne	Science	35	75	125	100	Nobel Physics 1924
Siegel & Shuster	Cartoonist	175			400	Superman/Signed by Both
Siegel, Don	Ent	20	50		40	Film Director
Siegel, Jerry 1915-96	Cartoonist	25			75	Superman Co-Creator
Siegel, Joel	Ent	5			10	TV Film Reviewer
Siegfried and Roy	Ent	20			40	Magicians
Siegmeister, Elie	Music	25	75		40	Composer
Siems, Margarethe	Music	45			125	Opera
Sigall, Joseph	Art	100	200	400		Pres and Royal Portraits
Sigel, Franz 1824-1902	Civil War	75	125	200		Union General
Sighele, Mietta	Music	15			30	Opera
Signac, Paul	Art	75	150	300		Watercolor Seascapes
Signoret, Simone	Ent	75	125		150	AA Winner
Sigsbee, Charles D.	Military	50	100	150	75	Capt. USN The Maine
Sihanouk, Norodom	Political	35	75	125	75	Cambodia
Sikes, Cynthia	Ent	5			15	
Sikorsky, Igor 1889-1972	Aviation	100	225	300	275	Designed 1st Helicopter
Silja, Anja	Music	15			40	Opera
Silliman, Benjamin	Science	35	75	100		Am.Chemist
Sills, Beverly	Music	15			35	Am. Soprano
Sills, Milton 1882-1930	Ent	30		75	75	Silent Films
Silver, Ron	Ent	15			40	Veronica's Closet
Silvera, Frank	Ent	10			20	
Silverheels, Jay	Ent	200	300		350	Tonto/Lone Ranger
Silverman, Fred	Business	5	20		10	Broadcasting Executive
Silverman, Jonathan	Ent	10			25	The Single Guy
Silverman, Robert	Music	15			45	Contemporary Pianist
Silvers, Phil 1912-85	Ent	50		125	175	Sgt. Bilko
Silverstone, Alicia	Ent	30			60	Batgirl/Batman Movie
Silvstedt, Victoria	Ent	25			50	Model/Playboy
Simenon, Georges	Author	75	125	275	125	1903-1989
Simmons, Gene	Music	25			45	KISS member

Name	Field	SIG	DS	ALS	SP	Remarks
Simmons, Jean	Ent	10		20	20	
Simmons, Richard	Business	5			15	Excercise Guru
Simmons, Richard	Ent	15			35	
Simms, Ginny	Music	10			20	Band Vocalist
Simms, William G.	Author	50	75	125		Lawyer
Simon and Garfunkel	Music	50			100	Signed by Both
Simon, Carly	Music	25	50		50	
Simon, Claude	Author	150				Nobel Literature 1985
Simon, Herbert A.	Science	20		50	25	Nobel Economics
Simon, Neil	Author	25	50		50	Playwright, Screenwriter
Simon, Paul	Music	25	50		50	
Simon, Simone	Ent	20			45	
Simpson, James H.	Civil War	35	75			Union General/1813-83
Simpson, James Y.	Science	25	75	150		
Simpson, Louis	Author	25			75	Am. Poet
Simpson, Russell	Ent	50			100	
Simpson, Wallis W.	Political	150		450		Duchess of Windsor
Simpson, William H.	Military	25		200	75	Gen.WWII
Sims, William S. 1858-36	Military	30		125	50	Adm.USN WWI/Pulitzer
Sinatra, Frank	Ent	200	500		500	Rat Pack
Sinatra, Nancy	Ent	5	20		20	
Sinbad	Ent	10			20	
Sinclair, Harry F.	Business	125	175	300	200	Teapot Dome
Sinclair, Upton	Author	50		150	125	Am. Writer
Sinding, Christian A.	Music	50		175		
Singer, Isaac Bashevis	Author	45		225	150	Nobel Literature 1978
Singer, Isaac M. 1811-75	Science	600	2,000	RARE	RARE	Singer Sewing Machine
Singer, Lori	Ent	15			30	
Singer, Marc	Ent	10			30	
Singlaub, John K.	Military	10	25	35	20	GeneralWWII
Singleton, Penny	Ent	5			20	Blondie
Sinise, Gary	Ent	25			50	AA Winner
Sinopoli, Giuseppe	Music	15			35	Conductor
Sioli, Franco	Music	5			15	Opera
Siple, Paul A.	Aviation	20	45			
Sirica, John J.	Political	20	35		50	Watergate Judge
Siroky, Villiam	Political	50				Premier Czech.
Sirtis, Marina	Ent	15			35	Star Trek/ Next Generation
Siskel, Gene	Ent	5			15	Film Critic
Sisley, Alfred 1839-99	Art	175	400	1,200		Fr. Impressionist
Sissle, Noble	Music	25			50	Big Band Leader
Sitgreaves, John	RevWar	35	75	125		
Sitting Bull 1831-1890	Western	5,750	RARE	RARE	15,000	Sioux Indian Leader
Sitwell, Edith Dame	Author	75	125	175		British Poet
Sitwell, Osbert Sir	Author	35	75	150		Playwright/Novelist
Skaggs, Ricky	Music	10			20	
Skala, Lilia	Ent	10	25		30	

Name	Field	SIG	DS	ALS	SP	Remarks
Skelly, William Grove	Business	300				Founder Skelly Oil
Skelton, Red	Ent	35		100	75	
Skerrit, Tom	Ent	10			30	
Skinner, B. F.	Author	25		50	75	Behavioral Psychology
Skinner, Cornelia Otis	Ent	15			25	1901-1950
Skinner, Cortlandt	Military	50	75	150		Born NJ. Loyalist General
Skinner, Otis	Ent	35		75	65	
Skinner, Stella	Art	25	40	75		
Skipworth, Alison	Ent	15		30	25	
Skorzeny, Otto 1908-75	Military	250		450	500	Nazi SS Officer & Adventurer
Skouras, Spyros 1893-71	Business	50			175	Fndr/20th Century Fox
Skovhus, Boje	Music	10			25	Opera
Skye, Ione	Ent	15			30	
Slater, Christian	Ent	20	50		50	
Slater, Helen	Ent	20			45	SuperGirl
Slaughter, Frank G.	Author	10		35	20	
Slayton, Donald K.	Space	35	150		125	Mercury Seven "Deke"
Sledd, Patsy	Music	5			15	
Slezak, Leo 1873-1946	Music	45			125	Tenor/Opera
Slezak, Walter	Ent	35			75	
Slick, Grace	Music	25			50	
Slidell, John 1793-1871	Civil War	75		200		Statesman/CSA Diplomat
Slim, Wm. Joseph, Sir	Military	30	75	125	75	Br. General WWII
Sliwinski, Josef	Ent	25		100	75	Pianist
Sloan, Alfred P. Jr.	Business	50		100	75	Sloan-Kettering Inst.
Sloan, John	Art	100	200	400		Am Painter/Illustrator
Sloan, John 1779-1856	Political	25		75		Fillmore Treasurer of U.S.
Sloane, Everett	Ent	30			50	
Sloat, John Drake	Civil War	50	100	125		Union Naval Officer
Slocum, Henry Warner	Civil War	75		150		Union General/1827-94
Slough, John P.	Civil War	200		600		Union General/1829-67
Smallens, Alexander	Music	20			50	Conductor/Porgy and Bess
Smallwood, Norma	Ent	20			50	Miss America 1926
Smart, Jean	Ent	15			45	Designing Women
Smedley, Richard	Ent	5			10	
Smetana, Bedrich	Music	1,500	RARE	RARE	RARE	Composer
Smiley, Delores	Music	10			20	
Smirnoff, Yakov	Ent	10			15	Comedian
Smith, Anna Nicole	Ent	20			50	Playboy/Model
Smith, Al	Cartoonist	15			45	Mutt & Jeff
Smith, Alexis	Ent	15	30		35	
Smith, Alfred E.	Political	50			125	Presidential Candidate
Smith, Armistead B.	Aviation	10		25	30	WWII Navy ACE
Smith, Ashbel	Civil War	150		450		
Smith, Bernie	Ent	10			15	
Smith, Betty	Author	40		75		
Smith, Buffalo Bob	Ent	35			75	Howdy Doody

Name	Field	SIG	DS	ALS	SP	Remarks
Smith, C. Aubrey	Ent	35			75	
Smith, C.R.	Military	25		75		Adm. Flagship Fleet
Smith, Caleb 1808-64	Political	50	150	250		Lincoln Attorney General
Smith, Carl	Music	5			15	
Smith, Charles E.	Political	15		25	20	P.M. General 1898
Smith, Charles M.	Ent	10			25	
Smith, Connie	Music	5			15	
Smith, Edmund K.	Civil War	400	900	1,250		CSA General/War Dated
Smith, Edmund Kirby	Civil War	300		600		CSA General/1824-93
Smith, Elinor	Aviation	50	100	150	125	
Smith, Elizabeth Oakes	Political	100	200	325		Womens Suffrage
Smith, Francis Hopkinson	Art	15	20	35		Am. Engineer/Artist
Smith, Francis M. Borax	Business	30	60	75		Founder U.S. Borax Co.
Smith, Frederick W.	Business	15	30	45	25	Fndr Federal Express
Smith, Garrett	Political	25		100		Abolitionist
Smith, Gerrit 1797-1874	Political	100		300		Abolitionist
Smith, Green Clay	Civil War	50		125		Union General/1832-95
Smith, Gustavus W.	Civil War	125	250	550		CSA General/1822-96
Smith, Hamilton	Science	15	35	45	25	Nobel Medicine 1978
Smith, Harry	Ent	5	15		10	Broadcast Journalist
Smith, Hoke 1855-1931	Political	10	35		30	
Smith, Ian	Political	15		45	30	
Smith, Ida B. Wise	Political	30	50	75		Temperance Advocate
Smith, Jaclyn	Ent	10	25		25	Charlie Angels
Smith, James 1719-1806	RevWar	250	750	1,600		Signer Decl. of Indepen.
Smith, James Y.	Civil War	35	75			Civil War Gov. RI/1809-76
Smith, Joe	Ent	15			45	
Smith, John	Political	RARE	RARE	RARE	RARE	
Smith, Joseph 1805-44	Clergy	750	1,500			Founder Morman Church
Smith, Julia Holmes, Dr.	Science	100		300		
Smith, Kate 1909-1986	Music	50	125	175	100	God Bless America Singer
Smith, Keely	Music	10			30	Band Vocalist
Smith, Kent	Ent	5			15	
Smith, Maggie	Ent	15	30		30	AA Winner
Smith, Margaret Chase	Political	10	25	45	25	
Smith, Martha	Ent	5			15	
Smith, Martin Luther	Civil War	75	125	200		CSA General/1819-66
Smith, Matthew	RevWar	25	75			
Smith, Melancton	RevWar	75	125			Continental Congress
Smith, Michael J.	Space	200			300	Died on Challenger
Smith, R.T.	Aviation	15		45	35	WWII Flying Tiger ACE
Smith, Rex	Ent	10			20	
Smith, Richard	RevWar	50	125	250		Continental Congress
Smith, Robert 1757-1842	Political	50	150	300		Att'y Gen./Sec'y Navy
Smith, Robert H. Snuffy	Aviation	15		45	35	WWII Flying Tiger ACE
Smith, Roger	Ent	10			20	
Smith, Samuel 1752-1839	RevWar	50	125	200		Senator MD

Name	Field	SIG	DS	ALS	SP	Remarks
Smith, Samuel Francis	Music	200		450		America"/1808-1895
Smith, Stanley	Ent	10		25		
Smith, Sydney	Cartoonist	30			60	The Gumps
Smith, Thomas A.	Military	100		250		General
Smith, Thomas Church	Civil War	30	50	75		Union General/1819-97
Smith, Tom E.	Business	10	25	30	25	Pres. Food Lion Grocery
Smith, Truman 1791-1884	Political	10	25	45		
Smith, Walter Bedell	Military	35	50	75	45	WWII General
Smith, William 1797-1887	Civil War	100	225	300		CSA General
Smith, William Farrar	Civil War	50		175		Union General/1824-1903
Smith, William S.	RevWar	50		175		RevWar Soldier
Smith, William Sidney	Military	50		150		Br.Adm. Napoleonic War
Smith, Willie The Lion	Music	75			125	Jazz
Smithers, Jan	Ent	5			15	
Smits, Jimmy	Ent	15			45	NYPD Blue
Smothers Brothers	Ent	15	45		45	Signed by Both
Smothers, Dick	Ent	10			25	Smothers Brothers
Smothers, Tommy	Ent	10			25	Smothers Brothers
Smucker, Paul	Business	10			25	Smuckers Jams & Jellies
Smuts, Jan Christian	Political	50	100	300	250	Fld. Marshal. Pres.
Smythe, Reg	Cartoonist	10			30	Andy Capp
Snell, George D., Dr.	Science	15	30	45	45	Nobel Medicine 1980
Snipes, Wesley	Ent	25	75		50	
Snow, Charles Percy	Author	25	75	150	75	
Snow, Hank	Music	20			45	
Soddy, Frederick, Dr.	Science	75	150	225	125	Nobel Chemistry 1921
Soglow, Otto	Cartoonist	25			75	The Little King
Sohn, Lee	Music	10			20	Singer
Sokoloff, Vladimir	Ent	25			50	
Solow, Robert M., Dr.	Science	20	30		25	Nobel Economics 1987
Solti, Georg, Sir	Music	30	45		75	Conductor
Solzhenitsyn, Alex.	Author	100	275		175	Sov. Novelist. Nobel Lit
Somers, Suzanne	Ent	20			45	Three's Company
Somervell, Arthur, Sir	Music	25	50	75		Composer
Somervell, Brehon B.	Military	35	100			Gen.WWII
Sommer, Elke	Ent	10	20		25	
Sommers, Joanne	Ent	5			10	
Somoza, Anastasio	Political	25			75	Nicaragua
Sondergaard, Gale	Ent	30			65	AA Winner/1899-1985
Sondheim, Stephen	Music	50	100		125	Composer
Sonic Youth	Music	25			50	Signed by all
Sonny & Cher	Music	100	200		200	Signed by Both
Sontag, Henrietta Rossi	Music	100			375	Opera
Sontag, Susan	Author	10	25	45	20	
Soo, Jack	Ent	100	150		150	Barney Miller/Scarce
Sopwith, Thos. Sir	Aviation	50		150	100	British Pioneer
Sorbo, Kevin	Ent	25			50	TV's Hercules

Name	Field	SIG	DS	ALS	SP	Remarks
Sorrel, Gilbert M.	Civil War	300	RARE	RARE	RARE	CSA General/War Dated
Sorrel, Gilbert Moxley	Civil War	150	300	400		CSA General/1838-1901
Sorrvia, Agnes	Music	20			45	Opera
Sorvino, Mira	Ent	25			50	AA Winner
Sorvino, Paul	Ent	15			35	Mira's Father
Sothern, Ann	Ent	20		35	35	
Sothern, E. A.	Ent	35	75	125		19th Century Romantic Idol
Soto, Talisa	Ent	25			50	
Soucek, Appolo, Lt .	Aviation	15			25	World Altitude Records
Soul Asylum	Music	45			100	Signed by Entire Group
Soul, David	Ent	10	35		35	Starskey and Hutch
Soule, Pierre	Civil War	75	150	250		CSA General/1802-70
Soult, Nicolas Jean de	Military	100	225	300		Nap.Marshal of France
Sousa, John Philip	Music	125	400	400	900	Composer/1854-1932
Soustelle, Jacques	Political	5	20	30	15	
Souter, David H.	SuprCt	40			60	
Southampton, 1st Earl	Royalty	75	200	350		
Southey, Robert 1774-43	Author	100	225	350		Br. Poet Laureate
Sovine, Red	Music	15			35	
Soyer, Raphael 1899-87	Art	25	50	125	100	
Spaak, Paul-Henri	Political	15	30	40	25	
Spaatz, Carl Tooey	Military	75	100		125	General WWII
Spacek, Sissy	Ent	15			40	AA Winner/Carrie
Spacey, Kevin	Ent	20			50	AA Winner
Spader, James	Ent	15			30	
Spaight, Richard Dobbs	RevWar	100	250			Signer Constitution
Spalding, Albert	Music	35			75	Violinist/1888-1953
Spalding, J. Walter	Business	25		100	50	
Spallanzani, Lazzaro	Science	150	300	600		Artificial Insemination
Sparks, Jared 1789-1866	Author	20	35	65		US Historian
Sparks, Ned	Ent	25	35	75	65	
Sparks, William E.	Military	20	35	50		
Spate, Wolfgang	Aviation	50			85	German WWII ACE
Spaulding, Albert	Music	25			65	Composer
Spaulding, R.Z.	Business	15	40	50	25	
Speaks, Oley	Music	50	75	100		Composer
Spector, Phil	Music	60	100		75	
Speed, James 1812-87	Political	50	75	125		Lincoln Att'y Gen.
Speer, Albert 1905-1981	Military	50	150	225	150	Hitler's Architect
Speidel, Hans	Military	35	75		75	Nazi General
Spelling, Aaron	Ent	10			25	Film Producer
Spelling, Tori	Ent	25	50		50	
Spencer, George E.	Civil War	40	75	150		Union Officer
Spencer, Herbert, Sir	Author	50	125	200		Br. Philosopher
Spencer, John C.	Political	25	50	100		Tyler Sec'y War
Spender, Stephen	Author	50	150	200	75	British Poet
Spenser, Tim	Music	15			35	Sons of the Pioneers

Name	Field	SIG	DS	ALS	SP	Remarks
Sperry, Elmer A,	Science	125	350	450	225	Inventor Gyroscope
Sperry, Roger W.	Science	20	30	35	30	Nobel Medicine 1981
Spice Girls	Music	65			125	Signed by All FIVE
Spice Girls	Music	75			150	Signed by all five
Spiegle, Dan	Cartoonist	35			75	Hoppy cartoon strip
Spielberg, Steven	Ent	40	150		75	Director
Spillane, Mickey	Author	40	75	100	125	Detective Fiction
Spin Doctors	Music	35			65	Signed by all
Spiner, Brent	Ent	15			35	Star Trek/Next Gen/Data
Spinner, Francis E.	Political	25		45		Treasurer for 4 Presidents
Spitz, Mark	Sports	10			30	Olympic Swimmer
Spivak, Charlie	Music	20			40	Big Band Leader-Trumpet
Spock, Benjamin, Dr.	Science	35	75	100	50	Am. Pediatrician
Spofford, Harriet P.	Author	15	25	40		Am. Poet/Novelist
Spong, Hilda	Ent	15			40	
Spontini, Gaspare	Music	100		300		Composer
Sprague, Frank Julian	Science	50	100	150	100	Asst. to Edison
Sprague, William	Civil War	75		100		Union General/1830-1915
Springfield, Rick	Music	20			40	
Springfield, Sherry	Ent	20			50	ER
Springsteen, Bruce	Music	35			75	The Boss
Spruance, Raymond A.	Military	25	125	125	65	1886-1969
Squibb, Edward R.	Business	75	150	200		Pharmaceuticals
St. Clair, Arthur 1734-18	Military	150	250	700		Pres Continental Congress
St. Cyr, Lily	Ent	15			30	
St. Denis, Ruth 1878-1968	Ent	50	125	225	300	Dancer, Choreographer
St. Jacques, Ramond	Ent	15			45	
St. John, Isaac M.	Civil War	100		250		CSA General
St. John, Jill	Ent	10			20	
St. Johns, Adela Rogers	Author	10	25	35	25	Star Hearst Reporter
St. Laurent, Louis	Political	20			45	P. M. Canada
St. Vincent, John Jervis	Military	35	65	125		Br. Adm. 1735-1823
Stabile, Dick	Music	20			40	Big Band Leader
Stacey Q	Music	15			30	
Stack, Robert	Ent	10	20		20	Untouchables
Stael, Anne-Louise	Author	75	150			Fr. Writer
Stafford, Jo	Music	5	20		15	Country
Stafford, Susan	Ent	10			25	
Stager, Anson	Civil War	20	50	100		Union Officer/1825-85
Stahl, Leslie	Ent	5			10	TV's 60 Minutes
Stalin, Joseph 1879-1953	Political	3,500	7,500	20,000	RARE	USSR
Stalin, Svetlana	Political	35	100	150	75	Daughter of Stalin
Stallone, Sylvester	Ent	25	75		50	
Stamos, John	Ent	15			35	Full House
Stamp, Terence	Ent	20			35	
Stanbery, Henry	Political	10		45		Att'y General 1866
Stander, Lionel	Ent	20	30		35	Hart To Hart

Name	Field	SIG	DS	ALS	SP	Remarks
Standing, Guy Sir	Ent	25			50	
Standish, Miles	Political	RARE	RARE	RARE	RARE	Mayflower Colonist
Stanford, Leland 1824-93	Business	225	1,750	2,500	400	Calif. Gov.
Stang, Arnold	Ent	5			15	Voice of Top Cat
Stanhope, Edward	Military	10	20	30		
Stanhope, Hester, Lady	Political	15	45	75		
Stanhope, Phil.H.5th Earl	Author	10	20	25		
Stanhope, Phil.H.7th Earl	Author	10	20	35		
Stanhope, Philip D.	Author	125				4th Earl Chesterfield
Stanislavski, Konstantin	Ent	275				
Stanislaw, Augustus P.	Royalty	100	300	600		Last King of Poland
Stanley, David Sloane	Civil War	25	75	75		Union General/1828-1902
Stanley, Freelan	Science	350		1,200		Stanley Steamer/Auto
Stanley, Henry M. Sir	Explorer	275		550	750	Am Journalist
Stanley, Wendell M.	Science	20	25	60	30	Nobel Chemistry 1946
Stanton, Edwin M.	Political	100	150	300		Sect of War/1814-69
Stanton, Elizabeth Cady	Political	150	225	400		Pres. Womans Suffrage
Stanton, Frank L.	Author	5		25		Am. Poet/Journalist
Stanton, Frank, Dr.	Business	15	50	75	30	Pres. CBS
Stanton, Harry Dean	Ent	10			20	
Stanwyck, Barbara	Ent	30	100		100	1907-1990
Stapleton, Jean	Ent	5	20		20	Edith/All in the Family
Stapleton, Maureen	Ent	10			25	
Stapp, Olivia	Music	15			35	Opera
Stark, Harold R.	Military	15	45	75	40	
Stark, John	RevWar	400	600	1,250		Often Quoted General
Starr, Belle	Western	2,500	RARE	RARE	RARE	Early West Bandit Queen
Starr, Blaze	Ent	15		45	30	
Starr, Kay	Music	20			30	Big Band Singer
Starr, Leonard	Cartoonist	25			40	Little Orphan Annie
Starr, Ringo	Music	125	250		200	Beatles Drummer
Starrett, Charles	Ent	25	45		65	Cowboy Star "Durango"
Statlers, The	Music	25			50	
Stead, Wm. Thomas	Author	30	75	100		Died on Titanic
Steber, Eleanor	Music	25			75	Opera
Stedman, Edmund C.	Author	20	35			Poet/Publisher
Steel, Danielle	Author	10			25	Novelist
Steele, Barbara	Ent	20			35	
Steele, Bob	Ent	25			55	Cowboy Star
Steele, Frederick	Civil War	50	100	150		Union General/1819-68
Steele, Richard, Sir	Author	200	600	1,200		1672-1729
Steele, Tom	Ent	15			25	
Steely Dan	Music	25			50	Signed by Both
Steenburgen, Mary	Ent	15			40	
Stefani, Gwen	Music	25			50	No Doubt
Stefansson, Vilhjalmur	Explorer	75	150	225	275	Arctic Explorer
Steffens, Lincoln 1866-36	Author	40	100	150		Journalist

Name	Field	SIG	DS	ALS	SP	Remarks
Stegner, Wallace	Author	20		45		Am. Novelist. Pulitzer
Steichen, Edward J.	Art	100	200	300	400	Pioneer Photgraphy as Art
Steig, William	Cartoonist	20			40	New Yorker Cartoonist
Steiger, Rod	Ent	10			25	
Stein, Gertrude 1874-46	Author	400	550	750	675	Expatriot Am. Writer
Stein, Jules	Political	50	100			Founder MCA
Steinbeck, John 1902-68	Author	400	1,450	2,250	1,250	Pulitzer and Nobel in Lit.
Steinem, Gloria	Political	15	25	30	25	Editor
Steinhoff, J. 'Mickey'	Aviation	15	25	40	30	
Steinmetz, Charles P.	Science	75	150	300		Electrical Engineer
Steinway, Henry Z.	Business	20	50	75	35	Steinway Piano
Stella, Antonietta	Music	25			50	Opera
Stemple, Robert	Business	25			40	Pres. General Motors
Sten, Anna	Ent	15		30	35	
Stephanie, Princess	Royalty	10			25	Princess of Monaco
Stephen, Adam 1730-91	RevWar	75	150	250		General
Stephens, Alexander H.	Civil War	250		500		VP CSA/1812-83
Stephenson, George	Science	225	350	750		Steam Locomotive
Stephenson, Henry	Ent	35			75	
Stephenson, Robert	Science	100	200	350		Br. Railroad Engineer
Steppenwolf	Music	75	125		125	Signed by Entire Group
Sterling, Andrew B.	Music	25	50	100		Composer
Sterling, Robert	Ent	10			20	
Sterling, Robert	Ent	10			20	
Stern, Daniel	Ent	15			25	
Stern, Howard	Ent	25			55	Syndicated Radio Show
Stern, Isaac	Music	20	35	45	60	
Sterrett, Cliff	Cartoonist	35			65	Polly And Her Pals
Stettinius, Edward R. Jr.	Political	30	100	150	55	FRD & Trumans Sect/State
Steuben, Friedrich von	RevWar	1,400	RARE	RARE	RARE	1730-94
Stevens, Albert W., Capt.	Aviation	25	35			Aviator-Balloonist
Stevens, Andrew	Ent	10	20		20	
Stevens, Brinke	Ent	5			15	Scream Queen
Stevens, Cat	Music	35	100		75	
Stevens, Clement H.	Civil War	250	1,500	2,500		CSA General/1821-64
Stevens, Connie	Ent	5			15	
Stevens, Craig	Ent	10			20	
Stevens, Ebenezer	RevWar	75	175			Boston Tea Party
Stevens, Fisher	Ent	15			25	
Stevens, George	Ent	30			60	Director
Stevens, Inger	Ent	75			150	Scarce
Stevens, James F.	Author	125	250			Paul Bunyan Stories
Stevens, John 1748-1838	RevWar	25	45	75		Engineer/Steam Engine
Stevens, John Paul, III	SuprCt	40	100		150	
Stevens, K.T.	Ent	5			10	
Stevens, Onslow	Ent	35			75	
Stevens, Ray	Music	5			10	Country

Name	Field	SIG	DS	ALS	SP	Remarks
Stevens, Rise	Music	20			40	Opera
Stevens, Stella	Ent	5			20	Nutty Professor
Stevens, Thaddeus	Political	35	100	150		
Stevens, Wallace	Author	250	750	RARE	RARE	Am. Poet/Pulitzer
Stevens, Walter Husted	Civil War	250				CSA General
Stevens, Warren	Ent	5			15	Forbidden Planet
Stevenson, Adlai E.	Vice Pres	50	150	200	150	Cleveland Vice Pres.
Stevenson, Carter L.	Civil War	100	200	400		CSA General/1817-88
Stevenson, McLean	Ent	35	75		75	MASH
Stevenson, Parker	Ent	15			25	Hardy Boys
Stevenson, R. H.	Civil War	10		30		Union Officer
Stevenson, Robert Louis	Author	300	750	1,400	RARE	Novelist
Stewart, Alexander P.	Civil War	250		600		CSA General/War Dated
Stewart, Alexander P.	Civil War	150	300	350		CSA General/1821-1908
Stewart, Catherine Mary	Ent	5			15	
Stewart, Charles	Military	100	250			Cmdr. USS Constitution
Stewart, Elaine	Ent	5			10	
Stewart, James (Jimmy)	Ent	45	150	225	150	
Stewart, James C.	Aviation	15	25	40	30	WWII ACE
Stewart, Jon	Ent	15			25	
Stewart, Lisa	Ent	5			15	
Stewart, Paul	Ent	10			30	
Stewart, Peggy	Ent	5			10	
Stewart, Potter	SuprCt	35			75	
Stewart, Rex	Music	75	100		150	
Stewart, Rod	Music	25			50	
Stewart, William	Political	30	50	75		Drafted US Mining Law
Stewart, Wynn	Music	10			20	
Stiborik, Joe	Aviation	30			50	Enola Gay Radar Operator
Stieglitz, Alfred 1864-46	Art	200	450	600		Rev. Camera Techniques
Stiers, David Ogden	Ent	40			75	MASH/Scarce Signer
Stigler, George J.	Science	20		40	25	Nobel Economics 1982
Still, William Grant	Music	125		300	250	
Stills, Stephen	Ent	40			65	
Stilwell, Joseph W.	Military	175			400	WWII General
Stimson, Henry L.	Political	40	125		50	1867-1950
Sting	Music	25			50	
Stirling, Linda	Ent	20			45	
Stirling, Wm. Alex.	RevWar	450		1,500		General Continental Army
Stock, Frederick A.	Music	25	50		45	
Stockdale, James B.	Military	20			25	WWII Adm.
Stockton, Frank R.	Author	25			35	Juvenile Fiction
Stockton, Richard	RevWar	500	1,000	RARE	RARE	Signer Decl. of Indepen.
Stockton, Robert Field	Military	125	250	350		
Stockwell, Dean	Ent	15			30	Quantum Leap
Stockwell, Guy	Ent	10			30	
Stockwell, Harry	Ent	50			100	

Name	Field	SIG	DS	ALS	SP	Remarks
Stoddard, Richard H.	Author	20	30	45		Poet/Writer
Stoddart, James H.	Ent	20			40	Vintage Actor
Stoddert, Benjamin	RevWar	100	250	400		Ist Sec'y Navy 1798
Stoica, Chivu	Political	50				Romanian Premier
Stoker, Bram 1847-1912	Author	200		450		Dracula
Stokes, William	Civil War	75				Union Officer
Stokowski, Leopold	Music	65	125	150	150	Conductor
Stollery, David	Ent	10			20	
Stoloff, Morris	Music	10			30	Conductor
Stoltz, Eric	Ent	10		20	25	
Stolz, Robert 1880-1975	Music	25	75			Conductor/Composer
Stolz, Teresa	Ent	40	75			
Stone Temple Pilots	Music	40			90	Signed by Entire Group
Stone, Ezra	Ent	25	40		50	
Stone, Fred	Ent	30		50		Scarecrow in Broadway Oz
Stone, George E.	Ent	20			45	
Stone, Harlan Fiske	SuprCt	75	200	250	225	Chief Justice
Stone, Irving	Author	20	45	100	40	Historical Novelist
Stone, Lewis	Ent	30	40	75	65	
Stone, Lucy (Blackwell)	Political	100		350		Womans Rights/Suffragette
Stone, Marcus	Art	15		30		Illustrated for Dickens
Stone, Matt	Cartoonist	25			50	Co-Creator of South Park
Stone, Milburn	Ent	75	100		125	Doc in TV's Gunsmoke
Stone, Oliver	Ent	10	25		25	AA Film Director
Stone, Paula	Ent	25			40	Western Heroine
Stone, Sharon	Ent	25	75		50	
Stone, Thomas 1743-87	RevWar	500	775	1,400		Signer Decl. of Indepen.
Stoneman, George	Civil War	75	200			Union General/1822-94
Stooges, The Three	Ent	1,500			3,500	Signed by Orig Three
Stoopnagle, Colonel L.	Ent	15		30	30	Radio
Stoppard, Tom	Author	30	75	125	35	Br Playwright
Storch, Larry	Ent	5			15	F Troop
Stordahl, Axel	Music	25			65	Conductor
Storey, June	Ent	15			45	Western Actress
Storm, Gale	Ent	10			20	Star of Early TV Series
Storm, Tempest	Ent	10		30	25	
Story, Joseph	SuprCt	100	175	250		1779 - 1845
Stoughton, William	Political	450	950			1632-1701
Stout, Rex 1886-1975	Author	35	100	200	45	Nero Wolf
Stowe, Harriet Beecher	Author	275		550	RARE	1811-96/Uncle Toms Cabin
Stowe, Madeline	Ent	25			50	
Strachey, Lytton	Author	75	150			
Stradlin, Izzy	Music	20			45	Guns N' Roses
Straight, Beatrice	Ent	10			20	AA Winner
Strait, Donald G.	Aviation	15		40	35	WWII ACE
Strait, George	Music	20			45	Country
Stranahan, Robert A, Jr.	Business	5			10	CEO/Champion Spark Plugs

Name	Field	SIG	DS	ALS	SP	Remarks
Strand, Paul	Art	25	75	200		
Strange, Glenn	Ent	150	200	250	250	Frankenstein
Strangis, Judy	Ent	10			20	
Strasberg, Lee 1901-82	Ent	25	35		75	
Strasberg, Susan	Ent	15		35	20	
Stratas, Teresa	Music	25			50	Opera
Stratemeyer, George F.	Military	30			50	
Stratten, Dorothy	Ent	125			250	Playboy Model/Killed
Stratton, Chas. S.	Ent	250		375	450	General Tom Thumb
Straus, Nathan 1848-1931	Business	100				Owner R.H. Macy Co. Dept
Straus, Oscar 1870-1954	Music	150		250	200	The Chocolate Soldier
Strause, Charles	Music	10		30	25	
Strauss, Franz Josef	Political	15	45	75	35	
Strauss, Johann 1804-49	Music	250	450	1,200	RARE	Aus. Waltzes
Strauss, Johann, Jr.	Music	450	750	900	RARE	The Waltz King
Strauss, Levi	Business	RARE	RARE	RARE	RARE	1850 Establ'd Levi Strauss
Strauss, Peter	Ent	15			45	
Strauss, Richard	Music	225	450	750	700	
Strauss, Robert	Ent	25			45	
Stravinsky, Igor 1882-71	Music	325	550	750	750	Composer
Strawberry, Darryl	Sports	35			75	Baseball
Stray Cats	Music	40	100		75	Signed by Entire Band
Strayhorn, Billy	Music	RARE	RARE	RARE	RARE	Jazz Musician
Streep, Meryl	Ent	20	30	45	50	AA Winner
Street, Julian	Author	25			75	
Streib, Werner	Aviation	25			60	German ACE WWII
Streich, Rita	Music	10			25	Opera
Streicher, Julius	Political	50	125			Nazi Anti-Semetic, Hanged
Streight, Abel	Civil War	50	150			Union Gen. Escaped Libby
Streisand, Barbra	Ent	150	400		250	
Stribling, Thomas S.	Author	15		45		Am. Novelist/Pulitzer
Strindberg, August	Author	275		750	900	1849-1912
Stringfield, Sherry	Ent	20			40	ER
Stringham, Silas Horton	Civil War	50	100			Union Admiral
Stroheim, Eric von	Ent	150	300		450	Classic Film Director
Stroll, Edson	Ent	10			20	
Stromberg, Hunt	Ent	10			30	Film Producer, Director
Strong, Caleb 1745-1819	RevWar	75	200	400		1st US Senator
Strong, George C.	Civil War	350	550			Union General/KIA
Strong, Susan	Ent	10			20	Vintage Actress
Strong, William	SuprCt	80	160	250		
Stroud, Robert	Criminal	200	RARE	550	RARE	Birdman of Alcatraz
Strouse, Charles	Music	15			30	Composer
Struck, Heinz	Science	10			35	Rocket Pioneer
Struthers, Sally	Ent	15	25		25	All in the Family
Stryker	Music	30			65	Signed by All Four
Stuart, Alexander H. H.	Political	25	60	75		Fillmore Sec'y Interior

Name	Field	SIG	DS	ALS	SP	Remarks
Stuart, Gilbert 1755-1828	Art	200	500	750		Pres and Royalty Portraits
Stuart, Gloria	Ent	20			50	Titanic
Stuart, J. E. B. 1833-64	Civil War	2,500	4,500	RARE	RARE	CSA General
Stuart, J.E.B.	Civil War	RARE	RARE	RARE	RARE	CSA General/War Dated
Stuart, Marty	Music	10			25	Country
Studebaker, Clement	Business	200	500	650		Studebaker Bros.
Studebaker, Jr., Clement	Business	40	80	150	75	Studebaker Bros. Mfg. Co,
Studer, Cheryl	Music	15			35	Opera
Stultz, Wilmer	Aviation	75			250	Pioneer Aviator
Stump, Felix B.	Military	25			50	WWII Adm.
Sturge, Joseph	Political	10		45		1793 - 1859
Sturgeon, Daniel	Political	25	75	125		
Sturges, John	Ent	5			15	
Sturges, Preston	Ent	20			50	Director/Writer
Sturgis, Samuel D.	Civil War	50	100			Union General/1822-89
Styne, Jule 1905-1994	Music	25			50	Composer
Styron, William	Author	15	35		60	
Styx	Music	40			80	Signed by Entire Band
Suchet, David	Ent	10			30	Br. Actor. Poirot
Suchet, Louis G. Duc	Military	100	200	300		Marshal of Napoleon
Sucre, Antonio de	Military	300	650			
Sues, Alan	Ent	10			20	Laugh In
Sugar Ray	Music	25			50	
Sullivan, Anne (Annie)	Science	200		400		
Sullivan, Arthur, Sir	Music	175	400	650	1,000	1842-1900
Sullivan, Barry	Ent	10			25	
Sullivan, Ed 1902-1974	Ent	30	50		125	Columnist, TV Host
Sullivan, Francis L.	Ent	10	25		25	
Sullivan, James	RevWar	50	100	200		Continental Congress
Sullivan, John 1740-95	RevWar	150	400	550		Continental Congress/Gen
Sullivan, John L.	Sports	600			1,250	Boxer
Sullivan, Kathleen	Ent	10			20	TV Hostess
Sullivan, Kathryn D.	Aviation	10	25	45	30	
Sullivan, Margaret	Ent	60	75		125	Suicide
Sullivan, Pat	Cartoonist	75			250	Felix The Cat
Sullivan, Peter John	Civil War	60	100	150		Union General/1821-83
Sullivan, Susan	Ent	5		20	15	
Sullivan, William	Author	20	40	75		Politician
Sully, Alfred	Civil War	50	100	100	150	Union General/1821-79
Sully, Thomas 1783-1872	Art	175	350	450		Portraits
Sully-Prudhomme, Ren.	Author	50	125	200		Fr. Poet/Nobel
Sulzberger, Art Ochs, Jr.	Business	10	25	30	20	NY Times
Summer, Donna	Music	20			45	Disco Queen
Summerall, Charles P.	Military	15	25	35	25	Gen/Pres.Citadel 1931-53
Summerfield, Arthur E.	Political	15		30	25	
Summers, Yale	Ent	10			25	
Summersby, Kay	Military	75			125	D.D. Eisenhower's WWII

Name	Field	SIG	DS	ALS	SP	Remarks
Sumner, Charles 1811-74	Civil War	100		225		Abolitionist
Sumner, Increase	Political	75	175			Rev. War Jurist /1746-99
Sumter, Thomas	RevWar	400	900			Soldier
Sun Yat-Sen 1866-1975	Political	6,000	900	1,250	2,000	Ist Pres. Chinese Republic
Sunday, William A.	Clergy	100		200	400	Evangelist
Sung, Kim II	Political	50			150	North Viet Nam
Supertramp	Music	40			75	Signed by Entire Group
Susann,Jacqueline	Author	20	35	45	40	Valley of the Dolls etc.
Sutherland, Donald	Ent	10	20		20	MASH movie
Sutherland, George	SuprCt	75	150		250	
Sutherland, Joan	Music	15		35	35	Opera
Sutherland, Keifer	Ent	15			45	
Sutro, Adolph H. J.	Business	35	90	150		Mining Magnate
Sutter, John A. 1803-80	Western	1,200	RARE	2,700	RARE	Ca. Gold Rush on his Farm
Sutton, Frank	Ent	75	100		100	Sgt. Carter/Gomer Pyle
Sutton, Grady	Ent	10			15	
Sutton, John	Ent	10			25	Suave Br. Co-Star
Suvari, Mena	Ent	25			50	American Beauty
Svanholm, Set	Music	20			45	Opera
Svenson, Bo	Ent	5			10	
Swaggart, Jimmy	Clergy	10		35	30	Evangelist
Swan, James	RevWar	200	450	600		Financial Speculator
Swanson, Gloria 1897-83	Ent	50	100		150	
Swanson, J.	Civil War	75	125	175		
Swanson, Kristy	Ent	20			50	
Swarthout, Gladys	Music	25	75		75	Opera and Film Star
Swasey, Ambrose	Business	50	75			
Swayne, Noah H.	SuprCt	45	125	200		
Swayne, Wager	Civil War	25	50	100		Union General/1834-1902
Swayze, John Cameron	Ent	5			10	TV Newsman
Swayze, Patrick	Ent	25			50	Dirty Dancing/Ghost
Sweeney, Walter C.	Military	5	15	25	15	Gen/Tactical Air Command
Sweet, Blanche	Ent	20		35	35	
Sweet, John H.	Business	5			10	
Swenson, Ruth Ann	Music	10			25	Opera
Swett, James E.	Aviation	15	30		45	WWII ACE
Swift, Frederic W.	Civil War	65	125	175		Union Officer
Swift, George B.	Political	10	25			Mayor of Chicago
Swift, Harold Higgins	Business	20	50	75	35	Swift and Co.
Swift, John W. 1750-1819	RevWar	75	150			Soldier/Merchant
Swift, Jonathan 1667-45	Author	2,500	RARE	RARE	RARE	Poet
Swigert, John L. Jr.	Space	40	75		125	Astronaut
Swinburne, Algernon C.	Author	150	200	450		British Poet
Swinnerton, Frank	Author	25	50	85		British Novelist
Swinton, Ernest D.	Military	50	100	200		British Inventor of Tank
Swit, Loretta	Ent	15			30	MASH/Hotlips
Switzer, Carl "Alfalfa"	Ent	400	RARE	RARE	900	Our Gang

Name	Field	SIG	DS	ALS	SP	Remarks
Swope, Herbert Bayard	Author	10		60	25	War Correspondence
Swope, James S.	Aviation	15		40	30	WWII ACE
Sykes, Jerome H.	Music	15			30	Opera
Sylvia	Music	15			30	
Symmes, John Cleves	RevWar	125	275	450		Patriot/Cont. Congress
Szell, George	Music	25			75	Hungarian Conductor
Szent-Gyorgyi, Albert	Science	30	75	100	50	Nobel Medicine 1937
Szigeti, Joseph	Music	75			200	Violinist
Szold, Henrietta 1860-45	Political	150	450	600		
Szymanowski, Karol M.	Music	150		450		Composer

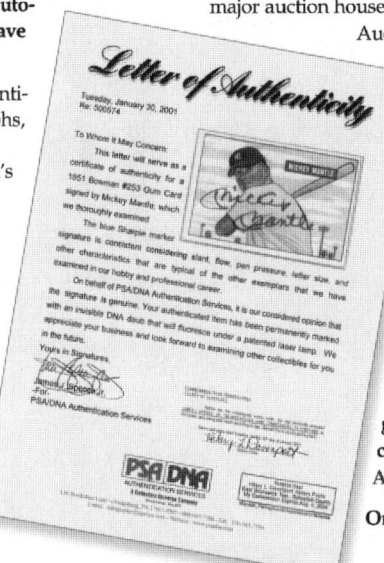

Name	Field	SIG	DS	ALS	SP	Remarks
Taft, Charles P.	Business	10		25	10	
Taft, Helen Herron	First Lady	100	200	450	850	1861-1943
Taft, Helen Manning	First Lady	75	150	300	500	Daughter
Taft, Lorado 1860-1936	Art	75	125			Am Sculptor/Author
Taft, William Howard	President	175	450	650	450	1857-1930
Tagliabue, Carlo	Music	50			150	Opera
Tagliavini, Feruccio	Music	35			75	Opera
Taglioni, Marie 1804-1884	Music	300		RARE	RARE	It. Premier Ballerina
Tagore, Rabindranath	Author	100	250	350	350	Poet/Nobel
Takei, George	Ent	15		40	30	Star Trek
Talbot, Gloria	Ent	10			20	
Talbot, Helen	Ent	10			25	
Talbot, Lyle	Ent	10	25	25	20	
Talbot, Nita	Ent	10			20	
Talbot, Wm. Henry Fox	Science	300		900		Inv. Photographic Process
Talcott, Joseph	Political	35	75	150		Colonial Gov.CT/1669-1741
Talese, Gay	Author	10			25	Am. Novelist
Taliaferro, William B.	Civil War	175	400	650		CSA General/War Dated
Taliaferro, William B.	Civil War	90		300		CSA General/1822-98
Talking Heads	Music	35			65	Signed by Entire Group
Tallchief, Maria	Ent	15	20	35	30	Ballerina
Talley, Marion	Music	15		45	50	Am. Soprano
Talleyrand, Charles M.	Political	200	600	750		Chancellor of Napoleon
Talmadge, Benjamin	RevWar	225	400			1754-1835
Talmadge, Constance	Ent	35			75	Silent Star
Talmadge, Norma	Ent	75			175	
Talman, William	Ent	50	75	150	125	Perry Mason
Talvela, Marti	Music	30			75	Opera
Tamblyn, Russ	Ent	10			20	
Tambor, Jeffrey	Ent	10			20	
Tamiroff, Akim	Ent	30	45	75	75	
Tandy, Jessica 1904-94	Ent	25	45	60	60	AA Winner
Taney, Roger B.1777-64	SuprCt	100	275	350		
Tanner, Henry Ossawa	Art	275		600		Religious Subjects
Tansman, Alexandre	Music	50	125		250	
Tappan, Arthur	Political	25	65	100		Merchant/1786-1865
Tappan, James C.	Civil War	35	75	100		CSA General
Tarantino, Quentin	Ent	20			50	AA Writer/Director
Tarbell, Ida M. 1857-1944	Author	20	45	75	30	
Tarkington, Booth	Author	50	150	175	125	Playwright/Nobel
Tarleton, Banastre, Sir	RevWar	150	300	600		British General
Tashlin, Frank	Ent	25			35	Director

Name	Field	SIG	DS	ALS	SP	Remarks
Tashman, Lilyan	Ent	30	45	75	75	
Tassigny, J.M.G. de	Military	35	75	125		
Tate, Allen 1899-1979	Author	10	30	75		Am.Poet/Biographer
Tate, Henry, Sir	Business	50	100	175		
Tate, Jackson R.	Military	10		30	25	Adm. WWII
Tate, Sharon	Ent	275		550	775	Murdered/Manson Gang
Tattersall, Richard	Business	25	50	75		1724-95
Tattnall, Josiah	Civil War			650		CSA Naval Captain
Tatum, Edward L.	Science	45	75	125		Nobel Medicine 1958
Taube, Henry, Dr.	Science	20	35		30	Nobel Chemistry 1983
Tauber, Richard	Music	50			150	Opera
Taufflieb, Gen.	Military	50	125	150	100	
Taurog, Norman	Ent	50			150	Film Director
Taveling Wilbury's	Music	100	200		200	Signed by all four
Tayback, Vic	Ent	35	60		50	Alice
Taylor, Bayard 1825-78	Author	25	75	125		Journalist
Taylor, Deems	Music	40	75		60	Musicologist
Taylor, Don	Ent	10			20	Actor/Director
Taylor, Dub	Ent	15			40	
Taylor, Elizabeth	Ent	175	400		350	AA Winner
Taylor, Estelle	Ent	15		45	45	
Taylor, George 1716-81	RevWar	7,500	20,000	45,000	RARE	Signer
Taylor, James	Music	35	100		65	Singer/Writer
Taylor, Joseph P.	Civil War	65	150			Union General
Taylor, Kent	Ent	5			15	
Taylor, Laurette	Ent	15		40	35	
Taylor, Margaret	First Lady	RARE	RARE	RARE	RARE	
Taylor, Mary	Music	10			20	
Taylor, Maxwell D.	Military	25	75	100	65	Gen. WWII
Taylor, Meshach	Ent	15			35	Designing Women
Taylor, Niki	Ent	20			50	Super-Model
Taylor, Richard	Civil War	375	1,400			CSA General/War Dated
Taylor, Richard 1826-79	Civil War	225	675			CSA General
Taylor, Richard E., Dr.	Science	20	50			Nobel Physics 1990
Taylor, Robert 1911-69	Ent	50	100	125	150	
Taylor, Rod	Ent	5	20	20	20	
Taylor, Thomas H.	Civil War	75	100	200		CSA General/1825-1901
Taylor, Thomas H.	Civil War	125	200	450		CSA General/War Dated
Taylor, Vaughn	Ent	20			50	
Taylor, Walter H.	Civil War	50	100			Aide to Robt E. Lee
Taylor, Zachary	President	525	1,500	3,000		1784-1850
Taylor-Young, Leigh	Ent	5	20		15	
Tchaikovsky, Piotr I.	Music	2,000	3,000	RARE	RARE	Russian Opera/1840-93
Tchernihovsky, Saul	Author	175		450		Poet
Teagarden, Charlie	Music	10			25	Jazz Trumpet
Teagarden, Jack	Music	65	100		125	Big Band Leader
Teal, Ray	Ent	50			150	

Name	Field	SIG	DS	ALS	SP	Remarks
Tearle, Conway	Ent	15			40	Vintage Br. Actor
Tearle, Godfrey, Sir	Ent	20			50	British Actor
Tebaidi, Renata	Music	20			45	Opera
Telfair, Edward	RevWar	40	80	150		Continental Congress
Teller, Edward, Dr.	Science	35	125	250	90	1908-1994
Telva, Marion	Music	15			45	Opera
Temin, Howard M., Dr.	Science	20	35	56	35	Nobel Medicine 1975
Tempest, Marie	Ent	25	45	50	75	
Temple, Shirley	Ent	200	450	600	450	Signature as a Child
Temple, Shirley (Black)	Ent	20	75	75	45	Adult Signature
Templeton, Alec	Music	20			50	Br. Blind Jazz Pianist
Templeton, Ben	Cartoonist	10			20	Motley's Crew
Templeton, Faye	Music	25	50		65	
Temptations	Music	45	125		125	Signed by Entire Group
Ten Broeck, Abraham	RevWar	100	125			General/Judge
Tenant, Victoria	Ent	10			25	
Tenniel, John, Sir	Art	75	150	250		Illustr. Alice in Wonderland
Tennille, Toni	Music	5			15	Captain and Tennille
Tennyson, Alfred, Lord	Author	200		700	950	Br. Poet Laureate
Tennyson, Jean	Music	10			20	Am. Soprano
Teresa, Mother 1910-97	Clergy	125	250	RARE	275	Nobel Peace Prize
Tereshkova, Valentina	Space	200	250		250	1st Woman in Space
Terfel, Bryn	Music	15			35	Welsh Operatic Baritone
Terhune, Alfred Payson	Author	25	65	75	50	Writer of Dog Stories
Terhune, Max	Ent	100			225	
Terkel, Studs	Author	10		25	20	TV Biographer
Ternina, Milka	Music	25		125		Opera
Terry, Alfred Howe	Civil War	150	350	475		Union General/1827-90
Terry, Ellen, Dame	Ent	35	65	100	75	
Terry, Fred 1864-1933	Ent	15		25	25	Br. Stage & Film Star
Terry, Henry D.	Civil War	45	100	150		Union General/1812-69
Terry, Paul	Cartoonist	50			100	Animator-Mighty Mouse
Terry, Phillip	Ent	5		20	15	
Terry, William H.	Civil War	73		225		CSA General/1824-88
Terry, William Richard	Civil War	75	150	250		CSA General/1817-97
Tesla, Nikola, Dr.	Science	400	850	1,250	1,250	Physicist
Tetard, J.	Aviation	50	75	150	100	
Tetrazzini, Luisa	Music	75	125	200	225	Opera/1871-1940
Teyte, Maggie	Music	50			125	Opera
Thacher, James, Dr.	RevWar	50		250		Revolutionary War Surgeon
Thackeray, Wm. M.	Author	100	300	550		Br. Novelist/1811-63
Thalberg, Irving	Ent	250	450	600	450	MGM Producer
Tharp, Twyla	Ent	20	25		40	Dancer-Choreographer
Thatcher, Henry Knox	Civil War	50	100	150		Union Naval Commander
Thatcher, Margaret	Political	50	150	225	135	Prime Minister
Thaw, Harry K.	Business	50	100	200	75	
Thaxter, Celia 1835-94	Author	25	45	90	125	Am. Poet

Name	Field	SIG	DS	ALS	SP	Remarks
Thaxter, Phyllis	Ent	10			25	
Thayer, Abbott	Art	15	35	65		Am. Landscapes
Thayer, Celia	Author	5		15		Am. Novelist
Thayer, John Milton	Civil War	45	75	150		Union General
Thayer, Silvanus	Military	75	125	200		
Thebaw	Political	125				Burma
Thebom, Blanche	Music	25	45		75	Opera
Theissen, Tiffany Amber	Ent	20			50	
Thelen, Bob	Aviation	15		40	35	WWII ACE
Theron, Charlize	Ent	25			50	
Thicke, Alan	Ent	15	25		25	Growing Pains
Thiers, Louis-Adolphe	Military	35	65	150		Ist Pres. 3rd Republic
Thieu, Nguyen Van	Political	25	60	125	45	South Vietnam
Thinnis, Roy	Ent	5		20	15	
Thomas, Ambroise	Music			450		Composer/1811-1896
Thomas, B.J.	Music	10	20		15	Writer
Thomas, Betty	Ent	5		15	10	
Thomas, C.-L.-Ambroise	Music	75	125	250		Composer
Thomas, Charles	Military		600			Union General/1840-1878
Thomas, Clarence	SuprCt	25			40	
Thomas, Danny	Ent	25	55		60	1914 - 1991
Thomas, Dave	Business	10	25		25	Founder of Wendy's
Thomas, Dave	Ent	10			20	Grace Under Fire
Thomas, Dylan 1914-53	Author	500		1,500	1,500	Welsh Poet/Playwright
Thomas, E. Donnall, Dr.	Science	15	25		30	Nobel Medicine 1990
Thomas, Frankie	Ent	10			20	
Thomas, George Henry	Civil War	125	300	500		Union General/1818-70
Thomas, Heather	Ent	15	30		35	
Thomas, Isaiah 1749-31	Business	150	300	750		
Thomas, Jess	Music	15			40	Opera
Thomas, John 1724-76	RevWar	500	750	1,400		Am. Physician & Gen.
Thomas, John Charles	Ent	25	45	55	45	Am. Baritone
Thomas, Jonathan T.	Ent	20			50	Home Improvement
Thomas, Kurt	Ent	5			15	
Thomas, Lorenzo	Civil War	75	140	250		Union General/1804-75
Thomas, Lowell	Ent	35			125	
Thomas, Marlo	Ent	10	20		20	That Girl
Thomas, Michael Tilson	Music	20			45	Am. Conductor
Thomas, Norman	Political	35	100	200	75	6 Presidential Attempts
Thomas, Richard	Ent	5			15	
Thomas, Robert Bailey	Author	25	45	80		
Thomas, Samuel	Civil War	45				Union General
Thomas, Seth E.	Business	125	250	400		Fndr Seth Thomas Clock
Thomas, Seth E. Jr.	Business	75	175	350		Cont'd Seth Thomas Clock Co.
Thomas, Terry	Ent	50		100	150	
Thomas, Theodore	Ent	15			30	Conductor
Thompson Twins	Music	30			65	Signed by Both

Name	Field	SIG	DS	ALS	SP	Remarks
Thompson, Benj. von	RevWar	275	450	1,400		Br.Physicist/Inventor
Thompson, Denman	Ent	10			30	Stage Actor
Thompson, Dorothy	Author	35	50	75	75	Journalist/1894-1961
Thompson, Emma	Ent	25			50	Br. Actress-Playwright AA
Thompson, Ernest Seton	Author	50	100	200		Wild Life Stories
Thompson, Gordon	Ent	10			20	
Thompson, Hank	Music	5			15	
Thompson, J. Walter	Business	100	750			Father/Modern Advertising
Thompson, Jacob	Civil War	150	300	RARE	RARE	CSA Secret Service Agent
Thompson, John P.	Business	15	35	50	25	Pres. Southland Corp.
Thompson, John T.	Science	100	300	RARE	RARE	Arms Inventor
Thompson, Lea	Ent	20			45	Caroline in the City
Thompson, Linda	Ent	5			10	
Thompson, Merriwether	Civil War	125	275	400		CSA General/1826-76
Thompson, Richard W.	Political	25	45	65		Sec'y Navy 1809
Thompson, Ruth Plumly	Author	450		RARE	RARE	
Thompson, Smith	SuprCt	75	150	175		1768 - 1843
Thompson, Wm. H. Big	Political	125				
Thomson, Charles	RevWar	700	1,400			1729-1824
Thomson, Elihu 1853-37	Science	500	950			Electrical Engineer-Inventor
Thomson, Geo. Paget	Science	50				Nobel Physics 1937
Thomson, Virgil	Music	50	75	150	125	1896-1989
Thor, Jerome	Ent	10			20	
Thorborg, Kerstin	Music	25			75	Opera
Thoreau, Henry David	Author	3,000	6,000	8,500	RARE	Am. Naturalist
Thorndike, Sybil, Dame	Ent	30	45		75	
Thornhill, Claude	Music	15			45	Bandleader
Thornton, Billy Bob	Ent	25			50	AA Winner
Thornton, Matthew	RevWar	625	1,400	1,650		Signer/1714-1803
Thornton, William	RevWar	150	300			Am. Architect
Thornton, William A.	Civil War	35				Union General/1803-66
Thorpe, Jim	Sports	400			1,250	1963 Football HOF
Thorvaldsen, Bertel	Art	100	250			Sculptor Lion of Lucerne
Three Stooges, The	Ent	1,400	2,750		2,550	With Moe, Curly and Larry
Thruston, Gates P.	Civil War	25		55		Union General
Thurber, James	Cartoonist	100		450	400	New Yorker Illustrator
Thurman, Uma	Ent	25			50	
Thurmond, J. Strom	Political	10		25	15	SC Senator
Thurston, Howard	Ent	200	600	600	475	Magician/1869-1936
Tibbett, Lawrence	Music	50	100		125	Opera
Tibbetts, Paul W.	Aviation	25		100	75	Pilot of Enola Gay
Tidball, John C.	Civil War	60	125	175		Union Officer
Tiegs, Cheryl	Ent	10			20	Model
Tierney, Gene	Ent	25		50	45	
Tierney, Harry	Music	50	100	200		Composer
Tietjens, Therese	Music	45			125	German Soprano/Opera
Tiffany, Charles Lewis	Business	200	400	RARE	1,500	Founder Tiffany and Co.

Name	Field	SIG	DS	ALS	SP	Remarks
Tiffany, Louis Comfort	Art	400	750	RARE	1,500	Stain Glass Artist
Tiffin, Pamela	Ent	5		20	15	
Tilden, Samuel J.	Political	75	150	250		Presidential Candidate
Tilghman, James	RevWar	40	75	150		
Tilghman, Lloyd 1816-63	Civil War	150	300	450		CSA General/KIA/RARE
Tilghman, Matthew	RevWar	200		650		Cont. Congress
Tilghman, William M.	Western	200	850	1,250		Early Western Sheriff
Tilkin-Servais, Ernest	Music	35			85	Opera
Tillinghast, Charles C.	Business	10	20	30	15	
Tillis, Mel	Music	5			15	Country
Tillis, Pam	Music	15			35	
Tilly, Jennifer	Ent	15			35	
Tilly, Meg	Ent	15			35	
Tilton, Charlene	Ent	15	35		40	
Tilton, Wm. Stowell	Civil War	50	100			Union Officer
Tim, Tiny	Music	20			45	Tiptoe through the Tulips
Timken, William Robert	Business	30	75	100	60	
Ting, Samuel C., Dr.	Science	20	35	50	25	Nobel Physics 1976
Tingey, Thomas	Military	75	150	200		Continental Navy
Tinker, Grant C.	Ent	10			15	TV Film Producer
Tiny Tim	Music	25	35		45	Tiptoe Thru the Tulips
Tiomkin, Dimitri	Music	45		175	100	Composer/1894-1979
Tippett, Michael Sir	Music	50			150	Composer
Tisch, Laurence A.	Business	15			35	CEO of CBS
Tissot, James	Art	75	150	225		
Tito, Marshal	Political	75	175	250	250	1892 - 1980
TLC	Music	35			75	Signed by all three
Tobey, Ken	Ent	10	25		25	
Tobias, George	Ent	50			150	
Tobin, Genevieve	Ent	15		35	35	
Tocqueville, Alexis de	Author	50	125	275		Fr. Writer/Politician
Todd, Alexander R.	Science	30	75		45	Nobel Chemistry 1957
Todd, Ann	Ent	20			40	
Todd, Richard	Ent	75			125	
Todd, Robert	Aviation	15	30	45	25	
Todd, Thelma 1905-35	Ent	175	250	350	475	Mysterious Death at 30
Togo, Heihachiro	Military	100	300	450	200	Jap. Adm. Sino-Jap. War
Togo, Shigenori	Political	250			400	
Tojo, Hideki 1884-1948	Military	250	550	1,500	1,500	Jap Adm/Pearl Harbour
Toklas, Alice B. 1877-67	Author	50	100	RARE	RARE	
Tokody, Ilona	Music	10			25	Opera
Tokyo Rose (Iva,Toguri)	Military	250			400	WWII
Toler, Sidney	Ent	150			300	Charlie Chan
Tolkien, John R.R.	Author	500	1,500	2,500	RARE	Br. Lord of the Rings
Tolstoy, Leo, Count	Author	1,200	RARE	RARE	2,200	Rus. Novelist
Tombaugh, Clyde W.	Science	30	65	125	125	Astronomer/Discov. Pluto
Tomei, Marissa	Ent	25			50	AA Winning Actress

Name	Field	SIG	DS	ALS	SP	Remarks
Tomlin, Lily	Ent	10	20		20	
Tomlin, Pinky	Music	15			35	Scat Singer
Tompkins, Angel	Ent	10		20	25	
Tompkins, Daniel	Vice Pres	100	125	150		Monroe's VP
Tone, Franchot 1905-68	Ent	25	50	55	50	
Toombs, Robert A.	Civil War	125	200	200		CSA General/1810-85
Toomey, Regis	Ent	15	25		45	
Toones, Fred Snowflake	Ent	150			300	
Topal	Ent	15			30	
Topp, Erich	Military	35			100	Ger. U Boat Cmdr. WWII
Topping, Dan	Business	10		30	15	Owner NY Yankees
Torisu, Kennosuke	Military	50		150	75	
Tork, Peter	Music	20			45	The Monkees
Torme, Mel	Music	25			50	Singer/Writer
Torn, Rip	Ent	15			35	Easy Rider
Torrance, Ernest 1878-33	Ent	75			150	Silent Films
Torrence, Ridgely	Author	25	35	75		Am. Poet/1875-1950
Torres, Raquel	Ent	25			45	
Tors, Ivan	Ent	15			35	Producer-Director
Toscanini, Arturo	Music	300	550	750	700	Conductor/1867-1957
Tosti, Paolo	Music	25	60	125		Composer
Toto	Music	65			150	Signed by Entire Band
Totten, Jos. G.	Civil War	20	35	65		Union General/1788-1864
Totter, Audrey	Ent	5	15		15	
Toucey, Isaac 1792-1869	Political	25	75	125		
Toulouse-Lautrec, Henri	Art	1,200	2,500	RARE	RARE	
Toumanova, Tamara	Ent	35			100	Rus-Am Ballerina
Tourel, Jennie	Music	25			50	Opera
Tourgee, Albion W.	Author	15	25	40		Lawyer/Judge
Tower, Zealous B.	Civil War	20	35	50		Union General/1819-1900
Townes, Charles Hanson	Science	25	35	65		Inventor
Townsend, Edward D.	Civil War	30	55	60		Union Officer/1817-93
Townsend, Francis E.	Science	50			150	Physician
Townsend, Frederick	Civil War	15	30	45		Union General
Townsend, George A.	Author	15		40		War Correspondent
Townsend, Lynn	Business	10		35	20	CEO Chrysler Corporation
Townsend, Pete	Music	30			65	The Who
Townsend, Robert	Ent	10			20	Director
Toynbee, Arnold 1852-83	Author	25	105	190	75	Br, Historian, Sociologist
Tozzi, Giorgio	Music	20			40	Opera
Tracy, Doreen	Ent	5			15	Mouseketeer
Tracy, Edward Dorr	Civil War	150	450	750		CSA General/KIA
Tracy, Lee	Ent	10			25	
Tracy, Spencer 1900-67	Ent	125	250	350	300	AA Winning Actor
Train, Arthur	Author	10		35		
Trapier, James H.	Civil War	125	200	325		CSA General/1815-65
Trask, Diana	Music	10			20	

Name	Field	SIG	DS	ALS	SP	Remarks
Traubel, Helen 1899-72	Music	40			90	Opera
Trautloft, Hannes	Aviation	25			50	Ger. Ace WWII
Travalena, Fred	Ent	5			15	Comedian
Travanti, Daniel J.	Ent	10			20	
Traven, Berwick	Author	275	650	1,250		German Novelist
Travers, Henry	Ent	250	RARE	RARE	400	Angel/Its a Wonderful Life
Travers, Patricia	Ent	5			15	
Traverso, Giuseppe	Music	15			45	Opera
Travis, Kylie	Ent	10			20	
Travis, Merle	Music	20			40	
Travis, Nancy	Ent	20			45	
Travis, Randy	Music	20			40	Country
Travis, Richard	Ent	10			20	
Travis, William Barret	Military	2,500	RARE	RARE	RARE	Co-Cmdr Alamo
Travolta, John	Ent	25			50	
Treacher, Arthur	Ent	20			45	1894 - 1975
Treadwell, John	RevWar	25	60	75		
Trebek, Alex	Ent	10		20	25	Host/Jeopardy
Tree, Herbert Beerbohm	Ent	35	75	100	75	
Treen, Mary	Ent	10		30	25	
Treilhard, Jean-Baptiste	Military	15	25	50		Fr. Politician
Trelawny, Edward	Author	175	400	750		Br.Author-Adventurer
Trenholm, George A.	Civil War	100	200	450		CSA Sec'y Treasury
Trettner, Henrich 'Heniz	Aviation	20	50		50	
Trevelyan, George Otto	Author	15		75		Br. Historian
Treves, Frederick, Dr.	Science	200		400		Dr. To Elephant Man
Trevor, Claire	Ent	30	45		45	AA Winner
Trilling, Lionel	Author	10	25	45		Am. Lit. Critic. Professor
Trimble, Isaac Ridgeway	Civil War	175		400		CSA General/1802-88
Tripler, Charles E.	Science	75	150			Inventor Liquid Air
Tripplehorn, Jeanne	Ent	15			45	
Tritt, Travis	Music	20			45	Country
Tritton, William Ashbee	Science	25	65	100	45	Developed Military Tank
Trollope, Anthony	Author	100	225			Br. Novelist. 50 Novels
Trollope, Frances	Author	35	100	200		Br. Novelist
Trollope, Thomas A.	Author		25	45		Novelist/1810-92
Trotsky, Leon 1879-1940	Political	650	1,500	2,250	950	Communist Leader
Troubridge, Thomas, Sir	Military	75		250		Br Admiral
Troup, Bobby	Music	10			20	Composer
Trow, Bob	Ent	10			20	
Trower, Robin	Ent	15			30	
Troyanos, Tatiana	Music	15			40	Opera
Truax, Ernest	Ent	10		40	30	
Trudeau, Gary	Cartoonist	30			65	Doonesbury
Trudeau, Pierre	Political	25	65	90	65	Prime Minister Canada
Truffaut, Frangois	Ent	50	150			
Trujillo, Rafael 1891-1961	Political	75			250	Dominican Republic

Name	Field	SIG	DS	ALS	SP	Remarks
Truman, Bess W.	First Lady	75	125	200	175	1885-1982
Truman, Harry S.	President	150	450	1,200	400	1884-1972
Truman, Harry S.	President	300	1,200	3,500	800	As President
Truman, Margaret	Political	25	65	80	30	Daughter of Truman
Trumbo, Dalton	Author	50			75	Blacklisted Oscar Winner
Trumbull, John 1750-31	Author	75		200		CT Poet & Lawyer
Trumbull, John 1756-43	Art	100	300	750		
Trumbull, Jonathan	Military	125	300	450		Sec'y Washington's Staff
Trumbull, Jonathan	RevWar	300		900		1710-85
Trump, Donald J.	Business	15	50	75	40	Millionaire Entrepreneur
Trump, Ivana	Business	10			35	Ex Mrs. Donald Trump
Truth, Sojourner	Political	30,000	RARE	RARE	RARE	Abolitionist
Truxton, Thomas	RevWar	125	300	550		Cmdr. USS Constellation
Truxton, William Talbot	Civil War	20	45	75		Union Admiral
Tryon, William	RevWar	150	300	600		Colonial Governor NC/NY
Tsiolkovsky, Konstantin	Science	RARE	RARE	2,500	RARE	Rus. Space Program
Tubb, Ernest	Music	15			35	
Tuchman, Barbara W.	Author	35	100	150	45	Historian
Tucker, Forrest	Ent	25		40	45	
Tucker, John R.	Civil War	125	200			CSA Commdr. 1812-83
Tucker, Orrin	Music	15			25	Big Band Leader
Tucker, Richard	Music	35	75		120	Opera
Tucker, Samuel	RevWar	125	250	550		Am. Naval Hero
Tucker, Sophie	Ent	25		60	60	Vaudeville
Tucker, Tanya	Music	20			50	Country
Tucker, Thomas T.	RevWar	50	150	175		Soldier/Statesman
Tucker, Tommy	Music	20			45	Bandleader
Tudor, Anthony	Ent	35	45		90	Dancer/Choreagrapher
Tufts, Cotton 1734-1815	RevWar	75	150	250		Physician
Tufts, Sonny	Ent	20	25		35	
Tully, Tom	Ent	25			45	
Tune, Tommy	Music	10			20	Dancer/Choreagrapher
Turgenev, Ivan 1818-33	Author	200	450	900	1,200	Russian Novelist
Turkel, Ann	Ent	5			15	
Turkel, Studs	Author	10	25	35	20	TV Commentator
Turlington, Christy	Ent	20			45	Super-Model
Turner, Edward	Science	25		125		Chemist/Atomic Weight
Turner, Frederick J.	Author	50		200		Pulitzer Prize. Historian
Turner, J. M. W. 1775-51	Art	200	500	900		Br. Landscape Painter
Turner, Janine	Ent	25			60	
Turner, John Wesley	Civil War	100	125	300		Union General/1833-99
Turner, Kathleen	Ent	15			35	
Turner, Lana	Ent	40	75	100	80	
Turner, Philip	RevWar	65	125	225		Surgeon During War
Turner, Roscoe, Col.	Aviation	75			125	Pioneer Aviator
Turner, Ted	Business	10		40	30	
Turner, Tina	Music	25			50	

Name	Field	SIG	DS	ALS	SP	Remarks
Turpin, Ben	Ent	150			375	
Turreau de Garambouville	Military	25		75		French Revolution
Turtles	Music	35			75	Signed by Entire Group
Turturro, Nick	Ent	10			25	
Tusmayan, Barsag	Music	10			25	Opera
Tuttle, Lurene	Ent	5		20	15	Radio Dramatic Star
Tuttle, Wes & Marilyn	Music	15			30	
Tutu, Desmond, Bishop	Clergy	50	100	200	75	Nobel Peace Prize
Tuve, Merle Antony	Science	35	75	150	50	Radar
Twain, Mark	Author	500		1,500		
Twain, Shania	Music	25			50	Country/Pop Star
Tweed, Shannon	Ent	10		30	25	
Tweed, William Marcy	Political	125	200	350	750	
Twiggs, David E.	Civil War	150	300	750		CSA General/1790-1862
Twiggy (Leslie Hornsby)	Ent	15		40	35	60's Brit. Fashion Model
Twining, Nathan F.	Aviation	45	125	175	65	General WWII
Twiss, Peter	Aviation	10		30	20	
Twitty, Conway	Music	40	60		65	Country
Two Guns White Calf	Western	750	RARE	RARE	2,000	Buffalo Nickel Model
Tyler, Bonnie	Music	15			35	
Tyler, Daniel 1799-1882	Civil War	35	75	125		Union General
Tyler, Edward Burnett	Science	15	35	50		
Tyler, Gerald E.	Aviation	15		40	30	ACE WWII
Tyler, John 1790-1862	President	400	750	1,200		
Tyler, Judy	Ent	10			20	
Tyler, Julia Gardiner	First Lady	200	450		650	
Tyler, Liv	Ent	25			50	
Tyler, Moses Coit	Author	10		25		Am. Historian
Tyler, Robert 1816-77	Military	100		250		President's Son. Mex War
Tyler, Robert C.	Civil War	250	500	800		CSA General
Tyler, Royall	RevWar	25	50	100		Jurist/Author
Tyler, Tom	Ent	100	200		200	GWTW...Phantom
Tyndale, Hector	Civil War	35	55	75	150	Union General/1821-80
Tyndall, John 1820-93	Science	50	125	150		Physicist/Philosopher
Tyner, James N.	Political	15	40	75		P. M. General 1876
Tyner, McCoy	Music	10	20		30	Jazz Pianist-Composer
Tyson, Cicely	Ent	10		30	20	
Tyson, Mike	Sports	30			75	Boxer

U

Name	Field	SIG	DS	ALS	SP	Remarks
U-2	Music	75			175	Signed by entire group
Udet, Ernst 1896-1941	Aviation	225	375	450	500	WWI German ACE
Ueberroth, Peter	Business	10	25	25	15	
Uggams, Leslie	Ent	10	20		20	
Ullman, Liv	Ent	15		40	35	
Ullman, Tracey	Ent	25			50	
Umberto I	Royalty	60	150	275		King Italy
Umeki, Miyoshi	Ent	200			400	
Underwood, Blair	Ent	15			25	
Underwood, J. T.	Science	45	125	200		Underwood Typewriter
Undset, Sigrid 1882-1949	Author	100			300	Nobel Prize Winner
Unger, Jim	Cartoonist	15			25	Henry
Ungher, Caroline 1803-77	Music	50		150		Opera
Unitas, Johnny	Sports	15			45	1979 Football HOF
Unreal, Minerva	Ent	25			60	
Untermeyer, Louis	Author	20	40	75	25	Am. Poet/Critic
Updike, John	Author	25	75	125	45	Am. Novelist
Upjohn, E. Gifford, Dr.	Business	125	250			Upjohn Pharmaceuticals
Upshaw, Dawn	Music	10			25	Opera
Upshur, Abel Parker	Political	25	50	75		Tyler Sec'y Navy
Upton, Emory	Civil War	25	50	75		Union General/1839-81
Urbanowicz, Witold A.	Aviation	35	70	125	60	WWII Polish ACE
Urey, Harold C. 1893-81	Science	100		350		Nobel in Chemistry 1934
Urich, Robert	Ent	10	25		30	
Uris, Leon	Author	30	75	125	65	Am. Novelist
Urso, Camilla	Music	25			40	Fr. Violinist
Urvanowicz, Witold A.	Aviation	25		75	50	WWII Polish ACE
Usher, John P.	Political	40	90	175		Sec'y Interior 1863-65
Ustinov, Peter	Ent	25	65		65	AA Actor/Author
Utrillo, Maurice 1833-55	Art	450	550	650		Fr. Paris Scenes

Name	Field	SIG	DS	ALS	SP	Remarks
Vaccaro, Brenda	Ent	5	20	15	10	
Vadim, Roger	Ent	20			50	
Vague, Vera	Ent	35			65	Disney Voice
Valdengo, Giuseppe	Music	15			40	Opera
Vale, Virginia	Ent	15			35	
Valens, Richie	Music	450			900	
Valenti, Jack	Ent	5	10		15	Pres/Motion Pix Assoc.
Valentine, Karen	Ent	10	20		20	Room 222
Valentine, Lewis	Political	35	75		50	
Valentino, Rudolph	Ent	900	1,500		2,000	
Valenzuela, Fernando	Sports	10			25	Baseball
Valery, Paul A, 1871-45	Author	50	100	150		Poet/Philosopher
Valette, A.J.M.	Military	25		75		French Revolution
Valetti, Cesare	Music	25			50	Opera
Vallandigham, Clement	Civil War	125		250		Civil War Copperhead
Vallee, Rudy	Ent	15	35	45	35	1901 - 1986
Vallejo, Mariano G.	Military	150	350			
Valli, Frankie	Music	15			45	
Valli, Virginia	Ent	15			40	Films From 1915-1931
Van Allan, Richard	Music	10			25	Opera
Van Allen, James	Science	40	100	200	100	Nobel Physics
Van Ark, Joan	Ent	5	15		15	
Van Buren, Abigail	Author	10	20	30	20	Am. Syndicated Columnist
Van Buren, Angelica	First Lady	RARE	RARE	RARE	RARE	
Van Buren, Hannah	First Lady	RARE	RARE	RARE	RARE	
Van Buren, Martin	President	350	900	900		1782 - 1862
Van Buren, Raeburn	Cartoonist	10			30	Abbie & Slats
Van Cleef, Lee	Ent	25			45	
Van Dam, Rip 1662-1736	Political	75	175	300		Colonial Governor
Van Devanter, Willis	SuprCt	50	125	150	75	
Van Dine, S.S.	Author	50	100	150	2,000	Created Philo Vance
Van Dongen, Kees	Art	30	45	90		Fauvist Painter
Van Doren, Carl	Author	15	45	75	25	Pulitzer in Biography
Van Doren, Mamie	Ent	10		25	25	
Van Doren, Mark 1894-73	Author	10	50	45	25	Poetry/Pulitzer
Van Dorn, Earl	Civil War	350		RARE	RARE	CSA General/Assasinated
Van Dorn, Earl 1820-63	Civil War	250		700		CSA General/Assasinated
Van Dresser, Marcia	Ent	15			40	
Van Druten, John W.	Author	10	20	35	15	Novelist/Playwright
Van Dyck, M, Ernest	Music	15	25		40	Tenor
Van Dyke, Dick	Ent	15	40		35	Dick Van Dyke Show
Van Dyke, Henry 1852-33	Political	25	50	75		

Name	Field	SIG	DS	ALS	SP	Remarks
Van Dyke, Jerry	Ent	10	20		20	Coach
Van Dyke, Nicholas	RevWar	125	250	450		Statesman/1738-89
Van Fleet, James, Gen.	Military	25	65	75	45	Gen. WWII
Van Fleet, Jo	Ent	15	20	40	35	AA Winner
Van Halen	Music	50			100	Signed by Four members
Van Halen, Alex	Music	20			50	Van Halen Musical Group
Van Halen, Eddie	Music	25	75		50	
Van Heusen, James	Music	50	75	150	75	Composer
Van Hoften, James D.	Space	10			20	Astronaut
Van Horne, David	RevWar	20		75		
Van Kirk, Theodore	Aviation	50	85		100	
Van Loon, Hendrik W.	Author	15	40	60	40	Historian/Journalist
Van Loon, William	Author	15		50		Journalist
Van Patten, Dick	Ent	5	20	20	15	Eight is Enough
Van Patten, Joyce	Ent	5			15	
Van Sloon, Edward	Ent	125			250	
Van Stade, Frederica	Music	15			45	Opera
Van Sweringen, Otis P.	Business	15	45	75	35	
Van Vechten, Carl	Author	40		150	75	Am. Novelist
Van Vleck, John H., Dr.	Science	30	50	75		Nobel Physics 1977
Van Vliet, Stewart	Civil War	50		200		Union General/1815-1901
Van Wyck, Charles Henry	Civil War	40	75	100		Union General/1824-95
Van Zandt, Philip	Ent	50			150	
Van Zant, Ronnie	Music	35			75	
Van Zealand, Paul	Political	15			35	Premier Belgium
Van, Bobby	Ent	10			20	
Van, Gloria	Ent	5			15	
Vance, A.T., Capt.	Aviation	15	25		35	Record Polar Flight
Vance, Cyrus	Political	10	20	35	25	Sec'y State/Sec'y Army
Vance, Jack	Author	10		20	15	Sci-Fi Writer
Vance, Louis Joseph	Author	15	35	65		Am. Novelist
Vance, Robert Brank	Civil War	75	150	225		CSA General/1828-1899
Vance, Vivian	Ent	150	200		225	I Love Lucy/Ethel
Vance, Zebulon Baird	Civil War	175		450		Gov NC/Opposed Davis
Vandamme, Dominique	Military	75	150	200		Battle of Waterloo
Vandamme, Jean-Claude	Ent	25			50	
Vandenberg, Hoyt S.	Aviation	25			75	
Vander Pyl, Jean	Ent	10			20	Voice/Wilma Flintstone ...
Vanderbilt, Alfred G.	Business	15	35	65	25	
Vanderbilt, Amy	Author	15	25	40	35	Authority on Manners
Vanderbilt, Cornelius	Business	600	2,000	3,500	3,000	Financier/1794-1877
Vanderbilt, Cornelius, Jr.	Business	200	750	1,500	450	Journalist/1843-1899
Vanderbilt, George W.	Business	200	500	900	350	Biltmore House/1862-1914
Vanderbilt, Gloria	Business	20	45	65	35	Fashion Designer
Vanderbilt, Jacob H.	Business	500	1,500	2,500		Brother of Cornelius
Vanderbilt, William H.	Business	250	750	1,500	500	Railroad Executive
Vanderbilt, William K.	Business	200	550	1,200	400	RR Exec/Financier

Name	Field	SIG	DS	ALS	SP	Remarks
Vandergrift, Alexander	Military	50	75	125	60	Marine Corps Gen. WWII
Vanderlyn, John 1775-52	Art	250		550		Am. Pres. Portraits
VanDien, Caspar	Ent	20			40	
Vane, John R., Dr.	Science	20		50	25	Nobel Medicine 1982
Vaness, Carol	Music	15			35	Opera
Vanili, Milli	Music	30			65	Both Signed
Vanilla Ice	Music	20			40	
Vanity	Ent	10			25	
Vanzetti, Bartolomeo	Criminal	600	1,500	RARE	RARE	Convicted Murderer
Varese, Edgard	Music	200	400	575		
Vargas, Alberto	Art	150		350	250	
Vargas, Getuilio	Political	50	100		75	Revolutionary Pres. Brazil.
Varick, Richard	RevWar	75	150	200		Soldier
Varmus, Harold E., Dr.	Science	25	50		35	Nobel Medicine 1989
Varney, Astrid	Music	10			25	Opera
Varney, Jim	Ent	10			20	
Vasarely, Victor	Art	40	125			
Vasquez, Roberta	Ent	5			15	Playboy Centerfold
Vassar, Matthew	Business	200	750	1,500		Founder Vassar College
Vaughan, Benjamin	Political	200	1,000			Br. Diplomat/1751-1835
Vaughn, Alfred J.	Civil War	100		300		CSA General/1830-99
Vaughn, George A.	Aviation	35	55	95	65	WWII ACE
Vaughn, John C.1824-75	Civil War	100	200			CSA General
Vaughn, Robert	Ent	15	25		25	Man from UNCLE
Vaughn, Sarah	Music	50	75	150	125	Jazz Vocalist-Pianist
Vaughn, Stevie Ray	Music	150			300	Died in air crash
Vaughn, Vince	Ent	20			40	Psycho re-make
Vaughn-Williams, Ralph	Music	75	200	350	150	
Vedrines, Jules	Aviation	175	300		275	
Vee, Bobby	Music	5			15	
Veidt, Conrad 1893-1950	Ent	75	150		250	
Velez, Lupe 1908 - 1944	Ent	70	125	200	175	Mexican Spitfire
Venable, Evelyn	Ent	65			85	Disney Voice
Vendela	Ent	20			45	SuperModel/Actress
Vendome, L.J., Duke de	Military	150		450		Marshal of France
Ventura, Charlie	Music	25			75	Bandleader
Vera Ellen	Ent	20			45	Dancer
Verdi, Giuseppe	Music	1,200	1,500	2,400	RARE	Composer/1813-1901
Verdin, James, Lt.Cdr.	Aviation	10	25			
Verdon, Gwen	Ent	5		20	15	
Verdugo, Elena	Ent	15			30	The Wolfman
Verdy, Violette	Music	10			30	Opera
Vereen, Ben	Ent	10			20	
Vereshchagin, Vassili V.	Art	50		150		Paintings of Russian Wars
Vergennes, Chas. G.,Le	Political	175	300			Fr Ambassador
Verlaine, Paul 1844-96	Author	175		500		Fr. Symbolist Poet
Vermehren, Werner	Aviation	20	35	55	60	Ger. Capt. WWI Zeppelin

Name	Field	SIG	DS	ALS	SP	Remarks
Verne, Jules 1828-1905	Author	250	650	900	RARE	20K Leagues Under Sea...
Vernier, Theodore	Military	35	100			French Revolution
Vessey, John W.	Military	10			30	
Vetch, Samuel 1668-1732	Political	100	225	400		Colonial Governor
Veverka, Jaroslav	Music	20			45	Opera
Vezzani, Cesare	Music	50			150	Opera
Vickers, Jon	Music	25			50	Opera
Victor and Mussolinni	Royalty		600			Signed by Both
Victor Emmanuel I	Royalty		350			King of Sardinia
Victor Emmanuel II	Royalty	100	250	450		
Victor Emmanuel III	Royalty	40				King Italy 1900-46
Victor, Claude Perrin	Military	125		150		Marshal of Napoleon
Victoria, Duchess/Kent	Royalty			125		Mother of Queen Victoria
Victoria, Empress	Royalty	45		125		Eldest Daughter of Queen
Victoria, Mary Louisa	Royalty	45	125	175		Mother of Q. Victoria
Victoria, Queen 1819-01	Royalty	175	350	550	900	Great Britain etc.
Victors, Henry	Ent	75			200	
Vidal, Gore	Author	10	20	30	20	Am. Novelist/Playwright
Vidor, Florence	Ent	40	35	65	60	
Vidor, King 1894-1982	Ent	30			100	AA Winning Director
Viele, Egbert L.	Civil War	25	40	55	65	Union General/1825-1902
Vigneaud, Vincent du	Science	10	25	45	25	
Vilas, William F.	Political	15	30	45	35	PM General
Viljoenk, B.J.	Military	35		125		
Villa, Francesco	Military	900	1,500	2,500	3,500	Pancho Villa
Villa-Lobos, Heitor	Music	100	200	400	250	Composer/1887-1959
Villechaize, Herve	Ent	45	75		75	Tatoo/Fantasy Island
Villepique, John B.	Civil War	250		550		CSA General/1830-62
Villiers, Frederic	Art	10		35	25	
Vinay, Ramon	Music	75			200	Opera
Vincent, Gene	Music	175			300	
Vincent, Jan-Michael	Ent	10		20	20	
Vincent, Thomas M.	Civil War	30	55	100		Union General/1832-1909
Vinci, Leonardo da	Art	RARE	RARE	RARE	RARE	
Vinson, Carl 1883-1991	Political	25	45		75	
Vinson, Frederick M.	SuprCt	75	150	300	300	Chief Justice
Vinson, Helen	Ent	15		40	35	
Vinton, Bobby	Music	5			15	
Vinton, David 1803-73	Civil War	125	250			Union General/First POW
Virchow, Rudolf 1821-02	Science	250				Founder Cellular Pathology
Vishinsky, Andrei	Political	75		150	125	
Visitor, Nana	Ent	15			35	Star Trek/Deep Space Nine
Vittor, Frank	Art	45		125		
Vivian, Richard H. Sir	RevWar	50	125	250		
Vlaminck, Maurice de	Art	125	200	450	325	Fr. Fauvist Painter
Voelker, John D.	Author	5		15	15	
Voight, Deborah	Music	10			25	Opera

Name	Field	SIG	DS	ALS	SP	Remarks
Voight, Jon	Ent	10	30		30	AA Winner
Voisin, Gabriel	Aviation	75	125	225	125	Fr. Airplane Mfg. Pioneer
Vokes, Christopher	Military	15		40	25	
Volkov, Vladislav	Space	75			150	Cosmonaut
Voll, John J.	Aviation	20	45	75	50	WWII ACE
Volstead, Andrew J.	Political	75	150	200		1860-1947
Volta, Alessandro	Science	600	1,400	2,500	RARE	Volt Unit Named for Him
Voltaire, Francois M.	Author	500	1,400	RARE	RARE	Fr. Writer/Philosopher
Von Behr, Henrich	Military	15			30	
Von Braun, Magnus	Science	15			45	Rocket Pioneer
Von Braun, Wernher	Science	150	400	550	400	German Rocket Pioneer
Von Bulow, H.	Music	20		65		German Pianist
Von Debizka, Hedwig	Music	40			150	Opera
Von der Chevaerie	Military	15			40	
Von Edelsheim, M.	Military	20			45	Panzer General
Von Gazen, Waldemar	Military	20			50	Panzer General
Von Gronau, Wolfgang	Aviation	200			500	WWI German ACE
Von Hesse-Nassau, A.	Royalty	100	200	300		Ist Duke of Luxembourg
Von Kleist, Paul	Military	50	100		100	German WWII Tank Comdr.
Von Kretchmer, Otto	Military	45	100			Top German U-Boat Cmdr. WWII
Von Oy, Jenna	Ent	15			35	Blossom/Six
Von Papen, Franz	Military	100	150	250	175	
Von Paulus, Friedrich	Military	175	350			Ger. WWII Field Marshal
Von Sauken, Dietrich	Military	25			75	Panzer General
Von Sternberg, Joseph	Ent	30	75		45	Director
Von Stroheim, Erich	Ent	150			450	Director
Von Tilzer, Albert	Music	30		150	45	Founder ASCAP
Von Trapp, Maria	Music	40	125	200	85	Sound of Music Fame
Von Zell, Harry	Ent	10		25	25	Radio Announcer
Vonnegut, Kurt, Jr.	Author	20	40		50	
Voronoff, Serge 1866-51	Science	25			50	
Vorster, Balthazar J.	Political	25	60	125	55	Prime Minister South Afr.
Voslo, Arnold	Ent	20			50	The Mummy/Darkman II
Vosseller, Aurelius B.	Military	35	75			
Vraciu, Alex	Aviation	15	25	50	35	WWII ACE
Vuillard, Edouard 1868-49	Art	150	300	450		French Painter

Name	Field	SIG	DS	ALS	SP	Remarks
Wachtel, Theodor	Music			195		Opera
Wade, Benjamin F.	Political	50	100	150		OH Senator
Wade, Leigh	Aviation	30	75	100	45	Pilot'24 Round The World
Wadopian, Eliot	Music	10			25	Bassist
Wadsworth, James S.	Civil War	50	100	200		Union General/1807-64
Wadsworth, Jeremiah	RevWar	150	300	450		Army Officer/1743-1804
Waesche, R.R.	Military	20	50			US Coast Guard Command
Wafterson, Henry 1840-21	Author	25		75	100	CSA Army/Pulitzer
Waggoner, Lyle	Ent	10			25	Carol Burnett Show
Wagner, Jane	Author	10			20	Playwright
Wagner, Lindsay	Ent	10	20		25	Bionic Woman
Wagner, Richard	Music	1,200	1,600	2,500	3,000	Composer/1813-1883
Wagner, Robert	Ent	15		25	35	Hart to Hart
Wagner, Robert F.	Political	30	75	125	50	1877-1953
Wagoner, Porter	Music	10			20	
Wahlberg, Mark	Ent	20			40	Marky-Mark
Wainwright, James	Ent	5			15	Actor
Wainwright, Jonathan	Military	100	225	250	225	Gen. WW II
Waite, H. Roy	Aviation	15	25	40		
Waite, Morrison R.	SuprCt	50	75		65	Chief Justice SuprCt
Waite, Ralph	Ent	5		20	15	
Wakely, Jimmy	Music	45			100	
Waksman, Selman A.	Science	45	75	100	75	Nobel Medicine 1952
Walburn, Raymond	Ent	15		45	35	
Walcott, Charleis F.	Civil War	15		45		Union Officer
Walcutt, Charles C.	Civil War	30		75		Union General/1838-98
Wald, George	Science	15	30	50	25	Nobel Medicine 1967
Wald, Jerry	Music	15	25		45	Bandleader
Wald, Lillian D. 1867-40	Political	30	60		50	Reformer
Waldheim, Kurt	Political	15	65	100	40	Prime Minister Austria
Waldo, Janet	Ent	5			15	Voice Judy Jetson...
Waldron, Hicks B.	Business	5			10	CEO Heublein Inc.
Walesa, Lech	Political	25	75		100	President of Poland
Walgreen, Charles R.	Business	35	75	100		Fndr. Walgreens
Walken, Christopher	Ent	20			50	
Walker, Alice	Author	25			50	The Color Purple
Walker, Benjamin	RevWar	100	250			Rev. Army Officer
Walker, Clint	Ent	20			35	Western TV Star
Walker, Francis Amasa	Civil War	45	90	145		Union General/1840-97
Walker, Frank C.	Political	5	15		10	P.M. General 1940
Walker, James J.	Political	25	60		45	Mayor NYC
Walker, Jimmy	Ent	10	20		20	Good Times

Name	Field	SIG	DS	ALS	SP	Remarks
Walker, John Brisben	Author	10	30			Editor Cosmopolitan
Walker, John George	Civil War	75	150	225		CSA General/1822-93
Walker, Leroy Pope	Civil War	250	400	600		CSA General/1817-84
Walker, Mary E. 1832-19	Civil War	300		550	RARE	Union Nurse/Surgeon
Walker, Mort	Cartoonist	15			35	Beetle Bailey
Walker, Nancy	Ent	30	40		45	Rhoda
Walker, Reuben L.	Civil War	100		250		CSA General/1827-90
Walker, Robert J.	Political	25	75	125		Polk Sec'y Treasury
Walker, Robert, Sr.	Ent	50		150	150	
Walker, T. Bone	Music	45			85	Jazz Guitar-Vocalist
Walker, Walton H.	Military	30	55	75	50	Gen./Killed in Korea 1950
Walker, William S.	Civil War	100		250		CSA General/1822-90
Walker, Wm Henry T.	Civil War	150	350	475		CSA General/KIA
Wallace, Alfred R.	Science	75	150	400		Theory of Evolution
Wallace, Dee	Ent	5		20	15	
Wallace, Edgar 1875-32	Author	75	225	300	350	
Wallace, Henry A.	Vice Pres	50	125	150	100	FDR V.P.
Wallace, Irving	Author	25	100	150	75	Am. Novelist
Wallace, Jean	Ent	10		20	25	
Wallace, John	Civil War	100	300			
Wallace, Lewis Lew	Civil War	150	300	450		Union General
Wallace, Marjorie	Ent	10			20	Miss USA/Actress
Wallace, Mike	Ent	5		20	15	60 Minutes
Wallace, William H.	Civil War	100	250			CSA General/1827-1905
Wallach, Eli	Ent	5	20		20	Batman villian "Mr.Freeze"
Wallburg, Donnie	Music	15			45	Marky Mark
Wallenda, Karl 1905-78	Ent	150	250		400	Flying Wallendas Circus
Wallenstein, Alfred, Dr.	Music	25			75	Conductor
Waller, Littleton	Military	100				Marine General 1880-1920
Waller, Thomas Fats	Music	125	275	RARE	400	Jazz Pianist/1904-43
Walley, Deborah	Ent	5		15	30	
Wallis, Barnes, Sir	Aviation	35	75			Br. Aircraft Designer
Wallis, Hal	Ent	20	45		40	Producer
Wallis, Ruth	Ent	10			25	
Walpole, Horace 1717-97	Author	150	450	900		Br. Novelist
Walpole, Hugh Seymour	Author	35	90	125		Novelist/Playwright
Walpole, Robert, Sir	Political	75		300		Prime Minister
Walsh, Blanche	Ent	15			35	
Walsh, John	Ent	5			10	Fox TV Host
Walsh, Kenneth	Aviation	15	25	50	35	WWII ACE
Walsh, M. Emmet	Ent	5			15	
Walsh, Raoul	Ent	35			75	Director
Walsh, Thomas J.	Political	15	40		25	1859-1933
Walston, Ray	Ent	15	25		30	My Favorite Martian
Walter, Bruno	Music	75		150	375	German Conductor
Walter, Jessica	Ent	10			15	
Walters, Barbara	Ent	10		20	20	TV Anchor

Name	Field	SIG	DS	ALS	SP	Remarks
Walters, Julie	Ent	5		20	15	
Walthall, Edward C.	Civil War	100	150	250		CSA General/1831-98
Walthall, Henry B.	Ent	25		55	65	
Walton, Ernest T.S.,Dr.	Science	75				Nobel Physics 1951
Walton, George 1740-04	RevWar	350	650	950		Signer
Walton, Sam M.	Business	50			80	Wal-Mart
Walton, William, Sir	Music	75		200	150	Composer/1902-83
Waltrip, Darrell	Sports	5			15	Auto Racing
Wambaugh, Joseph	Author	10		35	25	Novelist/Amercian
Wanamaker, John	Business	45	60	150	100	Department Store Pioneer
Wanger, Walter 1894-68	Ent	30	45			Producer
Wapner, Jos. A., Judge	Ent	5			15	TV Judge
War	Music	30			75	Signed by Entire Group
Ward, Aaron	Military	15	35	50		General/War of 1812
Ward, Artemas	Author	15	35	60	25	Humorist
Ward, Artemas 1727-00	RevWar	350	1,500			RevWar Commander
Ward, Burt	Ent	15	25		25	TV's Batman/Played Robin
Ward, David	Music	10			35	Opera
Ward, Henry 1732-97	RevWar	150	350	700		
Ward, Henry A.	Business	40		125		Merchant
Ward, J.H. Hobart	Civil War	35	60	75		Union General
Ward, John Q. Adams	Art	25	75	100	45	Am. Sculptor/1830-1910
Ward, Joseph, Sir	Political	15	25	60		PM New Zealand
Ward, Rachel	Ent	10			25	
Ward, Richard 1689-1763	Political	20	35			Colonial Governor of RI
Ward, Samuel 1725-1776	RevWar		550	775		Patriot/Merchant
Ward, Sela	Ent	15			30	
Warden, Jack	Ent	5			15	
Warfield, David	Ent	35	50	75	75	
Warfield, Marsha	Ent	10			25	Night Court
Warfield, William	Music	15			45	Baritone
Warhol, Andy 1930-87	Art	150	250	475	275	
Waring, Fred	Music	15	40		25	Big Band
Warner, Adoniram J.	Civil War	25		100		Union General/1834-1910
Warner, Charles Dudley	Author	20	65	100		1829-1911
Warner, H.B.	Business	40	125		125	Warner Brothers
Warner, Harry M.	Business	100	175		150	Fndr. Warner Bros.
Warner, Jack L.	Business	75	175		150	Fndr. Warner Bros)
Warner, Malcolm Jamal	Ent	15	30		30	Cosby Show
Warner, Seth 1743-84	RevWar	250				
Warnow, Mark	Music	10			25	Big Band Leader
Warrant	Music	45			80	Signed by Entire Group
Warren, Chas. Marquis	Author	5		25	10	
Warren, Earl 1891-1974	SuprCt	75	165		250	Chief Justice, Governor CA
Warren, Gouverneur K.	Civil War	125	250	400		Union General/1830-82
Warren, Harry	Music	25	75		50	Composer
Warren, James 1726-08	RevWar	125	350	750		Patriot/Merchant

Name	Field	SIG	DS	ALS	SP	Remarks
Warren, Jennifer	Music	10			25	
Warren, Joseph 1741-75	RevWar	6,000	RARE	RARE	RARE	Patriot/Doctor
Warren, Joseph, Sr.	Political	50	125	175		Colonial
Warren, Lavinia	Ent	75			225	Mrs.Tom Thumb
Warren, Leonard	Music	75			275	Opera
Warren, Leslie Ann	Ent	15	25		30	
Warren, Michael	Ent	5			15	
Warren, Robert Penn	Author	35	100	125	75	Am. Poet
Warren, Russell 1783-60	Science	35		150		Architect
Warren, William 1812-88	Ent	10		25		
Warrick, Ruth	Ent	10		20	25	
Warsitz, Erich	Aviation	15	35	45	45	
Washburn, Cadwallader	Civil War	45	75		85	Union General/1818-82
Washburne, Elihu B.	Political	25	50	75		Minister France
Washington, Booker T.	Author	300	450	700	1,500	1856-1915
Washington, Bushrod	SuprCt	125	350	700		1762 - 1829
Washington, Denzel	Ent	25	60		50	
Washington, Dinah	Music	125			200	Vocalist
Washington, George	President	4,500	10,000	14,000		1732-99
Washington, John A.	Civil War	125		450		CSA Lt. Colonel General
Washington, Martha	First Lady	RARE	RARE	RARE	RARE	
Washington, Ned	Music	50			100	
Washington, William	Military	65	165	250		General/Patriot
Wasserman, Dale	Music	15		35	30	
Waterhouse, Benjamin	Science	250	600	1,650		Small Pox Vaccination
Waterhouse, J. W.	Art	15		50		
Waterhouse, Richard	Civil War	150	275	450		CSA General/1832-76
Waterman, F.D.	Business	75	200			Waterman Pen
Waters, Ethel 1896-1977	Music	55	100	125	150	Stormy Weather
Waters, Muddy	Music	100	200		275	Jazz Musician
Waterston, Sam	Ent	15	35		30	Law & Order
Watkins, Henry George	Explorer	125		300		
Watson, Harold F.	Aviation	10	30	45	25	
Watson, J. Crittenden	Civil War	25	60	90		Union Commodore
Watson, James D., Dr.	Science	30	40	50	35	Nobel Medicine 1962
Watson, R.J. Doc	Aviation	15	25	40	30	USAF WWII ACE
Watson, Thomas A.	Science	75	225	275	RARE	
Watson, Thomas J., Jr.	Business	100	550	1,250	200	Chairman IBM
Watt, James	Political	10		20	25	Controversial Sec'y Interior
Watt, James 1736-1819	Science	400	750	1,400		Inventor/Steam Engine
Watt, James, Jr.	Science	40	85	160		
Watterson, Bill	Cartoonist	25			55	Calvin & Hobbes
Watts, George Frederick	Art	75	150	300		Br. Painter & Sculptor
Watts, Thomas H.	Civil War	50				CSA Att'y Gen./1819-92
Waugh, Evelyn 1903-66	Author	45	150	225	75	Brideshead Revisited
Wavell, Archibald, Sir	Military	50	150	175	65	Br. Field Marshal
Wayans, Keenen Ivory	Ent	15			35	

Name	Field	SIG	DS	ALS	SP	Remarks
Wayne, Anthony 1745-96	RevWar	750	1,500	RARE	RARE	Mad Anthony" Wayne
Wayne, Carol	Ent	35		125	150	
Wayne, David	Ent	20	45		45	1914 - 1996
Wayne, Henry C. 1815-83	Civil War	100	200	275	250	CSA General
Wayne, James M.	SuprCt	100	200	350		
Wayne, John 1907-79	Ent	400	800	1,000	800	
Weare, Meshech 1713-86	RevWar	35	100			Pres. of New Hampshire
Weathers, Carl	Ent	10			20	
Weaver, Dennis	Ent	10			25	
Weaver, Doodles	Ent	20	20		30	
Weaver, James B.	Civil War	30		140		Union General/1833-1912
Weaver, Sigourney	Ent	20			50	Aliens movies
Webb, Alexander S.	Civil War	25		55		Union General/1835-1911
Webb, Beatrice Potter	Political	40	125			Reformer
Webb, Charles Henry	Author	10		30		
Webb, Clifton	Ent	35			65	1891 - 1966
Webb, Del	Business	10		25	30	Desert Inn Casino
Webb, Jack	Ent	45	75		100	Dragnet
Webb, Jimmy	Music	25	35		65	Composer
Webb, Richard	Ent	15			35	Capt. Midnight
Webb, Samuel B.	RevWar	125	300	450		1753-1807
Webb, Sidney	Political	35		75	150	Br. Economist
Webb, W.R. Spider	Aviation	15	30	45	35	WWII ACE in One Day
Webber, Andrew Lloyd	Music	75		RARE	175	Br. Musical Theatre
Weber (Joe) and Fields	Ent	75			150	Vaudeville Comedians
Weber, Joe 1867-1942	Ent	20		45	45	
Weber, Karl Maria von	Music	375	900	1,200		Composer
Webster, Ben	Music	125				Tenor Sax-Arranger
Webster, Daniel 1782-52	Political	100	250	350	475	
Webster, Jean	Author	15	45	95		Am. Novelist
Webster, Noah 1758-1843	Author	500	750	1,400		Am. Lexicographer
Webster, Paul Francis	Music	25	50	75	45	Composer
Wedell, Jimmie	Aviation	15	30	40	35	
Wedemeyer, Albert C.	Military	45	150		150	Gen.WWII
Weed, Marian	Music	20			50	Opera
Weede, Robert	Music	10			35	Opera
Weeks, John W.	Political	15	35	65		Sec'y War 1921
Weems, Ted	Music	20	30	50	45	Big Band Leader
Weidler, Virginia	Ent	15		20	25	1927 - 1968
Weikl, Bernd	Music	10			20	Opera
Weill, Kurt	Music	250	500	900	375	Composer/1900-1950
Weinberg, Steven, Dr.	Science	25	35		30	Nobel Physics 1979
Weinberger, Casper	Political	5		25	15	Sec'y HEW, Sec'y Defense
Weingartner, Felix von	Music	50		200	150	Austrian Conductor
Weir, Julian Alden	Art	50	125	250		Am. Impressionist
Weir, Robert Walter	Art	50	125	225		
Weisbart, David	Ent	15			35	Director-Producer

Name	Field	SIG	DS	ALS	SP	Remarks
Weiser, Jan Conrad	Military	250	750	1,400		French Revolution
Weisiger, David A.	Civil War	100	225			CSA General/1818-1899
Weissmuller, Johnny	Ent	150	300		400	Tarzan/1904-84
Weitzel, Godfrey	Civil War	50	100	150		Union General/1835-84
Weizman, Vera	First Lady	25	75		35	Widow of lst Pres. Israel
Weizmann, Chaim	Political	450	1,200	2,200	900	lst Pres. Israel
Welby, Amelia	Author	450		RARE	RARE	Poet
Welch, Raquel	Ent	15	45		35	
Weld, Tuesday	Ent	10		30	25	
Welden, Ben	Ent	10			25	
Weldon, Felix de	Art	75				Iwo Jima Memorial Statue
Welk, Lawrence	Music	10		35	25	
Weller, Peter	Ent	10	20	25	35	Robocop
Weller, Thomas H., Dr.	Science	25	35	50	30	Nobel Medicine 1954
Welles, Gideon 1802-78	Political	100	200	300	675	Sect of Navy
Welles, Orson 1915-85	Ent	125	450		350	QQ Winner
Welles, Sumner 1892-61	Political	25	75	100	55	Ambassador
Wellington, 1st Duke of	Political	175	250	375		Prime Minister
Wellman, Manly Wade	Author	35	100		75	
Wellman, Walter	Aviation	60	150	225	75	Aviator-Explorer-Writer
Wells, Kitty	Music	5			15	
Wells, Carolyn	Author	10	25	35	15	
Wells, Carveth	Author	20	45	90	35	Explorer, Author
Wells, Dawn	Ent	10	20		20	Mary Ann/Gilligans Island
Wells, H.G. 1866-1946	Author	175		400	750	War of the Worlds
Wells, Henry & Fargo, J.	Business	850	1,250			Wells Fargo
Wells, Henry & Fargo, W.	Business		1,500			Wells Fargo/Amer Express
Wells, Henry 1805-78	Business	300	750	1,500		Wells Fargo/Amer Express
Wells, Junior	Music	5			10	
Welty, Eudora	Author	35	100	175	100	Am. Novelist
Wendelin, Rudolph	Cartoonist	25			45	Smokey the Bear
Wendorf, E.G. Wendy	Aviation	10	25	40	30	WWII Navy ACE
Wendt, George	Ent	15	30		35	Norm on "Cheers"
Wenrich, Percy	Music	55	100			Composer
Wentworth, Benning	Political	100	250	450		1696-1770
Wentworth, John 1737-20	RevWar	100	225	300		
Wermuth, Arthur W.	Military	15	35	50	25	WWII Hero
Werner, Oskar	Ent	25		45	50	
Werrenrath, Reinald	Music	25		45	50	Opera
Wesley, John	Clergy	500		2,500		Methodist Founder
Wessel, Corydon M., Dr.	Military	45	85	150	65	Missionary China.WWII
Wesselowsky, Aless.	Music	50			150	Opera
Wesson, Daniel B.	Science	400				Gunsmith
West, Adam	Ent	10	25		25	TV's Batman
West, Benjamin 1738-20	Art	200	700	1,250		Am. Historical Painter
West, Dottie	Music	15			40	
West, F. H.	Civil War	40	100			Union Officer

Name	Field	SIG	DS	ALS	SP	Remarks
West, Jessamyn	Author	15	30	35	25	Novelist
West, Joseph R. 1822-98	Civil War	40	75			Union General
West, Mae 1892-1980	Ent	55	115		250	
West, Morris L.	Author	15	45	80	30	
West, Rebecca, Dame	Author	15	45	75		Br. Novelist
Westall, William	Art	15	45	95		
Westheimer, Ruth, Dr.	Science	5	15	25	15	Sex Therapist
Westinghouse, George	Business	300	900			Fndr. Westinghouse Co
Westinghouse, George	Business	500	1,500			Fndr Westinghouse Corp.
Westminster, 2nd Earl	Royalty	25	50			Robert Grosvenor
Westmore, Wally	Ent	25			50	Makeup Director
Westmoreland, Wm. C.	Military	25		75	65	Gen. Korea. Viet Nam
Weston, Edward 1850-36	Business	45	125	300	75	
Weston, Edward 1886-58	Art	35				Am. Western Photographer
Weston, Paul	Music	15			45	Bandleader/Arranger
Westover, Russ 1887-66	Cartoonist	20		40	35	Tillie The Toiler
Weygand, Maxime	Military	40	75	150	125	Fr. Gen./ Chief of Staff
Weyman, Stanley J.	Author	15	35	65		Br. Novelist
Whalen, Michael	Ent	15		35	30	
Wharton, Edith N.	Author	225	475	950		Age of Innocence/Pulitzer
Wharton, Gabriel C.	Civil War	80		175		CSA General/1824-1906
Wharton, John A.	Civil War	200	450	900		CSA General/1828-65
Wharton, Thomas	RevWar	125	275	450		Governor PA
Wheaton, Wil	Ent	25			50	Star Trek/Wesley
Wheatstone, Charles, Sir	Science	100	300	450		Br. Physicist, Inventor
Wheeler, Bert	Ent	25			75	Wheeler and Woolsey
Wheeler, Earle G.	Military	20			50	
Wheeler, Ellie	Ent	10		25	25	
Wheeler, Joseph	Civil War	275	750	1,250		CSA General/War Dated
Wheeler, Joseph	Civil War	125	300	350	950	CSA General/1836-1906
Wheeler, William A.	Vice Pres	75	225			Hayes VP
Whelan, Arleen	Ent	10		25	20	
Whelchel, Lisa	Ent	10			25	Facts of Life
Whipple, Abraham	RevWar	250	750			Fired First Gun in RevWar
Whipple, Amiel Weeks	Civil War	125	225	300		Union General/1816-63
Whipple, George H.	Science	50	75	150		Nobel Medicine !934
Whipple, William	RevWar	750		1,500		Signer Decl. of Ind.
Whipple, William D.	Civil War	25		50		Union General/1826-1902
Whirry, Shannon	Ent	10			25	
Whisner, William T.	Aviation	25	50	75	50	WWII ACE
Whistler, James McNeill	Art	300	450	600		Am. Painter
Whitaker, Johnnie	Ent	10			25	
White, Alice	Ent	25	45		75	
White, Anthony Walton	RevWar	55	150	250		Washington Aide de Camp
White, Betty	Ent	10	15	20	20	MTM/Golden Girls
White, Byron R.	SuprCt	55	125	150	75	
White, E.B.	Author	35	125			Charlotte's Web

Name	Field	SIG	DS	ALS	SP	Remarks
White, Edward D.	SuprCt	50	150	200	150	
White, Edward H.	Space	200	250	550	600	1st Am. To Walk In Space
White, George	Ent	60			100	
White, George Stuart	Military	40		75		Br.Fld.Marshal
White, Jesse	Ent	25	50		50	Harvey
White, Jim	Explorer	50		150		Discover Carlsbad Caverns
White, Josh	Music	65			225	Am. Folk Singer
White, Julius	Civil War	25	50	100		Union General/1816-90
White, Paul Dudley, Dr.	Science	45	100		80	Heart Specialist
White, Pearl	Ent	125		250	275	Silent Film
White, Robert, Maj.	Aviation	10	25		30	Speed & Altitude Record
White, Sanford	Science	100	200		150	
White, Stewart E.	Author	10	20	40	20	Am. Westernn Stories
White, Vanna	Ent	5		20	15	Wheel of Fortune
White, William Allen	Author	35	75	85	75	Pulitzer
White, Windsor T.	Business	125		350		Pioneer Auto-Truck Mfg,
Whitelaw, Billie	Ent	15			30	
Whiteman, Paul	Music	60		160	175	King of JAZZ
Whitestone, Heather	Ent	20			40	Miss America/1995
Whiting, Jack	Ent	5			15	
Whiting, John D.	Political	10		20		Jerusalem
Whiting, Margaret	Music	10			15	Vocalist
Whiting, Richard	Music	50		125	100	Composer
Whiting, William Henry	Civil War	200				CSA General/1824-65
Whitlam, Gough	Political	10			25	Prime Minister Australia
Whitley, Ray	Music	10			35	Cowboy Movies
Whitman, Slim	Music	5			15	
Whitman, Walt 1819-92	Author	1,200	2,000	2,400	2,750	Am. Poet
Whitmore, James	Ent	5		20	15	
Whitney, Asa 1797-1872	Business	35		100		Transcontinental Railroad
Whitney, Casper	Business	10	25	35		Publisher
Whitney, Courtney	Military	15	40	75	35	WWII General
Whitney, Eli 1765-1825	Science	750	2,500	3,500	RARE	Am. Inventor Cotton Gin
Whitney, Grace Lee	Ent	15	25	30	25	Star Trek
Whitney, Josiah D.	Science	75		250		1819-1896
Whitney, Richard	Business	35	50			Pres. NY Stock Exchange
Whitney, William Collins	Political	20	45	65	35	1841-1904
Whittaker, Charles E.	SuprCt	50	75	150	85	
Whitten-Brown, Arthur	Aviation	250	375			Pioneer Aviator
Whittier, John Greenleaf	Author	100	250	350		Quaker Poet
Whittle, Frank, Sir	Aviation	15			45	
Whittlesey, Elisha	Political	15		45		Founder of Whig Party
Who, The	Music	350			600	Signed by Four Originals
Wickersham, George W.	Political	15	45	60	45	Taft Att'y Gen.
Wickes, Mary	Ent	20	30		30	
Wickham, William C.	Civil War	80	250			CSA General/1820-88
Wickliffe, Charles A.	Political	30	65	100		P.M. General

Name	Field	SIG	DS	ALS	SP	Remarks
Widmark, Richard	Ent	10		20	25	
Widor, Charles Marie	Music	65		150		Composer
Wieghorst, Olaf	Art	75	225	250	200	Dean of Western Art
Wiemann, Ernst	Music	10			20	Opera
Wiesel, Elie	Author	20	45	55	25	Nobel Peace Prize 1986
Wiesel, Torsten S., Dr.	Science	20	30	45	25	Nobel Medicine 1981
Wiesenthal, Simon	Political	20	45	90	35	Famed Nazi Hunter
Wiest, Diane	Ent	20	45		45	AA Winner
Wigfall, Louis T. 1816-74	Civil War	125	225			CSA General
Wiggin, Kate Douglas	Author	95		165	125	
Wigner, Eugene P. Dr.	Science	15	25	45	25	Nobel Physics 1963
Wihan, Hanus	Music	35		100		Czech Violinist/Cellist
Wilberforce, William	Political	50	145	250		Br. Anti-Slavery Politician
Wilbur, Curtis D,	Political	10	25	35	25	Sec'y Navy
Wilbur, Ray Lyman	Political	20	25	35	25	Sec'y Interior
Wilbur, Richard	Author	5		35	10	U.S. Poet Laureate
Wilcox, Cadmus M.	Civil War	100	200	300		CSA General/1824-90
Wilcox, Cadmus M.	Civil War	175	400			CSA General/War Dated
Wilcox, Ella Wheeler	Author	20	35	75		Journalist/Poet
Wilcoxon, Henry	Ent	20		35	45	
Wild, Edward A.	Civil War	75	150	200		Union General/1825-91
Wilde, Cornel	Ent	15	25	40	35	
Wilde, Oscar 1856-1900	Author	675	1,500	2,500	2,250	Ir. Poet/Playwright
Wilde, Percival	Author	25	50	100		Playwright/Novelist
Wilder, Billy	Ent	20	50		50	AA Winning Director
Wilder, Gene	Ent	15	30		30	Young Frankenstein
Wilder, Thornton	Author	75	150	350	200	Pulitzer/1897-1975
Wilding, Michael	Ent	30			55	
Wilhelm I (Ger) 1797- 88	Royalty	75	250	350		King of Prussia
Wilhelm II (Kaiser)(Ger)	Royalty	175	375	450	300	1859-1941
Wilhelmj, August	Music	25			75	German Violinist
Wilke, Robert J.	Ent	10			25	
Wilkerson, Guy	Ent	25			65	
Wilkes, Charles	Civil War	50	100	200		Union Admiral/1798-1877
Wilkes, Earle	Military	20			50	
Wilkie, David, Sir	Art	40	80	125		Br.Genre Paintings
Wilkins, Geo. Hubert,Sir	Explorer	30	50	90	55	1888-1958
Wilkins, Roy	Political	15	35	45	25	Statesman/Civil Rights
Wilkinson, Geoffrey	Science	15	25	40	25	Nobel Chemistry 1985
Wilkinson, James	RevWar	125	275	350		
Wilkinson, June	Ent	5		20	20	
Willard, Edward S.	Ent	15		35	30	
Willard, Frances E.	Political	40	65	125		Temperence Movement
Willard, Frank	Cartoonist	35			65	Moon Mullins
Willard, Fred	Ent	5			15	
Willard, John	Ent	10			25	Playwright
Willcox, Orlando B.	Civil War	40	75	150		Union General/1823-1907

Name	Field	SIG	DS	ALS	SP	Remarks
Willem VI & I, 1772-1848	Royalty		600			King Netherlands
Willett, Marinus 1740-30	RevWar	75	150	250		Cont. Army Officer
William III (Eng)	Royalty	650	1,400	2,250		
William IV (Eng) 1765-37	Royalty	100	300	400		The Sailor King
William, 4th Duke of	Political	75	175	300		Prime Minister 1756
William, Warren	Ent	10		40	45	
Williams, Andy	Music	20			45	
Williams, Barry	Ent	20	50			Brady Bunch
Williams, Ben Ames	Author	15	25	40	25	Am. Novelist
Williams, Bill	Ent	10			25	
Williams, Billy Dee	Ent	10	25		25	Empire Strikes Back
Williams, Cindy	Ent	5		20	20	Laverne and Shirley
Williams, Clarence	Ent	15			30	Mod Squad
Williams, Edward M.	Business	35	75	125		
Williams, Edy	Ent	10			20	
Williams, Esther	Ent	10		20	20	
Williams, George H.	Political	10	25	40		Attorney General
Williams, Grant	Ent	45			125	
Williams, Gus	Ent	10			25	Showman
Williams, Guy 1924-89	Ent	150	250		250	Zorro/Lost in Space
Williams, Hal	Ent	5			15	
Williams, Hank	Music	650	1,200		1,200	
Williams, Hank Jr.	Music	20	25		35	
Williams, JoBeth	Ent	10			25	
Williams, Joe	Music	15			40	Jazz Vocalist
Williams, John	Music	20	75		50	Composer/Conductor
Williams, Jr., Alford J.	Aviation	35	45	75	125	
Williams, Mary Alice	Author	10			20	TV News Journalist
Williams, Mason	Music	10			20	Guitar Soloist
Williams, Otho	RevWar	150	400	600		1749 - 1800
Williams, Paul	Music	10			20	
Williams, Robin	Ent	20	50		50	
Williams, Roger	Music	10			35	Pianist
Williams, Roy	Ent	10			20	
Williams, Seth 1822-66	Civil War	35	65	85		Union General
Williams, Spencer	Ent	10			20	
Williams, Tennessee	Author	150	300	475	350	Cat on a Hot Tin Roof
Williams, Tex	Music	10			20	Big Band
Williams, Treat	Ent	10	20	25	20	
Williams, Van	Ent	15	25		25	TV's Green Hornet
Williams, Vanessa	Ent	25			50	Miss America
Williams, William	RevWar	300	450	600		Signer Decl. of Indepen.
Williams, William Carlos	Author	275			300	Am. Poet/Novelist
Williamson, Fred	Ent	10			20	
Willing, Foy	Music	10			20	(Riders of the Purple Sage)
Willing, Thomas	RevWar	75	200			Banker/Cont. Congress
Willis, Bruce	Ent	35	125		65	Tough Signer

Name	Field	SIG	DS	ALS	SP	Remarks
Willis, Nathaniel P.	Author	20	45	75		1806-67
Willkie, Wendell	Political	35	75		125	Pres. Candidate
Wills, Bob	Music	75			200	
Willson, Meredith	Music	25	75	125	80	Composer/The Music Man
Willys, John North	Business	60	100	125	90	Auto Pioneer, Diplomat
Wilson, Brian	Music	40			85	Beach Boys
Wilson, Bridget	Ent	10			30	
Wilson, Charles E.	Business	20	35	70	30	Pres. GM./Sec'y Defense
Wilson, Charles Edward	Business	20	75			Pres. General Electric
Wilson, Demond	Ent	25			45	Sanford and Son
Wilson, Dennis	Music	35			75	Beach Boys
Wilson, Dooley	Ent	400	500		800	Casablanca Sam
Wilson, Edith Bolling	First Lady	100	200	250	200	1872-1961
Wilson, Edmund	Author	25	75	150		
Wilson, Edmund B.	Science	350	450			Am. Biologist
Wilson, Ellen Louise	First Lady	100	300	550		1st Wife - Pres. Wilson
Wilson, Flip	Ent	25	50		50	
Wilson, Francis 1854-35	Ent	15			25	
Wilson, Gahan	Cartoonist	15			25	Magazine and Comic Book Artist
Wilson, Harold, Sir	Political	40	75		65	Br. Prime Minister
Wilson, Henry 1812-75	Vice Pres	85		125		Grant VP
Wilson, Jackie	Music	200	300		250	
Wilson, James 1742-98	SuprCt	700	900	1,400		Signer
Wilson, James 1835-1920	Political	25	50	75		Sec'y Agriculture 1897
Wilson, James G.	Civil War	100		275		Union General/1833-1914
Wilson, James H. 1837-25	Civil War	85	175	350		Union General Calvary
Wilson, Julie	Ent	15			35	
Wilson, Kemmons	Business	15	45		50	Founder Holiday Inn
Wilson, Lois	Ent	15		35	45	
Wilson, Marie	Ent	25	35	50	60	My Friend Irma Early TV
Wilson, Robert, Dr.	Science	15	25	35	25	Nobel Physics 1978
Wilson, Sloan	Author	15	35	50	25	Man in Grey Flannel Suit
Wilson, Teddy 1912-86	Music	40		75	100	Pianist-Arranger
Wilson, Tom	Cartoonist	10			30	Ziggy
Wilson, Woodrow	President	200	550	750	775	1856-1924
Winchell, Paul	Ent	10	25		35	Ventriloquist
Winchell, Walter	Author	35	40	45	45	1897-1972
Winchester, Oliver F.	Science	400	1,500	1,500		Winchester Repeating Arm
Winder, Charles S.	Civil War	RARE	RARE	RARE	RARE	CSA General/KIA
Winder, John Henry	Civil War	150		450		CSA General
Windgassen, Wolfgang	Music	15			45	Opera
Windsor, Claire	Ent	10			25	
Windsor, Duke/Duchess	Royalty	400			650	Edward & Wallis
Windsor, Marie	Ent	5	20	15	15	
Windsor, Wallis, Duchess	Royalty	125	250	450	175	
Winfield, Paul	Ent	15	30		35	Afr.-Am. Actor
Winfrey, Oprah	Ent	20			45	

Name	Field	SIG	DS	ALS	SP	Remarks
Wing, Toby	Ent	10		25	25	
Wingate, Francis R., Sir	Military	35	75	125	75	Gen. Succeeded Kitchener
Winger, Debra	Ent	15	50		45	
Winkler, Henry	Ent	5	20		20	The Fonz on "Happy Days"
Winner, Septimus	Music	100	200	350		Composer
Winninger, Charles	Ent	25		50	60	
Winningham, Mare	Ent	10			30	
Winslow, Edward	RevWar	25	50	100		Loyalist/1714-84
Winslow, John 1753-19	RevWar	25	50	100		Soldier/Hero
Winslow, John Ancrum	Military	100	275	375		Union Naval Officer
Winslow, John F.	Civil War	75	150	225		Builder of the Monitor
Winters, Jonathan	Ent	10	25	25	25	
Winters, Roland	Ent	30	45	75	75	Charlie Chan
Winters, Shelley	Ent	5	20		20	
Winthrop, John 1714-79	RevWar	200	600			Science
Winthrop, John, The	Political	800	1,600	RARE	RARE	Colonial Governor
Winthrop, Thomas L.	RevWar	25	50	90		Merchant
Winwood, Estelle	Ent	15	35		35	1883 - 1984
Wire, Calvin C.	Aviation	15		30	25	WWII ACE
Wirt, William 1772-1834	Political	40	90	125		Attorney General 1817
Wirz, Henry Hartmann	Civil War	600	RARE	RARE	RARE	CSA Officer
Wise, Henry A.	Civil War	100	200	250		CSA General/1806-76
Wise, Robert	Ent	15	30		30	Director
Wiseman, Joseph	Ent	35			65	Dr. No/James Bond film
Wister, Owen 1860-1938	Author	50	150	200	75	Novelist/The Virginian
Withers, Jane	Ent	10		25	20	Shirley Temple Sidekick
Withers, Robert E.	Civil War	25		75		CSA Colonel
Witherspoon, Jimmy	Music	15			30	Jazz Musician
Witherspoon, John	RevWar	600	1,500	RARE	RARE	Signer Decl. of Indepen.
Witte, Serge	Political	30		100		1st Premier of Russia
Wittig, Georg F.K.	Science	25	50		40	Nobel Chemistry 1979
Wixell, Ingvar	Music	20			45	Opera
Wodehouse, P. G.	Author	150		300	450	British Novelist
Wolcott, Derek	Author	15	20		25	Poet/Nobel
Wolcott, Oliver 1726-97	RevWar	200	450	1,200		Signer Decl. of Ind.
Wolcott, Oliver, Jr.	Political	75	250	350		Washington Sec'y Treas.
Wolf, Gary	Author	10			25	Who Framed Roger Rabbit?
Wolf, George	Political	35	75	150		Gov. PA 1829, Statesman
Wolf, Hugo 1860-1903	Music	250	RARE	RARE	RARE	Austrian Composer
Wolfe, James 1727-59	Military	1,500	RARE	RARE	RARE	Br.Gen/French/Indian War
Wolfe, Thomas 1900-38	Author	500	2,000	RARE	RARE	
Wolfe, Tom	Author	15	45	65	35	Am. Novelist
Wolff, Karl	Military	175		550		German SS General
Woll, Matthew	Political	20		75		Am. Labor Leader
Wolper, David	Ent	5			15	
Wolseley, Garnet J.	Military	25	75	100	35	Br.Field Marshal
Wolsey, Thomas	Political	RARE	7,500	RARE	RARE	Cardinal/Statesman

Name	Field	SIG	DS	ALS	SP	Remarks
Wonder, George	Cartoonist	15			35	Terry & The Pirates
Wonder, Stevie	Music	RARE	200	N/A	150	Only "Signs"w/Thumbprint
Wong, Anna May 1907-61	Ent	75	150	150	175	Chinese Film Star
Wood, Edward F.L.	Political	15	35	50	25	Diplomat/1881-1959
Wood, Evelyn, Sir	Military	20		55		Br.Fld.Marshal (Boer War)
Wood, Fernando 1812-81	Civil War	20	55	75		Civil War Mayor NYC
Wood, Garfield 'Gar'	Science	60		80	75	Boat Designer/Builder
Wood, Grant	Art	150	400	550		American Gothic
Wood, Haydn	Music	20	55	75	35	Composer
Wood, James 1750-1813	RevWar	50	75	125		Governor VA
Wood, Lana	Ent	10	20		25	James Bond Girl
Wood, Leonard, Dr.	Military	25	45	75	150	Roosevelt's Rough Riders
Wood, Murray	Ent	25	35		50	Munchkin in Wiz of Oz
Wood, Natalie 1938-81	Ent	150			400	Died Young
Wood, Peggy	Ent	20			35	
Wood, Robert	Space	5			15	Astronaut
Wood, Robert E.	Military	20	75			General WWII
Wood, Robert W.	Science	10	25		25	Manhatten Project
Wood, Sam	Ent	40			90	
Wood, Sterling Alex.	Civil War	100	200	300		CSA General
Wood, Thomas J.	Civil War	50	100	100		Union General/1823-1906
Wood, Thomas W.	Art	10	25	50		
Woodbury, Levi 1789-51	SuprCt	65	150	250		
Woodcock, Amos Walter	Military	10			20	General
Woodfill, Samuel	Military	10	30	50	25	WWI
Woodford, Stewart L.	Civil War	35	100	200		Union Officer/1835-1913
Woodhull, Victoria C.	Political	125	250	450		1870's Feminist
Woodring, Henry H.	Political	20	45	70	30	FDR Sect of War
Woods, Charles Robert	Civil War	30	50	75		Union General/1827-85
Woods, Donald	Ent	15	20	35	35	
Woods, James	Ent	20		25	45	
Woods, Phil	Music	15			45	Jazz Alto Sax-Clarinet
Woods, Rose Mary	Political	15		30		Nixon Sec'y. Watergate
Woods, William B.	SuprCt	40	85	150	125	
Woodward, Bob	Author	10	20	35	25	Watergate
Woodward, Edward	Ent	10	15	25	20	
Woodward, Joanne	Ent	15	40		30	AA Winner
Woodward, Robert Burns	Science	20	40	75	35	Nobel Chemistry 1965
Woodworth, Samuel	Author	50	150	275		
Wool, John E. 1789-1869	Civil War	100	200	350		Union General
Wooley, Sheb	Music	10			20	
Woolf, Virginia 1882-44	Author	450		1,500	RARE	British Novelist
Woolworth, Charles S.	Business	250	750	Scarce	Scarce	F.W. Woolworth Co.
Woolworth, Frank W.	Business	550	2,500	RARE	RARE	Fndr. F.W. Woolworth Co.
Woorinen, Charles	Music	10	25	40		Composer/Pulitzer
Wooster, David 1710-77	RevWar	250	600	RARE	RARE	General: Continental Army
Wopat, Tom	Ent	10			20	Dukes of Hazzard

Name	Field	SIG	DS	ALS	SP	Remarks
Worden, Hank	Ent	15				
Worden, John L.	Civil War	125	175	250		Union Naval Commander
Wordsworth, William	Author	225		1,200		Br. Poet Laureatte
Work, Hubert	Political	20	45	90	35	Sec'y Interior 1923
Worley, Jo Ann	Ent	5			15	Laugh In
Worth, Irene	Ent	10			25	
Worth, William J.	Military	35	75	125		General/Mexican War
Wouk, Herman	Author	45	100	150	125	Am. Novelist/Caine Mutiny
Wray, Fay	Ent	25			50	King Kong
Wren, Christopher	Science	1,500	RARE	RARE	RARE	
Wright, Bobby	Music	5			15	
Wright, Frank Lloyd	Science	900	1,550	RARE	RARE	Architect
Wright, Harold Bell	Author	25			50	Am. Novelist
Wright, Henry C.	Political	10	20	35		1797-1870
Wright, Horatio G.	Civil War	50	150	200		Union General/1820-99
Wright, Marcus J.	Civil War	125	150	175		CSA General/1831-1922
Wright, Orville 1871-1948	Aviation	500	1,250	1,750	2,000	
Wright, Richard	Author	75	225		375	
Wright, Robin	Ent	25	65		50	
Wright, Teresa	Ent	30			60	AA Winner
Wright, Turbutt 1741-83	RevWar	25	60	75		Continental Congress
Wright, Wilbur 1867-12	Aviation	775	2,000	5,000	4,500	
Wrigley, Philip K.	Business	75	150	200	150	Wrigley Gum; Chicago Cubs
Wrigley, William, Jr.	Business	150	350	400	350	Founder Wrigley Gum Mfg.
Wunderlich, Fritz	Music	150			400	Opera
Wunsche, Max	Military	50			125	Hitlers Adj/WWII
Wyant, Alexander H.	Art	100		300		
Wyatt, Jane	Ent	5			20	Spocks Mom/Star Trek
Wyeth, Andrew	Art	250	450	650	950	Am. Painter
Wyeth, Jamie	Art	125		300	300	Andrews Son
Wyeth, John A.	Science	75		250		Noted Surgeon
Wyeth, N. C. 1882-1945	Art	150	400	800		Am. Illustrator & Painter
Wyler, William	Ent	25	35		75	AA Winning Director
Wylie, Elinor	Author	65	125	250		Am. Poet/Novelist
Wylie, Noah	Ent	15			35	ER
Wylie, Robert 1839-1877	Art	50	150			
Wyllys, Samuel 1739-23	RevWar	20		45		Military. Sec'y State of CT
Wyman, Bill	Music	35		RARE	75	Rolling Stones Bassist
Wyman, Jane	Ent	15			35	
Wyman, Willard G.	Military	15	25	40	25	4 Star General WW II
Wyndham, Charles, Sir	Ent	15	35	45	60	1837-1919
Wynette, Tammy	Music	10			30	Country
Wynn, Ed	Ent	50	100		125	1886 - 1966
Wynn, Keenan	Ent	25	35		45	1916 - 1986
Wynter, Dana	Ent	5			15	
Wysong, Forrest R.	Aviation	10		30	20	
Wythe, George 1726-06	RevWar	450	650	RARE	RARE	Signer

Name	Field	SIG	DS	ALS	SP	Remarks
Xenia Alexandrova	Political	75		300		Russia

PIECE OF THE PAST

*MONTHLY(no min.bid)CATALOG/AUCTION

*WEEKLY Ebay AUCTIONS(piecepast2)

MONTHLY FIXED PRICE LISTS

9030 W.Sahara Dr.
Suite #448
LasVegas,NV.89117

Toll Free 888-689-7079

Over 15 Years Specializing in Entertainment...
*Autographs
*Props
*Costumes

Name	Field	SIG	DS	ALS	SP	Remarks
Yadin, Yigael	Science	55		85		Archaeologist
Yalow, Rosalyn S.	Science	15	25	40	25	Nobel Medicine 1972
Yamamoto, Isoroku	Military	150		450	475	Pearl Harbor Attack
Yamanashi, Hanzo	Military	100	250			
Yamashiro, Katsumari	Military	100			300	
Yamashita, Tomoyuki	Military	125	275	500	275	Jap. General. Hanged
Yang, Chen N.	Science	15	20	35	20	Nobel Physics 1957
Yang, Y. C.	Political	10			20	
Yankovic, Frank	Ent	5			10	
Yardbirds	Music	150	250		275	Entire Band Signed
Yarnell, Harry E.	Military	15	35		25	Adm. Fleet Commander
Yarnell, Lorine	Ent	5			10	Shields & Yarnell
Yates, Edmund 1831-94	Author	5		25		Br. Journalist-Novelist
Yates, Peter W., 1747-26	RevWar	45	125	175		Continental Congress
Yates, Richard 1815-73	Civil War	45	125	200		Civil War Governor IL 1861
Yaw, Ellen Beach	Music	45			175	Am. Soprano
Yeager, Chuck	Aviation	25	50	65	50	WWII ACE/Test Pilot
Yeager, Jeana	Aviation	15			35	
Yearwood, Trisha	Music	15			35	Country
Yeates, Jasper 1745-1817	RevWar	15	35	60		Jurist
Yeats, Jack Butler	Art	25	60	125		Brother/ Wm. Butler Yeats
Yeats, Wm. Butler	Author	200	600	900		Novelist/Poet
Yeltsin, Boris	Political	600	1,200			Russia
Yen, C.K.	Political	50	150			Pres. Republic China
Yeoh, Michelle	Ent	25			50	James Bond babe
Yerby, Frank G.	Author	35	75	150	45	Novelist
Yerkes, Charles	Business	35	100			Capitalist
Yes	Music	60	125		125	Signed by Entire Band
Yo Yo Ma	Music	25			45	Concert Cellist
Yokum, Dwight	Music	15			35	Country
York, Alvin, Sgt. 1887-64	Military	175	250	450	425	
York, Dick	Ent	25	60		50	Bewitched/Darren
York, Michael	Ent	10	25	25	25	Logans Run
York, Susanna	Ent	10			30	
Youmans, Vincent	Music	75	150	200	150	Composer/Tea for Two
Young, Alan	Ent	5	20	20	15	
Young, Art	Cartoonist	20			45	Political Cartoonist
Young, Brigham 1801-77	Clergy	650	1,500	RARE	RARE	Mormon Leader/Scarce
Young, Burt	Ent	10			20	
Young, Charles Augustus	Science	35	125	200		Am. Astronomer
Young, Chic 1901-73	Cartoonist	35			75	Blondie
Young, Clara Kimball	Ent	40			75	Vintage Stage Actress

Name	Field	SIG	DS	ALS	SP	Remarks
Young, David H.	Aviation	10	25		35	
Young, Faron	Music	5			15	
Young, Gig	Ent	30	50	75	75	1913 - 1978
Young, Henry E.	Civil War	25	45	70		CSA Officer
Young, John	Space	75			125	Moonwalker
Young, Lester	Music	75		150	150	JAZZ
Young, Loretta	Ent	20			45	
Young, Lyman	Cartoonist	10			25	Tim Tyler's Luck
Young, Neil	Music	25			50	
Young, Owen D. 1874-62	Business	15	25	35	20	
Young, Pierce M.B.	Civil War	100		300		CSA General/1836-96
Young, Robert	Ent	15			45	
Young, Roland	Ent	25			50	
Young, Samuel B.M.	Civil War	30	50	75		Union Officer
Young, Sean	Ent	15			35	
Young, Trummy	Music	15			45	Jazz Musician
Young, Whitney	Political	5	20	45	15	Am. Civil Rights Leader
Younger, Cole	Western	2,000		7,500		
Zadora, Pia	Ent	10			25	

Z

Name	Field	SIG	DS	ALS	SP	Remarks
Zane, Billy	Ent	25			50	Titanic/Phantom
Zanuck, Daryl F. 1902-79	Ent	50			85	Producer/20th Cent. Fox
Zapata, Emiliano	Military	500	1,500	RARE	RARE	Mexican Leader/1879-1919
Zappa, Frank 1940-1993	Music	100	200		200	
Zellwegger, Rene	Ent	25			50	
Zeman, Jacklyn	Ent	5			15	
Zemekis, Robert	Ent	20	50		45	Director/Back to the Future
Zemke, Hubert Hub	Aviation	15			45	WWII Triple ACE
Zeppelin, Ferdinand von	Aviation	275	475			Inventor Dirigible Air Ships
Zhukov, Georgi K.	Military	100			300	Soviet Hero in WWII
Ziegfield, Florenz	Ent	200	350	500	300	1869-1931
Ziegler, George M.	Civil War	40		100		Union General
Zimbalist, Efrem Jr.	Ent	5			15	
Zimbalist, Efrem Sr.	Music	50			150	Composer
Zimbalist, Stephanie	Ent	10			35	Remington Steele
Zinneman, Fred	Ent	35			75	Director/AA Winner
Zola, Emile 1840-1902	Author	200		450	1,500	Fr. Novelist
Zollicoffer, Felix K.	Civil War	300		750		CSA General/KIA
Zukor, Adolph 1873-1976	Ent	50		200	150	Founder Paramount Pix
Zumwalt, Elmo	Military	25	75	125	50	Admiral in WWII
Zweigert, Eugen Lt.	Aviation	100			300	German ACE WWII
Zworykin, Vladimir	Science	60			100	Inventor of the TV System
ZZ Top	Music	45			90	Signed by Entire Group

©©

BOOK COLLECTING BASICS

By Tim Miller

Since man first learned that knowledge was valuable, books have been considered true treasures of a lifetime! Prior to the advent of mass production, books were extremely expensive. Only the most wealthy could afford to have even a few books; far fewer could afford a true, personal library.

Most people believe that a "true first edition" is a book from the first print run from the publisher, published in the United States. Many people collect just "true first editions." Keep the following in mind when you believe you are buying a "true first edition."

Many publishers plan for buying patterns of both readers and collectors. For this reason, many times the "true first edition" is released in England (the UK printing). This was done recently with Lee Child's (award-winning author of *Killing Floor)* newest book *The Visitor,* which was released in the United States two months after the UK Edition. Other reasons include where the writer is from, schedules, and other book releases by the same publisher/author.

In addition, some publishers also claim that the "true first edition" is sometimes the leather-bound, slipcased and signed version of the title. These leather-bound collectibles are a fairly recent phenomenon, and it may actually be true that these were printed prior to what most of us collect, namely the "First Trade Printing." Keep these things in mind as you fill your collection.

What is a First Edition and how does it differ from a First Printing?

An edition is all the copies of a book printed from a single setting of type. Thus a first edition is all the copies of a book printed from the first setting of type. This definition is easy to understand when applied to the days when type was set by hand. When a book had been printed, the individual pieces of type were taken out of the press and used on another job. Now, however, type is set on computers, and an entire book can be stored in a single file and reprinted without being reset. Today, therefore, even books that are reprinted many times are frequently printed over and over from the same setting of type, technically making them all "First Editions."

When a book collector or dealer uses the term "first edition" he is almost always referring to the first printing of the first edition. A printing is all the copies of a book printed in a single run of the press. In other words, if a publisher orders a printer to print 15,000 copies of a new novel and then, several months later, orders another 10,000 copies to be printed without making any changes, the result is a first and second printing of the first edition. To most book collectors, however, only the first printing is considered desirable, and when they use the term "First Edition" without qualification, it is the first group of 15,000 to which they refer. The term "impression" is used by British dealers and publishers, and is synonymous with "printing."

It is possible for copies of a book from a single printing to differ from one another. There are two terms that are used to describe such variations: state and issue. A separate *state* of a printing occurs when a change is made during the press run, but all the books are still published simultaneously. For example, if, after 2,000 copies of our first printing of 15,000 copies had been printed, someone discovered a typographical error in the text, the press might be stopped, the error corrected, and the remaining 13,000 copies printed. All the books would then be sent to the publisher for distribution. This scenario would create a first and second state of the first edition. For a collector, the first state would be much more desirable. This would hold true even if the first state consisted of 13,000 copies and the second state only 2,000. That's because the collector nearly always prefers the earliest version of a book, even if it is not the rarest. Of course, many collectors are acquisitive enough that they would want examples of both states.

A separate *issue* of an edition is similar to a separate state, with the exception that it involves the two groups of books being issued by the publisher at two different times. For example, if the dedication page of a book were improperly printed and the mistake not discovered until 10,000 copies of our first edition had been sent to bookstores, the publisher might return the remaining 5,000 copies to the printer, have the faulty page cut out and a new page pasted in, and then issue the remaining copies at a later date, thus creating a first and second issue of the edition. Dust jackets, too, can have different issues or states. The state can be difficult to discern, and some dealers use the terms interchangeably. The differences between the various issues and states of an edition are called "points of issue," or just "points," and are described in bibliographies and some price guides.

In some cases, variants of a book have been noted, but bibliographers have been unable to determine which variant came first. Occasionally, variants are even published simultaneously, as in the case of some 19th century books, which were available in several colors of binding. In such cases, books often will be described with the notation "no known priority," which means there is no way to determine whether or not the issue described is the first.

How do we know which books to buy and which books will increase in value?

In a nutshell, we don't know for sure. However, we can certainly improve our chances by being smart collectors. Some of the things to watch for are covered in this article. Always remember to collect what YOU enjoy! That way you will always have a wonderful collection whether book values go up or down!

One of the surest signs that a book will go up in value is when that particular title wins a prominent award. This may be a national book award like the Shamus or a worldwide award like the Pulitzer Prize. An author whose first book is recognized both by peers and by an award committee like the Pulitzer would see his or her book escalate in value exponentially. A good example of this recently was Frank McCourt's *Angela's Ashes,* a true milestone in literature.

Other signs of particular interest when buying books for long-term value would be those that have already held their own during decades of collecting. Examples of these would be books by Hemingway, Steinbeck, Fitzgerald and Faulkner. These books will experience less volatility in the marketplace since they have withstood the test of time. More recent books are much more likely to have large price swings.

As for best values, always pay close attention to new authors and their new books. If you are able to get a MINT Hardcover Signed First Printing for $50 or less, what have you got to lose? At worst, $50! There is no doubt that some of today's newcomers will be the literary giants of our future!

Here are a few general rules to follow in keeping your rare and collectible books in perfect condition:

- Keep away from direct sunlight.
- Keep them on their foot or base, just as they would be in a bookstore or library standing totally upright and straight. Never lay them down flat, or on top of each other.
- Keep the area free of high moisture and high heat.
- Keep them on a slick-surfaced bookshelf, not felt or anything rough.
- Keep the books snug, between each other, not too tight, not too loose!

Follow these simple steps and you are certain to maintain the condition and value of your collection forever!

Is collecting books a good investment? What should the collector/investor watch out for?

Collecting books as an investment is not new! Investors and collectors have been speculating and investing in collectibles of all types for decades! While many collectibles like baseball cards and beanie babies have large followings, they have provided a relatively unstable market. But certain collectible books have enjoyed relatively upward-spiraling increases in value.

There are two things to be very mindful of when purchasing a book for both collecting and/or investment: condition of the book and popularity of the title. It is not unusual to find that collectible books in MINT/NEAR MINT condition command a premium price in the market. Books of superior condition sometimes bring double the price of a book in even very good condition! It is especially true of what we call "hyper-modern" books that condition plays an incredibly important role in determining value. By "hyper-modern," we mean in the last 10 years. Although condition is still extremely important, it is not unusual to find just Good condition copies of titles in demand by such legends as Hemingway or Salinger that still command prices of $1,000.

The title of the collectible book is almost as important as its condition. Look for an example of John Steinbeck's work. While there certainly is some consideration given to the number of copies produced, it is not unusual to find titles like *The Wayward Bus* or *The Pearl* far less expensive than his more famous and noteworthy titles like *The Grapes of Wrath* and *Of Mice and Men*. In the case of a more modern example, there were fewer copies of Stephen King's *Thinner* produced than there were *Skeleton Crew,* yet the market price for *Thinner* is actually less, if in the same MINT condition! Remember, the market price for collectible books is set just like the market price for gold, corn or homes – it all goes back to supply and demand. If there are only 10 copies of a book in the world and there is NO demand, its rarity means absolutely nothing!

HOW TO USE THE BOOK PRICE GUIDE

The following section is provided for those collectors who are interested in collecting signed books. The prices that follow represent the approximate values of books in above average condition and complete in their presentation. This section is simply a sampling of the more popular titles.

The term "flatsigned" was originally used by the world's most popular living author, Stephen King. He stumbled upon this new word when he needed to differentiate between personal requests from his fans versus those from dealers or resellers while signing their books. King now believes that this term was already was already common in the book collecting vernacular when he first began using it.

As an educational and marketing phrase, the term was originally used by Tim Miller to describe the most desirable type of collectible book. FLATSIGNED® means – Signed by the author, directly on the book itself without being inscribed to a specific autograph requester. Most importantly, it is not signed on a bookplate and then affixed to your book!

* denotes Limited Edition

Tim has been collecting books all his life and began his large collection in its current form over 10 years ago. He began to promote the now internationally-recognized phrase FLATSIGNED® when he began selling his books directly to collectors. The word has since become a popular term for describing these desirable books. In fact, most collectors prefer a FLATSIGNED® book as opposed to an inscribed copy.

Author	Title	Publisher	Year Published	Flatsigned	Signed & Inscribed	Signed on Bookplate
Aaron, Hank	Going Against the Wind	Long Street Press	*1992	349	296	261
Aikman, Troy	Reaching For the Stars	Tyler Publishing	*1993	249	211	186
Albee, Edward	Everything in the Garden			98	83	73
Allison, Dorothy	Bastard Out Of Carolina	Dutton	1992	289	245	216
Ami, Bel	Perfect Couples	Bruno Gmunder	1999	89	75	66
Ami, Bel	Photos of Johan	Bruno Gmunder	1997	99	84	74
Anderson, Kevin	The X-Files: Ground Zero	HarperPrism	*1995	149	126	111
Asimov, Isaac	Asimov's Sherlockian Limericks	Mysterious Press	*1978	389	330	291
Asimov, Isaac	Fantastic Voyage II	Doubleday	*1987	249	211	186
Asimov, Isaac	Foundation and Earth	Doubleday	1986	149	126	111
Asimov, Isaac	Foundation and Earth	Doubleday	*1986	249	211	186
Asimov, Isaac	Foundation's Edge	Whispers Press	*1982	289	245	216
Asimov, Isaac	Nemesis	Doubleday	*1989	249	211	186
Asimov, Isaac	Prelude to Foundation	Doubleday	*1988	289	245	216
Asimov, Isaac	The Asimov Chronicles	Dark Harvest	*1989	249	211	186
Asimov, Isaac	The Best of Isaac Asimov	Doubleday	1974	249	211	186
Asimov, Isaac	The Robots of Dawn	Phantasia	*1983	249	211	186
Bachman, Richard	The Regulators	Dutton	1996	349	296	261
Bacon, David	The Beatles' England	910 Press	1982	89	75	66
Barker, Clive	Cabal	Poseidon Press	1988	89	75	66
Barker, Clive	Everville	Harper Collins	1994	89	75	66
Barker, Clive	In the Flesh	Poseidon Press	1986	89	75	66
Barker, Clive	Night Visions 4	Dark Harvest	*1987	249	211	186
Barker, Clive	Sacrament	Harper Collins	1996	89	75	66
Barker, Clive	The Books of Blood	Ace / Putnam	1988	149	126	111
Barker, Clive	The Damnation Game	Ace / Putnam	1987	89	75	66
Barker, Clive	The Great and Secret Show	Harper & Row	1989	109	92	81
Barker, Clive	Weaveworld	Poseidon Press	1987	129	109	96
Barr, Nevada	A Superior Death	Putnam	1994	129	109	96
Barr, Nevada	Deep South	Putnam	2000	89	75	66
Barr, Nevada	Firestorm	Putnam	1996	89	75	66
Bellow, Saul	The Actual	Viking	1997	129	109	96
Benson, Raymond	High Time to Kill	Putnam	1999	89	75	66
Berendt, John	Midnight In The Garden Of Good And Evil	Random House	1994	289	245	216
Berger, Robert James	The Gerald Ford Letters	Lyle Stuart	1974	349	296	261
Block, Lawrence	A Dance at the Slaughterhouse	Morrow	1991	89	75	66
Block, Lawrence	A Long Line of Dead Men	Morrow	1994	129	109	96
Block, Lawrence	A Walk Among the Tombstones	Morrow	1992	89	75	66
Block, Lawrence	After Hours	New Mexico Press	1995	149	126	111
Block, Lawrence	Ariel	G&G Books	*1980	249	211	186

Author	Title	Publisher	Year Published	Flatsigned	Signed & Inscribed	Signed on Bookplate
Block, Lawrence	Burglars Can't be Choosers	Dutton	1995	89	75	66
Block, Lawrence	Code of Arms	Marek	1981	149	126	111
Block, Lawrence	In the Midst of Death	G & G Books	1995	89	75	66
Block, Lawrence	Random Walk	Tom Doherty Assoc.	1988	89	75	66
Block, Lawrence	The Burglar in the Library	Dutton	1997	129	109	96
Block, Lawrence	The Burglar Who Painted Like Mondrain	Arbor House	1983	199	169	149
Block, Lawrence	The Burglar Who Studied Spinoza	Random House	1980	249	211	186
Block, Lawrence	The Burglar who Traded Ted Williams	Dutton	1994	89	75	66
Block, Lawrence	The Devil Knows You're Dead	Morrow	1993	89	75	66
Block, Lawrence	The Sins of the Fathers	Dark Harvest	*1992	299	254	224
Block, Lawrence	The Specialists	Cahill	*1996	129	109	96
Block, Lawrence	The Thief who Couldn't Sleep	Armchair Detective Lib.	1994	89	75	66
Block, Lawrence	Threesome	Subterranean Press	*1999	179	152	134
Block, Robert	Psycho II	Whispers Press	*1982	189	160	141
Brackett, Leigh	No Good from a Corpse	Dennis McMillan Pub.	1999	149	126	111
Bradbury, Ray	A Graveyard for Lunatics	Knopf	1990	149	126	111
Bradbury, Ray	Ahmed and the Oblivion Machines	Avon Books	1998	89	75	66
Bradbury, Ray	Death Has Lost Its Charm For Me	Lord John Press	*1987	225	191	168
Bradbury, Ray	Death Is A Lonely Business	Knopf	1985	189	160	141
Bradbury, Ray	Fahrenheit 451	Simon & Schuster	1993	249	211	186
Bradbury, Ray	Fahrenheit 451	Simon & Schuster	*1993	249	211	186
Bradbury, Ray	Green Shadows White Whale	Knopf	1992	195	165	146
Bradbury, Ray	Review	Graham	*1988	249	211	186
Bradbury, Ray	Something Wicked This Way Comes	Gauntlet	*1999	249	211	186
Bradbury, Ray	The Halloween Tree	Knopf	1972	349	296	261
Bradbury, Ray	The Last Circus & the Execution	Lord John Press	1980	179	152	134
Bradbury, Ray	The Last Circus & the Execution	Lord John Press	*1980	249	211	186
Bradbury, Ray	The Love Affair	Lord John Press	*1982	175	148	131
Bradbury, Ray	The Martian Chronicles	Avon Books	*1999	189	160	141
Bradbury, Ray	The October Country	Avon Books	1997	189	160	141
Bradbury, Ray	The October Country	Gauntlet	*1997	249	211	186
Bradbury, Ray	Toynbee Convector	Knopf	1988	149	126	111
Bradbury, Ray	Twin Hieroglyphs That Swim the River Dust	Lord John Press	*1978	175	148	131
Bradbury, Ray	With Cat for Comforter	Gibbs Smith	1997	89	75	66
Bradley, Bill	Time Present, Time Past : A Memoir	Knopf	1996	189	160	141
Bradley, Bill	Values of the Games	Artisan Publishing	1998	149	126	111
Bruce, J. Campbell	Escape From Alcatraz	McGraw Hill	1963	329	279	246
Buchanan, Thomas	Who Killed Kennedy?	Putnam	1964	189	160	141
Buck, Pearl S.	America	Bartholomew	*1971	129	109	96
Buck, Pearl S.	Once Upon a Christmas	John Day Co.	*1972	129	109	96
Burke, Billie	With A Feather On My Nose	Appleton Century	1949	129	109	96
Burke, James Lee	A Stained White Radiance	Hyperion	1992	89	75	66
Burke, James Lee	Black Cherry Blues	Little Brown	1989	129	109	96

Author	Title	Publisher	Year Published	Flatsigned	Signed & Inscribed	Signed on Bookplate
Burke, James Lee	Burning Angel	Hyperion	*1995	289	245	216
Burke, James Lee	Dixie City Jam	Hyperion	1994	99	75	66
Burke, James Lee	Dixie City Jam	Hyperion	*1994	149	126	111
Burke, James Lee	Heaven's Prisoners	Henry Holt	1988	249	211	186
Burke, James Lee	In the Electric Mist With Confederate Dead	Hyperion	*1993	249	211	186
Burke, James Lee	Lay Down My Sword And Shield	Crowell	1971	2400	2,040	1,800
Burke, James Lee	Neon Rain	Henry Holt	1987	369	313	276
Burke, James Lee	The Lost Get-Back Boogie	Louisiana St. Univ. Press	1986	789	670	591
Burke, James Lee	The Lost Get-Back Boogie	LSU Press	1986	689	585	516
Burke, James Lee	To The Bright and Shining Sun	Scibner	1970	2799	679	599
Burke, James Lee	Two for Texas	Cahill	*1992	149	126	111
Burke, James Lee	Winter Light	Cahill	*1992	149	126	111
Burroughs, Edgar Rice	Tarzan and the Foreign Legion	Burroughs	1947	589	500	441
Burroughs, Edgar Rice	Tarzan Lord Of The Jungle	Grosset and Dunlap	1928	1,589	1,350	1,191
Burroughs, Edgar Rice	Tarzan of the Apes	Grosset and Dunlap	1914	1,289	1,095	966
Burroughs, Edgar Rice	Tarzan The Invincible	Grosset and Dunlap	1931	2,889	2,455	2,166
Burroughs, Edgar Rice	The Return of Tarzan	Grosset and Dunlap	1915	589	500	441
Bush, Barbara	A Memoir	Scribner	1994	149	126	111
Bush, George	All The Best	Scribner	1999	789	670	591
Bush, George W.	A Charge To Keep	Morrow	1999	289	245	216
Butler, Robert Olen	A Good Scent From a Strange Mountain	Henry Holt	1992	249	211	186
Butler, Robert Olen	Sun Dogs	Horizon Press	1982	189	160	141
Butler, Robert Olen	The Alleys of Eden	Horizon Press	1981	249	211	186
Butler, Robert Olen	They Whisper	Henry Holt	1994	98	83	73
Butler, Robert Olen	Wabash	Knopf	1987	179	152	134
Byrd, Richard E.	Little America	G.P. Putnams	1930	249	211	186
Caldwell, Erskine	God's Little Acre	N.A.L	1933	249	211	186
Cannell, Stephen J.	The Devel's Workshop	Morrow	1999	89	75	66
Cannell, Stephen J.	The Plan	Morrow	1995	89	75	66
Capote, Truman	A Christmas Memory	Random House	*1956	1,249	1,061	936
Capote, Truman	A Christmas Memory	Random House	1956	589	500	441
Capote, Truman	A Tree Of Night	Random House	1949	789	670	591
Capote, Truman	In Cold Blood	Random House	1965	650	552	487
Capote, Truman	In Cold Blood	Random House	*1965	1,450	1,232	1,087
Capote, Truman	Music for Chameleons	Random House	1980	649	551	486
Capote, Truman	The Grass Harp	Random House	1951	549	466	411
Capote, Truman	The Thanksgiving Visitor	Random House	*1967	1,249	1,061	936
Capote, Truman	The Thanksgiving Visitor	Random House	1967	589	500	441
Card, Orson Scott	Treasure Box	Harper Collins	1996	89	75	66
Carre, John Le	The Secret Pilgrim	Knopf	1990	158	134	118
Carroll, James	Fault Lines	Little Brown	1980	189	160	141
Carroll, James	Mortal Friends	Little Brown & Co.	1978	89	75	66
Carter, Jimmy	A New Spirit A New Commitment A New America	Duobooks	1977	489	415	366

Author	Title	Publisher	Year Published	Flatsigned	Signed & Inscribed	Signed on Bookplate
Carter, Jimmy	Always A Reckoning	Random House	1995	189	160	141
Carter, Jimmy	Always A Reckoning	Times Books	1995	289	245	216
Carter, Jimmy	An Hour Before Daylight	Simon & Schuster	2001	89	75	66
Carter, Jimmy	An Outdoor Journal	Bantam	1988	129	109	96
Carter, Jimmy	Everything to Gain	Random House	1987	349	296	261
Carter, Jimmy	Keeping Faith	Bantam	1982	145	123	108
Carter, Jimmy	Keeping Faith	Easton Press	1982	295	250	221
Carter, Jimmy	Keeping Faith	Bantam Books	*1982	349	296	261
Carter, Jimmy	Keeping the Faith	Bantam	1982	289	245	216
Carter, Jimmy	Sources of Strength	Times Books	1997	189	160	141
Carter, Jimmy	Talking Peace	Dutton Children's Books	1993	189	160	141
Carter, Jimmy	The Blood Of Abraham	Houghton Mifflin	1985	489	415	366
Carter, Jimmy	The Candidacy Of Carter	Strawberry Hill	1976	289	245	216
Carter, Jimmy	The Little Baby Snoogle-Fleejer	Times Books	1995	489	415	366
Carter, Jimmy	The Virtues of Aging	Ballantine Pub. Group	1998	129	109	96
Carter, Jimmy	Turning Point	Times Books	1992	209	177	156
Carter, Jimmy	Why Not the Best	Broadman Press	1975	189	160	141
Cascone, A.G.	Deadtime: Terror in Tiny Town	Troll	1996	89	75	66
Chabon, Michael	The Amazing Adventures of Kavalier and Clay	Random House	2000	389	330	291
Cher, Cher	The First Time	Simon & Schuster	1998	169	143	126
Child, Lee	Die Trying	Putnam	1998	89	75	66
Child, Lee	Running Blind	Putnam	2000	129	109	96
Child, Lee	Tripwire	Putnam	1999	129	109	96
Chopra, Deepak	The Seven Spiritual Law of Success	Amber/Alan Publishing	1994	89	75	66
Clancy, Tom	Clear and Present Danger	Putnam	1989	249	211	186
Clancy, Tom	Debt of Honor	Putnam	1994	189	160	141
Clancy, Tom	Debt of Honor	Putnam	*1994	249	211	186
Clancy, Tom	Executive Orders	Putnam	1996	129	109	96
Clancy, Tom	Fighter Wing	Berkley	1995	89	75	66
Clancy, Tom	Into the Storm	Putnam	1997	89	75	66
Clancy, Tom	Rainbow Six	Putnam	1998	149	126	111
Clancy, Tom	Red Storm Rising	Putnam	1986	129	109	96
Clancy, Tom	SSN	Berkley	1996	189	160	141
Clancy, Tom	Submarine	Putnam	*	289	245	216
Clancy, Tom	The Bear and the Dragon	Putnam	2000	129	109	96
Clancy, Tom	The Cardinal of the Kremlin	Putnam	1988	249	211	186
Clancy, Tom	The Hunt For Red October	Naval Institute Press	1984	2,000	1,700	1,500
Clancy, Tom	The Sum of All Fears	Putnam	1991	129	109	96
Clancy, Tom	The Sum of All Fears	Putnam's Sons	*1991	149	126	111
Clancy, Tom	Without Remorse	Putnam	1993	249	211	186
Clark, Mary Higgins	Anastasia Syndrome	Simon & Schuster	1989	149	126	111
Clark, Mary Higgins	While My Pretty One Sleeps	Simon & Schuster	1989	189	160	141
Clark, Mary Higgins	You Belong to Me	Simon & Schuster	1998	89	75	66
Clarke, Arthur C.	2010 Odyssey Two	Phantasia Press	*1982	129	109	96

Author	Title	Publisher	Year Published	Flatsigned	Signed & Inscribed	Signed on Bookplate
Clavell, James	Gai-Jin	Delacorte Press	*1993	199	169	149
Clavell, James	Whirlwind	Morrow	1986	149	126	111
Clinton, Bill	Between Hope and History	Times Books	1996	189	160	141
Cole, Nat King	An Intimate Biography by Maria Cole	Morrow	1971	89	75	66
Colfer, Eoin	Artemis Fowl	Hyperion	2001	189	160	141
Colfer, Eoin	Artemis Fowl	Hyperion	2001	139	118	104
Colfer, Eoin	Artemis Fowl	Viking	2001	289	245	216
Collins, Judy	Singing Lessons	Simon & Schuster	1998	89	75	66
Connell, Evan S.	Saint Augustine's Pigeon; The					
	Selected Stories of Evan S. Connell	North Point Press	1980	115	97	86
Connelly, Michael	Blood Work	Little Brown & Co.	1998	89	75	66
Connelly, Michael	Blood Work	Little Brown & Co.	*1998	349	296	261
Connelly, Michael	The Black Echo	Little Brown & Co.	1992	249	211	186
Connelly, Michael	The Black Ice	Little Brown & Co.	1993	129	109	96
Connelly, Michael	The Last Coyote	Little Brown & Co.	1995	89	75	66
Connelly, Michael	Void Moon	Little Brown & Co.	2000	89	75	66
Connelly, Michael	Void Moon		*	189	160	141
Conroy, Pat	Beach Music	Doubleday	1999	129	109	96
Conroy, Pat	The Prince of Tides	Houghton Mifflin Co.	1986	229	194	171
Coonts, Stephen	Cuba	St. Martin's Press	1999	89	75	66
Coonts, Stephen	Final Flight	Doubleday	1988	89	75	66
Coonts, Stephen	Flight of the Intruder	Naval Institute Press	1986	149	126	111
Coonts, Stephen	The Cannibal Queen	Pocket Books	1992	89	75	66
Coonts, Stephen	The Monitor	Doubleday	1989	89	75	66
Coonts, Stephen	Under Seige	Pocket Books	1998	89	75	66
Cornwell, Patricia	All That Remains	Scribner	1992	89	75	66
Cornwell, Patricia	Black Notice	Putnam	1999	89	75	66
Cornwell, Patricia	Body Farm	Scribner	1994	149	126	111
Cornwell, Patricia	Body Of Evidence	Scribner	1991	289	245	216
Cornwell, Patricia	Cause of Death	Putnam	1996	129	109	96
Cornwell, Patricia	Cruel and Unusual	Scribner	1993	129	109	96
Cornwell, Patricia	From Potter's Field	Scribner	1995	89	75	66
Cornwell, Patricia	Point of Origin	Putnam	1998	89	75	66
Cornwell, Patricia	Point of Origin	Putnam	*1998	249	211	186
Cornwell, Patricia	Southern Cross	Putnam	1998	99	75	66
Cornwell, Patricia	Unnatural Exposure	Putnam	1997	89	75	66
Crais, Robert	Free Fall	Bantam Press	1993	289	245	216
Crais, Robert	L.A. Requiem	Doubleday	1999	89	75	66
Crais, Robert	L.A. Requiem	Scorpion Press	*1999	249	211	186
Crais, Robert	Lulllaby Town	Bantam	1992	789	670	591
Crais, Robert	Stalking The Angel	Bantam Press	1989	289	245	216
Crais, Robert	Sunset Express	Cahill	*1996	189	160	141
Crais, Robert	The Monkey's Raincoat	Doubleday	1987	289	245	216
Crichton, Michael	Airframe	Knopf	1996	129	109	96
Crichton, Michael	Disclosure	Knopf	1993	89	75	66

Author	Title	Publisher	Year Published	Flatsigned	Signed & Inscribed	Signed on Bookplate
Crichton, Michael	Sphere	Knopf	1987	149	126	111
Crichton, Michael	The Lost World: Jurassic Park	Knopf	1995	289	245	216
Crichton, Michael	Timeline	Knopf	1999	89	75	66
Crumley, James	Whores	Dennis MacMillian	*1988	249	211	186
Cussler, Clive	Atlantis Found	Putnam	1999	89	75	66
Cussler, Clive	Dragon	Simon & Schuster	1990	129	109	96
Cussler, Clive	Flood Tide	Simon & Schuster	1997	89	75	66
Cussler, Clive	Raise the Titanic	Viking	1976	389	330	291
Cussler, Clive	Sahara	Simon & Schuster	1992	149	126	111
Cussler, Clive	Vixen 03	Viking	1978	289	245	216
Dart, Iris Rainer	Beaches	Bantam Press	1985	89	75	66
Devlin, Dean	Independence Day	Harper Prism	*1996	249	211	186
Dickey, James	Deliverance	Houghton Mifflin	1970	489	415	366
Dickey, Rufus Needham	The Sermon On The Mount	The Kelvie Press	1936	489	415	366
Doctorow, E.L.	Welcome To Hard Times	Simon & Schuster	1960	989	840	741
Downs, Hugh	Fifty to Forever	Nelson	1994	89	75	66
Drury, Allen	Adivse and Consent		*	158	134	118
Dunning, John	Deadline	Cahill	1995	249	211	186
Dunning, John	Deadline	Cahill	*1995	189	160	141
Dunning, John	On the Air	Oxford	1998	289	245	216
Dunning, John	The Bookman's Wake	Scribner	1995	89	75	66
Dunning, John	Tune In Yesterday	Prentice Hall	1976	189	160	141
Dunning, John	Two O'Clock Eastern Wartime	Scribner	2001	89	75	66
Evanovich, Janet	Four To Score	Scribner	1998	99	75	66
Evanovich, Janet	High Five	Scribner	1999	149	126	111
Evanovich, Janet	Hot Six	Scribner	2000	99	84	74
Evanovich, Janet	One for the Money	Scribner	1994	349	296	261
Evanovich, Janet	Three To Get Deadly	Scribner	1997	149	126	111
Evanovich, Janet	Two for the Dough	Scribner	1996	249	211	186
Evanovich, Janet	Two for the Dough	Scribner	*1996	349	296	261
Evans, Nicholas	The Horse Whisperer	Delacorte Press	1995	99	84	74
Fairstein, Linda	Cold Hit	Scribner	1999	129	109	96
Fairstein, Linda	Final Jeopardy	Scribner	1996	249	211	186
Ferguson, Sarah (Duchess of York)	Reinventing Yourself With the Duchess of York	Simon & Schuster	2001	89	75	66
Ford, Gerald	A Time To Heal	Harper and Row	1979	489	415	366
Ford, Gerald	Gerald Ford and the Future of the Presidency	The Third Press	1974	349	296	261
Ford, Gerald	Grand Rapids	Towery Publishing Inc.	1998	249	211	186
Ford, Gerald	Humor and the Presidency	Arbor House	1987	495	420	371
Ford, Gerald	JFK Death Report-Warren Commission	Doubleday	1964	389	330	291
Ford, Gerald	The American Adventure		1976	289	245	216
Ford, Richard	A Piece Of My Heart	Harper & Row	1976	89	75	66
Ford, Richard	Independence Day	Knopf	1995	389	330	291

Author	Title	Publisher	Year Published	Flatsigned	Signed & Inscribed	Signed on Bookplate
Ford, Richard	Wildlife	Atlantic Monthly Press	1990	89	75	66
Francis, Dick	10lb Penalty	Putnam	1997	189	160	141
Frazier, Charles	Cold Mountain	Atlantic Monthly Press	1997	289	245	216
Frost, David	I Gave Them a Sword	Morrow	1978	129	109	96
Gallico, Paul	Love Let Me Not Hunger	Doubleday	1963	89	75	66
Gash, Jonathan	Spend Game	Ticknor & Fields	1981	175	148	131
George, Elizabeth	A Great Deliverance	Bantam	1988	175	148	131
Gingrich, Newt	To Renew America	Harper Collins	1995	89	75	66
Glenn, John	A Memoir	Bantam	1999	189	160	141
Glenn, John	John Glenn : A Memoir	Easton Press	1999	289	245	216
Golden, Arthur	Memorirs of a Geisha	Knopf	1997	349	296	261
Golden, Harry	Carl Sandburg	World Publishing Co.	1961	189	160	141
Goldwater, Barry M.	With No Apologies	Morrow	1979	249	211	186
Gore, Al (JR)	Earth In the Balance	Houghton Mifflin	1992	549	466	411
Gore, Al (JR)	Earth In the Balance	Houghton Mifflin	1992	689	585	516
Gore, Al (JR)	His Life And Career	Birch Lane Press	1992	549	466	411
Gore, Al (SR)	Let the Glory Out	Viking	1972	289	245	216
Gore, Albert	The Eye Of The Storm	Herder	1970	189	160	141
Gore, Tipper	Raising PG Kids In an X-Rated Society	Abingdon Press	1987	149	126	111
Grafton, Sue	A is for Alibi	Henry Holt	1982	1,999	1,699	1,499
Grafton, Sue	B is for Burglar	Henry Holt	1985	1,485	1,262	1,113
Grafton, Sue	C is for Corpse	Henry Holt	1986	1,485	1,262	1,113
Grafton, Sue	D is for Deadbeat	Henry Holt	1987	550	467	412
Grafton, Sue	E is for Evidence	Henry Holt and Co.	1988	289	245	216
Grafton, Sue	F is for Fugitive	Henry Holt and Co.	1989	149	126	111
Grafton, Sue	G is for Grafton	Henry Holt	1997	289	245	216
Grafton, Sue	G is for Gumshoe	Henry Holt and Co.	1990	129	109	96
Grafton, Sue	H is for Homicide	Henry Holt and Co.	1991	89	75	66
Grafton, Sue	I is for Innocent	Henry Holt and Co.	1992	89	75	66
Grafton, Sue	Keziah Dane	Macmillan	1967	1,750	1,487	1,312
Grafton, Sue	M is for Malice	Henry Holt and Co.	1996	89	75	66
Grafton, Sue	P is for Peril	Henry Holt	2001	79	67	59
Grisham, John	A Painted House	Doubleday	2001	249	211	186
Grisham, John	A Time To Kill	Wynwood	1989	4,889	4,155	3,666
Grisham, John	A Time To Kill	Doubleday	1993	589	500	441
Grisham, John	A Time To Kill		*	1,489	1,265	1,116
Grisham, John	The Brethren	Doubleday	2000	129	109	96
Grisham, John	The Brethren	Doubleday	*2000	349	296	261
Grisham, John	The Chamber	Doubleday	*1994	689	585	516
Grisham, John	The Chamber	Doubleday	1994	289	245	216
Grisham, John	The Client	Doubleday	1993	389	330	291
Grisham, John	The Client	Doubleday	*1993	1,449	1,231	1,086
Grisham, John	The Firm	Doubleday	1991	749	636	561
Grisham, John	The Firm	Doubleday	*1992	1,449	1,231	1,086
Grisham, John	The Partner	Doubleday	1997	189	160	141

Author	Title	Publisher	Year Published	Flatsigned	Signed & Inscribed	Signed on Bookplate
Grisham, John	The Partner	Doubleday	*1997	489	415	366
Grisham, John	The Pelican Brief	Doubleday	1992	389	330	291
Grisham, John	The Pelican Brief	Doubleday	*1992	1,289	1,095	966
Grisham, John	The Rainmaker	Doubleday	*1995	649	551	486
Grisham, John	The Rainmaker	Doubleday	1995	489	415	366
Grisham, John	The Runaway Jury	Doubleday	*1996	449	381	336
Grisham, John	The Street Lawyer	Doubleday	1998	179	152	134
Grisham, John	The Street Lawyer	Doubleday	*1998	349	296	261
Grisham, John	The Testament	Doubleday	1999	149	126	111
Grisham, John	The Testament	Doubleday	*1999	349	296	261
Guest, Judith	Ordinary People	Viking	1976	179	152	134
Gurganus, Allan	White People	Knopf	1990	89	75	66
Guterson, David	Snow Falling On Cedars	Harcourt Brace	1994	349	296	261
Hailey, Arthur	Airport	Random House	1968	189	160	141
Haley, Alex	A Different Kind of Christmas	Doubleday	1988	149	126	111
Haley, Alex	The Autobiograpy Of Malcolm X	Grove Press	1965	389	330	291
Harris, Thomas	Black Sunday	Putnam	1975	689	585	516
Harris, Thomas	Hannibal	Delacorte Press	1999	649	551	486
Harris, Thomas	Red Dragon	Putnam	1981	589	500	441
Harris, Thomas	The Silence of the Lambs	St. Martin's Press	1988	1,229	1,044	921
Harrison, Jim	The Road Home			98	83	73
Hayes, Helen	On Reflection	Evans-Lippincott	1968	129	109	96
Heinemann, Larry	Paco's Story	Farrar Straus & Giroux	1986	89	75	66
Heller, Joseph	Catch-22			349	296	261
Heller, Joseph	Something Happened	Knopf	1974	189	160	141
Heyerdahl, Thor	The RA Expeditions	Doubleday	1971	89	75	66
Hiaasen, Carl	Double Whammy	Putnam	1987	89	75	66
Hiaasen, Carl	Kick Ass	University Press of Florida	1999	149	126	111
Hiaasen, Carl	Lucky You	Knopf	*1997	189	160	141
Hiaasen, Carl	Native Tongue	Knopf	1991	89	75	66
Hiaasen, Carl	Skin Tight	Putnam	1989	129	109	96
Hiaasen, Carl	Stormy Weather	Knopf	1995	89	75	66
Hiassen, Carl	Double Whammy	Putnam	1987	389	330	291
Hiassen, Carl	Sick Puppy	Knopf	1999	129	109	96
Hiassen, Carl	Skintight	Putnam	1989	349	296	261
Hiassen, Carl	Tourist Season	Putnam	1986	389	330	291
Highsmith, Particia	People Who Knock On The Door	Penzler	1985	289	245	216
Highsmith, Patricia	People Who Knock On the Door	Penzler Books	*1997	249	211	186
Hillerman, Tony	A Thief Of Time	Harper and Row	1988	389	330	291
Hillerman, Tony	Coyote Waits	Harper & Row	1990	129	109	96
Hillerman, Tony	Dance Hall of the Dead	Armchair Detective Lib.	1992	149	126	111
Hillerman, Tony	Dance Hall of the Dead	Armchair Detective Lib.	*1991	149	126	111
Hillerman, Tony	Dance Hall Of The Dead	Pluto Crime	1973	289	245	216
Hillerman, Tony	Finding Moon	Harper Collins	1995	149	126	111
Hillerman, Tony	Hunting Badger	Harper Collins	1999	129	109	96

Author	Title	Publisher	Year Published	Flatsigned	Signed & Inscribed	Signed on Bookplate
Hillerman, Tony	Sacred Clowns	Harper Collins	1993	189	160	141
Hillerman, Tony	Skinwalkers	Harper and Row	1986	389	330	291
Hillerman, Tony	Talking God	Harper & Row	1989	149	126	111
Hillerman, Tony	Talking Mysteries	Univ. of New Mexico	1991	289	245	216
Hillerman, Tony	The Dark Wind	Harper & Row	1982	289	245	216
Hillerman, Tony	The First Eagle	Harper & Row	1998	89	75	66
Hirsch, James S.	Hurricane	Houghton Mifflin	2000	189	160	141
Hitchcock, Champion Ingraham	The Dead Man's Song	C.I. Hitchcock	1914	399	339	299
Hope, Bob	Don't Shoot It's Only Me	Putnam	1990	129	109	96
Hunter, Stephen	Black Light	Doubleday	1996	89	75	66
Hunter, Stephen	Dirty White Boys	Random House	1994	89	75	66
Hunter, Stephen	Point of Impact	Bantam Press	1993	289	245	216
Hunter, Stephen	The Day Before Midnight	Bantam Press	1989	129	109	96
Hunter, Stephen	The Master Sniper	Morrow	1980	389	330	291
Hunter, Stephen	The Second Saladin	Morrow	1982	249	211	186
Hunter, Stephen	The Spanish Gambit	Crown	1985	189	160	141
Hunter, Stephen	Time to Hunt	Doubleday	1998	89	75	66
Irving, John	A Widow for One Year	Unicycle Press	*1998	249	211	186
Irving, John	Cider House Rules	Morrow	1985	449	381	336
Irving, John	The World According To Garp	Dutton	1978	289	245	216
Jackson, Bo	Bo Knows Bo	Doubleday	1990	149	126	111
James, Maureen	Except the Dying	St. Martin's Press	1997	89	75	66
James, P.D.	A Certain Justice	Knopf	1997	89	75	66
James, P.D.	A Taste For Death	Knopf	1986	129	109	96
James, P.D.	Devices and Desires	Knopf	1989	249	211	186
James, P.D.	Devices and Desires	Frankiln Library	*1990	249	211	186
James, P.D.	Devices and Desires	Knopf	1990	149	126	111
James, P.D.	Innocent Blood	Scribner	1980	89	75	66
James, P.D.	Original Sin	Knopf	1994	129	109	96
James, P.D.	The Maul and the Pear Tree	Mysterious Press	1971	189	160	141
James, P.D.	The Skull Beneath The Skin	Scribner	1982	149	126	111
Jennings, William	The Cowboys	Stein and Day	1971	389	330	291
Johnson, Lyndon	The Professional	Houghton Mifflin	1964	589	500	441
Johnson, Lyndon B.	The Vantage Point	Holt Rinehart & Winston	1971	749	636	561
Johnston, Ollie	The Disney Villain	Hyperion	1993	249	211	186
Jones, Tristan	The Incredible Voyage	Cheed Andrews	1977	89	75	66
Kennedy, Jackie	Jacqueline Bouvier Kennedy	Doubleday	1961	1,750	1,487	1,312
Kennedy, John	Profiles In Courage	Harper and Brothers	1956	3,889	3,305	2,916
Kennedy, John	The Strategy of Peace	Harper	1960	3,889	3,305	2,916
Kennedy, Robert	The Riverkeepers	Scribner	1997	349	296	261
Kerouac, Jack	Door Wide Open	Viking	2000	89	75	66
Kesey, Ken	One Flew Over The Cuckoo's Nest	Penguin Books	1999	149	126	111
Kesey, Ken	One Flew Over the Cuckoo's Nest			4,449	3,781	3,336

Author	Title	Publisher	Year Published	Flatsigned	Signed & Inscribed	Signed on Bookplate
Ketchum, Jack	The Girl Next Door	Overlooked Connection Press	*1989	289	245	216
Kidder, Tracy	House	Houghton & Mifflin Co	1985	129	109	96
Kijweski, Karen	Wild Kat	Cahill	1994	89	75	66
Kilcher, Jewel	A Night Without Armor	Harpercollins	1998	89	75	66
King, Coretta Scott	My Life With Martin Luther King, JR	Holt Rhinehart Winston	1969	389	330	291
King, Laurie	A Letter of Mary	St. Martin's Press	1996	89	75	66
King, Laurie	Night Work	Bantam Press	2000	89	75	66
King, Martin Luther	Stride Toward Freedoom	Harper & Bros	1958	6,449	5,481	4,836
King, Martin Luther	Where Do We Go From Here	Harper & Row	1967	6,449	5,481	4,836
King, Stephen	Bag of Bones	Scribner	1998	329	279	246
King, Stephen	Carrie	Doubleday	1974	1489	415	366
King, Stephen	Christine	Viking	1983	489	415	366
King, Stephen	Christine	Grant	*1983	449	381	336
King, Stephen	Cujo	Viking	1981	289	245	216
King, Stephen	Danse Macabre	Everest House	1981	449	381	336
King, Stephen	Desperation	Grant	*1996	349	296	261
King, Stephen	Different Seasons	Viking	1982	349	296	261
King, Stephen	Dolores Claiborne	Viking	1993	249	211	186
King, Stephen	Firestarter	Viking	1980	389	330	291
King, Stephen	Gerald's Game	Viking	1992	349	296	261
King, Stephen	Insomnia	Viking	1994	249	211	186
King, Stephen	It	Viking	1986	225	191	168
King, Stephen	Kingdom of Fear	Underwood Miller	*1986	249	211	186
King, Stephen	Misery	Viking	1987	289	245	216
King, Stephen	Needful Things	Viking	1991	189	160	141
King, Stephen	Night Shift	Doubleday	1978	999	849	749
King, Stephen	Night Visions 5	Dark Harvest	*1988	249	211	186
King, Stephen	Nightmares & Dreamscapes	Viking	1993	349	296	261
King, Stephen	On Writing	Scribner	2000	489	415	366
King, Stephen	Pet Semetary	Doubleday	1983	289	245	216
King, Stephen	Rose Madder	Viking	1995	349	296	261
King, Stephen	Salem's Lot	Doubleday	1975	1,249	1,061	936
King, Stephen	Skeleton Crew	Putnam	1985	289	245	216
King, Stephen	The Dark Half	Viking	1989	379	322	284
King, Stephen	The Dark Tower II: The Drawing of the Three	Grant	1987	649	551	486
King, Stephen	The Dark Tower III: The Waste Lands	Grant	1991	449	381	336
King, Stephen	The Dark Tower: Gunslinger	Grant	1982	749	636	561
King, Stephen	The Dark Tower: Gunslinger	Grant	*1982	889	755	666
King, Stephen	The Eyes of the Dragon	Viking	1987	489	415	366
King, Stephen	The Stand	Doubleday	*1978	1,589	1,350	1,191
King, Stephen	The Talisman	Viking	1984	389	330	291
King, Stephen	The Tommyknockers	Putnam	1987	489	415	366
King, Stephen	Weird Tales	Weinberg Books	1990	289	245	216

Author	Title	Publisher	Year Published	Flatsigned	Signed & Inscribed	Signed on Bookplate
King, Stephen	Whispers	Underwood Miller	1982	389	330	291
Kingsolver, Barbara	Pigs In Heaven	Harper Collins	1993	89	75	66
Kissinger, Henry	Observations	Little Brown	1985	389	330	291
Koenig, Laird	The Little Girl Who Lives Down the Lane	Coward; McCann; & Geoghegan	1974	95	80	71
Koontz, Dean	Cold Fire	Putnam	1991	89	75	66
Koontz, Dean	Dark Rivers of the Heart	Knopf	1994	89	75	66
Koontz, Dean	Fear Nothing	Bantam Books	1998	89	75	66
Koontz, Dean	Fear Nothing	Cemetary Dance	*1998	289	245	216
Koontz, Dean	Hanging On	Evans	1973	489	415	366
Koontz, Dean	Hideaway	Putnam	1992	89	75	66
Koontz, Dean	Intensity	Knopf	1996	89	75	66
Koontz, Dean	Lightning	Putnam	1988	129	109	96
Koontz, Dean	Mr. Murder	Putnam	1993	89	75	66
Koontz, Dean	Oddkins	Warner Books	1988	129	109	96
Koontz, Dean	Shadowfires	Dark Harvest	*	249	211	186
Koontz, Dean	Sole Survivor	Knopf	1997	89	75	66
Koontz, Dean	The Bad Place	Putnam	1990	89	75	66
Koontz, Dean	The Bad Place	Headline	1990	89	75	66
Koontz, Dean	The Difinitive Best of the Horror Show	C. D. Publications	*1992	249	211	186
Koontz, Dean	The Key to Midnight	Dark Harvest	*1989	249	211	186
Koontz, Dean	The Servants of Twilight	Dark Harvest	*	249	211	186
Koontz, Dean	Twilight Eyes	Christopher Zavisa	1985	189	160	141
Koontz, Dean	Watchers	Putnam	1987	129	109	96
Krueger, William Kent	Iron Lake	Pocket Books	1998	89	75	66
Kuralt, Charles	A Life on the Road	Putnam	1990	129	109	96
Kuralt, Charles	On The Road	Easton Press	1990	249	211	186
Lahiri, Jhumpa	Interpreter of Maladies	Houghton Mifflin	1999	89	75	66
LaLanne, Jack	The Jack La Lanne Way to Vibrant Good Health	Prentice Hall	1960	89	75	66
Lama, Dahai	Ethics for the New Millennium	Riverhead Books	1999	129	109	96
Lawson, Ted W. (Capt.)	Thirty Seconds Over Tokyo	Blue Bibbon Books	1943	129	109	96
Lee, Harper	To Kill A Mockingbird	Lippincott	1960	17,500	14,875	13,125
Lee, Harper	To Kill a Mockingbird - 40th Anniversary	HarperCollins	2000	289	245	216
Lehane, Dennis	A Drink Before the War	Harcourt-Brace	1994	189	160	141
Lehane, Dennis	Gone Baby Gone	Morrow	1998	89	75	66
Lehane, Dennis	Sacred	Morrow	1997	89	75	66
Leno, Jay	Leading With My Chin	Harper Collins	1996	99	84	74
Leonard, Elmore	Be Cool	Delacorte Press	1999	89	75	66
Leonard, Elmore	Cat Chaser	Arbor House	1982	129	109	96
Leonard, Elmore	City Primeval	Arbor House	1980	129	109	96
Leonard, Elmore	Cuba Libre	Delacorte Press	1988	89	75	66
Leonard, Elmore	Double Dutch Treat	Arbor House	1980	129	109	96
Leonard, Elmore	Dutch Treat	Mysterious Press	*1977	249	211	186
Leonard, Elmore	Freaky Deaky	Arbor House	1988	129	109	96

Author	Title	Publisher	Year Published	Flatsigned	Signed & Inscribed	Signed on Bookplate
Leonard, Elmore	Get Shorty	Delacorte Press	1990	99	84	74
Leonard, Elmore	Glitz	Mysterious Press	*1985	149	126	111
Leonard, Elmore	Glitz	Arbor House	1985	249	211	186
Leonard, Elmore	Hombre	Armchair Detective Lib.	*1961	249	211	186
Leonard, Elmore	Killshot	Morrow	1989	89	75	66
Leonard, Elmore	LaBrava	Arbor House	1983	89	75	66
Leonard, Elmore	Maximum Bob	Delacorte Press	1991	89	75	66
Leonard, Elmore	Naked Came the Manatee	Putnam	1996	249	211	186
Leonard, Elmore	Notebooks	Lord John Press	*1991	149	126	111
Leonard, Elmore	Out of Sight	Delacorte Press	1996	99	84	74
Leonard, Elmore	Pronto	Delacorte Press	1993	89	75	66
Leonard, Elmore	Riding the Rap	Delacorte Press	1995	89	75	66
Leonard, Elmore	Rum Punch	Delacorte Press	1992	89	75	66
Leonard, Elmore	Split Images	Arbor House	1981	129	109	96
Leonard, Elmore	Stick	Arbor House	1983	89	75	66
Leonard, Elmore	Touch	Arbor House	1987	89	75	66
Lewis, Sinclair	Cass Timberlane	Random House	1945	129	109	96
Lewis, Wyndham	The Apes Of God	McBride	1932	389	330	291
Lovell, Jim	Lost Moon	Houghton & Mifflin	1994	129	109	96
Ludlum, Robert	The Bourne Supremacy	Random House	1986	189	160	141
Ludlum, Robert	The Bourne Ultimatum	Random House	1990	89	75	66
Ludlum, Robert	The Holcroft Covenent	Marek	1978	139	118	104
Ludlum, Robert	The Icarus Agenda	Random House	1988	99	84	74
Ludlum, Robert	The Road to Omaha	Random House	1992	89	75	66
MacDonald, Ross	A Collection of Reviews	Lord John Press	1979	375	318	281
MacKinlay, Kantor	Spirit Lake	World Publighing Co.	1961	389	330	291
Maclaine, Shirley	Dance While you Can	Bantam	1991	129	109	96
Maguire, Jack	The Presidents Country	Alcalde	1964	889	755	666
Mailer, Norman	The Time of Our Time	Random House	1998	128	108	96
Mailer, Norman	Tough Guys Don't Dance	Random House	*1984	129	109	96
Mandela, Nelson	Long Walk to Freedom	Easton Press	2001	389	330	291
Mann, Thomas	Nocturnes	Equinox Coop Press Inc	*1934	249	211	186
Margolin, Phillip	The Burning Man	Doubleday	1996	89	75	66
Margret, Ann	My Story			98	83	73
Marquez, Gabriel Garcia	News of a Kidnapping	Knopf	1997	349	296	261
Maso, Carole	Defiance	Dutton	1998	89	75	66
Mason, Herman (JR)	Going Against The Wind	Longstreet Press	1992	489	415	366
Matlin, Mary	All's Fair	Random House	1994	129	109	96
Matthiessen, Peter	Under the Mountain Wall	Viking	1962	149	126	111
McAuley, Paul F.	Making History	PS Publishing	2000	89	75	66
McBain, Ed	And All Through the House	Warner Books	1984	89	75	66
McCain, John	Faith of My Fathers	Random House	1999	129	109	96
McCammon, Robert	Night Visions 8	Dark Harvest	1990	249	211	186
McCarthy, Cormac	Ecco	Ecco Press	1994	689	585	516

Author	Title	Publisher	Year Published	Flatsigned	Signed & Inscribed	Signed on Bookplate
McCarthy, Cormac	The Crossing	Knopf	1994	589	500	441
McCarthy, Cormac	The Gardener's Son	The Ecco Press	1996	589	500	441
McCarthy, Cormac	The Stonemason	Ecco Press	1994	59	50	44
McCourt, Frank	Angela's Ashes	Harper Collins	1996	489	415	366
McCourt, Frank	Angela's Ashes	Scribner	1996	689	585	516
McCourt, Frank	Tis	Scribner	1999	89	75	66
McCullough, Colleen	Morgan's Run	Simon & Schuster	2000	289	245	216
McGovern, George	Grassroots: The Autobiography of George McGovern	Random House	1977	189	160	141
McGovern, George	The Third Freedom	Simon & Schuster	2001	89	75	66
McGuane, Thomas	Nothing but Blue Skies	Houghton Mifflin & Co.	1992	98	83	73
McGuane, Thomas	The Longest Silence	Knopf	1999	98	83	73
McMurtry, Larry	All My Friends Are Going To Be Strangers	Simon & Schuster	1972	349	296	261
McMurtry, Larry	Anything for Billy	Simon & Schuster	1988	129	109	96
McMurtry, Larry	Buffalo Girls	Simon & Schuster	1990	179	152	134
McMurtry, Larry	Cadillac Jack	Simon & Schuster	1982	449	381	336
McMurtry, Larry	Comanche Moon	Simon & Schuster	1997	349	296	261
McMurtry, Larry	Dead Man's Walk	Simon & Schuster	1995	89	75	66
McMurtry, Larry	Desert Rose	Simon & Schuster	1983	129	109	96
McMurtry, Larry	Duane's Depressed	Simon & Schuster	1999	249	211	186
McMurtry, Larry	Flim Flam	Simon & Schuster	1987	389	330	291
McMurtry, Larry	Horesman Pass By	Harper & Bros	1961	3,489	2,965	2,616
McMurtry, Larry	In A Narrow Grave	Encino Press	1968	2,889	2,455	2,166
McMurtry, Larry	Leaving Cheyenne	Harper & Row	1963	2,400	2,040	1,800
McMurtry, Larry	Lonesome Dove	Simon & Schuster	1985	889	755	666
McMurtry, Larry	Moving On	Simon & Schuster	1970	489	415	366
McMurtry, Larry	Pretty Boy Floyd	Simon & Schuster	1994	179	152	134
McMurtry, Larry	Roads	Simon & Schuster	2000	89	75	66
McMurtry, Larry	Some Can Whistle	Simon & Schuster	1989	179	152	134
McMurtry, Larry	Somebody's Darling	Simon & Schuster	1978	449	381	336
McMurtry, Larry	Still Wild	Simon & Schuster	2000	189	160	141
McMurtry, Larry	Streets of Laredo	Simon & Schuster	1993	289	245	216
McMurtry, Larry	Terms of Endearment	Simon & Schuster	1975	479	407	359
McMurtry, Larry	Texasville	Simon & Schuster	1987	229	194	171
McMurtry, Larry	The Evening Star	Simon & Schuster	1992	89	75	66
McMurtry, Larry	The Last Picture Show	Simon & Schuster	1989	189	160	141
McMurtry, Larry	The Last Picture Show	The Dial Press	1966	789	670	591
McMurtry, Larry	The Late Child	Simon & Schuster	1995	129	109	96
McMurtry, Larry	Zeke and Ned	Simon & Schuster	1997	89	75	66
McPhee, John	Giving Good Weight	Farrar Straus and Giroux	1979	889	755	666
McPhee, John	Looking For A Ship	Farrar Straus Giroux	1991	89	75	66
Michener, James	A Michener Miscellany	Random House	1973	289	245	216
Michener, James	Hawaii	Random House	1959	289	245	216
Michener, James	Iberia	Random House	*1968	649	551	486

Author	Title	Publisher	Year Published	Flatsigned	Signed & Inscribed	Signed on Bookplate
Michener, James	Poland	Random House	1983	89	75	66
Michener, James	Presidential Lottery	Random House	1969	449	381	336
Michener, James	Tales Of The South Pacific	MacMillan	1947	2,449	2,081	1,836
Michener, James	The Bridges at Toko-ri	Random House	1953	49	41	36
Michener, James A.	Recessional	The Franklin Library	1994	289	245	216
Michener, James A.	Recessional	Random House	*1994	249	211	186
Michener, James A.	The Covenant	Random House	1980	279	237	209
Michener, James A.	Ventures In Editing	Cahill	*1995	189	160	141
Mieville, China	King Rat	Tom Doherty Assoc.	1998	89	75	66
Miller, Arthur	Salesman In Beijing	Viking	1984	149	126	111
Miller, Arthur	After the Fall	Viking	*1964	189	160	141
Miller, Arthur	Conversations With Arthur Miller	Mississippi Press	1987	189	160	141
Miller, Arthur	Echoes Down the Corridor	Viking	2000	189	160	141
Miller, Arthur	Homely Girl A life and Other Stories	Viking	1992	129	109	96
Miller, Diane Disney	The Story of Walt Disney	Holt	1957	6,400	5,440	4,800
Milne, A.A.	The House At Pooh Corner	Methuen	1928	489	415	366
Milne, A.A.	The Secret	The Fountain Press	1929	489	415	366
Milne, A.A.	Year In, Year Out	Methuen	1952	489	415	366
Monsarrat, Nicholas	The Tribe That Lost Its Head	Sloane	1956	289	245	216
Morris, Edmund	Dutch: A Memoir of Ronald Reagan	Random House	1999	129	109	96
Morrison, Toni	Beloved	Knopf	1987	389	330	291
Morrison, Toni	Song of Solomon	Knopf	1977	289	245	216
Morrison, Toni	Sula	Knopf	1974	589	500	441
Morton, Andrew	Diana - Her True Story	Simon & Schuster	1992	129	109	96
Morton, Andrew	Monica's Story	St. Martin's Press	1999	189	160	141
Mosley, Walter	A Red Death	Norton & Co.	1991	149	126	111
Mosley, Walter	Black Betty	Norton & Co.	1994	89	75	66
Mosley, Walter	Blue Light	Little Brown	1998	89	75	66
Mosley, Walter	Devil in a Blue Dress	Norton	1990	169	143	126
Mosley, Walter	RL's Dream	Norton & Co.	1995	89	75	66
Mosley, Walter	White Butterfly	Norton	1992	375	318	281
Muller, Marcia	Beyond the Grave	Walker	1986	335	284	251
Muller, Marcia	The Tree of Death	Walker	1983	195	165	146
Muller, Marcia	There's Something in a Sunday	Mysterious Press	1989	115	97	86
Muller, Marcia	Till the Butchers Cut Him Down	Mysterious Press/ Time Warner	1994	95	80	71
Muller, Marcia	Where Echoes Live	Mysterious Press	1991	95	80	71
Murphy, Audie	To Hell And Back	Holt	1949	389	330	291
Nevin, David	Muskie of Maine	Random House	1972	89	75	66
Nixon, Richard	Six Crises	Doubleday	1962	589	500	441
Nixon, Richard	The Memoirs of Richard Nixon	Grosset & Dunnlap	*1978	449	381	336
Nolan, William F.	Helltracks	Cemetary Dance Pub.	*2000	89	75	66
North, Oliver	Under Fire	Harper Collins	1991	129	109	96
Novak, William	Man of the House	Random House	1987	89	75	66
Palahniuk, Chuck	Choke	Doubleday	2001	89	75	66

Author	Title	Publisher	Year Published	Flatsigned	Signed & Inscribed	Signed on Bookplate
Palahniuk, Chuck	Fightclub	Norton	1996	129	109	96
Parker, Robert B.	A Catskill Evil	Delacorte Press	1985	129	109	96
Parker, Robert B.	Pale Kings and Princes	Delacorte Press	1987	129	109	96
Parker, Robert B.	Sudden Mischief	Putnam	1998	89	75	66
Parker, Robert B.	Taming a Sea-Horse	Delacorte Press	1986	89	75	66
Parker, Robert B.	The Widening Gyre	Delacorte Press	1983	89	75	66
Parker, Robert B.	Valediction	Delacorte Press	1984	89	75	66
Passos, John Dos	Most Likely To Succeed	Prentice Hall	1954	289	245	216
Pasternak, Boris	Doctor Zhivago	Pantheon	1958	249	211	186
Peale, Norman Vincent	Enthusiasm Makes the Difference	Prentice-Hall	1967	129	109	96
Perry, Anne	The Face of a Stranger	Fawcett Columbine	1990	89	75	66
Philbin, Regis	I'm Only One Man	Hyperion	1995	89	75	66
Phillips, Scott	The Ice Harvest	Ballantine Books	2000	89	75	66
Podrug, Junius	Frost of Heaven	Dark Harvest	*1992	189	160	141
Pohl, Frederik	The Gateway Trip	Del Rey Books	1990	89	75	66
Powell, Colin	My American Journey	Random House	1995	289	245	216
Powell, Colin	My American Journey	Random House	*1995	289	245	216
Powers, Jim	The Drawing of the Dark	Hypatia Press	*1991	149	126	111
Price, Eugenia	Lighthouse	Lippincott	1971	89	75	66
Proulx, E. Annie	Accordion Crimes	Scribner	1996	129	109	96
Proulx, E. Annie	Accordion Crimes	Scribner	*1996	249	211	186
Proulx, E. Annie	The Shipping News	Scribner	1993	889	755	666
Prouty, L. Fletcher	The Secret Team	Prentice-Hall	1973	129	109	96
Reagan, Nancy	I Love You Ronnie	Random House	2000	189	160	141
Reagan, Nancy	My Turn	Random House	1989	129	109	96
Reagan, Nancy	Nancy	Morrow	1980	249	211	186
Reagan, Ronald	An American Life	Simon & Schuster	1990	1,489	1,265	1,116
Reagan, Ronald	Speaking My Mind	Simon & Schuster	1989	1,849	1,571	1,386
Rice, Anne	Beauty's Punishment	MacDonald	1984	489	415	366
Rice, Anne	Belinda	Arbor House	1986	389	330	291
Rice, Anne	Cry To Heaven	Knopf	1982	389	330	291
Rice, Anne	Exit to Eden	Arbor House	1985	289	245	216
Rice, Anne	Interview with the Vampire	Knopf	1976	1,289	1,095	966
Rice, Anne	Interview With the Vampire	Knopf	*1996	149	126	111
Rice, Anne	Interview with the Vampire	Knopf	*1992	489	415	366
Rice, Anne	Lasher	Knopf	1993	149	126	111
Rice, Anne	Memnoch the Devil	Knopf	1995	129	109	96
Rice, Anne	Memnoch the Devil	B.E. Trice	*	249	211	186
Rice, Anne	Pandora	Knopf	*1998	279	237	209
Rice, Anne	Servant of the Bones	Knopf	1996	99	84	74
Rice, Anne	Taltos	Knopf	1994	99	84	74
Rice, Anne	Taltos	Knopf	*1994	249	211	186
Rice, Anne	The Feast of All Saints	Simon & Schuster	1979	289	245	216
Rice, Anne	The Mummy	Chatto & Winclus	1989	289	245	216

Author	Title	Publisher	Year Published	Flatsigned	Signed & Inscribed	Signed on Bookplate
Rice, Anne	The Queen of the Damned	Knopf	1988	389	330	291
Rice, Anne	The Tale of the Body Thief	Knopf	1992	99	84	74
Rice, Anne	The Tale of the Body Thief	Knopf	1992	89	75	66
Rice, Anne	The Vampire Armand	Knopf	1998	99	84	74
Rice, Anne	The Vampire Lestat	Knopf	1985	349	296	261
Rice, Anne	The Witching Hour	Knopf	1990	189	160	141
Rice, Anne	Violin	Knopf	1997	149	126	111
Rice, Anne	Vittorio the Vampire	Knopf	1999	89	75	66
Rice, Anne	Witching Hour	Knopf	1990	189	160	141
Ripley, Alexandra	Scarlett: The Sequel to Gone With the Wind	Warner Books	1991	175	148	131
Roberts, Cokie & Steve	From This Day Forward	Morrow	2000	89	75	66
Roth, Philip	Sabbath's Theater	Houghton Mifflin	1995	129	109	96
Roth, Philip	The Dying Animal	Houghton Mifflin	2001	89	75	66
Rowling, J.K.	Harry Potter and the Chamber of Secrets	Scholastic	1998	789	670	591
Rowling, J.K.	Harry Potter and the Chamber of Secrets	Scholastic	1999	289	245	216
Rowling, J.K.	Harry Potter and the Goblet of Fire	Scholastic	2000	129	109	96
Rowling, J.K.	Harry Potter and the Prisoner of Azkaban	Scholastic	1999	789	670	591
Salinger, J.D.	Franny And Zooey	Little and Brown	1961	389	330	291
Salinger, Pierre	With Kennedy	Doubleday	1966	34	28	25
Sandburg, Carl	Always the Young Stranger	Harcourt Brace	1953	129	109	96
Sandford, John	Easy Prey	Putnam	2000	89	75	66
Sandford, John	Rules of Prey	Putnam	1989	249	211	186
Sandford, John	Secret Prey	Putnam	1998	89	75	66
Sandford, John	Shadow Prey	Putnam	1990	89	75	66
Sandford, John	Silent Prey	Putnam	1992	129	109	96
Sandford, John	Sudden Prey	Putnam	1996	89	75	66
Sandford, John	The Devil's Code	Putnam	2000	89	75	66
Sandford, John	The Night Crew	Putnam	1997	89	75	66
Sandford, John	Winter Prey	Putnam	1993	99	75	66
Schwarzkopf, Norman	The Autobiography: It Doesn't Take a Hero	Bantam	1992	149	126	111
Segal, Erich	Man Women and Child	Harper & Row	1980	89	75	66
Settle, Mary Lee	Celebration			98	83	73
Shula, Don	Everyone's a Coach	HarperBusiness	1995	149	126	111
Siddons, Anne Rivers	The House Next Door	Old New York Book Shop	*1993	279	237	209
Smiley, Jane	A Thousand Acres	Knopf	1991	249	211	186
Snow, C.P.	Strangers and Brothers	Scribner Sons	1972	749	636	561
Sparks, Nicholas	The Notebook	Warner Books	1996	99	84	74
Spillane, Mickey	Black Alley	Dutton	1996	129	109	96
Spillane, Mickey	The Killing Man	Dutton	1989	149	126	111

Author	Title	Publisher	Year Published	Flatsigned	Signed & Inscribed	Signed on Bookplate
Spillane, Mickey	Tomorrow I Die	The Mysterious Press	*1984	179	152	134
Springer, Jerry	Ringmaster	St. Martins Press	1998	89	75	66
Staubach, Roger	Reaching For the Stars	Tyler Publishing	*1993	249	211	186
Steel, Danielle	No Greater Love	Delacorte Press	*1991	199	169	149
Steel, Danielle	Silent Honor	Delacorte Press	*1996	199	169	149
Steel, Danielle	The Long Road Home	Delacorte Press	*1998	199	169	149
Steel, Danielle	Zoya	Delacorte Press	*1988	199	169	149
Steinbeck, John	The Moon Is Down	Viking	1942	289	245	216
Steinbeck, John	Travels With Charley	The Viking Press	1962	6,889	5,855	5,166
Stern, Howard	Private Parts	Simon & Schuster	1993	149	126	111
Stone, Robert	A Flag for Sunrise	Knopf	1981	128	108	96
Stone, Robert	Children of Light	Knopf	1986	98	83	73
Stone, Robert	Damascus Gate			98	83	73
Stone, Robert	Outerbridge Reach	Ticknor & Fields	1992	98	83	73
Straub, Peter	Mystery	Dutton	1990	189	160	141
Styron, William	Sophie's Choice	Modern Library	1999	389	330	291
Talese, Gay	Honor Thy Father	World Publishing Co.	1971	99	84	74
Talese, Gay	The Kingdom and the Power	World Publishing Co.	1969	89	75	66
Talese, Gay	Unto the Sons	Knopf	1992	89	75	66
Tan, Amy	The Hundred Secret Senses	Putnam	*1995	249	211	186
Tan, Amy	The Joy Luck Club	Putnam	1989	389	330	291
Tarkington, Booth	The Midlander	Doubleday	1923	289	245	216
Tessier, Thomas	Ghost Music	Cemetary Dance Pub.	*2000	89	75	66
Thatcher, Margaret	DOWNING STREET YEARS	HarperCollins	*1993	395	335	296
Thomas, D.M.	Alexander Solzhenitsyn			98	83	73
Thompson, Jim	The Killer Inside Me	Blood & Guts Press	*1989	249	211	186
Thoreau, Henry David	A Yankee In Canada	Ticknor and Fields	1866	189	160	141
Townsend, Jimmy	Wait Just A Cotton Pickin' Minute!	Advocate Press	1983	129	109	96
Trapp, Maria Von	Yesterday Today and Forever	New Leaf Press	1975	89	75	66
Treece, Henry	The Magic Wood	Harper Collins		89	75	66
Truman, Harry S.	Mr. Citizen	Bernard Geis Assoc.	1960	449	381	336
Trump, Donald	The Art of the Comeback	Random House	1997	179	152	134
Trump, Donald	Trump: The Art of the Deal	Random House	1987	189	160	141
Turow, Scott	One L	Putnam	1977	489	415	366
Turow, Scott	Personal Injuries	Farrar Straus Giroux	1999	89	75	66
Turow, Scott	Presumed Innocent	Farrar Straus Giroux	1987	289	245	216
Turow, Scott	The Burden of Proof	Farrar Straus Giroux	1990	99	84	74
Tyler, Anne	A Patchwork Planet	Knopf	1998	89	75	66
Tyler, Anne	Breathing Lessons	Knopf	1988	129	109	96
Tyler, Anne	Dinner At The Homesick Restaurant	Knopf	1982	249	211	186
Tyler, Anne	Ladder of Years	Knopf	1995	89	75	66
Tyler, Anne	Morgan's Passing	Knopf	1980	289	245	216
Tyler, Anne	Saint Maybe	Knopf	1991	129	109	96
Tyler, Anne	The Accidental Tourist	Knopf	1985	179	152	134
Updike, John	A Month of Sundays	Knopf	*1975	229	194	171

Author	Title	Publisher	Year Published	Flatsigned	Signed & Inscribed	Signed on Bookplate
Updike, John	Memories of the Ford Administration	Knopf	1992	149	126	111
Updike, John	Problems and Other Stories	Knopf	1979	129	109	96
Updike, John	Rabbit Run		*	249	211	186
Updike, John	Rabbit At Rest	Knopf	1990	189	160	141
Updike, John	Rabbit At Rest	The Franklin Library	1990	249	211	186
Updike, John	Rabbit is Rich	Knopf	1981	675	573	506
Updike, John	S.	Knopf	1988	129	109	96
Updike, John	The Beloved	Lord John Press	1982	229	194	171
Updike, John	The Coup	Knopf	1978	149	126	111
Updike, John	The Music School	Knopf	1966	89	75	66
Updike, John	The Witches of Eastwick	Knopf	1984	149	126	111
Updike, John	Toward the End of Time	Knopf	1997	129	109	96
Ventura, Jesse	Do I Stand Alone?	Pocket Books	2000	89	75	66
Vidal, Gore	The Golden Age	Doubleday	2000	149	126	111
Vollmann, William T.	The Royal Family	Putnam	2000	99	84	74
Vonnegut, Kurt	Bagombo Snuff Box	Putnam	*	249	211	186
Vonnegut, Kurt	Bluebeard	Delacorte Press	1987	249	211	186
Vonnegut, Kurt	Breakfast of Champions	Delacorte Press	1973	289	245	216
Vonnegut, Kurt	Deadeye Dick	Delacorte Press	*1982	129	109	96
Vonnegut, Kurt	Galapagos	Delacorte Press	1985	249	211	186
Vonnegut, Kurt	Jailbird	Delacorte Press	1979	149	126	111
Vonnegut, Kurt	Palm Sunday	Delacorte Press	1981	159	135	119
Vonnegut, Kurt	Palm Sunday	Delacorte Press	*1981	129	109	96
Vonnegut, Kurt	Slapstick	Delacorte Press	1976	189	160	141
Vonnegut, Kurt	Slaughterhouse-Five	The Easton Press	2001	289	245	216
Vonnegut, Kurt	Timequake	Putnam	1997	99	84	74
Vonnegut, Kurt	Wampeters Foma & Granfalloons	Delacorte Press	1974	249	211	186
Wahlen, John	Shoot To Miss	Sunrise	1981	89	75	66
Walker, Alice	Anything We Love Can Be Saved	Random House	1997	89	75	66
Walker, Alice	In Search Of Our Mothers' Gardens	Harcourt Brace	1983	589	500	441
Walker, Alice	Living By the Word	Harcourt Brace	1981	89	75	66
Walker, Alice	The Color Purple	Harcourt Brace	1982	889	755	666
Walker, Alice	The Temple of My Familiar	Harcourt Brace	1989	289	245	216
Walker, Alice	The Way Forward Is With a Broken Heart	Random House	2000	89	75	66
Wallace, Chris	First Lady - A Portrait of Nancy Reagan	St. Martin's Press	1986	589	500	441
Wallace, Irving	The Plot	Simon & Schuster	1967	89	75	66
Wallace, Robert	The World of Rembrandt 1606-1669	Time Life Books	1968	249	211	186
Walters, Minette	The Ice-House	St. Martin's Press	1992	589	500	441
Wambaugh, Joseph	Finnegan's Week	Morrow	1993	89	75	66
Wambaugh, Joseph	Floaters	Bantam	1996	89	75	66
Wambaugh, Joseph	The Choirboys	Delacorte Press	1975	149	126	111
Watson, Lawrence	In A Dark Time	Scribner	1980	549	466	411
Welty, Eudora	The Collected Stories Of Eudora Welty	Harcourt Brace	1980	379	322	284
White, Randy Wayne	Captiva	Putnam	1996	95	80	71

Author	Title	Publisher	Year Published	Flatsigned	Signed & Inscribed	Signed on Bookplate
White, Randy Wayne	Shark River	Putnam	2001	89	75	66
White, Randy Wayne	Ten Thousand Islands	Putnam	2000	89	75	66
White, William	The Citadel	Harper	1957	49	41	36
Wicker, Tom	Facing the Lions	Viking	1973	89	75	66
Williams, Tennesse	Steps Must Be Gentle	Targ Editions	1980	389	330	291
Winfrey, Oprah	Journey To Beloved	Hyperion	1998	249	211	186
Woodford, Jack	Possessed	The Woodford Press	1946	89	75	66
Wouk, Herman	The Caine Mutiny	The Franklin Library	1977	389	330	291
Wright, Frank Lloyd	When Democracy Builds	Cambridge Press:				
		London	1945	389	330	291
Wyland	Whale Tales	Wyland Studios	1995	149	126	111

HOW TO USE THE SPORTS GUIDE

This guide should be used for authenticated items only. The guide provides pricing for items that have already been certified by a respected third party authenticator. Regardless, the prices listed in this guide represent what the items should approximately sell for if in fact they were certified. For autographs acquired prior to 1980, the guide reflects pricing for what would be considered an "8" signature. For autographs acquired after 1980, the guide reflects pricing for mint condition autographs. Remember, although SMR does its absolute best to reflect the current market for autograph prices, the prices listed should only be used as a guide when buying and selling autographed items. Please refer to the autograph chart and to the section below, "A Note about Autograph Pricing," for further explanation.

A Note About Autograph Pricing

Autograph pricing can be, at times, a difficult task. There are many factors to consider when placing a value on an autographed item. Condition, rarity, eye appeal and age are just some of the factors used in evaluating autograph pricing. For example, when you have an autographed team ball, many collectors assume that you simply add all the individual signatures to come up with the value. That is not the case. While team signed baseballs are great collectibles, single signed items are considered more desirable than those items that are signed by multiple players. Another pricing dilemma occurs when the condition of the autograph and the item itself differ. A baseball maybe in mint condition but the autograph may only grade a 4 or 5 on a scale of 1 to 10.

The situation is the same for items that are signed perfectly but the items themselves may be in poor condition. In addition, a player may rarely sign certain items such as game-used equipment or the player may not sign often with inscriptions. All in all, there is a lot to consider when determining the value of autographed items. I have provided a general condition guide that should be used as a base only because, as it was stated above, autograph pricing can vary a great deal.

Valuation Factors

Baseballs - There are several factors that contribute to the value of autographed baseballs. First, as a general rule, baseballs are valued higher if they are signed on the sweet spot as opposed to the side panel. Sweet spot autographs are much easier to display and therefore command a premium price. On the other hand, many players, especially those from the vintage era, signed on the side panel often. Baseballs signed on the side panel offer an affordable alternative to those on the sweet spot.

Second, official league baseballs are generally valued higher than non-league baseballs. Third, baseballs that are harder to locate such as World Series baseballs or scarce versions of regular season baseballs command a premium. Fourth, personalized baseballs such as "To Jack" are valued less than non-personalized baseballs. Finally, the condition of the baseball itself, regardless of the condition of the autograph, is also a major factor in determining the value. Coloring (whiteness), scuffing, shellacking (a glossy coat to preserve the autograph), staining and overall wear are all key factors in determining the value of autographed baseballs. The general and simple rule is the better the eye appeal, the higher the value.

Photos - When determining the value of an autographed photo, there are a few factors to consider. The photo may have corner wear or slight edge wear without detracting significantly from the value but any wear or damage that detracts from the image itself will lower the value considerably. Also, as with baseballs, personalized autographs will lower the overall value. Other major factors include rarity of the photo, historical importance, picture quality and overall eye appeal. Photos are usually used as display items so the eye appeal is very important. The prices in this guide are for 8x10 (modern) or smaller (vintage) photos.

Documents - The keys to determining the value of an autographed document are over-all condition and content. Many letters will have folds or bends in them because of the mailing process so, as long as there are no major flaws such as tears or staining that affect the content, the value won't be affected very much. Content is another major factor. As a general rule, the more sports related content, the higher the value. There are instances where non-sports content may be worth more; it simply comes down to how interesting the content is.

Another content-related factor revolves around the amount of handwriting found in the document. With all other things being equal, if a letter is handwritten, it is usually worth more than a letter that is typed. Collectors seem to like the personal touch the handwritten pieces offer.

Bats, Gloves, Helmets and Jerseys - This guide should be used for non-game equipment. Autographed game-issued or game-used equipment would command a much higher premium than the prices listed in this guide. The autographed bat, glove, helmet and jersey prices listed are for replica or commemorative-type items. General condition principles apply.

Flats - General condition principles apply to all other miscellaneous flat items.

Final Note

As stated earlier, autograph pricing is a very difficult task when you consider the amount of subjectivity involved. At SMR, we will do our very best to track the market on all of the items listed and add new items as needed. **Remember that autographs authenticated in the presence of the signer will usually sell for a premium price, sometimes a major one, when the service provided includes certification (usually accompanied by a sticker, hologram or DNA) from a respected company in the industry. The bottom line in auto-graph collecting or any other area of collecting is that you get what you pay for. There is great value in buying authenticated autographs. Not only are they more liquid when it comes time to sell them but you absolutely know you are getting the real thing. Major premium prices may apply to autographs of this quality and for very good reason.** We hope this information proves to be useful in determining the values of your prized autographed items.

Legend

HOF	Hall of Fame Induction
3X5	Index Card
ACTIVE	Still Playing
A/P	Album Page
GLAC	Goal Line Art Card
HOF PLAQ-B/W	Hall of Fame Plaque

Black & White issued before 1963.

HOF PLAQ-Gold	Hall of Fame Plaque

Gold card issued after 1963.

IMP	Impossible

For instance, it is impossible for Grover Alexander to have signed a Gold Hall of Fame plaque card because he passed away prior to issuance.

N/A	Not Applicable

For instance, Gil Hodges was never inducted into the Hall of Fame, therefore the Hall of Fame plaque cards will not apply to him.

SS BALL	Single Signed Official Baseball
SS BAT	Single Signed Bat
SSF	Single Signed Official Football
SSJ	Single Signed Jersey
UNK	Unknown
*	Deceased

Name	HOF	3x5 A/P	Gum Card	Photo	Check	HOF Plaq B/W	HOF Plaq COLOR	Letter	SS Bat	SSBall
Aaron, Hank	1982	35	40	55	100	IMP	30	150	150	80
Alexander, Grover*	1938	700	1000	1000	UNK	3000	IMP	1200	UNK	4000
Alomar, Roberto		25	30	30	UNK	ACTIVE	ACTIVE	125	100	40
Alston, Walter*	1983	50	50	85	150	IMP	150	100	UNK	600
Anderson, Sparky	2000	10	20	25	UNK	IMP	30	200	80	35
Anson,"Cap"*	1939	2000	5000	9000	UNK	IMP	IMP	2500	UNK	25000
Aparico, Luis	1984	25	30	25	300	IMP	25	200	80	40
Appling, Luke*	1964	10	20	20	UNK	IMP	20	250	250	100
Ashburn, Richie*	1995	15	25	25	75	IMP	50	125	175	80
Averill, Earl*	1975	15	30	75	UNK	IMP	25	150	UNK	800
Bagwell, Jeff		20	25	35	UNK	ACTIVE	ACTIVE	100	100	55
Baker, Frank "Home Run"*	1955	275	500	700	2500	2000	IMP	1500	UNK	3500
Bancroft, David*	1971	150	175	250	UNK	IMP	1100	350	UNK	1800
Banks,"Ernie"	1977	15	30	35	75	IMP	25	200	75	45
Barlick, Al*	1989	10	25	25	35	IMP	25	200	75	40
Barrow, Edward*	1953	200	N/A	400	135	IMP	IMP	150	UNK	2500
Beckley, Jacob*	1971	4000	6000	N/A	4500	IMP	IMP	6000	UNK	UNK
Bell, James "Cool Papa"*	1974	25	35	65	700	IMP	35	250	UNK	175
Belle, Albert		25	35	30	UNK	IMP	N/A	UNK	100	30
Bench, Johnny	1989	25	30	35	200	IMP	30	175	125	45
Bender,"Chief"*	1953	275	500	600	900	IMP	IMP	600	UNK	2700
Berg, Moe*		200	500	700	250	N/A	N/A	800	UNK	UNK
Berra, Lawrence "Yogi"	1972	15	25	40	200	IMP	25	200	100	55
Biggio, Craig		15	20	25	UNK	ACTIVE	ACTIVE	100	80	35
Boggs, Wade		20	25	35	UNK	IMP	N/A	150	100	40
Bonds, Barry		20	30	50	UNK	ACTIVE	ACTIVE	200	175	75
Bottomley, Jim*	1974	350	500	700	2500	IMP	IMP	700	80	2500
Boudreau, Lou*	1970	5	10	15	50	IMP	10	50	UNK	30
Bresnahan, Roger*	1945	700	1200	1500	UNK	IMP	IMP	3000	UNK	5000
Brett, George	1999	25	30	40	UNK	N/A	40	150	125	55
Brock,"Lou"	1970	15	20	35	UNK	IMP	15	250	80	45
Brouthers, Dan*	1945	1500	UNK	UNK	UNK	IMP	IMP	4500	UNK	UNK
Brown, Kevin		15	25	30	UNK	ACTIVE	ACTIVE	100	90	35
Brown, Mordecai "3 Finger"*	1949	500	900	1800	UNK	IMP	IMP	1200	UNK	4500
Bulkeley, Morgan*	1937	1200	N/A	UNK	1500	IMP	IMP	1500	UNK	UNK
Bunning, Jim	1996	15	25	25	200	IMP	25	100	70	40
Burkett, Jesse*	1946	800	1000	1800	31000	2500	IMP	4000	UNK	4500
Campanella, Roy*	1969	450	500	1000	UNK	IMP	500 (post)	2000	2500	4500
Canseco, Jose		20	25	30	100	ACTIVE	ACTIVE	150	90	40
Carew, Rod	1991	20	30	30	UNK	IMP	30	300	100	40
Carey, Max*	1961	25	50	75	50	150	100	150	UNK	1300
Carlton, Steve	1994	20	25	30	100	IMP	25	150	80	45

Name	HOF	3x5 A/P	Gum Card	Photo	Check	HOF Plaq B/W	HOF Plaq COLOR	Letter	SS Bat	SS Ball
Carter, Joe		15	20	25	UNK	IMP	N/A	100	80	35
Cartwright, Alexander*	1938	1200	N/A	UNK	2000	IMP	IMP	2000	UNK	UNK
Cash, Norm*		45	50	60	UNK	N/A	N/A	200	250	350
Cepeda, Orlando	2000	12	15	20	45	N/A	30	85	85	40
Chadwick, Henry*	1938	3000	N/A	UNK	UNK	IMP	IMP	4000	UNK	UNK
Chance, Frank*	1946	1800	2500	UNK	UNK	IMP	IMP	4000	UNK	UNK
Chandler, Albert*	1982	25	35	50	150	IMP	20	100	200	150
Carhleston, Oscar*	1976	4500	N/A	UNK	UNK	IMP	IMP	UNK	UNK	UNK
Chesbro, Jack*	1946	2500	UNK	UNK	6000	IMP	IMP	6000	UNK	UNK
Ciotte, Ed*		350	600	600	UNK	N/A	N/A	1000	UNK	2000
Clark, Will		20	25	25	UNK	IMP	N/A	100	100	35
Clarke, Fred*	1945	250	400	500	UNK	850	IMP	500	UNK	2000
Clarkson, John*	1963	UNK	UNK	8000	UNK	IMP	IMP	UNK	UNK	UNK
Clemens, Roger		30	40	60	UNK	ACTIVE	ACTIVE	250	150	75
Clemente, Roberto*	1973	400	550	800	1000	IMP	IMP	1500	2000	3500
Cobb, Ty*	1936	500	1000	1500	800	2200	IMP	2000	2500	5000
Cochrane, Mickey*	1947	250	400	500	250	900	IMP	500	UNK	2750
Colavito, "Rocky"		10	25	30	35	N/A	N/A	150	100	35
Collins, Edward*	1939	400	1000	1200	2500	2750	IMP	500	UNK	3500
Collins, Jimmy*	1945	2000	2000	3000	UNK	IMP	IMP	5000	UNK	UNK
Combs, Earle*	1970	70	100	275	150	IMP	150	400	UNK	1500
Comiskey, Charles*	1939	700	N/A	2000	3500	IMP	IMP	1500	UNK	15000
Cone, David		20	25	30	UNK	ACTIVE	ACTIVE	150	90	35
Conigaliaro, Tony*		100	150	250	N/A	N/A	N/A	300	500	700
Conian, John*	1974	20	35	50	UNK	IMP	25	65	250	175
Connolly, Tom*	1953	500	1000	1200	UNK	1500	IMP	1000	UNK	2700
Conner, Roger*	1976	3000	UNK	6000	UNK	IMP	IMP	UNK	UNK	UNK
Coveleski, Stan*	1969	15	40	75	UNK	IMP	30	125	UNK	500
Crawford, Sam*	1957	250	150	250	UNK	450	375	375	UNK	2500
Cronin, Joe*	1956	30	65	65	200	150	50	100	UNK	400
Cummings, William*	1939	3700	UNK	UNK	UNK	IMP	IMP	7000	UNK	UNK
Cuyler, Hazen*	1968	500	700	900	2500	IMP	IMP	1000	UNK	2500
Dandridge, Ray*	1987	35	35	60	50	IMP	35	250	225	100
Davis, George*	1998	UNK	UNK	UNK	UNK	IMP	IMP	7000	UNK	UNK
Dawson, Andre		10	15	20	35	N/A	N/A	100	70	35
Day, Leon*	1995	50	50	50	125	IMP	IMP	300	200	125
Dean,"Dizzy"*	1953	100	150	300	UNK	250	150	500	UNK	1300
Delahanty, Ed*	1945	4000	UNK	UNK	UNK	IMP	IMP	10000	UNK	UNK
Dickey, Bill*	1954	35	60	60	150	125	60	200	350	175
Dihigo, Martin*	1977	1200	UNK	2500	UNK	IMP	IMP	2500	UNK	2500
Dimaggio, Dom		15	25	25	50	N/A	N/A	100	70	40
Dimaggio, Joe*	1955	200	20	200	1500	275	200	1500	2500	375
Dimaggio, Vince*		50	85	150	UNK	N/A	N/A	250	400	700
Doby, Larry	1998	20	25	25	UNK	IMP	35	150	100	35
Doerr, Bobby	1986	5	20	20	25	IMP	10	75	70	30
Drysdale, Don*	1984	30	40	65	200	IMP	30	150	225	125

Name	HOF	3x5 A/P	Gum Card	Photo	Check	HOF Plaq B/W	HOF Plaq COLOR	Letter	SS Bat	SS Ball
Duffy, Hugh*	1945	400	600	800	UNK	2250	IMP	800	UNK	3000
Durocher, Leo*	1994	25	35	50	500	IMP	IMP	150	250	175
Evans, Billy*	1973	400	700	900	UNK	IMP	IMP	400	UNK	3000
Evers, John*	1946	700	1500	1500	3000	IMP	IMP	1300	UNK	10000
Ewing,"Buck"*	1939	2000	UNK	UNK	UNK	IMP	IMP	6000	UNK	UNK
Faber,"Red"*	1964	45	75	125	UNK	IMP	85	200	UNK	1500
Feller, Robert	1962	10	20	20	150	50	15	125	60	25
Ferrell, Rick*	1984	10	20	25	35	IMP	15	85	125	60
Fingers, Rollie	1992	15	20	30	50	IMP	15	100	75	35
Fisk, Carlton	2000	30	35	40	UNK	N/A	35	150	125	45
Flick, Elmer*	1963	65	150	250	UNK	750	375	250	UNK	2000
Ford,"Whitey"	1974	20	25	30	35	IMP	20	150	90	50
Foster, Rube*	1981	3000	N/A	UNK	UNK	IMP	IMP	7000	UNK	UNK
Foster, Willie*	1996	3000	N/A	UNK	UNK	IMP	IMP	UNK	UNK	UNK
Fox,"Nellie"*	1997	225	250	350	900	IMP	IMP	400	500	3000
Foxx, Jimmie*	1951	450	650	2000	UNK	1600	4000	2000	UNK	13000
Frick, Ford*	1970	45	75	175	1000	IMP	150	150	UNK	1600
Frisch, Frankie*	1947	75	150	175	250	375	175	250	UNK	2000
Furillo, Carl*		35	50	85	UNK	N/A	N/A	150	250	350
Galarraga, Andres		20	30	30	UNK	ACTIVE	ACTIVE	150	90	40
Galvin, James*	1965	3500	UNK	UNK	UNK	IMP	IMP	8000	UNK	UNK
Garciaparra, Nomar		25	35	55	UNK	ACTIVE	ACTIVE	150	150	75
Gehrig, Lou*	1939	1500	5000	7500	13000	IMP	IMP	7500	10000	32000
Gehringer, Charles*	1949	15	25	25	400	75	25	125	300	100
Gibson, Josh*	1981	5500	N/A	12000	UNK	IMP	IMP	16000	UNK	33000
Gibson, Bob	1972	20	25	30	UNK	IMP	30	500	80	45
Giles, Warren*	1979	45	90	250	500	IMP	IMP	150	UNK	1200
Gilliam, Jim*		90	100	150	UNK	N/A	N/A	200	UNK	2000
Glavine, Tom		20	30	35	UNK	ACTIVE	ACTIVE	125	80	40
Gomez, Lefty*	1972	20	50	75	UNK	IMP	30	150	250	175
Gonzalez, Juan		35	40	45	UNK	ACTIVE	ACTIVE	200	100	50
Goslin, Goose*	1968	150	250	500	UNK	IMP	3000	350	UNK	2000
Grace, Mark		20	30	35	UNK	ACTIVE	ACTIVE	125	90	40
Greenberg, Hank*	1956	60	90	300	500	200	85	300	UNK	800
Griffey, Ken Jr.		35	50	65	UNK	ACTIVE	ACTIVE	500	300	85
Griffith, Clark*	1946	175	350	500	650	1250	IMP	350	UNK	2000
Grimes, Burleigh*	1964	20	35	85	75	100	25	150	UNK	275
Grove, Lefty*	1947	45	100	175	150	200	120	200	UNK	1300
Guerrero, Vladimir		20	30	35	UNK	ACTIVE	ACTIVE	150	125	50
Gwynn, Tony		25	35	40	UNK	N/A	N/A	200	125	55
Haley, Charles*	1971	50	100	250	UNK	IMP	375	300	UNK	2500
Haines, Jesse*	1970	25	85	175	100	IMP	85	275	UNK	1500
Hamilton, Billy*	1961	2500	UNK	UNK	UNK	IMP	IMP	UNK	UNK	8000
Hanlon, Ned*	1996	2500	UNK	UNK	UNK	IMP	IMP	3500	UNK	UNK
Harridge, William*	1972	150	300	250	UNK	IMP	IMP	125	UNK	2000
Harris, Bucky*	1975	75	125	150	UNK	IMP	175	250	UNK	1500

Name	HOF	3x5 A/P	Gum Card	Photo	Check	HOF Plaq B/W	HOF Plaq COLOR	Letter	SS Bat	SS Ball
Hartnett, Gabby*	1955	75	100	400	375	550	375	600	UNK	2000
Hellmann, Harry*	1952	450	700	800	800	IMP	IMP	800	UNK	2800
Henderson, Rickey		25	35	40	UNK	ACTIVE	ACTIVE	250	125	45
Herman, William*	1975	15	25	35	100	IMP	15	125	200	90
Hodges, Gil*		300	350	400	600	N/A	N/A	600	750	2000
Hooper, Harry*	1971	30	60	125	100	IMP	100	150	UNK	1800
Homsby, Rogers*	1942	350	500	700	UNK	1150	IMP	600	UNK	3200
Howard, Elston*		90	100	300	UNK	N/A	N/A	275	2500	2000
Hoyt, Waite*	1969	20	35	75	150	N/A	35	125	UNK	450
Hubbard, Cal*	1976	60	200	250	150	IMP	750	150	UNK	1300
Hubbell, Carl*	1947	15	30	60	90	IMP	35	100	300	150
Hubbs, Ken*		200	300	350	500	50	N/A	700	UNK	1000
Huggins, Miller*	1964	1200	3000	400	3000	N/A	IMP	3500	UNK	5000
Hubert, William*	1995	UNK	N/A	UNK	UNK	IMP	IMP	10000	UNK	UNK
Hunter,"Catfish"	1987	15	25	25	150	IMP	20	200	110	45
Irvin,"Monte"	1973	10	20	25	35	IMP	15	75	75	30
Jackson, Joe "Shoeless"*		5000	UNK	20000	15000	IMP	N/A	UNK	UNK	UNK
Jackson, Reggie	1993	35	50	55	200	N/A	60	150	175	70
Jackson, Travis*	1982	30	35	50	1000	IMP	50	200	500	275
Jenkins, Fergie	1991	10	20	25	30	IMP	15	150	80	30
Jennings, Hugh*	1945	1500	2500	2500	UNK	IMP	IMP	3000	UNK	6000
Jensen, Jackie*		25	75	150	100	IMP	N/A	150	UNK	350
Jeter, Derek		25	35	80	UNK	ACTIVE	ACTIVE	250	250	110
Johnson, Ban*	1937	500	N/A	1500	2500	IMP	IMP	500	UNK	UNK
Johnson, Charles		20	25	30	UNK	ACTIVE	ACTIVE	100	80	35
Johnson, Randy		25	35	40	UNK	ACTIVE	ACTIVE	150	100	50
Johnson, Walter*	1936	750	1200	1300	1200	IMP	IMP	1500	UNK	25000
Johnson, William*	1975	25	50	50	500	IMP	35	350	UNK	250
Jones, Andruw		20	35	35	UNK	ACTIVE	ACTIVE	150	100	45
Jones, Chipper		20	30	40	UNK	ACTIVE	ACTIVE	150	125	50
Joss, Addie*	1978	4000	UNK	UNK	UNK	IMP	IMP	UNK	UNK	UNK
Kaline, Al	1980	15	25	30	150	IMP	15	150	90	40
Karros, Eric		20	25	30	UNK	ACTIVE	ACTIVE	100	70	40
Keffe, Timothy*	1964	UNK	UNK	UNK	UNK	IMP	IMP	UNK	UNK	UNK
Keeler, Willie*	1939	1500	UNK	UNK	UNK	IMP	IMP	UNK	UNK	UNK
Kell, George	1983	5	20	20	35	IMP	15	70	60	30
Kelly, George*	1973	20	35	75	100	IMP	40	150	UNK	400
Kelly, Joseph.*	1971	2000	UNK	UNK	2500	IMP	IMP	6000	UNK	UNK
Kelly,"King"*	1945	2700	UNK	UNK	UNK	IMP	IMP	UNK	UNK	UNK
Killebrew, Harmon	1984	15	30	35	200	IMP	25	150	125	55
Kiner, Ralph	1975	10	20	25	50	IMP	15	125	80	35
Klein, Chuck	1980	400	600	750	UNK	IMP	IMP	800	UNK	2500
Klem, Bill*	1953	600	800	900	UNK	IMP	IMP	1200	UNK	5000
Kluszewskl,Ted*		25	45	75	100	N/A	N/A	150	UNK	275
Knoblauch, Chuck		25	30	35	UNK	ACTIVE	ACTIVE	125	90	35
Koufax, Sandy	1972	45	50	70	UNK	IMP	65	500	175	85

Name	HOF	3x5 A/P	Gum Card	Photo	Check	HOF Plaq B/W	HOF Plaq COLOR	Letter	SS Bat	SS Ball
Lajoie, Napoleon "Larry"*	1937	375	800	800	UNK	1300	IMP	1800	UNK	6000
Landis,"Judge"*	1944	450	N/A	700	3000	IMP	IMP	400	UNK	4000
Larkin, Barry		20	30	35	UNK	ACTIVE	ACTIVE	125	20	40
Lasorda, Tommy	1997	20	25	30	200	IMP	40	200	80	40
Lazzeri, Tony*	1991	575	900	900	2500	IMP	IMP	1800	UNK	3500
Lemon, Bob*	1976	5	15	15	200	IMP	10	175	70	30
Leonard,"Buck"*	1972	20	35	40	50	IMP	40	200	150	60
Lindstrom, Fred.*	1976	30	40	75	1000	IMP	75	200	UNK	1800
Lloyd, John*	1977	5000	N/A	UNK	UNK	IMP	IMP	UNK	UNK	UNK
Lofton, Kenny		25	35	35	UNK	ACTIVE	ACTIVE	150	90	50
Lombardi, Ernie*	1986	50	100	175	UNK	IMP	IMP	200	UNK	2000
Lopez,"Al"	1977	15	30	30	UNK	IMP	30	150	125	65
Lopez, Javy		20	30	35	UNK	ACTIVE	ACTIVE	125	80	40
Lyons, Ted*	1955	15	35	60	65	85	35	125	UNK	275
Mack, Connie*	1937	250	500	800	UNK	1200	IMP	350	UNK	1200
MacPhail, Larry	1978	200	N/A	700	1500	IMP	IMP	375	UNK	75
MacPhail, Lee	1998	25	N/A	50	200	IMP	35	150	100	100
Maddux, Greg		25	35	45	UNK	ACTIVE	ACTIVE	250	150	70
Maglie, Sal*		25	50	75	65	N/A	N/A	125	UNK	375
Mantle, Mickey*	1974	275	300	200	2500	IMP	250	1200	1500	375
Manush, Heinie*	1964	65	100	250	275	IMP	375	250	UNK	2000
Maranville,"Rabbit"*	1954	400	6100	750	UNK	IMP	IMP	1000	UNK	2500
Marichal, Juan	1983	20	25	25	200	IMP	25	200	80	40
Maris, Roger*		225	300	600	1500	N/A	N/A	700	850	1700
Marquard, Rube*	1971	30	75	100	UNK	IMP	40	150	UNK	800
Martin, Billy*		100	125	150	UNK	N/A	N/A	200	500	200
Martin,"Pepper"*		175	275	350	UNK	N/A	N/A	250	UNK	1800
Martinez, Pedro		25	30	125	UNK	ACTIVE	ACTIVE	150	150	225
Martinez, Tino		25	35	35	UNK	ACTIVE	ACTIVE	125	125	45
Mathews, Edwin*	1978	20	30	45	UNK	IMP	25	400	125	60
Mathewson, Christy*	1936	1500	UNK	6500	7500	IMP	IMP	5500	UNK	28000
Mattingly, Don		25	35	40	UNK	N/A	N/A	250	125	50
Mays, Willie	1979	40	50	55	1000	IMP	60	700	150	80
Mazeroski, Bill	2001	10	15	25	150	IMP	15	85	80	30
McCarthy, Joseph*	1957	35	100	175	500	150	75	200	UNK	900
McCarthy, Thomas*	1946	2000	UNK	UNK	UNK	IMP	IMP	250	UNK	UNK
McCovey, Willie	1986	20	30	35	50	IMP	30	250	100	50
McGinnity, Joseph*	1946	UNK	UNK	UNK	UNK	IMP	IMP	8000	UNK	UNK
McGowan, Bill*	1992	450	750	850	UNK	IMP	IMP	800	UNK	4000
McGraw, John*	1937	800	UNK	1500	3000	IMP	IMP	2000	UNK	6000
McGwire, Mark		75	100	250	UNK	ACTIVE	ACTIVE	500	850	900
McKechnie, Deacon*	1962	200	275	350	UNK	900	IMP	500	UNK	1800
Medwick, Joe "Ducky"*	1968	50	90	175	UNK	IMP	150	350	UNK	1500
Mize,Johnny*	1981	15	25	25	150	IMP	25	150	250	75
Molitor, Paul		25	30	40	100	N/A	N/A	150	150	50
Mondesi, Raul		20	25	30	UNK	ACTIVE	ACTIVE	100	70	30

Name	HOF	3x5 A/P	Gum Card	Photo	Check	HOF Plaq B/W	HOF Plaq COLOR	Letter	SS Bat	SS Ball
Morgan, Joe	1990	20	30	35	200	IMP	30	150	90	40
Musial, Stan	1969	20	35	45	100	IMP	35	200	150	70
Mussina, Mike		20	25	30	UNK	ACTIVE	ACTIVE	150	80	45
Newhouser, Hal*	1992	12	20	25	50	IMP	20	100	85	35
Nichols,"Kid"*	1949	400	9100	1000	3500	1750	IMP	900	UNK	4000
Niekro, Phil	1997	10	20	25	UNK	IMP	30	200	80	35
Nomo, Hideo		35	40	50	UNK	ACTIVE	ACTIVE	200	100	60
O'Doul, Lefty*		85	UNK	250	100	IMP	IMP	200	UNK	1000
O'Rourke, James*	1945	2500	750	UNK	UNK	IMP	IMP	8000	UNK	UNK
Ott, Mel*	1951	450	200	1000	UNK	1400	IMP	1500	UNK	9000
Paige, Satchel*	1971	125	30	250	UNK	IMP	150	1000	UNK	1000
Palmeiro, Rafael		25	25	35	UNK	ACTIVE	ACTIVE	150	90	40
Palmer, Jim	1990	15	25	30	200	IMP	20	150	70	35
Pennock, Herbert*	1948	450	20	1000	900	IMP	IMP	700	UNK	3000
Perez, Tony	2000	20	30	35	200	IMP	30	150	90	35
Perry Gaylord	1991	10	20	25	25	IMP	25	100	60	35
Petitte, Andy		20	25	40	UNK	ACTIVE	ACTIVE	150	125	50
Piazza, Mike		25	35	65	UNK	ACTIVE	ACTIVE	200	150	90
Plan, Edward*	1946	2000	UNK	UNK	UNK	IMP	IMP	7500	UNK	UNK
Puckett, Kirby	2001	25	30	35	UNK	IMP	25	200	125	50
Radbourn, Charles*	1939	UNK	UNK	UNK	UNK	IMP	IMP	20000	UNK	UNK
Ramirez, Manny		20	35	40	UNK	ACTIVE	ACTIVE	150	100	60
Reese, "Pee Wee"*	1984	30	35	45	200	IMP	30	200	100	55
Rice,"Sam"*	1963	45	125	200	1500	220	125	250	UNK	1500
Rickey, Branch*	1967	350	400	600	650	IMP	IMP	400	UNK	2500
Ripken Jr., Cal		35	55	75	UNK	ACTIVE	ACTIVE	500	200	100
Rixey, Eppa*	1963	275	350	650	225	IMP	IMP	375	UNK	2500
Rizzuto, Phil	1994	15	30	35	200	IMP	20	150	90	40
Roberts, Robin	1976	10	25	25	200	IMP	10	150	80	30
Robinson, Brooks	1983	10	20	30	30	IMP	15	100	100	40
Robinson, Frank	1982	25	30	40	200	IMP	25	350	125	45
Robinson, Jackie*	1962	375	550	900	650	1250	1000	1200	UNK	3500
Robinson, Wilbert*	1945	1000	UNK	1500	UNK	IMP	IMP	1500	UNK	6000
Rodriguez, Alex		30	35	55	UNK	ACTIVE	ACTIVE	200	150	70
Rodriguez, Ivan		25	35	40	UNK	ACTIVE	ACTIVE	200	100	55
Rogan, Wilber*	1998	UNK	N/A	UNK	UNK	IMP	IMP	UNK	UNK	UNK
Rolen, Scott		20	30	35	UNK	ACTIVE	ACTIVE	125	90	45
Rose, Pete		25	30	35	375	N/A	N/A	500	100	50
Roush, Edd*	1962	15	35	60	175	85	25	150	UNK	300
Ruffing,"Red"*	1967	35	60	100	UNK	IMP	75	300	UNK	600
Rusie, Amos*	1977	800	UNK	UNK	UNK	IMP	IMP	2500	UNK	UNK
Ruth, George "Babe"*	1936	1200	3500	4000	2200	IMP	IMP	4200	15000	20000
Ryan, Nolan	1999	35	40	60	UNK	N/A	50	500	200	75
Salmon, Tim		20	30	35	UNK	ACTIVE	ACTIVE	125	80	35
Schalk, Ray*	1955	85	150	800	UNK	550	375	350	UNK	2000
Schmidt, Michael	1995	35	40	50	UNK	IMP	40	300	125	60

Name	HOF	3x5 A/P	Gum Card	Photo	Check	HOF Plaq B/W	HOF Plaq COLOR	Letter	SS Bat	SS Ball
Schoendiest, Red	1989	15	20	25	200	IMP	15	125	70	35
Seaver,"Tom"	1992	30	35	40	350	IMP	40	300	100	50
Sewell, Joe*	1977	15	40	50	30	IMP	15	75	250	150
Simmons, Al*	1953	350	600	750	400	1000	IMP	600	UNK	2500
Sisler, George*	1939	60	150	275	375	225	150	375	UNK	2000
Slaughter, Enos	1985	5	15	20	30	IMP	10	75	60	30
Smith, Ozzie		20	30	35	UNK	IMP	N/A	150	125	45
Snider,"Duke"	1980	15	30	35	75	IMP	25	125	100	50
Sosa, Sammy		50	60	75	UNK	ACTIVE	ACTIVE	500	250	110
Spahn, Warren	1973	10	20	25	100	IMP	15	100	80	40
Spalding, Al*	1939	1500	N/A	2000	UNK	IMP	IMP	2500	UNK	UNK
Speaker, Tris*	1937	375	600	800	UNK	1000	IMP	900	UNK	4500
Stargell, Willie*	1988	15	25	30	150	IMP	20	200	100	45
Stengel, Casey*	1966	125	250	300	700	IMP	175	500	UNK	1200
Sutton, Don	1998	20	25	30	UNK	IMP	35	200	70	40
Terry, Bill*	1954	15	30	75	90	85	30	125	UNK	150
Thomas, Frank		25	40	50	UNK	ACTIVE	ACTIVE	200	150	50
Thompson, Sam	1974	UNK	UNK	UNK	UNK	IMP	IMP	UNK	UNK	UNK
Thomson, Bobby		10	15	20	35	N/A	N/A	100	80	35
Tinker, Joe*	1946	700	1200	1500	3000	UNK	IMP	2000	UNK	3500
Traynor,"Pie"*	1948	175	275	375	400	750	1000	400	UNK	1500
Vance,"Dazzy"*	1955	300	500	6000	UNK	1350	IMP	700	UNK	2800
VanderMeer, Johnny*		15	5	35	45	N/A	N/A	125	150	60
Vaughan, Arky*	1985	500	800	1000	UNK	IMP	IMP	1800	UNK	3000
Vaughn, Mo		25	30	35	UNK	ACTIVE	ACTIVE	200	125	50
Veeck, Bill*	1991	135	UNK	350	UNK	IMP	IMP	200	UNK	800
Waddell, Rube*	1946	UNK	UNK	UNK	UNK	IMP	IMP	UNK	UNK	UNK
Wagner, Honus*	1936	550	800	1000	1700	1500	IMP	1500	UNK	5500
Walker, Larry		25	30	35	UNK	ACTIVE	ACTIVE	125	100	35
Wallace, Bobby*	1953	550	750	1200	UNK	1200	IMP	1200	UNK	3500
Walsh, Ed*	1946	275	500	700	UNK	900	IMP	800	UNK	4000
Waner, Lloyd*	1967	20	40	75	UNK	IMP	35	250	UNK	750
Waner, Paul*	1952	375	500	600	UNK	850	IMP	800	UNK	3000
Ward, Monte*	1964	UNK	UNK	UNK	UNK	IMP	IMP	6500	UNK	UNK
Weaver, Earl	1996	15	25	30	200	IMP	30	150	70	40
Weiss, George*	1971	100	UNK	300	500	IMP	4000	150	UNK	1800
Welch, Mickey*	1973	2500	UNK	UNK	UNK	IMP	IMP	UNK	UNK	20000
Wells, Willie*	1997	350	500	800	UNK	IMP	IMP	900	UNK	2200
Wheat, Zach*	1959	85	150	350	900	550	375	400	UNK	2500
Wilhelm, Hoyt	1985	10	20	25	40	IMP	10	150	70	35
Williams, Bernie		25	30	40	UNK	ACTIVE	ACTIVE	200	80	50
Williams, Billy	1987	15	25	30	200	IMP	15	175	80	35
Williams, Ted	1966	175	200	225	1000	IMP	175	1000	1500	325
Willis, Vic*	1995	3000	UNK	UNK	UNK	IMP	IMP	6000	UNK	UNK
Wilson,"Hack"*	1979	650	900	1000	1600	IMP	IMP	1500	UNK	4000
Winfield, Dave	2001	20	30	35	UNK	N/A	N/A	150	100	45

Name	HOF	3x5 A/P	Gum Card	Photo	Check	HOF Plaq B/W	HOF Plaq COLOR	Letter	SS Bat	SS Ball
Wood, "Smokey" Joe*		25	75	100	25	IMP	20	150	UNK	350
Wood, Kerry		25	35	40	UNK	ACTIVE	ACTIVE	150	125	50
Wright, George*	1937	900	UNK	2000	UNK	IMP	IMP	1800	UNK	UNK
Wright, Harry*	1953	1500	UNK	UNK	UNK	IMP	IMP	3500	UNK	UNK
Wynn, Early	1972	25	30	30	75	IMP	15	150	125	50
Yastrzemski, Carl	1989	30	35	40	500	IMP	40	250	125	50
Yawkey, Thomas*	1980	250	UNK	450	UNK	IMP	IMP	375	UNK	2300
Young, Cy*	1937	500	1000	800	UNK	1400	IMP	1500	UNK	6000
Youngs, Ross*	1973	1500	UNK	3000	UNK	IMP	IMP	UNK	UNK	UNK
Yount, Robin	1999	30	35	40	200	IMP	35	150	150	50

Name	3X5	8X10	Ball	Jersey
Abdul-Jabaar, Kareem	60	75	175	400
Archibald, Nate	15	20	125	175
Arizin, Paul	10	25	150	200
Auerbach, Red	15	30	150	175
Barkley, Charles	35	45	175	315
Barry, Rick	10	20	125	175
Baylor, Elgin	15	25	150	200
Bellamy, Walt	10	20	125	175
Bing, Dave	10	25	150	200
Bird, Larry	50	55	250	350
Bradley, Bill	75	90	175	225
Bryant, Kobe	40	65	250	350
Carter, Vince	30	45	200	300
Chamberlain, Wilt*	150	175	325	475
Cousy, Bob	10	40	175	225
Cowens, Dave	15	20	125	175
Cunningham, Billy	10	20	125	175
Davies, Bob*	50	75	275	350
DeBusschere, Dave	10	20	125	175
Duncan, Tim	25	45	125	200
Erving, Julius	30	75	250	300
Ewing, Patrick	35	50	200	300
Frazier, Walt	15	20	125	175
Fulks, Joe*	25	125	unk	unk
Garnett, Kevin	35	50	175	325
Gervin, George	10	20	125	175
Gola. Tom	10	25	150	200
Greer, Hal	10	20	100	150
Hagan, Cliff	10	25	125	175
Havlicek, John	15	25	175	225
Hawkins, Connie	15	20	125	175
Hayes, Elvin	15	20	100	150
Heinsohn, Tom	12	30	165	225
Hill, Grant	35	45	175	250
Holman, Nat*	20	35	175	275
Holzman, Red*	25	40	200	300
Issel, Dan	10	25	125	175
Iverson, Allen	30	45	200	275
Jeanette, Buddy	10	20	125	175
Johnson, Magic	50	135	300	350
Jones, K.C.	10	20	125	175
Jones, Sam	10	20	125	175

Name	3X5	8X10	Ball	Jersey
Jordan, Michael	100	400	750	1250
Lanier, Bob	10	20	100	150
Lovellette, Clyde	10	20	100	150
Lucas, Jerry	15	20	100	150
Macauley, Ed	10	20	150	175
Malone, Karl	35	45	215	295
Maravich, Pete*	250	500	2500	3000
Martin, Slater	10	25	150	200
Mikan, George	12	35	175	250
Monroe, Earl	15	20	125	175
O'Neal, Shaquille	50	85	250	325
Olajuwon, Hakeem	25	45	175	250
Pippen, Scottie	30	50	215	300
Reed, Willis	15	25	150	200
Robertson, Oscar	50	65	175	250
Robinson, David	35	45	150	225
Rodman, Dennis	30	40	125	200
Russell, Bill	100	200	500	600
Schayes, Dolph	12	20	150	200
Stockton, John	25	45	175	250
Thomas, Isiah	10	25	125	175
Walton, Bill	10	25	150	200
West, Jerry	15	25	150	225
Wilkens, Lenny	10	15	125	175
Wilkins, Dominique	10	25	125	175

Name	HOF	3 X 5 AP	Letter/Doc	Photo	Glove
Ali, Muhammad	Yes	45	350	200	350
(Vintage Cassius Clay signatures sell for a premium)					
Ambers, Lou*	Yes	10	UNK	35	110
Angott, Sammy*	Yes	25	UNK	65	UNK
Arcel, Ray*	Yes	20	UNK	100	200
Arguello, Alexis	Yes	10	UNK	25	100
Armstrog, Henry*	Yes	65	150	350	800
Attell, Abe*	Yes	150	250	350	725
Baer, Max*	Yes	100	200	275	1000
Basilio, Carmen	Yes	10	UNK	35	100
Benitez, Wilfred	Yes	15	UNK	50	150
Benvenuti, Nino	Yes	15	UNK	45	175
Berg, Jackie Kid*	Yes	25	50	65	165
Blackburn, Jack*	Yes	150	250	350	UNK
Braddock, James J.*		125	UNK	400	1500
Brenner, Teddy	Yes	5	UNK	15	45
Britlon, Jack*	Yes	85	150	250	UNK
Brown, Joe*	Yes	10	UNK	25	100
Brown, Panama Al*	Yes	150	250	350	UNK
Burley, Charley*	Yes	15	UNK	35	100
Burns, Tommy*	Yes	250	650	1500	6000
Canto, Miguel	Yes	10	UNK	25	75
Canzoneri, Tony*	Yes	150	250	250	1000
Carnera, Primo*	Yes	150	350	450	2250
Carpentier, Georges*	Yes	150	250	275	1100
Cerdan, Marcel*	Yes	400	1000	800	1000
Cervantes, Antionio	Yes	15	UNK	35	150
Charles, Ezzard*	Yes	150	250	450	1000
Chavez, Julio Cesar		15	UNK	45	150
Chocolate, Kid*	Yes	150	250	450	UNK
Clancy, Gil	Yes	5	UNK	15	45
Commacho, Hector "Macho"		10	UNK	25	75
Conn, Billy*	Yes	25	UNK	150	350
Corbett, James J.*	Yes	250	500	800	12000
D'Amato, Gus*	Yes	35	100	75	UNK
Darcey, Les*	Yes	450	1800	2500	UNK
DeJesus, Esteban*	Yes	75	UNK	250	UNK
De la Hoya, Oscar		12	UNK	65	150
Delaney, Jack*	Yes	175	350	350	UNK
Dempsey, Jack*	Yes	75	150	250	1000
Dempsey, Nonpareil*	Yes	350	850	1500	UNK
Dixon, George*	Yes	650	1800	3500	UNK

Name	HOF	3 X 5 AP	Letter/Doc	Photo	Glove
Donovan, Arthur*	Yes	25	65	75	UNK
Douglas, Buster		10	UNK	25	65
Dundee, Chris	Yes	10	UNK	35	125
Dundee, Angelo	Yes	8	UNK	15	45
Dundee, Johnny*	Yes	75	UNK	150	450
Dunphy, Don*	Yes	15	UNK	35	50
Duran, Roberto	Yes	12	UNK	35	100
Duva, Lou	Yes	5	UNK	15	45
Elorde, Flash*	Yes	65	UNK	150	250
Fitzsimmons, Bob*	Yes	1500	3500	4500	10000
Fleischer, Nathaniel S.*	Yes	25	45	65	135
Flowers, Tiger*	Yes	250	650	950	UNK
Foreman, George	Yes	25	UNK	75	225
Foster, Bob	Yes	5	UNK	15	65
Frazier, Joe	Yes	10	UNK	75	175
Fullmer, Gene	Yes	5	UNK	15	50
Futch, Eddie	Yes	8	UNK	15	50
Galaxy, Khozsai	Yes	10	UNK	25	75
Galento,Tony*	Yes	35	UNK	200	400
Gans, Joe*	Yes	250	1800	2500	3000
Gavilan, Kid	Yes	15	UNK	40	150
Genaro, Frankie*	Yes	5	UNK	45	UNK
Giardello, Joey	Yes	10	UNK	15	45
Gibbons, Mike*	Yes	100	UNK	250	UNK
Gibbons, Tommy*	Yes	50	UNK	150	UNK
Goldstein, Ruby*	Yes	10	UNK	35	UNK
Gomez, Wilfredo	Yes	10	UNK	35	100
Graham, Billy*	Yes	15	UNK	45	100
Graziano, Rocky*	Yes	45	UNK	150	250
Greb, Harry*	Yes	800	2000	3500	UNK
Griffith, Emile	Yes	5	UNK	15	45
Griffo, Young*	Yes	250	350	450	UNK
Hagler, Marvin	Yes	25	UNK	65	125
Harada, Fighting	Yes	10	UNK	25	75
Hart, Marvin*	Yes	1500	3500	6500	9000
Herman, Pete*	Yes	25	UNK	85	UNK
Holmes, Larry	Yes	10	UNK	35	75
Holyfield, Evander		25	UNK	75	250
Jack, Beau	Yes	10	UNK	35	75
Jackson, Peter*	Yes	350	650	1500	UNK
Jacobs, Mike*	Yes	15	35	45	UNK
Jeanette, Joe*	Yes	650	1800	2500	UNK
Jeffries, James J.*	Yes	350	750	1500	8000
Jofre, Eder	Yes	10	UNK	25	100
Johnson, Harold	Yes	5	UNK	15	45
Johnson, Jack*	Yes	350	850	2500	5500

Name	HOF	3 X 5 AP	Letter/Doc	Photo	Glove
Ketchel, Stanley*	Yes	1500	3500	4500	UNK
Kilbane, Johnny*	Yes	75	UNK	250	UNK
King, Don	Yes	10	UNK	25	65
La Barba, Fidel*	Yes	10	UNK	45	85
LaMotta, Jake	Yes	10	UNK	35	100
Langford, Sam*	Yes	650	1500	2500	UNK
Leonard, Benny*	Yes	150	250	350	1800
Leonard, Sugar Ray	Yes	15	UNK	35	125
Lewis, John Henry*	Yes	45	UNK	175	750
Lewis, Lennox		12	UNK	65	150
Lewis, Ted "Kid"*	Yes	45	UNK	150	UNK
Liston, Sonny*	Yes	550	UNK	2000	4000
Loughran, Tommy*	Yes	75	125	150	400
Louis, Joe*	Yes	150	250	475	3000
Lynch, Benny*	Yes	175	400	400	UNK
Marciano, Rocky*	Yes	250	350	800	5000
Markson, Harry	Yes	250	750	1000	UNK
Maxim, Joey	Yes	10	UNK	25	75
McCoy, Charles"Kid*	Yes	5	UNK	15	65
McGovern, Terry*	Yes	150	UNK	350	UNK
McLarnin, Jimmy	Yes	1000	2500	3500	UNK
Mercante, Arthur	Yes	5	UNK	35	UNK
Miller, Freddie*	Yes	5	UNK	15	45
Montgomery, Bob*	Yes	45	UNK	150	UNK
Monzon, Carlos*	Yes	30	UNK	150	250
Moore, Archie*	Yes	50	UNK	150	250
Muhammad, Matthe Saad	Yes	15	UNK	45	100
Napoles, Jose	Yes	5	UNK	20	55
Nelson, Battling*	Yes	40	UNK	95	500
Norton, Ken	Yes	15	UNK	30	85
O'Brien, Phila. Jack*	Yes	10	UNK	35	100
Odd, Gilbert	Yes	75	175	250	UNK
Olivares, Ruben	Yes	5	UNK	15	70
Ortiz, Carlos	Yes	8	UNK	25	75
Ortiz, Manuel*	Yes	5	UNK	15	45
Papke, Billy*		350	UNK	700	2500
Parnassus, George*	Yes	25	UNK	150	UNK
Patterson, Floyd	Yes	10	UNK	50	175
Pedroza, Eusebio	Yes	5	UNK	25	75
Pep, Willie	Yes	15	UNK	45	125
Perez, Pascual*	Yes	8	UNK	25	75
Pryor, Aaron	Yes	15	UNK	30	125
Quarry, Jerry*	Yes	10	UNK	60	200
Rickard, George "Tex"*	Yes	150	UNK	425	1250
Robinson, Sugar Ray*	Yes	35	UNK	400	1500
Rodriguez, Luis*	Yes	15	UNK	75	250

Name	HOF	3 X 5 AP	Letter/Doc	Photo	Glove
Rosario, Edwin*		10	75	100	250
Rosenbloom, Maxie*	Yes	30	UNK	75	1500
Ross, Barney*	Yes	25	UNK	200	325
Saddler, Sandy	Yes	15	UNK	75	125
Sanchez, Salvador*	Yes	500	UNK	1000	1800
Schmeling, Max	Yes	50	150	110	225
Sharkey, Jack*	Yes	50	UNK	175	525
Spinks, Michael	Yes	15	UNK	25	125
Stevenson, Teofilio	Yes	10	UNK	75	200
Steward, Emanuel	Yes	15	UNK	35	100
Stribling, Young*	Yes	10	UNK	25	65
Sullivan, John L.*	Yes	450	UNK	2000	15000
Tiger, Dick*	Yes	125	UNK	275	400
Torres, Jose	Yes	50	UNK	150	125
Trinidad, Felix		10	UNK	75	125
Tunney, Gene*	Yes	100	250	300	700
Tyson, Mike		75	150	150	250
Villa, Pancho	Yes	50	UNK	125	250
Walcott, Barbados Joe*	Yes	75	UNK	250	UNK
Walcott, Jersey Joe*	Yes	50	200	100	350
Walker, Mickey*	Yes	40	UNK	140	1000
Welsh, Freddie*	Yes	65	UNK	250	UNK
Whitaker, Pernel		15	UNK	25	125
Wilde, Jimmy*	Yes	10	UNK	25	400
Willard, Jess*		375	UNK	600	2250
Williams, Ike*	Yes	15	UNK	35	125
Wills, Harry*	Yes	10	UNK	35	3000
Wright, Chalky*	Yes	150	UNK	350	UNK
Zale, Tony*	Yes	20	UNK	40	350
Zarate, Carlos	Yes	25	UNK	75	175
Zivic, Fritzie*	Yes	35	UNK	150	600

Name	HOF	3x5-A/P	Gum Card	Photo	Check	GLAC	Letter	SSJ	SSF
Adderley, Herb	1980	10	15	20	UNK	25	50	150	75
Aikman, Troy		10	15	40	UNK	N/A	75	325	225
Allen, Marcus		10	15	30	UNK	N/A	50	200	150
Alworth, Lance	1978	15	25	30	UNK	40	60	175	90
Atkins, Doug	1982	10	15	20	25	25	50	150	75
Badgro, Morris "Red"*	1981	10	20	25	UNK	50	50	200	100
Barney, Lem	1992	10	15	20	UNK	25	50	150	75
Battles, Cliff*	1968	75	150	200	UNK	IMP	150	UNK	UNK
Baugh, Sammy	1963	15	25	35	UNK	50	75	300	200
Bednarik, Chuck	1967	10	15	20	30	25	50	150	75
Bell, Bert [owner, commissioner]*	1963	350	IMP	1000	UNK	IMP	750	IMP	UNK
Bell, Bobby	1983	10	15	20	UNK	25	50	150	75
Berry, Raymond	1973	10	15	20	75	25	50	150	75
Bidwill, Charles Sr. [owner]*	1967	1000	IMP	UNK	UNK	IMP	2000	IMP	UNK
Biletnikoff, Fred	1988	10	15	25	UNK	30	50	150	75
Blanda, George	1981	10	15	20	UNK	25	50	150	75
Bledsoe, Drew		10	15	30	UNK	N/A	50	275	200
Bloudt, Mel	1989	10	15	20	UNK	30	50	UNK	75
Bradshaw, Terry	1989	15	20	35	UNK	40	75	265	160
Brown, Jim	1971	25	35	50	UNK	40	150	250	160
Brown, Paul [coach]*	1967	35	40	50	UNK	100	75	IMP	UNK
Brown, Roosevelt	1975	10	15	20	UNK	30	50	150	75
Brown, Willie	1984	10	15	20	UNK	25	50	150	75
Buchanan, Buck*	1990	35	50	60	UNK	200	100	350	250
Buoniconti, Nick	2001	10	15	20	UNK	25	50	150	75
Butkus, Dick	1979	20	25	30	UNK	35	75	225	150
Campbell, Earl	1991	15	20	25	UNK	35	75	200	100
Canadeo, Tony	1974	10	15	20	30	25	50	150	75
Carr, Joe [president]*	1963	1500	IMP	UNK	UNK	IMP	2000	IMP	UNK
Carter, Chris		10	15	25	UNK	N/A	50	150	125
Chamberlin, Guy*	1965	300	UNK	500	UNK	IMP	500	UNK	UNK
Christiansen, Jack*	1970	35	65	100	UNK	IMP	75	UNK	UNK
Clark, Earl "Dutch"*	1963	75	150	250	UNK	IMP	200	UNK	UNK
Connor, George	1975	10	15	20	UNK	25	50	150	75
Conzelman, Jimmy*	1964	250	350	500	UNK	IMP	500	UNK	UNK
Creekmur,"Lou"	1996	10	15	20	UNK	30	50	150	75
Csonka, Larry	1987	20	25	30	UNK	40	75	225	125
Culpepper, Daunte		10	15	40	UNK	N/A	50	250	175
Cunningham, Randall		10	10	25	UNK	N/A	50	175	125
Davis, Al [owner]	1992	75	100	150	UNK	250	150	UNK	250
Davis, Terrell		10	25	55	UNK	N/A	50	325	225
Davis, Willie	1981	10	15	20	UNK	30	50	150	75

Name	HOF	3x5-A/P	Gum Card	Photo	Check	GLAC	Letter	SSJ	SSF
Dawson, Len	1987	10	15	20	UNK	25	50	200	100
Dayne, Ron		10	15	35	UNK	N/A	50	200	150
Dickerson, Eric	1999	25	35	40	UNK	N/A	100	250	150
Dierdorf, Daniel	1996	10	15	20	UNK	25	50	150	75
Ditka, Mike	1988	15	20	25	UNK	35	75	200	100
Donovan, Art	1968	10	15	20	UNK	30	50	150	75
Dorsett, Tony	1994	25	35	40	UNK	40	60	225	135
Driscoll, John*	1965	250	UNK	400	UNK	IMP	600	UNK	UNK
Dudley, William	1966	10	15	20	UNK	30	50	150	75
Edwards, Albert "Turk"*	1969	200	250	300	UNK	IMP	600	UNK	UNK
Elway, John		15	20	45	UNK	N/A	150	350	240
Ewbank, Weeb [coach]*	1978	15	20	25	75	35	50	225	100
Faulk, Marshall		10	10	30	UNK	N/A	50	155	150
Favre, Brett		10	15	60	UNK	N/A	75	325	275
Fears, Tom	1970	10	15	20	35	30	50	150	75
Finks, Jim*	1995	125	150	250	UNK	IMP	200	UNK	UNK
Flaherty, Raymond "Red"*	1976	15	25	35	UNK	50	60	UNK	125
Ford,"Len"*	1976	175	200	350	UNK	IMP	300	UNK	UNK
Fortmann, Danny*	1965	40	65	100	UNK	IMP	150	UNK	UNK
Fouts,"Dan"	1993	15	20	35	UNK	35	50	225	150
Gatski, Frank	1985	10	15	20	UNK	25	50	150	75
George, Bill*	1974	100	150	250	UNK	IMP	200	UNK	UNK
Gibbs, Joe [coach]	1996	15	20	25	UNK	50	50	225	125
Gifford, Frank	1977	30	40	50	UNK	50	100	200	150
Gillman, Sid [coach]	1983	10	15	20	UNK	25	50	150	75
Graham, Otto	1965	10	15	20	UNK	40	50	200	125
Grange, Red*	1963	50	75	100	UNK	150	300	750	500
Grant, Bud [coach]	1994	15	20	25	UNK	35	50	200	125
Greene, Joe	1987	15	20	25	UNK	35	75	200	125
Gregg, Alvis	1977	10	15	20	UNK	25	50	150	75
Griese, Bob	1990	20	25	30	UNK	40	75	200	125
Groza, Lou	1974	10	15	20	UNK	30	50	150	75
Guyon, Joe*	1966	200	250	300	UNK	IMP	300	UNK	UNK
Halas, George*	1963	75	100	150	UNK	IMP	200	UNK	UNK
Ham, Jack	1988	10	15	20	UNK	25	50	150	75
Hannah, John	1991	10	15	20	UNK	25	50	250	125
Harris, Franco	1990	20	25	30	UNK	40	100	250	125
Haynes, Mike	1997	10	15	20	UNK	25	50	150	75
Healey, Ed*	1964	75	125	150	UNK	IMP	150	UNK	UNK
Hein, Mel*	1963	15	20	50	UNK	IMP	75	250	150
Hendricks, Ted	1990	10	15	20	UNK	30	50	150	75
Henry, Wilbur "Pete"*	1963	600	UNK	1000	500	IMP	750	UNK	UNK
Herber, Arnie*	1966	125	175	250	UNK	IMP	200	UNK	UNK
Hewitt, Bill*	1971	1500	UNK	UNK	UNK	IMP	2000	UNK	UNK
Hinkle, William*	1964	35	75	150	UNK	IMP	100	UNK	UNK
Hirsch, Elroy	1968	10	15	20	UNK	30	40	175	75

Name	HOF	3x5-A/P	Gum Card	Photo	Check	GLAC	Letter	SSJ	SSF
Hornung, Paul	1986	20	25	30	UNK	40	75	200	125
Houston,"Ken"	1986	10	15	20	UNK	25	50	150	75
Hubbard, Robert "Cal"*	1963	60	200	250	150	IMP	250	UNK	UNK
Huff, Robert "Sam"	1982	15	20	25	UNK	35	60	200	100
Hunt, Lamar [owner]	1972	10	15	20	UNK	25	50	150	75
Hutson, Don*	1963	35	45	50	UNK	75	75	300	175
James, Edgerrin		10	15	30	UNK	N/A	50	200	150
Johnson, Jimmy [coach]	1994	10	15	20	UNK	25	50	150	75
Johnson, John	1987	10	15	20	UNK	30	75	150	75
Joiner, Charlie	1996	10	15	20	UNK	30	50	150	75
Jones, Deacon	1980	10	15	20	UNK	30	75	175	90
Jones, Stan	1991	10	15	20	UNK	25	50	150	75
Jordan, Henry*	1995	200	250	350	UNK	IMP	400	UNK	UNK
Jurgensen, Sonny	1983	10	15	20	UNK	30	50	175	100
Kelly, Jim		10	15	40	UNK	N/A	50	200	150
Kelly, Leroy	1994	10	15	20	UNK	25	50	150	75
Kemp, Jack		10	15	35	UNK	N/A	60	150	100
Kiesling, Walt "Babe"*	1966	1200	UNK	UNK	1500	IMP	1500	UNK	UNK
Kinard, Frank*	1971	100	150	250	UNK	IMP	200	UNK	UNK
Krause, Paul	1998	10	15	20	UNK	30	50	150	75
Lambeau, Earle*	1963	600	UNK	1000	UNK	IMP	1000	UNK	UNK
Lambert, Jack	1990	10	15	25	UNK	30	50	225	125
Landry, Tom*	1990	10	15	25	UNK	35	75	200	125
Lane, Dick	1974	10	15	25	UNK	30	50	150	75
Langer, Jim	1987	10	15	20	UNK	30	50	150	75
Lanier, Willie	1986	10	15	20	UNK	25	50	150	75
Largent, Steve	1995	15	20	30	UNK	35	60	200	125
Lary, Robert Jr. "Yale"	1979	10	15	20	30	25	50	150	75
Lavelli, Dante	1975	10	15	20	UNK	25	50	150	75
Layne, Bobby*	1967	75	100	150	UNK	IMP	125	UNK	UNK
Leemans, Alphonse*	1978	250	300	350	UNK	IMP	300	UNK	UNK
Levy, Marv	2001	10	15	20	UNK	25	50	150	75
Lilly, Bob	1980	10	15	20	UNK	30	50	175	90
Little, Larry	1993	10	15	20	UNK	25	50	150	75
Lombardi, Vince [coach]*	1971	250	UNK	700	250	IMP	700	UNK	UNK
Long, Howie	2000	10	15	35	UNK	40	50	150	125
Lott, Ronnie	2000	10	15	25	UNK	30	50	150	125
Luckman, Sid*	1965	20	30	40	UNK	60	50	225	125
Lyman, William*	1964	125	200	275	UNK	IMP	225	UNK	UNK
Mack, Tom	1999	10	15	20	UNK	N/A	50	150	75
Mackey, John	1992	15	20	25	UNK	25	50	150	75
Manning, Peyton		15	20	50	UNK	N/A	100	235	150
Mara, Tim [owner]*	1963	UNK	IMP	UNK	UNK	IMP	1500	UNK	UNK
Mara, Wellington [owner]	1997	15	30	35	UNK	50	75	150	75
Marchetti, Gino	1972	10	15	20	UNK	25	50	150	75
Marino, Dan		15	30	55	UNK	N/A	150	350	225

Name	HOF	3x5-A/P	Gum Card	Photo	Check	GLAC	Letter	SSJ	SSF
Marshall, George Preston [owner]*	1963	275	IMP	750	IMP	IMP	500	UNK	UNK
Martin, Curtis		10	10	25	UNK	N/A	50	165	110
Matson, Ollie	1972	10	15	20	UNK	25	50	150	75
Maynard, Don	1987	10	15	20	UNK	25	50	150	75
McAfee, George	1966	10	15	20	UNK	25	50	150	75
McCormack, Mike	1984	10	15	20	UNK	25	50	150	75
McDonald, Tommy	1998	10	15	20	UNK	25	50	150	75
McElhenny, Hugh	1970	15	20	25	UNK	30	50	175	90
McNally, Johnny*	1963	100	175	250	UNK	IMP	250	UNK	UNK
Michalske, Mike*	1964	50	75	150	UNK	IMP	125	UNK	UNK
Millner, Wayne*	1968	75	100	175	UNK	IMP	125	UNK	UNK
Mitchell, Bobby	1983	10	15	20	UNK	25	50	150	75
Mix,"Ron"	1979	10	15	20	25	25	50	150	75
Monk, Art		10	15	30	UNK	N/A	50	150	125
Montana, Joe		15	20	65	UNK	N/A	150	325	200
Moon, Warren		10	15	25	UNK	N/A	50	190	125
Moore, Lenny	1975	10	15	20	25	25	50	150	75
Moss, Randy		10	15	50	UNK	N/A	50	275	200
Motley, Marion	1968	15	20	25	UNK	35	50	150	75
Muchak, Mike	2001	10	15	20	UNK	25	50	150	75
Munoz, Anthony	1998	15	20	25	UNK	35	50	150	75
Musso, George	1982	10	15	20	UNK	25	50	150	75
Nagurski,"Bronko"*	1963	50	75	100	150	IMP	100	500	350
Namath, Joe	1985	40	50	70	UNK	60	500	300	225
Neale, Earl [coach]*	1969	175	200	300	UNK	IMP	200	UNK	UNK
Nevers, Ernie*	1963	75	125	200	UNK	IMP	150	UNK	UNK
Newsome, Ozzie	1999	10	15	20	UNK	N/A	50	150	75
Nitschke, Ray*	1978	15	20	25	UNK	60	50	200	100
Noll, Chuck [coach]	1993	10	15	25	UNK	35	50	150	75
Nomellini, Leo	1969	10	15	20	UNK	25	50	150	75
Olsen, Merlin	1982	15	20	25	UNK	40	75	200	100
Otto, Jim	1980	10	15	20	UNK	30	50	150	75
Owen, Stephen [coach]*	1966	350	IMP	700	UNK	IMP	600	IMP	UNK
Page, Alan	1988	10	15	20	UNK	30	50	175	90
Parker, Clarence	1972	10	15	20	UNK	25	40	150	75
Parker, Jim	1973	10	15	20	75	25	40	150	75
Payton, Walter*	1993	25	30	70	UNK	45	100	350	275
Perry, Fletcher "Joe"	1969	15	20	25	UNK	35	50	150	75
Pihos, Pete	1970	15	20	25	UNK	35	60	150	75
Ray, Hugh [official]*	1966	2500	IMP	UNK	UNK	IMP	UNK	IMP	UNK
Reeves, Dan [owner]*	1967	350	IMP	600	UNK	IMP	500	IMP	UNK
Renfro, Mel	1996	10	15	20	UNK	25	50	150	75
Rice, Jerry		10	25	65	UNK	N/A	50	275	215
Riggins,John	1992	40	50	50	UNK	100	100	250	150
Ringo, Jim	1981	10	15	20	UNK	30	50	150	75
Robustelli, Andy	1971	10	15	20	UNK	30	50	150	75

Name	HOF	3x5-A/P	Gum Card	Photo	Check	GLAC	Letter	SSJ	SSF
Rockne, Knute*		450	UNK	2500	UNK	IMP	2500	UNK	UNK
Rooney, Art [owner]	1964	40	75	100	UNK	IMP	125	IMP	350
Rozelle, Pete [commissioner]*	1985	40	50	100	200	100	100	IMP	175
Sanders, Barry		10	25	75	UNK	N/A	50	320	235
Sanders, Deion		15	20	45	UNK	N/A	75	225	150
Sayers, Gale	1977	25	30	35	UNK	40	75	200	125
Schmidt, Joe	1973	10	15	20	UNK	25	50	150	75
Schramm, Tex [general manager]	1991	10	15	25	UNK	30	50	175	90
Selmon, Lee	1995	10	15	25	UNK	30	50	150	75
Sharpe, Shannon		10	15	25	UNK	N/A	50	200	150
Shaw, Billy	1999	10	15	20	UNK	N/A	50	150	75
Shell,"Art"	1989	15	20	25	UNK	35	50	175	100
Shula, Don	1997	15	20	30	UNK	40	60	200	100
Simpson,O.J.	1985	35	40	50	UNK	75	200	300	200
Singletary, Mike	1998	10	15	20	UNK	35	50	200	90
Slater, Jackie	2001	10	15	20	UNK	25	50	150	75
Smith, Bruce		10	15	40	UNK	N/A	50	190	125
Smith, Emmitt		10	25	45	UNK	N/A	50	295	200
Smith, Jackie	1994	10	15	20	UNK	25	50	175	100
St. Clair, Bob	1990	15	20	25	UNK	35	50	175	90
Starr,"Bart"	1977	15	25	40	UNK	35	75	250	150
Staubach, Roger	1985	20	25	40	UNK	40	75	250	150
Stautner,"Ernie"	1969	10	15	20	UNK	25	50	150	75
Stenerud, Jan	1991	10	15	20	UNK	25	50	150	75
Stephenson, Dwight	1998	10	15	20	UNK	30	50	150	75
Strong,"Ken"*	1967	90	150	200	100	IMP	125	UNK	UNK
Stydahar, Joseph*	1967	75	100	200	UNK	IMP	150	UNK	UNK
Swann, Lynn	2001	15	25	35	UNK	35	75	175	90
Tarkenton, Fran	1986	15	20	35	UNK	40	60	200	150
Taylor,"Charles"	1984	10	15	20	UNK	25	50	150	75
Taylor, Jim	1976	10	15	20	UNK	30	50	150	75
Taylor, Lawrence	1999	30	40	50	UNK	N/A	150	250	150
Thomas, Thurman		10	15	25	UNK	N/A	50	185	135
Thorpe, Jim*	1963	750	1500	2000	UNK	IMP	1500	UNK	UNK
Tittle, Y.A.	1971	10	15	20	UNK	30	50	200	100
Trafton, George*	1964	150	200	300	150	IMP	200	UNK	UNK
Trippi, Charles	1968	10	15	20	40	25	50	150	75
Tunnell, Emlen*	1967	90	150	200	UNK	IMP	150	UNK	UNK
Turner, Clyde*	1966	25	30	35	50	75	75	225	125
Unitas,"Johnny"	1979	15	25	35	UNK	40	100	250	150
Upshaw, Gene	1987	10	15	20	UNK	25	50	150	85
VanBrocklin, Norm*	1971	75	125	150	UNK	IMP	150	UNK	UNK
VanBuren, Steve	1965	10	15	20	UNK	25	50	150	75
Walker, Ewell*	1986	15	20	25	UNK	50	50	225	125
Walsh, Bill [coach]	1993	15	20	25	UNK	40	50	200	125
Warfield, Paul	1983	10	15	20	UNK	30	50	175	90

Name	HOF	3x5-A/P	Gum Card	Photo	Check	GLAC	Letter	SSJ	SSF
Warner, Kurt		12	20	55	UNK	N/A	75	275	225
Waterfield, Bob*	1965	75	100	200	UNK	IMP	150	UNK	UNK
Webster, Mike	1997	10	15	20	UNK	30	50	150	75
Weinmeister,"Arnie"	1984	10	15	20	UNK	25	50	150	75
White, Randy	1994	10	15	20	UNK	30	50	200	100
White, Reggie		10	20	45	UNK	N/A	50	235	170
Willis,"Bill"	1977	10	15	20	UNK	25	50	150	75
Wilson,"Larry"	1978	10	15	20	UNK	30	50	175	90
Winslow, Kellen	1995	10	15	20	UNK	30	50	175	100
Wojciechowicz, Alex*	1968	20	30	40	UNK	500	50	300	200
Wood,"Willie"	1989	10	15	20	UNK	30	50	150	75
Yary, Ron	2001	10	15	20	UNK	30	50	150	75
Young, Steve		10	15	40	UNK	N/A	75	200	150
Youngblood, Jack	2001	10	15	25	UNK	30	50	150	75

Name	HOF	Card	Photo	Puck
Amonte, Tony		8	25	30
Barber, Bill	1990	8	20	25
Belfour, Ed		15	55	60
Beliveau, Jean	1972	10	25	30
Bourque, Ray		15	55	60
Bossy, Mike	1991	10	25	30
Brodeur, Martin		18	65	70
Bure, Pavel		12	35	40
Chelios, Chris		12	45	50
Cherry, Don		15	30	35
Clarke, Bobby	1987	15	45	50
Coffey, Paul		10	25	30
Dionne, Marcel	1992	8	18	20
Dryden, Ken	1983	45	150	150
Esposito, Phil	1984	12	30	35
Esposito, Tony	1988	10	25	30
Fedorov, Sergei		15	55	60
Forsberg, Peter		12	45	50
Gainey, Bob	1992	12	35	40
Gartner, Mike		12	35	40
Geoffrion, Bernie	1972	8	20	25
Giacomin, Ed	1987	8	20	25
Gretzky, Wayne	1999	60	225	250
Hall, Glenn	1975	8	20	25
Hasek, Dominik		25	85	90
Howe, Gordie	1972	25	75	80
Hull, Bobby	1983	12	30	35
Hull, Brett		20	65	70
Jagr, Jaromir		18	60	65
Joseph, Curtis		12	40	45
Kariya, Paul		12	40	45
Konstantinov, Vladimir		20	50	55
Kurri, Jari		10	22	25
Lafleur, Guy	1988	10	22	25
Leetch, Brian		12	40	45
Lemaire, Jacques	1984	10	22	25
Lemieux, Mario	1997	45	125	150
Lindros, Eric		12	40	45
Mahovlich, Frank	1981	6	18	20
Messier, Mark		30	100	120
Mikita, Stan	1983	8	25	30
Modano, Mike		15	40	45

Name	HOF	Card	Photo	Puck
Neely, Cam		12	30	35
Orr, Bobby	1979	20	65	70
Parent, Bernie	1984	8	22	25
Plante, Jacques*	1978	40	175	125
Richard, Henri	1979	6	18	20
Richard, Maurice*	1961	25	75	80
Richter, Mike		15	50	55
Roy, Patrick		15	55	60
Sakic, Joe		10	35	40
Sawchuk, Terry*	1971	50	400	225
Shanahan, Brendan		15	40	45
Shore, Eddie*	1947	40	275	UNK
Sittler, Darryl	1989	10	22	25
Stevens, Scott		15	50	55
Thorton, Joe		8	25	30
Trottier, Bryan	1997	8	22	25
Worsley, Gump	1980	8	20	22
Yzerman, Steve		25	80	85

HOW TO USE THE GAME-USED BAT GUIDE

This guide should be used for professional game-used bats. The term "game-used" has been defined in many different ways over the years by different hobbyists. In my opinion, the best definition of the term game-used bat, as it relates to this guide is: A **professional player bat that was used by a roster player, during their major league career.** The pricing in this guide refers to bats of this nature and this nature only.

Before you read the prices in this guide, it is very important that you first familiarize yourself with all of the valuation factors listed below because each of these factors play a significant role in determining the ultimate value of a bat. Please refer to the game-used bat guide below entitled "A Note about Game-Used Bat Pricing" for further explanation about the valuation and appeal of different bats.

A Note About Game-Used Bat Pricing

There are many factors that affect the value of game-used bats. Rarity, eye-appeal, age, provenance and historical importance are just some of the key factors that can help determine the value of a particular bat. In many cases, it eventually comes down to personal taste. For instance, one collector might prefer the look of a Mizuno model bat to the look of a Cooper model bat. It becomes very subjective. There are, however, some basic elements that need to be addressed. Below is a breakdown of some important aspects to game-used bat collecting.

Valuation Factors

Autograph – Many game-used bat collectors like to acquire autographs on their prized gamers. The effect an autograph can have on the valuation of a bat can really vary depending on the player. Some players rarely sign game-used equipment while others sign routinely. For instance, the cost of having your Ted Williams gamer signed might cost you around $5,000 while the cost to have Hank Aaron sign your bat is approximately $150. Placement, content and strength of the autograph can also be factors.

Cracked versus Uncracked – There is no rule stating that an uncracked bat is more valuable than a cracked bat or vice versa, it simply is a matter of taste. Some collectors prefer cracked bats because they believe it adds authenticity to the bat while others like uncracked bats for aesthetic reasons. As long as the crack does not affect the overall eye-appeal of the bat, it should not detract from the value. Severe cracks that affect the labeling or bats that exhibit missing pieces can lower the value of the lumber significantly if the eye-appeal if dramatically affected.

Deadwood – This term refers to the flaking or raising of the wood grain due to repeated contact of a ball on the hitting surface. Most collectors feel the same about deadwood as they do cracks. As long as the deadwood is not too severe and thus damaging the visual appeal of the bat, it is not seen as a detractor.

Missing Piece or Pieces – A missing piece or pieces to a bat may detract from the visual appeal significantly depending on the size of the piece in question. As a result, these bats are valued less than bats that are fully intact. On the other hand, bats with missing pieces that do not detract from the overall displayability will not detract significantly. For instance, if the missing piece is extremely small or on the back of the barrel where it is not highly noticeable.

Repairs – Many cracked bats or bats with missing pieces are, at some point, repaired in one of two ways. There is professional repair and non-professional repair. When a crack is repaired professionally, most collectors cannot detect it. Unlike the sportscard market, professional repair is not frowned upon in the bat market because condition is not viewed in the same light. In fact, professional repair can really improve the eye-appeal of a gamer. Non-professional repair such as batboy repair or collector repair may also be a factor. Batboys, in days past, were routinely instructed to repair player bats in the dugout by using nails. Many collectors feel that the presence of batboy repairs adds a vintage feel to the piece while others may not like the look. Collector repairs are, for the most part, accepted as long as the repair was not done in a reckless manner.

Usage – The topic of bat usage inevitably comes down to personal taste. Collectors who prefer bats with heavy game use value the fact that the bat was in the player's hands for a long period of time. These collectors look for strong evidence of ball, seam, bat rack, and cleat marks along with unique player characteristics such as shaved or taped handles and grooving. Other collectors, who prefer light use, enjoy the eye-appeal that a virtually untouched bat offers. One important thing to keep in mind is that vintage bats do not show use as clearly as the modern bats do. This is due to the difference in wood type and qualtiy. For example, the old hickory bats simply do not reveal wear like the modern white ash does. Again, it really comes down to personal taste but a clear showing of some use is essential. Remember that these are not baseball cards, they are supposed to have wear from game use. More use means that the bat was in the players hands for a longer period of time and that is where a lot of the value comes from.

Game-issued bats – Some professional model bats never make it into the game. These bats are simply called game-issued bats. They were made for game use but were left in the locker room or the bat bag. These bats do have value but the value is somewhat lower than that of game-used bats. Much of the value turns on the fact that the bat saw game action.

Postseason and All-Star bats – Due to extreme limited production, bats that were made for postseason or All-Star play command a significant premium over regular issue bats. These bats will exhibit distinctive labeling such as the city the All-Star Game was played in or the year and series the bat was made for. Every bat manufacturer has a different way of labeling these special bats so it is imperative that you familiarize yourself with each company's label design.

Special bats – Some players will mark bats with special notations such as home run bats or significant hit bats. This can be true for vintage as well as modern player bats. These bats usually sell for a significant premium depending on the importance of the notation or rarity of such an occurrence.

Manufacturers – In the older days of the game, there were very few bat manufacturers. H&B (now Louisville Slugger) and Adirondack were among the handful. Today, there are several bat companies and each company has its own distinct style. Some companies have come and gone such as Worth while others have recently started like Sam and Young. The importance of bat brand is two-fold.

First, some players are commonly associated with particular bat companies like Mark McGwire and some are not. McGwire has used Rawlings model bats for the great majority of his at-bats. As a result, many collectors prefer Rawlings gamers over any other brand McGwire may have tried during his career. A great way to check what bat players are using is by looking at baseball cards, photos and television broadcasts. Usually, by doing this, you can get a good idea of what bats the player uses the most. Other collectors like the rarity of a bat not commonly associated with a player but beware, just because a bat was made for a player does not mean the player used it.

Second, and just as important, is the difference in visual appeal between the brands. Some collectors prefer the classic look of a Louisville Slugger while others are drawn to the unique designs attributed to modern KC Slammers or vintage beauties like the white lettered, caramel colored Adirondacks of the 1950's and 60's. In addition, some bats include the team name on the barrel while others do not. Some collectors prefer bats that include the team name in the labeling for display purposes. Keep in mind that most vintage bats never included the team name as part of the labeling. The bottom line is visual appeal. Each brand offers a different look but some bats are clearly better looking than others.

Rarity – Like most collectibles, bats are judged by rarity. For example, a 1950's Mickey Mantle game-used bat is far more rare than a Mantle bat from the 1960's. The same can be said for other players such as Willie Mays and Hank Aaron. Rarity can have a major effect on pricing. For example, Monte Irvin bats are virtually impossible to find, therefore, the rarity is reflected in the price. Even though Frank Robinson was a superior player to Irvin, his bats are more common so the difference in price is apparent.

In addition, modern bats are manufactured at a much higher rate than they were in the past. For example, Ken Griffey Jr. has had more bats made in two years than Mantle received in his entire career. On the other hand, some modern players are very protective of their equipment. Finding a true gamer from these players can be very tough because their bats rarely escape from the clubhouse. A significant premium is usually applied to those bats that exhibit unique qualities or true rarity.

Side Written or Vault Marked Bats – Some vintage bats, primarily during the pre-war era, may exhibit what is referred to as side writing or vault marks. When players would crack their bats and needed to order more of the same model, they would return the bat to the factory. After arrival, bats were labeled with grease pencil to confirm the order. The player's name, city, and date were usually placed on the barrel in fairly large letters. The side writing pinpoints the time when the bat was returned and what player was returning the bats. In some rare instances, players would return another player's bat in hopes of getting the same model made for them. Vault marks can also be identified on some vintage bats. These marks were made as a result of the handling process at the factory. Bats that exhibit either of these distinctive marks are valued significantly higher than bats without the marks.

Provenance – Professional player bats, due to the distinct labeling and unique usage characteristics, can be clearly identified by bat experts but provenance may add a significant premium to a particular bat. Provenance is probably best described as evidence of origin; however, the strength of evidence is what matters. For instance, strong provenance might be shown by the existence of a letter from a former teammate, batboy, umpire, family member or baseball organization. These are just some examples. The fact that a bat once resided in a particular collection should not, in itself, play a significant part in the valuation of the piece. The bat is what it is regardless of who owned it but, if the collection the bat came from can help show a chain of custody or an important relationship that can help explain the acquisition of the bat, it may be a factor.

Teams – Many collectors focus on particular teams or prefer a bat that links a player to a certain team. For example, a Reggie Jackson game-used bat that was used during his stint with the Yankees would sell for a slight premium over a bat used during his time with the Angels. Whether a player accomplished more from an individual standpoint or from a team standpoint, the bat price will be affected. Another example would be Mark McGwire. His Cardinals bats sell for more than his Athletics bats do, even though he won a World Series with Oakland, because of the fact that he emerged as a star as a member of the St. Louis team. In Oakland, he was slightly overshadowed by other star players.

The affect a team might have on values can be dramatic in some instances. Game-used bats from legendary or World Championship teams can be highly desirable even if the bats are from common players. The team factor can turn a common player bat into a highly valuable one depending on the year. For example, any bat from the 1927 New York Yankees is highly desirable due to the historical importance of that squad. Significant premiums for star or common player bats should be added when applicable.

Pitcher Bats – Bats that were used by pitchers are highly desirable and very rare in many cases. Key Hall of Fame pitcher bats such as Sandy Koufax and Walter Johnson are amongst the most valuable in the market. Pitchers have very few bats made for them and only occasionally make plate appearances. These factors really limit the available number of game-used pitcher bats, especially from the vintage era. Due to the extreme rarity of many of these pitcher bats, much like the special bats listed above, the price guide does not include price listings for these examples.

      Authentication – Like for most important pieces of memorabilia, authentication of bats is key. It is important, before you purchase a game-used bat, that you consult a bat expert that is nationally recognized by advanced sports memorabilia hobbyists. I would recommend that collectors ask around the hobby, at its highest levels, to find the bat expert that is best qualified to authenticate your bat. The reality is that there are very few individuals qualified to render an expert opinion regarding the authenticity of game-used bats but, the experts who are qualified, provide a highly valuable service for collectors. Having your game-used bat properly authenticated will ensure that other potential buyers will accept the bat as being legitimate in case you ever have to sell and it can prevent a collector from losing money on a bat that fails industry standards.

Final Note

      As stated above, there are many factors that help determine the value of a game-use bat. As a result, pricing can be difficult at times. SMR does it absolute best to keep up to date on the game-used bat market and we will add players as demand dictates. Remember that this price list should be used as a guide because each bat is unique in its own way. We hope this information proves to be useful in determining values on professional game-used bats. **Finally, and most importantly, this price guide refers to the approximate values of standard game-used bats only and should not be used for any of the rarities or special bats mentioned in the aforementioned guide.** Premiums should apply when applicable.

Hall of Famers	Approximate Value
Hank Aaron	4500
(1950's examples are very tough)	
(a 1957 All-Star example sold for $21,300)	
Louis Aparicio	625
Luke Appling	3250
Richie Ashburn	3250
Earl Averill	3500
Frank Baker	7500
Dave Bancroft	3250
Ernie Banks	3500
Johnny Bench	900
Yogi Berra	4000
(pre-1960 examples sell for a premium)	
Jim Bottomley	3250
Lou Boudreau	2500
Roger Bresnahan	6500
George Brett	850
Lou Brock	950
Roy Campanella	5000
(Campy bats are very tough)	
Rod Carew	600
Max Carey	3250
Orlando Cepeda	800
Frank Chance	9000
Oscar Charleston	10500
Fred Clarke	5000
Bob Clemente	4000
(grooving of barrel is sought after)	
Ty Cobb	40000
(early examples are very scarce)	
(high-end examples sell for $60-$80,000)	
Mickey Cochrane	5500
Eddie Collins	7500
Earle Combs	6500
Stan Coveleski	6000
Sam Crawford	4500
Joe Cronin	1200
Kiki Cuyler	2000
Ray Dandridge	3500
Bill Dickey	7000
Joe DiMaggio	15000
Larry Doby	2500
Bobby Doerr	700
John Evers	7500
Rick Ferrell	1500
Carlton Fisk	400

Hall of Famers	Approximate Value
Nellie Fox	1500
Elmer Flick	7500
Jimmie Foxx	9750
(a vault marked example sold for $31,189)	
Frankie Frisch	3000
Lou Gehrig	35000
(side written examples have sold for $75,000 and up)	
Charlie Gehringer	5500
Goose Goslin	4000
Hank Greenberg	7500
(Greenberg has a very strong following)	
Chick Hafey	2500
Bucky Harris	1500
Gabby Hartnett	5000
Harry Heilmann	2000
Billy Herman	2000
Harry Hooper	5500
Rogers Hornsby	10000
(high-end examples have sold for $17,500 and up)	
Monte Irvin	4000
(only a few are known to exist)	
Reggie Jackson	750
(Yankee era bats and early examples sell for a premium)	
Travis Jackson	4000
Al Kaline	1100
George Kell	1100
George Kelly	1500
Harmon Killebrew	2500
(pre-1960 examples are very tough)	
Ralph Kiner	750
Chuck Klein	2500
Nap Lajoie	12500
Tony Lazzeri	6000
Fred Lindstrom	3500
John "Pop" Lloyd	6000
Ernie Lombardi	3000
Al Lopez	2500
Ted Lyons	4000
Mickey Mantle	17500
(high-end examples sell for a major premium)	
(a 1955 World Series bat sold for $51,518)	
Heinie Manush	2750
Rabbit Maranville	3000

Hall of Famers	Approximate Value
Ed Mathews	2850
(pre-1960 bats are very desirable)	
Willie Mays	5500
(early Mays bats sell for a premium)	
Bill Mazeroski	1500
Willie McCovey	1000
Joe Medwick	5000
Johnny Mize	2500
Joe Morgan	500
(early examples sell for a premium)	
Stan Musial	5250
(pre-1960 examples are very desirable)	
Mel Ott	15000
(a 1933 example sold for $30,925)	
Tony Perez	450
Kirby Puckett	425
Hal "Pee Wee" Rees	2750
Sam Rice	5000
Phil Rizzuto	2750
Brooks Robinson	1000
(early examples sell for a premium)	
Frank Robinson	1850
(a pre-1960 example sold for $10,000)	
Jackie Robinson	19000
(top notch examples sell for $30,000 and up)	
Edd Roush	1250
Babe Ruth	30000
(high-end and early examples sell for $50,000 and up)	
Ray Schalk	4000
Mike Schmidt	800
(home run bats sell in the $3,500-$6,000 range)	
Red Schoendienst	700
Joe Sewell	4000
Al Simmons	2500
George Sisler	2500
Enos Slaughter	1200
Duke Snider	3750
(pre-1960 examples are very desirable)	
(look for evidence of handle tape)	
Tris Speaker	8500
Willie Stargell	600
Casey Stengel	4250
Bill Terry	2500
Joe Tinker	7500
Pie Traynor	3500
Arky Vaughan	3500
Honus Wagner	35000
Bobby Wallace	5000
Lloyd Waner	5000
Paul Waner	3000

Hall of Famers	Approximate Value
Zack Wheat	4500
Billy Williams	800
Ted Williams	12500
(high-end examples sell for $20,000 and up)	
Hack Wilson	5000
Dave Winfield	450
Carl Yastrzemski	750
Ross Youngs	3500
Robin Yount	500

Vintage Stars	Approximate Value
Richie Allen	600
Sandy Amoros	750
Hank Bauer	600
Benny Bengough	2500
Moe Berg	5000
Bobby Bonds	250
Ken Boyer	600
Lew Burdette	400
Chico Carrasquel	1000
Norm Cash	650
Ray Chapman	4500
Hal Chase	5000
Rocky Colavito	900
Dave Conception	200
Tony Conigliaro	1100
Chuck Connors	2000
Frank Crosetti	1500
Alvin Dark	300
Tommy Davis	275
Dom DiMaggio	1200
Vince DiMaggio	1500
Chuck Dressen	400
Joe Dugan	1200
Dale Ennis	400
Darrell Evans	200
Dwight Evans	225
Curt Flood	450
George Foster	175
Bill Freehan	400
Carl Furillo	2000
Chick Gandil	6500
Steve Garvey	200
Jim Gilliam	1400
Joe Gordon	1500
Dick Groat	600
Heinie Groh	1000
Tommy Henrich	750
Babe Herman	750
Gil Hodges	2500
Elston Howard	550

Vintage Stars	Approximate Value
Frank Howard	450
Joe Jackson	
Playing Days	75000
Post-Ban Signature	20000
Post-Ban Block	10000
Jackie Jensen	400
Ken Keltner	1000
Dave Kingman	250
Ted Kluszewski	525
Mark Koenig	2500
Tony Kubek	1200
Harvey Kuenn	450
Davey Lopes	150
Greg Luzinski	175
Fred Lynn	150
Bill Madlock	175
Marty Marion	600
Roger Maris	3000
Billy Martin	1750
Pepper Martin	1500
Tim McCarver	300
Bob Meusel	2500
Minnie Minoso	650
Thurman Munson	1250
Graig Nettles	225
Tony Oliva	400
Al Oliver	250
Dave Parker	150
Joe Pepitone	350
Johnny Pesky	225
Jim Piersall	400
Lou Pinella	200
Vada Pinson	350
Wally Pipp	2000
Boog Powell	350
Pete Reiser	550
Bobby Richardson	1750
Swede Risberg	6000
Pete Rose	1500
Al Rosen	600
Ron Santo	850
Ted Simmons	175
Dick Sisler	400
Bill Skowron	600
Rusty Staub	275
Vern Stephens	300
Riggs Stephenson	1000
Dick Stuart	250
Bobby Thompson	700
Joe Torre	400
Alan Trammell	200

Vintage Stars	Approximate Value
Mickey Vernon	400
Bill Wambsganss	4000
Buck Weaver	6000
Vic Wertz	300
Lou Whitaker	250
Bill White	400
Maury Wills	300
Gus Zernial	350

Modern Stars	Approximate Value
Edgardo Alfonzo	225
Roberto Alomar	300
Jeff Bagwell	550
Harold Baines	250
Albert Belle	250
Craig Biggio	300
Wade Boggs	450
Barry Bonds	1200
Jose Canseco	400
Gary Carter	250
Joe Carter	175
Andre Dawson	350
Carlos Delgado	450
Jim Edmonds	225
Cecil Fielder	150
Andres Galarraga	200
Nomar Garciaparra	1750
Jason Giambi	450
Troy Glaus	750
Juan Gonzalez	325
Mark Grace	275
Ken Griffey Jr.	1300
Shawn Green	300
Vladimir Guerrero	850
Tony Gwynn	575
Todd Helton	400
Rickey Henderson	350
Bo Jackson	175
Derek Jeter	2750
Andruw Jones	350
Chipper Jones	450
Jeff Kent	150
Edgar Martinez	350
Don Mattingly	650
Fred McGriff	200
Mark McGwire (A's)	1500
Mark McGwire (Card	3000
Paul Molitor	450
Dale Murphy	350
Eddie Murray	550

Modern Stars	Approximate Value	Modern Stars	Approximate Value
Rafael Palmeiro	250	Sammy Sosa	1100
Mike Piazza	900	Ichiro Suzuki	
Jorge Posada	325	(limited supply has caused Ichiro bats to sell for	
Tim Raines	150	$1,000's)	
Manny Ramirez	500	(one example sold for over $7,000, the market	
Jim Rice	300	is volatile)	
Cal Ripken	1850	Frank Thomas	400
Alex Rodriguez	650	Bernie Williams	450
Ivan Rodriguez	425	Mo Vaughn	225
Ryne Sandberg	450		

Note: The prices listed above are approximate average prices for standard game-used bats and do not apply to bats which exhibit special or exceptional qualities as described in the Valuation Factors section. Significant premiums may apply to bats that exhibit these qualities.

HOW TO USE THE GAME-USED JERSEY GUIDE

This guide should be used for professional game-used jerseys. The term "game-used" has been defined in many different ways over the years by different hobbyists. In my opinion, the best definition of the term game-used jersey, as it relates to this guide is: A **professional game jersey that was used by a roster player, during their professional career.** The pricing in this guide refers to jerseys of this nature and this nature only.

Before you view the prices in this guide, it is very important that you first familiarize yourself with all of the valuation factors listed below because each of these factors plays a significant role in determining the ultimate value of a jersey. Please refer to the game-used jersey guide below entitled "A Note about Game-Used Jersey Pricing" for further explanation about the valuation and appeal of different jerseys.

A Note About Game-Used Jersey Pricing

There are many factors that affect the value of game-used jerseys. Rarity, event significance, age, provenance, alterations, eye-appeal and team affiliation are just some of the key factors that can help determine the value of a particular jersey. In many cases, it eventually comes down to personal taste. For instance, one collector might prefer the look of a Mickey Mantle road flannel to the pinstripe design of a home example. It becomes very subjective at times. There are, however, some basic elements that need to be addressed. Below is a breakdown of some important aspects to game-used jersey collecting.

Valuation Factors

Autographs – Many game-used jersey collectors will attempt to acquire autographs on their prized game-used jerseys. The effect an autograph can have on the valuation of a jersey can really vary depending on the player but, for the most part, the presence of an autograph on a jersey will not have nearly the significance that an autograph on a bat will. For the most part, game-used jerseys are significantly more expensive than game-used bats. An autograph on a Mickey Mantle game-used bat might increase the value from $15,000 to $20,000 so the effect is great. That is an increase of over 30%. The autograph on a jersey, on the other hand, may not have nearly the effect because a 1958 Mickey Mantle game-used jersey might sell for $90,000. Even if you add $5,000 for the additional autograph, it becomes less significant to the overall price increase. Placement, content and strength of the autograph can also be factors.

Restoration and Repairs – This issue is complex and certainly controversial to some degree. When it comes to restoration, like the replacement of patches or the name on the back, the collecting world is somewhat split. While mild restoration is not taboo by any means, it can lower the value of a jersey in certain cases. Some collectors are afraid to buy a jersey that shows any evidence of restoration because of the concern of authenticity. Other collectors don't cringe at restoration at all. They realize that jerseys were reused in many cases so restoration, in their minds, shouldn't affect the price. For instance, once a major league team received new jerseys, the old ones were often reused in the minor leagues so, in turn, the name was changed in some cases. Situations like this were commonplace in days past, it was just the way things worked and it is sometimes literally unavoidable. Still, other collectors prefer all-original jerseys.

Repairs are entirely different. The word repair should be used when referring to a jersey that has had a tear fixed or a stain removed. There are still those collectors who prefer that their jerseys be left in the original condition that they were found in but repairs do not, in any way, affect the authenticity of a jersey. The jersey was either worn by Lou Gehrig or not. Fixing a tear would simply be for aesthetic reasons; it has nothing to do with the authenticity of the game use. Assuming that the repair is minor, it should not have a dramatic affect on the value of the jersey. In many cases, the area of restoration and repair is entirely subjective. Remember that this price guide refers to all-original jerseys only. Evidence of repairs or restoration could lower the price depending on the severity of the alteration.

Usage – The topic of usage inevitably comes down to personal taste. Collectors who prefer jerseys with heavy game use value the fact that the jersey was worn for a long period of time. These collectors look for strong evidence of sweat marks on various areas of the jersey, general wear and tear throughout the shirt, pad or brace evidence, and genuine player characteristics such as pine tar stains along the shoulder where a player might rest his bat in between swings. Other collectors, who prefer light use, enjoy the eye-appeal that that "fresh looking" jerseys offer. Most collectors want at least some legitimate showing of true game wear but the taste, in regards to the amount of wear, varies. Some jerseys, due to the color and materials, make wear much easier to locate than on other jerseys. For example, sweat stains will be much more visible on a white home jersey than a grey road example. Remember, while the taste may vary, these are not sportscards, they are supposed to have wear from game use. More use means that the player wore the jersey for more games and thus increasing the odds that the player may have accomplished more on the field.

Game-issued Jerseys – Some professional player jerseys never see game action. These jerseys are simply called game-issued jerseys. They were made for game use but were left in the locker room on a hanger. These jerseys do have value but the value is somewhat lower than that of game-used jerseys. Much of the value turns on the fact that the jersey saw game action. Unused bats seem to retain more value, at least with regards to the vintage examples, than do jerseys. In almost every case, you want to see some legitimate game use.

Rookie Jerseys – Rookie jerseys, much like rookie cards in sportscard collecting, command a premium in the marketplace. In some cases, depending on the importance of the jersey and the player, rookie jerseys can command significantly more than standard game-used jerseys from an athlete's career. In cases where any jersey is difficult to obtain, such as a jersey worn by Ted Williams, a rookie jersey may not carry a significant premium. In other

words, since any Williams jersey is rare, collectors will pay nearly as strong for a Williams jersey worn during any season. A rookie Ted Williams jersey may sell for somewhat of a premium but, due to overall scarcity, the urgency for a rookie example is not as strong. On the other hand, a rookie example of someone such as Reggie Jackson will sell for significantly more than a jersey from later in his career due to the availability of 1980's knits.

Postseason and All-Star Jerseys – Due to extremely limited production, jerseys that exhibit attributes of postseason or All-Star action command a significant premium over regular issue jerseys. These jerseys will exhibit unique characteristics such as distinctive patches commemorating the event in question. Some jerseys may not have distinctive patches but they may have an autograph or letter explaining the significance of the jersey. Due to the varying styles of the patches that signify these events, it is important that you do as much research as you can by analyzing auction catalogues and photographs when you get the chance. You might even be able to contact the team equipment manager who can offer quality assistance.

Special Jerseys – Some players will mark jerseys with special notations. The signature might relate to a significant accomplishment such as a record breaking touchdown or no-hitter. The jersey may not even exhibit a special notation but it can be placed at a certain event in sports history. This can be found on vintage and modern player jerseys. These jerseys usually sell for a significant premium depending on the importance of the notation or accomplishment and the rarity of such an occurrence.

College, Minor League Jerseys or Practice Jerseys – There is certainly a market for college, minor league and practice jerseys but this guide and pricing section deals with professional game(for football, basketball, etc.) or Major League game jerseys (for baseball) only. Some jerseys, like minor league and college jerseys, have brought tremendous prices at auction but they are so rare and the market is so thin in this area that it is virtually impossible to establish any type of legitimate guide or price structure for them. On the whole, these jerseys sell for somewhat less than the type of jerseys discussed in this guide. Practice jerseys, such as the ones used for batting practice or spring training in baseball, are worth significantly less than actual game jerseys.

Flannels versus Knits – Until the early 1970's, flannel jerseys were the norm throughout baseball. A brief experiment with knit jerseys in 1970 led to all teams using knits in 1973. Flannels are very scarce in comparison to most knit jerseys and, as expected, more desirable where there is a choice. For example, a Hank Aaron flannel is far more desirable than a knit from the mid-1970's. In addition, players wore far fewer flannels throughout their career than they did knits. Knits, especially today, are produced and worn at a much higher rate than flannels were 30 or so years ago. Finally, the potential for fraud

is much, much greater with knits than it is with regards to flannels due to the comparable ease in which a knit can be replicated or altered. As you may notice in the price guide, the difference between a flannel value and a knit value can be significant in some cases.

Rarity – Like most collectibles, jerseys are often judged by rarity. For example, a Willie Mays game-used jersey from the 1950's is much tougher to find than a later shirt from the 1970's. Other times, a jersey may be rare because the player had a brief stay with a particular team or the team itself has stringent policies regarding access to team equipment. The bottom line is that rarity can make a very significant difference when it comes to price.

Provenance – Jerseys can be affected by provenance significantly. There are respected authenticators within the hobby but, when a jersey is accompanied by some legitimate provenance, a significant premium usually follows. Provenance is probably best described as evidence of origin; however, the strength of evidence is what matters. For instance, the existence of a letter from a former teammate, official, umpire, family member, sports organization or the player might show strong provenance. These are just some examples. The fact that a jersey once resided in a particular collection should not, in itself, play a significant part in the valuation of the piece. The jersey is what it is regardless of who owned it but, if the collection the jersey came from can help show a chain of custody or an important relationship that can help explain the acquisition of the jersey, it may be a factor.

Fraud – The potential for fraud, in regards to game-used jerseys, is far greater than it is for game-used bats. The bottom line is that jerseys can be more easily manipulated, copied or altered than just about any other piece of professional sports equipment. Again, knits are where the majority of fraud occurs because they can be recreated much easier than flannels can. The other area where fraud can occur is in the game use itself. In modern times, athletes receive many times more jerseys than they did as recently as 10-15 years ago.

There are a few different reasons for the production explosion but the most significant reason might be the development of the jersey market as a whole. Collectors desire jerseys whether they are in one piece or cut into 1,000 pieces to be used as part of a sportscard. Demand alone has caused a great increase in production. For this reason, more game-issued jerseys are available. If unethical individuals acquire game-issued jerseys, game use can then be manufactured on the shirt to make it appear as if it saw true game action. Remember, this is not a major problem with the majority of flannels and even most knits, but it can occur and collectors need to be aware of the problem. It is primarily a modern one.

Salesman Sample – This is a problem that can affect both modern and vintage jerseys. Salesman Samples are jerseys that are produced by the manufacturers and are basically exact replicas of the real thing. When these jerseys get out into the hobby, some of them are unfortunately sold as real gamers. They are detectable but that is why provenance and expert authentication are so important.

Teams – Many collectors focus on particular teams or prefer a jersey that links a player to a certain team. For example, a Reggie Jackson game-used jerseys that was used during his stint with the Yankees would sell for a slight premium over a jersey used during his time with the Angels. Whether a player accomplished more from an individual standpoint or from a team standpoint, the jersey price will be affected. Another example would be Mark McGwire. His St. Louis jerseys sell for more than his Oakland jerseys do, even though he won a World Series with Oakland, because of the fact that he emerged as a star as a member of the St. Louis team. In Oakland, he was slightly overshadowed by other star players.

The affect a team might have on values can be dramatic in some instances. Game-used jerseys from legendary or World Championship teams can be highly desirable even if the jerseys are from common players. The team factor can turn a common player jersey into a highly valuable one depending on the year. For example, any jersey from the 1927 New York Yankees is highly desirable due to the historical importance of that squad. Significant premiums for star or common player jersey should be added when applicable.

Authentication – This, like provenance, is extremely important. There are a few different ways you can have your jerseys authenticated. There is authentication that comes directly from the player or team and 3rd party authentication. Team letters or player letters carry a great deal of weight in the hobby and for obvious reasons. In fact, some equipment managers will actually authenticate your items for a small fee. The majority of the time, however, a jersey will not come with such iron clad documentation.

It is important, before you purchase a game-used jersey which is absent of direct source documentation, that you consult a jersey expert that is nationally recognized by advanced sports memorabilia hobbyists. I would recommend that collectors ask around the hobby, at its highest levels, to find the jersey expert that is best qualified to authenticate your jersey. The reality is that there are very few individuals qualified to render an expert opinion regarding the authenticity of game-used jerseys but, the experts who are qualified, provide a highly valuable service for collectors. Having your game-used jersey properly authenticated will ensure that other potential buyers will accept the jersey as being legitimate in case you ever have to sell and it can prevent a collector from losing money on a jersey that fails industry standards.

Final Note

As stated above, there are many factors that help determine the value of a game-use jersey. As a result, pricing can be difficult at times because jerseys, especially vintage examples, are very rare. SMR does its absolute best to keep up to date on the game-used jersey market and we will add players as demand dictates. The price range listed will be a reflection of a confirmed range of average sales that have occurred within the last few years. Each price range refers to flannels unless noted. Remember that this price list should be used as a guide because each jersey is unique in its own way and, therefore, will command a price based on its unique characteristics. We hope this information proves to be useful in determining values of professional game-used jerseys. **Finally, and most importantly, this price guide refers to the approximate values of all-original standard game-used jerseys only and should not be used for any of the special jerseys mentioned in the aforementioned guide.** Premiums should apply when applicable.

Retired Baseball Stars

Hank Aaron
Flannel - $20,000 and up
Knits - $7,500-$15,000
(a 1973 knit sold for $19,607)
(a 1971 flannel sold for $31,859)

Richie Ashburn
any - $6,000-$20,000

Ernie Banks
any - $15,000-$30,000
(a 1968 example sold for $23,830)
(a 1969 example sold for $18,511)

Johnny Bench
Flannel - $12,000-$20,000
Knit - $2,000-$4,000

Yogi Berra
any - $15,000-$40,000

Wade Boggs
any - $1,200-$2,500

George Brett
any - $2,000-$6,000

Lou Brock
Flannel - $12,000-$20,000
Knits - $4,000-$7,000

Roy Campanella
any - $20,000-$40,000
(a 1957 example sold for $46,856)

Rod Carew
Flannel - $10,000-$15,000
Knit - $1,750-$3,000

Steve Carlton
Flannel -$15,000-$25,000
Knit- $2,500-$5,000

Gary Carter
any - $1,000-$3,500

Orlando Cepeda
Flannel - $5,000-$10,000
Knit - $2,500-$4,000

Retired Baseball Stars

Bob Clemente
Flannel -$30,000-$40,000
Knit - $12,000-$20,000

Ty Cobb
any - $150,000 and up
(One sold for $332,500 (1928))
(same jersey resold for $240,000)

Rocky Colavito
any - $1,000-$3,000

Tony Conigliaro
Flannel - $5,000-$7,500
Knit - $2,500-$5,000

Andre Dawson
any - $1,000-$3,000

Joe DiMaggio
any - $75,000 and up

Don Drysdale
any - $10,000-$20,000

Dwight Evans
any - $750-$1,750

Bob Feller
any - $20,000-$30,000

Rollie Fingers
Flannel - $2,500-$5,000
Knit - $1,000-$2,000

Carlton Fisk
Flannel - $6,000-$7,500
Knit - $1,750-$3,500
(a rookie flannel sold for $9,487)

Whitey Ford
any - $15,000-$20,000

Nellie Fox
any - $5,000-$10,000

Jimmie Foxx
any - $90,000 and up

Lou Gehrig
any - $110,000 and up
(His Farewell Jersey sold $400,00)
(A 1927 jersey sold for $305,00)
(same jersey resold for $187,000)

Charlie Gehringer
any - $10,000-$15,000

Bob Gibson
Flannel - $15,000-$25,000
Knits - $7,500-$12,000
(a 1970 example sold for $27,610)

Hank Greenberg
any - $40,000-$60,000

Lefty Gomez
any - $20,000-$25,000

Goose Goslin
any - $8,000-$15,000

Lefty Grove
Philadeplhia - $60,000-$140,000
Boston $25,000-$40,000
(a 1931 example sold for $140,488)

Gil Hodges
Dodgers -$12,000-$20,000
Mets - $6,000-$12,000
(a 1952 example sold for $18,485)

Rogers Hornsby
any - $40,000-$60,000

Carl Hubbell
any - $20,000-$40,000
(a 1937 example sold for $48,048)

Catfish Hunter
Flannel -$5,000-$10,000
Knit - $2,500-$5,000

Monte Irvin
any - $8,000-$12,000

Reggie Jackson
Flannel - $10,000-$20,000
Knit - $2,000-$10,000
(Yankee knits sell at the high end of range)

Fergie Jenkins
Flannel - $5,000-$8,000
Knit - $1,000-$3,000

Al Kaline
Flannel - $10,000-$20,000
Knit - $2,500-$5,000
(a 1964 example sold for $14,115)

Harmon Killebrew
Flannel - $15,000-$25,000
Knit - $2,500-$5,000

Ralph Kiner
any - $15,000-$25,000

Ted Kluszewski
any - $3,500-$6,000

Sandy Koufax
Brooklyn - $50,000-$90,000
L.A. - $30,000-$50,000
(a 1963 example sold for $46,000)
(a 1955 example sold for $82,885)

Mickey Mantle
any - $75,000 and up
(a 1958 example for $91,649)
(a 1963 example sold for $110,000)

Juan Marichal
Flannel - $8,000-$15,000
Knit - $2,000-$4,000
(a 1967 example sold for $8,140)

Roger Maris
any - $12,000 and up
(Yankee jerseys would sell for a significant premium)
(a Yankee jersey from 1961 would be worth multiple times the listed price)

Ed Mathews
any - $12,500-$25,000
(early Braves jerseys sell at higher end of range)
(a 1959 example sold for $20,872)

Don Mattingly
any - $4,000-$7,500
(a rookie jersey sold for $9,604)

Willie Mays
Flannel - $30,000-$65,000
Knit - $8,000-$12,500
(a 1957 example sold for $54,231)

Willie McCovey
Flannel - $10,000-$17,500
Knit - $1,000-$5,000

Paul Molitor
any - $1,500-$3,500

Joe Morgan
Flannel - $7,500-$15,000
Knit - $1,000-$5,000
(Reds knits sell at higher end of range)

Thurman Munson
Flannel - $15,000-$20,000
Knit - $5,000-$12,500

Dale Murphy
any - $1,000-$2,000

Eddie Murray
1970's - $3,000-$5,000
1980's/1990's - $1,000-$2,500
(Early Baltimore jerseys sell for a premium)

Stan Musial
any - $30,000-$50,000
(a 1949 example sold for $35,186)

Phil Niekro
Flannel - $3,000-$5,000
Knit - $1,000-$1,500

Mel Ott
any - $40,000-$60,000
(a 1946 example sold for $46,000)

Jim Palmer
Flannels - $9,000-$15,000
Knit - $2,500-$7,500

Tony Perez
Flannels - $4,000-$8,000
Knits - $1,000-$3,000

Gaylord Perry
Flannel - $3,000-$5,000
Knit - $750-$1,500

Pee Wee Reese
any - $10,000-$25,000
(a 1952 example sold for $18,040)

Phil Rizzuto
any - $12,000-$20,000

Kirby Puckett
any - $2,000-$3,500

Brooks Robinson
Flannel - $12,000-$20,000
Knit - $3,000-$6,000

Frank Robinson
Flannel - $15,000-$25,000
Knit - $3,000-$6,000

Jackie Robinson
any - $75,000 and up

Pete Rose
Flannel - $15,000-$35,000
Knit - $2,000-$7,500
(a rookie jersey sold for $39,312)

Babe Ruth
any - $200,000 and up
(a 1930 example sold for $325,000)

Nolan Ryan
Flannel - $25,000-$50,000
Knit - $4,000-$15,000
(a 1984 example sold for $7,396)
(a 1970's knit sold for $10,350)
(a 1969 example sold for $52,806)

Ryne Sandberg
any - $1,500-$3,000
(a 1991 example sold for $4,539)

Mike Schmidt
any - $5,000-$10,000

Tom Seaver
Flannel - $20,000-$40,000
Knit - $3,000-$8,000

Ozzie Smith
1970's - $2,500-$3,500
1980's/1990's - $1,500-$2,500

Duke Snider
Brooklyn - $30,000-$50,000
L.A. - $15,000-$20,000
(a 1951 example sold for $66,125)

Warren Spahn
any - $30,000-$45,000

Willie Stargell
Flannel - $5,000-$10,000
Knit - $1,500-$3,000
(a 1968 example sold for $8,625)

Don Sutton
Flannel - $10,000-$15,000
Knit - $1,200-$3,500

Billy Williams
Flannel - $7,500-$12,000
Knit - $3,000-$5,000
(a 1966 example sold for $10,330)

Ted Williams
any - $50,000 and up
(a 1946 WS example sold for $123,000)
(a 1948 example sold for $66,312)

Dave Winfield
any - $1,500-$7,500
(Yankee jerseys sell at high end of range)

Carl Yastrzemski
Flannel - $7,500-$12,500
Knit - $2,500-$6,000

Robin Yount
any - $2,000-$4,000

Modern Baseball Stars	Value Range
Roberto Alomar	$1,200-$1,500
Jeff Bagwell	$1,400-$2,000
Albert Belle	$800-$1,000
Barry Bonds	$3,500-$5,000
Jose Canseco	$1,500-$2,200
Roger Clemens	$2,500-$4,000
Carlos Delgado	$1,750-$2,500
Darin Erstad	$1,000-$1,500
Nomar Garciaparra	$3,000-$4,000
Jason Giambi	$1,200-$1,500
Juan Gonzalez	$1,100-$1,300
Ken Griffey Jr.	$3,000-$3,500
Vladimir Guerrero	$1,500-$2,000
Tony Gwynn	$1,300-$2,500
Todd Helton	$1,250-$1,750
Rickey Henderson	$1,500-$4,000
Derek Jeter	$4,000-$7,500
Randy Johnson	$1,750-$3,500
Andruw Jones	$1,750-$2,500
Chipper Jones	$1,500-$2,000
Greg Maddux	$3,000-$4,000
Pedro Martinez	$4,000-$6,000
Fred McGriff	$800-$1,000
Mark McGwire (A's)	$5000-$5,500
Mark McGwire (Cards)	$9,000-$12,000
Rafael Palmeiro	$1,200-$1,500
Mike Piazza	$2,000-$2,500
Manny Ramirez	$1,500-$1,750
Cal Ripken	$3,500-$5,500
Alex Rodriguez	$2,000-$2,500
Ivan Rodriguez	$1,200-$1,500
Ryne Sandberg	$1,500-$2,500
Sammy Sosa (Sox/Rangers)	$1,500-$1,750
Sammy Sosa (Cubs)	$3,000-$5,000
Frank Thomas	$1,200-$1,500
Bernie Williams	$1,750-$3,000
Mo Vaughn	$1,000-$1,200

Basketball Players Approximate Values

Kareem Abdul-Jabaar
Milwaukee -$10,000 and up
LA - $3,000 and up

Charles Barkley
Philly - $2,500 and up
other - $1,000 and up

Rick Barry
ABA - $7,500 and up
NBA - $5,000 and up

Elgin Baylor
any - $20,000 and up

Larry Bird
any - $3,000 and up
(a 1989 example sold for $4,870)

Kobe Bryant
any - $4,000 and up

Vince Carter
any - $2,500 and up

Wilt Chamberlain
Philly - $25,000 and up
LA - $20,000 and up
(a 1971 example sold for $22,411)
(a 1962 example sold for $33,613)

Bob Cousy
any - $15,000 and up

Clyde Drexler
any - $750 and up

Tim Duncan
any - $1,500 and up

Julius Erving
NY - $20,000 and up
Philly - $4,000 and up

Patrick Ewing
any - $1,250 and up

Walt Frazier
any - $5,000 and up
(a 1972-73 example sold for $9,614)

Basketball Players Approximate Values

Kevin Garnett
any - $2,000 and up

John Havlicek
any - $7,500 and up
(a 1973-74 example sold for $20,372)

Connie Hawkins
ABA - $10,000 and up
NBA - $2,500 and up

Tom Heinsohn
any - $7,500 and up

Allen Iverson
any - $1,500 and up

Magic Johnson
any - $3,500 and up

Sam Jones
any - $5,000 and up

Michael Jordan
any - $9,000 and up
(a 1991/92 example $21,846)

Karl Malone
any - $1,000 and up

Pete Maravich
Hawks - $12,500 and up
other - $5,000 and up

Kevin McHale
any - $1,000 and up

George Mikan
any - $45,000 and up

Earl Monroe
Baltimore - $15,000 and up
New York - $5,000 and up

Shaquille O'Neal
any - $2,000 and up
(Lakers jerseys sell for a premium)

Hakeem Olajuwon
any - $1,500 and up

Robert Parrish
any - $1,250 and up

Scottie Pippen
any - $1,250 and up
(premium for Bulls jerseys)

Willis Reed
any - $10,000 and up

Oscar Robertson
Milwaukee - $10,000 and up
Cincy - $20,000 and up

David Robinson
any - $1,000 and up

Bill Russell
any - $40,000 and up
(a 1960's example sold for $63,393)

Dolph Schayes
any - $20,000 and up

John Stockton
any - $1,000 and up

Isiah Thomas
any - $1,250 and up

Bill Walton
any - $5,000 and up

Jerry West
any - $15,000 and up

James Worthy
any - $1,000 and up

Pricing Note: This guide provides average pricing for standard game-used jerseys and not for those jerseys that exhibit exceptional qualities. Jerseys of that nature might sell for a significant premium above the listed price. In addition, unlike baseball jerseys, All-Star basketball jerseys might sell for less than standard examples.

Football Players Approximate Values

Marcus Allen
any - $1,500 and up

Troy Aikman
any - $5,000 and up
(a 1994 example sold for $8,625)

Sammy Baugh
any - $40,000 and up

George Blanda
any - $2,500 and up

Drew Bledsoe
any - $2,500 and up

Terry Bradshaw
any - $8,000 and up

Jim Brown
any - $25,000 and up
(one sold for $40,745-1960's)

Dick Butkus
any - $15,000 and up

Earl Campbell
any - $3,500 and up
(a late-1970's example sold for $8,538)

Chris Carter
any - $2,500 and up

Tim Couch
any - $4,000 and up

Larry Csonka
any - $5,000 and up

Daunte Culpepper
any - $4,500 and up

Randall Cunningham
any - $1,500 and up

Terrel Davis
any - $4,000 and up

Eric Dickerson
any - $2,500 and up

Football Players Approximate Values

Mike Ditka
any - $10,000 and up

Tony Dorsett
any - $3,000 and up

John Elway
any - $4,000 and up
(a 1997 example sold for $8,857)
(a 1994 example sold for $9,300)

Marshall Faulk
any - $3,000 and up

Brett Favre
any - $5,000 and up

Tom Fears
any - $4,000 and up

Dan Fouts
any - $2,500 and up

Frank Gifford
any - $10,000 and up

Otto Graham
any - $30,000 and up

Red Grange
any - $50,000 and up

Joe Greene
any - $7,500 and up

Bob Griese
any - $5,000 and up

Franco Harris
any - $6,000 and up

Paul Hornung
any - $15,000 and up

Edgerrin James
any - $3,500 and up

Deacon Jones
any - $3,000 and up

Jim Kelly
any - $1,500 and up

Jack Kemp
any - $5,000 and up

Jack Lambert
any - $5,000 and up

Dick Lane
any - $10,000 and up

Steve Largent
any - $3,000 and up

Bobby Layne
any - $5,000 and up

Howie Long
any - $2,500 and up

Ronnie Lott
any - $2,000 and up

Sid Luckman
any - $40,000 and up

Peyton Manning
any - $4,000 and up

Dan Marino
any - $5,000 and up

Steve McNair
any - $4,000 and up

Cade McNown
any - $2,500 and up

Art Monk
any - $1,500 and up

Joe Montana
any - $6,000 and up
(a 1988 example sold for $9,900)

Warren Moon
any - $1,500 and up

Randy Moss
any - $4,000 and up

Joe Namath
any - $20,000 and up
(one sold for $32,535-1968)

Merlin Olsen
any - $1,500 and up

Walter Payton
any - $8,000 and up
(a 1975 example sold for $28,327)
(a 1985 example sold for $11,827)

Jerry Rice
any - $3,000 and up
(a 1989 Super Bowl jersey sold for $10,634)

John Riggins
any - $3,000 and up

Barry Sanders
any - $7,000 and up

Gale Sayers
any - $10,000 and up

Shannon Sharpe
any - $1,500 and up

O.J. Simpson
any - $3,000 and up

Mike Singletary
any - $2,000 and up

Bruce Smith
any - $1,250 and up

Emmitt Smith
any - $5,000 and up

Bart Starr
any - $15,000 and up

Roger Staubach
any - $15,000 and up
(one sold for $20,240-1975)

Lynn Swann
any- $4,000 and up

Fran Tarkenton
any - $4,000 and up

Lawrence Taylor
any - $3,000 and up

Thurman Thomas
any - $2,000 and up

Football Players Approximate Values

Y.A. Tittle
any - $20,000 and up
(one sold for $26,409-1960's)

Johnny Unitas
any - $25,000 and up
(one sold for $30,560- last)
(one sold for $22,000- 1970-72)

Norm Van Brocklin
any - $15,000 and up

Steve Van Buren
any - $7,500 and up

Football Players Approximate Values

Kurt Warner
any - $5,000 and up

Reggie White
any - $2,500 and up

Ricky Williams
any - $5,000 and up

Steve Young
any - $2,000 and up

Pricing Note: This guide provides average pricing for standard game-used jerseys and not for those jerseys that exhibit exceptional qualities. Jerseys of that nature might sell for a significant premium above the listed price. In addition, unlike baseball jerseys, Pro Bowl football jerseys usually sell for less than regualr season gamers.

Hockey Players Approximate Values

Jean Beliveau
any - $12,000 and up

Marcel Dionne
any - $4,500 and up

Phil Esposito
Bruins - $8,000 and up
Rangers - $6,500 and up

Wayne Gretzky
Oilers - $25,000 and up
others - $10,000 and up
(a 1991-92 example sold for $12,952)

Gordie Howe
Detroit - $25,000 and up
WHA - $13,500 and up
Whalers - $14,500 and up

Bobby Hull
Chicago - $25,000 and up
Jets - $9,500 and up
Whalers - $7,000 and up

Brett Hull
any - $3,500 and up

Jaromir Jagr
any - $4,500 and up

Paul Kariya
any - $3,500 and up

Mario Lemieux
any - $8,000 and up

Hockey Players Approximate Values

Frank Mahovlich
any NHL - $8,000 and up
WHA - $5,500 and up

Mark Messier
Oilers - $7,000 and up
others - $5,500 and up

Stan Mikita
any - $5,500 and up

Mike Modano
any - $3,000 and up

Bobby Orr
Boston - $25,000 and up
Chicago - $12,500 and up
(a 1967-68 example sold for $44,820)

Jacques Plante
any - $10,000 and up

Henri Richard
any - $7,500 and up

Maurice Richard
any - $25,000 and up

Patrick Roy
any - $4,500 and up

Terry Sawchuk
any - $22,000 and up

Steve Yzerman
any - $4,500 and up

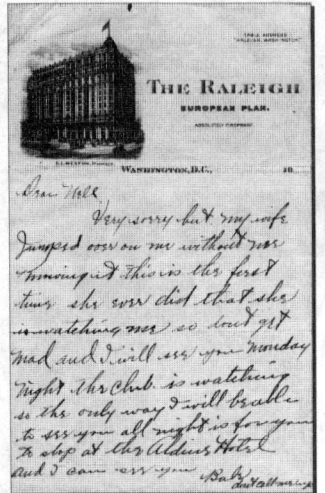

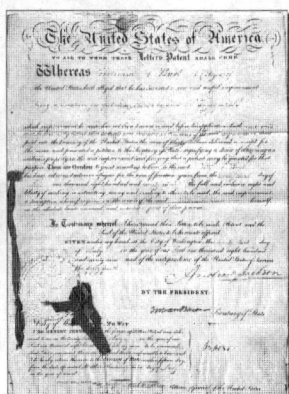

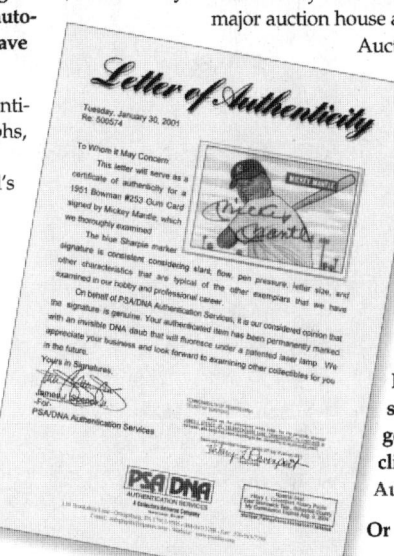

ATTENTION ALL AUTOGRAPH COLLECTORS
international
autograph collectors club

P.O. Box 848486
Hollywood, FL 33084

The Original Autograph Collector/Dealer Association

Web Site: www.iacc-da.org

PRESIDENT
John Reznikoff
University Archives
49 Richmondville Ave.
Westport, CT 06880

VICE PRESIDENT
Scott Winslow
Scott J. Winslow Assoc. Inc.
P.O.B. 10240
Bedford, N.H. 03110

TREASURER
Mike Frost
4575 Sheridan St.
Suite #111
Hollywood, FL 33021

EXECUTIVE DIRECTOR
Stephen Koschal
P.O. Box 1581
Boynton Beach, FL 33425

**DIRECTOR
INTERNATIONAL
RELATIONS**
Thomas Kotte
Kotte Autographs
Kirschenweg 9, 86916
Kaufering, Germany

ETHICS BOARD
Larry Rosenbaum
EAC Gallery
99 Powerhouse Rd., Ste. 204
Roslyn Heights, NY 11577

LEGAL COUNCIL
Daniel Brams

AUTOGRAPH COLLECTORS
YOUR INVITATION TO JOIN THE IACC

The IACC is the most unique and progressive autograph organization in existence today. A non-profit corporation, it is the first organization of its kind which includes separate categories for collectors and dealers. We feel this marriage is a vital one; as it assures that collectors and dealers can join forces in ways previously impossible. Additionally, we are the largest group **DEDICATED** exclusively to autograph collecting. By keeping this as our focus, we can concentrate our efforts only on this field. In our dedication to educate and inform, we feel that the measures we have taken as an organization will revolutionize the autograph world.

Our club has on hand one of the largest and most comprehensive collection of authentic "standards" for perusal by members. You are invited to interact with board members. We also offer material that is a result of our private signings to our members at prices below market value.

Our club publication *Eyes, Ears and Voice of the Hobby* is published six times annually. It has been called by many "the best in the business" due to the inclusion of informative articles, biographies of member dealers and our landmark signature studies. All news is timely and fresh. The low cost of your membership includes this publication, your membership card, the "2001 IACC/DA Dealers Directory", discount admission at all IACC/DA endorsed events and much more. Educational courses are available at most events and the instructors are among the flagship names in this field.

Membership in the IACC is open to all interested in autographs.

2001 Collector Membership (U.S. zip codes) $24.00
2001 All Foreign Countries USD $32.00
Lifetime Membership (U.S. zip codes) USD $375.00

Please send membership checks to:
IACC, P.O. Box 848486, Hollywood, FL 33084

The Professional Autograph Dealers Association™

🖊 The Leading Source for *authentic* autographs and for autograph dealers who are:
- ☞ Experienced, Knowledgeable and Ethical

🖊 Visit Our Website, *www.PADAweb.org* to:
- ☞ Learn About PADA, Our Members, and Our Shows

🖊 Visit Our Shows, *the Nation's Premier Autograph Shows*
- ☞ April—New York City
- ☞ September—California

For a free brochure and membership directory
or for other information write to:

Professional Autograph Dealers Association, Inc.
P.O. Box 1729-A, Murray Hill Station,
New York, NY 10156
or call 1-888-338-4338
or visit the web site: *www.PADAweb.org*

For the only guarantee you will ever need,
look for the PADA logo

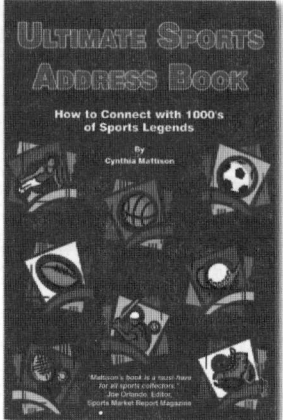

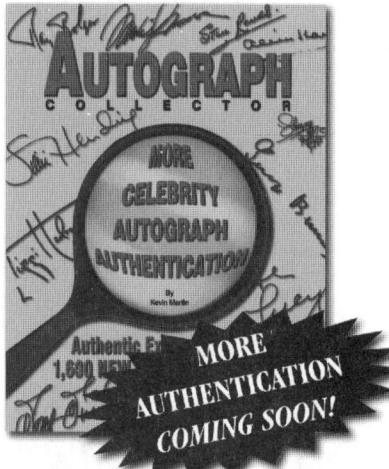

PIECE OF THE PAST

*MONTHLY(no min.bid)CATALOG/AUCTION

*WEEKLY Ebay AUCTIONS(piecepast2)

MONTHLY FIXED PRICE LISTS

9030 W.Sahara Dr.
Suite #448
LasVegas,NV.89117

Toll Free 888-689-7079

Over 15 Years Specializing in Entertainment...
*Autographs
*Props
*Costumes

Sterncastle Collectibles

Old-Fashioned Service & Integrity

WE BUY & SELL

★ Vintage Hollywood Autographs ★

★ Original Vintage Hollywood Photos ★

★ Contemporary Hollywood & Television Autographs ★

MADONNA

The Push for
CHANGE

Stepping into Possibility

By Joe Roberts

with Marie Marcoux-Roberts

Published by Joe Roberts Speaking Inc.
Vancouver, British Columbia
skidrowceo.com

Printed and bound in Canada by Friesens Corporation

ISBN 978-09732482-4-1

TABLE OF CONTENTS

DEDICATION

This book is dedicated to the love of my life, Marie.

We were sweethearts first in high school
and then you reappeared in my life 30 years later
to walk this crazy road together.

No one will ever know the pain and sacrifice you
endured to ensure *The Push for Change* was successful.
My job was easy, walk, talk, and repeat.
You managed everything else.

I said from the beginning that if we experienced
any level of success it would be because of you.

Every single person and community that
was impacted has you to thank.

You made a little boys dream come true
and I'm not talking about walking across Canada.

I love you.

FOREWORD

How much has the word "purpose" been showing up in your life lately?

Perhaps it has been floating across your social media feed or working its way into your workplace conversations? Maybe it has been touted as the key to great leadership, or simply identified as a requirement for happiness?

Simon Sinek, in his (now famous) TED talk, reminds us that to build great companies, develop great leadership or achieve anything in life, we need to start with "WHY" to discover our purpose.

Purpose seems to be everywhere… and for good reason. As a performance psychologist, I have studied the brain science of why purpose is important for humans to achieve almost anything. I have also worked with individuals and teams to harness the power of purpose to create extraordinary results in their own lives and the lives of others.

Purpose is like rocket fuel for most things we do as human beings. Tapping into, growing and acting on our sense of purpose can provide the inspiration to do things we might once have thought impossible.

In the ever accelerating, always-on, digitized and automated world we live in, while our need for purpose continues to grow, it is also easier than ever to disconnect from anything meaningful in our lives.

Recent studies of workplace engagement confirm this ever-increasing desire to do work that is personally meaningful, but at the same time we see a growing dissatisfaction with life for those who feel disconnected from purpose.

It seems we have reached a critical point in our existence – while we are looking for more meaning and we want to know how we can make a difference with that meaning - we might be a little lost in our search for purpose and how to apply it in a meaningful way.

What I know is, often, the greatest sense of purpose is developed when we step out of our prototypically human self-focus and step into a world of service to others.

To connect to your purpose and understand how to bring it to life, there may be no better place to start than to step into the shoes of another who has gone before you, someone who has wrestled with their own questions about purpose, capability, and self-worth and found a way (driven by purpose), to triumph against the odds and break free from the voices of doubt.

It is not common to meet someone who is truly connected to a deep sense of purpose, that sense of "I know what I am meant to do with my life." It is even rarer to find someone who is acting on that meaning and truly fulfilling their purpose. When you do find them, however, you want to connect to them, grab onto their energy, learn about their story and let yourself be inspired by their journey.

Joe Roberts is not just a man who is deeply connected to his purpose; he is someone who has pushed himself beyond all limits to bring that purpose to life.

Joe's story, the story of *The Push for Change*, is one that will inspire anyone to believe they can turn their doubts into extraordinary possibilities and their dreams into reality.

Over the past decade as I have gotten to know Joe well and worked alongside him, I have been constantly reminded and inspired by the possibilities that live within us and what it takes to bring them to life.

This book will take you on his incredible journey from roadblocks to purpose to action: understanding the very human roadblocks that can stop any of us in life (and keep possibility and purpose hidden from view); connecting to a purpose that is big enough to get you out of your own way and a simple action plan to achieve the seemingly impossible.

I am blessed to have been touched by Joe's life, his energy and inspiration. Reading this book, I hope you will experience the magic too!

Dr. Sean Richardson

INTRODUCTION

The Push for Change almost didn't happen, but then again I almost didn't happen. In the late 1980s I struggled with addiction, mental health and homelessness on the streets of Vancouver's Downtown Eastside. My life was in such a state of chaos that I'm certain I would have died on the streets if something didn't change.

One day as I sat on a park bench (completely lost, homeless and looking to score my next fix) I met a man named Gus. In those days I was consumed with my own needs and I saw Gus as nothing more than an opportunity to get a few dollars. Gus obliged and handed me a couple of bucks, but he also gave me something else. As we sat there, he told me something that would eventually help me to build the most extraordinary life and achieve more amazing things than I could have ever imagined.

Looking back, I can honestly say at that time I was the least likely person to discover the key to success. Before I met Gus, the entire scope of my life's accomplishments had been pitifully below average.

Gus taught me that we have infinitely more potential than we could ever imagine, but it's something that most of us never put to the test. I did and three decades later I can tell you that Gus was right. That potential exists in me and it also exists in you.

This book is for the underdog and the overachiever in all of us and it is my hope that it will inspire you to see that we all pretty much share the same struggles, hopes and dreams.

As we travel together, I will share my lowest point on the mean streets of Vancouver in the 1980s and the transformation that took me from habitual failure to graduating college with honours, transitioning into business and rising to the rank of CEO. Despite all of my success, I never forgot the bargain I had struck. When I was on the streets in Vancouver, I made a promise to pay it forward if I ever escaped.

The Push for Change was born out of my desire to give something back after all of the help and support I had received in my own recovery and to shine a light on all of the young people across Canada who are struggling as I did.

So how does a homeless drug addict turned CEO manage to walk 9,000 kilometres across Canada? I did it by using the inspiration that Gus gave me almost 30 years ago on that park bench and I want to share those thoughts with you.

How do you get into action and stay there? How do you overcome and succeed despite the roadblocks you face? How can you accomplish anything you set your mind to?

It starts with inspiration and a few small steps; that's what this book is all about.

THE PURPOSE

The purpose of this book is to ignite your imagination to discover what is truly possible.

Often, we limit our achievements because we hold a number of normal and predictable human beliefs. However, what I have learned as a result of my own failures and transformation is that most of our limitations are "mind made."

What would your life look like if you were no longer afraid to fail? If you no longer worried about what others thought? What if you had the courage to risk everything? What's really possible for you, your business, your family or your community?

As you read these experiences and become inspired, I want you to see how your life relates to the stories we will share with you. It's not just *The Push for Change* story, it's everyone's story: how each and every one of us face adversity, challenge and change and how each of us aspires, hopes and dreams for a more purposeful life. Surprisingly, adversity (that thing we try so hard to avoid), often holds the seeds to enormous personal growth when we emerge on the other side, triumphant.

What I know for sure is that actions connected to purpose-driven emotion can lead to an extraordinary life. So, don't just read this book, read it and get inspired to do something. Take action, even if it's a small action like getting off the couch and going for a walk. Who knows where that walk may lead you?

Your dreams are waiting for you; all you need is a little "push" to discover what you're capable of. That's what this book is pointing to, the infinite possibility that is YOU!

THE PUSH FOR CHANGE

PART ONE
EARLY LIFE

1

As I sat on a bench in Pigeon Park, smack in the middle of Vancouver's Downtown Eastside on a cold, rainy day just weeks before Christmas 1989, I couldn't stop running the events of my life back and forth in my head. How in the world had a happy-go-lucky young boy from Ontario ended up on the streets of Vancouver trapped in the vicious cycle of homelessness and addiction? It was completely baffling to me. Yet as bad as that day was, it would end up being the day my life was forever changed.

Desperate, broken and descending into a state of withdrawal, I had done the unthinkable and sold the only item I had left in the world that was worth 10 dollars for a fix of heroin. A friend of mine, John, had given me the boots with very explicit instructions, "Whatever you do, don't sell them."

It was obvious to everyone around me that my life had disintegrated into an addict's existence and I can't honestly say I was really even living at that point; I was just surviving from one fix to the next trying to avoid the dread of withdrawal.

After I sold the boots, I headed back into the streets. It was raining hard, the kind of cold, late November rain Vancouverites are accustomed to. My feet were covered in a thin pair of ragged socks that I had been wearing for over a month, so when my foot touched the sidewalk it sent a chill up my spine. Fiercely cold and wet, I began walking towards Main and Hastings, through the poorest postal code in Canada. A wave of despair and sadness hit me like a bus.

"How did my life end up like this?" I cried out.

I was a good kid from a good mother. How did I end up on the streets of Vancouver, a homeless junkie? Tears began to well up and I wept as I walked aimlessly through the streets. I had nothing left. I was 22 years old, homeless, hopeless and now shoeless on the streets of East Vancouver.

I truly believe that our toughest experiences in life have the power to transform us, but it usually isn't until we are backed into a corner or completely and utterly desperate that we become willing to make the painful, scary changes that put us on a better path. Anguish can be a powerful catalyst for inspired change and it was in that moment of despair when I made a decision that would change everything for me. I cried out for help. I looked up to the heavens and begged God for a second chance. I had always been a bit of a hustler, so even in the midst of misery I struck a deal with my sidewalk petition.

In asking God to give me a second chance, I promised if it was granted, I would "pay it forward" and do something to help others. Of course, only God and I knew about this little deal, but that didn't matter because even in what was certainly my darkest moment of personal bankruptcy, I still had my honour and I knew my word meant something, at least to me. So it was, on that park bench with what was left of my fragile honour, that I made a solemn promise that would change my life forever.

2

2

Growing up in Midland, Ontario, I had been the middle of three children. I have very fond memories of my early childhood. I was an energetic, curious and rambunctious child. I loved the outdoors and I especially loved riding my bicycle and exploring the woods and back trails of the small town of my birth. I was entrepreneurial as a child, working every possible odd job imaginable; I shoveled snow, raked leaves, collected empty pop bottles and even ran a seasonal "Kool-Aid" stand. We weren't poor as a family, but we also weren't catered to as children. We each received one big gift at Christmas and on our birthday, but if our desires overflowed, we were encouraged to make our own money to buy the things a child yearns for. It was a good lesson and one that I took to heart. I liked earning my own money and found it deeply fulfilling finding creative ways to do it.

As I mentioned, I had a lot of energy as a kid and that presented some challenges. I was a bigger handful for Mom and Dad as well as my teachers and, well, basically anyone that knew me. I was outspoken and naturally led in anything I was involved in and I always sought more attention. In school I was the class clown. If I couldn't garner attention with good grades, I would get it by acting the fool, it suited me well.

It's funny, but as a little boy I always felt different. Different from my brother and sister and different from the other kids, I just felt I didn't fit in. Teachers would get frustrated with me and soon I began to feel I was being labeled as the "bad" kid. I truly believed at an early age that I wasn't as good as the other kids and it is from that distorted perspective that I began making self-compromising choices, something that would define the trajectory of the next decade or more of my life.

Today, I'm the father of an extraordinary little girl who is just like me. My job is to nurture and welcome all the wonderful and crazy ways she shows up in this world. I applaud her outspoken nature, celebrate her genius, have time for her performances and praise her individuality. The difference between a "genius" and a "bad seed" is in the story a child tells to themselves about how they fit into the world. If you can get a kid to believe a lie about who they are, you can predict some of the poor choices they will make.

Awkward and uncertain, I fumbled my way through my early childhood, trying to figure out how I fit into this big world where I felt like such an outsider and then the unimaginable happened, my father died suddenly at the age of 35. As a family we were stunned, my Mom lost the love of her life and all three of us kids lost our hero. Our family also lost its main breadwinner. When I look back at my life trajectory, there are several key moments where I'd say, "That's when everything changed." Dad dying was a big one for me. I was already struggling with a number of issues that were guaranteed to give me challenges later in life, but the devastating blow of losing my Dad thrust me over the edge. I was eight years old.

3

After Dad died, my mom started dating a man that would later become my stepfather. He had his work cut out for him; my father had left some pretty big shoes to fill. I have a lot of empathy for stepparents, it's a tough role for anyone to try and fill. The problem was that "Dad 2.0" wasn't at all interested in being a role model, a supporter, or for that matter, even a good example. In the beginning while they were dating, he was super nice to us kids and to our mom, but shortly after moving into our home, his true colours were revealed. He had a lifetime of his own demons and they manifested in the form of alcoholism and violence.

It wasn't long before our home became a war zone. I can distinctly remember the sound of his Cadillac Eldorado slowly rolling into our stone driveway on Dominion Avenue late one evening in 1977. The family was always on edge when he returned from a night of drinking at the local Legion Hall. You just never knew if he would explode, so the house was always filled with tension. That night, as on so many others, Mom would bear the brunt of it. As kids, we had to deal with the terror and emotional abuse, but it was Mom who dealt with his fists. I can still hear her screams today. If I could have killed him, I would have, but I was only nine at the time. It took me years to understand how a good woman like my mom could get trapped in a vicious cycle of domestic abusive. To this day, I don't like bullies.

Life in Midland, a town located 150 km North of Toronto, was very much like life in any other small town in Canada in the late 1970s. Trouble didn't usually come looking but you could find it if you wanted. With everything going on at home I preferred to stay away as much as possible. My brother was three years older than me and had a gaggle of friends that I desperately wanted to be part of and I was willing to do anything to fit in, including compromising my own self worth. One afternoon in a park off Woodland Drive, some older boys asked me if I wanted to get high. I hesitated, nervous, but inside I think I had already made up my mind. The truth of the matter was that I was willing to do just about ANYTHING they asked to be accepted by these boys! They explained to me that if I sniffed the air in the bag, the fumes would get me stoned. I thought at first that they were teasing (or lying to me), but four deep breathes later my head was spinning like the blades on a helicopter. It felt amazing and for a moment I was catapulted away from the problems in my life. I felt invincible, joyous and carefree. On top of the extraordinary feeling in my body, I was also celebrating the fact that I was being welcomed into the inner circle of these older boys. It was perfect!

At home later that day, I was still quite buzzed as I sat on the edge of my mother's green plaid chesterfield in the front room, when my stepfather began one of his berating tirades. As he belittled and attempted to intimidate me, I sat there grinning like a Cheshire Cat. For the first time in my life he couldn't get me. I was stoned in a bubble of protection and for the first time since my father died, I wasn't afraid anymore.

Drugs aren't the cause of human suffering that we often make them out to be (more often, addiction is a by-product of trauma as opposed to being the cause). In fact, as a recovering addict with decades of sobriety, I would suggest that drugs and alcohol serve a very important role. For me they provided emotional protection and stability in an uncertain world. I didn't become an addict on a whim; as a teenager drugs helped me to escape from things that I felt powerless to control. I believe many

5

of the events of my early childhood, including the trauma of losing my dad and subsequent exposure to a violent alcoholic (along with the resulting low self esteem and self loathing I experienced), paved the way for potential addiction. At the time I started using drugs, all I knew was that getting high felt good and I was in no mood to follow rules any longer for the simple reason that I didn't trust or respect the rule makers.

For the next two years I sniffed glue, then I smoked pot, then I dropped acid, snorted coke, popped pills, ate mushrooms and injected cocaine. If it got me high, I was going to try it. Inside I was a scared little boy but what the world saw was an angry, rebellious teenager. By the time I was 15, my stepfather and I were fighting regularly and the environment at home went from bad to worse. I was defiant in the face of his presumed authority. I had spent over five years watching this dickhead emotionally and physically abuse my family. I was done. One afternoon, in a fit of rage following yet another fight, I stormed out vowing never to return to my mom's house as long as he was present.

4

My first apartment was set up for me by my employer. I worked weekends at the local flea market and the guy I worked a booth for offered to rent me a room in his basement. It helped that he was a drug dealer. Although I was only in grade 10, already I had my independence, access to drugs and a place to party; what more could a guy want?

Despite being out of the house, I continued to attend school and had no intention of quitting. I still valued learning and I wanted to finish high school. The problem was I was working evenings at the local Ponderosa Steak House as a cook, going to classes during the day and partying far too much on the weekends. After a while, work started getting in the way of my lifestyle and I found I could earn just as much money selling drugs to my friends. School too was starting to get in the way of my weekday partying and there came a point when I realized I might be in trouble. I had gone to school to write a math exam after a night of drinking and just two hours of sleep. I walked into the exam room smelling viciously of BO and alcohol sweat and was promptly escorted out and asked to leave. I argued that I wasn't drunk and I had a right to finish the test. I wrote the exam inside the principal's office under careful watch. However, instead of seeing this as a warning sign, I ignored the fact that none of the other grade 10 kids had been drunk in the exam room and continued on my downward trajectory.

By this time booze, drugs and partying had taken over my life. I was 17 years old and hell-bent on solidifying my reputation as a dropout druggie. On the outside, I presented myself to the world as a rebel and a carefree stoner. Inside, I was alone, afraid and aching for love and attention.

One night, before my departure from my job at the Ponderosa, I caught the eye of a very pretty girl named Marie. She had beautiful, innocent eyes and lovely blonde hair but what attracted me to her the most is she seemed to think I was funny. When I performed for her (in the way that young men do to get attention) she would blush, giggle and smile shyly. What's more, I would often catch her looking my way and I had all these "funny" feelings inside. With zero girl experience and a shattered sense of self worth, I approached with caution. One night I asked Marie if I could walk her to the bus stop and she accepted. We shared a cigarette along the way and it was both terrifying and exciting. She liked me too, I could tell.

Slowly, as in every bad teen romance, I edged myself closer to her favour until one day many weeks later, I asked if she would "go steady" with me. She said yes as she flung her arms around my neck and kissed me. She was pretty and I was smitten. It was January 1984 and I was 17 and in love.

Marie was my first love and our relationship lasted much longer than a typical teen romance. Our days together were carefree, at least for a while. My drug and alcohol use increased and as school and work evaporated from my life, they were replaced with petty crime, drug dealing and aimlessness. Eventually, Marie became tired of my instability and self-destructive behaviour and one night after I had been arrested, she broke up with me. I was devastated. I swore, begged and promised her things would be different, to no avail. We were splitsville.

Living in a small town with a shared group of friends, the breakup was particularly tough for me. All I wanted was to be reunited, but Marie went her own way and connected with a cool guy who had a Trans Am and played in a rock and roll band. I simply couldn't compete. I was depressed and lonely and fell deeper into drugs and alcohol to cope.

By the time I was 19 years old, not only was I a high school dropout with a rampant drug problem, I was also a convicted criminal. Barrie had little more to offer me, so I decided to cut my losses and head west. Before I left town, I had one last meeting with Marie. I asked her if maybe at some later time in life (if the stars aligned) perhaps we could try again. In sympathy, she said "sure" then kissed me on the cheek and said goodbye.

Marie

I was 15 when I got my first job at the Ponderosa Steakhouse in Barrie; I was a bus girl. I was shy and quiet, almost withdrawn. There were quite a few teenagers working at Ponderosa but I mostly kept to myself, which was easier for me than trying to fit in. Most of the others didn't pay me any attention, but there was a tall, outspoken boy from the kitchen who often did funny (and sometimes weird) things just to catch my attention. I soon learned his name was Joe. He was the complete opposite of me, very bold and self-expressed, not afraid to be the centre of attention. To my surprise, I was attracted to this behaviour, maybe because deep inside I wanted to be more outgoing. Although he lived nowhere near me, one day he asked to walk me home. That walk was really the beginning of our life-long relationship.

As the third youngest in a family with nine siblings (my mom gave birth to 10 children in a span of 12 years), my parents were busy! Trying to find my "place" in a busy household was tough. In most situations I found it was simpler to just accept things as they were rather than try to fight against the current. Not that my childhood was hard; I had all the necessities of life, definitely food, water, education, love and nurturing (we were a close family and my mom and dad showed their love to all of us), it was just never me alone. I never got one-on-one time with my mom the way I wanted. I looked up to her and loved her so much, but she worked full-time, took care of 10 kids and did all the cooking and cleaning and everything else that is required of a mom. She simply didn't have time to spend alone with me. I never blamed her for that, but it did make it easy for me to fade into the background.

I loved the attention I got from Joe. From the very first time he walked me home, I was thrilled that he was interested in me. He asked me questions about my life; my likes and dislikes, my family, my school, my friends. I warmed to him instantly and several weeks later, on another "walk home" it was easy for me to say, "YES!" when he asked if I would go steady with him. I could tell he was surprised by my quick reply; it revealed a vulnerable side to Joe that I hadn't seen before. This boy had a humble softness inside of him that wasn't on display for everyone to see.

I loved spending time with Joe and Joe loved to shine his light. During one of our walks down a pretty busy street, we were walking side-by-side chatting when suddenly I realized that Joe was no longer beside me. When I looked back, I couldn't see him anywhere, but then I looked up. Joe had shimmied up a hydro pole like a monkey climbing a tree and was almost at the very top, waving. The drivers of cars passing by couldn't believe their eyes as they slowed down to check out the crazy guy on a hydro pole. That was a typical date with Joe (and I loved it). I loved his carefree attitude and his brave nature. He was fun, the most fun I had ever experienced and although his actions sometimes embarrassed me a bit, they endeared him to me even more. Finding someone who didn't care what others thought was an eye opener and something I envied.

It didn't take long for the two of us to become inseparable. We both attended Barrie Central Collegiate and we both worked at the Ponderosa Steakhouse, however, I soon realized that he didn't live with his mom or dad. While it should have been a shocker to me, for some reason, it wasn't. His living arrangements in a townhouse with two other guys just seemed rather normal. Oddly enough, I don't remember asking him why he didn't live with his parents, it just seemed natural for Joe to be on his own, even though he was only 16. He certainly appeared mature enough to be on his own and it gave us the opportunity to spend a lot of time together at his house. His house was also the party house to be at and I jumped in with both feet. It was a chance for me to express myself and be my own person. Joining the party, I found I could drink my fair share of beer and I felt like I belonged with this fun group who seemed to have no worries in the world.

Weekends in the townhouse at 28 Donald Street, Unit 48 (which quickly won the nickname 28-48) became the highlight of our existence.

I knew that I was Joe's first girlfriend and within a few short months I could see that he was falling for me in a big way, he even told me he loved me. At 16, I didn't know what true love was or what it was supposed to feel like, I just wanted to have fun and I was enjoying this new environment and all of the friends I'd met at 28-48. I liked the crazy atmosphere of the party house, but Joe tried to pull me away from his parties so we could be alone. I wasn't interested in that at all and found myself starting to pull away from him. After a year of dating I'd had enough of feeling attached to Joe and decided I should let him know I didn't want to be his girlfriend anymore.

Although I knew Joe was going to take it hard, I finally got up the nerve to drop him. I wrote a short goodbye note and gave it to him in the hallway between classes. I stood beside him as he read it, although in hindsight, I should have passed it to him and kept going because I had to watch him break down and plead with me to give him a second chance. I felt so bad for blindsiding him; I could see he wasn't expecting it and I had hurt him deeply. I also knew I didn't want to continue with the relationship, so I stubbornly told him it was over and walked away.

It didn't take long for me to find another boyfriend but Joe didn't give up easily. One afternoon while I was sitting on the couch at my new boyfriend's apartment, I spotted Joe walking up the street. Sure enough, he stopped and there was a knock at the door. My boyfriend's roommate answered the door and I could hear Joe ask for me. I had told my boyfriend and his roommate to tell Joe I wasn't there, I didn't want to see him because I was afraid to face Joe's pain again. Even though he was told I wasn't there, I could hear Joe say, "I know she is in there, let me talk to her." They wouldn't and the door closed. As I sat and watched Joe walk away with his head down, I felt extremely sad to see him so broken.

5

As my Greyhound bus cruised past the wheat fields of Saskatchewan, I was relieved that all of my troubles were behind me now. I truly believed that all of my problems were related to my stepfather, the police, the government, my high school and the town I had been living in. At no time did I see that the mess I had made of my life was solely my responsibility. I was a master at deflecting responsibility and smart enough to debate the issue *ad nauseam*. I really thought that all I needed was a change of venue and everything would be A-OK. It was 1986 and Expo (the World's Fair) was taking place in Vancouver. I figured I could easily find a job, start making some money and set myself up quite nicely on the West Coast.

I stepped off the bus early in the morning and made my way to a small city park where I watched the sun rise over East Vancouver. I had this incredible feeling of aspiration, that this was the place where my life was going to really take off. I felt like Mary Tyler Moore and wanted to spin around and throw my hat in the air (for anyone under 40 reading this, Google the Mary Tyler Moore Show from the 1970s). Little did I know that within weeks of arriving in Vancouver, I would find myself homeless and living under the viaduct directly adjacent to the park where I was currently celebrating my arrival in BC.

The next several years were bad. As a small town kid I had no real understanding of how life in a big city worked. My fear led me to more drug and alcohol use and more petty crime. I was in and out of jail cells. I wasn't a threat to society as much as I was a nuisance due to my drug consumption. My days of smoking grass and getting drunk had been replaced with injecting cocaine and heroin and things began to get very serious, very fast. I'm not sure exactly when I graduated from being a carefree teenager getting high to becoming a dedicated drug addict, but it happened nonetheless. I spiralled down into a world of violence, criminal behaviour, disease, poverty and hopelessness.

I was injecting heroin multiple times a day and "needed" the drug to survive. If I skipped getting high I faced withdrawal, an experience I can only describe as hell on earth. It starts with aches and pains, a runny nose and an inability to sleep or eat, then comes diarrhoea and a pounding headache, followed by anxiety and panic, until finally you are immobilized into a useless ball of flesh, curled in the fetal position. The only way I can describe this to folks in a way they get is it's like having the worst flu virus you've ever had 20 times over. Imagine the worst flu in the world, then imagine you're homeless and on the streets trying to deal with it, all the while knowing that $20 will make it go away. It's not something that I ask folks to condone, but rather I hope they can begin to understand how that vicious cycle gets created and how it is almost impossible to break the cycle without outside help.

In 1989, I reached my lowest point. Chronically homeless, I chose to get high over having a safe, warm place to live. My self esteem was so low I felt I didn't deserve to sleep anywhere but outside on the ground, like a dog. I had completely lost perspective on any potential I may have once had as a young man. I lived from day to day, eating in soup kitchens, begging for change and cigarettes and looking for a scheme that would help get me that next hit of heroin. I was unemployed and on welfare with a rap sheet of petty crimes as long as my arm. I cycled in and out of emergency rooms and city holding cells and visited mental health units. I was a high-volume consumer of social services, food banks, drop-in centres and a frequent visitor to organizations like The Salvation Army.

I felt like a bum. I was a broken failure. If you'd run into me on the street in 1989, I would have been pushing a shopping cart and collecting cans and bottles. I was a "dumpster diver" and yes, I did eat from trash bins. My appearance was unsettling as well; I was 6'2" tall but only weighed 170lbs. I had dirty, matted, unwashed hair; a scruffy unkempt beard; yellow, broken teeth; blackened fingernails and clothes that were filthy and worthy of the dumpsters I was jumping in and out of. All of that, combined with the scent of failure, piss and BO from not showering for months at a time. If I would have approached you on the street back then, my appearance and behaviour would likely have repulsed you and possibly even scared you a bit. Yet somewhere deep down, all of my possibility and potential was still there, dormant and waiting.

It's so easy and normal for us as human beings to perceive the things around us as fixed in a certain way. We see ourselves this way, we see institutions this way and we see other people this way. It's normal for us to view the world through the lens of a probability mindset. Our brains look for simple ways to interpret things and the best predictor of something is its history. If it was like that yesterday, it will be like that tomorrow. The only problem with this fixed way of thinking is we fail to see what could be, what might be, or any of a million other possibilities. Without opening this creative part of our mind, we will always and only see the world in ways that seem probable. With a fixed mindset, we kill off both creativity and possibility. There is another option. Great thought leaders and many who have become world renowned icons tend to see the world in terms of what could be and what is possible. In so doing, they invite themselves and others into a world where new solutions can be discovered through exploration and create a space for possibilities to grow.

Let me explain what I mean. When children are small all we see is their potential; it's easy to dream of what possibilities their life will hold and the options seem utterly endless, open and infinite. Now, consider how different the view that we hold is when we encounter that same child, now 16 years old, looking disheveled and sitting on a piece of cardboard in front of the liquor store asking if we can spare some change. Has their possibility disappeared? Does their life no longer hold potential? No. History is full of examples of individuals who have risen from the ashes to achieve great things. It's just that due to probability thinking, their potential is more difficult for us to see. And if you think it's tough for you to see their potential, imagine how hard it is for them to see it. Great coaches, managers, parents and mentors share one thing in common. They see your potential, your possibility, and they work with you until you discover it for yourself.

In my life, the most important developments have happened when people saw my potential and then helped me to discover it for myself. One of those experiences happened just a few weeks before I sold my boots, while I was sitting (as I often did those days) on a bench in East Vancouver's notorious Pigeon Park. It was towards the end of my days on the street so I looked pretty much how I described earlier. Dirty and dishevelled, I approached a man whose name I would later learn was Gus, and accosted him for a cigarette. He obliged, so I took it a step further and asked him for a couple of dollars. He obliged again and gave me two dollars, yet these gifts would pale in comparison to what he gave me next. As I sat on the bench, destitute, homeless and deep in the throes of my drug addiction, Gus saw something different. He looked into me and saw my possibility and he said to me, "Joe you have this

13

homeless/addiction thing going on, but if you were to ever make a decision to get clean you could do amazing things with your life." He followed this with, "There's so much more to you than you can see."

"There's more to me than I can see," I mumbled. I certainly didn't feel that way. In fact I thought there was much less to me than most people saw. But as I gazed into this man I felt his warmth and sincerity. He had these piercing blue eyes with a joy-filled smile that lit up his face. I had long lost sight of my potential, but for the first time since I was a child, someone saw and spoke my potential into reality. Gus spoke to my possibility.

All of us at some point lose sight of our potential. Maybe not to the extreme of living on the streets addicted to drugs, but think for a minute about the limiting stories you tell yourself about what you can or cannot do. If fear were not in our path, what possibilities might we all achieve? I have learned not only through a very tough set of personal circumstances, but also through my many achievements, that life is no more than a reflection of the conversation that we have going on in our head. Our potential NEVER goes away, but the narrative to access it can. If you want power in your life, if you want to change any negative aspect of your life, change the story you tell yourself, because in the end each and every one of us is infinitely more than we can see. Gus gave me more than a smoke and two bucks, he gave me my life's mantra, one that I have been testing and proving again and again for more than 30 years now.

A word about panhandling, the most common question I get asked is, "Should I give money to those who ask me for it on the street?" My answer is simple, give if you feel like it but understand that any gift of money, food, or even warm mittens is an act of compassion. Sometimes I give and sometimes I don't, it really depends for me personally. However, if you want to support the issue in a deeper way, I suggest you and your family regularly donate to an organization that supports street involved individuals. By that, I mean support organizations whose mandate it is to help the folks who are most vulnerable. Our family supports Raising the Roof and The Salvation Army. We like them because they are fiscally responsible and are supporting organizations all across Canada. Find an organization in your community that is managing their money well and reaching people every day, wherever they're at.

So what can you give that person on the street? Ask them their name, give them encouragement, speak to their potential, tell them not to give up, and if you feel comfortable give them a hug and tell them they have value and worth. Give the gift of engagement and see them for who they are. Help collapse the stigma and acknowledge those who feel invisible. Tell them that there is more to them than they can see. If nothing else, send them a silent blessing and see for them a new possibility.

6

There was more to me than I could see, but accessing my potential was a problem. As I walked aimlessly along the street without my boots in a deluge of rain and misery, I wondered how a good kid from a good mother could end up a heroin addict on the streets of Vancouver. I began to think about what my next move was going to be.

Today when I reflect back on my life I'm reminded of the movie, Saving Private Ryan. Out of so many that I met during my time on the streets, including friends that died from overdoes, those who were sent to the penitentiary or contracted HIV, why was I one of the very few to survive? It's not like I did anything to deserve my second chance. The one thing I did have going for me was my mom. Mom loved and supported me through everything. That said, after years of me asking for help, she had finally reached the end of her rope and instituted a tough love approach when she told me she didn't want me to call for "bail outs" anymore. Even I understood that I had taxed my mom beyond anything reasonable. Since I was 10, Mom was the person who got called every time I was in trouble, did something stupid or needed help. Hundreds, if not thousands of times, Mom was there.

As I continued up the street I saw a familiar place, the Salvation Army, which had a drop-in centre that I frequented. I ducked inside and connected with a gentleman who knew me. I was a regular. He asked how he could help me and I told him I wanted help to try and get sober.

I was finally ready to take those first fearful steps towards change. I asked if he would help me connect with my mother in Ontario. Within a short period of time I had Mom on the line. In a tear-filled plea I asked if she would help me. Naturally, Mom was hesitant and asked, "Why will this time be any different?" I'm not sure if it was the words or the desperation in my voice, but Mom agreed and said, "Ok, but I swear this is it."

Within three days Mom was in Vancouver. I instructed her to take a cab downtown and meet me at Main and Hastings, the epicentre of Vancouver's notorious Downtown Eastside. When she saw me, she began to cry. I was emaciated and barely recognizable to her. She wrapped her arms around me, giving me a really tight "Mom" hug and whispered in my ear, "Let's get you the help you need son."

I have often reflected on the question, "Where would I have ended up without Mom?" I truly believe that if I didn't have a champion, someone who still believed in me, I wouldn't have made it off the streets of Vancouver. Never underestimate the power that you have to see and support someone's possibility, it can make a world of difference.

A couple of days later, we were back in Ontario at mom's home in Midhurst, a community just north of Barrie. I would love to tell you that sobriety began immediately, but it did not. My life had improved tremendously by getting off the streets, I had clean clothes, I was eating regularly, my health improved and I was no longer using street drugs, so things were definitely moving in the right direction, but I still hadn't made a commitment to get sober. Instead of using heroin and cocaine I substituted with alcohol and prescription pills.

My brother-in-law worked for a local drugstore chain that also sold groceries and discount food. He offered me a job working nights stocking shelves and I took it. The work was hard, but I've never shied away from hard work. In the beginning, I worked diligently all week and drank on the weekends. On the surface, my life had improved tremendously but without addressing my addiction, disaster was lurking just around the corner.

One night I showed up for work after drinking all day. With no one else in the building, during a break I was emboldened to rummage around behind the pharmacy counter. What I found there were expired narcotics and other pills I was familiar with from my time on the streets. This would prove to be a step backwards for me.

Over the next several months my life began to slide out of control. I was addicted to opiates once again. Although it wasn't heroin, it was basically the same thing in pill form. My life began to spiral out of control. I was a master at hiding things, so no one around me really knew anything was wrong until it spiralled out of control.

One day, I was called into the boss's office at work and the next thing I knew I was fired. Not much was offered in terms of cause, but I knew enough not to press the issue. As my narcotics supplies dried up I took to drinking more heavily and taking all sorts of other kinds of pills, a combination that often has lethal consequences. Alcohol and pills seldom produce positive results; for me the result was a downward spiral of self destruction, depression and thoughts of suicide.

Sometime during the previous year I had purchased a 9mm pistol off someone I barely knew. I'm not sure what I was thinking other than it would be cool to own a gun, but now, in my state of depression, having a gun close at hand, together with the deadly cocktail of chemicals I was ingesting, created the elements for a perfect storm of self destruction.

One evening in the spring of 1991, I sat on the edge of my bed in my mom's basement completely wasted on Diazepam, Halcyon, Secanol, Demerol and whiskey. I was at the end of my rope and the only solution I could see was suicide. It hadn't taken much of an argument, but I had convinced myself that I was an abject failure and would be better off dead. Mom walked into my bedroom that night and saw me sitting there with the gun, at which point she completely lost it. Petrified, she ran out of the room and called the Ontario Provincial Police. The last person I wanted to see was a cop, but within minutes the police arrived. The only thing the police were told was that there was an armed, suicidal male located in a "hard to approach" room in the basement.

Knowing what I know today about such interactions, this was a very dangerous situation for everyone. A different day or another cop and this could have turned out tragically. Too often stories like this have tragic outcomes. We tend to only hear about the ones where things go horribly wrong, but that night the OPP got it right. The first officer on the scene was Constable Scott MacLeod of the Barrie OPP. Scott's only objective was to deescalate the situation peacefully. When he called me out of my room, I opened the door and walked towards him. That night I was wearing a blue terrycloth housecoat with deep pockets. My right hand was sunk deep into one pocket where I was gripping a handful of pills. Scott, of course, didn't know this and demanded to see my hand.

It really could have ended right there. He didn't know I was gripping pills; all he knew was there was a gun somewhere. What I distinctly remember about that night was how well Scott talked me down and (pardon the pun), disarmed the situation. He treated me with respect and once he saw that I wasn't armed, his next objective was to find and remove the gun from the premises.

Earlier, when my mom had run out of the room in hysterics, I had panicked and tossed the gun into a spot within the wooden frame of the house that would make it very difficult to retrieve. Even if they searched for hours, they would never have found the gun where I stashed it. Realizing I wasn't going to budge and tell him where it was, Scott offered me a deal. In exchange for the location of the gun, he would drop all of the drug charges that they could lay against me (given the hundreds of pills I had in my possession without any legal prescriptions). I knew I was beat and gave up the gun.

Once the gun was located, I was whisked off to RVH hospital to deal with the side effects of potential overdose and undergo psychiatric assessment. I wasn't sent to jail.

Since the early 90s I have watched police across Canada take on the challenge of finding better ways to deal with mental health, addictions and dangerous situations like the one I was in. With millions and millions of interactions, there are always bad examples to point to. In my situation the police got it right and it would forever change the trajectory of my life. When I speak to police leaders today, I always emphasize that there are no average calls and that every interaction has the potential to be one that defines your career.

7

After my release from the hospital I still had weapons charges hanging over my head and Mom had finally reached her limit. She told me that if I wasn't willing to enter treatment, I had to leave her house. Together we worked on a plan and with a lot of hard work on her end; I was admitted into Serenity House in Belleville, Ontario.

My first few days were pretty rough, although I had gone through an initial detox in Kingston before arriving in Belleville; I wasn't used to life without the crutch of alcohol and drugs. I had to relearn everything, how to interact with people, how to be responsible for chores, how to honestly share my feelings, it was a scary time. One of the reasons I think it's easier to use drugs than to get clean is that the prospect of change is incredibly frightening. Humans don't do well with any kind of change and here I was trapped in a position where I had to give up the only things that had helped to numb my fear. Drugs and alcohol had been the medicine that allowed me to function in a world I couldn't control, but the cure almost killed me.

Even though rehab was scary, the prospect of going back to the streets or using drugs frightened me even more. I was 24 years old and the carefree "party" days of my life were over. For me, drug and alcohol use wasn't about the party anymore; I used drugs to numb my senses in order to make life somewhat bearable. What I really needed was to go much deeper and discover what I was hiding from. Why did I start doing drugs in the first place and how could I put the past behind me and focus on a future that was drug free by making new meaning out of the tough experiences I had been through?

When I went to my first recovery meeting I felt like an alien, it was so completely uncomfortable. As I sat and listened what became quickly evident is that I was hearing stories very similar to my own from people with a fractured sense of self-worth who had chosen to cope with life by using drugs. I heard many stories of degradation and shame, but I also heard something else, I heard a story about a new way to live. I was eager to learn how to deal with all the scary stuff in life and not use drugs and they encouraged me to keep coming around. I did, and before long I learned how I too, could live clean.

Recovery isn't a one and done situation though, even today, I continue to be part of a community of like-minded people who choose to live clean and be that example to others. I may have accomplished a few interesting things in life but none that I can take sole credit for. I am a by-product of the courage and influence of thousands of people; their ideas, their non judgement, and their investment of time and energy. We grow in community, we wither by ourselves. I'm fairly certain I will always seek the company of others to keep me honest and grounded and give me a place to belong where I can have an impact on others who are struggling to find their way. It's one of the promises I have made and hope to keep for the rest of my life.

8

With a solid foundation in recovery, I decided to go back to school even though I wasn't completely sure it was the place for me. I truly believed I was dumb and when I dropped out of high school in Barrie, I had resigned myself to being a truck driver. My addictions councillor Brian convinced me to give college a try and he made me a deal that if I applied for classes at the local college he would get me an extension to stay in the treatment centre. The truth was I already had the extension, I just didn't know it. Twenty years later at a convention for addictions councillors in the Belleville area, I told this story. Unbeknownst to me Brian was in the audience and I had the opportunity to thank him publicly for helping me take a step that I never would have taken on my own.

School was a scary prospect for me, I was 24 years old and much more experienced than most of my classmates. Yet, even though I had life experience, there was still a nagging voice that said, "You're not good enough, you're not smart enough!" It was a battle in the beginning and the only thing to my credit was that I kept going. I reminded myself that success is rarely the result of one or two key decisions; rather, it is built on the foundation of a million small, deliberate steps in the right direction. It's simple though not necessarily easy; just keep moving forward no matter what.

At Loyalist College I began to flourish, I started to get A's and although I was a mature student, I really felt I was starting to fit in. Things were going really well until the middle of my second semester when I suddenly found myself in the grip of fear and depression. I became convinced school was not for me and I went to my professor, Tom Thorne and asked to be released from the program. It was a Thursday afternoon and he asked me to take Friday and the weekend to think about it and wait until Monday to decide.

On Monday morning I went to his office still convinced to quit and assertively asked him to sign off on the papers. He asked to me sit down and proceeded to tell me that he was not going to let me quit (if in fact I did quit, it would have to be his signature that sealed the deal). Instead, he asked me what was going on and why my enthusiasm had faltered since the holiday break. He told me that he would be willing to work with me, to give me extra time on assignments and empower me in any way he could to assist in my success, but he wasn't going to quit on me. Tom knew my history and he explained that he was afraid of what would happen to me if I dropped out. I told him I was scared and he shared something that has stayed with me ever since, he said, "Joe it doesn't matter how you feel, it only matters what you do next. We live in an effort-based world." Then something extraordinary happened, he looked me straight in the eye and told me that he believed in me (that I had what it took to get this done). For a moment I felt like I was sitting on the bench with Gus once again and he was telling me (through Tom) that there's more to me than I can see, I just needed to keep trying.

On a bright sunny day in June of 1995, in the auditorium of Loyalist College they called out my name, "Joe Roberts, Dean's List." I graduated with a 3.94 GPA. With my goofy-looking mortar board, I walked proudly across the stage to accept my diploma as a roar went up at the back of the room (where my recovery friends sat). They knew this was no average achievement. Handing me that diploma was none other than Tom Thorn, the man who wouldn't let me quit. Reeling with emotion I worked my way back to my seat. In the seat beside me was my Mom, the woman who never gave up (who helped me and loved me no matter what). It was a special day for her as much as it was for me and both of us had tears in our eyes. Like Private Ryan, I mused at my good fortune as I asked myself, "Why me?" I was blessed indeed, but it wasn't because I was special; it was that I had people in my life like my Mom and Constable Scott MacLeod and my teacher, Tom Thorn. I truly believe all any person really needs is people that believe in them. To show them their unlimited possibility and to help them become the person they were always intended to be. That idea, of helping to unlock human possibility and create more second chances, is my life's work today.

After graduating from college, I tried to stay in the Belleville area but there wasn't much available for a Marketing/Business Sales graduate. I tried my hand at selling advertising for the local newspaper and then I sold freezer food plans (that was fun). I even sold magazines for Chatelaine, which involved a sales call being set up via a call centre, after which I would show up at your house and write an annual subscription for a whole bunch of dying publications that nobody really wanted. Not exactly fulfilling, but it provided the foundation for my next position selling photocopiers.

I was kind of done with Ontario and itching to make a move. I already had a brother in the Vancouver area, so I decided to take a risk and move out West again. It was a bold move. Vancouver hadn't really treated me well the first time, but I thought if I'm going to fail, may as well do it where the weather is nice.

I packed my U-Haul truck and my '82 Honda Civic and headed west for fame and fortune. Four days later I was on my brother's doorstep and with help from his wife at the time, I landed my first job. It was with Minolta Canada, selling copiers and fax machines.

I loved my job! I was crushing sales and doing all kinds of creative deals. The math was easy for me, so was dealing with customers and exploring their wants and needs. I quickly found success and I loved the idea that by working hard I could dramatically impact my salary. After a year at Minolta, I joined an American audio-visual company as a business development manager and a year after that; I left to work with a friend in a business start-up developing websites and online content.

One day years later, as I drove through the Downtown Eastside on my way to the office in a large, ostentatious German sedan, I stopped at the light at the corner of Hastings and Dunlevy where I saw a young man pushing a shopping cart along the sidewalk. In that moment, it hit me just how far I had come. When I got to the office that day sitting on my desk was a copy of Canadian Business Magazine and I was the featured story on the cover. In less than 12 years I went from being a homeless junkie pushing a shopping cart and collecting cans and bottles, to achieving more success than I could have ever thought possible.

What I love to share with the people I meet is that we are all made of the same stuff and each and every one of us (to some extent) is held prisoner by limiting beliefs about what we can or cannot do. We are blinded by our fears, misled by our stories and held back by indecision. The greatest tragedy is not that life ends too soon, it's that we wait too long to really get going. My life and my story are a testament to what anyone can do if only they keep taking steps forward. My failure was my inspiration to change and take action. What failures have you faced that have forced change in your life?

Later that same year, MacLean's magazine interviewed me for the Honour Roll Issue on Canada Day (it was a special piece titled, 10 Canadians Who Are Making A Difference). During the interview the reporter said to me, "You're successful despite being a former homeless drug addict." However, I explained that my success didn't come in spite of my experience, but because of my experience. My time on the streets had given me a number of transferable skills that helped me to accelerate my success. These are the top five:

1. **Hard work** – being a homeless drug addict was hard work. Full time, on call 24/7, no days off.
2. **Street smarts** – it's hard to explain but it includes the ability to read people, predict the next move, trust your gut and smell out a rat. My life was in a survival modality for years and my instincts had to be sharp. In many situations in the world I lived in, if you forgot this one rule you could get seriously hurt.
3. **Communications** – In order to shape behaviour and get what I needed to survive on any given day, I needed to be able to articulate and sell my position. I needed to be very adept at empathy, the ability to

understand where someone else is coming from and shape my message for maximum conversion potential.

4. Innovation - I worked overtime using the right hemisphere of my mind to develop and employ creative solutions to impossible problems. If I asked any corporate executive to hit the street for 10 days and come up with $200 per day using nothing but their wits, I'm not sure many would survive the challenge. Through my time on the streets I developed well worn neural pathways of creative thinking. I own a mind today that was built for breaking rules and problem solving, a perfect fit for the tech sector.

5. Perspective – I know what a bad day looks like, it's not a 300 point drop in the Dow. A bad day is watching your friend's body being removed from a garbage dumpster, or the scream of an ambulance hauling away someone you just had a conversation with, or pointing out the women you knew who were on Robert Pickton's list of victims. Life is not as bad as we make it out to be. Having been cold and hungry enough to dine from a dumpster, I am blessed to have that contrast when I get to whining today. In all honesty, I haven't had a really bad day in a long time.

9

My life had hit a nice stride and then one day out of nowhere, life took me out at the knees. I found myself seriously ill and it was pretty tense for a couple of weeks. I was diagnosed with a degenerative colon disease called diverticulitis. I went into the hospital on December 31 and didn't come out until shortly before Feb 14. It was a long stay and one I almost didn't survive. I had five surgeries in three weeks, including both a colostomy and an ileostomy. I had contracted MRSA (antibiotic-resistant bacteria) and developed an internal infection called peritonitis, yet somehow I ended up walking away from another brush with death. It was after getting out of the hospital I started to really question who I wanted to be when I grew up. Maybe it was time for me to get serious about what I wanted in life. Business was fun, but the idea of being chained to a money-making machine for the rest of my life bored me.

Don't get me wrong, I love business, but going through a near death experience has a way of forcing deeper ideas up into your neocortex.

I wanted to do things I was good at, but also things that had purpose and meaning (all the better if I could help others in the process). At this point in life, mostly due to the media exposure around my story, I was getting a lot of requests to speak to young people in schools about my life experiences. As an impact speaker, I was presented with the gift of access to young minds. Young people lean forward when I share in a transparent way how I ended up homeless and addicted to drugs. The story is honest and authentic. When I was a teenager I hated condescending speakers that waggled their fingers and said, "Don't do drugs children, drugs are bad. Just say no!" I vowed to never talk down to kids, but rather, just to be honest and open and give them the information to make an informed decision.

Schools started to call and make requests, then businesses wanted me to speak at sales gatherings and then conference planners started to call. I was getting far more fulfillment from speaking to an auditorium filled with students than I was from attending boardroom meetings, so I decided to quit the business world.

I developed marketing materials, set up a website, wrote a book and became a motivational speaker. My life was going better than good. I was doing work that was deeply fulfilling, I was making a difference and I felt happy. It was around this time that my life was blessed with the birth of my daughter, Loren. Could life get any better?

More than a year after my health scare, I returned to the hospital for a routine follow-up surgery. After the surgery, I began abusing the medication I'd been given and in no time my life began to spiral out of control once more. I couldn't believe that after 12 years of continuous sobriety, I was stuck in that old familiar vicious cycle of addiction. The only difference this time was that I knew what to do about it. I reached out and connected with my recovery friends for help and began to rebuild my life anew.

This time around, my recovery seemed much easier and as my life filled up with wonderful things once again, I stopped making recovery a priority and as a result I relapsed a second time (which was something I felt ashamed about for many years afterwards). I let myself down and chose drugs over being a father. I also abandoned my commitments and destroyed a lot of valuable business relationships. I felt like a fraud and a hypocrite and I was deeply ashamed of myself.

Often the really tough stuff is what provides us with the most profound life lessons. That relapse was over 12 years ago now and once I finally realigned my sails, I managed to stay on an even keel. More than anything my last relapse helped me to understand what was most important to me (and all that I had to lose) and that life lesson continues to guide many of my big life decisions.

Despite all my business experience and success, I was advised by people who knew and loved me not to jump back into the business world too fast. My recovery friends advised me to do work that would tire me out and keep me humble, but they never said I couldn't be entrepreneurial, so after working for another guy for a few weeks watching how he ran an odd job operation, I went out on my own. I bought a van, a pressure washer, window cleaning equipment and two extended ladders. I called the company Joe Jobs, and if you lived in Surrey or Coquitlam, BC in 2008, I may have been the guy you hired to clean your rain gutters. We cleaned windows, pressure washed concrete and vinyl siding, emptied rain gutters and a host of other home maintenance tasks. I wasn't satisfied just keeping myself busy, however, so I devised a marketing plan, put together a flyer and strategically targeted sections of the city I knew we could be successful in. The plan worked and it kept me busy for over a year until I was ready to go back to speaking.

I have to tell you, this was a humbling experience, but here's the funny part. I hate ladders and heights, yet on any given day it was my job to scurry 40 feet up a ladder and slip and slide across a moss-covered rooftop or teeter off the side of a house hanging onto a 40lb bucket of wet leaves. I have to admit I loved pushing myself and doing stuff that was scary. Also somewhat amusing is the fact that I am the least handy handyman you will ever meet. Fixing things has never been one of my strengths; in fact last month I had to hire someone to put together my IKEA closet. Ha!

My support friends were right however; physical work was exactly what I needed to do. After a year of hard work and with a nice nest egg saved, I began moving back towards what I loved to do most, speaking. My first event was an alternative school in the Fraser Valley. Being back in front of those young people and connecting, I knew exactly what I wanted to do. Armed with a new website, new brochures and a new video, I began the process of self-promotion to get my story out there. I took any and all speaking engagements that would get me exposure: chambers of commerce, service clubs, high schools. My strategy worked and within a few short months I was getting requests to speak at large conferences and major corporations.

THE PUSH FOR CHANGE

PART TWO

INSPIRATION

10

In the spring of 2011, I received a rather intriguing call with a request. It was from a meeting planner in Montreal who was organizing a community responsibility event for Aeroplan, one of the world's largest reward program operators. Each year Aeroplan would use their conference time to connect with team leaders and staff, but they also had a tradition of doing something that would positively impact the community and teach their people something important. The previous year they focused on the environment, this year it was homelessness.

The company orchestrating the event had a grand vision. The theme of the event would be youth homelessness and they wanted participants from Aeroplan to have an immersive experience to truly understand what street-involved teens face every day. The plan was to conduct multiple exercises that would incorporate learning objectives to give delegates a better insight into street life. The three experiences were designed to illuminate the problems of food scarcity, money scarcity and the lack of adequate housing.

As a facilitator, they wanted me to begin by sharing my story as a former homeless youth and then, over the next 35 hours, take delegates through some of the experiences that street youth go through every day. This was the first time as a professional speaker where I had been asked to do more than just speak and share an inspiring story. If we executed it properly, I believed this event had the power to be truly transformational.

The event kicked off with 450 delegates. Aeroplan had partnered with Dans la rue, a Montreal-based youth homelessness advocate, whose mandate was to serve the needs of up to 5,000 homeless young people on the streets of Montreal on any given night. After Dan made a few comments, I was asked to share my story. The purpose of my presentation was to inspire people into seeing possibility and I ended my keynote with a simple question. I asked the 450 participants if they wanted to make a difference. They answered with a resounding, "Yes!" and we proceeded with the first of three exercises.

Exercise one was designed to teach how food scarcity impacts homeless youth. The attendees were divided into groups and challenged with making sandwiches. In less than 30 minutes, the teams produced 1,500 sandwiches, which were given to Dans la rue for distribution to those in need. It was a great way for us to start a conversation about how difficult it is for a young person to find food once they leave home. It was also a simple, low barrier exercise that left everyone feeling empowered and excited; they were energized and ready for exercise two.

Exercise two was a little more intense. It dealt with money scarcity. I asked the audience, "How many people in this room have ever had to pan handle?" The room went silent. Participants began to look at one another and I guessed that they were a little hesitant about what was coming next. We divided the participants into groups of 10 and sent each group out on a bus. The buses took the groups to assigned subway stations where they were instructed to panhandle. It had taken some creativity to get the permission to execute this exercise. The city of Montreal's bylaws prohibit panhandling, so the organizers had to approach the subway authorities to get permission. The exercise equipped each team with orange toques and scarves to help brand the group. They were given blank cardboard signs and instructed to write a compelling statement that would assist in getting people to donate. They were also given an empty paint can and very simple cards that could be handed out to passersby. The cards explained the group's mission and stated that 100% of the dollars raised were in support of Dans la rue and homeless youth in Montreal.

To be honest I wasn't sure how it would go, but I figured both failure and success would have teachable moments, so I was eager to see how each group would do. After the groups were loaded on the buses and taken to their prospective drop zones, I changed my clothes and jumped on the subway so I could ride from stop to stop incognito, watching how each group engaged the public. Some groups used music and chants, others created funnelling techniques, while others ran "hug me" campaigns. The goal was simple; engage people quickly and get their attention, explain why they were there and who they were supporting, then ask for a donation.

In all honesty I didn't think it would be anything more than a fun exercise, but it turned out to be utterly transformative for the people involved. We had to wait until everyone returned and the money was counted for the results but when they came, it blew everyone away. One group alone had raised over $1,500 in under two hours and when all the groups were added together, the participants had raised more than $13,000 in change after two hours in subway stations on the streets of Montreal. The feedback we received from the groups was that the people who donated felt they were getting something more in return for their small investment. The exercise inspired the communities of Montreal, which in turn inspired the team members creating a domino effect of inspiration that was kind of magical. What's more, it wasn't one big thing that did it but rather a collection of thousands of little things.

As the group celebrated the afternoon's success, there was an incredible buzz in the air. Something amazing had just happened and for me, it validated a long-held belief that human beings are their most beautiful when they are helping others. These individuals had pushed their boundaries, stepped into something uncomfortable and come out triumphant. In the process, they had inspired and engaged over 100,000 people in a very spontaneous way and the reward was far greater than any of us could have imagined.

Mealtime that evening was facilitated by street vendors (in keeping with the theme of the event) and the entertainment was provided by real, local street buskers. It was awesome mingling with folks and sharing inspired experiences. I was super proud, but I also knew what was coming next. Just up the street in an area outside the Bell Centre, a parking lot was being prepared for exercise number three.

Around 10:00 pm, everyone gathered and I led another short talk. The final exercise was designed to show people just how harsh sleeping outside on the street really is, especially during the colder months of the year. Given that it was October 10 and the weather was not particularly nice, it would be a true test for some of the participants who had all been given the same one item; a piece of cardboard. The area was secured but other than that, there was little in the way of comfort, no heat vents, benches or doorways to shelter on or in. Today, all over the world, "sleep outs" are organized to raise money and awareness, but in 2011 they weren't a regular thing.

I think it was around 2:00 am when I ran into Steve Allmen (a senior leader at Aeroplan) and struck up a conversation that would lead to a lifelong friendship. Steve was amazed with how engaged his colleagues were and truly impressed with how the day had gone. Little did I know that evening that Steve would end up being part of something much bigger that was inspired by the events of that day.

The next morning, everyone congregated to celebrate the successes of our time together, although I believe I might have been the only one who got to sleep the night before. It was a grand celebration; along with the $13,000 in change collected, there were additional donations tallying $25,000. The leadership of Aeroplan generously decided to match the total and a cheque for approximately $80,000 was presented to Dans la rue.

As a side note I want to thank the leadership of Aeroplan. It takes tremendous courage to lead a corporation into a learning experience of this nature, but Aeroplan was committed. It's also worth noting that during the three weeks before the event took place, Occupy Wall Street protests were happening in cities around the world. From a public relations perspective, this could have become a nightmare really quickly if the exercise had been misinterpreted. I'm proud to have worked on this project and impressed by the corporate courage it took to follow through in spite of the potential blowback.

During the wrap up event, people shared how insightful and inspiring the event was for them and as the group dispersed, I received heartfelt and earnest feedback from all kinds of people. The resonating theme behind their remarks was that this experience had forever changed the way they see homeless youth. The experience had transformed their view on a very important issue and I was excited by the notion that I hadn't just inspired the group, I had changed the way they saw the world.

One of the most profound comments came from the CEO, who told me that in over 20 years as a "C" level executive, working for two of the most corporately engaged companies on the planet, he had never had an experience as powerful as this. I was very happy to hear this, given that I always want clients to receive high value for their investment, but part of me was also troubled. For 20 years I had been sharing my story and I had never had this kind of transformative experience. As I returned home, one question bounced around in my head, "If we could transform the perspective of 400 conservative business leaders in just 35 hours and get them to see youth homelessness from a new viewpoint; what could we accomplish if we aimed higher?"

11

Back home in Vancouver, I couldn't help but share my experience and excitement with my friend and business colleague, Dr. Sean Richardson. Sean is an expert in high performance and also has a doctorate in sport psychology. He has personal experience training for two Olympic Games as well as a long history in competitive elite sports. Sean and I worked together as management consultants, teaching companies how to engage people and teams for high performance. We were, I guess, an odd team in that we came at performance from opposite sides. On one hand, Sean saw the world from the standpoint of what it takes to be the best in the world; while on the other, I understand why people underperform and what keeps them stuck. We had done some incredible work speaking together and consulting together.

One afternoon on a flight to Calgary, Alberta, to conduct workshops for a group of managers, I was talking with Sean about my experience in Montreal. I was getting pretty animated as I told him how absolutely crazy fun it had been and how inspired I was to engage and see so many people take action. Most importantly, I was excited about how in such a short period of time we had raised a ton of money AND changed people minds about a pressing issue that's very close to my heart.

I mused out loud, "How could we take what we did in Montreal and go across Canada with it? If we could change the perspective of 400 people in one day, imagine what we accomplish if we engaged the whole country."

As the airplane carried us along 35,000 feet in the sky, Sean and I engaged in some blue-sky thinking. I looked at Sean and asked him how we could replicate what was done in Montreal in cities across Canada. Our first idea was to put together a road show and do one event in each city. However, we quickly tossed that idea away given that it would require an enormous budget and a big team to execute. We needed something more grassroots that would be run by people who were as inspired as we were.

New ideas surfaced and were discarded as we continued our exercise of possibilities... until we hit gold.

"Why don't you run across Canada?" Sean asked, looking altogether serious about the idea.

"Why don't you run across Canada?" I quipped back.

I couldn't even imagine myself running across Canada, I wasn't the sporty type. I exercised of course, but the notion of running across the entire country was beyond my comprehension.

"Besides, it's been done," I told him.

As we soared through the sky, we stayed with the thought. Sean brought up the point that it's kind of a Canadian tradition to cross

Canada for a cause. Heroes like Terry Fox and Rick Hansen came to mind and we knew we were onto something. I pointed out to Sean that although these campaigns had been very successful, copying them wasn't an option. If we were going to consider anything even remotely similar, it would have to have an edge, something different and very unique that would tie it to youth homelessness.

Sean looked at me and said, "I've got it! Why don't you push a shopping cart across Canada? The shopping cart is a reflection of your life when you were homeless on the streets of East Vancouver; it's also an outcome you're trying to avoid for young people. And walking is a whole lot easier than running...."

A smile spread across my face as the hair on the back of my neck stood up. "Push a shopping cart across Canada for youth homelessness. Wow, that would be something," I agreed.

As huge as the idea was, surprisingly no part of my mind said that it wasn't possible (sometimes an idea just needs a little nurturing instead of being discarded out of hand). I truly believe that many of us tragically underestimate what we are capable of, so every day we throw away amazing ideas with the justification that they are impossible to achieve. The truth is nothing is impossible; it's only our beliefs that get in the way.

Our plane landed in Calgary; we crushed the event and flew home to Vancouver the next day. It was late November 2011 and *The Push for Change* idea was in the ether. Little did I know that this idea would consume the next seven years of my life and lead me to a deep understanding of possibility mindset and the power of a personal promise.

THE PUSH FOR CHANGE

PART THREE
PREPARATIONS

12

Back in BC, I couldn't let go of the idea of crossing Canada, it began to consume my every thought. One of the first realizations I had was that physically, I was in no shape to walk across the second widest country in the world. I was 46 years old, non-athletic and 289lbs (which meant I was about 79lbs overweight). I had spent too many days sitting in front of a computer and my fondness for drive-through meals had left me in a pretty unhealthy state. My physical condition alone should have been enough to disabuse me of such a crazy idea, but I've always liked a challenge and thinking about this one had me excited.

That weekend, I decided to put my fitness to the test. I owned a treadmill, although at the time I dusted it more than I used it, so I decided to get on and see what I could do. Over the next few weeks I started to walk longer and longer distances on the treadmill. First, I walked 5 km and then 10 (which wasn't too difficult since I had regularly done similar distances before when I was in better shape). One Saturday afternoon, I jumped on and managed to walk 21.2 km, the distance of a half marathon. On Sunday, although I'd woken up tired and very sore, I pushed myself to do ANOTHER half marathon. I proudly posted this achievement on my Facebook page and shortly after, my phone rang. On the other end was Sean, who asked me what I was doing walking that many kilometres in such a short time.

What I didn't tell you about Sean is that his doctoral thesis focused on over-training. He, more than anyone else on the planet, understands what happens to athletes who push too hard. They inevitably hurt themselves. Sean asked the question again, "Why have you logged so many kilometres this weekend?"

"Because I'm going to walk across Canada, just like we talked about on the airplane!" I announced, quite proudly.

"Are you out of your mind?" he asked.

"You're the psychologist," I retorted. "You tell me!"

There was a long pause and then he said something that moved my dream one step closer to reality. "If you're really going to do this, I'm going to help you, mate."

Once again, someone saw my possibility and offered help.

13

In the beginning, *The Push for Change* was nothing more than a fragile idea, but with encouragement and hard work it turned into something extraordinary. During those early days of the campaign's genesis, I believe if it hadn't been for the possibility mindset that both Sean and I brought to table, it might never have evolved past the point of being an inspiring idea. A wiser person would have discarded the foolish notion of walking across Canada, but wisdom has nothing to do with possibility!

As I began to prepare myself physically I was pretty determined to drive myself into the ground with exercise; in my mind I needed lots and lots of training. Thankfully, Sean was there to explain mind-body science and he told me that at the rate I was going, I was destined for injury. I didn't like hearing this, nor did I want to be told what to do, but Sean had something I didn't... experience. I reluctantly listened and learned as Sean explained the need for a detailed exercise program that allowed for rest and time to heal. He also started to add in stretching, cross-training and ice baths (I'll get into that one later). Given Sean's science background, his history working with some of the best athletes in the world, his personal experience as a former Olympic athlete and his doctorate in sports science, I did the smartest thing I could, I listened and I learned. I knew I was lucky to have Sean in my corner.

On top of all the body science he brought to the equation, Sean was also a confidante with whom I could share anything. As a psychologist, he helped me work through numerous mental challenges that came with *The Push for Change*. For a number of years, we had shared a dual relationship as friends and colleagues, but now Sean was also my psychologist and we went to some very vulnerable places together which undoubtedly unleashed demons from the past. In doing so, Sean taught me how to make new meaning out of the tough stuff from my past. He also filled my mind with great new ideas, taught me that most of what we humans do is normal and helped me to understand that feeling badly about yourself isn't all that productive. In many ways, who I am today can be attributed to the tools Sean gave me.

In life, if you're lucky you'll meet a handful of great people who will help to shape you and teach you about character and when you look back on the trajectory of your life you'll recognize that meeting those key people changed you. I believe coaches don't get enough credit for what they do. All my life, I had the possibility within me to be and do so much more, but it took people like Sean and Gus and Scott and my mom to show me what they saw before I could see if for myself.

Sean and I shared everything in the beginning of this journey and I think that kinship existed for a number of reasons. First and foremost, the cause behind PFC lit us both up, we shared a deep commitment to seeing young people grow up strong and avoid homelessness, mental health issues and addiction. I, of course, see it through the perspective of lived personal experience, while Sean, as a psychologist, understands how young minds are shaped by things like trauma, poor parenting and mental health. *The Push for Change* was a way for each of us to take positive action and that was very exciting.

Shortly after that first long weekend of walking, Sean and I sat down to discuss training. He explained that in the Olympics there's usually a qualifying race prior to the games that gives athletes an opportunity to test their readiness. He advised that in order to maximize our success, we needed to do a "pilot" or training walk, something long enough that it would give us a feel for the highway and long distances. This couldn't just be a weekend walk; it had to be more substantial. We also discussed the need to experience hills and tough terrain. Let's face it, Canada has some rugged geography to navigate and the more we could simulate that in training, the better.

Money was another issue; if we were going to cross the entire country we would need some serious sponsors. If the training project and trial run were successful and we documented the whole thing on film, we could use that success to attract sponsors and support. The next question was where and when we would do the trial run. It was already early January and we needed time to prepare, so we decided the best time to do a serious walk would be in the summer. We also needed to choose a route. We talked about walking from Vancouver to Whistler, but thought it would be too short. Hope to Vancouver? Better, but no hills. Then Sean said, "How about Calgary to Vancouver?"

We looked at each other and grinned. It would definitely be tough enough (with a few hills to conquer) and the distance was almost 1,100 kilometres, more than enough of a challenge. It was set, starting on Canada Day (July 1) 2012, I was going to attempt a walk starting from downtown Calgary with a 56-day deadline to finish in downtown Vancouver on August 25. The idea was to successfully complete the walk from Calgary to Vancouver and then prepare for a national walk, which would begin eight months later on May 1, 2013. That was the plan anyway.

14

Committing to a timeline was critical for creating urgency around the building blocks of the campaign. We immediately set up social media channels and started on a website, although we struggled with the name. In the beginning I wanted the campaign to be called *The Homeless Prophet*. I thought the name really reflected what we were trying to do. Sean disagreed and pushed back. Again, I got a little upset and we had a heated discussion about it. He explained that "Homeless Prophet" wasn't quite the brand we were looking for. As we struggled back and forth, Sean asked me a question. "What do you want to do with this campaign?"

Without thinking I blurted out, "I want to push for change, to get people to think differently about homelessness and how easily it can happen."

Sean repeated the words, *"Push for Change"* and just like that we had a name. Sean worked with an online company and in no time, we also had a logo and things really began to take shape.

Over the next five months I had just one job, train and focus on a successful trial campaign. I began walking long distances while listening to music and my walks took me through every corner of the Lower Mainland. Often, I walked more than 30 kilometres in one day, which was good since I would need to walk long distances day after day after day. One of the things that was never far from my mind during this time was the possibility of injury. It was something that scared me a lot; every time my knees hurt my mind would over-react and go to a place where I thought it was all over.

Sean gave me simple rules for training; if I was tired or sore, I was instructed to suck it up and get to work, however if I was hurt or in pain I was to stop immediately. Sean taught me that it's when athletes unnecessarily push themselves that they get hurt. Often, you don't know you've gone too far until it's too late, so it's important to listen closely to your body. As the weeks moved on, I began building a tolerance for long walks, sometimes as long as five or six hours. Some days it was lovely, other days the weather was terrible. When the weather was bad, I connected with the notion that this was hard to do and felt a kind of sadistic joy on those tougher days.

Another interesting thing about my training is that I travelled a great deal during those five months to speaking engagements all across Canada, so I had the opportunity to train in many different provinces. I trained in Ottawa, Toronto, Halifax, Edmonton, Winnipeg and even Yellowknife. One of the things I did to help motivate myself is to imagine that I was already on my trek and walking through those communities. I could see and feel what it would be like with people there to greet me and cheer me on. I used my imagination a lot in building a mental picture of the trek. I also used words a lot. On days when the campaign or the training and everything else felt overwhelming, I would repeat, "The campaign has already happened," over and over to myself, which might seem like a silly exercise, but what I was doing was harnessing the power of my mind by using a past tense. I would also repeatedly envision myself walking down East Hastings on the last few kilometres with a crowd of supporters surrounding me.

The mind is a powerful thing and I used these and a number of other techniques and tricks to condition my mind. We all have the ability to guide our mind, but the mind doesn't differentiate tomorrow from today when we give it commands. By visualizing the difficult task ahead of me as already completed, by seeing, hearing, and most importantly, FEELING the campaign's conclusion, I believe I accessed a deeper part of my mind to help achieve the goal.

Training wasn't always a fun time I'll admit, there were a lot of days when I fell short and felt terrible. Sean would always tell me to pick it up the next day and "don't try to make up the kilometres," which is something I struggled with. If I missed a day or two, my tendency was to go hard, but that's a no-no when training properly. It's when we "give it" on those make-up days that we can hurt ourselves. I had to dig deep a lot of days and there were a lot of adjustments along the way.

For example, in the beginning my footwear was all wrong and my feet started to shred, I literally had a blister on top of a blister. It took me some time before I found a sneaker that I could comfortably do 25 kilometres in day after day without getting sore, blistered feet. I also learned that blisters are just blisters. Suck it up and move on.

I had a "blister bag" filled with every kind of ointment, bandage, second skin and moleskin, but my trusted friend was a roll of grey duct tape. When I got a blister, I would drop, yank off my sock and wrap the area in duct tape. This protected the skin from additional friction and gave a little extra cushion. I made a painful mistake one day with a loonie-sized blister on the ball of my right foot. The shoes I had were striking wrong or too loose and I developed this massive blister. I used toenail clippers to drain the liquid out and then wrapped it tight with duct tape and kept trucking. The problem was that I didn't cover the loose, torn blister skin with gauze and when I took that duct tape off later, a chunk of skin came with it which was protecting a very sensitive and deeply exposed raw area on my foot. No biggie though, I only had a 30 km walk planned the following day, and 28 km after that and 24 km after that. I logged all those training days despite my tender foot and I learned that blisters are not as bad as I thought. Yes, they're uncomfortable, but not debilitating. Wrap them up and keep walking was my new mantra.

Blisters were just one of my challenges; sore, tight legs were another. There is an abundance of information on the internet about how to complete your first half or full marathon, but there isn't a whole lot on how to complete 400 half marathons in a row! That is in essence what we were up against, so testing my limits and building physical resilience were important. We also needed to identify things that would help me heal quickly and accelerate recovery after long walks, even if they seemed pretty far out.

It was during one of our early conversations about training when Sean suggested ice baths or cold water therapy, essentially immersing myself hip deep in water of 5-8 degrees Celsius for 10-15 minutes. I was reluctant at first, but I'm a gamer so I gave it a whirl. It was not a pleasant experience! If you've ever reached your hand deep into a cooler filled with ice to grab a beer or soda on a hot summer day and felt that stinging sensation, you can start to imagine how cold it was. Now think about being waist deep in there for 15 minutes! Think about that fellas! It was one of the most excruciatingly painful experiences of my life. So, after

43

walking 30 kilometres and feeling exhausted, hungry and tired I would run a bath with only cold water and fill the tub waist deep. Then I would dump in three or four bags of ice from the store, stir for five minutes and get in. If you want to seriously slow down time try it out, minutes will feel like hours.

After a few times doing this, I decided it would be simpler to set up an ice bath outdoors. My daughter Loren had an old miniature swimming pool, so I filled it with water and left it in my carport. Given that it was February in Vancouver, the water stayed quite cold and some days it even had a thin layer of ice on top. Following a long walk I would come home, shed my long pants and sit in the ice pool. After a couple of days it just seemed normal to me, however, one night as I was sitting in the cold water in my carport, the neighbours noticed me and I caught them curiously looking out of their windows. I can only wonder what they thought seeing me sitting in my driveway in a kiddie pool in February. It wasn't until several weeks later when we met in the street that I explained what I was doing. It wouldn't be the last of the funny looks I'd get throughout this extraordinary adventure.

Although the ice baths weren't much fun, what I noticed almost immediately were the results. I was feeling stronger, healing quicker and had fewer aches and pains. The science regarding cold water therapy isn't clear, but I can say it is something I used and it worked for me. It also came in very handy when I was walking from Calgary to Vancouver on those super hot days. The thinking behind ice baths is that they reduce inflammation, promote circulation, squeeze out lactic acid and stimulate the immune system. All I know is that after a 15-minute ice bath, I felt if I can endure this I can do anything, which really helped me to build mental resilience.

Ice baths weren't the only addition to my training; I was also instructed to incorporate strength training, core exercises, stretching and nutrition. Sean suggested I connect with his wife Kate, who is an extraordinary personal trainer, although I feel personal trainer is too broad and vague a title. Kate is obsessed with helping people understand what they need to do to experience extraordinary health. She and I had a sit down and talked about core workouts, strength training, stretching and most importantly, nutrition. Over the next several weeks she created a menu along with a detailed workout schedule and we booked time to train together.

In the beginning, I was intimidated. Unlike me Kate was in extraordinary shape and even though she was nothing but kind and encouraging, I felt self conscious. I wanted to work out at home, so together we created a list of exercises that I could do on my own and after some one-on-one coaching I left with my homework.

One of the challenges around things like core workouts and stretching is that I hated doing them, so they often got left undone and I felt bad that I wasn't doing all that I could each and every day to maximize my training. I have learned that missing an exercise or training day is not ideal, but it's okay in the long run. What isn't okay is to miss something and then beat yourself up for it. If I missed a day or was out of alignment with my training I could always start again the next day. Once I got good at this modality my stress level went down and I was actually able to get more consistency while leaving the guilt behind.

15

When Sean and I initially talked about crossing the country, it was assumed I would push a shopping cart for a number of reasons. First, it is a symbol of chronic homelessness, something no child in Canada should have to experience. Another reason we wanted to use a shopping cart is that it is related to my personal story of living on the streets, which is a story of transformation, resiliency and hope—a message we have used time and again to humanize the issue of homelessness and help collapse barriers and stigma. The third reason we wanted to use a shopping cart is that it is unique and therefore it would help our walk across Canada stand out and be noticed. One of the things both Sean and I recognized when we first starting playing with the idea was that no one had ever pushed a shopping cart across Canada, so not only was it symbolic, powerful and poignant, it would also turn some heads.

We had no idea where this shopping cart was going to come from, the notion of pushing a real shopping cart was out of the question. Not only would it be too heavy and poorly suited to winter conditions, with my luck I would end up picking a cart with a wobbly wheel and wouldn't get out of my driveway.

This was another example of being okay with not knowing and just letting things unfold. It was around this time I was in Toronto speaking at a CEO conference. I shared publicly what I was about to do and afterwards Phil White, the co-founder of Cervelo offered to help. He thought this was a project his engineers could get behind and build something really cool for me. At the time I didn't know what Cervelo was. I Googled them later that night and realized this company builds elite high-performance racing bikes. Their bikes have been ridden by the top cyclists around the world.

Shortly after meeting Phil we set up a call and laid out our vision. They had a ton of positive ideas, the only challenge we faced was time to design. Because this was a ground-up approach, the engineers would need time to develop a prototype. We needed a beta cart for the Calgary to Vancouver training launch for July 1. We also needed to train with it ASAP since we didn't know how my body was going to perform with the cart.

Needless to say, the shopping cart was a great idea but it presented many unknowns. What kinds of challenges would it add to a long distance walk, would it be durable enough, and how would it perform in wet or winter conditions? The shopping cart definitely presented some uncertainties.

One afternoon while training with Kate in her home studio, I noticed a baby carriage. It was a high-end model for active moms and dads, called the Chariot Carrier. During the workout I kept looking at it and it got me thinking, maybe we could transform the carriage into a shopping cart somehow and use it as a beta while Team Cervelo built a slick custom unit. I asked Kate if I could push it up and down the laneway to try it out. It was super light and smooth. This was the start of something.

Around the same time I met with a group of young people at Pinetree Secondary School in Coquitlam. The students wanted to be involved in *The Push for Change*, so I told them about the shopping cart problem. Our first line of thinking was to build a cart from the ground up, so the students went away and came back with some sketches. After my meeting with Kate and looking at the Chariot, the students strongly suggested we use the Chariot as a base and their design to modify it. I liked their thinking.

I researched Chariot and learned the head office was in Calgary where I had meetings scheduled a week later. I connected with the head of marketing and asked if we could meet briefly. What was really interesting is that on their website their slogan was, "Safely moving children from one place to another." The more I thought about it, the more I thought that's what *The Push for Change* is doing too! When we met a week later, I explained that we wanted to take their product, strip it down to its frame and transform it into a shopping cart for a cross-Canada walk. The idea resonated and I left the meeting with a firm commitment. One week later we had a 2 CX1 Chariot Carrier shipped to my home address. Once assembled, we looked at the design the kids made and began searching for a metal fabricator that could help us with our odd request.

Throughout the entire campaign one thing we experienced again and again was excellent timing. Every new champion we met and every new resource appeared just when we needed them. When we were looking for a metal fabricator our request was an odd one for any metal shop and I got a number of rejections. I think I confused the first three shops I called, but as I worked my way through the list I found someone that listened.

A&A Steel Fabricators had a small shop in Port Moody, which was relatively close to my place in Coquitlam. When I rang them up, I was put through to Ryan and I explained what I was trying to do. Ryan suggested I come by and bring the cart and he would see what he could do. I was so excited at the prospect of getting feedback I threw the Chariot into the car and drove there right away. Ryan asked questions about how the cart would be used and we determined it needed to be lightweight, durable and interchangeable. I showed Ryan the drawing the students from Pinetree developed and left it with him. Two weeks later I called Ryan and he told me, "It's all ready." Again, too excited to wait, I drove down immediately. When I saw what they had done I was emotional. It sounds silly, but what they created was a vision come true. They took the stroller Chariot had donated and using the drawings and information I provided, they welded together a lightweight aluminum frame that made the baby carriage look like a shopping cart. The dream was beginning to materialize before our eyes.

I took the beta cart home, stripped the baby carriage accessories out and headed down to speak with Andrew at Fast Signs in Coquitlam. Again, Andrew learned what we were doing and agreed to help in any way he could. I left the cart with Andrew and his team and came back three days later. Not only did the cart now have signage, he had also created pop up banners, stickers, business cards and committed to a vinyl wrap for the RV closer to launch.

I want to mention here that the students from Pinetree were connected to Odyssey of the Mind, an international education program that provides creative problem-solving opportunities for students. Odyssey Angels, which is a sub-group of the larger organization was created to help the "thinkers" of Odyssey of the Mind build projects that have significant community impact. Our project fell under this group's mandate. So, not only did Odyssey of the Mind students help us design a successful working prototype, they actually won a worldwide competition and were honoured in front of 20,000 students from around the world at the annual conference at Iowa State University.

The cart we developed in 2011 would eventually log over 12,000 kilometres, to include both training and the campaign across Canada.

16

From the time I got on the treadmill and began walking to the time we had a shopping cart was seven weeks. We were well on our way and had overcome some major roadblocks, but we still had enormous work ahead of us. We needed lots of help if the Calgary to Vancouver walk was to be successful. We needed events to be organized, as well as sponsors, volunteers and an RV. We also needed a professional driver and a videographer. We knew the most important part of doing the trial walk was capturing the journey so we could create additional sponsorship material to show potential partners what our national vision looked like. In order to do all these things, we needed money to operate, which came with its own challenges. As a charity, we created a governance rule that we could NOT use any public donations to operate with. In other words, we could only pay for operating expenses with sponsorship money. We wanted to be able to tell people who donated to us that 100% of that money was going to support the cause, not pay for our campaign. Transparency is incredibly important and we wanted to be squeaky clean in every financial decision. So now we had a new problem, who was going to sponsor us?

We put together a budget and the bare bones estimate for everything we needed to get from Calgary to Vancouver came in at $45,000. I started to get nervous; who was going to give us $45k to push a shopping cart from Calgary to Vancouver? The good news was we had already begun to develop a great team of people around us who were donating their time and expertise. Fast Signs had supported us with signage, a good friend had developed our web presence, Chariot donated the baby carriage and A&A Steel transformed the carts.

We put together a proposal and started asking for financial help, but this was a whole new world for me and I felt lost. I had zero experience in the charity sector and didn't even know how to create a sponsorship brief. We needed to learn fast and in the beginning we struggled, but things got better with action. The first two organizations that helped us were Cloverdale Paint and Elks of Canada. Cloverdale donated cash, but more importantly brought their people, as did Elks of Canada. Although these organizations were very different, both saw an opportunity to be involved in something that inspired their people.

We were encouraged but still far from being funded. At one point I said to Sean, "I don't care if I have to put the rest of it on my credit card we are doing this no matter what." The fact that we were 100% committed to doing the walk is what I believe pulled everything together. An energy began to build around the project and just like before, timing was everything.

When we initially put together the budget, we realized the RV rental was going to be expensive. July and August are prime months for rentals in the Rocky Mountains. We needed a C Class unit around 30ft long, something a team could live in and work from. This RV was going to be home for 56 days and 1,100 kilometres.

In the process of talking to people and trying to learn how a campaign like this works we ran into the mom of a young woman who just finished a cross-Canada tour for brain injury. When I connected with Melissa for coffee, I asked her a million excited questions. Her responses were helpful, but tinged with the fatigue and frustration of having just single-handedly managed a campaign across the entire country. "If I had to do it again, I wouldn't!" she told me emphatically. I learned a lot that day from Melissa, information that would come into clearer focus when we started planning the national campaign.

On the subject of RVs, Melissa told me Fraserway RV had helped them, so I called them up. Following a few conversations, I met with James Epp, the owner and operator. When I explained what we were doing he got behind us 100%. "Fraserway is a values-led company that believes in community support," James told me. Which is why they're involved in many different kinds of philanthropy. With a handshake we had our RV. I was so excited driving home, elated in fact, until I realized I still didn't have a driver.

I placed an ad for a professional driver on Craigslist with an explanation about what we were attempting to do. It had all the elements of a good, old-fashioned Canadian trek for charity. I didn't expect much but within a few days I got a hit from a guy named Jeremy. Jeremy had just completed Rick Hansen's 25th anniversary relay. To celebrate Rick's Man in Motion world tour in 1986/87, the foundation retraced his Canadian route and invited participants to take part and become medal carriers.

I decided to meet with Jeremy and found myself sitting across from someone who had knowledge of the inner workings of the Rick Hansen campaign. I learned a massive amount about cross-Canada treks for charity. I also learned that the team he worked on was mostly comprised of people who had just completed the 2010 Olympic torch campaign. Meeting Jeremy gave me insight into how huge campaigns are staffed, funded and run. Learning how well they ran things, I started feeling really small. These were multi-million dollar operations with so many people involved. I was excited to simply have an RV.

There's a serious danger when building your dream if you compare what you're doing to someone else's accomplishments. Learn from others and be teachable, but don't try and live up to anyone's expectations but your own.

When I was done with Jeremy, I realized how little I really knew about a cross-Canada trek. I also realized there was no way I could afford a professional driver. I simply didn't have the budget. I needed someone who could join the campaign, work for peanuts and be excited about what we were doing. I was desperate and decided to ask for help on Facebook.

Facebook is a funny thing, in a campaign like ours it was necessary to share with people what we were doing. Social justice campaigns like *The Push for Change* need exposure and Facebook has a way of getting the message to a much broader audience. One of the challenges for me was that I didn't personally know a lot of the people who were following. One guy in particular kept sending nice, encouraging messages that were written in a very familiar way, like he knew me. I decided to connect privately through direct messaging and thank him for his support. The gentleman's name was Rob Cook and he had been following the campaign for some time. Rob told me he was super inspired by what we had started and would be willing to help out. Curious, I asked him how he knew me and he said, "It's Cooter."

I couldn't believe this Rob Cook, aka "Cooter" was someone I had known on the streets of Vancouver in the mid 1980s. We had spent a lot of time back then looking out for each other and here we were more than 20 years later connecting on social media. I picked up the phone and called him directly. We had a quick catch-up and then I told him what we needed most now that we were less than three months to launch, was a driver; someone comfortable enough to drive an RV five kilometres an hour from Calgary to Vancouver who was willing to do it for cheap.

I heard a chuckle on the other end of the phone as Rob proceeded to explain that for the last number of years all he'd been doing was driving professionally. Delivering trucks, shuttling cars, moving furniture, you name it and Rob was driving it around. He told me he'd be more than happy to do the job and he would even do it for free if needed.

The next person to join the team was our videographer Ali Virk. We found Ali through an email I sent to Vancouver Film School, asking if they might have a practicum student interested in the project. They explained that their courses don't work that way but were happy to forward the email to recent grads.

Three days later we got an email from Ali saying he was interested in the job. We chatted on the phone, then met up in person a few weeks later and agreed that Ali would join us on the trek. Ali's job was to capture the essence of *The Push for Change* on film. Trying to comprehend a 1,100 km walk from Calgary to Vancouver is much easier with a video that actually shows the difficult weather, the steep, treacherous terrain and the community embrace.

The RV was in place and we had secured a driver as well as a videographer and three weeks before launch TELUS gave us $25,000 and technology to help push us over the top. All of the pieces were coming together. With our team assembled, training continued and campaign logistics progressed as we continued the countdown to July 1, 2012.

17

In the last couple months before the trial launch, the idea for a *Push for Change* theme song was born out of a caffeinated discussion between Sean Richardson, Cal Misener and me in a Vancouver coffee shop. Cal, a lifelong musician and music enthusiast, came up with the possibility of producing a theme song that would speak to the spirit of *The Push for Change*. We all liked the idea but couldn't imagine how we would do it on our budget. Through Cal's network we accessed a "song mentor," Jen Herschmann to facilitate a session with a group of young people who would help us develop the lyrics, melody and song wireframe. I met up with the group of young volunteers early one Saturday morning in Coquitlam and shared my story along with the story of *The Push for Change*. With coaching and leadership from Jen, the songsters quickly came up with draft lyrics and a melody that was absolutely amazing.

Now that we had a rough cut, we needed a lead vocalist. Sean's wife Kate Richardson was the perfect candidate (when you listen to the song you will understand why). Her voice is powerful, passionate, expressive and beautiful. It was amazing too, because Kate was pregnant and not feeling well the day they recorded, yet it didn't affect her performance one bit! With Kate leading and the songsters backing her up, *The Push for Change* single was recorded at Nimbus Studio in Vancouver. From concept to finished product, the PFC theme song was an exercise in possibility (from that first coffee shop discussion to the finished track took just three months).

We're very thankful to everyone who helped give PFC a theme song, including: Taylor Tibbles, Jacey Yu, Sarah Doyle, Ron Goodman, Jeremy Kevin Wong, Melanie Law, Jennifer Hershman, Sean Richardson, Kate Richardson, Cal Misener and Loren Roberts.

Momentum is everything when you're tackling a big goal but uncertainty and fear can sometimes stop you in your tracks. My secret was, I kept my feet moving all of the time and I was 100% committed, so although I had doubts about whether or not I would be successful, I knew that I would give it everything I had. Sean taught me that failure is fine as long as you give 100%. "Fail leaning forward," he advised.

With so much at stake I felt I needed a reminder of my commitment, something physical that would encourage me every day and help keep me focused. A friend of mine worked out a deal with a local tattoo artist to offer me a free tattoo. I liked the idea a lot and the next day I went down to the tattoo shop and got the PFC logo emblazoned on the top of my right arm.

Throughout my training and the entire PFC campaign, the tattoo was a constant reminder to me of what's possible if you just keep your feet moving. Today the tattoo reminds me of my unlimited potential, representing both possibility and personal transformation. It is the culmination of over 11 million steps and likely as many actions that were needed to accomplish what most people thought was impossible. Some days I still need to be reminded of the unlimited possibility we all possess and this tattoo is my reminder.

18

Perhaps the greatest lesson I learned from my experience with the PFC campaign was that as human beings we have the power to create anything. Up to that point in my life I had repeatedly underestimated what was possible and settled for whatever was available instead of reaching for something bigger. By taking action I discovered that we can take ideas and make them things. That dreams can become physical and that anything we can think, we can create. By falling in love with an idea and ramping up both my emotion and my actions I opened the portal to a unique perspective on how life really works. One that would teach me that anyone can do anything.

All of this may sound a little trite, but I have come to believe through personal testing and experience that thoughts are extremely powerful things that determine what we create in life. If we consistently marinate in negative thoughts (or what I call diminished thinking) we will inevitably create a poor reality for ourselves. This was (and sometimes still is) my greatest challenge, therefore, I strive to have discipline in what I think and hold every thought to account. My mind is always running and if I don't pay attention, I get stuck in a loop and repeat negative thought patterns that are unproductive. It's a very human thing to do.

It's so easy to procrastinate, or worry and manufacture reasons not to try... or be afraid of failing and give up after one or two minor setbacks. With *The Push for Change* campaign, I gave myself no choice but to follow through and in the process I discovered "possibility mindset."

I believe thinking is the most important thing we do (it's also the foundation for creating anything). Often I look at the world around me and marvel at the fact that EVERYTHING I see that is not part of nature was first created by someone thinking about it. Look around you right now. Everything you see, your computer, your furniture, the clothes you're wearing, your automobile, your home and all its possessions, were once just thoughts in someone's head. We affect the world around us far more than we realize.

Most of my life, I felt powerless about the way life impacted me. I was a "victim" of circumstances or the "product" of my environment. The truth is when I got up off that park bench and started taking different actions (combined with different thinking), the world around me shifted (different thinking and action changed everything). I realize now that my entire life I had unconsciously based my world view on

Newtonian physics (which is also known as classical mechanics). I'm no physicist but from what I have read and my experience of life, I would say that quantum mechanics better explains my reality.

What's the difference? Well, Newtonian physics simply states that everything is predictable. If you know about the parts, you can know about the whole. The world is made of matter and forces act on that matter. Therefore, the likelihood of a homeless drug addicted individual experiencing transformation is highly unlikely.

Quantum mechanics perspective purports that everything is energy and a single electron can exist simultaneously in more than one place. The variable in the equation is our observation; therefore everything exists in the form of pure potential or possibility. We learned that matter can be in two places at the same time, and matter can change from particle to wave based solely on whether it is viewed (watched) or not. It's truly mind boggling the things we're discovering, but what it all points to is that our reality can be any one of a zillion possibilities. The world around us is nothing more than a large chunk of clay waiting for our consciousness to mold our reality from it. Therefore, a homeless drug addicted individual can change his environment by changing thinking, energy and action.

For the science minded, please forgive me. I have taken some massive liberties here but I'm simply trying to make the point that there is far more in the realm of possibility than we understand. In time, science will be able to better define these ideas and explain how it all works. For now, all we need to do to make these ideas work for us is to believe that anything is possible and take action towards our desired outcomes. Personally, I don't understand all the science behind how electricity works but that doesn't stop me from accessing its power to transform my life in a thousand ways every day.

To summarize, the world around you and your reality is nothing but possibility (potential) waiting for the right thought and energy to create it. There is so much more to each of us than what we can see, just as Gus said.

So why do we get stuck and not fully realize our potential? Why do we desire great outcomes but come up short? Why are extraordinary results not the norm? I think its two things. First, our brains have evolved to help us survive, NOT to operate at peak performance. Secondly, our emotions stymie actions that would otherwise lead to extraordinary experiences and results.

Before Dr. Sean Richardson and I met, I had a few accomplishments under my belt. I had worked very hard and followed direction well in my recovery and in my business life, but I couldn't really identify and explain what had made me successful. When Sean and I began working together, he shared a model for personal development that I could really identify with. I saw my life through this model and it helped me better understand how to access more possibilities.

It's all well and fine to tell someone they have potential, but without instruction they are left to flounder. As a psychologist and an elite athlete, Sean understands what it takes to perform at a consistently high level; he also understands what gets people stuck. One afternoon we sat down over coffee to talk about mental resiliency and how I would need to condition my mind to prepare for the massive amount of work in front of me.

Sean took out a large folded sketch pad, it was sort of a portable blackboard and he wrote three letters on it: A I R. He then added a plus symbol in between the "A" and the "I" and a minus symbol between the "I" and the "R" and at the end of the "R" added an equal symbol and the word Performance. When he was done this is what I saw on the page:

$$A + I - R = \text{Performance.}$$

He looked at me and told me this idea, more than anything, was going to help me successfully walk across Canada. He called it the AIR Model. I was curiously amused.

Sean and I had a multi-faceted relationship at this point in the campaign. Not only was he a co-founder, trainer and shaper of the early stages of *The Push for Change*, he was also a business partner, a great friend and my psychologist. Together, we had worked closely on many things, including some very vulnerable issues I had not shared with anyone else, so my trust in Sean ran deep. He was a friend and confidante. I also respected him a great deal as a person and a professional who understood how the body and mind worked together.

I think because of this and the fact the AIR Model looked so simple, I was nodding my head as he explained it, soaking up the ideas and eager to put them to use.

Sean began to break down the AIR model, which was part of his PhD work and based on his own life experience, as a tool to help unlock possibility. In short, the AIR Model is the psychology of excellence.

Sean explained that understanding all the drivers (and inhibitors) of human performance is essential to achieving personal goals.

Without a clear understanding of what I was trying to achieve (and through assessment processes), he told me there would be gaps in my strategic problem solving which would result in mistakes that could hinder the development of my potential to walk across Canada.

In order to be successful, I would need to continuously maximize "action accountability" and "inspiration" while minimizing "roadblocks" and/or the impact they would have.

The formula looks like this:

$$[A_{max} + I_{max} - R_{min}]_{time} = \textbf{Performance}_{success}$$

A = Maximize accountability, action and achievement (related to mechanics such as training, nutrition, ice baths, as well as the sponsorship drive).

I = Maximize inspiration (having a clear purpose, vision and strategy, the "why" behind the campaign that would motivate me and the team).

R = Minimize roadblocks (barriers at either the team or individual level that would get me stuck mentally or physically) while increasing resiliency and resolution.

Having objective measures of performance in place (deliverables, project milestones and deadlines) helps to pinpoint roadblocks or performance deficiencies (what isn't working), allowing for adjustments so that over time, performance increases and success is achieved.

Success is simple: **P = A**

Performance = Action Accountability - choose what you want to achieve then get busy doing it and persist until you achieve it.

To get people performing, you start with the mechanics, so determine their responsibilities and deliverables and find a way to keep them accountable (that's the A-factor).

Of course, humans are not simple, we want a reason to perform:

$$P = A + I$$

Performance = Action Accountability + Inspiration/Purpose

Continuous high performance is abnormal - so we need to have purpose/inspiration (often driven by leadership) to keep us going. To keep people performing at optimum levels and accelerate their progress and productivity takes something that's a bit intangible. In a team environment, this comes from leadership and coaching. As a leader, you want to inspire your team. For an individual, the key is to find ways of connecting on a daily basis to your purpose, that's the big "why" that inspires action. The "I" factor can help reduce the amount of time it takes to achieve high level success. Humans are motivated to perform better when they are inspired.

Humans are fallible, however, and that too is part of the equation:

$$P = A + I - R$$

Performance =
Action Accountability + Inspiration/Purpose – Roadblocks

Individuals come with both personal and situational roadblocks that can get in the way of performance and often the biggest risks to performance success are things that aren't outwardly apparent. Great teams acknowledge and support the resolution of roadblocks; seeing them as challenges rather than problems. With good behavioural science, you can predict what some of the unseen roadblocks might be and prepare in advance to navigate them effectively when they occur. For individuals, dealing with roadblocks is about practicing a non-judgmental mindset towards your weaknesses and a possibility mindset for the things that get in the way - resolution often includes summoning the courage to ask others for help.

Great teams and high performing individuals drive "A," lead "I" and manage "R."

19

The ideas outlined in the previous chapter are from Dr. Sean Richardson's *AIR Model – The Psychology of Excellence*; brilliant stuff that I began applying immediately to help with the massive challenge ahead of me. I had a lot of work to do, not all of it physical. In fact, the greatest steps I would take in the years to come related to how I perceive myself and what I am capable of. Since learning about it from Sean, I have used the AIR Model in almost every area of my life; from parenting to business management, to health, wellness and running our charity. You can take any desired outcome and work it backwards through the AIR Model and you will discover an incredibly simple way of understanding what needs to happen to achieve success as well as what will potentially get in the way. I personally think that when we repeatedly fail at something it's not because of how we handled roadblocks, it's because we haven't connected our goals to an inspiration that resonates for us. Our "WHY" has to be big enough to stay in action and drive through the roadblocks.

In the beginning, I was dealing with a lot of leftover baggage. I had debilitating beliefs about myself. I had guilt, feelings of self hatred and a resonating belief that I wasn't worth it. When I look back at my life, these themes were the underpinning for many poor and destructive choices.

All of my humanness began to surface when I put my body and mind to the test. But I wasn't alone, I had the AIR Model to work with and Sean to help sort out the roadblocks as they arose.

As I began building my training regime, there were many days when feelings of uncertainty and fear would become overwhelming and it always played out the same way. The physical or mental roadblock would arise, followed by negative emotion which would stop me in my tracks. Sometimes I would be out of action for days in a row. Other times I simply didn't know what my next step should be and it would cause me to get out of action and once again the negative emotion would show up. Other times I just wasn't motivated enough to take action and I would flounder until I reconnected to what first inspired the actions.

In every situation whether I needed help understanding what to do next, motivation (or reconnection with my inspiration) or to overcome mental or physical roadblocks, the AIR Model had the answer. It provided me with a simplistic, yet powerful formula for success. At the start of my *Push for Change* journey I needed confidence, but confidence comes after action. I needed something to get me off the bench and taking steps to move forward.

Fortunately, the reasons why I wanted to walk across Canada were good ones. *The Push for Change* connected with a deeper purpose; my desire to help young people avoid the outcome I had experienced. I truly believe we can change outcomes for young people who are homeless and dealing with drug dependency, mental health and family conflict. I also believe we can create a world where our response to homelessness is different. It was from this deep desire to change things that I decided to walk across Canada, which made it easy to reconnect to my "WHY" and use it as inspiration. When I got out of action, Sean would remind me WHY I was doing this. Once connected to my WHY, I could take some action. Action always led to good feelings and over time, my confidence built.

At the beginning of the campaign my two most significant roadblocks were my physical and mental conditioning; I didn't think or act like an athlete. I was overweight, I ate poorly and I struggled to walk even 10 km; simply put, I had treated myself badly for decades and my body needed some work. Mentally, I felt guilty about being overweight and out of shape. This guilt, coupled with many failed attempts at fitness over the years led to a false belief that "I was no athlete" and probably deeper than that was a belief that, "I'm not worth it." Looking through the lens of the AIR Model, it's easy to see that most of my life I was out of action because I had no connection to a "WHY" that would make fitness a priority, so now I was faced with numerous mental and physical roadblocks.

Psychologically, a lot of different issues surfaced as I began training, particularly fear that I would fail and humiliate myself or that I would get injured and have to quit. I also had persistent doubts about tackling the biggest challenge of my life and anxiety that I was facing years of hard work to achieve my dream. There were many days when I would reach out to Sean freaking out about sponsorship, money issues, training challenges and anger or frustration that stuff wasn't moving along fast enough.

In each and every instance Sean would calmly coach me using the AIR Model:

"Are you out of action? If so, go train."

"Are you disconnected from why you're doing this? If so, remember the young people you are helping."

"Are you dealing with roadblocks such as fear and uncertainty? That's understandable, but you can work through those."

Whenever I got to beating myself up for not staying on track, Sean reassured me that it's normal for someone in my position to have those feelings and then he would ask, "What can you do right now to make a shift? What action can you take?" Sean's coaching was fundamental to my mental development as I prepared for the campaign.

When it came to the physical roadblocks, Sean and I simply strategized to figure out what I needed to do: take a day off, have an ice bath, do some stretching, go see an RMT or physiotherapist, etc. No matter what arose, the AIR Model captured it and helped me monitor my actions; it also enabled Sean to coach me forward.

With Sean and the AIR Model, I began to climb hills bigger than any I had scaled in my life. I learned that mental roadblocks are just noise and that fear is a boogeyman that disappears when you flick on the "light" of action. I learned that my greatest roadblocks were "MIND

MADE" and that when we use our brain in a responsible way, any one of us can take action that diminishes negative emotion and builds momentum. Most importantly, I learned that the body will do what the mind tells it to. The AIR Model was the mental nutrition I needed to reprogram 45 years of undisciplined, misaligned thinking.

How about you?

Are you stuck?

Do you want to change your life circumstances?

Do you feel like you can't move forward?

Maybe you're aspiring towards the next challenge in your life.

Believe me when I tell you, your mind is a powerful tool and when you harness that power through meditation, visualization and focus (followed by right action), you can make anything you desire a reality. All you have to do is get off the bench and take some steps forward. I'm not special or exceptional, but I met extraordinary people who helped me to understand that I have potential, I'm worth it and that each and every moment I can breathe the "AIR" of unlimited possibility. The same applies to you.

20

The launch date for the trial walk was fast approaching and I marvelled at what we had accomplished in six months. We had created a brand, built a website and launched our social media channels. Our sponsors and funding had been lined up; we'd built a successful shopping cart prototype, hired a driver and videographer, acquired permits and secured an RV. In addition, training was going well and we had surrounded ourselves with good people, including experts to guide and coach us. To think that all of this had happened as the result of an inspired, pie in the sky conversation on a flight to Calgary was amazing to me. Success was in the AIR!

I was ready to put the AIR Model and six months of training to the test. We arrived in Calgary the night before Canada Day and stayed in a hotel. When the clock buzzed at 6:00 am, I jumped out of bed excited and a little scared. We headed to The Salvation Army downtown for our kick-off event. The Salvation Army was gracious enough to support us by hosting events from Calgary to Vancouver.

As the morning progressed friends and supporters arrived. Our videographer Ali showed up with his father and we started to load his gear into the RV. I was glad I was there because Ali had seriously over packed and his dad was able to take back some of the large items he had intended to travel with. After loading Ali into the RV, we headed into the Salvation Army where we did a short presentation.

It's funny how something looks in your mind and then how it actually turns out. The walk from Calgary to Vancouver would teach us some extremely important lessons about engaging the public. There's a romantic notion that if you choose to conduct any kind of journey for a cause such as this, the public will be inspired and come out in droves to support you. That's simply not true. No one cares until you help them care.

Despite the lacklustre crowd and the absence of excitement, an hour or so later, with Bobby (aka Rob) behind me in the RV and Sean by my side, I started walking. It was the beginning of an epic journey that would first take me towards and then through the Rocky Mountains, followed by the Okanagan Valley, along Highway 3 to Manning Park and eventually back into Vancouver's downtown Eastside, covering a total of 1,071 kilometres.

It was Canada Day 2012 and my energy was peaked (I felt a sense of triumph for having made it to the start line). Too often in life we think about things but don't follow through, so all those crazy altruist ideas that roll through our brains end up getting dismissed as we continue on with our "normal lives." However, if you're lucky (like me in this case) every now and again you take a risk. Instead of "Why bother?" you say "Why not?" and throw caution to the wind as you step out of your comfort zone.

I had thrown caution to the wind alright and wind is exactly what I was feeling a few short hours into my trek. I walked along the Sarcee Trail SW as it merged with the Trans-Canada Highway. On my left were the ski jumps constructed for the 1988 Olympics and in front of me (way off in the distance) were the mountains that define Western Canada. The wind hit me as I crested the hill; it was fierce and powerful, yet warm and welcoming. It was a poignant moment that reminded me just how special Canada is (warm and welcoming, but also beautifully rugged and wild). By the end of day one, Bobby, Ali and I had reached Callaway RV Park and cleared the city. The next 55 days would be filled with experiences that we'd remember for the rest of our lives.

The goal of the trial walk was simple; we would walk from Calgary to Vancouver and learn everything we could to help us prepare for the national event. I honestly don't think we would have been successful with our national walk if we had not first done the walk from Calgary to Vancouver. Just the value of capturing the trek on video and in photos proved to be extremely valuable when we began to look for national sponsors.

We also needed to learn how my body would react, we needed to fail at engaging the public in order to better define our national engagement goals. We needed to learn how to support sponsors. We needed to understand all the things that go into a rolling nomadic operation. It was tough building a team environment while living in an RV. Tempers would flare and it was so important that each team member understood what we were doing and why we were doing it.

We had great support from friends like Cloverdale Paint and The Salvation Army, who hosted events and met up with us at different points along the journey. What we learned however was that we needed to do a better job at attracting public interest. We had several extraordinary events but we also had a number of poorly attended events that caused us to look hard at how to get people excited and engaged. This would become a huge question to solve for the national walk.

The physical challenges were incredibly difficult. Walking through the Rocky Mountains was extraordinarily beautiful but it was also extremely hard on my body. As we hit Canmore and Lake Louise things began to get steep. It took me longer to finish my 21 km minimum each day, but fortunately I had access to ice-cold glacial water for my ice baths.

I remember walking through Rogers Pass and having a surreal feeling as I crested the summit. It took me three days of uphill walking (about 80 km) from Golden, BC. I had only ever driven along that part of the Trans-Canada Highway and taking the time to walk it was amazing. I remember the summit sign and thinking to myself, "Holy crap, I just summited Rogers Pass with a shopping cart." It was definitely a day to remember.

Even though Rogers Pass was epic, it wasn't my toughest day by far. After successfully walking through the pass, we continued on through Revelstoke to Sicamous and straight down the Okanagan Valley. Just south of Penticton we headed west towards Princeton via the Crows Nest Highway 3. When we had originally applied for our permit from BC's Ministry of Highways we were told this was a "safer" route. If you know the highway or have ever driven it, you know that isn't really the case. It was far more likely that the government simply didn't want us on the main highway that links Kelowna to Merritt and Hope.

For someone walking, the highway between Princeton and Hope is just plain treacherous. It is highly populated with logging trucks and no shoulder to walk on in some places. Bobby couldn't safely travel behind me in the RV so he had to drive ahead. And then there were the elevation changes, constant ups and downs with extreme hair pin turns. On one day of walking, I encountered six hairpin turns. We embraced those extreme days with persistence and determination and eventually made it safely through the mountains to Hope.

The single most inspiring day of my journey was the day I walked just over the distance of a proper marathon (actually it was 44 kilometres). I started the day at Bromley Rock Provincial Park, 22 km east of Princeton, and made the town of Princeton in record time with lots of energy to spare, so I decided to soldier on and began walking out of Princeton heading west. Little did I know the highway leaving Princeton would be a steady climb upwards for over 20 kilometres. It takes you up from the valley, 550 meters to where the copper mine is. The highway has several steep hairpin turns that are a challenge for large trucks both ascending and descending this huge set of hills. By the time I hit the steepest part, I was 30 km into my walk. The hill grade was over 12% and the temperature was more than 85 degrees.

When I started walking that day, I had no intention of completing a marathon. In fact Sean, who was overseeing my efforts from a training perspective, forbade me to push my body for fear of injury. That day I didn't listen and sometime around 5:00 pm, I reached the summit with a spectacular view across the valley. I was exhausted and suffering from minor heat/sun stroke but there I was on the other side of an extraordinary accomplishment. Remembering the feeling I had that day, together with the accomplishment of completing the trial walk would provide me with the mental resilience needed to take on a walk across Canada. In the entire campaign, there would only be one other day when I would top this distance and effort.

Throughout the trial campaign we had so many positive encounters with people we met who came out to support us, make donations and cheer us on. I remember early one morning just outside of Enderby, BC; I met a couple of gentlemen in a red pickup truck. They were curious as to what I was doing. I explained my story, the significance of the shopping cart and why we were pushing for change. One of the gentlemen was aboriginal and when I told him our mission, he got out of the truck, walked back towards a very humble home beside the road and reappeared a few minutes later. He handed me a thermos and told me he was moved by what we were doing. Judging by how he was dressed and his modest home, I assumed he had little money and yet he gave us a thermos filled with loonies and toonies. I almost teared up when he gave me the thermos as I knew this man couldn't afford such a gift but the spirit of generosity had touched something close to his personal journey and he gave with his whole heart.

Interactions like this happened regularly throughout the trek. It inspired us and helped fuel our energy on tough days. We knew that we were doing something good and all we needed to do was keep moving down the road.

After almost two months of walking, we arrived in the Fraser Valley and were greeted in Abbotsford with a hero's welcome. The Salvation Army hosted an event that had the mayor, the Abbotsford police and the entire community turn out. It was everything we imagined it could be and were taken aback by how cool and organized the event was. We were grateful to our friend Deb Lowell, who worked tirelessly as a community champion to bring it all together. She even arranged to have us escorted through the streets by the police and when we arrived she had a live band playing for us. There was even a gigantic shopping cart onsite donated by Thrifty Foods. The day was truly magical with all the pieces we imagined when we began incubating *The Push for Change*. The challenge before us was how could we do events like this across the entire country?

21

It was a perfect summer morning when I walked the final leg into Vancouver on August 25. We started in Port Moody and were due to meet a number of supporters at Gore and Hastings at noon. I made fast work of my walk that morning and thanks to an email we had sent out, a whole bunch of supporters showed up to finish the walk into Vancouver.

As we approached the Downtown Eastside, we had support from Vancouver Police and a large gathering of friends from The Salvation Army Harbour Light as well as supporters, our sponsor's families and friends. As I slowly worked my way down through the old neighbourhood, I began to get emotional. After seven months of planning and 56 days of walking, I had covered 1,071 kilometres from downtown Calgary to downtown Vancouver. As I crossed over Main and Hastings, I hoisted the shopping cart in the air for an epic picture that would later be broadcast nationwide. A few steps from the finish line, my mom appeared and I gave her a huge hug. I felt so lucky and grateful not just for succeeding in the walk but for having the opportunity to change my life. It was a moment of triumph to be back in the neighbourhood I had escaped from 24 years earlier, doing something far more constructive and rewarding with my life.

We had our final event at The Salvation Army where I got to thank so many great friends and supporters. I also learned a valuable lesson; always make a list of friends to thank. In all of the emotion of the day, I forgot to thank Kate Richardson who had played a big role in our success (helping with training, nutrition, the shopping cart and as the lead voice for our PFC theme song). I felt really bad that I had missed an opportunity to acknowledge Kate's many contributions.

The test project was complete: we dreamed, we planned, we walked and we conquered. To be sure, we failed as much as we succeeded and it taught me that the road to success is one with many turns and setbacks. We learned a lot about what worked and what didn't and as a result had a much clearer idea of what challenges faced us in preparing to walk across Canada. As difficult as walking from Calgary to Vancouver had been, we knew it was nothing compared to traversing the entire country. Canada is massive and there's no way to cross it continuously on foot without encountering winter. Yet, for all the challenges it presented, I was confident I could do it. The trial campaign had done as much to prepare my mind as my body. I had successfully applied the AIR model and proved for myself that the impossible is only impossible for those who entertain that kind of limited thinking. I was infused with a possibility mindset.

Life is full of challenges and opportunities and through my personal experience of both; I've come to believe that we can make our own prosperity through our thinking and our actions. One of my greatest assets is my zest for life and eagerness to try new things. I like the sense of adventure and uncertainty that comes with new ideas. To many, I probably didn't look like the most likely person to be successful at walking across Canada (I wasn't particularly athletic and I had no idea how to tackle something so monumental). What I did have was a sense of wonder and a relentless appetite for action. When we first started to build the campaign, there were so many uncertainties that I just had to have faith that we would eventually figure them out. It was tough going in the early days, because both Sean and I were smart enough to know what needed to be done, we just didn't have the experience to do it all ourselves.

When I look back, all of the times I've succeeded in life wasn't because I was lucky or talented, or even because of good timing. I've succeeded because I refused to stop taking steps forward. The only times I've ever failed have been when I gave up trying. I wish I had known this when I was 16, when life was really scary. I might have taken more risks knowing that I could not fail. Something else I learned from my business experience is that when you find yourself in a situation where you don't know something, find someone that does know and borrow their insight. With our sights set on walking across the entire nation, we knew we were going to need help to understand all of the elements that went into such a campaign. We also knew the team needed to expand.

The success of the trial walk buoyed my confidence and for the first time in my life, I felt unstoppable. I knew in my core that walking across Canada pushing a shopping cart wasn't just possible; it was my mission and my spirits remained high in the weeks that followed. I was fired up and ready to go. We even had a sponsor ready to give us $100,000 in support, all we had to do was create the proposal, explain where our fundraising money was going and provide our vision and mission.

We began to unpack what we'd learned from the trial walk and how it would apply to our national efforts, but the more we unpacked the more questions we had (we started to feel overwhelmed). We decided to host a think tank and get advice from people we respected, friends who would ask the tough questions and give us honest feedback. We gathered together a group of business and charity leaders as well as folks who had been involved in the 2010 Olympic Torch Relay across Canada and the 25th Anniversary Rick Hansen Relay. The room was stacked with smart, seasoned people who understood what we needed to do to run a successful cross-Canada campaign.

We were buoyed with enthusiasm and energy as we laid out our plan for launching the national campaign on May 1, 2013 (only eight months away). Our goals were ambitious and our vision of success more than a little rose-colored. By the end of our four-hour session, our friends had asked over a hundred questions, 90 of which we had no answer for. I'm sure if you were in the room you could have heard the air being sucked out of my preverbal balloon. The last thing I wanted to do was stall the launch. We had been promised $100,000 and I was eager to drum up additional support and get going, nevertheless, the challenges brought up in the meeting stopped us in our tracks.

At the end of the think tank session, Cal Misener took me aside and offered some sage advice. He said, "Joe, you can leave in eight months and successfully walk across Canada, but if making an impact is what you want to measure success by, then wait, sort out the challenges you have and launch when you're ready."

Cal was right, but the truth hurt, this was my baby! The idea of waiting scared me and the mountain of roadblocks that stood in our way seemed insurmountable. As Cal's words sunk in, I thought the unthinkable, what if we couldn't pull it off and *The Push for Change* never happened? Everything we had planned and worked so hard towards hung in the balance.

22

Following the meeting, I hired a friend named Tyrone Lingley to help us dig into some of the deeper issues. Tyrone was a seasoned cross-Canada event specialist. He had worked on the 2010 Olympics and with the Rick Hansen 25th Anniversary campaign. Tyrone was smart and analytical and brought a wealth of knowledge and insight.

Tyrone and I worked out of the City in Focus offices in Vancouver, thanks to the generosity of Tom Cooper and every morning, we'd meet to pour over the many challenges that faced *The Push for Change*. Funding was a huge challenge and we made a decision early on to be fully funded by sponsors before we left for Newfoundland. That meant we had to create a budget, develop a sponsorship brief and sell the sponsorship package. We also needed to figure out what exactly we were raising money for and who our charitable partner would be. On Tyrone's advice, we transformed what had started out as a non-profit BC society into a CRA registered charity.

Despite making headway, there was still a long list of items to be dealt with: permits, uniforms, logistics, staffing, social media, community engagement and how the heck we were going to get permission to walk through Northern Ontario in the winter. We decided to focus first on creating a budget and a pitch deck for potential sponsors. Once we had those elements in place, we could send our information to a number of large Canadian organizations that we expected to salivate at the opportunity to partner with us.

Tyrone and I worked really hard for three months and produced a great set of documents that would end up helping us later in the campaign. Unfortunately, our efforts just weren't enough to get PFC off the ground. We had one really great meeting in Toronto thanks to our good friend Steve Allmen, who had been a supporter of PFC from the beginning. He had joined our board and helped us get a meeting with the head of CSR for Target Canada. The meeting went really well and the company seemed interested in our campaign. Unfortunately Target turned out to be just as ill prepared as we were and not long afterwards, the head office in the US announced that they were pulling out of the Canadian market.

By the time our national campaign finally launched nearly four years after the trial walk, *The Push for Change* had undergone a massive transformation that was integral to our success. Looking back, I realize that having the campaign stall the way it did was actually EXACTLY what we needed to get everything in place to get us to the start line.

23

What happened next can only be described as *The Push for Change* love story.

During the trial trek, I had received an unexpected email that turned out to be a sign of something big to come. I'd had a long, hot morning walking in the Okanagan sun and we were chilling out in the RV when I suddenly jumped up from my laptop, excited about a message that had just come in. Bobby asked me what I was so excited about and I explained that a girl I had dated in high school had found me through an online article and reached out to connect with me. It had been over two decades since we had been in contact. Bobby looked at me kind of puzzled and asked, "Why are you so happy about that?"

He had a point, what was I so excited about? After all, I had been reunited with dozens of old acquaintances over the years. Part of being featured repeatedly in the media is that it makes it easy for people from the past to reconnect after they've seen an article or TV coverage. It had happened quite a few times over the years, yet something felt different about this time.

Marie and I had dated in grade 10; she was my very first crush and my first girlfriend (we dated for over a year). At the time she connected with me, I was going through huge changes in my life. Not only was I struggling with the direction of *The Push for Change*, but my marriage had run its course and I was facing a divorce. Life was dark and then Marie came along.

When we initially connected it was purely platonic, she had read my story and asked how I was and we agreed to connect when I travelled to Ontario for a conference. Several weeks later, I found myself having a lovely dinner with an amazing person. It turned out she was also going through huge changes in her life and marriage. In many ways we were in the same boat. Yet for all of this, neither Marie nor I approached our re-connection romantically, that happened later.

We began to get to know each other again and shared our dreams and aspirations. We also talked about what was missing in our lives. It turned out that we not only shared a past but we saw potential for a future together and from there things began to bloom. There was only one challenge, I lived in BC and she was in Ontario. After several months of long-distance dating, I decided to move to Ontario. We had a plan to work together on *The Push for Change* and we would spend the next 18 months building out the campaign and implementing it together.

There was new energy as we came together and I was excited to see that Marie was 100% behind PFC. Not once did she have a discouraging word to say, even though the campaign was stalled and we were sorting out huge life changes, we were both committed to seeing PFC through...at some point.

Marie

One marriage, two children and twenty-eight years later, I found myself thinking about Joe again. I was having one of those days when I just felt grounded and satisfied with life, without a care in the world. It was a Saturday afternoon and my housework was done, my (teenage) kids were out and I was wandering around the house almost in a sentimental daze when I stopped at my laptop (which was sitting on the kitchen island). I opened it up and typed a name into the search bar: Joe Roberts.

Up until this point I hadn't thought much about Joe. I was still living close to Barrie, Ontario where we had hung out as teenagers and I assumed he was somewhere near the same area (although I hadn't seen or heard from him in over two decades). There were a lot of Google results for the search Joe Roberts, but the one that caught my eye was entitled, "A deal with God," and it linked to The Salvation Army. The long article detailed the journey of a young man who had roots in Ontario but had ended up a homeless heroin addict on the streets of East Vancouver. It also explained how, with the help of his mom and The Salvation Army, he was able to turn his life around. I sat looking at my computer screen in shock! Could this be the same Joe Roberts I had dated in high school? "There's no way," I thought to myself. "I don't believe he even left the Barrie region and Joe Roberts is a pretty common name, it must be a story about someone else." However, as I scrolled to the bottom of the article there was a picture of Joe (looking much older and a little heavier, too). What convinced me that it must be Joe was his smile, he had the kind of smile that was easy to identify. Bewildered at the story I had read, I knew I had to connect with him to see if this was really his story. I found an email address online and sent him a short brief email.

Hello Joe,

I Googled your name and was surprised to see your story, A deal with God, on the Salvation Army website.

Wow! How I love that story and am so happy for you that your life turned out so wonderful!

You are the Joe I once knew, correct? You'll remember me from the 28-48 days...

A friend from the past, Marie Marcoux

To my surprise, that same evening he replied assuring me he was the same Joe I had dated as a teenager. He told me he was currently in the middle of a trial walk from Calgary to Vancouver, and training in preparation for a walk across Canada that he called The Push for Change. More impressively, he had taken the time to recount dozens of memories

73

about our year-long teenage romance. There were so many details of our relationship he remembered that I had completely forgotten about; it was surreal to relive my teenage experiences through his words.

It wasn't long before our email exchanges warranted an in-person meeting. As it happened Joe planned to travel to Toronto shortly after his trial walk for a conference where he was scheduled to speak. We decided to meet in Brampton for a casual date and catch up. Ironically, it started with a five kilometre walk around the nearby park and ended with dinner at Vesuvio Ristorante. We talked easily and comfortably with each other, sharing everything life had given us in the past couple of decades. We discovered that we had a lot in common and wanted the same things out of life. I loved Joe's positive outlook despite the (seemingly) hopeless experiences he had lived through. I was not raised to believe in unlimited possibilities; I'd been taught that you got what you got and anything better was (really) an unreachable dream. Not that I lived a deprived life, but it was mediocre for sure. Listening to Joe, thoughts of infinite potential awakened inside of me and I was eager to learn more. Joe offered to be my long-distance mentor and from him I began to learn about the power of a "possibility" mindset.

During that first dinner date, Joe told me about his plans to walk across Canada to raise awareness about youth homelessness. I wasn't enamoured or even impressed with the idea of Joe physically walking across the country, what struck me was the passion with which he spoke about the project. The way he shared it was deeply inspiring and even contagious and over the next few months I couldn't help but feel drawn and connected to The Push for Change. So much so that I had this uncanny feeling it would become a huge part of my life, even though it seemed doubtful, given where my life was at and the fact that I lived in Ontario and Joe was in BC (little did I know how that feeling would transform into reality over the next several years).

Through our long distance communications, Joe and I helped each other. He mentored me using the AIR model, which he had mastered with the guidance of Dr. Sean Richardson and together, we worked through the issues that I believed were holding me back from my unlimited potential. I was ecstatic about this new knowledge and the discovery that my life could be anything I dreamed of, the only thing holding me back wasn't my background, my upbringing or my environment, it was me! On my side, with my long career and vast experience in business and accounting, I was well equipped to help Joe with the administration of The Push for Change Foundation. He had just acquired the foundation name and charitable status and needed someone to file society reports and annual returns. I loved this kind of work and it was simple for me to do, even remotely! I also worked with the Canada Revenue Agency to change the charity's purpose and in no time The Push for Change was ready to operate as a public foundation, meaning it could disburse funds to other charities (which would become an integral part of the trek's fundraising initiatives).

The national walk was initially proposed to start in May, 2013, however Joe found it difficult to create a proposal that answered the questions of the major funder, who had promised to support the trek. Given their limited experience, Joe and his team in BC didn't know what exactly was required to run a successful trek, so the campaign had been delayed to allow more time to research and plan. This would be one of those times we would look back on later and say, "Everything happens for a reason, it's all about timing."

Despite the distance that separated us, my relationship with Joe grew stronger by the day. We had a deep respect for each other's abilities and thoroughly enjoyed being in communication with one another. In the months that followed our first dinner date, Joe travelled to Ontario several times as a conference speaker which made it easy for us to meet up and get to know each other again. We found ourselves attracted to one other in ways that went beyond just business and we began falling in love. In no time, we were emailing, texting or talking on a daily basis and our bond grew stronger by the day. By the spring of 2013, we knew we wanted to be together and start our life anew so Joe took the plunge and moved back to Ontario. We purchased a house together and by mid-June of 2013, we were back together in our hometown of Barrie! I don't believe any of that would have happened if the campaign had gone ahead as planned.

While the two of us and our families adjusted to our new living situation, I continued to work at the public accounting firm where I had been employed for the past decade and Joe managed his speaking business from our home office. We loved our new life—being together every day instead of texting or talking on the phone, we both had so much gratitude for our reality! As for the PFC campaign, it was on hold and while we both knew it would eventually happen; this was not the time. Six months after we moved in together, we decided I would leave my career in accounting to join Joe in his speaking business and build The Push for Change together. It was a scary move for me, not just because I loved my job and enjoyed the company I worked for, I had always been the employee who put in the most hours during busy times and some might say I was addicted to my job. I also made good money and felt very secure in my position. Nonetheless, the idea of leaving my status as an "employee" to become self-employed with Joe and have time for The Push for Change was an exciting move I didn't want to pass up. In January of 2014 (just before tax season) I gave my notice and Joe and I joined forces. I'll be honest, I knew nothing about the speaking profession or managing a campaign, so I came into these new endeavours with a little apprehension.

24

Marie and I fell deeply in love and we worked well together, I can honestly say that without a doubt Marie was the missing link that was needed to launch the PFC national campaign. With the two of us working together and support from the extraordinary network we had built, over the next few years slowly but surely, we began building and working through every roadblock that had been brought up in our think tank discussion. Some problems were simple while others took months to solve. There were days when I thought we might never get to execute *The Push for Change* and others where we could see it getting closer. There were many days of doubt and uncertainty. I remember on more than one occasion listening to our national anthem or looking at a Canadian flag and wondering if I would ever get to walk across Canada like I had dreamed of doing. Being unclear and uncertain is a hard place to be, it's difficult to stay in action, to keep motivated and to stave off emotional roadblocks.

A number of key things happened that really helped the campaign regain momentum. One was Marie quitting her secure, well-paying job to support *The Push for Change*. We were able to achieve this move financially by splitting her time between building the PFC campaign and managing my professional speaking business; with the fees from paid speaking engagements helping to augment her salary.

The second thing that we did to accelerate our success was set a new launch date. There's something very powerful about making a commitment in stone. We chose May 1, 2016 as our new drop-dead launch date and we were determined to go, hell or high water. In fact, at this time we went to our bank and asked for the largest line of credit we could get. They gave us $60,000 and that's where we started. We believed in what we were doing, we were excited about the energy it created and we knew that no matter what, even if we could not secure sponsors or support, we were going to start walking across Canada from St. John's, Newfoundland on May 1, 2016.

With renewed energy, we reconnected with our early stakeholders and sponsors, essentially anyone who supported us in the beginning or was excited about PFC and what we were trying to do. What we didn't anticipate was the damage that had been done by pausing the campaign. Most of the folks we had initially worked with were not going to support the national campaign, so we were facing a tough set of roadblocks to get the campaign funded and sponsored. Thankfully, we had 18 months to build the campaign and get the support we needed. There was also a lot of tactical work to do, I needed to train and get my body ready and we had a thousand logistics issues to work out. We needed an RV to live in, a pace vehicle, uniforms, a website, fundraising tools, event materials and a social media strategy. We also needed a map, something that could tell us where we would be each day of the 517-day tour. This was crucial for building events and getting communities to support us. We also needed to put the map online so that anyone could find where we would be and what we had planned.

Once we got started and made the commitment to launch many long-standing issues began to get resolved. However, we still didn't have a charitable partner or an answer to the question, "Where is the money going and how are you going to make a difference?"

One morning Marie was reading an article in the Toronto Star that mentioned York University professor Dr. Stephen Gaetz, who was championing some really innovative youth homelessness prevention strategies. His ideas really resonated because they were prevention based. The idea is to stop youth homelessness BEFORE it happens, by re-thinking the approach and focusing on reducing the number of young people falling through the cracks.

We set up a meeting with Dr. Gaetz and over the next few months built a relationship with three organizations: The Canadian Observatory on Homelessness, A Way Home Canada and Raising the Roof Canada. In one of these meetings I asked them where the biggest need was, the resounding response was prevention. If we want to see a reduction in the number of young people becoming homeless, we need smart money to be invested into prevention models. The Canadian Observatory on Homelessness and A Way Home Canada had been working really hard on piloting a new idea called The Upstream Project, which focused on working with youth at risk inside the school system to get the supports they need, thereby minimizing their risk of becoming homeless in the future.

When PFC started, A Way Home Canada was a brand new organization created to help prevent, reduce and eventually end youth homelessness in Canada. Raising the Roof was the organization that would be administering The Upstream Project. It was a perfect fit for us. We wanted to champion a solution that took a different approach, with ideas that would have real impact and change the lives of young Canadians. What was also amazing is that we were now working with organizations that were at the centre of this issue nationally. The key to the whole thing working was collaboration. Stephen Gaetz introduced us to Melanie Redman from A Way Home Canada and after extensive discussions, it all came together. The question of where the money would go was solved; we were helping to fund a youth homelessness prevention model called The Upstream Project administered by Raising the Roof.

Marie

Joe and Sean had created the foundation for an extraordinary campaign and I loved the name The Push for Change (it was self-explanatory, catchy and relevant to a walk). The concept was also endearing; Joe walking across the country for youth homelessness to 'pay it forward' because he had been homeless as a youth. Who wouldn't be inspired by such a noble act? Nevertheless, as bold and great as their ideas were there were no solid plans for execution. From my perspective, it looked disorganized and a little out of control, but it just so happens that I'm an organizing queen and a bit of a perfectionist to boot! Everything must be in its place and done to the absolute best of my ability in order for me to feel a sense of purpose. Joe and I had discovered this while unpacking some of the limiting beliefs I had about myself. Those traits would prove useful in building the PFC campaign because I could effortlessly take all the moving parts (and there were dozens) and organize them in such a way that we could prioritize and tackle tasks efficiently.

Our first big challenge was to determine the purpose of doing a walk across Canada. Why were we doing it and what did we expect to accomplish? Joe had done a lot of work on this already, so it was easy to compile and document his answers. We had also put together a preliminary budget of $1 million to cover the campaign costs, including staff/labour, all travel-trek related expenses, marketing, web design, mapping, events, photography and videography. Our plan was to acquire sponsors to pay for the campaign so that all of the funds raised during the trek could go directly to the cause. However, we still didn't know who (or what organization) would receive the fundraising dollars and we quickly realized we couldn't prepare an effective proposal for potential sponsors without answering that question.

Turning to Google for assistance, it didn't take long for me to find the leading expert on youth homelessness in Canada, Dr. Stephen Gaetz of York University, who was also the Director of the Canadian Observatory on Homelessness. During our very first meeting with Dr. Gaetz, we discovered the answer we had been looking for, prevention! The key to ending youth homelessness was by intervening before it happened. As a result of numerous additional meetings with Dr. Gaetz, together with Melanie Redman of The Learning Community (a community of practice that focuses on youth homelessness) and key stakeholders from Raising the Roof (a national charity dedicated to long-term solutions to homelessness) as well as other reputable social agencies, we developed a much better understanding of the issues surrounding youth homelessness in Canada.

We also had a clearer idea of how we wanted our fundraising dollars to be used. We wanted to protect youth who were at risk of becoming homeless by wrapping services around them that would support them through their challenges.

Surprisingly, Joe had communicated with Raising the Roof back in 2013 and the Executive Director at the time turned down an offer of collaboration (perhaps she was unsure of the motive for the campaign or the direction Joe was going). Now Raising the Roof (with help from Dr. Gaetz and Melanie Redman) was developing a new program called The Upstream Project, a school-based, youth homeless prevention program that would be implemented in high schools across Canada. Given that Raising the Roof had previously rejected Joe's offer, he was uneasy about approaching them again. I, on the other hand, couldn't imagine any reason why they wouldn't take our fundraising dollars to support The Upstream Project. I insisted that we ask them again and we did. With the blessing of Dr. Gaetz, we signed a Letter of Agreement with Raising the Roof, making them the official charitable partner of PFC.

25

With that important question answered, we turned our attention to sponsorship and fundraising. Remember we made an agreement that we would use no donated money to pay for the walk. The operating expenses had to come from sponsors. The price tag was a whopping $1,000,000 and the question that kept me awake at night was who was going to give us a million dollars to push a shopping cart across Canada?

When I look back at how we systematically worked through every roadblock that stood in our way, the campaign was really three parts. Part one was preparing and executing the trial walk. Part two was preparing and planning for the national walk and part three was actually executing the walk across Canada. In a lot of ways, the work needed to get us to the starting point was by far the most difficult.

From the beginning, Sean and I had spent countless hours dreaming about a walk across Canada that would impact and inspire. Sean's role was absolutely critical in the genesis of the campaign and his impact was felt in each and every step I took in the early days. In addition to supporting the campaign in countless pitch meetings and with the development of the first sponsorship brief, he also helped us source the PFC logo that we still use today and was instrumental in countless partner meetings. Having a former Olympic athlete with a PhD in sports psychology as a founding member also helped to build our credibility when we went into meetings.

Without Sean's initial contribution I'm not sure I would have made it through the trial campaign, however, not long afterward Sean and his family relocated back to Australia and I moved to Ontario, we were a world apart. Shortly after choosing our new start date, I reached out to Sean and asked for his continued support, once again, without hesitation, he agreed to help in any way he could.

The challenges in the beginning were different from the ones we faced now. The sheer number of tasks to be completed was overwhelming. The time between the trial walk and the eventual launch date was approximately four years. In those four years we learned a great deal about what a campaign of this nature needed in order to effectively engage the country. We had knowledge, now we needed to put that knowledge into operation. I was really good at sharing my story and promoting PFC as well as doing interviews, corporate speaking engagements and school presentations. What I wasn't good at was managing the deluge of items that constituted the backbone of the campaign's success.

During the campaign and even today I am publicly acknowledged for having successfully walked across Canada, but I did far less work than one other person. I was the front guy in the band but it was our manager, our detail person and our hub that kept it all together; that person was Marie. Throughout the four-year incubation and the entire campaign, Marie personally managed every detail and she worked harder than I did most days. For months, she spent 14-16 hours a day working flat out. I was very good at being the face and voice of the campaign, but Marie was extremely good at managing everything else: accounting, website development, mapping, logistics, collateral development, charitable status, campaign communications, police liaisons, school coordination, event coordination, managing sponsor relationships, managing social media and traditional media, budgets, accommodation coordination, payroll and taxes.

When Marie joined the campaign, she took a massive risk in doing so. Before she joined full time, she worked as an accountant under the managing partner of a mid-sized accounting firm in Barrie. She was extremely valuable to that organization and had advanced her career through hard work and determination for 10 years. When she left the company, she was one of the highest paid employees in her field and could even boast that in the lean years following the 2007 economic downturn she was one of the only employees in the firm to receive a raise.

PFC was lucky to have her. I know what you're thinking, as Marie's husband its natural for me to brag about my wife's accomplishments and value. But I'm not writing this from the perspective of her husband, I'm writing from the perspective of a business leader. I have worked for two decades in the business world and have yet to find anyone quite like Marie. Her work ethic is above reproach, she is smart, a self starter and does not get emotional about roadblocks and challenges, she simply finds the solution and applies it. In many ways, Marie and I have opposite and complementary skills, which is what makes it a perfect fit.

As much as I get the attaboys, *The Push for Change* would not have happened without Marie and her team of doers; her direction, her systems, her hard work, her vision. Before I left Newfoundland on day one, I stated that if *The Push for Change* was to have any impact whatsoever, it would be thanks to Marie. She is the unsung hero of this story and sadly the one who gets overlooked when acknowledgements are handed out. I have never met anyone who can get stuff done quite as well as she can and for that I am grateful and blessed to be her husband and her business partner. With her endless energy and dedication, Marie is the heart behind *The Push for Change*.

The first of many problems that Marie helped to solve was sponsorship. Working with Tyrone had helped us to understand what our budget would look like as well as the moving pieces that would be needed inside a working campaign. We dug up the old documents we had put together, added in the current info we needed to include and within a few days Marie had a sharp-looking sponsorship package put together. One of the unique advantages we had in seeking sponsorship was that I was already doing both paid and pro-bono speaking engagements across the country. Marie and I were more or less already running a social enterprise in that I was booked throughout the country as an inspirational speaker. Industries of all kinds hired me to share my rags to riches story. Going from skid row to CEO had messages and context that resonated with a wide range of audiences and we found ourselves very busy going from event to event. In our down time, we continued to build *The Push for Change* campaign.

During one of my speeches I decided to tell people about my plan to walk across Canada, it was a scary but liberating experience. There is something extraordinarily powerful about a public declaration of your goals. People began to ask how they could help.

From that experience through the next 150 presentations, I told EVERYONE about *The Push for Change* as it was the perfect conclusion to a great speech. By doing this consistently we began to build a network of support across Canada that would eventually help us generate not just financial support, but also community support for when we trekked through their towns.

Marie

Landing $1 million in sponsorship to pay for the campaign trek was no small task. I knew we would get it. I don't know how I knew, but I was so confident that the campaign would happen that I could envision day one in my mind and I rejoiced at the thought of day 517. I told myself that it didn't matter if the sponsorship dollars came or not, we were going. We had saved some money and we had large credit limits on our credit cards; we also had a line of credit that could get us across the country if necessary (albeit it would be a bare-bones trek).

I started to apply for grants online: the Joyce Foundation, Home Depot, Motorola, Canada Post, RBC, Telus, Kiwanis Club, Rotary Club, etc. The applications were tedious and cumbersome to say the least, once you applied, you waited... and hoped. As time went on you couldn't help but lose hope. Much to my chagrin, not one grant was awarded to us. Meanwhile, we had produced a sponsorship proposal that could be customized for any company and we started to pitch to organizations including Walmart, Target, Canadian Tire, Ford and a few smaller companies. They all said they loved the idea, but they still turned us down.

26

We had a lot of ground to cover to get the campaign sponsored. We had lost momentum since the successful 2012 trial walk and the sponsor that promised us $100,000 had gone in another direction. Many of our initial supporters didn't have an appetite for what we were doing, so we basically had to start over from scratch.

As we began to share our vision for re-launching the campaign, we had the opportunity to connect with an international service club and things began to get exciting. There seemed to be a real interest within the organization to not only help us with sponsorship but also community engagement. At the time, it seemed like a perfect fit. Over the next nine months I spoke at a series of events to reach every potential stakeholder in the organization. I spoke in Ottawa, Toronto, Barrie, Sault Ste. Marie and even Thunder Bay. We drafted special proposal documents and with the help of two extraordinary gentlemen, championed *The Push for Change* through their organization.

It seemed to be going well, but the need to enrol support from so many people slowed the process down. Service clubs are typically autonomous and focused on their local community, so getting every group and every region to agree was proving difficult. One evening after we presented to one of their largest and wealthiest clubs in Ottawa, I received a call informing me that they had decided (at least at their group level) to support *The Push for Change* with $50,000. I was over the moon with excitement; things seemed to be moving in a positive direction.

The excitement was soon dashed as group members held an emergency meeting the next day and voted to rescind the offer. Over the next few months we got a real lesson on how internal politics and decentralized decision-making within service clubs can get in the way of trying to build a national partnership. It was a real bummer. Our two friends had worked so hard, but in the end they couldn't get their own members to see the value in supporting us.

What had seemed like a viable funding partner evaporated into thin air; we had lost almost a year chasing a parked car. Even though we never secured a national partnership with them, we did have extraordinary support from specific clubs across the country and several key events during the campaign had service clubs as our community champions.

As we headed towards the end of summer, we had some serious ground to cover.

By the way, chasing down opportunities was something we did a lot during the campaign, many folks said they would and could help, but when it came time to take action, it just never materialized. Many days I was frustrated that our efforts were not producing fruit, but in the midst of all the rejections we stayed in action and learned to shrug off every "no" and move forward.

In the fall of 2014 things began to pick up speed, I called Fraserway RV and asked if they would support us on the national campaign. After a number of calls and a short visit, we once again secured their support. Fast Signs in Coquitlam also agreed to provide collateral and printed material. We called a contact of Marie's in Barrie, Rick Schaly, who ran Mind to Muscle, Sports Medicine and Trainers Choice. Between these three organizations, Rick was able to support me with trainers, physiotherapists, a massage therapist and all the gear we would need throughout the trek. This was a huge win. Unbeknownst to us they also began to fundraise for *The Push for Change* and before our launch presented us with a cheque for $5,000.

Another friend in Toronto, Robert Pilon, invited us to a dinner where we met a connection to The Westin Foundation. After hearing our story and our plans we were granted $30,000 and we used this as leverage to approach Loblaws and with the help of Vice President Bob Chance we secured our grocery sponsor. Loblaws gave us $30,000 in gift cards to feed our team throughout the entire campaign. Then we had a friend in Vancouver anonymously donate $20,000. We were gaining momentum, but it was still nowhere close to what we needed and I felt powerless in the knowledge that I couldn't just pay for it myself and get on with the campaign.

27

The cost for staff, fuel and accommodations to have a team on the road for over 17 months was a million dollars but we had no idea where to turn for that kind of sponsorship. We had tried service clubs, we pitched every major Canadian company we could think of, but none seemed interested. Getting gifts in kind was easy, but we needed a large infusion of cash.

I remember creating multiple budgets. When I was afraid, I would create a "bare bones" budget that would get us started with a minimum amount of cash. I would show these to Marie and she would immediately reject them and say, "We are going to get the million dollars." I had doubts, but Marie didn't and I believe it was her steadfast possibility mindset that attracted our next sponsor.

In August of 2015, I was hired to speak at a national conference for the United Association of Canada, which represents the unionized pipe trades across Canada. My job was simple, go, speak and inspire them with a story of possibility. The president, John Telford, had heard me speak at another industry conference and asked if I would attend the UA conference. I approached this conference like any other I prepared by taking some time to understand their members and what their world looks like. I began to customize my content and when the day finally came, I went to the Sheraton in Downtown Toronto and shared my story. At this point my story had three components: 1. Being homeless and addicted, struggling to survive on the streets of Vancouver; 2. My triumphant transformation and rise to success and; 3. The plan to pay it forward and walk across Canada.

When I closed out my presentation I mentioned that a week prior, our friends at the Amalgamated Transit Union Local 113 (which represents bus and subway operators in Toronto) had made a cash donation. I said we were grateful for that support and it would be great to have theirs as well.

What happened next was one of the defining moments in our fundraising drive. With all of their representatives present, one member stood and put forward a vote to support *The Push for Change*. It passed unanimously, and then, John Telford stood up and announced that the national office would match any local contribution. When I stepped off the stage, Terry Snooks, president of Toronto's Local 46, gave me his card and told me to call him.

As I left the room I thought to myself, "Something big just happened here, I'm not sure exactly what, but it felt like something important." As I was leaving, Steve Morrison asked me how much money we needed. I didn't want to scare them off so I deferred the question and simply said there's a lot of room for help. Little did I know UA Canada was about to become our Presenting Partner.

I immediately followed up with Terry Snooks and scheduled a meeting. I was living in Barrie with Marie and Local 46 had a hall which is where Terry and I met. During our conversation Terry asked how he could help. I got really honest and told him the biggest thing we needed was money. We needed dollars to operate and hire people, to pay for gas, salaries and the countless expenses in our million-dollar budget.

I suggested that as the president of the largest local in Canada, he had an excellent opportunity to lead in a way that the other locals would follow. If Local 46 could support us in a significant way it would give us leverage with every local across the country. I left it in Terry hands and hoped for the best.

The next conversation we had was with President John Telford. Marie scheduled a call to discuss what sponsorship would look like. Marie had drafted a proposal that showed three levels of sponsorship: Silver, Gold and Presenting. I suggested that there was a real opportunity to have the entire campaign sponsored by UA Canada. If every local stepped up this could become a national UA project. That conversation went well and with the help of John's assistant, Annie, we sent out information to every local and donations began to trickle in.

Marie and I continued to work events across the country, speaking at conferences and schools. On a Friday afternoon, we found ourselves in Bancroft, Ontario following a presentation at a local high school. Before driving back to our hotel in nearby Belleville, I decided to check my email. I plugged my cell phone into the laptop in the car, connected to a hotspot, hit send/receive on my Outlook account and there is was. Terry Snooks and Local 46 came through in a huge way with a $100,000 donation! After four years of obsession, planning and thousands of hours of effort we were on our way to being funded. With the promised matching from head office we were looking at a minimum of $200k and we were just getting started.

This was the moment we had worked so hard for. All of our frustration melted away as the support from Local 46 created exactly the momentum we believed it would. Every local across the country stepped up and the donations began to role in. The support was much greater than even John Telford and head office had imagined. Annie built a spreadsheet so we could keep track of all the donations and by mid-November, UA Canada Locals committed over $250k and head office matched every dollar. We now had half of what we needed. What I found extremely refreshing about our newfound relationship with UA Canada was when I asked the question, "What do you want out of the partnership?" They looked at me funny and said they wanted what we wanted, to end youth homelessness. Unlike the business world CSR people I had spoken with, they had no expectations other than wanting to support a great cause. In fact, that was the case with all of our sponsors – they were on board for one reason, to help Push for Change.

Thanks to UA's leadership, other organizations that had an affiliation also began to step up. We received donations from building trades, the boilermakers, the HVAC folks, James Hogarth from the Ontario Pipe Trades Council (OPTC) stepped up, and Dave Griffiths from Quality Control Council of Canada (QCC) wrote a cheque. Dave would also become instrumental in a whole bunch of other things during the campaign.

Around this time a UA Member named Budrow Tozer from New Brunswick was involved in an organization called General President's Maintenance Committee (GPMC) which is associated with a number of prominent unions and contractors. I was asked to speak at their meeting at the Royal York in Toronto after which they presented us with $100,000. We could not believe how well UA Canada and their friends rallied around what we were doing.

Needless to say, we had finally broken through, the sponsorship money was flowing and once we had a little momentum everything else fell into place. In November I spoke in Hamilton at a Salvation Army event and met Walter Koppelaar. The Walters Group became a sponsor and in Calgary I also spoke for The Salvation Army and met Gerry Wood from Wood Automotive who ended up becoming our vehicle sponsor by leasing us a Ford Transit pace/safety vehicle.

The year was almost over and Marie and I were looking forward to an opportunity to relax over the holidays. I walked to the mailbox to retrieve the mail. Inside was a cheque from UA Canada and, as promised, John had matched every single Local donation. It was a huge cheque with lots of zeros and for the first time in four years we could see the campaign materializing before us. Needless to say, that was a great holiday.

Marie

All of the no's we received along the way were hard to take and they made us question our mission. Joe became impatient and several times he even threatened to cancel the walk altogether. He said if no one else cared about youth homelessness, what difference would we possibly make? At that point we had already invested so much heart and time into the campaign (especially Joe), I knew deep down if we cancelled he would be regretful for the rest of his life and I couldn't let that happen. After all, I was the one who had to live with him for the rest of his/my/our life! With each door that closed, I remained outwardly positive and encouraged Joe to remember that everything was happening just as it should, even if it wasn't necessarily when or how we expected. We just had to be patient; it would be worth the wait.

When the funding did come, it was a total shock to us and the most unexpected sponsors started to embrace our campaign. It was not like we planned, but we had done enough personal development to know staying positive and attracting exactly what you want or need will bring forth the results (if only you allow it to happen in its own time and way). Still, when we knew we were funded, we were blown away, we had finally broken the

barriers and made the impossible possible. Being restless and pushing for
change paid off. We were filled with gratitude to say the least.

For Christmas 2015, Joe and I decided to take some personal time and
go to Montreal for a few days. Little did I know he had planned a very
romantic getaway and intended to propose to me during an intimate
dinner at Europea in downtown Montreal. It was the fanciest restaurant
I'd ever been to and we had the best table in the house (secluded and set
inside windows to give us privacy with a view). Halfway through the meal,
he nonchalantly rose out of his seat, kneeled in front of me and proposed,
displaying the most beautiful diamond I had ever seen. It was cute and
romantic all at once and his love was so evident, visions of him as a
teenager flashed before my eyes. In that moment I loved him so much and
knew we were destined to spend the rest of our days together. I accepted his
proposal and we got married almost three months later on March 26, just
five weeks before the PFC campaign kicked off in Newfoundland. The
timing was perfect.

28

As Marie had envisioned, by the end of 2015 we had all of the
resources we needed. One of the things that we are extremely proud of
is that we were fully funded and had everything paid for BEFORE we
took one step. This was different than any other grassroots effort. By
having sponsorship to pay for the campaign, every dollar we raised
across Canada would go towards the cause. With the exception of
corporately run national campaigns, that had never been done before.

With funding out of the way, we turned our focus to creating
engaging events and excitement for our trek across the country. Marie
and I were still extremely busy speaking at conferences. One call for a
speaking event stood out. Chief Superintendent Rick Barnum from the
Ontario Provincial Police (OPP) had reached out to Marie inquiring
about a speaking opportunity at the upcoming commissioner's event at
the Deerhurst Resort in Huntsville. We had just reset our launch date
when I got an opportunity to connect directly with Rick. I gave him my
back-story and explained the connection to the OPP. I took Rick

through the night Scott MacLeod and I met and how that interaction changed the trajectory of my life. We talked about how we could share this at their conference and I suggested they invite me to do my usual presentation and then surprise the audience with this part of my story in an impactful, meaningful way.

On the day of the event, I spoke for 45 minutes about my life and the challenges I had growing up related to mental health and addiction. I emphasized the significance how one person, one interaction or one decision, can have for someone like me. This was something very relevant to every person in that room because over 25% of calls that come into police centres are related to mental health, addiction and/or suicide. I told them about my friend Scott who was there for me at a crucial time and who, in my opinion, had been instrumental in changing my life. It wasn't until the last few words of my speech that the audience learned Scott was actually OPP Constable Scott MacLeod. After a thunderous and emotional standing ovation, Scott surprised the audience by appearing on the side stage and sharing his perspective.

It was an opportunity to share a message that gets far too little attention; an example of what happens when the police get it right. On that night, Scott had got it right and I was standing there because of him. The execution of the event could not have gone better. The impact of the story and the emotion in the room was palpable. Thanks to the leadership of Rick Barnum, the event was a resounding success. Commissioner Vince Hawkes was there and I could tell from the post-event conversation, he was moved and inspired by the message we delivered. As was my habit, I mentioned *The Push for Change* as we debriefed the event and both Rick and Commissioner Hawkes asked how they could help.

Over the next year Rick, Marie and I met regularly to discuss how we could work together. At the time, the OPP was heavily invested in managing the Pan-Am Games in Toronto, so taking on a new community project wasn't likely going to happen quickly, but we knew if we were going to build a relationship, we needed an internal champion. Rick was our guy. A full year passed and the Pan-Am Games were wrapping up when I was once again asked to speak at the annual commissioner's event and give an update.

During this presentation I highlighted our success in raising the money we needed and securing vehicles for the campaign. I also talked about the national partnerships we had built. Towards the end of the presentation, I looked at Commissioner Hawkes and emphasized that I would give everything I had to this campaign, but I needed the OPP's help to get it right.

When I was done, the commissioner stood up in front of his senior leadership team and announced that they would support us and encouraged everyone else in the room to do so as well. Rick worked the room and in no time he had a list of qualified people to serve on a Push for Change/OPP committee, at which point, he began drawing up an org chart. Apparently, getting anything done in the OPP requires an org chart, according to Rick.

Something else happened in that meeting that would help us in Atlantic Canada; a very unassuming gentleman approached me and asked me who I knew in the East. I confessed that we had very few contacts and he said he might be able to help. I asked him his name. He said, "Assistant Commissioner Roger Brown of the New Brunswick RCMP." I later learned that Roger was something of a legend as an RCMP leader. He was commander and chief during the terrible Moncton shooting crisis and was beloved by police leaders around the world. Although Roger would be retired by the time we reached New Brunswick, his influence and support were felt by our campaign from Newfoundland to British Columbia.

A few weeks after the event, I got an email from Rick Barnum asking us to attend a meeting at OPP Headquarters in Orillia. Marie and I showed up and after clearing security we were escorted into the boardroom where we found ourselves a little intimidated by the collection of folks gathered for the meeting. Sitting around the table were senior leaders from across the province: Traffic Safety, Community Engagement, Communications and the Administration specialist, we had everyone in the room. Over the next 90 minutes, we discussed how we were going to execute PFC with the OPP in Ontario. After working our butts off for four years, I couldn't believe Marie and I were sitting in front of a leadership team that represented the second largest police force in North America and they were asking us what we wanted them to do. It truly was a "possibility" that had resulted from tireless action.

In the same way that our partnership with UA solved the money issue, the OPP helped us solve the community engagement issue. Over the months that followed, Marie worked closely with Rick and his team to build out the engagement strategy for Ontario. Initially the OPP planned to host 25 events; however by the time we were done they ended up supporting us in a way never before seen in the history of their organization. All together they hosted over 221 events. They were also instrumental in securing support from every municipal and provincial police force in Canada, as well as the RCMP. Given the level of commitment that had been pledged by the OPP we revised our map through Ontario to include an additional 800 kilometres.

Who would have imagined a guy like me (who had lived on the wrong side of the law half of his life and even been chased by the police), would be working with them to support young people and engage the community. It was just more proof that anything is possible.

29

With the OPP and UA Canada behind us, we focused on our campaign goals. We set a financial target to raise 50 cents from every Canadian. It was a lofty goal indeed, but we believed it was doable. The dollars we raised would go to support the Upstream Project through our charitable partner Raising the Roof. Our mission was simple: prevent, reduce and end youth homelessness by changing the way we approach the issue. To make it easy to ask for donations, we published the fact that 100% of every dollar raised would go directly towards the cause. Marie worked with a company in Vancouver called CHIMP to set up a web-based system that would allow people to donate online. The system also allowed our partners to set up individual pages to fund-raise.

We created unique fundraising opportunities including a Celebrity Shopping Cart. To push the celebrity cart along a portion of the road, an individual had to reach a certain fundraising goal. We also had a "Walk with Joe" campaign, a health and wellness promotion where organizations could match my steps and raise money. The OPP championed this one in a number of regions. Another event was the Sleepout Challenge, which encouraged organizations and schools to "sleep" out of their comfort zone to better understand the hardships a young person might experience while homeless. This was a national challenge and a number of schools, colleges and OPP detachments really got behind it. We also received general donations of money from businesses and associations including Rotary and Kiwanis; as well as from foundations, departments within the OPP, schools and private donors.

PART FOUR
COUNTDOWN TO THE CAMPAIGN

January 1, 2016 – 121 days to launch

With our goals set and our partners lined up, the calendar rolled over to 2016 and the countdown began. My job was to continue my training and help wherever I could to finish the long list of tasks that had to be completed by launch day on May 1.

Even though we were consistently clearing major roadblocks, we never had much time to celebrate. Once one big set of challenges was solved, we immediately shifted to the next. One of these was making sure I had all the right equipment including lots of running shoes, winter boots, jackets, gloves, balaclavas and rain gear. I needed to keep going, rain or shine, for 17 months across Canada, including five months of winter in Northern Ontario. Fortunately, the Ford Transit 250 that had been leased to us from Woodridge was on its way and my plan was to use it as a rolling closet.

Logistically, our time on the campaign was as follows: each day Bobby (who would once again be our driver) and I would wake up in our base camp. In the summer the base camp would be the RV donated by Fraserway RV and in the winter it would be a series of Best Western hotel rooms. Regardless, we would wake up, brew our coffee, grab our lunch kits and drive to where we had left off walking the previous day. I would start walking and log a minimum of 24 kilometres per day. After walking we would head to a scheduled event if there was one and later I would sort through the pictures and video that had been shot that day.

I would be walking a minimum of five days per week, with one day set aside just for community engagement and events (no walking) and one day as a day off where we didn't work on the campaign – although that proved to be tough some months. With the campaign carved up in this way, we mapped out a 17-month journey across Canada (517 days) that allowed us to know more or less where we would be on any given day so we'd never miss an event.

As January progressed, our preparations kicked into overdrive; we needed uniforms for the team and we had to transport an RV from BC and a Ford Transit from Calgary to the starting point. We needed to get vinyl wraps for our three vehicles and have the vehicles insured; we also had mapping to finish and Marie had 400 events to plan. Think about that one for a moment. If you've ever hosted an event, imagine being directly involved with 400 events that were all being organized simultaneously. We had police logistics to contend with, schools to liaison with and large-scale community events to coordinate. As more support for the campaign poured in and new events were added, the workload increased as did the pressure on our small team.

As the start date drew closer, Marie and I had some unique logistical problems of our own. In order for us to undertake this 17-month journey, we needed to become nomads ourselves. It was kind of ironic that in order to run a campaign to end youth homelessness, we needed to become homeless, at least symbolically. Not only did we need to pack and prepare to be on the road non-stop for 17 months, we also needed to figure out where our mail would go, where we would store our personal belongings, how we would access additional resources needed for the campaign and who was going to rent our house. Just sorting out a logistics plan for our personal stuff took half a day and a pot of coffee.

Once that was sorted, we tackled how to move three vehicles across the country with only two drivers (which was a bit of a head scratcher). During the fair weather (April-Oct), we planned to live in the RV but we would be in Ontario when winter hit. The RV carried so much stuff, we needed to downsize as we transitioned into hotel rooms for the winter and we still needed to fit gear for three people (along with a full office and kitchen) into one van and a car. I think you're probably beginning to see that we had our hands full just trying to build a plan that would enable us to move down the road efficiently. As we checked off the challenges one by one, a workable plan slowly emerged.

February 9, 2016 - 81 days to launch

I was in good spirits after completing 18 km on the treadmill. Outside, it was –15°C with blizzard conditions, so I didn't mind being indoors. My training has been going well despite a sore knee. I used ice to reduce the swelling but issues like this always caused anxiety. Once we had sponsors and the OPP behind us, my number one concern was, "Could I make it?" All I could do was focus on what I was trained to do and follow the plan Sean had given me. One of the compounding issues I faced with training was nutrition. I generally ate poorly and now that I was constantly hungry from training and stressed about the upcoming campaign, it only exacerbated my poor eating habits. If I was tired or anxious I habitually reached for the wrong food. It was a pattern that left me overweight, but more importantly, it caused me to feel that I wasn't doing everything I could to be successful. It was a constant battle.

On a positive note, we managed to fly the drone for the first time. Our vision was to be able to use the drone to capture key moments of the campaign and shoot videos. Getting it up and running for the first time was exciting.

One of the interesting things about our preparation days is that I had to spend a lot of hours on the treadmill while I was also working (sometimes for six hours or more, a day). There was no way for me to stop working, so many of my calls to clients or supporters were made from the treadmill. We also sourced out a laptop holder that sat on the treadmill so I could place my laptop in front of me to answer emails and take notes. It was kind of normal for Marie and me, but every now and then someone would come into the house and see me on the treadmill wearing a headset with a laptop strapped to the treadmill in front of me. I got some funny looks when that happened.

February 13, 2016 - 77 days to launch

I did some winter training and walked 18.5 km around Barrie. The temperature was -28°C with the wind-chill putting it at –35°C, which was perfect since it allowed us to test out different gear and understand what kinds of problems we would face in northern Ontario.

My feet stayed warm in the walking boots and the clothing layers also worked well. What needed improvement was my headgear; my ears and face were really cold by the end of my walk (there's a real danger of frostbite if we don't figure out a better solution). I also discovered that our iPhones won't work in the extreme cold. My phone lasted for less than five minutes when exposed to the cold and wind, the battery level dropped like a rock and the phone just stopped working. What's more, I learned that I needed to store my water in the truck when I'm walking. My water bottle froze solid which is not something I would have thought about. Without my usual volume of water, I was poorly hydrated and I also hadn't eaten well, so I paid the price for both. Walking in the cold takes more energy and calories which makes it's absolutely crucial to hydrate and eat well. I noticed walking and pushing the cart was a lot harder with the snow slowing us down, too.

All in all, it was a great day of learning; we got to do a long walk in seriously challenging winter conditions and we know what we need to change to improve performance.

February 14, 2016 - 76 days to launch

After what had already been a long week of training, I woke up and completed a 16 km day (which put my total for the week at over 80 kilometres). A number of those kilometres were in fierce Ontario winter weather (which was a bonus). I've been having some challenges with my knee and thanks to our friends at Sports Medicine, I was able to see a chiropractor and a massage therapist to get some input and advice.

Having Sports Medicine and Mind to Muscle support the campaign has been invaluable. The professional feedback on training and access to all of their experts has given me the confidence to push myself to be in my best shape before the walk.

Mind to Muscle also put me in touch with Greg, a nutrition expert at the University of Guelph. At the university, we did a sweat test where I was hooked up to a number of machines for 90 minutes to analyze how my body burns energy. When it was done, Greg gave me a long-term nutrition plan designed to meet my body's needs. It was cool using the absolute latest technology, which is normally reserved for elite athletes. It was also cool to learn exactly how my body works and how to hydrate and fuel it.

Our goal as we approach the start of the campaign is to build resiliency and avoid injury (which requires me to listen carefully to my body). If it's sore, adjust, if it's painful, STOP. The challenge with walking across Canada is if I ignore something painful, it could stop the campaign in its tracks and just like a million elite athletes who pushed too hard, I'll end up getting sidelined. With a tight schedule to adhere to, we can't afford downtime or time off once the campaign begins.

February 27, 2016 - 63 days to launch

Although I put in 22 km of training, I didn't feel great but I'm happy to say I got it done anyway. I'm eager to have those daily kilometres count towards my goal of walking across the country.

Last week we flew to Vancouver and spoke to Family Services of Greater Vancouver. It looks like they may be interested in supporting a PFC event when we reach the finish line.

This week we were in Fredericton at an event hosted by our friend, Assistant Commissioner Roger Brown. We conducted a town hall style meeting with the mayor, the Minister of Justice, Acting Deputy Premier Stephen Horsman and our friends from UA Local 325 and QCC Canada to talk about campaign logistics. Most importantly, we had police chiefs from every city in New Brunswick, who pledged to support us on the road throughout the province. Roger also reached out to the Royal Constabulary in Newfoundland and they committed to help us as well.

When the week was done we were looking at some serious support in Atlantic Canada and Marie and I were getting more excited by the day.

February 28, 2016 - 62 days to launch

Another great training day; after four and a half years of planning, dreaming and hard work, the campaign to *Push for Change* is in sight and I can finally see the start line. For years, this part of the vision was somewhat fuzzy in my mind but as details fall into place, it becomes clearer and clearer.

Thanks to our new partners and friends we're beginning to have important conversations with senior law enforcement officials as well as provincial and federal government representatives. We are connecting to a greater conversation and the opportunity for our campaign to make a real impact is growing. We even have friends working on making a connection in the Prime Minister's office and with luck we may get the opportunity to meet.

This week we also realized that we get to skip over a step that is required for so many campaigns like ours. By working directly with our law enforcement partners and building a strategic safety plan, in many cases we'll be able to forego the permit process. In the early stages of the campaign, both our friends from the 2010 Olympics campaign and Tyrone from the Rick Hansen campaign told us we would need a full-time person just to submit permits. As a grassroots campaign with limited resources, we couldn't see how that would be possible, so today we're feeling both clever and blessed. Clever for understanding how helpful a partner like the OPP could be, and blessed that the campaign led us to each other.

March 3, 2016 - 58 days to launch

Checking things off the campaign to-do list is very satisfying; it also gives us more breathing room. Marie has worked on creating logos we can use across all platforms. We've also created a version that is both French and English combined (which is important) and engaged a consultant who is translating our website to create a French version. This is important when engaging not just with Quebec but also New Brunswick and hundreds of additional communities across the country. It's also the kind of thing we didn't consider when we started planning four years ago. Marie was also successful in getting PFC logo secured as a registered trademark, which is just another example of her ability to take care of the detailed stuff.

This week I got in 88 kilometres of training and then pulled a muscle shovelling snow. The good news is I no longer consider a sore back a show stopper. I've learned that a pulled or sore muscle can be stretched and worked, so when I have a sore back now I go for a walk, then lay on a roller.

Later this afternoon I'm going to my Uncle Bruce's house, he's promised to introduce me to something called grounding. Without going down a wormhole trying to explain it, I'm told it can speed up recovery time for athletes by improving circulation. The science is incomplete but I'm guessing it can't be worse than sitting in a bath filled with ice and water and anything that can help prevent injury or speed up healing is worth a try.

March 10, 2016 - 51 days to launch

It was a difficult training day for me; I lacked motivation and drive but did it anyway. We also had a disappointing day yesterday, when we met with a potential PR specialist (the second one we've interviewed so far). After giving him some time to absorb the scope of the campaign, we were expecting some useful insights but he came back with a proposal that made zero sense. I had a hard time sitting through the meeting when I realized that his work was sloppy and filled with errors in both its message and direction. The kicker was he got the name of UA Canada (our main sponsor) wrong in the materials he showed us. Marie and I discussed it and told him we didn't want to move forward. Our team bench is really small and we're not willing to put our heart and soul into something and give someone else a pass. We only want to work with strong, dedicated people who are willing to work their tails off.

Something else we've experienced more than a few times recently is people who feel compelled to share negative opinions. They don't (or can't) see what we do and offer what seems like advice, but it's really just their inability to embrace our "possibility mindset." It's funny, in the past conversations like that would bother me and leave me feeling discouraged. Not anymore. When you've worked as long and hard on something as we have and seen so many pieces come together, it tends to give you a bounce in your step and a sense of confidence in what you're doing. These days, when we get "idea donations" from people (which are usually their opinions or a list of things we ought to do), we simply say, "Thank you," and move on.

I've spent a lot of time visualizing how I want the campaign to go lately, from launch to completion. I even created an audio mp3 to listen to that affirms my vision for success. There's one portion where I repeat that *The Push for Change* has already been successfully completed. I know elite athletes use this kind of positive affirmation so I thought, why not us?

We received news that the Ford Transit 250 is on its way. Once it gets to Ontario, we'll insure it for the campaign and then have it wrapped.

We had an event at a nearby university this week that was a total bust; which is another one of those things that used to discourage me, now I just shrug it off and move on.

April 1, 2016 - 29 days to launch

Marie and I decided to get married. With so much going on only weeks before the launch, we chose to do it really quietly and snuck away last weekend to the Briars on Lake Simcoe where we had our Rotary friend Karen officiate. The only people at our wedding were Russ and Martha. It was quiet, sweet and horribly romantic. I couldn't be happier about being married to Marie; my only regret is we got married at such a crazy time in our life. Now as husband and wife, we're ready to tackle the biggest thing either of us has ever done and we get to do it together.

Bobby picked up the RV from Fraserway this week, insured it and hit the road, he's due in Ontario in four days.

We hired a woman from St. Johns to be our PR specialist. She's going to take care of radio, print and media releases; we're excited to have her on board and it's one less thing for Marie to worry about.

Our to-do list was getting shorter by the minute. Once Bobby arrived we could send the RV in to be wrapped and then begin loading it with all the gear we'd need for the 17 months. At the same time, we started to pack up our house. A family friend agreed to rent the house while we're on the road. It's a perfect fit for us as it's someone we trust. We can keep the mail coming to the address and we can use one of the spare rooms to store our stuff. Sorting out the house was a huge challenge, so I'm happy it's solved.

With only four and a half weeks to go it's mind boggling to think how much work we've done over the past four years. I can truly say if Marie and I hadn't reconnected and I hadn't moved to Ontario and convinced her to join the campaign, there's no way the launch would be happening in just four weeks. Everything has come together and the list of things to do is getting shorter and shorter.

April 5, 2016 - 25 days to launch

This week was totally hijacked by issues with vehicle logistics and the nightmare of sourcing vehicles from two different provinces. The RV arrived safe and sound, but Marie spent several days sorting out how to insure a driver from BC and a vehicle from BC for a charity walk across Canada when the charity's address is in Ontario. Confused yet? Welcome to the club. Every insurance provider Marie talked to got confused, but practising patience as only Marie can (I would have lost my mind), it got sorted out and the RV is on its way to get the vinyl wrap thanks to Mario Design in Barrie. We pick it up in a week.

The FORD Transit was another story completely. The van was very generously leased to us by the Wood Automotive Group in Calgary and shipped to the Ford dealership in Barrie. Unfortunately, when it arrived nobody knew who the vehicle belonged to, so it sat there until we made some inquiries. The good news: we located the van; the bad news: no one knew where the keys were so we had to pay to get the vehicle unlocked, assuming the keys were somewhere inside. They weren't. After a day and a half of phoning and emailing, we finally learned the keys were hidden in the gas cap. With all the back and forth, we lost two days of valuable prep time.

After all that, the vehicle wouldn't start and had a number of engine lights that needed to be cleared. Long story short, the vehicle had sat for a long time and needed a little TLC. Our friends at Barrie Ford came to the rescue and in two days we finally had the vehicle ready to insure... or so we thought. The documents sent to us from Calgary hadn't been signed. Marie had to courier the docs to Calgary, have them couriered back overnight and then provide all of our foundation documentation before we could get insurance. Compared to this experience, walking across Canada should be a piece of cake.

But that wasn't the end of it; we still needed to insure a driver from BC for a vehicle in Ontario that originated from Alberta for a cross-Canada charity walk. After two weeks and four different insurance companies, we were at our wits end and facing critical deadlines.

Thankfully, Wayne Branchaud, our friend and community champion in Brantford, came to the rescue and connected us with some helpful folks at Co-operators Insurance, who agreed to write a policy for us.

Once the Ford is vinyl wrapped, Marie's nephew Jeff has offered to help us customize the inside so we can hang and pack everything.

The last step will be to install a car trailer on the back of the RV so we can take Marie's Mazda 3, which will be used by her for events and running around.

When the whole process is done we'll have all three vehicles transported to St. John's Newfoundland, where we begin our cross-Canada walk on May 1.

April 30, 2016 - One day to launch

Marie and I went to BC to speak at an HR conference this week while Bobby headed for the start point in the RV (with the Mazda in tow) and Marie's mom and her husband Neil drove the Ford Transit with all of our gear. When our conference ended, we flew from one end of the country to the other. How fitting considering that the next morning I would begin a walk back the other way. It's kind of funny how we were complaining about the eight hours or more of flights, yet walking is going to take 17 months. I promise I'll never complain about a flight time again.

All of the problems with the vehicles are behind us and everyone made it safely to the East Coast. As I record this, I am standing on a hillside near the city of St. John's with the brisk Atlantic breeze blowing in my face. After four and a half years of preparation, we finally made it to the beginning of this extraordinary odyssey. Tomorrow is the start of what will become a thousand memories and experiences.

Believing in a goal and staying in action is what brought us this far. Staying connected to purpose on days that were dark, keeping the dream alive... this is the moment I dreamt about for so many years and now it's here!

When Terry Fox left this very spot, he left with a bottle of water and the idea that he would dump his water from the Atlantic into the Pacific.

In keeping with that sentiment, I gathered a small number of pebbles that I will carry to remind myself of the place I'm standing in today.

The sky is bright blue and the ocean is vast, empty and beautiful. In front of me lies 9,000 kilometres of highway and the greatest challenge of my life. Tomorrow and every day after that, I will give my best and if I fail at least I can say I gave this everything I had and hold my head high.

As I stand here, I realize we have accomplished the impossible. So many people dream about the impossible, and unfortunately most dreams never become reality. Our dream was coming true.

So what is teachable about this accomplishment? It is that we relentlessly did the things that scared us and the things we didn't want to do. The world doesn't care how you feel, it responds to what you think and do.

How can you ever really know what your possibility is unless you test it?

I truly believe that our possibilities as human beings lie just beyond the courage to fail.

Follow the Journey online.

See the photos and videos.

www.thepushforchangebook.com

PART FIVE
THE CAMPAIGN

30

I'm not sure what time it was when I woke up but I knew what day it was. For four years, six months and 21 days I had obsessed about this day and now it was finally here. After a hearty breakfast of oatmeal, dates and walnuts along with three shots of strong espresso, I was as ready as I was ever going to be. The team assembled and we headed off to Cape Spear which is east of the city of St. John's. This is the most easterly point of North America. It is also the very spot that Rick Hansen left from and I thought it would be fitting for us to do the same.

We gathered the three vehicles: the RV, our support van and the event vehicle. They looked so cool all together, wrapped with our logo and sponsors. The weather was amazing; we had worried about wind, rain or even snow, but the day could not have been nicer.

Friends and supporters began to arrive as we set up the portable sound system we had purchased for staging events and we prepared for more folks to join us. As the crowd began to grow there were some familiar faces, including Dave Griffiths and Brent Hunt from QCC Canada and Terry Snooks from UA Canada. The RCMP had sent two officers dressed in their official red serge uniforms and Paula Walsh from the Royal Newfoundland Constabulary was also present, wearing her formal attire.

Marie's mom Jean was there with her husband Neil; they had driven the support van from Ontario for us. Russ and Martha from Barrie had flown out to join us as well. This was actually a big deal for Russ as he had never been on a plane before. I was impressed that the launch inspired him enough to push through his fear of flying to be here for this special day. Martha had her own reasons for coming. Not only was she our go to person at our bank, she had also conducted multiple events and fundraisers leading up to the launch and was truly a PFC champion. We were happy to see them both at the launch.

With about 40 people present, Marie stepped up and conducted a short ceremony that began with the Canadian national anthem. It was horribly patriotic (just the way we imagined it would be) and Marie's passion really shone through in her address. She will be the first to admit she's not a fan of public speaking, but as I stood on the sidelines watching her I couldn't help but get a lump in my throat. Marie had spent years pouring her heart and soul into every detail in order to get us here. She boldly took the microphone and I watched her mom look on with pride as Marie addressed the audience.

This humble gathering of friends, family and stakeholders was the official start of a 17-month, 9,064 km journey across the widest part of North America; a campaign that would cross ten provinces and two of the three northern territories and engage millions of people. *The Push for Change* trek would change our lives and the lives of many others whom we would meet along the way.

I took the microphone and said a few words, thanking our sponsors, supporters and everyone else that helped to us get to the starting line. After a few additional comments from our friends, the time had finally arrived. When pursuing impossible things in our lives there is a time to dream, a time to plan and a time to take action. The dreaming and planning were complete; it was time for the walking to begin.

We were really fortunate to have the CBC and the Newfoundland Television folks come out and cover the story. We also had the local radio station on location; in fact, their morning guy came and joined me for the first few kilometres which was really cool. The kick-off was exactly what we wanted; grassroots, not too glitzy, honest and authentic. It didn't feel like a well-oiled corporate machine, it felt like a small group of people dedicated to championing change.

Our videographer Brian had flown out to capture some interviews as well as the launch. He lined up the crowd to form a tunnel and the campaign launched with me walking through a crowd of cheering supporters as I headed out of the parking lot onto the road that led to St. John's, 13 kilometres away.

Marie

The support we received on launch day was overwhelming. Our sponsors, family, friends, and community champions from the area (who already had become fast friends) displayed such encouragement and enthusiasm for what we were embarking on, that we couldn't help but feel extremely proud to have made it this far. And that was before Joe had taken even one step of his walk for the day. I honestly felt a little out of my league and when high ranking officers from The Royal Newfoundland Constabulary (NL's provincial police), members of the RCMP, city councillors and other officials joined us to celebrate our kick-off from Cape Spear, I almost couldn't believe that our planning and action over the past three years made this happen.

With three events planned for the first day, there was no time to reminisce about how we made it here, it was time to be present and enjoy the ride. Joe had asked me to prepare a kick-off speech, and despite a life-long fear of public speaking, I knew I was in this too far and too deep to say no. The words I prepared were meant to bring meaning to our campaign even though I knew the supporters who joined us on that first day understood our purpose as they stood behind us. Nonetheless, I reminded the crowd that gathered with us at Cape Spear that whether we realize it or not, we all have a passion to help and love, and it is in this service to others that we find personal fulfillment. I also explained that The Push for Change endeavours to empower each and every person who hears Joe's story to believe in their own unlimited possibilities and tear down the limiting beliefs that lay between their own two ears. Standing in front of the crowd delivering the message that morning, and listening to Joe deliver the same message time and again over the 517 days that followed, I was honoured and humbled to play a part in unleashing human potential. On a personal level, I also discovered that day that my fear of public speaking was nothing more than a block between my own ears, and when I got out of my own way; I could stand up in front of a crowd and talk till the cows came home.

31

As the cheering faded behind me, the only sounds I heard were the rattling of my shopping cart and the crunching of tires as Bobby's support van followed me. Off in the distance waves crashed along the rugged shore and seagulls swooped through the air; the scene was surreal and beautiful. The road to St. John's was very hilly, with winding curves making up a coastline unique to Newfoundland. The air was filled with the fresh smell of the ocean; the wind pleasant and caressing, an anomaly for this place. The sun was warm on my face and each step revealed hidden pockets of coastline, ocean and cliffs. The waves crashed relentlessly as the Atlantic Ocean danced for me like it was in an audition.

In front of me lay 9,000 kilometres of Canadian splendour. The experience would be both exquisitely beautiful and ruthlessly unforgiving; nevertheless, I was committed to crossing the continent and my first day was a true gift of nature's magnificence.

Thirteen kilometres later, after scaling some serious hills that I was not completely ready for, I reached the outskirts of the city of St. John's. I was met by our friends from the Royal Newfoundland Constabulary (RNC) which is the local police force who escorted us into town for our second event at Choices for Youth. As we worked our way through the city I felt a sense of pride having the police usher us through the community with lights flashing. St. John's has some pretty steep hills and the final hill had to be a 20% grade. It would be one of the steepest I would climb during the entire campaign. Fortunately it was short. When we crested the hill, we found ourselves in the parking lot of Choices for Youth where we had a small gathering that included our friends from the RCMP and the RNC and featured some short speeches from the deputy mayor, city council and the local MHA.

With the goal of raising awareness and support for the prevention of youth homelessness across the country, it was crucial for us to engage as many advocacy and support agencies for youth at risk as possible. Choices for Youth provided an array of services to help young people in crisis, not just with emergency shelter, but all kinds of services that a young person might need to get back on their feet. Through our campaign, we wanted to champion solutions that would help young people get help and support before they became homeless. When implemented, such strategies have the added benefit of reducing the stress on emergency service providers and allowing frontline workers to be more effective. Probably the most powerful part of that morning was listening to comments from the youth present. There was one young woman who shared her personal story of homelessness and with tears of passion, emphasized the importance of our work for others like her. Her remarks moved me and fuelled the fire in my belly.

After a short reception we headed out to begin our walk through the city; our next stop was city hall. By now the wind had picked up a bit and the temperature was dropping. The weather in this part of Newfoundland can be windy and bitterly cold, which is not a problem if you keep moving but we found ourselves standing still waiting for the mayor of St. John's to show up. Our media liaison had promised that the mayor was going to meet us here and walk with us for a couple kilometres. After waiting 30 minutes the team grew restless and cold and we decided we had to keep moving. I was a little disappointed but thought, "At least it will give me something to write about later."

I don't want to shame the good mayor as I am sure he had pressing business that was necessary for him to cancel without notice. I don't want to mention his name because I wouldn't want to offend his worship Denis O'Keefe. In all honesty I wasn't offended at all and I share this with a very light and joking heart. It did teach us a valuable lesson that not all things that are planned go down as expected.

We headed out of downtown and up Route 2 towards the Trans-Canada and our next event. A few hours later at the off ramp in Mount Pleasant we were met by UA Local 740 and a crowd of enthusiastic supporters. This was our first "Walk with Joe," experience where I was joined by a group of people and we walked in solidarity to the training centre where we had our third event.

UA Canada and their locals across the country were our biggest supporters and when we arrived at UA 740 we were greeted with hugs and welcomed like family. They had put on a spread for the occasion and after I shared our story and the significance of UA's support they presented us with a generous donation.

After a very full day Marie, Bobby and I headed back to base camp, exhausted. I had walked 28 km, done three interviews and spoken at three events. The news coverage was amazing and social media was blowing up. Day One was officially behind us and it couldn't have been more perfect. The dream of *The Push for Change* was becoming reality, one that would take us across the country and into the hearts and minds of millions.

Marie

Crossing Canada with PFC helped me grow in so many ways. It also changed my outlook on homelessness from one of ignorance to empathy. To be honest, during most of my adult life, anytime I was confronted by homeless people, I was a little startled. I was under the impression that they wanted to steal from me or maybe even hurt me; not that it had ever happened, it was just my ignorance. PFC taught me that no one plans to be homeless. For the most part it happens because of circumstances that are beyond the individual's control: family conflict, childhood trauma, mental health issues, addiction, poverty, exclusion. Homelessness could happen to anyone.

Choices for Youth in St. John's, Newfoundland, was the first youth services agency to host one of our events. At the event, I met caring staff members (and the youth who were their clients) and I was in awe of the professional, yet personal relationships they had built and the sense of community. I started to see that homelessness was something that happened to people, but it didn't define who they were.

32

On day two we woke up at 5:00 am and were on the road by 6:00. Bobby and I were working out a routine; our goal was to get up and head out of the RV as quick as possible each morning so we could hit the road. The sooner we got me moving the better. Mornings always started with strong espresso from our machine, one of the few luxuries we brought with us. Next, we grabbed thermoses of coffee and lunch and headed out to the van. Once we arrived at the place we'd stopped the day before, I'd start walking.

Day two began on the Trans-Canada Highway in Mount Pleasant heading east and after only a few hours we found ourselves outside the city limits. For the next several weeks we would have more or less the same scenery, as we passed by small ponds and lakes, miles of bush land and the odd glimpse of ocean. Newfoundland is such a wild place; vast, beautiful and breathtaking. In May, it's also cold, windy and wet. We needed to adjust to the wet weather quickly. I was annoyed by chafing under my layers of clothes and I struggled to keep my feet dry. Wet feet can lead to serious problems. When your feet get wet they soften and that coupled with the heat generated by friction can create a perfect recipe for debilitating blisters.

At the end of day two I felt good but the hills were taking their toll on me. I had done lots of hill training in BC for the trial walk; unfortunately all my recent training had been in Barrie, Ontario where there weren't a lot of hills. I found myself making adjustments and trying to adapt at a time when I should have been completely prepared and I started to get scared as we moved away from St. John's towards Gander. That part of Newfoundland is known as the Peninsula and the hills for the next 150 km were going to be serious; up and down all day long. From a conditioning standpoint I was in great shape, my cardio, stamina and willpower were all excellent, it was just that my body wasn't used to the hills.

By day four I had hit a wall and walked just nine kilometres. The rain was killing me and the wind was over 40 kmh, but what had me more concerned was the pain in my right knee. In the morning I had been stiff and sore, but as the morning progressed the soreness turned to pain and then it became a sharp pain. I knew I was in trouble.

Fortunately, I also knew what to do and Sean's simple advice played in my head: "If you're tired suck it up; if you're in pain, STOP immediately." I trusted his advice, after all he'd written his PhD thesis on over-training. As Sean had often told me, "The only time you will know for sure that you have pushed too hard is after an injury and then it's too late." Not being able to complete the walk because of an injury was my biggest fear by far. With my fear manifesting right before my eyes, now I was dealing with two problems; the physical pain in my knee and the doubt that was building in my mind. We were fortunate that we had flexibility in the schedule to move events around, but we needed to get some help fast.

After a call to Sean, Marie booked me in with a local physiotherapist and RMT. The physiotherapist explained that the up and down on hills had caused my right IT band to tighten and pull my knee to the side, which put it out of alignment and resulted in inflammation and pain. I was given two things to help me, one was a series of six stretches designed to help release the muscles and reduce the pull on my knee. The second tool I was given was sports tape. Because my knee was pulling to the right, my entire leg and foot were rotating out. The tape brought the foot back to its normal position and helped correct my crooked step.

After my physio appointment, we met with Debbie, an amazing RMT whom we would have taken on the road with us in a heartbeat. She was really excited to hear about our campaign and ended up supporting us for more than half of our trek across Newfoundland. We set up a massage table inside the RV, which created a bit of a comedy act. To give Debbie enough room to work on my leg, Marie had to stay seated while Bobby was relegated to his sleeping quarters above the vehicle cab. Thanks to Debbie's magic hands, the sports tape and stretches; and a solid day of rest with a couple of ice baths thrown in, I was ready to tackle the road again.

Starting out, I was scared and went super slow, but the first six kilometres felt really good. In fact, that day I did an amazing 18 km and felt better than I had on day one. The following day I did 21 km and by the day following that, I was back up to my 24 km average. I had some severe blisters as a result of my foot being turned and then forced back with tape, but in comparison to a knee that didn't work it was a problem I was happy to manage. Blisters are simple to deal with; they require duct tape, gauze and indifference. They might slow you down but they can't stop you unless you let them. I was happy to be back up to 24 km which was my daily minimum to stay on schedule.

After a good injury scare, I was determined to do all the little things necessary to be successful. During all my years of training I had been lazy when it came to stretching; it was one of those things I balked at and avoided because I thought it was a waste of time. Sean, Marie and every RMT, chiropractor and physiotherapist I ever met had hounded me about it and I had ignored them all, not anymore.

I was also back to daily ice baths. Not surprisingly, it's easy to find cold water in natural settings in Newfoundland in May. I remember one night sitting waist-deep in lake water in the pouring rain. Ice baths really helped release muscle pain and reduce inflammation but they also got me a lot of strange looks from people. I got the same kind of looks on the highway; I can only imagine what those folks must have thought seeing a guy in the middle of nowhere pushing a shopping cart. Sometimes, all I could do was smile.

By the end of day nine we were approaching Terra Nova National Park with our walk through Newfoundland about 25% complete. We had hit our first real roadblock and managed through it; we were learning as we went.

The next challenge we encountered was one we hadn't anticipated. It turns out the tourism season in Newfoundland doesn't really get underway until the May long weekend so early May isn't a great time to be staying in an RV park. In fact Newfoundland can often experience serious snow storms in May. We were fortunate; the only snow we encountered was minor and didn't really slow us down. The RV parks didn't have a lot of services up and running however, and in a lot of parks that meant no laundry and no showers, so for the first month we were really roughing it.

Internet connection was another challenge, a lot of places were remote and not having internet brought our social media and other communications to a halt. This was particularly hard for Marie whose entire workday in the RV relied on the internet. Heating the RV was also a challenge. The RV was heated with propane but propane was hard to find. Because of safety measures and the pump upgrades needed to sell propane, there were only about ten places on the entire island where we could get a tank filled, this was a problem since we had to fill the RV every 3-4 days. It really took some creative thinking to keep things running during the first 30 days in Newfoundland and we gained a deeper understanding of how to problem solve and work smarter. Many days, after the walking was done, Marie and I would strategize while Bobby shopped, cooked, did laundry and maintained the vehicles. We were learning how to live and work together in an RV (which is a challenge all by itself); each of us had different skills and abilities and we were learning how to use them to grow stronger as a team.

Marie

When preparing the RV back at home, I hadn't been the least bit concerned about giving up the comforts of home. The RV we received from Fraserway was new and quite cozy; some might even say flamboyant. Joe and I had the bedroom at the back of the RV and luckily it had storage space for clothes and linens because apparently I had a lot; I was packing for 17 months on the road after all! In addition to my seasonal/current clothes, I had one tote full of shoes and boots (I couldn't decide which ones to leave at home so I packed most of them), one tote full of winter clothing and one tote full of outdoor gear. Bobby's bed was at the front of the RV, above the driver and passenger seats. The RV also had a couch that pulled out into an extra bed and a table with two bench seats that had storage space underneath. Across from the table and couch was the kitchen with a sink, microwave, stove and fridge with freezer. There were five cupboards above and five below the countertop. Between the kitchen and our bedroom there was a shower on one side of the aisle and a toilet/sink/mirror on the other. It was a beautiful, well equipped RV, not quite home, but considering we were advocating for homelessness prevention, it was more than sufficient.

Living with Joe and Bobby in a space that was less than 300 square feet was much easier than I expected. Of course Joe and I were already comfortable with each other, since we'd reconnected in 2012. We had pretty much been inseparable. Bobby proved to be a gem to live with; he was neat, quiet and very amiable. By the time we left Newfoundland 45 days later on June 14, we were all getting nicely accustomed to our shared space in the RV.

33

As we made our way towards Clarenville, I couldn't help but notice how similar this road was to BC's own Sea to Sky highway which runs from Vancouver to Whistler. With its big sweeping hills and vistas that look out towards the ocean, the entire Avalon Peninsula reminded me of BC. The hills, rocks, coniferous forests and ocean views reminded me of home, yet I couldn't have been farther from it.

As I mentioned earlier, our mornings generally started at 5:00 am when we would leave base camp and drive to the spot where we'd left off the day before. On day eight we saw our first moose, a huge, majestic creature. I marvelled that the first five to six feet of height is all leg. One of the biggest driving hazards in Newfoundland is hitting a moose, so we were extra careful in the early morning and at dusk. By the time we were halfway across Newfoundland we stopped counting how many we'd seen.

On the morning of May 9, I had already been up and down a few serious hills when I noticed an eagle circling way up in the sky. I wasn't sure if it was a bald eagle or not; it certainly looked like one. Having lived on the coast of BC where they nest in the winter months, I've seen a lot of eagles. Yet no matter how many times I see a bald eagle, they always take my breath away; maybe it's the reverence I've observed that First Nations have for them or maybe I just deeply respect these magnificent birds of prey.

As I walked I felt like this one was watching me or maybe even following me. It was odd, yet comforting. I lost sight of my friend as I crested a large hill flanked by a rock face on the left and a cliff on the right. The view was amazing as I looked out onto the Atlantic Ocean and a series of small inlets and coves. As the road took a little bend the wind started to blow pretty good and the ocean air filled my senses. Just at that moment I looked down and saw a huge eagle feather on the grass at my feet. As the wind whipped around me, I couldn't believe the feather was just sitting there. I'm not sure exactly what it meant, but I felt it was a sign of some kind. It felt significant. What was even more wondrous was that just a few hundred meters above me on the adjacent rock cliff, I saw the nest. As I walked a little further the combination of rain and sun produced a beautiful rainbow. It was too much beauty to take in, in one day. I was moved by the magic Mother Nature was performing for me.

Later that afternoon I remembered something my mother had posted on my Facebook page before I left BC. She said when you find a feather it will be a reminder that I am thinking and praying for your safe travel. I still have the feather and it is a special memento. What's very interesting is that I had never before found a feather in a natural setting like that. I have hiked and walked thousands of kilometres in BC's most remote places (which are filled with eagles, incidentally) and never found an eagle feather. The meaning I took out of this lucky find was that the universe and all that is good, natural and beautiful in this world was firmly behind me and *The Push for Change* campaign.

Before we left the Avalon Peninsula, we had one more very special thing happen. Our greatest support in those early days came from UA Local 740. Bruce Power was one of the leaders in this group and one morning I got a text from him asking if I would stop and meet with his kids. He wanted to share this with them and felt it was important. I shrugged it off, but he told me that in their eyes I was a hero and meeting me would be a special moment. Bobby and I arranged to meet Bruce at a gas station after we finished our walk for the day. We pulled in and shortly after I was introduced to Jake and Lilly, who had been following what we were doing through their mom's Facebook page. They had been watching as our campaign developed, knew when we left St. John's and even understood why we were doing this walk. Jake told me he had something for me and pulled out a $50 bill; it was his birthday money and he wanted to give it to *The Push for Change*. We posed for pictures and I gave both Lilly and Jake a few small gifts to thank them for their contribution. Later that afternoon it hit me just how big a deal this was; we had inspired these young people to do something to support the cause. It was an amazing interaction that would be repeated thousands of times as I walked across the country.

On May 10, we visited The Newfoundland Youth Detention Centre and did a presentation to the youth and staff. It was a powerful event. We also did some smaller presentations in Clarenville, for a faith-based youth club. Although the events were small they made an impact on us as a team and the groups we met. I have to say that Newfoundlanders welcomed us and were super supportive everywhere we went.

Shortly after Terra Nova National Park I started to hit my stride, my body was working really well and Bobby and I had developed a rhythm that made getting up to tackle 24 km each day easier. Not too easy though. In fact, some days were downright difficult due to weather. It's true the people of Newfoundland were warm and welcoming but I think that's to make up for their downright inhospitable weather. One morning I woke up at 5:30 am to the sound of rain pummelling the roof of the RV. It was thunderous and all I could think about was that I had to leave the warmth of my bed to go and walk in this slop for 6-7 hours. That morning I walked for 21 km straight without the rain letting up and 12 km of that was in a torrential downpour. The only good thing about the rain, wind and cold temperatures is it helped us figure out what gear worked and what we needed to adapt.

34

On day 16 we arrived in Gander; for anyone who has seen the musical *Come from Away*, this is the town it was set in. The community was warm and welcoming; we had an event with the mayor and local community stakeholders and donations were very generous. The local Rotary Club held a meeting for us and also made a donation. When we walked into town, Debbie the massage therapist from St. John's was waiting for us. She was so eager to help that she drove all the way to Gander to work on my tight legs and lower back and like so many other people we encountered, she wouldn't think of letting us pay her. I felt truly indebted to Debbie for helping me overcome my sore knee and I guess I praised her so much that Bobby and Marie were jealous, so I suggested Debbie work on them too. By the time we parted ways, the whole team was sad to say goodbye and Debbie told us that if she could, she would have joined us for the entire trip.

Gander was full of special moments but the biggest surprise was walking into the local fish and chip shop and seeing Wayne and Dee Branchaud. Wayne was an avid supporter and our community champion for Brantford, Ontario. The two of them decided to surprise us and drop in on the campaign. The following day Wayne joined me for a long walk on the Trans-Canada.

Our visit to Gander also coincided with a 5 km fundraising walk organized by NAV Canada (the organization in charge of air traffic control). They were holding simultaneous walks in major cities all across Canada with half of the money going to PFC. I had the pleasure of speaking to this organization prior to the campaign, which is when they had pledged their support. I joined the local group in a parking lot near the airport and said a few words before the walk got underway. They let us know that when *The Push for Change* campaign reached Ottawa, there would be a cheque presentation at their head office.

On day 26 we moved our base camp to Gateway to the North RV Park in Deer Lake, where we were greeted with hugs, two free nights, some homemade jam, a jar of pickled mussels, three moose steaks and a big "welcome bye." Newfoundland really is a unique place, where the people are as nice as the winter is long.

Shortly after leaving Gander we reached Grand Falls Windsor, the halfway mark for Newfoundland. I remember the sun was really nice the morning we hit the 500 km point along the highway (although our base camp hadn't reached this town yet). During the campaign our logistics plan was simple; we moved base camp every 150 km or so. Each time we set up a new camp, we would start the next day by backtracking to our previous day's completion point to begin the day's walk. It would usually take us 5-6 days to reach the town we were camped in. Once we reached our camp, we would walk away from that town for 5-6 days and then we would move again. It was kind of a leap frog approach and we set it up like that so we wouldn't have the extra work of moving more than we needed to. Moving days required a lot more work and took up valuable time. Thankfully, most of the work was done by Bobby; he was a master at moving and setting up. Our longest days were the ones when we had to drive 150 km just to get to our jump-off point.

Hitting the 500 km marker was one of our first milestones and I had stopped to take a picture for social media when a big black truck pulled up behind us. By now we had been on the island just shy of a month and although it's a big place, it's a close-knit community and news travels fast. We had been getting great coverage on TV, the radio and in local papers and folks were getting to know us. A man got out of the truck and walked up to me with his wallet in his hand. He pulled out a hundred dollar bill and thrust it into my hand. What struck me in that moment was the look on his face, he had big tears in his eyes and I think if he had tried to speak, he would have broken down. I thanked him and then I got emotional. Something about what we were doing had inspired this guy and although I will never know what his personal story was, I knew we were doing more than walking across Newfoundland; we were touching hearts and changing minds. This kind of thing happened so often during our trek that we had to create a separate column in Marie's fundraising ledger for "roadside" donations.

One of the commitments we made before the campaign started was to speak at a handful of conferences during our time on the road. In order to accommodate the conferences, we had to structure our days off in sequence, jump on a plane, do the event and fly right back so we wouldn't fall behind in the campaign. Thankfully, we were near a small regional airport. The first conference was with the Educational Computing Network of Ontario (ECNO) which provides IT services within the Ontario school system. What was very cool for us is that their conference theme was "Pushing for Change" and they had collectively decided to make PFC their charity this year. Following our presentation, Marie and I explained that it was our day off from the campaign and we had flown from Newfoundland, where we were about 600 km into our trek across Canada. Folks were inspired and moved by our commitment and by the end of the conference, they raised almost $12,000 for PFC. Marie and I drove back to Toronto, flew to Halifax and then on to Deer Lake, Newfoundland and with very little rest took up where we left off the next morning when the alarm buzzed at 5:00 am.

There were many times throughout the campaign where both Marie and I spread ourselves too thin, but we were excited that everything we had worked so hard to accomplish was actually happening and we didn't want to miss even one opportunity.

As we moved on from Deer Lake to Corner Brook, I was surprised at the landscape which again reminded me of BC with its mountains, water and huge views; it was breathtaking. When we reached the city of Corner Brook, the local Rotary hosted a meeting for us. We also visited a high school and had a meeting at the local youth drop-in centre. After Corner Brook we headed south and with one final event in Port Aux Basques, there was just 220 km remaining between us and the ferry that would take us to Sydney, Nova Scotia.

Walking so many kilometres day after day can get a little boring, so I was always excited when I spotted something on the side of the road. Bobby and I jokingly called this, "roadside treasure." One morning I looked into the ditch and saw a yellow Frisbee. When I picked it up I began to laugh uncontrollably and Bobby stopped the truck to see what the commotion was. Seeing the bright yellow Frisbee with the famous

1970's happy face laying there, I couldn't help but feel it was like a scene straight out of the movie *Forrest Gump*.

As we made our way to Port Aux Basques we had been warned about a particularly windy section of Newfoundland called Wreckhouse. Locals said that on any given day without warning the winds can climb to hurricane force. Bobby and I had finished our walk for the day and were just 50 km away so we decided to drive on and scout out the area. When we arrived, it was a beautiful, balmy day. Sure it was a little windy as one would expect, but certainly nothing to fuss about. I laughed off the warnings as exaggeration from the locals.

Two days later I understood exactly what they were talking about when we came face to face with wind speeds of 150 kmh. We had left our base camp at Pirate Haven RV Park in Robinson (where they had kindly given us free nights and a donation to the campaign) and were headed south towards our jump-off point near Wreckhouse. By the time we reached the end of the Codroy Valley near Doyles, the van was swerving from side to side. I asked Bobby why he was driving so erratically and he told me it wasn't him; the wind was literally pushing the van across the road. It was time to stop and re-evaluate, as it stood there was no way we could drive any further, let alone try to walk with the shopping cart. We stopped the vehicle near a warning sign that told us winds were expected to reach 160 kmh, which is technically hurricane force winds.

We headed back to base camp and checked the government weather channel. They were predicting the winds would subside by the following day and with some luck we would be able to make the final push to the ferry terminal through Wreckhouse and the community of Port Aux Basque. The next morning's weather showed promise so we cautiously headed out; it was still windy but not dangerously so. We got to the jump spot and proceeded through Wreckhouse to Port Aux Basque. The winds still topped 60-70 kmh and were strong enough to knock you down if you weren't sure-footed. We were only four kilometres from the ferry when the skies opened up and it began to pour. Marie was a real trooper and walked the last few kilometres with me despite the wind that slammed the rain into our faces. Cold and wet, we made our way to an event that was being hosted in the local hockey rink; the gathering was small but friendly and even the local RCMP came out to support us.

Afterwards, we said our goodbyes to Newfoundland and headed to the ferry, which boarded at night and took eight hours to cross the channel. Marie and I splurged for a cabin and managed to get a little sleep before we arrived in Sydney, Nova Scotia the next morning. After a month and a half of walking we now had 925 km and one big province behind us.

35

One of the most significant realizations about *The Push for Change* and the importance of our mission occurred to me at the side of a rainy, lonely highway one afternoon just before Corner Brook. As you can imagine, walking so many kilometres both during the campaign and while I was training, I found more than my share of coins. I'm not sure if I'm the only one; but I seem to find change everywhere. Quarters, nickels, dimes and the occasional loonie or toonie. In fact, I still have a large jar filled with coins that I picked up during my 17-month journey across Canada. Every time I looked down and saw a coin it reminded me of why we were pushing for change, in some kind of spiritual way it also felt like validation that something bigger was supporting our work.

As I wandered along the misty highway in one of my monotonous walking trances (let's face it, walking 24 km every day can get a little tedious) I wasn't thinking about anything in particular. It had been raining for several days and the portion of highway I was on was dirt and gravel, which made anything reflective stand out. As I turned my head something caught my eye and I bent down and dug out a half-buried penny from the dirt. It was amazing that I even saw it, the penny was so masterfully camouflaged (the identical colour of the dirt that surrounded it). It also had no earthly business being where I found it, given that we were a good 30 km from any kind of community. It could not have been a more remote location to discover this lonely penny.

The penny was caked in dirt and mud and I had to bang it on the side of my cart to clean off the chunks. I held the penny in my hand as I continued walking. I still had most of the day ahead of me and as I continued with the penny in my hand, I couldn't help but feel there was something significant about it. It meant something but I couldn't quite put my finger on it. As I walked on, reaching 12 km, 15 km and then 20 km; the meaning began to crystallize. I pulled out the penny and looked at it again. It was dirty, rough and corroded; it didn't look like the other pennies I had found. It was evident just by looking at it that it had definitely seen better days.

The clouds began to part and the sun poked through as the metaphor hit me with the same blinding clarity. I found this penny in the street; it had spent days, months or even years living outside in the cold and wet. At one time this penny had been shiny and new but that sparkle had long departed. Yet despite how it looked or what it had been through, this penny by its very nature could never, ever lose its value. And just like a penny, a person can't ever lose their value. What I held in my hand was something that represented every homeless young person; the brokenness, the heartache and the abuse, but also the hope. Hope that we could push for change and rethink our approach to youth homelessness, to see the value in every person despite their appearance or their circumstances. I clung to that penny on the ferry ride to Sydney knowing I needed to share this wonderful story and give this penny to someone that I thought could help us create the change we were pushing for.

36

Shortly after we arrived in Sydney we met Mel Gillis, the business manager for UA Local 682, who escorted us to our hotel. Marie and I were thrilled at the idea of having our own room. Living in an RV with three people takes coordination and patience. The hotel room was lovely and we settled in quickly. Later that day we had an event planned in downtown Sydney. It was well attended and we were excited to begin engagement into our second province. We had some friends from the mayor's office as well as local youth service providers and the Chief of Police, Peter McIsaac, in attendance. Thanks to RCMP Assistant Commissioner Roger Brown from Fredericton, New Brunswick, we received excellent support from law enforcement leaders throughout Atlantic Canada. After sharing our story and passing the can around we raised $1,000 and then Mel Gillis from UA Local 682 presented us with a cheque for $10,000! It was awesome knowing that we had such great support.

Before the day finished, Chief McIsaac took part in the PFC Barefoot Challenge. The concept was simple, shed your shoes and socks and make a donation to *The Push for Change*. The challenge was directly linked to my story of about how I had sold my shoes on the streets of Vancouver. When I had shared this at a speaking engagement in Fredericton it resonated so much that the Barefoot Challenge became a fundraising campaign. Fredericton Police Chief Leanne Fitch had taken part and she was the one who challenged Chief McIsaac. Some of the others taking part in the challenge were MP Matt DeCourcey, Deputy Premier Stephen Horsman, members of UA Local 325, and even Premier Brian Gallant of New Brunswick. It was cool for us to see the organic way people engaged with PFC beyond the walk.

After our event in downtown Sydney, we met a group of students from a local First Nation's school for a Walk with Joe. Thanks to Mel Gillis (who had connected us with the school), they were excited to have the students involved with PFC. After our walk, I had a chance to talk to the students. There's nothing I love more than being in front of young people telling my story. When I share my experience in an honest, authentic way, I can tell I've got their attention because they lean forward to listen and they ask questions. It's an incredible gift to be able to reach kids with a message.

During our time together, we talked about how I had ended up on the street. Then we talked about addiction, family violence, being bullied as a child and the negative impact of low self-esteem. We also talked about following your dreams and the importance of setting goals and going after them. It was a small group but they had so many questions for me about the campaign. They wanted to know where I slept and how many shoes I had worn out. They wanted to know about the shopping cart and how we moved around as a campaign. We left them with some small gifts including a pin and a PFC information card and after a group photo we headed to our last stop of the day.

The hotel that UA Local 682 put us up in was right across the street from an active job site where some of their members were working. We went over to the job site where we gathered a number of members together and told them how much we appreciated their support for PFC. Mel was happy we took the time to visit and before we left we gave everybody some chocolate. We had several cases of fundraising chocolate in the RV that was left over from a group of well-meaning supporters. When they couldn't sell the chocolate, we had bought it back and now it was sitting in our hot RV. We had no intention of eating 100 bars of chocolate and chocolate-covered almonds. The guys were super appreciative and I was happy to see the chocolate go.

37

The next morning Bobby and I headed back to the ferry terminal and began walking around the perimeter of Sydney. We were met by the Cape Breton Regional Police and over the next six hours we walked around the entire city. The only police support we'd had or needed so far was back in St. John's. We'd completed over 900 km across Newfoundland without support, so having a police escort in front and behind us was really cool, it felt like we were a big deal. Because of the media coverage and police escort we also received lots of supportive honks. The day whipped by and before we knew it we were wrapping up at Sydney Forks on Route 4. We took out our kilometre marker, wrote the current number on it and had the officers pose for a picture to post on social media. The kilometre marker was an idea I thought up and Marie made happen; it showed the number of kilometres walked to date along with the names of our sponsors. We thought it was absolutely brilliant!

When we arrived in the lot where the RV was parked, I jumped inside to grab a couple of things to take to the room. Marie and I had plans to go out for a nice dinner and enjoy some much-needed time together. As I grabbed my dress shirt from the back, I noticed a rotten smell and saw water on the floor near the fridge. When I opened the freezer it became apparent what the smell was. Everything in the freezer was melted and rotting. For some reason the fridge wasn't working either. I was concerned at first because I thought the whole unit might need to be replaced, but my concern turned to frustration when we traced the problem backwards. It turns out when RV tanks are filled at a gas station; they turn the propane valve off for safety reasons. Bobby had forgotten to turn the tanks back on and the fridge/freezer ran on propane; it also ran on electricity if you were plugged in, which we weren't. Without access to propane, the freezer/fridge stopped working.

I was frustrated at three things. One, we had wasted a lot of food. Two, this was completely avoidable. Three, Bobby would not take responsibility; he insisted it was the gas station's fault. It seemed that things like this were happening almost every day, not big things maybe, but small incidents that cost us time and sometimes inconvenienced and distracted the entire team. Bobby was incredibly loyal and helpful and he would do anything to support the campaign, but his mistakes left us scrambling and dealing with things that were completely avoidable. It was beginning to worry me as I saw that the coming months would be much, much busier and we needed the entire team to be on their game if we were going to make it through Ontario. I was both angry and concerned.

With Bobby working to resolve the problem, Marie and I headed out for the night we had promised to one another. It was a beautiful Sydney evening and buskers played their fiddles as we walked along the pier. We ended up at a lovely restaurant where we shared a huge seafood tower stacked high with lobster, shrimp, cod, halibut and an array of shellfish. We stuffed ourselves and enjoyed the local music as we watched the sun set. It was a lovely evening and I would go back to this place in a heartbeat. It's hard to describe the hospitality in Atlantic Canada, everywhere we went we were treated like family, the people are warm, sincere and honest. Marie and I fell in love with this part of the country and vowed to return.

Given the rough weather and sparse population, there had been a lot of lonely miles in Newfoundland and at times I questioned if we were making a difference. The greatest fear I had for the campaign was being irrelevant. When we arrived at our first stop in Nova Scotia it felt very different. There was excitement and engagement on so many levels. Every day that we walked, we posted on social media and every day we noticed that people from across the country and beyond were activating and responding to what we were doing. Our social media presence was growing and we were building an audience of support far beyond the roads we walked along.

As the sole person responsible for events, fundraising, media coordination and liaison with the Ontario Provincial Police (who would be hosting a large number of events for us); Marie's job was intensifying by the day. The campaign had massive things happening down the road and it was Marie's responsibility to coordinate it all. While my job was to walk, talk and compile video and pictures for social media (in addition to overseeing Bobby's role), everything else was Marie's responsibility. Looking back, we seriously underestimated her workload; she should have had a full-time assistant from day one.

Day 49 began in Sydney Forks and after an hour or so I found myself walking parallel to Bras d'Or Lake. I later learned this lake is a mix of salt and fresh water, one of the largest of its kind in the world. The day was perfect; the sun was shining brightly, the flowers were blooming and the fruit trees were covered with beautiful blossoms. The birds were singing and a warm breeze blew in my face; much different from a few days ago in Wreckhouse. I realized as I walked along that I needed to shed some layers. For the first time since the trek began I got rid of my winter shell and long pants and by the end of my walk it felt like summer; 25 degrees without a cloud in the sky. I decided to try an ice bath in the lake only to find the water warm. Well maybe not warm, but not cold. I was accustomed to submersing myself in 3-5°C water and this lake was warm in comparison. Fortunately, we had a large plastic tub in the van that we could use to create an ice bath. Maybe today would be a good day to try it out.

I was about 10 km into my morning walk when I heard someone calling out. I turned to see a woman running down her driveway. It was a steep driveway and she was not a young woman and I feared that I was about to watch her do a face-plant on the pavement. I turned to go meet her and she slowed down. In her hand she had something for me but it took her a minute to catch her breath. She explained that her husband had been at our event in Sydney the day before and she'd been watching out her window all morning for us. She gave Bobby and me a big bag of homemade treats, a special Nova Scotia recipe. I asked what they were and she said, "Oatcakes." I was a bit puzzled, I had never heard of oatcakes before so I took one out and had a big bite. They were delicious and not as sweet as an oatmeal cookie. They kind of reminded me of the oat bars they sell at Starbucks but way tastier. I thanked her and continued on.

The locals were really supportive as we made our way along Route 4 towards Port Hawkesbury and at the end of day 49 we reached the 989 km mark, almost four digits. Hard to believe we were nearly 1,000 km into our trek. During the Calgary to Vancouver walk that number had seemed huge, but in comparison to what we had left to go with this campaign, it was only a dent. One of the things I've learned from my experience so far is that if you set your goals really high and fail, you fail way above average. It's an interesting game to play. I have always set my goals really high and truthfully, most of the goals I've set I failed to reach. That said I have always outdone my previous year's goals, outperformed my previous personal best and broken through what I initially believed was impossible. So setting your goal high isn't such a bad strategy. It has consistently helped me to perform at my very best and that's something I feel good about. If you give something your best and fail at least you know deep down it was your best. If *The Push for Change* failed for some reason, if I got injured or, God forbid, there was an accident and I didn't make it, at least I knew I gave this campaign absolutely everything I had. That's my definition of success; being all in, completely committed, fearless, faith-filled and action-oriented, even in the face of uncertainty.

The next morning the weather was beautiful once again, sunshine, blue sky and flowers everywhere. Bobby and I were so fortunate, to wake up each morning with the sun and witness the start of the day; the mist, the scenery, and quiet mornings where the world slowly came to life in front of our eyes. To describe the natural wonders we observed would take another five volumes and there are some things that words and even pictures can't describe. Needless to say I was grateful for getting to see Canada in this way and witness nature from multiple angles.

One of the ways we promoted the PFC campaign was when I spoke at conferences. A year earlier, I had spoken in Halifax for the Association of Municipal Administrators of Nova Scotia (AMANS). This particular morning, I was about 14 km into my day when I was startled from behind. I had my headphones on when I felt someone come up behind me and I squealed as she touched my shoulder. After we laughed a bit she introduced herself and told me she had heard me speak at AMANS. She was out for a jog and asked if she could join me. I agreed happily. We spoke briefly about the challenges that face Sydney and the area and before we knew it our time together was done. We stopped for a short break in front of the late great Rita McNeal's tea house for a picture with our kilometre sign and said our farewells. I thought it was odd that we ran into each other like that but it was something that happened a lot on the trek. I ran into people I knew in every province and territory we visited. People say Canada is a big place, and in land mass it is but the country is actually small when you start to connect the relationships that we each have.

38

Our last few days on Cape Breton Island flew by. In the small town of Port Hawkesbury we received a warm reception from the local Rotary Club and shared the PFC story over lunch. Back on the road, our media rep had set up some interviews just before the causeway, first with a local newspaper and then the radio folks. After 30 minutes of interviews we left Cape Breton, which was sad because we loved this area so much. Marie and I vowed to return as tourists!

The Cano causeway links Cape Breton to the mainland portion of Nova Scotia. This long narrow causeway is very busy, with lots of big trucks. I didn't want to crowd the road and create a safety hazard so I took the shopping cart up over to the right of the metal guardrail and slowly walked across. It was slow going through the weeds and rocks but it was the only safe place I could walk.

When I reached the other side of the causeway I watched a lobster boat crew work their traps as I bent to pull the weeds out of the wheels of the shopping cart. It was beautiful to watch, the boat had a big front bow and long rectangle back. The captain steered as the first mate used a hook to pull up the lobster traps. Then he would clear out the catch, re-bait the trap and send it back over. In the few minutes I was there I watched them clean and re-bait at least a dozen traps. What was beautiful about it from my vantage point was how fluid it all was, like a Norman Rockwell painting come to life and so perfectly Nova Scotian.

With only six kilometres left in my day, I heard someone call out as I passed a gas station. I turned and met a man running up to me. "How you doing Joe?" he asked. I was a little surprised he knew my name. I asked where we'd met and he said I'd been the keynote speaker at the Home Hardware Spring Market conference. I remembered the event; in fact we were headed to a Home Hardware store in Truro that had a bunch of events planned. He thanked me, gave me a pat on the back and stuffed $20 in my hand. I walked away feeling so inspired, I was meeting so many people in random places that had either met me before or heard about us on the news. In fact, several times a day we were stopped on the highway by people who wanted to give a donation. As we approached Canada Day, I felt more patriotic than ever.

Bobby fuelled up the van at the gas station and we headed out to finish our day. I was inspired and full of energy and as we headed up the hill we passed in front of some guys who were working a boom lift with a sign for The Cove Motel & Restaurant. As we approached I looked up and saw this huge lobster and I had to get a picture with me beside this monster. I yelled up to the guys and they lowered the boom and came over to us. The lead guy had heard about us on the news and gave me an attaboy and a donation. I asked if he would let me in the boom and take me up to get a picture beside the lobster. He said, and I quote, "No problem bye." So up I went 40 ft in the air, smiling like a fool in front of this massive lobster; I felt a bit like Rick Mercer when he does crazy Canadian things. It was more fun than I deserved! I only wished Bobby had gotten a clearer picture of it. It was just a perfect finish to our day. I have many fond memories of Nova Scotia but that day was a good one. Before we left the area Bobby and I doubled back and bought three huge fresh lobsters from the same boat I had been watching earlier and brought them back to the RV to cook up.

Our base camp was located near a tiny community called Havre Boucher at an RV Park called Hyclass. As was customary when we checked in, we told the RV folks what we were doing and asked for a break. Bobby was really good at the asking, he was so excited and inspired about the campaign that most times people just gave him whatever he asked for so we were given free nights, meals, fuel and in some cases, even donations. We were very appreciative of these businesses, a lot of which were small family operations as this was their bread.

The lady at Hyclass was very accommodating and gave us a reduced rate. The manager asked if we also wanted to engage with a local 4H Club, so one evening Marie and I went to the community centre and spoke to a group of about 15 young ones. It was a special night and when we finished the club leader gave us the member dues from that evening. We didn't expect a donation when we agreed to do the event; as with many of the events that we did we didn't go in with the idea we would be leaving with money. The campaign was primarily to raise awareness and reduce stigma, so getting a chance to impact and inspire young minds was a true blessing and we were happy to be invited.

The next day Marie and I headed back to Ontario. Laurentian University had granted me an Honorary Doctorate of Letters and it was a big deal for me. We drove to Sydney, then flew to Toronto and drove to Barrie. The following day with all my family present, I delivered one of the most impassioned speeches of my life. The President and Chancellor both commented that it was the most inspiring speech they had ever heard at convocation. With the ink barely dry on my honorary doctorate we flew back to Halifax, then on to Sydney and the following morning I was back out walking, except now I could put "Dr." in front of my name. Although it was pretty cool, all I could think about was how I could leverage the accolade to get more attention for PFC.

The RV was spotless when we returned, which was something Bobby was very good at. He wasn't the best with logistics, mapping, directions or locating suitable RV parks, but he was amazing at cleaning the RV, shopping, cooking, maintaining the vehicles and keeping us properly stocked. His strengths made him the perfect guy for the campaign at this point, but I had reservations about how he would manage down the line.

The next UA Local event was super cool. Just off Route 104 heading towards Antigonish, UA Local 244 had arranged a lunch, meet and greet together with a show and shine. After a short talk, Business Manager

Ben Chisholm presented us with a $5,000 donation from the Local and $10,000 from Nova Scotia Pipe Trades. We were completely blown away by their generosity. We thanked everyone and gathered outside for a ceremonial run. Many of the UA members had brought their motorcycles and Ben had his Mustang so with Harleys thundering and muscle cars growling, we slowly made our way to the highway where they were happy to hit open road. As the bikes roared off we continued our walk for another couple of hours before our day was complete. We were $15,000 richer in donations thanks to UA and the Pipe Trades; it was a very good day.

After Antigonish we headed south towards the eastern shore. Instead of going directly across the top of the province and hitting New Brunswick near Amherst, we had opted to take a half circle route from Cape Breton to Antigonish, then down the eastern shore to Dartmouth and Halifax, then up to Truro and over to New Glasgow, ending up in Pictou where we would catch the ferry. It added an extra 244 km but we felt it was important to hit Halifax and also go to PEI. Unfortunately, it meant we left out the entire lower peninsula of Nova Scotia, but since we didn't have any planned events (and it would have taken an additional 40 days to cover that ground) it made sense logistically. Within a couple of days we found ourselves walking along the eastern shore, which was quiet and really beautiful. Taylor Bay Provincial Park had something I never thought I'd see on the east coast of Canada, crescent shaped beaches and crystal clear water; it reminded me of the Caribbean with one exception, the water was pretty cold.

Along this stretch my knee began to flare up again; it was the same problem, my IT band was tight and pulling my kneecap out of alignment. We got a recommendation from one of the UA members to see a chiropractor in Halifax and he was a miracle worker. He was a former NHL hockey player who had leveraged his experience into a career in sports medicine and he knew exactly what to do. Using a combination of acupuncture and electric tens therapy, in minutes my IT band was released. It was amazing. I also received some excellent RMT from the same office and I was set. I visited a few more times during the two weeks we were in the area and those treatments made a world of difference.

Around the same time, Sean introduced me to the Wim Hof breathing technique. Wim Hof was also an advocate of ice water submersion. I began to use the technique in addition to my ice baths and things began to improve greatly. The eastern shores of Nova Scotia were beautiful but they were also narrow and curvy which meant a lot of my walking was done with my right leg lower than my left (and my body on more of an angle). These small differences caused problems but thankfully, as we approached Dartmouth the highway levelled out again.

My daughter Loren came to join us for ten awesome days together. Whenever Loren was around, we tried to cram in as much fun as possible. One evening at the RV Park in Dartmouth we planned our own special Canada Day celebration with a huge bunch of fireworks. We tried to light them in the RV park, which was a no, no, so we kept them and lit them off over the lake together with some of the other campers.

Our arrival in Halifax and the days that followed were a blur. Don Farmer, a good friend that I had met years earlier through Brunswick Street Mission, helped us engage in the city. We joined a pancake breakfast with Mayor Rick Savage, followed by a Canada Day Parade with the Royal Nova Scotia Tattoo and over 60,000 spectators that ended with a speech in the park in front of a crowd. It was super fun, as was the BBQ hosted by our friends at UA Local 56. We also dropped in on a breakfast at Brunswick Street Mission, but my favourite event was inside a local youth shelter called Phoenix House. I shared my story, after which a young woman of about 17 who seemed inspired but skeptical asked me, "What advice would you give someone like me?" As she said it, I could see that something deep inside her was hurt. I could sense her brokenness, her pain and her sense of failure. I could see she might not have thought much of herself and that her possibilities were likely hidden from her view. I saw this as an opportunity. I said to her "Despite everything that has ever happened in your life, despite what people have said to you and what people may have done to you. Despite what you believe about yourself, despite all the crap that life has given you that you didn't deserve, in spite of all of that inside you is unlimited potential, there is more in you than you can see."

I'm not sure if it was what I said or how I said it, but what I told this girl is what's at the core of everything that PFC stands for. When she heard my words I could see it touched her in a deep and meaningful way. I knew in that moment that I had connected and given her the same gift Gus gave to me on that park bench 20 years earlier.

After some pizza and sweets, we left Halifax and headed north towards our next event in Truro.

39

On day 69 of the campaign, I was arguing with Bobby about something stupid when all of a sudden a pain shot up my back, then down my right arm and leg and dropped me to the floor of the RV like a sack of rocks. I lay there helpless for a few minutes during which even the slightest movement was painful. I pulled myself across the floor with my hands and tried to sit up. Marie managed to get me an emergency appointment at the clinic in Halifax; however after 60 minutes with the RMT I was still no better so I went back to the RV. The only thing I could think to do now was follow the advice Dr. Sean Richardson and others had been giving me for years; keep moving, stretch it out and don't let it seize up.

In the past this kind of thing would have landed me on the couch for two weeks on muscle relaxants. Unfortunately, I didn't have that luxury. The follow morning when the alarm went off, I turned on my stomach and slowly inched my way out of bed onto my hands and knees. From there, I gingerly stood up and stretched until I was limber enough to move. Bobby and I loaded up the RV with the stretch mat and my blue foam roller and headed out to the highway. At the jump-off point I stretched again and rolled my back out then started walking very slowly. After five kilometres my back loosened up and although it was very tender for the remainder of the day, I managed to get in 24 km.

The boxer Jack Dempsey is quoted as saying that a champion is someone who gets up when they can't. That day I was a champion, what got me out of bed that morning was the thought of that young girl and so many others like her who have lost sight of their possibility. I felt like my walk that day was for every kid that got dealt a crappy hand. I got up for them with determination and a resiliency I never knew I had.

On day 71, our camp moved to the Scotia Pines RV Park near Truro and we prepared for another extraordinary day engaging with the community. After walking in from the highway, we met James MacPherson from Home Hardware at the local McDonalds along with a member of the Truro Police Department. We took out the celebrity cart and began a walk through town. Bobby was in front and the officer was behind us as we slowly made our way through the community. After about five kilometres we came to a gathering point where we were joined by the Boys and Girls Club, the Truro Fire Department, the mayor and a large group from Home Hardware. They had made support placards and welcomed us to Truro. After a short speech we led the group back along the road through town; our plan was to finish at the Home Hardware store. This was the first time we had a parade of walkers that was organized just for us. As I walked beside Marie, I was inspired to look back over my shoulder and see a long string of people following. Thirty minutes later, we were greeted by a group of cheering supporters in the Home Hardware parking lot along with a BBQ and refreshments. The sign out front welcomed *The Push for Change*. The store owner gave a short talk and they presented us with a cheque for $5,692. I thanked everyone and told a condensed version of my story. It was very inspiring to have such enthusiastic support for PFC.

As we left Home Hardware we were approached by a woman who worked at the Nova Institute for Women and she asked us if we would consider going into the institution. I told her we would love to engage with the women, however Nova is a federal prison and I was doubtful that she would be able to get us security clearance. Amazingly, with help from Marie we were granted clearance in just three days. Marie and I arrived at the facility and were cleared through security along with my shopping cart. As I shared my story, I talked in depth about the challenges I had faced during my early life at home, my drug addiction and homelessness. I also shared the hope of recovery and what happened after I put my troubled life behind me. Marie and I also told them our love story and how we had reconnected 30 years after dating in high school. It was a beautiful and emotional day and when we were done a First Nations leader in the group presented us with dream catchers and a blanket. The blanket was a special gift and we accepted it with great reverence. As we left we were told that because we had secured access we could now visit any federal institution in the country; that was pretty cool.

Once we left Truro we headed east on Highway 104, which was counter intuitive but necessary if we were going to catch the ferry from Pictou to PEI. We had one more event to hit before leaving the province.

My back was feeling much better and my knee problems had diminished somewhat, partly because the highway shoulders were wider and flatter, but also because I was stretching regularly, doing ice baths and using the Wim Hof breathing technique. The best part about the breathing technique was that it completely eliminated my anxiety about injury. I liked the feeling of fearlessness that it inspired and continued to use the technique for the remainder of the campaign.

On the road to our last stop in New Glasgow we received a unique donation. I was walking under an overpass when a gentleman stopped his truck and began throwing change down to me. It made for a cool photo and Bobby managed to snap a shot. I loved these kinds of spontaneous interactions which happened most often in RV parks or on the side of the highway. I had mastered the "short explanation talk" to help people understand what we were doing and why; usually these talks ended with me giving folks a small card that explained our mission and a PFC pin.

The pin had a special significance. In 2012, I met Terry Fox's dad while I was doing my training walk from Calgary to Vancouver. I met him at an event in Chilliwack near the end of the walk and he personally gave me a Terry Fox commemorative pin. Remembering how special that was for me, I asked Marie to get pins for our campaign. The cards were also important because they gave folks something to take away and they directed traffic to the website. These were the kind of details that were critical in helping us reach a wider audience with the campaign.

On day 75 we took inventory of our shoes and calculated that I had worn out five pairs of sneakers so far. We also ran into a problem with the shopping cart when the right wheel broke on the way to the PEI ferry. Fortunately we had a contingency plan. One of the reasons we had brought the celebrity cart was to use it for spare parts. We took a wheel off the spare and were back up in five minutes. It was cool to see how our pre-trek planning and preparation was paying off as we moved down the road.

With Nova Scotia almost complete, we stopped in New Glasgow for one last event. An organization called Roots for Youth had organized an Amazing Race fundraiser with teams from various local organizations. Roots for Youth was an amazing organization that provided all kinds of services for young people under one roof, including housing, clothing, food, a drop-in community and an emergency shelter. During the previous year they had helped 13 kids get off the street! Folks showed up at the event wearing costumes and ready to go. My job was to simply talk about why their support for Roots for Youth was so important. This was such an easy event for us because all we needed to do was show up. When we were building the campaign, we were told by our friends from other campaigns to look for opportunities to join things that were already planned. This was one of those opportunities; it was also a perfect ending to our time in Nova Scotia. The next day I walked 30 km and ended up at the ferry from Pictou to Woods Island. We now had two provinces behind us.

Marie

As we settled into our routines, the bulk of my days (and evenings) were spent in front of my computer or on my phone. I had weekly phone conversations with the OPP/PFC committee and with our own team of specialists (Joe and Bobby, Social Media, Traditional Media, and Web Developer). Since we had the entire campaign mapped out, we already knew exactly where we would be on any given day during the 517 day trek, so I was already liaising with individuals and teams that had promised to host an event for us when we trekked through their city. We called these very valuable friends our "community champions." By the time we left Nova Scotia on July 16, 2016 (which was day 77 of 517), we had successfully engaged at 30 events. Trying to be present for current events and working with champions on upcoming events took all the time I had. As much as I promised each day that I would take some time for myself, each day was busier than the one before. I didn't much mind though; I thoroughly enjoyed my role and was inspired by the devotion of our

139

community champions and Joe's unrelenting commitment to walk 24km per day. No matter if he was fatigued or the weather wasn't cooperating; out he went every morning by 7:00 am. Some days he had to drive an hour or more to the drop point before he could start his walk.

Joe's role was much different from mine, but we both put a lot of pressure on ourselves to run the campaign as picture-perfect as possible. If we didn't have an event to attend, when Joe returned from his walk, he would put his feet up (mandatory recovery time) and organize pictures and videos from the day for social media. That alone could sometimes take 3-4 hours. For my part, given that I was working with community champions all across the country, my job never let up. Even though 5:00 pm EST was the end of the workday in Nova Scotia, it was only 1:00 pm in British Columbia. Emails and phone calls came in constantly and if I didn't stay on top of them, it would be close to impossible to catch up the next day. It was easier to just sit with my laptop open and my phone on all the time so I could manage correspondence as it came in. Almost every evening, either Joe or Bobby would make dinner (which was a huge blessing) and Bobby took on doing the dishes, which to my surprise he did to my satisfaction.

40

When we arrived in Prince Edward Island, we set up in an RV park east of Charlottetown and on the morning of day 78, Bobby and I woke up early and drove back to Woods Island to begin our walk across PEI. We arrived just as the morning sun was coming up over the Northumberland Straight. It was a perfect morning with no wind at all and we took some pictures for social media in front of the Welcome to Prince Edward Island sign and the lighthouse before we started to walk.

About four kilometres into my walk I realized I was under attack by bugs. It was a three-pronged assault; black flies, mosquitoes and something the locals called "no see ums," which are five times smaller than mosquitoes, but they still bite! I desperately tried to swat away the pests as they dive bombed me from every angle. It was so bad I had to keep my mouth shut tight although that still left my eyes, ears and nose as targets. I layered on more clothes to help protect my arms and legs but that only caused me to sweat. I was so frustrated I wanted to scream. Fortunately, around 18 km we crested a hill where a little breeze came along and blew away most of the bugs. By the time we reached the 24 km mark and headed home, my body was covered in bug bites. I counted over 100 bumps. Marie was aghast when she saw me step into the RV; I looked like I had been through a war.

I fell asleep that night wondering if this was how the rest of the summer would be. Fortunately, there were no other days quite like that one. Once I cleared the area I had little exposure to bugs due to a lack of rain. The only other place that would present a similar problem was along the shores of the St. Lawrence Seaway east of Quebec City.

The next few days I enjoyed strolling across rolling hills of red earth. The potato farms were in bloom and it was amazingly beautiful with row upon row of various kinds of potatoes. The route we took led us through both potato farms and sea farms. As we edged along the shoreline we got to see the oyster farms and lobster traps of the commercial fishing industry, another one of those uniquely Maritime landscapes.

One my second day of walking in PEI, I reached the city of Charlottetown. I approached the city from the east and ended my day at the city sign. We took a picture and headed off to a Rotary event where I was scheduled to speak. One of the members in the group was connected to The Salvation Army and they asked if I would drop by their lunch program the following day. Even though it was my day off I agreed. I have always found that my story has the most impact when I am sharing with people who are actively going through a struggle. I also find it resonates with the folks who work and volunteer in those sectors.

It was a short but meaningful event at a soup kitchen where I learned that Charlottetown (and PEI) provided very few resources to young people experiencing homelessness. It was really weird because just the day before at the Rotary event I met a retired businessman who proclaimed that Charlottetown had no homeless youth! Yet there I was talking to a young woman who was eight months pregnant and had nowhere to turn. I asked her about her housing situation and she told me she was "couch surfing" but as soon as the baby was born she would have to find other accommodations.

In many communities, youth homelessness isn't something that's visible, which makes it easy for young people who have experienced family conflict, mental health issues, abuse or addiction to find themselves living in unstable situations, cut off from the resources they need. By the time you actually see someone on the streets and visibly homeless, they have already cycled through a number of stages where there were opportunities for intervention. A lot of what we were trying to do with our campaign was to educate communities about what constitutes youth homelessness, so that collectively we can better understand the problems faced by youth and properly allocate resources so that 18-year-old pregnant girls get what they need to move forward. The Salvation Army event once again reminded me of why we were pushing for change and the next day I was back at it.

Taking care of my feet wasn't something that I paid a lot of attention to, but it was around this time in the campaign that I noticed I was causing some of my own discomfort by switching footwear too often. We had brought six different kinds of shoes as well as hiking shoes and assorted winter footwear that we were saving for the snow in Ontario. When I realized that some of my aches and pains were caused by changing footwear, I decided to stick to one specific kind of shoe and as long as it was working for me I wasn't going to change. This proved to be one of the wisest decisions I made in regard to injury prevention. I would later learn from a specialist that changing footwear is not wise at all, especially considering the amount of repetitive exercise I was doing. I also started to regularly wear the compression socks that Sports Medicine had provided, which really helped improve circulation and reduce recovery time.

These small adjustments made a big difference in how my body worked and now that I was stretching regularly as well as doing ice baths and breathing exercises, my focus was sharp and I felt more confident in my physical capabilities. Later on in the campaign, we would realize that PEI was our breakthrough province in terms of physical functioning.

Halfway through PEI, we got a call from the Local 721 UA business manager Gerry MacDonald, requesting to walk a full day with me. I was a little reluctant; I was a fast walker and hated slowing my pace. Every day I woke up ready to rock and the added stress of walking with someone for the whole day didn't appeal to me. I was glad I accepted though; as we started our day my fears of Gerry not being fit or able to walk the 24 km dissipated quickly and before we knew it our day together was coming to an end. After this positive experience, we challenged other UA business managers to walk a full day with us and it began a trend that continued as we crossed the country.

Before leaving PEI, we had a short visit with Don Famer at his cottage near Victoria; it was a pleasant and much needed break, not for Bobby and me but for Marie. My world had a slow and steady pace while Marie's world and her workload were becoming more chaotic by the day. With Ontario only a few months away, planning for hundreds of events was underway. We had received word that the police commissioner was going to meet us at the border of Ontario together with 26 schools that had been invited. We also learned Walter Gretzky was going to be in attendance and possibly even Bobby Orr.

The Ontario Provincial Police had asked every one of their 176 detachments to host an event with us and support for the campaign was building. Some of the events were huge, but no matter the size every event needed Marie's attention. As I watched her put in 16 hour days I felt bad. Some days Marie would wake up in her pajamas and at 9 o'clock at night she would still be wearing the same pajamas; she was that crazy busy. She received on average 150 emails per day, all of which needed her attention and care.

PEI was no different than the previous two provinces. I continued to find change along the roadway. I remember thinking one morning as I stopped to pick up a dime that these coins were like breadcrumbs or even coin shaped Inukshuks. Every time I found a coin it inspired me. Not only was I finding change everywhere, our donations were growing too. I was getting sometimes $100-$200 per day from motorists and that combined with other generous gifts from friends like UA and Home Hardware added up to over $80,000 to date. It was quite a lot considering that fundraising was not the primary goal of our campaign.

On Day 83, I found myself at the foot of the Confederation Bridge with 1,655 km completed. The CBC showed up to do an interview before we left PEI; it was the perfect send-off from province number three. We crossed the bridge into New Brunswick and set up the RV in Shediac.

In the early days when I was planning and building PFC, I read Rick Hansen's book, *Man in Motion*. It was a great read that gave me insights into some of the challenges Rick and his team faced as he toured the entire globe. One story in the book was about how Rick had fallen in love with his massage therapist Amanda and proposed marriage in Shediac, NB. At the time I read this I was really lonely and missing that kind of romance in my life. My first marriage was coming to an end and I yearned for that kind of deep connection with someone. I remember closing the book late one night alone in my bed thinking that I not only wanted to cross the country like Rick but I also wanted to find the kind of love that Rick had found; that special person to share my interests, my dreams and my goals. At the time *The Push for Change* was still years away from taking those first steps in Newfoundland, but I dared to dream.

As fate would have it, many things did change in my life and I remember feeling so blessed when we reached Shediac; not just because we were now in our fourth province but because all those dreams I had about meeting someone and falling deeply in love had come true for me. Marie and I had reconnected after years apart and we were a perfect fit for each other and now we were in Shediac together and living out my dream. I decided to celebrate and took Marie for a well-deserved dinner at Le Petit Paris, a quaint little French restaurant. The evening was perfect, it was a warm summer night, the food and the atmosphere were perfect too and I sat and thought about how lucky I was to be following my dreams with the girl of my dreams. In more ways than I can ever express, Marie is the biggest reason I succeed in life; she is my friend, my confidant and my right arm. As her daughter Cindi once said, "Marie is the heart behind the cart."

Marie

I fell in love with Prince Edward Island! It might have been because we were there at a perfect time of year (mid-July) or that the weather was absolutely lovely. It was my first time visiting the island and it just looked so beautiful; the grass was bright green, the water was bright blue and the sky was always sunny. I took some time away from my computer during our visit to be outdoors with Joe and enjoy the city. It was only 114 km from one end of the island to the other, so we trekked through it pretty quickly (we were in and out in under a week). We also had great engagement with three different Rotary Clubs on the island as well as the Salvation Army. I remember how inspired the Rotarians were after hearing Joe's message. Of course, the Rotary Clubs were already doing so much service in their communities (they certainly weren't oblivious to local homelessness issues), but by putting a "face" to homelessness Joe inspired many of them to think differently about how we address homelessness as a nation. Seeing firsthand the impact that Joe's message had from city to city, energized both Bobby and me in our roles and really connected us to a deeper purpose. We were committed to the success of the trek more than ever and stood strongly behind Joe in every step he took. He made it easy for us to put all that we had into our daily tasks because we wanted to succeed with him.

41

Marie was born in Moncton, New Brunswick so it was only fitting that we met some of her family on the side of the highway on our second day of walking in the province. We also ran into our friends Dave Griffiths and Brent Hunt from QCC Canada who met up with us just outside of Moncton and filled us in on all the events Dave was planning in his hometown of Guelph. Champions like Dave were the secret to our success. These were the folks with boots on the ground organizing and gathering volunteers so that when we reached their communities we would have events to attend, access to the media and the ability to engage schools. We left the meeting knowing Guelph, Ontario was going to be awesome!

By this time, the warm weather had eliminated any access to natural cold water for ice baths so we used the tub we carried in the van. We got the huge plastic tub from a TSC Farm store (it was actually meant for feeding or watering livestock). It was six feet long, 18 inches wide and 12 inches deep, which made for a perfect portable bathtub. When we flipped it over, the two shopping carts fit nice and snug on top of it inside the van, so it was also easy to transport. Every couple of days I would ask Bobby to pull out the tub, fill it with cold tap water and dump 3-5 bags of ice in so I could take an ice bath. It worked well but we got some funny looks from the adjacent campers.

In Moncton, we met a large group of supporters in a mall parking lot on the edge of town so we could walk together to an event in support of an organization called Youth Quest. Our friends from NAV Canada joined us for the walk and with the help of the RCMP we headed into town in high spirits. When we reached the event, we were met by local government representatives and MP Ginette Petitpas Taylor. The highlight for me was a group of young people associated with Youth Quest, who played music, read poetry and shared their views and experiences.

On day 89, I did another interview on the side of the road. It was interesting because the reporter tried to get me to make disparaging comments about a controversy that was brewing in St. John, New Brunswick with Safe Harbour. I have always believed that a spirit of inspiration has the ability to build bridges and create more collaboration so I NEVER say anything that could divide people. Although it may get more publicity, being divisive hurts the people we are trying to serve. If I say something from a place of anger or frustration I hurt someone on the street that really needs help. However, if I say something that's inspiring and inclusive I have a better chance of moving hearts and minds to a more compassionate position.

I truly believe that the way we create change in ourselves and others is first through inspiration. Our entire campaign was built on that idea; inspire sponsors, inspire community supporters, inspire youth, inspire the power brokers and government decision-makers. Whether the challenge is a personal one like weight loss or something bigger, like changing the world, action only lasts as long as inspiration. It's by repeatedly renewing our inspiration that we find the determination to keep taking steps forward. In my life, inspiration has always preceded motivation. It's worth pointing out that I learned this important lesson on the streets of Vancouver not at a college or in the business world.

I'm glad I kept my message positive because the following day our story was picked up by the CBC and broadcast across the country. We also got picked up by MSNBC and were popping up all over the internet. Horns were honking and roadside donations were up, which was one way we knew that our media efforts were paying off. People were aware of what we were doing.

On day 94 we drove down to Saint John for an event even though it wasn't on our walking route. Community engagement was our number one priority, so we were willing to go and engage anywhere if a local champion was willing to organize for us. Following a short presentation in the town square about homelessness and PFC, the youth in attendance were given chalk and a patch of sidewalk to decorate. What they created really touched our hearts. It was amazing to see how insightful and compassionate they were. Afterwards, the mayor said a few words and Chief John Bates from the Saint John Police welcomed us to the city. Next, we took the cart and the kids and walked the entire perimeter of the park and when we were done crossed the street to the Imperial Theatre where our friend and community champion Greg Bishop, had organized an event. Greg said a few words and then Marie got up to speak, which made me so proud. It takes a lot of courage for Marie to speak in public and I love seeing her tackle her fears. After I told my story, we collected donations and distributed pins and thanked everyone for their support.

Back on the road the next day, I felt something funny in my knee again, but this time I didn't let fear get in the way. We had developed a protocol for when my body acted up and within a day the problem was resolved. Since I had started the Wim Hof training, I had a deeper sense of confidence in myself and emotions were no longer running the show.

On day 93 we rolled into the city of Fredericton, which turned out to be our best city to date for a number of reasons. Approximately 24 km outside of town, we met up with the RCMP, Deputy Premier Stephen Horsman, the Minister of Community and Social Development and Katharine Horsman from UA Local 325. Fredericton had started planning immediately after the event hosted by RCMP Acting

Commissioner Roger Brown so they were well organized and the city council had officially proclaimed it *Push for Change* week.

Our morning together was spent walking towards the city limits of Fredericton with me pushing my cart and Katharine and Stephen taking turns pushing the "celebrity cart." The RCMP took us to the city limits and then Constable Jan Smith from the Fredericton Police took over. Jan was part of the planning committee and she was a ball of energy and fun. Our first stop was a surprise congregation at St. Thomas University where Susan Reid, another community champion who organized the "PFC Freddy" events, greeted us. From there we headed towards the river along a street that took us past the legislature and city hall through downtown Fredericton. UA Local 325 had paid for TV ads about PFC and the recognition we received as we walked through the downtown core was heartwarming.

We stopped briefly near the police station and collected a few more supporters from UA Local 325 before heading to Old Government House, a beautiful property that is home to the Lt. Governor of New Brunswick, the Honourable Jocelyne Roy-Vienneau. The driveway was a large semi-circle which allowed us to drive in the RV, the van and our event vehicle. On the other side of the semi-circle was the Fredericton Fire Department with a truck waiting to lead the parade that was going to commence as soon as our reception was over.

A large group was gathered in front of this beautiful historic building, including friends from all different community organizations as well as families and kids. As the Honourable Jocelyne Roy-Vienneau welcomed us to the province and thanked Marie and I for the work we were doing to make Canada a better, safer place for young people, I felt my heart brimming with pride. After sharing the PFC story, I attempted to thank everyone who had helped, which was no small task. There were always so many people to thank and when it was done I realized I had failed to acknowledge the efforts of Katharine Horsman from UA Local 325, who had worked tirelessly on these events for months. She was gracious but I felt bad.

After the formalities were complete, Marie and I met briefly with her Honour, posed for pictures and signed her guest book; it was a pretty big moment for us.

Meanwhile, out on the lawn everyone was assembled for a celebratory parade through Fredericton. With the fire truck in front, people walking in the middle and our three vehicles bringing up the rear, we slowly headed out to the street and exited the other side of the semi-circle driveway.

Leading the parade was Assistant Deputy Fire Chief David McKinley on the bagpipes. As someone who grew up in and around Scottish culture, the sound of the pipes touches something deep inside me that connects to all that was good about my childhood. As we marched through town, I had a tear in my eye and wished that my mom could see this. Our route ended at the fairgrounds where a carnival had been set up with bouncy castles, cotton candy, face painting and a BBQ hosted by UA Local 325. Jan and Susan stood smiling from ear to ear at their accomplishment.

"We said there would be bouncy castles and there are bouncy castles," said Susan. These two gals had given so much time to make this happen, it was inspiring to see their efforts rewarded.

The next day was packed with events, starting with a pancake breakfast set up by the local Kinsmen with proceeds going to Chrysalis House, a local facility committed to helping homeless youth. Next, we headed to St. Thomas University for a talk. During our time in Fredericton, a lot of energy was put behind the Barefoot Challenge to see if we could get it to go viral and after the talk, MP Matt DeCourcey got up and encouraged everyone to participate. Before we knew it everyone in the auditorium was barefoot. We moved our reception to the lobby where a silent auction was being held and posed for pictures before heading to the parking lot where the next event was already underway. This one was an annual event called Touch a Truck with vehicles and displays from all different agencies including fire, police, ambulance and military. The vehicles are available for kids and families to explore which is pretty cool. During the event the local Rotary Club used our RV to host a BBQ so we got to hang out and meet the community; although Marie got into trouble at the police table when she picked up a tear gas gun. The cop did NOT find it amusing and looking back, I probably shouldn't have encouraged her.

A great takeaway from our Fredericton experience was that piggybacking on an existing community event was much easier than building one from scratch and we looked for more opportunities to do just that across the country.

After Touch a Truck, Marie and I headed to the local youth shelter to do a presentation. Although they had known about our visit for months, when we arrived the leader told us that the kids were difficult to corral so we wouldn't be able to speak to them as a group. This was a completely different reception from what we'd experienced at Phoenix House in Halifax and I was puzzled. If I ran this house, I would have told the young people that they really needed to hear how this guy had been exactly where they are and managed to turn it all around. That's how we instructed other organizations and it always resulted in a better turn out and more buy in. Clearly, this leader wasn't inspired by what we were doing which is why she hadn't bothered to gather the clients for our message. I really didn't care that she was indifferent, what pissed me off is that because of her bias she had ripped off the kids in her charge.

Instead of giving in to resentment I hung out with one of the clients, a young man named Will, for the afternoon. I was scheduled to throw out the starting pitch for the Fredericton Royals that night at a ball park just up the street, so Will and I practised tossing the ball back and forth as we got to know one another. That evening in the ball park Marie, Will and I stood and sang, "Oh Canada" with the rest of the crowd and I realized how those words were taking on a deeper meaning as I walked across the country. After a brief introduction from the announcer, I walked onto the mound and threw the ball perfectly as the crowd cheered. No one wants to be the guy who throws a lame first pitch, so I was relieved it went well. As I exited the field I got high fives from the entire team and a few minutes later the GM gave me the ball (signed by all of the players). Will was standing beside me with a big smile and a few minutes later I passed the ball to him and told him he deserved it for helping me practise. At the end of the day, I was happy to have had the opportunity to connect with at least one young person.

Marie

We spent almost a month in New Brunswick, from July 22-August 19 and although we only had 10 events in the entire province, my communications with community champions all across the country had suddenly increased substantially. Our entrance into Ontario on September 22 was fast approaching and thanks to our partnership with the Ontario Provincial Police, (plus the fact that school started up again in September) we were about to be bombarded with events. Each school request required multiple emails and phone conversations and the sheer volume of events was simply too much for me to handle alone. I needed an event coordinator to help manage communications with my community champions. To understand just how much I had on my plate, I compiled a list of duties I was directly responsible for. It was a little overwhelming to look at.

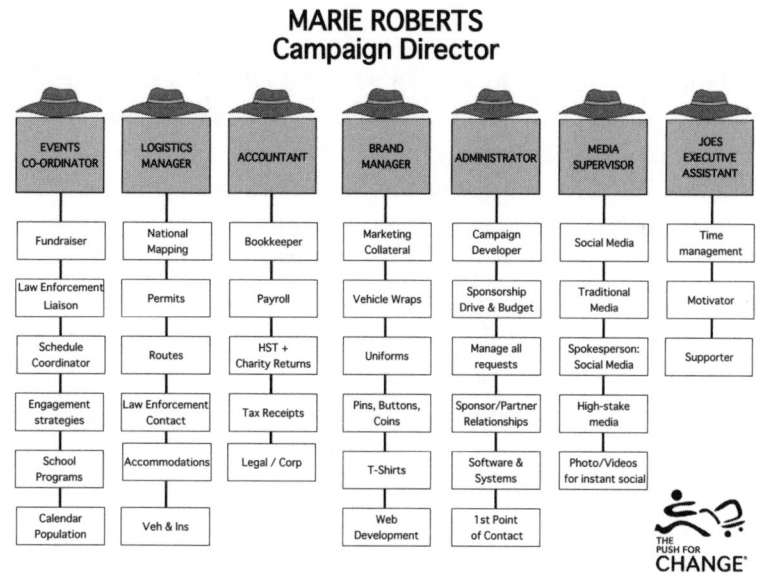

MARIE ROBERTS
Campaign Director

EVENTS CO-ORDINATOR	LOGISTICS MANAGER	ACCOUNTANT	BRAND MANAGER	ADMINISTRATOR	MEDIA SUPERVISOR	JOES EXECUTIVE ASSISTANT
Fundraiser	National Mapping	Bookkeeper	Marketing Collateral	Campaign Developer	Social Media	Time management
Law Enforcement Liaison	Permits	Payroll	Vehicle Wraps	Sponsorship Drive & Budget	Traditional Media	Motivator
Schedule Coordinator	Routes	HST + Charity Returns	Uniforms	Manage all requests	Spokesperson: Social Media	Supporter
Engagement strategies	Law Enforcement Contact	Tax Receipts	Pins, Buttons, Coins	Sponsor/Partner Relationships	High-stake media	
School Programs	Accommodations	Legal / Corp	T-Shirts	Software & Systems	Photo/Videos for instant social	
Calendar Population	Veh & Ins		Web Development	1st Point of Contact		

THE PUSH FOR CHANGE

Although we had both a social media and traditional media specialist, both roles required daily instruction and input from me. Our web developer was very capable, but also needed input from me about what needed to be changed or updated on a regular basis. It was clear that I was simply wearing too many hats.

Perusing my long list of duties convinced me that hiring some help was long overdue and I placed an ad for an event coordinator on Indeed.com. Hiring someone at this point in the campaign took time I really couldn't afford, but I was a little desperate. The event coordinator could work remotely from their home liaising with our community champions to help plan their events. After reviewing the resumes and interviewing four candidates, I hired a gentleman who seemed to have the skills I was looking for (although I realized that overseeing yet another contractor wasn't ideal). After some thought, I assigned him to just one project, working with the planning committee of our big Yonge/Dundas event, which was happening in Toronto on October 23. This event was by far one of our biggest and dealing with the City of Toronto as well as the Toronto Police Service was time consuming enough for me, never mind coordinating the volunteer duties, organizing the Walk with Joe route and organizing the pipe band, stage/seating setup, music, emcee, speakers, run of show, etc., etc. The list was endless. Thankfully, we had a very capable and dedicated committee planning the event in Toronto, but having another person to oversee all the details was a huge help.

Meanwhile, we were still in New Brunswick where our main events were managed by very capable teams, one of which labelled themselves, "PFC Freddy." Attending their four events in Fredericton (which took place back to back over two days) provided me with a much needed break from the admin role that I was playing from the RV. These champions, like all of our community champions, worked tirelessly for months in advance to plan well thought-out events aimed at maximizing awareness within their community. Being able to witness months of planning come to fruition with our champions was such a joy for me, because as much as I had worked tirelessly alongside them, they had freely given so much of themselves to our campaign and we were deeply grateful. Given the nature of a cross-Canada trek, the one regret Joe and I both had after each event, is that there wasn't enough time to properly thank our champions before we had to move on. We remain indebted to their generosity and amazing community spirit.

42

In Fredericton, the team was fortunate to stay in a hotel thanks to the generosity of UA Local 325. Marie and I thoroughly enjoyed being out of the RV and with the hotel's ice machine it was so much easier to do regular ice baths. We had a wrap up lunch with Jan and Susan before we left; they had worked so hard to bring PFC to the community and now that is was all over, we all felt a little sad. I was learning to get over things quickly though, as my focus turned back to walking and grinding out the kilometres needed to get to the next province. Our pace often shifted like that during the campaign, we would hit a community and go nuts for a couple days with back to back events and then head back out on the road where our pace was much slower.

One of our biggest supporters from the area was the UA Atlantic representative Bruce Myles. Bruce hadn't been able to join us for any events because he'd been attending an international conference in San Diego, but he was back in town and wanted to take up the challenge to walk with us for a full day. Katharine Horsman (who was also with Local 325) had challenged Bruce on social media after her walk and he was ready to make good. Bruce brought along one of his business agents, George Estey and we met early in the morning outside Fredericton. At the end of our day together, Bruce's dad also came out to meet us and Bruce told me he was truly inspired by what we were doing.

As always, while I was out walking Marie was dealing with event details and happenings in communities all across the country and we received word that The House of Commons would officially receive us when we arrived in Ottawa on October 23. We also learned that the Barrie Huronia Rotary Club had raised $5,000, so we arranged for friends from our OPP team to accept the cheque on our behalf. In other good news, NAV Canada had raised a total of $26,000 across the country and we were scheduled to meet with their group in Ottawa for a cheque presentation in September. Last but not least, we got confirmation of our appearance at WE Day in Toronto. I was scheduled to speak on October 19 and they had even made it possible for us to have the shopping cart on stage with me while I spoke. The icing on the cake was that both MacLean's Magazine and the Canadian Press were running national editorial content on *The Push for Change* in their Labour Day issue, thanks to our extraordinary relationship with UA Canada.

Marie was also involved in planning two really huge events that required daily attention. One was when we hit the Ontario Border. The other was the Yonge and Dundas downtown Toronto event. Marie received information that Walter Gretzky was confirmed to walk with me as I entered Ontario and they were even trying to get Bobby Orr.

The event in Toronto had Rod Black from TSN and CTV Sports confirmed as the MC and Robert Pilon was going to sing for us. The Stars from Degrassi were confirmed and we had just learned that Michael "Pinball" Clemons was confirmed to walk with us and speak at the event. These were just the highlights Marie was sharing with me. The only bad news we received was that despite trying we could not find anyone in Iqaluit, Nunavut to host an event. We always envisioned going to every province and territory but without any scheduled events we decided the huge cost of going up north wasn't worth it if we didn't have a community champion to help organize something. We decided to wait and see if we could do something later in the campaign. All of the good news made it really easy to get up every day and walk, even though some days I was sore and tired.

The toughest days for me were when it rained. On day 103, close to Perth, New Brunswick, it rained so hard that even with really good rain gear, I was soaked most of the day and the rain didn't let up for nearly a week. Rain was always more difficult, mostly because it was never constant. I would put rain gear on, then take it off, then put it back on. It always slowed down the pace and made for a longer day. It also made my feet heavier, which meant my body had to work harder.

Although my body was doing really well, we were always in the market for good therapy. We made an appointment to see an RMT in Edmundston, but I left disappointed. Instead of getting a deep tissue massage, I got a relaxing massage. To me the mark of a good RMT is someone who goes deep enough that I have to "tap out" or say ouch. Good RMT people know how to find the tight spots and work them out. If they are any good at what they do it feels good when it's done but when you're in the middle of it, it should be intense. Many days throughout the campaign I wished I could have taken the excellent team of RMTs and physiotherapists from Sports Medicine and Mind to Muscle on the road with me.

Edmundston was to be our last stop before we moved camp into Quebec and with New Brunswick almost behind us, we had a few days to regroup and do some team evaluation. Marie was busier than both Bobby and I put together so it was imperative that we pick up the slack to allow her to focus on upcoming events in Ontario. Unfortunately, Bobby hadn't risen to the occasion and I had become increasingly frustrated with his poor performance. After three months on the road together, we were also starting to get on each other's nerves. I wish I could say this was one of my finest moments as a leader but it wasn't. With so much riding on the campaign when we hit Ontario, I was gravely concerned that Bobby wouldn't be able to manage the new tasks that would be added to his role. His job was about to get much harder, but often when I checked his work it needed additional attention, coaching or correction and I no longer felt confident that things were being done right.

The situation came to a head one day when I caught Bobby in a lie about a very important task. When I confronted him, he adamantly defended the lie which was a head scratcher for me. My problem at this point was we were one province away from absolute mayhem and I had zero faith in our key support person. It was too bad, we liked Bobby a lot. He was easy to get along with, he was engaged and he loved the campaign, he was also super loyal and the things he did well were amazing. Truth be told, he was the best driver I had ever met. But while he was perfect for this part of the job, he wasn't well suited for what lay ahead and that was a fact we needed to face.

43

For some reason, walking into Quebec was emotional for me. I'm not sure why, maybe because I was moving closer to my home province or perhaps because I was amazed that I had completed my fourth province.

The first person we engaged with was a member of the Sûreté du Québec, the police force for most of the rural parts of Quebec. They are also responsible for provincial highways. Because the RCMP in Atlantic Canada knew who we were (and that we had a strict safety protocol) we had been given a pass, however when we reached Quebec we were told we could not walk on the highway. Although I couldn't know for sure what the officer had to say, we got the gist of the message from his tone and gestures... I so wished I had paid more attention in French class.

Later that day back at the RV park, we adjusted our route to stay on secondary roads and we were good to go. In two days, we planned to move camp to Rivière-du-Loup, but for now we were still closer to Edmundston, which was a good thing because I wanted to watch a concert that was going to be aired live from Kingston, Ontario.

Some of the questions I got asked most often during the campaign were: How many shoes have you worn out? How long does it take you to walk 24 km? What do you eat? And of course, what kind of music do you listen to while you're walking?

One of my all-time favourite bands will always be The Tragically Hip; partly because I lived in the Kingston area when they were first taking off as a band and partly because they are definitively and unapologetically Canadian. I also think that Gord Downie's lyrics smack of poetic genius, being both clever and multi-layered. To my mind, there's never been a musical outfit quite like The Hip, although I kind of think you have to be Canadian to get what they're about. The Hip got me through my early recovery from addiction as well as the highs and lows of my 30s and 40s and now they were with me every step of the way across Canada. When I learned about their farewell concert all I wanted was to be a part of it in some small way, even if from afar. I was so grateful the CBC decided to broadcast the concert and they did it for free (which I thought was a smart move).

There are a handful of experiences that I would describe as truly iconic Canadian moments and The Hip's final concert together was one of them. It would prove to be the greatest concert I never attended. I'm sure I must have looked silly in the back of the RV with my computer on my lap and tears streaming down my face feeling patriotic and a deep sense of admiration for a man saying goodbye with his music... and singing his heart out to a nation that loved him. During the second encore I lost it when they played the song *Grace Too*. To this day, it's the best concert I have ever been to and I wasn't even there.

The next day I was back on the road and still feeling patriotic. I pulled out the Canadian flag that I kept tucked into the inside of my shopping cart for photo ops and wrapped it around myself. As I strolled along the side of the highway, motorists honked and cheered. It's amazing how as Canadians, we all share a love of the flag for whatever it represents to each of us. We are after all, the True North Strong and Free!

The next few days were nice, I remember walking by a tree laden with fruit and picking some lovely ripe apples. It seemed like just yesterday that I had been walking through Cape Breton where the trees were just starting to blossom. It was cool to see the seasons change. In no time at all, I found myself walking parallel to the St. Lawrence Seaway moving west towards Quebec City. The weather was lovely; there were a lot of bugs but most days the wind kept them from being bothersome. There was no doubt however that the weather was changing and I remember having a foreboding feeling in the pit of my stomach. It was only August but soon it would be fall and then winter! The thought of winter had all of us a little scared; so many things would need to be adjusted. My greatest fear was how my body was going to hold up; it's not like we picked the best place to walk through the winter, in fact it was the worst. Our winter months would be between Sudbury and Kenora. Northern Lake Superior is one of the most treacherous places to be in the winter with unforgiving temperatures and heaps of snow; all of which would be conjured up every time a cool wind hit my face.

On day 124 we reached Montmagny and moved our camp; shortly after our arrival we noticed the hot water wasn't working. Having walked 24 km in the morning I was tired and didn't want to deal with mechanical problems. I really relied on Bobby for this kind of thing but he wasn't very helpful and now we were all frustrated and cranky. I finally decided that instead of guessing and arguing, we would take the RV to a dealer and get it diagnosed. The good news was they found the problem. The other good news was it was fixable and they had the part. The bad news was it cost $1,400. We would also learn later on that the problem was the result of user error.

The next day I hit the 2,200 km mark and the campaign was officially 25% complete, which got me thinking that if we decided to go back to Newfoundland, it would take us at least 22 hours to drive, not including the ferry.

Marie was busy coordinating events in Quebec City and Montreal when we got word that when we reached Kingston, Ontario we would be presented with a cheque for $25,000 from our community champion there! We were excited with how Ontario was shaping up.

44

On the day of our event in Quebec City I was a little anxious. I didn't speak French which meant we needed to use an interpreter. The event went better than expected; it turns out most Quebecers do far better with English than I do with French, so my message carried well. Afterwards we did a Walk with Joe through the city. It was about five kilometres and we had a great turnout. We were surprised that our friend from UA Local 144 drove all the way from Montreal to join us and we also had a number of big media folks turn up.

The following day we were all over the newspapers in Quebec City and the English radio station. I was in a small town called Levis just about to cross over the St. Lawrence River into the city. Most times our events didn't line up perfectly with where I was on the highway which was fine for us. As I approached the bridge, there were oodles of cyclists and pedestrians and I began to get a lot of encouragement and friendly remarks, most of which I didn't understand. I recall one cyclist yelled, "Bonne chance!" as he rode past, which I knew meant good luck. A number of people who spoke English stopped to chat as they offered donations and thanked us for what we were doing. As always, the press coverage was tremendously helpful in getting our message out and we learned from this experience that inspiration cuts across the boundaries of culture and language and is more about actions than words.

On day 130 we were 70 kilometres east of Trois-Rivières and after lots of discussion, Marie and I decided we had to let Bobby go. Marie was in the midst of changing out someone who worked media relations for us as well, so in one day we made decisions that changed 50% of our team. We were both so busy it was insane. Marie was either on the phone or answering emails 16 hours a day. I was busy walking, doing interviews, managing social media, and creating all of our video content while also sorting through the thousands of pictures we'd taken. Even so, we knew the team had to change if we were going to be successful.

When we reached Montreal we had quite a few events stacked up. UA Local 144 hosted an event on a job site in the northeast corner of the island where a large L&G facility was under construction for Linde. Thanks to Business Manager Stephane Favron, who coordinated the event, we were presented with cheques from Black and MacDonald, Metro Gaz, Linde and UA Local 144. In total, we raised over $15,000. The CBC also had us on the radio and Breakfast TV shot a morning bit with us. Later, we had a Walk with Joe event in downtown Montreal with friends from AMJ Campbell and Five Days for the Homeless before heading off to Dans la rue.

Dans la rue is an organization that serves homeless youth throughout Montreal. In fact, it's the same organization that Aeroplan had partnered with for the event I facilitated in 2011, when I first got the inspiration for *The Push for Change*. Following a facility tour that ended in the back parking lot with a BBQ, I was asked to say a few words. Once again, I was nervous that my message wouldn't translate but it did and we had the amazing experience of connecting with 30-40 street involved youth who were going through many of the same things I had been through when I was homeless in Vancouver.

After the event a young man named Jean came up and said he wanted to walk with me. "I would love to walk with you," I told him. However, when I got the full interpretation, I realized he wanted to finish the entire walk across Canada with me. I had so inspired this young man that he wanted to finish the trek with me. It was truly amazing to see how we were impacting people and although I would have loved to take Jean with us, I explained how horribly impractical it would be. I made a concession though. If he was willing, I would be more than happy to meet him the next day and let him show me around the city of Montreal. I had only one rule, we would have to walk a minimum of 24 kilometres. The interpreter also reluctantly agreed to join us to help with communication and the next day we hit Montreal.

I have to say it was one of the best guided tours of my life. Jean took me to all the places you wouldn't see or dare to go as a tourist. I enjoyed my walk and I especially enjoyed getting to know this young man whose story was familiar. He had left home due to conflict with his parents and the friend he rented an apartment with robbed him of the rent which left him homeless and sleeping in a park at the age of 18. This kid was smart and engaging and had everything going for him in life except for circumstances. Our day ended too early and I was sad to say goodbye. It was one of the best days of *The Push for Change* campaign and I didn't even have my cart with me.

Although I was strung out from back to back events and daily walks, when I learned about a big UA gathering in Ottawa I decided I had to make the extra effort to attend. I was glad I did. At an earlier event in San Diego, some big changes had been announced. Terry Snooks, our good friend from Local 46 was being moved up to the international office and Steve Morrison would be the incoming Director of Canadian Affairs, replacing John Telford, who was retiring. It was a great opportunity to shake some hands and update everyone on the campaign while we thanked them for their continued support. I was so exhausted afterwards that when I tried to drive back to Montreal, I couldn't and we ended up getting a hotel room where Marie and I crashed.

During our time in Quebec, we conducted several interviews and thought we'd found a perfect candidate to do Bobby's job. It was going to be tough to let Bobby go because we liked him and he was a really hard worker, but we knew it was necessary as things were about to get much, much busier. When we finally broke the news to Bobby he seemed almost relieved. We drove him to the airport where we had a flight prearranged for him to return to BC. On the way to the airport Bobby thanked us for the opportunity and apologized for letting us down; although to my mind there was nothing to apologize for. He asked if he could take part in the final day in Vancouver when we got there and I said, "Yes, of course." At the airport we said our goodbyes; I was sad to see Bobby go but the mission had to come first.

The next morning our new driver arrived and we began training, we'd met Mike through a friend and we felt he would be a really good fit. He had been a police officer for over 20 years and understood logistics. He also had personal experience with addiction, recovery and mental health and he seemed eager to join us and get started.

Mike picked up some key parts of the job quickly, which was good given that Marie's world was coming undone. Her workload was so staggering she was losing sleep, there were hundreds of school visits and community events in various stages of development and she was involved in all of them. She tried hiring someone to help her but in the end they caused her more work than they took away. One afternoon we went out together for her to get her hair done. We weren't gone more than three hours and when we returned she had 60 new emails. That night while scrolling through social media, I found a video from Michael "Pinball" Clemons promoting our event, which would take place at Yonge and Dundas in Toronto in a little less than a month. One of the things I learned from the campaign was that with success comes great pressure and both Marie and I were feeling it. Ontario was going to take every ounce of energy we had.

Marie

From August 19 to September 21, we trekked through Quebec and by this time Joe could see that I was overworked and out of balance. More often than not, when he returned from his daily walk, it was obvious that I hadn't moved from my seat at the table in the RV. He encouraged me to get back into some sort of fitness routine and he took me out on date nights for dinner or a walk around the lake or to see a new city we had never been to. He also brought home lots of "roadside treasures" that he had found while walking. Some of them made me laugh and others I discarded. There were a few that I kept, like a beautiful yellow and white gold linked bracelet that he found in a ditch in Nova Scotia. It's one of the bracelets I wear the most! Joe had an eye for anything that didn't belong on the road and he stopped and looked at most of these roadside treasures in case something was of value. I loved his sense of adventure and boyish nature. He was always so proud of every item he brought home. We still have two huge totes crammed full of random license plates that he found in ditches during the trek (who knows when they may come in handy!)

Joe's presence itself helped to balance me in that it reminded me to be present and enjoy the moment. Some days I even pulled myself away from my computer and joined him on his walk, which gave me the opportunity to see the trek from his perspective. But I didn't allow myself to join him very often, there was much too much to do planning the next day, and the next, and the next. Of the 9,064 kilometres that Joe walked, I may have walked 500 with him.

45

On day 144 we completed our walk through Quebec, ending the day in Grenville, with Hawkesbury, Ontario just on the other side of the bridge. We had successfully campaigned across five provinces and the momentum was building as we prepared to enter Ontario. The phone was ringing off the hook as a result of national media releases sent out by the OPP; we already had 17 interview requests and had been scheduled to appear on the CTV National News in Ottawa.

As I stood on a small grassy area on the Quebec side looking across the bridge to Ontario, I reflected on my journey so far. I thought about how I had put into action the things Sean had taught me about turning every challenge into a game and how to live the AIR model by connecting action and inspiration to smash through roadblocks. I thought about how I had turned every rainy day, every sore muscle and every setback into fuel to drive myself forward. I also thought about every crappy part of my early life and how every mistake and hardship had been a building block. I thought about how my experience being homeless and addicted to drugs had become my greatest asset because it gave me a story that touched people's hearts and minds. It also gave me access to young people and a platform from which to drive change. As I stood looking towards Ontario, I realized that adversity really is the greatest teacher of all.

In addition to all of the amazing support we received along this crazy journey, we also heard from many people who didn't get it. They couldn't see our vision and so they told us it couldn't be done. We ignored them and did it anyway. Sometimes it's better to follow your gut and ignore the so-called "voice of reason." Sometimes you need to bend some rules and go for it despite conventional thinking. In the end if you want something, I mean really want it as badly as a junkie craves their next fix, then it will be yours. I guarantee it. After 4.5 years of planning and with over 2,300 kilometres already behind us we were about to enter Ontario with thunder. Waiting for us on the other side was the full support and engagement of the Ontario Provincial Police, the second largest police force in Canada. We had accomplished the impossible.

When we started this campaign, all I wanted was to create change. In my mind, PFC was for every young person who didn't have a voice, every kid huddled in a doorway and every kid who, like me, had felt like they weren't good enough. It was also for every kid that'd been kicked in the teeth before they learned how to fight back, every kid who'd been discriminated against, or whose sexuality had caused them to feel alienated, for every kid that had been bullied and every kid that struggled with mental health. This campaign was all about them and tomorrow as we took on Ontario; it would be a day for the underdogs!

Follow the Journey online.

See the photos and videos.

www.thepushforchangebook.com

PART SIX
ONTARIO

46

The feeling I had walking over the bridge into Ontario was like the climax in an emotional movie where the hero emerges triumphant, you know, the scene that causes tears to flow as you feel a connection to the underdog character and their journey to triumph. It was a day I had only ever pictured in my mind, now it was a reality.

My sleep the night before entering Ontario had been terrible; I got four hours at best. I was exhausted before the day even started, but this was organized to be the biggest day in the campaign so far. Marie, Mike and I stopped on the Quebec side of the river and waited for everyone to show up. Initially the OPP wanted to shut down the entire bridge for our crossing but the Quebec Police didn't want that to happen.

The bridge into Ontario is a long arch over the Ottawa River. We departed from our holding area with Mike behind me and the OPP bringing up the rear. I walked alone as I slowly ascended the bridge deck. As I reached the mid-point there was a small marker that signified Ontario, and I heard the buzz of the OPP's drone overhead. They wanted to capture video of my arrival in Ontario. Looking down, I saw the OPP's safety boat in the water below and I waved at them as I passed. As I looked forward again, I got a lump in my throat. All of our hard work and months of walking had led to this, waiting to welcome me into Ontario were hundreds of students and supporters along with our friends from UA Canada and the OPP. I could hear them cheering as I got closer and my emotions got the best of me as I walked down the bridge deck to a hero's welcome into Hawkesbury.

The streets were lined with hundreds of students carrying signs and cheering as I walked by. Supporters from UA Canada and friends from QCC Canada were prepared to walk with us. As I approached the holding area I was met by Commissioner Vince Hawkes of the OPP, Deputy Commissioner Rick Barnum and the greatest hockey dad in the world, Walter Gretzky. The town's mayor was there too, along with service clubs and all kinds of supporters from local agencies. What shocked me was how many senior OPP members had turned up. We took some group photos and did a quick TV interview and then assembled for our walk through town and on to the community centre where our first events were to be held.

The group was led by the Commissioner's Own Pipe and Drums as we began the 4 km walk. Flanking me were Marie, Walter Gretzky and the commissioner along with Rob Jamieson of the OPP Association (representing the union); it was nothing short of spectacular. About halfway through the walk, I became concerned for Walter Gretzky. It was a hot day and he was determined to walk the entire route so I asked Marie to keep an eye on him. At the community centre, we were officially piped in and there were remarks from all of the dignitaries and I got up and did my small speech; then we had several cheque presentations. The Wayne Gretzky Foundation gave us $10,000, OPPA gave us $6,000, QCC Canada gave us $40,000 and UA Canada gave us $500,000. Of course, the UA money had been received a long time before but because we never did an official cheque presentation this was an opportunity to acknowledge them.

Sergeant Kerry Schmidt was there to cover us on social media and we also had support from the entire OPP communications team. The execution of the event was flawless and with a Canadian-wide media release from the OPP, our campaign was starting to get noticed.

The best part of our day was a question and answer session with the students which was really cool for a couple of reasons. Hawkesbury is predominantly a French speaking community so we needed to navigate some of that process in our presentation. But what really struck me was how intuitive and thoughtful the questions were. It was a great beginning to Ontario. After more interviews we broke for the afternoon with an evening fundraiser planned for a smaller group of supporters.

June Dobson and Frankie Campisi from the OPP were our coordinators in that area and after a short break and a chance to rest (which I desperately needed), we headed to the evening event. One of the creative things the OPP did to help raise money was to create customized Push for Change/OPP t-shirts and everyone was wearing them. It was so cool to see our brands together. We had a lot of fun at the evening event; June and Frankie presented us with a cake and there was entertainment and a silent auction with all kinds of cool stuff. June Dobson was our connection to Walter Gretzky as well as Bobby Orr. Mr. Orr couldn't make it but there was a pile of his signed memorabilia. Our local champions from Rotary were also in attendance and half of everything we raised in Hawkesbury would be dedicated to their projects related to youth at risk.

That evening I had the pleasure of sitting with Walter Gretzky. Walter was so gracious with his time and he even brought a small stack of paper to give out autographs. When I had a moment, I leaned in and asked him what piece of advice he would give someone like me who is taking on such a huge challenge or facing huge adversity. He looked at me with light in his eyes and a huge broad smile like I was tapping into something deep within him and I was ecstatic to be accessing the same wisdom and mentorship that helped produce one of the greatest hockey players on earth.

He smiled at me and said, "Don't quit." At the time I thought to myself, "I was hoping for something a little deeper Walter," but the following day as I walked, I marinated on his instruction. It was simple, it was profound and it was real. I began to think about all of the people who needed to hear that message just as much as I had. I thought about all the reasons why we were pushing for change and that if more kids had someone like Walter in their life, maybe we wouldn't need to. Walter was right, we don't fail at things in life, we just quit before we succeed.

Understanding just how big a deal supporting our campaign was for the OPP was made clear one day when we were getting gas near Hawkesbury. An OPP officer was filling his cruiser when he spotted us and came over to make a donation. I thanked him and asked if he was part of the planning committee and he said no. I asked how he knew about *The Push for Change* and he laughed and said, "Are you kidding me? You guys are famous. *The Push for Change* is the screensaver on every OPP computer in the province. Everyone knows who you guys are now."

The days that followed our entry into Ontario were a whirlwind. In Quebec, we had had much more time on our hands. With the exception of Montreal and Quebec City our engagement there had been minimal. It's not that we didn't want to engage in Quebec, it's just that it was summer time and we had only a few local champions to help us coordinate. Ontario was proving to be an entirely different experience. Every day for weeks we had events and appearances booked, media interviews, school events and walks through communities. A buzz was building and it was fun, but it was also a whole lot more work.

For one thing, our days started much earlier because now we had to coordinate each morning with a local volunteer OPP member who would be with us as our community support liaison. The OPP had committed to see us through the entire province, which meant a person and vehicle were assigned to us every day that we walked.

Marie

Entering Ontario was a game changer for the campaign. Since May I had been in consistent communication with the OPP at all levels. We had weekly conference calls that were billed as PFC Operations Committee meetings. The calls had participants from all departments and levels of the OPP, including OPP members from General Headquarters, logistics, communications, administration, all (5) regional detachments as well as me. These weekly teleconferences, as well as other daily calls with OPP members as required, would prove to be integral to the success of our trek through Ontario as we ironed out every conceivable hindrance. We also ensured that every detachment, and there were over 150, were ready to host a successful OPP/PFC event. We established plans and procedures for the volunteer officers who would accompany Joe on the road every kilometre that he walked (where and when they would meet Joe, the exact route, stops along the way, other walkers joining Joe). Every detail for every day in Ontario (200 days in total) was worked through. We also outlined key messages for traditional and social media so that we were aligned publicly and created itineraries and run of show documents for all of the major OPP/PFC events.

I very quickly learned I was working with some of the best people on the planet! The OPP members I worked with were professional, organized, efficient, diligent, logical and they had integrity! If they said they would do something, it happened. Working with such high-quality people was a blessing I didn't take for granted, I was grateful every day for their amazing support.

The leaders in the Eastern Region were excited to welcome us to Hawkesbury, Ontario from the Quebec border. Their enthusiasm was contagious and in the days leading up to our arrival into Ontario, I couldn't help but feel relieved to be entering Ontario where I would have daily support from such capable and caring individuals.

The Hawkesbury events hosted by the OPP Eastern Region were a huge success. Not only did we engage citizens, municipal leaders and officials in the small communities around the Quebec border, we also inspired thousands of students to think differently about youth homelessness. More importantly, through our interactions with them it became evident that we had changed the perspective of the OPP members *themselves on social issues related to homelessness, mental health and addiction. This was something we heard firsthand from numerous members who spoke about how their perceptions had shifted as a result of their time with us.*

47

The first few days in Ontario were so inspiring for me. After the huge event in Hawkesbury, we embarked on a series of community engagements that would lead us towards Ottawa. The first community was Rockland and when we arrived at the local park they were all set up for a community BBQ along with a PA system for my talk. I spoke briefly about my experiences and why it was so important for us to actively engage and help those who are less fortunate. The kids from this community had been gathering needed items that could be used at a homeless shelter and they had several shopping carts filled with food, clothing and non-perishables. We gathered near the entrance to the park and headed off through town in procession. In front of us the OPP were leading the way and taking intersections to ensure our safety. Over my shoulder I could see this mass gathering of locals parading with their shopping carts; it was exactly how I had seen it in my mind, a sort of pied piper kind of thing. I was really proud of the work Marie had done to bring the campaign this far.

We walked for three kilometres and ended up back at the park where I said a few more words and we took some great group photos. Because the community was informed that we were coming and took action to support the campaign they were already super excited when we got there which made all the difference in the way the day turned out. This format for community engagement served us well and provided the opportunity to reach a lot of young people. Typically, schools would host some kind of activity to support PFC and when we arrived in the community, the OPP would coordinate a walk through the town. By the time the campaign was complete, Walk with Joe events took place in hundreds of towns and engaged tens of thousands of students.

When we got close to the city of Ottawa, there were a number of events lined up. First, I spoke at Recovery Day Ottawa; then The Alliance to End Homelessness hosted an event at city hall. Our friend from Kiwanis, Peter Charboneau also coordinated a number of school presentations and the Kiwanis Club of Orleans dedicated a unique local event to us. Each year they operate a Haunted House which is open to the public. It's extremely well organized and runs for the entire month of October. The students who volunteer for the event are responsible for everything from running concessions to playing zombies; it's a lot of fun for the kids and a great way to generate money for the Kiwanis to fund community projects.

The student volunteers needed to attend an orientation to work at the event and we took the opportunity to go speak to these young people. After my presentation all of the students took part in a sleep out. It was amazing to see over a hundred young people taking action and I was happy to be able to inspire them and thank them. As the campaign gained momentum, events like this were beginning to happen not just on the campaign trail but in many cases all over the province. The day after the event we got an emotional letter from a young lady who took part in the sleep out. Having experienced homelessness personally, she explained that the event meant a lot to her.

The day I walked into Ottawa was very special; we had started the day in Orleans and followed the river route into the city. We had some friends from the Ottawa Police with us on motorcycles to help navigate through traffic safely. We slowly worked our way towards the city centre passing Rideau Hall and 26 Sussex Drive, the official residence of the Prime Minister, along the way. We continued past the Canadian Mint and the Ottawa Museum and the next time I looked up, I caught my first sight of the House of Commons. Parliament is of course where national decisions are made and if we were ever going to make change it needed to happen here.

When we reached the Château Laurier, we were expecting a large group from the Kiwanis Club of Ottawa. In the planning phase, this group had told us they were really keen to come out and support *The Push for Change*. Our friends from Ottawa had also told us it was a really active club; in fact I had done a talk for this group in the lead up to the campaign. To our bewilderment, when we arrived in front of the hotel our friends were nowhere to be seen. Due to the heavy traffic congestion in the area we had to keep moving; we found out later that they had got the meet-up time confused.

As I walked up the long hill over the Rideau Canal, I spotted Marie waiting on the side of the road, I was proud and so excited to know we had come this far! Together we finished our walk up onto the lawn in front of Parliament. As we arrived on the front lawn the huge clock that is situated in the massive Peace Tower struck 12 noon. It was perfect timing and waiting for us were friends from the RCMP who had been informed we were coming. Although the group was small, the sense of accomplishment I felt was massive. I had stood in this very spot years earlier dreaming about reaching this point one day and here we were.

A few days later we were invited back to Ottawa to meet with Minister Jean-Yves Duclos and MP Adam Vaughan. They wanted to know what our specific ask was and we told them we were championing youth homelessness prevention and that our partners A Way Home Canada and Homeless HUB were the deeper thinking behind what we specifically needed the government to do. Our new friends committed to a meeting where we could all sit down and discuss details. I could never have imagined what would end up coming from this but it turned out the Government of Canada was really looking for new ways to address homelessness in Canada and just like when the tower bell had rung upon our arrival, our timing was perfect.

Shortly after arriving in downtown Ottawa we had a corporate event to attend with our friends at NAV Canada so we headed down the street to their head office where I gave a short speech and their CEO presented us with a cheque for over $13,000. Because they had committed to match funds raised by their people across Canada, an additional $13,000 stayed in the communities that hosted events. We were humbled to think we inspired this extraordinary organization to get involved across the entire country.

As we got closer to the west side of the city, we attended an event in our honour hosted by the Kanata Kiwanis Club who did an amazing job of mobilizing the community including both community stakeholders and students. The event raised $5,000 and we were really starting to enjoy the momentum that was building.

On day 152, our route led us out of the city of Ottawa and along the Ottawa River once again. The weather was amazing and my body felt good. I was adapting to the increased workload and seemed to have the energy needed for community events and interviews as well as my daily walk. It was exhausting but extremely rewarding. In contrast, Marie was buried in work and never seemed to get everything she wanted done. At this point she wasn't even going to events anymore, if she had she'd come back to 100 new emails. I was sad about how hard she was working. She really needed help but we were moving so fast it seemed all but impossible to try to find someone and bring them up to speed while juggling everything else that was going on. It was easier for her to do it all herself.

We did a couple of drop-in events as we passed through communities like Barry's Bay where we had the OPP coordinate school stops and a Walk with Joe event. Renfrew also hosted a community walk, BBQ and school presentation.

Our route was taking us down towards Kingston and as we approached Lanark County, we had tremendous support from the United Way and our friends at the OPP. Early one morning we were walking through Carlton Place when a bunch of high school students came running out of a house to meet us. They were all in their pajamas and had heard about us on TV and the radio. They were excited to meet us and even more excited that we would be at their school the next day. We took some selfies with them and were on our way. Roadside engagement like this happened all across the country, but in Ontario it was crazy. We actually needed to add additional time to the daily walk because so many people stopped us and some days it seriously slowed down our pace.

We had a couple of great events in Carlton Place. Bean Chevrolet hosted a BBQ and made a generous donation and the school events were fun. Then it was on to Perth where we walked through town with students from the local high school and stopped to do a speech on the steps of city hall before making our way to the farmer's market for another short speech and community gathering. Something that caught my attention was a teenager who had set up a treadmill so he could walk to match my steps and raise money for PFC; it was all very small town organic and we loved the imagination and enthusiasm. We had Fraser Scantlebury from United Way and Greg Streng from the OPP to thank for the great success we were experiencing along this stretch of our route. The media exposure and community engagement that had been initiated before our arrival were the primary reasons it worked out so well and we were grateful.

In Perth, I met a gentleman named Chris who walked with us through town; he owned and managed a few drug treatment centres. Moved by the work we were doing, he gave me a very large personal donation. It was beyond generous and I could tell he was moved by the momentum of the campaign. I asked him if he would like us to visit his treatment centre and talk to the staff and clients. He agreed and later in the year we travelled to Caledon, Ontario to do an event. It was a special day talking to people in early recovery and encouraging them to stay sober one day at a time. Anytime I share my story to a group of people in recovery something magical happens. It's hard to explain, but I know from many such experiences that the sharing of a personal story and words of encouragement have the power to change people's lives. It's a special thing.

When I finished my talk, Chris's young son said he had a $20 bill that he wanted to give me. I could tell he wasn't sure whether he wanted to part with it or not; I let him make his own choice and when he finally made the decision, I was so proud of him. Not because the campaign was $20 richer, but because this young man learned about how good it feels to give.

At Smith Falls we had our first opportunity to visit an OPP Communications Centre, thanks to our champion Glenda Reid. It was one of five centres in the province that receives emergency police calls. The folks who worked in these centres were huge *Push for Change* supporters; they were also an important part of my story. One of the biggest crises in my life began with a call to one of these centres. As we wandered through the centre, I thanked everyone for their commitment. It was fascinating to see what they do firsthand. Every single emergency call to the OPP goes through a centre like this and it is then routed to a person who manages a specific geographic area. At that point, police and other agencies are dispatched as needed and the call is monitored until cleared. On a daily basis, the people who work at these centres are exposed to every horrific event, accident, suicide, shooting and domestic violence call in the province. I met each person very briefly as they worked the calls and shared a micro version of my story and thanked them for what they do. Like other OPP groups, they had raised money, collected items and matched steps in several fun and engaging ways. It was cool to see how much they did to support *The Push for Change*.

As we travelled through Carlton Place, Perth, Smith Falls and Kemptville we had the pleasure of working with Greg Streng, who accompanied us every morning on the route. In addition to working really hard to support the traffic safety component of our campaign, Greg did an awesome job connecting to schools including a number of impromptu school presentations that he arranged. On one such day in Almonte, the kids from the local elementary school lined up all along the fence facing the highway. We pulled up and used a loudspeaker from the police car to do a short speech. They were all so excited and chanting and I carried that amazing energy with me for the rest of the day. At another elementary school we went into the gym to talk to the kids.

Because we were doing so many elementary schools, I was constantly working on ways that I could get the really young kids to understand what we were doing. I asked them if they thought it was good to share – and they yelled, "Yes!" I asked if they thought giving people a second chance was good, they yelled, "Yes!" I asked if they thought everyone deserved a warm bed and a home to sleep in and they yelled, "Yes!" It was amazing how grade four students understood the fundamentals of a social contract better than most adults. One afternoon as I tried to share the essence of my story without going into the more graphic details that I'm able to share with older groups, I asked the question: "How many of you have every felt that you were not good enough?" I used this question to talk about self esteem and how it related to the poor life choices I had made. I was heartbroken when 60% of those honest little people put up their hands. It really emphasized the importance of the prevention work we were pushing for.

Shortly after hitting the 3,000 km mark on Day 154, we visited the town of Kemptville thanks to a very special and eccentric community champion named Craig. Craig worked for the OPP and had reached out to us really early to request an event in his town. Our campaign route wasn't supposed to take us anywhere near Kemptville, but we decided engagement was more important than our route and made an adjustment. We did the same with a number of cities throughout the country. Some we walked into and some we drove or flew to just to attend events. That's essentially how we were able to fit in places like Yellowknife, Whitehorse, Prince Albert, Moosonee, and Norway House.

Craig was super energetic and passionate. He was the first of many to actually create a customized shopping cart to join us. He even sold advertising on it and did an amazing job of mobilizing the community to come out and support us. On the day of our walk, Greg Streng led us into Kemptville. It was a Sunday and the local farmer's market was in full swing as we headed downtown. Someone yelled out, "Here he comes, get your money out!" In an instant I was swarmed by well wishers offering hugs and handfuls of cash. We raised $300 in two minutes. When the event was over, we had raised over $8,600 thanks to Craig and his supporters. Small towns were way more fun for us throughout the campaign, not just because of the donations, but also for the amazing community engagement.

48

On September 30, we moved our base camp to Kingston KOA. The folks were super nice and the spot they gave us was really close to showers and laundry. We had learned from experience that proximity to amenities (along with good cell coverage), was the most important thing with any accommodation. Without good cell coverage we weren't able to post on social media, send or receive email or use the internet. Fortunately, Kingston was a great location and they gave us a break as a charity.

When we reached Kingston, we realized it was the end of the campaign road for Mike who was struggling with the increased activity and responsibility. His driving was excellent but as the campaign intensified in Ontario, cracks began to show. As we sat to chat at the picnic table at our camp site, I learned about a whole pile of personal matters going on back home that had his attention diverted. We both agreed it would be best for him to leave the campaign and within the hour his things were packed and we headed to the bus station. Although it was best for all it left Marie and I with a massive problem. We had no driver and no time to find a new one. We reached out to friends and supporters and even interviewed a fellow named Roy, but in the end it didn't work out. Fortunately, Glenda Reid from the OPP stepped up to help us as a volunteer driver for our next set of events as we approached the city of Kingston. Prior to the launch we had met a really friendly guy name Peter Kostogiannis from Kingston. Peter ran the Cushman Wakefield office and coordinated a team of volunteers to host events and make sure we had impact in Kingston. Peter and his team had been working for months to arrange over ten different engagements, many of which were in partnership with United Way of Kingston. On the day we arrived, we were met at the city limits by our friends from The Kingston Police Service. We picked up some walkers and headed toward Fort Henry where we met Peter and his staff. Peter had created special *Push for Change* water bottles along with customized t-shirts for Kingston which gave the campaign good visibility.

Our time in Kingston was a whirlwind, when we arrived on the steps of city hall; we were met by the mayor and the chief of police as well as the executive director from the United Way and a representative from organized labour. After a short speech and the presentation of challenge coins we headed to a local high school and then off to a private reception that evening where Peter presented us with a cheque for $25,000. The next day was a luncheon sponsored by Peter and coordinated by United Way with several hundred people including MPP Sophie Kiwala. United Way Kingston is a strong champion for homeless youth and the awareness and work we were championing linked really well to their projects.

Even though our Kingston engagement was really good, the fact that we were still without a driver was weighing on me. The role was so critical to our success but I didn't know where to turn. I decided the only way I could solve the problem was to start with a possibility mindset. As I sat in the control booth of a local radio station answering questions live on-air, I got the opportunity I needed. With only seconds left in the interview, the announcer asked, "What has been your greatest challenge so far?" I pounced on the opportunity and used it as a chance to recruit a driver. I explained how difficult the past few days had been and told listeners we needed to hire someone ASAP.

My radio appeal brought a call from a fellow named Jaime. As a front-line worker in the Downtown Eastside of Vancouver (who had since moved to Kingston), Jaime was intrigued by the interview and reached out to learn more. After a couple calls and some concessions on our end we struck a deal, Jaime would be the new full-time driver for *The Push for Change*.

On our last night in Kingston, Peter treated us to a lovely dinner with his family and then we headed out to meet former Toronto Maple Leaf legend Doug Gilmour and drop the puck at the Kingston Frontenacs game.

As a footnote to Kingston, at one of the schools where I spoke we met a young man who followed up with us and hosted a benefit concert several months later with his band City of Stone, which raised over $1,000. As we trekked across the countryside, we were excited by the fact that we were inspiring young people to initiate projects that supported our message. It was pretty special to watch these events popping up all over the country.

It was cold, windy and pouring rain when we left Kingston and headed towards Napanee on a route that took us past two notorious penitentiaries; Collins Bay and Millhaven. The skies opened up and even with my rain gear, I was soaked in no time. When I reached kilometre 19 for the day, I met with a number of members from UA Local 401 and we walked together for the last 6 km. As we walked along, one of the guys pointed to a house and said, "That's Bathhouse Recording Studio where The Tragically Hip recorded." I stopped and took a picture and after a really nice lunch with the guys we wrapped up for the day.

49

Jaime joined the campaign just outside of Belleville, Ontario and we decided to go off the route to a less crowded highway to do his orientation while I got in my kilometres for the day. That's where we were when a vehicle pulled over and my college professor Bernie Belange, stepped out to greet me. I had lost touch with Bernie some ten years prior but never forgot the impact he had on me and the friendship we had built. Bernie was a former prison guard who had quit his job to become a teacher; I was a former street addict with a history of criminal activity. In our old worlds we would never had become friends and yet we did at Loyalist College which I had attended in 1991. I loved that kind of serendipitous meeting; it was as if the universe was in sync with everything we were doing and every now and then it would spontaneously reveal a bit of its tapestry.

The fall colours were bold and vibrant as we arrived in Belleville, headed to a reception at city hall that had been organized by my college friend John Wendling. The Belleville police escorted us down Highway 2 and as we arrived we were greeted by the local MPP, the federal MP, my old friend Joan and our local fuel sponsor Fergusson Energy. I had to laugh when we experienced our first PFC distracted driving incident. As he watched our "walking parade," a guy driving in the lane next to us rear ended the car in front of him. Fortunately there wasn't any damage done and both drivers laughed and carried on. In the back of my mind I was aware of my own vulnerability, spending six hours a day walking alongside heavy traffic.

We finished Belleville with a visit to my alma mater Loyalist College, where Brad Baragar, another friend and professor of mine, hosted a series of events. We spoke to the students, followed by an interview on their in-house radio station and then had a gathering with the college leadership as well as the chief of police and local agencies. We even had time to visit Serenity House, the treatment centre where I got clean and say a few words to the clients. It was humbling to be back at the place where my life really began. Belleville wasn't just the place where I spent the first five years of my recovery; it was where I actually grew up and began taking responsibility for myself. I owe a deep debt of gratitude to Belleville, Serenity House and Loyalist College; together they provided exactly what I needed to move on and rebuild my life.

Before we left Belleville, we took a picture in front of the huge flower bed facing Highway 401 in the north of the city and then headed towards Trenton. When we arrived, we were greeted at the local high school where we had a wonderful event. We had been at this school before we launched *The Push for Change* so coming back was really cool for some of the students who had heard me talk a year earlier.

Even though we weren't scheduled to walk through Peterborough we visited for the afternoon and attended a community gathering hosted by the OPP. At the event, we were presented with yet another *Push for Change* cake. The funny thing about social media is that when we posted about the first cake, events all down the line got the impression that we liked cake – I loved it! Marie abstained; she's always had more discipline than I have when it comes to sweets. Speaking of treats, we had another unscheduled stop at the Enniskillen Ice Cream Shop in Hampton. We had met these folks at a Rotary event in Toronto some time ago and ever since the campaign launched, they had been collecting money in a jar beside the till. When we arrived, we got to meet the entire Sheehan family and were treated to a MASSIVE ice cream cone and $300 in donations. It was too cool, pardon the pun.

As we made our way west towards Toronto the campaign continued to pick up momentum. When we hit Durham, we were greeted by the local police as was the case in every community we went through. If an area wasn't served by the OPP, they had reached out to ensure we had support from whichever police service was in charge. When we originally created our map, we never in our wildest dreams thought that we would have police support in every major city in the country, but we did. Following a community event hosted by the Murray McKinnon Foundation, we moved on from Durham.

One of our biggest days around this time occurred as we walked from Bowmanville through Oshawa to Whitby. The day was planned and executed by our friend Terry Caputo from the Whitby Rotary Club. Previously, I had spoken in Toronto and met Terry when he invited me to speak at his club. That was before the campaign so it gave them lots of time to organize and get ready. Normally, I did most of my walking in the morning, but this was an afternoon event and my energy was low. It was also pouring rain so my spirit wasn't in the game until I arrived at the start location and saw how many people had shown up to walk the entire 24 km with us.

We had both police and fire department support as we departed Bowmanville and the crowd continued to grow as we went along. As we passed through Oshawa, we were joined by more community leaders and local officials and when we arrived at the Whitby Public Library there was a huge community gathering. The mayor, the police chief, the area's federal MP and provincial MPP as well as Rotary Clubs from all around the area had made commitments and we were presented with a cheque for over $10,000. Even though it was raining the community support warmed our hearts. This whole day was such a great example of how one champion could mobilize and bring together three cities. That evening a group of young people conducted a sleep out at the library in support of PFC. The campaign was firing on all cylinders and it felt great despite our fatigue.

50

Toronto proved to be one of the most intense weeks of the campaign. The logistics required for the Yonge and Dundas event alone almost killed Marie; she was literally having sleepless nights over it. The venue, which is Canada's version of Times Square, is one of the most iconic outdoor venues in the country and together with her team Marie had been working for months on this one massive event which involved coordinating hundreds of people. As a non-profit, we simply weren't staffed properly to coordinate huge events AND run the day to day logistics of a cross-Canada trek. Most of the events we had during the campaign were successful because of community champions like Terry in Whitby, who coordinated working committees to do most of the heavy lifting (so that all we had to do was show up).

Yonge and Dundas was our event and once we were committed Marie wasn't backing down, although working with the coordinator from the organization that manages the venue wasn't easy. One afternoon Marie got screamed at because our permits and other details were not according to their "process" since we were working directly with the Toronto Police Service and the coordinator didn't like that we bypassed her. We were told in no uncertain terms that our event was NOT going to happen and it left us with a sick feeling in the pit of our stomachs. This was one of the biggest events that we had planned in the country and we couldn't let it fail. We contacted a friend who had personal contacts with the Mayor John Tory and in one phone call the problem was solved. That phone call did NOT improve Marie's relationship with the coordinator but everything was set for a huge welcome into Toronto!

While Marie was busy with our downtown Toronto event, I rushed around doing media interviews (live in studio with CP24 and then AM 680). I also did a segment on Breakfast Television and was invited to appear on The Social on CTV. Coverage of PFC had gone national and the evening before our big arrival in Toronto, I spoke before a crowd of 20,000 people at WE Day Family at the Air Canada Centre. I was exhausted and exhilarated at the same time. As a side note, even if you think you're a confident speaker, a crowd of 20,000 will shake that resolve. As I walked out onto that stage with my PFC uniform and my shopping cart, I couldn't help but reflect on how much work had gone into that one moment. It was surreal to be speaking on stage with one of the biggest youth empowerment organizations in the world. It was definitely a "pinch me" moment.

As I wandered backstage, we got pictures with Colonel Chris Hadfield, Paula Abdul, Mark and Craig Kielburger and my old friend Rick Hansen, but my biggest thrill had to have been when Gord Downie walked past. He was gaunt and had his head down as he walked by wearing a jean jacket and his signature fedora adorned with feathers. We had been told prior to the event not to bother Gord if we saw him as he was very sick. Despite his illness, Gord was at WE Day to perform excerpts from Secret Path, the story of Chanie Wenjack who died trying to leave a residential school. The project had been created to bring awareness to the abuse suffered by more than 150,000 First Nations children in Canada.

Gord Downie died on October 17, 2017, eighteen days after I finished walking across Canada and if I have one regret, it was not stopping him in the hallway and thanking him for everything he gave us. Gord was a big hero of mine; a word shaman whose art captured our imagination and whose soul pierced our consciousness. Gord Downie defined what it is to be Canadian and he did it with grace and courage.

The next day, my *Push for Change* co-founder Sean Richardson was waiting for us at our hotel. He had flown in from Australia and our plan for the day was to walk across the top of Toronto from Don Mills to the 404 Highway on Steeles Avenue. It was a beautiful day despite being extremely windy, as we slowly worked our way across the city with Jaime driving in front along with a police escort. The following day was our big event in downtown Toronto so we were enjoying the quiet before the storm. When we finished up our walk we doubled back to Finch and Steeles, where there was a nice Welcome to Toronto sign, to take a picture for social media.

With nowhere to park, we ventured into a nearby housing project and parked illegally as our intention was to just stay a few minutes. We took our picture and headed back to the van only to realize we had locked ourselves out; that's when we started to panic. My phone only had 10% battery and we needed Marie to come over from the hotel and help us (like she didn't have anything else to do). I remember thinking as I stood waiting in the shadow of those huge low-rent housing towers that this probably hadn't been the smartest decision. I didn't bother telling anyone else in our party since I didn't want to alarm them, but we were in a North Toronto neighbourhood that had a reputation for gun and gang violence. After Marie rescued us and we were driving back to the hotel, I explained to the guys where we had been. Back at the hotel we were chilling in the lounge when the news came on with a story about a shooting in the neighbourhood we had just left. If they hadn't believed me in the van, they certainly believed me after watching the news.

That night Sean, Marie and I headed out together for dinner. As we got seated, I noticed someone's head bobbing in the booth behind us and to my amazement it was my mom, my little sister Roberta and my uncle Jimmy (who had come out to surprise me).

51

On day 175, the agenda was jam packed as we prepared to engage the city of Toronto. Today was the Yonge and Dundas event and the plan was for the team to convene behind the old Maple Leaf Gardens and lead a procession down Church to the back of the square at Yonge and Dundas where we had a large event planned.

The morning was cold as the crowd started to gather. The Glen Healy Pipe Band had agreed to lead the procession and we had huge support on the ground from the Toronto Police Service. The Toronto Police Service had done more than just provide traffic support; they also raised money and presented us with a cheque. The media was out to cover the event and the excitement in the air was palpable.

John Joseph and a number of friends from UA Local 46 arrived with the Hammer Heads. The Hammer Heads is an apprentice program sponsored by UA Local 46 that's offered to youth in impoverished parts of the city. The apprentices were all in their beige coveralls and looked quite impressive. Melanie Redman and Steve Gaetz also came down to walk with us and leading the way was former NHLer Glen Healy and his Pipe Band. My sister Roberta was also with us and after a few short words we headed out.

I remember looking at the rather formidable crowd and thinking back to the days when we were just planning; this was exactly what I imagined the campaign would look like. As we were about to start walking, Sergeant Elizabeth Byrnes from Toronto Police asked me if I would like to go down Yonge Street instead of Church. I said I would love to go down Yonge Street and just like that another dream came true. When we were planning the campaign back in Vancouver years earlier, we talked about walking down Yonge Street and our friends who represented both the Rick Hansen Campaign and the 2010 Olympic Torch Campaign balked and told us it would never happen. The logistics required to walk down one of the busiest streets in Canada were just too daunting. I believe in their hearts they were really trying to help us, but something important that I've learned from this journey is that just because someone can't see the possibility doesn't mean it can't be done.

The bagpipes were howling as the crowd surged forward and the narrow city street opened up into the massive open-air space that is Yonge and Dundas. The feeling of having achieved something that was so utterly difficult was unbelievable. It wasn't just about the campaign and walking several thousand kilometres; it was executing this huge event. We had a large group on the street as we edged closer but an even larger crowd was waiting for us at the square. I turned to Sean and said, "Remember when they told us this couldn't be done?" We shared a moment and then for the next few hours just took it all in.

When we arrived at the square, my mom and my uncle Jimmy were waiting and it was about as magical a moment as you can imagine. After walking for more than 3,000 kilometres (most of it quiet and alone) I found myself in one of the most extraordinary venues in the country surrounded by thousands of supporters.

It was not lost on me the amount of work that had gone into this day. There were food vendors and friends from Raising the Roof and 360 Kids; in fact, the entire square was set up with booths featuring organizations from all across the city. We also arranged to have the RV, the Mazda and the van present on the square so they would be visible during the festivities (the logistics on that alone could be a chapter in this story).

We posed for pictures and did a live social media feed with Sergeant Kerry Schmidt from the OPP, as well as media interviews with Global and City TV before we got pulled onstage. For the next few hours the celebrities and entertainers put on a spectacular show. The Glen Healey Band opened the show and The Salvation Army Kettle Band also played. Our very special friends Robert and Patti Pilon brought some talented friends to perform including the entire Laura Secord Choir. The Emcee for the night was Rod Black from TSN and Dr. Draw performed (playing the electric violin) as well as international recording artist Julie Black, who sang *The Push for Change* song. Garrick the DJ kept the music moving and Robert Pilon (with his extraordinary voice) sang a number of beautiful songs, which was a real highlight for me. Robert is a gifted performer and one of the songs he covers extremely well is *The Circle of Life* from *The Lion King*. I remember sitting onstage with Sean, Marie, Pinball Clemons and Rod Black as Robert belted out that song; the music filled the city streets and the emotion was incredibly uplifting. It was by far my favourite moment of the day. As I looked out into the audience, I saw so many friends and family: Martha and Russ from Barrie; my mom, my sister and Uncle Jimmy; the kids from Degrassi Junior High; and Terry Snooks and the brothers and sisters from UA Local 46.

It was amazing to hear all of these entertainers and influential people saying nice things about *The Push for Change* and showering me with accolades. Pinball Clemons got up and fired everyone up with an impassioned speech and then he brought me on stage and thanked me for the work we were doing. He also called me a hero and made a donation to PFC. I was deeply moved, not only because Pinball agreed to volunteer his time he also donated his own money to the cause.

Sean got up to share his message next and then it was my turn. I talked about why I was walking across Canada, what it meant to me and how grateful I was to everyone who supported us. One huge regret from that night is that I didn't directly acknowledge Dr. Steven Gaetz and Melanie Redman for all of their support of PFC and the amazing work they had championed all across the country.

After months of sleepless nights and thousands of hours of work, Marie and her small team had pulled off the impossible; coordinating and executing a world class event in one of the biggest cities in North America. This event alone should have had a team of 15-20 people and Marie had done so much of it herself, so I felt a little heartsick that she was left out when we were introduced onstage by the emcee. Marie was the person who had given her heart and soul to making Yonge and Dundas happen and I couldn't imagine what it must have felt like to not be acknowledged. When it was my turn to speak, I raved about the work she had done to make not only this event happen, but the entire PFC campaign! No words will ever be enough to give her credit for the time and energy she poured into *The Push for Change*.

After our big event, we had one more day in Toronto. We had engaged the public and now it was time to engage the government. Instead of walking away from Toronto we reversed our route so we would finish our daily walk in front of Queens Park, where the provincial government meets. We started in the dark but as the morning wore on, the sun rose directly in front of us and it was a picture perfect day. The commuter traffic was thick as we made our way along Lakeshore Boulevard. As we slowly approached the city, the iconic CN Tower was getting closer and closer and I could not believe what we were doing. It was all so surreal. We reached York Street and walked past The Royal York Hotel, then headed down University Avenue. The Toronto Police were taking each intersection in preparation for our procession using both motorcycles and police cars. It was amazing to watch how they blocked traffic and took lights with precision. I couldn't help but feel important as we made our way through the congested streets.

A funny coincidence that morning was that a friend who had inadvertently been stuck behind us in the traffic congestion that we had caused was none other than Steve Allmen. Steve was at the original event that inspired *The Push for Change* and he managed to jump out of his car to greet me as I walked through an intersection. He later told me how proud he was seeing the campaign grow from a dream to a reality. Catching up to us while we were walking into Toronto was just the icing on the cake.

When we reached University Avenue, we were met by the Minister of Housing Chris Ballard who walked with us to the steps of Queens Park. On the steps of the Provincial Parliament, we were greeted by a number of MPP's from all three parties, while inside Queens Park we were met by Premier Kathleen Wynne and officially acknowledged by the provincial government.

After a very short break we were whisked through an underground tunnel to the OPP's Toronto headquarters where yet another event was scheduled. A group of Ontario Public Service Students had raised food, money and needed items to donate. I gave a short speech and we thanked everyone for their support. Looking back on the events around Toronto, it was amazing how much we fit in, in such a short period of time. Most of our support from police initially came from the OPP, so it was always great to have events that included them. With that said, the Toronto Police were also extraordinarily supportive. When we initially drew up our route for the campaign, we didn't include major cities because we knew it would take a lot of work to coordinate so it was really cool to be in Toronto and have so much support from local agencies. We were especially grateful to Garfield Dunlop, who opened so many government doors for us at Queens Park.

We were really excited to have PFC acknowledged in the legislature by various MPPs from around the province. So were our law enforcement friends, who made the mistake of standing and clapping. I had to smile when the Speaker of the House asked them to respect the House protocol and refrain from applauding.

Engaging Ontario's provincial government had been a cool experience and on October 25, we headed to Ottawa where the same kind of thing happened in the House of Commons. Thanks again to Garfield who connected with MP Bruce Stanton and asked him to read a statement from the floor of the House of Commons. Having our hard work acknowledged by the federal government was incredibly gratifying, but what was even more important to us was the private meeting we had with MP Adam Vaughan. We managed to broker a meeting with Adam, together with Melanie Redman and Dr. Stephen Gaetz to talk about what was needed for us to get beyond just an emergency response for homeless youth. That meeting would prove to be very important.

Marie

Of the 453 events we hosted during the campaign, 266 were in Ontario, and of those, 221 involved the OPP. In Ontario, I was now in the deep end of the campaign working with dozens of community champions on the logistics of their events. As much as I loved attending every event (and needed this social interaction), there wasn't enough time to go to events and plan for what was coming next. I also didn't have time to feel left out as we had some pretty big events in October, including Joe's appearance at WeDay Family, our Yonge-Dundas event in Toronto, the Richmond Hill Rotary breakfast fundraiser, a Rotary Walk with Joe Rally in Whitby, several United Way events in Kingston. The list, although impressive, seemed endless. Before each event I would brief Joe on the specific details: who was hosting, who was attending, relevant community issues, media coverage, interview times, etc. My job was to protect his time so he could focus on his health and walking. Everything was shared on a need to know basis and our briefing time immediately before an event was always thorough and efficient.

October 25 was a special day for us; we had been invited to Ottawa's Parliament Hill to hear MP Bruce Stanton read a statement in The House of Commons endorsing The Push for Change. This was followed by an important meeting with MP Adam Vaughan, which was led by Melanie Redman from A Way Home and Dr. Stephen Gaetz from The Canadian Observatory on Homelessness. At the meeting we talked about youth homelessness prevention models that we hoped the government would support along with The Push for Change. This meeting proved successful as we later learned when the government released their 2017 budget.

At six months into the campaign, we were definitely in our groove and running the operation like an experienced team. The daily routes and meeting places were easy to navigate for both our driver and the OPP officer accompanying Joe. The events were well planned and executed and Joe's body was performing well. The RV was being parked for the winter and we easily changed gears to hotel living. I had booked our accommodations up to a year in advance, and as with the RV, we spent anywhere from six nights to two weeks in one place. Moving from place to place was just another aspect of the campaign and in many ways it was refreshing to see a new city almost every week! With 32 events in the calendar, October was one of our busiest months and we were thrilled to raise over $100,000. Even more inspiring was the impact of sharing Joe's message with thousands of people across Eastern and Central Ontario. It was uplifting to hear so many different people say, "I will never look down at youth homelessness again."

52

After Toronto we moved on to Brampton where we met with students representing ten local high schools (thanks to our community champion Regeneration Outreach Community). Our walk through town started off with a rally in downtown Brampton which was attended by the newly elected mayor, the chief of police and dozens of students who had raised over $1,000. The students had created handmade signs that they carried and each sign contained statistics related to homeless issues. What was incredible to me was that Brampton didn't have a youth shelter but they were trying really hard to get one up and running. We learned a few months later that they had successfully opened a youth shelter and our campaign had really helped to drive the project forward.

We had fun events in both Peel and Mississauga. The one in Peel was organized by a friend from the United Way and included a walk through the community with local schoolchildren supported by the Peel Regional Police. It all went very well, however, I remember when we were preparing to go to the event we received an email that had been forwarded to Marie by mistake. It was a long string and in it were some private thoughts on why the Peel Regional Police were assisting us. I chuckled when I read, "I don't know, it's some guy pushing a shopping cart that the OPP are in love with, so we need to help when he comes to Mississauga." In the end, the Peel Regional Police were awesome, but I found that email hilarious.

Moving on to Halton, I was joined by Tina Blatchford, the Executive Director from Halton Children's Aid Society for the day. Tina's organization had collaborated with the CEO of the Halton Schools District to get ready for us and when we arrived in Halton it was pure pandemonium. The local schools had spent weeks engaged in activities in preparation for our arrival and when we reached the first school, the kids were losing their minds. They were clamouring at the windows yelling, "It's him, it's him!" Our plan was to gather the first group of students and walk to a neighbouring school 3 km away where a rally was planned. After a short speech using a megaphone (which I am certain no one could hear over the kids), we headed out to the road, which is precisely when the skies opened up and it poured rain. It was an absolute downpour and the kids got soaked. By the time we got to the second school and joined up with the second group of kids the energy in the crowd was electric. It was like a concert and I was the rock star. My favourite moment was letting a shy young woman wearing a hijab push the cart the last 500 meters into the school. She acted like this was the greatest honour she had ever been given. I thanked her from the stage when the schools presented us with a cheque for $10,000 and I could tell she was thrilled to be acknowledged in front of her entire school. It was a magical day.

After the school event we headed to a hockey game organized by the Burlington OPP. Everyone at the game brought items to donate to a local shelter. Kerry Schmidt was there along with senior leaders and the game was great fun, although I have no idea who won.

The difference between Halton and our next stop in Hamilton was like night and day. Being dependant on community champions to organize events meant that sometimes there was little engagement in places that needed our message. It kind of bummed me out because Hamilton was home to the Walters Group, one of our big supporters and we had really hoped to put together a meaningful event. Instead of a big community event, I spoke to a group at a drop-in centre and spent a Saturday morning doing multiple presentations for City Kidz, an awesome program for inner city youth supported by the Walters Group.

We did have complete support from the Hamilton Police and I walked through the entire city early one morning, but instead of people running out to give us donations we got funny looks. I also had someone get really mad at me. As I walked along the road, the police cruiser hugged the right lane and the cars went around us on the left (fortunately, there were two lanes). The problem arose when the city bus went around us and in doing so it skipped a stop. A lady who was waiting for the bus realized what had happened and she was thoroughly unimpressed. As I walked by she glared at me. It didn't feel like a glare of support.

By the end of the day we found ourselves close to Grimsby at kilometre 3,471. The next day we would be picked up by the Niagara

Regional Police who would accompany us for several days as we made our way towards St. Catharines and Niagara Falls. There was little doubt at this point that fall was almost over and it was time to move out of the RV. After a day of purging and reorganization we loaded everything we needed into totes that could be carried in and out of hotel rooms and Jaime drove the RV up to Cookstown where our friends from Fraserway winterized and stored it for the winter.

Using hotels as our base for the winter had both good and bad elements to it. Marie and I had our privacy which was really nice and the heating was more reliable than in the RV; which Marie definitely liked, but lugging six totes around every time we moved was a lot of work. As with everything else, eventually we improvised and adapted and soon it just became the norm.

With the Niagara Police beside us, on November 1, 2016 (day 185 in our campaign) we made our way through Grimsby and on to St. Catharines. The Niagara guys were super accommodating and when we walked into St. Catharines we literally took over the entire bridge. It was another hero's welcome as we were met by the mayor and throngs of supporters who were waiting for us on the other side with signs and warm wishes. We walked through the downtown core to an event hosted by The Raft, a forward-thinking local agency that supported homeless youth. Mike Lethby, Executive Director of The Raft walked along with us, as did members of the Amalgamated Transit Union. Cindy Mewhinney from the local Rotary Club had coordinated a donation campaign in support of PFC and when it was done, we received over $10,000.

Marie and I had known Mike Lethby for a while, he had really helped us understand the issues around youth homelessness and his organization was one of the few in Canada that were getting really great results by working in schools and providing early detection and intervention strategies. By working with kids before they became homeless, they were actually seeing the number of youth on the street drop. This was the model we were pushing for every community across Canada to adopt.

We'd been on the road for a full six months and covered over 3,600 kilometres; with 11 months to go I was anxious about the approach of winter. We really had no idea how tough it was going to be and the thought was always in the back of my head that I would be pushing a shopping cart along the shore of Lake Superior in February. It was unsettling to say the least.

53

When you reflect back on a journey like *The Push for Change* it's not unusual for a lot of days to melt together, while other more significant moments really stand out and resonate in your memory. Day 187 was definitely one of those days. Given that we had the support of the Niagara Police we were told we could walk right up alongside Niagara Falls if we wanted to. During planning stages this was another one of those items we had been told by folks who had done treks across Canada to forget. They said the process to get permission to walk along the roadway that traverses the falls was simply out of reach for a small grassroots campaign like ours.

The morning we started towards Niagara Falls it was raining hard and all of the motorcycle officers were dressed in their rain gear. They also brought along a cruiser for additional support. As the day progressed the weather improved and so did my mood. There are several landmarks that define Canada. If you think about the images that accompany our National Anthem, they usually include the lighthouses of Atlantic Canada, the Rocky Mountains, the endless wheat fields of Saskatchewan and Niagara Falls. As we got closer to the falls my heart began to flutter and I was overwhelmed with emotion. Flanked by the full support of the Niagara Police, we were led up to the edge of the falls at Table Rock and I had this amazing feeling that anything was possible. I had dreamed about this moment and my dream had come true. We were even permitted to drive our vehicles up onto the pedestrian walkway where the Sergeant arranged to have a picture taken from the rooftop with the falls behind us. Those pictures are some of my favourites of the entire trek. We created so much buzz that people in the restaurant started coming out to make a donation. We even had

Japanese tourists wanting to take pictures with us although I'm not sure they knew why.

While we were at Table Rock, I had the opportunity to thank Staff Sergeant Romolo Diegidio of the Niagara Falls Police Service and give him one of our challenge coins. We had the challenge coins minted to give to special folks we met along the way as a small symbol of gratitude to thank them for being part of our team. They mean a lot in police and military culture and it was the least we could do to honour the volunteers who supported us.

On our day off Marie and I headed to London where the Canadian Alliance to End Homelessness was holding their annual conference. It was awesome to see our friends from all across Canada gathered in one place. I was given ten minutes to speak and even with that limited amount of time, I managed to bring everyone to their feet. What was really cool about the event was how quickly people recognized us. Given that we had already been through the entire east coast, the province of Quebec and a large chunk of Ontario, there were a lot of people we had encountered during the campaign that came up and said hello. Our time at the conference was short and sweet and we headed back to Niagara Falls to prepare to walk down towards Fort Erie.

On Day 188 we had another classic Canadian moment. Still supported by our friends from Niagara Police we were about 6 km into our morning walk when we decided to stop at the local Tim Hortons. With an entourage of three motorcycles and a police vehicle escorting us, it may as well have been the Queen coming in for coffee. There were cheers and applause as we walked into the parking lot. I don't think I have ever or will ever again acquire my morning coffee with quite the same pomp and circumstance.

It was a warm fall afternoon when we reached Fort Erie and stopped at the memorial near the water for some photos; after which Jaime and I headed off to the local high school for a presentation. Jaime was proving to be a real asset to the campaign; he was smart and worked well with the police. He was also an excellent photographer and intuitive in his thinking and actions. I didn't have to ask Jaime to take care of things, he knew without instruction and the campaign was running really smoothly as a result.

194

Before we left the Niagara region we attended a huge gala held in our honour along with a ribbon cutting ceremony for a local housing project. With little sleep we were up and out the next morning walking with our friends from UA Local 67 out of Hamilton. The guys were really accommodating and made us feel really welcome. They presented us with a cheque and a bunch of nice swag. We were even invited back for a BBQ but had to decline. It was really tough when people invited us into their lives. I was so exhausted at the end of the day I didn't have any energy left to socialize. I basically went back, showered, did social media or interviews and crashed. I always felt bad but I just didn't have anything left at the end of the day.

At kilometre 3,615 we said goodbye to our friends from the Niagara Regional Police, they had been a pleasure to work with and we had a few laughs along the way. Even though it was nearing the end of fall the entire week or so that we were together was done mostly with the motorcycles.

54

The strangest day of the campaign happened somewhere between Welland and Cayuga. It was a beautiful crisp November morning and we stopped for our first break. It was customary for me to walk a minimum of 6 km before we took a break. During our break I grabbed a handful of red raspberry candies which were left over from the previous night's event. I was always putting quick sugar snacks in the van for times when I needed a fast energy boost. After the break I popped a half dozen candies into my mouth as I began walking again, at which point I noticed something extremely unsettling happening inside my mouth. It felt like I had a mouthful of rocks. Instinctively I spit out the candies into my hand only to discover they had dislodged my bridge and two crowns. The entire back section of my right jaw was toothless.

As jarring as that was, standing on the side of the road with my dental work in my hand I looked up and to my utter shock saw Cal Misener walking up out of the ditch to greet me. My brain was having a really hard time processing everything because Cal was from Vancouver and had absolutely no business whatsoever being near Welland. Turns out he had a conference in Toronto and sneakily hatched a plan with Marie to find out where I was so he could surprise me on the road. Cal walked over 20 km with us that day and was rewarded at the end with a group of elementary students who were waiting for us in a small community. The group was full of energy and chanted at us when we got close. It was one of those magical moments that happened often but were difficult to describe.

We finished up the day in Jarvis which is in Haldimand County and after a brief event in Cayuga; we headed back to Welland for rest. We were going to need it to get through the next few days.

In Norfolk County we connected with the OPP's Ed Sanchuk who had been preparing for months. Ed had approached every business along the roads on our walking route and asked them to create a welcome sign for *The Push for Change*. McDonald's, Shoppers Drug Mart, the BP gas station, the Blue Elephant and even the Brew House had customized their signs for us (I found the Brew House support particularly ironic considering I haven't had a drink in decades). But it wasn't just the businesses that were ready for us, the schools were too. Ed had rallied every school in Simcoe and Port Dover to participate so when we walked through town the entire school population lined the streets. There were thousands of kids chanting and waving as we progressed along our route and I remember thinking it was a lot like Halton County. They had welcome signs and had collected donations, but most of all they were just excited to be a part of the campaign.

In Port Dover we teamed up with Mac's Milk to help them launch their positive ticketing program called Project Heat. Essentially, Mac's provided the OPP with free drink coupons that they could distribute to youth when they were "caught" exhibiting positive behaviour or doing good things in the community. The idea was to increase positive interactions between police and local youth. Each coupon was good for one hot chocolate and on the back of the ticket was information about *The Push for Change*, which was great exposure for us.

The launch event was held in front of the Mac's Milk store and after a few words from the mayor a group of students from a local school for the deaf presented us with a cheque for $367; money the young people raised all by themselves. It was truly inspiring. After the ceremony we walked down to the local community centre for our official PFC event. I remember leaving the event feeling completely exhausted, which happened a lot when the energy was really high. As we walked out of the centre, I noticed there were several shopping carts filled with food, toiletries and clothing that had been gathered by the OPP and community members and I was thankful to Ed, the hero who had mobilized an entire community and drummed up a huge amount of support in what was a pretty small place. What was even more extraordinary is that this kind of thing was happening all around the province, not just in communities we visited. For example, the Kawartha Lakes OPP detachment hosted an event in the community of Lindsay called "Sleep Walk for Change" that raised $8,317 and every day we learned about more events in various parts of the province and the country.

On Nov 12, Terry Gough from Ingersoll Rotary stepped in as our volunteer driver, which allowed us to give Jaime some extra time off. The landscape was very pretty as we walked along a single lane country road in Oxford County heading towards Aylmer and Tillsonburg. By now there was frost on the crops and the first snow could come at any time. I had grown accustomed to the feeling of impending doom that overtook me when I thought about it. The media was carrying us well in the small towns so roadside donations were frequent and generous. Just before we wrapped up that afternoon, a local electrician pulled his truck over and gave us a crisp $100 bill. Small towns were the best!

We moved our base camp to the Best Western in St. Thomas and an amazingly comfortable bed that was just what my tired body craved. It would be a well-deserved day off, or so I thought. As it turned out, I spent the entire day in the dentist's chair getting a root canal. After my crowns had fallen out, we went to a dentist in Niagara Falls, however by the time we could schedule it in we were 300 km down the road. I wasn't happy about getting a root canal, but at least I got to sleep in that morning and I was happy to have it fixed.

Down in West Elgin we visited several schools and did a walk through Aylmer followed by a short gathering in front of city hall, but the highlight was our visit to the Aylmer Police College and the opportunity to speak to students who would soon be joining police forces all around Ontario. The story of how Constable MacLeod had impacted my life was something I felt was extremely important for me to share with these young people at the beginning of their careers. It was also very cool getting a tour of the facility.

One evening on the way back from a particularly long day, Marie and I were looking forward to some rest when the phone rang and our friends at the St. Thomas YMCA asked if we were still coming. Ooooops! It was the very first, and only time, that Marie forgot an event. Luckily, we were already in the car and they were kind enough to wait. Despite the screw up, the gathering was amazing and we had the opportunity to meet with a group of young people who represented the LGBTQ community which is a group that is disproportionately represented on the street. I could tell *The Push for Change* story and my personal experience on the streets really resonated with them.

On day 202, we moved our base camp to Chatham and MPP Rick Nicholls, whom we'd originally met in Toronto, was there to greet us and walk through town. It was unseasonably warm and the walk was easy. The community did a really great job of coming together and a restaurant owner in downtown Chatham partnered with Rick's office to host a luncheon from which we received the proceeds. It was another excellent example of small communities pulling together.

The next day we attended a large annual event for the Salvation Army where I had been asked to speak. It was events like this that kept us going. It was also really important for us to focus on these regional engagements because for the most part we weren't really breaching the national consciousness with our campaign. The response was up and down; in some towns it was off the charts and in other communities it was really quiet.

55

As we moved through November; I knew it was just a matter of time before I would be facing snow. I stumbled across a Farmer's Almanac that promised a tough winter ahead. It had been a very long and unseasonably warm fall and the pessimist in me believed that for every day I got off easy I was going to have to pay double down the line.

The mayors of both Leamington and Kingsville came out and walked with me one morning. Our morning included a "walk by" with elementary students cheering us on, which was always a great way to start the day. Later that evening we hosted a community Town Hall to discuss issues around youth homelessness. This meeting would prove important in the coming months when policy was to be voted on. With a better understanding of what youth homelessness really is, the mayors and councils would be empowered to make better policy decisions to protect young people. It was a small win but that's often how change comes about. It was around this time that we learned there were also some really positive things happening in Ottawa on the federal front.

Just before we hit Windsor, we arranged to have a volunteer driver relieve Jaime for a few days so he could go home and be with his family. Retired OPP officer Tim O'Hagan jumped in to help us. When we arrived in Windsor, we had a number of schools lined up to meet us including George P Vanier, a French immersion elementary school. One of the teachers had heard about *The Push for Change* and called Marie and pleaded to have PFC come by their school. Apparently, the teacher was using *The Push for Change* to educate a class of fourth graders and when they found out there were young people in Canada that were homeless, they began fundraising and wanted to be involved.

We considered driving to the school, but decided it would have more impact if we walked and gave the kids the experience of seeing us arrive with our police escort. We were right. As we approached the corner where the school was, with the sirens periodically sounding off, the kids knew we were getting close and when we finally arrived, the entire school was waiting for us outside. The children were so inspired; they were holding support signs hand printed in French. The principal welcomed us and the kids recited a small welcome they had rehearsed. Using a portable microphone I thanked everyone and the kids began to cheer and chant. I remember looking over the heads of the youngsters and seeing a look in Tim O'Hagan's eyes; it was a special day indeed.

On day 206 we headed into Windsor supported by members of the Windsor Police; we had five vehicles taking intersections as we headed towards the downtown core. As we travelled through Walkerville, we had a spectacular view of both the Detroit skyline and the Detroit River and I recalled how a reporter near Leamington had asked me why we bothered to walk all the way down to Windsor. The answer was simple, not only did we not want to exclude Southwestern Ontario, we also decided to make the most of the tremendous support from the OPP and extended our route to include a huge loop through Southern Ontario so we could engage as many communities as possible. We ended up adding 800 km to the campaign and I was glad we did.

During one of our breaks, Tim and I were in a parking lot when he presented me with a special gift. Tim was a retired OPP member and as he handed me what looked like a faded blue mail bag, he shared a story. Before electronic mail existed, the mail bag was used by the OPP to transfer important documents around the province. These bags had been particularly important during a mail strike in the 1970s as that was the only means of sending mail critical to the operations of the OPP. He gave me the bag and told me it wasn't my job to "carry the mail." It was an inspiring gesture and the sentiment wasn't lost on me. I thanked Tim and in to return I gave him one of our challenge coins.

Tim had a funny smile on his face as he instructed me to open the bag. Inside was a large manila envelope which contained something that hangs on my wall today. Over the years, Tim visited the OPP headquarters in Orillia a lot and one afternoon he walked into a boardroom where he saw hundreds of 10x12 original photos of Terry Fox that had been taken in Northern Ontario. He convinced the guy in charge of the photos to part with two of them. Tim told me that the one in the envelope was now mine. Words can hardly explain how this gesture made me feel. Terry Fox is my hero. I met Terry when he came through Barrie in 1982 and his passion and the example he set was one of the greatest influences in my life. It was also one of the reasons we considered a walk across Canada. The photo Tim gave me was taken two days before Terry had to stop. It was taken on a huge hill east of Nipigon and in time I would face that very hill myself.

This gift was exactly the motivation I needed to face my fears about the winter weather that was coming. Later that night I shared the story with Marie and created a little goal to help myself stay focused. We had been walking for more than half a year and we weren't even close to the halfway mark. What's more, we had no idea how we would deal with severe conditions. There was still so much work to do that some days it was overwhelming. That night I calculated how far it was to the Terry Fox Monument in Thunder Bay and made that my new goal. It was 1,890 kilometres away and if I could get there, the toughest part of the journey would be behind me.

Windsor was an amazing series of events including a Walk with Joe through downtown and along Lakeshore Boulevard. During our walk we ran into some friends from UA Canada working on a job site. It was an awesome shout out and one of those really cool organic encounters. The weather was blustery; it was windy and really wet. We finished our walk at Charles Clark Square with a bunch of diehard supporters. Everyone was wet but spirits were high. After a few words from the police and the mayor followed by interviews with the Windsor Star, CBC and CTV, we were off. The following morning, we had an event with 700 students who had been bussed in for a youth rally. We also visited our friends at the Salvation Army where we spoke to clients and staff and then headed to Essex Children's Aid where we connected with a group of young people. Someone at Children's Aid found out it was my birthday so they had a cake ready for us. It was the big 5-0 and I could hardly believe I'd spent the past seven months walking across Canada.

While I celebrated my birthday, we invited communities to take part in the Sleep Out Challenge. The challenge offered youth and community leaders the opportunity to sleep out of their comfort zone and experience what it might be like to be homeless. The challenge was eagerly adopted by a number of organizations and community groups and started to blow up on social media with images being posted of sleep outs all around the province and beyond. The OPP were particularly engaged and shared photos from North Bay and Orillia of people outside trying to keep warm. Although it took me a minute to recognize him, there was even a photo of the deputy commissioner in a green jacket and black toque trying to stay warm and dry under a blue tarp. This was exactly the kind of community engagement we had hoped for and as I quietly turned 50, throughout the province and across Canada people were taking action and joining in *The Push for Change*.

Leaving Windsor, the weather was unusually warm. On the day we reached the community of Lakeside it was 20°C. As we left Windsor we were walking east, which meant it was one of only a very few times during the campaign when we faced the sun during our morning walk. For the next month or so we would be heading back toward central Ontario before turning north through Orillia on our way to Sault Ste. Marie.

At the community of Lakeside we were met by a small group of walkers and the community welcomed us by hosting a town meeting. We also had a visit from my relatives Tom and Joanne Williams.

Marie

Joe's 50th birthday was November 25 and I knew we couldn't celebrate it in a typical way with his family and friends. PFC was our life and right now it revolved around 24 km daily walks and community engagements. Social media was also a big part of our life, so I decided I would organize a surprise birthday video for Joe. I reached out to dozens of people in our network and asked them to send me a short clip wishing Joe a happy birthday. Before long, I had a file folder full of mp4 videos and with help from my son Curtis we created a wonderful surprise birthday video. I posted the video on our Facebook page and made sure Joe went to the page first thing in the morning on November 25. As he watched the video with people from all over the country wishing him birthday blessings, I could see he was touched in a deep way. Usually Joe was the instigator of inspiration, but this was a chance for him to see how he had touched others in a profound way.

As we celebrated his birthday together in our room at the Holiday Inn in Chatham-Kent, I couldn't help but feel honoured to be part of a trek where my own husband, a 50 year old man, sacrificed 17 months of his life to walk 24 km a day (often in adverse weather conditions), to raise awareness for youth homelessness. All in the hopes that no youth would have to experience what he did; living outside and stuck in a vicious cycle of drug addiction, disconnected from not only family, but community. As a mom of two young adults, the thought of them battling with addiction or struggling with mental health issues to the extent that they disconnected from family was heartbreaking to say the least. If we saved even one person from such circumstances, it would be worth it. I felt privileged to be leading a national campaign advocating for prevention and I felt blessed to be Joe's biggest fan, motivating him when he was tired and reminding him of the countless people he had already touched by sharing his most personal and life-changing experience of homelessness.

Follow the Journey online.

See the photos and videos.

www.thepushforchangebook.com

PART SEVEN
WINTER IS COMING

56

In Tilbury, we hit the 4,000 km mark as our route headed north for a few days to visit Sarnia. By day 213, winter had finally begun to catch up to us; there was no snow but the wind gusts were over 50 kmh and with the wind chill it was below zero. What made the day even more difficult was the fact there was no variation in the direction I was walking all day; I walked directly into the wind for 24 km. When I got back to base camp that night, I had severe wind burn on my face and ears which were both beet red. Marie noticed it the moment I walked through the door.

We reached Sarnia on day 218. UA Local 663 had been organizing for a while and we anticipated a huge walk with hundreds of participants. The meeting point was a car dealership approximately 24 km outside of town and it was still dark as two buses showed up full of caffeinated UA members. The Local had created their own customized shopping cart equipped with a set of lights, which really stood out in the dark! The cart was well put together and emblazoned with Local 663 signage supporting *The Push for Change*. It was an awesome start to a memorable morning. Led by Russ Jessop and Jim Hogarth, we spent the next several hours walking towards Sarnia and the union hall for an event. It was quite the sight to see hundreds of people walking down the highway flanked by the OPP and our support vehicles. No detail had been spared; they even had the foresight to wrangle a portable toilet that was in the back of a pickup truck behind the caravan of people. It was a sight to see.

The walk wasn't easy for everyone so our pace was slower than usual to ensure that we all stayed together. When we reached the city we made a brief stop at the Salvation Army and then headed to the union hall where the local hockey team was waiting for us with their sticks held in the air to create a hero's welcome into the hall. The event itself went really well, the community had gathered donations and purchased Christmas presents for local needy families. On the way into town Russ had made a phone call and helped secure a $10,000 donation so our trip to Sarnia was worth the detour. They even had a customized *Push for Change* cake for everyone to enjoy; I think it was the fifth cake we'd received.

We weren't quite halfway done the campaign and we had participated in over 100 events and raised $280,000, what we were doing was definitely working and yet I often had the feeling we weren't doing enough. No matter how successful we were I found myself comparing our campaign to other great cross-Canada campaigns and it was a foolish thing to do as it always left me feeling dissatisfied. It was difficult not to compare our accomplishments to those of others, but I knew that doing so was not a good use of my time or energy.

The next morning we were back to the routine of walking and with the help of the Sarnia Police we circled the entire city. It was a walking day with no events and towards the end of my walk I came face to face with the reason we were pushing for change. As I walked through an impoverished area of the city, I saw a young woman up ahead with a shopping cart. When she saw the police behind me she started to act a little nervous so when I approached I told her to relax, the cop was not going to bother her.

As I stood in the street with that young woman who was no doubt struggling with addiction and mental health issues (as well as poverty and homelessness) it was a stark reminder of the thousands just like her that needed help and support and thousands more that we could prevent from ever hitting the streets. I told her what we were doing and she thought that is was cool. After a few words of encouragement, we parted ways. Interactions like this really helped me when I felt tired or discouraged along the road. Thinking about a specific person or event helped me reconnect to my "why" and find the energy to soldier on.

One of our community champions in Sarnia was a young man named Jacob Pullen from Lambton College; Jacob was studying to become a police officer and had heard about us through law enforcement channels. Leading up to our visit, the college had organized hockey games, sleep outs and other activities to raise awareness about PFC, so when we arrived in Sarnia we visited the college for an organized event. At the event, I was presented with a jersey signed by all of the volunteers and the crew at Lambton even arranged for us to take part in a Santa Claus parade in Petrolia. It was awesome to see such enthusiasm from future community leaders and I made a point to formally acknowledge and thank Jacob for his commitment and present him with one of our challenge coins.

After Sarnia we headed east again and made a stopover in Strathroy where we walked with the chief of police and about 1,000 students to a local school auditorium for a huge event. The weather was getting colder and there were some minor snow flurries as we approached the city of London. Glenda Reid arranged for us to visit a second OPP Communications Centre where we witnessed all kinds of shows of support. The communications staff had created a Health and Wellness

Challenge to match my steps, they also filled several shopping carts with food and donated items and one officer even started a program to collect and distribute winter boots. The impact we were having (as evidenced by the notes and emails that both OPP civilians and officers sent to us) was truly inspiring. We weren't just having an impact on the issue of homelessness we were also impacting the organizational culture of the OPP and forever changing their perception of an important social issue.

As we approached the city of London, we stopped for a short chat with the London Police Department then headed off to Legacy Partners of London. Their company had been fundraising for PFC and they presented us with a cheque for $2,800. This kind of quick visit happened more and more as awareness spread across the country. We were thankful for every gift received and made a point to stop and thank as many organizations as we could along our route.

A rather strange coincidence happened while we were in London. The McIntosh Gallery at Western University was promoting The Unity Project, an organization dedicated to providing emergency shelter and transitional housing. The gallery's exhibition featured the work of artist Kelly Wood and the presentation was built around a series of photographs of shopping carts from the downtown Eastside of Vancouver. She had also created a book filled with pictures she had taken over many years depicting life on the streets of Vancouver. I thought it was only fitting that we attend the event and when I met the artist, I shared my personal experience as well as the story of *The Push for Change*. Not surprisingly, I could identify the exact location in Vancouver where a number of the photos had been taken and looking at pictures of neighbourhoods that were seared into my memory brought up a lot of emotions for me.

We had a great event in London with Youth Opportunity Unlimited (YOU), at their annual gala. YOU was perfectly aligned with what we were championing and the event was well attended by the city's stakeholders, which gave me the perfect platform to share my story and emphasize the need to continue to provide the best opportunities possible for marginalized youth. At the event we met a staff member from the Elgin Middlesex Detention Centre and with a bit of rescheduling we managed to get inside the facility the next day to speak to the inmates. The contrast between our audiences during *The Push for Change* was stark. One day we would be at a fancy catered event with city leaders and philanthropists and the next, we would be inside prison walls. In every case, our message of hope (and the need to invest in young people) transcended the differences. The message worked no matter where we went; it was something everyone could agree on. In addition to giving us an audience with the inmates, the staff at Elgin also raised $600 for the cause and we shared our thanks.

Leaving the outskirts of London the next morning, I encountered my first snow plow of the season as we headed towards Ingersoll. With very little snow to clear, the plow made a loud menacing noise as it scraped by me. It was like an eerie scene for a Stephen King movie as the grinding continued on down the road. The following day, we awoke to a huge dump of snow, winter was finally here.

In Ingersoll we intended to meet up with a group of enthusiastic young people from the local high school, unfortunately, the weather wasn't cooperating. Thanks to the heavy snow, the school buses had been cancelled; however, the event was still on for the community and OPP. That morning we learned how snow slowed everything; we took extra time to prep the vehicle in the morning, extra time travelling to the drop point, and it took a lot more time to walk in the sloppy, wet snow. We also ended up getting the van stuck, which was kind of my fault. Jaime was new to driving in snow and when he attempted a three-point turn in a driveway, the heavy van slid sideways. Wanting to help, I jumped in the driver's seat and within a couple minutes had the van pinned against the homeowner's gate. I still had to get my kilometres in, so I left Jaime to wait for help. Kudos to him, he managed to find a tow truck and they pulled him free.

With that small mishap behind us, our first stop in Ingersoll was a site visit with Fusion, an organization that supported youth in the community with a wide range of programs and services. Next, we headed to the local high school and even though the students weren't there we still had a great presentation with the few dozen folks that could make it. The local Rotary Club presented us with a cheque and to make up for not seeing the kids we recorded a cool video and left it behind for them to play later. I really felt bad for Terry Gough, who was our contact for Rotary and the schools; he had worked so hard to engage his community, unfortunately Mother Nature had a different plan.

The following day there was terrible weather as well and by the time we reached the city of Woodstock, we were walking in blizzard conditions. In fact, the picture on the cover of this book is from that day. We finished our walk at the local fire hall and prepared for an event at the community centre. St. Mary's Catholic School hosted the event and raised $711 for us. After a short speech from centre ice (another horribly Canadian thing), we headed off to help out with a community booth at the Kitchener Rangers OHL hockey game. We even got some coverage on the big screen during the game, which was an added bonus.

57

Despite being out of the way, the one city that we absolutely had to visit in Ontario was Brantford. Wayne Branchaud was a champion of ours from the beginning of the campaign. He and his wife Dee had hosted events for us, led fundraising efforts, connected us with people that helped solve our insurance problems and even flew out to Newfoundland to walk with us on the rock.

Wayne had committed to walk the entire day with me and he came through on that promise. We started early in the morning and by mid day we arrived in town and the city of Brantford was waiting for us. Wayne had a great organizing committee and as we made our way through town, I looked over my shoulder to see fire, ambulance, police, and hundreds of supporters walking with us. It was still snowing and we got some epic pictures of everyone walking through downtown towards an event at the Sanderson Centre. Thanks to Wayne we received a pile of donations from individuals and organizations, including our friends from the Lions Club, who stopped by our room at the Best Western to present us with a cheque for $1,000. Another day, I remember it was very cold on my walk and I stopped into a local Husky gas station where the owner gave me a $100 bill. That's just how good Brantford was to us. During our walk through Brantford we ran into a friend from the Walters Group who worked at a facility close by. Word got back to the

CEO and once again the stars aligned and we were asked to join them in Hamilton a couple of days later for their annual Christmas dinner. Although we were there simply to thank the organization for their support, in true generous fashion they presented us with a cheque for the cause.

After leaving Brantford, we visited the Six Nations Council and took part in a number of events they had planned, including a sleep out. We were welcomed into the community and shared our story before doing a community walk. It was a very special moment walking with the Chief and the elders discussing what we share in common.

On day 233 we awoke to a foot of fresh snow and a temperature of -12°C. My iPhone wouldn't work at all in the cold, the wind and snow brutally slammed into my face with every step and the battery in the van died; it was a perfect storm.

One of the greatest lessons I learned during the campaign was that no matter what life threw at us, there was always something we could do to keep moving forward. Once we made the public declaration that we were going to push a shopping cart across Canada, there was no backing out, which meant that we simply needed to deal with every problem that came our way until we accomplished our goal. Whatever roadblocks we faced, there was always a next positive action. I'm not saying it will always be fun, but I can tell you there is always something you can do to move forward. You can quit (that's always a choice) or you can complain (which just delays the inevitable), but the smart choice is to skip the drama and get busy on the next action you can take to reach your goal.

The next day, winter conditions were downright dangerous; the roads were extremely slippery and several cars had gone into the ditch. We were eager to get media coverage but only for the right reasons. We certainly didn't want to be on the news for causing an accident, so after discussing the situation with the OPP and Cambridge Police, we decided to cancel the day's walk from Cambridge to Kitchener. We still had a community event scheduled at city hall with the mayors of Kitchener, Cambridge and Waterloo, along with MPs, MPPs and lots of community supporters. I was happy because all of my nieces showed up too. As we left the event someone had a brilliant idea, since we'd been walking in all kinds of weather, why not ask The Weather Network to come out and cover our story. So, we reached out and told them about the crazy conditions we had encountered so far on our trek and they sent Storm Hunter Mark Robinson to cover our story. Much to our surprise, the piece ended up getting national coverage. How's that for taking advantage of a bad set of circumstances?

In Kitchener, we had engagements organized with more than 15 schools. Prior to the campaign, the Waterloo Catholic District School Board had committed to work with us and they were well organized when we arrived in the area. Over the course of several days we had thousands of students from schools including St. Margaret, St. Mary's and St. Benedict walk with us and attend hosted events. They had also done a great job of raising money and we were presented with donations at every school we visited. One morning we met at one school and arranged to have the kids walk with us to a neighbouring school for an event. The roads were filled with snow that day so in one section we took the sidewalk.

The route took us down a long hill and up the other side. When I got to the top, I turned and took a picture of the students as they marched and chanted behind me. The line was blocks long and it made for a surreal photo. On another day we were in Dave Griffiths neighbourhood. Dave had coordinated a whole bunch of events in Guelph so walking past his house was a kind of tribute to say thanks. The OPP pulled out all the stops for the occasion and showed up with eight police vehicles for the walk past. I chuckled to myself because it looked a lot like a scene from the OJ Simpson police chase from the 1990s. Dave had worked extremely hard to rally his community and make *The Push for Change* well known in the city of Guelph and he deserved all the recognition we could give him.

Winter walking presented some new problems as we headed into Guelph. The snow had begun to pile up and we were concerned about drivers swerving or sliding into us. The shopping cart was holding up well and so was my body, although it was significantly harder to walk 24 km in sloppy snow. My lower legs were working hard to adjust and my calves in particular were sore from plowing through wet, thick snow. When the snow was wet it also slowed down the shopping cart as the wheels picked up snow; it wasn't ideal, but we learned from each new challenge and made adjustments. In many ways we were making it up as we went along and the knowledge we accumulated as a result was amazing. We also learned that showing up every day and taking action (no matter how you feel) builds resiliency and provides the practise needed to solve any challenge.

When we reached Guelph, we thanked Dave Griffiths and QCC Canada who put us up in a really nice hotel. It was wonderful to be pampered given that winter conditions had made it much harder to walk every day and our level of community engagement had increased substantially. A typical day started with the daily walk, after which I would speak at one or two schools and then do media (which could include posting on our social media channels or doing interviews). When it was over, we would head back to our home base to shower, do laundry, cook, eat and sleep; only to wake up the next morning and do it all over again (and hope the weather would cooperate). Don't get me wrong, it was exactly what we wanted the campaign to be like, but it was also a continuous stream of work with no end in sight. Given my experience thus far walking in the snow with my shopping cart, the thought of walking in Northern Ontario was even more daunting, yet that's where we were headed.

Dave had hired a coordinator to put together a series of impactful events in Guelph and they were executed with precision. The first event was held at the hotel where we stayed and was attended by the OPP, community stakeholders, the mayors of several surrounding communities, senior leadership from UA Canada and QCC Canada as well as Michael Pinball Clemons, who gave an inspirational address. In addition to the money raised at the event, there were several shopping carts in the lobby that were filled up during the event with items to be donated. We also received a cheque from Cooperators Insurance for $5,000.

One of the fun things that Dave and his team came up with to raise money for the cause was PFC socks. They ordered thousands of pairs to sell at local hockey games and in the community. The idea was very successful and raised thousands of dollars. Our days in Guelph were jam packed, in addition to walking with students from several schools, we hosted a public skating event where I got to put skis on the shopping cart and skate around with the mascot from the Guelph Storm OHL hockey club. On another day we visited the local homeless mission and shared a message of hope, but my favourite event took place early one morning at a local diner. The restaurant had volunteered to donate and serve breakfast for a ticketed event attended by the mayor, the local MP and our friends and clients from the Wyndham House Youth Shelter. I remember watching as the OPP and Guelph Police Service members served the young people breakfast. It was an inspiring demonstration of leadership and unity and everyone had a great time. There was also lots of money donated. It was really touching how Dave had committed so much time and effort to the success of the campaign right from the beginning, brainstorming ideas, organizing events, visiting us at several points during our trek and hosting us in his hometown. He was a true PFC champion.

Several weeks after leaving Guelph, we received a letter from the Executive Director of Wyndham House thanking us. In her 27 years working in the business of helping young people, she had never before experienced such a fantastic outpouring of support. Not only had the attitude of the local police changed, but local businesses were calling her to ask how they could help and social justice classes from schools throughout the area were offering support of all kinds. All of the attention had also made youth in the community more aware of the resources available to them. Although our time in each community was short, the power of connecting people and inspiring them to work together produced a wave of positive side effects that continued to ripple long after we had moved on.

Looking back, we were amazed at how well Guelph did in hosting so many events just before Christmas; it's a tough time to get folks out and they really came through. In the lobby of the hotel just before we parted ways, Dave presented us with one final gift. He was heading off for a well-deserved holiday, but before he left he pulled out his smart phone and shared a short video with me. On the screen was Don Cherry in the Hockey Night in Canada studio doing a shout out for PFC. I couldn't believe my eyes. Canadian icon (and legend) Don Cherry was supporting us publicly. I gave Dave a teary-eyed hug and thanked him for being such a champion. Dave explained that he knew Don Cherry through some other business and had asked if he would help us. Don was more than happy to help and we got a lot of airplay out of that video. As Dave left for the holidays, we headed to St. Thomas Aquinas in Tottenham to pack up and then moved our base to Newmarket.

58

We reached Newmarket on the edge of the Christmas holidays and gave Jaime some time off to be with his family. Russ from Barrie, who is Martha Baker's significant other, agreed to volunteer for the next couple of days. Both Russ and Martha were such great supporters of the campaign that they were game for any task, so when we told them we needed a driver for Christmas day they were more than willing to help.

On Christmas morning we started our walk in the parking lot of the York Regional Police with the same officer who had accompanied us through the top of Toronto. It was a quiet morning and Russ followed behind as we walked through the quiet city streets. Marie didn't often have time to walk with me, but today she joined me and it was so wonderful to share Christmas morning with her. The scene couldn't have been more peaceful and serene, when all of a sudden we were bombarded with the loud grinding of heavy metal music (cranked and blaring) from the support van. At first, I thought he was just playing a joke but after two blocks of noise I had to go back and ask him to dial it down. What Russ didn't realize was that the van's largely hollow interior amplified the music much more than in a normal vehicle. The kids in the neighbourhood must have thought Satan had come to town instead of Santa; on our break we had a good laugh about that.

By late morning, we had made our way out of Newmarket and onto Highway 11 heading north towards Bradford. At one point a vehicle stopped and I was surprised to see my mom and my uncle Jimmy, who jumped out to give me a hug. We were getting close to Barrie where they lived, so it was nice that they could drive out and visit me on Christmas. Before the end of our walking day my niece Emma and her husband Kawlin also joined us as we finished with a walk through Bradford.

Back at the hotel we got to spend some family time together. My daughter Loren was just waking up and it was not a traditional Christmas family morning but it was pretty cool as we enjoyed food and gift exchange. One of the toughest things I had to manage was how to juggle so many roles and partition time as best as I could. Yet no matter how well I did, I also felt that my daughter and Marie were not getting enough of my attention. It was one of the harder things I had to reconcile during the entire campaign.

The next day started in Innisfil and we reached Barrie, the town where both Marie and I grew up. The weather had been cold, then warm, then cold again and the sides of the road were solid ice although the roads themselves were dry. I was wearing a pair of new boots that had special grip soles, but it was still slow going on the ice. We made our way down Highway 11 into the south end of Barrie where we met a large group of people waiting for us in front of Zehrs. It was kind of funny being back home. Marie and I had planned the entire campaign from our home in Barrie, so walking this far across Canada had a sentimental quality to it.

59

Barrie held two distinct sets of memories for me. First, it was the city I lived in when I was young and making a lot of mistakes. It was also the city where Marie and I had developed our plans to build *The Push for Change* campaign. We had family and a lot of community connections in Barrie and on the morning when we arrived at Zehrs, a lot of them were waiting to greet us including Mayor Jeff Leman, Barrie Police Chief, Scott MacLeod, and OPP Deputy Commissioner Rick Barnum. Our friends from Youth Haven also came out to support us.

We left the Zehrs parking lot with the goal of reaching Kempenfelt Centre, where the Rotary Club was hosting a large luncheon for us. As we walked down Yonge Street with a large group of people, I had a flashback to one of my training days. When I lived in Barrie prior to the campaign, I walked thousands of kilometres as part of my training regimen. One summer afternoon I was walking near Yonge Street and

Little Avenue when a large procession flanked by police and support vehicles entered, then moved through the intersection. I had no idea what campaign it was, but I was so inspired to see them moving down the road supported by the community and police. As I stood there, I told myself, "That's what I want our campaign to look like when we reach Barrie." A smile came to my face as I walked through that very same intersection. My dream had been realized; even better the support we received in Barrie was a lot more substantial than I had imagined it would be.

The event at the Kempenfelt Centre was very moving; Scott MacLeod was there along with my mom, Marie's mom, her husband Neil and my daughter Loren. It was a homecoming of sorts and with speeches from MP's and the mayor, we had ourselves a pretty inspiring afternoon. The day finished up with a cheque presentation from Rotary and then a couple of local musicians performed *The Push for Change* song. Martha Baker had arranged the performance and when they started to sing, I got emotional; it was a perfect homecoming. Barrie had also been the scene of my early addiction and it was a city I had fled from trying to find myself. To be back decades later, receiving accolades and support from community leaders for the work we were doing to help youth who were struggling as I had struggled; it was a point of great pride for me.

Walking into Barrie had been difficult on the ice but walking out the following day was even harder. Overnight we'd received 30cm of snow. It was wet and slippery and it made walking tough. The OPP's Steve Martel was behind me, with the Barrie City Police in front. We started in the downtown core and when we hit the main street, I ran into another gentleman with a shopping cart. It was freezing cold with 30cm of fresh snow and this man was out collecting empty bottles and cans to earn a few dollars. We spoke briefly and I told him my story. The shopping cart I was pushing represented an outcome we were trying to avoid for young people. This man's shopping cart represented his need to survive. It was a stark reminder of the importance of our campaign and also of all that I have to be thankful for today; I was both humbled and grateful for running into this man.

Our route took us up and down some very steep, slippery hills and Jaime got the van stuck a couple of times. We worked our way through the community and then walked out of town and through Midhurst (a community my family had lived in for short time). We ended our day back in Barrie at Georgian College.

The OPP coordinated a very cool breakfast event where OPP members and their families came out to serve a community breakfast. It was open for anyone but geared towards supporting the poor and homeless in downtown Barrie. Again, it was great to see the police and their families coming together to support vulnerable people.

The following day was December 29, and with the help of Steve Martel from the OPP we made it to ORO Station. Unfortunately, most of the walk had to be cancelled due to blizzard conditions. Thankfully, the short walk we had planned with the community was still on. We met at the community centre with the goal of walking up to the fire hall and back. As always, the OPP was very well represented and our good friend (and ardent supporter) Chief Superintendent Ken Leppert drove all the way down from North Bay to attend. We were also joined by a number of senior officials from Orillia, Deputy Commissioner Rick Barnum and Opposition Leader Patrick Brown, who brought his mother to join our walk.

The biggest highlight from our time in Oro was Tania, otherwise known as the "Soup Lady." Tania worked as a civilian for the OPP and was one of our biggest supporters. She was determined to raise $1,000 so she could push our celebrity shopping cart. Tania had worked tirelessly to support us and when she hit her goal, we proudly pulled the cart out and publicly acknowledged her for all her hard work. She was as happy as I've seen; grinning from ear to ear she was so proud to be a part of the walk and the campaign. You see Tania had a special connection to the homeless community. For years she has been known in Barrie for her Big Black Soup Truck or as the Soup Lady. Tania started feeding the homeless years ago; it began with her making a large bowl of soup that she served from the back of her truck. When we met Tania, she had been serving the community by providing food and clothing for over a decade, so when she heard about *The Push for Change* she wanted to help in any way she could. Not only did Tania proudly take part in our walk that morning, she also served us all a nice bowl of healthy soup when we returned to the community centre and gave us the leftovers for the next day!

Our last event for the year was a large outdoor New Year's Eve celebration hosted by the City of Barrie which had two parts. First, the family portion (for those with kids) ran until nine o'clock followed by an adult celebration with live bands and fireworks to ring in the New Year. I was asked to speak to the kids and it was a really great crowd but my energy was low and I hadn't really prepared anything. I was given 12 minutes to speak but only spoke for about eight which left a hole in the program since the fireworks were scheduled for a pre-set time. Fortunately, Mayor Jeff Lehman rescued me and we rang in the New Year together.

That night back in the hotel, we crashed; it had been an incredible couple of weeks. We were all exhausted and needed rest even though we knew none would be coming. 2016 was officially behind us and we had succeeded beyond anything we could have imagined. We had successfully made our way along the Ontario route, executed hundreds of events, raised hundreds of thousands of dollars and successfully adapted to winter. With 2016 behind us, it was time to really test our resilience as we headed into northern Ontario in January.

Marie

As 2016 drew to a close it was hard for me to focus on the accomplishments of our campaign thus far. Since I was very young, I had been driven to do my best at everything I took on and my work as campaign director was no different. With every detail and decision, I noticed what was missing and what could have been better. Although many details were beyond my control, I unnecessarily beat myself up when an event didn't have enough people in attendance, or it wasn't covered by media, or didn't raise a lot of funds. Instead of patting myself on the back for all of the successes of the campaign, I judged myself for the things that didn't measure up to my self-imposed standards.

Something that Joe and I had in common and loved about our reconnection was our shared enthusiasm for personal development. We were always reading books, watching self-help videos and working to develop qualities that would improve our well-being. One day when I was feeling disconnected, I pulled myself away from my laptop and phone and sat on the bed in our hotel room to contemplate my feelings of inadequacy. I had learned somewhere that as humans our brains have evolved to survive and that the tendency to dwell on negative issues more so than positive ones is my brain's way of keeping me safe. Psychologists call it the negative bias. Historically, humans had to be on the lookout for things that were dangerous or threatening and this instinct had been passed from generation to generation.

Well, I knew there was no imminent threat for me to worry about, so what strategies could I employ to overcome the negative bias that was making me feel inadequate? I decided the best place to start was by being more mindful of my thoughts. When I found myself dwelling on a negative thought, I made a point to mentally stop and consider, "Was there something to learn from this thought and how could I reframe it or replace it with something more positive?" I also decided to focus more attention on the positives that happened (and there were definitely tons of positive to dwell on).

I pulled out a sheet of paper and listed every accomplishment that I had managed or overseen thus far in the campaign:

1 — I had planned and successfully executed 196 events

2 — We had raised funds in excess of $400,000

3 — I had coordinated 162 media interviews

4 — There were no injuries or major hiccups to report after six months on the road

5 — We had been successful in getting an S031 statement endorsing The Push for Change read out in the House of Commons

6 — We had instigated collaboration between social work and service providers in multiple cities

The list went on and on and by all accounts I should have been damn proud of my achievements.

Over the next few weeks, I focused on adjusting my expectations to be more realistic and practiced the power of acceptance while also verbally acknowledging what I was grateful for. It didn't take long before I noticed how shifting my focus to the positive emitted feel-good chemicals in my brain. It sounds so simple when I write it on paper, but boy do I know how easy it is to be caught up in negativity and get stuck there. It was refreshing to know I could stimulate my own happy chemicals instead of relying on the world to do it for me. Maybe I was in control after all.

60

On January 1, 2017, we arrived in Orillia. The city had been preparing for our visit for a long time and Inspector Pat Morris from the OPP had been organizing events with local schools. Students from a variety of schools had taken part in sleep outs and Patrick Fogarty Catholic Secondary School had hosted a ping pong tournament. The original plan had been to bus the students from all of the local schools to the Opera House and have a huge community rally so we could meet the students and thank them for their support. Unfortunately, the weather was horrible and all of the buses had been cancelled due to freezing rain. It was a little heartbreaking considering how much work had gone into organizing the event, not to mention months of fundraising by the students.

Despite the weather, we decided to go ahead with the presentation at the Opera House for anyone who could make it and with the help of Mayor Steve Clarke we connected with several dozen folks from the community. The OPP, the Orillia Fire Department and several other local agencies also came out to support us and one mom brought three young girls who were about 11 years old. After our presentation we had a chance to chat with the girls and even though the other 700 students hadn't been able to make it, we made the most of the opportunity.

Later that night the mom sent us a video of what happened when they left the Opera House. On the way home the girls spotted a man sitting on the corner holding a sign. He was homeless and they wanted to help him. The video showed the girls get out of the truck and go to the man; as they approached him, they said some kind words and offered the man help. As I watched the video, it warmed my heart to see these young ladies inspired to take compassionate action. One of our most pressing goals during the campaign was to get people to see those who are homeless through a different lens. It's not that I advocate giving money or food to every homeless person you see on the street, but rather to view them as fellow human beings with a heart of kindness and compassion. If we can do that, we will be able to find solutions that serve them and also help us. These young ladies and the video their mom made really inspired me on that cold, blustery day.

Orillia had other surprises in store for me as well. When we arrived in the city, Marie told me we had an event to attend at OPP General Headquarters. When I asked how many people would be there she said, "Maybe 30-40," so I assumed it was going to be a small reception with a few folks to mark the beginning of a new year and our halfway point through Ontario. We had been given directions to OPP Headquarters and instructed to wait at the end of their big driveway. The building was an impressive modern structure where thousands of people work every day keeping the province safe. The driveway was a huge one-way semi-circle that led to the entrance. As we stood waiting as we had been instructed, the building began to empty and hundreds of people poured out to greet us. Eventually, the commissioner and the deputy commissioners came out to formerly greet us and accompany us into the building.

By this time, the semi-circle was lined with a contingent of uniformed police officers and as we walked with the commissioner towards the building's entrance they began to clap rhythmically to welcome *The Push for Change*. The clapping sounded like drums and had such resonance that I could feel it in my heart. "How cool is that?" I thought to myself as I moved along. There were a lot of familiar faces in the crowd; folks who had been helping and supporting us for months as we travelled through Eastern Canada and across Ontario including members of our traffic safety support team, executive committees and the engagement teams who worked with us in the schools. It was ironic to think that at one point in my life I had been living on the wrong side of the law, struggling with all sorts of personal issues and now, I had successfully inspired and engaged one of the largest police forces in the world to help support an important issue. Walking into Ontario had been amazing, but this was my new favourite day. I truly felt like a hero.

Once everyone was back inside the building, we held a presentation in the cafeteria (later we learned that there had never been that many people in the cafeteria at one time). As I spoke, I could feel that my message was resonating around the room and I remember thinking, "This is not the 30-40 people Marie said it would be." It was a huge gathering and I was inspired to see the entire senior leadership team there standing side by side with the cadets. In fact, the group that lined the driveway were all new cadets, so I took the opportunity to share the story of how as a young officer, Scott MacLeod had impacted my life. I explained that in their career they too might have an opportunity to change someone's life and encouraged them to be on the lookout for their "Joe." Following a cheque presentation and photos, we headed back to the Best Western Mariposa where our friend Michelle was taking really great care of us. Best Western was one of our generous "in kind" supporters throughout the campaign and we were thankful to be very well taken care of wherever we went.

Our visit to OPP Headquarters was definitely one of those uniquely memorable days that stick out in retrospect. We were so fortunate to have garnered the support of the OPP and to have them embrace us in the way that they did was something we could never have predicted. What was truly amazing is that from the very beginning, we had intended to walk through Northern Ontario in the winter and yet we did so without ever considering the logistics of such a thing. When we planned the trek, it was four years before we had our first meeting with the OPP. How bold was that thinking? The truth is, if we hadn't forged this relationship we would have probably been removed from the highway on day one and that would have been the end of it. The goal to walk across Canada was really created with that *Field of Dreams* mentality that, "If you build it, they will come." I think any big audacious goal has to have some element of that kind of thinking. Any time you tackle something big, there are always going to be huge unknowns and in order to get the answers you need to move forward, you're going to have to step out of your comfort zone and take a few risks. By continuing to take action while staying focused on our vision, we found our way to the help we needed to get the job done.

On January 2, we hit the halfway point of the campaign (kilometre 4,500) as we left Orillia and headed towards Coldwater and Midland. The weather was cold. It was -9°C with a wind that felt much colder. I had to cover my whole face for fear of exposure and frost bite. The thing about that kind of cold is you could easily freeze up and not know it. My body was always well protected (with the right gear and gloves to protect my hands) but my face was usually exposed. At one point when I jumped in the van, I realized I had lost feeling in my cheeks and ears, so I warmed them up and put on additional layers of protection before I headed out to continue. Spending 4-6 hours a day on the side of a windy highway was a challenge when the weather was this cold. One advantage of the cold was that the usually sloppy snow became crunchy, which made it much easier to walk. I would much rather walk on top of hard snow than trudge through wet stuff. It was interesting that with every kind of weather, there were both good points and challenging ones. Given that I couldn't control the weather (or choose where I would walk on any given day based on the forecast), it helped to look for the positives.

When we reached Coldwater, Garfield Dunlop and his wife Jane had a nice little event planned for us and Russ and Martha from Barrie presented us with a cheque (which was just another example of how much these two wonderful people supported us). Russ and Martha really deserved a medal for their dedication; they were always there when we needed them. Marie's mom and Neil stopped in as well and some kids from the local area came out so we had a small chat on the ice rink. It was really cool to be in Coldwater because the bridge over the little river was dedicated to Rick Hansen and Garfield had actually been there when Rick's Man in Motion World Tour came through town decades earlier.

Switching up my footwear to walk in the cold and snow wasn't as easy as I'd anticipated. To date, my training and campaign walking added up to more than 10,000 kilometres, all of which I'd done in shoes (and mostly just one kind of shoe). As I switched to winter boots I began to experience problems; my hip flexor started to act up and my shins started to hurt, a lot. After a day of walking, I found myself lying on the bed with both shins throbbing in pain. I also noticed that when I woke up in the morning and climbed out of bed, the simple act of standing up caused my shins to ache. It was concerning and something I knew I would eventually have to deal with. All in all, my body was feeling a little beat up with the onset of winter and the challenges brought on by blizzards and snow squalls. The area around Georgian Bay (especially on the road to Parry Sound) was notorious for winter storms and lake-effect streamers, which often came out of nowhere to wreak havoc.

On January 3, we walked along the west side of Lake Couchiching near Fern Resort. Russ had once again stepped in for Jaime, so Martha joined us as well and with support from the Rama Police we had a really great day. A few days later we weren't as lucky with the weather. As we approached the Parry Sound area, we found ourselves suddenly enveloped in white-out conditions. I was eager to reach the community since I'd learned that the local first responders had hosted a sleep out the night before on the fire station roof. That in itself was not remarkable; what really impressed me is that it had been -30 Celsius, so I don't imagine anyone got any real sleep. I couldn't believe the grit this community showed to support PFC and I wanted them to know how much it meant to us.

When we arrived in town, the roads were extremely icy and dangerous but we managed to get in a portion of our daily walk and towards the end of the morning we connected with the local OPP leadership and did a community walk that finished up at the Fire/Police station. When we got to the station there was another group of folks waiting with a fire truck boom extended, which made for a great photo. Of course, when I saw the boom I knew I had to ask if I could go up in it (just like any little kid would!) "No problem," they said and up I went. As the boom rose higher and higher, I got an awesome view of the water as well as the town of Parry Sound. Not about to miss a photo opportunity, I took out my Canadian flag and extended it in the wind while Jaime snapped a really great picture. It was moments like this that made the cold and the pain in my legs worth it.

In a marathon campaign like PFC, it's not often that there is a desire to go backwards or retrace your steps; however, on the road through Ontario there was one instance that I felt warranted it. The town of Midland (which is where I was born) wanted to host an event that both of the local schools could participate in, however because we were there during the holidays it simply wasn't possible to schedule. So, after Parry Sound, we decided to choose a day and go back to spend a day in Midland.

The route we took through the Midland area was a giant loop, which was unlike a typical day on the highway where I would start at one point and finish 24 km down the road. The route was designed to circle all of Midland and Penetanguishene and bring me back to meet with a group of students from St. Theresa's for a walk down King Street, then on to a huge school rally.

61

It was a powerful day being back where I spent the first 10 years of my life. At one point, I realized we were just two blocks from the house I grew up in so I asked the officers if we could alter the route slightly to walk by my old house. It was emotional walking up Dominion Avenue that afternoon and catching sight of the big blue water tower that had been like a beacon to us as kids. As I crested the hill and found myself in front of the house a flood of emotions hit me. I'm sure a lot of that had to do with the pain of losing my father at a young age (and the tough times that my family went through afterwards); it was kind of cathartic standing in front of my old house thinking about how my life had come full circle. After walking around the entire community we met the kids and headed to the school where we had a pizza reception and then I addressed the entire school. As we headed back to Parry Sound, I was glad I'd taken the time to circle back.

We reached North Bay on January 12, which also happened to be Marie's birthday. Our first stop of the day was a visit to the OPP Communications Centre where the campaign received a cheque and Marie was presented with a surprise birthday cake. Next up, Canadore College hosted an amazing event with students, members of the OPP and the local community, which they live-streamed to allow other colleges in the area to join in. It was a powerful event with a great turnout. That evening we attended an OHL hockey game and this time, Marie and I got to drop the puck together.

Our visit to North Bay went by quickly and the next stop on our itinerary was Sudbury. The winter weather had really set in, with daytime temperatures that regularly dropped below -20C. With all of the adjustments in gear, I struggled more and more with my boots and the pain in my legs. When I wore my shoes, my feet didn't hurt, but now that the weather was so much colder, I was wearing boots all of the time to protect my feet from the cold and wet. Unfortunately, my body didn't adjust well to the new footwear and there was an ongoing concern that I might sustain an injury. I tried switching it up and tested out all of the different boots we'd brought (and there were a lot of them), but none of the alternatives worked and my shins continued to ache.

When we reached Sudbury, we spent a frigid day making our way around the city's perimeter alongside a number of Sudbury Police vehicles and our friends from the OPP. As we worked our way back towards town, we took the off ramp that led to the Science North facility and were surprised to be greeted by cheers from a large crowd as we approached. I immediately noticed that Terry Snooks from UA was in the group and I stopped to give him a huge hug. Nick Warus, together with a whole contingent of UA supporters was also there to cheer us on. The chief of police made a speech which included a public declaration about not making homelessness a criminal issue in Sudbury, which was an excellent thing for a police leader to declare. After I'd said a few words as well, we gathered the group together to walk into downtown Sudbury. The walk was several kilometres in length and police vehicles blocked the entire road for us, which made for an amazing video as the large group spread out and wound its way up the long, curving hill towards town.

In Sudbury, there's a bridge called the Bridge of Nations that you cross as you go into the downtown area. The bridge is lined with flags from all over the world. Approximately two years after *The Push for Change* campaign, I spoke at an event in Ontario where I met one of the workers who had been present on the day we walked over the bridge. He shared how *The Push for Change* had impacted him and also the huge impact it had on the population of homeless people who actually lived under that bridge. He told me that PFC had given them hope for the future, which was something they hadn't had for a long time.

I walked alongside Marie and Laurentian University President Dominic Giroux as we crossed over the bridge (it seemed like only a few weeks earlier I had walked across the stage to accept my honorary doctorate at Laurentian University's Barrie convocation). The local newspaper took a great photograph of our entourage as we crossed the bridge and I was happy to get the opportunity to share a part of the walk with Mr. Giroux and other delegates from Laurentian.

That evening, we were invited once again to drop the puck at an OHL hockey game; although this puck drop was different. They had a long red carpet rolled out and all of the officials and special guests (including me), walked out and lined the carpet. We then turned and faced the flag to sing, "Oh Canada." This was my third puck-dropping experience and it was pretty amazing. I felt really humbled to be standing in that huge arena with my hand over my heart while our police friends saluted the flag and our national anthem played. I also felt really proud and lucky to be Canadian. As "Oh Canada" played, I quietly reflected on all of the parts of this country I had walked across; from Newfoundland through Atlantic Canada and down the St. Lawrence to Quebec City; then into Ontario where I had visited Toronto, Niagara Falls, Windsor and now Sudbury. I had enough mental imagery to make me really smile as I thought about what a vast and amazing country we live in. When the music finished the announcer introduced me by name, at which point I dropped the puck then headed for the exit. Tomorrow would be another busy day.

The United Way was very supportive of PFC in Sudbury and they worked really hard to host a series of events. Similar to our time in Windsor, we started the day with a morning event where students had been bused in from several local schools and École Secondaire Hanmer presented us with a cheque for $400. Rallies like this (with the kids) were always a lot of fun. That evening the United Way and Blue Door served chilli in the park for the community and friends. They had a great turnout and the chilli was really good.

One thing that was never missing during my walk across Canada was my appetite. I was constantly eating and I was always hungry, which wasn't surprising since I burned an average of 3,000 calories every day. It would have made for a great weight loss program had I been more mindful about what I ate, but I wasn't. The truth is, I was horribly indiscriminate about what I stuffed in my face. I may have exhibited the physical behaviour and output of an elite athlete but I certainly didn't eat like an elite athlete. In fact, here's a piece of personal trivia worth sharing. I walked 9,064 kilometres across Canada, that's approximately 35,000 steps a day, six days a week, for 17 months...and I didn't lose one pound! So, if you think exercise alone will drop weight, you're wrong. It wasn't until I got home and switched to a plant-based diet that the weight fell off. Maintaining a healthy weight is primarily about diet, not exercise!

Speaking of diet, during the campaign Marie switched her diet to vegetarian and then she went full vegan. I honestly don't know how she did it, it was tough to prepare good meals while living in an RV or jumping from hotel to hotel. That was one of my excuses why I ate crap. Marie was and is much more disciplined when it comes to food and one night in our search for healthy food we decided to walk to a local eatery that offered healthy choices. I complained; not about the food, but about the walk. As we trucked along, we noticed a newspaper at the end of someone's driveway and when we picked it up, guess who was on the cover? *The Push for Change* had made the front page of the Northern Life. It was a great picture of Marie and me with a huge crowd as we walked over the Bridge of Nations into Sudbury.

Between Sudbury and Blind River, the roads were solid ice so we decided to go along the back route. One day we walked the entire 24 km on ice. Like our visits to so many out of the way places, walking into the small town of Espanola was amazing; the kids were so inspired they chanted as we walked along and the community gathering was a spirited event. They even made their own signs and had raised money for us. They were so happy we took the time to go see them and we were moved by their community spirit.

On day 269, we celebrated the 5,000 kilometre campaign milestone with a presentation at the high school in Blind River alongside local MPP Michael Mantha.

Hockey Day in Canada was one of many community events that took place during our time in Ontario, which we were able to benefit from. While we were in North Bay, we'd been asked to do an interview with CTV's Sportsnet (which is a national broadcast) to promote Hockey Day in Canada, primarily because the OPP had coordinated 28 Hockey Day in Canada tournaments around the province. One community's HDIC activities in particular caught our attention. Not only had the folks in the little town of Geraldton hosted a game at the local rink to rally the community and raise thousands of dollars for *The Push for Change*, they also put the PFC logo on the surface of the ice and had a homemade Stanley Cup to present to the winning team. We hadn't planned a visit to Geraldton, but when we saw how well the community came together, we decided we had to fit one in at some point if we could. Marie and I were always inspired by the lengths to which some people went to get involved in PFC. That kind of organization and engagement was what made the campaign easier on the days when the walking was tough. I was inspired on a daily basis by the volunteerism that I witnessed in communities big and small and by the enthusiasm of the kids we met along the way; that's what really kept my feet moving.

62

As you might have guessed, not every day was filled with community events and celebrations. A lot of my kilometres were logged in remote and quiet places. In Sudbury, I was happy to be joined by a gentleman named Sergeant Struan Frederiksen, who wanted to walk with us for several days as a personal challenge. After he'd accomplished his goal, Straun challenged other OPP officers to match or beat his steps (it was a kind of informal OPP Challenge).

Sometimes, the best places that we ended up walking weren't even on our route. Walking along Highway 17 towards Sault St. Marie we decided to take some secondary roads in order to avoid dangerous traffic. This took us through some truly beautiful First Nations communities where we interacted with the Anishinabek people. On one occasion I met with the Chief and we walked together to the band office where we chatted and shared ideas. Another time we were invited to speak at a daycare centre where I had the opportunity to sit down on the floor and try to explain to itty bitty children what we were doing. Mostly we talked about sharing and helping one another, simple ideas that small children understood instinctively.

One of the skills I really honed as a result of *The Push for Change* was the ability to speak to different groups and tailor my message and its delivery to different environments. In one instance, it could be a 30-second chat with a motorist, in another it might be a 45-minute keynote at a conference, or possibly a four-minute pep talk in a school parking lot. I adjusted the words and tone to whatever was needed and it was always fun.

My body was rebelling against winter and we needed to do something about it. I was still doing the deep breathing technique, which helped but I felt it was time to reintroduce regular ice baths. While we were in Blind River, I scouted the lake for an area where I could get into the water safely. Although most of the lake was covered in ice, there was one place where I could get into the water. "What the heck, I have to try something!" I thought to myself as I lowered my shivering body into the water. Needless to say, this was no ordinary ice bath; it was the northern passage of Lake Huron in January and it was damn cold!

Marie and I had decided if I was going to endure a 15-minute soak in an ice-cold lake in January, we needed to record it on video. As I sat in the freezing water with Marie filming, a woman who lived across the street from the little park we were in opened her door and yelled out, "I saw you on the news last night!" and gave us a big thumbs up. It was just the kind of warm encouragement I needed to get me through the painful submersion.

The trickiest part about doing an ice bath outside, especially in the winter, is getting back to the vehicle without wiping out. The cold had taken away most of my dexterity and my body felt rigid as I negotiated my way back to the truck. Thankfully I didn't wipe out and end up face down in a snow bank. As I shivered in my seat, I felt a strange sense of satisfaction and pride in my commitment to do whatever it took to succeed. Marie looked down at my legs and feet (which were lobster red from the cold), and commented that she couldn't for a minute imagine herself doing such a thing. We posted the video of my ice bath online and the reactions we got were hilarious. People could not believe the footage of me sitting in the water surrounded by ice and snow. The ice bath was good social media fodder and it was also good for my body; although the shin pain continued for several more weeks.

As we approached the end of January, whatever fears we'd had about walking in the winter were long gone. By this point, we'd been hammered with everything Mother Nature could throw at us; freezing rain, wet slush, blizzards, ice and -30 temperatures with 50 kmh winds. Nothing was slowing us down anymore and just like the US Marines we were "embracing the suck." In other words, everything that was hard just made us stronger. When it looked like things were getting tougher or conditions were challenging, I would just grin and keep moving, perseverance in action. Nothing was going to stop me from reaching Vancouver, nothing.

This part of the trek took us through places like Thessalon, Bruce Mines and a number of other small communities. Along the way we visited elementary schools and high schools and were met with similar enthusiasm at both. Smaller communities always welcomed us warmly and we relished the opportunity to share our message and hold events in places that probably wouldn't have even heard about the campaign if we didn't visit. As we got closer to Sault St. Marie, I did some calculations and realized we had already walked 2,200 kilometres in Ontario. That was roughly equal to the distance from Newfoundland to the Ontario border. We had another 850 kilometres to go to reach the Terry Fox Monument and 1,400 to finish up our trek through Ontario.

Whenever I had time on my hands at the hotel, I would play around on Google Maps to figure out the distance to different points along the way. This was important because during the walk I never focused on Vancouver as a final destination, I found it more helpful to set mini goals to keep myself motivated. This kept me from feeling overwhelmed and it also helped me to focus. In Ontario I had a number of mini goals. Finishing the entire province was more than a mini goal however; I knew Ontario was going to be my greatest challenge of the campaign by far. In total Ontario accounted for 3,600 kilometres, which was six full months of walking. More importantly, it represented winter—a

Northern Ontario, Lake Superior kind of winter. So, in theory if I could make it to Kenora, which was our last town before the Manitoba border, there would be plenty to celebrate. That's one of the reasons Marie was working feverishly behind the scenes while we were still 1,400 kilometres away; together with the OPP, she was planning our Ontario send-off event in Kenora. It was going to be huge. We had also received news that the RCMP in Manitoba were going to help us to engage as we travelled through that province, so the next leg of our journey was starting to take shape.

On January 31, (day 294) we hit the last of the little communities before Sault St. Marie. Echo Bay is home to the Canadian loonie (the coin's designer lives in Echo Bay), and just like the big nickel in Sudbury the town has a huge loonie coin, so we had to stop and take a picture of it. When we reached the community meeting place it was filled with rambunctious children from the local elementary school. With help from the OPP we marched down the street with the children chanting, "Push for Change! Push for Change! Push for Change!" and the video we posted on social media was priceless. When we got to the local elementary school, we had a short rally. Because I had been walking all morning, I wanted to change my shirt so I quickly ducked behind the curtain on the auditorium stage and swapped out what I was wearing. As I stood there I noticed a massive pile of snowshoes stacked against the wall. It was a stark reminder of what I had to look forward to for the next couple of months. I knew that once we left Sault St. Marie and headed north along the shores of Lake Superior, the weather was going to get wilder than anything we'd experienced so far and the snowshoes were a grim reminder of that.

I rejoined the rally, which was in full swing in the auditorium. The kids were awesome and the event was so full of energy, it almost made me forget about the road ahead where our next stop was Sault St Marie.

Marie
By the end of January we had already had the pleasure of engaging with over a dozen UA Locals from Newfoundland to Sault Ste Marie, as

well as members from their partner organizations QCCC and OPTC. Having had no previous experience working with unions, I was unaware of their loyal commitment to community-building and charity work. Members who supported PFC did so fervently and with solidarity. Where one member jumped in to support, the whole union stepped in behind them. Locals planned their PFC event months in advance of our arrival and their organizational skills and ability to mobilize shone through time and time again. Every organizer seemed to make their event happen almost as if by magic; the atmosphere they created allowed members to bring energy and spread enthusiasm to all participants. Whether their PFC event was at the Local Union itself, on a job site, at a community centre or school, or on the street with a Walk with Joe parade, every member that attended did so enthusiastically. As I worked with individual members in preparation for their event, I was steadily impressed by their pledge to PFC and the hours and effort they so obviously put into making their events as successful as possible. This success didn't just benefit our charity and cause; it was also a source of pride for their thousands of members, who felt good for giving of themselves and serving others.

Before this experience with UA, I had accepted the false belief that unions weren't really positive for our society, culture or employers. What a wonderful eye-opening experience to learn that unions not only make a substantial contribution to member wellbeing in the workplace, but their involvement in local charitable and social issues is well above par. UA Canada and their partners deserve to be recognized for the positive energy they bring to not only their members, but to every community where they have a presence.

63

Reaching Sault St. Marie was a huge milestone for us; we could hardly believe we'd made it this far. As we approached the city limits, we stopped and took a picture of the welcome sign and posted it on social media. Our time in "The Soo" turned out to be a week we wouldn't soon forget. Because I'd spoken in the city a few years earlier and they had been anticipating our visit for some time, there was an enthusiastic and well-organized planning committee in place with all sorts of fun events lined up.

The biggest event planned for us was a downtown street party, for which they had closed off two city blocks to traffic. The party included an outdoor hockey game and there was a stage set up for speeches and entertainment. The local youth shelter, Pauline's Place would receive 50% of funds raised by the event. We encouraged this kind of sharing wherever we could because it was important to us to leave dollars in the communities we visited. The mayor of Sault St. Marie said a few kind words to kick off the event and then a young man who had lived on the streets shared his story. I followed that up with a talk about *The Push for Change*. After the short presentations were out of the way (they needed to be short because it was -20°C), the real fun began. The Soo created this crazy game called Shopping Cart Wars with real shopping carts. Each competitor had to race through a series of challenges with their shopping cart and the winners took home a prize. Everyone had a lot of fun and we raised some good money for the campaign. It was a unique approach to fundraising and one that really tied in with PFC.

If you're wondering how much it snows around Sault St. Marie, the answer is, a lot! The lake effect that happens down around Georgian Bay is even more pronounced off the shores of Lake Superior. I found out it's not uncommon at all to get a good foot of snow in 24 hours in Sault St. Marie (that's over 30cm by the way). During the first two weeks of February we received at least 60-90cm. I couldn't believe how much it snowed, yet to my surprise nothing was closed down. I think the Soo gets so much snow that they're just used to it, so it doesn't disrupt everyday life much.

On the day that had been set aside to walk the perimeter of the city, we were joined by the OPP's, Monique Baker. Monique had been challenged by Straun back in Sudbury and she was determined to try and walk more than 100 km with us during our time in the area. As we walked through the community we were joined by more and more walkers, including the chief of police and a whole bunch of folks from Ontario Works. Mike Nadeau (who we had met a couple years earlier) was one of our biggest local champions and when we reached downtown he joined us along with a number of new walkers. We made a short stop at the local Tim Hortons, where we were offered free drinks along with an armful of branded mitts and toques (which we were more than happy to accept). It was just another awesome Canadian moment.

The snow continued to fall throughout the day until it was complete mayhem. On top of the snow we had people joining the walk at every turn throughout the city. We had kids and dogs and at one point it felt like people were jumping out of the snow banks to join us. Thank goodness we had such excellent support from both the OPP and the Sault St. Marie Police; otherwise the walk could have been downright dangerous. With their help directing traffic on the roads and through intersections everything flowed really smoothly. We ended our walk at the Sault St. Marie Police Headquarters where we exchanged challenge coins with the chief. Months later we read in the paper how this particular chief had won an award for community engagement.

Monique had completed her first full day of walking, but our day wasn't quite over. Nick Warus from UA Local 800 had been supporting us nonstop from North Bay through Sudbury to the Soo, so it was important for us to stop by the local union hall. Nick and the boys had a BBQ set up for us and it was a good thing since Jaime and I were both starving. Marie joined us as well and we had a nice celebration as we thanked the local members for their ongoing support. The funniest part of the night was when Marie put on one of the welder's masks and we all laughed and took pictures. Even in a welder's mask Marie was cute as a bug's ear.

Being on the road for 17 months, there were a lot of moving parts so it was inevitable that once in a while we would be caught off guard by an event. One that we almost missed was hosted by our friend Mike Nadeau. We were just finishing up after the downtown street party when Mike stopped by and said, "I'll see you tonight!" which caused both Marie and I to do a double take. Apparently, months earlier, an event had been discussed but it was never confirmed with us. It was tough news to hear as I was so looking forward to getting back to the hotel and simply crashing. The combination of long days of walking, back-to-back engagements and tough winter conditions, together with persistent pain in my legs had me really looking forward to an evening of doing absolutely nothing. Instead I found some strong coffee and soldiered on.

The event turned out to be a really good one for us. It was a Christmas-style dinner hosted by Ontario Works at the Quattro Hotel for low income families. When I shared my story of overcoming hardship I could tell that it resonated. It was truly an inspired event and everyone enjoyed the delicious meal; I was grateful we hadn't missed it. When I finished my speech, the hotel owner asked me where we were staying and what we were paying and then offered us free accommodations in his hotel. The next day we moved everything over and for the next week we lived in absolute comfort. Marie and I had a king suite and it was just the luxury we needed for a well-deserved day off.

Marie

February in Ontario is typically the month that feels the longest, even though it has the least number of days. As someone who grew up in Barrie, I remember the winter blues and those long dark days that never went by fast enough. February 2017 had me feeling quite the opposite. We had been in Ontario for 159 days and with only 41 to go, I felt like time was moving much too quickly. The wonderful events, the amazing engagement and the tremendous support from the OPP made me want to hold still and savour the experience. On a daily basis, I was astounded by all of those around me who stood by our side, committing their time and energy to a PFC event in their town or pledging to accompany Joe in the OPP's Chevy Tahoe...or the thousands of students and individuals who walked with Joe, championed fundraising campaigns or sat intently listening to his personal story and powerful message. All of these people were our community champions, supporting our cause whole-heartedly and selflessly. Who doesn't want to be in the company of such noble and considerate people? I was in constant appreciation of the collaborative community effort that had risen up around us. In a world where self-interest is encouraged it can be easy to assume everyone is out to fulfill their own agenda. However, I discovered that there are many among us who know the value of living in community and have felt pure joy and love in giving to and doing for others. These are the people we were surrounded by and if I could, I would have frozen time to preserve that incredible sense of belonging.

64

The snow continued the entire week we were in Sault St. Marie, yet nothing closed and life went on. Snow might have been no big deal for this community, but for me the snow made it harder to walk and with each passing day the problem with my shins and sore legs got worse. Each morning when I got out of bed and put pressure on my legs, I experienced sharp pains shooting up both legs. To say I was worried would be an enormous understatement. I was facing 700 kilometres to Thunder Bay along one of the most unforgiving highways in Canada (with long, steep hills like I had encountered in BC, except with winter weather conditions). My biggest concern was that something serious was going to happen that would stop me from finishing the campaign. If I didn't figure this out soon, serious injury wasn't just possible, it was imminent. With 4,000 kilometres still to go, there was no way I was going to make it in the shape I was in.

Thankfully, a call with the OPP's Detective Superintendent Ken Leppert a short time later put me on the path to solving my problem. Ken and I were talking about my recovery routine and ice baths when I mentioned the problems I was having with my legs and shins. He advised me to think about switching to trail shoes. As someone who lived in North Bay and often ran in winter conditions, he suggested that my problems were likely caused by the footwear I was wearing. Ever since the snow came, I had been trying different kinds of boots to adjust to the snow and cold. He told me to get rid of the boots and just wear shoes with two pairs of socks for warmth.

"If your feet get wet, just change your shoes throughout the day," he suggested. "As long as you've got a few extra pairs, you can just rotate them as needed." I definitely had enough pairs of shoes to give it a try, so immediately following the call I set the boots aside and switched to shoes. With the wet snow, my feet got soaked after about 12 km, but it was easy enough for me to change socks and shoes and continue on my way. At the end of every day we had two or three pairs of wet shoes but fortunately we had so many shoes it didn't matter if they took a day or two to dry. After only three days in shoes I started to notice a difference; walking wasn't as hard and the pain was beginning to recede.

"Was it really that simple?" I wondered.

As a matter of fact it was and that small tip from Ken changed everything just in time for us to move on from Sault St. Marie and head north up Highway 17 towards Wawa (and eventually on to Thunder Bay). The King's Highway as it is also known, is an epically beautiful stretch of highway with huge rolling hills along the exposed shores of Lake Superior. The road itself is single lane in many places and in the winter it's one of the most treacherous roads in Canada to drive, let alone push a shopping cart. Just like the fall leaves changing colour had made me nervous about the onset of winter, I had that same foreboding feeling about wandering through the wilderness in a blizzard as we left Sault St. Marie on a journey to the Manitoba border that would take us 1,300 kilometres to the northwest. This part of the trek would test my resolve in ways I could only imagine.

Monique Baker was an awesome companion as we headed north on the first day. She had committed to walk a minimum of 100 km with the campaign and I was happy to have someone to distract me from my own thoughts. It was the first time that I was really nervous as I set out on the road, despite assurances from the locals at our morning safety briefing. This was something we did every morning to ensure we all knew the plan for the day and how to be safe on the road. On that particular day, there was a snowstorm rolling in. I asked if they thought everything was going to be OK. The answer was a resounding, "Absolutely, no problem." I think when you live in the snow-belt and travel in treacherous conditions all the time you just get used to it; so I figured if they thought it was safe I could rely on their judgement and experience.

The first stretch out of the city took us down a massive slope called "One Mile Hill" and as I walked down this very long hill all I could think about was that there would be many, many more just like this one and some of them would undoubtedly be uphill. If that thought didn't cause me enough concern, the logging truck that had become stuck on the hill certainly did. Apparently, the grade on One Mile Hill is so steep that if the trucks going uphill towards Sault St. Marie don't have enough speed, they end up literally stuck on the hill spinning their wheels and going nowhere. The OPP told us it's something that happens quite frequently. In fact, it happens so frequently that you can actually see tire marks carved into the road's surface around the mid-point of the hill.

Despite the steep grade, Monique didn't miss a beat; she matched me step for step as we slowly made our way north along the highway and when we stopped to take a picture of the sign that read, "Wawa 227 km," it suddenly dawned on me how utterly amazing this experience was. Although the snow continued to fall, we managed to keep moving until we reached Mountain View Public School in Goulais River. It was a tiny little community but one that Monique knew very well. She had been eager for us to visit the community to share our message with several high-risk youth. Ever since I started sharing my life story and seeing the impact that it had, I've found speaking to youth who are dealing with serious life issues is the most rewarding kind of interaction. If I can inspire even one young person to see past their circumstances and reach for a possibility then I have been successful. That's why I never turn down those kinds of opportunities.

I'm not sure what the name of the community was the next day. We had just walked down a big hill and when we rounded the corner we spotted a group of people waiting for us on the other side of the road. I had a rule that I followed whenever I encountered well-wishers or people offering donations on the highway. I would always cross the road and go to meet them rather than waiting for them to cross over to me. We stopped for a brief chat and received a $20 donation from every person in the group. We also got an amazing photo of the group of eight or so people, all bundled up in their winter clothes on the side of the highway standing around a shopping cart.

It was around this time that Sergeant Manuela Byrnes from Wawa joined us. Manuela had been challenged by Monique who had been challenged by Straun and so every day I had fresh walkers to join me, not just a few kilometres, but for the whole day. I welcomed the company, especially along these really quiet roadways. Manuela had come up with her own unique way to engage with the PFC campaign and also support a local shelter. She created a campaign called, "Sock it to Youth Homelessness." Her goal had been to walk 100 km and collect 100 pair of socks. In the end she walked much further and collected 500 pair of socks!

65

With 200 kilometres still to go to reach Wawa, it felt like weeks since we'd left Sault St. Marie. There were a lot of hills along this stretch of highway and the winter scenery was spectacular, the tree branches were heavy with freshly fallen snow and the embankments on either side of the road were covered in animal tracks. The moose tracks, which seemed to be everywhere, reminded me that even though it was quiet, we were far from alone in this wilderness. There were also tracks from other types of animals that were indistinguishable to me, but together, the way they criss-crossed the fresh snow created a kind of mosaic that was intensely beautiful. Breathing in the crisp winter air as we walked along each day was invigorating and with both Monique and Manuela making treats to share, we were well fed and enjoyed logging the kilometres together.

Even though the Soo was behind us, just like with Guelph, we later learned that our engagements in the community opened eyes and created the kind of awareness that brought additional corporate support. As an example, the summer following our visit, the committees that had formed to support PFC organized a golf tournament and raised $50,000. *The Push for Change* helped to mobilize the community to address local needs and new stakeholders were inspired to step up and help as a result. This kind of news was deeply encouraging as we continued our campaign across the country.

Back on the highway we encountered a dad and his sons getting ready to go out on their snowmobiles. The kids remembered us from a visit we'd made to their school, which lifted our spirits, but the best part of the day came when the wind picked up and (with the snow blowing in our faces) we could barely see two feet ahead. Getting in the spirit of the moment, the OPP support vehicle that trailed us began to howl out ACDC's *Highway to Hell*. OPP Staff Sergeant Michael Maville, who had been steadfastly following behind us since the Soo, had loaded up the song and proceeded to blare it through the loud speaker on his police cruiser. At first, I thought I was imagining it, until I turned around to see his grinning face as he rode along warm and cozy in the car while Monique, Manuela and I trudged through the snow.

It was a slow walk through Batchawana and Pancake Bay on our way to Montreal River, with snow flurries on and off all day. When the sun did come out it was magnificently beautiful as the snow-laden pine trees glistened and sparkled. When the weather wasn't knocking us down, the scenery really was spectacular. The highway took us up long hills (some as much as a kilometre long) that would open up into breathtakingly expansive views of the lake and its shoreline. When we were close to the water, I could hear the pounding of the waves and see the ice pushed up onto the beach. The rock cuts along the side of the highway were adorned with icicles that were 10 meters long. It was a magical time to be in the area and I often mused as we made our way through what was undoubtedly an unforgiving landscape, that I was truly fortunate to be seeing this part of the country at this time of year. Most people visit northern Ontario in the summer and the opportunity to witness the harsh, yet beautiful winter landscape left me awestruck.

The Montreal River hill was infamous, another one of those hills that is closed periodically due to poor road conditions. The steep grade, combined with heavy snow is known to trap trucks on the hill and completely shut down the highway. It's also a very long hill that gains about 300m in elevation. From the direction we approached, the first portion is steep for about 5 km. The hill first gained infamy when Terry Fox ran up it in 1980 during his Marathon of Hope. I was fortunate to have a bunch of folks with me as I tackled the behemoth. In addition to Monique and Manuela, a friend of theirs had joined us for this epic adventure, along with Marie. The weather was actually really nice; it was cold but not too windy and there was no snow in the forecast, which was good. Together we worked our way up the hill and entered Lake Superior Provincial Park. The grade of the hill had our hearts pumping for sure, but the camaraderie within the group kept our spirits high.

Around midday, we stopped for lunch and a bathroom break. When it came to taking a pee, I was lucky I could simply duck behind the van. In fact, Jaime and I had a system; he would pull over to the side of the road at an angle so that when the front door of the van opened it would shield me from traffic in both directions. Bathroom breaks became a little more complicated in a mixed group. Marie needed a little privacy and the van was not going to work for her so she decided to walk down a little road that was near where we'd stopped.

The road had a sharp turn in it and dropped down the hill (and it was in the middle of nowhere), so we figured there was a pretty slim chance that anyone would drive by. We agreed to signal if any vehicles were coming our way, but no one was really concerned. The thing that made what happened next so funny is the clothing Marie had chosen to wear that day. She was definitely dressed for the cold and one of the layers she had put on in the morning was a pair of neon pink yoga pants. As she was dressing, I had commented that she could safely go hunting with those pants on. So, you know what's coming next right?

Marie headed down the path for some privacy, only to get caught with her pants down. Fortunately, the hunter that surprised her as she was yanking up her bright pink pants didn't really see anything, but he did surprise her enough that she returned with her face as pink as her pants. I'm not sure what the hunter's name was, but I like to think of him as "Slim."

66

The next morning, our day began deep inside the provincial park where we witnessed a spectacular sunrise over Lake Superior in a tiny place called Old Woman Bay. The sunrise was a spectacular hue of pinks and orange and as we left the shore and climbed up our first hill the view improved with every step until we were on top of the hill looking back as the sun continued to climb and shine its glory across the partially ice-covered lake and shoreline. The temperature was -30°C, so I needed to keep moving in order to stay warm, but Jaime captured some beautiful photos of the morning.

As the day progressed the weather turned stormy as snow blew in and the sun disappeared. With no one to accompany me, the hills were unrelenting and my entire day's walk felt like it was uphill. It was tough going and my energy dragged; I felt worn out. I knew one of the reasons was my diet. I could have been eating better and fueling my body more effectively, but I didn't have that much discipline when it came to food. I also needed more rest but I knew I wasn't going to get it; there was too much road to cover to stay on track with our itinerary. After a few moments of feeling down, I did what I knew needed to be done; I put my headphones on, cranked up the tunes and buckled down to do my kilometres (and tried not to look at my watch too often). Throughout the campaign I wore a Garmin watch that tracked me on GPS and gave me accurate numbers so I knew when my 24 km was up each day. I also used it to schedule breaks and chart my progress. The problem with looking at my watch too often was that some days when I looked and it read 3 km, or 4 km, it just made me more tired thinking that I still had 20 or 21 km to walk. That's why on days when I already felt tired, I tried not to check my watch too often.

As I continued to put one foot in front of the other my mood improved and I began to feel better. The endorphins that came from exercise and the satisfaction of doing something tough always brought me renewed energy. The snow was blowing hard in the last few kilometres so I kept my head down. Days like this tested my resolve but I knew there was no backing down, not even for one second. I was on a mission and no matter what roadblocks lay ahead; I was determined to see the campaign through.

Despite the blizzard conditions, as I reached the edge of town something told me I needed to stop and look up. As I brushed off my snow-covered toque and tilted my head back, I found myself staring directly at a famous roadside attraction that for some reason captures the essence of our country. I had made it to the Wawa Goose! For anyone who has driven the Trans-Canada Highway through Ontario, this is an important stop. The Wawa Goose is about as Canadian as Niagara Falls or the Lighthouses of Nova Scotia.

I'm not sure why it happened, perhaps it was a result of extreme fatigue or maybe it was something more, but as I stood in the shadow of that landmark, I felt the emotion welling up in me and tears flowed down my cheeks. I marvelled at how far I'd come. Having pushed a shopping cart from Newfoundland to Wawa, I was over halfway done the campaign and given that I was currently walking through Northern Ontario in February, whatever lay in front of me couldn't be any more difficult than what I had already accomplished. I knew in that moment that I was going to make it all the way to Vancouver and I felt an overwhelming sense of gratitude for being lucky enough to have been born in Canada. As I stood there looking up at a symbol of this great country, I was reminded of the many blessings in my life.

I live in a country that afforded me a second chance.

I live in a country that paid for my detox and my treatment as well as my college education.

It is a country that is filled with beauty, both in its natural wonders and in its people and their values.

It is a country where someone like me can go from skid row to CEO.

As I stood at the base of the Wawa Goose, I was reminded of what I have known for a very long time; this really is one of the best places on planet earth, "The True North Strong and Free."

"My name is Joe and I am Canadian!" I shouted out loud as I stood with my arms stretched high in the air like Rocky. I was a champion and I knew nothing was going to stop me or *The Push for Change*. Coincidentally, that was also the day that my legs finally stopped hurting.

The next day the weather was so bad we all decided it would be best if we didn't walk on Highway 17, so we turned onto a secondary road that led to the Michipicoten reserve. From time to time throughout the campaign we moved our walk off the pre-determined route. Sometimes, we did so to engage a community that wanted us to visit. Other times it was because of weather or highway conditions. What was more important than "where" we walked, was that we recorded the actual kilometres walked and added them together to make up the 9,064km total.

The road to Michipicoten was nothing like the highway. There were really steep hills, so steep that the van got stuck several times and Jaime would have to take a run at them to get up. The steep grades and the slippery snow made it a lot harder to walk too, so our progress was slow. Interestingly, people driving by us headed in the other direction kept stopping to ask when I would be arriving. We didn't have a planned event in Michipicoten, but apparently they were waiting for us. Eventually we made our way into the community, which was really very pretty. The village was at the end of a road that looped around to the shore of Lake Superior. We were invited into the band hall where we were served chicken soup and bannock. The Chief said a few words and I said a few words and before we left one of the elders gave me a small pouch of tobacco which she asked me to carry to BC and put in the ocean. I was happy to accept this honour and promised I would do as she asked.

The next day we had a series of events in Wawa. First, we visited the local hockey rink where students had been brought in on buses. Our new friends from the Michipicoten First Nation were also there to drum and sing a traditional song. Afterwards, they presented me with a genuine Canadian beaver-pelt hat and the chief gave me a blessing. OPP Sergeant Manuela Byrne also said a few words and was acknowledged for collecting more than 500 pairs of socks. In the afternoon, we walked over to the local high school where we joined the students for a formal presentation and a school rally. We stayed in Wawa for several days and despite the cold temperatures, the folks were welcoming and happy to engage with us.

On our day off from walking we decided to take the OPP up on an offer to visit a remote fly-in community on the shores of James Bay, situated just below Hudson's Bay. The plan was to drive to Sault St. Marie where we would meet up with OPP Deputy Commissioner Rick Barnum and Detective Superintendent Ken Leppert and load the shopping cart into their Pilatus PC-12/NG. The flight took us up over the Northern Ontario ice highway into the communities of Moosonee and Moose Factory. We had several events scheduled for the day to make the most of the time we had. The first stop was Northern Lights Secondary School where we received a warm welcome. After a short speech, we did a walk through the community escorted by snowmobiles which was a really cool experience.

Next, we travelled across the frozen river to Moose Factory where we engaged with the Moose Cree First Nation. They booked me into their local radio station for an interview and after another short presentation we headed out for a walk along the ice road. In the winter, the river between Moosonee and Moose Factory freezes over making it possible to drive across between the two communities. We gathered a group of volunteers and I changed the tires on the cart to skis before we headed out. It was a really big deal for the community that we came all this way and their support was amazing. At one point during the walk I looked over my shoulder to see about eight police vehicles and four snowmobiles accompanying the crowd. When we reached the other side, the local fire department had set up for a BBQ and there was a large bonfire. We had a nice meal together and then it was time to head back to the airport.

On the plane ride back to Sault St. Marie, I thought about how remarkable it was that the OPP were that invested in community engagement to go to the trouble of bringing us that far north. We were amazed by the resilience of the people living in these remote communities and grateful for the experience. It was dark when we returned to Sault St. Marie, so rather than drive back to Wawa, we decided to stay the night. Joe at the Quattro was only too happy to oblige and comped us a room yet again.

Back on the road I spent a few days in the middle of nowhere as I walked between Wawa and White River. While I walked communities across the country celebrated Hockey Day in Canada. In Ontario, there were more than 30 hockey games in communities around the province. As had been promised, throughout the day Sportsnet ran our interview from coast to coast. Our videographer (and friend) Brian had also put together a *Push for Change* commercial that was being broadcast throughout British Columbia, so we were getting some excellent media coverage.

The route between Wawa and White River was relatively easy, in sharp contrast to the big hills we'd encountered around Montreal River. There was a lot of bush and rock and not much else. On Day 297, I arrived in the town of White River, famous for being the home of the black bear cub that inspired the Winnie-the-Pooh children's stories. Angelo Bazzoni, who is a local businessman and also the mayor, held a reception for us. It was a nice gathering with food and a small group of friendly faces. Before we left White River, we said goodbye to Sergeant Manuela Byrnes and thanked her for her amazing effort. She had been determined to beat Monique's mileage and ended up walking an amazing 160 km with me. No one else would come near that number during the entire campaign, except of course Marie!

67

We moved our base camp from Wawa to Marathon just as the weather turned unseasonably warm and instead of snow we got a big dump of rain, which I didn't mind at all. It helped melt down some of the massive snow piles on the side of the road that narrowed the space where I could walk. It also brought some challenges though as I found myself walking in thick, sticky dirt. For a couple days it felt like walking through sand on a beach; it was really hard on my calves. It also didn't help that I was sick.

At one point near Crocker Lake, I recall looking at my reflection in the mirror and being shocked by what I saw. I had deep dark circles under my eyes and I looked pale and emaciated. The tough part about getting sick during a non-stop campaign was, it didn't matter how I felt, I still had to get up every day and walk; and if there were engagements to attend, I still had to go and "bring the energy." There was no time off for being sick. All I could do is try to get to sleep early, drink lots of coffee and make the most of downtime when we had it. The soft dirt and my sluggish body made for a couple of really long days but eventually we got through it and reached the border of the OPP Northwest Region where we were welcomed by OPP members from Marathon.

On day 304, we found ourselves approaching Marathon, Ontario. The OPP had coordinated events with several local schools. At one elementary school we visited a grade one classroom and served lunch to the children. At Margaret Twomey Public School we gathered everyone in front of the school and did a walk through the community followed by a presentation in the gym. When it came time to ask questions, a young boy who was in grade three said something incredibly wise. He said, "It's important that we don't judge people about whether they have a home or not. It's better to be kind and generous." Out of the mouth of babes (as they say), this eight-year-old boy understood something that we were desperately trying to get national leaders to grasp.

Before we left the school, the OPP presented me with an awesome gift. An OPP member (who also happened to be a gifted caricature artist), drew a cartoon depiction of me arriving in Marathon with some angry bears scowling at me. It's an amazing drawing that still hangs in our living room as a memento of our visit.

Marathon was a warm welcome, however, the impending storm and the highway ahead wouldn't prove to be so kind. Just outside of Marathon we entered Nays Provincial Park where the terrain changed dramatically. The highway from Marathon to Nipigon had many long sweeping hills and tight corners that required guard rails. If you were powering up and down the hills with your own energy (as I was) it's a lot of hard work. The road was narrow and dangerous and the hills were unforgiving but the views on this section of Highway 17 were nothing short of spectacular. Even though I had spent many kilometres walking through this spectacular landscape, the scenery still took my breath away. After walking 2-3 kilometres up a long steep hill, the road would turn and take me through a massive ice-laden auburn rock cut which would open up to a sweeping view of Lake Superior with its wave-crashed shoreline. It was wild, untamed beauty and I stopped often, just to take it all in. It was never warm, in fact the wind was always in my face; but it was so amazing that it was worth taking the time to stop and appreciate this natural wonder.

On February 28, with 5,586 kilometres on the campaign odometer, we visited the communities of Terrace Bay and Schreiber. The walk into Terrace Bay was epic. We started the day at Jackfish Lake and proceeded to climb the long, steep hill into town. As we left the relative safety of the protected valley and began to gain altitude, the wind picked up off the lake until it was a fierce 50 kmh headwind. The day had started at −44°C and later warmed up to −37°C (I have no idea what it was with the wind-chill factored in but I was wearing seven or eight layers of clothing that morning. When we arrived in town, Holy Angels School hosted an event and Lake Superior High School had scheduled a hockey game. We got to speak to the students before the game and by the time we left, we had raised several hundred dollars in these two small communities.

The next day things got a little more interesting on the road. We were about 5 km into our walk near Ross Port when the OPP officer got out of his car and told us we had to move off the road and suspend our walk. Fortunately, we were close to a Ministry of Highways outpost where snowplows and trucks were stored so we just pulled over and stopped. There was a note of urgency in the officer's request so I asked what was going on. Although he was vague about the details, he told me there was a police chase underway just up the highway and it was headed our way. We needed to get off the road in case the chase made it this far (he didn't want us to be caught in the middle of a dangerous situation). I watched and listened and tried to absorb as much information as I could. This was exciting; definitely more exciting than the last 1,000 kilometres of rocks, trees and lakes I had been staring at. We might get to witness a real-life police chase.

Jaime and I got ready for the action, him with the camera and me with my iPhone. We fixed our eyes on the curve in the road to the west of us and waited. The OPP officer accompanying us originally thought the incident wouldn't make it this far since he'd heard on the radio that the police had laid out spike strips 10 km back. The spike strips are meant to flatten the tires of the vehicle and cause it to stop, but they didn't stop this guy! With our eyes focused on the road, we saw him approach.

It turned out the chase was after a stolen flatbed tow truck with a car on the back of the flatbed. The evening before, the accused driver had been stopped and arrested in Nipigon for a traffic violation and the police had impounded his car. In the morning when the man was released from custody he decided it would be a good idea to go down to where the tow truck was parked with his car on the back and steal the whole rig. Clearly, he hadn't put a lot of thought into his plan. I had just walked from Sault St. Marie along 600 km of lonely, desolate highway. There was nowhere to run and definitely nowhere to hide. Had he really thought he would go unnoticed?

As the truck careened around the corner towards us a large chunk of his shredded front tire fell off and rolled into the ditch. The truck didn't even slow down as he continued on with just the rim on asphalt and flew past Jaime and me on the highway. Chasing the tow truck were three or four OPP cruisers and the officer that was with us peeled out immediately to join the chase. Later on, we found out that they managed to stop the vehicle and apprehend the driver just a few kilometres past us without anyone getting hurt.

It was one of the coolest things Jaime and I had experienced on the trek so far and we were like two little boys watching a live episode of, "Cops Northern Ontario." I took Jaime's video and my video and edited them together into a really cool montage that I thought would be an excellent post for social media. To my disappointment, when I showed it to Marie she advised against it. It didn't reflect anything to do with the campaign and the only way we were able to capture the film was with the foreknowledge we gained from the OPP member. So, it's one of those videos that no one ever saw, lost forever in the PFC media vault.

Funnily enough when we got to Nipigon, the event vehicle Marie had been driving wouldn't start. I had no idea what was wrong so I looked up the local tow service and gave them a call to see if they could tow the vehicle to their shop and see what was going on. The guy on the phone told me, "No can do." Apparently, their tow truck had been stolen and damaged. I had to laugh! Left to my own devices, I removed the battery from the vehicle, replaced it, and we were up and running in an hour.

68

On day 313, Marie and I were staying in Nipigon when we received news that the federal government (through Minister Patty Hajdu) had announced $8 million dollars in funding for a youth employment initiative called Making the Shift. The program was established to pilot a number of projects that directly impacted youth at risk and actively engaged homeless youth. The funding and the projects were critical for establishing a research-based understanding of what kinds of programs work and what to fund and replicate. Our partners from A Way Home Canada, Homeless Hub and York University now had the resources needed to run projects that would impact young people's lives and also gather the evidence needed to drive additional funding. For the first time, the federal government was investing in the prevention of youth homelessness and it had happened during *The Push for Change*. It was a huge win for our partners and we felt proud of the small role we played.

At the time we heard the news, I was in the midst of the last really difficult hilly portion of the highway before Nipigon, so the news was a welcome distraction. The next day as I walked through a long rock-cut section of highway, the sun cast a shadow of me and my shopping cart on the deep, beautiful red rock formation and I remembered what Cal Misener had said years before, "If you want to have real impact, wait and do it right." Our goal from inception had always been to engage the country in a conversation about what we could do to better address youth homelessness through prevention. We had always envisioned connecting with students, community stakeholders, police, and of course, politicians. We had succeeded and the announcement from the federal government was proof of that.

With the tough hills of the past few weeks finally behind me, I enjoyed my time in Nipigon. The community had worked really hard to prepare for our visit and planned a number of really inspiring events. We started off our visit with a walk through town with a group of students followed by an event where the Superior North Catholic School District, the Red Rock Indian Band and the Superior-Greenstone District School Board presented us with $1,400. The kids in the community were so enthusiastic with fundraising for us that even the people who ran the local coffee shop knew exactly who we were when we stopped in.

Something special happened in Nipigon that had a lasting impact on both Marie and me. Months before PFC was scheduled to arrive in their community, the local music teacher Shy-Anne Hovorka talked with her students about what we were doing and why it was important. She asked them if they would like to take on the project of writing and performing a song for us. As part of the welcome when we arrived at the school, these creative and inspired young people got up in front of their peers (and community leaders) to perform the song they had written. It left me speechless and filled with emotion; the lyrics were beautiful and heartwarming. These young people had really put their hearts into the project and I could not have been more honoured by their gesture.

Staying in Nipigon, we were near the intersection of the highway that led north towards Geraldton, the community that had organized a hockey tournament and put the PFC and OPP logos into their ice surface. We decided to take a day to go north and walk through the community to thank the people for their fundraising and support of the campaign. When we arrived in Geraldton, we were met by a huge crowd waiting in front of the school. Following a walk through town, we gathered at the community centre for a talk about PFC and a cheque presentation. It never ceased to amaze us how these small, remote communities were able to mobilize and fundraise the way they did. It was inspiring.

As we crossed over the big bridge through Nipigon, our route turned southwest towards Thunder Bay. My goal to reach the Terry Fox Monument was coming to fruition. I had spent many months walking since I set the goal way back in Windsor; as we crossed the bridge in Nipigon we stepped onto the Hope Courage Highway which had been named after Terry Fox. The steps I was walking in were some of Terry's last on his Marathon of Hope. It was sad, yet inspiring.

Near the town of Shuniah we were met by an OPP auxiliary officer who was to be our escort on the road. We had travelled together about 10 km when I heard a loud pop behind me. I walked back to the officer's car and discovered he had run over a large metal bolt, which was firmly lodged in his tire. He looked at me and said, "Should I pull it out?" I just smiled, when what I should have done was pull out my phone and record what happened next. He slowly pulled the bolt away from the rubber and when the end popped out, the tire hissed and went completely flat in a matter of seconds. What was left was a huge tear in the rubber and a very flat tire. Our day ended there and we picked up the following morning after the tire was repaired.

69

Closer to Thunder Bay, my little sister Roberta volunteered to drive the van to allow Jaime some time off with his family. Roberta lived in Thunder Bay, so it was a great opportunity for us to spend some time together. Our first couple of days were spent on the approach to Thunder Bay from the east. One morning we crested a large hill to a wonderful view of Sleeping Giant Provincial Park off in the distance. The morning was crisp and cold but cloudless as the sun rose overtop the lake. It was a magnificent sight; we could see for miles. The large rock cuts along the highways made it easy for me to scramble up and I took some extraordinary pictures as the bright orange sunlight collided with the red rocks. I began to understand why my sister loved living here, the landscape was spectacular. We ended the day 25 km from the Terry Fox Monument. The following day would be a big one.

When I was 13 years old, Terry Fox ran through Barrie during his Marathon of Hope and my mom took me to Centennial Park to meet him, I even got his autograph. At the time, although I thought meeting Terry Fox was really cool no one could have predicted the impact he would have on a nation. Because of his incredible courage, Terry would end up becoming one of the most celebrated Canadians who ever lived. Terry's example awakened our hearts and inspired hope in millions of people. Terry also showed us something about ourselves as a nation. He showed us that Canadians embrace change makers; we embrace and support those who dare to take on unbelievable challenges to try to make the world a better place.

Throughout my adolescence and early adult life I would often reflect back on meeting the hero, Terry Fox. As his legacy grew, my meeting him became more important and although I could never identify with Terry or living with cancer, I could identify with the struggle, in fact I think we all can. Ironically, when I was at my very lowest point living under the Georgia Street viaduct in Vancouver, not more than a block away (in front of BC Place Stadium) stood a massive statue of Terry Fox.

Terry moved our nation and gave everything he had, including his life. He was the very essence of a hero, selfless, courageous and visionary. During *The Push for Change* I was always concerned when reporters or other people compared me (or the campaign) to Terry Fox. Not that I wasn't flattered, I just didn't want to tread on something that I believed was sacred. Terry's example was definitely the inspiration behind why we chose to walk across Canada. The whole concept of crossing Canada was just one of the legacies he gave us. Terry showed us how to engage Canadians and raise awareness while tackling something so hard it left people awestruck.

I truly believe without Terry Fox there likely would never have been a *Push for Change*, but that's where the similarities end. Terry was a pioneer and a trailblazer; he had no example to follow. I couldn't begin to imagine the challenges he endured on his run. Every day I woke up and walked 24 km. Every day Terry woke up, he **ran** 42 km. I had two strong legs to propel me forward; Terry had one and because of the way he ran it created severe pain and blistering. Terry Fox covered 5,373 km in 143 days. It had taken me 317 days to cover 5,817km. What I was doing was easy compared to the intensity and physical output that Terry gave every day. Terry also didn't take days off, he was a physical monster with the heart of a thousand Olympic champions. When you study what he really did, as I have, you gain a deeper appreciation of how much of a legend he really was. But I think the biggest difference is the ultimate price Terry paid. Many have speculated that his run across Canada may have been the reason his cancer returned and ultimately cost him his life. Terry gave everything for the cause and if I had to be honest, I wasn't prepared to give that much.

On a lonely piece of highway several kilometres before the large monument and the park, is a signpost that marks the place where Terry Fox had to stop his Marathon of Hope (he lost his battle with cancer less than a year later). As I stood next to the marker, I was deeply grateful to have personally met this man who had inspired so many millions of people world-wide to take action and fight for causes they believed in. It was humbling to walk in his footsteps.

My little sister jumped out of the van and we took some pictures. I think she knew what a big deal this was for me. A few kilometres later, we arrived at the pull-out for the Terry Fox memorial where there is a statue of him that overlooks Lake Superior and Sleeping Giant Park. Marie was waiting to give me a big hug. We took lots of pictures and basked in the many accomplishments of the campaign so far. I was proud to have completed over 5,800 kilometres of my walk across Canada and walked in the footsteps of heroes, to have engaged with so many communities knowing that we had made a difference. This was what we always imagined *The Push for Change* could be and this day was a celebration of the hero who had inspired a lot of it.

The road to Thunder Bay was quiet, however when we reached the city we had numerous events to attend. We planned to make Thunder Bay our base for a number of weeks, so we were grateful to the folks at the Valhalla Inn, who provided us with very nice accommodations. I had spoken at a Salvation Army event a few years earlier and they had told us they would be happy to comp our accommodations when we reached that point in the campaign.

Marie

While we had hundreds of community champions who directly impacted the success of our campaign on a day to day basis, we also had incredible support behind the scenes.

For me, a huge amount of this support came from family; especially my mom and her husband Neil and my kids, Cindi and Curtis (who were young adults in post-secondary school at the time). We were very tight-knit and I knew that me being absent physically from their lives for 17 months would play havoc on all of us.

Thankfully, they supported me from the very beginning. Right from the time we started building the PFC campaign, they could see I was giving it my all and "in it to win it!" With their support and encouragement, I pushed through my feelings of guilt for deciding to leave home and go on the road for 17 months. I explained that I didn't want to feel I was sacrificing my family life to advocate for youth homelessness; I wanted to feel like my family was with me in the campaign and they rose to the occasion when I discussed my feelings with them. They reassured me that they fully supported me and were proud of my commitment. On my birthday they even wrote a special poem that I cherish:

The Heart Behind the Cart
The cart that travels from the eastern provinces
to the Pacific Ocean and everywhere in between.
The heart behind every community champion, inspired child,
teacher and police officer.
The heart behind every phone call, email and event.
The heart behind the man pushing to end youth homelessness.
But most importantly, the heart behind the kids who are
overwhelmed with joy, inspiration and hope
that their mom is changing the world.
Happy Birthday to the Heart Behind the Cart.

As a family, we found ways to connect even though we were apart, through texts, phone calls, social media and even postcards. What's more, for every PFC event that was even remotely close to them, they attended to support us in person. My blessings were not overlooked, I was grateful every day to have so much love and support all around me.

70

Our time in Thunder Bay started off with a number of events at local high schools. The Salvation Army also hosted an event for us and we were given an opportunity to visit a local youth detention facility. As always, it was a powerful experience talking to youth at the facility. The OPP held a special reception for us following a tour of our last Communications Call Centre; we were fortunate to visit all five throughout the province. We were also excited to share the news with our friends and supporters that we had received a special invitation to go to Ottawa and meet with Prime Minister Trudeau and members of his cabinet.

We had two more special events during our time in Thunder Bay. One was hosted by the Amalgamated Transit Union, ATU Local 966.

Some of the members had heard me speak at an event and thanks to the ATU Local in Toronto they learned about *The Push for Change* campaign and wanted to host a rally and walk. The community walk was awesome and we ended back at the venue where we had lunch and presentations. At the end of a perfect day they presented us with a cheque for $1,400.

The next day's event at city hall was a reception attended by OPP officials, the mayor, members of the media, front-line workers from local agencies and youth who had lived on the streets. Weeks earlier, the young people who would be attending the event had been given cameras and asked to take part in a project called Photo Voice. They were asked to take pictures and capture life in Thunder Bay through their eyes to give the public a perspective of the stark realities that youth who are street involved must face. The photos, together with written essays, were unveiled at the event and we could tell it was a real eye opener for the public and the media. The stories these young people shared and the pictures that reflected how they saw the world around them provided a powerful perspective and offered an excellent way to engage these young people in a dialogue about issues that impact them directly.

The most powerful part of the event was when several youth stood up and courageously shared their personal stories. One of the people present that morning was Minister Patty Hajdu, who was working behind the scenes on the "Making the Shift Project" for which the federal government had announced funding. We had the chance to speak with Minister Hajdu and we invited her to come and walk with us in a few days. She was happy to oblige and a few days later she met us for a walk together on a cold afternoon. We were inspired by the traction we were beginning to see from federal politicians and we thanked the Minister for taking the time to learn about *The Push for Change* and how we were raising awareness at a grassroots level. We arranged to walk over to Shelter House (a local homeless shelter) and have a tour of the facility. It was an amazing day and kind of fortuitous as only a few days later we would see Patty Hajdu again, in Ottawa.

For months Marie had been working patiently with MP Adam Vaughan to try and get us a meeting with Prime Minister Trudeau and now it was finally happening. Marie and I flew to Ottawa the following day. We had some time on our hands so Marie decided she wanted to get her hair done. After we left the salon, we headed up Metcalfe Street towards Parliament. Along the way we encountered a young man sitting on a piece of cardboard (not more than half a block from Parliament). He was wearing a blue hat and holding a Tim Hortons cup, asking passersby for change. The idea that I was about to meet with the leader of Canada to advocate for services that could very well affect this young man struck me. I asked the young man what his name was and he told me it was Todd. I gave him a few bucks and some words of encouragement and then we headed to Parliament.

To access the building, we had to go through an elaborate screening process and once inside we had to go through another screening process before we were in the queue to meet the Prime Minister. He was scheduled to come and visit with us after Question Period was over for the day, so we waited patiently. As I paced back and forth in the holding area, I knew I had one job, to inspire the Prime Minister with my words. I instinctively knew that I would have precious little time, so I needed to be concise and clear.

As much as I wanted to meet the Prime Minister, I was also interested in influencing this leader in hopes that it would produce a policy shift that would really benefit vulnerable youth in this country. Finally, there was a slight commotion and we saw several RCMP walking towards us followed by the Prime Minister. With the Prime Minister were Minister Patty Hajdu, MP Adam Vaughan and Minister Jean-Yves Duclos. Marie had brought a copy of the Prime Minister's book and wished him a belated happy birthday. She presented the Prime Minister with a *Push for Change* t-shirt, which he graciously held up for a photo and then it was my turn to speak.

I nervously clutched the penny I had found in Newfoundland in my hand. I had purchased a little plastic case for the penny so I could present it to the Prime Minister. I leaned in and told him the story of how I had found the penny outside in the street, how it had travelled a tough road, how it wasn't as pretty and shiny as the other pennies, but despite its outward appearance by the very nature of what it was, it could never ever lose its value. I told the Prime Minister that this penny represented every young person in this country that needed support and protection. This penny represented the vulnerable, voiceless and invisible young people in every city and small community across Canada and they were the reason we were pushing for change.

I handed the penny to the Prime Minister and saw that he was visibly moved by my words. In fact, Mr. Trudeau was a bit emotional as he turned to me and gave me a hug. He told me that on behalf of all Canadians he was proud of the work Marie and I were doing and he made me a promise. He told me as long as he was Prime Minster; he was going to keep this penny on his desk to remind him of the importance of Canadian youth. The last thing the Prime Minister said to me was a whisper in my ear as I left. He said "Joe, you're really going to like the federal budget announcement tomorrow." It just so happened the government was about to unveil their federal spending budget the following afternoon with an address from Finance Minister Bill Morneau.

One of the greatest lessons that I had reconfirmed to me time and again during the PFC campaign was that we *can* change the world, but first we must inspire the world to change. All Marie and I did to make *The Push for Change* happen was to stay in action and continuously tell a story that inspired people. The right people heard that story and provided everything we needed to be successful. The penny story inspired the Prime Minister, it inspired our sponsors and it inspired the OPP. It was a story that opened people's hearts and allowed new ideas to be grafted. Those new ideas opened up new possibilities, but the story was the key. In an ever more divisive world, we need to lead with the heart, sell our ideas with emotion and lead with the why. Once you touch a powerful person's heart, they will move mountains to do the right thing. Divisive conversations lead nowhere. Choosing sides and yelling at each other never produces positive results. Throughout the campaign I was goaded by reporters and advocates to pick a side but in the end that accomplishes nothing. Instead I chose to focus on inspiring people to see things differently. In my experience, inspiration is the greatest motivator of all.

Back in Thunder Bay the next day, we packed up our gear and headed towards our next base in Ignace. With the Prime Minister's words rolling around in my head, I kept the radio station tuned to the

CBC as they prepared to announce the details of the 2017 Federal Budget. Marie and I both listened intently as the details of Bill Morneau's budget announcement were explained.

As pine trees, snow banks, rocks and lakes whizzed by, the CBC commentator announced that the federal government was going to invest $11.2 billion over the next 11 years to dramatically reduce homelessness in Canada. After years of committee reports and groups across the country making recommendations; all petitioning the government to seriously invest in ending homelessness, the government was finally listening. Marie and I were ecstatic; it was like the home team just won the championship. There was much hooting and yelling in the car; I even had a small tear of joy. $11 BILLION!!! It was the largest investment the government had made in decades. We were so thrilled; and although it was still unclear what all this meant specifically for youth regarding things like prevention and early intervention, this was undoubtedly really good news for us.

I leaned back in the car seat, ruminating on what the Prime Minster had said to me, "You're going to like the budget news tomorrow." Right he was! It felt amazing to have played a small role in this positive result. *The Push for Change* was always about awareness because we understood that if we could raise enough awareness, we would garner the attention of politicians who have the power to change and fund new policy. What was really ironic for me was that as the budget news was winding down, the reporter commented that there was nothing really big to announce. In his estimation, the budget was underwhelming and didn't really favour any business sector. He also mentioned that inside of the House of Commons there was no real excitement generated by the announcements.

The only reason no one in the House of Commons was excited about this news was it didn't impact them. The people who ought to have been excited were young men like Todd who was sitting less than a block away on Metcalfe Street. Little did Todd know that inside the building behind which he sat and begged for change, real change had been committed to; the funding announced that afternoon could very well support Todd and many others with transitional housing. Our efforts and those of like-minded organizations were starting to pay off; this was indeed progress.

As we continued down the road I was reminded of something I heard Jimmy Pattison say once, "If I knew how successful I was going to be I would have set bigger goals."

71

When we arrived in Ignace on March 25, our accommodations weren't as nice as in Thunder Bay but we had everything we needed. The good thing about the places we stayed was that it was always temporary. With the onset of spring, we were seeing a lot more wildlife on our daily walks. One morning we saw a Lynx squatting down in a driveway. I thought it was a large domestic cat until it stood up; the distinct back legs combined with its pointed ears gave it away. It was super cool because Jaime had his camera ready and snapped a few shots. Later that same day we saw a fox and on the way home I spotted a bald eagle at the top of a pine tree. I mentioned the eagle to Jaime at which point he wanted to go back for some pictures. Jaime got out his distance lens and snapped some great shots; he even captured a couple when the eagle decided to fly away. When he showed them to me later, they looked like professional quality images to me. The amount of wildlife we encountered during the campaign was so incredible; every day we had the opportunity to see something new.

As we walked through the area towards Dryden, we had a few schools to visit along the way. My favourite was in Upsala where we were met at the doorway by five young kids. We spoke with them very briefly and then took a really cool picture with the kids, the cart and a Canadian flag. Although some events were small, I really enjoyed meeting the people in tiny, out of the way communities.

Our next base camp at the Dryden Best Western was in stark contrast to our accommodations in Ignace. We had contacted the manager months before our arrival and they had set aside their honeymoon suite for us. It was a huge suite that had recently been remodelled and it was like walking into a fancy suite in Las Vegas. Marie and I were in heaven.

Our time in Dryden was organized by OPP Sergeant Brian Eschbach (aka Sergeant Xbox), who really worked hard to support us. Long before we arrived, he had hosted community events, done media interviews, organized a huge community walk through town and also came out to support us on the highway for several days. In addition, like so many of the OPP staff we'd met, he did all of this on his own time as a volunteer.

The day we walked into Dryden it felt like we were operating *The Push for Change* Express. On the edge of town, we were met by a group of walkers along with a member of the Dryden Police Service. Together we walked with this group up over the bridge into town and then worked our way through the community. As we walked through town, I believe we passed by four different schools and with each school our crowd of walkers increased until we arrived at the auditorium with about 700 kids. I felt really bad for the first group of kids who had showed up in running gear. It was cold. Someone had given them bad information (they thought it was supposed to be a run) and they spent at least 40 minutes in the freezing cold.

They weren't the only ones dealing with adversity either. During one of the photos, I kneeled down the wrong way and put out my back. I felt a sharp pain shoot down my leg, just like what happened near Dartmouth, Nova Scotia. The pain almost had me on the ground, but somehow I managed to pull myself back up. Fortunately, I had the shopping cart to hang onto as we continued on into the auditorium where I tried to lie down and stretch out my back before I addressed the crowd (it was getting tighter and tighter by the minute). If this had been any other time, I might have gone back to the hotel but this was *The Push for Change* and I wasn't going to let this community down. They were excited to have us so the show had to go on. After the event I managed to stretch a little bit more and got some much-needed sleep. The one thing I had learned from other times was that the best thing for a sore back was a 24 km walk and that's exactly what I did the following day and after a couple more days I was back to normal.

Another community that really wanted us to visit was Sioux Lookout, which was northwest of Dryden. Because of how well the community had come together we decided that, as we had done in

Geraldton, we would go and walk in Sioux Lookout. We headed up early one morning and met with Constable Ben Bye, who walked with us. We arrived at Queen Elizabeth high school where a group of social justice students, who were working through the WE Day program, had collected shopping carts full of food and other needed items. They had also collected clothing for the Suits for Change program (which had been organized by the OPP) and they even raised $500 in cash, which they presented to us.

Our next stop was a very special school called Pelican Falls First Nations High School. Once a residential school run by the Government of Canada it was now a fly-in high school for indigenous youth from remote communities in Northern Ontario. Students that attended PFFNHS were flown in every September and stayed for the whole school year with a break at Christmas to go home.

The challenges that impact some of these remote communities are horrendous and the roadblocks facing some of the kids are huge. First Nations are disproportionately represented within all age groups when it comes to homeless statistics right across Canada, so the stuff we were talking about was very relevant. The students listened intently and when we were done, they presented us with a cheque representing money they had raised. The opportunity to visit this remote school was worth the extra time and effort it took to get to look Sioux Lookout.

72

On day 340, we reached Vermillion Bay and the weather was so nice I had to get rid of my big winter jacket. It was a sign that spring was on its way. If you've ever driven through Vermillion Bay, you'll probably remember it as the small town with a big gorilla as a roadside attraction. I'm not sure what the significance of the gorilla is, but that's where we intended to meet up with students from Lillian Berg Elementary School. As we approached, they were waiting with homemade signs and little jars of change. It was absolutely adorable. Elementary schools were so much fun because the kids were always full of energy and excitement when we arrived. After our presentation with them and with the help and support of Sergeant Xbox we managed to use the video conferencing technology available at the school to link into a remote school in Red Lake, Ontario. It was such a different way to communicate; one that I wasn't used to. I discovered pretty quickly that my dry humour didn't translate well over video.

When we reached Wabigoon the following day, I got a blister on my foot for the first time in a long while. I think with things warming up, my feet got a little sweaty and the next thing I knew I had a fat old blister. I may have caused Sergeant Xbox to squirm a little when I peeled off my sock and casually sliced open the blister with a utility knife. Once I had drained the blister, I threw on some gauze, wrapped my foot in duct tape and was back on my feet in five minutes. I learned in training that blisters are no big deal; wrap them tight in duct tape (which eliminates friction) and keep them clean so you don't get an infection.

With my blister in healing mode, we covered the remaining distance to Kenora, which was a big deal for a number of reasons. This was our last Ontario city before we reached Manitoba so we were almost done the entire province. Kenora was also the place where we were going to say goodbye to the OPP. Since the day we'd walked into the province, Marie and the OPP had been planning a series of events that were designed to send us off in style.

Just at the edge of Kenora, we were met by two amazing young boys named Caleb and Seth, also known as the Philanthro Brothers. These two brilliant young boys were fundraisers extraordinaire. With a little help from their mom and her Facebook page, these two young men had successfully organized a number of innovative campaigns and raised thousands for local charities. When they heard PFC was coming to town, they decided they wanted to raise some money to support us and what they did was amazingly creative. Using their mom's Facebook, they asked friends and family to send in photos that they could convert into colouring books. With the help of a local printer they created their own colouring book with the photos and sold them at an event that was held before we reached Kenora. They collected over $800 so when we reached town, I really wanted to acknowledge their efforts by having them walk with me and push the celebrity cart.

265

It was a nice, sunny afternoon when I met up with Caleb, Seth and their mom. Beaming like a couple of heroes, the two proud young men pushed the "celebrity cart" right through the community, finishing up the afternoon in front of the downtown OPP station. Marie and I had a special thank you swag bag for each of them. This was the kind of youth engagement that really inspired both Marie and me.

Now that we were in Kenora, it was hard to believe we were just 75 kilometres from the Manitoba border. It was also becoming more apparent that we were going to have support from the RCMP. Over the months that she had been preparing for the campaign beyond Ontario, Marie had been in contact with the RCMP and it looked like we would have their support as we travelled through Manitoba. We were also informed that there was going to be an official hand off from the OPP to the RCMP in Kenora with leadership from the RCMP and the OPP in attendance. Marie also briefed me that events and school visits were being confirmed throughout Manitoba and beyond and that the Regina RCMP J Division wanted us to come and speak to all of the new cadets at their Regiment Dinner (which takes place at their special training centre at RCMP Academy, Depot Division).

In Kenora, we had two main events planned and both were elaborate. The first was a walk through the community followed by a large public event at the Cultural Centre. The second was a luncheon and "Farewell to Ontario" event at the Kenora Tourism Centre. These events had taken a long time to plan and they were really important to the OPP and the community.

Prior to the first event, we gathered a few kilometres from the venue for a rally and then walked together through Kenora to the venue. We picked a spot right in front of the famous "Husky the Muskie" landmark by the water in downtown Kenora as the meeting point. Students from the local high schools showed up with homemade support signs and were soon joined by local OPP supporters, representatives of the city (including the mayor) and friends from the school board, as well as the senior leadership from the OPP (who had flown in from across the province just for these events). We had Commissioner Vince Hawkes, Deputy Commissioner Brad Blair, Detective Superintendent Ken Leppert and even Glenda Reid, who helped coordinate all the communication centre events. We also had the entire communications team with Brad and Jeanie, Rob Jamieson from the OPPA and of course we invited Scott MacLeod to come and take part. There were people from all over Ontario who had worked hard to make *The Push for Change* happen and we were thankful they had taken the time to come to Kenora to say goodbye.

There was a light, happy feeling in the air and as we walked through the community, I saw a lot of smiling faces. Completing *The Push for Change* through Ontario (with the help of so many community-minded individuals) had been no small feat and we had a lot to celebrate.

The day before our event at the Cultural Centre, we had been told that something very special was going to happen upon our arrival. The chief, elders and a local First Nations drummer were there to perform a drumming ceremony and prayer. Sharing in the traditional way, the chief spoke to the community and talked about youth and the importance of helping them find their way. There was a blessing made and a food offering and then they asked me to come and be prayed over. Speaking in his native language, the chief prayed over me and then said some very kind words about the work *The Push for Change* was doing in English. Next, he blessed a blanket which the elders from the group placed over my shoulders and then we sang and danced in a circle as the drummers drummed.

In the days leading up to the event, when the chief and elders in the community had learned about PFC, they decided they wanted to bless me with a traditional Thunder Bird Star Blanket. This was a massive honour. Star blankets are a symbol of deep respect, generosity and honour. To be given a blanket is a high honour and to be given one so publicly was the greatest honour of all. I was deeply moved by the gesture. After the event, back at the hotel I was speaking with the Treaty Three Police Chief who had attended the event and he told me that the Thunder Bird on the blanket represents leadership and that they saw me as a leader. He also told me the blanket had healing powers and I could use it to stay strong and heal myself when things got challenging.

That evening we had a private dinner with our OPP and RCMP friends together with 60-80 people who had worked on the campaign. What I really loved about the event is when the Commissioner Hawkes got up and said some very kind words (not to me but to Marie), acknowledging her whole-hearted commitment to the campaign. This meant a lot to me because I knew how hard Marie worked every day; most people couldn't see or understand the kind of commitment she had made.

The next day we had our provincial hand-off and farewell to Ontario event at the Kenora Welcoming Centre on the way out of town. Even though we still had a few days of walking to do before we reached the provincial border, we decided this was the best venue for us to celebrate the completion of Ontario. The event was a little smaller but with lots of familiar faces. My goal was to somehow condense and thank the OPP for everything they had done to get us through the toughest part of the journey. The commissioner and senior level OPP from around the province were there along with Kenora's mayor and a large showing of senior level RCMP from Manitoba. RCMP Assistant Commissioner Scott Kolody was a great friend of the OPP and made a point of attending and welcoming us into Manitoba. Marie had been working with the RCMP to plan a number of engagements in the province but there was still no solid commitment from them to provide vehicle support.

To thank our OPP supporters, we put together a video featuring significant moments from our six months trekking through the province. Literally thousands of OPP members had supported us in hundreds of communities and as the video came to an end, the emotion in the room was palpable. Unfortunately, our biggest OPP supporter and internal champion, Deputy Commissioner Rick Barnum was unable to make it (he had some serious health issues at the time). It was a real bummer because Rick's support had been a crucial part of the OPP/PFC relationship. After watching the video while standing side by side, RCMP Assistant Commissioner Kolody turned to retired Constable Kelly Harder and asked him if he would be interested in following us across Manitoba for the next several weeks. Harder said yes and just like that we had vehicle support for all of Manitoba.

The food served at the event was amazing; Marie and I still talk about how good it was. There was a massive fish-fry set up and loaves of freshly baked bread to go with the deep-fried pickerel. It was by far, the best fish-fry I had ever been to. The rice salad was made with wild rice that grew in the area, and to top everything off, there was delicious home-made bannock. I was in heaven.

After lunch we went outside and posed for some official photos after which the crowd began to disperse. It was a bittersweet moment as we said goodbye to people we had forged strong friendships with over the past many months. I remember one moment particularly, after everyone had gone and it was just me and OPP Ken Leppert standing in the empty room. We looked at each other and I could tell we both felt the same way; we were really going to miss working together. Ken was one of so many people who had worked tirelessly to ensure that PFC was a success and I was grateful. We said our goodbyes and just like that, our Ontario campaign was over.

Marie

After six months of outstanding OPP support, it was time to say goodbye to our friends in Ontario and I did so with trepidation. The OPP had protected Joe along every kilometre he walked in Ontario and it quickly became evident that they weren't just committed to safety, security and prevention protocols, they were dedicated to the wellbeing of their communities. They hosted events for us, they walked with us, they connected us to other police services and they even put out media releases for us. They became more than just valuable community partners, they were our friends and I valued the relationship we had built with OPP members across the province.

Our final event in Kenora on April 8 (which was hosted by the OPP North West Region with help from headquarters), was beyond extraordinary. Both Joe and I were humbled and honoured as the OPP shared what The Push for Change had meant from their perspective. We were thrilled to hear the massive impact the campaign had, not only for their communities but with their members. Many OPP officers across the province told us how we had changed their perspective on homelessness (and its causes), and helped them to see addiction and mental health in a new and empathetic way. This was a massive shift in their culture and one that's necessary in order to change how we address youth homelessness in

Canada. As the second largest policing service in the country, I honestly feel without the support and connections of the OPP behind us, The Push for Change would have been irrelevant, just another charity walk across Canada.

73

Even though the events were over and we had officially wrapped up the province we still had some kilometres to cover before we were done walking through Ontario. As I walked out of Kenora and reconnected with Highway 17, I spotted more roadside pennies; two of them. It was almost like they were put there for me to find. It was a reminder of what we had left to do; Western Canada still lay before us and these pennies were an inspiration of why we had to keep going.

Day 346 was our last day in Ontario and the weather was bright, sunny and mild. As we got closer to the Manitoba border I spotted a large collection of eagles near a small lake. There were more than ten bald eagles and three Golden eagles. As we walked, the majestic birds circled overhead, following us all the way down the hill and around the corner. It was almost like the eagles had come to officially bless the blanket I had received two days earlier. It was odd to see so many eagles clustered together and I took it as a good omen for our transition to the next part of our journey.

Something even more mysterious happened when I was about ten kilometres from the provincial border. I had an eerie feeling that I was being watched and when I looked up to the tree line on the opposite side of the road there was a dog following along with me. When I would stop, he would stop; when I began walking again, he would walk. He was extremely curious and had his attention keenly focused on me as he shadowed me for over a kilometre. Just before he disappeared into the bushes it occurred to me that we were nowhere near any houses and this wasn't a dog, it was a timber wolf. I couldn't help but think that the pennies, the eagles and the timber wolf were all part of some kind of validation from the universe. I was on the right path; I had weathered the storms. The great plains were in front of us with our goal almost in sight.

There is a slight hill to climb as you approach the Manitoba border. I could see twinkling lights up ahead where a large group of RCMP from D Division waited to officially welcome us. As each step brought me closer, a feeling of accomplishment washed over me. There was absolutely no doubt that Ontario was the hardest challenge we would face on the entire campaign. Walking around Lake Superior in the winter had been difficult beyond description but it wasn't just the north that had been hard. Ontario accounted for over 3,600 kilometres of the campaign and we had spent six months trekking the long way through this massive province which added up to over three million steps. I felt extremely proud of this accomplishment. I had faced my fears and emerged victorious, I felt like a champion. Marie and I had successfully accomplished what so many people said was impossible. I had walked through Northern Ontario (in the midst of a fierce Canadian winter) pushing a shopping cart and with the incredible support from the OPP, we had raised hundreds of thousands of dollars and inspired tens of thousands of people. I had a huge smile on my face as I approached the flashing police lights. One of the RCMP officials stepped forward and extended her hand, "Congratulations Mr. Roberts; welcome to the Province of Manitoba."

Follow the Journey online.

———

See the photos and videos.

———

www.thepushforchangebook.com

PART EIGHT
MANITOBA AND THE WEST

74

Our first day in Manitoba was beautiful. The sun was bright and warm; spring was definitely in the air. Kelly Harder was our volunteer RCMP escort. His job was simply to drive along behind us and keep us and the motoring public safe. We had become accustomed to having the OPP accompany us, so working with Kelly was easy. In fact it was really easy because he stayed with us throughout the whole province so we only needed to brief him once on how we conduct ourselves on the highway.

For some reason, I thought as soon as we crossed the Manitoba border the highway would be split into a divided highway, but Kelly told me that wasn't for another 16 km. Jaime and I had really been looking forward to a divided highway. For most of the previous 4,000 plus kilometres we had travelled on roads that varied from four lanes with wide shoulders to a single lane with narrow (sometimes non-existent) shoulders. We'd experienced some intense days with traffic (particularly commercial trucks) whizzing by us at high speed. The idea of having a big, comfy two lane highway with a wide shoulder for the next three provinces was a comforting thought indeed.

The first tiny community we encountered in Manitoba was Whiteshell and already the landscape was different. The further we got away from the border of Ontario, the more the geography changed. After months spent walking across the Canadian Shield (a landscape littered with lakes, hills, rocks and forest) we were headed to the sweeping plains of southern Manitoba.

In the early afternoon, we reached the beginning of the divided highway and celebrated; from here to the BC border we would have a lot more roadside space to work with.

As we moved west over the next few days, the trees we saw along the way were noticeably smaller and the land began to flatten out. The snow was melting and before we knew it, we were walking on the edge of the Great Plains and spring was upon us. What was absolutely astonishing to me was how much life existed all around me. I always thought the prairies were barren and somewhat lifeless, yet as I walked along I was mesmerized by the number of birds and other wildlife I encountered every day. The land and its inhabitants were waking up after a long winter and the place was teeming with life.

Thanks to the RCMP and their engagement team, school events were being set up throughout the province for us. Two of the first places we visited were Steinbach and Selkirk. We were also invited by the Dakota Ojibway Police Service to visit a remote First Nations community southeast of Winnipeg called Rousseau River. We broke from our normal walking routine for the day and conducted a Walk with Joe from the highway into the community, where we held an event. As we got closer to the community, we picked up more and more walkers along the way. It was a rainy day, so everyone was getting a little wet, although the rain never bothered me. By this point in the campaign, I had seen it all and my philosophy was that weather only impacted what gear you needed to use, it didn't need to impact your mood. Truth be told, some of my happiest days on the campaign were days when the weather was challenging.

At the end of our event, the Chief from Rousseau River along with the Dakota Ojibway Police Service presented us with gifts and said some kind words about the campaign. They also presented me with another star blanket. In the eyes of our First Nation's friends and partners, what *The Push for Change* stood for was deeply personal within their communities. I was humbled by their generosity and support.

It only took us about six days of walking before we reached Winnipeg, where we received a huge welcome from the city and prepared for a series of events. I had visited Winnipeg many times in the past as an inspirational speaker at various conferences which were often located in the downtown core. This time I was escorted by the RCMP and the Winnipeg Police Service as we made our way through Main and Portage on our way to city hall, where a collection of supporters were waiting to participate in a rally, along with various media outlets that were there to cover the event.

Mayor Brian Bowman met us at city hall along with RCMP Assistant Commissioner Scott Kolody and Grand Chief Jerry Daniels. Friends from End Homelessness Winnipeg were also there, along with various other community supporters and city leaders. A First Nation's elder said a prayer, smudged the area and made a tobacco offering after which she gave me an eagle feather that had been blessed. I held the feather as I told the leaders of Winnipeg why I had walked over 6,000 kilometres to their great city. I spoke of collaboration, the need to prevent homelessness and the vital need to see possibility, especially where possibility is hard to see.

After the media interviews, we dispersed for the day to prepare for an early start the next morning. Every year End Homelessness Winnipeg hosts a CEO Sleepout and even though the event was not scheduled to happen until the fall, they chose to get an early start and kick off the campaign in the spring. The timing could not have been better for us to spread our message. The morning was well attended by local business leaders and I had the opportunity to share my story (as a former homeless youth who was provided with a second chance and became a successful business leader). I also talked about how you don't have to walk across Canada to push for change, we can all do something and the CEO Sleepout was a perfect example of that. It was a great event and after a snack we headed to Vincent Massey High School for a presentation to the students.

The assistant commissioner had coordinated a private event for RCMP, Justice and other police services to come hear me speak at their Winnipeg headquarters. It was well attended by police and justice leaders and when it was complete the assistant commissioner and I exchanged challenge coins. One of the interesting contrasts during the campaign was the wide variety of groups we spoke to. We could be at a shelter in the morning sharing coffee with people who were homeless and meeting provincial politicians in the afternoon. It was an excellent opportunity for me to craft different ways to contextualize what we were trying to accomplish and make it meaningful for different groups. It was something that I found both challenging and fun.

Our last big event in Winnipeg was coordinated by RAY, which is an acronym for Resource Access for Youth. The Executive Director, Kelly had connected with Marie months earlier and committed to host an event that would raise awareness about youth homelessness and also directly involve youth that she worked with through her organization. RAY is one of those amazing front line groups that meet youth in crisis wherever they are at and offers help and support in a multitude of ways. What was cool was that Kelly was like a surrogate mom to many of these young people and RAY was their home.

We started the day at the University of Winnipeg where a large crowd had gathered with signs and banners and proceeded through the city with the help of the Winnipeg Police. When we arrived at RAY, there was a parking lot reception. We had a number of friends and supporters join us on the walk including our friends from UA Local 254 (who also presented us with a cheque at the event). We were joined by local NAV Canada staff, who had been part of that organization's fundraising for PFC all across Canada the previous year.

When we got to the parking lot the youth were waiting for us. They had been working hard since the previous day preparing chicken soup and homemade bannock for the event. It was a great feast and even though it was raining lightly, it didn't dampen our spirits. After lunch we headed inside the facility where the kids had set up music equipment and were preparing to perform. There were a lot of people in the room and I could see that it was a bit intimidating for the youth who normally had this place to themselves. I was quite impressed with their courage when they started to perform songs they had written themselves. One of the performers was a young girl, who first shared her heartbreaking story and then sang a song and dedicated it to *The Push for Change*. It was powerful and hit me right in the heart.

75

So far during the campaign, we had spent a lot of time walking across Canada, building campaign support, doing media interviews and talking to politicians. What we hadn't done much was to connect with street-involved youth and listen to their perspective; which is not as easy a thing to do as you might think. First you need to be invited by someone like Kelly from RAY. But even then, there's no guarantee the young people are going to want to talk with you or listen to what you have to say. Because of Kelly's strong relationship with the kids, they trusted me and we felt privileged to be invited into their space. I think my favourite part of the day was towards the end when we went downstairs and hung out for over an hour and just talked.

I shared some of my story, they shared some of their stories and we talked about what gets us stuck and what we can do to move forward. It was an opportunity to share the AIR model and how I used PFC to overcome my own barriers and many of the things I was afraid of. Connecting directly with youth who are where I was, is one of my favourite things to do. Because my life experience is raw and authentic, I have the ability to connect and bond with them. I earn respect quickly and it opens lines of communication that are closed to 99% of the people they encounter on a daily basis. It is because of this that I am grateful for the challenges I've had to endure in my life. It has given me a voice in places where no other voices can be heard.

Thanks in part to our visit to RCMP Headquarters (which must have inspired their leadership), we were asked if we wanted to visit a northern community. As had happened in Ontario, when we arrived at the airfield, the shopping cart was loaded into the RCMP jet and we headed to Norway House, which is a small, remote community. When we landed, our first stop was the local high school where we were welcomed by the First Nations Chief. For 45 minutes as I shared my story, the entire school population was dead quiet.

Afterwards, we had both school counsellors and teachers tell us they had never seen the kids so dialed in. Following the presentation, we were invited to join in a feast that the local culinary students had worked really hard to prepare. As we entered the big hall, we were met by a group of smiling young people who had laid out a huge, long table filled with goose, pickerel and bannock. The meal was amazing and the hospitality was especially warm and welcoming. We flew back to Winnipeg the same day and the next morning we were back on the road heading west towards Brandon, where a huge committee had been building events for us for more than a year.

On day 357, we were west of Winnipeg heading towards Portage la Prairie where we planned to join up with AC Scott Kolody and walk into town for a local school presentation. It was super cool because Scott had brought a bunch of senior RCMP people with him and one of the RCMP members was even in Red Serge (which is the RCMP's traditional dress uniform which includes a signature bright scarlet tunic and wide-brimmed felt campaign hat).

On April 27, we received sad family news; my uncle Jimmy had passed away. Uncle Jim had remained active, curious and full of adventure throughout his retirement and he was an avid supporter of PFC. I remember his big smile as he greeted me when I arrived at Yonge and Dundas in Toronto. PFC inspired him, in fact he made of point of telling me he already had his ticket for Vancouver and was going to be there when I rolled in.

Maybe it was coincidence but on the same day that my uncle Jim passed away I received a unique donation on the side of the Trans-

Canada Highway west of Brandon. Placed on the side of the highway were two bright blue five dollar bills held down by rocks to prevent them from blowing away. Although the anonymous donation was most likely from a motorist who knew I would be headed that way, it felt like a touch point from another dimension. In 9,064 kilometres it was the one and only time that money was left on the road for me to find and I chose to take it as a sign that Uncle Jimmy was watching over me. If there's one thing I learned from my uncle Jim it was to never grow old and frail. No matter what, stay active, adventurous and curious about the world... and never, ever stop smiling.

76

When we walked into the city of Brandon on May 1, we had officially been on the road for over a year. Thanks to the media attention we'd received in Winnipeg (and the fact that the Trans-Canada Highway is practically the only major road in the region), we received lots of donations and cars honking their support as we walked. The donations were also extremely generous; on multiple occasions people stopped and handed us hundred-dollar bills. It really was "Friendly Manitoba."

As spring progressed, the weather grew warm and the landscape took on hues of green. Every day we encountered wildlife including coyotes, deer, muskrat, ducks, geese, hawks, eagles and what seemed like ten thousand other birds I'd never seen before. Every day I walked by ponds and waterholes filled with ducks and other birds of all shapes and sizes. I also seemed to meet several hawks on a daily basis. They would be perched atop a hydro pole or tall tree watching me as I passed by. Other birds, especially the crows, would grow curious and fly ahead and sit on a pole and then do it again as I passed. Even when there were no people around, I always felt I was being watched when I was out on that highway; it was a reminder that the prairies were full of life. Just like I had been grateful for the opportunity to see northern Ontario in the winter, I felt blessed to be in Manitoba in the spring. Unless you live there you likely wouldn't get to experience the visceral experience of witnessing the plains come alive as summer edged ever closer.

Our quiet days walking the prairie ended when we reached Brandon; the city was prepared for our visit and the days that followed were filled with events. Brandon was also a key stop on our route for another reason. Since November 1 of the previous year we had been leapfrogging from one hotel to another, all the way from Welland, Ontario to Brandon, Manitoba. Now that the weather was consistently warm, it was time to move back into the RV. Fraserway RV had stored the RV at their location in Cookstown for the winter, so now we had to get it to Brandon. Scott MacLeod (who was a friend and former OPP member) and his wife Pam volunteered to drive it up from Cookstown and join us as surprise guests at the Brandon Fundraising Gala (which was taking place later that week). There was only one problem. The weather wasn't cooperating. When Scott and Pam reached Thunder Bay they were stopped in their tracks by freezing rain, which had caused the highways to shut down completely. When Scott was finally able to get the RV rolling again, driving conditions were treacherous and his progress was slow. For Scott and Pam to drive through freezing rain from Marathon to Dryden was heroic and brave. They arrived the night before the big event and we were thankful they made it safely.

During the entire PFC campaign (and even during the trial walk from Calgary to Vancouver), I never drove the RV myself. At 31 feet long, plus a car trailer, it wasn't something I felt comfortable with so I left the driving to others. Given that he'd joined us after the RV had been stored for the winter, I was interested to see how well Jaime managed the RV once we got it back on the campaign trail.

The day of the gala, we did our walk through the community of Brandon, which was followed by a big BBQ in the city park. We gathered near the university with community supporters and our friends from Kiwanis (who had been organized by our local community champion, Dr. Hamid Mumin) and proceeded through Brandon with the chief of police leading the way. Students from the university brought their own decorated shopping cart and were accompanied by staff from local shelters and community youth workers. When we rounded the corner and headed towards city hall, we were joined by Mayor Rick Chrest, who pushed my cart the rest of the way to the park.

Although it was primarily a fundraiser, the BBQ was organized to make it accessible for everyone in the community to attend so those who wanted to could buy a ticket for themselves and sponsor a ticket for someone else who might not be able to afford it. This allowed everyone to join the celebration. The park was also set up with a series of fun events for all ages. They even had a car smash, where you got to take a big sledgehammer to an old car from the junkyard. With headgear and body protection on (just in case any parts came flying off) I went at the car like an angry teenager; it was even more fun than I imagined.

The bandstand was set up for music and speeches and I did a short presentation and then handed it over to the mayor, who thanked us for our efforts on behalf of Canadian youth. After the speeches, the local Rotary and Kiwanis Clubs presented us with cheques. We also received a surprise donation from James Shearer a star player on the Brandon Wheat Kings hockey team. As part of the celebration of Canada's 150th birthday, the Royal Bank of Canada had given 150 community leaders across Canada $150 to "do something that makes their community a better place." James decided PFC was a worthy cause and presented us with the gift in front of the community. Our time in Brandon was a lot of fun; although it was laid back, it was also very well organized and we enjoyed the people immensely.

The Gala banquet that evening was amazing. As we walked into the huge ballroom, we were flabbergasted that the entire event had been put together by volunteers. Hamid and the Kiwanis members had really knocked themselves out. Not only was the venue perfect but the room was packed by the time we got started; we had local officials, MPs MLAs, the chief of police, students and a couple hundred community supporters. We also had two surprises for the audience; both my mom and Scott MacLeod were in the room. As I shared the story of my struggle back from the brink of addiction and homelessness, when I got to the part about how Scott (as a young police officer) had intervened in my life, I invited him up onto the stage to say a few words. As the one person who never gave up on me no matter what, it was equally powerful to have my mom in the room as I told my story and then introduced her to the audience.

THE PUSH FOR CHANGE

Thanks to the wonderful organizers who also put together a silent auction for the event, the gala raised over $15,000 for PFC, an amazing accomplishment for a city of less than 50,000 people.

77

Once our events in Brandon were over, we focused on getting the RV organized and ready for the road. When we'd prepared the RV for storage the previous fall the campaign had been chaotic, so when we opened up the RV and began to organize things, we realized just how much work we had ahead of us. What I thought would take a few hours, ended up taking an entire day. When Bobby was with the campaign, everything had been spotless; he had been amazing at managing the RV and the vehicles, but I wasn't sure how Jaime was going to do with the added responsibility. Jaime had encountered some challenges adjusting to winter driving conditions and he had managed, but a 31ft RV towing a car was a different beast. It required more than just a steady hand, it required confidence.

Getting our gear sorted out was our first challenge. Throughout the winter, we'd been using six large totes to move our stuff from hotel to hotel. In addition to packing away the winter gear (organizing our summer gear) we also needed to do a major purge and eliminate anything that wasn't needed.

Jaime and I set to the task. First, we dumped everything from the RV, the van and the totes on the grass and meticulously sorted through the lot. What I wanted when we were done was a clean and organized set of totes (that we could carry in the van) filled with the gear we needed to finish the campaign.

"Transition Organization Day" or TOD as I called it, was long but when we were done, we were lean and organized. We also got rid of a lot of stuff we didn't need. In fact, our RCMP escort Kelly Harder took away an RCMP cruiser filled to the brim with goodies that we donated. So many things we would no longer need that could help someone else. There is something about a purge that I really like. It's empowering to get rid of stuff you don't use or need. Marie and I love doing this in our house too. What's more, after a purge I rarely ever really miss anything that's gone. I think when we let go of the stuff we don't use anymore it restores energy in us. After a long, cold winter, we needed to have our energy restored. We had three and a half provinces still to go, so getting organized and doing our spring cleaning really helped set us on the right path.

When we opened the RV for the first time, we were in for a few surprises. First off, we hadn't properly drained the water line to the toilet in the fall, so when we hooked up the water the toilet began to spray water all over the place. Until we got it repaired we couldn't turn on the water. Due to a mouse infestation over the winter, we also had to scrub the RV from top to bottom (there were traces of the little critters in every nook and cranny). People in the park told us not to worry about the mice, it was a common problem and they would disappear once we got rolling. I wasn't so sure and it still left us with lots of cleaning to do.

Something about being back in the RV felt great. It wasn't as comfortable as staying in a hotel but it was easier in a lot of ways. We didn't have to move all our belongings in and out of a different room every week and it was easier to walk and work out of one location. Granted, it wasn't as comfortable, but it was easier.

In the year that we had been on the road, I had walked the equivalent of 322 half marathons while Marie had managed over 300 events. As a team, we were well seasoned and organized and for the first time since the beginning of the campaign, things felt like they were getting easier rather than harder.

As spring turned to summer, I reflected on how much mental toughness it had taken to stay the course; I reminded myself daily to keep a possibility mindset. Getting to Manitoba, heck even getting to Newfoundland and taking that first step, was a massive achievement. I learned that when tackling big goals you have to be really mindful of your own thoughts and also what influences you allow into your experience. Probability mindset is everywhere. A lot of people live in fear and they are more than happy to tell you about all of the bad things that *could* happen. I've learned that it's really helpful to listen to the potential ideas that may come out of those conversations but to leave the negative energy behind. When we were planning the PFC campaign we heard from many doubters; people who were unable to envision what we were doing. Some of them told us it couldn't be done. I would always thank them for their perspective and then carry on and find my own way around the roadblocks that stood in my path. My vision of PFC was always crystal clear; I saw the finish line in Vancouver before I even began walking.

I believe that without trailblazers and mavericks who challenge the status quo, we would never change or grow. Having lived on the street I was used to ignoring conventional wisdom and doing things my way. In this situation it had paid off, the campaign was everything I had dreamed it would be and more. The trick to listening to others when your goals are big is to take the potentially useful bits of advice but leave the doubt and fear alone.

Marie

After six months in Ontario, our 25 days in Manitoba went by in a flash. Thanks to the OPP, we had full support from Assistant Commissioner Scott Kolody, who was the Commanding Officer of the Manitoba RCMP. I remember Scott telling me at our Kenora event that he wished he had known about our campaign sooner, so he could have done more...but he did so much for us! In addition to providing Joe with an Auxiliary Officer to accompany him every kilometre along the Manitoba highways, he put together a small team to coordinate school and community events for us. He also flew us to Norway House to engage with the local First Nations community. After hearing Joe's story at our Kenora event, Scott knew Joe's message needed to be heard by as many people as possible and he quickly mobilized the province.

With only five months left in the trek (and summer ahead of us), my duties with community champions lessened a little, allowing me to attend more events and even walk with Joe some days. I was always thrilled to watch the faces of those who heard Joe's message. They were always inspired and mesmerized by his story of overcoming adversity. He had such a gift, not just for presenting, but also for being able to read his audience and deliver exactly what they needed. He would add in little tidbits or local facts here and there for good measure, to make the story more relatable. It didn't matter the age or the venue, he nailed it every time and I witnessed one audience after another being moved to a more empathetic understanding of homelessness. When events had time for Q&A, Joe easily and naturally answered the questions with the kind of self assurance and knowledge that comes from decades of experience.

Joe walked 24 km every day with confidence and determination and he talked to hundreds of people every day with conviction and purpose so I thought it was pretty fitting when I labelled him the official PFC Walkie Talkie.

78

As we approached the Saskatchewan border on day 373, our friends from the RCMP showed up in full regalia. Assistant Commissioner Scott Kolody had brought along four RCMP members in Red Serge and we walked the last few kilometres of Manitoba together. Although the prairie winds were getting stronger as we moved west, they were nothing when compared to our experience in Northern Ontario. It was hard to believe we were almost done walking across our seventh province; only three more to go.

Waiting to welcome us at the border was a contingent of RCMP officials from Saskatchewan. Considering we hadn't arranged anything in advance, we were thrilled by the support we were getting from the RCMP as we made our way from one province to the next. Although it was an informal hand off, the assistant commissioner had some very kind words and gave me a crisp salute as we said our goodbyes. I was sad to be leaving Manitoba behind and even sadder to say goodbye to Kelly Harder, who had accompanied us across the entire province. I thanked him for his support and camaraderie.

With 6,800 km behind me, my feet were doing great, the walking temperature was pleasant and aside from some strong winds now and then, things were pretty easy. After sitting down for a live CBC interview which gave us some great exposure in Saskatchewan, I was done for the day and actually had the opportunity to relax a bit. It was something that didn't happen often so we celebrated with a big communal meal.

In Saskatchewan we were fortunate to have our good friend Rand Teed step up at the eleventh hour and book a bunch of school events for us. Although we had connected with a community champion months earlier and thought we had it covered, when we arrived in the province we discovered that nothing had been organized. Thankfully, we were in good hands with Rand who had an extensive background working with schools. He made some calls and got us booked around the province. Rand was also a huge supporter of all the events that had been organized for Regina.

Our first school visit was in the small town of Maryfield. The students met up with us at the town's welcome sign and walked with us to their school. It was a small, but mighty group. After the school presentation was over, we found a huge wide-open field with large, round hay bales and took some very prairie PFC photos. The wind was blowing really hard so we got the Canadian flag out and got some great shots to share with our supporters on social media.

We ended our day with some good news; Marie received confirmation from the RCMP at J Division that Assistant Commissioner Curtis Zablocki had invited us to attend their annual Regimental Dinner. The dinners are a tradition that goes back to the earliest days of the Northwest Mounted Police and this one was going to be held at Depot (the RCMP Training Centre located in Regina) which was founded in 1885 and has been training the best and brightest of the RCMP ever since. Since we were attending the dinner, Marie was working with Assistant Commissioner Brenda Lucki to see if we could arrange a series of engagements with the staff and cadets during our time in Regina.

The first half of our walk through Saskatchewan featured a series of small towns. On day 377, we visited Whitewood where we engaged with the local school and then it was on to Broadview and Indian Head. We loved walking through town with the students in each community and they seemed happy to have a break from their regular routine. The RCMP were great at making sure we had whatever support was needed as we moved along. For our part, Marie and I were like little kids in a foreign land, taking selfies in front of the grain elevators. In one small town, Marie and I parked the car in front of some absolutely massive grain elevators and took a picture of Marie standing inside the car with her body coming out the sun roof. A group of locals drove by and laughed at our touristy antics.

Although he had been a great member of the team up to this point, it was becoming clear as we moved through Saskatchewan that Jaime wasn't very comfortable with his new responsibilities related to the RV. As our one-man road crew, he was now in charge of the operation and maintenance of both the RV and the van (which included camp set-up and takedown) as we moved from site to site. Neither Marie nor I had time to manage the vehicles or help with moving and setting up of the RV, we were simply too busy doing everything else to keep the campaign on track. That meant a huge number of new responsibilities had been added to Jaime's role, (including safety procedures related to the RV) and I grew more concerned by the day as I noticed more and more inconsistencies. To top it off, the three of us were all living in the RV together, sharing the same 300 square feet of space.

When we reached Regina, thanks to the efforts of Street Culture Kidz, Carmichael Outreach and Rand Teed, we had a full day of events to attend. We started the day at the Street Culture facility where we were officially welcomed by the mayor as well as the local MP and MLA. Rod Pedersen, who is the voice of the Saskatchewan Rough Riders, was our emcee and after a prayer was offered by a local First Nations elder, we gathered out front for a walk through downtown Regina. As we started off, I thanked Rand for his commitment to helping us engage the city.

We had a pretty big crowd join us for the walk including our friends from UA Local 179, so we were thankful to the Regina Police Service for providing traffic support. One of my concerns when walking through city streets with a large group was slow walkers. Anytime the walk was longer than a few kilometres the line of people would get thin in spots as the faster walkers moved ahead and slower walkers straggled behind. This created a hazard when impatient drivers decided to cut in between walkers. Jaime had a tough job trying to keep the whole group moving together. As the procession became more spread out, Jaime asked the two slowest walkers if they wanted a ride, but when they declined he felt he had no choice but to drive around them and rejoin the main part of the group.

At the end of the walk, everyone gathered at Carmichael Outreach for a BBQ. Global News was there and shot a quick piece for the six o'clock news after which I sat down to enjoy my meal. As I started to eat my hamburger, suddenly a very angry man approached and started yelling at me, it was bizarre and really caught me off guard. His attack was clearly aimed at me personally, however I couldn't understand what he was angry about so I let him unwind a bit until he calmed down enough to explain that Jaime had gone around him and left him and his companion to walk the rest of the way on their own (essentially, the parade had gone on without them). I understood that he was angry but I also understood Jaime's position. After the dust settled, I had an opportunity to really talk with the man and I tried to explain that we're all on the same team. We don't take an "us and them" perspective, we are all "us." He expressed his remorse for his outburst and we shook hands and put it behind us.

Later, as I reflected on what had transpired, it reminded me of so many other conversations going on in the world today. Sometimes it seems the only kind of conversations we know how to have are divisive ones. I prefer to take the approach of, "inspire first, then work together to look for solutions." It's not that the issues around homelessness and children being vulnerable in this country don't infuriate me, they do, but we can't expect to make progress if we let our anger get the better of us. Too often I have seen people who support social justice causes draw distinct lines between themselves and others and then everyone's yelling and no one is listening. I get that we need to take action and stand up for what we believe in, I also believe we have to try and find common ground to work from (so we're united against the problem, not the people). If we could teach these skills to everyone who has a passionate mission, we might actually make some progress. Anger simply begets more anger and it's rare that anything good ever comes from a place of anger.

The day after our community event I walked the perimeter of Regina. Although we didn't have an RCMP escort for every kilometre across Saskatchewan, we had been told we would have them where we needed them most. As I walked around the city, I was joined by Constable Rick Hutchinson from the RCMP, who was very excited to be part of the campaign. I also had the pleasure of walking and talking with Rod Pedersen. Rod was most famous for being the official announcer for the Saskatchewan Rough Riders CFL team. If you live in Saskatchewan, you already know the Riders are a pretty big deal. Heck you don't even have to be from Saskatchewan to love the Riders. Rod and I had a great chat and we did one more interview with CTV News before heading west out of the city. The following morning, we had a long walk with a group from the Canadian Indian Affairs office in Regina. I'm not sure how they heard about us but they had been inspired to raise money for PFC and asked if they could join us for a walk while we were in the area.

79

Marie and I were really excited by the opportunity to attend the RCMP Regimental Dinner at Depot Centre, which provided us with a chance to get dressed up (no *Push for Change* sweats for this event). The official picture from the event was of me and Marie sitting side by side surrounded by RCMP and other Police and military leaders from across the province. What I loved about the picture was the big beautiful tree behind us. It was some kind of fruit tree and it reminded me of the cherry blossoms in Vancouver with its bright pink petals. The dinner was lovely, the protocol was interesting and the history behind it all was fascinating. It was quite something to get a peek behind the curtain into a world that I knew nothing about. Assistant Commissioner Zablocki from Saskatchewan and Assistant Commissioner Lucki from RCMP Depot were both in attendance. Although my speech was short I made it count and by the end I brought everyone in the room to their feet (maybe it was my unbridled patriotism or the fact that I had walked over 7,100 km across Canada so far, I'm not sure).

Shortly after my presentation, I was standing next to Marie when a smartly dressed gentleman approached and shook my hand. He told me how impressed he was with my commitment and asked when I was going to be near Moose Jaw or Swift Current. I did a quick calculation in my head and told him we would be in Swift Current in about 12 days. I asked him what his interest was in PFC. He said he wanted to send a fly over while we were in the area. I must have looked really puzzled, at which point he stuck out his hand and introduced himself as Colonel Denis O'Reilly of the Royal Canadian Air Force. What he was talking about was sending a pair of CF-18's to fly over us as we walked along the road! I was floored, but what happened next was even better. The Colonel invited us for a private tour of the Airbase at 15 Wing Moose Jaw; home of the CF 18s, the BAE Hawks and of course the Tutors (more commonly known as the Canadian Snowbirds). It was a once in a lifetime opportunity and we were happy to accept the Colonel's invitation.

Later that week we visited the UA Local 179 Union Hall for a short chat and a cheque presentation. Just like their counterparts across the country, the UA guys were super supportive of the campaign.

On the way back to our base camp (which was just outside of Regina) Jaime's performance weighed heavy on my heart. The combination of his inability to handle the increased work load, safety concerns and his general disconnection from the campaign led Marie and I to make a tough decision. I was concerned about safety and work not getting done, Marie was concerned that Jaime didn't seem to be inspired or interested in the campaign. We agreed that it was pretty important for every member of the team to care about what we were doing, after all this wasn't just a job it was evangelism. If he'd lost his faith, there really wasn't any place for him in *The Push for Change*, so, we asked Jaime to go home. He seemed sad when we talked about it, but I think he was also relieved and after we'd talked it through, we all agreed that it was for the best.

Based on our previous experience, we knew that finding a new driver who could start immediately might be a challenge, so we decided to call Bobby and see what he was doing. Despite the challenges that we'd run into in Ontario, we knew Bobby was good at managing the RV and keeping everything clean and in good order. We also knew Bobby was really comfortable driving the RV and towing the car and the really challenging part of the campaign was now behind us. What Marie and I also really liked about Bobby was he felt like family, we knew and trusted him and didn't mind sharing our space with him. He was also super excited about PFC and because we had left things with Bobby on good terms, we thought, "What the heck!" I called him and to our shock and delight he was available and dropped everything to rejoin the campaign. Jaime left us on May 23, 2017 and Bobby arrived on May 26.

No sooner had Bobby returned and the place was spotless; the cars were detailed, the RV was super clean and all the chores were done. Bobby had even washed and folded all of my laundry. What's more, Bobby always had a huge smile on his face, he was just happy to be along for the ride. On day 394 we drove up to Prince Albert to do a school presentation. We were supposed to have engagements with schools in Saskatoon but that hadn't worked out. The drive up to Prince Albert was nice and Bobby and I used the time to review his role and talk about what hadn't worked out in the past. I took some of those responsibilities away from him so he could focus on what he did best.

Bobby arrived just in time for our visit to the airbase in Moose Jaw. It was such a great tour. Marie got to sit in the ejection seat simulator and have the wits scared out of her. We got to see the CF-18s and sit inside a BAE Hawk fighter jet. We also climbed the stairs to visit the air control tower but the greatest thrill was being inside the hanger where the Canadian Snowbird Squadron was. We saw engines being repaired and when they asked if we wanted a picture inside the cockpit, we all said, "Hell yes!" I was like a little kid just soaking it all in and so was Bobby.

We were invited back to the airbase a few weeks later to give a presentation as part of the base's wellness day. I was more than happy to speak to the group as a way to thank the Colonel for the amazing tour. The talk took place inside a lecture theatre and it was definitely a conservative group, but I remember thinking as I left the base that afternoon, that I had just addressed a group of the finest pilots and military leaders in our country. It was an honour to be invited and welcomed in this way.

Before I left the Colonel asked if, when I finished walking across Canada, he could have me return and share the whole story with his troops. He also said that in exchange for the presentation he would give Marie and me a ride in a Canadian fighter jet. I couldn't believe my luck.

The next few days of walking seemed really easy and we experienced our first taste of the prairie heat. On day 401, the temperature rose over 35°C for the first time since we hit the campaign trail. Bobby asked me which I preferred, heat or cold. I told him I'd take heat any day because there are lots of ways to cool down. Our strategy for dealing with the heat was simple; Bobby and I just got up earlier and hit the road. On days when we started by 5:30 am, we could sometimes finish our walking by 10:30 or 11:00 am.

As we approached the end of the school year, our engagements slowed temporarily and we were able to relax a bit. I still had lots of work to take care of; sorting pictures, doing media interviews and posting on social media, but the events dropped off for a while.

80

One of the things I really noticed walking from Regina to Swift Current was that Saskatchewan is not flat. All my life I'd heard jokes about how flat Saskatchewan is and although it's true that it is dead flat between Regina and Moose Jaw, the rest of the province is quite varied. As I walked into Swift Current, I encountered rolling green hills like the ones on my computer's screensaver (soft, gentle hills that went on for kilometres). They were majestic and beautiful, but they were not flat and the closer we got to the Alberta border, the more the landscape transformed. I also noticed as I got closer to the Alberta border to the south was a massive ridgeline called Cypress Hills where the topography changes a lot. Little did I know I would end up doing an impromptu *Push for Change* event in those foothills.

Maple Creek was our last RV park before we headed into Alberta. One afternoon I was walking on the highway nearby when a car pulled up behind me, which wasn't unusual. Most often it was a kind motorist offering a donation or someone who was curious as to why I was pushing a shopping cart along the Trans-Canada Highway. Either way I always stopped to chat and gave them an information card and a pin. It was simple to provide people with a way they could learn more and possibly support the campaign.

The gentleman who stopped on this occasion was neither of those; he was Captain Ed Dean from the Maple Creek Salvation Army. We chatted for about 30 minutes before I had to head out and finish my walk for the day, However I told him I would be very open to speaking at his church if there was an opportunity to do so. Marie followed up and the next Sunday we attended the morning service and met Ed's wife, Captain Charlotte Dean and the entire congregation. I shared my story and how it intersected with the Salvation Army. I also talked about my faith and what I was doing to try and make life safer for young people in Canada. We could not believe how much these kind people supported us. When the day was done the small group had collected and given us $600 in donations.

My presentation to the Salvation Army in Maple Creek certainly wasn't a planned event and neither was the next event we did. When Ed found out that Marie and I had clearance to visit federal correctional institutions, he invited us to speak at the Federal Women's Prison, the Okimaw Ohci Healing Lodge in Kikawinaw. We left the small town late in the afternoon in Ed's truck and bounced down the dusty road until it disappeared into rolling hills. Eventually, we arrived at the entrance, which had a bunch of Government of Canada stuff printed on it.

Even though it was definitely a prison, the way it was set up, it didn't look or feel like one. It was a minimum-security facility and felt more like a healing retreat. The room we met in was shaped like a huge wooden teepee. The meeting began with a smudge and a fire was lit in the centre of the room. I shared my story like I would at a recovery meeting. Nothing fancy, just the way it was, what happened and the way it is today. We also shared the PFC message and that seemed to inspire them quite a bit. I was struck by the fact that this was a prison, yet the staff looked no different from the clients. There was a strong emphasis on First Nations culture, healing and traditional ways. I found the community very open and receptive to change. It wasn't like any jail I was ever in, that's for sure.

On Day 408, we gathered about 5 km from the Alberta border with a group of supporters for our send-off from Saskatchewan. Once again, we had support from the RCMP and our friends from the Salvation Army as we made our way towards the sign that read, "Welcome to

Alberta." Off in the distance I noticed an antelope watching us curiously and then running away. As we got close to the provincial border, a train approached on our right and gave us a huge blare from his horn. After a few photos with our friends from the Saskatchewan RCMP, we ended our day on the other side of the border.

Marie

Our second summer of the trek was upon us but this time I could see the finish line. With only a few months to go I began to focus on our final event in Vancouver on September 29, 2017. We had a great committee that was meeting regularly in Vancouver to plan the Walk with Joe and the celebration at the Vancouver Public Library, but there was still much to do from my end. Before the campaign even started, we had envisioned how our final day would look. We wanted the final Walk with Joe to be led by a marching pipe band and we would walk down East Hastings, the street where Joe had spent much of his time as a homeless youth. We also wanted a public event attended by community members, police, students, municipal officials, partners and sponsors and to have Kate Richardson sing The Push for Change theme song. The finale at the library would be emceed by someone who was well known in the Lower Mainland and we would have a slide show on a big screen to show highlights from the 17-month trek.

All these things came to be, but not without perseverance as we encountered unforeseen obstacles at every turn. The venue the planning committee had chosen was outdoors in the square at the Vancouver Public Library, which meant we would need an outdoor screen that could handle any weather. We also needed tents and chairs to seat guests and provide cover for the music equipment. Kate had moved to Australia; would she come back to sing for us? Members of marching pipe bands are mostly volunteers (who work other full time jobs); finding one to accommodate us on a Friday afternoon was no easy task. Because our walk started in Burnaby and ended in Vancouver, we had to coordinate with both the Vancouver Police Department and the Burnaby detachment of the RCMP. They had to agree on the routes, the process and the hand-off at Boundary Road.

Setting these goal years in advance paid off. Because we had envisioned the finale so clearly and given ourselves plenty of time to work through the obstacles, in the end it all came together just as we imagined.

81

As we moved into Alberta, grain fields gave way to rolling foothills and wide-open pastures. Time and again, we tried to capture the beauty with photos but they never did the landscape justice, even with the panorama feature. There was something magical about being there and absorbing it all in the moment.

Our days with Bobby were easy. He was super supportive and took care of so many things that it allowed Marie and me to focus on our most important responsibilities, planning events and walking. Everything was going smoothly and that made me happy despite the fact that our everyday community engagement had slowed with the approach of summer.

Our next base camp was a really nice RV site in Medicine Hat (not all of them were nice). The timing of our arrival in Medicine Hat couldn't have been better as it coincided perfectly with their annual Housing First conference. Marie contacted the conference organizers and I was asked to speak. What's more, Medicine Hat made the news when they agreed to adopt a housing first strategy that effectively eliminated chronic homelessness in their community. The concept of housing first is simple. Communities make a commitment to build housing and support services to help the most vulnerable street-involved individuals and the savings (in terms of healthcare, police and other emergency services), far outweigh the cost to build and operate the housing. Most studies show a 4-1 return on investment. For example, one housing unit costs $40,000 per year, whereas a homeless individual (with all of the interactions they have with health care, emergency services, police, courts, hospitals etc.) can cost the community upwards of $200,000 per year. It made sense and Medicine Hat was leading the way. The event went really well, I had the pleasure and opportunity to meet and chat with Mayor Ted Clugston and the entire committee responsible for the direction and example Medicine Hat has given the country.

We had the opportunity to film and take some pictures under the large teepee monument in town and while we were there, we ran into an employee from the local correctional facility. He was curious about what we were doing and when he heard our story, he agreed to try and get us in to visit the local jail.

When we reached Redcliff, we had a cool little event at the Redcliff Youth Centre, which provides drop in programs for the young people in the area. We talked for a bit and then walked through town together. It was a small group but we had fun together; the kids had homemade signs and brought their own shopping carts.

With only a few days left in the school year, we had the pleasure of connecting with a local school when we reached Brooks, Alberta. We met up with the students at a park on the edge of town and I gave a little speech before we walked through the community. It was a bigger crowd than I anticipated in such a small community; I was surprised to look over my shoulder and see about 500 students walking down the road behind us. The school was super excited to have us and the energy from the kids reminded me of our days in Ontario.

With only 100 days left in the campaign, as we walked closer to the city of Calgary I was excited that any day now (if the weather was clear) I would catch a glimpse of the Rocky Mountains looming up ahead. On day 421, we reached the town of Bassano. My body was feeling great although with the onset of summer, spending six hours a day outdoors had its own challenges, including dealing with bugs, heat, sunburn and dehydration. Fortunately, we'd had lots of experience managing adjustments so it wasn't a difficult transition

The landscape through this section of our route was amazing, especially along the riverbanks where there were these incredible canyon-like formations called coulees. As I approached Strathmore and Chestermere on Day 422, I saw the mountains for the first time! I could just barely make them out on the horizon, but they were there. I remember when I was in Newfoundland, I day-dreamed about walking into the Rockies and how good that would feel. It was also noteworthy as I got closer to the city of Calgary, that I was reaching a point where I had "technically" walked across the entire country (given that I had already walked from Calgary to Vancouver during the trial walk in 2012).

82

As we approached Calgary, I had several moments of reflection regarding all of the challenges we had faced. *The Push for Change* almost didn't happen. We fumbled a lot in the first few years to work out the logistics of a big campaign and gleaned what we could from the experience of others, then we stalled due to funding problems, but we were 100% committed and eventually we overcame it all. Although it was a frustrating lesson, I learned that big goals take time and a lot of effort and it doesn't really matter what you think, it only matters what you do. You've got to wake up every day, put your shoes on and get out there.

There were a lot of days in the build-up to the campaign, as well as during the campaign, when I didn't feel like doing it. When that happened, I stubbornly refused to give in and did it anyway. Doing what you need to do despite negative emotion is what creates legendary results. Something else I learned is that success doesn't always look successful and it's never a straight line to the top.

Our plan when we reached Calgary was to set up camp to the west of the city (near Cochrane). Part of the reason we ended up so far from the city was that we had waited too long to book our RV site and all of the good spots had been reserved by people who were in town for the Calgary Stampede. When we arrived at the city limits, we took some photos in front of the "Welcome to Calgary" sign and then headed to our new base camp. Once we were set up, we had a series of events scheduled that would take us to Edmonton, Whitehorse and Yellowknife before we returned to Calgary where we planned to celebrate Canada's 150th birthday with our friends from UA.

Although we never walked to Edmonton, it was crucial for us to visit the city. Edmonton had a strong organizing committee in place and we had a really great event planned with the community.

At the end of June, we held a huge event at the Westin Hotel in Edmonton together with some amazing supporters including David French, (who is a dedicated advocate for homeless youth) from A Way Home Canada. We were also joined by I Human, E4C, REACH Edmonton and numerous officials from the city including the chief of police and members of the fire department and RCMP. The organizing committee for the event was hosted by Homeward Trust and even Lois Mitchell, the Lieutenant Governor of Alberta, attended the event. At the gala, our friends Jerry Cordeiro and Lorna Dancey (who were very keen PFC supporters) had set up a photo display depicting the various faces of Edmonton's homeless community. Their work was designed to break down the stigma around homelessness and help us see each person as an individual, despite their circumstances. Leslie Cleary, who had worked with us on another project, had been instrumental in connecting us with these two amazing photographers. Jerry and Lorna offered to join me and take some pictures as I entered the Rockies in a few days and we agreed to meet near Kananaskis.

The next morning we had another event in Edmonton, but this one was outside in the park. UA Local 488 had worked really hard to put together the event and they had the BBQ set up to feed the crowds that showed up. There was also a stage set up and I had the chance to thank Edmontonians for their support, including one very special young man who had come to our attention. When Marie and I were in Ontario we read a story about a little boy who took it upon himself to start a knapsack program for the homeless in Edmonton. We loved his initiative and reached out to his mom to see if he could attend our event. We brought him up on stage to be recognized and he got a standing ovation for his efforts. It was inspiring to see such a little guy take on such a compassionate project.

Once we wrapped up our event in Edmonton, the plan was to head to the Northwest Territories for an event in Yellowknife. We had met a wonderful youth champion named Iris who wanted to do a walk and then host an event with her organization The Side Door. Everything was going smoothly until we hit the airport and lost seven hours as a result of flight delays. Both Marie and I had been counting on a quick flight and some time to relax before the event, but we lost it all in the airport.

Although we were thrilled at the opportunity to visit amazing places like Yellowknife and participate in so many amazing events, after more than a year on the road, we were a little weary from travel. Even with scheduled rest days it was still this kind of relentless grind to keep going no matter what. We both agreed that a year on the road would have been plenty but now that we were this far in, there was nothing else to do but smile and keep going.

Not surprisingly, Yellowknife was an amazing experience. We gathered in front of city hall and took an amazing group photo of all of the young people and supporters from The Side Door. From there we walked through the city with the help of the RCMP and finished up at The Side Door for a community BBQ. When we reached the parking lot a fellow introduced himself as a member of UA Local 46. He was in the Northwest Territories working on a project. I really enjoyed it when UA members approached us to say hi as we travelled around and it was quite inspiring to meet a UA member from Toronto in Yellowknife. We thanked our host, Iris for her hospitality and jumped on our plane back to Calgary. Bobby was waiting for us at the airport. We'd been going all-out for four days in a row and things weren't going to slow down anytime soon, but Calgary would prove to be a ton of fun.

Marie

It had always been our intention to visit all three of Canada's northern territories during the trek. It was important to us because we knew aboriginal and First Nations people were at a disproportionately higher risk of becoming homeless and the community needed to hear the message.

Planning our visit to the Yukon was simpler than we imagined, as soon as the UA Local in Whitehorse heard that we wanted to visit, they stepped up and offered to host an event. I connected their Business Manager with staff from a few local youth agencies and just like that we had a strong team of champions planning our Yukon events.

We were equally fortunate in the Northwest Territories. We had met Iris from The Side Door (a youth agency in Yellowknife) at two different conferences and after she learned that we wanted to visit the north, she became our champion for The Northwest Territories. Iris had a lot of

299

friends in the city that she activated to put on a memorable event for us in Yellowknife and even took it a step further to find a sponsor to pay for our flight and hotel accommodations.

Sadly, we weren't as lucky trying to get to Nunavut. We hadn't met anyone personally who was from Nunavut, so we relied on referrals and were introduced via email to the executive directors of the two homeless shelters in Iqaluit. Both EDs were very kind and wanted to engage, but did not have the time or the means to put on any kind of community event. I also connected with a city council and the mayor but nothing worked out. We also had introductions to people in Cambridge Bay, unfortunately, that didn't pan out either. It was the first time during the campaign that we experienced doors shutting without others opening for us. Eventually, we realized that Nunavut just wasn't in the cards for us this time around and moved on with the rest of the trek.

83

Our first day back in Calgary, we partnered with The Boys and Girls Club of Calgary for an event and walked through downtown. In addition to the after school programs that they are best known for, this organization is also heavily involved in preventing youth homelessness which made them a perfect community champion for us. We gathered at their facility where the event was well attended. After a short speech and some refreshments, we gathered outside for a walk through Calgary that took us to city hall. We had some EMS friends follow us on the walk in an ambulance as well as full support from members of the Calgary Police Service who had brought their bikes.

The local MP, a couple of MLAs and several city councillors joined us for the walk along with a number of youth and other supporters. After walking only a short distance, the skyline of downtown Calgary came into view. It was exciting to see all of the tall buildings and have such a spectacular view of the city. Coincidentally, one of the tallest and most prominent buildings in Calgary is the Bow Tower which our friends and supporters from Walters Group played a major role in developing.

We crossed the river into the downtown core and passed a huge building called KEY, which happens to be one of the largest homeless shelters in Canada, housing over 1,000 people. Our walk through downtown Calgary ended at city hall where Jeff from The Boys and Girls Club had arranged a special tribute. On behalf of Mayor Nenshi, a city official presented me with a signature Smithbilt white hat and made me an honorary Calgarian (I even had to recite an oath); it was so much fun. Given that the Calgary Stampede was in full swing, the streets were swarming with people and alive with energy. It was a perfect day to be in the city and after a photo op we headed out to enjoy the festivities.

Marie and I got cleaned up back at the RV site before hitting the town. Neither of us had been to the Calgary Stampede before and if I were to try to describe it, I would say it was like a fall fair on steroids. It was amazing. We started off by watching a show that had been put together as a special Canada 150 tribute with songs and dancing. As we watched the show, I felt really proud. Walking across the country gave me a much deeper sense of who we are as Canadians and all that I am grateful for. It also made me feel more Canadian, if that makes any sense.

On July 1, 2017, Canada officially celebrated its 150th anniversary as a country and our friends from UA Local 496 held a pancake breakfast in our honour. The event took place outside, next to the union hall and it was packed with members and their families. UA Business Manager, Trevor Robertson welcomed us with some very kind words and presented us with a cheque, after which the party really got started. We got some great footage of the celebration which we later used in a tribute to Canada video that we posted on social media. It was a great end to a week of intense engagement that had taken us to three separate cities.

On day 430, we had our last engagement before heading west towards the mountains. It was a special day planned with the Wood Automotive Group and Woodridge Ford Lincoln. Gerry Wood was our friend and he had generously sponsored the Ford Connect van that we used as our pace vehicle. What was amazing about this company's commitment to the campaign was that they sponsored us because they really believed in our cause, not because they would get a lot of exposure from it. PFC was not an Alberta or Calgary specific event. We travelled all across Canada and so I thought it was really generous of Gerry and the team to help us in such an extraordinary way. While we were at the dealership we got to meet everyone, take some photos and get the van serviced. We even got the shopping cart into the shop to get it cleaned up, remove some winter corrosion and oil anything that had started to squeak.

They filmed me walking into the service bay with the shopping cart and then leaving with it looking all shiny and new. It was a hoot. From the time we first met them (way back before we started the tour); the people at Woodridge had always treated us well. They were a proud supporter of what we were doing and after a year of walking across Canada, we were happy to be able to stop by and properly thank the team for their generosity.

On the fourth of July, while our friends in America were celebrating their independence my computer crashed and I went into panic mode. All of the pictures and video we'd recorded of the campaign were on that hard drive along with all of the content we'd posted on social media. I was in a full blown panic until Marie reminded me that we had everything backed up. I still had to swap out my computer, which was no fun at all but it was better than losing everything.

By day 431 (after more than a year of continuous walking), I could finally see the Rocky Mountains clearly and it occurred to me that I had officially crossed the second widest country on earth by foot. Not only that, the campaign had raised over $450,000, impacted more than a hundred thousand people and included over 400 events and yet with all of the successes, I felt it wasn't enough.

Despite having accomplished something that was truly amazing, I felt I just didn't measure up; I hadn't done "good enough." I felt sad that when Canada 150 was being celebrated all over the country, PFC hadn't received an invitation to any of the big national events. Our campaign never made it to the national stage, yet I know both Marie and I gave it everything we had. Although it was far more awesome than we had ever imagined, I was stuck comparing our campaign to Terry Fox and Rick Hansen (two of my personal heroes) even though I knew it was a foolish thing to do.

I guess what I was really grappling with was how much is enough? As humans, we have a tendency to base our happiness on conditional things (such as possessions or accomplishments), which can leave us perpetually wanting more. We sacrifice love, family, health and relationships in the pursuit of more, but maybe what we need is less. I suspect the key to true and lasting happiness is choosing to be happy with less (whether that means fewer possessions, a smaller house or car, or less money) and focusing more time and energy on simple pleasures and the relationships that help us feel connected with each other.

As we got closer and closer to Kananaskis, the mountains loomed in the distance, they were truly magnificent. I forgot how small you can feel as a mere human in the shadow of those giant rocks. Just before we reached Lac de Acres we connected with our friends Jerry and Lorna from Edmonton and they took some amazing photos. It was very kind of them to drive all the way from Edmonton to help capture this part of our journey. I was happy that Marie was free to participate in the photo shoot with me.

We were having a spectacular stretch of weather and the day after our photo shoot we walked through Canmore. Surrounded by the majestic Rockies, it was dream-like to once again be pushing my shopping cart along this extraordinary piece of highway. The air was clear and clean, the mountains were snow-capped and no matter what direction you looked in, the scenery took your breath away. The film footage we captured of the area was absolutely amazing.

84

We were nearing 7,950 kilometres on the campaign odometer when we reached the entrance to Banff National Park and I looked forward to the opportunity to walk through this beautiful place at the height of summer. One of the highlights was spending an entire day walking along the Bow River where the water was turquoise blue. The sediment in the runoff from glaciers is what gives it that special colour. We managed to get an RV spot in Banff, but only for one night; the park was packed with tourists from all over the world.

Although we weren't done walking in Alberta, our next base camp was in Golden, BC, so the commute over the next couple of days back and forth to the jump point was a long one. When we reached Lake Louise, we were joined by Marie's son Curtis, who had just graduated with a digital photography diploma. Over the next few weeks we would be travelling through some of the most spectacular mountain passes in the Rockies and I wanted Curtis to help us capture the beauty of the area.

While we were in the parking lot of Lake Louise, two school kids that we'd met at a presentation at their school in Ottawa, came up to say hello. It was cool for us and for them. The parking lot was extremely full and all of the scenic viewpoints were crowded with visitors but we got the pictures we wanted. We even got to squeeze in a canoe paddle on the water with Marie and Curtis.

There was one more iconic place in the area that I wanted to visit, but it was highly unlikely we were going to get access. One of the side roads near Lake Louise takes you to a place called Moraine Lake. It's a 12 km drive off the main route and only has a tiny parking lot, so it fills up fast and when it's full, they simply turn people away. As I watched the traffic control guy up ahead turning cars away, I was sure we would suffer the same fate, until Bobby pulled a genius move. When we got to the front of the line, Bobby told the traffic guy that we were there for a commercial video shoot and they let us through. I was flabbergasted; he didn't even ask for proof. As we made our way towards the lake, we couldn't stop laughing at the boldness of Bobby's actions and our good fortune.

Moraine Lake did not disappoint; the reflection of the mountains in the crystal-clear turquoise water was postcard perfect. No wonder this was once the image on the back of the Canadian $20 bill. There were breathtaking views everywhere you looked. We scrambled up some rocks to the mini summit and took some amazing team photos. It was a perfect bluebird day with clean, clear air and visibility for at least 30 km. Little did we know, that was about to change in a big way.

The wild fires in BC were getting more and more out of control and a good deal of smoke had made its way into Alberta. By the time we were finished up in Alberta, the skies where thick with a yellow orange haze. Initially, I wasn't very worried because I figured it would pass. As it turned out, the wildfires in BC would end up being the last major challenge we would have to navigate before we made it home.

85

On July 14, we walked across the border to the tenth and final province of our campaign, Beautiful British Columbia. We had completed nine provinces so far and all we had to do now was walk across five mountain ranges, visit Vancouver Island, do a quick tour of the Lower Mainland and finish up in Vancouver. It sounded simple enough.

The day we reached the provincial border and the Alberta RCMP handed us off to their counterparts in BC the smoke wasn't too bad, but soon it would get much worse. The Alberta Mounties had been awesome and we thanked them and exchanged some challenges coins before we left. As I embarked on my first day of walking in BC, I developed a distinct tingling in my throat and a dull headache from the thick yellow smog-like smoke. It was a little foreboding to think that I would be breathing this every day as I pushed my cart up and down mountain passes.

In BC, the road conditions were much different from what we had experienced during our month in Alberta. No more divided highway and not nearly as much room on the side of the road for us to walk. The shoulders were narrow, the roads were steep and the tight, blind corners made things dangerous. The road into Field (the first town after the border), was filled with construction zones and other hazards so we detoured past the dangerous stuff.

The Kicking Horse River runs right through Field, which is a beautiful peaceful little town situated at the bottom of the tallest mountain pass in BC. It is also the location of the Continental Divide, which means that all of the water (from rivers, streams and such) from this point westward empties in the Pacific Ocean whereas all of the water behind us (to the east) flows to the Atlantic Ocean. The Kicking Horse River was crystal clear and I felt it calling me into the water for an ice swim. The mountains that flank this tiny town tower over it on both sides and from Field the highway twists and turns through the Kicking Horse Pass and all the way to Golden.

One afternoon as I was slowly making my way towards Golden, a car pulled over right beside me and my daughter Loren jumped out. It was so great to see her; I immediately gave her a big hug. I had no idea she was in the area but apparently, she was on holidays with her mom and travelling through BC. I was excited for a number of reasons, the first being that I was back in BC and we would get to see each other a lot more and secondly, we had planned to have her come and stay with us for a couple of weeks when we got to Hope, which wasn't that far off. After a short catch-up on the side of the road, they were off and I was back to climbing mountains.

Kicking Horse Pass is a piece of highway that has always been really treacherous. As you approach Golden you basically have to hug the cliff-side 1,000 feet in the air along hairpin corners where the big trucks coming towards you barely slow down as they take the corner. Cages run up the sides of the vertical cliffs to catch the falling rocks that would otherwise land on the road below. I had no choice but to take my life in my hands walking this stretch as it is the only road in and out of Golden.

Curtis joined me on the walk through this section so we could share it with our followers and supporters. It was the kind of place that has to be seen to be believed so we wanted to capture it with pictures and film. We were really lucky as we entered BC to have support from the BC Conservation folks. The RCMP had been overwhelmed with the forest fires and couldn't spare personnel to help us. Thankfully, the Golden BC Conservation Office had an officer that was willing to help. It meant a lot to us through the mountain pass where the highway was fast and dangerous.

The Park Bridge that crosses the Kicking Horse River is a feat of engineering all on its own. To build the highway through the area they had to create two massive rock cuts 90 meters high. Surrounded by rocks that towered more than 30 stories above me as I walked along; I felt like I had been miniaturized. The rock cuts give way to the bridge deck which turns and drops elevation quickly to a truck rest area at the bottom of the hill. As I walked towards the bridge, I could see commercial trucks at the bottom of the hill shifting gears to climb this massive hill. They looked tiny in comparison to the bridge and the surrounding topography. The hill was long and steep and the trucks had to give it everything they had to get up over the bridge and through the rock cuts.

As I walked along marvelling at how big everything was and how utterly small I felt, I looked up to see a mountain goat standing on the top of the rock cut above me. To be honest, I'm not sure if it was a mountain goat or a big-horned sheep but he was definitely looking right at me. I smiled back at him, it was the first time I'd ever seen one of these guys.

86

Reaching Golden was a real milestone for me and harder than I'd remembered from my trial walk. The adjustment from walking across flat plains to hiking up and down huge mountains was taking a toll on me. It also didn't help that the air quality continued to degrade as a result of the wildfires. It was getting so bad I could taste the smoke and almost every day I woke up with a sore throat and sometimes a headache, too. I started to worry about our route and what would happen if we couldn't continue because of the smoke.

The smoke was particularly concerning given that we had one of our biggest challenges in front of us, Rogers Pass. Rogers Pass is infamous as a gateway to the rest of BC. Had the pass not been discovered back when the railroad was being built, some people say the history and geography of our country might be very different today. Fortunately, they did find the pass and built the railroad right through it; now it was my job to climb over it. From Golden to the summit of Rogers Pass is 80 km and most of it is uphill. I knew from my previous experience that it would take me three gruelling days to climb and it wasn't going to be fun. To make matters worse, as we approached Donald Bridge (which is where the climb begins) there were flashing information boards warning of fires in the area. The sign read: EXTREME FIRE HAZARD – WILD FIRES IN AREA. Before leaving Golden we had purchased smoke masks; we got the really good ones because there was really nowhere for us to go to get a break from the smoke (people with any sort of respiratory issue were being told to stay indoors) and we honestly didn't know how bad it would get.

On day 445, I crossed the Donald Bridge and began the ascent to the top of Rogers Pass. I remember at first I was hesitant to move forward. I was paralyzed with fear regarding what might lay ahead and not wanting to take action. All I wanted to do was stay in Golden.

In the end, climbing Rogers Pass was just a bunch of little steps; one foot forward and then the other. It requires courage to keep moving when all you see before you is uncertainty. After three days and four avalanche snow tunnels, I summited the most iconic transportation pass in the country on day 447. I had completed 8,180 kilometres of my journey and once again, the timing could not have been better. In celebration of Canada 150, Shaw Communications had recognized me as one of 50 Outstanding Canadians. The intention of the award was to acknowledge Canadians who had done something extraordinary to support children and youth across Canada. The award included a $1,500 donation to PFC which was really nice.

The reason the timing was perfect is because they had sent a film crew from Edmonton to capture footage of the walk as we finished up the pass. It was really cool being in this incredibly remote location shadowed by professional videographers. We took a break to do an interview at the monument situated at the top of the pass. We were fortunate that the wind had shifted, giving us respite from the smoke for a couple of days which allowed them to capture footage of me walking past the large wooden archways. Later, when the interview and footage were edited together we were able to share them on our social media channels.

Just like it had taken three days to climb up to Rogers Pass, it took another three days to descend into the town of Revelstoke. The highway from the BC border took us in and out of several national parks and the scenery was spectacular (at least what we could see of it through the smoke). Rogers Pass was in Glacier National Park, so the mountains and scenery were unspoiled by human development of any kind. It was all very wild and majestic.

On day 450, we started our day 42 km east of Revelstoke in Canyon Springs at 5:00 am. Bobby and I knew this stretch of highway would be fast, narrow and congested so we decided to try and get the bulk of our walk done before the traffic got heavy. We had learned some really sad news the night before; Budrow Tozer from UA Canada had passed away from cancer. Budrow had been instrumental in getting us a $100,000 commitment from the General Presidents Maintenance Committee (GPMC); which was a pivotal donation for the campaign. I'm not sure why but that day I went against all of the advice I had been given and decided to keep walking even after I'd reached my mandated 24 km for the day. Despite stern warnings from Sean not to push myself beyond what I had trained for (given that it could lead to serious problems, especially if I injured myself) I ignored the rules and by the time I reached 37 km the heat was really starting to come on, as was the traffic. By early afternoon, I had walked 42 km and completed a full marathon.

Up to that point I had never walked more than 45 km in a day, but that day I decided to test my body and really push myself. I was battling heat, traffic, blisters and a raging headache but I kept going. As the day got longer and longer, I realized that this experience was a micro version of what we had experienced as we built and executed on the entire *Push for Change* odyssey. I realized that most of the things that hold us back are in our mind and we rarely get outside our comfort zone to really test what's possible. We spend our lives allowing our potential to be burglarized by fear.

With Budrow heavy on my heart I realized I have only one life in which to give it my best. I realized it's not that life ends too soon, but that most of us wait too long to do the things we want because of fear. I spent the entire first half of my life thinking I needed to become something that I already was; a worthwhile person deserving of love and other good things. I knew I needed to push myself to the limit because I didn't want to die knowing I could have done more, been more and achieved more.

When day 450 was done, I had pushed my shopping cart 60 km and even Bobby was exhausted. I dedicated the longest walk of PFC to our friend Budrow Tozer, who had gone the extra mile for us.

87

By the time we reached Sicamous at the north end of the Okanagan Valley, it was blistering hot with daytime temperatures soaring to 39°C. In addition to things like heat and exhaustion, I needed to beware of dehydration, sunburn and heatstroke on my daily walk. A few times on the highway I got dizzy and had to jump in the van to take advantage of the air conditioning.

We were excited to move our base camp from Revelstoke to Enderby. Riverside RV Park in Enderby was a special place where we had friends who had been supporting us since the trial trek. Brandy and Denny had been following the campaign on social media and made it clear they wanted to help us when we came through the area. They held a special RV spot just for us and let us know we could stay for as long as we needed, free of charge. It was good to be back in Enderby.

After walking from Enderby to Vernon, our intention was to walk along Highway 97 towards Kamloops, however, the wind had changed again and the entire Okanagan was filled with thick orange smoke. It was even worse than it had been back in Golden, you could barely see down the road and the scenery was completed obliterated by the smoke. We knew we were getting closer to the epicentre of the wildfires when we reached Vernon because there were roadside signs directing fire evacuees. They had also set up emergency shelters and facilities for people who had been displaced due to evacuations.

On August 3, we started along Highway 97 North towards Salmon Arm. By this point I was wearing a fully ventilated safety mask to try and reduce the amount of polluted air I had to breathe but it simply wasn't working. The smoke was so thick my eyes and throat hurt, I couldn't sleep at night and my lungs were aching. On our last day before we finally decided to change our route, I walked through an area that had been severely burned near Falkland. We got as far as Monte Lake, where the earth had been scorched black and, in some areas, there was still smoke rising from the smouldering ashes. It was like walking through Armageddon. Everything was burned, including the sides of entire mountains. The air had turned from thick orange to an auburn brown with a tinge of dark yellow.

On the news, we heard that the air quality was currently five times worse than in Beijing, China. That day the interior of BC had the worst air quality on the entire planet. What was scary for me is that I was exercising in this crap every day and the route we were currently on would require us to spend the next month breathing this unsafe air.

After the campaign was over, I looked up some stats on the wildfires and learned that more than 1,300 fires had engulfed the province between April and November, costing BC more than $564 million. The 2017 wildfire season also saw the longest state of emergency in the province's history, lasting a total of 10 weeks. The destructive fires displaced thousands of British Columbians and burned more than 1.2 million hectares of forest.

The problem we faced was that there was nowhere we could get out of the smoke. It's one thing to stay indoors and wait for the wind to shift and hopefully clear the air; it's another to have to exercise all day long in smoky conditions. I was going to sleep with a sore throat, stinging eyes and a headache. My lungs hurt and I also noticed the time that it took me to complete a 24 km walk increased dramatically. In general, it sucked and the sky looked like Armageddon had arrived.

On Day 464 we decided to alter our route and go through Kelowna, Penticton and Princeton and then on to Hope via Highway 3. It wasn't ideal but it had to be better than walking headlong into a million acres of burning forest. Even though we'd changed our walking route, we still had an event planned in Kamloops that we had committed to attend. It was a community breakfast hosted by A Way Home Kamloops. These guys had done such amazing work that we really needed to show up regardless of the fires and the state of emergency in the area.

The event went well but to give you an idea of just how close we were to the fires, when we returned to the car to drive back towards the Okanagan, it was covered in a fine grey ash and when you looked up into the sky over Kamloops, it appeared to be snowing. You could have caught ash on your tongue (like kids do with snowflakes) if you were so inclined. We were happy we made it to the event, but even happier to leave the area when it was over.

88

On the ride back to our latest camp location in the South Okanagan, Marie caught me up to date on all the exciting things she was working on as we got closer to Vancouver. She had managed to secure the support of an RCMP Sergeant who would be coordinating all of our traffic support throughout the Lower Mainland and on Vancouver Island, which was awesome.

Marie was also working on myriad details for the final day of the campaign, which had a lot of moving parts. With the experience from Toronto under her belt, she was much better prepared for this event. She also had a planning committee behind her which included Cal Misener and our friends from Family Services of Greater Vancouver. The details of our closing event sounded really exciting, it was going to be an excellent finale.

Our initial intention had been to visit Kamloops and then walk straight down the Coquihalla Highway to Hope. Before the fires started, the RCMP had given us clearance for the route and from a logistical point of view it made the most sense. It was a hard route to climb but it was direct and it offered a lot more room on the side of the highway for us to work with.

When we changed our route, we found ourselves walking along Highway 97C towards Kelowna at the height of summer, a time when it is one of the busiest and most dangerous highways in the country. The commercial traffic wasn't the problem though; it was the weekend warriors towing boats and trailers that made me nervous. Because of the fires we were without a police support vehicle as well, since all of the local RCMP members had been asked to put in a number of days in the affected areas. We were thankful to make it to Kelowna without incident.

In Kelowna we had an event scheduled with The Boys and Girls Club which also operated a facility supporting homeless youth. With the support of police we met for a brief rally together with our local community champion Winmar and our friend Adria. As a group, we made our way through town and ended our walk at the youth shelter. As we were walking through a poor area of Kelowna where the homeless gathered, a man approached us and gave me a bag of small change, mostly nickels and dimes. I was touched that this man who was clearly homeless and had next to nothing was willing to give us what little he had. He told me he was a big fan of what we were doing and wanted to give what little he could to support our cause.

After Kelowna, our base camp moved to Keremeos where Marie and I enjoyed all the fresh fruit we could eat. It was late summer and every kind of delicious fruit you could think of was ripe and ready. We had a short event in Penticton and then made our way along the infamous Hope Princeton Highway. As far as roads go, this one is about as tough as they come; not even northern Ontario compared to Highway 3. Its steep inclines and descents coupled with numerous hair pins turns (as it takes you up through Manning Park and on to Hope) are enough to make any driver dizzy. Although the hills were tough and the weather was hot, I paid the conditions no attention whatsoever. I was seasoned at tackling tough challenges and this was just one more. The one thing that did bother me however was the air quality. Even though we were now hundreds of kilometres away from the fires, the air throughout these mountains was thick and orange. We were hoping and praying every day that the wind would shift direction, but it never really did. The smoke from the fires in BC was affecting air quality as far away as Edmonton and Calgary and apparently from space, the plume of smoke could be seen reaching as far as Winnipeg. It was the worst wildfire season in BC's history.

On August 16 we arrived in Hope and even though we still had a month and a half to go we were pretty much done the hardest parts of the campaign. We moved our base camp to a really nice RV park in Hope and started to finalize our plans for the Lower Mainland and Vancouver Island.

The route was set. We were going to walk as far as Maple Ridge and stop. We would then take two days to fly north to visit Whitehorse and then south to Nanaimo for a planned walk to Victoria. Once we reached downtown Victoria, we would circle back to Sidney and take the ferry back to the mainland. The final weeks of the campaign would include a huge loop through the Lower Mainland and on the last day we would walk from Burnaby to finish in downtown Vancouver where we would have our closing celebrations. Although we could have finished up much quicker, we wanted to stretch out the campaign for two reasons. First, we wanted to include schools, which would be starting back up in three weeks and second, since we had incubated *The Push for Change* in BC, we wanted to engage as many municipalities as possible.

Despite the increased number of events and all the work that needed to be done for the final few days, Marie and I still found time to find a house to move into at the end of the campaign. After 17 months of voluntarily homelessness, we were looking forward to having a home again, although all of our belongings were in Barrie and we needed to move them to BC. It was always our intention to stay in BC when the trek finished up, so we had been using our rest days to look at houses and coordinate the logistics of a move.

Marie

It was time to think about life after the trek, the campaign was coming to an end and we didn't have a place to call home when the walk ended on September 29. We knew before the trek began that we were going to rent out our house in Barrie and move to Vancouver. My daughter had already moved to the Lower Mainland with her husband (who was posted with the RCMP in BC) and my son had moved with them. Joe's daughter was also already in Vancouver, living with her mom and stepdad. All of the family was there and now it was our turn, but first we needed to find a place.

I started to look at houses in the Lower Mainland to rent for a few months so we could take the time to search properly for a house to purchase, but rental prices were ridiculously high. We decided renting was out of the question, but how would we find a house to purchase with a closing date at the beginning of October; it was already the end of August. I started to search for houses on MLS. Vancouver prices were steep, so I adjusted my search to surrounding cities; Burnaby, Pitt Meadows, Langley. I found a few and set up viewings for the Labour Day weekend. When we looked at houses in Langley, I immediately loved the city and the neighbourhood. It was bright, clean, close to the highway and overall it just had a good vibe. We spent the entire weekend looking at places and finally found the perfect one to put an offer on. Following a short negotiation, both parties signed off with a closing date of October 6 and amazingly, over the course of one weekend we found and purchased the house we still live in today.

89

Leaving Hope, our route took us along Highway 7 on the north side of the Fraser River. From this point forward, we would have roadside support from the RCMP for the remainder of the campaign. On my second day of walking along the long road towards Mission, I looked down and found my second eagle feather. I remember feeling a spiritual connection as I picked it up. It reminded me of the first feather that was gifted to me in Newfoundland. This bald eagle feather was unique and must have been one of the primary feathers, since it was long and very skinny. The timing seemed auspicious; I had found my first feather near the beginning of my long journey and this feather presented itself very close to the end of my journey. It felt like a sign.

Upon my arrival in Mission, the campaign odometer read 8,700 kilometres. As I walked toward Mission and crossed the railroad tracks for the last time I remember looking up and seeing the iconic bell tower of the Westminster Abbey high up on the hillside. When we finished up for the day we were met by the mayor of Mission and several city councillors. The following day we drove out to the Fraser Valley and visited Cyrus Centre in Chilliwack and Abbottsford. It was really hot and the events were short. We really appreciated the opportunity to visit but I had hoped to engage more people. Maybe it was because of the heat or perhaps people just wanted to get away and enjoy the last few weeks of summer, but our events weren't attracting anything like the massive crowds we had experienced in Ontario. I felt a little sad that after walking all the way across Canada we never really blew up like I thought we would.

After we left Mission, we had one more community to engage with before we left for Whitehorse. The morning was bright and sunny as I started to walk and the traffic was just beginning to pick up. Now that we were back in highly populated municipalities I was concerned about safety. Inside the cities was fine, our RCMP escort always slowed down approaching traffic, however the highways were fast and busy. As we approached Maple Ridge that afternoon a truck pulling a trailer with two jet skis in it skirted around me and pulled over really abruptly.

The guy got out of the truck really fast and initially I thought he was extremely angry. To my surprise, when he reached me, he handed over a whole handful of $20 bills and told me how inspired he was by what we were doing. He also told me he used to be homeless but now his life was excellent thanks to the right supports and getting sober. His show of support and words of encouragement were just the shot in the arm that I needed at that moment as I'd been feeling a little disconnected since we arrived in Hope. His story reminded me of the reason I was pushing my cart.

We had a couple of fun events in Maple Ridge. The first was with a group of students who met us at a recreation centre outside of town and joined in as we walked to city hall. At city hall we met up with more supporters and had an informal event in the park. The following morning we had a larger event at the community centre and the young people unveiled an amazingly huge sign that read: We are Possibility! The students had also done some fundraising and presented us with a cheque. My friends from Manion and Associates were also present. Tom Manion is a friend of mine who had posted a pledge on social media that he would donate $100 for every province I made it through. His son Christian was there to present the cheque on behalf of the team. Tom was one of those people who had believed in me right from the beginning and throughout the campaign he had been a cheerleader for PFC encouraging us via social media.

When the Maple Ridge event was over Bobby and I drove all the way back to Hope and struck camp. This move would take us to our very last RV park of the trek. What was really exciting for Marie and me (probably more for Marie) was that we were about to be done with communal living. Not that Bobby was hard to live with or that the RV wasn't comfortable. We loved our time in the RV, but it would be so nice to have more space and privacy. We were both looking forward to it.

90

Perhaps not surprisingly, as we neared the end of the road, I started to feel a little let down with the campaign. The momentum had slowed for a number of reasons, a big one being that it was summer and students were out of school. Most of our big events in Ontario had revolved around school involvement and that wasn't happening in BC. We were having good events but they were much more spread out and didn't have the powerful energy that we'd felt in Ontario. I lamented that the best was behind us and that included the physical challenge. Everything now seemed too easy. I would have liked it much better if we had ended the campaign doing something really physically demanding but that's not how we planned it.

There was also the fact that we had not really broken through nationally. Although we had some really huge highlights during the campaign, it was more like peaks and valleys than a powerful surge. We went to one event (I won't say where it was), where there was just one person. I walked approximately 9,000 km across Canada and one person showed up. What was strange to me is that the facility in question worked directly with homeless youth, yet they didn't seem to care that we had taken the time to come and share our journey. It's not that my ego was hurt; it's just that I figured BC was going to be huge considering it's where I lived when I started *The Push for Change*. It's also where we had the most contacts and a province where the issues related to homelessness are visible in virtually every community.

Although we gave it our best, for reasons that were beyond my comprehension we failed to gain a massive national following for PFC and I kept going over and over in my head what I could have done better. I began to think about my management style. As someone with a perfectionist streak, I knew I had not always been easy to work with during the campaign. I thought too, about how we could have done better with traditional PR as well as social media. Our media coverage wasn't what I'd hoped it would be. I felt in a lot of ways we had failed to execute properly and I felt like I failed as a manager. I was also frustrated with all the people that had promised to help and never showed up but I realized in the end this wasn't their dream, it was ours.

I realized finally that I had to accept that some things were beyond my control. We had accomplished so much and we were going to finish what we started. We had left everything we had on the field of play and managed to pull off the impossible. Measuring ourselves against iconic campaigns from decades past or comparing our work to corporately-managed events was completely unfair. Besides it wasn't over yet, we still had a few weeks to go and anything could happen.

91

We had promised to visit the Yukon and the trip turned out to be well worth our time. Marc Gagne from UA Local 310 was our friend and support contact in the city of Whitehorse and he set up several schools for us to visit. The kids were awesome and it was great to be back in front of young people and able to express our passion for them and all young people across Canada. We weren't able to bring my shopping cart but we had a couple of loaners. After the three school events, there was a community gathering and walk organized. The event started with a reception and ceremony at the centre of town under a huge totem pole. The mayor said a few words and one of the First Nations elders welcomed us and said a prayer. Doug Phillips, who is the Commissioner of the Yukon, also joined us. The commissioner's role is equivalent to being a Lieutenant Governor of a province.

Our goal was to walk through the community with the borrowed shopping carts and finish at a large banquet hall. As we walked I felt really excited again and the feelings of doubt and disappointment from a few days earlier simply melted away. Marie and I were in the Yukon connecting with the local community and sharing the PFC message of hope and inspiration just like we imagined. We had always said we wanted to come up north, but had no idea how to make it happen. As I looked over my shoulder and saw all of the people behind me, including first nations dancers wearing full regalia and a long line of youngsters (many of them also dressed in ceremonial clothes) who were going to sing and dance for us at the feast, I felt intensely happy and blessed.

The food and the celebration in the Yukon were both amazing and we were sad to leave; but the next day we were on a plane once again and headed to Nanaimo where we would pick up the campaign.

When we originally considered ending the campaign in Vancouver, I was concerned about overlooking all of the communities on Vancouver Island, especially Victoria (which has one of the biggest homeless problems in the whole country). In order to include Vancouver Island and still end where it all began, we decided to walk from Nanaimo to Victoria and then return to the mainland for our final series of events ending in Vancouver on Sept 29.

We were so lucky to have RCMP John Stein support us as we made our way along the Island Highway towards Victoria. John spent several days coordinating our route with Bobby as we moved from Nanaimo to Victoria and then up to Saanich. The only thing John did that I really wish he hadn't was to introduce Bobby and me to bacon maple eclairs in Cobble Hill. We ate so many that our stomachs hurt!

On the morning of day 502, we started our walk into Victoria with John as our escort and when we got closer to the downtown area the Victoria Police joined as well. The weather was perfect and something stirred inside me as we turned the corner to see the beautiful Fairmont Empress Hotel on the right and the BC Legislature straight ahead. A small crowd had gathered to welcome us and cheer us on as we made our way to the provincial legislature. When we arrived in front of the building, we took some photos and were greeted by our friends from UA Local 324 and Threshold Housing, an organization that works with homeless youth in Victoria. We were also greeted by provincial leaders and invited to join them inside the legislature later that day to be formally recognized by the government for the work we had accomplished.

Before we did that however, we had a walk planned with the community. The group had grown substantially since our arrival and we were led by Chief Del Manic from the Victoria Police Department as we headed towards the water. This wasn't supposed to be a big deal, since the trek still had several days before we officially finished in Vancouver, but the day was still pretty special when I reached the end of our walk and found myself standing in front of the Mile Zero sign. I had walked all the way from the Mile Zero sign in Newfoundland to the Mile Zero sign in Victoria. Logistically, we had crossed Canada. When we gathered in the park at the end of our walk, there was a statue of Terry Fox and the Chief had some very flattering words for Marie and me. I was happier than I had anticipated. When I pictured Victoria in my mind, I never considered it to be the end, but in some ways it really was.

Later the next day, UA Local 324 invited us to their union hall where I got to say a few words and thank them. They voted and presented us with a nice donation and some swag and promised to join us in Vancouver for the final day.

While we were in Victoria, I also had the privilege to speak at the city's annual End Homelessness Coalition. Just like with so many of the other events across the country that had lined up perfectly with the walk, we were happy to get to be a part of their conference and share a message of hope and solidarity.

The next day we headed towards the ferry terminal and made one last stop for an event hosted by the Saanich Police. Marie did an amazing job as the event host even though giving speeches is something she dreads. In reality, she's a great presenter and every time she's had the courage to push through her discomfort and do a presentation, she's been amazing. In Saanich she really knocked it out of the park and the event raised $860.

92

Our route for the final ten days of our trek across Canada would take us from Tsawwassen to Richmond and then on to Delta and Surrey, followed by White Rock, Cloverdale and Langley. After that, we would head over to New Westminster for a day; then walk through Burnaby and Vancouver to celebrate the final day of the campaign.

On September 20, we left the ferry terminal early in the morning and after a short ride through the tunnel, we started down the highway towards Richmond. Our goal was to finish up in Delta by the end of the day. We walked around the city of Richmond and since we didn't have any events planned, we headed east towards Delta. The next morning, we started early once again and this time we were near the bottom of Nordel Way, leading up into Delta. By 11:00 am, we were at 120th and Scott Road where we were joined by the Delta Police Service and Chief Neil Dubord.

On day 509 we were excited to take part in *The Push for Change* Art Rapture event (which included a funky art show hosted at a gallery in downtown Vancouver). Art Rapture (with the help of Tyrone Lingley) had raised $5,000 for us with a gala event and auction the year before while we were on the road in Ontario and this year they were doing it again. In addition to the artworks up for bidding, there were a number of specific items auctioned off just for PFC. In fact; we auctioned off a pair of the sneakers that I wore when I walked through the BC Rockies for over $500. The auction was full of energy and I asked if we could present a video and do a short presentation. It was a little tough getting everyone's attention in such a busy venue, but I managed to pull it off and when the numbers were tallied for the night the organizers told us that they'd raised $15,000 for PFC. We were ecstatic.

I wasn't feeling quite as rapturous the next morning. Normally, I didn't like being up past 9:00 pm on a walk night but, I'd already missed the event the first time around and I hadn't wanted to miss the opportunity to thank Tyrone and friends for their support a second time around.

As we counted down the days, Marie had all kinds of great news to share about our closing event and I started to get really excited. Being on the road every day walking and focused on attending events, I seldom knew what was being planned behind the scenes. Marie and her community champions and planning committees were in charge of that and I was only told what I needed to know as we moved along. Much like a professional athlete, I was only focused on the game I was in, not the game that was still two days away. I had to think that way otherwise I would have lost my mind with all of the activity that was going on. One really great piece of news, UA Canada announced that they would be hosting a private, invitation-only dinner event for us in Stanley Park on the last day of the campaign. They planned to take care of the food, the venue and all of the expenses, which took a weight off of our shoulders while providing us with the opportunity to thank all of the amazing people who had contributed to the campaign. Marie and UA had been working on the details for a while and it sounded amazing.

Day 510 started off early in White Rock with the Tallest Mountie in Canada, who was 7-foot 7 inches tall. The guy was a giant with a huge heart to boot! We started on the east side of White Rock and walked our way around the community and then down the hill towards the beach. Along the way, we met lots of folks who had heard about us on the news and wanted to make a donation. The views from up on the hill in White Rock were amazing and the weather was warm but not overbearing. We were also happy to have a respite from wildfire smoke. We thought for sure once we hit Hope that we wouldn't have to deal with forest fire smoke anymore, but it had infiltrated the entire Lower Mainland and some days the air was as bad in Vancouver as it was in the Okanagan.

We left White Rock and headed northeast towards our next event in Cloverdale. When we stopped at a gas station I felt kind of bad for the Mountie who was accompanying us. He was dressed in his traditional Red Serge riding uniform and we arrived at the gas station at the same time as a busload of tourists who were headed across the border to the US. When they spotted the Mountie, everyone poured off the bus and wanted to take a selfie with him.

Following a community walk later that afternoon in Cloverdale, we attended a fun event hosted by the folks at Community Living BC. They had a dunk tank and I got up in the seat and taunted everyone. With the trek almost done, it was time to unwind and have some fun. For some reason, Bobby wanted to be the first guy to dunk me in the tank (possibly some kind of payback for the boss after all those months on the road). He bought 20 bucks worth of balls and it wasn't long before he got his wish. I was expecting the water to be warm when I finally went in and boy did I get a shock; it was ice cold.

The next day wasn't a walking day but we agreed to a short visit with the City of Langley. The local Rotary Club organized an event at city hall and we walked through town to Langley Secondary School. The crowd was small but enthusiastic and afterwards I had the opportunity to do a presentation to the students.

Our walk through New Westminster (which was our second last community event) began in front of the police Station on Columbia Street, where the chief welcomed us to the city and gave us some swag. I reciprocated with a challenge coin. The gathering was an impromptu group of people who worked for the city and I did a brief presentation about our journey before we headed off together to walk up the steep hills of New Westminster towards the city's border with Burnaby at 10th Avenue. It was a short, yet meaningful walk and I thanked the chief and did a few media interviews before heading back to base camp to get ready for the most important day of the campaign.

We had one day left and I was excited. Marie and her team had been working really hard and if BC was to have only one big event, we were going to make sure it was memorable. After 4.5 years of planning and 17 months of walking we were one day away from making history.

93

On the last morning I was tired, but still excited. The long months of relentless activity had taken a toll on me. I was worn out and happy to see the end in sight. It was mind blowing to think about what we had been through over the past 17 months; the lives we had touched and the impact we had created. When we started we had no idea how things were going to turn out, but in some ways that was the fun part. The uncertainty created a lot of pleasant surprises. So many times during the campaign we were inspired by the enthusiastic response we got from communities, especially some of the small ones. We could aspire and work hard but what happened in each community was really out of our hands.

We began our final morning early at our accommodations in Burnaby, waiting for Bobby to drive us to the start point. The day's events would begin at a rec centre in Burnaby with a short talk before we headed towards downtown Vancouver. Our second stop was a rally point at No Frills on Hastings near Clarke. There we had a short event planned where we would be joined by more people who would walk with us through the Downtown Eastside to our next meeting point at Victory Square. This portion of the walk would take us through the infamous neighbourhood I once called home. It was where I had experienced my greatest struggles in life and also the location of the bench I sat on when I made my solemn promise to pay it forward. From Victory Square it was exactly one kilometre to the Vancouver Public Library where our final event would take place. Marie, Cal and Family Services had been working together for months on all the details. It was going to be an extraordinary day to mark an extraordinary achievement.

Something I learned during *The Push for Change* is that there are always going to be elements that are out of your control, (like the weather or traffic) in which case you just have to adjust. The weather didn't look like it wanted to cooperate and to top it off, Bobby was late. Bobby was never late but today he had underestimated the traffic and travel time and was running almost 30 minutes behind. I was stressed. I wanted the last day to go perfectly and this did not help. After a short discussion, we decided to meet Bobby at the first rally point. As for the rain, I was hoping it would subside and we would escape a serious downpour.

When we arrived at the rally point, a small group of people had already gathered and that's when it hit me. These people were not from Burnaby, they were from New Brunswick, Ontario, Newfoundland and Manitoba. They were friends, community champions and people we had inspired along the way who had decided they wanted to be there at the end and share in the final, inspiring kilometres. How fitting that the people who helped us the most all across Canada were going to share this special moment. I was touched that PFC had inspired these people enough for them to get on airplanes and come all the way across the country just to share this special moment with us.

Some of those present included Deputy Commissioner Rick Barnum and Commissioner Vince Hawkes from the OPP. We also had supporters from UA Canada from all across Canada as well as James Hogarth from OPTC and Dave Griffiths from QCC Canada. There was a tap on my shoulder and when I turned around it was Scott MacLeod (the former OPP member who had a huge impact on my life). Marie's adult children, Cindi and Curtis had both made massive contributions to the campaign and we were happy they could join us. Cindi had helped us with social media and Curtis had supported us with photography and video. Cindi's husband Nate was also there as one of our RCMP escorts. The RCMP had helped us with traffic and roadside logistics all across Canada, which was no small commitment and they were an important part of the campaign.

As the crowd gathered it felt like a *Push for Change* family reunion and I stood there for a moment just taking it all in. Steve Morrison and Terry Snooks had come to represent the leadership team of UA Canada. It was great to see Terry, who'd had a habit of showing up all across Canada during the campaign. It was also great to see Steve who had been behind us since our very first meeting with UA at the Sheraton in Toronto. We also had UA members from Locals across Canada, many of whom we had met when we were in their communities.

Behind me was a large group of police waiting for instruction so I went and introduced myself. We were fortunate to have a team of RCMP and Vancouver City Police that would take us across the Burnaby/Vancouver border and into the downtown core. I took a few minutes to meet with the police and briefly told my story and gave each of them a challenge coin. The story was the same one I had shared with each and every police officer I met along the way. I told them that I was here thanks to Scott MacLeod (a police officer who got it right), and that I was deeply grateful for the work they do and what they represent. The challenge coins were a small but significant way for us to say thank you. It was the least we could do considering the amount of help we received.

94

After a short speech, the plan was to leave the recreation centre and walk towards Boundary Road. Once we entered Vancouver, we would continue along Hastings Street and walk the final 8 km (stopping at two rally points along the way) to finish at the Vancouver Public Library.

It was hard to believe but this was it, our last day. I looked around in wonder, inspired by all of the smiling faces, reflected back on all those long cold days of walking, the hot summer sun in Calgary and Atlantic Canada, the blistering winter winds of Northern Ontario and the majesty of the snow-capped Rocky Mountains. We did it! We did what they told us couldn't be done. We committed to walk across Canada and engage the country and we achieved that and much more. Today was our day to bask in our collective accomplishment.

Although I hadn't prepared a speech beforehand, when the time came to get things started, I thanked everyone for their help and support and told them how proud I was of their commitment and contributions to the campaign. *The Push for Change* was successful because each person present that morning, along with tens of thousands of other people had believed in our vision. As we began walking again, I realized just how many people it had taken to make this dream of walking across Canada a reality.

As we headed towards Vancouver, the city's skyline rose up before us. It was like seeing the emerald city and I felt a wave of emotion well up in me. It was so inspiring to finally be home. As we came down the hill we were joined by Terry and Deb Russell who lived close by. Deb was taking pictures for us and Terry was going to play the role of Town Crier when we reached the library. Marie had worked with Vancouver Mayor Gregor Robertson's office to decree this *Push for Change* day in Vancouver and Terry was going to read the proclamation. It was great to have him join us as he had watched the campaign build over the years.

95

When we crossed Boundary Road, the Vancouver Police took over and escorted us along the busy Hastings Street route. When we were initially planning the route, the Vancouver Police weren't very enthusiastic about going down Hastings Street since it's an arterial route through the city. However, after we explained the significance of the street and the neighbourhoods we wanted to visit, they agreed to the route plan. As we reached Nanaimo Street we were surprised by a group of students. Marie had coordinated with a local school to have students line the sidewalk and cheer us on. It was a reminder of the 100,000 plus students we had met along the journey, the hundreds of schools we had visited and the change and inspiration we had left in our wake. It was a special treat for the people who were walking with us for the first time as they got to experience something I had experienced hundreds of times; the power of young people supporting a worthwhile cause. I looked over my shoulder and saw Commissioner Hawkes smiling broadly; Steve Morrison was also grinning.

Our next stop was No Frills where the Vancouver planning committee had coordinated a rally with support from the store manager. It was a perfect fit for us too, since Loblaws was our grocery sponsor and we had received a nice donation from the W. Garfield Weston Foundation (which is directly connected to Loblaws group of companies). In the parking lot, tents were set up with food and drinks and the store manager presented us with a cheque. Using a bullhorn I thanked the growing crowd for all their support. I was delighted to see that Walter Koppelaar and his wife Carolyn had joined us (they had flown in from Hamilton). Walters Group had been a big contributor to the campaign. I also noticed our OPP group had grown and Tania, the Soup truck lady from Barrie, Ontario was in the crowd, as was Steve Allmen. Steve was at the Aeroplan event in Montreal back in 2011 that had been the inspiration behind the whole campaign. I remember us eating hotdogs at 2:00 am talking about how cool that event had turned out.

As we left No Frills, we headed into the Downtown Eastside. This was an emotional mile for me; I knew every corner of this neighbourhood intimately from my time on the streets in the late 1980s. With police motorcycles in front managing traffic and hundreds of people walking along behind, we took in the sights, sounds and smells of one of Vancouver's toughest neighbourhoods.

If you've never been to Vancouver's Downtown Eastside, I can only describe it as a war zone. It consists of several congested blocks, heavily populated by the homeless and those struggling with mental illness, where open-air drug consumption is an everyday activity. It's not a sight most regular folks would be used to, seeing an addict injecting drugs in a doorway or smoking crack cocaine at a bus stop, yet it is painfully commonplace in this stretch of Hastings. The neighbourhood is littered with makeshift camps and blue-tarped shopping carts that serve as makeshift homes. The despair and hopelessness are palpable. It's a scene that makes most people uncomfortable when they find themselves in the neighbourhood by accident. I remember looking back at the faces behind me and they had changed. Smiles and laughter had been replaced with expressions of sadness, disgust and fear. They were seeing people at their lowest point and addiction and chronic homelessness at its worst (this is what happens when a country falls down on its social contract with its most vulnerable members). It was a sharp reminder of why I had walked across Canada and why we all needed to continue to push for change. Most parents wouldn't want their children to travel through this neighbourhood on a bus, let alone live here. But if we couldn't prevent youth homelessness, undoubtedly, this is where some of the most vulnerable would end up.

We arrived at the corner of Main and Hastings (the epicentre of the Downtown Eastside) and as the Vancouver Police fired up their sirens, I took the intersection. I paused for a moment and hoisted the shopping cart over my head in victory. This was the corner where I hit bottom and called my mom in a plea for help; this was the corner where I walked away from my life as an addict. A little further on was the park bench where I had made my promise to pay it forward. I looked over and then looked back at Scott MacLeod and thought what a long, strange trip it had been. It's truly amazing where life can take you when you make a commitment and follow through with action.

As we passed Pigeon Park and continued west, I could see and hear a crowd cheering up ahead. Victory Square at the corner of Cambie and Hastings was our last rally point before we walked the last kilometre to the Vancouver Public Library. When we arrived at Victory Square we were greeted with cheers and as I scanned the crowd, I saw many familiar faces. The first person I noticed was my daughter Loren, who was acting as *The Push for Change* Youth Ambassador. I was so proud of Loren and happy that as a father I was able to give her such a powerful example of what we can accomplish if we put our mind to it.

Other familiar faces stood out in the crowd including our partners: Melanie Redman from A Way Home Canada, Dr. Stephen Gaetz from Homeless Hub and Michael Braithwaite from Raising the Roof. I also noticed our dear friend Lorne Segal had shown up and off to my right were Sean and Kate Richardson, who had flown all the way from Australia. We were also joined by the JP Fell Pipe Band, a Scottish pipe and drum team for the last kilometre. What was so interesting for me was that it had taken so many years to get to this place and now it was going by really fast.

96

As we prepared for the final push, Marie addressed the group using the bullhorn. No longer the quiet, reserved accountant I had met for dinner in 2012, she commanded their attention.

We wanted the OPP and UA Canada to join us at the front of the procession. They had supported us the most and we wanted to ensure they were acknowledged and properly honoured. With the striking of the drums and the howl of bagpipes, the parade began. As we turned off Hastings and walked along Cambie Street, I felt both joy and elation and tears began to flow as I realized, "We did it!" We walked over 9,000 km, visited hundreds of communities and engaged tens of thousands of Canadians from coast to coast. It was amazing to look behind me and see the faces of so many friends and supporters from all across the country.

As we crossed over Georgia Street I looked east. One block from where we stood was the Georgia Street viaduct, a place I used to call home. Pausing to think about it, I was astounded by the contrast between then and now. I went from living under that bridge (and battling with addiction and mental health issues) to finding recovery, succeeding in school and achieving great success in business. And today, I was completing something so extraordinarily special, it was hard to believe. Yet I remember a time when my life was so dark all I wanted was to die. I couldn't see a way out of my despair and I wrestled daily with thoughts of suicide. I believe the only reason I survived is because I eventually summoned the courage to ask for help. The hardest thing I ever did was to admit that I was in trouble and when I found the courage to do that, everything in life began to move forward. I took a few small steps and then a few more and now, years later, all of those steps added up to something pretty incredible.

I don't consider myself an extraordinary person, I simply found the key to unlock my possibility and I believe that anyone can do special things in their life if they follow these simple guidelines:

1. Ask for help when you need it.
2. Connect to your reason for wanting to change.
3. Get into action.
4. Focus on the results you want and build a contingency plan for managing roadblocks.

If a homeless heroin addict can turn their life around and produce extraordinary results, anyone can!

We walked past Georgia Street and turned right onto Robson and as I turned the corner I knew the memorial to Terry Fox at BC Place Stadium was behind me. Terry had been a hero to me since my teens and I was grateful to have borrowed some of the ideas he used to inspire a nation (and to have humbly walked in his massive shadow). As I turned the corner the library came into view. As I got closer, I noticed Russ and Martha from Barrie, as well as a very old friend named Dean Bernard, whom I had grown up with in Barrie. Out of the corner of my eye I also spotted my mom. I wanted to run over and hug her, but the crowd was huge and its forward momentum was strong. In her hands she had a picture of my uncle Jim who had passed away while I was walking through Manitoba. I knew how much he wanted to be part of this celebration with us and it made me smile. My brother Jeff was also with my mom and my sister Roberta (who was next to me) had flown from Thunder Bay to walk the last 12 km with us! I was happy to be surrounded by family.

As I walked onto the steps of the Vancouver Public Library, I was overwhelmed with tears of joy and I broke down. All those days of hard work had brought us to this extraordinary moment of achievement and celebration. It was a really special moment for me and I took the time to hug and thank as many folks as I could. I could hear myself repeating over and over, "We did it! We did it!" I think up until that very moment, it hadn't really hit me what we had accomplished.

97

The final event featured a series of speakers and acknowledgements from numerous officials and agencies that had supported the campaign. Kate Richardson and Cal Misener had pulled together a band to perform for us. Fortunately, the band's equipment and the PA system were under a tarp, because almost immediately the skies opened up and it began to pour rain, cold, hard rain that lasted for almost the entire reception. Although the rain put a bit of a damper on the celebration, in many ways it was a perfect example of what 40,000 youth across Canada deal with when they find themselves without shelter. Standing there in the rain gear that I had regularly worn on the road, I may have been the only one who was really prepared for the rain.

Family Services of Greater Vancouver and Cal Misener (working together with Marie), had done an excellent job of coordinating the final event. The turnout was awesome and so was the lineup of speakers. The final ceremony began with our friend Laurie DeGrace, who hushed the crowd and introduced the JP Fell Pipe Band, who played Amazing Grace as a tribute to all those who were lost and struggling, still trying to find their way home. The song was followed by an acknowledgement of the traditional First Nations territory and some words from Chief Ian Campbell of the Squamish Nation.

Next, our town crier Terry Russell read out a proclamation from the mayor of Vancouver declaring it Push for Change Day. It was fun to see Terry ringing the bell and yelling, "Hear ye! Hear ye!" He always cracked me up and I don't think we could have found a better town crier.

Peter Legge, who is a dear friend of mine, agreed to emcee the event for us. Peter was a polished presenter as well as a long-time mentor and friend and he was masterful at emceeing high profile events. Everyone in the crowd had been outfitted with a custom t-shirt provided by UA Canada with the slogan, "We are Stronger Together," which was the theme of the celebration.

Over the next 60 minutes we heard from an amazing lineup of stakeholders, friends and supporters including the Deputy Police Chief of Vancouver, the City of Vancouver, Family Services of Greater Vancouver, Dr. Stephen Gaetz from Homeless Hub, Melanie Redman from A way Home Canada and Michael Braithwaite from Raising the Roof. We also had a special address from the Commissioner of the OPP, who had taken the time to come all this way to be part of a campaign that had finished in his province six months earlier. We were thrilled that the OPP were supporting us through to the end. It was so important for us to demonstrate that *The Push for Change* wasn't just about walking across the country. It was about bringing people together and looking for common ground upon which to build collaborative relationships and work towards shared goals. Most importantly, it was about finding ways to better protect vulnerable young people.

Following the speeches, we shared a five-minute video showcasing our journey and all of the different places we had been in the previous 17 months, which garnered a huge cheer from the crowd at the end. Two of my favourite parts included Don Cherry doing a shout out from Hockey Night in Canada and a personal message from the Prime Minster of Canada, congratulating us on the success of our mission.

In between the different segments of the program, we were blessed to have Kate Richardson and Cal's band perform for us. The highlight was when Kate sang The Push for Change song (which had been created back in 2012). It was amazing to hear it performed live by the original artist. Several people had covered the song during our trek across Canada, but no one could sing it like Kate. Even though the weather was terrible the moment could not have been more perfect.

Marie and I both had short speeches and I followed mine with a video montage and a song (that I had secretly commissioned from Kate – *Wind Beneath My Wings*) dedicated to Marie for being the true "heart behind the cart." So much of PFC's success was thanks to Marie and I wanted everyone to know it.

The next speaker was my daughter Loren. Even though she was just 13, Loren had always been an outspoken leader, so she was the perfect youth ambassador for PFC and she delivered a speech that brought everyone to their feet. I couldn't have been more proud. She nailed her speech and even Lorne Segal, who is the chair of WE DAY Vancouver, turned to me and said, "That was amazing." WE DAY was a showcase for some pretty amazing young speakers so this was a huge compliment.

There was one presentation left before the campaign was officially over. Although the rain had caused the crowd to thin a bit, nothing could put a damper on what happened next. President of UA Canada Steve Morrison, UA International Representative Terry Snooks, UA Special Representative Stephane Favron and Bruce Miles from QCC Canada took the stage and stood together. Steve Morrison talked about why UA Canada chose to get behind *The Push for Change*. They also talked about how PFC had inspired their members and their affiliates QCC Canada, OPTC and the Boilermakers. As he was acknowledging PFC and thanking all of the members and Locals across Canada (many of whom were in the crowd) I made eye contact with Dave Griffiths, who grinned at me like the Cheshire Cat. Something big was about to happen. Although I was mentally tracking Steve Morrison's speech, I couldn't believe my ears when he announced that UA Canada and QCC Canada, together with the Boilermakers and OPTC, were committing a million dollars to support *The Push for Change*.

The crowd erupted in excitement at the news; it was a storybook finish to a dream that had been born out of "possibility thinking."

98

The final event of the day was a celebratory dinner hosted by UA Canada in Stanley Park for all of our friends, family and key stakeholders. The commissioner of the OPP honoured me with the organization's highest civilian award. We were also invited to return to Ontario for the commissioner's event in three days where we would meet the Lieutenant Governor of Ontario.

As we celebrated PFC's success, we took the opportunity to thank our families and our many friends (including our dear friend David Ash and his wife Lise), for their encouragement and support throughout the campaign. Before the night was over there was one last surprise. Deputy

Commissioner Rick Barnum handed me a phone and told me Senator Gwen Boniface was on the line.

I put the phone up to the microphone to share her message with the audience as the senator announced that she was putting my name forward to receive the Senate of Canada's 150th Anniversary Medal. The crowd cheered and after that the rest of the evening was a whirlwind.

When it was all over Marie and I jumped into the van with Bobby. Marie thought we were heading back to the house but I had other plans, we were booked into the Pan Pacific Hotel for some much-needed rest.

Marie

After our VIP dinner at The Stanley Park Pavilion, Joe had a surprise for me. Instead of driving to the Airbnb rental we had stayed at for the month of September, we drove downtown to the Pan Pacific Hotel. He had booked two nights' accommodations so we could unwind without any distractions. It was a beautiful room with amazing views of the harbour and mountains. Plush pillows and a thick, comfy mattress were just what the doctor ordered. After staying in the RV for months and then an Airbnb rental, this was heaven. Sleep came fast for both of us; we barely even finished our conversation about how hastily the trek had ended.

When we awoke the next morning, our first impulse was to do a reality check: "Did UA Canada really just fund The Push for Change for the next three years to further our work?" We had met with them while we were in Kamloops and presented a proposal to build on the success of PFC by doing a road tour of school presentations across the country. We never heard back about that proposal, so their announcement at our Grand Finale came as a big surprise to both Joe and me. While I should have been lit up with excitement, I couldn't help but feel anxiety at the thought of another campaign across Canada, albeit a road tour.

When I shared my thoughts with Joe it brought him down from the high he was rightfully experiencing after completing a 17 month, 9,000 km continuous walk across Canada. He heard me though and understood what I was saying; it was much too soon to be contemplating another stint on the road. But, we'd established some amazing relationships with advocacy groups, elected officials and other stakeholders across the country as a result of the campaign and we wanted to continue to build on that momentum to ensure that good prevention measures are developed for youth. We had come this far, how could we not continue to Push for Change!

With our honeymoon already planned for November and December, we knew we would have six weeks to rest up from the walk and we would be ready to go again. It is just who we are! We eased back into the present moment and reflected on the generosity and kindness of our partners and community champions who helped the campaign get this far. We were reminded of the joy we felt during the last 17 months working with others to create a safety net for vulnerable youth. We knew if we were to walk away and not continue the work we started, we would have life-long regret. We looked at each other as we shared the emotion of happiness that we know comes from being of service to others and we made a promise to Push for Change for as long as we could. Serving others is an honourable thing to do for our country, but it's also what we feel we need to do for our own inner peace.

99

Several days after the event, I returned to the bench where it all began. Filled with a sense of accomplishment I sat on the bench not as a broken homeless young person but as a champion. As I sat there I thought about my conversation with Gus all those years earlier. He was right, "There was more to me than I could see." I finally truly understood what he meant. The campaign was officially over; I had walked across Canada. Marie and I were exhausted but we had proved something to ourselves and to anyone who was watching. You really can push for change if you have the willingness to create a vision, connect to passion and get off the bench and take a few steps with intention.

And who knows where those steps might take you. The PFC journey led me in some unexpected directions and took far longer than I ever imagined, but those experiences were all part of the adventure. Although there's never a guarantee about the outcome, one thing I know for sure is if you don't get off your bench, nothing in your life will ever change.

As for me, I'm back to wondering what my next adventure will be. But I am no longer afraid to try. Whatever I had been afraid of for so many years, whatever it was that had plagued me and stifled my ability to take action, it was gone. I left that anxiety and fear somewhere on the Trans-Canada Highway. Today, the sky is the limit as I continue to employ the AIR model in every area of my life and I know I can do or be anything I choose. Anything is possible if you first dare to dream and then actively pursue those dreams. In many ways I feel like at 52 years old, I'm just getting started.

ACCOMPLISHMENTS

What we accomplished during *The Push for Change* far exceeded our expectations. In the beginning our only aspiration was to actually make it across the country. The idea of a non-athletic 50-year-old pushing a shopping cart across the second widest country on the planet was daunting enough. What's more, in a world that's become congested with charitable causes and events, we were uncertain of the impact we would actually have. We dared to dream nonetheless about the possibility of engaging a nation... although (to be honest), we held onto those expectations loosely.

Below is a list of the extraordinary milestones and accomplishments (along with a few fun facts) that resulted from our walk across Canada:

MILESTONES AND ACCOMPLISHMENTS

- PFC raised $1 million in sponsorship (operating money) before we took our first step in Newfoundland.

- Joe successfully pushed a shopping cart 9,064 km or 11,375,000 steps across Canada and walked continuously for 17 months through ten provinces (and also visited two northern territories). He also walked through Northern Ontario during a Canadian winter (and lived to talk about it).

- PFC raised $575,000 from Canadians and 100% of every dollar raised went to support youth homelessness.

- We were invited to a private meeting with the Prime Minister of Canada. Together with other advocates, PFC participated in conversations that led to an $11.2 billion investment in addressing homelessness across Canada – the largest investment of its kind from the federal government in decades.

- We played a role in the announcement of the Making a Shift proposal which included an $8 million investment in youth homelessness prevention research – the first of its kind in Canadian history.

- PFC invested and participated in the implementation of The Upstream Project, an innovative approach to early detection and prevention of youth homelessness.

- PFC inspired millions of Canadians through our rallies and events (with over 450 events across Canada).

- We directly connected with over 100,000 students and held 190 school presentations.

- Tens of thousands of students walked with Joe as he made his way through their communities.

- We inspired dozens of communities to host events in support of PFC including sleep outs, hockey games, fundraisers, sports events, awareness events and arts and culture events.

- Thousands of pounds of food, clothing, socks, winter coats and footwear were collected for local homeless shelters and emergency service providers during the campaign.

- We commissioned and professionally produced our own PFC theme song and also inspired students in Nipigon to write and produce a PFC tribute song and video.

- We spoke to more than 16,000 students and parents at WE Day Family in Toronto.

- PFC secured a National Partnership and Support Agreement with United Association (UA) of Canada and UA Locals hosted fundraising events all across Canada.

- PFC built an extraordinary community partnership with the Ontario Provincial Police (OPP) during the six months we spent in the province.

- The OPP ran a Suits for Change campaign, which collected thousands of gently-used dress clothes. They also conducted Sleep Outs for PFC in multiple communities during the winter and conducted 27 community hockey games to coincide with Hockey Day in Canada.

- PFC inspired the largest volunteer effort in the OPP's history (the OPP hosted over 220 of their own PFC events) and deeply impacted the internal culture of the organization.

- PFC had full support from the RCMP and countless municipal police forces across Canada.

- In total PFC received over 6,000 km of police escort and traffic safety support during the campaign.

- PFC received support letters from provincial Premiers, MP's, MLA's, mayors, police chiefs and the Prime Minister of Canada.

- PFC received a $1 million legacy donation from UA Canada, OPTC and QCCC.

- Thousands of volunteers donated over 50,000 volunteer hours during the campaign.

- PFC received support from and walked with celebrities including Robert Pilon, Don Cherry, Michael Pinball Clemens, Walter Gretzky, Rod Black, Rod Pedersen and the cast from Degrassi.

- NAV Canada hosted events in every city where they had a presence and raised $26,000.

- Marie managed PFC's entire charity office and operations centre from an RV or hotel room for 18 months.

- PFC shared fundraising dollars with local communities and agencies all across Canada.

- We were flown in the OPP Pilatus jet (with Joe's shopping

cart) to the remote communities of Moose Factory and Moosonee, Ontario where we walked on the ice highway supported by the OPP (in vehicles and on snow machines).

• We flew into the remote community of Norway House, Manitoba in the RCMP jet (with Joe's shopping cart) and were honoured with a feast by the First Nations community (who served us Canadian goose).

• PFC engaged and walked through dozens of First Nations communities, where we were honoured by chiefs and elders and received a number of handmade gifts including deer skin gloves, a beaver pelt hat, eagle feathers, tobacco and sage. Joe was also honoured with a blanket ceremony when we left Ontario.

• PFC engaged in a wide range of presentations from kindergarten classes to retirement centres.

• PFC had a private audience with Ontario Premier Kathleen Wynne.

• The federal Minister of Employment, Patty Hajdu, walked with us in Thunder Bay.

• We gained security clearance in Nova Scotia and visited several federal penitentiaries – we even brought the shopping cart inside the prison.

• We were given a private tour of RCMP Depot in Regina and participated in training simulations on the firing range and in the police chase simulator.

• We had a private tour of CFB 15 Wing Moose Jaw by Colonel Denis O'Reilly and were granted permission to sit in the Snow Bird and CT 155 Hawk cockpits.

• We were invited back to 15 Wing by Colonel Denis O'Reilly after the trek and given the honour of flying in formation (both Marie and Joe) in the CT-156 Harvard II with two of the best pilot instructors in Canada, doing aerobatics and dog-fight manoeuvres. This is a rare thing for any civilian to experience.

• PFC was welcomed into every province in Western Canada by RCMP leaders along with members dressed in formal Red Serge.

• Joe walked an entire day with the Deputy Premier of New Brunswick.

• We were received and acknowledged at both Queens Park in Ontario and the BC Legislature in Victoria. We were also received in the House of Commons in Ottawa, where a members' statement was read aloud acknowledging *The Push for Change* (with the Prime Minster present).

• PFC had a private meeting with the Federal Minister of Families, Children and Social Development Jean-Yves Duclos and MP Adam Vaughan to discuss the government's response to homelessness.

• The city of Fredericton, New Brunswick declared it, "*Push for Change* Week" when we arrived.

• Deputy Mayor Mark Taylor of the city of Ottawa declared September 29, 2016 "Joe Roberts – Push for Change Day."

• Mayor Gregor Robertson of the city of Vancouver declared September 29, 2017 "Push for Change Day."

- Joe was received and publicly acknowledged by the Lieutenant Governors of New Brunswick, Ontario, Alberta and the Yukon.

- Joe received the John Graves Simcoe Medal of Excellence.

- Joe was recognized as one of Shaw Media's 50 Outstanding Canadians.

- Joe was given an Honorary Doctorate of Letters from Laurentian University.

- Joe received the Senate of Canada's 150 Medal.

- Joe was presented with the OPP Commissioner's Badge by acting Commissioner Vince Hawkes.

- Joe was awarded the Meritorious Service Medal of Canada by the Governor General.

Fun Facts

- Joe wore through approximately 23 pair of shoes during the PFC trek across Canada.

- Joe consumed over 500 bowls of oatmeal and approximately 2,500 shots of espresso.

- According to Bobby and Marie, Joe did no dishes during the trek… ever!

- Joe and Marie were technically "homeless" for over 18

months with no fixed address.

- Joe and Marie were married just 36 days before the walk began, and often joked that the campaign was their honeymoon.

- PFC had 214 hotel nights and 303 RV nights. Despite over 300 nights in RV campgrounds, only two campfires were ever made.

- *The Push for Change* team moved 75 times during the campaign.

- PFC struck a limited number of challenge coins to present to special champions across Canada.

- Joe picked up a handful of rocks in Cape Spear and gave them away to very special contributors he met along the way.

- Joe has a large container of pennies and other coins he found on the side of the road – he gives the pennies away and plans to make something artistic with the other coins.

- Joe and Bobby collected over 100 license plates from the side of the road. Newfoundland yielded the most plates.

- The PFC shopping cart is retired and hangs in Joe and Marie's garage.

- Everything for the entire 17-month campaign (including all winter gear, kitchen gear, personal belongings and the entire office) was packed and followed us for the entire trek.

- The direct distance across Canada is approximately 7,500 km. Our route was 9,064 km (the extra kilometres were added to make a loop around Nova Scotia so we could include PEI).

- We also added an additional 800+ km to include southwestern Ontario after the OPP became our community safety partner.

- PFC was initially going to be called The Homeless Profit, but it changed after Dr. Sean Richardson adamantly opposed the name. Good thing!

- *The Push for Change* was stalled for almost three years due to multiple challenges.

- Joe was a non athlete when the planning to walk across Canada began.

- Marie's diet changed from modern, to pescatarian, to fully vegan during the 17-month trek.

- Several OPP members were scolded by the Chair of the Ontario Legislature in Queens Park for cheering when PFC was acknowledged (it's against parliamentary rules for guests to make any noise in the chamber).

- Only two planned events were cancelled, both due to "snow day" weather conditions that were beyond our control.

- There were only two (extremely minor) accidents during the entire campaign.

- The route through BC had to be changed due to wildfire smoke.

- Joe had to wear a mask through most of BC but still suffered due to the poor air quality.

- Out of over 450 events, only one was forgotten, however we were still able to get there and engage at the last minute.

- Despite Marie's fear of public speaking, she spoke at least 50 times at events.

- We planned our walk in Northern Ontario four years before we had a working relationship with the OPP.

- Surprisingly, Joe had very few blisters during the campaign.

- Joe had the flu three times during the campaign but didn't take any days off for illness.

- Including the trial walk from Calgary to Vancouver (and four years of training) Joe walked a total of over 20,000 km.

- Joe had over 150 RMT appointments and countless meetings with nutritionists, chiropractors and physiotherapists during the trek.

- Joe was "sweat tested" by Sports Medicine Nutrition professionals at the University of Guelph.

- Joe threw an opening pitch for a baseball game and dropped four ceremonial hockey pucks.

- PFC's digital catalogue includes over 40,000 pictures, thousands of hours of video footage and hundreds of media articles.

- Joe met Terry Fox's dad, Rolly Fox, on his trial walk in 2012.

- Joe was given one of 150 customized red refrigerators from Molson Canadian.

Thank You

What's harder than pushing a shopping cart across Canada? Listing by name all of the people who helped to make it possible.

For everyone who sponsored us, cheered us on, worked as a volunteer, walked with us or donated time, money and talent, we want to say thank you from the bottom of our hearts!

The Push for Change was successful because tens of thousands of good people believed in what we were doing and took action to make it happen.

Together we created change and our work has contributed to a larger movement that will continue to impact young people for generations to come.

For every vulnerable young person who has found themselves in need of help or huddled in a doorway exhausted and afraid, not knowing what their next move will be; they are why we *Pushed for Change*. And although you may never meet them or know their names, *The Push for Change* wants to thank you for your contribution and commitment and for giving these young people both a face and a voice.

PHILOSOPHERS NOTE

Writing a book to inspire people undoubtedly means that some of the really honest stuff gets left out, so while the PFC story and all the events are accurate there's also another side to the story. The truth is there were days when the campaign sucked and times when we were simply depressed, disengaged or burned out. There were also a lot of things we didn't do well and although the narrative is one of inspired triumph, there were days (before, during and after the campaign) when I questioned whether it was all worth it.

Walking across Canada gives you a lot of time to really think. The thrust of this book and everything I talk about when I speak publicly revolves around inspired human achievement through a resiliency mindset. It's true we can do or be anything, but the bigger question we should always ask is, "Why are we doing it?" I have a confession to make, the never-ending treadmill and drive for success, status and acquisition brought me no closer to happiness. It simply kept me busy long enough to sidestep the sense of emptiness that can lead to asking those hard questions.

As humans, ever since the industrial revolution we've judged our success in life on more, faster and better. But even at a time of unprecedented quality, production and innovation we are left empty, unfulfilled and yearning for something deeper.

We can spend our whole lives chasing success, money and achievement and in the end completely miss the point. It's true we can do anything we want and achieve things that are simply mind-boggling, but the currency we trade to accomplish those ambitions is our time.

Life can go by really quickly, so choose wisely how you want to invest your time. Just because you can do something doesn't mean you should. As for me, after 17 months on the road, with little time for the people that I love most in the world, I'm learning to enjoy "what's now" instead of always looking for "what's next."

ABOUT JOE

Joe Roberts, aka The Skidrow CEO, is an expert on resiliency and change. Having experienced both catastrophic failure and extraordinary success, Joe teaches how anyone can overcome perceived limitations and create high performance results.

Joe's business solutions have made millions of dollars for his clients across a wide variety of business sectors. It is this experience that Joe draws from when addressing Fortune 500 companies, professional associations and organizations internationally.

To inquire about Joe's availability as your next keynote speaker, contact our office today.

Marie Roberts - Business Manager
Email: marie@skidrowceo.com
Website: www.skidrowceo.com

Joe is also the author of:

Don't Buy the Lie about Getting High
Fred the Cat – The eyes and soul of an addict
7 Secrets to Profit from Adversity

To learn more or to purchase these books visit our website
www.skidrowceo.com